DICTIONARY *OF* FICTIONAL CHARACTERS

Dictionary
of
Fictional Characters

Completely Revised Edition

Martin Seymour-Smith

Boston
THE WRITER, INC.
Publishers

Library of Congress Cataloging-in-Publication Data

```
Seymour-Smith, Martin.
  Dictionary of fictional characters / Martin Seymour-Smith. --
Rev.ed.
    p.  cm.
  Originally published: London : Dent, 1974.
  ISBN 0-87116-166-4
  1. Characters and characteristics in literature--Dictionaries.
I. Freeman, William, 1880-    Dictionary of fictional characters.
II. Title.
PN56.4.S49    1992
820'.3--dc20                                          92-5025
                                                        CIP
```

Printed in the United States of America

TO
Christie Hickman and Shena Mackay

CONTENTS

INTRODUCTION

In 1963 the late J. E. Freeman published the first edition of *Everyman's Dictionary of Fictional Characters*. Its inclusion in the Everyman series made the term 'dictionary' mandatory, and in this completely new version it has been retained. But Freeman's was, and this is, really, like most self-styled dictionaries, a list – a selection. Otherwise one could go on adding to it indefinitely – and with little point. And, as Freeman wrote, 'selection, even when tersely and colourlessly recorded, is bound to reflect the likes, dislikes and general make-up of the recorder . . . .' My own approach has been historical: on the whole, I have included characters in books which have been read by other people, rather than merely liked by me. I have not left out the works of writers whom I personally dislike, or who bore me, or who (like most of Thackeray) are blind spots with me. Nonetheless, when all is said and done, my selection reflects what some will call prejudices (unless they agree with them). Like Freeman, I have left out junk; but I do not expect much criticism on that score.

Freeman's was, so far as I can ascertain, the first work of its kind. For its time – when there were many readers of popular but not reprinted Victorian books still living – it was excellently done. But when Fred Urquhart came to revise it, in 1973, he was critical. He thought that Freeman's 'overpowering fondness' for all Kipling's characters was a 'quirk', and made it clear that, had time and expense allowed it, he would have severely pruned them. He 'ruthlessly eliminated about four hundred characters from novels by Madame Albanesi, Walter Besant, Rosa N. Carey, Mary Cholmondeley . . .'. He then added 1614 new references of his own.

I have retained Fred's 1614 additions; but I have also restored a few of the characters from Victorian novels which he excised. My own taste has little to do with this: a few of the novels of Mary Cholmondeley, and even some of Besant's, have now been seen to be of interest (if not exclusively literary), after all. Not a few Victorian novels by women have been reprinted – and quite widely read.

I have retained, too, for the most part, Freeman's selections – they might be felt by some to be over-abundant – from the following authors: Sir Walter Scott, Thackeray, Dickens (I have added a few in this case), H. G. Wells, Gilbert and Sullivan, George Bernard Shaw. I have also, after much consultation and opinion-taking, retained the Kipling characters in more or less their entirety. Such lists are not easily obtainable elsewhere; all these authors (except perhaps Shaw?) are still widely read; and it would have been wasteful to consign all the industry of Freeman and his helpers to oblivion.

But this is a new work. The information in it has been differently presented, and the clumsy system of indentation used in the original printing has been dropped. I have also dropped hundreds of Freeman's entries from novels and, in particular, plays that are unavailable, of little or no merit or even interest, and are unlikely ever to see the light of day in any form. Of course I have had to use my judgement here, but I do not believe that this has been any more idiosyncratic than anyone else's would have been. I have picked up on many characters Freeman missed (there is, for example, more from Trollope here, more from early fiction, very much more from America, more from Commonwealth fiction, more from women), and I have added a small selection from non-English literatures.

I have followed Freeman in his descriptions of the characters where these could not be bettered; but I have also added some annotations of my own. They seldom express my own opinions.

The key to the abbreviations is given immediately below; a short appendix gives details of some more or less technical terms.

Let me conclude by quoting from the admirable Freeman's introduction of 1963: the reader, he wrote, 'will assuredly discover . . . variations in style and in the presentation of details'. Like him, I have tried to be as consistent as I can; but different kinds of books and characters have at times demanded slightly different treatments; in the interests of clarity they have therefore received them. Above all, I have tried to produce a book that can be perused in bed (it is light enough), and which will lead readers to new, good books.

Martin Seymour-Smith
Bexhill-on-sea
3 August 1990

ABBREVIATIONS

cc: *a* (not necessarily *the*) central character

ccs: central characters

hist.: historical character

legd.: legendary character

m.: married

myth.: mythological character

rev.: revised

rn: real name

ss: short story

tr.: translated

*: referred to in a separate entry, or, if a technical term, briefly explained in the appendix

†: and in other works

For ease of reference, names beginning with Mc have been grouped with those beginning with Mac. See p. 298ff.

NB Every effort has been made to discover the Christian names of wives, parents, etc., but in most cases these have not been available in the works themselves.

APPENDIX

I have used a few technical terms in my annotations. Here are brief explanations.

Saved character. I have taken this useful term over from an early phase of Northrop Frye's work. A saved character is one whose view of the events, or possibly action upon them, or both, represents the author's own moral (or amoral) view. Thus Mrs Moore is obviously the saved character in Forster's *A Passage to India*. Needless to say, this does not imply that the author is 'right'. But he or she thinks so.

Public service. I have called novels or plays of more than mere competence *public service* if they drew attention to abuses, or to inhumane or unjust conditions, which led – directly or indirectly – to reforms of bad conditions. Obvious examples that will be found here are works by Upton Sinclair* (the meat industry), John Galsworthy* (prison conditions). A slightly less obvious one is Cronin's* *The Citadel* (the practice of medicine by money-grubbing charlatans). There is a public service element, of course, in the fiction of Charles Dickens*; but there is also much more than that. When the term is used it implies that the impact on the readership was decisive, that the psychology is sound rather than distorted or sentimental, but that the writing in itself is somewhat, although not necessarily very, drab or uninteresting. One therefore would not want to use it of Dickens or Shaw*, and I have not sought to introduce controversy in my use of it.

Picaresque. *Picaro* is a Spanish word meaning, approximately, a rogue – a rogue almost always at least superficially likable or engaging. The paradigmatic picaresque text is *Lazarillo de Tormes*, although the term was not coined until long after it appeared. The first-person narratives of its successors (such as *Guzman**), which were translated and then imitated throughout Europe, told the story of the adventures of people from the lower orders who made good by luck, trickery and opportunism, or by all three; these central characters might finally prosper, or they might not. These texts varied in the degree of their ostensible cynicism, and in the direction of their social criticism. The form influenced Tobias Smollett*, whose work influenced Dickens. But Dickens was not a picaresque novelist, and we do not see the form again until this century, when it was revived for purposes of social criticism – and simply as a convenient, loose form.

Realism. Of course, the aim of all literature has always been to describe, and to draw attention to, reality. But *realism* was a specific movement in European letters towards the deliberate depiction of a broad spectrum of social conditions, of human psychology as it actually was rather than as it may have been felt it ought to have been. *Realism* as a movement is best defined as a reflection – but not always necessarily a precise one – of the tendency away from religious observance, or the contemplation of the beautiful (and, it was felt, upper class), and towards a positivist view of existence. Realism has its birth in the Enlightenment and its culmination in Flaubert*, whose opponents found him *nasty* and *gloomy*, but whose supporters found him equally illuminating and enlightening. He was himself an opponent of the merely programmatic realism advanced by such lesser lights as his contemporary, Champfleury, whose own exercises in it would now fail to stand reissue except as critical curiosities.

Naturalism was a specific offshoot of realism which is associated with Zola in France, with Norris*, Dreiser* and Farrell* in America, and (more nebulously) with Gissing*, Moore* (who alone of British novelists started by taking it up as a creed), Morrison* and others in England. Naturalism was more coherent as a movement: it sought to analyse society, and thus (or so it announced) to improve it. Naturalists were usually, unless merely trivial, in effect symbolistic and pessimistic. But they worked on the raw material, especially the urban raw materials, of the then new science of sociology; they were almost obsessed with then current notions of heredity – from whose bad influence (e.g. venereal disease, alcoholism) they felt human beings could not escape; and many of them were concerned with what was then felt to be the inescapably 'neurasthenic' nature of the 'interesting' individual.

Silver-fork; *dandy*; *fashionable*. These more or less interchangeable terms belong to the early nineteenth-century English novel, and are in themselves less important. A publisher called Colburn exploited the readership's fascination with Regency high life by issuing novels purporting to 'give away' all the secrets of the aristocracy. Good examples of such books to be found here are by Mrs Gore*, Robert Plumer Ward* and even Hook* and Disraeli*. Thackeray* parodied the genre and put an end to it; but the versatile Lytton* had taken full advantage of it in *Pelham**, perhaps the best of its kind.

Provincial. The nature of this kind of fiction, which is sometimes called *regional* – and in America *local color*, and in Spain *costumbristo* – is self-evident. It culminated, of course, in Hardy*, who wrote about what he called Wessex; and it has not died out, especially in so huge a country as America.

Newgate; sensation; Gothic; neo-Gothic. These terms are not synonymous, although there is considerable overlap. *Newgate* novels usually had plots based on the *Newgate Calendar* and the like, which recorded notorious crimes. Fielding's* *Jonathan Wild** comes into this category, but the term only came into vogue with Lytton's* title *Pelham**. Novels of *sensation*, which were attacked by certain clergymen and others for their immoral tendencies, dealt with lurid and implausible events. Dickens* exploited the vein, and Collins*, like Mrs Braddon* and Mrs Wood*, was recognized as a *sensation* novelist. The *Gothic* novel, with its wild settings and fantastic – often occult – plot, began with Walpole's* title *Castle of Otranto**, and came into fashion from the 1790s onwards: it was mocked by Austen* and Peacock* and gradually degenerated, through *Dracula**, into the 'horror tale', contemporary examples of which are puerile and entirely lack the genuine *frisson* of the earlier books. The term *neo-Gothic* is sometimes applied to serious fiction which contains elements of *Gothic*, as have been alleged in Faulkner* and exist in John Gardner*.

ACKNOWLEDGEMENTS

I am grateful to many people who helped me to compile this book. Chief amongst them is the late William Freeman, and Fred Urquhart – to whose pioneer work I have, however, alluded in my introduction.

Then there are the countless dictionaries of literature of which I have made use, to all the editors of which, and contributors to, I am duly thankful.

Arnor Ltd., whose *Protext* word processor I used to set this book, provided me with help far beyond the call of normal sales service. I am grateful to Mark Tilley for both writing to me, and talking to me on the telephone, about the problems involved in arranging and sorting such a massive amount of data. *Protext* is already well-known as one of the best (as well as one of the least expensive) programmes for journalists and writers. Unsolicited, I endorse that.

I am grateful, too, to: my wife, the London Library, the East Sussex County Library (particularly to my old friend Richard Acam, who always does all he can to get me the books I need) Robin Sisman, Imogen Taylor, Malcolm Gerratt, Shena Mackay, Christie Hickman, Giles Gordon, Michael Thorn, Peter Davies and many others who wish to remain nameless. Judith Hart made some helpful editorial comments at an early stage, and I am indebted to her. Mark Redhall spent sleepless nights doing an invaluable job in sorting the index, and I am beholden to him. Above all, I am indebted to Lesley Baxter, the final editor and indexer: an ideal one, who understood exactly what was needed. Errors remain my own.

A

A-Water, John Mayor of Cork
Perkin Warbeck play (1634) John Ford

A.D. resurrected suicide, hermaphrodite in neo-Gothic* novel that is of interest in the history of early radical feminism
The One Who is Legion, or A.D.'s After-Life (1930) Natalie Barney

A; B; C; D four thus named assassins in ingenious hist. novel set in late 18th-century Sweden (the same circumstances as those in Verdi's opera *Un Ballo in Maschera*) that has always fascinated its readers
The King With Two Faces (1897) Mary Coleridge

Aardvaark, Captain ('Old Arfie')
Catch-22 (1961) Joseph Heller

Aaron Moor loved by Tamora*
Titus Andronicus play (1623) William Shakespeare

Aaron see 'Riah

Abarak hunchback magician
The Shaving of Shagpat (1856) George Meredith

Abbeville, Horace
Cannery Row (1945) John Steinbeck

Abbott, Caroline with whom Lilia Herriton* goes to Italy
Where Angels Fear to Tread (1905) E. M. Forster

Abbotts, The family; cousins of the Dodsons*
The Mill on the Floss (1860) George Eliot (rn Mary Anne, later Marian, Evans)

Abdalla Saracen slave
Ivanhoe (1819) Walter Scott

Abdallah el Hadgi ('The Pilgrim') Saladin's* ambassador
The Talisman (1825) Walter Scott

Abdil priest in whose being the function called conscience had not quite atrophied
All and Everything: Beelzebub's Tales to His Grandson (1950) G. I. Gurdjieff

Abdulla chief of Syed Arab trading post
Almayer's Folly (1895) Joseph Conrad

(rn Josef Teodor Konrad Korzeniowski)

Abdullah Khan one of the 'Four'
The Sign of Four (1890) Arthur Conan Doyle

Abdy, John ('Old John') gout-ridden old man, ex-clerk to late Revd Bates
John his son, head man at the *Crown*
Emma (1816) Jane Austen

Abednego, Moses clerk to Independent W. Diddlesex Insurance Co.
The Great Hoggarty Diamond (1841) W. M. Thackeray

Abel farmer
Middlemarch (1871–2) George Eliot (rn Mary Anne, later Marian, Evans)

Abel, Guevez de Argensola narrator cc
Green Mansions (1904) W. H. Hudson

Abelard (hist.) cc
Heloise and Abelard (1921) George Moore

Abershaw
Elizabeth his wife
The Revenge for Love (1937) Wyndham Lewis

Abergavenny, Lord
King Henry VIII play (1623) William Shakespeare and John Fletcher

Abetz German official who fights Alphonse de Châteaubriant*
D'un Château l'autre (Castle to Castle) (1957) Louis-Ferdinand Céline (rn Louis-Ferdinand Destouches)

Abhorson executioner
Measure for Measure play (1623) William Shakespeare

Abigail waiting gentlewoman
The Scornful Lady play (1616) Francis Beaumont and John Fletcher

Abinger, Colonel
Mary his daughter m. Rob Angus*
When a Man's Single (1888) J. M. Barrie

Ablett, Mr
Trelawny of the Wells play (1898) Arthur Wing Pinero

Ablewhite, Godfrey swindler

The Moonstone (1868) Wilkie Collins
Abney, Mr
ss 'Lost Hearts'
Ghost Stories of an Antiquary (1910)
M. R. James
Abou Taher Achmed Emir of Masre
Vathek (1786) William Beckford
Abra girl loved by Aron Trask*
East of Eden (1952) John Steinbeck
Abrahamson, Jake 'old, subtle, sensual'
You Can't Go Home Again (1947)
Thomas Wolfe
Abram servant to Montague*
Romeo and Juliet play (1623) William
Shakespeare
Abrams, Moss usurer
Pendennis (1848) W. M. Thackeray
Abreskov, Paul Bolshevik enemy of
Saskia*
Huntingtower (1922) John Buchan
Absolute, Jack, Captain alias Ensign Be-
verley
Sir Anthony his father
The Rivals play (1775) Richard Brinsley
Sheridan
Acheson double-crossing solicitor
Campbell's Kingdom (1952) Hammond
Innes
Achilles
Caesar and Cleopatra play (1900)
George Bernard Shaw
Achilles Grecian commander
Troilus and Cressida play (1623) William
Shakespeare
Achilles Tatius ('The Follower') head of
the imperial bodyguard
Count Robert of Paris (1832) Walter
Scott
Achitophel satirical portrait of the Earl of
Shaftesbury
Absalom and Achitophel poem (1681)
John Dryden
Achsah mad wife of Sadrach* in book that
made its author hated throughout Wales
ss 'A Father in Sion'
My People (1915) Caradoc Evans (rn
David Evans)
Achthar, Anophel, Lord villainous peer
Melincourt, or Sir Oran Haut-on (1817)
Thomas Love Peacock
Ackerdocke Faust's* monkey
Faust (1980) Robert Nye
Ackley, Robert Caulfield's* fellow pupil

The Catcher in the Rye (1951) J. D.
Salinger
Acland, Thomas, Sir, cavalier
Woodstock (1826) Walter Scott
Acres, Bob
The Rivals play (1775) Richard Brinsley
Sheridan
Acton, Robert the Wentworths'* neigh-
bour, admirer of Baroness Mun-
ster*
The Europeans (1878) Henry James
Ada graduate
Princess Ida opera (1884) W. S. Gilbert
and Arthur Sullivan
Ada maidservant to Mr Asprey*
ss 'The House'
The Wind Blows Over (1936) Walter de
la Mare
Adaile, Mrs woman adored by Conrad
when he was very young
Conrad in Search of His Youth (1919)
Leonard Merrick
Adair, Robert, The Hon.
ss 'The Empty House'
The Return of Sherlock Holmes (1905)
Arthur Conan Doyle
Adalmar son to Melveric*
Death's Jest Book, or The Fool's Tragedy
play (1850) Thomas Lovell Beddoes
Adam Olivia's* servant
As You Like It play (1623) William
Shakespeare
Adam, Big eccentric hired man
The Story of a Country Town (1883)
E. W. Howe
Adam, Miss landlady
Daniel Deronda (1876) George Eliot (rn
Mary Anne, later Marian, Evans)
Adams seaman, foster-father of William
Peters*
The King's Own (1830) Captain Marryat
Adams, Evalina cc one of the best but least
known of the American author's writings
ss 'Evalina's Garden'
Silence and Other Stories (1898) Mary E.
Wilkins Freeman
Adams, Jack ('W.P.')
Dombey and Son (1848) Charles Dickens
Adams, John
Mary his wife, ccs of novel satirizing the
absurd divorce laws of its time
Holy Deadlock (1934) A. P. Herbert
Adams, Nick part-autobiographical cc of

short stories onwards from
In Our Time (1925) Ernest Hemingway
Adams, Rev. Abraham
Joseph Andrews (1742) Henry Fielding
Adams, Will (hist.) first Englishman to visit Japan, cc
Lord of the Golden Fan (1973) Christopher Nicole
Addams, F. Jasmine ('Frankie') twelve-year-old cc
Royal Quincy her father
Jarvis her brother
Janice Evans Jarvis's bride
The Member of the Wedding (1946) Carson McCullers
Addenbrooke, Bennett lawyer
Raffles (1899–1901) E. W. Hornung
Addlepot, Simon, Sir 'a coxcomb, always in pursuit of women of great fortunes'
Love in a Wood, or St James's Park comedy (1672) William Wycherley
Aderyn the Bird Queen, mother of Llew*
M.F. (1971) Anthony Burgess (rn John Burgess Wilson)
Adhemar, Prior 'an exemplary prelate'
The Antiquary (1816) Walter Scott
Adolph Negro dandy and major-domo to St Clare*
Uncle Tom's Cabin (1851) Harriet Beecher Stowe
Adolphe cc of classic French novel
Adolphe (1816) Benjamin Constant
Adolphe, Monsieur reception manager, Imperial Palace Hotel
Imperial Palace (1930) Arnold Bennett
Adonais name for Keats in the elegy written for him
Adonais poem (1821) Percy Bysshe Shelley
Adorni follower of Camiola's* father
The Maid of Honour play (1632) Philip Massinger
Adrastus essayist
The Impressions of Theophrastus Such (1879) George Eliot (rn Mary Anne, later Marian, Evans)
Adrian portrait, to a very limited extent, of the author's late husband
The Last Man (1826) Mary Shelley
Adriana wife to Antipholus of Syracuse
A Comedy of Errors play (1623) William Shakespeare
Adverse, Anthony cc popular historical

novel of Napoleonic era described by one critic as a 'mountain of trash'
Anthony Adverse (1934) Hervey Allen
Aëcius a general
Valentinian play (1647) John Fletcher
Aegeon merchant of Syracuse
Aemelia his wife
A Comedy of Errors play (1623) William Shakespeare
Aegisthus lover of Clytemnestra*, murdered by Orestes*
The Orestia trilogy of tragedies (458 BC) Aeschylus
Aclucva, The Lady see **Dalyngridge, Richard, Sir**
Aemelia see **Aegeon**
Aemelius nobleman
Titus Andronicus play (1623) William Shakespeare
Aeneas Trojan commander
Troilus and Cressida play (1623) William Shakespeare
Aeschere counsellor of Hrothgar* carried off by Grendel*
Beowulf (c. 745)
Agamemnon brother of Menelaus*
The Orestia trilogy of tragedies (458 BC) Aeschylus
Agamemnon Greek general
Troilus and Cressida play (1623) William Shakespeare
Agatha wronged woman
Lovers' Vows play (1798) Elizabeth Inchbald
Agathon foul-mouthed Spartan seer in satirical dialogue novel
The Wreckage of Agathon (1970) John Gardner
Agatson part-portrait of legendary Beat Bill Cannastra, drunken humiliator of women
Go (1952) John Clellon Holmes
Agelastes, Michael 'aged and adroit sycophant'
Count Robert of Paris (1832) Walter Scott
Ager, Lady sister of Russell*
Captain Ager her son
A Fair Quarrel play (1617) Thomas Middleton and William Rowley
Agnes Arnolphe's* ward
L'École des Femmes (The School for Wives) (1662) Molière (rn Jean-Baptiste

Poquelin)

Agnes ill-tempered Flemish maid to Mme Walravens*
Villette (1853) Charlotte Brontë

Agnes, Sister penitent nun formerly Lady Laurentini
The Mysteries of Udolpho (1794) Mrs Ann Radcliffe

Agrippa friend to Octavius*
Antony and Cleopatra play (1623) William Shakespeare

Agrippa, Cornelius (hist.)
ss 'The Mortal Immortal'
Tales and Stories (1891) Mary Shelley

Aguecheek, Andrew, Sir
Twelfth Night play (1623) William Shakespeare

Agurion representing the vice of greed for money
Cynthia's Revels, or The Fountain of Self-Love play (1601) Ben Jonson

Agustin
For Whom the Bell Tolls (1940) Ernest Hemingway

Ah Fe Chinese servant
ss 'An Episode of Fiddletown'
The Luck of Roaring Camp (1868) Bret Harte

Ah Loi
Gallions Reach (1927) H. M. Tomlinson

Ah Sin the 'Heathen Chinee': innocent-seeming card player
Plain Language From Truthful James narrative light verse (1870) Bret Harte
Ah Sin play (1877) Bret Harte and Mark Twain (rn Samuel Langhorne Clemens)

Ahab, Captain one-legged monomaniac cc
Moby Dick, or The Whale (1851) Herman Melville

Ahoon Beelzebub's* devoted servant
All and Everything: Beelzebub's Tales to His Grandson (1950) G. I. Gurdjieff

Ai, Genly male chauvinist envoy of Ekuman to planet Gethen (Winter)
The Left Hand of Darkness (1969) Ursula Le Guin

Aigredpoux, Mme Paulina Home's* former schoolmistress
Villette (1853) Charlotte Brontë

Aikwood, Ringan 'a sable personage'
Saunders his father
The Antiquary (1816) Walter Scott

Aimwell, Thomas
The Beaux' Stratagem (1707) George Farquhar

Ainsley, Mary Ann very ugly old maid of fifty, unselfish and Christ-like
Shirley (1849) Charlotte Brontë

Ainslie, Andrew robber
Deacon Brodie play (1892) W. E. Henley and Robert Louis Stevenson

Aisgill, Alice Joe Lampton's* lover
George her husband
Room at the Top (1957) John Braine

Aissa cc half-bred Fulani; maid to Miss Carr*
Aissa Saved (1932) Joyce Cary

Aitken friend to Tam Dyke*
Prester John (1910) John Buchan

Ajax 'blockish' Greek commander
Troilus and Cressida play (1623) William Shakespeare

Akela Lone Wolf, leader of the Seonee pack
Jungle Books† (1894–5) Rudyard Kipling

Akens, Julius cc, journalist seeking escape from a stultifying middle-class marriage
A Man Reprieved (1949) Arthur Calder-Marshall

Akershem, Sophronia m. Mr Lammle*
Our Mutual Friend (1865) Charles Dickens

Alabama, Red Temple Drake's* lover
Pete his brother, blackmailer; also Temple's lover
Sanctuary† (1931) William Faulkner

Alabaster, A. W.
The Horse's Mouth (1944) Joyce Cary

Alan member of the crew of the *Hispaniola*
Treasure Island (1883) Robert Louis Stevenson

Alarbus son to Tamora*
Titus Andronicus play (1623) William Shakespeare

Alaric the Goth (hist.)
Antonina (1850) Wilkie Collins

Alasi narrator cc, Prince of Kharezme
Vathek (1786) William Beckford

Alba, the
ss 'What a Misfortune'
More Pricks That Kicks (1934)
poem 'Alba'
Echo's Bones and Other Precipitates (1935) Samuel Beckett

Albanact son to King Brutus*, brother to Camber* and Locrine*
Locrine play (1595) 'W. S.' (?George Peele; ?Robert Green)

Albani music master
ss 'Mr Gilfil's Love Story'
Scenes of Clerical Life (1857) George Eliot (rn Mary Anne, later Marian, Evans)

Albany, Duke of
King Lear play (1623) William Shakespeare

Albany, Joseph student and practical joker, later called 'Joseph Rochecliffe'
Woodstock (1826) Walter Scott

Albert assistant to Charley Raunce*
Loving (1945) Henry Green (rn Henry Yorke)

Albey, Kate name under which Cathy Trask (*née* Ames*) joins the brothel in Salinas
East of Eden (1952) John Steinbeck

Albo, Captain a pandar
A Fair Quarrel play (1617) Thomas Middleton and William Rowley

Alcander
The Bee (1759–60) Oliver Goldsmith

Alcharisi see **Halm-Eberstein**

Alcibiades Athenian general
Timon of Athens play (1623) William Shakespeare

Alconleigh, Lord Matthew (family name **Radlett**)
Sadie his wife
Louisa; Linda; Jassy; Robin; Matt; Victoria; their children
David a relative
Emily David's wife; onwards from
The Pursuit of Love† (1945) Nancy Mitford

Aldclyffe, Cytherea in love with Ambrose Graye* and then with his daughter Cytherea Graye* (named after her); Manston* is her bastard son by her cousin, a 'wild officer'; in author's first (published) novel
Captain Aldclyffe her father, formerly **Bradleigh**
Desperate Remedies (1870) Thomas Hardy

Alddiborontiphoscophornio king of Queerummania in 'the most Tragical Tragedy that ever war was Tragediz'd by any company of Tragedians'
Chrononhothologos burlesque stage farce (1734) Henry Carey

Alden, Bessie sister to Mrs Westgate*
An International Episode (1879) Henry James

Alden, John who woos and eventually m. Priscilla* on behalf of Miles Standish*
The Courtship of Miles Standish poem (1858) Henry Wadsworth Longfellow

Alden, Oliver cc in whom 'puritanism worked itself out to its logical end': failed in love, killed in First World War
Peter his father, wealthy, effete drug addict and suicide
Nathaniel his puritanical uncle
Harriet his conventional and cold mother
– in novel by philosopher that unexpectedly became bestseller
The Last Puritan (1936) George Santayana

Alden, Roberta for whose murder (but was it?) Clyde Griffiths* dies in the electric chair
Mr and Mrs Titus Alden her parents
Tom; Gifford; Emily her brothers and sister
An American Tragedy (1925) Theodore Dreiser

Aldermanbury young tallow merchant
The Book of Snobs (1847) W. M. Thackeray

Alderney, Mrs and Master
Vanity Fair (1847–8) W. M. Thackeray

Aldington, Lord press genius
Mr Apollo: A Just Possible Story (1908) Ford Madox Ford

Aldobranfalconieri, Princess Florio's* kinswoman
Count Florio and Phyllis K. (1910) Reginald Turner

Aldrick the Countess of Derby's* Jesuit confessor
Peveril of the Peak (1822) Walter Scott

Aldrovan, Father chaplain to Sir R. Berenger*
The Betrothed (1825) Walter Scott

Aldwinkle, Lilian, Mrs
Irene her niece m. Lord Hovenden*
Those Barren Leaves (1925) Aldous Huxley

Alençon, Duke of
King Henry VI plays (1623) William

Shakespeare

Alex psychopathic music-loving cc
A Clockwork Orange (1962) Anthony
Burgess (rn John Burgess Wilson)

Alexandros Arab curio dealer in Jerusalem
The Mandelbaum Gate (1965) Muriel
Spark

Alexeyev 'Nature had not bestowed upon
him a single, striking, noticeable characteristic, good or bad'
Oblomov (1859) Ivan Goncharov

Alexievna, Anna Russian prostitute
The Research Magnificent (1915) H. G.
Wells

Alexis
The Faithful Shepherdess play (*c.* 1609)
John Fletcher

Alf, Ferdinand editor of the *Evening Pulpit*
The Way We Live Now (1875) Anthony
Trollope

Alfagi, Hamet relapsed convert
Ivanhoe (1820) Walter Scott

Algadi, Freddy, Count Italian who
enchants Mary Anne Gogan*
ss 'Liars'
The Talking Trees (1971) Sean O'Faolain

Alhambra del Bolero, Don
The Gondoliers opera (1889) W. S.
Gilbert and Arthur Sullivan

Ali, Ameer Thug, narrator (confessor to a
'sahib'), cc of well-informed and influen-
tial novel
Azima his wife (who is ignorant of his
Thuggism)
Confessions of a Thug (1839) Captain
Meadows Taylor

Alibi Ike (Frank X. Farrell) baseball player
the **X** in whose real name must have
stood for 'Excuse Me'
ss 'Alibi Ike'
You Know Me Al (1916) Ring Lardner

Alibi, Tom Grubbet's* solicitor
Waverley (1814) Walter Scott

Albius doctor who undertakes to cure
fools and madmen
Isabella his wife
The Changeling play (1653) Thomas
Middleton and William Rowley

Alice cc
Alice in Wonderland (1865)
*Through the Looking-Glass and What
Alice Found There* (1872) Lewis Carroll
(rn Charles Lutwidge Dodgson)

Alice lady to Katherine*
King Henry V play (1623) William
Shakespeare

Alice maid to Countess Czerlaski* m.
Edmund Bridmaine*
ss 'The Sad Fortunes of the Rev. Amos
Barton'
Scenes of Clerical Life (1857) George
Eliot (rn Mary Anne, later Marian,
Evans)

Alice maid to the Deanes*
The Mill on the Floss (1860) George Eliot
(rn Mary Anne, later Marian, Evans)

Alice mistress o' the game
Bartholomew Fair play (1631) Ben
Jonson

Alice servant
ss 'Prelude'
Bliss (1920) Katherine Mansfield (rn
Katherine Mansfield Beauchamp)

Alicia, Lady
Persuasion (1818) Jane Austen

Alick shepherd and head-man to Martin
Poyser*
Adam Bede (1859) George Eliot (rn
Mary Anne, later Marian, Evans)

Alicompayne eldest son of the Earl of
Brandyball*
The Book of Snobs (1847) W. M.
Thackeray

Alimony, Agatha 'dusky and deep-voiced'
Marriage† (1912) H. G. Wells

Aliris Sultan of Lower Bucharia m. Lalla
Rookh* in frame story of this once
popular series of oriental tales in verse
connected by a frame story
Lalla Rookh poems (1817) Thomas
Moore

Alissa high-minded protestant daughter of
a banker and an amorous Creole; loves
Jérôme* but cannot resolve the struggle
in her between sacred and profane love;
based by author in part on his own wife
Juliette her sister, in love with Jérôme
La Porte étroite (1909) André Gide

Allaby, Revd rector of Crampsford
Mrs Allaby his wife
Christina one of his nine children, m.
Theobald Pontifex*
The Way of All Flesh (1903) Samuel
Butler

Allan, Jack
The House with the Green Shutters

(1901) George Douglas (rn George Douglas Brown)

Allan, Mrs Colonel Mannering's housekeeper
Guy Mannering (1815) Walter Scott

Allan, William see Eustace, Father

Allan-a-Dale northern minstrel
Ivanhoe (1820) Walter Scott

Allande, Maria de Italian Cardinal
Death Comes for the Archbishop (1927) Willa Cather

Allard, Rives Kentuckian Confederate spy, cc epic novel of American Civil War; m. Lucy Churchill
None Shall Look Back (1937) Caroline Gordon

Allaster minstrel
Rob Roy (1818) Walter Scott

Albee, Kirby
The Victim (1947) Saul Bellow

Allegra beautiful Italian girl cheated of Simon Warre* by Anne Delaware, but m. Lord Wickenham*
The Gods, Some Mortals And Lord Wickenham (1895) John Oliver Hobbes (rn Pearl Craigie)

Allegre, Henry art connoisseur
The Arrow of Gold (1919) Joseph Conrad (rn Josef Teodor Konrad Korzeniowski)

Allen, Arabella attractive brunette m. Nathaniel Winkle*
Benjamin her brother
The Pickwick Papers (1837) Charles Dickens

Allen, Lord i.e. Lord Rosebery
The New Republic, or *Culture, Faith and Philosophy in an English Country House* (1877; edition by John Lucas, 1975, lists originals of characters) William Hurrell Mallock

Allen, Madge keeper of an animal farm
The Postman Always Rings Twice (1934) James M. Cain

Allen, Major 'officer of experience'
Old Mortality (1816) Walter Scott

Allen, Mr sensible owner of most of the property about Fullerton
his wife, who has neither beauty, genius, accomplishment nor manner, but does have the air of a gentle woman
Northanger Abbey (1818) Jane Austen

Allen, Revd Mr scoundrelly tutor to Richard Carvel*
Richard Carvel (1899) Winston Churchill

Allen, Samantha cute homilizing cc of series of humorous books that for a time rivalled Twain's* in popularity
Josiah her acquiescent husband; onwards from
Samantha at the Centennial† (1870) Marietta Holley

Allen, Sister
Adam Bede (1859) George Eliot (rn Mary Anne, later Marian, Evans)

Allestree, John, Sir his wife
Sir Charles Grandison (1754) Samuel Richardson

Alleyn, Roderick Eton-educated detective by New Zealand writer onwards from
A Man Lay Dead† (1934) Ngaio Marsh

Allingham Australian gunnery officer, the *Saltash*
The Cruel Sea (1951) Nicholas Monsarrat

Allison, Clive seeking information leading to the conviction of whoever was responsible for the death of Harold Godwen-Austen
Girl with Red Hair (1974) Giles Gordon

Allison, Howard lawyer whose father was a slave
Nigger Heaven (1926) Carl Van Vechten

Allitsen, Robert surly cc called 'the disagreeble man'; goes to die in Swiss sanatorium after failing to declare his love for Bernadine Holme*
Ships That Pass in the Night (1893) Beatrice Harraden

Allnutt, Charlie ne'er-do-well engineer
The African Queen (1935) C. S. Forrester

Allo a Pict
ss 'On the Great Wall'
ss 'The Winged Hats'
Puck of Pook's Hill (1906) Rudyard Kipling

Alloa, Lord
The Thirty-nine Steps (1915) John Buchan

Allwit a contented and complacent cuckold
Mistress Allwit his wife and one of Sir

Walter Whorehound's* mistresses
A Chaste Maid in Cheapside play (1630)
Thomas Middleton
Allworth a young gentleman, page to Lord
Lovell*
Lady Allworth a rich widow, his step-
mother
A New Way to Pay Old Debts play
(1633) Philip Massinger
Allworthy, Squire
Bridget his sister m. Captain Blifil*;
mother to Tom Jones*
Tom Jones (1749) Henry Fielding
Almanac doctor in physic, and jeerer
The Staple of News play (1631) Ben
Jonson
Almathea sister to Argeleon*
Marriage à la Mode play (1673) John
Dryden
Almayer, Kaspar cc, European trader in
Dutch East Indies in author's first novel
Almayer's Folly (1895) Joseph Conrad
(rn Josef Teodor Konrad Korzeniowski)
Almeira cc of this author's only tragedy
The Mourning Bride play (1697) William
Congreve
Almond, Julia cc, portrait of the judicially
murdered Mrs Edith Thompson in recon-
struction of the case
A Pin to See the Peep-Show (1934)
F. Tennyson Jesse
Almond, Julian
Daisy *née* Beaumont*, his wife
Bryony their daughter
A Bowl of Cherries (1984) Shena
Mackay
Almond, Mrs sister to Dr Sloper*
Marian her daughter, engaged to Arthur
Townsend*
Washington Square (1880) Henry James
Alone, Kitty cc of exciting historical novel
(*c.* 1820) taking in Dartmoor rick-
burning and Brunel's 'Atmospheric Rail-
way'
Kitty Alone: A Story of Three Fires
(1895) Sabine Baring-Gould
Alonso King of Naples
The Tempest play (1623) William Shake-
speare
Aloysha saddlemaker
Tobit Transplanted (1931) Stella Benson
Aloysius, Brother see **Meats, Henry**
Alpine, Frankie cc, robs a Jew but then

repents and becomes one, in order to win
Helen Bober*, whom he had previously
insulted
The Assistant (1957) Bernard Malamud
Alquist, Paula
Gaslight play (1939) Patrick Hamilton
Alrui Jewish conqueror, cc of romance set
in 12th-century Azerbaijan
Alroy (1833) Benjamin Disraeli
Alsemero loved by Beatrice-Joanna*
The Changeling play (1653) Thomas
Middleton and William Rowley
Alsop, Gerald friend to George Webber*
The Web and the Rock (1929) Thomas
Wolfe
Altamont, Jack, Colonel alias **Armstrong**
and **Amory**; bigamist and ex-felon; first
husband of Lady Clavering*
Blanch known as **Amory** their daughter
Pendennis (1848) W. M. Thackeray
Altangi, Lien Chi imaginary Chinese
philosopher residing in London who
wrote letters for Newberry's *Public
Ledger*, later reprinted in
The Citizen of the World (1762) Oliver
Goldsmith
Alter, Wingfield, O. M. great author
The Gunroom (1919) Charles Morgan
Altifiorla, Francesca feminist she-dragon
'born in poor circumstances, but with an
exalted opinion as to her own blood'
Kept in the Dark (1882) Anthony
Trollope
Altisidora wanton
Don Quixote (1605–15) Miguel de
Cervantes
Altofronto, Duke of Genoa see **Malevole**
Alvarado, Captain
The Bridge of San Luis Rey (1927)
Thornton Wilder
Alvaro, Don jailer
The Revenge for Love (1937) Wyndham
Lewis
Alveric son of the Lord of Erl* m. Lirazel*
Orion their son
The King of Elfland's Daughter (1924)
Lord Dunsany
Alving, Mrs woman in revolt against
falsity
Oswald her son, suffering from syphilis
which he has inherited from his father
Ghosts play (1881) Henrik Ibsen
Alwyn, Nicholas cc, goldsmith, foster-

brother to Marmaduke Nevile*
The Last of the Barons (1843) Edward Bulwer Lytton

Alyface, Annot maiden to Dame Custance*
Ralph Roister Doister play (1551) Nicholas Udall

Amal a Dane
ss: 'The Winged Hats'
Puck of Pook's Hill (1906) Rudyard Kipling

Amala Thorwold's* daughter
Death's Jest Book, or The Fool's Tragedy play (1850) Thomas Lovell Beddoes

Amalfi, Giovanna, Duchess of
Antonio Bologna her second husband
Ferdinand, Duke of Calabria her jealous brother
The Cardinal another of her brothers
The Duchess of Malfi play (1613) John Webster

Amalia a cook
Barry Lyndon (1844) W. M. Thackeray

Amanda wife to Loveless*
The Relapse, or Virtue in Danger play (1697) John Vanbrugh

Amaranta wife to Bartolus
The Spanish Curate play (1647) John Fletcher and Philip Massinger

Amarillis
The Faithful Shepherdess play (1609) John Fletcher

Amarinth, Esmé supposed portrait of Oscar Wilde*; the author was here aided by Max Beerbohm*, who probably virtually rewrote the first draft
The Green Carnation (1894) Robert Hichens

Amaury, Giles Grand Master of the Templars
The Talisman (1825) Walter Scott

Amberley, Mary, Lady drug-ridden alcoholic
Eyeless in Gaza (1936) Aldous Huxley

Ambermere, Lady
Queen Lucia (1920) E. F. Benson

Ambient, Mark eminent writer with whose work the American narrator is entranced
his wife, a 'blandly detached' philistine (in part based on Mrs John Addington Symonds)
Dolcino their angelic son, whom his mother prefers to allow to die rather than to be exposed to the peril to his soul latent in his father's prose
Miss Ambient his sister, 'restless romantic disappointed spinster'
ss 'The Author of "Beltraffio"'
Stories Revived (1885) Henry James

Ambitioso brother to Lussurioso*
The Revenger's Tragedy (1607/8) ?Thomas Middleton; ?Cyril Tourneur

Amble man to Lady Allworth*
A New Way to Pay Old Debts play (1633) Philip Massinger

Amboyne, Dr ('Jack Doubleface') philanthropist and peacemaker
Put Yourself in His Place (1870) Charles Reade

Ambrose builds a cathedral, climbs the spire, falls and flies; canonized after his death
Ambrose's Vision: Sketches Towards the Creation of a Cathedral (1980) Giles Gordon

Ambrose, Nelly cc of early socialist novel much admired by Engels, m. George*
her Roman Catholic parents, who turn her out after Arthur Grant* has seduced her
A City Girl (1887) John Law (rn Margaret Harkness)

Ambrosio evil and eventually damned Spanish monk in paradigmatic Gothic novel*
The Monk: A Romance (1796) Matthew Lewis

Amedroz, Clara independent girl of no wealth who chooses man she loves, Will Belton*
The Belton Estate (1866) Anthony Trollope

Ameera Indian mistress of John Holden*
Toto their son who dies
ss 'Without Benefit of Clergy'
Life's Handicap (1891) Rudyard Kipling

Amélie wife of unnamed narrator, a pastor in love with Gertrude*
Jacques their son, also in love with Gertrude
La Symphonie Pastorale (1921) André Gide

Amelot page to Damian de Lacy*
The Betrothed (1825) Walter Scott

Amelus friend to Nearchus*
The Broken Heart play (1633) John Ford

Amenartas wife of Kallikrates*, ancestor of Leo Vincey*
She (1887) Henry Rider Haggard

Americy mulatto half-sister of Theodosia Bell*
Lethe her sister
My Heart and My Flesh (1927) Elizabeth Madox Roberts

Amerigo, Prince impoverished Italian aristocrat whose fine but flawed (and eventually smashed) character is throughout symbolized by the title; m. Maggie Verver*
The Golden Bowl (1904) Henry James

Ames, Anros
Louisa his wife
Mourning Becomes Electra play (1931) Eugene O'Neill

Ames, Cathy m. Adam Trask*; changes her name to Kate Albey*; prostitute and murderess
East of Eden (1952) John Steinbeck

Ames, Harry black cocksman, an attempt at a portrait of Richard Wright*
Charlotte his wife
The Man Who Cried I Am (1967) John Williams

Amethus cousin to Palador*
The Lover's Melancholy play (1629) John Ford

Amherst, John assistant manager of a mill
Bessy *née* Langhope his first wife and owner of the mill
Justine *née* Brent nurse, his second wife
The Fruit of the Tree (1907) Edith Wharton

Amiens lord attendant on the duke
As You Like It play (1623) William Shakespeare

Aminadab Aylmer's* servant
ss 'The Birthmark'
Mosses from an Old Manse (1846) Nathaniel Hawthorne

Aminadab sheriff's officer
The Great Hoggarty Diamond (1841) W. M. Thackeray

Amintor betrothed to Aspatia*
The Maid's Tragedy play (1619) Francis Beaumont and John Fletcher

Amlet, Dick gambler and thief in comedy adapted from the French
Mrs Amlet his mother, seller of all sorts of private affairs to ladies and with whom Gripe's* wife Clarissa* has pawned a necklace
The Confederacy play (1705) John Vanbrugh

Ammen, Jasper cc
King Coffin (1935) Conrad Aiken

Ammersfoot
The Thirty-nine Steps (1915) John Buchan

Amorous La Foole, Sir snob
Epicene, or The Silent Woman play (1609) Ben Jonson

Amorphus who has lost his shape through too much travel
Cynthia's Revels, or The Fountain of Self-Love play (1601) Ben Jonson

Amory see **Flint, Gertrude**

Amory, Blanche christened **Betsy**; daughter of Lady Clavering* by her first marriage m. Count Montmerenci de Valentinois*
Pendennis (1848) W. M. Thackeray

Amphialus
The Arcadia (1890) Philip Sydney

Amphigenia cc complex romance with which the author became bored, and ended: 'Let those that are not pleased with this Conclusion, let them throw away as many idle hours as I have done, and they may compleat that story which hath now quite jaded and dull'd my pen'
Pandion and Amphigenia (1665) John Crowne

Amyclas King of Laconia
The Broken Heart play (1633) John Ford

Anacleto Filipino servant to Alison Langdon*
Reflections in a Golden Eye (1940) Carson McCullers

Anaides representing the vice of impudence
Cynthia's Revels, or The Fountain of Self-Love play (1601) Ben Jonson

Anastasius young Greek cc ruined by 'injudicious indulgence' whose adventures 'dizzy the arithmetic of memory' before he dies young and wasted – he is by turns thief, killer and beggar; in novel admired by Byron and many others
Anastasius, or The Memoirs of a Modern Greek, Written at the Close of the Eighteenth Century (1819) Thomas Hope

Anatole valet to Henry Foker*
Pendennis (1848) W. M. Thackeray
Anderson
ss 'No 13'
Ghost Stories of an Antiquary (1910)
M. R. James
Anderson, Charles friend to Tom
Bertram*
Mansfield Park (1814) Jane Austen
Anderson, Charley plane manufacturer
U.S.A. (1930–6) John Dos Passos
Anderson, Donovan civil servant; first
boyfriend of Martha Quest*
The *Martha Quest* series (1952–69)
Doris Lessing
Anderson, Gilbert, Dr psychiatrist
The Return of the Soldier (1918) Rebecca
West (rn Cecily Fairfield)
Anderson, Eppie one of Meg Dod's* maids
St Ronan's Well (1824) Walter Scott
Anderson, Harvey
Edward his brother
Fanny his sister
The Daisy Chain (1856) Charlotte M.
Yonge
Anderson, Job member of the crew of the
Hispaniola
Treasure Island (1883) Robert Louis
Stevenson
Anderson, John tramp
his wife
ss 'Tramps'
The Uncommercial Traveller (1860–8)
Charles Dickens
Anderson, Revd Anthony
Judith his wife
The Devil's Disciple play (1899) George
Bernard Shaw
Anderson, Walter bookshop assistant
George his brother
Jim their father
Bella *née* Gillespie their mother
Time Will Knit (1938) Fred Urquhart
Andrada, Manuel servant to Trujillo told
to bring back or kill Justo de
Villamayor*; but drawn to him and
changed by him
The Exiles (1962) Albert Guerard
Andreson, Ole intended victim paralysed
by fear
ss 'The Killers'
Men Without Women (1927) Ernest
Hemingway

Andrews, John cc, Harvard-graduate
musician from Virginia who wants to be
composer; deserts with Chrisfield*
Three Soldiers (1921) John Dos Passos
Andrews, Joseph cc of satire on *Pamela**
Joseph Andrews (1742) Henry Fielding
Andrews, Miss sweet girl who reads all the
horrid novels she can get hold of, but
cannot manage even the first volume of
*Sir Charles Grandison**
Northanger Abbey (1818) Jane Austen
Andrews, Nurse
ss 'The Daughters of the Late Colonel'
The Garden Party (1922) Katherine
Mansfield (rn Katherine Mansfield Beau-
champ)
Andrews, Pamela favourite maid of
wealthy Lady B—, who recounts in
letters to her parents her rejection of the
attempts of Squire B—* to seduce her un-
til he marries her
John her father
Elizabeth her mother
Pamela or *Virtue Rewarded* (1740–1)
Samuel Richardson
Andrews, Polly graduate of Vassar
The Group (1963) Mary McCarthy
Andriaovsky, Michael 'little Polish
painter'
Maschka his sister
ss 'Hic Jacet: A Tale of Artistic Con-
science'
Widdershins (1911) Oliver Onions
Andromache wife of Hector*
Troilus and Cressida play (1623) William
Shakespeare
Andross, John cc American novel (a 'grim
and powerful etching') – of political
corruption
John Andross (1874) Rebecca Harding
Davis
Anemolius laureate of Utopia
Utopia (1515–16) Thomas More
Angel based on physician and television
hypnotist Stephen Black, whom the
author for a time believed was
persecuting him by telepathy
The Ordeal of Gilbert Pinfold (1957)
Evelyn Waugh
Angel dead-end kid
Dead End play (1936) Sidney Kingsley
Angel, Hosmer see Windibank
Angel, Lady a rapturous maiden m. Major

Murgatroyd*
Patience opera (1881) W. S. Gilbert and Arthur Sullivan

Angel, Lucasta bastard daughter of Sir Claude Mulhammer*, m. Barnabas Kaghan*
The Confidential Clerk play (1954) T. S. Eliot

Angelica rich niece to Foresight
Love for Love comedy (1710) William Congreve

Angelina daughter to Lewis* m. Charles Brisac*
The Elder Brother play (1635) John Fletcher and Philip Massinger

Angelo friend to Leandro*
The Spanish Curate play (1647) John Fletcher and Philip Massinger

Angelo friend to Lord Paulo*
The Case is Altered play (1609) Ben Jonson

Angelo goldsmith
A Comedy of Errors play (1623) William Shakespeare

Angelo treacherous and lustful puritan, Deputy to the Lord of Vienna, betrothed to Mariana*
Measure for Measure play (1623) William Shakespeare

Angelus, Dr
Iris his wife
Dr Angelus play (1947) James Bridie (rn O. H. Mavor)

Angry Snake nickname of enemy Indians
Settlers in Canada (1844) Captain Marryat

Angstrom, Harry ('Rabbit') once a high-school basketball champion; a Babbitt-type*
Rabbit, Run (1960); *Rabbit Redux* (1971); *Rabbit is Rich* (1981) John Updike

Angus nobleman of Scotland
Macbeth play (1623) William Shakespeare

Angus, Rob cc, saw-miller, late leader-writer the *Wire* m. Mary Abinger*
When a Man's Single (1888) J. M. Barrie

Animula female sprite caught in microscope with whom Lindley* falls in love
ss 'The Diamond Lens' (1858); *Poems and Stories* (1881) Fitz-James O'Brien

Ann saved character*

Outward Bound play (1923) Sutton Vane

Anna cc domineering, kindly German servant in early and masterly *conte* partly modelled on *Trois Contes*
ss 'Anna'
Three Lives (1909) Gertrude Stein

Anna Frau Ebermann's* maid
ss 'Swept and Garnished'
A Diversity of Creatures (1917) Rudyard Kipling

Anna old friend of Deeley's* wife Kate*
Old Times play (1971) Harold Pinter

Anna servant whose mistress writes her love letters for her, m. Raye*
ss 'On the Western Circuit'
Life's Little Ironies (1894) Thomas Hardy

Annabella incestuous cc, daughter to Florio*
'Tis Pity She's a Whore play (1633) John Ford

Annable gamekeeper
The White Peacock (1911) D. H. Lawrence

Anne Dombey's* housemaid
Dombey and Son (1848) Charles Dickens

Anne, Lady widow of Edward Prince of Wales later m. Richard III*
King Richard III play (1623) William Shakespeare

Annesley, Harry m. Florence Scarborough*
Mr Scarborough's Family (1883) Anthony Trollope

Annesley, Mrs companion to Georgiana Darcy*
Pride and Prejudice (1813) Jane Austen

Annette maid to Emily St Aubert*
The Mysteries of Udolpho (1794) Mrs Ann Radcliffe

Annibale a gondolier
The Gondoliers opera (1889) W. S. Gilbert and Arthur Sullivan

Annipe maid to Zenocrate*
Tamburlaine play (1587) Christopher Marlowe

Anodos twenty-one-year-old narrator
his father
Phantastes (1858) George Macdonald

Anscam, Mr headmaster who confiscates stories by Maupassant* from Blaize*
David Blaize (1916) E. F. Benson

Ansell, Moses pious Jew
Esther his daughter
Children of the Ghetto (1892) Israel Zangwill
Ansell, Stewart Cambridge friend of Rickie Eliott*
The Longest Journey (1907) E. M. Forster
Anselm, Prior confessor to King Robert
The Fair Maid of Perth (1828) Walter Scott
Anselmo old Spaniard
For Whom the Bell Tolls (1940) Ernest Hemingway
Anstey, Sybil m. (1) Charles Herbert*, (2) Harry Jardine*
The Ballad and the Source (1944) Rosamond Lehmann
Anstruther, Nigel, Sir beastly depraved Englishman, m. Rosalie Vanderpool to restore fortunes shattered by dissipation; horsewhipped; perishes of stroke
The Shuttle (1907) Frances Hodgson Burnett
Anthony Meg Dod's* humpbacked postilion
St Ronan's Well (1824) Walter Scott
Anthony, Brother
ss 'The Janeites'
Debits and Credits (1926) Rudyard Kipling
Anthony, John founder of Trengartha Tin Plate Works, whose employees are on strike
Strife play (1909) John Galsworthy
Anticant, Pessimist, Dr
The Warden (1855) Anthony Trollope
Antigonus Sicilian lord
A Winter's Tale play (1623) William Shakespeare
Antijack, Anyside caricature of the politician George Canning
Melincourt (1817) Thomas Love Peacock
Antiochus King of Antioch
Pericles play (1609) William Shakespeare
Antiphila waiting-woman to Aspatia*
The Maid's Tragedy (1619) Francis Beaumont and John Fletcher
Antipholus of Ephesus and Antipholus of Syracuse twin sons of Aegeon*
A Comedy of Errors play (1623) William Shakespeare

Antirosa guardian of Dick Heldar* and Maisie*
The Light that Failed (1890) Rudyard Kipling
Antoine fellow-employee of Ferdinand* who bumps into people with his erect penis: he is looking for butter with which to sodomize his boss's wife
Mort à crédit (*Death on the Instalment Plan*) (1936) Louis-Ferdinand Céline (rn Louis-Ferdinand Destouches)
Antolini schoolteacher
The Catcher in the Rye (1951) J. D. Salinger
Anton, Gregory
Gaslight play (1939) Patrick Hamilton
Antonapoulos, Spiros dumb man
The Heart is a Lonely Hunter (1940) Carson McCullers
Antonia, Donna sister of Ambrosio* m. Don Lorenzo de Medina
Elvira her mother
Leonella her aunt
The Monk: A Romance (1796) Matthew Lewis
Antonina daughter of Numarian, a Roman Christian; in 5th-century romance
Antonina (1850) Wilkie Collins
Antonio
Anne of Geierstein (1829) Walter Scott
Antonio a gondolier
The Gondoliers opera (1889) W. S. Gilbert and Arthur Sullivan
Antonio a merchant, victim of Shylock
The Merchant of Venice play (1623) William Shakespeare
Antonio a pretended changeling
The Changeling play (1653) Thomas Middleton and William Rowley
Antonio an old lord
The Revenger's Tragedy (1607/8) ?Thomas Middleton; ?Cyril Tourneur
Antonio brother to Leonato*
Much Ado About Nothing play (1623) William Shakespeare
Antonio father to Proteus*
The Two Gentlemen of Verona play (1623) William Shakespeare
Antonio sea captain who rescues Sebastian*
Twelfth Night play (1623) William Shakespeare
Antonio son of Andrugio*, cc of two-part

play mocked by Ben Jonson*
Antonio and Mellida play (1602) John Marston

Antonio usurping Duke of Milan
The Tempest play (1623) William Shakespeare

Antonio young Spanish guitar player
ss 'Poor Mercantile Jack'
The Uncommercial Traveller (1860–8) Charles Dickens

Antony, Mark
Julius Caesar play; *Antony and Cleopatra* play (1623) William Shakespeare

Antrim, Colonel
Mrs Antrim his wife
Roger their son
Violet their daughter m. Alec Peacock*
The Well of Loneliness (1928) Radclyffe Hall

Antrobus, George Mr Everybody
Mrs Antrobus his wife
The Skin of Our Teeth play (1942) Thornton Wilder

Antrobus, Mrs
Piggy; Goosie her daughters
Queen Lucia (1920) E. F. Benson

Anville, Evelina cc
Evelina, or The History of a Young Lady's Entrance Into the World (1778) Fanny Burney

Ap-Llymry, Mr and Mrs
Crotchet Castle (1831) Thomas Love Peacock

Ape, Melrose, Mrs evangelist
Vile Bodies (1930) Evelyn Waugh

Apemantus ill-tempered philosopher
Timon of Athens play (1623) William Shakespeare

Apis fighting bull
ss 'The Bull That Thought'
Debits and Credits (1926) Rudyard Kipling

Apley, George rich Bostonian cc
Catherine his wife
John; Eleanor their children
The Late George Apley (1937) John P. Marquand

Apollo, Phoebus, Mr (sometimes **Prince**), a divine godhead; cc of the author's only overtly religious novel
Mr Apollo: A Just Possible Story (1908) Ford Madox Ford

Apollos, Revd Mr popular Congregationalist preacher
The Impressions of Theophrastus Such (1879) George Eliot (rn Mary Anne, later Marian, Evans)

Apolonius duke and lover of 'a certain natural allurement'; in story that served as source for *Twelfth Night**
novella 'Of Apolonius and Silla'
Farewell to Militarie Profession (1581) Barnabe Rich

Appin, Cornelius Englishman who teaches animals to speak; killed by elephant in Dresden zoo
ss 'Tobermory'
The Chronicles of Clovis (1911) Saki (rn Hector Hugh Munro)

Appleton, Adam, Sir
The Roaring Girl play (1611) Thomas Middleton and Thomas Dekker

Appleton, Stella Witla's* first love
The Genius (1915) Theodore Dreiser

Appleton, Will
Tom his father
Fred his brother
Kate his sister
ss 'The Sad Horn Blowers'
Horses and Men (1924) Sherwood Anderson

Appleyard, Nick
The Black Arrow (1888) Robert Louis Stevenson

Appolodorus
Caesar and Cleopatra play (1900) George Bernard Shaw

Appolyon 'The foul fiend'
The Pilgrim's Progress (1678–84) John Bunyan

April giant Gullah Negro foreman on a South Carolina cotton plantation
Leah his wife
Breeze one of his many illegitimate children, through whom the tale is told
Black April (1927) Julia Peterkin

Apthorpe fellow officer of Guy Crouchback*
Men at Arms (1952) Evelyn Waugh

Aquila conversational trifler
The Impressions of Theophrastus Such (1879) George Eliot (rn Mary Anne, later Marian, Evans)

Aquila, Felix cc proto-ecological novel of the far distant future in which Great Britain has descended into an age of

barbarism
After London (1885) Richard Jeffries
Arabia, King of
Tamburlaine play (1587) Christopher Marlowe
Arabin, Very Revd Francis Dean of Barchester m. Eleanor Bold *née* Harding*
Barchester Towers (1857) Anthony Trollope
Aram, Eugene (hist.) murderer, cc of a 'Newgate novel'*
Eugene Aram (1832) Edward Bulwer Lytton
Araminta in love with Vainlove*
The Old Bachelor comedy (1793) William Congreve
Araminta wife to Moneytrap,* very intimate with Clarissa*
The Confederacy play (1705) John Vanbrugh
Aramis one of the original three musketeers
Les Trois Mousquetaires (*The Three Musketeers*) (1844); *Vingt ans après* (*Twenty Years After*) (1845); *Le Vicomte de Bragelonne* (*The Viscount of Bragelonne*) (1848–50) Alexandre Dumas (père)
Arane Queen Mother
A King and No King play (1619) Francis Beaumont and John Fletcher
Arb, Mrs confectioner m. Henry Earlforward*
Riceyman's Steps (1923) Arnold Bennett
Arbaces King of Iberia
A King and No King play (1619) Francis Beaumont and John Fletcher
Arble, Eric fruit farmer m. Iseult Smith*
Eva Trout (1969) Elizabeth Bowen
Arbuthnot, Patience, Mrs grandmother of Henrietta Mountjoy*
The House in Paris (1935) Elizabeth Bowen
Arbuthnot, Mrs the woman of no importance, ruined by Lord Illingworth* when he was a young man
Gerald her son
A Woman of No Importance play (1893) Oscar Wilde
Arcati, Madame medium
Blithe Spirit play (1941) Noël Coward
Archbold, Edith, Mrs reformed 'female rake' m. Frank Beverley*

Hard Cash (1863) Charles Reade
Archdale, Alan
Porgy (1925) Du Bose Heyward
Archer 'literary man' and humbug
Pendennis (1848) W. M. Thackeray
Archer 'unworthy friend' to Colonel Mannering*
Guy Mannering (1815) Walter Scott
Archer, Brendan, Major civilized and faithful man in bad circumstances
Troubles (1970); *The Singapore Grip* (1978) J. G. Farrell
Archer, Francis
The Beaux' Stratagem (1707) George Farquhar
Archer, Gloria ex-mistress of James Flitestone*
ss 'The Skeleton'
Blind Love (1969) V. S. Pritchett
Archer, Helen (Mère Marie Hélène)
Henry her father
The Land of Spices (1941) Kate O'Brien
Archer, Isabel American heiress m. Gilbert Osmund*
The Portrait of a Lady (1881) Henry James
Archer, Lew private-eye in mystery novels onwards from
The Moving Target (1949) Ross Macdonald (rn Kenneth Millar)
Archer, Miles Spade's* murdered partner
The Maltese Falcon (1930) Dashiell Hammett
Archer, Mrs malevolent servant
The Lifted Veil (1879) George Eliot (rn Mary Anne, later Marian, Evans)
Archer, Newland m. May Welland* in novel of an 1870s New York marriage afflicted by high society
Dallas his son
The Age of Innocence (1920) Edith Wharton
Archibald, John groom of the Chambers to the Duke of Argyll*
Heart of Midlothian (1818) Walter Scott
Archidamus a Bohemian lord
A Winter's Tale play (1623) William Shakespeare
Archie, Howard, Dr friend and advisor to Thea Kronborg*
The Song of the Lark (1915) Willa Cather
archy typing cockroach in popular light

verse, onwards from
archy and mehitabel† verse (1927) Don
Marquis
Arcite one of the two noble kinsmen, both
being in love with Emelia*
The Two Noble Kinsmen play (1634)
William Shakespeare and John Fletcher
(?with Francis Beaumont)
Arcoll, James, Captain
Prester John (1910) John Buchan
Ardale, Hugh, Captain former lover of
Paula Tanqueray*
The Second Mrs Tanqueray play (1893)
A. W. Pinero
Ardell, Sergeant
The Basic Training of Pavlo Hummel
play (1973) David W. Rabe
Arden, Julia schoolmate of Catherine
Furze*
Catherine Furze (1893) Mark Ruther-
ford (rn William Hale White)
Ardorix of Curdun, Guemoné his wife and
children
Caltane his cousin
The Conquered (1923) Naomi Mitchison
Arena, Mary engaged to Marcus
Macauley*
The Human Comedy (1943) William
Saroyan
Aresby, Captain
Cecilia (1782) Fanny Burney
Arethusa daughter to the king
Philaster (1620) Francis Beaumont and
John Fletcher
Aretus eunuch promoted into the service of
Valentinian*
Valentinian play (1647) John Fletcher
Aretus tutor to Palador*
The Lover's Melancholy play (1629)
John Ford
Argallo, Felix 'a genius for pity'
ss 'Argallo and Ledgett'
Seven Men (1919) Max Beerbohm
Argeleon favourite to Polydamus*
Marriage à la Mode play (1673) John
Dryden
Argentine, Lord Helen Vaughan's* victim
The Great God Pan (1894) Arthur
Machen
Argento, Stiano Sicilian refugee from
fascism
his wife and daughter
The Ship and the Flame (1948) Jerre

Mangione
Argier, King of
Tamburlaine play (1590) Christopher
Marlowe
Argyll, Duke of
Heart of Midlothian (1818) Walter
Scott
Arhoonilo, the Great once famous prophet
from the planet Desagroanskrad
*All and Everything: Beelzebub's Tales to
His Grandson* (1950) G. I. Gurdjieff
Ariel an air spirit
The Tempest play (1612) William Shake-
speare
Arkansas, the Big Bear of unhuntable bear
in Southwest tall story
ss 'The Big Bear of Arkansas' (1841)
The Hive of the Bee Hunter (1854) T. B.
Thorpe
Armadale, Allan refers to no less than five
characters, in complexly plotted psycho-
logical thriller which is nonetheless only a
little behind the author's two more
widely acknowledged masterpieces
Armadale (1866) Wilkie Collins
Armado, Don Adriano a fantastical Span-
iard
Love's Labour's Lost play (1623)
William Shakespeare
Armine, 'Uncle'
Bella his wife
ss 'A Madonna of the Trenches'
Debits and Credits (1926) Rudyard Kipl-
ing
Armine, Ferdinand reckless soldier in debt
who becomes engaged to Henrietta
Temple*, whom he loves, and to
Katherine Grandison*, his cousin, for her
wealth; m. Henrietta Temple
Henrietta Temple: A Love Story (1837)
Benjamin Disraeli
Armitage, Humphrey
Ethel his daughter
ss 'A Capitalist'
The House of Cobwebs (1906) George
Gissing
Armitage, Jacob servant and friend to the
Beverleys*
The Children of the New Forest (1847)
Captain Marryat
Armitage, Leonard blind lawyer
ss 'Blind Love'
Blind Love (1969) V. S. Pritchett

Armitage, Mr mill owner
his six daughters
Shirley (1849) Charlotte Brontë
Armostes a counsellor of state
The Broken Heart play (1633) John Ford
Armsby, Mrs
ss 'Tea at Mrs Armsby's'
The Owl in the Attic (1931) James
Thurber
Armstrong companion to Richard Wade*
and John Brent*
John Brent (1862) Theodore Winthrop
Armstrong wealthy client of Robert
Dempster*
ss 'Janet's Repentance'
Scenes of Clerical Life (1857) George
Eliot (rn Mary Anne, later Marian,
Evans)
Armstrong, Archie court jester
The Fortunes of Nigel (1822) Walter
Scott
Armstrong, Grace m. Hobbie Elliot*
The Black Dwarf (1816) Walter Scott
Armstrong, Jane m. Stephen Monk*
The World in the Evening (1954) Chris-
topher Isherwood
Armstrong, Kate journalist cc
The Middle Ground (1980) Margaret
Drabble
Armstrong, Robert farming student, ex-
drunkard, of vile temper, m. Rhoda
Fleming*
Rhoda Fleming (1865) George Meredith
Arnheim, Baron and Baroness von grand-
parents of Anne*
Sybilla their daughter
Anne of Geierstein (1829) Walter Scott
Arnold, Ida
Tom her husband
Brighton Rock (1938) Graham Greene
Arnold, J. trusted servant turned spy
Pamela, or *Virtue Rewarded* (1740–1)
Samuel Richardson
Arnold, Madeline in love with Gordon
Leeds*
Strange Interlude play (1927) Eugene
O'Neill
Arnold, Michael
Julie *née* Hempel his wife
Eugene their son
Paula their daughter m. Theodore
Storm*
So Big (1924) Edna Ferber

Arnold, Mr and Mrs temporary hosts to
the Primrose* family
The Vicar of Wakefield (1766) Oliver
Goldsmith
Arnolphe middle-aged jealous guardian of
Agnes*
L'École des Femmes (*The School for
Wives*) (1662) Molière (rn Jean-Baptiste
Poquelin)
Arnott, Mrs sister of Mrs May*
The Daisy Chain (1856) Charlotte M.
Yonge
Arnott, Priscilla
Cecilia (1782) Fanny Burney
Arnoux, M. shady art dealer, and, later,
owner of a factory turning out china
Marie his wife, loved by Moreau* and in
love with him
their baby
L'Education sentimentale (1869) Gust-
ave Flaubert
Arowhena daughter of Nosnibor*
Erewhon (1872) Samuel Butler
Arpajon, Mother Superior of unnamed
lesbian nun who seduces Suzanne Simo-
nin* but is then driven mad by the latter's
refusal to consent to her demands
La Religieuse (*The Nun*) (1796) Denis
Diderot
Arragon, Prince of unsuccessful suitor of
Portia*
The Merchant of Venice play (1623)
William Shakespeare
Arrow, Mr member of crew of *Hispaniola*
Treasure Island (1883) Robert Louis
Stevenson
Arrowhead Tuscarora Indian
The Pathfinder (1840) James Fenimore
Cooper
Arrowpoint a 'perfect gentleman'
his wife
Catherine their daughter m. Julius
Klesmer*
Daniel Deronda (1876) George Eliot (rn
Mary Anne, later Marian, Evans)
Arrowsmith, Martin, Dr cc with a passion
for what was then called 'pure science';
m. (2) Joyce Lanyon*
Leora *née* Tozer his first wife
Arrowsmith (1925) Sinclair Lewis
Arsene man who mysteriously appears
Watt (1953) Samuel Beckett
Arsenio friend to Leandro*

The Spanish Curate play (1647) John
Fletcher and Philip Massinger
Artemidorus a sophist
Julius Caesar play (1623) William Shakespeare
Artemis, Melissa Greek dancer and prostitute
The Alexandria Quartet (1957–61)
Lawrence Durrell
Arthur nephew to King John*
King John play (1623) William Shakespeare
Arthur, George new boy, protégé of Tom Brown*
Tom Brown's Schooldays (1857)
Thomas Hughes
Arthur, King (hist.; legd.) cc set of medieval romances written up in extremely influential form (e.g. Spenser*, Tennyson) by knight of whom little is known except that he died in jail
Le Morte d'Arthur (c. 1469) Thomas Malory
Arthuret, Misses Seraphina and Angelica 'the Vestals of Fair-ladies'
Redgauntlet (1824) Walter Scott
Artie brash good-hearted young man created in humorous columns of the Chicago Morning News and later in the Record
Artie (1896) George Ade
Artie not totally incorrect perception of the compiler of this dictionary when at a tender stage of development
The Island (1963) Robert Creeley
Arundel, Lewis cc
Rose his sister, m. Richard Frere*
Lewis Arundel (1852) F. E. Smedley
Arundel, Myra
Hay Fever play (1925) Noël Coward
Arviragus (Cadwal) Cymbeline's* son
Cymbeline play (1623) William Shakespeare
Asano Japanese attendant on Graham*
When the Sleeper Wakes (1899) H. G. Wells
Asbury romantic invalid
Mary George his sister
ss 'The Enduring Chill'
Everything That Rises Must Converge (1965) Flannery O'Connor
Ascanio son to Don Henrique by Jacintha*
The Spanish Curate play (1647) John

Fletcher and Philip Massinger
Aschenbach, Gustav von writer cc
Der Tod in Venedig (Death in Venice) (1913) Thomas Mann
Ashburnam, Edward ('Teddy'), Captain good soldier, Hampshire magistrate, landowner and compulsive pursuer of women
Leonora, née Powys his wife
The Good Soldier (1915) Ford Madox Ford
Ashburton, Mr becomes MP for Carlingford
Miss Marjoribanks (1866) Mrs Margaret Oliphant
Ashby, Thomas, Sir brutal husband to Rosalie Murray*
Agnes Grey (1847) Anne Brontë
Ashcroft, Mrs
Arthur her grandson
ss 'The Wish House'
Debits and Credits (1926) Rudyard Kipling
Ashe, William heir to title of Tranmore; modelled on Lord Melbourne; m. Lady Kitty Bristol*
The Marriage of William Ashe (1905) Mrs Humphry Ward
Asher, Owen, Sir 'Berkeley Square hedonist' in love with Evelyn Innes*
Evelyn Innes (1898) George Moore
Ashford, Nettie 'aged half-past six', author of the romance of Mrs Orange and Mrs Alicumpane
A Holiday Romance (1868) Charles Dickens
Ashiata Shiemash one of the Highest Most Very Saintly common-cosmic Sacred Individuals
All and Everything: Beelzebub's Tales to His Grandson (1950) G. I. Gurdjieff
Ashley, Henry unpleasant and scheming writer, cc
Rogue Elephant (1946) Walter Allen
Ashley, Rachel enigmatic heroine by adroit romantic author
My Cousin Rachel (1951) Daphne du Maurier
Ashted, Billy old narrator of his life
All in a Lifetime; in America as Threescore and Ten (1959) Walter Allen
Ashton, Roland
Hester (1883) Mrs Margaret Oliphant

Ashton, William, Sir lawyer and politician
The Bride of Lammermoor (1819)
Walter Scott
Ashurst, Frank
Stella his wife
ss 'The Apple-Tree'
Five Tales (1918) John Galsworthy
Asiman, Brother the alchemist
All and Everything: Beelzebub's Tales to His Grandson (1950) G. I. Gurdjieff
Askerton, Colonel
Mary his wife
The Belton Estate (1866) Anthony Trollope
Askew cousin to Lacy*
The Shoemaker's Holiday (1600) Thomas Dekker
Asotus representing the vice of prodigality
Cynthia's Revels, or The Fountain of Self-Love play (1601) Ben Jonson
Aspent, Caroline m. Ned Hipcroft*
ss 'The Fiddler of the Reels'
Life's Little Ironies (1894) Thomas Hardy
Asper the presenter, 'without fear controlling the world's abuses'
Every Man Out of His Humour play (1599) Ben Jonson
Aspern, Jeffry deceased early 19th-century American romantic poet whose letters to his mistress are sought from latter, Miss Bordereau*, by editor who narrates the tale
The Aspern Papers (1888) Henry James
Aspinall, Laurence wily rival to Jabez Clegg*, m. Augusta Aston*, but dies
The Manchester Man (1876) Mrs G. Linnaeus Banks
Asprey, Mr cc old man leaving his house
ss 'The House'
The Wind Blows Over (1936) Walter de la Mare
Assarachus brother to King Brutus* and Corineus*
Locrine play (1595) 'W. S.' (?George Peele; ?Robert Green)
Assher, Lady widow of Sir John
Beatrice her daughter, beautiful and cold-hearted engaged to Anthony Whybrow*
ss 'Mr Gilfil's Love Story'
Scenes of Clerical Life (1857) George Eliot (rn Mary Anne, later Marian,

Evans)
Astarte, Queen of the Ansaray
Tancred (1847) Benjamin Disraeli
Aston, Mr small-ware manufacturer
Augusta his daughter, m. (1) Laurence Aspinall*, (2) Jabez Clegg*
The Manchester Man (1976) Mrs G. Linnaeus Banks
Astrea 'investigator' (with a bow to Mrs Behn*) of 'customs' on 'Mediterranean' island (i.e. England) in underrated satirical scandal-novel written with poker-faced moral indignation; when the first part was suppressed (and the publishers arrested for libel) the author asserted that she was unaware that her characters had any resemblance to real people, although she had issued a 'key'
Secret Memoirs and Manners of Several Persons of Quality of Both Sexes from the New Atlantis, an Island in the Mediterranean (1709)
Memoirs of Europe, Towards the Close of the Eighth Century (1710) Mrs Delarivière Manley (Also known as Mary Manley)
Astrée ('Dike') beloved of Céladon*, cc
L'Astrée (1607–27) Honoré d'Urfé
Astutio a counsellor of state
The Maid of Honour play (1632) Philip Massinger
Asunción, Josefa de la
The Revenge for Love (1937) Wyndham Lewis
Atarnakh Kurd philosopher who wrote *Why do Wars Occur on the Earth?*; truly learned though very proud and self loving, he revived the ancient custom of sacrificial offerings
All and Everything: Beelzebub's Tales to His Grandson (1950) G. I. Gurdjieff
Atheist
The Pilgrim's Progress (1678–84) John Bunyan
Atheist, The
The Adventures of David Simple (1744–53) Sarah Fielding
Athelney, Thorpe good friend to Philip Carey*
Betty his 'unmarried wife'
Sally the one of their nine children who m. Philip Carey*
Of Human Bondage (1915) W. Somerset

Maugham

Athos one of the original three musketeers
Les Trois Mousquetaires (*The Three Musketeers*) (1844); *Vingt ans après* (*Twenty Years After*) (1845); *Le Vicomte de Bragelonne* (*The Viscount of Bragelonne*) (1848–50) Alexandre Dumas (père)

Athelstane King of England
Agripyne his daughter
Old Fortunatus play (1600) Thomas Dekker

Athena Goddess of Wisdom
The Orestia trilogy of tragedies (458 BC) Aeschylus

Athulf son to Melveric
Death's Jest Book, or *The Fool's Tragedy* play (1850) Thomas Lovell Beddoes

Atkins, Miss whom Harley* rescues from a brothel
The Man of Feeling (1771) Henry Mackenzie

Atkins, Ruth unhappy wife of Robert Mayo*
Beyond the Horizon play (1920) Eugene O'Neill

Attentive, Mr friend of Mr Wiseman*
The Life and Death of Mr Badman (1680) John Bunyan

Attlee, Joe cc and hero
Lord Kilgoblin (1872) Charles Lever

Aubreys, the family cheated of inheritance by Quirk*, Gammon* and Snap*, and by Tittlebat Titmouse*, in early Dickensian sensation novel* also influenced by Hook*
Ten Thousand a Year (1841) Samuel Warren

Aucassin yellow-haired youth in famous 13th-century French *cante-fable*: the story goes back at least to Byzantine times (e.g. *Flore et Blanchefleur*)
Aucassin and Nicolette Anon.

Auclaire, Euclide Parisian apothecary who goes to Canada at end of 17th century
Cecile, his daughter
Shadows on The rock (1932) Willa Cather

Audley, Michael, Sir, Baronet
Lady Audley his supposed wife, legally Mrs George Talbot, originally calling herself **Lucy Graham**, murderess in novel admired by Thackeray* and Hardy*
Lady Audley's Secret (1862) Mary Elizabeth Braddon

Augusta German seamstress who saves Professor St Peter's* life
The Professor's House (1925) Willa Cather

Aurelia cousin to Graciana*, in love with Col. Bruce*
The Comical Revenge, or *Love in a Tub* play (1664) George Etherege

Aurelia daughter to Count Ferneze and sister to Lord Paulo* and Phoenixella*
The Case is Altered play (1609) Ben Jonson

Aurelia Duchess of Siena
The Maid of Honour play (1632) Philip Massinger

Aurelian accomplished young Florentine
Don Fabio his father
Incognita (1692) William Congreve

Aurigans, The strange beings from outer space
The Saliva Tree (1966) Brian W. Aldiss

Aurore Eugénie Besançon's* slave. m. Rutherford*
The Quadroon (1856) Thomas Mayne Reid
The Octoroon play (1859) Dion Boucicault

Austin, Jinny jealous cc: 'I want to be Brunhilde, and I'm only Frou-Frou!'
Jack her husband
The Girl With the Green Eyes play (1905) Clyde Fitch

Avarice
Pierce Penilesse his Supplication to the Devil (1592) Thomas Nashe

Avenal, Mary see **Glendenning, Halbert, Sir**

Axelrod, Moe one-legged war veteran, lover of Hennie Berger*
Awake and Sing! play (1935) Clifford Odets

Aylmer misguided perfectionist scientist who removes birthmark from face of
Georgiana his wife who dies
ss 'The Birthmark'
Mosses from an Old Manse (1846) Nathaniel Hawthorne

Aylmer, M. P., Captain boring cousin to Clara Amedroz* to whom she is betrothed but finally rejects
Lady Aylmer his unpleasant and con-

descending mother
The Belton Estate (1866) Anthony Trollope

Aylmers, The agreeable family
Mansfield Park (1814) Jane Austen

Ayloffe, Captain (hist. executed for his part in Rye House Plot, 1685); it is unlikely that the letters published as by him were in fact his: in them we 'detect the beginning of the revolt against the gallant game of love'
Letters of Wit, Politicks and Morality . . . (1701) Abel Boyer (editor)

Aylwin, Henry cc
Aylwin (1899) Theodore Watts-Dunton

Azrielke, Rabbi
Der Dibuk (*The Dybbuk*) play (1918) S. Ansky (rn Shloyome Zanvil Rappoport)

B

B, Squire would-be seducer of Pamela Andrews*
Dacre, Lady his sister
Pamela, or Virtue Rewarded (1740–1) Samuel Richardson
Bårdsson, Erle Skule self-questioning pretender to Norwegian throne; killed by mob
Margaret his daughter m. Håkon Håkonsson
Kongs-emmnerne (The Pretenders) play (1863) Henrik Ibsen
B. de, M. whose mistress Manon Lescaut* becomes
Manon Lescaut (1731, rev. 1753) Abbé Prévost
Baba, Hajji, of Isaphan
Hajji Baba (1824) J. J. Morier
Babalatchi, Mahmat head of Almayer's* household
Almayer's Folly (1895) Joseph Conrad (rn Josef Teodor Konrad Korzeniowski)
Babberley, Fancourt, Lord undergraduate
Charley's Aunt stage farce (1892) Brandon Thomas
Babbie, Lady ('The Egyptian')
The Little Minister (1891) J. M. Barrie
Babbitt, George Folansbee real-estate agent, hopelessly middle class, who gave a name to the language
Myra *née* Thompson his wife
Verona their daughter m. Kenneth Escott*
Theodore Roosevelt ('Ted') their son m. Eunice Littlefield*
Katherine ('Tinka') their younger daughter
Babbitt† (1923) Sinclair Lewis
Babley, Richard always known as **Mr Dick**; amiable old gentleman
David Copperfield (1850) Charles Dickens
Babo servant to Benito Cereno*, who leads a mutiny, foiled by his master, and is eventually executed

ss 'Benito Cereno'
The Piazza Tales (1856) Herman Melville
Babraham, Henry, Marquess of, ('The Emir') m. Jane Palfrey
Antigua Penny Puce (1936) Robert Graves
Babulo a clown, servant to Janicola*
The Pleasant Commedye of Patient Grissill play (1603) Thomas Dekker
Backbite, Benjamin, Sir
The School for Scandal play (1777) Richard Brinsley Sheridan
Backystopper coachman to Lady Kew
The History of Pendennis: His Fortunes and Misfortunes, His Friends and His Greatest Enemy (1850) W. M. Thackeray
Bacon publisher; partner and then rival to Bungay
The History of Pendennis: His Fortunes and Misfortunes, His Friends and His Greatest Enemy (1850) W. M. Thackeray
Bacurius a lord
A King and No King (1619) Francis Beaumont (mainly) and John Fletcher
Baddeley Sir Thomas Bertram's* butler
Mansfield Park (1814) Jane Austen
Badebec mother to Pantagruel*
Gargantua, Pantagruel, Tiers Quart, Quart Part (1532–54) François Rabelais
Badge, Miss daughter of a wealthy soap-boiler
The Virginians (1857–9) W. M. Thackeray
Badger, Bayham, Dr Kenge's* cousin
Laura his wife, previously twice widowed
Bleak House (1853) Charles Dickens
Badger, Mr a badger
The Wind in the Willows (1908) Kenneth Grahame
Badger, Will huntsman and servant of Sir Hugh Rosbart*
Kenilworth (1821) Walter Scott

Badgery, Edmund, Lord
ss 'The Tillotson Banquet'
Mortal Coils (1922) Aldous Huxley
Badman, Mr eldest and wickedest of family, cc
The Life and Death of Mr Badman (1680) John Bunyan
Bagarag, Shibli chief barber to the court of Persia
The Shaving of Shagpat (1856) George Meredith
Bagenhall, James friend of Sir Hargrave Pollexfen*
Sir Charles Grandison (1754) Samuel Richardson
Bagg, Miss heiress with whom Towrowski* eloped
The Book of Snobs (1847) W. M. Thackeray
Baggins, Bilbo finder of the One Ring
Frodo his young kinsman and heir
The Lord of the Rings (1954–5) J. R. R. Tolkien
Baglione, Paulo uncle to the Duchess Bianca of Pavia*
Love's Sacrifice play (1633) John Ford
Baglioni, Pietro student who tries to save Beatrice Rappaccini* from results of her father Giacomo's* experimentation
ss 'Rappaccini's Daughter' 1844
Mosses from an Old Manse (1846) Nathaniel Hawthorne
Bagnet, Matthew ex-artilleryman and owner of music shop
Mrs Bagnet his wife
Malta, Quebec their daughters
Woolwich their son
Bleak House (1853) Charles Dickens
Bagot creature to the King
King Richard II play (1623) William Shakespeare
Bagot, William ('Little Billie') art student
Mrs Bagot his mother, m. Sandy McAllister*
Blanche Bagot his sister
The Revd T. Bagot his uncle
Trilby (1894) George du Maurier
Bagshaw, Cyril Boom, Revd
If Winter Comes (1921) A. S. M. Hutchinson
Bagshot highwayman
The Beaux' Stratagem play (1707) George Farquhar

Bagshot MP for a Norfolk borough
The Newcomes (1853–5) W. M. Thackeray
Bagster Whig MP for Middlemarch
Middlemarch (1871–2) George Eliot (rn Mary Anne, later Marian, Evans)
Bagster, Florrie
Hilda Lessways (1911) Arnold Bennett
Bagster, Freddie in love with Helen Rolt*
The Heart of the Matter (1948) Graham Greene
Bagstock, Major
Dombey and Son (1848) Charles Dickens
Baguenault, Michael
Catherine his half-sister
Seven Poor Men of Sydney (1934) Christina Stead
Bahadur Khan Imray's* servant and murderer
ss 'The Return of Imray'
Life's Handicap (1891) Rudyard Kipling
Bailey, Captain
David Copperfield (1850) Charles Dickens
Bailey, Master bailiff in second-oldest English comedy
Gammer Gurton's Needle play (1575) ?William Stevenson
Bailey, Oscar political journalist
Altiora his wife
The New Machiavelli (1911) H. G. Wells
Bailey, Thomas cc of partly autobiographical novel
The Story of a Bad Boy (1870) Thomas Bailey Aldrich
Baillie, A. and his family
The Pickwick Papers (1837) Charles Dickens
Baillie, Gabriel (known also as Faa, or Tod or Hunter Gabbie)
Giles his father
Guy Mannering (1815) Walter Scott
Baines of Holly & Baines, Newcome's* bankers
Euphemia; Flora his daughters
The Newcomes (1853–5) W. M. Thackeray
Baines, Constance m. Samuel Povey*
Sophia her sister m. Gerald Scales*, later known as Mrs Frensham, keeper of a boarding-house in Paris
John their father, draper of Bursley
The Old Wives' Tale (1908) Arnold

Bennett
Baines, Mrs
Major Barbara play (1905) George Bernard Shaw
Bains, Lulu Elmer Gantry's* mistress
Elmer Gantry (1927) Sinclair Lewis
Baird, Angus fence and blackmailer
Raffles (1899–1901) E. W. Hornung
Baird, Revd Mr
ss 'The Sad Fortunes of the Rev. Amos Barton'
Scenes of Clerical Life (1857) George Eliot (rn Mary Anne, later Marian, Evans)
Bajazet
Tamerlane play (1701) Nicholas Rowe
Bajazeth Turkish emperor
Zabina his wife
Tamburlaine play (1587) Christopher Marlowe
Baker, Henry and his wife
ss 'The Blue Carbuncle'
The Adventures of Sherlock Holmes (1892) Arthur Conan Doyle
Baker, Jordan Nick Carraway's* girl
The Great Gatsby (1925) F. Scott Fitzgerald
Baker, Lady widow, mother-in-law of Lovel*
Captain Clarence her son
Lovel the Widower (1860) W. M. Thackeray
Baker, Tom, Lieutenant
The Cruel Sea (1951) Nicholas Monsarrat
Baker, Steve actor m. Julie Dozier*
Show Boat (1926) Edna Ferber
Bakewell, Thomas ploughman accused of arson
The Ordeal of Richard Feverel: A History of Father and Son (1859, rev. 1878) George Meredith
Balaam and his wife
The Virginian (1902) Owen Wister
Balchristie, Janet, Mrs mistress of the Laird of Dumbledikes*
Heart of Midlothian (1818) Walter Scott
Balcombe, Caroline, Lady Secretary of State for Foreign Affairs
But Soft – We are Observed! (1928) Hilaire Belloc
Balderstone, Caleb sole manservant of the Ravenswood* family

The Bride of Lammermoor (1819) Walter Scott
Balderstone, T.
Sketches by Boz (1836) Charles Dickens
Baldock, Lord
his wife; onwards from
Phineas Finn† (1869) Anthony Trollope
Baldrick Saxon hero
Vanda his wife
The Betrothed (1825) Walter Scott
Baldringham, Lady of (Ermengarde)
The Betrothed (1825) Walter Scott
Baldry, Captain Chris
Kitty his wife
Oliver their dead son
Jenny his cousin
The Return of the Soldier (1918) Rebecca West (rn Cecily Fairfield)
Baldwin, Admirable a deplorable-looking personage, looks sixty but is only forty
Persuasion (1818) Jane Austen
Baldwin, George lawyer
Cicely his wife
Manhattan Transfer (1925) John Dos Passos
Balfour of Kinloch, John leader of the army of the Covenanters
Old Mortality (1816) Walter Scott
Balfour of Pilrig cousin of David Balfour*
Catriona (1893) Robert Louis Stevenson
Balfour of Shaws, David cc and narrator m. Catriona Drummond*
Alexander his father
Ebenezer his uncle
Kidnapped† (1886) Robert Louis Stevenson
Balibari, Chevalier de assumed name of uncle of Barry Lyndon*, cardsharper
The Luck of Barry Lyndon (1844 in *Fraser's Magazine*) as *The Memoirs of Barry Lyndon, by Himself* (1852) W. M. Thackeray
Balim, Mr
Sketches of Young Gentlemen (1838) Charles Dickens
Baliol, Martha Bethune whose recollections Chrystal Croftangry* draws upon
The Chronicles of the Canongate (*The Fair Maid of Perth, The Two Drovers* and *The Highland Widow*) (1827) Walter Scott
Balkan, Max young Jewish misfit in minor classic of the Depression in New York

Homage to Blenholt (1936) Daniel Fuchs

Balkis Solomon's Queen
ss 'The Butterfly that Stamped'
Just So Stories (1902) Rudyard Kipling

Ball, John, Sir m. (1) Rachel, (2) Margaret
Mackenzie*
Jack his son – and three sisters
Lady Ball his mother, aunt to Margaret
Mackenzie
Miss Mackenzie (1863) Anthony
Trollope

Balladino, Antonio pageant poet
The Case is Altered play (1609) Ben
Jonson

Ballam, Thomas
ss 'The Distracted Preacher'
Wessex Tales (1888) Thomas Hardy

Ballantrae see **Durrisdeer**

Ballenger, Major
Jorrocks's Jaunts and Jollities (1838) R.
S. Surtees

Ballenkeiroch clansman of Fergus McIvor
Waverley (1814) Walter Scott

Ballinger, Mrs member of the Lunch Club,
a ladies' literary discussion group
ss 'Xingu'
Roman Fever (1911) Edith Wharton

Balliol, the Misses friends to Clive
Newcome*
The Newcomes (1853–5) W. M.
Thackeray

Baloo the Brown bear, teacher of Mowgli*
Jungle Books (1894–5) Rudyard Kipling

Balthasar see **Portia**

Balthazar
The Spanish Tragedy play (1592)
Thomas Kyd

Balthazar man known to the police only
under this 'terrible pseudonym', with a
'terrific penis' that makes him especially
popular with the ladies
Voyage au bout de la nuit (*Journey to the
End of Night*) (1932) Louis-Ferdinand
Céline (rn Louis-Ferdinand Destouches)

Balthazar merchant
A Comedy of Errors play (1623) William
Shakespeare

Balthazar servant to Don Pedro*
Much Ado About Nothing play (1623)
William Shakespeare

Balthazar servant to Romeo*
Romeo and Juliet play (1623) William
Shakespeare

Balthazar, S. Jewish doctor and mystic
The Alexandria Quartet (1957–61)
Lawrence Durrell

Balue, John of Cardinal and Bishop of
Auxerre
Quentin Durward (1823) Walter Scott

Balveeny, Lord Kinsman to the Earl of
Douglas
The Fair Maid of Perth (1828) Walter
Scott

Balwhidder, Micah solemn self-important
Ayrshire parish minister narrator; from
this novel John Stuart Mill adopted the
term 'utilitarianism'
Betty *née* Lanshaw his first wife
Lizy *née* Lubbock his second wife
Mrs Nugent widow, his third wife
Annals of the Parish (1821) John Galt

Bamber, Jack attorney's clerk
The Pickwick Papers (1837) Charles
Dickens

Bambini, Doctor
*All and Everything: Beelzebub's Tales to
His Grandson* (1950) G. I. Gurdjieff

Bamboo Miami Mouth's* fisherman
lover; eaten by a shark
Prancing Nigger (1924) Ronald Firbank

Bamborough, Lord 'Descendant of the
Hotspurs'
The Virginians (1857–9) W. M.
Thackeray

Bambridge horse dealer
Middlemarch (1871–2) George Eliot (rn
Mary Anne, later Marian, Evans)

Bamforth, Rosina (Rozzy) one of
Jimson's* 'wives'; onwards from
Herself Surprised† (1941) Joyce Cary

Ban, King of Benwick father to Launcelot*
Le Morte D'Arthur (1485) Thomas Malory

Banahan, Catherine mistress to Studs
Lonigan*
The Studs Lonigan trilogy (1932–5)
James T. Farrell

Band second woman
The Staple of News play (1631) Ben
Jonson

Bandar-Log, The monkey-people, vain
and empty-headed
Jungle Books (1894–5) Rudyard Kipling

Bandello, Pico ('Little Caesar') prohibition
gangster in early hard-boiled novel
Little Caesar (1929) W. R. Burnett

Bando, Dai miner and boxer, friend of Huw Morgan*
How Green Was My Valley (1939) Richard Llewellyn

Banford, Miss cc killed by Grenfel*, half purposely
ss 'The Fox'
The Captain's Doll (1923) (in UK, *The Ladybird*) D. H. Lawrence

Bangham, Mrs charwoman
Little Dorrit (1857) Charles Dickens

Banghurst unscrupulous journalist
ss 'Filmer'†
Twelve Stories and a Dream (1903) H. G. Wells

Bangs, Tommy m. Dora West*
Little Men (1871); *Jo's Boys* (1886) Louisa M. Alcott

Bantext, Salathiel, Captain 'a godly gentleman'
Heart of Midlothian (1818) Walter Scott

Banjo, Burton leader of a pop group
Army his brother, guitarist
Barefoot in the Head (1969) Brian W. Aldiss

Bankes, William elderly scientist
To the Lighthouse (1927) Virginia Woolf

Banks bailiff to Sir H. Mallinger*
Daniel Deronda (1876) George Eliot (rn Mary Anne, later Marian, Evans)

Banks miller of Waltham in comedy once ascribed to Shakespeare*
The Merry Devil of Edmonton play (1608) ?Thomas Dekker

Banks trampled to death by horses
Margaret his wife, the beating to death of whom, with a truncheon, brings Thick* to orgasm
The Lime Twig (1961) John Hawkes

Banks, Joey
Pilgrimage (1915–38) Dorothy M. Richardson

Banks, Major (alias **Meltham**) old East India director
Hunted Down (1860) Charles Dickens

Banks, Randy Black Councilman in American town
The Grand Parade (1961) Julian Mayfield

Bannal
Fanny's First Play play (1905) George Bernard Shaw

Bannerbridge lawyer

The Adventures of Harry Richmond (1871) George Meredith

Bannerman, Alec
ss 'The Man Who was Unlucky With Women'
Unlucky for Pringle (1973) Wyndham Lewis

Bannerman, Mabel friend to Sylvia Scarlett*
Sylvia Scarlett (1918) Compton Mackenzie

Bannister actor at Budmouth theatre
The Trumpet Major (1880) Thomas Hardy

Bannmann, Baroness acrid characterization of German leader of woman's movement
Is He Popenjoy? (1878) Anthony Trollope

Banquo general of King Duncan's* army
Macbeth play (1623) William Shakespeare

Bantam, Angelo Cyrus
The Pickwick Papers (1837) Charles Dickens

Bantam, Hong Kong, Sir
The Impressions of Theophrastus Such (1879) George Eliot (rn Mary Anne, later Marian, Evans)

Baps dancing master at Dr Blimber's*
Dombey and Son (1848) Charles Dickens

Baptsita rich gentleman of Padua, father to Katharine* and Bianca*
The Taming of the Shrew play (1623) William Shakespeare

Barabas cc, rich Jew in tragi-farce
Abigail his daughter
The Jew of Malta play (1633) Christopher Marlowe

Barabbas swindler
The Impressions of Theophrastus Such (1879) George Eliot (rn Mary Anne, later Marian, Evans)

Baran, Tomek forester cc of characteristic novella by Polish author
Tomek Baran (1897) Wladyslaw Reymont

Barban, Tommy war hero
Tender Is the Night (1934) F. Scott Fitzgerald

Barbara the Garlands' maid, m. Kit Nubbles*
her mother

The Old Curiosity Shop (1841) Charles Dickens

Bárbara, Doña cc seminal Venezuelan novel: barbaric ruler of a large domain, on the *llanos*, who believes that she possesses supernatural powers: in part a caricature of the mad dictator Juan Vicente Gómez; later the author, who wrote other fiction, became democratic president, but was deposed
Doña Bárbara (1929) Rómulo Gallegos

Barbary, Miss aunt and godmother of Esther Summerson*
Bleak House (1853) Charles Dickens

Barbason, Claude Colin March's* rival in the army
ss 'Honours Easy'
Fiery Particles (1923) C. E. Montague

Barber, Nicol friend to Dorothy Glover*
The Fair Maid of Perth (1828) Walter Scott

Barber, Tom cc of trilogy by gifted Ulster novelist
Uncle Stephen (1931); *The Retreat* (1934); *Young Tom* (1944) (all three together as *Tom Barber*, 1955) Forrest Reid

Barbi, Enrico Ottavia, Marchese
ss 'Bluebeard's Keys'
Bluebeard's Keys (1874) Anne Thackeray

Barbon, 'Nosy' art student
The Horse's Mouth (1944) Joyce Cary

Barclay, James, Colonel
ss 'The Crooked Man'
The Memoirs of Sherlock Holmes (1892) Arthur Conan Doyle

Barclay, Wildred well-known English novelist
The Paper Men (1984) William Golding

Bardamu, Ferdinand cc, narrator, 'only young after the fashion of boils because of the pus that hurts from the inside and swells them up' ('an enormous hatred keeps me alive. I'd live a million years if I could be sure I'd see the world croak' – wrote the author)
Voyage au bout de la nuit (*Journey to the End of Night*) (1932) Louis-Ferdinand Céline (rn Louis-Ferdinand Destouches)

Bardell, Mrs Martha Pickwick's* landlady
Tommy her son
The Pickwick Papers (1837) Charles Dickens

Bardi, Romola de m. Tito Melema*
Bardo her blind father
Bernardino ('Dino') her brother (Fra Luca)
Romola (1863) George Eliot (rn Mary Anne, later Marian, Evans)

Bardolph crony of Falstaff*, tapster at the Garter Inn; later, as a soldier, hanged for looting
The Merry Wives of Windsor, King Henry IV, King Henry V plays (1623) William Shakespeare

Bardon, Hugh scoutmaster to Prince John*
Ivanhoe (1820) Walter Scott

Bardshare, Mr and Mrs
ss 'The Sad Horn Blowers'
Horses and Men (1924) Sherwood Anderson

Bardwell, Olga Jane, Lady freak-show bearded lady with a fourth husband
McSorley's Wonderful Saloon (1943) Joseph Mitchell

Bareacres, Earl of (George) impoverished peer; family name Thistlewood
his wife
Lady Blanche their daughter m. Lord Gaunt*
Lady Angela their daughter m. George Silvertop*
Vanity Fair† (1847–8) W. M. Thackeray

Barentz, Wilhelm captain of the *Vrow Katerina*
The Phantom Ship (1839) Captain Marryat

Barfield, Arthur
his father, 'the gaffer'
Esther Waters (1894) George Moore

Barfield, Major
ss 'Tobemory'
The Chronicles of Clovis (1911) Saki (rn Hector Hugh Munro)

Barfoot, Captain town councillor
Ellen *née* Coppard, his wife
Jacob's Room (1922) Virginia Woolf

Barfoot, Mary gentle feminist; partner to Rhoda Nunn* in management of clerical training school for young women
Everard her cousin, m. Agnes Brissenden*
Tom Everard's dying brother
Tom's wife

The Odd Women (1893) George Gissing

Bargrave, Mrs close friend to Mrs Veal*
ss (pamphlet) 'A True Relation of the Apparition of one Mrs Veal, the next Day after her Death, to one Mrs Bargrave at Canterbury, the 8th of September, 1705' (1706) Daniel Defoe

Barker, Betty
Cranford (1853) Mrs Gaskell

Barker, James, The Hon. Provost of North Kensington
The Napoleon of Notting Hill (1904) G. K. Chesterton

Barker, Jeremiah cab driver
Polly his wife
Black Beauty (1877) Anna Sewell

Barker, Phil
Oliver Twist (1838) Charles Dickens

Barkiarokh, Prince youngest son of a fisherman
Homaiouna his wife, a disguised peri
Vathek (1786) William Beckford

Barkis carrier m. Clara Peggoty*
David Copperfield (1850) Charles Dickens

Barkley, Nurse Catherine cc who dies in childbirth
A Farewell to Arms (1929) Ernest Hemingway

Barlasch, Sergeant cc, French army veteran in once popular novel now to be found only in Army hospitals
Barlasch of the Guard (1903) H. Seton Merriman

Barley, Clara
Old Barley her father
Great Expectations (1861) Charles Dickens

Barley, Daisy (Mrs Fillans) ex-music-hall artiste, landlady Dog and Bell, m. Tommy Tiverton*
Let the People Sing (1939) J. B. Priestley

Barlow, Christine m. Andrew Manson*
The Citadel (1937) A. J. Cronin

Barlow, Edith old writer and friend of Claire Temple*
There Were No Windows (1944) Norah Hoult

Barlow, Mr and Mrs
Love on the Dole (1933) Walter Greenwood

Barlow, Revd Mr tutor to Sandford* and Merton* in novel trying to promote more enlightened methods
Sandford and Merton (1783–9) Thomas Day

Barmby, Samuel Bennett ('The Prophet') self-opinionated and pompous suitor to Nancy Lord*
his father, partner to Stephen Lord*
his mother and sisters
In the Year of Jubilee (1894) George Gissing

Barnabas, Revd Mr
Joseph Andrews (1742) Henry Fielding

Barnaby a hired coachman
The New Inn, or The Light Heart play (1629) Ben Jonson

Barnacle
The Gamester play (1637) James Shirley

Barnacle Family, The
Lord Decimus Tite-Barnacle and others, all of the Circumlocution Office
Little Dorrit (1857) Charles Dickens

Barnaclough, Lady
The Thinking Reed (1936) Rebecca West (rn Cecily Fairfield)

Barnadine a friar
The Jew of Malta play (1633) Christopher Marlowe

Barnard
The Cruel Sea (1951) Nicholas Monsarrat

Bernard, Thomas, Dr friend and guardian of Denis Duval*
his wife
Denis Duval (1861) W. M. Thackeray

Barnardson, Barnard portrait of the art historian Bernard Berenson
Count Florio and Phyllis K. (1910) Reginald Turner

Barnes see **Meats, Henry**

Barnes, George brother to the Earl of Kew*
Lady Julia his sister
The Newcomes (1853–5) W. M. Thackeray

Barnes, Jake American newspaperman in Europe; incapable of sexual intercourse owing to war wound
The Sun Also Rises (in England, *Fiesta*) (1926) Ernest Hemingway

Barnes, Jonathan
Belle; Maddie his daughters
Robbery Under Arms: A Story of Life and Adventure in the Bush and in the

Goldfields of Australia (1888, rev. 1889) Rolf Boldrewood (rn Thomas Alexander Browne)

Barnes, Miss journalist
The Winslow Boy play (1946) Terence Rattigan

Barnes, Mr ('of New York') wealthy American master of every situation in popular novel by English-born engineer and stockbroker
Mr Barnes of New York (1887) Archibald Clavering Gunter

Barnes, Stevie m. Dolly Targett*
The Sailor's Return (1925) David Garnett

Barnes, Will country gallant
Tom Jones (1749) Henry Fielding

Barnet, Frederick infantry officer and wireless employer
The World Set Free (1914) H. G. Wells

Barnet, George gentleman-burgher
his wife
ss 'Fellow Townsman'
Wessex Tales (1888) Thomas Hardy

Barnet, Mr nephew to Lady Allestree*
Sir Charles Grandison (1754) Samuel Richardson

Barney waiter; friend to Fagin*
Oliver Twist (1838) Charles Dickens

Barney, Peg, Private
ss 'The Big Drunk Draf'
Soldiers Three (1888) Rudyard Kipling

Barnstable, Alfred sub-editor, *The Liberal*
Men Like Gods (1923) H. G. Wells

Barois, Jean cc novel by (1937) French winner of Nobel Prize: it covers its period (of the Dreyfus case); and deals with the naturalist* theme of heredity in a new way
Jean Barois (1913) Roger Martin du Gard

Baron, Jack de
Is He Popenjoy? (1878) Anthony Trollope

Baroni Eastern servant to Lord Montacute
Tancred (1847) Benjamin Disraeli

Baroski, Benjamin, Signor ('The Ravenswing')
Men's Wives (1843) W. M. Thackeray

Barr-Saggott, Antony Commissioner
ss 'Cupid's Arrows'
Plain Tales from the Hills (1888) Rudyard Kipling

Barrack, Elihu, Dr of Sundering-on-sea

The Undying Fire (1919) H. G. Wells

Barraclough, Moses hypocritical Methodist preacher with wooden leg; transported
Shirley (1849) Charlotte Brontë

Barralonga, Lord
Men Like Gods (1923) H. G. Wells

Barratter Counsellor, an old Templar
The Fortunes of Nigel (1822) Walter Scott

Barraway, Mrs nurse-secretary to Sir Henry Harcourt-Reilly*
The Cocktail Party play (1950) T. S. Eliot

Barrett, Edward Moulton (hist.), here not accurately but powerfully depicted in successful well-made play*
Elizabeth his daughter m. Robert Browning*
Henrietta her sympathetic younger sister
her six brothers
The Barretts of Wimpole Street play (1930) Rudolf Besier

Barrett, Mr and Mrs
ss 'The Beckoning Fair One'
Widdershins (1911) Oliver Onions

Barrett, Williston Bibb cc, ex-dehumidification engineer with telescope, madman
The Last Gentleman (1966) Walker Percy

Barron, Deacon
Heart of Midlothian (1818) Walter Scott

Barron, Wilkie fortunate opportunist in reconstruction of 19th-century murder case
World Enough and Time (1950) Robert Penn Warren

Barroneau see **Rigaud**

Barry, Redmond Barry Lyndon's* original name
Mrs Barry his mother
Sir Charles diplomat and roué
Barry Lyndon (1852) W. M. Thackeray

Barry, Tom m. Rose Phelan*
Without My Cloak (1931) Kate O'Brien

Barrymore caretaker at Baskerville Hall
his wife, sister to Selden*
The Hound of the Baskervilles (1902) Arthur Conan Doyle

Barsad, John see **Pross, Solomon**

Barstow, Captain see **Fenwicke**

Bartels, Schoffer owner of galliot *Johannes Karl* his son

The Riddle of the Sands (1903) Erskine Childers

Barter, Hussell, Revd rector at Worsted Skeynes
The Country House (1907) John Galsworthy

Barter, Tom Philip Crow's* manager
A Glastonbury Romance (1932) John Cowper Powys

Bartleby scrivener who prefers not to do anything and dies in prison
ss 'Bartleby the Scrivener: A Wall Street Story' (1853)
Piazza Tales (1856) Herman Melville

Bartlett, Miss Charlotte
A Room With a View (1908) E. M. Forster

Bartlett, Mr and Mrs and their family
Crewe Train (1926) Rose Macaulay

Bartolus a lawyer
The Spanish Curate play (1647) John Fletcher and Philip Massinger

Barton, Amos, Rev. commonplace curate of Shepperton
Amelia (Milly) his wife
Frederick; Patty; Sophy; Walter and two others, their children
ss 'The Sad Fortunes of the Rev. Amos Barton'
Scenes of Clerical Life (1857) George Eliot (rn Mary Anne, later Marian, Evans)

Barton, Andrew, Sir pirate gunrunner
ss 'Hal o' the Draft'
Puck of Pook's Hill (1906) Rudyard Kipling

Barton, Arthur artist
Anna: Olive; Alice their daughters, the last-named m. Dr Reed*
A Drama in Muslin (1886) George Moore

Barton, Herminia cc of notorious 'new woman' novel: woman who seeks to emancipate herself from bonds of matrimony
The Dean of Dunwich her father
Dolores her bastard daughter by Alan Merrick*; she becomes a conventional woman
The Woman Who Did (1895) Grant Allen

Barton, Jacob grocer
his wife

Sketches by Boz (1836) Charles Dickens

Barton, Mary cc of one of first novels to deal with factory life; m. Jem Nilson*
John her honest weaver father, a Chartist, who is picked by lot to carry out the assassination of young Carson*
Mary her mother
Mary Barton (1848) Mrs Gaskell

Barton, Mr
Tom Burke of Ours (1844) Charles Lever

Bartram, George nephew to Andrew Vanstone*
Admiral Arthur Bartram his uncle
No Name (1862) Wilkie Collins

Bascombe, Maury L. brother to Mrs Compson*
The Sound and the Fury (1931) William Faulkner

Basil cc narrator, m. Margaret Sherwin*
Ralph his elder brother
Clara his sister
his father, an MP
Basil (1852) Wilkie Collins

Basil changes his name to Mahood
Molloy (1951); *Malone meurt* (*Malone Dies*) (1951) (tr. 1956); *L'Innommable* (1953) (*The Unnamable*) (tr. 1958) trilogy Samuel Beckett

Basil, Mrs
The Good Soldier (1915) Ford Madox Ford

Basildon, Olivia, Lady
An Ideal Husband play (1895) Oscar Wilde

Basilios, Prince
The Gates of Summer play (1956) John Whiting

Basingfield, Eustace old bore
Museum Pieces (1952) William Plomer

Baskerville see Stapleton

Baskerville, Charles, Sir deceased
Sir Henry his nephew and successor
The Hound of the Baskervilles (1902) Arthur Conan Doyle

Basket-Hilts man to Squire Tub
A Tale of a Tub play (1640) Ben Jonson

Bass poacher
Middlemarch (1871–2) George Eliot (rn Mary Anne, later Marian, Evans)

Bassanes a jealous nobleman
The Broken Heart play (1633) John Ford

Bassanio friend to Antonio*, m. Portia*
The Merchant of Venice play (1623)

William Shakespeare
Basset, Antony attorney
  Nelly his niece
  Tom Burke of Ours (1844) Charles Lever
Basset-Holmer, Captain
  ss 'The Man Who Was'
  Life's Handicap (1891) Rudyard Kipling
Bassett gardener, partner with Paul*
  ss 'The Rocking Horse Winner'
  The Lovely Lady (1932) D. H. Lawrence
Bassianus in love with Lavinia*
  Titus Andronicus play (1623) William
  Shakespeare
Bassington, Comus cc
  Francesca his mother
  The Unbearable Bassington (1912) Saki
  (rn Hector Hugh Munro)
Bassompierre, Count father to Paulina
  Home*
  Villette (1853) Charlotte Brontë
Bast, Leonard clerk, lover of Helen
  Schlegel*
  Jacky his mistress and later wife
  Howard's End (1910) E. M. Forster
Bastable, Raymond KC, Sir ('Beefy') m.
  Barbara Crowe*
  Cocktail Time (1958) P. G. Wodehouse
Bastable, Richard
  Dora: Oswald; Dicky; Alice and Noel
  twins **Horace Octavius** (**H.O.**) his children
  The Treasure Seekers (1899); *The
  Would-be-Goods* (1901) E. Nesbit
Bat Burst a broken citizen, and in-and-out-
  man
  The New Inn, or *The Light Heart* play
  (1629) Ben Jonson
Batch, Katie landlady's daughter
  Clarence her brother
  Zuleika Dobson (1911) Max Beerbohm
Batchelor, Barbie retired missionary
  teacher
  The Raj Quartet (1976) Paul Scott
Batchelor, Charles friend to Lovel*
  Lovel the Widower (1860) W. M.
  Thackeray
Bates head of United Services College
  Stalky and Co. (1899) Rudyard Kipling
Bates, Belinda
  ss 'The Haunted House'
  Christmas Stories (1859) Charles
  Dickens
Bates, Bill (Alias **Alan Beverley**) m. Ann-

ette Brougham*
  The Man Upstairs (1914) P. G. Wode-
  house
Bates, Charley one-time pupil to Fagin*
  Oliver Twist (1838) Charles Dickens
Bates, Farmer
  The Hampdenshire Wonder (1911) J. D.
  Beresford
Bates, Hetty happy good-tempered
  woman
  Mrs Bates her mother, widow of Revd
  Bates, Vicar of Highbury and mother of
  Mrs Jane Fairfax*
  Emma (1816) Jane Austen
Bates, Mr surgeon
  Jane Eyre (1847) Charlotte Brontë
Bates, William m. Jane Packard*
  ss 'Rodney Fails to Qualify'
  The Heart of a Goof (1926) P. G. Wode-
  house
Bateshaw mad scientist
  The Adventures of Augie March (1953)
  Saul Bellow
Batherbolt, Revd Mr curate, m. Georgiana
  Longestaffe*
  The Way We Live Now (1875) Anthony
  Trollope
Bathgate, Noel 'Watson' to Roderick
  Alleyn* onwards from
  A Man Lay Dead† (1934) Ngaio Marsh
Bathurst, Mrs hotel keeper and *femme
  fatale*
  ss 'Mrs Bathurst'
  Traffics and Discoveries (1904) Rudyard
  Kipling
Bathwick, Miss Boon's* secretary
  Boon (1915) H. G. Wells
Batsby, Captain vulgar hunting man who
  wishes to m. Ayala Dormer*
  Ayala's Angel (1881) Anthony Trollope
Batt & Cowley lawyers of the Bycliffes*
  Felix Holt (1866) George Eliot (rn Mary
  Anne, later Marian, Evans)
Batt, A. J., Mr Mrs Tuke's* ancient lodger
  Miss Gomez and the Brethren (1971)
  William Trevor
Battens, Mr old pensioner
  ss 'Titbull's Alms-houses'
  The Uncommercial Traveller (1860–8)
  Charles Dickens
Battle, Sarah, Mrs devotee of whist
  Essays of Elia (1823) Charles Lamb
Batts, Captain adventurer

The Virginians (1857–9) W. M. Thackeray

Baudricourt, Robert de (hist.)
St Joan play (1924) George Bernard Shaw

Bauer servant to von Tarlenheim*
Rupert of Hentzau (1898) Anthony Hope

Bauer, Karl the *Blackgauntlet*
The Bird of Dawning (1933) John Masefield

Bauersch, Mr American book-buyer
Riceyman Steps (1923) Arnold Bennett

Baughton, Curry, Sir
his wife and daughter
The Newcomes (1853–5) W. M. Thackeray

Bauldie old shepherd storyteller
The Black Dwarf (1816) Walter Scott

Baumert, Old
his crippled wife and family
Die Weber (The Weavers) play (1892) Gerhart Hauptmann

Baviaan wise baboon
ss 'How the Leopard Got His Spots'
Just So Stories (1902) Rudyard Kipling

Bawdber a pandar
Thierry and Theodoret play (1621) John Fletcher, Philip Massinger ?and Francis Beaumont

Baxby, Lord and Lady
ss 'Old Audrey's Experience'
Life's Little Ironies (1894) Thomas Hardy

Baxter, J. M. M. solicitor haunted by the truth behind apparently evil actions
ss 'The House Surgeon'
Actions and Reactions (1909) Rudyard Kipling

Baxter, Jody cc
Ezra Ezekiel his father
Ory his mother
The Yearling (1938) Marjorie Kinnan Rawlings

Baxter, Timothy tool of Squire Thornhill*, abductor of Olive Primrose*
The Vicar of Wakefield (1766) Oliver Goldsmith

Baxter, William Sylvanus ('Silly Billy') adolescent in throes of first love affair, 'the funniest novel I ever read' (F. Scott Fitzgerald*)
Seventeen (1915) Booth Tarkington

Bayer friend of Mr Norris*
Mr Norris Changes Trains (1935) Christopher Isherwood

Bayham, Frederick eccentric journalist and mimic; friend to Colonel Newcome
The Newcomes (1853–5) W. M. Thackeray

Bayham, Rodney Leonora Ashburnham's* second husband, described by Dowell* as rather like a rabbit
The Good Soldier (1915) Ford Madox Ford

Bayley, Colonel ('Boy')
ss 'The Army of a Dream'
Traffics and Discoveries (1904) Rudyard Kipling

Baynard
his wife, an extravagant vixen
The Expedition of Humphrey Clinker (1771) Tobias Smollett

Bayne foreman of works
Put Yourself in his Place (1870) Charles Reade

Baynes, Charles, General henpecked retired Indian officer, Philip Firmin's* trustee
his wife
Charlotte m. Philip Firmin*; **Jany; Mary; Moira; Ochterlong; M.'Grigor; Carrick** their children
The Adventures of Philip (1862) W. M. Thackeray

Baynes, Frederick Peak young poetaster
Love and Mr Lewisham (1900) H. G. Wells

Bazalgette, Reginald, Captain of *Vulture*, cousin to Captain Dodd*
Hard Cash (1863) Charles Reade

Bazano Consuelo's* fellow performer and partner, in love with her
Tot, kto poluchaet poshchochiny (He Who Gets Slapped; once tr. as *The Painted Laugh*) play (1916) Leonid Andreyev

Bazardo Spanish painter
The Spanish Tragedy play (1594) Thomas Kyd

Bazarov, Evgeni tender-hearted 'nihilist' cc
his old parents
Otsy i Deti (Fathers and Sons) (1862) Ivan Turgenev

Bazzard clerk to Grewgious*

Edwin Drood (1870) Charles Dickens

Beach, Esther
The Trumpet Major (1880) Thomas Hardy

Beach-Mandarin, Lady friend to Lady Harman*
The Wife of Sir Isaac Harman (1914) H. G. Wells

Beacon, Tone groom attached to Tom Chiffinch*
Peveril of the Peak (1822) Walter Scott

Beadles, Harriet see **Tattycoram**

Beagle-Boy unpleasant half-witted foxhound in the Gihon Hunt
ss 'Little Foxes'
Actions and Reactions (1909) Rudyard Kipling

Beaker, Sheila ('Sheikie') m. Trevor Artworth*
The Little Girls (1964) Elizabeth Bowen

Beaksby magistrate
The Adventures of Philip (1862) W. M. Thackeray

Beale 'hired retainer'
his wife
Love Among the Chickens (1906) P. G. Wodehouse

Beale, Edith m. Sir Mosley Monteith* and dies in childbirth
her father, a bishop
The Heavenly Twins (1893) Sarah Grand (rn Frances McFall)

Beamish, Giles, Alderman
Harry Lorrequer (1839) Charles Lever

Beamish, Mrs landlady
Tilly her daughter m. (1) Mr Ocock* (2) Purdy Smith*
Jinny her daughter m. John Turnham*
The Fortunes of Richard Mahoney (1917–30) Henry Handel Richardson (rn Ethel Florence Lindesay Richardson Robertson)

Bean of Wilson & Bean, solicitors
Kipps (1909) H. G. Wells

Beaney, Esther
A Bowl of Cherries (1984) Shena Mackay

Bear, Edward see **Winnie the Pooh**

Bear, Prince Russia
ss 'Prince Bull'
Reprinted Pieces (1858) Charles Dickens

Bearcliff, Deacon
Guy Mannering (1815) Walter Scott

Beardsall, Cyril cc
Frank his father
Rebecca his mother
Lettice his sister m. Leslie Tempest*
The White Peacock (1911) D. H. Lawrence

Beatrice niece to Leonato* m. Benedick*
Much Ado About Nothing play (1623) William Shakespeare

Beauchamp, Henry
Passages from the Diary of a Late Physician (1832) Samuel Warren

Beauchamp, Lucas ageing black farmer, son of Carothers McCaslin* (white) and a slave woman; unjustly accused of killing Vinson Gowrie*
Intruder in the Dust (1948) William Faulkner

Beauchamp, Nevil humourless and impetuous cc of the author's most political novel; British naval officer, m. Jenny Denham*, dies saving a child from drowning
Beauchamp's Career (1875) George Meredith

Beauchamp, Edward, Sir
Sir Charles Grandison (1754) Samuel Richardson

Beauchampe, Jeroboam (hist.) see **Beaumont, Jeremiah**

Beaufere, Claudia, Mrs
The Human Comedy (1942) William Saroyan

Beauffet butler to Mrs Bethune Baliol*
The Highland Widow (1827) Walter Scott

Beaufort, Edward originally an ambitious writer, but later a sponger off his wife, Lady Caroline Lindores*
The Ladies Lindores† (1883) Mrs Margaret Oliphant

Beaufort, Lord
The Comical Revenge, or *Love in a Tub* play (1664) George Etherege

Beaufort, Lord a young Lord
The New Inn, or *The Light Heart* play (1629) Ben Jonson

Beaufoy, Philip of the Playgoers Club
Mina his wife
Ulysses (1922) James Joyce

Beaugard, Captain soldier of fortune
The Soldier's Fortune play (1681) Thomas Otway

Beaujeu, Count de of the Young Chevalier's* bodyguard
Waverley (1814) Walter Scott

Beaujeu, Monsieur de 'King of the Card-pack, Duke of the Dice-box'
The Fortunes of Nigel (1822) Walter Scott

Beaumanoir, Lucas de Grand Master of the Templars
Ivanhoe (1820) Walter Scott

Beaumont, Jeremiah ('Ned') gambler and amateur detective
The Glass Key (1931) Dashiell Hammett

Beaumont, Jeremiah murderer in reconstruction of 1826 crime, based on the confession of the murderer (whose real name was Jeroboam O. Beauchamp)
Rachel his wife, whom Fort* had seduced before the marriage; her real name was Anna Cooke
World Enough and Time (1950) Robert Penn Warren

Beaumont, Stanley *pauvre type*, writer, author of unpublished book of poems, *The Profane Comedy*
Rex his brother, novelist, m. Daphne, also a novelist
Major 'The Boy' Beaumont his father
Ronnie his mother
A Bowl of Cherries (1984) Shena Mackay

Beaumoris, 'Beau' 'a sort of Grand Seigneur'
Vanity Fair† (1847–8) W. M. Thackeray

Beaver captain of frigate
Waverley (1814) Walter Scott

Beaver, Mrs interior decorator
John her son
A Handful of Dust (1934) Evelyn Waugh

Beavers, Wesley lover of Rosacoke Mustian*
A Long and Happy Life (1962) Reynolds Price

Beavis, Anthony modest philosopher
Eyeless in Gaza (1936) Aldous Huxley

Bébert (hist.) who accompanied the author on his travels
Féerie pour un autre fois (*Fairy Play for Another Time*) (1952–4) Louis-Ferdinand Céline (rn Louis-Ferdinand Destouches)

Beca wife of Simon*
ss 'The Way of the Earth'

My People (1915) Caradoc Evans (rn David Evans)

Bech, Henry Jewish author, of New York
Bech: A Book (1970); *Bech is Back* (1982) John Updike

Bechamel odious art-critic and adversary of Hoopdriver*
The Wheels of Chance (1896) H. G. Wells

Beck, Marie Modeste *née* Kint headmistress of school in Rue Fossette, a 'compact little pony', jealous, tyrannical and prosperous
Desirée; Georgette; Fifine her daughters
Villette (1853) Charlotte Brontë

Beck, Martin, Chief Inspector sleuth cc of superior, disenchanted Swedish detective stories onwards from
Roseanna (1965) Maj Sjöwall and Per Wahlöö

Beck, Mrs lodging-house keeper
Middlemarch (1871–2) George Eliot (rn Mary Anne, later Marian, Evans)

Beck, Mrs maid to Countess of Rockminster*
Pendennis (1848) W. M. Thackeray

Beck, Paul
Paul his son; detective pair in crime novels by Irish nationalist barrister who wrote much other fiction; onwards from
Paul Beck, the Rule of Thumb Detective† (1898) M. McDonnell Bodkin

Beckett, Bob carpenter's mate
HMS Pinafore opera (1878) W. S. Gilbert and Arthur Sullivan

Beckett, Mr
ss 'Ding Dong'
More Pricks That Kicks (1934) Samuel Beckett

Beckett, Mr and Mrs
Lucy their daughter
Fanny By Gaslight (1940) Michael Sadleir

Beckmann, Sergeant cc, crippled old soldier rejected by River Elbe (presented as an old hag) when he throws himself into it; in play by opponent of Nazis who did not long survive their ill-treatment of him
his wife
Draussen vor der Tür (*The Man Outside*) play (1947) Wolfgang Borchert

Beckwith see **Meltham**

Beckwith, Seth
  Mourning Becomes Electra play (1931) Eugene O'Neill
Beddows, Mrs Emma, alderman
  Jim her husband
  Willie a widower, their son; **Chloe; Sybil** their daughters
  Wendy Willie's daughter
  South Riding (1936) Winifred Holtby
Bedford playwright, bankrupt, narrator; later alias Blake*
  The First Men in the Moon (1901) H. G. Wells
Bedford, Dick butler to Lovel*
  Mary *née* Pinhorn his wife
  Lovel the Widower (1860) W. M. Thackeray
Bedford, Duke of (John of Lancaster) in the last of the plays below he is Regent of France; his appearance at Agincourt as Duke of Bedford is historically impossible
  King Henry IV; King Henry V; King Henry VI plays (1623) William Shakespeare
Bedloe, Augustus ('Oldeb')
  ss 'A Tale of the Ragged Mountains'
  Tales of the Grotesque and Arabesque (1840) Edgar Allan Poe
Bedonebyasyoudid, Mrs
  The Water Babies (1863) Charles Kingsley
Bedrooket, Lady
  Redgauntlet (1824) Walter Scott
Bedwin, Mrs housekeeper to Brownlow*
  Oliver Twist (1838) Charles Dickens
Beebe, Arthur, Revd
  A Room With a View (1908) E. M. Forster
Beechamp, Mrs
  Mrs Dukes' Million (1977) Wyndham Lewis
Beeder, William, Sir
  his wife
  The Horse's Mouth (1944) Joyce Cary
Beekman, Francis, Sir
  his wife
  Gentlemen Prefer Blondes (1925) Anita Loos
Beel friend to Kenn*
  Highland River (1937) Neil M. Gunn
Beelzebub 'chief hero' of this 'Impartial Criticism of the History of Man'

All and Everything: Beelzebub's Tales to His Grandson (1950) G. I. Gurdjieff
Beere, John solicitor
  Angela his daughter
  A Glastonbury Romance (1932) J. C. Powys
Beesley friend of Jim Dixon* and possibly based on an Oxford character of that name now deceased
  Lucky Jim (1953) Kingsley Amis
Beetle the author's nickname for himself
  Stalky and Co.† (1899) Rudyard Kipling
Beetle, Mrs
  Agony her husband
  Meriam their daughter, hired girl, mother of four; in satire on Mary Webb*, Naomi Royde-Smith, Constance Holme*, D. H. Lawrence* and other 'something nasty in the woodshed' practitioners
  Cold Comfort Farm (1932) Stella Gibbons
Beeton Helder's* landlord
  his wife
  The Light that Failed (1890) Rudyard Kipling
Beevor, Mrs stepdaughter of Lord Grinsell*
  Middlemarch (1871–2) George Eliot (rn Mary Anne, later Marian, Evans)
Begs, Ridger, Mrs *née* Micawber
  David Copperfield (1850) Charles Dickens
Beguildy, Jancis
  Felix ('Wizard') her father
  Hephzibah her mother
  Precious Bane (1924) Mary Webb
Behrens Oxford don and physicist
  Marriage (1912) H. G. Wells
Beighton, Kitty
  ss 'Cupid's Arrows'
  Plain Tales from the Hills (1888) Rudyard Kipling
Beilby, Mr millionaire co-partner in Beilby & Burton*, civil engineers, to which 'great house' Harry Clavering* makes himself pupil
  The Claverings (1866–7) Anthony Trollope
Bel the Harper
  ss 'The Melancholy of Ulad'
  Spiritual Tales (1903) Fiona Macleod (rn William Sharp)

Bela young Circassian girl
Geroi Nas hego Vremeni (*A Hero of Our Time*) (1841) Mikhail Lermontov

Belarius banished lord
Cymbeline play (1623) William Shakespeare

Belch, Toby, Sir comic character, uncle to Olivia*
Twelfth Night play (1623) William Shakespeare

Belfield, Duke of
Evan Harrington (1861) George Meredith

Belford
The Clandestine Marriage comedy (1766) George Colman the Elder and David Garrick

Belforest a baron
The Atheist's Tragedy, or The Honest Man's Revenge play (1611/12) Cyril Tourneur

Belinda cousin to Araminta*, an affected lady in love with Bellmour*
The Old Bachelor comedy (1793) William Congreve

Belinda niece to Lady Brute*
The Provok'd Wife play (1697) John Vanbrugh

Belisarius, Count (hist.); cc of novel about his attempts to win back Roman territory in 6th century
Count Belisarius (1938) Robert Graves

Belknap, Alvin Clyde Griffiths'* defence lawyer
An American Tragedy (1925) Theodore Dreiser

Bell skipper of the *Kite*
ss 'Bread Upon the Waters'
The Day's Work (1898) Rudyard Kipling

Bell, Adam godfather and benefactor to Margaret Hale*
North and South (1855) Mrs Gaskell

Bell, Charlie cc of farcical American novel; spends a night in a left-luggage locker
The Man in the Middle (1954) David Wagoner

Bell, David cc
Americana (1971) Don DeLillo

Bell, Francis, Revd chaplain, Coventry Island
Martha *née* Coacher his ill-tempered wife
Helen Laura their daughter, adopted by Helen Pendennis* m. Arthur Pendennis*

Pendennis† (1848) W. M. Thackeray

Bell, Gladys widowed sister of Bob Tallow* engaged to Jim Watts*
The Cruel Sea (1951) Nicholas Monsarrat

Belladonna, Countess of mistress of Lord Steyn, superseding Becky Sharp*
Vanity Fair (1847–8) W. M. Thackeray

Bellair
The Man of Mode comedy (1676) George Etherege

Bellair, Lady
The Marquis of Lossie (1877) George Macdonald

Bellairs, Mrs 'fortune-teller' and spy
The Ministry of Fear (1943) Graham Greene

Bellamine courtesan
The Jew of Malta play (1633) Christopher Marlowe

Bellamont, George, Duke of
Katherine his wife
Lord Montacute Tancred their son
Tancred (1847) Benjamin Disraeli

Bellamour, Lady see Celestina

Bellamy farmer
his wife
Catherine Furze (1893) Mark Rutherford (rn William Hale White)

Bellamy, Ernest, Revd m. Camilla Christy*
Men and Wives (1931) Ivy Compton-Burnett

Bellamy, Mr and Mrs butler and housekeeper to Sir Charles Cheverel*
ss 'Mr Gilfil's Love Story'
Scenes of Clerical Life (1857) George Eliot (rn Mary Anne, later Marian, Evans)

Bellario see Euphrasia

Bellasis, Lord murdered father of Rufus Dawes* (Richard Devine*)
His Natural Life (1870–2; abridged by the author 1874; in 1885 as *For the Term of His Natural Life* – thus evading the author's irony; original text edited by Stephen Murray-Smith, 1970) Marcus Clarke

Bellaston, Lady
Tom Jones (1749) Henry Fielding

Bellasys, Flora flirts with Guy Livingston' in novel more 'Muscular' than Christian, but much admired and popular in

its time
Guy Livingston, or Thorough (1857)
George Alfred Lawrence
Bellcour, Old employer of Stockwell*
his daughter, m. Stockwell
Young Belcour his grandson, cc, noble
savage, m. Louisa Dudley*
The West Indian play (1771) Richard
Cumberland
Belle Afris
Caesar and Cleopatra play (1900)
George Bernard Shaw
Bellefield, Lord worldling and gambler,
evil genius of spirited novel
Lewis Arundel (1852) Francis Smedley
Bellefontaine, Evangeline cc once much-
read American narrative poem
Benedict her father
Evangeline poem (1847) Henry
Wadsworth Longfellow
Bellegarde, Urbain, Marquis de ungrac-
ious brother to Mme de Cintré*, opposed
to her marriage to Christopher New-
man*
his wife
Valentin his younger brother
The Marquise his mother, murderess of
her husband
The American (1876) Henry James
Bellenden, Margaret, Lady
Willie her dead son
Edith his daughter
Old Mortality (1816) Walter Scott
Bellendon, Bessie of the Princes Theatre
(stage name of Elizabeth Prior*)
Lovel the Widower (1860) W. M.
Thackeray
Bellette, Amy
The Ghost Writer (1979) Philip Roth
Belleur companion to Mirabel* and
Pinac*
The Wild-Goose Chase play (1652) John
Fletcher
Bellew, Christopher ('Smoke') cc
adventure story set in Klondike
Smoke Bellew (1912) Jack London
Bellew, Helen, Mrs separated from
Captain Bellew her husband
The Country House (1907) John
Galsworthy
Bellew, Louisa m. Jack Hinton*
Sir Simon, Baronet her father
Jack Hinton (1843) Charles Lever

Bellimperia sister of Lorenzo*
The Spanish Tragedy play (1594)
Thomas Kyd
Belling, Master pupil of Squeers*
Nicholas Nickleby (1839) Charles
Dickens
Bellingham governor of Boston
The Scarlet Letter (1850) Nathaniel
Hawthorne
Bellman, Baptist Chief Registrar, Calcutta
Tape and Sealing Wax Office
The Newcomes (1853-5) W. M.
Thackeray
Bellmour friend to Vainlove*, in love with
Belinda*
The Old Bachelor comedy (1793)
William Congreve
Belmaine, Mr and Mrs friends to the
Doncastles*
The Hand of Ethelberta (1876) Thomas
Hardy
Belmont, John, Sir father to Evelina*
Evelina (1778) Fanny Burney
Belpher, Lord see Marshmoreton
Belrose, Charlie confectioner
his wife
Riceyman Steps (1923) Arnold Bennett
Belsize, Charles ('Jack') the Hon. later
Lord Highgate one of Lord Kew's*
cronies
The Newcomes (1855) W. M. Thackeray
Beltham, Squire
Dorothy, his daughter
Marion his daughter m. Augustus F. G.
Roy Richmond*
The Adventures of Harry Richmond
(1871) George Meredith
Belton, James ('Howieglass') Sir surgeon
ss 'Tender Achilles'
Limits and Renewals (1932) Rudyard
Kipling
Beluncle, Mr furniture manufacturer who
has held many religious beliefs, but is
now a member of the Church of the Last
Purification, Toronto, a sect which denies
the objective existence of evil
Mr Beluncle (1951) V. S. Pritchett
Belvawney, Miss member of Crummles'*
Theatrical Company
Nicholas Nickleby (1839) Charles
Dickens
Belzanor
Caesar and Cleopatra play (1900)

George Bernard Shaw

Belzebub
Doctor Faustus play (1604) Christopher Marlowe

Ben governor of a province in Ethiopia and *ex officio* master of the Gibon Hunt
ss 'Little Foxes'
Actions and Reactions (1909) Rudyard Kipling

Ben, Old bear
ss 'The Bear'
Go Down Moses (1942) William Faulkner

Benarbuck, Laird of 'second sight'
The Black Dwarf (1816) Walter Scott

Benassis, Dr beloved doctor and mayor in Grande Chartreuse region near Grenoble
Le Médecin de campagne (The Country Doctor) (1833) Honoré de Balzac

Benbow 'deem'd injurious to himself alone;/Gen'rous and free, he paid but small regard/To trade, and fail'd'
The Borough poem (1810) George Crabbe

Benbow, Albert m. Clara Clayhanger*
Bert; Flossie; Amy; Lucy; Rupert their children
Clayhanger (1910); *Hilda Lessways* (1911); *These Twain* (1916) Arnold Bennett

Benbow Horace ('Horry') lawyer m. Belle Mitchell
Narcissus ('Narcy') his sister m. Bayard Sartoris*
Sartoris (1929); *Sanctuary* (1931) William Faulkner

Bencombe, Marcia m. (1) Leverre*, (2) Jocelyn Pierston*
The Well Beloved (1897) Thomas Hardy

Bendien, Cornelius
You Can't Go Home Again (1940) Thomas Wolfe

Bendix, Joan murderee in classic work of detection
The Poisoned Chocolates Case (1929) Anthony Berkeley (rn Anthony Berkeley Cox)

Bendrix, Maurice narrator: novelist, and lover of Sarah Miles*
The End of the Affair (1951) Graham Greene

Benedetto Italian conspirator
ss 'The Wrong Thing'

Rewards and Fairies (1910) Rudyard Kipling

Benedetto, Don anti-fascist priest
Pan e vino (rev. as *Vino e pane* in 1962)
Bread and Wine (1937) Ignacio Silone

Benedick
The Merry Devil of Edmonton play (1602) ?Thomas Dekker

Benedick m. Beatrice*
Much Ado About Nothing play (1623) William Shakespeare

Bengough, Elsie Paul Oleron's friend, to have been 'his Beatrice, his vision!'
ss 'The Beckoning Fair One'
Widdershins (1911) Oliver Onions

Benham, William Porphyry cc, m. Amanda Morris*
Revd Harold his father, first husband of Lady Marayne*
his mother
The Research Magnificent (1915) H. G. Wells

Benito peasant of Agna Secreta
Josepha; Salvatore his daughter and son
José; Santiago his grandsons
Death Comes for the Archbishop (1927) Willa Cather

Benjamin Bunny
his father; onwards from
The Tale of Benjamin Bunny (1904) Beatrix Potter

Benjamin jeweller of Harter & Benjamin, friend to Lady Eustace*
The Eustace Diamonds (1873) Anthony Trollope

Benjamin Jorrocks's* boy
Jorrocks's Jaunts and Jollities (1838) R. S. Surtees

Benjamin Ram harp-playing ram
Uncle Remus (1895) Joel Chandler Harris

Benlian mad sculptor who cannot be X-rayed
ss 'Benlian'
Widdershins (1911) Oliver Onions

Bennet, Mr owner of Longbourne
his wife, *née* Gardiner*
Jane m. Charles Bingley;* **Elizabeth** m. Fitzwilliam Darcy;* **Mary; Kitty; Lydia** their daughters
Pride and Prejudice (1813) Jane Austen

Bennett, ('Bobbie') niece and heiress of Handcock

Some Experiences of an Irish R.M. (1899) O. E. Somerville and Martin Ross (rn Edith Somerville and Violet Martin)

Bennett, Arthur, Revd chaplain
Kim (1901) Rudyard Kipling

Bennett, Captain master of the *Altair*
Gallions Reach (1927) H. M. Tomlinson

Bennett, Mr a communist
It's a Battlefield (1935) Graham Greene

Bennett, Mrs learned widow, once seduced by My Lord*; secures Captain Booth's* commission for her own husband
Amelia (1752) Henry Fielding

Benoit Mrs Rouse's* man
Minty Alley (1936) C. L. R. James

Bensey, Lou m. Pearl Lester
Tobacco Road (1948) Erskine Caldwell

Benshaw, Farmer strawberry grower
Bealby (1915) H. G. Wells

Bensington, F. R. S. joint discoverer of the food
Jane his cousin and housekeeper
The Food of the Gods (1904) H. G. Wells

Benson, Jan
his mother
ss 'The Well'
The Lady of the Barge (1902) W. W. Jacobs

Benson, Miss heiress courted by Dr Firmin*
The Adventures of Philip (1862) W. M. Thackeray

Benson, Molly m. Colonel Martin Lambert*
The Virginians (1857–9) W. M. Thackeray

Bent, Bill
Violet his wife, aunt of Karen Michaelis*
The House in Paris (1935) Elizabeth Bowen

Bent, Mr 'The Dancing Master'
ss 'A Second-rate Woman'
Wee Willie Winkie (1888) Rudyard Kipling

Benteen, Will
Gone With the Wind (1936) Margaret Mitchell

Bentham, Charlie schoolmaster
Juno and the Paycock play (1925) Sean O'Casey (rn John Casey)

Bentivolio cc 'allegorical-religious romance', 'its unillumined profundity swarms with low forms of life; poly-syllabic abstractions crowd its pages, and deposit their explanatory spawn in the margin' (Sir Walter Raleigh); but it ran through four editions, just as some much worse run through more now
Bentivolio and Urania (1660) Nathaniel Ingelo

Bentley, Bert musical director
Red Peppers play (1936) Noël Coward

Bentley, Geoffrey publisher
Put Out More Flags (1942) Evelyn Waugh

Benton sailor on the torpedoed *Aurora*
The Ocean (1946) James Hanley

Benton, Miss housekeeper to Master Humphrey*
Master Humphrey's Clock (1840–1) Charles Dickens

Benvolio cc
ss 'Benvolio' (1875) Henry James

Benvolio friend to Romeo*
Romeo and Juliet play (1623) William Shakespeare

Benvolio, Countess
Jorrocks's Jaunts and Jollities (1838) R. S. Surtees

Benwick, Captain excellent young man, 'he must love somebody', guest of the Harvilles' at Lyme Regis
Persuasion (1818) Jane Austen

Benyon, Butcher
Bess his wife
Gossamer their daughter, schoolmistress
Billy their son
Under Milk Wood play (1954) Dylan Thomas

Benyon, Mrs Davy Morgan's* landlady
Evan her husband
Tegwen their daughter
How Green Was My Valley (1939) Richard Llewellyn

Benzaguen, Vidal actress
her mother
ss 'The Village that Voted the Earth was Flat'
A Diversity of Creatures (1917)
ss 'Dayspring Mishandled'
Limits and Renewals (1932) Rudyard Kipling

Bérenge, Mme concierge
Mort à credit (*Death on the Instalment Plan*) (1936) Louis-Ferdinand Céline (rn Louis-Ferdinand Destouches)

Berenger, Raymond, Sir
Eveline his daughter, betrothed to Sir
Hugo de Lacy*
The Betrothed (1825) Walter Scott
Berenice whose brightly white teeth are
drawn by Egaeus* while she is in a trance
ss 'Berenice'
Tales of the Grotesque and Arabesque
(1840) Edgar Allan Poe
Beresford, Lady passenger in the *Agra*
Hard Cash (1863) Charles Kingsley
Beresin officer
ss 'The War Baby'
Blasting and Bombadiering (1967); *Un-*
lucky for Pringle (1973) Wyndham Lewis
Berg, Howard
Wickford Point (1939) John P.
Marquand
Berg, Teddy the greatest living American
composer
Real People (1969) Alison Lurie
Bergerac, Gabrielle de cc very early tale
ss 'Gabrielle de Bergerac' (1868) Henry
James
Bergetto nephew to Donato*
'Tis Pity She's a Whore play (1633) John
Ford
Bergfeld, Anna
her husband
The Silver Spoon (1926) John
Galsworthy
Bergmann, Clara and **Emma**
Pilgrimage (1915–67) Dorothy M.
Richardson
Bergotte writer
A la recherche du temps perdu (*In Search*
of Lost Time) (1913–27) Marcel Proust
Berinthia a widow
A Trip to Scarborough play (1777)
Richard Brinsley Sheridan
Berinthia niece to Mrs Pipchin*
Dombey and Son (1848) Charles Dickens
Berinthia young widow, cousin to
Amanda*
The Relapse, or *Virtue in Danger* play
(1697) John Vanbrugh
Berkeley, Viscount
The American Claimant (1892) Mark
Twain (rn Samuel Langhorne Clemens)
Berkely, Augusta of, Lady
Castle Dangerous (1832) Walter Scott
Berman, Joe cc, plumber, a modern Job
settled in America out of Russia

Ruthie one of his daughters
his dead wife and son (killed in the war)
The Human Season (1960) Edward
Lewis Wallant
Berman, O. J. Hollywood agent
Breakfast at Tiffany's (1958) Truman
Capote
Bernadine poet to Montoni*
The Mysteries of Udolpho (1794) Mrs
Ann Radcliffe
Bernard writer, one of the characters
whose interior monologue* makes up
this variously ('boring and pretentious';
'masterpiece') regarded novel
The Waves (1931) Virginia Woolf
Bernard, Captain gluttonous Frenchman
Pending Heaven (1930) William
Gerhardie
Bernard, John friend to Basil*
Basil (1852) Wilkie Collins
Bernardo an officer
Hamlet play (1623) William Shakespeare
Bernardo in 'bibliographic romance'
Bibliomania (1809) T. F. Dibdin
Bernenstein
The Prisoner of Zenda (1894); *Rupert of*
Hentzau (1898) Anthony Hope
Berners, Isopel ('**Belle**') 'woman of the
road', Lavengro's* companion
Lavengro (1851) George Borrow
Berners, Mrs cancer patient
ss 'Unprofessional'
Limits and Renewals (1932) Rudyard
Kipling
Bernstein dissolute German baron, ex-
valet, m. Beatrix Esmond*
The Virginians (1857–9) W. M.
Thackeray
Berrendo, Lieutenant Francoist officer
For Whom the Bell Tolls (1940) Ernest
Hemingway
Berridge, Mrs the narrator's landlady
The Hampdenshire Wonder (1911) J. D.
Beresford
Berry, Mrs
The Ordeal of Richard Feverel: A
History of Father and Son (1859, rev.
1878) George Meredith
Berry, Mrs whose companion Maggie
Grey* becomes
The Wooing O't (1873) Mrs Hector
Alexander
Berryl, John, Sir

Arthur his son
The Absentee (1812) Maria Edgeworth
Bertha orphan, m. Faust*
ss 'The Mortal Immortal'
Tales and Stories (1891) Mary Shelley
Bertha Scandinavian servant girl who sinks lower and lower but has 'greatness of soul' in immensely popular novel, which was both filmed and dramatized
Lummox (1923) Fannie Hurst
Berthelini, Léon strolling player
Elvira his wife
ss 'Providence and the Guitar'
The New Arabian Nights (1882) Robert Louis Stevenson
Bertie and Bellair, Lady
Tancred (1847) Benjamin Disraeli
Bertoldo natural brother to Robert*, King of Sicily
The Maid of Honour play (1632) Philip Massinger
Bertram faithful minstrel
Castle Dangerous (1832) Walter Scott
Bertram, Allan Laird of Ellangowan
Dennis his son
Donahoe son of Dennis
Lewis son of Donahoe
Godfrey son of Lewis
wife to Godfrey
Harry ('Vanbeest Brown') son to Godfrey: kidnapped and taken to Holland and then India, m. Julia Mannering*
Lucy daughter of Harry and Julia
Commissioner Bertram cousin
Guy Mannering (1815) Walter Scott
Bertram, Count of Rousillon
All's Well That Ends Well play (1623) William Shakespeare
Bertram, Mrs mother to Sarah Miles*
The End of the Affair (1951) Graham Greene
Bertram, Thomas, Sir Baronet and MP 'grave, stately, oratorical'
Maria *née* Ward, his wife, who though she does not think deeply, thinks justly
Thomas; Revd Edmund m. Fanny Price*; **Maria** m. James Rushworth*; **Julia** m. John Yates*, their children
Mansfield Park (1814) Jane Austen
Bertram, Lionel, Lieutenant-Colonel, Sir soldier of fortune
George cc, his son, m. Caroline Harcourt *née* Waddington*

George his brother, to whom he entrusts his son's welfare
The Bertrams (1859) Anthony Trollope
Bertran French naturalist
ss 'Bertran and Bimi'
Life's Handicap (1891) Rudyard Kipling
Bertrand, Archie the author's attempt to reply to Maugham's* devastating portrait of him as Alroy Kear*
John Cornelius (1937) Hugh Walpole
Berwick, Arabella, Duchess of
Lady Windermere's Fan play (1892) Oscar Wilde
Beryl assistant to Myrtle Bagot*
Brief Encounter play (1945) Noël Coward
Besnard Commissioner of Police
At the Villa Rose (1910) A. E. W. Mason
Bess Black ex-prostitute and drug-taker, cc
Porgy (1925) Du Bose Heyward
Bessie girl recovering from serious illness
ss 'Io'
Widdershins (1911) Oliver Onions
Bessie nurse to the Reed* children; m. Robert Leavens*
Revd J. Boyer suitor of Eliza Wharton* who gives her up because she is entranced by the libertine Major Sanford*; in once popular American novel
The Coquette (1797) Mrs Hannah Foster
Besso, Hillel and his wife; foster-parents of Emir Fakredeen*
Tancred (1847) Benjamin Disraeli
Bessus
A King and No King play (1611) Francis Beaumont and John Fletcher
Beste-Chetwynde, Mrs Margot, the Hon. m. (2) Viscount Metroland*
Peter her son by her first marriage; later Earl of Pastmaster; m. Lady Mary Meadows*
Decline and Fall (1928) Evelyn Waugh
Bethany, Revd Mr
The Return (1910) Walter de la Mare
Bethel, Otway, Colonel
East Lynne (1861) Mrs Henry Wood
Bethia maid to the Edgeworths*
A House and its Head (1935) Ivy Compton-Burnett
Bethune, Richard, Sir father to Martha Baliol*
ss 'Lady of Quality'
The Highland Widow (1827) Walter

Scott

Betsey Jane Mrs Wickham's* uncle's daughter
Dombey and Son (1848) Charles Dickens

Betsey maid to Bob Sawyer*
The Pickwick Papers (1837) Charles Dickens

Betteridge, Gabriel house steward to Lady Verinder*
Selena his dead wife
Penelope their daughter
The Moonstone (1868) Wilkie Collins

Betterton, Mr
Coming Up For Air (1936) George Orwell (rn Eric Blair)

Bettesworth, Mr cc
The Portrait (1910) Ford Madox Ford

Bettisher, Tony close friend to Dick Munt*
ss 'The Travelling Grave'
The Travelling Grave (1948) L. P. Hartley

Betts, Mrs nurse
ss 'A Habitation Enforced'
Actions and Reactions (1909) Rudyard Kipling

Betty maid, Sancho Panza* to Dorcas Sheldon*
Female Quixotism (1801) Tabitha Tenney

Betty waiting-woman to Mrs Rich*
The Comical Revenge, or Love in a Tub play (1664) George Etherege

Bevan, George song composer; m. Lady Maud Marsh*
A Damsel in Distress (1919) P. G. Wodehouse

Bevan, Ralph Waddington's former secretary, sacked for trying to write Waddington's book, *Ramblings Through the Cotswolds*, for him
Mr Waddington of Wyck (1921) May Sinclair

Bevan, Theodore cc, sexual predator who violates women's minds and bodies
The Fowler (1899) Beatrice Harraden

Beveridge, Lady cc who has lost brother and sons in Great War
Daphne her daughter, society beauty
Daphne's husband
ss 'The Ladybird'
The Captain's Doll (1923) (in UK, *The Ladybird*) D. H. Lawrence

Beverley gambler cc of tragedy (not to be confused with plays by Shirley* and Mrs Centlivre*) that was adapted by Diderot*; it has been called 'the most modern tragedy written in the eighteenth century'
his wife
The Gamester play (1753) Edward Moore

Beverley horrible beautician
Laurence her husband; in 'devised theatre' play, i.e. the actors improvise on the basis of their own interactions
Abigail's Party play (1977) Mike Leigh

Beverley, Archdeacon Broad Church cleric who visits Carlingford and is attracted to Rose Lake*
Miss Marjoribanks (1866) Mrs Margaret Oliphant

Beverley, Cecilia cc who cannot inherit unless her husband takes her name; m. Mortimer Delvile*; in novel, immensely popular in its time, and admired by Johnson*, Burke and others
Cecilia, or Memoirs of an Heiress (1782) Fanny Burney

Beverley, Colonel
his wife *née* Villiers
Edward m. Patience Heatherstone*; **Humphrey; Edith; Alice** their children
The Children of the New Forest (1847) Captain Marryat

Beverley, Ensign see **Absolute, Captain**

Beverley, Frank one-time lunatic m. Edith Archbold*
Hard Cash (1863) Charles Reade

Bevil
The Conscious Lovers play (1722) Richard Steele

Bevill, Lord
The Comical Revenge, or Love in a Tub play (1664) George Etherege

Bevin ex-sergeant and chicken farmer
ss 'A Friend of the Family'
Debits and Credits (1926) Rudyard Kipling

Bevis contemptible would-be seducer of Monica Widdowson (*née* Madden*)
The Odd Women (1893) George Gissing

Bevis, Henry *Times's* special correspondent
The Gates of Summer play (1956) John Whiting

Bhaer, Friedrich m. Jo March*
Rob; Teddy their sons
Franz Friedrich's nephew, merchant
Emil Friedrich's nephew, sailor, m. Mary Hardy*
Little Men (1871); *Jo's Boys* (1886) Louisa M. Alcott

Bhanavar the Beautiful
The Shaving of Shagpat (1856) George Meredith

Bhanipur, Nabob of see Singh, Hurree Jamset Ram

Bi-coloured Rock Snake, The
ss 'The Elephant's Child'
Just So Stories (1902) Rudyard Kipling

Bianca Isabella of Vicenza's* maid
The Castle of Otranto (1765) Horace Walpole

Bianca Katherine's* sister
The Taming of the Shrew play (1623) William Shakespeare

Bianchon doctor
La Cousine Bette† (1847) Honoré de Balzac

Bias a Vi-Politic, or Sub-Secretary
The Magnetic Lady, or *Humours Reconciled* play (1641) Ben Jonson

Bibbet secretary to General Harrison*
Woodstock (1826) Walter Scott

Bibot, Sergeant
The Scarlet Pimpernel (1905) Baroness Orczy

Biche, La Indian mistress of Museau*
The Virginians (1857–9) W. M. Thackeray

Bichelonne 'monster spermatozoon, all head!'; dies under surgery
D'un Château l'autre (*Castle to Castle*) (1957) Louis-Ferdinand Céline (rn Louis-Ferdinand Destouches)

Bickerton editor *Pall Mall Gazette*; supercilious snob
The Adventures of Philip (1862) W. M. Thackeray

Bickerton, Miss boarder at Miss Goddard's* who runs from gipsies
Emma (1816) Jane Austen

Bickerton, Mrs of Castle Gate, York
Moses her husband
Heart of Midlothian (1818) Walter Scott

Bicket, Tony packer at Darby & Winter
The White Monkey† (1924) John Galsworthy

Bickleigh, Dr murderer and fantasist
Malice Aforethought (1931) Francis Iles (rn Anthony Berkeley Cox)

Bicknell, Miss friend to Elfride Swancourt*
A Pair of Blue Eyes (1873) Thomas Hardy

Bidderman Flemish nobleman
The Bee (1759–60) Oliver Goldsmith

Biddlecombe schoolchum to Bultitude*
Vice Versa (1882) F. Anstey (rn Thomas Anstey Guthrie)

Biddulph villainous husband to Hannah Owen*
St Ronan's Well (1824) Walter Scott

Biddums, Miss Toby Austell's* governess
ss 'His Majesty the King'
Wee Willie Winkie (1895) Rudyard Kipling

Bide-the-Bent, Peter minister
The Bride of Lammermoor (1819) Walter Scott

Bideawhile the Trevelyans'* 'ancient family lawyer'
He Knew He Was Right (1869) Anthony Trollope

Bidlake, Elinor m. Philip Quarles*
John her father
her mother
Walter her brother
Point Counter Point (1928) Aldous Huxley

Bidmore, Lord
Augustus his son
Augusta his daughter
St Ronan's Well (1824) Walter Scott

Biederman, Arnold rightfully Count of Geierstein
Bertha his wife
Rudiger; Ernst; Sigismond; Ulrick his sons
Anne of Geierstein (1829) Walter Scott

Biel
ss 'The Bronckhorst Divorce Case'
Plain Tales from the Hills (1888) Rudyard Kipling

Big Daddy (Pollitt) wealthy Mississippi landowner
Big Mama his wife
Cooper ('Brother Man') their son
Mae ('Sister Woman') Cooper's wife
Brick Big Daddy's drunkard son
Margaret ('The Cat') Brick's wife

Cat on a Hot Tin Roof play (1955) Tennessee Williams (rn Thomas Lanier Williams)

Biggidy, Dicky Big-Bag alias **Blue Rabbit**
Uncle Remus (1880–95) Joel Chandler Harris

Bigglesworth, Air Detective Inspector ('**Biggles**') popular cc of series of boys' books onwards from
The Camels Are Coming (1932) W. E. Johns

Biggs bosun HMS *Harpy*
Mr Midshipman Easy (1836) Captain Marryat

Biggs, Jno. Horatio Mayor of Tooting East
Gladys his daughter m. Clarence Mulliner*
Meet Mr Mulliner (1927) P. G. Wodehouse

Bighead, Bessie
Under Milk Wood play (1954) Dylan Thomas

Bigot, Francois Intendant, leader of the corrupt Grand Company
The Golden Dog (unauthorized 1887, 1896) William Kirby

Bigstaff, John constable
Peveril of the Peak (1822) Walter Scott

Bilbo
The Merry Devil of Edmonton play (1602) ?Thomas Dekker

Bildad, Captain retired whaler, Quaker, part-owner of the *Pequod*
Moby Dick, or *The Whale* (1851) Herman Melville

Biles, Hezekiah rustic
Two on a Tower (1882) Thomas Hardy

Biles, John
ss 'Absent-mindedness in a Parish Choir'
Life's Little Ironies (1894) Thomas Hardy

Bill, Buffalo (hist.: William Cody) cc of innumerable westerns of which none is worse than this; by drunkard, temperance lecturer, murderer, lynched (but rescued at the point of death), riot leader, liar, founder of the anti-Catholic Know Nothing party, and much else
Buffalo Bill, the King of the Border Men (1869) E. Z. C. Judson (or 'The Great Rascal')

Billali aged chief; servant to 'She'*
She (1887) Henry Rider Haggard

Billickin, Mrs cousin to Mr Bazzard*, lodging-house keeper
Edwin Drood (1870) Charles Dickens

Billson, Wilberforce ('**Battling Billson**') boxer
Uckridge (1924) P. G. Wodehouse

Billy a battery mule
ss 'Her Majesty's Servants'
Jungle Books (1894–5) Rudyard Kipling

Billy Bluetail ('**Mr Hawk**')
Uncle Remus (1880–95) Joel Chandler Harris

Billy Hedgehog
The Wind in the Willows (1908) Kenneth Grahame

Billy the Boy
Robbery Under Arms: A Story of Life and Adventure in the Bush and in the Goldfields of Australia (1888, rev. 1889) Rolf Boldrewood (rn Thomas Alexander Browne)

Bilsiter, Leonard 'one of those people who have failed to find this world attractive or interesting, and who have sought compensation in an "unseen world"'; turns Mrs Hampton* into a wolf but does not get the glory
ss 'The She Wolf'
Beasts and Super Beasts (1914) Saki (rn Hector Hugh Munro)

Bimala Nikhil's* wife and, for the author, symbol of Bengal
The Home and the World (1916) Rabindranath Tagore

Bimi jealous orang-outang which kills
ss 'Bertran and Bimi'
Life's Handicap (1891) Rudyard Kipling

Binat French landlord in Port Said; drunken ex-artist
The Light that Failed (1890) Rudyard Kipling

Bindloose copper-nosed sheriff-clerk
St Ronan's Well (1824) Walter Scott

Bindon-Botting, Mrs socialite, friend to the Walsinghams*
Kipps (1905) H. G. Wells

Binet, Captain tax collector
Madame Bovary (1857) Gustave Flaubert

Bingham ex-bank manager turned thief
ss 'Mr Leadbetter's Vocation' (and elsewhere)
Tales of Life and Adventure (1923) H. G. Wells

Bingley actor-manager, Chatteris Theatre
his wife
Pendennis (1848) W. M. Thackeray
Bingley, Charles m. Bennet*
Caroline his sister
Pride and Prejudice (1813) Jane Austen
Bingley, Mr and Mrs employers of Esther
Waters*
Esther Waters (1894) George Moore
Binkie Torpenhow's* dog
The Light that Failed (1890) Rudyard
Kipling
Binkie, Grizzel m. Sir Pitt Crawley*
Vanity Fair (1847–8) W. M. Thackeray
Binks, Bingo, Sir
St Ronan's Well (1824) Walter Scott
Binnie, James civil servant, friend to Col-
onel Newcome*
The Newcomes (1853–5) W. M.
Thackeray
Binny, Beilby, Revd curate and keeper of
small school m. Miss Grits*
his sister and housekeeper
Vanity Fair (1847–8) W. M. Thackeray
Birberry, Leon, Sir massacred as a Jew
ss 'The Unrest-Cure'
The Chronicles of Clovis (1911) Saki (rn
Hector Hugh Munro)
Birch, Dr flogger cc, head of Archbishop
Wigsby's College of Rodwell Regis
Doctor Birch and His Young Friends
(1849) W. M. Thackeray
Birch, Inspector
The Red House Mystery (1922) A. A.
Milne
Birch, Milly maid to Paula Power*
A Laodicean (1881) Thomas Hardy
Birchfield, Marilyn
The Pawnbroker (1961) Edward Lewis
Wallant
Bird Woman, The friend of Freckles* in
almost unprecedentedly popular senti-
mental book by, not an author, but 'an
institution, like Yellowstone Park'
Freckles (1904) Gene Stratton Porter
Bird, Luke
Mr Weston's Good Wine (1927) T. F.
Powys
Bird, Senator and his wife; helpers of
Eliza*
Uncle Tom's Cabin (1851) Harriet
Beecher Stowe
Birdseye, Miss 'celebrated abolitionist'

The Bostonians (1886) Henry James
Birdseye, Nellie young girl narrator, later
Mrs Casey
Lydia her aunt
Lydia's three sisters
My Mortal Enemy (1926) Willa Cather
Birkin sympathetic portrait of the British
fascist, Sir Oswald Mosley (for fuller
details see Maddison, Philip)
Chronicles of Ancient Sunlight
(1951–69) Henry Williamson
Birkin, Rupert schools inspector m. Ursula
Brangwen*
Women in Love (1921) D. H. Lawrence
Birkland schoolmaster
Mr Perrin and Mr Traill (1911) Hugh
Walpole
Birnam, Don repressed homosexual,
alcoholic cc of five-day saga in the life of a
drunken author-manqué
Wick his brother
The Lost Weekend (1944) Charles
Jackson
Bishop, The who proposes a massacre of
all Jews in James P. Huddle's district
ss 'The Unrest-Cure'
The Chronicles of Clovis (1911) Saki (rn
Hector Hugh Munro)
Biswas, Mohun cc
A House for Mr Biswas (1961) V. S.
Naipaul
Black Will murderer, with Shakebag*, of
Arden*: 'For a cross word of a tapster I
have pierced one barrel after another
with my dagger till all the beer hath run
out'
*The Lamentable and Terrible Tragedy of
Arden of Feversham in Kent* play (1592)
Anon.
Black, Dick aspiring writer cc, from
Cincinnati
The Big Cage (1949) Robert Lowry
Blackett, Nancy (Ruth)
Peggy her sister
Swallows and Amazons (1930) Arthur
Ransome
Blackhall victim of Allan, Lord
Ravenswood*
The Bride of Lammermoor (1819)
Walter Scott
Blackland gambling friend to Colonel
Altamont*
Pendennis (1848) W. M. Thackeray

Blacklees, Tomalin warder
The Talisman (1825) Walter Scott
Blackmore manager, Bundelcund Bank
The Newcomes (1853–5) W. M.
Thackeray
Blackmore, Honour ('Mrs Honour') maid
to Sophia Western*
Tom Jones (1749) Henry Fielding
Blackpool, Stephen cc, honest mill-hand
unjustly accused of stealing
Hard Times (1854) Charles Dickens
Blackstick, Fairy
The Rose and the Ring (1855) W. M.
Thackeray
Bladderskate, Lord judge
Redgauntlet (1824) Walter Scott
Bladen ('Boy')
Campbell's Kingdom (1952) Hammond
Innes
Blague innkeeper
The Merry Devil of Edmonton play
(1608) ?Thomas Dekker
Blaine, Amory wealthy playboy, cc
This Side of Paradise (1920) F. Scott
Fitzgerald
Blaine, Elizabeth ('Fanny') m. Nicholas
Forstye*
The Forsyte series (1906–33) John
Galsworthy
Blaise friend and servant to Lord
Castlewood*
Henry Esmond (1852) W. M. Thackeray
Blaise Northumberland-dwelling master
of Merlin*
Le Morte D'Arthur (1485) Thomas Malory
Blaize, Lucy m. Richard Feverel*
Tom her father
Tom ('Young Tom') her brother
The Ordeal of Richard Feverel (1859,
rev. 1878) George Meredith
Blake alias of Bedford* after return to
earth
The First Men in the Moon (1901) H. G.
Wells
Blake, Audrey governess to Ogden Ford*
m. (1) Sheridan* (2) Peter Burns*
The Little Nugget (1913) P. G. Wodehouse
Blake, Baldur old sculptor, mystic
Baldur's Gate (1970) Eleanor Clark
Blake, Darrell
The Moon in the Yellow River play

(1932) Denis Johnston
Blake, Dennis commuter, newcomer to the
village, in love with Coral Fairbrother*
Joan his wife
Clara their cold and unpleasant daughter
Old Crow (1967) Shena Mackay
Blake, Franklin cc and part narrator m.
Rachel Verinder*
The Moonstone (1868) Wilkie Collins
Blake, Fred young Australian in Far East
The Narrow Corner (1932) W. Somerset
Maugham
Blake, Honor
The Playboy of the Western World play
(1907) J. M. Synge
Blake, Joseph, Dr
Mourning Becomes Electra play (1931)
Eugene O'Neill
Blake, Joseph, Revd formerly in English
army in America
Joseph Clinton his son m. Theodosia
Warrington*
The Virginians (1857–9) W. M.
Thackeray
Blake, Miss governess to Una* and Dan*
Puck of Pook's Hill (1906) Rudyard
Kipling
Blake, Mr
ss 'A. V. Laider'
Seven Men (1919) Max Beerbohm
Blake, Nat violinist m. Daisy Brooke*
Little Men (1871); *Jo's Boys* (1886)
Louisa M. Alcott
Blake, Philip
his wife
Nora; Matthew their children
Charles O'Malley (1841) Charles Lever
Blakeley, Dennis socialist
Kathleen his daughter
Radcliffe (1963) David Storey
Blakely, Constance, Mrs
ss 'Pish-Tush'
Unlucky for Pringle (1973) Wyndham
Lewis
Blakeney, Felicia m. Chester Meredith*
Crispin her brother
ss 'Chester Forgets Himself'
The Heart of a Goof (1926) P. G. Wodehouse
Blakeney, Percy, Sir 'The Scarlet
Pimpernel'
Marguerite *née* St Just his wife; in
swashbucklers that still just endure;

onwards from
The Scarlet Pimpernel† (1905) Baroness
Orczy
Blakeston, Jim lover of Liza Kemp*
his wife
Liza of Lambeth (1897) W. Somerset
Maugham
Blanchard, Augusta, Miss artist
Roderick Hudson (1875) Henry James
Blanchard, Emmy
Jenny her younger sister, in love with
Keith Redington*
Alf her father
Nocturne (1917) Frank Swinnerton
Blanche, Anthony 'aesthete'
Brideshead Revisited (1945) Evelyn
Waugh
Blanche, Lady Professor of Abstract
Science
Melissa her daughter m. Florian*
Princess Ida opera (1884) W. S. Gilbert
and Arthur Sullivan
Blancove, William, Sir m. (2) Mrs Lovell*
Edward his son, law student
Algernon his nephew, in love with Mrs
Lovell
Rhoda Fleming (1895) George Meredith
Bland, Dr Lady Tiptoff's* physician
The Great Hoggarty Diamond (1841) W.
M. Thackeray
Bland, Pigling
Alexander; Chinchin; Stumpy children
The Tale of Pigling Bland (1913) Beatrix
Potter
Blandeville, Emily, Lady m. Colonel
Talbot*
Waverley (1814) Walter Scott
Blandish cc
ss 'Spoils of Mr Blandish': read by Boon*
in book which upset the by-then seri-
ously ill Henry James* because of its
caricature of him
Boon (1915) H. G. Wells
Blandish, Lady friend to the Feverels*
*The Ordeal of Richard Feverel: A
History of Father and Son* (1859, rev.
1878) George Meredith
Blandois see **Rigaud**
Blandesbury, Cyril, Sir
his wife
The Hand of Ethelberta (1876) Thomas
Hardy
Blandy, Peregrine, Sir successor to

Rawdon Crawley* as governor of Cov-
entry Island
The Newcomes (1853–5) W. M.
Thackeray
Blane, Neil town piper
Jenny his daughter
Old Mortality (1816) Walter Scott
Blaney 'Observe that tall pale veteran!
what a look/Of shame and guilt! . . . a
wealthy heir at twenty-one./At
twenty-five was ruined and undone'
The Borough poem (1810) George
Crabbe
Blanquart schoolmaster and secretary to
the Mairie
Cécile his daughter
his sister
The Spanish Farm trilogy (1927) R. H.
Mottram
Blathers Bow Street Officer
Oliver Twist (1838) Charles Dickens
Blatherwick attorney
The Great Hoggarty Diamond (1841) W.
M. Thackeray
Blattergrowl, Dr dull and prosy minister of
Trotcosey
The Antiquary (1816) Walter Scott
Blayds, Oliver just deceased much vener-
ated 'last Victorian', so eminent that his
daughter's husband took his name, yet a
complete humbug who stole all the
poetry he published from a fellow-poet
who died in youth
Marian Blayds-Conway his daughter,
who wants to cover up the truth because
it would embarrass her husband,
William*, who is writing a biography
Isobel his younger daughter, who wants
to renounce the fortune the family has
acquired, and make the facts public
(*Blayds* was the original name of the light
poet C. S. Calverley)
The Truth About Blayds in *Three Plays*
(1923) A. A. Milne
Blemont, Caroline de pupil at Mlle
Reuter's* School; devoid of morals
The Professor (1857) Charlotte Brontë
Blend, Miss writes poetry; mistress of
Arthur Stubland*
Joan and Peter (1918) H. G. Wells
Blenkensop, Lady close confederate of
Sarah, Duchess of Marlborough*
The Bride of Lammermoor (1819)

Walter Scott

Blenkins, Bonaparte English sadist and scoundrel
The Story of an African Farm (1883) Olive Schreiner

Blenkinsop, Dr
The Doctor's Dilemma play (1906) George Bernard Shaw

Blenkinsop, Miss 'actress of high quality'
Pendennis (1848) W. M. Thackeray

Blenkinsop, Samuel bank clerk m. Hannah Mole*
Miss Mole (1930) E. H. Young

Bless, Christopher
ss 'The Melancholy Hussar'
Life's Little Ironies (1894) Thomas Hardy

Bletson, Joshua Parliamentary Commissioner
Woodstock (1826) Walter Scott

Blettsworthy, Mr the 'Sacred Lunatic' in dystopia modelled on Candide*
Mr Blettsworthy on Rampole Island (1933) H. G. Wells

Blewett, Richard partner with Deuceace* in swindling Dawkins*
ss 'The Amours of Dr Deuceace'
The Yellowplush Papers (1852) W. M. Thackeray

Blick, Detective representative of evil
The Time of Your Life play (1939) William Saroyan

Blifil, Dr
his brother, the Captain, m. Bridget Allworthy*
their son
Tom Jones (1749) Henry Fielding

Blifil-Gordon Conservative MP
A Clergyman's Daughter (1935) George Orwell (rn Eric Blair)

Bligh
ss 'Phantas'
Widdershins (1911) Oliver Onions

Bligh family name of **Lord Rockage**

Blimber, Dr sadistic schoolmaster
his wife
Cornelia his daughter, m. Feeder*
Dombey and Son (1848) Charles Dickens

Blinkhoolie see **Boniface**

Blinkhorn housemaster at St Grimstone's
Vice Versa (1882) F. Anstey (rn Thomas Anstey Guthrie)

Blinkinsop, Colonel old soldier

The Virginians (1857–9) W. M. Thackeray

Bliss, Judith
David her husband
Sorel: Simon their children
Hay Fever play (1925) Noël Coward

Bliss, Reginald friend and literary executor to George Boon*
Boon (1915) H. G. Wells

Blitch, Mabel school friend to Undine Spragg* m. Henry Lipscombe*
The Custom of the Country (1913) Edith Wharton

Bloat, Teddy
Gravity's Rainbow (1973) Thomas Pynchon

Bloch ill-mannered friend to Marcel*
A la recherche du temps perdu (*In Search of Lost Time*) (1913–27) Marcel Proust

Block, Martin butcher of Dijon
Anne of Geierstein (1829) Walter Scott

Bloeckman, Joseph vice-president of film company
The Beautiful and Damned (1922) F. Scott Fitzgerald

Blogg, William late master of Boniface
Pendennis (1848) W. M. Thackeray

Bloggs, Thelma fairly young person with expectations, Belacqua Shuah's second wife, dies on honeymoon
Otto Olaf Bloggs her brother or husband or namesake
Mrs Bridie Bloggs perhaps some relation to her
ss 'What a Misfortune'
ss 'Draff'
More Pricks That Kicks (1934) Samuel Beckett

Blois, Chevalier de aristocratic *émigré*, Thomas Newcome's* French master
The Newcomes (1853–5) W. M. Thackeray

Blok, Nikkel butcher of Liège
Quentin Durward (1823) Walter Scott

Blomefield, Revd Mr Vicar of Birtwick
Black Beauty (1877) Anna Sewell

Blood, Lydia New England teacher, 'lady of nature's own making', cc who goes on a sea voyage and is courted by James Staniford* (after his initial misgivings), whom she m.
A Lady of the Aroostook (1879) William Dean Howells

Blood, Mr wealthy landowner of vast intelligence
Mr Fleight (1913) Ford Madox Ford
Bloodenough, Victor, V.C., General Chairman of Governors, Harchester College
Meet Mr Mulliner (1927) P. G. Wodehouse
Bloom, Leopold journalist m. Marion Tweedy*
Milly their daughter
Ulysses (1922) James Joyce
Bloomfield, Edward Hugh uncle to Gideon Forsythe*
The Wrong Box (1889) Robert Louis Stevenson and Lloyd Osbourne
Bloomfield, Mr
his wife, *née* Robson
his mother
Tom who tortures animals; **Mary; Ann; Fanny** their children and Agnes Grey's* pupils
Agnes Grey (1847) Anne Brontë
Blore the Monts'* butler
The Forsyte series (1906–33) John Galsworthy
Blore, Sammy farm labourer
Two on a Tower (1882) Thomas Hardy
Blotton member of the Pickwick Club
The Pickwick Papers (1837) Charles Dickens
Bloundell (also called **Bloundell Bloundell**) gambler
Pendennis (1848) W. M. Thackeray
Blount, Jake frustrated idealist
The Heart is a Lonely Hunter (1940) Carson McCullers
Blount, Nicholas, Sir Master of the Horse to the Earl of Sussex
Kenilworth (1821) Walter Scott
Blount, Nina fiancée of Adam Fenwick-Symes*
Colonel Blount her father
Vile Bodies (1930) Evelyn Waugh
Blowater, Pennyfather, Revd democratic vicar
Mr Fleight (1913) Ford Madox Ford
Blower, Peggy, Mrs
John her dead husband
St Ronan's Well (1824) Walter Scott
Blowselinda chambermaid at the Red Lion
The House With the Green Shutters (1901) George Douglas (rn George Douglas Brown)
Bludyer, Roger, General Sir
Lady Bludyer his wife
Vanity Fair (1847–8) W. M. Thackeray
Blue Rabbit see **Biggidy, Dicky Big-Bag**
Blue, Angela schoolteacher m. Eugene Witla*; in autobiographical novel (the author's wife's maiden name was Sara White)
The Genius (1915) Theodore Dreiser
Blueskin rogue
Jonathan Wild (1743) Henry Fielding
Bluff, Sylvanus
Rosamund his wife
Hawbuck Grange (1847) R. S. Surtees
Bluffe, Captain cowardly bully
The Old Bachelor comedy (1793) William Congreve
Blumine woman with whom Herr Teufelsdröckh falls in love, based on a woman once admired by the author
Sartor Resartus (1833–4) Thomas Carlyle
Blundell, Zoe cc 'problem play'* influenced by Ibsen*
her broker husband
Mid-Channel play (1910) Arthur Wing Pinero
Blunt, Captain Captain of the *Pretty Mary*, seduced and drugged by Sarah Purfoy*
His Natural Life (1870–2; abridged by the author 1874; in 1885 as *For the Term of His Natural Life* – thus evading the author's irony; orignal text edited by Stephen Murray-Smith, 1970) Marcus Clarke
Blunt, Captain J. K.
The Arrow of Gold (1919) Joseph Conrad (rn Josef Teodor Konrad Korzeniowski)
Blunt, Inspector
The Stolen White Elephant (1882) Mark Twain (rn Samuel Langhorne Clemens)
Blunt, Sir Thomas
Julia his wife; uncle and aunt of Lord Dreever*
A Gentleman of Leisure (1910) P. G. Wodehouse
Blunt, Sir Walter friend to the King
King Henry IV plays (1623) William Shakespeare
Bluntschli, Captain ('The Chocolate Soldier')

Arms and the Man play (1894) George Bernard Shaw

Blushington elderly rouged dandy
Pendennis (1848) W. M. Thackeray

Blythe, Pevensea editor of *The Outpost*
The *Forsyte* series (1906–33) John Galsworthy

Boabdil Saracen ruler
Ivanhoe (1820) Walter Scott

Boaler Paul Bultitude's* butler
Vice Versa (1882) F. Anstey (rn Thomas Anstey Guthrie)

Boam cockney constable
ss 'Another Temple Gone'
Fiery Particles (1923) C. E. Montague

Boanerges
The Apple Cart play (1929) George Bernard Shaw

Boatright, Moses young black in prison accused of eating a white man (which he has done, since he gives an account to Reddick* of what he tasted like)
The Man Who Cried I Am (1967) John Williams

Bobadil cowardly braggart, master of bomphilogy, one of the first (in English: the type originates in classical literature) in a long line (e.g. Pistol*)
Every Man in His Humour play (1598) Ben Jonson

Bobbe socialist friend to George Winterbourne*
Death of a Hero (1929) Richard Aldington

Bober, Morris Jewish grocer
Ida his wife
Helen his daughter
The Assistant (1957) Bernard Malamud

Bobsborough, Bishop of see Eustace and Greystock

Bobstay, Bill bosun's mate
H.M.S. Pinafore opera (1878) W. S. Gilbert and Arthur Sullivan

Bobster, Mr
Cecilia his daughter
Nicholas Nickleby (1839) Charles Dickens

Bode, Mr and Mrs
Almeric: Dulcia their son and daughter
A House and its Head (1935) Ivy Compton-Burnett

Bodfish, Martin ex-policeman, uncle of Mrs Negget*

ss 'Cupboard Love'
The Lady of the Barge (1902) W. W. Jacobs

Bodkin, Elias, Dr Dr Finn's* partner
Phineas Finn (1869) Anthony Trollope

Boffin, Nicodemus ('Noddy') formerly servant to John Harmon Sr.*
Henrietta his wife
Our Mutual Friend (1865) Charles Dickens

Bohemia, King of
ss 'A Scandal in Bohemia'
The Adventures of Sherlock Holmes (1892) Arthur Conan Doyle

Bohemond of Tartentum son of Robert Guiscard*: leader in the First Crusade
Count Robert of Paris (1832) Walter Scott

Bohun, Norman, the Hon. Colonel
Revd and the Hon. Wilfred his brother
ss 'The Hammer of God'
The Innocence of Father Brown (1911) G. K. Chesterton

Bohun, Walter son of Walter Boon* ('William')
You Never Can Tell play (1894) George Bernard Shaw

Boielle, Paul waiter and artist
ss 'Rough-hew them how we Will'
The Man Upstairs (1914) P. G. Wodehouse

Boileau, 'Tick' subaltern
ss 'A Conference of the Powers'
Many Inventions (1894) Rudyard Kipling

Bois-Guilbert, Brian de Commander of the Knights Templars
Ivanhoe (1820) Walter Scott

Boisgelin, Comtesse de
Anne of Geierstein (1829) Walter Scott

Boissec pedantic professor
Villette (1853) Charlotte Brontë

Boito, Arrigo (hist.)
Verdi: Roman der Oper (*Verdi: A Novel of the Opera*) (1924) Franz Werfel

Bojanus tailor
Antic Hay (1923) Aldous Huxley

Bok, Yakov a Kiev Jewish handyman framed for ritual child murder
The Fixer (1966) Bernard Malamud

Bokonan
Cat's Cradle (1963) Kurt Vonnegut

Boland, Con dentist

Mary his daughter, and other children
The Citadel (1937) A. J. Cronin

Bold, John surgeon m. Eleanor Harding*
Mary his sister
The Warden† (1855) Anthony Trollope

Boldero capitalist
Antic Hay (1923) Aldous Huxley

Boldero, the Hon. Mrs adventuress
Brenda; Minna her daughters
The Adventures of Philip (1862) W. M.
Thackeray

Boldheart, Captain
A Holiday Romance (1868) Charles
Dickens

Boldwig, Captain
The Pickwick Papers (1837) Charles
Dickens

Boldwood, William in love with Bathsheba
Everdene*; shoots Sergeant Troy*
Far From the Madding Crowd (1874)
Thomas Hardy

Bolfry 'Duke and General of Legions'
summoned from hell; character posited
as necessary to the maintenance of God
Mr Bolfry play (1943) James Bridie (rn
O. H. Mavor)

Bolingbroke, Duke of (later Henry IV) hist.
King Richard II; King Henry IV plays
(1623) William Shakespeare

Bollen, Mr farmer m. Adelaide Hinton*
Desperate Remedies (1871) Thomas
Hardy

Boller, Jacob ('Pennsylvania') preacher
and later seaman on *We're Here*
Captains Courageous (1897) Rudyard
Kipling

Bolling, Binx cc who lives in and for
movies, whose only reading is *Arabia
Deserta*, m. Kate Cutrer*
his mother
The Moviegoer (1961) Walker Percy

Bologna, Antonio second husband to the
Duchess of Malfi*
The Duchess of Malfi play (1623) John
Webster

Bolt, Ben ballad hero
'Ben Bolt' ballad (1843) T. D. English

Bolt, Henry Henry Little's* partner
Put Yourself in his Place (1870) Charles
Reade

Bolt, Tom
his wife
Charlie; Jack; Annie, Polly their children

All Our Yesterdays (1930) H. M.
Tomlinson

Boltby clerk to Hobson Bros
The Newcomes (1853–5) W. M.
Thackeray

Bolter, Jack friend to Barry Lyndon*
Barry Lyndon (1844) W. M. Thackeray

Bolter, Morris see Claypole

Bolton, Harry spendthrift aristocrat,
friend to Redburn*
Redburn: His First Voyage (1849) Herman Melville

Bolton, Lieutenant of the *Indefatigable* in
Hornblower series onwards from
The Happy Return† (1937) C. S.
Forrester

Bolton, Mrs 'portress' of Shepherds Inn
Barney; Amelia, Betsy; Fanny her children
Pendennis (1848) W. M. Thackeray

Bolton, Starworth, Captain
The Monastery (1820) Walter Scott

Bolus, Ovid chronic liar in sketch by
American jurist
sketch 'Ovid Bolus Esq'
Flush Times of Alabama and Mississippi
(1853) Joseph G. Baldwin

Bonaparte, Joe young boxer-violinist in
American play, the author's most successful
his father
his brother
Golden Boy play (1937) Clifford Odets

Bonaventura, Friar Giovanni's* tutor and
confessor
'Tis Pity She's a Whore play (1633) John
Ford

Boncinelli 'did know what he was saying.
He did know that knowing what one is
saying is something having meaning'
ss 'A Long Gay Book'
GMP (1932) Gertrude Stein

Bond, Hamish old man of New Orleans;
buys Amantha Starr*, at sixteen, from
her father; makes her his mistress, then
frees her
Band of Angels (1955) Robert Penn Warren

Bond, James Agent 007: cc successful
popular espionage series onwards from
Casino Royale† (1953) Ian Fleming

Bond, May comedy actress
Prisoner of Grace (1952) Joyce Cary

Bonduca i.e. **Boadicea** hist.
  Bonduca play (1647) John Fletcher
Bone, George Harvey tragic disturbed cc
  Hangover Square (1941) Patrick
  Hamilton
Bone, Malachi Canadian guide
  Settlers in Canada (1844) Captain
  Marryat
Bones, Billy, Captain of the *Hispaniola*
  Treasure Island (1883) Robert Louis
  Stevenson
Bones, Brom (Brom Van Brunt) reckless
  horseman and Ichabod Crane's* rival for
  Katrina Van Tassel*, whom he m.
  ss 'The Legend of Sleepy Hollow'
  The Sketch Book of Geoffrey Crayon,
  Gent (1820) Washington Irving
Bonewell, Thomas, Sir
  Aretina his wife
  The Lady of Pleasure play (1635) James
  Shirley
Boney a yellow horse preaching sedition
  ss 'A Walking Delegate'
  The Day's Work (1898) Rudyard Kipling
Bonfante, Arturo old revolutionary in
  Paris
  Birds of America (1971) Mary McCarthy
Bongolam courtier in Lilliput
  Gulliver's Travels (1726) Jonathan Swift
Boniface a landlord
  Cherry his daughter
  The Beaux' Strategem play (1707)
  George Farquhar
Boniface Lord Abbot of St Mary's
  The Monastery (1820) later **Blink-**
  hoolie *The Abbot* (1820) Walter
  Scott
Bonington, Ralph Bloomfield, Sir
  The Doctor's Dilemma play (1906)
  George Bernard Shaw
Bonner, Carl young lawyer, originally
  footballer and youngest Eagle Scout in
  the history of the State of Georgia: 'part
  of the way people thought about them-
  selves and the place they lived'
  Paris Trout (1988) Pete Dexter
Bonner, Dolly Milton Loftis'* mistress
  Lie Down in Darkness (1951) William
  Styron
Bonner, Mrs
  Lady Jocelyn; Juliana her daughters
  Evan Harrington (1861) George
  Meredith

Bonner, Susan maid to Lady Clavering* m.
  Lightfoot*
  Pendennis (1848) W. M. Thackeray
Bonner, Edmund rich Sydney draper, one
  of Voss' sponsors
  his wife
  Voss (1957) Patrick White
Bonnet, Madame *pensionnaire*
  Leontine her niece
  Fanny By Gaslight (1940) Michael
  Sadleir
Bonney company promoter
  Nicholas Nickleby (1839) Charles
  Dickens
Bonnington, Revd Mr second husband of
  Mrs Lovel*
  Lovel the Widower (1860) W. M.
  Thackeray
Bonnycastle a schoolmaster
  Mr Midshipman Easy (1836) Captain
  Marryat
Bonnyface, Mrs pretty landlady of the
  Swan, Exeter
  Barry Lyndon (1844) W. M. Thackeray
Bonover, George headmaster of Whortley
  Preparatory School
  Love and Mr Lewisham (1900) H. G.
  Wells
Bonteen, Mr Liberal MP
  his wife
  Phineas Finn † (1869) Anthony Trol-
  lope
Bonthron, Antony Sir J. Romorny's* 'dark
  satellite'
  The Fair Maid of Perth (1828) Walter
  Scott
Bonville, Katherine, Lady
  The Last of the Barons (1843) Edward
  Bulwer Lytton
Bonzig ('Le Grand Bonzig') head of boys'
  school in Paris
  The Martian (1897) George du Maurier
Booby, Thomas, Sir
  his wife; one-time employers of Joseph
  Andrews*
  Joseph Andrews (1742) Henry Fielding
Booch, Mrs pensioner of Lady Drew*
  Tono Bungay (1909) H. G. Wells
Booker, Alfred publisher
  The Way We Live Now (1875) Anthony
  Trollope
Boom, Hilary divorce solicitor for John
  Adam*

Holy Deadlock (1934) A. P. Herbert

Boom, Lord newspaper proprietor; opponent to Ponderevo*
Tono Bungay (1909) H. G. Wells

Boomer captain of the Fishbourne Fire Brigade
The History of Mr Polly (1910) H. G. Wells

Boomer the kangaroo
ss 'The Sing-Song of Old Man Kangaroo'
Just So Stories (1902) Rudyard Kipling

Boon, George cc, popular writer
Boon (1915) H. G. Wells

Boon, Percy young murderer cc of, in its time, very popular novel
Clarice his mother
London Belongs to Me (1945) Norman Collins

Boone, Daniel (hist.) American frontiersman (1734–1820) who explored and settled Kentucky and whose exploits were fictionalized in an allegedly 'autobiographical' account
Discovery, Settlement and Present State of Kentucky (1784) John Filson

Booth, James ('Old James') gardener at Fieldhead
Shirley (1849) Charlotte Brontë

Bootham, Harry nephew to Ted Gould , private secretary to Chester Nimmo*
Prisoner of Grace (1952) Joyce Cary

Booty, Fred friend to John Ransome*
The Combined Maze (1913) May Sinclair

Borachio D'Amville's* instrument
The Atheist's Tragedy, or The Honest Man's Revenge play (1611/12) Cyril Tourneur

Borden, Josiah
Emma his wife
Mourning Becomes Electra play (1931) Eugene O'Neill

Borden, Lizzie (hist.) acquitted of the murder of her father and mother, which may indeed have been committed by her elder sister Emma; none of the novels or plays based on the case has been successful, but that listed below is the most competent and readable
Lizzie Borden (1939) Marie Belloc Lowndes

Bordereau, Miss old lady living in Venice who was the mistress of Jeffry Aspern*

The Aspern Papers (1888) Henry James

Boreas, Nicholas film producer
Barefoot in the Head (1969) Brian W. Aldiss

Borel, Monsieur pastor of the French Church at Winchelsea
Denis Duval (1864) W. M. Thackeray

Borg, Isabelle
This Side of Paradise (1920) F. Scott Fitzgerald

Borkman, John Gabriel crooked tycoon cc; he has paced his study for eight years since his release from gaol
his wife, whom he refuses to see
Erhart their son
John Gabriel Borkman play (1896) Henrik Ibsen

Bornwell, Thomas, Sir
Aretina his wife, spendthrift
The Lady of Pleasure play (1635) James Shirley

Borodino, Countess of keeper of a Brussels *pension*
Vanity Fair (1847–8) W. M. Thackeray

Borokrom anarchist and murderer, with Ferdinand*, of Van Claben*
Guignol's band (1944) Louis-Ferdinand Céline (rn Louis-Ferdinand Destouches)

Bortz, Professor editor of a drama about the Tristero
The Crying of Lot 49 (1966) Thomas Pynchon

Bosola, Daniel de master of horse, and villain who repents
The Duchess of Malfi (1623) John Webster

Bossnowl, Lord, Earl of Foolincourt friend to MacCrotchet*
Crotchet Castle (1831) Thomas Love Peacock

Boswell all-in wrestler, cc
Boswell (1964) Stanley Elkin

Boswell, Joe handsome gipsy
The Virgin and the Gipsy (1930) D. H. Lawrence

Botell, Captain cc, master of *Oroya*
Captain Botell (1933) James Hanley

Bothwell, Francis Stewart, Sergeant
Old Mortality (1816) Walter Scott

Bott, Gladstone
ss 'High Stakes'
The Heart of a Goof (1926) P. G. Wodehouse

Bottleby friend of Talbot Twysden*
The Adventures of Philip (1862) W. M. Thackeray
Bottom weaver
A Midsummer Night's Dream play (1623) William Shakespeare
Boucher, Colonel m. Mrs Weston*
Queen Lucia† (1920) E. F. Benson
Boulanger, Rodolphe young landowner and lover of Emma Bovary*
Madame Bovary (1857) Gustave Flaubert
Boulby, Mrs innkeeper, the Pilot
Rhoda Fleming (1865) George Meredith
Boultby, Thomas, Dr hot-tempered rector of Whinbury
his wife and admirer
Grace possibly Mrs Boultby's daughter
Shirley (1849) Charlotte Brontë
Boulte engineer
his wife
ss 'A Wayside Comedy'
Wee Willie Winkie (1888) Rudyard Kipling
Boulter, George, the Hon. son of Lord Levant*
his wife, *née* Mango
Vanity Fair (1847–8) W. M. Thackeray
Bouncer landlord
Box and Cox play (1847) J. M. Morton
Bouncer, Henry m. Fanny Green*
The Adventures of Mr Verdant Green (1853, repr. 1982) Cuthbert Bede (rn Edward Bradley)
Bounderby, Josiah banker m. Louisa Gradgrind*
Hard Times (1854) Charles Dickens
Bountiful, Lady mother of Squire Sullen*
Dorinda her daughter
The Beaux' Strategem play (1707) George Farquhar
Bourbon, Duke of
King Henry V play (1623) William Shakespeare
Bourchier, Cardinal (hist.) Archbishop of Canterbury
King Richard III play (1623) William Shakespeare
Bourgh, Catherine de, Lady *patronne* of William Collins*; impertinent, her pride being a ridiculous exaggeration of that of her nephew Fitzwilliam Darcy*
Pride and Prejudice (1813) Jane Austen

Bournisien, Abbé consulted by Emma Bovary*, but he cannot be bothered with her
Madame Bovary (1857) Gustave Flaubert
Bovary, Charles inept physician
Emma his wife, cc
Berthe their daughter
Charles's mother
Madame Bovary (1857) Gustave Flaubert
Bowen, Evalina Colville's* friend
Effie her daughter
Indian Summer (1886) William Dean Howells
Bowen, Garnet author
Barbara his wife
Sandra; David; Mark their children
I Like It Here (1958) Kingsley Amis
Bowen, Laura
Charles her husband
The Custom of the Country (1913) Edith Wharton
Bowerbank, Mrs
The Princess Casamassima (1866) Henry James
Bowers, Captain uncle to Prudence Drewitt*
Dialstone Lane (1904) W. W. Jacobs
Bowles Corcoran's* landlord
Ukridge (1924) P. G. Wodehouse
Bowles missionary
The Heart of the Matter (1948) Graham Greene
Bowles, Beppo
Eyeless in Gaza (1926) Aldous Huxley
Bowles, Sally would-be *demi-mondaine*; singer
Goodbye to Berlin (1939) Christopher Isherwood
Bowling, George ('Fatty'; 'Tubby') insurance man, cc and narrator; when novel begins has just obtained new teeth
Hilda his wife, always looked like a hare – also, by now, an old gipsy woman over her fire; gets her kicks by foreseeing disasters
their children
Coming Up For Air (1936) George Orwell (rn Eric Blair)
Bowling, Lieutenant Roderick Random's* uncle
Roderick Random (1748) Tobias Smollett

Bowls butler to the Crawleys*
Vanity Fair (1847–8) W. M. Thackeray
Bows crippled fiddler
Pendennis (1848) W. M. Thackeray
Bowyer usher
Kenilworth (1821) Walter Scott
Bowyer, 'Honest' usurer
Alice his daughter
Master Humphrey's Clock (1841)
Charles Dickens
Box printer
Box and Cox play (1847) J. M. Morton
Box, Joe ('Chunks') of the *Jolly Bargee*
Fanny By Gaslight (1945) Michael
Sadleir
Box-Bender, Arthur MP m. Angela
Crouchback
Men at Arms (1952) Evelyn Waugh
Boxton, Dorothy m. 'Young' Nicholas
Forsyte*
The *Forsyte* series (1906–33) John
Galsworthy
Boy, The
ss 'Thrown Away'
Plain Tales from the Hills (1888) Rud-
yard Kipling
Boyce, Marcella, cc, social worker m.
Aldous Raeburn*
Richard her father
Evelyn her mother
Marcella (1894) Mrs Humphry Ward
Boyce, Selina daughter of Barbadian
immigrants to New York who finds
strength to combat racism through realiz-
ing herself in dance; by foremost
chronicler of West Indian experience in
America
Deighton her father
Brown Girl, Brownstones (1959) Paule
Marshall
Boylan, Hugh ('Blazes') Molly Bloom's*
lover
Ulysses (1922) James Joyce
Boyle, 'Captain' Jack
Juno his wife
Johnny; Mary their children
Juno and the Paycock play (1925) Sean
O'Casey (rn John Casey)
Boyle, Kevin, Professor murdered Pro-
fessor of English and poet; in outstanding
American crime novel by author who is
also one of the best living translators
The Horizontal Man (1958) Helen Eustis

Boyle, Revd Dr parson at Oakhurst
The Virginians (1857–9) W. M.
Thackeray
Boyne, Dr 'Protestant champion'
Pendennis (1848) W. M. Thackeray
Boynton, Dr 'honest charlatan' cc of novel
about evils of spiritualism and natural
honesty of the Shakers, whose com-
munity is sympathetically portrayed
Egeria his daughter, brought up by him as
a medium; James* told the author that he
thought the Shakers were described too
'unironically', 'as if you were a Shaker
yourself. (Perhaps you are . . .)'
The Undiscovered Country (1880)
William Dean Howells
Boythorne, Lawrence friend to Jarndyce*
Bleak House (1853) Charles Dickens
Bozzle, S. retired policeman
Maryanne his wife
He Knew He Was Right (1869) Anthony
Trollope
Brabantio senator
Othello play (1623) William Shake-
speare
Brabazon, Julia young cynic loved by and
in love with Harry Clavering*; m. Lord
Ogden* for his money and rank; later his
widow
Hermione ('Hermie') her sister m. Sir
Hugh Clavering*
Lord Brabazon their impoverished
deceased father
The Claverings (1866–7) Anthony
Trollope
Brace, Willie one of Angelica Deverell's*
publishers
Elspeth his wife
Angel (1957) Elizabeth Taylor
Bracebridge, Squire
Frank; Guy m. Julia Templeton – his sons
Simon ('Master Simon') his bachelor
cousin
The Sketch Book (1819); *Bracebridge
Hall* (1822) Washington Irving
Bracegirdle, Mary repressed young
woman
Chrome Yellow (1922) Aldous Huxley
Bracely, Olga prima donna
Queen Lucia (1920) E. F. Benson
Brack, Coralie, Madam horse rider
Pendennis (1848) W. M. Thackeray
Brackett Boston jailer

The Scarlet Letter (1850) Nathaniel
Hawthorne
Brackley, Daniel, Sir
The Black Arrow (1888) Robert Louis
Stevenson
Bracknel, Mr
his wife
Alfred sports lover; **Dennis** neurotic;
May; Amy their children
The Bracknels (1911) Forrest Reid
Bracknell, Lady
The Importance of Being Earnest play
(1895) Oscar Wilde
Bracy, Maurice de leader of mercenaries
Ivanhoe (1820) Walter Scott
Bradbourne, Lilias handmaiden to Lady
Mary Avenal*
The Abbot (1820) Walter Scott
Bradbourne, Paul aged gentleman-jockey
Before the Bombardment (1926) Osbert
Sitwell
Bradgate assistant officer, Yanrin
Aissa Saved (1932) Joyce Cary
Bradgate of Bradgate, Smith & Barrow,
lawyers
The Adventures of Philip (1862) W. M.
Thackeray
Bradleigh see Aldclyffe
Bradman, George, Dr
Violet his wife
Blithe Spirit play (1941) Noël Coward
Bradshaw, Revd lynch victim
A Different Drummer (1962) William
Melvin Kelley
Bradshaw, William friend to Mr Norris,*
narrator
Mr Norris Changes Trains (1935) Chris-
topher Isherwood
Bradshaw, William, Sir Harley Street
specialist
Mrs Dalloway (1925) Virginia Woolf
Bradwardine, Baron Cosmo of Comyne
Rose his daughter
Malcolm of Inchgrabbit his heir
Waverley (1814) Walter Scott
Brady, Caithleen (Kate) cc. m. Eugene
Galliard*
Kate her son
The Country Girls (1960); *The Lonely
Girl* (1962); *Girls in Their Married Bliss*
(1964) Edna O'Brien
Brady, Cecilia narrator
The Last Tycoon (1941) F. Scott

Fitzgerald
Brady, Michael uncle of Barry Lyndon*
his wife
Honoria his daughter
Barry Lyndon (1844) W. M. Thackeray
Brady, Pat treacherous estate manager
The Macdermots of Ballcloran (1847)
Anthony Trollope
Brady, Susan
The Playboy of the Western World play
(1907) J. M. Synge
Braggioni revolutionary
ss 'Flowering Judas'
Flowering Judas (1930, rev. 1935)
Katherine Anne Porter
Bragin, Colour-Sergeant
Annie his wife
ss 'The Solid Muldoon'
Soldiers Three (1888) Rudyard Kipling
Braiding, Mr and Mrs servants to G. J.
Hoape*
The Pretty Lady (1918) Arnold Bennett
Brainard, Erasmus nasty banker
The Cliff Dwellers (1893) Henry Blake
Fuller
Brainworm who manipulates the action
Every Man in His Humour play (1598)
Ben Jonson
Braithewaite, Maurice rugby player
This Sporting Life (1960) David Storey
Bramber, Miss
Sally her sister
Sir Charles Grandison (1754) Samuel
Richardson
Bramble, Lord employer of John Julip*
The Dream (1924) H. G. Wells
Bramble, Matthew travelling in search of
health, father of Humphrey Clinker*
Tabitha his 'starched, vain, ridiculous'
sister m. Lismahago*
The Expedition of Humphrey Clinker
(1771) Tobias Smollett
Bramble, Robert, Sir
The Poor Gentleman play (1802) George
Colman the Younger
Bramley, Miss Teresa ('Tibbets') cc; com-
panion to Miss Collier-Floodgaye*
Before the Bombardment (1926) Osbert
Sitwell
Bramsley, Caryl ('C') cc
Lord Charles Hengrave his father
his mother
Marjorie m. Sir Harold Ducane; **Julia** m.

Tommy Holden; **Edward; Gilbert; Harry** his brothers and sisters
C (1924) Maurice Baring
Brand, Admiral a shabby fellow
his brother
Persuasion (1818) Jane Austen
Brand, Fanny (cf. Fanny Brawne) John Shaynor's* girl
ss 'Wireless'
Traffics and Discoveries (1904) Rudyard Kipling
Brand, Mr minister, m. Charlotte Wentworth
The Europeans (1878) Henry James
Brander, Captain
ss 'His Private Honour'
Many Inventions (1893) Rudyard Kipling
Brander, Frank degenerate artist
Eric Dorn (1921) Ben Hecht
Brander, Hans portrait of the author's beloved friend, Max Beerbohm*, 'great, though slightly exiguous English man of letters'
Castles in Kensington (1904) Reginald Turner
Brander, Senator Jennie Gerhardt's* first lover
Jennie Gerhardt (1911) Theodore Dreiser
Brandon
King Henry VIII play (1623) William Shakespeare and John Fletcher
Brandon, Colonel owner of Delaford, m. Marianne Dashwood*
Mr Brandon his brother m. Eliza
Sense and Sensibility (1811) Jane Austen
Brandon, David in love with Hannah Jacob*
Children of the Ghetto (1892) Israel Zangwill
Brandon, Dorcas beautiful but apathetic heiress, cousin to, and formerly engaged to, Mark Wylder*
Wylder's Hand (1864) J. Sheridan Le Fanu
Brandon, Dr American alias of Dr Firmin*
Caroline, *née* Gann*, his wife ('The Little Sister') tricked into marrying him
The Adventures of Philip (1861–2); *A Shabby Genteel Story* (1840) W. M. Thackeray
Brandon, Joseph

Lucy his daughter m. Paul Clifford*
Sir William his brother, father of Paul; in 'Newgate novel'*
Paul Clifford (1930) Edward Bulwer Lytton
Brandon, Stanley, Revd Vicar of Lower Briskett-in-the-Midden
Jane his daughter m. Mulliner*
Meet Mr Mulliner (1927) P. G. Wodehouse
Brandt, Dr
ss 'Music'
A Beginning (1955) Walter de la Mare
Brandt, Margaret beloved of Gerard Eliasson*, and bearer of his child
The Cloister and the Hearth (1861) Charles Reade
Brandybuck, Meriadoc ('Merry') cousin to Frodo Baggins*
The Lord of the Rings (1954–5) J. R. R. Tolkien
Brangwen, Tom farmer
Lydia widow of a Pole, Lensky
Anna Lydia's daughter of her first marriage
Will handicrafts instructor, Tom's nephew m. Anna Lensky (above)
Ursula m. Rupert Birkin*; **Gudrun** art student; Will and Anna's daughters
The Rainbow (1915); *Women in Love* (1921) D. H. Lawrence
Brannon, Bill café owner
The Heart is a Lonely Hunter (1940) Carson McCullers
Bransdon, Simon leaves the colony and becomes a popular playwright
Ophelia his daughter
The Simple Life Limited (1911) Daniel Chaucer (rn Ford Madox Ford)
Branston butler to Austin Ruthyn*
Uncle Silas (1864) J. Sheridan Le Fanu
Brant, Adam, Captain lover of Christine Mannon*, murdered by Orin Mannon*
Mourning Becomes Electra play (1931) Eugene O'Neill
Brant, Joseph (hist.) Mohawk Chief who participated in atrocities and tr. St Mark's Gospel into Mohawk; in lively novel by author who became insane thirty-five years before he died
Greyslaer (1840) Charles Fenno Hoffman
Brasher, Phil founder of a new religion; in

novel evidently suggested by writings of P. D. Ouspensky
Angeline his wife
Barefoot in the Head (1969) Brian W. Aldiss
Bräsig, Zacharias kind-hearted steward, 'little man with the reddish face and stately nose', who befriends Havermann* after he has been sold up by Pomuchelskopp*
Ut mine Stromtid (An Old Story of my Farming Days) (1862–4) Fritz Reuter
Brass companion to Dick*
The Confederacy play (1705) John Vanbrugh
Brass, Sampson Quilp's* lawyer
Sally his sister
The Old Curiosity Shop (1841) Charles Dickens
Brassbound, Captain
Captain Brassbound's Conversion play (1900) George Bernard Shaw
Brassett college scout
Charley's Aunt play (1892) Brandon Thomas
Braun, Anna worthy teacher of German
Villette (1853) Charlotte Brontë
Bravassa, Miss actress
Nicholas Nickleby (1839) Charles Dickens
Braverman, Leslie young writer
To an Early Grave (1964) Wallace Markfield
Braxton, Stephen rival writer to Maltby*
ss 'Maltby and Braxton'
Seven Men (1919) Max Beerbohm
Bray, James, Colonel cc
Olivia his wife
A Guest of Honour (1971) Nadine Gordimer
Bray, Madeline m. Nicholas Nickleby*
Nicholas Nickleby (1939) Charles Dickens
Brayton, Harker
ss 'The Man and the Snake'
In the Midst of Life (1898) Ambrose Bierce
Brazen, Molly
Polly opera (1729) John Gay
Brazill, Eddy cc
ss 'Asylum'
Felo de Se (1960) (finally rev. as *Asylum*, 1979) Aidan Higgins

Bread, Dai
his two wives
Under Milk Wood play (1954) Dylan Thomas
Bread, Mrs maid to the old Marquise de Bellegarde*
The American (1876) Henry James
Breck, Alan (Stewart) cc, friend to David Balfour*; alias Stewart
Kidnapped (1886); *Catriona* (1893) Robert Louis Stevenson
Breck, Alison fishwife
The Antiquary (1816) Walter Scott
Breckinridge poultry dealer
ss 'The Blue Carbuncle'
The Adventures of Sherlock Holmes (1892) Arthur Conan Doyle
Brede, Clara cc, 'hemmed in Jamesian puritan', cultivated, thirty, her life cabined by endless duty
Revd Brede her half-demented father
The Benefactor (1905) Ford Madox Ford
Breedlove, Pecola eleven-year-old girl
her father, who rapes her
her mother
The Bluest Eye (1970) Toni Morrison
Breen, Dr woman doctor, cc
Dr Breen's Practice (1881) William Dean Howells
Brengwain childless wife of Gwenwyn*
The Betrothed (1825) Walter Scott
Brennan waxworks proprietor
ss 'propos des bottes'
Fiery Particles (1923) C. E. Montague
Brennan, Captain Irish Citizen Army
The Plough and the Stars play (1926) Sean O'Casey (rn John Casey)
Brennan, Malachi, Father
Harry Lorrequer (1830) Charles Lever
Brent, Henry cc, trying (and failing) to exorcise the evil of the title, an ancestor, Major Brent
A Name for Evil (1947) Andrew Lytle
Brent, John roving genius cc of melodramatic adventure story with vivid chase sequence, by writer killed at the big Bethel engagement in Virginia; m. Ellen Clitheroe*
John Brent (1862) Theodore Winthrop
Brent-Foster, Edward cc of author's only thoroughgoing farce, which contains much parody of Henry James*; the youngest major in the British army; m.

Lady Mary Savylle*
his aunt
The Panel (1912) (in UK as *Ring for Nancy*, 1913) Ford Madox Ford
Brentford, Earl of father of Lord Chiltern* and Lady Laura Standish*
Phineas Finn† (1869) Anthony Trollope
Brentmoor, Lord who decides to live like a working-class man
No. 5 John Street (1902) Richard Whiteing
Breton, Captain
The Wonder play (1714) Susannah Centlivre
Brett, Mrs maid to Mme Beatrix Bernstein*
The Virginians (1857–9) W. M. Thackeray
Brett, Sergeant-Master-Tailor friend to John Loveday*
The Trumpet Major (1880) Thomas Hardy
Bretton, Harry, CBE famous artist and devotee of 'the simple life'
Rachel his wife
Rose their daughter m. Joe MacPhail*
Cressida their granddaughter m. David Little*
The Wedding Group (1968) Elizabeth Taylor
Bretton, Louisa widow*
John Graham her handsome son, becomes a doctor m. Pauline Home*; impressionable but unimpressible
Villette (1853) Charlotte Brontë
Breville Peter cc of novel by St Lucia writer; returning to St Lucia after eight years
Phyllis his wife, whom he hardly knows, having m. her because she was pregnant, eight years earlier – and with whom he travels back to Europe
Paul his brother
Michael Paul's son by a girl who committed suicide because he refused to m. her – adopted by Peter and Phyllis
Nor Any Country (1969); *J—, Black Bam and the Masqueraders* (1972) Garth St Omer
Brewer member of Pinkie's* gang
Brighton Rock (1938) Graham Greene
Brewster, Maud writer m. Humphrey van Weyden*

The Sea Wolf (1904) Jack London
Brian
The Merry Devil of Edmonton play (1608) ?Thomas Dekker
Brice butler to Dr Firmin*
The Adventures of Philip (1862) W. M. Thackeray
Brick, Jefferson war correspondent
Martin Chuzzlewit (1844) Charles Dickens
Bridehead, Earl of see **Marchmain**
Bridehead, Susanna Florence Mary ('Sue') cc; cousin and lover of Jude Fawley* m. Richard Phillotson*
Jude the Obscure (1896) Thomas Hardy
Bridge, Mr
his wife and children; in American novels on a Babbitt* theme
Mrs Bridge (1959); *Mr Bridge* (1969) Evan S. Connell
Bridgenorth, Ralph, Major
Alice Christian his dead wife
Alice their daughter
Peveril of the Peak (1822) Walter Scott
Bridges, Ronald assistant curator in a museum
The Bachelors (1961) Muriel Spark
Bridget, Mother Abbess of St Catherine
The Abbot (1820) Walter Scott
Bridget, Mrs servant to the Widow Wadman* m. Corporal Trim*
Tristram Shandy (1767) Laurence Sterne
Bridgett, William tramp and thief
Bealby (1915) H. G. Wells
Bridmain, Edmund Countess Czerlaski's* half-brother; m. her maid Alice*
Scenes of Clerical Life (1857) George Eliot (rn Mary Anne, later Marian, Evans)
Brierly, Captain
Lord Jim (1900) Joseph Conrad (rn Josef Teodor Konrad Korzeniowski)
Brigge, Malte Laurids Danish poet in Paris; cc of autobiographical novel
Aufzeichnungen des Malte Laurids Brigge (*The Notebook of Malte Laurids Brigge*) (1908) Rainer Maria Rilke
Briggs miserly trustee
his wife
Cecilia (1782) Fanny Burney
Briggs pupil of Dr Blimber*
Dombey and Son (1848) Charles Dickens
Briggs shop assistant with Hoopdriver*

The Wheels of Chance (1896) H. G. Wells

Briggs solicitor who interrupts Rochester's bigamous wedding
Jane Eyre (1847) Charlotte Brontë

Briggs, Arabella companion to Miss Crawley*
Vanity Fair (1847–8) W. M. Thackeray

Briggs, Hortense Clyde Griffith's* girl for a short time
An American Tragedy (1925) Theodore Dreiser

Bright, Effie
If Winter Comes (1920) A. S. M. Hutchinson

Bright, Flossie draper's assistant; Grubb's* girl
War in the Air (1908) H. G. Wells

Brigson 'ulcer to the school', incited other pupils to throw crusts; in unintentionally hilarious novel (mocked in *Stalky**) by good-hearted dean whose message should instantly be heeded by contemporary teenagers
Eric, or Little by Little (1858) F. W. Farrar

Brimblecombe, Vindex schoolmaster and later curate
Westward Ho! (1855) Charles Kingsley

Brimsley, Jessy smallholder, m. Barnabas Holly*
South Riding (1936) Winifred Holtby

Brindle, Mrs village charlady
The Wedding Group (1968) Elizabeth Taylor

Brine, Dr organic chemist
The Small Back Room (1943) Nigel Balchin

Brinkley one-time manservant to Bertie Wooster*
Thank you, Jeeves (1934) P. G. Wodehouse

Brinkworth, Arnold m. Blanche Lundie*
Man and Wife (1870) Wilkie Collins

Briquet, Louis, ('Papa') circus manager
Tot, kto poluchaet poshchochiny (*He Who Gets Slapped*; once tr. as *The Painted Laugh*) play (1916) Leonid Andreyev

Brisac rich country gentleman
Charles; Eustace his sons, the elder his heir
The Elder Brother play (1635) John Fletcher and Philip Massinger

Briscoe, Lily painter
To the Lighthouse (1927) Virginia Woolf

Brisher, Mr
Jane his one-time fiancée
ss 'Mr Brisher's Treasure'
Tales of Life and Adventure (1923) H. G. Wells

Brisk a pert coxcomb
The Double-Dealer play (1710) William Congreve

Brisk, Fastidious
Every Man Out of His Humour play (1599) Ben Jonson

Brisk, Mr suitor of Mercy*
The Pilgrim's Progress (1678–84) John Bunyan

Brisket, Captain
Dialstone Lane (1904) W. W. Jacobs

Brissenden, Grace hostess of the nameless narrator, who appears to him to draw vitality from her husband
Guy her husband, younger than she
The Sacred Fount (1901) Henry James

Brissenden, Russ socialist poet, friend to Martin Eden*, suicide
Martin Eden (1909) Jack London

Brissendon, Agnes m. Everard Barfoot*
her mother and sisters
The Odd Women (1893) George Gissing

Bristle watchman
Bartholomew Fair play (1631) Ben Jonson

Bristol, Kitty, Lady modelled by author on Lady Caroline Lamb; m. William Ashe*
The Marriage of William Ashe (1905) Mrs Humphry Ward

Britannus
Caesar and Cleopatra play (1900) George Bernard Shaw

Brithwood, Richard rich young snob in very popular novel set c. 1780–1820
John Halifax, Gentleman (1856) Mrs Craik

Britling, Hugh author, art critic, cc
Mary his first wife
Hugh their son
Edith his second wife
their sons
Mr Britling Sees It Through (1916) H. G. Wells

Briton, Jules communist
It's a Battlefield (1935) Graham Greene

Britten-Close friend to Remington*

The New Machiavelli (1911) H. G. Wells
Brixham, Mrs landlady of Major Pendennis*
Pendennis (1848) W. M. Thackeray
Broadback, Esau innkeeper
Hawbuck Grange (1847) R. S. Surtees
Broadbent, Dr beautiful speaker at Bible meeting, but looks like a butcher
Shirley (1849) Charlotte Brontë
Broadbent, Thomas civil engineer
John Bull's Other Island play (1904) George Bernard Shaw
Broadwheel, Joe wagoner
Heart of Midlothian (1818) Walter Scott
Broc, Marie exhausting, dim pupil at Mme Beck's*
Villette (1853) Charlotte Brontë
Brock, Arthur in love with Elizabeth Caldwell*
The Beth Book (1897) Sarah Grand (rn Frances McFall)
Brocken, Henry cc narrator
The Diary of Henry Brocken (1904) Walter de la Mare
Brockett, Jimmy Falstaffian cc of Australian novel
Jimmy Brockett: Portrait of a Notable Australian (1951) Dal Stivens
Brockett, Jonathan playwright
The Well of Loneliness (1928) Radclyffe Hall
Brocklehurst, Earl of
Emily his wife
The Admirable Crichton play (1902) J. M. Barrie
Brocklehurst, Robert clergyman, treasurer of Lowood School, a 'black column', starves pupils and causes epidemic of typhus
his wife, richly dressed and interfering
Naomi his dead mother
Augusta; Broughton two of his children, the eldest being the well-dressed pupil Miss Brocklehurst
Jane Eyre (1847) Charlotte Brontë
Broderick, Isabel niece to Indefer Jones*, m. William Owen*
Cousin Henry (1879) Anthony Trollope
Brodie, Bennett m. Sarah Henderson*
Pilgrimage (1915–67) Dorothy M. Richardson
Brodie, James cc
Mary his mother

Margaret his wife
Matthew; Mary; Nessie their children
Hatter's Castle (1931) A. J. Cronin
Brodie, Jean schoolteacher in Edinburgh
The Prime of Miss Jean Brodie (1961) Muriel Spark
Brodie, William
Old Brodie his father
Mary his sister
Deacon Brodie play (1892) W. E. Henley and Robert Louis Stevenson
Brogley broker
Dombey and Son (1848) Charles Dickens
Broke, Bessie, model who destroys Heldar's* picture
The Light that Failed (1890) Rudyard Kipling
Bronwen cc, m. Ivor Morgan*
How Green Was My Valley (1939) Richard Llewellyn
Bronzomarte Launcelot Greaves's* horse
Sir Launcelot Greaves (1762) Tobias Smollett
Brook, Rhoda milkmaid
ss 'The Withered Arm'
Wessex Tales (1888) Thomas Hardy
Brooke head of school at Rugby
Tom Brown's Schooldays (1857) Thomas Hughes
Brooke, Catherine friend to Esther Dudley*
Esther (1884) Frances Snow Compton (rn Henry Adams)
Brooke, Dorothea cc m. (1) Edward Casaubon* (2) Will Ladislaw*
Celia her sister m. Sir James Chettam*
Middlemarch (1871 2) George Eliot (rn Mary Anne, later Marian, Evans)
Brooke, John m. Meg March*
John; Daisy; Josie their children
Little Women (1868); *Little Men* (1871); *Jo's Boys* (1886) Louisa M. Alcott
Brookfield, Jack keeper of gambling dive, possessor of telepathic powers who gets Helen Whipple's son* acquitted of murder by hypnotizing an attorney
The Witching Hour play (1916) A. M. Thomas
Brooksmith butler
ss 'Brooksmith'
The Lesson of the Master (1882) Henry James

Broom, Grace
Florrie her sister
Pilgrimage (1915–67) Dorothy M. Richardson
Broome, Arthur Anglican clergyman in Killala
The Year of the French (1979) Thomas Flanagan
Broster, Reggie tutor to Ogden Ford*
The Little Nugget (1913) P. G. Wodehouse
Brotherton, Marquis of hedonist who returns to England from Italy
his Italian wife
Lord Popenjoy his supposed heir
The Dowager Countess his mother
his three unmarried sisters
Lord George Germain his brother m. Mary Lovelace*
Is He Popenjoy? (1878) Anthony Trollope
Brough, John swindler
Isabella his wife
Belinda their ill-bred daughter
The Great Hoggarty Diamond (1841) W. M. Thackeray
Brougham, Annette alias **Brown** m. Bill Bates*
ss 'The Man Upstairs'
The Man Upstairs (1914) P. G. Wodehouse
Broun, Jessie one-time mistress of James Durie*
The Master of Ballantrae (1889) Robert Louis Stevenson
Broune, Nicholas editor of the *Morning Breakfast Table* m. Lady Carbury*
The Way We Live Now (1875) Anthony Trollope
Broussard, Monsieur
Louis his son
Gentlemen Prefer Blondes (1925) Anita Loos
Browdie, John Yorkshire farmer m. 'Tilda Price*
Nicholas Nickleby (1839) Charles Dickens
Browell, Bishop
Clare his daughter
Right Off the Map (1927) C. E. Montague
Brower, Dierich
The Cloister and the Hearth (1861)

Charles Reade
Brown ('Gentleman' Brown)
Lord Jim (1900) Joseph Conrad (rn Josef Teodor Konrad Korzeniowski)
Brown, Abraham old lodging-house keeper
Desperate Remedies (1871) Thomas Hardy
Brown, Berenice Sadie black cook with a glass eye, m. four times
Big Mama her fortune-telling mother
Honey Camden Brown her brother
The Member of the Wedding (1946) Carson McCullers
Brown, Captain
Miss Brown his daughter
Miss Jessie his daughter m. Major Gordon*
Cranford (1853) Mrs Gaskell
Brown, Charmian see **Sefton, Sophia, Lady**
Brown, Danny ('Cinnamon') sailor
Time Will Knit (1938) Fred Urquhart
Brown, Dolores farmer
Hawbuck Grange (1847) R. S. Surtees
Brown, Father priest-detective, cc of many stories
The Innocence of Father Brown† (1911) G. K. Chesterton
Brown, Henrietta cc
ss 'The Clerk's Quest'
The Untilled Field (1903) George Moore
Brown, Jenny mistress to David Scott*
Ship of Fools (1962) Katherine Anne Porter
Brown, John (hist.) cc
John Brown and Heroes of Harper's Ferry verse (1886) William Ellery Channing
Brown, John hired man forced by Dorcas Sheldon* to woo her because she has read *Roderick Random*￼
Female Quixotism (1801) Tabitha Tenney
Brown, Kate forty-five-year-old mother of four children
her husband, a neurologist
The Summer Before the Dark (1971) Doris Lessing
Brown, Ladbroke author of the funniest 'Shakespearian' play in any language
ss 'Savonarola Brown'
Seven Men (1919) Max Beerbohm

Brown, Lovell young reporter
South Riding (1936) Winifred Holtby

Brown, Mr elderly gentleman and gossip, teacher at M. Pelet's School
The Professor (1857) Charlotte Brontë

Brown, Mrs disreputable rag-and-bone merchant
Alice her daughter
Dombey and Son (1848) Charles Dickens

Brown, Puggy head of religious sect m. Lucy Wilcher*
Robert their son m. Ann Wilcher*
To Be a Pilgrim (1942) Joyce Cary

Brown, Rosamund harpsichordist; mother of Peter Levi*
Birds of America (1971) Mary McCarthy

Brown, Silas Lord Backwater's* trainer
ss 'Silver Blaze'
The Memoirs of Sherlock Holmes (1894) Arthur Conan Doyle

Brown, Susan m. Joe Lampton*
Room at the Top (1957) John Braine

Brown, Thomas (Tom) cc
Squire Brown his father
Tom Brown's Schooldays (1857) Thomas Hughes

Brown, Vanbeest see Bertram

Brown, Velvet Grand National winner
William her butcher father
Araminta her mother, a former channel swimmer
Edwina; Malvolia (Mally); Meredith (Merry); Donald her sisters and brother
National Velvet (1935) Enid Bagnold

Browne, 'Nosey'
Jorrocks's Jaunts and Jollities (1838) R S Surtees

Browne, Mrs widow
Edward her son
Maggie her daughter m. Frank Buxton*
The Moorland Cottage (1850) Mrs Gaskell

Browne, Richard, General friend to Lord Woodville*
The Tapestried Chamber (1828) Walter Scott

Brownell, 'Mister' schoolmaster in a late 'Stalky'* tale
ss 'The United Idolaters'
Debits and Credits (1926) Rudyard Kipling

Browner, James
ss 'The Cardboard Box'

His Last Bow (1917) Arthur Conan Doyle

Browning, Jack, Major persona of half-literate Yankee know-all adopted by the author in satirical letters attacking local customs and the presidency
Portland *Courier* (periodical) (1830) Seba Smith

Browning, Miss
Phoebe her sister
Wives and Daughters (1866) Mrs Gaskell

Browning, Robert (hist.) here dramatized in immensely popular play, m. Elizabeth Moulton Barrett*
The Barretts of Wimpole Street play (1930) Rudolf Besier

Brownlow, Mr
Oliver Twist (1838) Charles Dickens

Bruce, Colonel
The Comical Revenge, or *Love in a Tub* play (1664) George Etherege

Bruckner, Barbara engaged to Höfgen*
Mephisto (1936) Klaus Mann

Brudenell, Revd Mr (hist.)
The Devil's Disciple play (1899) George Bernard Shaw

Bruff family solicitor to the Herncastle* family; part-narrator
The Moonstone (1868) Wilkie Collins

Brugglesmith corruption of 'Brook Street, Hammersmith', and the only means by which a drunkard can be identified
ss 'Brugglesmith'
Many Inventions (1893) Rudyard Kipling

Brumby, Mrs wealthy widow
The Newcomes (1853–5) W. M. Thackeray

Brumfit, Norman, Dr 'wild man' of the medical school
Arrowsmith (1925) Sinclair Lewis

Brumley, George essayist and traveller
The Wife of Sir Isaac Harman (1914) H. G. Wells

Brundit, Courtenay ('Joe') baritone of the Dinky Doos
Stella Cavendish his wife, actress
The Good Companions (1929) J. B. Priestley

Brunhalt mother to Thierry* and Theodoret*

Thierry and Theodoret play (1621) John Fletcher, Philip Massinger ?and Francis Beaumont

Brunoni, Signor conjuror
Cranford (1853) Mrs Gaskell

Brunt jockey robbed of race by a low trick
ss 'The Broken Link Handicap'
Plain Tales from the Hills (1888) Rudyard Kipling

Brunton, Molly friend to Sylvia Robson*
Bessie her sister
Sylvia's Lovers (1863) Mrs Gaskell

Brush
The Clandestine Marriage play (1766) George Colman the Elder

Brush valet to Lord Sedley*
Vanity Fair (1847-8) W. M. Thackeray

Brush, George Marvin travelling salesman cc; 'holy fool'
Heaven's My Destination (1935) Thornton Wilder

Brush, Milly
Mrs Dalloway (1925) Virginia Woolf

Brustein, Sidney New York Jewish intellectual who has to learn that people are more important than abstractions
The Sign in Sidney Brustein's Window play (1965) Lorraine Hansberry

Brute, John, Sir
Lady Brute his wife
The Provok'd Wife play (1697) John Vanbrugh

Brutt, Major retired
The Death of the Heart (1938) Elizabeth Bowen

Brutus Australian 'bad hat' see also **Mephistopheles**
It is Never Too Late To Mend (1856) Charles Reade

Brutus, Junius tribune
Coriolanus play (1623) William Shakespeare

Brutus, King of Britain
Locrine play (1595) 'W.S.' (?George Peele; ?Robert Green)

Brutus, Marcus cc, assassin of Julius Caesar*
Julius Caesar play (1623) William Shakespeare

Bryan, Terry
South Riding (1936) Winifred Holtby

Bryan, Viscount see **Lyndon, Barry**

Brydon, Spencer who meets the Spencer Brydon, a 'hideous billionaire' who remained in New York, when he returns there from Europe; in tale of the uncanny
ss 'The Jolly Corner'
The Finer Grain (1910) Henry James

Bryerly, Dr Swedenborgian priest and friend to Austin Ruthyn*
Uncle Silas (1864) J. Sheridan Le Fanu

Brygandine, Bob clerk
ss 'The Wrong Thing'
Rewards and Fairies (1910) Rudyard Kipling

Bub
Second Skin (1964) John Hawkes

Bubb, Mrs landlady
The Town Traveller (1898) George Gissing

Bubble, Madame witch, temptress of Standfast*
The Pilgrim's Progress (1678-84) John Bunyan

Bubbleton, George Frederick Augustus, Captain later Lieutenant-General
Anna Maria his sister
Tom Burke of Ours (1844) Charles Lever

Bubenberg, Adrian de knight of Berne
Anne of Geierstein (1829) Walter Scott

Buchanan, Mr chief engineer of the *Dimbula*
ss 'The Ship that Found Herself'
The Day's Work (1898) Rudyard Kipling

Buchanan, Tom proto-fascist
Daisy his wife, lover of Gatsby*, cousin to Nick Carroway*
The Great Gatsby (1925) F. Scott Fitzgerald

Buck provost of North Kensington
The Napoleon of Notting Hill (1904) G. K. Chesterton

Buck trumpeter, friend to John Loveday*
The Trumpet Major (1880) Thomas Hardy

Buck, Joe lonely Texan
Midnight Cowboy (1966) James Leo Herlihy

Bucket, Inspector
Bleak House (1853) Charles Dickens

Buckhurst, Charles, Sir friend to Coningsby*
Coningsby (1844) Benjamin Disraeli

Buckie, Dr resident at Denbury Hospital
Let the People Sing (1939) J. B. Priestley

Buckingham, Duke of

King Richard III; *King Henry VI* plays (1623) William Shakespeare
Buckland, Widow Aglaura
  ss 'Piffingcap'
  Adam and Eve and Pinch Me (1921) A. E. Coppard
Bucklaw, Laird of see **Hayston, Frank**
Buckram, Lord son of Marquess of Bigwig*
  The Book of Snobs (1847) W. M. Thackeray
Bucksteed, Philadelphia
  Squire Bucksteed her father
  ss 'Marklake Witches'
  Rewards and Fairies (1910) Rudyard Kipling
Bud, Rosa pupil at Nun's College, betrothed as a child to Edwin Drood*
  Edwin Drood (1870) Charles Dickens
Budd, Billy young English sailor cc, hanged
  Billy Budd (1924) Herman Melville
Budd, Lanny trouble-shooting cc of political romances, by dear old Utopian, onwards from
  Dragon's Teeth (1942) Upton Sinclair
Budden, Octavius
  Amelia his wife
  Alexander Augustus their son
  Sketches by Boz (1836) Charles Dickens
Buddenbrook, Johann, Sr. the patrician; in epic novel — 1835–80 — of corn-factor's family in Lübeck, the author's native town
  Madame Antoinette his wife
  Johann, Jr. the Consul, their son
  Elizabeth *née* Kröger Johann's wife
  Gotthold Johann Sr.'s eldest son, by an earlier marriage
  Thomas; Johann; Antonie ('Toni'); Christian Johann Jr. and Elizabeth's children
  Gerda *née* Arnoldsen, Thomas' Dutch wife
  Justus Johann Kaspar ('Hanno') Thomas and Gerda's son
  Buddenbrooks, Verfall einer Familie (tr. as *Buddenbrooks*) (1901) Thomas Mann
Buddy assistant to Mr Conner*
  The Poorhouse Fair (1959) John Updike
Buffers fellow tenant of Philip Firmin* in Parchment Buildings
  The Adventures of Philip (1862) W. M. Thackeray

Buford, Chadwick cc, captain in Federal army, m. Margaret Dean*
  Chadwick his father
  Mary his mother
  Major Calvin relative who takes him in after his adopted parents have died
  Lucy his sister; in once very popular sentimental American Civil War romance set in Kentucky
  The Little Shepherd of Kingdom Come (1903) John Fox Jr.
Buggins shop-assistant friend to Kipps*
  Kipps (1905) H. G. Wells
Bugsby, Mrs lodging-house keeper
  The Newcomes (1853–5) W. M. Thackeray
Bukta native officer
  ss 'The Tomb of his Ancestors'
  The Day's Work (1898) Rudyard Kipling
Bulbo, Prince heir of Padella
  The Rose and the Ring (1855) W. M. Thackeray
Bulby chorister
  Pendennis (1848) W. M. Thackeray
Buldeo village hunter
  Jungle Books (1894–5) Rudyard Kipling
Bulders friend to Revd Lawrence Veal*
  Vanity Fair (1847–8) W. M. Thackeray
Bulgruddery, Dennis
  his wife
  John Bull play (1805) George Colman the Younger
Bull chaplain to Sir Tunbelly Clumsey*
  The Relapse, or Virtue in Danger play (1697) John Vanbrugh
Bull, Captain
  The Book of Snobs (1847) W. M. Thackeray
Bull, Dr (Saturday)
  The Man Who Was Thursday (1908) G. K. Chesterton
Bull, Johnny one of the famous five, onwards from
  The Magnet† periodical (1908) Frank Richards (rn Charles Hamilton)
Bull, Mrs
  Love on the Dole (1933) Walter Greenwood
Bull, Prince antagonist of Prince Bear, representing England in the Crimean War
  ss 'Prince Bull'

Reprinted Pieces (1858) Charles Dickens

Bullamy porter in Loan and Life Assurance Office
Martin Chuzzlewit (1844) Charles Dickens

Bullar, Mary, Dame prime minister
But Soft – We are Observed! (1928) Hilaire Belloc

Bullen, Anne (hist.)
King Henry VIII play (1623) William Shakespeare and John Fletcher

Bullfinch friend to the Uncommercial Traveller
ss 'A Little Dinner in an Hour'
The Uncommercial Traveller (1860–8) Charles Dickens

Bullington, Viscount enemy to Barry Lyndon*
Barry Lyndon (1844) W. M. Thackeray

Bullivant butler cc
Manservant and Maidservant (1947) Ivy Compton-Burnett

Bullivant, Walter, Sir
The Thirty-nine Steps (1915) John Buchan

Bullock 'gouty, bald-headed, bottle-nosed banker'
Francis his son m. Maria Osborn*
Vanity Fair (1847–8) W. M. Thackeray

Bullock master's mate
The King's Own (1830) Captain Marryat

Bullock, John, Private Everyman cc of bitter 1914–18 War book
The Patriot's Progress: Being the Vicissitudes of Pte. John Bullock (1930) Henry Williamson

Bullocksmithy, Bishop of
The Newcomes† (1853–5) W. M. Thackeray

Bullsegg Laird of Killancursit, 'cowardly half-bred swine'
Waverley (1814) Walter Scott

Bully, Colonel companion to Sir John Brute*
The Provok'd Wife play (1697) John Vanbrugh

Bulmer, Thomas, Sergeant
ss 'The Biter Bit'
The Queen of Hearts (1859) Wilkie Collins

Bulmer, Valentine m. Clara Mowbray*
St Ronan's Well (1824) Walter Scott

Bulminster, John, Sir

his wife
Vanity Fair (1847–8) W. M. Thackeray

Bulpitt, Samuel ex-waiter, millionaire, brother to Lady Abbot*
Summer Moonshine (1938) P. G. Wodehouse

Bulstead, William, Captain, RN of *Polyphemus*
Squire Gregory his brother
The Adventures of Harry Richmond (1871) George Meredith

Bulstrode, Nicholas banker
his first wife, formerly Mrs Dunkirk*
Harriet his second wife, sister of Mr Vincy*
Kate; Ellen their daughters
Middlemarch (1871–2) George Eliot (rn Mary Anne, later Marian, Evans)

Bulstrode, Talbot attractive young swine who loves and deserts Aurora Floyd*
Aurora Floyd (1863) Mary Braddon

Bultitude, Paul colonial produce merchant
Richard ('Dick') his son
Barbara; 'Roly' his other children
Vice Versa (1882) F. Anstey (rn Thomas Anstey Guthrie)

Bulwig, Mistaw Edward Lytton caricature of the well-known writer
The Yellowplush Papers (1852) W. M. Thackeray

Bumble workhouse beadle m. Mrs Corney*
Oliver Twist (1838) Charles Dickens

Bumpas, Dickie don who wrote the novel which Nicholas Herrick* tries to pass off as his own
Pastors and Masters (1925) Ivy Compton-Burnett

Bumper, Harry, Sir
The School for Scandal play (1777) Richard Brinsley Sheridan

Bumppo, Natty deerslayer, cc
The Leatherstocking Tales (1823–46) James Fenimore Cooper

Bumpshire, George, MP wealthy wholesale stationer
his wife, overdressed and three times his size
Bryanstone their son
Our Street (1848) W. M. Thackeray

Bumptious, Sergeant
Jorrocks's Jaunts and Jollities (1838) R. S. Surtees

Bumpus, Beatrice woman's suffrage worker
The Dream (1924) H. G. Wells
Bunce inmate of Hiram's Hospital
The Warden (1855) Anthony Trollope
Bunce MP for Newcome
The Newcomes (1853–5) W. M. Thackeray
Bunce, Jack, Lieutenant, *Fortune's Favourite*
The Pirate (1822) Walter Scott
Bunce, Jacob copying journeyman
Jane his wife, Finn's* landlady
Phineas Finn† (1869) Anthony Trollope
Bunce, Thomas innkeeper
Bessy his wife
Jenny their daughter
Mr Weston's Good Wine (1927) T. F. Powys
Bunch, Byron millworker and choir leader
Light in August (1932) William Faulkner
Buncle servant and secret messenger of Sir J. Ramorny*
The Fair Maid of Perth (1828) Walter Scott
Buncle, John cc essay-novel by 'Christian deist' which in some respects anticipates *Tristram Shandy*; it is encumbered with many footnotes; the narrator is in search of two things – a good country girl as wife, and money; he m. eight times; this has been called a 'comic masterpiece' – but 'no entirely sane person could ever read *John Buncle* from end to end without plentiful skipping'; one of the best episodes is a fight between a louse and a flea – who fixes a 'flashing eye' on his foe – seen through a microscope.
The Life and Opinions of John Buncle Esq. (1756–66) Thomas Amory
Bundren, Addie dying and then, for most of the novel, dead cc
Anse her husband
Cash; Darl; Jewel; Dewey Dell; Vardaman her children – the third-named by the Reverend Whitfield*
As I Lay Dying (1930) William Faulkner
Bunfit eminent detective
The Eustace Diamonds (1872) Anthony Trollope
Bung wine merchant, member of Sarcophagus Club
The Book of Snobs (1847) W. M. Thackeray

Bungay publisher of the *Pall Mall Gazette*, at enmity with his former partner, Bacon*
his wife
Pendennis (1848) W. M. Thackeray
Bunion, Miss writer of sentimental love poetry
Pendennis (1848) W. M. Thackeray
Bunner, Calvin C. American secretary to Sigsbee Manderson*
Trent's Last Case (1912) E. C. Bentley
'Bunny'
ss 'Aunt Ellen'
Limits and Renewals (1932) Rudyard Kipling
'Bunny' intimate of Raffles*; narrator of the series, onwards from
The Amateur Cracksman† (1899) E. W. Hornung
Bunny Bushtail squirrel; onwards from
Uncle Remus, His Songs and His Sayings† (1880) Joel Chandler Harris
Bunsby, Captain
his wife, formerly Mrs MacStinger
Dombey and Son (1848) Charles Dickens
Bunter, George William ('Billy') fat boy of Greyfriars, onwards from
Bessie his sister (featured in another publication by the same author)
The Magnet† periodical (1908) Frank Richards (rn Charles Hamilton)
Bunter, Mervyn manservant to Lord Peter Wimsey* in series onwards from
Whose Body?† (1923) Dorothy L. Sayers
Bunthorne, Edna m. Bert Smallways*
The War in the Air (1908) H. G. Wells
Bunthorne, Reginald fleshly poet
Patience opera (1881) W. S. Gilbert and Arthur Sullivan
Bunting, Mr and Mrs
Fred; Betty; Netty their children
The Sea Lady (1902) H. G. Wells
Bunting, Revd Vicar of Iping
The Invisible Man (1897) H. G. Wells
Buonaventure, Father alias of Bonnie Prince Charlie
Redgauntlet (1824) Walter Scott
Burbo wine seller, retired gladiator
The Last Days of Pompeii (1834) Edward Bulwer Lytton
Burch, Lucas ('Joe Brown') bootlegger and seducer, in the city, of Lena Grove*

Light in August (1932) William Faulkner
Burchell alias of Sir William Thornhill
The Vicar of Wakefield (1766) Oliver
Goldsmith
Burckheim, Honoré cc, owner of family
ironworks in Alsace village
his first wife
Caroline his second wife, from Boston
Cousin Honoré (1940) Storm Jameson
Burden victim in Orwellian* American
novel
One (1953) reissued as *Escape to No-
where* (1955) David Karp
Burden, Jack journalist, repentant political
lackey, narrator
All the King's Men (1946) Robert Penn
Warren
Burden, Jim narrator
My Antonia (1918) Willa Cather
Burden, Joanna Joe Christmas's* reclusive
white lover; killed by him
Light in August (1932) William Faulkner
Burden, Simon pensioner
The Trumpet Major (1880) Thomas
Hardy
Burdener, Michael maverick Englishman
Ama his African wife; in Canadian novel
set in West African country akin to
Nkrumah's Ghana
The New Ancestors (1970) Dave
Godfrey
Burdock, James country servant of Ernest
Vane*
Peg Woffington (1853) Charles Reade
Burdock, Miss runs the Rimini Hotel
The Old Boys (1964) William Trevor
Burge, Jonathan employer of Adam* and
Seth Bede*
Adam Bede (1859) George Eliot (rn
Mary Anne, later Marian, Evans)
Burges, Lewis Holroyd tobacconist and
freemason
ss 'In the Interests of the Brethren'
Debits and Credits† (1926) Rudyard
Kipling
Burgess Candida Morell's father
Candida play (1894) George Bernard
Shaw
Burgess, Bessie street fruit vendor
The Plough and the Stars play (1926)
Sean O'Casey (rn John Casey)
Burgess, Brooke employed at Somerset
House

Revd Barty his father
He Knew He Was Right (1869) Anthony
Trollope
Burgess, Ted farmer, Marian Maudsley's*
lover
The Go-Between (1953) L. P. Hartley
Burgoyne, General (hist.)
The Devil's Disciple (1899) George
Bernard Shaw
Burgundy, Duke of
King Henry V; *King Henry VI* plays
(1623) William Shakespeare
Burgundy, Duke of
King Lear play (1623) William Shake-
speare
Burjoyce printer
Vanity Fair (1847–8) W. M. Thackeray
Burke, Captain 'professional promoter of
revolutions'
Soldiers of Fortune (1897) Richard
Harding Davis
Burke, Chevalier de (Francis) Irish colonel
in service of the Pretender
The Master of Ballantrae (1889) Robert
Louis Stevenson
Burke, Dan
Nora his wife
In the Shadow of the Glen play (1903)
John Millington Synge
Burke, Mat
Anna Christie play (1922) Eugene
O'Neill
Burke, Miss Emma Greatheart's* com-
panion
Mother and Son (1954) Ivy Compton-
Burnett
Burke, Pat horse thief
*Robbery Under Arms: A Story of Life
and Adventure in the Bush and in the
Goldfields of Australia* (1888, rev. 1889)
Rolf Boldrewood (rn Thomas Alexander
Browne)
Burke, Reginald bank manager
ss 'A Bank Fraud'
Plain Tales from the Hills (1888) Rud-
yard Kipling
Burke, Sadie Willie Stark's mistress
All the King's Men (1946) Robert Penn
Warren
Burke, Tom cc narrator m. Marie
d'Auvergne*
Matthew his father
George his elder brother

Tom Burke of Ours (1844) Charles Lever
Burke, Ulick gentleman jockey and spy
Jack Hinton (1838) Charles Lever
Burkett, Dinah Dorothea m. Jo. Hermann*
Madeleine her sister m. Rickie Masters*
The Echoing Grove (1953) Rosamond Lehmann
Burkin, George peeping Tom
Heaven's My Destination (1935) Thornton Wilder
Burkin-Jones, Clare ('Mumbo') who is also **Mopsie Pye**, owner of gift shops
The Little Girls (1964) Elizabeth Bowen
Burkle, Matthew cc, man who hates sex and diverts his energy into money-making
Nothing Like Leather (1935) V. S. Pritchett
Burlap editor
Point Counter Point (1928) Aldous Huxley
Burleigh, Burton policeman
An American Tragedy (1925) Theodore Dreiser
Burleigh, Cecil
Men Like Gods (1923) H. G. Wells
Burleigh, Trayton murderer
ss 'In the Library'
The Lady of the Barge (1902) W. W. Jacobs
Burley, John in Shandean* novel supposedly written by Pisistratus Caxton*
My Novel, or Varieties in English Life (1850–3) Edward Bulwer Lytton
Burnage, Cecil editor, *The Voice*
Rose his wife
Right Off the Map (1927) C. E. Montague
Burnea cockney
ss 'The Woman in his Life'
Limits and Renewals (1932) Rudyard Kipling
Burnell, Linda née Fairfield
Stanley her husband
Isabel; Lottie; Kezia their daughters
Beryl her sister
ss 'Prelude'
Bliss (1920) Katherine Mansfield (rn Katherine Mansfield Beauchamp)
Burnet, Susan furniture renovator
The Wife of Sir Isaac Harman (1914) H. G. Wells

Burnet, Vincent
Cormorant Crag (1895) G. Manville Fenn
Burnett, Arabella, the Hon. ('Balmy Jane')
But Soft – We Are Observed! (1928) Hilaire Belloc
Burnett, James first lieutenant, *Compass Rose*
The Cruel Sea (1951) Nicholas Monsarrat
Burnham, Leicester, Dr Jeremiah Beaumont's* teacher
World Enough and Time (1950) Robert Penn Warren
Burns, Gerald ('Shifty') scaler in Liverpool docks
Ebb and Flood (1932) James Hanley
Burns, Helen pupil at Lowood who befriends Jane Eyre*
Jane Eyre (1847) Charlotte Brontë
Burns, Peter part-narrator, cc; m. Audrey Sheridan née Blake*
The Little Nugget (1913) P. G. Wodehouse
Burns, Summer professional barfly
Count Florio and Phyllis K. (1910) Reginald Turner
Burnside, Reggie
Death of a Hero (1929) Richard Aldington
Burnwell, George, Sir
ss 'The Beryl Coronet'
The Adventures of Sherlock Holmes (1892) Arthur Conan Doyle
Burrage, Mrs socialite
The Bostonians (1886) Henry James
Burrows, Eliphaz, Sir governor of Woldingstanton School
The Undying Fire (1919) H. G. Wells
Burt negro
ss 'I'm a Fool' and elsewhere
Horses and Men (1924) Sherwood Anderson
Burtenshaw, Alexander
Rosamund his daughter
A House and Its Head (1935) Ivy Compton-Burnett
Burton, Hannah maid to Clarissa Harlowe*
Clarissa (1748) Samuel Richardson
Burton, Millicent, Lady
Mrs Dalloway (1925) Virginia Woolf
Burton, Mr poorer and less ostentatious

co-partner in Beilby* & Burton
Theodore his son, who will succeed him; dusts his thick shoes with his handkerchief and is therefore not, in Harry Clavering's eyes, the paragon Florence thinks him
Cecilia Theodore's wife *née* Jones
Florence his youngest daughter m. Harry Clavering*
his wife
The Claverings (1866–7) Anthony Trollope
Burton, Reginald crooked millionaire
At His Gates (1872) Mrs Margaret Oliphant
Burton, Sarah cc, formidable headmistress of Kiplington High School
Pattie her married sister
South Riding (1936) Winifred Holtby
Burwen-Fossilton actor
The Diary of a Nobody (1902) George and Weedon Grossmith
Bury, Caroline, Mrs
It's a Battlefield (1935) Graham Greene
Buryan, John Thomas Cornish farmer
Kangaroo (1923) D. H. Lawrence
Busby, Mortimer shady publisher
Summer Moonshine (1938) P. G. Wodehouse
Bushman, Anse cc of Kentucky novel
Tarvin his son
Trees of Heaven (1940) Jesse Stuart
Bushy creature to King Richard
King Richard II play (1623) William Shakespeare
Buskbody, Martha mantua-maker of Gandercleugh
Old Mortality (1816) Walter Scott
Bussens, M. de tyrannical husband
Mme de Bussens his wife, cc, in love with Pastor Tremblez*; sent away for 'infidelity'
Maurice their son, who loves his mother's generosity of spirit and fears his father
Les Roches blanches (*The White Rocks*) (1895) Édouard Rod
Bustington, Lord
The Newcomes (1853–5) W. M. Thackeray
Busy, Zeal-Of-The-Land a Banbury man, suitor to Dame Purecraft*
Bartholomew Fair play (1631) Ben Jonson
Bute war correspondent
ss 'Two or Three Witnesses'
Fiery Particles (1923) C. E. Montague
Butler, Edward contractor and local politico
Aileen his daughter
The Financier (1912) Theodore Dreiser
Butler, Julius, Lieutenant later Captain
Waverley (1814) Walter Scott
Butler, Rhett blockader m. (as third husband) Scarlett O'Hara*
Bonnie their daughter, killed by a fall from pony
Gone With the Wind (1936) Margaret Mitchell
Butler, Stephen corporal in Cromwell's dragoons
Judith his wife
Benjamin their son
Reuben his grandson m. Jeanie Deans*
David; Reuben; Femie Reuben and Jeanie's children
Heart of Midlothian (1818) Walter Scott
Butt, Gregory, Sir
Dr Angelus play (1947) James Bridie (rn O. H. Mavor)
Buttercup bumboat woman (Mrs Cripps) m. Captain Corcoran*
H.M.S. Pinafore opera (1878) W. S. Gilbert and Arthur Sullivan
Butteridge, Alfred loud-mouthed fraud who claims to have invented airship
The War in the Air (1908) H. G. Wells
Buttermere family retainer
Men and Wives (1931) Ivy Compton-Burnett
Butters, Mrs missionary's wife, Manchuria
Tobit Transplanted (1931) Stella Benson
Butterworth, Clara m. Hugh McVey*
Tom her father
Poor White (1920) Sherwood Anderson
Button late research dynamiter (Monday)
The Man Who Was Thursday (1908) G. K. Chesterton
Butts, Dr physician to the King
King Henry VIII play (1623) William Shakespeare and John Fletcher
Buxton, Frank m. Maggie Browne*
Lawrence his father
his mother
Ermina ('**Minnie**') his cousin

The Moorland Cottage (1850) Mrs Gaskell

Buzfuz, Sergeant barrister for Mrs Bardell*

The Pickwick Papers (1837) Charles Dickens

Buzzford general dealer at Casterbridge

The Mayor of Casterbridge (1886) Thomas Hardy

Bycliffe, Maurice Christian claimant to the Transome estates

Annette *née* Ledru his wife

Esther their daughter; adopted by Revd Lyon*

Felix Holt (1866) George Eliot (rn Mary Anne, later Marian, Evans)

Byers, Jessie

The Story of Ragged Robyn (1943) Oliver Onions

Byfield, Professor balloonist

St Ives (1897) Robert Louis Stevenson

Bygrave alias of Mrs Wragge*; in novel about illegitimacy by author who had several children outside the wedlock he refused to contemplate

No Name (1862) Wilkie Collins

Bygrave, Miss see **Vanstone, Magdalen**

Byles, Cockle, Sir

The Book of Snobs (1847) W. M. Thackeray

Byng, Admiral (hist.) executed to encourage the others

Candide (1759) Voltaire (rn François-Marie Arouet)

Byng, Alexander

Sarah; Jane; Bill his siblings

Cautionary Tales (1907) Hilaire Belloc

Byng, Caroline, Lady sister of Lord Marshmoreton*

Clifford her dead husband

Reginald ('Reggie') her stepson m. Alice Faraday*

A Damsel in Distress (1919) P. G. Wodehouse

Byng, Robert cc of novel set in failed pseudo-medieval university (Chrysalis College) by author who was killed in the American Civil War

Cecil Dreeme (1862) Theodore Winthrop

Byrne, Michael tinker

Mary his mother

The Tinker's Wedding play (1909) John Millington Synge

Byron, Harriet cc, and the most prolific writer of letters, m. Sir Charles Grandison*

Sir Charles Grandison (1754) Samuel Richardson

C

Caballacu guerilla leader, murderer
  Doña Perfecta(1876)Benito Pérez Galdós
Cabestainy, William troubadour
  Anne of Geierstein (1829) Walter Scott
Cabot, Ephraim farmer
  Simeon, Peter and Eben his sons, the last
  of whom is seduced by Abbie
  Abbie his third wife
  Desire Under the Elms play (1924)
  Eugene O'Neill
Cabot, Lionel friend to Ulysses Macaulay*
  The Human Comedy (1943) William
  Saroyan
Cacafogo, Dr
  A Citizen of the World (1762) Oliver
  Goldsmith
Cacambo half-breed servant to Candide*
  Candide (1759) Voltaire (rn François-
  Marie Arouet)
Cackle assistant surgeon in George
  Osborne's* regiment
  Vanity Fair (1847–8) W. M. Thackeray
Caddles, Albert Edward giant child
  The Food of the Gods (1904) H. G. Wells
Cade, Jack (hist.) rebel
  King Henry IV; *King Henry VI* plays
  (1623) William Shakespeare
Cadogan, Mrs Yeates's* housekeeper
  Peter her nephew
  Some Experiences of an Irish R.M.
  (1899) O. E. Somerville and Martin Ross
  (rn Edith Somerville and Violet Martin)
Cadwal see Arvigarus
Cadwallader, Elinor, Mrs gossip addicted
  to notions of social rank
  Revd Humphrey her good-hearted hus-
  band
  Middlemarch (1871–2) George Eliot (rn
  Mary Anne, later Marian, Evans)
Cadwallon Gwenwyn's bard
  The Betrothed (1825) Walter Scott
Cady, Gladys and her family
  Beggar on Horseback play with music
  (1924) George S. Kaufman and Marc
  Connelly

Caelistine bride to Sir Walter Terrill*
  Satiromastix, or *The Untrussing of the
  Humorous Poet* play (1602) Thomas
  Dekker ?and John Marston
Caerleon, Mary, Lady m. the Marquis of
  Steyne*
  Pendennis (1848) W. M. Thackeray
Caesar, James cowardly grocer, almost m.
  Hannah Ferguson* but she thinks him a
  'spiritless old collie' until she believes he
  killed Witherow*
  John Ferguson play (1915) St John Ervine
Caesar, Julius (hist.) cc
  Calpurnia his wife
  Julius Caesar play (1623) William Shake-
  speare
  Caesar and Cleopatra play (1900)
  George Bernard Shaw
Cahel, Delia
  Kathleen ni Houlihan verse play (1902)
  W. B. Yeats
Cahill storekeeper and New York gangster
  (highwayman, the 'Red Rider') to ensure
  his daughter's fortune
  Mary his daughter
  Ranson's Folly (1902) Richard Harding
  Davis
Cairn, Rob
  ss 'The French Poodle'
  Unlucky for Pringle (1973) Wyndham
  Lewis
Cairns, Kitty
  Fanny By Gaslight (1940) Michael
  Sadleir
Cairo, Joel former agent of Casper Gut-
  man*
  The Maltese Falcon (1930) Dashiell
  Hammett
Caitlin daughter of MacMurrachu; a shep-
  herd girl
  The Crock of Gold (1912) James Steph-
  ens
Caius, Dr French physician
  The Merry Wives of Windsor play (1623)
  William Shakespeare

Caius Lucius Roman general
Cymbeline play (1623) William Shakespeare
Caius Marcius see **Coriolanus**
Calabria, Ferdinand, Duke of
The Cardinal his brother
The Duchess of Malfi play (1623) John Webster
Calamy
Those Barren Leaves (1925) Aldous Huxley
Calandrino a merry fellow
The Great Duke of Florence play (1636) James Shirley
Calantha daughter to Amyclas*
The Broken Heart play (1633) John Ford
Calder, James narrator m. Pat Leighton*
Wickford Point (1939) John P. Marquand
Caldwell, George science teacher; also **Chiron**
Cassie *née* Kramer his wife
Peter their teenage son
The Centaur (1963) John Updike
Calianax father of Aspatia*
The Maid's Tragedy play (1611) Francis Beaumont and John Fletcher
Caliban savage and deformed slave
The Tempest play (1623) William Shakespeare
Caliban, Mrs cc of energetic but chaotic surrealistic novel which became a brief sensation when chosen in 1986 by the British Book Marketing Council as one of the top twenty American novels of the post-war period
Mrs Caliban (1982) Rachel Ingalls
Caliban, Tucker cc
A Different Drummer (1962) William Melvin Kelley
Calidore, Mrs R. with a passion for private theatricals
Our Street (1848) W. M. Thackeray
Caligula (hist.)
Lazarus Laughed play (1927) Eugene O'Neill
Calipolis
The Battle of Alcazar play (1594) George Peele
Calista of Montfaucon chief 'bower-woman' of Queen Berengia
The Talisman (1825) Walter Scott
Calkin, Agatha

Men and Wives (1931) Ivy Compton-Burnett
Callaghan, Bat
Mrs Callaghan his mother
Some Experiences of an Irish R.M. (1899) O. E. Somerville and Martin Ross (rn Edith Somerville and Violet Martin)
Callard, Mrs
The Lie play (1923) Henry Arthur Jones
Callaway, Lew fisherman cc of novel that established this Australian author, first encouraged by A. R. Orage, m. Lena Christensen
Peter their son
The Passage (1930) Vance Palmer
Callcome, Nat best man at Dick Dewey's* wedding
Under the Greenwood Tree (1872) Thomas Hardy
Callcott, Jack neighbour to Somers*
Kangaroo (1923) D. H. Lawrence
Callendar, Major
A Passage to India (1924) E. M. Forster
Callender, Miss Daisy matron
The Good Companions (1929) J. B. Priestley
Callonby, Earl of
Lord Kilkee his son
Lady Catherine his daughter
Lady Jane his daughter m. Harry Lorrequer*
Harry Lorrequer (1839) Charles Lever
Caloveglia, Count
South Wind (1917) Norman Douglas
Calsabigi lottery contractor
Barry Lyndon (1844) W. M. Thackeray
Calton boarder at Mrs Tibbs's*
Sketches by Boz (1836) Charles Dickens
Calverley, Colonel Dragoon Guards, m. Lady Saphir*
Patience opera (1881) W. S. Gilbert and Arthur Sullivan
Calverley, Hugh, Sir
The White Company (1891) Arthur Conan Doyle
Calvert, Belle prostitute and witness to murder
The Private Memoirs and Confessions of a Justified Sinner (1824) as *The Suicide's Grave* (1828) as *Confessions of a Fanatic* in *Tales and Sketches* (1837) James Hogg
Calvert, Cathleen
Cade her brother

Gone With the Wind (1936) Margaret Mitchell

Calvert, Herbert property owner
The Card (1911) Arnold Bennett

Calvert, Roy confidant and close friend to Lewis Eliot*
Strangers and Brothers† sequence, onwards from 1949, C. P. Snow

Calvo, Baldassare adoptive father of Tito Melema*
Romola (1863) George Eliot (rn Mary Anne, later Marian, Evans)

Calymatch, Selim son of the Grand Seignior
The Jew of Malta (1633) Christopher Marlowe

Camber son to King Brutus*, brother to Locrine* and Albanact*
Locrine play (1595) 'W.S.' (?George Peel; ?Robert Green)

Cameron Highland boatman, later minister
Mary Rose play (1920) J. M. Barrie

Cameron, Brian
Gaslight play (1939) Patrick Hamilton

Cameron, Dr Finlay's senior colleague in sketches later made into long-running radio and tv series called *Dr Finlay's Casebook*
Beyond This Place (1953) A. J. Cronin

Cameron, Evelyn beautiful English girl loved by Ernest Maltravers
Ernest Maltravers (1837)
Alice, or The Mysteries (1838) Edward Bulwer Lytton

Cameron, Mary mistress to Dr Phillips*, m. Charlie Doveton*
Nita her daughter by Phillips
Doctor Phillips (1887) Frank Danby (rn Julia Frankeau)

Cameron, Rachel sexually frustrated spinster in Canadian prairie town
her mother, widow of an undertaker
A Jest of God (1966) Margaret Lawrence

Camilla m. David Simple* in tragi-comic novel in line of *Don Quixote**
Valentine her brother m. Cynthia*
The Adventures of David Simple (1744–53) Sarah Fielding

Camillo Sicilian lord, m. Perdita*
A Winter's Tale play (1623) William Shakespeare

Camiola maid of honour

The Maid of Honour play (1632) Philip Massinger

Cammysole, Mrs Titmarsh's* extortionate landlady
Our Street (1848) W. M. Thackeray

Campaspe
Alexander and Campaspe play (1584) John Lyly

Campbell ('Barcaldine') commander of troop
The Highland Widow (1827) Walter Scott

Campbell, Alan
The Picture of Dorian Gray (1891) Oscar Wilde

Campbell, Bessie see Hipkiss

Campbell, Colonel friend to Jane Fairfax's* father
his wife; parents of Mrs Dixon*
Emma (1816) Jane Austen

Campbell, Helen wife to Rob Roy*
Rob Roy (1818) Walter Scott

Campbell, Henry surgeon
Emily his wife
Henry, Jnr.; Alfred; Percival; John their sons
Emma, Mary adopted nieces
Douglas successful claimant to his estate
The Settlers in Canada (1844) Captain Marryat

Campbell, Johnny eighty-seven-year-old narrator of Jamaican dialect novel covering the period from the Morant Bay Rebellion (1865) until the reinstitution of constitutional rule (1944)
New Day (1949) Vic Reid

Campbell, Mike Brett Ashley's* fiancée
The Sun Also Rises (in England, *Fiesta*) (1926) Ernest Hemingway

Campbell, Mr surgeon of the *Thrush*
Mansfield Park (1814) Jane Austen

Campbell, Mrs ('The Polar') school cleaner, preacher
ss 'Washed in the Blood'
The Clouds Are Big With Mercy (1946) Fred Urquhart

Campbell, Charlotte, Mrs commits adultery with Adam Blair*
Some Passages in the Life of Adam Blair (1822) John Gibson Lockhart

Campbell, Mrs sister to Brookfield*
Viola her daughter
The Witching Hour play (1907) Ambrose

M. Thomas

Campbell, Duncan, Sir Knight of Ardenvohr
Lady Campbell his wife
Annot Lyle his daughter
The Legend of Montrose (1819) Walter Scott

Campbell, Stuart grandfather to Bruce Wetheral*, founder of 'Campbell's Kingdom'
Campbell's Kingdom (1952) Hammond Innes

Campeius, Cardinal
King Henry VIII (1623) William Shakespeare and John Fletcher

Camperdown Sir Florian Eustace's* lawyer; opponent to Lady Eustace*
John his son and partner
The Eustace Diamonds (1873) Anthony Trollope

Camperton, Major of Captain de Stancy's* battery
his wife: 'dapper little lady'
A Laodicean (1881) Thomas Hardy

Campian Jesuit priest
Westward Ho! (1855) Charles Kingsley

Campion, Albert detective – much altered in his later incarnation – in popular stories onwards from
Look to the Lady (1931) Margery Allingham

Campion, General godfather to Christopher Tietjens*, with whom his wife Sylvia* tries to ruin him while he is at the front
No More Parades (1925) Ford Madox Ford

Campion, Gladys mistress of Major Knott*
The Widow (1957) Francis King

Campion, Edward, Lieutenant-General Lord, V.C.
Last Post (1928) Ford Madox Ford

Campion, Victor, Jr. fop egged on by Lucy Hawthorne*
The Perennial Bachelor (1925) Anne Parrish

Campo-Gasso, Count
Quentin Durward (1823); *Anne of Geierstein* (1829) Walter Scott

Canby saloon-keeper
The Ox-Bow Incident (1940) Walter Van Tilburg Clark

Cancellarius Chancellor of Grunewald
Prince Otto (1885) Robert Louis Stevenson

Candace Paulina Home's* doll
Villette (1853) Charlotte Brontë

Candide cc, illegitimate son of the sister of Baron Thunder-ten-tronckh*
Candide (1759) Voltaire (rn François-Marie Arouet)

Candour, Mrs
The School for Scandal play (1777) Richard Brinsley Sheridan

Candover handiman
Let the People Sing (1939) J. B. Priestley

Candy, Dr
The Moonstone (1868) Wilkie Collins

Cann, Miss brisk and cheerful ex-governess
The Newcomes (1853–5) W. M. Thackeray

Cannan, David cc of Canadian novel of very high reputation; sensitive Nova Scotian boy who dies at thirty
his parents
his grandmother
The Mountain and the Valley (1952) Ernest Buckler

Cannister, Gilbert ('Jaffa Codling')
Mildred his wife
Adam; Eve; Gabriel their children
ss 'Adam and Eve and Pinch Me'
Adam and Eve and Pinch Me (1921) A. E. Coppard

Cannister, Martin sexton at Endelstowe
A Pair of Blue Eyes (1873) Thomas Hardy

Cannon, George bigamous husband of Hilda Lessways*
Charlotte his wife
Clayhanger (1910); *Hilda Lessways* (1911); *These Twain* (1916) Arnold Bennett

Canonbury, Fanny, Lady, daughter of 'Old Lady Kew'
The Newcomes (1853–5) W. M. Thackeray

Cantabile, Ronald (Rinaldo) hoodlum
Humboldt's Gift (1975) Saul Bellow

Cantacute, Verity one-time fiancée of Lionel de Lyndesay*
Crump Folk Going Home (1913) Constance Holme

Cantelupe, Charles, Lord

Waste play (1907) Harley Granville Barker

Canter, Simon Edward Christian's* alias when travelling with Peveril*
Peveril of the Peak (1822) Walter Scott

Canterbury, Archbishop of
King Henry V play (1623) William Shakespeare

Canterville, Lord
ss 'The Canterville Ghost' (1887)
Lord Arthur Savile's Crime (1891) Oscar Wilde

Cantle, Grandfer 'wrinkled reveller', was in the Bang-Up Locals in 1804
Christian his son, a simpleton
The Return of the Native (1878); *The Dynasts* poetic drama (1897–1907) Thomas Hardy

Cantleman
The Ideal Giant; *The Code of a Herdsman*; *Cantleman's Spring-mate* (1917); *Blasting and Bombadiering* (autobiography) (1937, rev. 1967)
ss 'The Countryhouse Party, Scotland'
Unlucky for Pringle (1973) Wyndham Lewis

Canton valet to Lord Ogleby*
The Clandestine Marriage play (1766) George Colman the Elder and David Garrick

Cantrell, Richard, Colonel cc
Across the River and Into the Trees (1950) Ernest Hemingway

Cantrip, Earl of Colonial Secretary in Palliser series onwards from
Phineas Finn† (1869) Anthony Trollope

Cantrips, Jess pickpocket
Redgauntlet (1824) Walter Scott

Canty, James farmer
Some Experiences of an Irish R.M. (1899) O. E. Somerville and Martin Ross (rn Edith Somerville and Violet Martin)

Canty, Tom boy cc
John his thieving and drunken father
Mrs Canty his mother, a beggar
Bet and **Nan** his sisters
The Prince and the Pauper (1882) Mark Twain (rn Samuel Langhorne Clemens)

Canynge, General
Loyalties play (1922) John Galsworthy

Cape, Michael
Eleanor his wife: ccs

Welded play (1924) Eugene O'Neill

Capes, Godwin biologist and dramatist (as 'Thomas More') m. Ann Veronica Stanley*
Ann Veronica (1909) H. G. Wells

Caplan, Robert
Freda his wife
Martin his dead brother
Dangerous Corner play (1932) J. B. Priestley

Capolin Egyptian captain
Tamburlaine play (1587) Christopher Marlowe

Capstern, Captain
The Surgeon's Daughter (1827) Walter Scott

Captain otter hound
Tarka the Otter (1927) Henry Williamson

Captain see **Skipper**

Captain, The Edward's* friend
Walhlverwandschaften (*Elective Affinities*) (1809) Johann Wolfgang Goethe

Captain, the Black
Jackanapes (1879) Juliana Ewing

Caption, Mr W. S.
Janet *née* Pawkie, his wife
The Provost (1822) John Galt

Capuchin, The Old venerable recluse
ss 'Mad Monkton'
The Queen of Hearts (1859) Wilkie Collins

Capucius ambassador of Charles V
King Henry VIII play (1623) William Shakespeare and John Fletcher

Capulet
Lady Capulet his wife
Juliet their daughter
Romeo and Juliet play (1623) William Shakespeare

Cara Lord Marchmain's* mistress
Brideshead Revisited (1945) Evelyn Waugh

Carabas, Marquess of bankrupt supersnob
The Book of Snobs (1847) W. M. Thackeray

Caraffa, Philippo Duke of Pavia
Love's Sacrifice play (1633) John Ford

Caramel, Richard novelist
The Beautiful and Damned (1922) F. Scott Fitzgerald

Caratach cousin to Bonduca*

Bonduca play (1614) Francis Beaumont and John Fletcher

Caraway, Earle
Wickford Point (1939) John P. Marquand

Caraze, Delphine quadroon cc of novela by New Orleans author
Olive her daughter by her dead white husband; Delphine pretends that she is not her mother in order to secure her happiness; m. Ursin Lemaitre*
Madame Delphine (1881) George Washington Cable

Carbuncle, Jane, Mrs 'wonderful woman'
The Eustace Diamonds (1873) Anthony Trollope

Carbury, Roger spokesman for the author
Sir Felix his second cousin
Henrietta Sir Felix's sister m. Paul Montagu*
Matilda, Lady Carbury mother of Felix and Henrietta m. (2) Nicholas Broune*
The Way We Live Now (1875) Anthony Trollope

Cardan, Tom 'one of the obscure great'
Those Barren Leaves (1925) Aldous Huxley

Carden, Lieutenant Colonel commanding Lorrequer's* regiment
Harry Lorrequer (1839) Charles Lever

Cardew, Cecily Jack Worthing's* ward, m. Algernon Moncrieff*
The Importance of Being Earnest play (1895) Oscar Wilde

Cardew, Theophilus, Revd gloomy preacher who saves Catherine Furze* from decline
Jane his wife
Catherine Furze (1893) Mark Rutherford (rn William Hale White)

Cardigan, Jack
Imogen *née* Dartie*, his wife
The *Forsyte* series (1906–33) John Galsworthy

Careless
The School for Scandal play (1777) Richard Brinsley Sheridan

Careless friend to Mellefont*
The Double-Dealer play (1710) William Congreve

Carella, Gino dentist's son, second husband of Lilia Herriton*
Where Angels Fear to Tread (1905) E. M. Forster

Carella, Steve Detective Second Grade (killed off in third novel of series but revived) on the squad of the 87th Precinct in 'an imaginary city' (New York)
Teddy his beautiful deaf-mute wife; onwards from
Cop Hater† (1956) Ed McBain (rn Evan Hunter)

Carew, Fred liberal journalist, editor of *The Eagle*, 'the workingman's friend', who continues to combat the greedy rich despite reverses
The Money-Makers (1885) H. F. Keenan

Carew, Sir Danvers MP murdered by Mr Hyde*
Dr Jekyll and Mr Hyde (1886) Robert Louis Stevenson

Carey, Philip club-footed cc
Stephen; Helen his dead parents
Revd William Carey his selfish hypocritical uncle
Aunt Louisa Revd William's wife
Of Human Bondage (1915) W. Somerset Maugham

Carcy, Widow
Sybil (1845) Benjamin Disraeli

Carfax, Frances, Lady
ss 'The Disappearance of Lady Frances Carfax'
His Last Bow (1917) Arthur Conan Doyle

Cargill, Revd Josiah
St Ronan's Well (1824) Walter Scott

Carker, James Dombey's heartless confidential assistant, who ruins him; killed by passing train
Dombey and Son (1848) Charles Dickens

Carlavero, Giovanni keeper of a wine shop
ss 'The Italian Prisoner'
The Uncommercial Traveller (1860–8) Charles Dickens

Carlo Buffone a public, scurrilous and profane jester whose religion is railing and whose discourse is ribaldry
Every Man Out of His Humour play (1599) Ben Jonson

Carlyle lawyer to Ballantrae*
The Master of Ballantrae (1889) Robert Louis Stevenson

Carlyle, Archibald forgiving hero, m. (1) Lady Isabel Vane*, (2) Barbara Hare*

Isabel; William; Archibald his children by Lady Isabel
Cornelia his half-sister
East Lynne (1861) Mrs Henry Wood
Carlyle, Louis 'Watson'* to Max Carrados*; solicitor who was unjustly struck off the rolls
Max Carrados (1914) Ernest Bramah (rn Ernest Bramah Smith)
Carlyle, Poppy
Sinister Street† (1913) Compton Mackenzie
Carlyon, Jimmy Australian social worker, cc
his mother, an 'old fake', whom he 'really likes'
A Stranger and Afraid† (1961) George Turner
Carmen
Carmen (1847) Prosper Merimée
Carmichael, Augustus poet
To the Lighthouse (1927) Virginia Woolf
Carmichael, William David alcoholic solicitor
Edna his wife
Madge; Norman their children
Time, Gentlemen! Time! (1930) Norah Hoult
Carmilla female vampire
ss 'Carmilla'
In a Glass Darkly (1872) J. Sheridan Le Fanu
Carmine, Lawrence, Captain friend to Britling*
Mr Britling Sees It Through (1916) H. G. Wells
Carnaby, Earl of brilliant roué
Tono Bungay (1909) H. G. Wells
Carnal, Lord suicide cc of early blockbuster
To Have and To Hold (1900) Mary Johnston
Carne, Robert sporting farmer, cc
Muriel his wife, who is confined to a mental hospital
Midge their daughter
William his architect brother
Mavis William's wife
South Riding (1936) Winifred Holtby
Carnehan, Peachey Taliaferro
ss 'The Man who would be King'
Wee Willie Winkie (1888) Rudyard Kipling

Caro, Avice the first of the Avices admired by Jocelyn Pierston*; m. Jim Caro, her cousin, a quarryman
Caro, Ann Avice Avice II, her granddaughter, washerwoman, servant to Jocelyn Pierston* until he learns that she is secretly married to Isaac Pierston*
Caro, Avice Avice III, m. Isaac Pierston*
The Well Beloved (1897) Thomas Hardy
Carpenter, Captain modern Don Quixote in classic poem
poem 'Captain Carpenter'
Two Gentlemen in Bonds (1927) John Crowe Ransom
Carr American thief
his wife, posing as 'Miss Grant', fiancée to Ralph Danvers
The Danvers Jewels† (1887) Mary Cholmondeley
Carr missioner, Yanrin
his wife
Aissa Saved (1932) Joyce Cary
Carr, Hugo cc in popular tale by fashionably clever author whose appeal did not last
ss 'When the Nightingale Sang in Berkeley Square'
These Charming People (1920) Michael Arlen (originally Dirkan Kuyumjian)
Carr, Katherine cc of popular American series
Dr Philip her father
Elsie; Clover; Johnnie; Phil; Dorry her sisters and brothers
Helen her cousin; onwards from
What Katy Did† (1872) Susan Coolidge (rn Sarah Chauncey Woolsey)
Carr, Wilfred cc
ss 'The Well'
The Lady of the Barge (1902) W. W. Jacobs
Carrados, Max (rn **Max Wynn**) blind (possibly owing to sexual excess) and therefore super-sensitive detective; onwards from
Max Carrados† (1914) Ernest Bramah (rn Ernest Bramah Smith)
Carrasco, Ramon, Don mystic revolutionary leader and reviver of cult of Quetzalcoatl
The Plumed Serpent (1926) D. H. Lawrence
Carraway, Nick narrator; cousin to Daisy

Buchanan*
The Great Gatsby (1925) F. Scott Fitzgerald

Carraze, Delphine
Olive her daughter
ss 'Madame Delphine'
Old Creole Days (1879) George Washington Cable

Carrel, M. head of art school, artist
Trilby (1894) George du Maurier

Carrickfergus, Marianne Caroline Matilda, Mrs rich, vulgar and kind widow m. Andrew Montfitchet*
A Shabby Genteel Story† (1840) W. M. Thackeray

Carrington, Henry, Sir ('Rico') Australian artist, m. Lou Witt*
St Mawr (1925) D. H. Lawrence

Carrington, Lukey science teacher
The Food of the Gods (1904) H. G. Wells

Carroll, William, Sir (later **Lord**) head of shipping line
Diana his wife
All Our Yesterdays (1930) H. M. Tomlinson

Carruthers narrator, cc
The Riddle of the Sands (1903) Erskine Childers

Carruthers, Dame housekeeper to Tower of London, m. Sergeant Meryll*
The Yeoman of the Guard opera (1888) W. S. Gilbert and Arthur Sullivan

Carruthers, Mabel
her mother
Sinister Street† (1913) Compton Mackenzie

Carslogie, Laird of
The Abbot (1820) Walter Scott

Carson trying to find secret of Krakatit; employer of George Thomas*
Krakatit (1924) Karel Capek

Carson, Harry rival to Jem Wilson*
Sophia; Helen; Amy his sisters
Mary Barton (1848) Mrs Gaskell

Carson, Kit (hist.) American hunter who assists Vaillant* and Latour* in their mission
Death Comes for the Archbishop (1927) Willa Cather

Carson, Louis
ss 'the Villa Desirée'
Uncanny Stories (1923) May Sinclair

Carson, Mrs nasty-minded sadistic woman confounded
ss 'Lily Daw and the Three Ladies'
A Curtain of Green (1941) Eudora Welty

Carson, Robert, Revd bigoted clergyman
Sanchia his wife, whose work in a birth-control clinic upsets her husband
Bob his son by his first marriage
Robert's Wife play (1937) St John Ervine

Carson, Thelma loved by Eddie Ryan*
The Silence of History (1963) James T. Farrell

Carstairs, Johnnie horse-dealer and 'packer'
Campbell's Kingdom (1952) Hammond Innes

Carstairs, Lord young rip expelled from Eton who gave, and would continue to give, Mary Wortle* trouble
Dr Wortle's School (1881) Anthony Trollope

Carstone, Richard ward in chancery, m. Ada Clare*
Bleak House (1853) Charles Dickens

Cartaret, Colonel ('Cold Steel Cartaret')
Rose Maynard's* guardian
Meet Mr Mulliner (1927) P. G. Wodehouse

Cartaret, Julian friend to Harry Somerford*
Fanny By Gaslight (1940) Michael Sadleir

Carter, Gil ranch hand
The Ox-Bow Incident (1940) Walter Van Tilberg Clark

Carter, Mr surgeon who amputates Rochester's* right arm
Jane Eyre (1847) Charlotte Brontë

Carter, Nick American dime novel* detective invented, probably, by John R. Coryell, T. C. Harbaugh and F. Van Rensselaer, onwards from
The Old Detective's Pupil† (1886)

Carter, Philip engineer wrongly imprisoned for embezzlement
Hazel his wife
Timmie their young son
The Glass Cell (1965) Patricia Highsmith

Carter, Simon secretary of the London Zoo
The Old Men at the Zoo (1961) Angus Wilson

Carter, Sylvia retired small hotel manager
her husband, a card-playing sponger

Harold her recently widowed son, a progressive headmaster
Harold's three teenaged daughters
Late Call (1964) Angus Wilson
Carteret, the Hon. Miss daughter of the Viscountess Dalrymple*, plain and awkward
Persuasion (1818) Jane Austen
Carthew, Maud governess to the Fanes m. Kenneth Ross*
Enid her mother
Joan; May; Nancy her sisters
Sinister Street† (1913) Compton Mackenzie
Carthew, Miss m. Sid Galer*
Mrs Galer's Business (1905) W. Pett Ridge
Cartlett, Mr bloated hotel keeper, 'with a globular stomach and small legs, resembling a top on two pegs', in Sydney; m. Arabella Fawley* *née* Donn (first bigamously)
Jude the Obscure (1896) Thomas Hardy
Carton, Sidney cc, guillotined to save Charles Darnay*
A Tale of Two Cities (1859) Charles Dickens
Cartwheel, Catherine the narrator's 'poor dreaming' mother
Miss MacIntosh, My Darling (1965) Marguerite Young
Cartwright, Evelina owner of tourist gift-shop who dominates the town of Escondido in novel set on the day of the assassination of Kennedy
Alec her daughter, freedom rider in the Deep South
One Day (1965) Wright Morris
Carver, Captain retired
The Kickleburys on the Rhine (1850) W. M. Thackeray
Carvil, Josiah blind boat-builder
Bessie his daughter
ss 'Tomorrow'
Typhoon (1903) Joseph Conrad (rn Josef Teodor Konrad Korzeniowski)
Carwell, Flora see Pyneweck, Flora
Carwin evil ventriloquist who menaces the family, the Wielands*
Wieland, or The Transformation: An American Tale (1798) Charles Brockden Browne
Cary, Mr of Clovelly Court

Will his son
Westward Ho! (1855) Charles Kingsley
Carysbrooke distant relative of the Earl of Ilbury*
Uncle Silas (1864) J. Sheridan Le Fanu
Casamassima, Prince m. Christina Light*
Roderick Hudson (1875) Henry James
Casanova i.e. Giovanni Jacopo Casanova de Seingalt: largely fictional character invented by himself in autobiography
Mémoires (1826–38)
Casaubon, Edward, Revd author of the never-to-be finished *Key to All Mythologies*; m. Dorothea Brooke*
Middlemarch (1871–2) George Eliot (rn Mary Anne, later Marian, Evans)
Casby, Christopher landlord of Bleeding Heart Yard, father of Flora Finching*
Little Dorrit (1857) Charles Dickens
Casca conspirator against Julius Caesar*
Julius Caesar play (1623) William Shakespeare
Cascade
Guignol's band (1944) Louis-Ferdinand Céline (rn Louis-Ferdinand Destouches)
Case island trader, villain, enemy of Wiltshire*
ss 'The Beach of Falesa'
Island Nights' Entertainments (1893) Robert Louis Stevenson
Casey mock-hero of popular baseball poem
ballad 'Casey at the Bat' (San Francisco *Examiner*, 3 June 1888) Ernest Lawrence Sayer
Casey, Jack first husband of Emma Newcome*
The Newcomes (1853–5) W. M. Thackeray
Casey, James m. Matty Dwyer*
Handy Andy (1842) Samuel Lover
Casey, Nellie, Mrs *née* Birdseye
My Mortal Enemy (1928) Willa Cather
Casey, Sarah who does *not* get married to Michael Byrne* with whom she lives
The Tinker's Wedding play (1908) John Millington Synge
Cashel, Roland cc, m. Mary Leicester*
Godfrey his father
Roland Cashel (1850) Charles Lever
Cashell, Mr ('**Young Mr Cashell**') young wireless enthusiast who carries out experiment while his father, a chemist,

lies ill upstairs
ss 'Wireless'
Traffics and Discoveries (1904) Rudyard
Kipling
Caspar, Sol really **Salvatore Gasparro**
small-town racketeer of whom a charac-
ter says: 'if that crook ever squatted hot,
that would be doing something for the
country'
Love's Lovely Counterfeit (1942) James
M. Cain
Cass, Miss personal secretary to Evelyn
Orcham*
Imperial Palace (1930) Arnold Bennett
Cass, Squire
Godfrey his son m. (1) Molly Farren*,
(2) Nancy Lammeter*
Eppie Godfrey's daughter by his first
marriage, adopted by Silas Marner*, m.
Aaron Winthrop*
Dunstan; Bob his other sons, the former a
thief and wastrel
Silas Marner (1861) George Eliot (rn
Mary Anne, later Marian, Evans)
Cassandra prophetess
Troilus and Cressida play (1623) William
Shakespeare
Cassandra young painter
Vive Le Roy (1936) Ford Madox Ford
Casse-une-Croute quadroon courtesan
Moths (1880) Ouida (rn Marie Louise de
la Ramée)
Cassidy, 'Hopalong' cowboy hero in
juvenile series created by New York
municipal clerk who did not visit the
scenes of his tales until 1924; onwards
from
Bar-20† (1907) Clarence E. Mulford
Cassilis, Frank cc, narrator, m. Clara
Huddlestone*
ss 'The Pavilion on the Links'
The New Arabian Nights (1882) Robert
Louis Stevenson
Cassilis, George
Tancred (1847) Benjamin Disraeli
Cassini, Stephen, Dr prison doctor who
gives drugs to Philip Carter*
The Glass Cell (1965) Patricia Highsmith
Cassio Othello's lieutenant
Othello play (1623) William Shake-
speare
Cassius conspirator against Julius Caesar*
Julius Caesar play (1623) William Shake-

speare
Cassius see **Concaverty**
Cassy slave of Legree*
Uncle Tom's Cabin (1851) Harriet
Beecher Stowe
Casterley, Countess of
Lady Gertrude Semmering her daughter
m. Lord Valleys*
The Patrician (1911) John Galsworthy
Castillones, Victor de né Cabasse snobbish
and bragging poet
The Newcomes (1853–5) W. M.
Thackeray
Castle-Cuddy, Lord friend to Captain
Craigengelt*
The Bride of Lammermoor (1819)
Walter Scott
Castleton friend to Michael Fane*
Sinister Street† (1913) Compton
Mackenzie
**Castlewood, Francis Edward, Baronet,
First Viscount**
George, Second Viscount his son
Thomas, Third Viscount his son; m.
(1) Gertrude Maes*, (2) Isabel, his
cousin, daughter of Second Viscount
Francis, Fourth Viscount wrongful
successor (should have been Henry Es-
mond*); m. Rachel née Armstrong*
Francis, Fifth Viscount, First Earl son of
Fourth Viscount; m. (1) Clotilda de
Wertheim, (2) Anna
Eugene, Second Earl son of First Earl; m.
Lydia van den Bosch
Thomas; Revd Francis sons of First
Viscount
Eustace; Isabel children of Second
Viscount
Beatrix daughter of Fourth Viscount
Maia daughter of First Earl by Clotilda
de Wertheim
William; Fanny children of First Earl by
Anna
The History of Henry Esmond (1852);
The Virginians (1857–9) W. M.
Thackeray
Caston degenerate American artist shot for
cowardice
The Secret Places of the Heart (1922) H.
G. Wells
Castorley, Alured subject of a terrible
revenge at the hands of Manallace*, for
what he did to, or said or implied about,

Vidal Benjaguen's* mother
ss 'Dayspring Mishandled'
Limits and Renewals (1932) Rudyard Kipling

Castries, Miss
ss 'Kidnapped'
Plain Tales from the Hills (1888) Rudyard Kipling

Castro, Mrs mysterious widow
Shall We Join the Ladies? play (1921) J. M. Barrie

Casy, Jim, Revd ex-preacher
The Grapes of Wrath (1939) John Steinbeck

Cat, Jack, Captain
Under Milk Wood play (1954) Dylan Thomas

Cataline, L. Sergius cc
Cataline play (1611) Ben Jonson

Catanach, Mrs midwife
The Marquis of Lossie (1877) George Macdonald

Catchpole, Mike loses his sight in accident at Mr Furze's* factory
Tom Catchpole, a clerk, his son, loves Catherine Furze* but is rejected by her
Catherine Furze (1893) Mark Rutherford (rn William Hale White)

Caterham John prominent politician
The Food of the Gods (1904) H. G. Wells

Cathcart, Captain commander of air base on Pianosa
Catch-22 (1961) Joseph Heller

Catherick, Mrs sister of Mrs Kempe*, part narrator
Anne her daughter
The Woman in White (1860) Wilkie Collins

Catherine of Newport mistress of Julian Avenel* and mother of his son; see **Graeme, Roland**
The Monastery (1820) Walter Scott

Catherine wife of Elias*, mother to Gerard*
The Cloister and the Hearth (1861) Charles Reade

Cathleen, the Countess sells her soul to the devil for the sake of starving peasants
The Countess Cathleen play (1891) W. B. Yeats

Cathro, Dominie
Sentimental Tommy (1896) J. M. Barrie

Catskill, Rupert Secretary of State for War

Men Like Gods (1923) H. G. Wells

Cattleman, Paul philanderer, writing the history of the Nutting Research and Development Corporation, Los Angeles
Katherine his neurotic wife
The Nowhere City (1965) Alison Lurie

Cauchon, Peter, Bishop of Beauvais (hist.)
St Joan play (1924) George Bernard Shaw

Caudill, Boone 'man without a home' cc of popular American historical novel
The Big Sky (1947) A. B. Guthrie

Cauldwell, Frank self-effacing narrator
The Firewalkers: A Memoir (1956) novelist (and pseudonymous author of *The Firewalkers* on its initial publication);
The Japanese Umbrella (1964) Francis King

Caulfield, Holden 16-year-old schoolboy, cc
Phoebe his small sister
The Catcher in the Rye (1951) J. D. Salinger

Cavan, Edward Harvard professor, in novel studying the effects of his suicide on his colleagues
Faithful are the Wounds (1955) May Sarton

Cave, Mary silent beauty, m. Revd Matthewson Helstone*
Shirley (1849) Charlotte Brontë

Cavender pushed his wife off a cliff for infidelity but worries, twelve years later, if she really had been unfaithful
Laramie his wife
Cavender's House poem (1929) Edwin Arlington Robinson

Cavendish, Mr popular Carlingford figure, but has shadow over his antecedents, the discovery of which threatens his sister Mrs Woodburn*
Miss Marjoribanks (1866) Mrs Margaret Oliphant

Caversham, Earl of, KG father of Lord Goring*
An Ideal Husband play (1895) Oscar Wilde

Cavor inventor of the gravity-resistant Cavorite
The First Men in the Moon (1901) H. G. Wells

Cawtree farmer
The Woodlanders (1887) Thomas Hardy

Cawwawkee
Polly opera (1729) John Gay
Caxon, Jacob barber
Jenny his daughter
The Antiquary (1816) Walter Scott
Caxton, Pisistratus narrator of only novel even faintly to 'capture flavour of *Tristram Shandy**'
The Caxtons: A Family Picture (1849) Edward Bulwer Lytton
Cayenne, Mr industrialist
Annals of the Parish (1821) John Galt
Cayley, Matthew cousin and secretary of Mark Ablett*
The Red House Mystery (1922) A. A. Milne
Cecco pirate
Peter Pan play (1904) J. M. Barrie
Ceci beatnik waitress with whom Paul Cattleman* has an affair
The Nowhere City (1965) Alison Lurie
Cecil cc of one of the best of the 'silver fork'* novels preceding *Vanity Fair**: a mixture of wit and knowingness, and consciously contrived self-styled 'rubbish', parodied by Thackeray* in *Novels by Eminent Hands*
Cecil, or The Adventures of a Coxcomb (1841)
Cecil A Peer (1841, as *Ormington*, 1842) Catherine Gore
Cecil, Mr lawyer for Lady Constantine*
Two on a Tower (1882) Thomas Hardy
Cedric of Rotherfield 'proud, fierce, jealous and irritable'
Ivanhoe (1820) Walter Scott
Céladon shepherd, cc of novel now seldom read, but loved and regarded as first French novel
L'Astrée (1607–26) Honoré d'Urfé
Celestina, Lady Bellamour to whom Sir Thomas Bornwell* pretends to pay attention in order to cure his wife Aretina* of extravagance
The Lady of Pleasure play (1635) James Shirley
Celestine maid to Mrs Manderson*
Trent's Last Case (1912) E. C. Bentley
Celia a fairy
Iolanthe opera (1882) W. S. Gilbert and Arthur Sullivan
Celia daughter of Duke Frederick*, m. Oliver*

As You Like It play (1623) William Shakespeare
Celia Irish prostitute in London
Murphy (1938) Samuel Beckett
Celie suffering child cc
The Color Purple (1982) Alice Walker
Celinda victim of Ferdinand*
The Adventures of Ferdinand, Count Fathom (1753) Tobias Smollett
Céline 'slobbering has-been' – in novel whose author told the Consul-General of Sweden, Raoul Nordling, that it ought to have won him the Nobel Prizes for Peace *and* Literature
D'un Château l'autre (*Castle to Castle*) (1957) Louis-Ferdinand Céline (rn Louis-Ferdinand Destouches)
Cellini, Mr leaves Velvet Brown* five horses
National Velvet (1935) Enid Bagnold
Cenci, Beatrice cc in verse tragedy her father
The Cenci play (1819) Percy Bysshe Shelley
Ceneus a Persian lord
Tamburlaine play (1587) Christopher Marlowe
Censorious Young Gentleman, The
Sketches of Young Gentlemen (1838) Charles Dickens
Cereno, Benito sick young sailor
ss 'Benito Cereno'
The Piazza Tales (1856) Herman Melville
Ceres a spirit
The Tempest play (1623) William Shakespeare
Ceria in charge of grill-room
Imperial Palace (1930) Arnold Bennett
Cerr-Norr, Charlie
Revd Cerr-Norr Vicar of Rookhurst, his father; in early novel of Devonshire childhood, much influenced by Richard Jeffries*, first of tetralogy called *The Flax of Dreams*
The Beautiful Years (1921, rev. 1929) Henry Williamson
Cesar the Writing Man
The Narrows (1953) Ann Petry
Cesarini, Castruccio envious Italian poetaster and murderer
Ernest Maltravers (1837)
Alice, or The Mysteries (1838) Edward

Bulwer Lytton

Cesario see Viola

Cethegus, Caius
Cataline play (1611) Ben Jonson

Chadband, Revd Mr ranting hypocrite
Bleak House (1852) Charles Dickens

Chadwick, Ellen wealthy invalid, m. Jabez Clegg*
The Manchester Man (1876) Mrs G. Linnaeus Banks

Chadwick, Jocelyn land agent
Famine (1937) Liam O'Flaherty

Chadwick, Mr
The Warden (1955) Anthony Trollope

Chaffanbrass, Mr brilliant lawyer for Lady Mason*
Orley Farm (1862) Anthony Trollope

Chaffery, James fraudulent medium, embezzler, stepfather to Ethel Henderson*
Love and Mr Lewisham (1900) H. G. Wells

Chainmail fond of poetry; a poet himself
Crotchet Castle (1831) Thomas Love Peacock

Charmot, Rose young girl brought before directors of Orphan Asylum of Bielle for having 'gone astray', and supported only by Pastor Tremblez* and Mme Bussens* in novel by Swiss (French) writer
Les Roches blanches (*The White Rocks* (1895) Édouard Rod

Chair midwife
The Magnetic Lady, or *Humours Reconciled* play (1641) Ben Jonson

Chaka (hist.) Zulu chief
Nada the Lily (1892) Henry Rider Haggard

Chakchek Greenland falcon
Tarka the Otter (1927) Henry Williamson

Charlaran, M.
Mme Charalan his wife
ss 'Unlucky for Pringle'
Unlucky for Pringle (1973) Wyndham Lewis

Chalk
his wife
Dialstone Lane (1904) W. W. Jacobs

Chalkfield Mayor, but not *the* Mayor, of Casterbridge (Dorchester)
The Mayor of Casterbridge (1886) Thomas Hardy

Challenger, G. E., Professor cc scientist and explorer
his wife
The Lost World (1912); *The Poison Belt* (1913) Arthur Conan Doyle

Challis, Henry anthropologist and local magnate
The Hampdenshire Wonder (1911) J. D. Beresford

Challong Oran-laut
ss 'The Disturber of Traffic'
Many Inventions (1893) Rudyard Kipling

Chambers, Frank murderer executed for a murder he did not commit in effective, ironic and popular hard-boiled tale
The Postman Always Rings Twice (1934) James M. Cain

Chamberlyne, Edward
Lavinia his wife
The Cocktail Party play (1950) T. S. Eliot

Chamont
The Orphan play (1680) Thomas Otway

Chamont friend to Gasper*
The Case is Altered play (1609) Ben Jonson

Champagne, Henry, Earl of vassal of King Philip*
The Talisman (1825) Walter Scott

Champignac, M. de attaché, French Embassy, London
Vanity Fair (1847–8) W. M. Thackeray

Champion, Brenda temporary mistress to Rex Mottram*
Brideshead Revisited (1945) Evelyn Waugh

Chan Hung mandarin of the eighth grade in deliberately stilted travesty of Chinese thought and speech
The Wallet of Kai Lung (1900) Ernest Bramah (rn Ernest Bramah Smith)

Chan, Charlie Chinese detective living in Hawaii who became most famous when his exploits were made into a series of films; his formula was that character is fate, and so he could therefore predict what anyone would do; onwards from
The House Without a Key† (1925) Earl Derr Biggers

Chance gardener brought up by the Old Man, called Chauncey Gardener by a misunderstanding; presidential advisor
Being There (1971) Jerzy Kosinski

Chance, Elizabeth, Miss sister of murderess, m. Tenbruggen*
The Legacy of Cain (1889) Wilkie Collins

Chancellor, Olive tyrannical feminist; her smile is like 'a thin ray of moonlight resting upon the wall of a prison'
The Bostonians (1886) Henry James

Chancellor, the Lord husband to Iolanthe* and father to Strephon*
Iolanthe opera (1882) W. S. Gilbert and Arthur Sullivan

Chand, Hukum government commissioner trying to prevent violence in novel about the division of India
Train to Pakistan (1956) Khushwant Singh

Chandler carrier
The Wrong Box (1889) Robert Louis Stevenson and Lloyd Osbourne

Chandler, Tommy friend to Ignatius Gallagher*
Annie his wife
ss 'A Little Cloud'
Dubliners (1914) James Joyce

Chang-Ch'un 'one of the wealthiest men in Canton'
The Wallet of Kai Lung (1900) Ernest Bramah (rn Ernest Bramah Smith)

Chant, Mercy
Dr Chant her father
Tess of the D'Urbervilles (1891) Thomas Hardy

Chantry-Pigg, Hugh, Revd the Hon. Father 'an ancient bigot'
The Towers of Trebizond (1956) Rose Macaulay

Chapel, Arnold novelist; partner to Peter Gresham*, m. Denham Dobie*
Crewe Train (1926) Rose Macaulay

Chapin, George American millionaire
Sophie his wife
ss 'An Habitation Enforced'
Actions and Reactions (1909) Rudyard Kipling

Chapman, Nat rustic
Two on a Tower (1882) Thomas Hardy

Chapman, Stephen, Captain
Alice Lorraine (1875) R. D. Blackmore

Charalois
The Fatal Dowry play (1632) Philip Massinger

Charcot, Professor (hist.) manager of hysterics and director of their performances; here has 'the typical properties of a mama's darling'
All and Everything: Beelzebub's Tales to His Grandson (1950) G. I. Gurdjieff

Chardon, Lucien cc
Illusions perdues† (Lost Illusions) (1843) Honoré de Balzac

Charegite a religious fanatic
The Talisman (1825) Walter Scott

Chariclea Ethiopian Princess, born white, whose adventures are traced in ten books in Greek prose romance by Syrian writer; influential from Renaissance to 18th century in translations; loves and eventually m. Theagenes
Aethiopica (3rd century AD) Heliodorus of Emesa

Charis Greek slave, narrator
ss 'The Story of the Greek Slave'
The Pacha of Many Tales (1836) Captain Marryat

Charisi, Daniel
Ephraim his son, father of Daniel Deronda*
Daniel Deronda (1876) George Eliot (rn Mary Anne, later Marian, Evans)

Charity see **Prudence**

Charles cc and phallic hero of Victorian pornographic classic by a team of quite good writers; the best episodes take place in King's College, London
The Romance of Lust (1873–6) William Simpson Potter (editor)

Charles the Bold (hist.) of Burgundy, enemy and vassal to Louis XI*
Quentin Durward (1823) Walter Scott

Charles VI of France (hist.)
King Henry V play (1623) William Shakespeare

Charles wrestler
As You Like It play (1623) William Shakespeare

Charles, Dauphin later Charles VII of France
King Henry VI plays (1623) William Shakespeare
St Joan play (1924) George Bernard Shaw

Charles, Helena friend to Alison Porter* and lover of Jimmy Porter*
Look Back in Anger play (1956) John Osborne

Charles, Nick private detective in series
Nora his wife; onwards from
The Thin Man (1932) Dashiell Hammett
Charley bashful man in love with Angela
Leath*
The Holly Tree (1855) Charles Dickens
Charley marine store dealer
David Copperfield (1850) Charles
Dickens
Charlie boy attached to Eustacia Vye* and
employed by her on errands
The Return of the Native (1878) Thomas
Hardy
Charlotte ('Lotte')
Die Leiden des Jungen Werthers (The
Sufferings of Young Werther) (1774)
Johann Wolfgang Goethe
Charlotte Edward's* wife
Walhlverwandschaften (Elective Affin-
ities) (1809) Johann Wolfgang Goethe
Charlson, Dr of Port Bredy (Bridport)
ss 'Fellow Townsman'
Wessex Tales (1888) Thomas Hardy
Charmazel see Ziska, Princess
Charmian attendant to Cleopatra*
Antony and Cleopatra play (1623)
William Shakespeare
Caesar and Cleopatra play (1900)
George Bernard Shaw
Charmond, Felice bored, vain ex-actress
widow who goes off with Dr Fitzpiers*
and is eventually shot
The Woodlanders (1887) Thomas Hardy
Charney, Ed big-shot gangster
Appointment in Samarra (1935) John
O'Hara
Charomonte, Carolo tutor to Giovanni*
The Great Duke of Florence play (1636)
James Shirley
Charrington, Mr of the Thought Police
1984 (1949) George Orwell (rn Eric
Blair)
Charron, Pierre fur trader
Shadows on the Rock (1932) Willa
Cather
Charteris, Colin Serbian 'saint' who leads
a hippy crusade
Barefoot in the Head (1969) Brian W.
Aldiss
Charteris, Leonard
The Philanderer play (1893) George
Bernard Shaw
Charteris, Patrick, Sir baron of Kinfauns,

Provost of Perth
The Fair Maid of Perth (1828) Walter
Scott
Charters, Magnus, Lord college friend to
Arthur Pendennis*
Pendennis (1848) W. M. Thackeray
Chartres, de, Mlle cc, m. the Prince de
Clèves*
her mother
La Princesse de Clèves (1678) Comtesse
de Lafayette
Chartres, John, Sir nerve specialist
ss 'In the Same Boat'
A Diversity of Creatures (1917) Rudyard
Kipling
Charwell, Cuthbert, Rt Revd Bishop of
Porthminster, cc
Elizabeth his wife
General Sir Conway, KCB, CMG; Ad-
rian; Lionel judge; **Wilmet; Revd Hilary**
their five children
Hubert, DSO son of General Charwell,
m. Jean Tarsbrugh*
Dinna daughter of General Charwell, cc
of final volumes, m. Eustace Dornford,
QC*
Clare daughter of General Charwell, m.
Sir Gerald Corven*, later mistress of
Tony Croom*
Mary wife to Revd Hilary
Lady Alison wife to Lionel
The Forsyte series (1906–33) John
Galsworthy
Chase, Elyot cc
Sibyl his wife
Private Lives play (1930) Noël Coward
Chase, Jack petty officer, 'our noble first
captain of the top', 'incomparable'; in
partly autobiographical novel of sea life
White-Jacket (1850) Herman Melville
Chateaubriant, Alphonse de (hist.) novel-
ist who became an enthusiastic Nazi
D'un Château l'autre (Castle to Castle)
(1957) Louis-Ferdinand Céline (rn Louis-
Ferdinand Destouches)
Chatterley, Clifford, Sir baronet paralysed
from the waist down
Constance his wife
Lady Chatterley's Lover (1928) D. H.
Lawrence
Chatterlitz language teacher
All and Everything: Beelzebub's Tales to
His Grandson (1950) G. I. Gurdjieff

Chauncey, Miss lonely and half-crazy resident of East Parrish
Deephaven sketches (1877) Sarah Orne Jewett

Chavez, Ignacio Yucatanian dog-catcher
One Day (1965) Wright Morris

Chawner school chum to Dick Bultitude*
Vice Versa (1882) F. Anstey (rn Thomas Anstey Guthrie)

Chawner wholesale stationer, Bursley
The Old Wives' Tale (1908) Arnold Bennett

Chedglow, Percy apprentice, *Blackgauntlet*
The Bird of Dawning (1933) John Masefield

Cheeryble, Ned and Charles brothers
Frank their nephew m. Kate Nickleby*
Nicholas Nickleby (1839) Charles Dickens

Cheetham, John wood carver
Put Yourself in his Place (1870) Charles Reade

Cheever, Eustace famous novelist
ss 'A Conference of the Powers'
Many Inventions (1893) Rudyard Kipling

Cheggs, Alick m. Sophia Wackles*
The Old Curiosity Shop (1841) Charles Dickens

Chelford, Lord and Lady
Wylder's Hand (1864) J. Sheridan Le Fanu

Chelifer, Francis editor of a livestock paper
his mother
Those Barren Leaves (1925) Aldous Huxley

Chell, Countess of
The Earl her husband 'ornamental' mayor of Bursley
The Card (1911) Arnold Bennett

Chelles, Raymond, Marquis of third husband to Undine Spragg*
The Custom of the Country (1913) Edith Wharton

Cheron, Mme sister of St Aubert* m. (2) Montoni*
The Mysteries of Udolpho (1790) Mrs Ann Radcliffe

Cherrington, Eustace and Hilda brother and (bullying) sister in trilogy
Alfred their father
Sarah their aunt
The Shrimp and the Anemone (1944); *The Sixth Heaven* (1946); *Eustace and Hilda* (1947) L. P. Hartley

Cherry, Bob one of the famous five, onwards from
The Magnet† periodical (1908) Frank Richards (rn Charles Hamilton)

Cheshire, Cecil, Duke of m. Virginia Otis*
ss 'The Canterville Ghost'
Lord Arthur Savile's Crime (1891) Oscar Wilde

Chesney, Francis, Baronet late Indian service
Jack his son, Oxford undergraduate
Charley's Aunt play (1892) Brandon Thomas

Chesney, Stella showgirl m. Augie March*
The Adventures of Augie March (1953) Saul Bellow

Chester Noble at the Court of England
Old Fortunatus play (1600) Thomas Dekker

Chester pearler, wrecker, whaler
Lord Jim (1900) Joseph Conrad (rn Josef Teodor Konrad Korzeniowski)

Chester, John, Sir
Edward his son, m. Emma Haredale*
Barnaby Rudge (1841) Charles Dickens

Chester, Nicholas portrait of the author's lover, Gerald O'Donovan
What Not: A Prophetic Comedy (1918) Rose Macaulay

Cheswardine, Stephen
Vera his wife
These Twain (1916) Arnold Bennett

Chettam, James, Sir m. Celia Brooke*
Middlemarch (1871–?) George Eliot (rn Mary Anne, later Marian, Evans)

Chetwynd, Aline, Miss schoolteacher
Elizabeth her sister
The Old Wives' Tale (1908) Arnold Bennett

Cheveley, Laura, Mrs
An Ideal Husband play (1895) Oscar Wilde

Chevenix, Major
St Ives (1897) Robert Louis Stevenson

Cheverel, Christopher, Sir
ss 'Mr Gilfil's Love Story'
Scenes of Clerical Life (1857) George Eliot (rn Mary Anne, later Marian, Evans)

Chew, Wilfred (Chu-wei-fu) Chinese bar-

rister
Tobit Transplanted (1931) Stella Benson
Cheyne, Harvey spoiled boy reformed
Harvey his father
Constance his mother
Captains Courageous (1897) Rudyard Kipling
Cheyne, Reginald servant to Lord Glenallen*
Elspeth his daughter, m. Mucklebackit*
The Antiquary (1816) Walter Scott
Cheyney, Mrs thief, cc
The Last of Mrs Cheyney play (1925) Frederick Lonsdale
Cheyneys, Simon shipbuilder
ss 'Simple Simon'
Rewards and Fairies (1910) Rudyard Kipling
Chichely coroner
Middlemarch (1871–2) George Eliot (rn Mary Anne, later Marian, Evans)
Chichikov, Pavel swindling cc
Myortvye dushi (*Dead Souls*) (1842) Nicolai Gogol
Chick, John
Louisa his wife, *née* Dombey
Dombey and Son (1848) Charles Dickens
Chicken, the Game prizefighter
Dombey and Son (1848) Charles Dickens
Chickenstalker, Anne shopkeeper
A Christmas Carol (1943) Charles Dickens
Chickerel, Ethelberta cc daughter of a butler called Chickerel; becomes pupil-teacher and a 'lady', 'Professed Story-teller', governess in Lady Petherwin's house, jilts Christopher Julian* to marry son of Sir Ralph and Lady Petherwin, but he dies; m. Lord Mountclere*, whom she reforms
The Hand of Ethelberta (1876) Thomas Hardy
Chickney, Lord
Bealby (1915) H. G. Wells
Chickweed, Conkey burglar
Oliver Twist (1838) Charles Dickens
Chiffinch, Tom 'prime minister of the King's pleasure'
Kate his mistress, granted wifely status
Peveril of the Peak (1822) Walter Scott
Chil the kite, 'to whom all things came in the end'
ss 'How Fear Came'

Jungle Books (1894–5) Rudyard Kipling
Chilcote, John, MP drug addict
Eve his wife
John Chilcote MP (1904) Katherine Thurston
Chilcox parliamentary candidate
The Patrician (1911) John Galsworthy
Child, Joshua, Sir merchant, fortune hunter
Henry Esmond (1852) W. M. Thackeray
Childers, E. W. B. member of Sleary's Circus
Hard Times (1854) Charles Dickens
Chiles, John
ss 'The Superstitious Man's Story'
Life's Little Ironies (1894) Thomas Hardy
Chiley, Mrs confidante to Lucilla Marjoribanks*
Miss Marjoribanks (1866) Mrs Margaret Oliphant
Chillingford, Thomas, Revd
his wife
Dorothy their daughter
The Good Companions (1929) J. B. Priestley
Chillingworth, Roger name assumed by aged husband of Hester Prynne* (see Dimmesdale*)
The Scarlet Letter (1850) Nathaniel Hawthorne
Chillion foster brother to Margaret* who is hanged for killing a lout who molests Margaret at behest of Rose*; in American novel by Calvinist turned Unitarian
Margaret (1845, rev. 1851) Sylvester Judd
Chillip, Dr the Copperfield* family doctor
David Copperfield (1850) Charles Dickens
Chilson, Hetty brothel keeper
Show Boat (1926) Edna Ferber
Chiltern, Lord (Oswald Standish) son of Earl of Brentford* m. Violet Effingham* onwards from
Phineas Finn† (1869) Anthony Trollope
Chiltern, Robert, Sir
Gertrude his wife
Mabel his sister
An Ideal Husband play (1895) Oscar Wilde
Chinaski, Henry self-portrait of author –

elsewhere described as having attitudes of 'a lowbrow outsider, egocentric, and interested in drink, sex and violence'
Ham on Rye (1982) Charles Bukowski

Chingachgook Mohican chief
the *Leatherstocking* series (1823–46) J. Fenimore Cooper

Chinnery, Elmer
Summer Moonshine (1938) P. G. Wodehouse

Chinnery, Joseph porter
Desperate Remedies (1871) Thomas Hardy

Chinnock, Bet madwoman
A Glastonbury Romance (1932) John Cooper Powys

Chinston, Dr in mystery novel by New Zealand author
The Mystery of a Hansom Cab (1886) Fergus Hume

Chiply, Elly actress known as Lenore La Verne, m. Harold Westbrook*
Show Boat (1912) Edna Ferber

Chips shipwright
ss 'Nurse's Stories'
The Uncommercial Traveller (1860–8) Charles Dickens

Chirac, Father friend to Gerald Scales*
The Old Wives' Tale (1908) Arnold Bennett

Chiron Tamora's* son
Titus Andronicus play (1623) William Shakespeare

Chisholm, Eustace ('Ace') poet in Chicago
Carla his wife
Eustace Chisholm and the Works (1960) James Purdy

Chisom, Fay thirty-year-old typist m. seventy-year-old Judge McKelva*; 'with out any powers of passion or imagination in herself and had no way to see it or reach the other person'
The Optimist's Daughter (1972) Eudora Welty

Chitterlow, Henry playwright, friend to Kipps*, whose fortune he makes
his wife
Kipps (1905) H. G. Wells

Chivery, John
his father, non-resident turnkey at Marshalsea
his mother, tobacconist

Little Dorrit (1857) Charles Dickens

Chloe a girl graduate
Princess Ida opera (1884) W. S. Gilbert and Arthur Sullivan

Chloe shepherdess
Daphnis and Chloe (1598; Greek text, 1587) Longus
The Pastoral Loves of Daphnis and Chloe (1924) George Moore

Choke, Cyrus, General 'one of the most remarkable men in the country', of the American militia
Martin Chuzzlewit (1844) Charles Dickens

Chollop, Hannibal
Martin Chuzzlewit (1844) Charles Dickens

Cholmondeley of Vale Royal
Peveril of the Peak (1822) Walter Scott

Cholmondeley, Richard, Sir Lieutenant of the Tower
The Yeoman of the Guard opera (1888) W. S. Gilbert and Arthur Sullivan

Cholmondely, Mrs fashionable lady
Villette (1853) Charlotte Brontë

Choon-Kil-Tez; Choon-Tro-Pel twin Chinese princes
All and Everything: Beelzebub's Tales to His Grandson (1950) G. I. Gurdjieff

Chops dwarf in Toby Magsman's* show; his real name is Stakes, and his professional one is Major Tpschoffski
Going Into Society (1858) Charles Dickens

Chorley, Dick ('Pepperbox') English renegade sea captain who aids Sanutee* in his rebellion against the British
The Yemassee (1835) William Gilmore Simms

Chowbok native chief
Erewhon (1872) Samuel Butler

Chowne, Farmer
his wife
Adam Bede (1859) George Eliot (rn Mary Anne, later Marian, Evans)

Chremes learned Greek
ss 'The Wonderful History of Titus and Gisippus' (1640) Sir Thomas Elyot

Chrisfield gentle farm-boy from Indiana goaded into killing an officer
Three Soldiers (1921) John Dos Passos

Christ, Jesus (hist.) cc who (literally) survives the cross in both instances
The Brook Kerith (1916) George Moore
King Jesus (1944) Robert Graves

Christabel enigmatic maiden
Christabel poem (1816) Samuel Taylor Coleridge

Christal 'broker and appraiser'
Peveril of the Peak (1823) Walter Scott

Christalla maid of honour
The Broken Heart play (1633) John Ford

Christian formerly **Graceless,** cc
  Christiana his penitent wife
The Pilgrim's Progress (1678–84) John Bunyan

Christian, Edward 'demon of vengeance', all-round villain; also known as Dick Gaulesse and Simon Canter
  William his brother
  Dame Christian William's widow
  Fenella daughter of Edward, brought up to believe that she was William's daughter; posed for years as deaf mute
Peveril of the Peak (1823) Walter Scott

Christian, Mary, Lady m. Justin*
  Philip her brother
The Passionate Friends (1913) H. G. Wells

Christian, Maurice adventurer whose real name is Henry Scaddon
Felix Holt (1866) George Eliot (rn Mary Anne, later Marian, Evans)

Christian, Mr friend and neighbour to Percy Munn*
Night Rider (1939) Robert Penn Warren

Christianson, Robert of Fen Farm, rival to Orchardson*
  Christian his son, m. Priscilla Sefton*
God and the Man (1881) Robert Buchanan

Christie of Clinthill 'henchman' of Julian Avenal*
The Monastery (1820) Walter Scott

Christie, Anna see **Christopherson, Anna**

Christie, John ship's chandler
  Nelly his jolly wife
  Sandie his father
The Fortunes of Nigel (1822) Walter Scott

Christina Alberta see **Preemby**

Christine ('The Pretty Lady') 'accidental daughter of a prostitute'
The Pretty Lady (1918) Arnold Bennett

Christmas, Joe lynched man whose father *may* have been black
  Doc Hines his grandfather
Light in August (1932) William Faulkner

Christophe herdsman
ss 'The Bull that Thought'
Debits and Credits (1926) Rudyard Kipling

Christophero Count Ferneze's* steward
The Case is Altered play (1609) Ben Jonson

Christopherson, Chris
  Anna his daughter
Anna Christie play (1922) Eugene O'Neill

Christy, Camila m. (1) Revd Ernest Bellamy*, (2) Matthew Haslam*, (3) Dominic Spong*
  her mother
Men and Wives (1931) Ivy Compton-Burnett

Chuang Tzu (hist.) who awoke and did not know if he were Chuang Tzu dreaming of a butterfly or a butterfly dreaming of Chuang Tzu
Chuang Tzu traditionally 3rd century BC

Chubb, William landlord of the Sugar Loaf, Sprexton
Felix Holt (1866) George Eliot (rn Mary Anne, later Marian, Evans)

Chubinov, Vassili Iulievitch revolutionary son of a lawyer
The Birds Fall Down (1966) Rebecca West (rn Cecily Fairfield)

Chubley, John, Revd, DD deceased Vicar of Huddleston
  his wife, also deceased
  Miss Chubley ('**Miss Dolly**') their daughter, an old maid
Wylder's Hand (1864) J. Sheridan Le Fanu

Chucks, Mr snobbish boatswain
Peter Simple (1834) Captain Marryat

Chuckster clerk to Mr Witherden*
The Old Curiosity Shop (1841) Charles Dickens

Chuffey clerk to Anthony Chuzzlewit*
Martin Chuzzlewit (1844) Charles Dickens

Chuffnell, Marmaduke, Lord m. Maureen Stoker*
  The Dowager Lady Chuffnell his Aunt Myrtle

Seabury Aunt Myrtle's son by her first marriage
Thank You, Jeeves (1934) P. G. Wodehouse

Church, Aurora
her mother
ss 'The Pension Beaurepas'
The Point of View (1883) Henry James

Churchill owner of Enscombe, brother of Mr Weston's* first wife
his dominating, possessive and bad-tempered wife; they bring up Frank Churchill*
Frank son of Mr Weston* and his first wife, takes the name Churchill at his maturity, m. Jane Fairfax*
Emma (1816) Jane Austen

Churchill, Belinda cc in romance by author who was aware that she had sold out her intelligence for the sake of sales ('I began as Zola, and end as Miss Yonge'); m. James Forth*
Sarah her sister
their grandmother
Belinda (1883) Rhoda Broughton

Churchill, Florence cc, m. Lewis Dodd*
Charles her father
The Constant Nymph (1924) Margaret Kennedy

Churm, John old friend to Byng's* father
Cecil Dreeme (1862) Theodore Winthrop

Churton
ss 'The Bisara of Pooree'
Plain Tales from the Hills (1888) Rudyard Kipling

Chuzzlewit, Martin the Younger cc, m. Mary Graham*
Martin his misanthropic grandfather, cousin to Pecksniff*
Anthony brother to old Martin
Jonas Anthony's evil son m. Mercy Pecksniff*
Martin Chuzzlewit (1844) Charles Dickens

Cicero (hist.) senator
Julius Caesar play (1623) William Shakespeare

Cigarette a *vivandière*
Under Two Flags (1867) Ouida (rn Marie Louise de la Ramée)

Cinna conspirator against Caesar*
Julius Caesar play (1623) William Shakespeare

Cinqbars, Viscount Second Earl of Ringwood, dissipated and despicable
A Shabby Genteel Story (1840) W. M. Thackeray

Cintré, Claire de widow, sister to the Marquis Urbain de Bellegarde*, affianced to Christopher Newman*
The American (1876) Henry James

Cissie nurse to Philadelphia Bucksteed*
ss 'Marklake Witches'
Rewards and Fairies (1910) Rudyard Kipling

Citrine, Charlie literary man, cc
Humboldt's Gift (1975) Saul Bellow

Civility see **Legality**

Claben, Van pawnbroker murdered by Ferdinand* and Borokrom* after he has been able to eat money
Delphine his governess
Guignol's band (1944) Louis-Ferdinand Céline (rn Louis-Ferdinand Destouches)

Clack, Drusilla niece of the late Sir J. Verinder; part narrator
The Moonstone (168) Wilkie Collins

Claelia, Princess patroness of Gerard Eliasson*
The Cloister and the Hearth (1861) Charles Reade

Claggart, John sadistic master-at-arms on HMS *Indomitable*
Billy Budd (1924) Herman Melville

Claiborne, Constance m. Martin Faber*
Martin Faber (1833, rev. as *Martin Faber, the Story of a Criminal*, 1837) William Gilmore Simms

Clairval, Mme Valencourt's* aunt
The Mysteries of Udolpho (1794) Mrs Ann Radcliffe

Clall, Eglantine, Mrs cook
The Sailor's Return (1925) David Garnett

Clancy drover in poems of Australian balladeer, author of 'Waltzing Matilda' ('Clancy's gone to Queensland droving, and we don't know where he are'); now part of Australian folklore
Collected Verse (1921) A. B. ('Banjo') Paterson

Clandon, Lanerey, Mrs wife of Fergus Crampton*
Gloria; Dorothy; Philip her children
You Never Can Tell play (1895) George

Bernard Shaw

Clane, Fox fat and senile judge
Johnny his dead son
John (Jester) his teenage grandson
Clock Without Hands (1961) Carson McCullers

Clanronald Highland chief
Waverley (1814) Walter Scott

Clapp faithful old clerk with whom the Sedleys* sheltered after their downfall
his wife
Mary their daughter, devoted to Amelia Sedley*
Vanity Fair (1847–8) W. M. Thackeray

Clapperclaw, Miss Mrs Cammysole's* first-floor lodger
Our Street (1848) W. M. Thackeray

Clara beloved of Captain Breton*
The Wonder play (1714) Susannah Centlivre

Clara companion to Lady Franklin*
Money play (1840) Edward Bulwer Lytton

Clara Rochester's* third mistress
Jane Eyre (1847) Charlotte Brontë

Clare, Ada ward of Mr Jarndyce* m. Richard Carstone*
Bleak House (1853) Charles Dickens

Clare, Angel whose love for Tess* was 'rather bright than hot', cc
Revd James his father, Vicar of Emminster (Beaminster)
his mother, the vicar's second wife
Revd Felix; Revd Cuthbert his brothers
Tess of the D'Urbervilles (1891) Thomas Hardy

Clare, Arthur, Sir
Lady Dorcas his wife
Millicent; Harry their children
The Merry Devil of Edmonton play (1608) Thomas Dekker

Clare, Francis neighbour of the Vanstones*
Frank; Cecil; Arthur his sons, the first-named being a weak fortune hunter, once engaged to Magdalen Vanstone*
No Name (1862) Wilkie Collins

Clare, Mother Abbess of Imber Abbey
The Bell (1958) Iris Murdoch

Clarel American theology student visiting Jerusalem in poem of 3500 octosyllabic couplets about faith and doubt – inspired by its author's visit to the Holy Land in

1856
Clarel poem (1876) Herman Melville

Claremont
Philaster play (1611) Francis Beaumont and John Fletcher

clarence the ghost
archy and mehitabel verse (1927) Don Marquis

Clarence, Duke of
King Henry VI; *King Richard III* plays (1623) William Shakespeare

Claret, Captain 'a Harry the Eighth afloat, bluff and hearty'
White-Jacket (1850) Herman Melville

Clarinda a young unmarried lady
A Journey to London play (1728) John Vanbrugh

Clarissa wife to Gripe*, an expensive luxurious woman, a great admirer of quality
The Confederacy play (1705) John Vanbrugh

Clark stout man in a wharfinger's office who gave Florence Dombey* into the charge of Mr Walter Gay* when she was lost
Dombey and Son (1848) Charles Dickens

Clark, Bernard 'sinister son of Queen Victora', m. Ethel Monticue*
The Young Visiters (1919) Daisy Ashford

Clark, George aged art collector
ss 'The Skeleton'
Blind Love (1969) V. S. Pritchett

Clark, Mark employed on farm at Weatherbury
Far From the Madding Crowd (1874) Thomas Hardy

Clarke first husband of Mrs Susan Weller*
The Pickwick Papers (1837) Charles Dickens

Clarke friend to Dr Raymond*
The Great God Pan (1894) Arthur Machen

Clarke, Jim smuggler
ss 'The Distracted Preacher'
Wessex Tales (1888) Thomas Hardy

Clarke, Mrs see **Weller, Tony**

Clarke, Thomas attorney, nephew to Sam Crowe*, m. Dorothy Greaves*
Will his father
Crowe his nautical uncle, who says, 'I think for my part one half of the nation is mad, and the other half not very sound'

Sir Launcelot Greaves (1762) Tobias Smollett

Clarkson bailiff's son
Phineas Finn (1869) Anthony Trollope

Claude cc of epistolary poem in hexameters
Amours du Voyage poem (1858) Arthur Hugh Clough

Claudio young gentleman
Much Ado About Nothing play (1623) William Shakespeare

Claudio young lord about to be executed, brother to Isabella*
Measure for Measure (1623) William Shakespeare

Claudius King of Denmark, repentant murderer, uncle to Hamlet*
Hamlet play (1623) William Shakespeare

Clavering, Francis, Sir, Baronet impoverished and unscrupulous gambler
'The Begum', his wife, rich, uneducated widow of Colonel John Altamont
Francis his son
wife of the above
Pendennis (1848) W. M. Thackeray

Clavering, Harry cc; one of the earliest characters in English fiction to choose science after studying arts; schoolmaster, then engineer; m. Florence Burton*
Revd Mr Clavering his idle but witty and genial father, Vicar of Clavering
Fanny; Mary his sisters
his mother
Sir Hugh Clavering m. Hermione Brabazon*; his first cousin and his father's nephew; mean, rude and inconsiderate
Captain Archibald Clavering Sir Hugh's brother
The Claverings (1867) Anthony Trollope

Clavering, Lee journalist who is disappointed of marriage with Countess Zattiany*
Black Oxen (1923) Gertrude Atherton

Clavers, Mary, Mrs purported author of sketches about frontier Michigan in the 1830s
A New Home – Who'll Follow? (reissued as *Our New Home in the West* in 1874) (1839) Mary Clavers (rn Caroline Kirkland)

Claverton, Lord terrified by loneliness
Michael Claverton-Ferry his son

Monica Claverton-Ferry his daughter; in attempt to put Sophocles into drawing-room terms
The Elder Statesman play (1959) T. S. Eliot

Clawson, Clif doctor
Arrowsmith (1925) Sinclair Lewis

Clay naive black man
Dutchman play (1964) LeRoi Jones (later Amiri Baraka)

Clay, John alias Vincent Spaulding, half-mad criminal
ss 'The Red-headed League'
The Adventures of Sherlock Holmes (1892) Arthur Conan Doyle

Clay, John tilemaker, the bridegroom
A Tale of a Tub play (1640) Ben Jonson

Clay, Parry black boy
Minerva his mother
Abel his father
In This Our Life (1941) Ellen Glasgow

Clay, Penelope, Mrs widowed daughter to John Shepherd*, designs to m. Mr Walter Elliot*
Persuasion (1818) Jane Austen

Clay, Robert adventurer and engineer m. Hope Langham*; in romance partly imitated from Anthony Hope's *Prisoner of Zenda**
Soldiers of Fortune (1897) Richard Harding Davis

Clayhanger, Edwin cc, frustrated architect, m. Hilda Lessways*
Darius his father, dictatorial printer
Maggie; Clara his sisters
Clayhanger (1910); *Hilda Lessways* (1911); *These Twain* (1916); *The Roll Call* (1918) Arnold Bennett

Claypole, Noah (alias **Bolter**) charity boy, thief calling himself Morris Bolter, under Fagin*
Oliver Twist (1838) Charles Dickens

Claypole, Tom dull son to a baronet
Flora his wife, *née* Warrington*
The Virginians (1857–9) W. M. Thackeray

Clayton, John see **Greystoke, Lord**

Cleave, Milton, Mrs one of those in the chain of false gossip about Sigismund Zaluski*
The Autobiography of a Slander (1887) Edna Lyall (rn A. E. Bayly)

Cleaver, Fanny (Jenny Wren) dolls'

dressmaker
her father
Our Mutual Friend (1865) Charles Dickens

Clegg, Harry archeologist
The Mandelbaum Gate (1965) Muriel Spark

Clegg, Jane long-suffering cc
Henry her lying and philandering husband
her mother-in-law
Johnnie; Jenny their children
Jane Clegg play (1914) St John Ervine

Clegg, Simon cotton spinner who adopts foundling
Jabez cc, waif, rises to be the 'Manchester Man', m. (1) Ellen Chadwick*, (2) Augusta Aspinall* *née* Ashton*; in novel which gives a valuable account of Manchester at the beginning of the 19th century
The Manchester Man (1876) Mrs G. Linnaeus Banks

Cleishbotham, Jebediah schoolmaster and parish clerk, Gandercleugh, nominal recorder of the tales
Tales of my Landlord (1816–32) Walter Scott

Clemency maid to Dr Jeddler*
The Battle of Life (1846) Charles Dickens

Clemens, Mrs landlady
James her husband
Farewell to Youth (1928) Storm Jameson

Clement, Brother
The Cloister and the Hearth (1861) Charles Reade

Clement, Father accused of 'seven rank heresies'
The Fair Maid of Perth (1828) Walter Scott

Clement, Joseph, Sir, Baronet parliamentary candidate for North Loamshire
Felix Holt (1866) George Eliot (rn Mary Anne, later Marian, Evans)

Clements, Mrs friend to Anne Catherick*
The Woman in White (1860) Wilkie Collins

Clemmens solicitor
Middlemarch (1871–2) George Eliot (rn Mary Anne, later Marian, Evans)

Clench, Rasi' farrier and petty constable
A Tale of a Tub play (1640) Ben Jonson

Clennam, Arthur m. Little Dorrit*
his widowed mother (who adopted him: he was the son of her husband's mistress), a brilliant business-woman, although crippled; always 'balancing her bargain with the Majesty of heaven'
Little Dorrit (1857) Charles Dickens

Cleomenes a Sicilian lord
A Winter's Tale play (1623) William Shakespeare

Cleon
The Maid's Tragedy play (1611) Francis Beaumont and John Fletcher

Cleon Governor of Tharsus
Pericles play (1609) William Shakespeare

Cleopatra Queen of Egypt
Antony and Cleopatra play (1623) William Shakespeare
Caesar and Cleopatra (1900) George Bernard Shaw

Cleopatra *see* **Skewton, Mrs**

Cleophila daughter to Meleander*, sister to Eroclea*
The Lover's Melancholy play (1629) John Ford

Clephane, Kate impulsive and selfish cc in novel depicting wealthy and idle Riviera folk who imagine they have fulfilled themselves through war work
Anne her daughter by the husband she deserted for another man
The Mother's Recompense (1925) Edith Wharton

Clergyman, The
ss 'The Shipwreck'
The Uncommercial Traveller (1860–8) Charles Dickens

Clergyman, The
The Adventures of David Simple (1744–53) Sarah Fielding

Clerval, Henry close friend to Victor Frankenstein*
Frankenstein (1818) Mary Shelley

Cleveland, Clement, Captain pirate, son of Basil Mertoun* and Ulla Troil*
The Pirate (1821) Walter Scott

Cleverly, Susannah Mormon emigrant
William her brother
ss 'Bound for the Great Salt Lake'
The Uncommercial Traveller (1860–8) Charles Dickens

Cleves, Helena Ormond's* mistress
Ormond, or The Secret Witness (1799)

Charles Brockden Brown

Cleves, Martin, Revd Rector of Tripple-
gate, friend to Amos Barton*
ss 'The Revd Amos Barton'
Scenes of Clerical Life (1857) George
Eliot (rn Mary Anne, later Marian,
Evans)

Clèves, Prince de m. Mlle de Chartres*
La Princesse de Clèves (1678) Comtesse
de Lafayette

Cleves, Prince of (Adolf)
Helen his daughter
A Legend of the Rhine (1845) W. M.
Thackeray

Clickett orphan girl who said she was an
'orfling'
David Copperfield (1850) Charles
Dickens

Cliff retired tailor
Silas Marner (1861) George Eliot (rn
Mary Anne, later Marian, Evans)

Cliff, Jasper m. Netty Sargent*
ss 'Netty Sargent's Copyhold'
Life's Little Ironies (1894) Thomas
Hardy

Cliffe, Geoffrey modelled by author on
Lord Byron*
The Marriage of William Ashe (1905)
Mrs Humphry Ward

Clifford, Jane college instructor
The Odd Woman (1974) Gail Godwin

Clifford, Lord
King Henry VI plays (1623) William
Shakespeare

Clifford, Paul cc, illegitimate son of Sir
William Brandon*, m. Lucy Brandon*;
Robin-Hood style highwayman cc of
novel written in part to expose harshness
of British justice; at suggestion of
Godwin* the author satirized political
leaders as criminals in manner of
Beggar's Opera – a 'Newgate novel'*
Judith his mother
Paul Clifford (1830) Edward Bulwer
Lytton

Clifford, Robert, Sir
Perkin Warbeck play (1634) John Ford

Clifton, Coke villainously lecherous and
witty aristocratic rake on lines of
Lovelace* ('Should I be obliged to come
like Jove to Semele in flames and should
we both be reduced to ashes in the
conflict I will enjoy her!') eventually

converted to high-minded radicalism
Anna St Ives (1792) Thomas Holcroft

Clincham, Earl of
The Young Visiters (1919) Daisy Ashford

Clink, Corporal
Vanity Fair (1847–8) W. M. Thackeray

Clink, Jem turnkey at Newgate
Peveril of the Peak (1822) Walter Scott

Clinker, Humphrey cc, ragged ostler taken
on by Matthew Bramble* as coachman
who turns out to be his bastard, m.
Winifred Jenkins*
The Expedition of Humphrey Clinker
(1771) Tobias Smollett

Clintock, Archdeacon
Daniel Deronda (1876) George Eliot (rn
Mary Anne, later Marian, Evans)

Clinton schoolmaster
Mr Perrin and Mr Traill (1911) Hugh
Walpole

Clinton, Harry ('Henry, Earl of Moreland)
cc of very popular novel in which an ideal
nobleman is educated by his businessman
uncle **Mr Clinton (Fenton)**; the novel
was admired (and abridged) by John
Wesley, and was later a favourite of
Kingsley*
The Fool of Quality, or *The History of
Henry Earl of Moreland* (1766–70)
Henry Brooke

Clintup nurseryman
Middlemarch (1871–2) George Eliot (rn
Mary Anne, later Marian, Evans)

Clip goldsmith
The Confederacy play (1705) John
Vanbrugh

Clippurse the Waverleys'* lawyer
Waverley (1814) Walter Scott

Clitheroe, Jack bricklayer
Nora his wife
The Plough and the Stars play (1926)
Sean O'Casey (rn John Casey)

Clitheroe, Mr English gentleman, half-
reluctant Mormon, in power of Sizzum*
Ellen his daughter, painter of Wild West
scenes, m. John Brent*
John Brent (1862) Theodore Winthrop

Clitoressa, Duchess
Ladies Almanack (1928) Djuna Barnes

Clive clerk in Circumlocution Office
Little Dorrit (1857) Charles Dickens

Cliveden-Banks, Mrs snobbish woman
condemned to live with her husband until

she learns to be a good wife, which she has not been
Outward Bound play (1924) Sutton Vane

Clodovitz anarchist
Guignol's band (1944) Louis-Ferdinand Céline (rn Louis-Ferdinand Destouches)

Cloggit neighbour to Mrs Amlet*
The Confederacy play (1705) John Vanbrugh

Cloke, Mr farmer
Mary his wife
ss 'An Habitation Enforced'
Actions and Reactions (1909) Rudyard Kipling

Clonbrony, Lord and **Lady** the absentees from their estate
Lord Colambre their son, who refuses to marry to their wishes
The Absentee (1812) Maria Edgeworth

Clootz, de, Baron student and successful gambler
Barry Lyndon (1844) W. M. Thackeray

Cloten son to Cymbeline's* Queen
Cymbeline play (1623) William Shakespeare

Clouston, Janet reputed witch
Kidnapped (1886) Robert Louis Stevenson

Clout, Colin
The Faërie Queen poem (1590)
Colin Clout's Come Home Again poem (1595) Edmund Spenser

Clov servant of Hamm* to whom he imparts information about the disintegrating world
Endgame play *Fin de partie* (1957) Samuel Beckett

Clove insufferable coxcomb inseparable from Orange*
Every Man Out of His Humour play (1599) Ben Jonson

Clover, Charles m. Sally Pickle*
Peregrine Pickle (1751) Tobias Smollett

Clover, Louisa 'china and glass for hire'
The Town Traveller (1898) George Gissing

Clovis cc
The Chronicles of Clovis (1911) Saki (rn Hector Hugh Munro)

Clubber, Bob Virginian with whom Warrington* quarrels
The Virginians (1857–9) W. M. Thackeray

Clubber, Thomas, Sir head of Chatham Dockyard, guest at the Bull Inn ball
his wife and daughter
The Pickwick Papers (1837) Charles Dickens

Clues, Alexander deacon; cousin to James Pawkie*
The Provost (1822) John Galt

Cluff-Trench
A Bowl of Cherries (1984) Shena Mackay

Clumber, Duke and **Duchess of**
Henry Sidney their son, school friend to Coningsby*
Coningsby (1844) Benjamin Disraeli

Clumly, Fred cc, police chief
his wife
The Sunlight Dialogues (1972) John Gardner

Clump apothecary to Miss Crawley*
Vanity Fair (1847–8) W. M. Thackeray

Clumsy, Tunbelly, Sir
The Relapse play (1696) Sir John Vanbrugh
A Trip to Scarborough play (1777) Richard Brinsley Sheridan

Cluppins, Elizabeth, Mrs 'a little, brisk, busy-looking' friend to Mrs Bardell*, sister to Mrs Raddle*
The Pickwick Papers (1837) Charles Dickens

Clutterbuck, Ann, Lady
Clementina her daughter, cadaverous red-haired poetess, author of 'The Death-Shriek'
The Book of Snobs (1847) W. M. Thackeray

Cly, Roger former servant to Darnay* who gave evidence against him at his trial; given sham burial; became spy; eventually guillotined
A Tale of Two Cities (1859) Charles Dickens

Clytemnestra wife to Agamemnon*, and his murderer; mother of Orestes* and Electra*; murdered by Orestes
The Orestia trilogy of tragedies (458 BC) Aeschylus

Clytie, Miss psychotic who kills herself
ss 'Clytie'
A Curtain of Green (1941) Eudora Welty

Coacher private secretary to Revd F. Bell*

Martha his ill-tempered daughter m. the reluctant Bell
Pendennis (1848) W. M. Thackeray

Coates, Bob m. Milly
Mrs Galer's Business (1905) W. Pett Ridge

Coavinses see Neckett

Coaxer, Mrs
Polly opera (1729) John Gay

Cob water carrier
Every Man in His Humour play (1598) Ben Jonson

Cobb, Tom a dull dog
Barnaby Rudge (1841) Charles Dickens

Cobbler, Reginald self-portrait of one of the most engaging of the British *inverti* exiled in Italy, here seen in Mouleville (Dieppe), where he had been with Oscar Wilde* when he died in 1900 (having himself just been victim of 'an unproven morals charge')
Castles in Kensington (1904) Reginald Turner

Coburn, Arthur, Revd Protestant minister
his wife
Famine (1937) Liam O'Flaherty

Cock Gammer Gurton's boy
Gammer Gurton's Needle play (1575) ?William Stevenson

Cockburn landlord of the George, near Bristoport
Guy Mannering (1815) Walter Scott

Cocker, Indignation, Mr
ss 'A Little Dinner in an Hour'
The Uncommercial Traveller (1860–8) Charles Dickens

Cockton a draughtsman
A Laodicean (1881) Thomas Hardy

Codelyn, Mrs widow whose rent collector Denry Machin* becomes
The Card (1911) Arnold Bennett

Codger tutor at Trinity
The New Machiavelli (1911) H. G. Wells

Codger, Miss literary lady: 'Codger's the lady . . . The oldest inhabitant who never remembers anything'
Martin Chuzzlewit (1844) Charles Dickens

Codlin, Thomas Punch and Judy showman, surly and grumbling
The Old Curiosity Shop (1841) Charles Dickens

Cody, Dan old man (of significant name), idealized by Gatsby*
The Great Gatsby (1925) F. Scott Fitzgerald

Coeur de Lion, Duke
The Book of Snobs (1847) W. M. Thackeray

Coffee, James Francis (Ginger) cc of modern picaresque novel set in Canada
The Luck of Ginger Coffey (1960) Brian Moore

Coffin, Peter landlord of the Spouter Inn
Moby Dick, or The Whale (1851) Herman Melville

Coffinkey, Captain specialist in punchmaking
Rob Roy (1818) Walter Scott

Coggan, Jan employed at Weatherbury (Puddletown)
Far From the Madding Crowd (1874) Thomas Hardy

Cogglesby, Andrew m. Harriet Harrington*
Tom his brother
Evan Harrington (1861) George Meredith

Coggs school chum of Dick Bultitude*
Vice Versa (1882) F. Anstey (rn Thomas Anstey Guthrie)

Cohen, Aaron cc of notable part public-service* novel against Victorian race prejudice
Rachel his wife
Joseph their son
Aaron the Jew (1894) Benjamin L. Farjeon

Cohen, Bella
Ulysses (1922) James Joyce

Cohen, Ezra pawnbroker
Addy his wife
Daniel Deronda (1876) George Eliot (rn Mary Anne, later Marian, Evans)

Cohen, Mirah beautiful young singer m. Daniel Deronda*
her father alias Lapidoth: a villainous actor
Sara her mother
Mordecai her brother
Daniel Deronda (1876) George Eliot (rn Mary Anne, later Marian, Evans)

Cohn, Robert man who does not understand the Hemingway 'code', once a middleweight champion
The Sun Also Rises (in England, *Fiesta*)

(1926) Ernest Hemingway

Coiler, Mrs widow
Silas Marner (1861) George Eliot (rn Mary Anne, later Marian, Evans)

Cokane, William de Burgh
Widowers' Houses play (1892) George Bernard Shaw

Coker, D. barmaid
her mother
The Horse's Mouth (1944) Joyce Cary

Cokes, Bartholomew an esquire of Harrow
Bartholomew Fair play (1631) Ben Jonson

Cokeson, Robert kindly office manager whose humanity does not prevail
Justice play (1910) John Galsworthy

Colambre see **Clonbrony, Lord**

Colander supercilious servant to Ernest Vane*
Peg Woffington (1853) Charles Reade

Colbert, Sapphire mistress of Nancy*, mid-19th-century black slave
Sapphira and the Slave-girl (1940) Willa Cather

Colbrand Swiss servant
Pamela (1740) Samuel Richardson

Colchicum, Viscount elderly and dissipated friend to Pendennis*
Pendennis (1848) W. M. Thackeray

Coldfoot, Harry, Sir Liberal Home Secretary
Phineas Finn† (1869) Anthony Trollope

Cole, Mr friendly man whose origins are in trade, making him only moderately genteel; has a bad stomach
his wife and children
Emma (1816) Jane Austen

Cole, Mrs
The Minor play (1760) Samuel Foote

Cole, Sam tool of Frederick Coventry*
Put Yourself in his Place (1870) Charles Reade

Cole, Thomas (legd.) cc; published earlier than date given below, but no copy extant
Thomas of Reading, or *The Six Worthie Yeomen of the West* (1612) Thomas Delaney

Coleman
Zoe his wife
Antic Hay (1923) Aldous Huxley

Colenso, Reuben of the *Lady Nepean*

St Ives (1897) Robert Louis Stevenson

Colepepper, Captain yachtsman
Phineas Finn† (1869) Anthony Trollope

Colepepper, Jack, Captain 'cowardly rascal'
The Fortunes of Nigel (1822) Walter Scott

Coles, Barney cousin to Jesse Piggot*
The Oriel Window (1896) Mrs Molesworth

Colet, James staff manager at Perriani's, later purser, the *Altair*, cc
Gallions Reach (1927) H. M. Tomlinson

Colford, Major
Loyalties play (1922) John Galsworthy

Colin of Glenure ('The Red Fox') (hist.) King's Factor of Appin
Kidnapped (1886) Robert Louis Stevenson

Colin, Dr atheist serving in leper colony
A Burnt-Out Case (1961) Graham Greene

Colleoni gang leader
Brighton Rock (1938) Graham Greene

Colles, Mr
Prester John (1910) John Buchan

Collett, Mary
John Inglesant (1881) J. H. Shorthouse

Colley-Mahoney, Father Mrs Hurstpierpoint's* chaplain
Valmouth (1919) Ronald Firbank

Collier-Floodgaye, Cecilia, Miss
Before the Bombardment (1926) Osbert Sitwell

Collin, Jacques see **Vautrin**

Collins, John, Master gunsmith
ss 'Hal o' the Draft'
Puck of Pook's Hill (1906) Rudyard Kipling

Collins, Mr not a sensible man, m. Charlotte Lucas*
Pride and Prejudice (1813) Jane Austen

Collins, Rupe bully
Penrod (1914); *Penrod and Sam* (1916); *Penrod Jashber* (1929) Booth Tarkington

Collins, Tom solitary wanderer, narrator of 'diary', published as by him, which liberated the Australian novel from the English tradition; contains 'offensively Australian' parodies of such novels as *Geoffrey Hamlyn*
Such is Life (1903) Joseph Furphy

Collins, William, Revd obsequious clergy-

man and prototype, since his creation, for pomposity and complacency
Pride and Prejudice (1813) Jane Austen

Collinson, General, KCB school governor ss 'The Flag of their Country'
Stalky & Co. (1899) Rudyard Kipling

Collonia, Francisco
The Case is Altered play (1609) Ben Jonson

Colocynth, Dr
Peregrine Pickle (1751) Tobias Smollett

Colona daughter to Petruchio*, a counsellor of state at Pavia
Love's Sacrifice play (1633) John Ford

Colquhoun, Robert, Revd second husband to Chris Guthrie*
A Scots Quair trilogy: *Sunset Song* (1932); *Cloud Howe* (1934); *Grey Granite* (1935) Lewis Grassic Gibbon (rn James Leslie Mitchell)

Colston, Godfrey rich active octogenarian
Charmian his wife
Dame Lettie his sister
Memento Mori (1959) Muriel Spark

Colston, Leo boy messenger between lovers
The Go-Between (1953) L. P. Hartley

Colston, Mrs brewer's wife
Charlie her son
Catherine Furze (1893) Mark Rutherford (rn William Hale White)

Coltherd, Benjie 'impudent urchin'
Redgauntlet (1824) Walter Scott

Coltrone magician and leader of Scalognati*
The Mountain Giants play (1938) Luigi Pirandello

Columbine in love with Harlequin*
Los intereses creados (*The Bonds of Interest*) (1908) Jacinto Benavente

Colville, Theodore American journalist who seeks to recapture his lost youth in early novel on theme of Americans in Europe
Indian Summer (1886) William Dean Howells

Colvin, Henry Master of Artillery
Anne of Geierstein (1829) Walter Scott

Colwan, George, Laird of Dalcastle Tory, 'droll, careless chap, with a very limited proportion of the fear of God in his heart, and very nearly as little of the fear of man'
Rabina, Lady Dalcastle née Orde, his

wife, religious fanatic of extreme Whig views
George; Robert their sons, brought up separately, the latter becoming known as Robert Wringhim; he murders George, and escapes; narrator of second part; in metaphysical thriller, dealing with the Calvinist mentality – Wringhim has been assured that no sin can rob him of election
The Private Memoirs and Confessions of a Justified Sinner (1824) as *The Suicide's Grave* (1828) as *Confessions of a Fanatic* in *Tales and Sketches* (1837) James Hogg

Comandine, Lord
Our Street (1848) W. M. Thackeray

Comber, Freddie schoolmaster
his wife
Mr Perrin and Mr Traill (1911) Hugh Walpole

Comfort, James blacksmith
his wife
The Trumpet Major (1880) Thomas Hardy

Cominius Roman general
Coriolanus play (1623) William Shakespeare

Commase, Rosaline loved by Amory Blaine*; but she rejects him for a wealthier man; in novel of 'jazz age'
This Side of Paradise (1920) F. Scott Fitzgerald

Communist, Gillian ('Jill')
The Revenge for Love (1937) Wyndham Lewis

Compass a Scholar Mathematic
The Magnetic Lady, or *Humours Reconciled* play (1641) Ben Jonson

Compeyson villain who led Magwitch* into crime, and who deserted Miss Haversham on the day they were to be m.; drowned in struggle with Magwitch
Great Expectations (1861) Charles Dickens

Compson, Quentin MacLachan to whom this family is traced back: came from Scotland to Carolina in the 18th century
Charles Stuart his son, fought with British in 1778
Jason Lycurgus Charles Stuart's grandson, builds estate around which Jefferson grows
Quentin Machlachan II son to Jason; Governor of Mississippi

Jason Lycurgus II son to Quentin II, Confederate General, helps build railway to Jefferson
Jason III son to Jason II, lawyer, recluse, drinker, reader of the classics, m. Caroline, née Bascombe
Candace ('Caddy'); Quentin III; Benjy originally Maury, castrated idiot; Jason IV children to Jason III and Caroline
Quentin illegitimate daughter to Caddy
The Sound and the Fury† (1929) William Faulkner

Conant, Walter, Sir landowner
ss 'An Habitation Enforced'
Actions and Reactions (1909) Rudyard Kipling

Conder journalist
It's a Battlefield (1935) Graham Greene

Condiddle, Coolie, Sir
The Bride of Lammermoor (1819) Walter Scott

Condomine, Charles writer
Ruth his second wife
Elvira ghost of his first wife
Blithe Spirit play (1941) Noël Coward

Condor, Charley auditor, Bundecund Bank
The Newcomes (1853–5) W. M. Thackeray

Condron, Michael scaler, riveter, in Liverpool docks
Mrs Condron his deaf and dumb mother
Ebb and Flood (1932) James Hanley

Coney, Christopher drunken rustic
The Mayor of Casterbridge (1886) Thomas Hardy

Conigsburgh, (Athelstane), Lord descendant of the Saxon King
Ivanhoe (1820) Walter Scott

Coningsby, Harry cc, m. Edith Millbank*
Coningsby (1844) Benjamin Disraeli

Conington, Donald barrister
Tom his brother
Death of a Hero (1929) Richard Aldington

Conklin, Jim veteran soldier
The Red Badge of Courage (1895) Stephen Crane

Conmee, John, Very Revd, SJ
Ulysses (1922) James Joyce

Connage, Rosalind loved by Amory Blaine*

This Side of Paradise (1920) F. Scott Fitzgerald

Conneau, Georges see Renauld, Paul

Conner, Mr superintendent of home for the aged
The Poorhouse Fair (1959) John Updike

Connolly, Doris; Micky; Marlene evacuee children
Put Out More Flags (1942) Evelyn Waugh

Connolly, Mr
Love Among the Artists (1900) George Bernard Shaw

Connor, Tommy
The Informer (1925) Liam O'Flaherty

Conrad cc of the chief work of a once popular – and skilful – bitter-sweet novelist; 'a man is young as often as he falls in love'
Conrad in Search of His Youth (1919) Leonard Merrick

Conrad, Father monk 'who seems purposely introduced . . . to cast an odium upon religion and its ministers'
Santa Maria, or The Mysterious Pregnancy (1798) J. Fox

Conroy
ss 'In the Same Boat'
A Diversity of Creatures (1917) Rudyard Kipling

Conroy city missionary
No. 5 John Street (1902) Richard Whiteing

Conroy, Gabriel Irish teacher
Gretta his wife
ss 'The Dead'
Dubliners (1914) James Joyce

Considine, Anthony
Molly his wife
Denis; Joey; Jack; Mary; Paddy; Tess; Floss; Jim their children
John his father, founder of the Considines
Sophia née Quillihey, his mother
Joe; Victor; Millicent; Agnes; Tom; Mary; Caroline; Teresa; Eddy his brothers and sisters
Without My Cloak (1931) Kate O'Brien

Considine, Count ('Billy')
Charles O'Malley (1841) Charles Lever

Constable, Yvonne divorced wife of Geoffrey Firmin*
Under the Volcano (1947) Malcolm

Lowry

Constance mother to Arthur*
King John play (1623) William Shakespeare

Constant a gentleman of the town
The Provok'd Wife play (1697) John Vanbrugh

Constantine, Lady Viviette *née* Glanville, noble cc of comi-tragedy who is broken by her too great concern for people's opinion of her; m. (1) Sir Blount Constantine, (2) Swithin St Cleeve* (believing Sir Blount to be then deceased: Sir Blount 'married a native princess according to the rites of the tribe' but drank too much and shot himself); still later, to legitimize her son by Swithin, she m. the arrogant Bishop Helmsdale*
Two on a Tower (1882) Thomas Hardy

Constantius, Emperor (hist.) mad Emperor, cousin to Julian* and Gallus*
Helena his sister m. Julian
Keiser og Gallilaeer (Emperor and Galilean) (1873) Henrik Ibsen

Consuelo cc, beautiful bare-backed rider in a circus, 'The Equestrian Tango Queen'; thus called, explains 'He Who gets Slapped'*, from a character in a book by George Sand*: consolation
Tot, kto poluchaet poshchochiny (He Who Gets Slapped; once tr. as *The Painted Laugh*) play (1916) Leonid Andreyev

Contarino secretary to Cozimo*
The Great Duke of Florence play (1636) James Shirley

Conti gaoler
Clélia his daughter, in love with Fabrice de Dongo*, m. Marchese Crescenzi
La Chartreuse de Parme (1839) Stendhal (rn Henri Bayle)

Continental Op., The anonymous detective with subtly distinctive moral code in tough crime tales
The Dain Curse (1929); *Red Harvest* (1929); *Blood Money* (1943); *(The Continental Op.* selected and edited by Steven Marcus, 1974) Dashiell Hammett

Conway, General (hist.) soldier and politician
Barnaby Rudge (1841) Charles Dickens

Conway, William see **Blayds-Conway**

Conyers, James villainous groom, m. (and blackmails) Aurora Floyd*; murdered by Hargraves*
Aurora Floyd (1863) Mary Braddon

Cook, Nelly
monstrous vital loquacious egotist
Cotters' England (1967) Christina Stead

Cookie' and **'R.J.C.'** otherwise unidentified narrator of novel-thriller about Sukarno's* last year of power
The Year of Living Dangerously (1978) C. J. Koch

Cookson pirate
Peter Pan play (1904) J. M. Barrie

Cooley, Benjamin ('**Kangeroo**') political leader in Sydney
Kangaroo (1923) D. H. Lawrence

Cooley, Hubert black superintendent of four Harlem tenaments trying to escape from his wife by making a successful bet (which he does make, but the numbers runner, John Lewis*, welshes)
Gertrude his troublesome wife
James Lee his son
The Hit (1957) Julian Mayfield

Coombe, Eliah marine store dealer
The Silver King play (1882) Henry Arthur Jones

Cooper Neary's* man-of-all work, sent to London to discover if Murphy* is dead
Murphy (1938) Samuel Beckett

Cooper, Augustus young gentleman in the oil and colour line
his 'little mother', who manages him, but not well enough to prevent the father of a Miss Billsmethie extracting £20 from him for breach of promise
Sketches by Boz (1836) Charles Dickens

Cooper, Marlene, Miss patron
The Bachelors (1961) Muriel Spark

Cooper, Sally friend to Liza Kemp*
her mother
Liza of Lambeth (1897) W. Somerset Maugham

Coote, Chester house agent, social climber
Kipps (1905) H. G. Wells

Coote, J. G. ('**Looney Coote**') friend to Corcoran* and Uckridge*
Uckridge (1924) P. G. Wodehouse

Cope, Percival, Revd fiancé of Frances Falkland*
ss 'For Conscience' Sake'
Life's Little Ironies (1894) Thomas Hardy

Copeland, Benedict, Dr black doctor
Willie; Portia his children
The Heart is a Lonely Hunter (1940)
Carson McCullers
Copleigh, Edith
Maud her sister
ss 'False Dawn'
Plain Tales from the Hills (1888) Rudyard Kipling
Coplestone, Celia cc
The Cocktail Party play (1950) T. S. Eliot
Coppard, George
Gertrude his daughter m. Walter Morel*
Sons and Lovers (1913) D. H. Lawrence
Coppard, James mayor and local bigwig, father to Ellen Barfoot*
Jacob's Room (1922) Virginia Woolf
Copper militant young son of white plantation owner and black field hand
ss 'Bloodline'
Bloodline (1978) Ernest J. Gaines
Copperfield, David cc, narrator, m. (1) Dora Spenlow*, (2) Agnes Wickfield*
Clara his mother, m. (2) Edward Murdstone*
David Copperfield (1850) Charles Dickens
Copperfield, Frieda cc innovatory novel: in search of self-fulfilment as distinct from Christina Goering's* search for sainthood; she achieves it through a Panamanian prostitute
Two Serious Ladies (1943) Jane Bowles
Coppinger, Curll, Captain ('Cruel Coppinger') smuggler m. Judith Trevisa*
In the Roar of the Sea (1892) Sabine Baring-Gould
Coquelin young tutor and lover of Gabrielle de Bergerac* in early unreprinted tale
ss 'Gabrielle de Bergerac' (1868) Henry James
Coral, Mrs
The Little Girls (1964) Elizabeth Bowen
Coralie premiere *danseuse*, Ludwiglust Court Theatre
Barry Lyndon (1844) W. M. Thackeray
Coralie, Mlle horse rider at Franconi's
Pendennis (1848) W. M. Thackeray
Corax a physician
The Lover's Melancholy play (1629) John Ford

Corbet lawyer
Henry Esmond (1852) W. M. Thackeray
Corbett, Cassandra cc, Oxford don
The Game (1967) A. S. Byatt
Corby survivor of the wreck of the *Warren Hastings*
Ravenshoe (1861) Henry Kingsley
Corcoran narrator, friend to Uckridge*
Uckridge (1922) P. G. Wodehouse
Corcoran, Captain m. Buttercup*
Josephine his daughter, m. Ralph Rackstraw*
H.M.S. Pinafore opera (1878) W. S. Gilbert and Arthur Sullivan
Cordatus the author's friend
Every Man Out of His Humour play (1599) Ben Jonson
Corde, Albert dean of men at a Chicago college, cc
Minna his Rumanian-born wife, an astronomer
The Dean's December (1981) Saul Bellow
Corder, Robert minister
Howard; Ethel; Ruth his children
Wilfred his nephew
Miss Mole (1930) E. H. Young
Coreb a spirit
The Merry Devil of Edmonton play (1608) ?Thomas Dekker
Corey, Bromfield artist
Anna his wife
Tom; Lily; Nanny their children, the first of whom m. Penelope Lapham*
The Rise of Silas Lapham (1885) William Dean Howells
Corin shepherd
As You Like It play (1623) William Shakespeare
Corineus brother to King Brutus*, father to Guendoline*
Locrine play (1595) 'W.S.' (?George Peele; ?Robert Green)
Corinna
Sacharissa her sister
The Adventures of David Simple (1744–53) Sarah Fielding
Corinna daughter to Gripe*, kept very close by her father
The Confederacy play (1705) John Vanbrugh
Corinne famous beautiful poet, half-sister to Lucille Edgermond*, in novel by the

lover (1794–1811) of Constant*
Corinne (1807) Madame de Staël
Corkery, Phil friend to Ida Arnold*
Brighton Rock (1938) Graham Greene
Corkett, Henry clerk to Geoffrey Ware*
The Silver King play (1882) Henry
Arthur Jones
Corkran, Arthur ('Stalky') cc based – to his
displeasure – on the author's schoolchum
Dunsterville, who became a general
Stalky & Co. (1899) Rudyard Kipling
Corley, Mr
ss 'Two Gallants'
Dubliners (1914) James Joyce
Corliss, Bud evil murderer
A Kiss Before Dying (1953) Ira Levin
Corliss, Vance noble cc: 'chaste, loyal,
morally courageous'
A Daughter of the Snows (1902) Jack
London
Cornelius see Oldacre, Jonas
Corner, Cicely remote cousin to Direck*
Letty her sister
Mr Britling Sees It Through (1916) H. G.
Wells
Corney, Mrs
Nelly her mother
Bessie her sister
Sylvia's Lovers (1863) Mrs Gaskell
Corney, Mrs matron of the workhouse
where Oliver Twist* was born, thief, m.
Bumble*; eventually inmate with her
husband of the same workhouse
Oliver Twist (1838) Charles Dickens
Cornichon, M. French architect
Barry Lyndon (1844) W. M. Thackeray
Cornichon, Mme calling herself
Valentinois, keeper of *pension* in Paris
The Adventures of Philip (1862) W. M.
Thackeray
Cornplanter American Indian
ss 'Brother Square Toes'
Rewards and Fairies (1910) Rudyard
Kipling
Cornu, Mme widow whom Barry
Lyndon* almost m.
Barry Lyndon (1844) W. M. Thackeray
Cornwall noble at the Court of England
Old Fortunatus play (1600) Thomas
Dekker
Cornwall, Duke of
King Lear play (1623) William Shake-
speare

Cornwell, Christine widow
Gwyneth doctor; **Tim** m. Maureen
Phillibrand* – her children
Larry her stepson
The Widow (1957) Francis King
Corombona, Vittoria Venetian
Camillo her husband
Flamineo; Marcello her brothers
The White Devil play (1612) John
Webster
Corporate, Christopher whose single
bought vote sees Haut-on* into Parlia-
ment
Melincourt, or *Sir Oran Haut-on* (1817)
Thomas Love Peacock
Corrie, Rollo, Mrs employer of Miriam
Henderson*
Felix her husband
Pilgrimage (1915–68) Dorothy M.
Richardson
Corrigan, Cornelius
Miles his grandfather
Roland Cashel (1850) Charles Lever
Corthell, Sheldon rich dilettante; artist; has
affair with Laura Jadwin *née* Dearborn*
The Pit (1903) Frank Norris
Cortright, Edith refined American woman
living in Italy, (presumably) m. Sam
Dodsworth*
Dodsworth (1929) Sinclair Lewis
Corven, Gerald, Sir husband of Claire
Charwell*
Over the River (1933) John Galsworthy
Corvick experienced critic, m. Gwendolyn
Erme*, who possibly murders him
ss 'The Figure in the Carpet'
Embarrassments (1896) Henry James
Corvino greedy merchant
Celia his wife
Volpone, or *The Fox* play (1606) Ben
Jonson
Corydon, Jackie
Hay Fever play (1925) Noël Coward
Cosroe brother to Mycetes*
Tamburlaine play (1587) Christopher
Marlowe
Cosser civil engineer
The Food of the Gods (1904) H. G. Wells
Cost (alias **Travers**) member of spy ring
The Ministry of Fear (1943) Graham
Greene
Costard a clown
Love's Labour's Lost play (1623)

William Shakespeare

Costigan, J. Chesterfield, Captain 'disreputable jolly Irishman'
Emily his daughter (see Fotheringay)
Pendennis (1848) W. M. Thackeray

Costlett, Captain Cavalier turncoat
Rob Roy (1818) Walter Scott

Cosway, Antoinette Creole, m. Mr Rochester*
her mother
Pierre her brother
Wide Sargasso Sea (1966) Jean Rhys

Cothorpe
Tono Bungay (1909) H. G. Wells

Cottar, George, Major, DSO 'The Brushwood Boy'; m. Miriam Lacy*
ss 'The Brushwood Boy'
The Day's Work (1898) Rudyard Kipling

Cottard, Dr
A la recherche du temps perdu (*In Search of Lost Time*) (1913–27) Marcel Proust

Cotterill, Nellie m. Denry Machin*
Councillor Cotterill her father
The Card (1911) Arnold Bennett

Coulson, William friend to Philip Hepburn*
Sylvia's Lovers (1863) Mrs Gaskell

Counihan, Miss depraved Cork County young lady who loves Murphy*
Murphy (1938) Samuel Beckett

Coupé, Bras African ex-prince who allows himself to be tortured to death rather than be a slave
The Grandissimes: A Story of Creole Life (1880) George Washington Cable

Coupler matchmaker
The Relapse, or Virtue in Danger play (1697) John Vanbrugh

Coupler, Mrs
A Trip to Scarborough play (1777) Richard Brinsley Sheridan

Cour, de la, Capitaine commander of French town
Somebody's Luggage (1862) Charles Dickens

Courcelles, de Canon of Paris
St Joan play (1921) George Bernard Shaw

Court, Landry young stockbroker m. Page Dearborn*
The Pit (1903) Frank Norris

Courtier freelance politician
The Patrician (1911) John Galsworthy

Courtine friend to Captain Beaugard*
The Soldier's Fortune play (1681) Thomas Otway

Courtly, Colonel
A Journey to London play (1728) John Vanbrugh

Courtney, Harry wealthy Australian who buys Hurtle Duffield* from his parents for £500
Alfreda his wife
Rhoda their daughter, a hunchback
The Vivisector (1970) Patrick White

Coutell, Lane boyfriend of Franny Glass*
Franny and Zooey (1961) J. D. Salinger

Cova, Arturo poet cc of influential Colombian novel about the primitive depths of the Amazonian basin, in which, mad, he perishes
La Vorágine (*The Vortex*) (1924) José Eustacio Rivera

Coventry, Frederick 'villain'
Put Yourself in his Place (1870) Charles Reade

Coverdale, Miles narrator of novel based on the 'Transcendental Picnic', the idealistic experiment in community living experienced by the author at Brook Farm
The Blithedale Romance (1852) Nathaniel Hawthorne

Covey working-class friend to Lord Brentmoor*
No. 5 John Street (1902) Richard Whiteing

Covey, The Young fitter, cousin to Jack Clitheroe*
The Plough and the Stars play (1926) Sean O'Casey (rn John Casey)

Cowdray, Walter, Sir
ss 'The Man in the Passage'
The Wisdom of Father Brown (1914) G. K. Chesterton

Cowie, Harold veterinarian
One Day (1965) Wright Morris

Cowlard, Laura
The Constant Nymph (1924) Margaret Kennedy

Cowley cashier
Justice play (1910) John Galsworthy

Cowper-Cooper, Mrs
Lady Windermere's Fan play (1892) Oscar Wilde

Cowperwood, Frank ruthless businessman cc based mostly on Charles Tyson

Yerkes, crooked American financier who invested in the London Underground (as is related), in 'Trilogy of Desire'; the final volume was 'fixed up' (i.e. rewritten by someone else, an editor) as the author admitted, and is inferior
Lillian *née* Semple his first wife
Aileen *née* Butler his second wife
Berenice Fleming his mistress and ideal, daughter of a brothel-keeper
Henry his father
The Financier (1912 revised 1927); *The Titan* (1914); *The Stoic* (1947) Theodore Dreiser
Cowslip, Dolly (rn **Dolly Greaves**)
Sir Lancelot Greaves (1762) Tobias Smollett
Cox journeyman hatter
Box and Cox play (1847) J. M. Morton
Cox, John suicide
The Life and Death of Mr Badman (1670) John Bunyan
Cox, Mr an astrologer
Malcolm (1959) James Purdy
Cox, Mr cook to Sir Gulliver Deniston*
The World My Wilderness (1950) Rose Macaulay
Cox, Sam barber
Jemima his snobbish wife
Jemima Ann their daughter m. Orlando Crump*
Barber Cox (1847) W. M. Thackeray
Coxe, Captain Director of Pageants, Kenilworth Castle
Kenilworth (1821) Walter Scott
Coxe, Mr
Wives and Daughters (1866) Mrs Gaskell
Coyne, Aurora cc of unfinished novel; promises to m. Ralph Pendrel* if he can resist returning from Europe to America to claim her
The Sense of the Past (1917) Henry James
Cozimo Duke of Florence
The Great Duke of Florence play (1636) James Shirley
Crab, Launcelot surgeon
Roderick Random (1748) Tobias Smollett
Crabb, Jack ancient frontiersman, cc
Little Big Man (1964) Thomas Berger
Crabb, Mrs mother to Juliana Gann*
A Shabby Genteel Story (1840) W. M.

Thackeray
Crabbe, Victor cc of trilogy set in Malaya
Time for a Tiger (1956); *The Enemy in the Blanket* (1958); *Beds in the East* (1959) Anthony Burgess (rn John Burgess Wilson)
Crabble, Inspector
The Last Revolution (1951) Lord Dunsany
Crabs, 13th Earl of (Gustavus Adolphus) scoundrel in high favour with the king
Barry Lyndon (1844) W. M. Thackeray
Crabs, Earl of (John A. A. P.) dissipated elderly scoundrel m. Lady Griffin*
The Great Hoggarty Diamond† (1841) W. M. Thackeray
Crabshaw Launcelot Greaves's* mad uncle
Sir Launcelot Greaves (1762) Tobias Smollett
Crabtree uncle to Sir Benjamin Backbite*
The School for Scandal play (1777) Richard Brinsley Sheridan
Crabtree, Cadwallader deaf and elderly
Peregrine Pickle (1751) Tobias Smollett
Crackenbury, Lady of shabby repute
Vanity Fair (1847–8) W. M. Thackeray
Crackenthorp, Revd Mr Rector of Raveloe
Silas Marner (1861) George Eliot (rn Mary Anne, later Marian, Evans)
Crackenthorpe, Joe landlord
his wife
Redgauntlet (1824) Walter Scott
Crackenthorpe, Miss
Sinister Street (1913) Compton Mackenzie
Crackit, Toby partner to Fagin*
Oliver Twist (1838) Charles Dickens
Crackthorpe Captain friend to Clive Newcome*
The Newcomes (1853–5) W. M. Thackeray
Craddock, Eric bookshop assistant
Celia his mother
Hemlock and After (1952) Angus Wilson
Craddock, Mrs landlady, Bath
The Pickwick Papers (1837) Charles Dickens
Cradock, Jack meat-buyer for Imperial
Imperial Palace (1930) Arnold Bennett
Craggs of Snitchey and Craggs, Dr Jeddler's* lawyers, 'white, like a flint'
The Battle of Life (1846) Charles

Dickens
Cragstone, Lady gambler
Daniel Deronda (1876) George Eliot (rn Mary Anne, later Marian, Evans)
Craig gardener in love with Hetty Sorrell*
Adam Bede (1859) George Eliot (rn Mary Anne, later Marian, Evans)
Craig, Thomas embezzler; friend to Ormond*; murderer
Ormond, or The Secret Witness (1799) Charles Brockden Brown
Craigdallie, Bailie Adam
The Fair Maid of Perth (1828) Walter Scott
Craigengelt, Captain gambler and informer
The Bride of Lammermoor (1819) Walter Scott
Crail, Captain
The Master of Ballantrae (1889) Robert Louis Stevenson
Crambagge, Paul, Sir 'a sour fanatic knight'
The Fortunes of Nigel (1822) Walter Scott
Cramchild, Cousin
The Water Babies (1863) Charles Kingsley
Cramp cabinet maker
Last Post (1928) Ford Madox Ford
Crampton, Fergus husband to Mrs Clandon*
You Never Can Tell play (1895) George Bernard Shaw
Crampton, Jack
Famine (1937) Liam O'Flaherty
Crampton, Josiah politician
The Bedford Row Conspiracy (1840) W. M. Thackeray
Cranage, Ben ('Wiry Ben') carpenter, rustic dancer
Adam Bede (1859) George Eliot (rn Mary Anne, later Marian, Evans)
Cranbourne, Jasper, Sir old cavalier
Peveril of the Peak (1822) Walter Scott
Cranch, Matilda, Mrs
Tom her son
Middlemarch (1871–2) George Eliot (rn Mary Anne, later Marian, Evans)
Crandall, R., Lieutenant old boy
ss 'A Little Prep'
Stalky and Co. (1899) Rudyard Kipling
Crane of the Surrey Hunt

Jorrocks's Jaunts and Jollities (1838) R. S. Surtees
Crane, Ichabod schoolmaster resembling 'some scarecrow eloped from a field' who is driven from the town by a 'headless horseman'
ss 'The Legend of Sleepy Hollow'
The Sketch Book of Geoffrey Crayon, Gent (1820) Washington Irving
Crane, Alison, Dame
Kenilworth (1821) Walter Scott
Crang, Joe village blacksmith
Perlycross (1894) R. D. Blackmore
Cranmer, Emile grocer's boy
The Wapshot Scandal (1963) John Cheever
Cranmer, Thomas (hist.) Archbishop of Canterbury
King Henry VIII play (1623) William Shakespeare and John Fletcher
Cranston, Bertine friend to Sondra Finchley*
An American Tragedy (1925) Theodore Dreiser
Craon, Pierre de leprous architect of cathedrals, kissed in pity by Violaine Vercors*
L'Annonce faite à Marie play (*The Tidings Brought to Mary*) (1912, rev. 1948) Paul Claudel
Crashaw, Percy, Revd
The Hampdenshire Wonder (1911) J. D. Beresford
Crashaw, Sidney victim of Helen Vaughan*
The Great God Pan (1894) Arthur Machen
Crasweller, Gabriel candidate for euthanasia in speculative fantasy which is essentially a retelling of the author's *The Warden*, set in Britannula, a future republic off Australia
The Fixed Period (1882) Anthony Trollope
Cratchit, Bob clerk to Scrooge
his wife
Martha; Belinda; Peter; Tiny Tim their children, the last a cripple
A Christmas Carol (1843) Charles Dickens
Craven, Daniel, Colonel
Julia; Sylvia his daughters
The Philanderer play (1893) George Bernard Shaw

Craven, Governor see Harrison, Gabriel
Crawford, Earl of
his wife
Perkin Warbeck play (1634) John Ford
Crawford, Henry ruined by early in-
dulgence and bad domestic example
Mary his sister, m. Edmund Bertram*
Admiral Crawford their uncle and
guardian, a man of vicious conduct
his ill-treated wife
Mansfield Park (1814) Jane Austen
Crawford, Miles journalist
Ulysses (1922) James Joyce
Crawfurd, David cc narrator
Prester John (1910) John Buchan
Crawley, Josiah, Revd perpetual curate of
Hogglestock, accused of stealing a
cheque
Kate his wife
their children
Framley Parsonage (1861) Anthony
Trollope
Crawley, Pitt, Sir, Baronet, MP cunning,
mean, selfish m. (1) Lady Grizzel Binkie,
(2) Rose Dawson
Pitt m. Lady Jane Sheepshanks; Rawdon
m. Becky Sharp* – children to Pitt and
Lady Grizzel
Pitt Binkie; Matilda children to Pitt and
Lady Jane
Bute his brother
Bute's wife née McTavish
James; Frank; Emma; Fanny; Kate;
Louisa; Martha Bute's children
Vanity Fair (1847–8) W. M. Thackeray
Crawley, Wilmot, Sir neighbour to the
Castlewoods
Wilmot his son
Henry Esmond (1852) W. M. Thackeray
Cray, Ailie schoolteacher, m. Ivie
McClean*
Kitty her sister
Sentimental Tommy (1896) J. M. Barrie
Cray, Colonel
ss 'The Salad of Colonel Cray'
The Wisdom of Father Brown (1914)
G. K. Chesterton
Crayton, Captain m. Mlle La Rue
Charlotte: A Tale of Truth (1791; in
America as *Charlotte Temple*, 1794) Mrs
Susannah Rowson
Crazy Ivar hired man
O Pioneers! (1913) Willa Cather

Crazy, Sheila girl loved by Max Fisher*
Pending Heaven (1930) William
Gerhardie
Creakle headmaster of Salem House who
delights in beating boys; later a magis-
trate
David Copperfield (1850) Charles
Dickens
Crebbin, Dr Darley's* doctor
A Certain Man (1931) Oliver Onions
Crécy, Odette de m. Swann*
A la recherche du temps perdu (*In Search
of Lost Time*) (1913–27) Marcel Proust
Credulous, Justice
Bridget his wife
Lauretta their daughter
St Patrick's Day play (1775) Richard
Brinsley Sheridan
Cree, Lucius cc novel held by many (e.g.
Caroline Gordon*) to be a masterpiece of
American fiction dealing with the South
The Velvet Horn (1957) Andrew Lytle
Creed landlord, White Hart, Margate
Jorrocks's Jaunts and Jollities (1838) R.
S. Surtees
Creedle, Robert old man working for Giles
Winterbourne*
The Woodlanders (1887) Thomas Hardy
Cregan, Hardress hapless cc of Irish novel
– the basis of Boucicault's play *The
Colleen Bawn*
The Collegians, or *The Colleen Bawn: A
Tale of Garryowen* (1829) Gerald Griffin
Cregeen owner of old lifeboat
The Card (1911) Arnold Bennett
Creighton, William, Colonel secret service
Kim (1901) Rudyard Kipling
Crespin, Antony hard drinking and bump
tious major
Lucilla his unhappy wife, invited by Raja
of Rukh* to enter his harem; priests plan
to sacrifice them to the Green Goddess
The Green Goddess play (1921) William
Archer
Cressida daughter of Calchas
Troilus and Cressida play (1623) William
Shakespeare
Cressler, Charles wheat speculator
The Pit (1903) Frank Norris
Cresswell, Oscar Paul's* uncle
ss 'The Rocking Horse Winner'
The Lovely Lady (1932) D. H. Lawrence
Crèvecoeur de Cordes, Philip, Count

French counsellor
Quentin Durward (1823) Walter Scott
Crevel ex-perfume salesman and debauchee
his daughter, m. Victorin Hulot*
La Cousine Bette (1847) Honoré de Balzac
Crewe, Luckworth originally a foundling, so-called by himself; vulgar and successful advertising man, suitor to Nancy Lord*
In the Year of Jubilee (1894) George Gissing
Crewe, Revd Mr curate of Milby
ss 'Janet's Repentance'
Scenes of Clerical Life (1857) George Eliot (rn Mary Anne, later Marian, Evans)
Crewler, Sophie m. Thomas Traddles*, 'the dearest girl in the world'
David Copperfield (1850) Charles Dickens
Crich, Gerald owner of a coal-mine
Thomas his father
Winifred his sister
Women in Love (1921) D. H. Lawrence
Crichley, Revd Mr Rector of Cumbermoor
ss 'Mr Gilfil's Love Story'
Scenes of Clerical Life (1857) George Eliot (rn Mary Anne, later Marian, Evans)
Crichton, Bill cc, butler to Lord Loam*
The Admirable Crichton play (1902) J. M. Barrie
Crick, Richard dairy farmer, employer of Tess Durbeyfield*
Christiana his wife
Tess of the D'Urbervilles (1891) Thomas Hardy
Crickett, Richard parish clerk of Carriford
his wife
Desperate Remedies (1871) Thomas Hardy
Cridley ex-public schoolboy
The Old Boys (1964) William Trevor
Crim, Sarah great-aunt to Penrod Schofield*, the only one who understands him
Penrod (1914); *Penrod and Sam* (1916); *Penrod Jashber* (1929) Booth Tarkington
Crim-Con, Lord sodomite by preference, flogger, dies in mid-orgy
Lady Pokingham, or *They All Do It*

(1880) Anon.
Crimple, David originally called Crimp; Secretary and resident Director of Tigg Montague's* bogus assurance company; absconded with the funds
Martin Chuzzlewit (1844) Charles Dickens
Crimsworth, William the professor, English teacher at M. Pelet's*, cc m. Frances Evans Henri*
Victor their son, eventually due to be sent to Eton for hardening off
Edward his elder brother
Edward's ill-treated wife
uncle to Edward and William, blackmailer
The Professor (1857) Charlotte Brontë
Cringer, Mr
Roderick Random (1748) Tobias Smollett
Cringle, Thomas, Captain narrator of naval episodes; opens in Baltic but mostly concerned with West Indies
Tom Cringle's Log (1836) Michael Scott
Cripples, Mr proprietor of a night school
Little Dorrit (1857) Charles Dickens
Cripplestraw, Anthony Mr Derriman's* odd man
The Trumpet Major (1880) Thomas Hardy
Cripps, Zacchary ('Zak') cc, carrier (of the post: before 1839 and the institution of the national postal service); rescuer of Grace Oglander*
Cripps the Carrier: A Woodland Tale (1876) R. D. Blackmore
Crisp, Revd Mr
Vanity Fair (1847–8) W. M. Thackeray
Crisparkle, Septimus, Revd minor canon
Edwin Drood (1870) Charles Dickens
Crispin cc of most highly regarded play by Spanish Nobel Prizewinning author; posing as servant to Leander*
Los intereses creados (The Bonds of Interest) (1908) Jacinto Benavente
Crispinus the poetaster, representative of John Marston*
The Poetaster play (1602) Ben Jonson
Satiromastix, or *The Untrussing of the Humorous Poet* play (1602) Thomas Dekker ?and John Marston
Crisson, Frances first wife of Young Jolyon

Forsyte*
The *Forsyte* series (1906–33) John Galsworthy
Critchlow chemist, Burslem
The Old Wives' Tale (1908) Arnold Bennett
Crites wise poet who devises the masque
Cynthia's Revels, or *The Fountain of Self-Love* play (1601) Ben Jonson
critics 'Not respect critics? . . . Such a man could only be GOOD FOR NOTHING'
'A Mammal's Notebook' (1921) Erik Satie
Crock, Adrian, Revd
The Sailor's Return (1925) David Garnett
Crocker-Harris, Andrew unhappily m. housemaster
Millie his unfaithful wife
The Browning Version play (1948) Terence Rattigan
Croft, Admiral of the White
his wife, *née* Wentworth, tenants of Kellynch Hall
Persuasion (1818) Jane Austen
Croft, Art narrator
The Ox-Bow Incident (1940) Walter Van Tilburg Clark
Croft, Denman m. Stanley Garden*
Told By an Idiot (1923) Rose Macaulay
Croftangry, Chrystal fictitious editor
The Chronicles of the Canongate (The Fair Maid of Perth*, The Two Drovers* and *The Highland Widow**) (1827) Walter Scott
Crofts, George, Sir
Mrs Warren's Profession (1902) George Bernard Shaw
Crofts, Montague, Captain
Tom Burke of Ours (1844) Charles Lever
Crome, Revd Mr
his grandson
ss 'The Ash-tree'
Ghost Stories of an Antiquary (1910) M. R. James
Cromlech, David friend to Sherston*: a portrait of Robert Graves* as a soldier
Memoirs of an Infantry Officer (1930) Siegfried Sassoon
Cromwell, Thomas (hist.)
King Henry VIII play (1623) William Shakespeare and John Fletcher

Cronkshaw see Carey, Philip
Cronshaw indigent poet ('An artist would let his mother go to the workhouse') to whom Carey* gives shelter
Of Human Bondage (1915) W. Somerset Maugham
Crookey waiter at Namby's lock-up
The Pickwick Papers (1837) Charles Dickens
Crookhill, George
ss 'An Incident in the Life of Mr George Crookhill'
Life's Little Ironies (1894) Thomas Hardy
Crooklyn, Professor
The Egoist (1879) George Meredith
Croom, James Bernard (Tony) lover of Clare Corven*
The Forsyte series (1906–33) John Galsworthy
Croop shoemaker
Daniel Deronda (1876) George Eliot (rn Mary Anne, later Marian, Evans)
Crosbie, William Provost of Dumfries
Jenny his wife
Redgauntlet (1824) Walter Scott
Crosby maid in the Pargiter* household
The Years (1937) Virginia Woolf
Crosnel, Renée de loved by Nevile Beauchamp* who loses her by his gallantry after she has fled her husband; the author's favourite of his women characters
Beauchamp's Career (1876) George Meredith
Cross Patch see Patch, Adam
Crossfield, Ursula, Mrs sister to Jim Beddows*
her husband
Rose their daughter
South Riding (1936) Winifred Holtby
Crossjay poor relation, officer of Marines
The Egoist (1879) George Meredith
Crotolon a counsellor of state, father to Orgilus*
The Broken Heart play (1633) John Ford
Crouchback, Guy cc, romantic who goes to war
his father
Angela his sister m. Arthur Box-Bender, MP
Men at Arms (1952) Evelyn Waugh
Crow High Constable of Treby

Felix Holt (1866) George Eliot (rn Mary Anne, later Marian, Evans)

Crow steward to Chris Glowry*
Nightmare Abbey (1818) Thomas Love Peacock

Crow, Jonathan cold-hearted egoist
The Man Who Loved Children (1940) Christina Stead

Crow, Philip industrialist, owner of dye works
Tilly his wife
John; Mary his cousins
A Glastonbury Romance (1932) John Cowper Powys

Crowborough, Thisbe, Lady
ss 'Maltby and Braxton'
Seven Men (1919) Max Beerbohm

Crowe, Mrs in love with Pope Hadrian
Hadrian the Seventh (1904) Frederick W. Rolfe

Crowe, Sam, Captain seaman, uncle of Thomas Clarke*
Sir Launcelot Greaves (1762) Tobias Smollett

Crowhurst, Phoebe maid to the Furzes*
Catherine Furze (1893) Mark Rutherford (rn William Hale White)

Crowl incredible selfish fellow, lodger of Newman Noggs*
Nicholas Nickleby (1839) Charles Dickens

Crown stevedore, murderer
Porgy (1925) Du Bose Heyward

Crowne, Lenina Alpha worker
Brave New World (1932) Aldous Huxley

Crowse, Revd Mr curate
Middlemarch (1871–2) George Eliot (rn Mary Anne, later Marian, Evans)

Croy, Kate unscrupulous young Englishwoman
The Wings of a Dove (1902) Henry James

Croye, Countess de
Reinhold her father
Hameline her aunt
Quentin Durward (1823) Walter Scott

Cruchecassé, Baroness de la of dubious reputation
Vanity Fair (1847–8) W. M. Thackeray

Cruickshanks, Ebenezer landlord of the Seven-branched Golden Candlesticks
Waverley (1814) Walter Scott

Cruickshanks, Joe

The Little Minister (1891) J. M. Barrie

Cruler, Captain insane murderer in novel by Welsh author
All in a Month (1908) Allen Raine (rn Mrs Benyon Puddlecombe)

Crumb, John m. Ruby Ruggles*
The Way We Live Now (1875) Anthony Trollope

Crummles, Vincent
The Pilgrims of the Thames in Search of the National (1838) Pierce Egan

Crummles, Vincent manager of touring theatrical company
his wife, a stout portly female
Ninetta the Infant Phenomenon, ten years of age for the last five years
Percy; Charles Ninetta's brothers
Nicholas Nickleby (1839) Charles Dickens

Crumms, Cynthia Allen, Mrs
Bob her husband, a ponderous six-footer
ss 'The Weeping Man'
Unlucky for Pringle (1973) Wyndham Lewis

Crump landlord of the Bootjack Hotel
his wife, an ex-dancer
Morgiana their daughter, 'the Ravenswing', m. Howard Walker*
ss 'The Ravenswing'
Men's Wives (1843) W. M. Thackeray

Crump super-snob
The Book of Snobs (1847) W. M. Thackeray

Crump, Dr of Siddermorton
The Wonderful Visit (1895) H. G. Wells

Crump, Lottie hotel proprietress
Vile Bodies (1930) Evelyn Waugh

Crump, Orlando m. Jemima Ann Cox*
Barber Cox (1847) W. M. Thackeray

Crumpton, Amelia and Mary keepers of ladies' seminary at Hammersmith
Sketches by Boz† (1836) Charles Dickens

Crunch, Abbie
her husband
Link their adopted son, cc
The Narrows (1953) Ann Petry

Cruncher, Jerry outdoor messenger of Tellson's Bank; a Resurrection Man by night, interested in funerals
his wife, pious and of orderly appearance
Young Jerry their son
A Tale of Two Cities (1859) Charles Dickens

Crupp, Mrs landlady of rooms in which David Copperfield* sets up as bachelor, subject to the spazzums
David Copperfield (1850) Charles Dickens

Crushton, The Hon. Mr
The Pickwick Papers (1837) Charles Dickens

Crusoe, Robinson cc and narrator
Robinson Crusoe (1719) Daniel Defoe

Cruze, Jack
The Revenge for Love (1937) Wyndham Lewis

Crystal Utopian youth
Men Like Gods (1923) H. G. Wells

Cubitt, Hilton
Elsie his American wife
ss 'The Dancing Men'
The Return of Sherlock Holmes (1905) Arthur Conan Doyle

Cuchulain, King (legd.) cc 'heroic farce' in verse
Emer his wife
The Green Helmet play (1910) William Butler Yeats

Cuculus foolish courtier
The Lover's Melancholy play (1629) John Ford

Cudjoe slave of Senator Bird*
Uncle Tom's Cabin (1851) Harriet Beecher Stowe

Cudmore, Garret
Harry Lorrequer (1839) Charles Lever

Cuff, Richard, Detective-Sergeant first full-scale fictional Scotland Yard detective
The Moonstone (1868) Wilkie Collins

Cuff, Jacob 'charity man'
Felix Holt (1866) George Eliot (rn Mary Anne, later Marian, Evans)

Cuff, Reginald school bully, thrashed by William Dobbin*
Vanity Fair (1847–8) W. M. Thackeray

Cullen, Mr and Mrs
The Pilgrim Hawk (1940) Glenway Westcott

Cullen, Patrick, Sir
The Doctor's Dilemma play (1906) George Bernard Shaw

Cullen, Philly farmer
The Playboy of the Western World play (1907) John Millington Synge

Culling, Rosamund housekeeper to Romfrey*
Beauchamp's Career (1875) George Meredith

Cully, Nicholas, Sir knighted under Oliver Cromwell
The Comical Revenge, or *Love in a Tub* play (1664) George Etherege

Culverin
Polly opera (1729) John Gay

Cummings friend to the Pooters*
The Diary of a Nobody (1892) George and Weedon Grossmith

Cumnor, Lord
his wife
Lady Harriet his daughter
Wives and Daughters (1866) Mrs Gaskell

Cunégonde
Candide, ou L'Optimisme (1759) Voltaire (rn François-Marie Arouet)

Cunningham, Avis narrator, m. Ernest Everhard*
Professor John her father
The Iron Heel (1908) Jack London

Cupid sadistic cop
My Uncle Dudley (1942) Wright Morris

Curdle, Mr who has written a pamphlet of sixty-four pages and is a literary man
his wife
Nicholas Nickleby (1839) Charles Dickens

Current, Isabella (Aunt Bel)
Evan Harrington (1861) George Meredith

Curry, Mrs
Hemlock and After (1952) Angus Wilson

Curtain, Michael cc, sailor torpedoed on the *Aurora*
The Ocean (1946) James Hanley

Curtenty, Jos
Clayhanger (1910) Arnold Bennett

Curtis, Henry, Sir (native name **Incubu**) one of the explorers
Neville his missing brother
King Solomon's Mines (1885) Henry Rider Haggard

Curtleaxe a sergeant
The Roaring Girl play (1611) Thomas Middleton and Thomas Dekker

Curzon, Charles adjutant
Harry Lorrequer (1839) Charles Lever

Cushing, Sarah
ss 'The Cardboard Box'

His Last Bow (1917) Arthur Conan Doyle

Cuss, Dr of Iping
The Invisible Man (1897) H. G. Wells

Custance, Christian, Dame widow affianced to Gawyn Goodluck*
Ralph Roister Doister play (1551) Nicholas Udall

Cut-Glass, Lord
Under Milk Wood play (1954) Dylan Thomas

Cute, Alderman magistrate determined to put down any nonsense from the poor, such as cant about starvation; understands the common people
The Chimes (1844) Charles Dickens

Cuticle, Surgeon ship's surgeon indifferent to suffering and humanity, unnecessarily amputates seaman's leg, and kills him
White-Jacket (1850) Herman Melville

Cutlace
Polly opera (1729) John Gay

Cutler, Dr regimental surgeon
Vanity Fair (1847-8) W. M. Thackeray

Cutrer, Kate cousin to Binx Bolling*, whom she m.
The Moviegoer (1961) Walker Percy

Cutter
Cutter of Colman Street play (1661) Abraham Cowley

Cutter, Wick amorous old man
My Antonia (1918) Willa Cather

Cutting, Val a roarer and bully
Bartholomew Fair play (1631) Ben Jonson

Cuttle, Ned, Captain lovable retired pilot-skipper, with a hook instead of a hand, famous for 'when found, make a note of'
Dombey and Son (1848) Charles Dickens

Cuxsom, Mother
The Mayor of Casterbridge (1886) Thomas Hardy

Cuzac, Anton m. Antonia Shimerda*
My Antonia (1918) Willa Cather

Cymbal master of the Staple
The Staple of News play (1631) Ben Jonson

Cymbeline King of Britain
his Queen
Cymbeline play (1623) William Shakespeare

Cynara 'I have been faithful to thee, Cynara, in my fashion'
poem 'Non Sum Qualis Eram' verses (1896) Ernest Dowson

Cynthia transformed 'from a Wit into a Toad-eater, without any visible Change, in either her Person or Behaviour'; m. Valentine, brother to Camilla*
The Adventures of David Simple (1744-53) Sarah Fielding

Cynthia cc
Cynthia's Revels, or The Fountain of Self-Love play (1601) Ben Jonson

Cynthia daughter to Sir Paul Plyant* by a former wife, promised to Mellefont*
The Double-Dealer play (1710) William Congreve

Cynthia girl in Demarest's* past
Blue Voyage (1927) Conrad Aiken

Cypress, Mr caricature of Byron
Nightmare Abbey (1818) Thomas Love Peacock

Cyprus, Prince of suitor for Agripyne*
Old Fortunatus play (1600) Thomas Dekker

Cyril friend to Hilarion*, m. Psyche*
Princess Ida opera (1844) W. S. Gilbert and Arthur Sullivan

Cyril, Bishop patriarch and arch-fanatic based on St Cyril, patriarch of Alexandria
Hypatia, or New Foes with an Old Face (1853) Charles Kingsley

Cyril, Uncle 'deported for a homosexual crime'
Ulysses (1922) James Joyce

Czerlaski, Countess husband-hunting widow
Scenes of Clerical Life (1857) George Eliot (rn Mary Anne, later Marian, Evans)

D

D. the artist hero
Ushant: an Essay (1952) Conrad Aiken

D'abbémar, Delphine often described as the 'first modern woman in French fiction'; in part a self-portrait; in epistolary novel
Delphine (1802) Madame de Staël

Dabber, Dingleby, Sir author existing only in Mrs Nickleby's* imagination
Nicholas Nickleby (1839) Charles Dickens

Dabis, Geraldine sister to Agatha Calkin*
Kate their half-sister
Men and Wives (1931) Ivy Compton-Burnett

Dabney, Colonel who demands Dolliver's* elixir of life for purely selfish reasons; when Dolliver refuses to give it to him he takes it at pistol-point, regains his youth, but then dies of the overdose he has swallowed
The Dolliver Romance (1876) Nathaniel Hawthorne

Dabney, G. M., Colonel, JP
ss 'In Ambush'
Stalky & Co. (1899) Rudyard Kipling

Dacey, Lord
his wife
Adam Bede (1859) George Eliot (rn Mary Anne, later Marian, Evans)

Dacier, Percy politician in love with Diana Warwick*
Diana of the Crossways (1885) George Meredith

Da Costa, Manasseh
Deborah his daughter m. Yankele ben Yitzchok*
The King of Schnorrers (1894) Israel Zangwill

Dacre, Lady aunt to Rita*, and responsible for her education
Rita (1856) Charles Aidé

Dacre, Lady see Andrews, Pamela

Dacres, Sim head hind
Gillian his wife

Polly their daughter
The Story of Ragged Robyn (1945) Oliver Onions

D'Acunha, Teresa accomplice of E. G. Neville*
The Antiquary (1816) Walter Scott

Dad, William governor of Woldingstanton School
The Undying Fire (1919) H. G. Wells

Dadson writing master
Sketches by Boz† (1836) Charles Dickens

Dafhu chief of the Wariri tribe
Henderson the Rain King (1959) Saul Bellow

Dagenham, Charles writer killed by shark
The Towers of Trebizond (1956) Rose Macaulay

Dagge, Joel blacksmith's son
Daniel Deronda (1876) George Eliot (rn Mary Anne, later Marian, Evans)

Daggoo African crew-member
Moby Dick, or The Whale (1851) Herman Melville

Dagley, Farmer
his wife
Jacob their son
Middlemarch (1871–2) George Eliot (rn Mary Anne, later Marian, Evans)

Dagonet King Arthur's* fool
Le Morte d'Arthur (c.1469) Thomas Malory

Dagonet, Clare m. Peter van Degen*
The Custom of the Country (1913) Edith Wharton

Dain, Oliver barber to Louis XI
Quentin Durward (1823) Walter Scott

Dain, Waris chief of Patusan
Lord Jim (1900) Joseph Conrad (rn Josef Teodor Konrad Korzeniowski)

Daintwich, Madeleine two girls, one called 'Madie'
ss 'The Man Who Was Unlucky With Women'

Unlucky for Pringle (1973) Wyndham Lewis

Dainty, Lady
The Double Gallant play (1707) Colly Cibber

Daisy, Solomon parish clerk of Chigwell
Barnaby Rudge (1841) Charles Dickens

Dale, Andrew ('**Black Andie**') shepherd and gamekeeper of the Bass
Catriona (1893) Robert Louis Stevenson

Dale, Dr
The Soul of a Bishop (1917) H. G. Wells

Dale, Dr Congregationalist minister
South Riding (1936) Winifred Holtby

Dale, Edward stockbroker
Louisa *née* Cutts, his wife
Vanity Fair (1847–8) W. M. Thackeray

Dale, Jack horse trader
Romany Rye (1857) George Borrow

Dale, Laetitia worshipper of Sir Willougby Patterne*, used by and then m. to him
The Egoist (1879) George Meredith

Dale, Parson simple Anglican of his times
My Novel, or Varieties in English Life (1850–3) Edward Bulwer Lytton

Dale, Suzanne young woman in love with Witla*
Emily her mother, who believed that she had caught her bad ideas from *Anna Karenina* – based on eighteen-year-old Thelma Cudlip
The Genius (1915) Theodore Dreiser

Dalgarno, Lord raffish son of Earl of Huntinglen*
The Fortunes of Nigel (1822) Walter Scott

Dalgetty, Dugald captain in Montrose's army
The Legend of Montrose (1819) Walter Scott

Dalgleish, Adam Scotland Yard man who writes poetry in whodunnits, onwards from
Cover Her Face† (1962) P. D. James

Dalison, Hilary class-bound painter, in contrast to his father-in-law Sylvanus Stone*
Bianca his wife, *née* Stone*
Fraternity (1909) John Galsworthy

Dallow, Julia *née* Sherringham, cc; political widow in love with Nick Dormer*
The Tragic Muse (1890) Henry James

Dalloway, Clarissa cc

Richard her husband
Elizabeth their daughter
Mrs Dalloway (1925) Virginia Woolf

D'Almanza, Clara, Donna
The Duenna play (1775) Richard Brinsley Sheridan

D'Alperoussa, Mme
The Thinking Reed (1936) Rebecca West (rn Cecily Fairfield)

Dalrymple, Major regimental paymaster
his wife
Matilda; Fanny their daughters
Charles O'Malley (1841) Charles Lever

Dalrymple, the Dowager Viscountess a charming woman but without any superiority
Persuasion (1818) Jane Austen

Daly, 'Joxer'
Juno and the Paycock play (1925) Sean O'Casey (rn John Casey)

D'Alvadorez, Lucia, Donna from Brazil
Charley's Aunt play (1892) Brandon Thomas

Daly, Dr, DD Vicar of Ploverleigh, m. Constance Partlet*
The Sorcerer opera (1877) W. S. Gilbert and Arthur Sullivan

Daly, Patsey horse thief
Robbery Under Arms: A Story of Life and Adventure in the Bush and in the Goldfields of Australia (1888, rev. 1889) Rolf Boldrewood (rn Thomas Alexander Browne)

Dalyell, Lord
Perkin Warbeck play (1634) John Ford

Dalyngridge, Richard, Sir Norman knight
Lady Aelueva his wife
Puck of Pook's Hill (1906); *Rewards and Fairies* (1910) Rudyard Kipling

Dambreuse crooked financier
L'Education sentimentale (1869) Gustave Flaubert

Damerel, Mrs mysterious widow, in fact Mrs Stephen Tarrant* – she left him; mother to Nancy and Horace Lord*
In the Year of Jubilee (1894) George Gissing

Damport, Rafe journeyman to Eyre*
Jane his wife
The Shoemaker's Holiday (1600) Thomas Dekker

Damson, Suke 'hoydenish maiden'
The Woodlanders (1887) Thomas Hardy

Dan
Una his sister: ccs, visited by Puck* and others
Puck of Pook's Hill (1906); *Rewards and Fairies* (1910) Rudyard Kipling
Dan murderer
Night Must Fall play (1935) Emlyn Williams
Dana Da
ss 'The Sending of Dana Da'
Soldiers Three (1888) Rudyard Kipling
Danagher, Bridget aunt and guardian to Christian Roche*
Without My Cloak (1931) Kate O'Brien
Danby, Philip Norman head of Danby & Winter, publishers, 'always right'
The *Forsyte* series (1906–33) John Galsworthy
Danceny, Chevalier
Les Liaisons dangereuses (1782) Pierre-Ambroise-François Choderlos de Laclos
Dancer, Daniel notorious 18th-century miser studied by Mr Boffin*
Our Mutual Friend (1865) Charles Dickens
Dancey, Revd Mr and Mrs
Catrina; Louise; Henry; Andrew their children
Eva Trout (1969) Elizabeth Bowen
Dancy, Ronald, Captain thief and suicide
Mabel his adoring wife who remains loyal to him
Loyalties play (1922) John Galsworthy
Dando, Roland Welsh Attorney-General of newly independent African state
A Guest of Honour (1971) Nadine Gordimer
Dandolo self-styled count, Professor of Dancing; has affair with Adeliza Grampus*
The Professor (1837) W. M. Thackeray
Dandy, Mick Trade Union Leader
Sybil (1845) Benjamin Disraeli
Dane, George successful author who has a dream; in revealing tale
ss 'The Great Good Place'
The Soft Side (1900) Henry James
Dane, Osric pseudonym of female author of *The Wings of Death*, a 'deep' book
ss 'Xingu'
Roman Fever (1911) Edith Wharton
Dane, William treacherous friend to Silas

Marner*
Silas Marner (1861) George Eliot (rn Mary Anne, later Marian, Evans)
Danesbury, John twice-m. head of drink-ravaged family
Robert; Lionel; William; Isabel; Arthur only the last of the sons, two by the second marriage, is not a drunkard; the girl m. one, who (however) reforms, in novel published by Temperance Society
Danesbury House (1860) Mrs Henry Wood
Danforth, Robert oppressor of the delicate spirit of Owen Warland*, m. Anne Hovenden*
ss 'The Artist of the Beautiful' (1844)
Mosses from an Old Manse (1846) Nathaniel Hawthorne
Dangerfield cowardly bully
Bellamira play (1687) Charles Sedley
Dangerfield, Captain spy, informer
Peveril of the Peak (1822) Walter Scott
Dangerfield, Sebastian cc
The Ginger Man (1958) J. P. Donleavy
Dangle
his wife
The Critic play (1779) Richard Brinsley Sheridan
Dangle, Mr friend to Mrs Hetty Milton*
The Wheels of Chance (1896) H. G. Wells
Dannisborough, Lord friend to Diana Warwick*, whom Augustus Warwick* mistakenly cites as co-respondent; drawn from Lord Melbourne
Diana of the Crossways (1885) George Meredith
Danvers, Mrs evil housekeeper
Rebecca (1938) Daphne du Maurier
Danvers, Ralph robbed cc
The Danvers Jewels† (1887) Mary Cholmondeley
Daphnis shepherd in Greek pastoral romance of late second century by author about whom nothing is known; in love with Chloe*; the latter item here is an adaptation of Amyot's French text of 1559
Daphnis and Chloe (1598 – Greek text published; 1587) Longus
The Pastoral Loves of Daphnis and Chloe (1924) George Moore
Dapper imprisoned clerk

The Alchemist play (1612) Ben Jonson
Dapper, Sir Davy
Jack his son
The Roaring Girl play (1611) Thomas Middleton and Thomas Dekker
Dara, Michael
The Shadow of the Glen play (1903) John Millington Synge
Darch, Car mistress of Alec D'Urberville*
Nancy her sister
Tess of the D'Urbervilles (1891) Thomas Hardy
D'Archeville, Baron owner of the Spanish Farm
Eugénie his wife
Georges their son
The Spanish Farm (1924) R. H. Mottram
Darcy, Fitzwilliam friend to Charles Bingley*, m. Elizabeth Bennet*, by whom his manners would hopefully be softened and improved
Lady Anne his mother
The late Mr Darcy his father
Georgiana his sister, seems proud but it is really shyness
Pride and Prejudice (1813) Jane Austen
D'Arcy, T. artist, friend of Henry Aylwin, in still readable novel by solicitor who enslaved but saved life of Swinburne*
Aylwin (1899) Theodore Watts-Dunton
Dare, William Captain de Stancy's* illegitimate son
A Laodicean (1881) Thomas Hardy
d'Arfay, Toby 'museum piece', Edwardian who will not adapt himself
Museum Pieces (1952) William Plomer
D'Argens, Marquis
Barry Lyndon (1844) W. M. Thackeray
D'Argent, Louise Eugénie French *emigrée*, governess, m. Edward Halifax*
John Halifax, Gentleman (1856) Mrs Craik
Daricoeus seer who prophesies destruction of Aulis, unless temples to the gods are built
Aphrodite in Aulis (1931) George Moore
Darkwell, Violet niece to Miss Dinah Perfect*, who interferes in her marriage choices, in ghost tale
All in the Dark (1866) J. Sheridan Le Fanu
Darley, Christopher cc, £1200-a-year man, with villa and greenhouse, at Slough

Hilda his wife
Nicky their son, sent down from Merton for wildness and insubordination
Jill their daughter, 'finished' in Paris
A Certain Man (1931) Oliver Onions
Darley, Helen schoolmistress
Elsie Venner (1861) Oliver Wendell Holmes
Darley, L. G. schoolteacher and would-be writer
The Alexandria Quartet (1957–61) Lawrence Durrell
Darling, Dora
Fanny's First Play play (1905) George Bernard Shaw
Darling, Mr and Mrs
Wendy Moira Angela who gave the English a new Christian name; **John; Michael** their children
Peter Pan play (1904) J. M. Barrie
Darlington, Lord
Lady Windermere's Fan play (1892) Oscar Wilde
Darnay, Charles name adopted in England by Charles St Evremond*
A Tale of Two Cities (1859) Charles Dickens
Darnel, Aurelia m. Launcelot Greaves*
her father
Anthony her uncle
Launcelot Greaves (1762) Tobias Smollett
Darnford, Lady daughter to Lady Jones*
Pamela (1740) Samuel Richardson
Darnley, Jim Oliver Alden's* unscrupulous paid companion
Rose his sister who rejects Oliver's love
The Last Puritan (1936) George Santayana
Darrell, Edmund, Dr lover of Nina Leeds*
Strange Interlude play (1928) Eugene O'Neill
Darrow, George American diplomat in London engaged to Anna Leath*
The Reef (1912) Edith Wharton
D'Artagnan, Charles de Baatz Guardsman and eventually Marshall of France based on memoirs of historical personage of that name in romances
Les Trois Mousquetaires (The Three Musketeers) (1844); *Vingt ans après (Twenty Years After)* (1845); *Le Vicomte*

de Bragelonne (The Viscount of Bragelonne) (1848–50) Alexandre Dumas (père)

Dartie, Montague m. Winifred Forsyte*
Publius Valerius ('Val'); Imogen m. Jack Cardigan*; **Maud; Benedict** their children
The Forsyte series (1906–33) John Galsworthy

Dartle, Rosa companion to Mrs Steerforth*
David Copperfield (1850) Charles Dickens

Darton, Charles
ss 'Interlopers at the Knap'
Wessex Tales (1888) Thomas Hardy

Darty, Emily m. (1) Steve Hardcome*, (2) James Hardcome*
ss 'The History of the Hardcombes'
Life's Little Ironies (1894) Thomas Hardy

Darvas, Mrs mother-in-law to Eugene Marsay*, described as 'the most moving and authentic portrait of a working woman in American letters'
You Can't Sleep Here (1934); *This is Your Day* (1937) Edward Newhouse

Darvil, Alice undeveloped young woman who learns virtue from Maltravers*
Luke Darvil her evil father
Ernest Maltravers (1837); *Alice, or The Mysteries* (1838) Edward Bulwer Lytton

Darzee the tailor-bird
ss 'Ricki Tikki Tavi'
Jungle Books (1894–5) Rudyard Kipling

Dashfort, Lady
The Absentee (1812) Maria Edgeworth

Dashwood, George, General Sir
Captain Dashwood his son
Lucy his daughter
Charles O'Malley (1841) Charles Lever

Dashwood, Henry
his wife
John his son by his first wife
Fanny John's wife, *née* Ferrars*
Harry son of John and Fanny
Elinor m. Edward Ferrars*; **Marianne** m. Colonel Brandon*; **Margaret** children of Henry Dashwood by his second marriage
Sense and Sensibility (1811) Jane Austen

Da Silva, da Silva painter cc of novels by Guyanese novelist
Da Silva da Silva's Cultivated Wilder-

ness† (1977) Wilson Harris

Dass, Secundra Indian friend to James Ballantrae*
The Master of Ballantrae (1889) Robert Louis Stevenson

Dass; Durga; Ram twins
ss 'Gemini'
Soldiers Three (1888) Rudyard Kipling

Datchery, Dick white-haired personage with black eyebrows; his identity is vexed, and it has been variously suggested that he was Drood*, Bazzard*, Helena Landless* or Tartar*
Edwin Drood (1870) Charles Dickens

Datchet, Mary idealistic political worker
Night and Day (1919) Virginia Woolf

Daubeny ('Dubby') Tory leader onwards from
Phineas Finn† (1869) Anthony Trollope

D'Aulnais maiden name of Charles Darnay's* mother, from which he takes his English name
A Tale of Two Cities (1859) Charles Dickens

Dauntless, Richard foster-brother of Sir Ruthven Murgatroyd*, m. Rose Maybud*
Ruddigore opera (1887) W. S. Gilbert and Arthur Sullivan

Dauphin, The (Prince Louis)
King Henry V play (1623) William Shakespeare

D'Auvergne, General m. Marie de Meudon*
Tom Burke of Ours (1844) Charles Lever

D'Avalos treacherous secretary to Duke of Pavia* who lays trap for Fernando* and Bianca* at behest of Fiormonda*
Love's Sacrifice play (1633) John Ford

Davenport, Lucy, Lady
Waste play (1907) Harley Granville Barker

Davers, Lady sister to Mr B*
her husband
Pamela (1740) Samuel Richardson

David (hist. and legd.) cc novel of the Biblical David
God Knows (1984) Joseph Heller

David butler to the Cheeryble Brothers*
Nicholas Nickleby (1839) Charles Dickens

David employed by Miller Loveday*
The Trumpet Major (1880) Thomas

Hardy
David servant to Bob Acres*
The Rivals play (1775) Richard Brinsley
Sheridan
David, David white biographer of Jack
Trap*
Trap (1970) Peter Mathers
David, Megan in love with Frank Ashurst*
The Apple Tree (1918) John Galsworthy
Davidge, Lucia ('Loo') Coventry girl on
holiday in Stockholm
England Made Me (1935) Graham
Greene
Davidson, Alfred, Revd missionary
his wife
The Trembling of a Leaf (1921) W.
Somerset Maugham
Rain play (1922) John Colton and Clem-
ence Randolph
Davidson, Captain
Victory (1915) Joseph Conrad (rn Josef
Teodor Konrad Korzeniowski)
Davidson, Sergeant
The Little Minister (1891) J. M. Barrie
Davies, Andrew ('Dago') scaler in
Liverpool docks
Ebb and Flood (1932) James Hanley
Davies, Arthur H. owner of yacht
Dulcibella
The Riddle of the Sands (1903) Erskine
Childers
Davies, John Superintendent of Tidenet
Fishing Company's station
Redgauntlet (1824) Walter Scott
Davies, Ken amateur actor
That Uncertain Feeling (1955) Kingsley
Amis
Davies, Mr old and rich; m. Ginevra
Fanshawe*
Villette (1853) Charlotte Brontë
Davilla follower of Pizarro* in drama
adapted from Kotzebue*
Pizarro play (1799) Richard Brinsley
Sheridan
Davilow, Captain stepfather of Gwen
Harleth*
Fanny his wife
Alice; Bertha; Fanny; Isobel their daugh-
ters
Daniel Deronda (1876) George Eliot (rn
Mary Anne, later Marian, Evans)
Da Vinci, Leonardo (hist.) inventor of a
bicycle in *tour de force* by American

author who believes that 'history is a
dream that strays into innocent sleep'
Da Vinci's Bicycle: Ten Stories (1979)
Guy Davenport
Davis doorkeeper at the Silver Vaults
Ellen his sister
Dust Falls on Eugene Schlumberger
(1964) Shena Mackay
Davison, Helena graduate of Vassar, ex-
room-mate of Kay Strong*
The Group (1963) Mary McCarthy
Davray, Richard rising novelist
Helen his wife
Davray's Affairs (1906) Reginald Turner
Daw, John pretentious pseudo-classicist
Epicene, or The Silent Woman verse play
(1609) Ben Jonson
Daw, Lily feeble-minded girl who con-
founds three nasty ladies (Watts*,
Slocum* and Carson*) by getting marr-
ied to a xylophone player when they had
planned to send her to Ellisville Institute
for the Feeble-Minded of Mississippi at
their own expense
ss 'Lily Daw and the Three Ladies'
A Curtain of Green (1941) Eudora Welty
Dawbeney, Lord
Perkin Warbeck play (1634) John Ford
Dawe, Harry, Sir
ss 'Hal o' the Draft'†
Puck of Pook's Hill (1906) Rudyard
Kipling
Dawes, Alice waitress, mistress of Patrick
Seton*
The Bachelors (1961) Muriel Spark
Dawes, Baxter m. Clara Redford*
Sons and Lovers (1913) D. H. Lawrence
Dawes, Gerald dies from injury playing
football, engaged to Agnes Pembroke*
The Longest Journey (1907) E. M.
Forster
Dawes, Marion an attempt at a part-
portrait of James Baldwin*
The Man Who Cried I Am (1967) John
Williams
Dawes, Mary nurse in household in which
Miss Wade* was governess
Little Dorrit (1857) Charles Dickens
Dawes, Rufus (Richard Divine) convict
and survivor in novel by brilliant journa-
list described by his schoolfriend, Gerard
Manley Hopkins, as a 'kaleidoscopic,
particoloured, harliquinesque, thaumo-

tropic being'; a book, it has been said, that has an assured place in 'the evolution of the literature of evil', and which has some features deserving comparison with *Crime and Punishment**
His Natural Life (1870–2; abridged by the author 1874; in 1885 as *For the Term of His Natural Life* – thus evading the author's irony; original text edited by Stephen Murray-Smith, 1970) Marcus Clarke

Dawkins, Jack ('The Artful Dodger') thief, pupil of Fagin*, transported
Oliver Twist (1838) Charles Dickens

Dawkins Thomas Smith swindled by Deuceace and Blewett*
ss 'The Amours of Mr Deuceace'
The Yellowplush Papers (1838) W. M. Thackeray

Dawley, Frank cc
Dean William his son
The Death of William Posters† (1965) Alan Sillitoe

Daws, Mary Mr Dombey's* kitchenmaid
Dombey and Son (1848) Charles Dickens

Dawson conspirator whose evidence eventually saves Sir Reginald Glanville*
Pelham, or *The Adventures of a Gentleman* (1828, rev. 1839) Edward Bulwer Lytton

Dawson family ccs in the *Twentieth-Century Cycle* – series of plays by Black American playwright, producer and director onwards from
In New England Winter play (1968) Ed Bullins

Dawson, Dave albino
God's Little Acre (1933) Erskine Caldwell

Dawson, Dinah and Hannah pastry-cooks
Cousin Phillis (1864) Mrs Gaskell

Dawson, Dr
The Woman in White (1860) Wilkie Collins

Dawson, Edward cc, dissatisfied with an existence devoted wholly to pleasure
Monk Dawson (1969) Piers Paul Read

Dawson, Louise
High Wind in Jamaica (1929) Richard Hughes

Dawson, Major
Dick ('The Devil') his son
Fanny his daughter, m. Edward

O'Connor*
Handy Andy (1842) Samuel Lover

Dawson, Rose m. Sir Pitt Crawley*
Vanity Fair (1847–8) W. M. Thackeray

Dawtry, Oliver, Sir financier
Caprice (1917) Ronald Firbank

Day, Fancy schoolteacher, m. Dick Dewy*
Geoffrey her father
Jane her stepmother
Under the Greenwood Tree (1872) Thomas Hardy

Day, Ferquhardh of the Clan Chattan
The Fair Maid of Perth (1828) Walter Scott

Daygo, Joe old fisherman
Cormorant Crag (1895) G. Manville Fenn

Dayson, Arthur
Hilda Lessways (1911) Arnold Bennett

D'Cruze, Michele
ss 'His Chance in Life'
Plain Tales from the Hills (1888) Rudyard Kipling

De Aquila, Gilbert Lord of Pevensea
ss 'Young Men at the Manor'†
Puck of Pook's Hill (1906) Rudyard Kipling

De Avila, Pedro Spaniard
ss 'Gloriana' (1910) Rudyard Kipling

De Beaulieu, Denis m. Blanch de Melétroit
Guichard his brother
ss 'The Sire de Melétroit's Door'
The New Arabian Nights (1882) Robert Louis Stevenson

De Beauvais, Henry
Tom Burke of Ours (1844) Charles Lever

De Charleu, Jean Albert, Colonel
his seven daughters
ss 'Belles Demoiselles Plantation'
Old Creole Days (1879) George Washington Cable

De Clancy, Phelim (*né* Clancy)
The Book of Snobs (1847) W. M. Thackeray

De Courcy, Admiral capricious and violent
William; Edward his sons, the latter enlisted in Navy as D. Peters
The King's Own (1830) Captain Marryat

De Courcy, Countess
Lord Porlock; George; John; Amelia m. Mortimer Gazebee*; **Rosina; Margaretta; Alexandrina** her children
Dr Thorne (1858) Anthony Trollope

De Courcy, Susan, Lady, widow of Mrs Vernon's* elder brother; beautiful, selfish and unscrupulous; writer of letters to Mrs Johnson*; m. Sir James Martin*
Lady de Courcy mother to Mrs Vernon* and to Reginald de Courcy*, mother-in-law to Lady Susan; author of many of the letters of which this posthumously published epistolary novel consists
Reginald de Courcy
Frederica her sixteen-year-old daughter, m. Sir Reginald de Courcy* (in time)
Lady Susan (1871) Jane Austen
De Coverley, Roger, Sir, JP, Baronet bachelor
Essays in the *Spectator* (1911–14) Joseph Addison
De Craye, Horace
The Egoist (1879) George Meredith
de Croisnel, Renée in love with Nevil Beauchamp*, but prevented from eloping with him by Rosamund Culling*
Roland her brother
Beauchamp's Career (1875) George Meredith
De Duvarney elder brother of Count of Valancourt*
The Mysteries of Udolpho (1794) Mrs Ann Radcliffe
De Ferrars, Compton, Lord
Cecilia (1782) Fanny Burney
De Flouncy, Mr and Mrs dancing instructors
Before the Bombardment (1926) Osbert Sitwell
De Foenix, Clare
her husband
Trelawny of the Wells play (1898) Arthur Wing Pinero
De Foley, Alicia, Dame prioress
Thomas her cousin, prior; in novel set in 14th century
The Corner That Held Them (1948) Sylvia Townsend Warner
De Forest of the Aerial Board of Control ss 'As Easy as ABC'
A Diversity of Creatures (1917) Rudyard Kipling
De Frey, Elaine heiress
The Unbearable Bassington (1912) Saki (rn Hector Hugh Munro)
De Frontenac, Count Governor-General of Canada

Shadows on the Rock (1932) Willa Cather
De Gard a noble gentleman, that, being newly lighted from his travels, assists his sister Oriana* in her chase of Mirabel* the Wild Goose
The Wild-Goose Chase play (1652) John Fletcher
De Grapions, Nancanou
Aurora his beautiful widow
Clothilde their daughter with whom Aurora lives in seclusion
The Grandissimes: A Story of Creole Life (1880) George Washington Cable
De Hamal, Alfred, Colonel shallow little dandy who disguises himself as a nun in order to meet Ginevra Fanshawe, whom he m.
Alfred Fanshawe de Bassompierre de Hamal their son
Villette (1853) Charlotte Brontë
De Horter, M. consul, Boulogne
Jorrocks's Jaunts and Jollities (1838) R. S. Surtees
De Jongh grog-shop owner
Lord Jim (1900) Joseph Conrad (rn Josef Teodor Konrad Korzeniowski)
De La Casternas, Marquis (alias d'Averada) m. Agnes de Medina*
The Monk (1796) Matthew G. Lewis
De La Touche, Mehée (Leon Guichard)
Tom Burke of Ours (1844) Charles Lever
De La Zouch, Lord friend to C. Aubrey*
Ten Thousand a Year (1839) Samuel Warren
De Lacey
Agatha; Felix his children
Frankenstein (1818) Mary Shelley
De Laval, Bishop
Shadows on the Rock (1932) Willa Cather
De Levis, Ferdinand Jewish cc in play about anti-Semitism cast in form of crime-thriller ('I've nothing against them, but the fact is – they get *on* so' says one character)
Loyalties play (1922) John Galsworthy
De Leyva, Miguel hidalgo
Carlotta his youngest daughter
Emilia his sister m. Piranha*
Odtaa (1926) John Masefield
De Lyndesay, Alicia cc, m. (1) Egbert (of another branch of the family),

(2) **William** Egbert's cousin
Stanley ('Slinker') son to Alicia and Egbert, m. Nettie Stone*
Christian son to Alicia and William, m. Deborah de Lyndesay (another branch)
Roger Deborah's father
Lionel ('Larupper') another cousin
Crump Folk Going Home (1913) Constance Holme
De Maine, Mme
Delina Delaney (1897) Amanda Ros
De Mendez Portuguese captain of ship that rescued Gulliver*
Gulliver's Travels (1726) Jonathan Swift
De Meudon, Charles Gustave
Marie his sister m. (1) General D'Auvergne*, (2) Tom Burke*
Tom Burke of Ours (1844) Charles Lever
De Nanjac, Vicomte de attaché
An Ideal Husband play (1895) Oscar Wilde
De Peters see **Sussman, Kenneth**
De Retteville, Adela, Dame half-witted nun
The Corner That Held Them (1948) Sylvia Townsend Warner
De Ribera, Andres, Don Viceroy of Peru
Don Jaime his son by Camila Perichole*
The Bridge of San Luis Rey (1927) Thornton Wilder
de Rodiencourt, Sosthène
Pépé his wife, whose nipple he has torn off
Guignol's band (1944) Louis-Ferdinand Céline (rn Louis-Ferdinand Destouches)
de Rouaillat, Marquis old aristocrat to whom Renée de Crosinel* is betrothed against her wishes
Beauchamp's Career (1875) George Meredith
De Saldar, Silva Diaz, Conde m. Louise Harrington*
Evan Harrington (1861) George Meredith
De Spain, Cassius, Major Confederate cavalry soldier, sheriff; in Yoknapatawpha saga
Manfred his son, mayor of Jefferson
Absalom!, Absalom! (1936) William Faulkner
De St Vallier, Bishop
Shadows on the Rock (1932) Willa Cather

De Stancy, Captain father of William Dare*
Sir William his father
Charlotte his sister
A Laodicean (1881) Thomas Hardy
De Stapledon, Matilda, Dame princess
Dame Lovisa her ambitious (illegitimate) relative
The Corner That Held Them (1948) Sylvia Townsend Warner
De Sussa, Miss
as 'Private Learoyd's Story'
Soldiers Three (1888) Rudyard Kipling
De Terrier, Lord Tory prime minister
Phineas Finn (1869) Anthony Trollope
De Thierry, Charles, Baron real-life eccentric who purchased 40,000 acres (1822) in New Zealand and failed (1837) to establish a Utopia for English settlers and Maoris with himself as Sovereign Chief: cc near masterpiece demanding revival by New Zealand poet and writer of true genius driven to the end of her tether at age only thirty-three, but not before she had written five novels and four books of poetry
Check to Your King: The Life History of Charles, Baron de Thierry (1936) Robin Hyde (rn Iris Wilkinson)
De Ventadour, Valerie, Mme old friend to Ernest Maltravers*, loved for a time by him
her husband
Ernest Maltravers (1837); *Alice, or The Mysteries* (1838) Edward Bulwer Lytton
De Vere, Dudley, Lord society adventurer
Jack Hinton (1843) Charles Lever
De Verviers, André
The Thinking Reed (1936) Rebecca West (rn Cecily Fairfield)
De Villeroi, Marquis
Lady Blanche his daughter
The Mysteries of Udolpho (1790) Mrs Ann Radcliffe
De Vionnet, Comtesse 'wicked woman', in love with Chadwick Newsome*
The Ambassadors (1903) Henry James
De Winter, Maximilian m. (1) Rebecca, whom he kills, (2) the mousy little heroine and (anonymous) narrator, who has captured so many hearts
Beatrice his sister, m. Giles Lacy*
his grandmother

Rebecca (1939) Daphne du Maurier

De Worms, Professor (Friday)
The Man Who Was Thursday (1908) G. K. Chesterton

De, Grish Chunder, M. A.
ss 'The Head of the District'
The Day's Work (1898) Rudyard Kipling

Deacon, Ina sister of Miss Lulu Bett* who treats her as servant
Dwight her husband
Ninian his brother who m. Miss Lulu Bett but then tells her that he does not know if his first wife is dead
Miss Lulu Bett (1920) Zona Gale

Deacon, The horse
ss 'A walking delegate'
The Day's Work (1898) Rudyard Kipling

Dead, Macon
Ruth his wife
'Milkman' their son
Song of Solomon (1977) Toni Morrison

Deadeye, Dick
H.M.S. Pinafore opera (1878) W. S. Gilbert and Arthur Sullivan

Deadlock otter-hound
Tarka the Otter (1927) Henry Williamson

Deakins, Jim Boone's* friend, but lover of Teal Eye*; murdered by Boone
The Big Sky (1947) A. B. Guthrie

Dean, Margaret m. Chad Buford*
The Little Shepherd of Kingdom Come (1903) John Fox

Dean, Nelly transmitter through Mr Lockwood* of the story, all of whose events only she has witnessed – interpreted by some as an evil genius
Wuthering Heights (1847) Emily Brontë

Dean, Richard ('Dickie') cc
ss 'The Man Who Was Unlucky With Women'
Unlucky for Pringle (1973) Wyndham Lewis

Dean, Susie comedienne
The Good Companions (1929) J. B. Priestley

Deane junior partner in Guest & Co
Susan his wife *née* Dodson*
Lucy their daughter, m. Stephen Guest*
The Mill on the Floss (1860) George Eliot (rn Mary Anne, later Marian, Evans)

Deane tutor to Vincent Burnet*
Cormorant Crag (1895) G. Manville Fenn

Deane, Drayton critic, m. Gwendolyn Erme*
ss 'The Figure in the Carpet'
Embarrassments (1896) Henry James

Deans, Davis
Christian his first wife
Jeanie their daughter, m. Reuben Butler*
Rebecca his second wife
Effie their daughter, m. George Staunton*
Heart of Midlothian (1818) Walter Scott

Dearborn, Laura m. Curtis Jadwin*
Page her younger sister, m. Landry Court*
The Pit (1903) Frank Norris

Dearsley, Sahib
ss 'The Incarnation of Krishna Mulvaney'
Life's Handicap (1891) Rudyard Kipling

Dearth, Will
Mabel his wife
Margaret his dream-daughter
Dear Brutus play (1917) J. M. Barrie

Deasy teacher
Ulysses (1922) James Joyce

Death name of escaped circus serpent
A Generous Man (1966) Reynolds Price

Death one of Miss Flite's* birds
Bleak House (1853) Charles Dickens

Deaudeuce, A. P., the Hon, son of Earl of Crabs (A. A. P.)* cardsharper m. Matilda Griffin*
The Great Hoggarty Diamond (1841) W. M. Thackeray

Debarry, Maximus, Sir
his wife
Philip; Harriet; Selina their children
Augustus his brother, Rector of Treby Magna
Felix Holt (1866) George Eliot (rn Mary Anne, later Marian, Evans)

Debbitch, Deborah nurse and guardian of Alice Bridgenorth*
Peveril of the Peak (1822) Walter Scott

Debenham, Joan cc, illegitimate daughter of Will Sydenham*, adopted by the Stublands*, m. Peter Stubland*
Joan and Peter (1918) H. G. Wells

Debon an old officer
Locrine play (1595) 'W.S.' (?George Peele; ?Robert Green)

Debriseau, Captain of the *Sainte Vierge*,

smuggler
The King's Own (1830) Captain Marryat
Decius Brutus (hist.) conspirator against Caesar*
Julius Caesar play (1623) William Shakespeare
Dedalus, Stephen
A Portrait of the Artist as a Young Man (1916); *Ulysses* (1922); *Stephen Hero* (1944) James Joyce
Dede, Inspector
Loyalties play (1922) John Galsworthy
Dedlock, Leicester, Sir, Baronet owner of Chesney Wold
Lady Honoria his wife, bearer (before m.) of the illegitimate Esther Summerson*, by Captain Hawdon*
Volumnia his elderly cousin
Bleak House (1853) Charles Dickens
Dee, Sam trainer
The Olympian (1969) Brian Glanville
Deedles banker and friend to Alderman Cute*
The Chimes (1844) Charles Dickens
Deeley film man
Kate his wife
Old Times play (1971) Harold Pinter
Deemes, Mrs
ss 'A Friend's Friend'
Plain Tales from the Hills (1888) Rudyard Kipling
Deepmere, Lord relation to the Bellegardes*
The American (1876) Henry James
Deercourt, Emma bosom friend to Minnie Gadsby*
The Story of the Gadsbys (1888) Rudyard Kipling
Deever, Danny killed a comrade sleeping poem 'Danny Deever'
Barrack-Room Ballads (1892) Rudyard Kipling
Defarge, Ernest proprietor of wine shop, once servant to Dr Manette*
Therese his wife, one of the women who knitted by the guillotine; shot by her own pistol in struggling with Miss Pross*
A Tale of Two Cities (1859) Charles Dickens
Deflores ugly servant and killer hired by Beatrice Joanna*, after whom he lusts
The Changeling play (c.1623) Thomas Middleton and William Rowley

Deipholos son of Priam*
Troilus and Cressida play (1623) William Shakespeare
Dekker, Matthew Vicar of Glastonbury
A Glastonbury Romance (1932) John Cowper Powys
Del Bosco, Martin Vice-Admiral of Spain
The Jew of Malta (1633) Christopher Marlowe
Del Lago, Alexandra alcoholic ex-movie queen
Sweet Bird of Youth play (1959) Tennessee Williams (rn Thomas Lanier Williams)
Delacour, Lady friend and hostess to Belinda Portman*
Belinda (1801) Maria Edgeworth
Delacroix, Dinah, Mrs formerly **Diana Piggott** (Dicey)
William; Roland her sons
The Little Girls (1964) Elizabeth Bowen
Delamayn, Geoffrey villainous brute interested only in athletics; m. Anne Silvester*
Man and Wife (1870) Wilkie Collins
Delane, Hayley decent elderly gentleman who 'stopped living' (or developing) after American Civil War
Leila his selfish and unfaithful wife
ss 'The Spark'
Old New York (1924) Edith Wharton
Delaney, Delina cc m. Lord Gifford* in unintentionally hilarious romance
Delina Delaney (1897) Amanda Ros
Delaney, Floss early girlfriend of Vance Weston*
Harrison her father, 'the byword of Euphoria'
Hudson River Bracketed (1929); *The Gods Arrive* (1932) Edith Wharton
Delano, Captain (hist.)
ss 'Benito Cereno'
The Piazza Tales (1856) Herman Melville
Delany, Cornelius ('**Corny**') Philip O'Grady's manservant
Jack Hinton (1843) Charles Lever
Delarey, General conqueror of the Rians
Right Off the Map (1927) C. E. Montague
Delaval, Fred (or **Frank**) cousin to the Honeywood's*, m. Kitty Honeywood
The Adventures of Mr Verdant Green (1853, repr. 1982) Cuthbert Bede (rn

Edward Bradley)
Deliro a good doting citizen, a fellow sincerely besotted on his own wife, and so wrapped with a conceit of her perfections, that he simply holds himself unworthy of her
Every Man Out of His Humour play (1599) Ben Jonson
Delisport, First Marquess of Captain of Industry
But Soft – We Are Observed! (1928) Hilaire Belloc
Delmour, Colonel cousin to Gertrude St Clair and engaged to her until she loses her inheritance
The Inheritance (1824) Susan Ferrier
Delvile, Mortimer hero in love with Cecilia Beverley*
The Hon. Compton his father; Cecilia's third guardian
Cecilia (1782) Fanny Burney
Delville, Mrs
ss 'A Second-rate Woman'
Wee Willie Winkie (1888) Rudyard Kipling
Del' Peyra, Ogier petty sieur
Noémi (1895) Sabine Baring-Gould
Demarest, William cc
Blue Voyage (1927) Conrad Aiken
Demas 'Son of Judas'
The Pilgrim's Progress (1678–84) John Bunyan
Demby, William cc of American novel set in Rome
The Catacombs (1965) William Demby
Demented Traveller, The passenger of the Paris Express who kept making errors
ss 'A Flight'
Reprinted Pieces (1858) Charles Dickens
Demetrius friend to Crispinus* and a representative of Thomas Dekker* – who returned to the attack in the second play
The Poetaster play (1602) Ben Jonson
Satiromastix, or The Untrussing of the Humorous Poet play (1602) Thomas Dekker ?and John Marston
Demetrius in love with Hermia*
A Midsummer Night's Dream play (1623) William Shakespeare
Demetrius son to Tamora*
Titus Andronicus play (1623) William Shakespeare
Demian, Max mysterious cc of influential

*Bildungsroman**
Demian (1919) Herman Hesse
Deming, Agnes young schoolteacher in Midwest novel that is a classic despite its stilted dialogue; long-lost daughter of Damon Barker*; m. Ned Westlock*
The Story of a Country Town (1883) E. W. Howe
Demodokos ('Peeker') companion and foil to Agathon*
The Wreckage of Agathon (1970) John Gardner
Demple, George pupil at Salem House
David Copperfield (1850) Charles Dickens
Dempsey, Constable
ss 'Brugglesmith'
Many Inventions (1893) Rudyard Kipling
Dempsey, Edward clerk
ss 'The Clerk's Quest'
The Untilled Field (1903) George Moore
Dempsey, Father
John Bull's Other Island play (1904) George Bernard Shaw
Dempsey, Corporal
ss 'The Courtship of Dinah Shadd'
Life's Handicap (1891) Rudyard Kipling
Dempster, Robert lawyer
Janet his ill-used wife
Old Mrs Dempster his mother
ss 'Janet's Repentance'
Scenes of Clerical Life (1857) George Eliot (rn Mary Anne, later Marian, Evans)
Denberry-Baxter, George, Sir
his nephew
Let the People Sing (1939) J. B. Priestley
Dence, Jael honest country girl, m. Guy Raby*
Martha her sister
her father
Put Yourself in his Place (1807) Charles Reade
Dench, Araminta
The Farmer's Wife play (1924) Eden Phillpotts
Dendreth evil friend to Robert Byng* from whom Cecil Dreeme* escapes
Cecil Dreeme (1862) Theodore Winthrop
Denham see **Longford, Edmund**
Denham, Jenny adopted daughter to Dr

Shrapnel*, m. Nevil Beauchamp*
Beauchamp's Career (1875) George Meredith
Denham, Ralph abrasive solicitor, m. Katharine Hilbery*
Night and Day (1919) Virginia Woolf
Denison, Mrs
Caleb Williams (1794) William Godwin
Deniston, Barbary cc
Sir Gulliver, K.C. her father
Richmond her brother
Helen her mother, later Michel
Pamela Sir Gulliver's second wife
David her half-brother, son of Sir Gulliver and Pamela
The World My Wilderness (1950) Rose Macaulay
Denman, Clara cc of interesting early transvestite novel who dresses up as male painter amongst New York artists under the name of **Cecil Dreeme** in order to escape marriage to the evil Dendreth*
her father
Emma her sister
Cecil Dreeme (1862) Theodore Winthrop
Denner maid to Mrs Transome*
Felix Holt (1866) George Eliot (rn Mary Anne, later Marian, Evans)
Denning, Ralph
ss 'The Weeping Man'
Unlucky for Pringle (1973) Wyndham Lewis
Dennis civil servant
ss 'A Conference of the Powers'
Many Inventions (1893) Rudyard Kipling
Dennis solicitor
Porgy (1925) Du Bose Heyward
Dennis young undertaker
Loot play (1966) Joe Orton
Dennis, Edward common hangman, based on a real person (who was not, however, hanged, as he is here)
Barnaby Rudge (1841) Charles Dickens
Dennis, Helen summer visitor from Boston to Maine seaport; the narrator of distinguished local-colour* tales
Deephaven (1877) Sarah Orne Jewett
Dennison, Charles friend to Matthew Bramble*

George his son m. Lydia Melford*, poses as actor, 'Wilson', to avoid arranged marriage
The Expedition of Humphrey Clinker (1771) Tobias Smollett
Dennison, Jenny maid to Edith Bellenden, m. Cuddie Headrigg*
Old Mortality (1816) Walter Scott
Dennistoun, Mr
ss 'Canon Alberic's Scrapbook'
Ghost Stories of an Antiquary (1910) M. R. James
Denny, Anthony, Sir
King Henry VIII play (1623) William Shakespeare and John Fletcher
Denny, Helen
Gallions Reach (1927) H. M. Tomlinson
Denny, Philip, Dr
The Citadel (1937) A. J. Cronin
Densher, Merton engaged to Kate Croy*, character in part based on Ford Madox Ford*
The Wings of a Dove (1902) Henry James
Denton, Ansel
Denton, Peace his daughter; in love with Shelley Ray*
The World of Chance (1893) William Dean Howells
Denzil, Somers poet, betrayer of Lady Feverel*
The Ordeal of Richard Feverel: A History of Father and Son (1859, rev. 1878) George Meredith
Deo Gratias Querry's native servant, burnt-out leper
A Burnt-Out Case (1961) Graham Greene
Depecarde, Archibald, Sir 'celebrated gambler'
Handley Cross (1843) R. S. Surtees
D'Ercilla, Don Antonio
The Duenna play (1775) Richard Brinsley Sheridan
D'Erfeuil witty superficial French *émigré* whose characteristics the author developed in *De l'Allemagne*
Corinne (1807) Madame de Staël
Dering, John cc
The Quick or the Dead (1889) Amélie Rives (later Princess Troubetzkoy)
Deronda, Daniel idealistic young Jew;

spiritual advisor to Gwendolen Harleth*; ward of Sir Hugo Mallinger*; m. Mirah Cohen*
Daniel Deronda (1876) George Eliot (rn Mary Anne, later Marian, Evans)

Derrick, Phyllis
Patrick her father
Love Amongst the Chickens (1906) P. G. Wodehouse

Derrick, Tom quartermaster of the *Fortune's Favourite*
The Pirate (1822) Walter Scott

Derriman, Benjamin owner of Oxwell Hall
Festus his nephew, m. Matilda Johnson*
The Trumpet Major (1880) Thomas Hardy

Dersingham, Mr
Angel Pavement (1930) J. B. Priestley

D'Ervan, Count
Tom Burke of Ours (1844) Charles Lever

Derwent, Irene m. Piers Otway*
The Crown of Life (1899) George Gissing

Des Grieux, Chevalier cc of highly influential French novel
Manon Lescaut (1753) L'Abbé Prevost

Des Pereires, Courtial suicide
Mort à credit (*Death on the Instalment Plan*) (1936) Louis-Ferdinand Céline (rn Louis-Ferdinand Destouches)

Desart, Fabian ('Carrots') cc of unaffected novel of 'ordinary' childhood
Captain Desart his father
Lucy his mother
Jack; Cecil; Louise; Maurice; Floss his brothers and sisters
Florence his aunt
Sybil her daughter
Carrots: Just a Little Boy (1876) Mrs Molesworth

Desart, Isabel m. Archie Traill*
Mr Perrin and Mr Traill (1911) Hugh Walpole

Desborough, Colonel parliamentary commissioner
Woodstock (1826) Walter Scott

Desborough, Lucy
The Ordeal of Richard Feverel: A History of Father and Son (1859, rev. 1878) George Meredith

Desdemona cc, wife to Othello
Othello play (1623) William Shakespeare

Desert, Wilfred, the Hon. in love with Fleur Mont*, then engaged to Dinny Cherwell*
The Forsyte series (1906–33) John Galsworthy

Deslauriers childhood friend to Moreau*, and author of his misfortunes; a shabby go-getter; m. Louise Rocque*
L'Education sentimentale (1869) Gustave Flaubert

Desmond, John friend (and tutor) to Max Hereford, murders a land agent
Doreen: The Story of a Singer (1894) Edna Lyall (rn A. E. Bayly)

Desmond, Theo, Captain, VC, intrepid hero of knowledgeable novel of Indian life characterized by its (unconsciously) resolute anti-feminism; by popular Anglo-Indian author
Evelyn his poor little wife
Honor née Meredith his second wife
Captain Desmond, VC (1906) Maud Diver

Desolation
Pierce Penilesse his Supplication to the Devil (1592) Thomas Nashe

Despain, Bernie gambler
The Glass Key (1931) Dashiell Hammett

Despair one of Miss Flite's* birds
Bleak House (1853) Charles Dickens

Despair, Giant
The Pilgrim's Progress (1678–84) John Bunyan

Destouches, Doctor 'he's the sensitive one!'; in unpleasant masterpiece whose nasty author is nearer to his readers than most of them would prefer to admit
Féerie pour un autre fois (*Fairy Play for Another Time*) (1952–4); *D'un Château l'autre* (*Castle to Castle*) (1957) Louis-Ferdinand Céline (rn Louis-Ferdinand Destouches)

Dethridge, Hester one of the author's best half-mad villainesses, homicidal keeper of Anne Silverster* in her captivity
Man and Wife (1870) Wilkie Collins

Deverell, Angelica romantic novelist m. Esmé Howe-Nevinson*
Mrs Emmie Deverell her mother
Lottie her aunt, a lady's maid
Angel (1957) Elizabeth Taylor

Devilsdust trade unionist

Sybil (1845) Benjamin Disraeli
Devine, Jerry
Juno and the Paycock play (1925) Sean O'Casey (rn John Casey)
Devine, Richard see **Dawes, Rufus**
Devizes, Wilfred mental specialist, cc, father of Christina Alberta*
Christina Alberta's Father (1925) H. G. Wells
Devore, Daisy Diana Dorothea middle-aged office worker who joins Mr Zero* in suicide; but they return from heaven, finding conditions there insufficiently enslaving
The Adding Machine play (1923) Elmer Rice
Devoy, Martin Jesuit master at Denis Considine's* school
Without My Cloak (1931) Kate O'Brien
Dewcy, Major
ss 'My Lord the Elephant'
Many Inventions (1893) Rudyard Kipling
Dewitt, George in love with Melalah Sharland*
Mehalah (1880) Sabine Baring-Gould
Dewsbury, Anastasia actress, mother to Augustus Richmond*
The Adventures of Harry Richmond (1871) George Meredith
Dewy, Dick cc, m. Fancy Day*
Reuben his father
Ann his mother
Susan; Jimmy; Bob; Bessy; Charley his brother and sisters
William his grandfather
Under the Greenwood Tree (1872) Thomas Hardy
Dgloz Armenian specialist in buying utterly worthless horses and skinning them (a reference to the author's teachings and his pupils)
All and Everything: Beelzebub's Tales to His Grandson (1950); G. I. Gurdjieff
D'Hemecourt refugee, café-owner
Pauline his daughter, m. Major Shaughnessy*
ss 'Café des Exiles'
Old Creole Days (1879) George Washington Cable
Di Leo, Paolo, Count gigolo
The Roman Spring of Mrs Stone (1950) Tennessee Williams (rn Thomas Lanier

Williams)
Di Mentoni, Aphrodite, Marchesa
her aged husband
ss 'The Visionary'
Tales of the Grotesque and Arabesque (1840) Edgar Allan Poe
Diabologh (or **Diavolo**), **Georges Hamlet Alexander** young Russian
Connie his father
Lucy his uncle
Molly his aunt, Lucy's wife
Teresa his aunt, m. Emmanuel Vanderflint*
The Polyglots (1925) William Gerhardie
Diadem, Harry villain
Eternal Fire (1963) Calder Willingham
Diamante woman of easy virtue
The Unfortunate Traveller, or *The Life of Jack Wilton* (1594) Thomas Nashe
Diamond, Captain cc of complex ghost tale
ss 'The Ghostly Rental' (1876) Henry James
Diana
All's Well That Ends Well play (1623) William Shakespeare
Diana elderly English waitress, second wife of Scripps O'Neil*
The Torrents of Spring (1933) Ernest Hemingway
Dibabs, Jane former friend of Mrs Nickleby*
Nicholas Nickleby (1839) Charles Dickens
Dibbitts chemist
Middlemarch (1871–2) George Eliot (rn Mary Anne, later Marian, Evans)
Dibble, Ferdinand m. Barbara Medway*
ss 'The Heart of a Goof'
The Heart of a Goof (1926) P. G. Wodehouse
Dibble, Sampson, Mr
Dorothy his wife
ss 'Bound for the Great Salt Lake'
The Uncommercial Traveller (1860–8) Charles Dickens
Diccon the Bedlem
Gammer Gurton's Needle play (1575) ?William Stevenson
Dick a gamester, son to Mrs Amlet*
The Confederacy play (1705) John Vanbrugh
Dick bootblack, friend and saviour of

Fauntleroy*
Little Lord Fauntleroy (1886) Frances
Hodgson Burnett
Dick mate of the *Seamew*
The Skipper's Wooing (1897) W. W.
Jacobs
Dick, Mr see **Babley**
Dickens, Martha housekeeper to Major
Bridgenorth*
Peveril of the Peak (1822) Walter Scott
Dickerman, Rita
An American Tragedy (1925) Theodore
Dreiser
Dickison landlord
The Mill on the Floss (1860) George Eliot
(rn Mary Anne, later Marian, Evans)
Diddler, Jeremy swindler
The Kickleburys on the Rhine (1850)
W. M. Thackeray
Diddler, Jeremy swindler
Raising the Wind play (1803) James
Kenney
Digby stage name given to Smike*
Nicholas Nickleby (1839) Charles
Dickens
Digby, Dr headmaster
Villette (1853) Charlotte Brontë
Dilber, Mrs laundry woman and thief
A Christmas Carol (1843) Charles
Dickens
Dilcey
Prissy her daughter; both slaves owned
by the O'Hara's*
Gone With the Wind (1936) Margaret
Mitchell
Dill barber
Middlemarch (1871–2) George Eliot (rn
Mary Anne, later Marian, Evans)
Dillon, Black villain
The House by the Churchyard (1863)
J. Sheridan Le Fanu
Dilsey black servant to the Compsons*
The Sound and the Fury (1931) William
Faulkner
Dimbula, The, SS
ss 'The Ship That Found Herself'
The Day's Work (1898) Rudyard Kipling
Dimmesdale, Arthur, Revd lover of Hester
Prynne* who is too cowardly to own up
to his guilt; but eventually confesses and
dies in her arms on the pillory on which
she suffered
The Scarlet Letter (1850) Nathaniel

Hawthorne
Dimple, Billy wealthy Anglophile hero of
first truly American drama
The Contrast play (1787) Royall Tyler
Dimple, Revd Vicar of Matchings Easy
Mr Britling Sees It Through (1916) H. G.
Wells
Din, Iman Strickland's* servant
ss 'A Deal in Cotton'
Actions and Reactions (1909) Rudyard
Kipling
Din, Muhammed
Imam Din his father
ss 'The Story of Muhammed Din'
Plain Tales from the Hills (1888) Rud-
yard Kipling
Dinah cc, Rastafarian prostitute who
attempts to break out of the Dungle, in
the slum world of Kingston, in enlighten-
ing novel by sociologist
The Children of Sisyphus (1964)
Orlando Patterson
Dinah head cook to St Clare*
Uncle Tom's Cabin (1851) Harriet
Beecher Stowe
Dinent, Abbé friend to Helen Michel*
The World My Wilderness (1950) Rose
Macaulay
Dingaan treacherous chief
Nada the Lily (1892) Henry Rider
Haggard
Dingo, Professor second husband to Mrs
Badger*, botanist of European repute
Bleak House (1840) Charles Dickens
Dingo, Yellow Dog
ss 'The Sing-Song of Old Man Kangeroo'
Just So Stories (1902) Rudyard Kipling
Dingwall, Cornelius Brook pompous MP
Sketches by Boz† (1836) Charles Dickens
Dingwall, David 'a sly, dry, shrewd
attorney'
The Bride of Lammermoor (1819)
Walter Scott
Dinmont, Andrew ('Dandy') store-farmer
Ailie his wife
Jenny their daughter
Guy Mannering (1815) Walter Scott
Dinsmore, Elsie priggish paragon of
virtue: Richardson's* Pamela* or
Clarissa* desexualized, and, in the first
instance, made adolescent – but the 'Elsie
books', typical of American 'happiness
novels', were so popular that in the

course of them she grew up, married and even became a grandmother; they fell out of favour at the turn of the century; onwards from 1867 (28 titles ceasing in 1905) Martha Farquharson (rn Martha Farquharson Finley)
Diogaras servant to Calianax*
  The Maid's Tragedy play (1611) Francis Beaumont and John Fletcher
Diogenes Mr Blimber's* dog, pet of Paul Dombey*
  Dombey and Son (1848) Charles Dickens
Diogenes slave to Agelastes*
  Count Robert of Paris (1832) Walter Scott
Diomedes Greek commander
  Troilus and Cressida play (1623) William Shakespeare
Dion a Lord
  Philaster play (1611) Francis Beaumont and John Fletcher
Dion a Sicilian Lord
  A Winter's Tale play (1623) William Shakespeare
Dionyza wife to Cleon*
  Pericles play (1609) William Shakespeare
Diphilus brother to Evadne*
  The Maid's Tragedy play (1611) Francis Beaumont and John Fletcher
Dippy dead-end kid in famous play and film
  Dead End play (1936) Sidney Kingsley
Dippy, Nell naive semi-prostitute
  Maggie her mother
  Truth her brother
  Time Will Knit (1938) Fred Urquhart
Direck, Mr secretary of a Massachusetts cultural society
  Mr Britling Sees It Through (1916) H. G. Wells
Dirkovitch Cossack officer
  ss 'The Man Who Was'
  Life's Handicap (1891) Rudyard Kipling
Discount and Shame encountered by Faithful*
  The Pilgrim's Progress (1678–84) John Bunyan
Dishart, Gavin, Revd m. Lady Babbie*
  Gavin; Gavina their children
  Margaret his mother
  The Little Minister† (1891) J. M. Barrie
Ditta Mull
  ss 'Tods' Amendment'

Plain Tales from the Hills (1888) Rudyard Kipling
Diver, Colonel editor of *New York Rowdy Journal*
  Martin Chuzzlewit (1844) Charles Dickens
Diver, Dick psychiatrist, cc
  Nicole his wife, insane murderess
  Tender is the Night (1934) F. Scott Fitzgerald
Diver, Jenny
  The Beggar's Opera opera (1728); *Polly* opera (1729) John Gay
D'Ivry, Duc
  his wife
  Antoinette their daughter
  The Newcomes (1853–5) W. M. Thackeray
Divver, Max self-loathing liberal journalist
  Boys and Girls Come Out to Play (in America as *A Sea Change*) (1949) Nigel Dennis
Dixon servant of the Hales*
  North and South (1855) Mrs Gaskell
Dixon, Anthony m. as second husband Nettie de Lyndesay* *née* Stone*
  Crump Folk Going Home (1913) Constance Holme
Dixon, Danby ex-guardsman, swindler
  Fanny his wife
  Our Street (1848) W. M. Thackeray
Dixon, James ('Lucky Jim') cc
  Lucky Jim (1953) Kingsley Amis
Dixon, Mrs farmer's wife
  Swallows and Amazons (1930) Arthur Ransome
Dixon, Mrs plain, friendly and lacking in envy; brought up with Jane Fairfax*
  her husband
  Emma (1816) Jane Austen
Di'monds and Pearls' loved by Larry Tighe*
  ss 'Love o' Women'
  Many Inventions (1893) Rudyard Kipling
Djinn, The, in Charge of All Deserts
  ss 'How the Camel got his Hump'
  Just So Stories (1902) Rudyard Kipling
Doane, Seneca
  Babbitt (1923) Sinclair Lewis
Doasyouwouldbedoneby, Mrs
  The Water Babies (1863) Charles Kingsley

Dobbin, William, Major awkward gallant, m. as second husband Amelia Osborn*, *née* Sedley*
Sir William his father, rich grocer
Vanity Fair (1847–8) W. M. Thackeray
Dobbins, Humphrey Sir Robert Bramble's* servant
The Poor Gentleman play (1802) George Colman the Younger
Dobble host of a party
Sketches by Boz† (1836) Charles Dickens
Dobbleton, Dowager Duchess of mysterious member of aristocracy resembling Mrs Tuggs*
Sketches by Boz† (1836) Charles Dickens
Dobelle, Mr
Blanaid; Columba his children
The Moon in the Yellow River play (1932) Denis Johnston
Dobie, Denham girl of nineteen, m. Arnold Chapel* 'savage captured by life trying to grasp its principles': transplanted from Andorra to London society in care of the Greshams*; could not see that it mattered what anyone said, wrote, or thought; wanted to save time, trouble, service, when giving dinners, by putting all the food on the table at once on one plate; lives in Cornish cave and goes around on motorcycle
her father, a retired clergyman
Sylvia her dead mother
her Andorran stepmother, with four children
Crewe Train (1926) Rose Macaulay
Doboobie, Demetrius, Dr 'bold, adventurous practitioner'
Kenilworth (1821) Walter Scott
Dobson farmer, in play not due for revival
The Promise of May play (1882) Alfred, Lord Tennyson
Dobson, Constable nephew of Sergeant Voules*
Thank You, Jeeves (1934) P. G. Wodehouse
Dobson, Zuleika cc
Zuleika Dobson (1911) Max Beerbohm
Doc cc, modelled on the marine biologist Edward F. Ricketts
Cannery Row (1945) John Steinbeck
Dockwrath, Samuel lawyer handling case against Lady Mason*
his wife

Orley Farm (1862) Anthony Trollope
Doctor, The who cures Arabella* of her romantic inclinations
The Female Quixote (1752) Mrs Charlotte Lennox
Dodd, David, Captain of the *Agra* (alias William Thompson of the Vulture)
Lucy his wife, *née* Fountain
Julia m. Alfred Hardie*; **Edward** their children
Hard Cash (1863) Charles Reade
Dodd, Edwin 'militant agnostic'
Boon (1915) H. G. Wells
Dodd, Lewis brutal don m. Florence Churchill, later runs off with Tessa Sanger*
The Constant Nymph (1924) Margaret Kennedy
Dodd, Tommy ('Deroulett')
ss 'The Head of the District'
Life's Handicap (1891) Rudyard Kipling
Dodge, William guest at the pageant
Between the Acts (1941) Virginia Woolf
Dodger, parasite to Earl of Lincoln*
The Shoemaker's Holiday (1600) Thomas Dekker
Dodger, the Artful see **Dawkins, Jack**
Dods, Meg landlady
St Ronan's Well (1824) Walter Scott
Dodson of Dodson & Fogg, shady attorneys for Mrs Bardell*
The Pickwick Papers (1837) Charles Dickens
Dodson, Jane m. Glegg*
Sophy m. Pullet*
Susan m. Deane*
Elizabeth m. Edward Tulliver*
The Mill on the Floss (1860) George Eliot (rn Mary Anne, later Marian, Evans)
Dodsworth, Sam successful automobile manufacturer of Zenith
Fran his spoiled wife
Dodsworth (1929) Sinclair Lewis
D'Ofort, Marquis sinister suitor to Rita*
Rita (1856) Charles Aidé
Dogberry a foolish officer
Much Ado About Nothing play (1623) William Shakespeare
Dogget prison warder
The Betrothed (1825) Walter Scott
Dogginson who has made up his mind about everything without knowing any-

thing about it: i.e. a 'regular John Bull'
ss 'Our Vestry'
Reprinted Pieces (1858) Charles Dickens
Doheny, Susie see **Hansa, Per**
Dohmann, Mathilde mistress of Dorn* in
Germany, communist
Eric Dorn (1921) Ben Hecht
Dol Common
The Alchemist play (1610) Ben Jonson
Dolabella friend to Octavius Caesar*
Antony and Cleopatra play (1623)
William Shakespeare
Dolbie, Rhoda maid
Charlie her illegitimate son
ss 'My Son's Wife'
A Diversity of Creatures (1917) Rudyard
Kipling
Doleful, Miserrimus half-pay captain
Handley Cross (1843) R. S. Surtees
Dolcman, Thomas friend to Lovelace*
Clarissa Harlowe (1748) Samuel
Richardson
Dolliver, Dr doctor who invents an elixir
of life in order that he might survive to
care for his great-granddaughter:
Pansie; in unfinished novel (the author
died whilst engaged on it)
The Dolliver Romance (1876) Nathaniel
Hawthorne
Dolloby old-clothes dealer
David Copperfield (1850) Charles
Dickens
Dolls, Mr name given by Eugene
Wrayburn* to Jenny Wren's drunken
father
Our Mutual Friend (1865) Charles
Dickens
Doloreine, Thomas
The Power House (1916) John Buchan
Dolores Catalan pupil at Mme Beck's*
Villette (1853) Charlotte Brontë
Dolour, Mark farm hand
Nancy his daughter
Cold Comfort Farm (1932) Stella
Gibbons
Dolphin theatre manager
Pendennis (1848); *Lovel the Widower*
(1860) W. M. Thackeray
Dombey, Paul pompous merchant, m.
(1) Fanny, (2) Edith Granger*, widow,
daughter to Mrs Skewton*
Florence m. Walter Gay*; **Paul** his and
Fanny's children

Louisa his sister, m. John Chick*
Dombey and Son (1848) Charles Dickens
Domingue assistant to Thomas Fowler*
The Quiet American (1955) Graham
Greene
Dominic valet and cook to Harold Tran-
some*
Felix Holt (1866) George Eliot (rn Mary
Anne, later Marian, Evans)
Don Ferdinand son to Don Jerome*
The Duenna play (1775) Richard
Brinsley Sheridan
Don Francesco Roman Catholic priest
North Wind (1917) Norman Douglas
Don Juan
Don Juan poem (1819–24) George
Gordon, Lord Byron
Don Lucifer
The Terrors of the Night (1594) Thomas
Nashe
Donado a citizen of Parma
'Tis Pity She's A Whore play (1633) John
Ford
Donalbain son of King Duncan*
Macbeth play (1623) William Shake-
speare
Donald, Nan Ord (of the Hammer), High-
land captain
The Abbot (1820) Walter Scott
Donatello, Count faun-like cc who finally
gives himself up to justice for murder
The Marble Faun first published in Eng-
land as *Transformation* (1860) Nathan-
iel Hawthorne
Doncastle, Mr and Mrs
The Hand of Ethelberta (1876) Thomas
Hardy
Dongo, de, Fabrice cc, eventually Arch-
bishop of Parma
La Chartreuse de Parme (1839) Stendhal
(rn Henri Bayle)
Donn, Arabella false wife of Jude Fawley*
her father and mother
Jude the Obscure (1896) Thomas Hardy
Donna Louisa daughter to Don Jerome*
The Duenna play (1775) Richard
Brinsley Sheridan
Donne, Joseph, Revd curate of Whinbury
Shirley (1849) Charlotte Brontë
Donnerhugel, Rudolph of Swiss deputy
Stephen his father
Theodore his uncle
Anne of Geierstein (1829) Walter Scott

Donnithorne, Arthur squire who seduces
Hetty Sorrel* but then intervenes to save
her from the gallows
Lydia his tyrannical daughter
Arthur his grandson
Adam Bede (1859) George Eliot (rn
Mary Anne, later Marian, Evans)
Donny, the Misses proprietresses of
Greenleaf, boarding-school where Esther
Summerson* was educated
Bleak House (1853) Charles Dickens
Donogan, Daniel Irish nationalist
Lord Kilgoblin (1872) Charles Lever
Donovan, Larry betrayer of Antonia
Shimerda*
My Antonia (1918) Willa Cather
Donovan, Mr doctor or apothecary
Sense and Sensibility (1811) Jane Austen
Donovon, Macy politician cc of Australian
trilogy
Golconda (1948); *Seedtime* (1957); *The
Big Fellow* (1959) Vance Palmer
Doolan journalist on staff of *Tom and
Jerry*
Pendennis (1848) W. M. Thackeray
Dooley, Mr Chicago-Irish barman in
humorous sketches onwards from
Mr Dooley in Peace in and War (1898)
Peter Finlay Dunne
Doolittle half-pay captain
The Monastery (1820) Walter Scott
Doolittle, Eliza
Alfred her father
Pygmalion play (1914) George Bernard
Shaw
Doom, Ada, Aunt see **Starkadder**
Doone, Lorna (really **Lady Lorna Dugal**,
daughter of the Earl of Dugal); cc of
popular romance; m. John Ridd*
Sir Ensor her supposed grandfather
Charlesworth; Counsellor and others, his
sons
Carver Doone villain, Counsellor's son
Lorna Doone (1869) R. D. Blackmore
Dor, Mme Jules Obenreizer's* Swiss
housekeeper
No Thoroughfare (1867) Charles
Dickens
Doramin 'big pot', murderer of Jim
Lord Jim (1900) Joseph Conrad (rn Josef
Teodor Konrad Korzeniowski)
Doran, Barney
John Bull's Other Island (1904) George

Bernard Shaw
Doran, Bob lover of Polly Mooney
ss 'The Boarding House'
Dubliners (1914) James Joyce
Doran, Hetty fiancée of Lord R. St
Simon*, m. Francis Moulton*
Aloysius her father
ss 'The Noble Bachelor '
The Adventures of Sherlock Holmes
(1892) Arthur Conan Doyle
Dorax a noble Portuguese
Don Sebastian play (1690) John Dryden
Dorbell, Mrs
Love on the Dole (1933) Walter
Greenwood
Dordan counsellor to Ferrex*, son to
Gorboduc*
Gorboduc play (1562) Thomas Sackville
and Thomas Norton
Dore, Billie actress, secretary, m. Lord
Marshmoreton*
A Damsel in Distress (1919) P. G. Wode-
house
Doria, Clare m. John Todhunter*
*The Ordeal of Richard Feverel: A
History of Father and Son* (1859, rev.
1878) George Meredith
Doricourt
The Belle's Stratagem play (1780) Mrs
Hannah Cowley
Dorimant
The Man of Mode play (1676) George
Etherege
Dorincourt, Earl of grim aristocrat with
heart of gold
Little Lord Fauntleroy (1886) Frances
Hodgson Burnett
Dorker pupil murdered by Squeers's* ill-
treatment
Nicholas Nickleby (1839) Charles
Dickens
Dorking, Earl of impoverished peer, family
name Pulleyn
his wife
Viscount Rooster; Lady Clara m. Barnes
Newcome*; **Lady Henrietta** m. Lord
Kew*; **Lady Belinda; Lady Adelaide** their
children
The Newcomes (1853–5) W. M.
Thackeray
Dormer attendant at the National Portrait
Gallery
Harold his son, m. Adelaide Moon*

Antigua Penny Puce (1936) Robert Graves

Dormer schoolmaster
Mr Perrin and Mr Traill (1911) Hugh Walpole

Dormer, Edgar deceased artist
Lucy; Ayala his daughters, ccs, for whom he fails to provide
Ayala's Angel (1881) Anthony Trollope

Dormer, Nick successful politician who gives up his career and marriage to Julia Dallow* in order to become a portrait painter
his ambitious and complaining mother
Lord Percy his selfish hunting brother
Bridget ('Biddy') his sister, the only person who understands him, in love with Peter Sherringham*
Grace his other, dull sister
The Tragic Muse (1890) Henry James

Dormer, Stephen Doughty, Captain trouble-shooting cc
The *Spanish Farm* Trilogy (1927); *Our Mr Dormer* (1927) R. H. Mottram

Dormouse, The
Alice in Wonderland (1865) Lewis Carroll (rn Charles Lutwidge Dodgson)

Dorn, Erik cynical journalist, cc
Anna his wife
Erik Dorn (1921) Ben Hecht

Dornford, Eustace, KC, MP
Over the River (1924) John Galsworthy

Dornton, Harry spendthrift
The Road to Ruin play (1792) Thomas Holcroft

Dornton, Sergeant one of the early detectives: told the story of the Adventures of a Carpet Bag (based on a Sergeant Thornton of Bow Street)
ss 'Detective Police'
Reprinted Pieces (1858) Charles Dickens

Dorotea, La the actress Elena Osorio in classic Spanish prose romance
La Dorotea (1632) Lope de Vega

Dorothy companion to Lorelei Lee*
Gentlemen Prefer Blondes (1925) Anita Loos

Dorothy imaginary housekeeper, being a caricature of the retainers of Gothic novels
Northanger Abbey (1818) Jane Austen

Dorriforth, Father priest who is made guardian of Miss Milner*, becomes Lord Elmwood, and m. her
A Simple Story (1791) Elizabeth Inchbald

Dorrit, Amy ('Little Dorrit') cc, m. Arthur Clennam*
William her father
her mother
Edward ('Tip') her ne'er-do-well brother
Fanny her frivolous elder sister
Frederick her uncle, down-at-heels clarinet-player at the Surrey Theatre
Little Dorrit (1857) Charles Dickens

Dorsay, von, Herr rich old sensualist who wants Fräulein Else* to strip for him, and thus save her father from prison
Fräulein Else (1926) Arthur Schnitzler

Dorset, Duke of undergraduate
Zuleika Dobson (1911) Max Beerbohm

Dorset, George
Bertha his treacherous wife, whose lies help to drive Lily Bart* to suicide
The House of Mirth (1905) Edith Wharton

Dorset, Marquis of
King Richard III play (1623) William Shakespeare

Dorward, Revd
Sylvia Scarlett (1910) Compton Mackenzie

Dosett, Reginald Admiralty clerk with whom Lucy Dormer* is sent to live at the death of her father
his wife
Ayala's Angel (1881) Anthony Trollope

D'Ossorio, Don Christoval Condé nephew of the Duke of Medina*
The Monk (1796) Matthew G. Lewis

Dost Akbar one of the 'Four'
The Sign of Four (1890) Arthur Conan Doyle

Dot, Aunt see ffoulkes-Corbett

Doubledick, Richard good-hearted scoundrel who turned over a new leaf; wounded at Waterloo, m. Mary Marshall*
Seven Poor Travellers (1854) Charles Dickens

Doublefree, Jacob agent of the Duke of Buckingham*
Peveril of the Peak (1822) Walter Scott

Dougal chief of the Gorbals diehards
Huntingtower (1922) John Buchan

Doughie, Dobinet 'boy' to Roister Doister*

Ralph Roister Doister play (1551)
Nicholas Udall
Douglas owner of the ms, narrator
The Turn of the Screw (1898) Henry
James
Douglas, Captain cousin to Lady Laxton*
Bealby (1915) H. G. Wells
Douglas, Charlotte
Lloyd her second husband
Marin her daughter, member of a radical
group
A Book of Common Prayer (1977) Joan
Didion
Douglas, Henry m. Lady Juliana*
Marriage (1818) Susan Ferrier
Douglas, Jane Lady Katherine Gordon's
attendant
Perkin Warbeck play (1634) John Ford
Douglas, Jim alias Greyman, English agent
during the Indian Mutiny, m. Alice
Erlton*
On the Face of the Waters (1896) Flora
Annie Steel
Douglas, Monica schoolgirl, member of
the 'Brodie set'
The Prime of Miss Jean Brodie (1961)
Muriel Spark
Douglas, Widow
Huckleberry Finn (1884) Mark Twain
(rn Samuel Langhorne Clemens)
Dounce, John retired glove-maker, jilted
by an oyster-lady, m. his cook
Sketches by Boz (1836) Charles Dickens
Dousterswivel, Hermann impudent and
crooked agent for the Glen Withershins
Mining works
The Antiquary (1816) Walter Scott
Dove, QC Camperdown's* consultant
concerning diamonds
The Eustace Diamonds (1873) Anthony
Trollope
Dovedale, Lord fleeced at cards by
Rawdon Crawley*
Vanity Fair (1847–8) W. M. Thackeray
Dover silversmith, chief creditor of Tertius
Lydgate*
Middlemarch (1871–2) George Eliot (rn
Mary Anne, later Marian, Evans)
Dover, Dennis chairman of directors, Im-
perial Palace
Imperial Palace (1930) Arnold Bennett
Doveton, Charlie m. Mary Cameron
Doctor Phillips (1887) Frank Danby (rn

Julia Frankeau)
Dow, Rob
Micah his son
The Little Minister (1891) J. M. Barrie
Dowden, Olly maker of heath brooms
The Return of the Native (1878) Thomas
Hardy
Dowdle, Robert clarinet player
'Absent-mindedness in a Parish Choir'
Life's Little Ironies (1894) Thomas
Hardy
Dowdles, Misses keepers of a school in
Devon, the 'most accomplished, elegant,
fascinating creatures' (Mrs Nickleby*)
Nicholas Nickleby (1839) Charles
Dickens
Dowell, John American millionaire
Florence *née* Hurlbird, his wife, the mis-
tress of Edward Ashburnam* the best
The Good Soldier (1915) Ford Madox
Ford
Dowlas farrier
Silas Marner (1861) George Eliot (rn
Mary Anne, later Marian, Evans)
Dowlas, Dick
Daniel his father
The Heir at Law play (1797) George
Colman the Younger
Dowler, Captain and Mrs who travelled
with Mr Pickwick* and his friends to
Bath
The Pickwick Papers (1837) Charles
Dickens
Dowler, Hetty one of Gantry's* mistresses
Elmer Gantry (1927) Sinclair Lewis
Dowling attorney
Tom Jones (1749) Henry Fielding
Dowling, Father cc
Such Is My Beloved (1934) Morley
Callaghan
Dowling, Margo film star
U.S.A. trilogy (1930–6) John Dos Passos
Downe, Charles struggling young lawyer
his drowned wife
ss 'Fellow-Townsmen'
Wessex Tales (1888) Thomas Hardy
Downey, Ella white woman m. Jim
Harris*, a black law student; her latent
prejudice emerges before she lapses into
madness
All God's Chillun Got Wings play (1924)
Eugene O'Neill
Downing, Jim

Dr Nikola (1896) Guy Boothby
Dowse lighthouse keeper
ss 'The Disturber of Traffic'
Many Inventions (1893) Rudyard Kipling
Dowse, H. L. housemaster
The Old Boys (1964) William Trevor
Dowsing, Abraham shepherd
Mehalah (1880) Sabine Baring-Gould
Dowton, Clement, Sir, Baronet
When a Man's Single (1888) J. M. Barrie
Doxy, Betty
Polly opera (1729) John Gay
Doyce, Daniel friend to Meagles*, inventor
Little Dorrit (1857) Charles Dickens
Doyle, Peter cripple who shoots Miss Lonelyhearts*
Fay his wife, 'a tent, hair-covered and veined'
Miss Lonelyhearts (1933) Nathanael West (rn Nathan Weinstein)
Doyle, Phil inspector of Irish schools
Abby his wife
Molly Abbey's sister, m. Fairley, Quigley, cabinet minister
ss 'Hymeneal'
The Talking Trees (1971) Sean O'Faolain
Dozier, Julie half-caste actress, m. Steve Baker*
Show Boat (1926) Edna Ferber
Do'em accomplice of Captain Fitzwhisker Fiercy*
The Pantomime of Life (1837) Charles Dickens
Dracula, Count cc, vampire
Dracula (1897) Bram Stoker
Draffin, Walter Italianate Irishman, formerly cicisbeo to Mrs Bridie Bloggs*, now a bureaucrat in the Land Commission, author of *Dream of Fair to Middling Women* (in fact at that time a typescript in possession of the author, and written by him)
ss 'What a Misfortune'
More Pricks That Kicks (1934) Samuel Beckett
Dragomiroff, Ivan of the Aerial Board of Control
ss 'As Easy as ABC'
A Diversity of Creatures (1917) Rudyard Kipling
Drake, Arthur friend to Michael Fane*

Sinister Street (1913) Compton Mackenzie
Drake, Dr Pinfold's doctor
The Ordeal of Gilbert Pinfold (1957) Evelyn Waugh
Drake, Temple college girl raped by Popeye Vitelli*; m. Gowan Stevens*
Sanctuary (1931); *Requiem for a Nun* (1950) William Faulkner
Draper London lawyer and agent
The Virginians (1857–9) W. M. Thackeray
Drassilis, Cynthia one-time fiancée of Peter Burns*, m. Lord Mountry*
The Hon. Hugo her father
The Little Nugget (1913) P. G. Wodehouse
Dravot, Daniel
ss 'The Man who would be King'
Wee Willie Winkie (1888) Rudyard Kipling
Drebber, Enoch
A Study in Scarlet (1887) Arthur Conan Doyle
Dred modelled on Nat Turner*
Dred: A Tale of the Great Dismal Swamp (1856) Harriet Beecher Stowe
Drede narrator
The Bowge of Court poem (1498) John Skelton
Dredlington, Earl of
Lady Cecilia his daughter, m. Tittlebat Titmouse*
Ten Thousand a Year (1841) Samuel Warren
Dreedle, General
Catch-22 (1961) Joseph Heller
Dreeme, Cecil see **Denman, Clara**
Dreissiger cruel manufacturer of cloth; in drama set in Silesia
Die Weber (The Weavers) play (1892) Gerhart Hauptmann
Drencher Lovel's family doctor
Lovel the Widower (1860) W. M. Thackeray
Drew, Euphemia elderly spinster
A Glastonbury Romance (1932) John Cowper Powys
Drew, Lady of Bladesover House
Tono Bungay (1909) H. G. Wells
Drewett, Andrew college friend to Miles Wallingford*
Afloat and Ashore (1844); *Miles Wall-*

ingford (1844) James Fenimore Cooper
Drewitt
Brighton Rock (1938) Graham Greene
Drewitt, Prudence termagant in tale of three landlubbers who are hoaxed into making a voyage to the South Seas
Dialstone Lane (1904) W. W. Jacobs
Driffield, Edward famous writer
Rose his first wife
Amy his second wife
Cakes and Ale (1930) W. Somerset Maugham
Drina sister to the dead-end kids
Dead End play (1936) Sidney Kingsley
Drinkwater, Felix
Captain Brassbound's Conversion (1900) George Bernard Shaw
Driscoll Yanks's* sailor friend and comforter
Bound East for Cardiff one-act play (1916) Eugene O'Neill
Driscoll, Myra m. Oswald Henshawe
John her great-uncle
My Mortal Enemy (1928) Willa Cather
Driscoll, Percy slaveowner at Dawson's Landing, Missouri
Tom his son
Judge Driscoll his brother; murdered by Chambers, Roxy's* son
The Tragedy of Pudd'nhead Wilson (1894) Mark Twain (rn Samuel Langhorne Clemens)
Driver clerk to Lawyer Pleydell*
Guy Mannering (1815) Walter Scott
Drizzle, Caroline English busybody
Black Venus (1944) Rhys Davies
Dromio of Ephesus; Dromio of Syracuse twin brothers
A Comedy of Errors (1623) William Shakespeare
Dronsart, Adele Belgian pupil at Mlle Reuter's*
The Professor (1857) Charlotte Brontë
Drooce, Sergeant Marines, the 'most tyrannical non-commissioned officer in Her Majesty's service'
The Perils of Certain English Prisoners (1857) Charles Dickens
Drood, Edwin cc unfinished novel, nephew of John Jasper*, betrothed to Rosa Bud*; disappeared to consternation of everyone ever since
Edwin Drood (1870) Charles Dickens

Drouet, Charles drummer (salesman) who rescues Carrie Meeber* and becomes her lover
Sister Carrie (1900) Theodore Dreiser
Drover, Jim condemned to death
Milly his wife, *née* Rimmer
Conrad his brother
It's a Battlefield (1935) Graham Greene
Drowvey, Miss Miss Grimmer's* partner in the school
A Holiday Romance (1868) Charles Dickens
Drudgeit, Saunders (or **Peter**) clerk to Lord Bladderskate*
Redgauntlet (1824) Walter Scott
Drugger, Abel artless and gullible tobacco seller
The Alchemist play (1610) Ben Jonson
Drum, Countess of wizen-faced dowager who alleges relationship with S. Titmarsh*
The Great Hoggarty Diamond (1841) W. M. Thackeray
Drum, Tony hunchbacked cockney butcher's boy in novel by sentimental realist of the 'Cockney School'
Michael his father
Honor his sister
Tony Drum, a Cockney Boy (1898) Edwin Pugh
Drummle, Bentley Pip's* fellow pupil at Matthew Pocket's*; his enemy; called by Mr Jaggers* 'The Spider'; m. and parted from Estella*; kicked to death by horse
Great Expectations (1861) Charles Dickens
Drummle, Cayley friend to Aubrey Tanqueray*
The Second Mrs Tanqueray play (1893) Arthur Wing Pinero
Drummond, Hugh, Captain cc series of thriller romances for teenagers
Bulldog Drummond (1920) Sapper (rn H. C. McNeile)
Drummons, Catriona cc, m. David Balfour* of Shaws
James her father
Catriona (1893) Robert Louis Stevenson
Dryasdust, Dr friend to The Antiquary, 'editor'
The Antiquary† (1816) Walter Scott
Dryesdale, Jasper steward of Lochleven Castle

The Abbot (1820) Walter Scott

Dryfoos farmer made into millionaire by discovery of natural gas on his property; orders March* to discharge Lindau*

Conrad his son

A Hazard of New Fortunes (1890) William Dean Howells

Du Bois, Blanche Stella Kowalski's* sister

A Streetcar Named Desire play (1949) Tennessee Williams (rn Thomas Lanier Williams)

Du Bois, M.

Evelina (1778) Fanny Burney

Duarte, Pascual killer of his dog, horse, mother etc., who tells his story in the death-cell in first important post-Spanish Civil War novel, called 'tremendista' ('tremendous') because of the frightful things that happen

La familia de Pascual Duarte (The Family of Pascual Duarte) (1942) Camilo José Cela

Dubbley helps Grummer* to arrest Pickwick*

The Pickwick Papers (1837) Charles Dickens

Dubbo, Alf aborigine; artist

Riders in the Chariot (1961) Patrick White

Dubin, William biographer of D. H. Lawrence*

Dubin's Lives (1979) Bernard Malamud

Dubourg French merchant

Clement his nephew

Rob Roy (1818) Walter Scott

Ducat, Mr

Polly opera (1729) John Gay

Duchess, The

Alice in Wonderland (1865) Lewis Carroll (rn Charles Lutwidge Dodgson)

Ducrosne

The Thirty-nine Steps (1915) John Buchan

Ducrow, Andrew (hist.) equestrian performer and mimic who went mad when Astley's Theatre was destroyed by fire, 1841

Sketches by Boz† (1936) Charles Dickens

Dudebat, Louis

Jennifer his wife

The Doctor's Dilemma play (1906) George Bernard Shaw

Dudeney shepherd

ss 'The Knife and the Naked Chalk'

Rewards and Fairies (1910) Rudyard Kipling

Dudgeon, Annie

Timothy her recently deceased husband

Richard; Christy their sons

William; Titus brothers to Timothy

The Devil's Disciple play (1899) George Bernard Shaw

Dudgeon, John, Mr attorney of Barford, in whose garden a fox took refuge

ss 'The Squire's Story'

Novels and Tales (1906–19) Mrs Gaskell

Dudgeon, Thomas clerk to Daniel Romaine*

St Ives (1897) Robert Louis Stevenson

Dudleigh, Henry ruined shipowner

his family

Passages From the Diary of a Late Physician (1832) Samuel Warren

Dudley, Bruce see **Stockton, John**

Dudley, Captain

Louisa his daughter, m. Young Belcour*

Charles her brother, m. Charlotte*

The West Indian play (1771) Richard Cumberland

Dudley, Esther cc, modelled on the author's wife

Esther (1884) Frances Snow Compton (rn Henry Adams)

Dudley, Herman narrator

ss 'The Man Who Became a Woman'

Horses and Men (1924) Sherwood Anderson

Dudley, Stephen temporarily blind, bankrupt Philadelphia merchant; murdered by Craig* at behest of Ormond*

Constantia his daughter, who becomes a seamstress

Ormond, or The Secret Witness (1799) Charles Brockden Brown

Dudley, Uncle con-man in novel by Nebraskan hardly known in Britain

My Uncle Dudley (1942) Wright Morris

Duenna, The (Margaret) cc

The Duenna play (1775) Richard Brinsley Sheridan

Duer, Angus Arrowsmith's* fellow medical student and later colleague

Arrowsmith (1925) Sinclair Lewis

Duff Bow Street officer

Oliver Twist (1838) Charles Dickens

Duff, Mrs housekeeper

The Last and the First (1971) Ivy Compton-Burnett

Dufferin, Anthony, Dr
Men and Wives (1931) Ivy Compton-Burnett

Duffield, Hurtle Australian artist, cc
The Vivisector (1970) Patrick White

Duffy, James bank clerk
ss 'A Painful Case'
Dubliners (1914) James Joyce

Duffy, John postmaster
Delia his daughter, engaged to Denis Geohegan*
The White-headed Boy play (1921) Lennox Robinson

Duffy, Tiny Stark's* fat yes-man
All the King's Men (1946) Robert Penn Warren

Dufoy a saucy impertinent Frenchman, servant to Sir Frederick Frolick*
The Comical Revenge, or *Love in a Tub* play (1664) George Etherege

Dufrayer, Louise Australian girl with whom Maurice Guest* has a tragic affair
Maurice Guest (1908) Henry Handel Richardson (rn Ethel Florence Lindesay Richardson Robertson)

Dugal, Lorna, Lady see **Doone, Lorna**

Duke Penrod Schofield's* mongrel dog
Penrod (1914); *Penrod and Sam* (1916); *Penrod Jashber* (1929) Booth Tarkington

Duke, Archibald, Revd
ss 'The Sad Fortunes of the Rev. Amos Barton'
Scenes of Clerical Life (1857) George Eliot (rn Mary Anne, later Marian, Evans)

Duke, Revd William sincere clergyman made immediate judge of the dead
Outward Bound play (1924) Sutton Vane

Duke, The living in exile
All's Well That Ends Well play (1623) William Shakespeare

Dukes, Mrs sixty-five-year-old cc of the author's first, but posthumously published, novel: will she ever learn of her million-pound inheritance, and will she be defrauded of it by Raza Khan*?
Arthur St Giles Dukes her late husband
Cole her son
Mrs Dukes' Million (1977) Wyndham Lewis

Dula waiting-woman to Evadne*
The Maid's Tragedy play (1611) Francis Beaumont and John Fletcher

Dull Vice-President of Umbugology and Ditchwateristics section of the Mudfog Association
The Mudfog Papers (1838) Charles Dickens

Dulver, Herbert m. Elsie Longstaff*
The Good Companions (1929) J. B. Priestley

Dumain lord attending on Ferdinand*
Love's Labour's Lost play (1623) William Shakespeare

Dumbello, Lord later **Lord Hartletop**, m. Griselda Grantly*
Framley Parsonage (1861) Anthony Trollope

Dumbledikes, Lord of grasping landlord
Jock his gawky son
Heart of Midlothian (1818) Walter Scott

Dumbledon 'idiotic goggle-eyed boy'
ss 'Our School'
Reprinted Pieces (1858) Charles Dickens

Dumby, Mr
Lady Windermere's Fan play (1892) Oscar Wilde

Dumetrius art dealer
The *Forsyte* series (1906–33) John Galsworthy

Dumkins one of the most renowned members of the All-Muggleton Cricket Club
The Pickwick Papers (1837) Charles Dickens

Dummerar, Revd Mr Vicar of Martindale-cum-Moultrassie
Peveril of the Peak (1822) Walter Scott

Dumoise surgeon
his wife
ss 'By Word of Mouth'
Plain Tales from the Hills (1888) Rudyard Kipling

Dumps, Nicodemus bank clerk: cross, cadaverous and ill-natured, Charles Kitterball's* uncle
Sketches by Boz† (1836) Charles Dickens

Dumtousie, Daniel lawyer, nephew of Lord Bladderskate*
Redgauntlet (1824) Walter Scott

Dun, Hughie body-servant of the Archbishop of St Andrews
The Fair Maid of Perth (1828) Walter

Scott

Dunboyne, Philip m. Eunice Gracedieu*
The Legacy of Cain (1889) Wilkie Collins

Duncalf town clerk of Bursley, Henry Machin's* first employer
The Card (1911) Arnold Bennett

Duncan King of Scotland
Macbeth play (1623) William Shakespeare

Duncan, Archibald
Middlemarch (1871–2) George Eliot (rn Mary Anne, later Marian, Evans)

Duncan, Long Rob miller
A Scots Quair trilogy: *Sunset Song* (1932); *Cloud Howe* (1934); *Grey Granite* (1935) Lewis Grassic Gibbon (rn James Leslie Mitchell)

Duncan, Major
The Pathfinder (1840) James Fenimore Cooper

Duncannon, Gregor landlord of the Highlander and the Hawick Gill
Waverley (1814) Walter Scott

Duncansby, Hector, Lieutenant
Catriona (1893) Robert Louis Stevenson

Duncanson, Neil
Catriona (1893) Robert Louis Stevenson

Dunce, Lady in love with Captain Beaugard*
Sir Davy her husband
Sylvia Dunce Sir Davy's niece
The Soldier's Fortune play (1681) Thomas Otway

Dundey, Dr Irish bank robber
ss 'Detective Police'
Reprinted Pieces (1858) Charles Dickens

Dunford, Walter, Bishop
Dame Sibilla his niece, a nun
The Corner That Held Them (1948) Sylvia Townsend Warner

Dungory, Earl of (family name Cullen)
Cecilia a cripple; **Jane**; **Sarah** his sisters
A Drama in Muslin (1886) George Moore

Dunham, Mabel m. Jasper Western*
Sergeant Dunham her father
'Cap' her uncle
The Pathfinder (1840) James Fenimore Cooper

Dunkerley senior assistant at Bonover School
Love and Mr Lewisham (1900) H. G. Wells

Dunkirk rich usurer with a disreputable past
his wife, later Mrs Bulstrode*
Sarah their daughter, mother to Will Ladislaw*
Middlemarch (1871–2) George Eliot (rn Mary Anne, later Marian, Evans)

Dunkle
Martin Chuzzlewit (1844) Charles Dickens

Dunmaya hill-woman
ss 'Yoked with an Unbeliever'
Plain Tales from the Hills (1888) Rudyard Kipling

Dunn draper in Milby
his wife
Mary their daughter
ss 'Janet's Repentance'
Scenes of Clerical Life (1857) George Eliot (rn Mary Anne, later Marian, Evans)

Dunne see Ryan, Eddie

Dunois bastard of Orleans
Saint Joan play (1924) George Bernard Shaw

Dunstable, Lieutenant, The Duke of Dragoon Guards, m. Lady Jane
Patience opera (1881) W. S. Gilbert and Arthur Sullivan

Dunstable, Miss heiress
Dr Thorne† (1858) Anthony Trollope

Dunstan, Mount, Lord impoverished honourable peer; horsewhips Sir Nigel Anstruther*; m. Betty Vanderpool*
The Shuttle (1907) Frances Hodgson Burnett

Dunstane, Emma, Lady friend to Diana Warwick*
Diana of the Crossways (1885) George Meredith

Dunster, Farmer
his wife
The Adventures of David Simple (1744–53) Sarah Fielding

Dunthorne, Major
The Woman in White (1860) Wilkie Collins

Dupin, Auguste C. detective who works solely by 'deductive' (in point of fact, like Holmes, *inductive*) methods, who became the prototype of later detectives such as those of Conan Doyle*; derived

from Vidocq's ghosted autobiography ss 'The Murders in the Rue Morgue't (1841)
Prose Tales of Edgar Allan Poe (1843)

Dupin, Martin mayor of Sémur, beleaguered by a strange mist after a public blasphemy
A Beleaguered City (1880) Mrs Margaret Oliphant

Dupont, Emil French journalist
Men Like Gods (1923) H. G. Wells

Dupont, M. cat with white spats
The Loving Eye (1956) William Sansom

Duport, Bob ex-husband to Jean Templer*
A Question of Upbringing† (1951) Anthony Powell

Dupuis, Léon notary's clerk who has an affair with Emma Bovary*
Madame Bovary (1857) Gustave Flaubert

Durango, Bishop of Santa Fé
Death Comes for the Archbishop (1927) Willa Cather

Durbeyfield, Tess cc
Sir Pagan D'Urberville founder of the D'Urberville and Durbeyfield families of which she is a member
Alexander ('Alec') D'Urberville seduces and later m. Tess
Alexander's mother
John Stoke D'Urberville Alec's father
John Durbeyfield Tess's father
Joan her mother
Eliza-Louisa ('Liza-Lu') her sister
her brothers and sisters
Tess of the D'Urbervilles (1891) Thomas Hardy

Durden, Dame see **Summerson, Esther**

Durdles drunken stonemason
Edwin Drood (1870) Charles Dickens

D'Urfe, Nicholas cc
The Magus (1965, rev. 1967) John Fowles

Durfey-Transome relations of earlier Transomes, to whom their estates passed
Felix Holt (1866) George Eliot (rn Mary Anne, later Marian, Evans)

Durfy of the *Rocket*,
Reginald Cruden (1894) Talbot Baines Reed

Durfy, Tom m. Kitty Flanagan*, *née* Riley
Handy Andy (1842) Samuel Lover

Durgan, Miss postmistress of Hickley-brow
The Food of the Gods (1904) H. G. Wells

Durgin, Jeff cc 'successful failure' who builds a fashionable hotel, m. Genevieve Vostrand*; character saved by circumstances from crime
The Landlord at Lion's Head (1897) William Dean Howells

Durham, Constantia who accepts Patterne's proposal but then elopes with Harry Oxford*
Sir John her father
The Egoist (1879) George Meredith

Durham, Maurice owner of Penge, barrister, platonic lover of Maurice Hill*
Maurice (1971) E. M. Forster

Durie family name of Lord Durrisdeer and Ballantrae

Durrance, John blinded hero who develops convincing powers of detection
The Four Feathers (1902) A. E. W. Mason

Durrisdeer and Ballantrae, Lord
James, Marquis of Ballantrae presumed killed at Culloden
Henry, Marquis of Ballantrae later Lord Durrisdeer, m. Alison Graeme*
Alexander; Katherine their children
The Master of Ballantrae (1889) Robert Louis Stevenson

Durward, Quentin of Louis XI's Scottish Guard, cc
Quentin Durward (1823); *Anne of Geierstein* (as M. de la Croye) (1829) Walter Scott

Dutcher, Rose reared by her widowed father on Wisconsin farm and, wishing to be an author, in revolt against her bleak life; in novel by pioneer of American realism who was influenced by the single tax theories of Henry George and by Howells*
her father
Rose of Dutcher's Cooly (1896) Hamlin Garland

Duthie, Jimsy poet, master printer, brewer
Jess his sister, m. Henry McQumpha*
A Window in Thrums (1889) J. M. Barrie

Dutton seaman on the *Sarah*
The Master of Ballantrae (1889) Robert Louis Stevenson

Dutton, Dolly dairymaid to Duke of Argyll*

Heart of Midlothian (1818) Walter Scott

Dutton, John slave master and father to all sixteen children of the mother of Vyry*

Big Missy Salina his wife

Johnny their son, young West Pointer killed in Civil War

Jubilee (1966) Margaret Walker

Duval, Denis smuggler and *perruquier*

Peter his grandfather, who taught him the trade

Ursule his mother

Denis Duval (1864) W. M. Thackeray

Duvallet

Fanny's First Play play (1905) George Bernard Shaw

Duveen, Praxis cc, woman who has served a prison sentence for killing an idiot baby

Praxis (1978) Fay Weldon

Dwining, Henbane 'a sneaking varlet'

The Fair Maid of Perth (1828) Walter Scott

Dwornitzchek, Heloise von and zu, Princess ex Mrs Franklin, *née* Bulpitt*, m. (3) Adrian Peake*

Summer Moonshine (1938) P. G. Wodehouse

Dwyer, Matty m. James Casey*

Handy Andy (1842) Samuel Lover

Dyke, Tam boyhood friend to David Crawford*

Prester John (1910) John Buchan

Dykes gamekeeper to Austin Ruthyn*

Uncle Silas (1864) J. Sheridan Le Fanu

Dylap, Lydia novelist, turned Bohemian

Museum Pieces (1952) William Plomer

Dylks (hist.) Ohio backwoodsman of 1840s who persuades himself and others that he is God

The Leatherwood God (1916) William Dean Howells

Dymond, Winnie ('Winkie') in love with John Ransome*

The Combined Maze (1913) May Sinclair

Dynever, Cecil, Mrs Lechmore's* granddaughter, m. Lionel Lincoln*

Lionel Lincoln (1825) James Fenimore Cooper

E

E23 Mahratta in Secret Service
Kim (1901) Rudyard Kipling
Eager, Cuthbert, Revd English chaplain, Florence
A Room With a View (1908) E. M. Forster
Eagles, Hook, Mrs at first patronizing and then cold-shouldering Becky Sharp*
Vanity Fair (1847–8) W. M. Thackeray
Eaglesham, Lord friend to Revd Micah Balwhidder*
Annals of the Parish (1821) John Galt
Eames subaltern
ss 'The Honours of War'
A Diversity of Creatures (1917) Rudyard Kipling
Eames, Ernest bibliographer
South Wind (1917) Norman Douglas
Earine with the 'most perfectly modelled bum in all Greece'
Aphrodite in Aulis (1931) George Moore
Earle, Edna owner of Hotel Beulah in Clay, Mississippi; narrator (of the story of her Uncle Daniel Ponder*)
The Ponder Heart (1954) Eudora Welty
Earle, Edna tamer of St Elmo Murray*
St Elmo (1866) Augusta Evans Wilson
Earlforward, Henry bookseller cc, miser
his wife, formerly Mrs Arb
Revd Augustus his brother
Riceyman Steps (1923) Arnold Bennett
Earnscliff, Patrick m. Isabel Vere*
The Black Dwarf (1816) Walter Scott
Earnshaw, Catherine cc novel that failed when first published (only Dobell and Swinburne* praised it) m. Edgar Linton*
Hindley her brother
Hindley's wife
Hareton son to Hindley; m. Cathy Heathcliff, *née* Linton
Wuthering Heights (1847) Emily Brontë
Earp, Ruth dancing-teacher, engaged to Denry Machin*, later Mrs Capron-Smith
The Card (1911) Arnold Bennett
Earwicker, Humphrey Chimpden Dublin publican (Here Comes Everybody; Haveth Childer Everywhere)
Ann (Anna Livia Plurabelle) his wife
Isabel their daughter
Kevin Shaun the Postman, Chuff, Yawn, Jaun; **Jerry** Shem the Penman, Dolph, Glugg – their twin sons
Finnegan's Wake (1939) James Joyce
East school chum of Tom Brown*
Tom Brown's Schooldays (1857) Thomas Hughes
Easthupp boatswain, purser's steward
Mr Midshipman Easy (1836) Captain Marryat
Eastlake, Elinor ('Lakey') graduate of Vassar
The Group (1963) Mary McCarthy
Easton, Lewis, Sir lover of Amanda Morris*
The Research Magnificent (1915) H. G. Wells
Eastwood, Charles, Major lover of Mrs Fawcett*
The Virgin and the Gipsy (1930) D. H. Lawrence
Easy, John cc
Nicodemus his father
Mr Midshipman Easy (1836) Captain Marryat
Easy, Lady
The Careless Husband play (1705) Colley Cibber
Eaves, Tom club gossip
Vanity Fair (1847–8) W. M. Thackeray
Ebea maid to Zabina*
Tamburlaine play (1587) Christopher Marlowe
Eben son to Hannah*
ss 'The Talent Thou Gavest'
My People (1915) Caradoc Evans (rn David Evans)
Ebermann, Frau selfish German housewife haunted by ghosts of children slaughtered by Germans
ss 'Swept and Garnished'

A Diversity of Creatures (1917) Rudyard Kipling

Eberson, Carl bastard son of William de la Marck*
Quentin Durward (1823) Walter Scott

Ebhart, Max engaged to Naomi Fisher
Leopold their bastard son, lover of Karen Michaelis*
The House in Paris (1935) Elizabeth Bowen

Eccles see **Skyrme**

Eccles tutor, scoundrel
Passages from the Diary of a Late Physician (1832) Samuel Warren

Eccles, John Scott
ss 'Wisteria Lodge'
His Last Bow (1917) Arthur Conan Doyle

Eccles, Robert
Jonathan his father
Rhoda Fleming (1865) George Meredith

Echo
Cynthia's Revels, or The Fountain of Self-Love play (1601) Ben Jonson

Eckdorf, Ivy photographer
Mrs Eckdorf in O'Neill's Hotel (1969) William Trevor

Ed
ss 'Io'
Widdershins (1911) Oliver Onions

Eddard intelligent donkey
Our Mutual Friend (1865) Charles Dickens

Eddi St Wilfrid's* priest
ss 'The Conversion of St Wilfrid'
Rewards and Fairies (1910) Rudyard Kipling

Eddie works in Tom Quayne's* advertising agency
The Death of the Heart (1938) Elizabeth Bowen

Eddin, Mullah Nassr legendary Arabic sage whose sayings are a frequent feature of this work
All and Everything: Beelzebub's Tales to His Grandson (1950) G. I. Gurdjieff

Ede, Kate cc, becomes an alcoholic; makes reputation as an actress under name of Kate D'Arcy; m. (2) Dick Lenox*
Ralph her first husband, m. (2) Hender, an assistant in his haberdasher's shop
Ralph's mother
A Mummer's Wife (1885) George Moore

Ede, Thomas farmer, former owner of Grand National 'Piebald'
National Velvet (1935) Enid Bagnold

Eden, Frank, Revd humane prison chaplain
It Is Never Too Late to Mend (1856) Charles Reade

Eden, Martin cc under whose muscled body lies a 'mass of sensibilities' – of questioning mind dedicated to ideas of Herbert Spencer, becomes a successful writer, but kills himself
Martin Eden (1909) Jack London

Eden, Nurse
ss 'Mary Postgate'
A Diversity of Creatures (1917) Rudyard Kipling

Ederic the Forester Saxon leader
Count Robert of Paris (1832) Walter Scott

Edgar Gloucester's son; also disguised as Poor Tom
King Lear play (1623) William Shakespeare

Edge, George Peter Waring's* uncle
Margaret his wife
George; Gordon; Thomas his sons
Alice his daughter, who puts a mouse in the soup
Peter Waring (1937) Forrest Reid

Edgehill
Dr Nikola (1896) Guy Boothby

Edgermond, Lucille m. Lord Nelvil*
Corinne (1807) Madame de Staël

Edgeworth, Duncan
Ellen his first wife
Nance m. Oscar Jekyll*; **Sybil** m. Grant Edgeworth – their daughters
Alison his second wife
Grant his nephew, m. Sybil (above)
A House and its Head (1935) Ivy Compton-Burnett

Edgeworth, Harold friend to Henry Maitland*
The Private Life of Henry Maitland (1912) Morley Roberts

Edgworth, Ezechiel cutpurse
Bartholomew Fair play (1631) Ben Jonson

Edith housemaid, runs away with Raunce*
Loving (1945) Henry Green (rn Henry Yorke)

Edlin, Mrs

Jude the Obscure (1896) Thomas Hardy

Edmonstone, Edward
his wife
Charles; Laura m. Philip Morville*; **Amy** m. Sir Guy Morville*; **Charlotte** their children
The Heir of Redclyffe (1853) Charlotte M. Yonge

Edmund bastard son to Gloucester
King Lear play (1623) William Shakespeare

Edmunds, George
The Village Coquette opera (1836) Charles Dickens

Edmunds, John subject of the Dingley Dell clergyman's story, 'The Returned Convict'
The Pickwick Papers (1837) Charles Dickens

Edny, Clithero morose maniac and attempted murderer and eventual suicide in American Gothic novel
Edgar Huntly, or *Memoirs of a Sleepwalker* (1799) Charles Brockden Brown

Edson lodger at Mrs Lirriper's*
Peggy his wife, whom he deserted
Mrs Lirriper's Lodgings and Legacy (1864) Charles Dickens

Edward II (hist.) cc
Edward II play (1594) Christopher Marlowe

Edward see **Skipper**

Edward V (hist.)
King Richard III play (1623) William Shakespeare

Edward wealthy nobleman
Walhlverwandschaften (*Elective Affinities*) (1809) Johann Wolfgang Goethe

Edward, Prince of Wales (hist.) son to Henry
King Henry VI plays (1623) William Shakespeare

Edward, Prince of Wales (hist.) son to Henry VIII, later King Edward IV
The Prince and the Pauper (1882) Mark Twain (rn Samuel Langhorne Clemens)

Edwards, Eleanor ('Magdalen')
Passages from the Diary of a Late Physician (1832) Samuel Warren

Edwards, Eurydice companion to Mme Ruiz*
Prancing Nigger (1924) Ronald Firbank

Edwards, Fox brilliant publisher's editor,
portrait of the author's mentor, Maxwell Perkins
You Can't Go Home Again (1941) Thomas Wolfe

Edwards, Jerome 'poor man' cc, m. Lucina Merritt*; in study of the 'New England' village character
Elmira his sister, m. Lawrence Prescott*
Abel his father
Ann his mother, *née* Lamb
Jerome (1897) Mary E. Wilkins

Edwards, Mog in love with Myfanwy Price*
Under Milk Wood play (1954) Dylan Thomas

Edwards, Rebecca mistress of James Bray*
Gordon her husband
A Guest of Honour (1971) Nadine Gordimer

Edwards, Tom
ss 'An Ohio Pagan'
Horses and Men (1924) Sherwood Anderson

Edwards, Miss pupil-teacher
The Old Curiosity Shop (1841) Charles Dickens

Edwin hermit cc of ballad read by Burchell*
The Vicar of Wakefield (1766) Oliver Goldsmith

Eeles, Julie actress and lover of Thomas and Edward Wilcher*
To Be a Pilgrim (1942) Joyce Cary

Eerith, Samuel oiler to the Monster
The Last Revolution (1951) Lord Dunsany

Effingham, Major alias Hawkeye
The Last of the Mohicans† (1826) James Fenimore Cooper

Effingham, Violet Lady Baldock's* niece, m. Lord Chiltern*
Phineas Finn† (1869) Anthony Trollope

Effrena, Stellio young poet maddened by his passion for La Foscarina* in sultry novel that was a *succès de scandale* of its time
Il fuoco (*The Fire*) (1900) Gabriele D'Annunzio

Egaeus youth of diseased mind
ss 'Berenice'
Tales of the Grotesque and Arabesque (1840) Edgar Allan Poe

Egan ('Horse') Irish private

ss 'The Mutiny of the Mavericks'
Life's Handicap (1891) Rudyard Kipling
Egan, Edward squire of Merryvale
Handy Andy (1842) Samuel Lover
Egan, Hugh cc of New Zealand novel about London expatriates struggling for meaning after 1939–45 war
The Sullen Bell (1956) Dan Davin
Egerton, Audley famous politician
My Novel, or Varieties in English Life (1850–3) Edward Bulwer Lytton
Egerton, Julia, Lady cousin to Jack Hinton*, m. Colonel Philip O'Grady*
Jack Hinton (1843) Charles Lever
Egeus father to Hermia*
A Midsummer Night's Dream play (1623) William Shakespeare
Eglantine barber and perfumer
ss 'The Ravenswing'
Men's Wives (1843) W. M. Thackeray
Ego, Pomponius
Handley Cross (1843) R. S. Surtees
Egremont, Charles, MP cc of novel appealing to reformist ideas of the 'Young England' group; younger brother to Earl of Marney*
Sybil (1845) Benjamin Disraeli
Egstrom & Blake ship's chandlers, employers of Jim
Lord Jim (1900) Joseph Conrad (rn Josef Teodor Konrad Korzeniowski)
Egypt, Soldan of
Tamburlaine play (1587) Christopher Marlowe
Einhorn, William brilliant, learned but corrupt crippled businessman who employs the young Augie March*, and instils into him a love of books
The Adventures of Augie March (1953) Saul Bellow
Einion, Father chaplain to Gwenwyn*
The Betrothed (1825) Walter Scott
Einsam, Isidore, Dr estranged husband to Glory Green*, doctor to Katherine Cattleman*; prescriber of multiple orgasms
The Nowhere City (1965) Alison Lurie
Eisman, Gus 'The Button King'
Gentlemen Prefer Blondes (1925) Anita Loos
Eitherside, Paul, Sir a lawyer and justice
Lady Eitherside his wife
The Devil is an Ass play (1616) Ben Jonson

Ek, Oscar athletics coach
The Human Comedy (1943) William Saroyan
Elbourne, Mr and Mrs
ss 'A.V.Laider'
Seven Men (1919) Max Beerbohm
Elderson, Robert insurance man who absconds with funds
The White Monkey (1924) John Galsworthy
Eldest Magician, The
ss 'The Crab that Played with the Sea'
Just So Stories (1902) Rudyard Kipling
Eldon, Hubert m. Adela Waltham*
Demos (1886) George Gissing
Eldridge, Mildred, Lady adopts Polly Monument*, who grows up as her own daughter
Beatrice ('Valentine') her daughter, m. Claude Monument*
Children of Gibeon (1886) Walter Besant
Elena; George; William
Odtaa (1926) John Masefield
Elenko maiden in title story of collection of oft-reprinted minor tales
ss 'The Twilight of the Gods'
The Twilight of the Gods (1888) Richard Garnett
Elenor driven by Ferdinand* to Bedlam
The Adventures of Ferdinand, Count Fathom (1753) Tobias Smollett
Eléonore
Adolphe (1816) Benjamin Constant
Elephant's Child, the
ss 'The Elephant's Child'
Just So Stories (1902) Rudyard Kipling
Elf grotesque barman, for a time engaged to Coral Fairbrother*
Old Crow (1967) Shena Mackay
Elias of Bury
Adah his wife
ss 'The Treasure and the Law'
Puck of Pook's Hill (1906) Rudyard Kipling
Elias of Tergou father to Gerard Eliasson*
Catherine his wife; ccs
The Cloister and the Hearth (1861) Charles Reade
Elias the Shop, Abishai
How Green Was My Valley (1861) Richard Llewellyn
Eliasson, Gerard cc, father of Erasmus (hist.); in novel occasioned by the

author's sexual frustration and based by him on his 1859 story 'A Good Fight'
The Cloister and the Hearth (1861) Charles Reade

Elinor, Queen mother of King John*
King John play (1623) William Shakespeare

Eliot, Helen
The Human Comedy (1943) William Saroyan

Eliot, Lewis barrister cc, narrator
The Strangers and Brothers† sequence (1940–70) C. P. Snow

Eliot, Meg poor widow, cc
Bill her husband, killed at Srem Panh airport in outbreak of political violence
The Middle Age of Mrs Eliot (1958) Angus Wilson

Elisa German servant of Miss Collier-Floodgate*
Before the Bombardment (1926) Osbert Sitwell

Eliza housemaid to Mrs Ingle*
The Last Revolution (1951) Lord Dunsany

Elizabeth, Queen (hist.)
ss 'Gloriana'
Rewards and Fairies (1910) Rudyard Kipling

Elizabeth, Queen (hist.) widow of Edward IV*
King Richard III play (1623) William Shakespeare

Elkin, Hester and her large Jewish family
Collected Stories (1975) Hortense Calisher

Ella, Lady rapturous maiden
Patience opera (1881) W. S. Gilbert and Arthur Sullivan

Ellen Presbyterian nurse, m. Thomas More*
Love Amongst the Ruins (1971) Walker Percy

Ellen servant to Theobald Pontifex*, m. **John** the Coachman*, later (bigamously) m. Ernest Pontifex*
Georgie; Alice her children
The Way of All Flesh (1903) Samuel Butler

Ellen servant to the Hares*
A Clergyman's Daughter (1935) George Orwell (rn Eric Blair)

Ellen, Aunt

The White-haired Boy play (1920) Lennox Robinson

Ellesmere, Mistress housekeeper at Martindale Castle
Peveril of the Peak (1822) Walter Scott

Ellieslaw see **Vere, Richard**

Ellinger, Frank has affair with Marian Forrester*
A Lost Lady (1923) Willa Cather

Elliot, Frederick ('Rickie') cc, sensitive, lame teacher, m. Agnes Pembroke*
The Longest Journey (1907) E. M. Forster

Elliot, Halbert ('Hobbie of the Heughfoot') m. Grace Armstrong*
John; Harry; Lilias; Joan; Annot his brother and sisters, the latter 'rustic coquettes'
The Black Dwarf (1816) Walter Scott

Elliot, Ralph (really **Richard Frampton**) bosom friend to Frank Fairlegh*
Frank Fairlegh (1850) Francis Smedley

Elliot, Walter, Sir of Kellynch Hall; vanity is the beginning and end of his character
his good wife
Elizabeth; Anne m. Captain Wentworth*; **Mary** their children
William Walter their nephew, not as pleasant as he seems; elopes with Mrs Clay*
Persuasion (1818) Jane Austen

Elliott, Christina cc
Gilbert her brother
Robert; Gilbert; Clement; Andrew: The Black Elliotts his four sons
Kirstie their sister
Weir of Hermiston (1896) Robert Louis Stevenson

Elliott, Henry merchant's clerk
Mary his wife
Passages from the Diary of a Late Physician (1832) Samuel Warren

Elliott, Liza fashion magazine editor-in-chief in musical with music by Kurt Weill
Lady in the Dark musical (1941) Moss Hart and Ira Gershwin (lyrics)

Elliott, Malcolm Protestant estate-holder in Ireland, with a social conscience
The Year of the French (1979) Thomas Flanagan

Elliott, Stephen orphan cousin of Mr Abney*
ss 'Lost Hearts'

Ghost Stories of an Antiquary (1910)
M. R. James

Ellis mean-minded manager of timber firm
Burmese Days (1935) George Orwell (rn
Eric Blair)

Ellis the Stable, Dai
How Green Was My Valley (1939)
Richard Llewellyn

Ellis, Sophy
ss 'The Wish House'
Debits and Credits (1926) Rudyard Kipling

Ellis, Steve Ida Scott's manager and lover
Another Country (1962) James Baldwin

Ellison, John manufacturer, partner to
John Manning*
Cousin Phillis (1864) Mrs Gaskell

Elmham, Bishop of
Mrs Yeld his wife
The Way We Live Now (1875) Anthony
Trollope

Elmslie, Mrs lived with the Monktons* on
strange terms
Ada her daughter, cc
cc 'Mad Monkton'
The Queen of Hearts (1859) Wilkie Collins

Elmwood, Lord see **Dorriforth, Father**

Eloi, The frail, exquisite inhabitants of the
upper world
The Time Machine (1895) H. G. Wells

Eloy (hist.) bandit, the night before whose
execution is here celebrated in Proustian*
style
Eloy (1960) Carlos Droguett

Elphinstone, Mr and Mrs
The War of the Worlds (1898) H. G.
Wells

Else, Fräulein cc, young girl invited to save
her father, an embezzler, by exposing
herself before von Dorsay* (at the request of her family); she rather kills
herself; in short narrative cast in form of
series of interior monologues*
her elderly aunt
Fräulein Else (1926) Arthur Schnitzler

Elshender see **Black Dwarf**

Elsing, Mrs
Hugh; Fanny her children, the latter m.
Tommy Wellburn*
Gone With the Wind (1936) Margaret
Mitchell

Elsinore Eva Trout's* room-mate at

school
Eva Trout (1969) Elizabeth Bowen

Elsmere, Robert young cc of bestselling
novel very influential in its time; loses his
faith; gives up family living and sets up
New Brotherhood of Christ in East End,
and dies of exhaustion
Catherine his wife, *née* Leyburn, who
does not understand his doubts
his parents
Robert Elsmere (1888) Mrs Humphrey
Ward

Elstir painter
A la recherche du temps perdu (*In Search
of Lost Time*) (1913–27) Marcel Proust

Elver
Grace his sister
These Barren Leaves (1925) Aldous
Huxley

Elvira Pizarro's* lover
Pizarro play (1799) Richard Brinsley
Sheridan

Elwood, Charles cc converted to Unitarianism as the (transcendentalist, radical,
anti-spiritualist) American author had
been (but he later became a Roman
Catholic)
Charles Elwood, or The Infidel Converted (1840) Orestes Brownson

Ely, Bishop of
King Henry V play (1623) William
Shakespeare

Ely, Revd of Milby
ss 'The Sad Fortunes of the Rev. Amos
Barton'
Scenes of Clerical Life (1857) George
Eliot (rn Mary Anne, later Marian,
Evans)

Em stepdaughter of Tant Sannie*
The Story of an African Farm (1883)
Olive Schreiner

Emanuel, Paul Carl David cc; **Mme
Beck's** cousin, visiting teacher at her
school
Josef his pianist brother
Villette (1853) Charlotte Brontë

Emelia sister to Theseus*; loved by the two
noble kinsmen, Palamon* and Arcite*
The Two Noble Kinsmen play (1634)
William Shakespeare and John Fletcher
(?with Francis Beaumont)

Emerson, George m. Lucy Honeychurch*
A Room With a View (1908) E. M.

Forster

Emerson, Jean m. Frank Gervais*
A Lamp for Nightfall (1952) Erskine Caldwell

Emery attorney
Manhattan Transfer (1925) John Dos Passos

Emery, Enoch zoo attendant; false prophet
Wise Blood (1952) Flannery O'Connor

Emilia Mrs Orange's* baby, with eight teeth
A Holiday Romance (1868) Charles Dickens

Emilia wife to Iago*
Othello play (1623) William Shakespeare

Emilius, 'The Revd' Jewish adventurer and blackmailer; 'greasy' but 'with something of poetry about him', m. Lady Eustace*
The Eustace Diamonds (1873) Anthony Trollope

Emily maidservant to Mr Asprey*
ss 'The House'
The Wind Blows Over (1936) Walter de la Mare

Emmanuel, Don
Inez his daughter, m. Frederick Powy*
Charles O'Malley (1841) Charles Lever

Emmeline dreamer
ss 'What Dreams May Come'
The Wind Blows Over (1936) Walter de la Mare

Emmeline quadroon sold to Legree* along with Uncle Tom*
Uncle Tom's Cabin (1851) Harriet Beecher Stowe

Emmersen English engineer and settler
The Settlers in Canada (1844) Captain Marryat

Emmett, Miss Catherine Faber's* guardian
M.F. (1971) Anthony Burgess (rn John Burgess Wilson)

Emmy, Aunt
Lolly Willowes (1926) Sylvia Townsend Warner

Emory, Julian B., Dr American doctor
ss 'My Sunday at Home'
The Day's Work (1898) Rudyard Kipling

Emulo a foolish gallant visiting Italy
The Pleasant Commedye of Patient Grissill play (1603) Thomas Dekker

Endal, Joan cc Catalan realist novel
Joan Endal (1909) Josep Folch i Torres

Endell, Martha unfortunate who emigrated with Peggotty* and m. a farm labourer
David Copperfield (1850) Charles Dickens

Enderby, F. X. cc, poet, lapsed Catholic
Inside Mr Enderby† (1963) Anthony Burgess (rn John Burgess Wilson)

Enderby, Maud virtuous woman loved by Osmund Waymark*
The Unclassed (1882) George Gissing

Endorfield, Elizabeth 'deep person', witch
Under the Greenwood Tree (1872) Thomas Hardy

Enfield, Richard kinsman and friend to Utterson*
Dr Jekyll and Mr Hyde (1886) Robert Louis Stevenson

Engelbrektsson, Engelbrecht folk hero, cc hist. play, 15th-century temporary liberator of Sweden from unjust union with Norway and Denmark
his wife and children
Engelbert play (1901) August Strindberg

Engeli, Cid Hamet ben Arab author of the story of *Don Quixote*
Don Quixote de la Mancha (1605–15) Miguel de Cervantes

Engelred one of the leaders of the Foresters, who fought against Rufus*
Bertha his daughter
Count Robert of Paris (1832) Walter Scott

Engine a broker
The Devil is an Ass play (1616) Ben Jonson

English, Julian cc, garage proprietor in Gibbsville
Caroline Walker English his wife
Dr William Dilworth English his father
Appointment in Samarra (1934) John O'Hara

Ennis, Richard (Ennis = Aeneas), cc, a sergeant in the Education Corps on Gibraltar (as was his creator)
A Vision of Battlements (1965) Anthony Burgess (rn John Burgess Wilson)

Enobarbus friend to Antony* who defects to Octavius Caesar*
Antony and Cleopatra play (1623) William Shakespeare

Entwhistle, Trevor, Revd headmaster of Harchester College
Meet Mr Mulliner (1927) P. G. Wodehouse

Envy; Superstition; Pickthank witnesses against Christian* and Faithful*
The Pilgrim's Progress (1678–84) John Bunyan

Ephrain Yahudi
ss 'Jews in Shushan'
Life's Handicap (1891) Rudyard Kipling

Epicene wife to Morose*
Epicene play (1609) Ben Jonson

Eppenwelzen-Sarkeld, Princess Ottilia, W. F. H. m. Prince Hermann*
The Margrave and Margravine her parents
Prince Otto her cousin
The Adventures of Harry Richmond (1871) George Meredith

Eppie servant to Revd Josiah Cargill*
St Ronan's Well (1824) Walter Scott

Erceldoun, Thomas of ('The Rhymer')
Castle Dangerous (1832) Walter Scott

Erich Elizabeth's* wealthy suitor and husband in German novella describing unhappy love and marriage
Immensée (1850, rev. 1851) Theodore Storm

Ericson, George E., Lieutenant-Commander Captain of the *Compass Rose*
Grace his wife
John their son
The Cruel Sea (1951) Nicholas Monsarrat

Erif Der the Spring Queen
Tarrik the Corn King, her husband
Berris Der her brother
The Corn King and The Spring Queen (1931) Naomi Mitchison

Erl, the Lord of
Alveric his son
The King of Elfland's Daughter (1924) Lord Dunsany

Erle, Barrington nephew to William Mildmay*
Phineas Finn† (1869) Anthony Trollope

Erle, Mary cc 'new woman' novel now claimed, by a reliable critic, to be the 'greatest unread novel' of its time; magazine editor and self-emancipated woman
James her brother

The Story of a Modern Woman (1894) Ella Hepworth Dixon

Erlton, Major cc of well-informed novel set in India at the time of the Mutiny
Kate his wife
On the Face of the Waters (1896) Flora Annie Steel

Erlynne, Margaret, Mrs mother of Lady Windermere*
Lady Windermere's Fan play (1892) Oscar Wilde

Erme, Gwendolyn m. (1) Corvick*, (2) Drayton Deane*
ss 'The Figure in the Carpet'
Embarrassments (1896) Henry James

Erring, Jo friend to Ned Westlock; younger brother of latter's mother; m. Mateel Shepherd*
The Story of a Country Town (1883) E. W. Howe

Errol, Cedric really Little Lord Fauntleroy*
Errol, the Hon. Mrs ('Dearest') his mother
Little Lord Fauntleroy (1886) Frances Hodgson Burnett

Erskine servant
Watt (1953) Samuel Beckett

Erskine, John young laird
The Ladies Lindores† (1883) Mrs Margaret Oliphant

Escalus Prince of Verona
Romeo and Juliet play (1623) William Shakespeare

Escanes a lord of Tyre
Pericles play (1609) William Shakespeare

Esclairmonde wife to Sir Huon*
ss 'Weland's Sword'†
Puck of Pook's Hill† (1906) Rudyard Kipling

Escott, Kenneth m. Verona Babbitt*
Babbitt (1923) Sinclair Lewis

Esdale friend to Adam Hartley*
The Surgeon's Daughter (1827) Walter Scott

Esdras philosophizing old Jew
Garth violinist; **Miriamne** his children
Winterset play (1935) Maxwell Anderson

Eshton, Mr magistrate
his well-preserved wife
Amy; Louisa two of her three daughters
Jane Eyre (1847) Charlotte Brontë

Eskdale, Lord
Coningsby (1844) Benjamin Disraeli

Eskelund, Julia sister to Cassandra Corbett*, novelist
her Norwegian husband
The Game (1967) A. S. Byatt

Esmond, Harry, Colonel cc, believed illegitimate but rightfully Viscount Castlewood*, m. Isabel*, widow of Lord Castlewood
his daughter and grandsons
Beatrix his second cousin, m. (1) Bishop Tusher*, (2) Baron Bernstein*
Lady Maria sister of the Earl of Castlewood, aged beauty, m. Geohegen Hagen*
Henry Esmond (1852); *The Virginians* (1857–9) W. M. Thackeray

Espinel, Thérèse mistress to Henry Maitland*, i.e. portrait of Gabrielle Fleury
her mother
The Private Life of Henry Maitland (1912) Morley Roberts

Essex, Earl of Chief Justice
King John play (1623) William Shakespeare

Essie illegitimate daughter to Peter Dudgeon, who was hanged as a rebel
The Devil's Disciple play (1899) George Bernard Shaw

Esteban foundling, twin brother to Manuel*
The Bridge of San Luis Rey (1927) Thornton Wilder

Estee, Claude successful screen writer
The Day of the Locust (1939) Nathanael West (rn Nathan Weinstein)

Estella daughter to Magwitch*, adopted by Mrs Havisham*, m. Bentley Drummle*
Great Expectations (1861) Charles Dickens

Estivet, d' Canon of Bayeux
Saint Joan play (1924) George Bernard Shaw

Estrella, Trock dying gangster cc popular verse play
Winterset play (1935) Maxwell Anderson

Estrild wife to Humber*
Locrine play (1595) 'W.S.' (?George Peele; ?Robert Green)

Etches, Harold 'wealthiest manufacturer of his years'
The Card (1911) Arnold Bennett

Ethelwyn ('Wyn') m. Davy Morgan*
How Green Was My Valley (1939) Richard Llewellyn

Etherington, Francis, Fifth Earl of m.
(1) Countess de Martigny* (in secret)
(2) Ann Bulmer*
Francis Tyrrel his son by his first wife
Valentine Bulmer Tyrrel his son by Ann, later Sixth Earl
St Ronan's Well (1824) Walter Scott

Ethiopian, The ('Sambo')
ss 'How the Leopard got his Spots'
Just So Stories (1902) Rudyard Kipling

Eubulus companion to Hermogenes*
Marriage à la Mode play (1673) John Dryden

Eudena mate to Ugh-Lomi*
ss 'A Story of the Stone Age'
Tales of Space and Time (1899) H. G. Wells

Eudoxia wife to Valentinian*
Valentinian play (1647) John Fletcher

Eugene, Charles Adolphe, M.
Jorrocks's Jaunts and Jollities (1838) R. S. Surtees

Euphranea daughter to Crotolon*, maid of honour
The Broken Heart play (1633) John Ford

Euphrasia daughter of Dion* disguised as a page, **Bellario**
Philaster play (1611) Francis Beaumont and John Fletcher

Euphues Athenian in romance whose affected, intricate, finicky style was both influential and much satirized
Euphues (1578–80) John Lyly

Eurgain, Miss piano teacher
Black Venus (1944) Rhys Davies

Eusabio Navajo Indian
Death Comes for the Archbishop (1927) Willa Cather

Eustace, Ethne m. Harry Feversham* after he has redeemed all the white feathers
The Four Feathers (1902) A. E. W. Mason

Eustace, Father formerly known as **William Allan**, sub-prior to St Mary's, Kennaquhair
The Monastery; *The Abbot* (1820) Walter Scott

Eustace, Lady (Elizabeth) *née* Greystock*

m. (2) Emilius*
Sir Florian her dead first husband
John, MP his brother
The Bishop of Bobsborough his uncle
The Eustace Diamonds (1873) Anthony Trollope
Eva servant who flirts with Ricketts*
The Pilgrim Hawk (1940) Glenway Westcott
Eva, Sister
ss 'The Record of Badalia Herodsfoot'
Many Inventions (1893) Rudyard Kipling
Evadne sister of Melantius* and Diphilus*
The Maid's Tragedy play (1611) Francis Beaumont and John Fletcher
Evan Dhu of Lochiel Highland chief
The Legend of Montrose (1819) Walter Scott
Evandale, Lord (William Maxwell) young and gallant fighter
Old Mortality (1816) Walter Scott
Evans humane warder
It Is Never Too Late To Mend (1856) Charles Reade
Evans the Death
Under Milk Wood play (1954) Dylan Thomas
Evans, Amelia, Miss tough owner of a store and still producing the best whiskey in the (Georgia) area; m. for ten days to Marvin Macy*, but refused to sleep with him and threw him out of the house
The Ballad of the Sad Café (1951) Carson McCullers
Evans, Franklin reformed drunkard in conventional temperance tract written with aid of liquor and later described by its author as 'damned rot'
Franklin Evans, or *The Inebriate* (1842) Walt Whitman
Evans, Hugh, Sir Welsh parson
The Merry Wives of Windsor play (1623) William Shakespeare
Evans, Iestyn m. Angharad Morgan*
Christmas his father
Blodwen his sister
How Green Was My Valley (1939) Richard Llewellyn
Evans, Janice see **Addams, F. Jasmine**
Evans, Jemima heroine of the scene in fight between Samuel Wilkins* and another
Sketches by Boz (1836) Charles Dickens

Evans, Marged m. Gwilym Morgan*
Sion her father
How Green Was My Valley (1939) Richard Llewellyn
Evans, Owen Welsh antiquary
A Glastonbury Romance (1932) John Cowper Powys
Evans, Sam silly decent boy who adores and m. Nina Leeds*; becomes successful businessman
Strange Interlude play (1927) Eugene O'Neill
Evans, Stephen, Sir
Colonel Jack (1722) Daniel Defoe
Evelina cc known as Miss Anville, actually daughter of Sir John Belmont*; m. Lord Orville*
Evelina (1778) Fanny Burney
Evelyn, Mr transcendentalist, m. Margaret* in American novel by Fourierist unitarian minister
Margaret (1845, rev. 1851) Sylvester Judd
Evenson, John a 'very morose and discontented' boarder at Mrs Tibbs*, who went to many public meetings in order to find fault with whatever was proposed
Sketches by Boz† (1836) Charles Dickens
Everard, Markham distinguished soldier
Woodstock (1826) Walter Scott
Everdene, Bathsheba cc, m. (1) Sergeant Troy, (2) Gabriel Oak*
Levi her father
Farmer Jones her uncle
Far From the Madding Crowd (1874) Thomas Hardy
Everett informer under Titus Oates*
Peveril of the Peak (1822) Walter Scott
Everhard, Ernest m. Avis Cunningham*
The Iron Heel (1908) Jack London
Everill champion of Meercraft*
The Devil is an Ass play (1616) Ben Jonson
Evers, Blanche 'pretty and prattling', m. Gordon Wright*
Confidence (1880) Henry James
Evesham eminent politician
The New Machiavelli† (1912) H. G. Wells
Evie daughter to Emily Frampton* by her first husband
Non-Combatants and Others (1916) Rose Macaulay

Eviot page to Sir John Ramorny*
The Fair Maid of Perth (1828) Walter Scott
Ewart 'monumental artist'
Millie his mistress
Tono Bungay (1909) H. G. Wells
Ewart, Anthony ('**Nanty**') captain of the *Jumping Jenny*
Redgauntlet (1824) Walter Scott
Exeter, Duke of uncle to the King
King Henry V play (1623) William Shakespeare
Exeter, Duke of
King Henry VI plays (1623) William Shakespeare
Exmoor, Duke of
ss 'The Purple Wig'

The Wisdom of Father Brown (1914) G. K. Chesterton
Eynsford-Hill, Freddy
his mother and sister
Pygmalion play (1914) George Bernard Shaw
Eyre, Jane cc, narrator, m. Edward Rochester*
John her uncle, wine merchant
Jane Eyre (1847) Charlotte Brontë
Eyre, Simon shoemaker cc, eventually Lord Mayor of London
Margery his wife; in major London comedy
The Shoemaker's Holiday (1600) Thomas Dekker

F

Faa, Gabriel see **Baillie, Gabriel**

Fabell, Peter 'The Merry Devil': magician who makes a compact with the devil
The Merry Devil of Edmonton play (1608) ?Thomas Dekker

Faber, Martin criminal cc, m. Constance Claiborne*, of early American quasi-psychological novel by Charleston author who was Cooper's rival ('The Cooper of the South') but who lost his popularity after the Civil War because he had been a Secessionist
Martin Faber (1833, rev. as *Martin Faber, the Story of a Criminal*, 1837) William Gilmore Simms

Faber, Miles college throw-out, heir to a fortune
Catherine his sister
Llew his double
M.F. (1971) Anthony Burgess (rn John Burgess Wilson)

Faber, Mrs neighbour to Britling*; food hoarder
Mr Britling Sees It Through (1916) H. G. Wells

Fabian servant to Olivia*
Twelfth Night play (1623) William Shakespeare

Face-maker, the fat man who impersonates characters at a Flemish fair
The Uncommercial Traveller (1860–8) Charles Dickens

Fadden, Fergus Irish novelist scriptwriting in Hollywood
Dr and Mrs Fadden his dead parents who reappear
Fergus (1971) Brian Moore

Fag servant to Captain Absolute*
The Rivals play (1775) Richard Brinsley Sheridan

Fagan, Augustus schoolmaster
Flossie; Diana ('Dingy') his daughters
Decline and Fall (1928) Evelyn Waugh

Faggus, Tom highwayman, cousin to John Ridd*
Lorna Doone (1869) R. D. Blackmore

Fagin thief, fence, villain
Oliver Twist (1838) Charles Dickens

Fagoni, Baron overseer of diamond mine
Martin Rattler (1858) R. M. Ballantyne

Failing, Mrs Rickie Elliot's* aunt
The Longest Journey (1907) E. M. Forster

Fainall
his wife, daughter to Lady Wishfort*
The Way of the World play (1700) William Congreve

Fainall, Colonel impersonates Simon Pure*
A Bold Stroke for a Wife comedy (1718) Susannah Centlivre

Fairbrother Effie Dean's* counsel
Heart of Midlothian (1818) Walter Scott

Fairbrother, Coral cc, village beauty turned scapegoat, persecuted, finally strangled when pursued by mob raised by Stella Oates*
Mr and Mrs Fairbrother her nasty and selfish grandparents
Paula; Ralph; Stephen her three children by different fathers
Old Crow (1967) Shena Mackay

Fairchild, Dabney beautiful girl about to be m. to Troy Flavin*
Battle; Ellen her parents
George her uncle, cc
Robbie George's wife, 'beneath' him socially, former shop-girl; leaves him but then rejoins him
Delta Wedding (1946) Eudora Welty

Fairchild, Dawson caricature of Sherwood Anderson* in slight work
Mosquitoes (1927) William Faulkner

Fairchild, Mr
his wife
Henry; Lucy; Emily their three children; pious series upon which most middle-class Victorians were brought up
The History of the Fairchild Family (1818–47) Martha Mary Sherwood

Fairchild, Seth newspaperman cc
Annie *née* Warren, his wife
Albert his corrupt politician brother
Isabel Albert's wife, who amuses herself
with 'young simpletons just to kill time'
John Seth's other brother
Seth's Brother's Wife (1887) Harold
Frederic
Fairfax censorious young gentleman
Sketches of Young Gentlemen (1838)
Charles Dickens
Fairfax, Alice widow of former Vicar of
Hay, keeps house for Mr Rochester*,
who pensions her off after his attempted
bigamy
Jane Eyre (1847) Charlotte Brontë
Fairfax, Colonel m. Elsie Maynard*
The Yeomen of the Guard opera (1888)
W. S. Gilbert and Arthur Sullivan
Fairfax, Gwendolen, the Hon. daughter of
Lady Bracknell*, m. Jack Worthing*
The Importance of Being Earnest play
(1895) Oscar Wilde
Fairfax, Jane, Mrs *née* Bates, youngest
daughter of Revd and Mrs Bates* of
Highbury, m. Lieutenant Fairfax who is
killed in action, she dying soon after-
wards
Jane their daughter, cc, taken into Col-
onel Campbell's* home, m. Frank
Churchill*
Emma (1816) Jane Austen
Fairfield, Leonard celebrated poet and
author
My Novel, or Varieties in English Life
(1850–3) Edward Bulwer Lytton
Fairfield, Mrs Linda Burnell's* mother
Beryl her daughter
ss 'Prelude'
Prelude (1918) Katherine Mansfield (rn
Katherine Mansfield Beauchamp)
Fairford, Alan friend to Darsie Latimer*
Saunders his father
Redgauntlet (1824) Walter Scott
Fairford, Charles second cousin to Flora
Poste*, whom he m.
Helen his mother
Cold Comfort Farm (1932) Stella
Gibbons
Fairford, Henley m. Clare Marvell*
The Custom of the Country (1913) Edith
Wharton
Fairies, Queen of the m. Private Willis*

Iolanthe opera (1882) W. S. Gilbert and
Arthur Sullivan
Fairlegh, Frank cc popular episodic novel,
illustrated by Cruikshank, set in Cam-
bridge; nearer to Hook* than Dickens*;
m. Clara Saville
Fanny his sister, m. Harry Oaklands
Frank Fairlegh (1850) Francis Smedley
Fairlie, Frederick of Limmeredge House,
part narrator
Laura his niece
Marion (Halcombe) his foster-daughter
Eleanor m. Count Fosco*; **Philip** his sister
and brother
The Woman in White (1860) Wilkie
Collins
Fairlight, Bruce
The Vortex play (1924) Noël Coward
Fairscribe solicitor
James his son
The Surgeon's Daughter (1827) Walter
Scott
Fairservice, Andrew gardener at Osbaldi-
stone Hall
Rob Roy (1818) Walter Scott
Fairway, Timothy furze cutter
The Return of the Native (1878) Thomas
Hardy
Fairweather Revd Dr
Elsie Venner (1861) Oliver Wendell
Holmes
Faith, Daddy who redeems the Loftis'*
servants
Lie Down in Darkness (1951) William
Styron
Faithful Christian's* fellow pilgrim, mar-
tyred at Vanity Fair
The Pilgrim's Progress (1678–84) John
Bunyan
**Faizanne, Henry Augustus Ramsay ('The
Worm')** subaltern who turns the tables
on a superior by acting the part of a
supposed deserted wife
ss 'His Wedded Wife'
Plain Tales from the Hills (1888) Rud-
yard Kipling
Fakrash-el-Aamash bad-tempered genie
who tries to help Ventimore* with his
architecture, with comic results
The Brass Bottle (1900) F. Anstey (rn
Thomas Anstey Guthrie)
Fakredeen, Shehaab dissembling Emir of
Canobia, m. Queen Astarte*

Tancred (1847) Benjamin Disraeli

Falconer Laird of Balmawhopple
Cornet his brother
Waverley (1814) Walter Scott

Falconer, Richard, Colonel betrayer of Jessie Gilbert*, whose brothers, the 'Hawks', seek revenge; in novel of the American Revolution by Whig novelist
Henry his nephew
The Hawks of Hawk Hollow (1835) Robert Montgomery Bird

Falconer, Sharon evangelist
Elmer Gantry (1927) Sinclair Lewis

Falder, William solicitor's clerk who commits forgery, cc of drama which caused Winston Churchill (as Home Secretary) to institute reforms
Justice play (1910) John Galsworthy

Falk Scandinavian pilot
ss 'Falk'
Typhoon (1903) Joseph Conrad (rn Josef Teodor Konrad Korzeniowski)

Falkiner, Frederick, Sir Recorder of Dublin
Ulysses (1922) James Joyce

Falkland cc, mysterious figure who persecutes Caleb Williams* but is finally obliged to confess to murder
Things as They Are, or *The Adventures of Caleb Williams* (1794) William Godwin
The Iron Chest dramatization (1796) George Colman the Younger

Falkland, Herbert 'big squatter'
Fanny his daughter
Robbery Under Arms: A Story of Life and Adventure in the Bush and in the Goldfields of Australia (1888, rev. 1889) Rolf Boldrewood (rn Thomas Alexander Browne)

Fall ('Conjuror') astrologer, weather prophet
The Mayor of Casterbridge (1886); *Tess of the D'Urbervilles* (1891) Thomas Hardy

Fallace Deliro's* wife, a proud mincing peat, and as perverse as he (Deliro) is officious
Every Man Out of His Humour play (1599) Ben Jonson

Fallic theatrical agent
Manhattan Transfer (1925) John Dos Passos

Fallon, Julia 'intuitive character', servant to Catherine Standish*

The Living and the Dead (1941) Patrick White

Falloux atheist schoolmaster
ss 'The Miracle of St Jubanus'
Limits and Renewals (1932) Rudyard Kipling

Falstaff, John, Sir
King Henry IV; The Merry Wives of Windsor; King Henry V (mentioned) plays (1623) William Shakespeare
Falstaff (1976) Robert Nye

Falx Labour leader, ex-engine driver
These Barren Leaves (1925) Aldous Huxley

Famine
Pierce Penilesse his Supplication to the Devil (1592) Thomas Nashe

Famish, Robert ensign, later promoted; a raffish and detestable snob
The Book of Snobs† (1847) W. M. Thackeray

Fancy, Patient, Sir
Sir Patient Fancy play (1678) Mrs Aphra Behn

Fancyful, Lady
The Provok'd Wife play (1697) John Vanbrugh

Fane 'raw-hand' war correspondent
ss 'Two or Three Witnesses'
Fiery Particles (1923) C. E. Montague

Fane clerk who coughs
Mrs Dukes' Million (1977) Wyndham Lewis

Fane, Michael
Stella, his sister; illegitimate children of wealthy parents
Sinister Street (1913); *Plashers Mead* (1917); *Sylvia Scarlett* (1918); *Sylvia and Michael* (1919) Compton Mackenzie

Fane, Paul painter cc of novel by American man of letters and editor, 'something between a remembrance of Count D'Orsay and an anticipation of Oscar Wilde' (Oliver Wendell Holmes*)
Paul Fane (1857) Nathaniel Parker Willis

Fane-Herbert, Hugh midshipman
Margaret his sister, loved by John Lynwood*
The Gunroom (1919) Charles Morgan

Fang overbearing magistrate who sentenced Oliver Twist*
Oliver Twist (1838) Charles Dickens

Fanny

Fanny's First Play play (1905) George
Bernard Shaw
Fanny maid to Lady Glyde*
The Woman in White (1860) Wilkie
Collins
Fanny sweetheart of Joseph Andrews*
Joseph Andrews (1742) Henry Fielding
Fansharpe, Miss Teresa Bramley's* first
employer
Before the Bombardment (1926) Osbert
Sitwell
Fanshaw ambisexual art instructor
Streets of Night (1923) John Dos Passos
Fanshawe, Ginevra pretty and vain, lives
'by proxy'; m. Colonel Alfred De
Hamal*
Captain Fanshawe her father, an officer
on half-pay
Augusta her sister, m. Mr Davies*
Villette (1853) Charlotte Brontë
Faraday, Alice Lord Marshmoreton's*
secretary, m. Reggie Byng*
A Damsel in Distress (1919) P. G. Wode-
house
Farag 'the fatherless', native kennel-boy to
the Gihon Hunt
ss 'Little Foxes'
Actions and Reactions (1909) Rudyard
Kipling
Faramond, Sophie
Selwyn her husband, archeologist
Caroline Traherne Selwyn's daughter
The Gates of Summer play (1956) John
Whiting
Farber, Jules character resembling the
comedian Lenny Bruce; has 'a terminal
sense of aggravation'
Marlene his estranged wife, undergoing
Christ Therapy
Mitchell his autistic son
You Could Live If They Let You (1974)
Wallace Markfield
Fardarougha Irish usurer torn between
love of money and of his son
Fardarougha, The Miser (1839) William
Carleton
Farebrother, Camden, Revd Vicar of St
Botolph's; plays cards for money; good
friend to Lydgate*
his wife
his mother
Middlemarch (1871–2) George Eliot (rn
Mary Anne, later Marian, Evans)

Farfrae, Donald cold and canny Scot, cc,
m. (1) Lucretta le Sueur* (2) Elizabeth
Jane Henchard*
The Mayor of Casterbridge (1886)
Thomas Hardy
Fargo, Professor odious charlatan and
mesmerist
ss 'Professor Fargo' (1874) Henry James
Fargus, Mrs neighbour to Mildred
Lawson, much blamed for influencing
her in the direction of women's
emancipation
her husband, asthma sufferer
ss 'Mildred Lawson'
Celibates (1895) George Moore
Farintosh, Marquess of wealthy brainless
dandy, once engaged to Ethel Newcome*
The Newcomes† (1853–5) W. M.
Thackeray
Farish, Gertrude cousin to Lawrence
Selden*
The House of Mirth (1905) Edith
Wharton
Farley, Mrs
Nathan her husband
Rollo their son, seduces Bertha*
Felix his son by Bertha
Lummox (1923) Fanny Hurst
Farll, Priam attends own funeral
Buried Alive (1908) Arnold Bennett
Farneze suitor to Julia*
*The Pleasant Commedye of Patient
Grissill* play (1603) Thomas Dekker
Farnham, Arthur well-bred hero of anti-
union novel that prompted replies,
chiefly *The Money-Makers**
The Bread-Winners (1884) John Hay
Farquar, Lois cc
The Last September (1929) Elizabeth
Bowen
Farquhar secondary squire, Shepperton
his wife
Arabella; Julia their daughters
ss 'The Sad Fortunes of the Rev. Amos
Barton'
Scenes of Clerical Life (1857) George
Eliot (rn Mary Anne, later Marian,
Evans)
Farquhar, Peyton confederate soldier
ss 'An Occurrence at Owl Creek Bridge'
In the Midst of Life (1898) Ambrose
Bierce
Farr, Joseph head of technical staff,

Woldingstanton
The Undying Fire (1919) H. G. Wells

Farrago, John, Captain cc, 'American Quixote' of influential satire on contemporary American life; mainly a constructive attack on failings of democracy – but 'What is the main characteristic of history?', '*Fiction*', 'Of novels?', '*Truth*'.
Modern Chivalry (1792–1805, rev. 1815, 1819)
(*A Brackenridge Reader*, edited Daniel Marder, 1970) Hugh Henry Brackenridge

Farragut, Ezekial in prison for the murder of his elder brother, Eben; escapes by pretending to be the corpse of his cellmate
Falconer (1977) John Cheever

Farran, William member of workers' deputation
Grace his wife
Shirley (1849) Charlotte Brontë

Farrand, Mim
Jim her son
Hermione (1981) H. D. (rn Hilda Doolittle)

Farrant, Anthony drifter in Stockholm
Kate his twin sister
England Made Me (1935) Graham Greene

Farrant, George
his wife
Waste play (1907) Harley Granville Barker

Farrel, Jimmy farmer
The Playboy of the Western World play (1907) John Millington Synge

Farrell, Patsy
John Bull's Other Island play (1904) George Bernard Shaw

Farrell, Peter chief accountant, Considines
Without My Cloak (1931) Kate O'Brien

Farrell, Tom farmer, owner of illicit still
ss 'Another Temple Gone'
Fiery Particles (1923) C. E. Montague

Farren, Molly m. Godfrey Cass*
Silas Marner (1861) George Eliot (rn Mary Anne, later Marian, Evans)

Farrinder, Mrs
The Bostonians (1886) Henry James

Fashion, Tom brother to Lord Foppington*
A Trip to Scarborough play (1777) Richard Brinsley Sheridan

Fashion, Young brother to Lord Foppington*
The Relapse, or *Virtue in Danger* play (1697) John Vanbrugh

Fashioner the tailor of the times
The Staple of News play (1631) Ben Jonson

Fashions, Novelty, Sir cc
Love's Last Shift play (1696) Colley Cibber

Fastidious Brisk a neat, spruce, affecting courtier; swears tersely, and with variety
Every Man Out of His Humour play (1599) Ben Jonson

Fat Boy, The see Joe

Fat Man 600lb cc who lives in an abandoned phosphorus mine, in first novel by American satirist
The Gospel Singer (1968) Harry Crews

Fathers, Sam
'The Bear'
Go Down Moses (1942) William Faulkner

Fatsolfe, John, Sir
King Henry VI plays (1623) William Shakespeare

Faugh, Mary an old woman
The Dutch Courtesan play (1605) John Marston

Faulconbridge, Robert
Philip bastard son of Richard I
Lady Faulconbridge their mother
King John play ((1623) William Shakespeare

Faulkland friend to Captain Absolute*
The Rivals play (1775) Richard Brinsley Sheridan

Fauntleroy, Lord see Erroll

Fauntley, Robert schoolmaster, colleague of Inigo Jollifant*
The Good Companions (1929) J. B. Priestley

Faust narrator, in 1833, as he completes 323rd year, m. Bertha*
ss 'The Mortal Immortal'
Tales and Stories (1891) Mary Shelley

Faustus (or **Faust, Dr**) (hist. but also legd.)
Dr Faustus play (1604) Christopher Marlowe
Faust play (1808–32) Wilhelm Goethe
Faust (1978) Robert Nye

Faux, David confectioner, thief (as

Edward Feely)
Jonathan his father
his mother
Jonathan Jr. his brother
Jacob his idiot brother who exposes him
ss 'Brother Jacob' (1864)
with *Silas Marner* in her *Works* (1878)
George Eliot (rn Mary Anne, later Marian, Evans)
Favell, Jack cousin and lover of Rebecca de
Winter*
Rebecca (1938) Daphne du Maurier
Faversham, Claude barrister acquitted of
murder, assistant to Edmund Melrose*,
m. Lydia Penfold*
The Mating of Lydia (1913) Mrs
Humphry Ward
Fawcett, Mrs
Mildred her daughter
ss 'The Dove's Nest'
The Dove's Nest (1923) Katherine
Mansfield (rn Katherine Mansfield Beauchamp)
Fawcett, Mrs lover of Charles Eastwood*
The Virgin and the Gipsy (1930) D. H.
Lawrence
Fawkes, Abigail schoolgirl friend to
Eugene Schlumberger*
her mother
Dust Falls on Eugene Schlumberger
(1964) Shena Mackay
Fawley, Catherine about to become a nun
Dick her drunken, malicious brother
The Bell (1958) Iris Murdoch
Fawley, Jude cc, m. Arabella *née* Donn*
Drusilla his great aunt
'Little Father Time' their son
Jude the Obscure (1896) Thomas Hardy
Fawn, Frederic, Lord rich peer, one-time
fiancée of Lady Eustace*
Clara m. Hittaway*; **Amelia; Georgiana;
Lydia; Cecilia; Nina** his sisters
Lady Fawn their mother, 'a miracle of
Virtue, Benevolence and Persistency'
Phineas Finn† (1869) Anthony Trollope
Fawn, Jasper bitter portrait of the
millionaire Joseph Duveen, who made
Berenson rich – when Berenson asked the
author what he thought of his collection,
he replied: 'Simply Duveen'
Samson Unshorn (1909) Reginald
Turner
Fawnia cc

Pandosto play (1588) Robert Green
Fax, Mr Malthusian economist
Melincourt, or Sir Oran Haut-on (1817)
Thomas Love Peacock
Fay, Father priest
My Mortal Enemy (1926) Willa Cather
Fay, Felix Illinois daydreamer of poor
family whose life is traced from his
adolescence until his literary success
in two, once popular semi-autobiographical novels
Moon-Calf (1920); *The Briary Bush*
(1921) Floyd Dell
Feathernest, Mr caricature of Southey
Melincourt (1817) Thomas Love
Peacock
Featherstone, Peter of Stone Court,
wealthy, malicious and miserly
Joshua Rigg his bastard son
Solomon his rich and greedy brother
Jonah his poor brother
Jane his sister, widow of Waule
Middlemarch (1871–2) George Eliot (rn
Mary Anne, later Marian, Evans)
Fedallah crew member
Moby-Dick, or The Whale (1851) Herman Melville
Federigo Ghent's* double
Federigo, or The Power of Love (1954)
Howard Nemerov
Federman, Lillian married sister to Jules
Farber*
You Could Live If They Let You (1974)
Wallace Markfield
Feeble-Mind
The Pilgrim's Progress (1678–84) John
Bunyan
Feeder, B. A. Blimber's* assistant, 'a kind
of human barrel organ'
Revd Alfred his brother, who m. him to
Cornelia Blimber*
Dombey and Son (1848) Charles Dickens
Feely, Edward see **Faux, David**
Feely, Innocent, Father innocent and childlike priest
Adam of Dublin (1920); *Adam and
Caroline* (1921); *In London* (1922);
Married Life (1924) Conal O'Connell
O'Reardon (rn F. Norreys Connell)
Feenix, Lord youthful-looking old man
who shelters Edith Dombey*
Dombey and Son (1848) Charles Dickens
Fielding, George young English officer, cc

of historical novel set in Napoleonic times
A Little Less Than Gods (1928) Ford Madox Ford

Feinschreiber, Sam immigrant, m. Hennie Berger*, who deserts him for Axelrod*
Awake and Sing! play (1935) Clifford Odets

Feldman, Leo entrepreneur
A Bad Man (1967) Stanley Elkin

Felise, Henrietta Faulkner secretary and lover to Notterdam*: 'Nicolete de clair visage'
When the Wicked Man (1931) Ford Madox Ford

Felix the umbrella man, whose extra limb serves in winter to fend off the rain, and in summer acts as a parasol
The Umbrella Man (1971) Giles Gordon

Felix, Don cc
The Wonder: A Woman Keeps a Secret play (1714) Susannah Centlivre

Fell, Charles, M., Dr
Barbara his sister
A Glastonbury Romance (1932) John Cowper Powys

Fell, Gideon, Dr mannered fat detective modelled by the author on G. K. Chesterton*, in once widely read series of detective stories; onwards from
Hag's Nook (1933) John Dickson Carr

Fell, Matthew, Sir deputy sheriff
Sir Matthew his son
Sir Richard his grandson
ss 'The Ash Tree'
Ghost Stories of an Antiquary (1910) M. R. James

Fellamar, Lord
Tom Jones (1749) Henry Fielding

Fellmer, Albert m. Rosa Halborough*
his mother
ss 'A Tragedy of Two Ambitions'
Life's Little Ironies (1894) Thomas Hardy

Fellowes, J. P. Revd Mr
ss 'The Sad Fortunes of the Rev. Amos Barton'
Scenes of Clerical Life (1857) George Eliot (rn Mary Anne, later Marian, Evans)

Fellows, Beatrice niece to Alexander Burtenshaw*
A House and Its Head (1935) Ivy Comp-

ton-Burnett

Felton, Harold schoolmaster, colleague of Inigo Jollifant*
The Good Companions (1929) J. B. Priestley

Fenchel, Thea wife of a rich man has an affair with Augie March* while hunting iguana in Mexico, and plans to divorce her husband
The Adventures of Augie March (1953) Saul Bellow

Fenerator the usuring bee
The Parliament of Bees play (?1607) John Day

Fenichka peasant girl, mistress to Nicolai Kirsanov*, who eventually m. her
Mitya her child by Kirsanov*
Otsy i deti (Fathers and Sons) (1862) Ivan Turgenev

Fenn MP for West Orchards
Daniel Deronda (1876) George Eliot (rn Mary Anne, later Marian, Evans)

Fenn, Burchell 'luscious rogue'
St Ives (1897) Robert Louis Stevenson

Fenno, Chris artist; old lover of Kate Clephane who m. Anne Clephane*
The Mother's Recompense (1925) Edith Wharton

Fenton
The Merry Wives of Windsor play (1623) William Shakespeare

Fenton see **Clinton**

Fenton, George blackmailer, 'meant no especial harm to his fellow-men save insofar as he meant uncompromising benefit to himself'; in the first novel of this author
Watch and Ward (1872) Henry James

Fenton, Mr educator and philanthropist in Rousseauist* novel
The Fool of Quality, or *The History of Henry Earl of Moreland* (1766–70) Henry Brooke

Fenwick lighthouse keeper
ss 'The Disturber of Traffic'
Many Inventions (1893) Rudyard Kipling

Fenwick, Boy commits suicide because he has syphilis; cc of immensely successful 'daring novel' of the 1920s
Iris his wife, cc
The Green Hat (1924) Michael Arlen (originally Dikrin Kuyumjian)

Fenwick, Dr narrator; author of pamphlet against Dr Lloyd's* pretensions
A Strange Story (1862, rev. 1863) Edward Bulwer Lytton

Fenwick-Symes, Adam young writer
Vile Bodies (1930) Evelyn Waugh

Fenwicke (Captain Barstow) Jesuit
Peveril of the Peak (1822) Walter Scott

Ferdinand Duke of Urbin
The Maid of Honour play (1632) Philip Massinger

Ferdinand King of Navarre
Love's Labour's Lost (1623) William Shakespeare

Ferdinand narrator, whose surname is not vouchsafed, a doctor of medicine; thinks of sending his patients to the slaughterhouse to drink warm blood; often vomits – on one occasion on his widowed mother's calves – cc highly influential novel written to 'resensitize the language'
Auguste; Clémence his parents – his mother is sure that he will end on the gallows
Mort à credit (Death on the Instalment Plan) (1936); *Guignol's band* (1944) Louis-Ferdinand Céline (rn Louis-Ferdinand Destouches)

Ferdinand son of Alonso
The Tempest play (1623) William Shakespeare

Ferdinand, Count Fathom 'deliberately created monster from the purlieus of treachery and fraud'; not a count but the son of a camp follower of Marlborough's army; cc of late picaresque* novel; 'unmitigated scoundrel'
The Adventures of Ferdinand, Count Fathom (1753) Tobias Smollett

Ferdinand, Don
The Duenna play (1775) Richard Brinsley Sheridan

Ferentes a wanton courtier
Love's Sacrifice play (1633) John Ford

Ferguson, Helen nurse
A Farewell to Arms (1929) Ernest Hemingway

Ferguson, John kindly invalided old Protestant farmer
his wife
Andrew their son, who murders Witherow*
Hannah their daughter

Andrew his brother in America (unseen) who is late sending him a cheque that will secure him from dispossession by Witherow
John Ferguson play (1915) St John Ervine

Fermor, George, Lord uncle to Lord Henry Wotton*
The Picture of Dorian Gray (1891) Oscar Wilde

Fernandez, Margaret
Jimmy; Harry her brothers
High Wind in Jamaica (1929) Richard Hughes

Fernando favourite of Philippo Caraffa, the Duke of Pavia*
Love's Sacrifice play (1633) John Ford

Ferneze Governor of Malta
Lodowick his son
The Jew of Malta play (1633) Christopher Marlowe

Ferneze, Count
Lord Paulo Ferneze his son
Camillo his lost son, at court as Gasper*
The Case is Altered play (1609) Ben Jonson

Feroce bathing-machine operator
ss 'Our French Watering Place'
Reprinted Pieces (1858) Charles Dickens

Ferraby, Gordon sub-lieutenant, *Compass Rose*
Mavis his wife
Ursula their baby
The Cruel Sea (1951) Nicholas Monsarrat

Ferraby, William, Sir
Fanny By Gaslight (1940) Michael Sadleir

Ferrand, Bishop missionary
Death Comes for the Archbishop (1927) Willa Cather

Ferrar, Marjorie rival of Fleur Forsyte*
Lord Charles her father
The Silver Spoon (1926) John Galsworthy

Ferrar, Nicholas (hist.) leader of religious community at Little Gidding, in which this novel revived interest
John Inglesant (1881) J. H. Shorthouse

Ferrars, Edward clergyman, m. Elinor Dashwood*
Robert his brother, elopes with Lucy Steele*
their ill-natured mother, widow of a rich

man
Sense and Sensibility (1811) Jane Austen
Ferrars, Endymion sweet-tempered cc; finally is asked to form a government
Myra his twin
Pitt young politician, their father; kills himself when he realizes that he will not achieve cabinet rank; in novel characterized by James* to Howells* as 'contemptible' – 'Can the novel be a thing of virtue when [*Endymion*] can be written and read?'
Endymion (1880) Benjamin Disraeli
Ferrers, Lumley unscrupulous enemy of Maltravers* finally murdered by his own instrument, Cesarini*
Ernest Maltravers (1837); *Alice, or The Mysteries* (1838) Edward Bulwer Lytton
Ferret also called Stote and Vermin: Lovel's* servant
The New Inn, or The Light Heart play (1629) Ben Jonson
Ferret misanthropic charlatan
Bridget *née* Maple, his wife
Sir Launcelot Greaves (1762) Tobias Smollett
Ferrex brother to Porrex* and son to Gorboduc*
Gorboduc play (1562) Thomas Norton and Thomas Sackville
Ferris, Henry American consul and painter, in love with and eventually m. Florida Vervain*, but only when he can overcome his jealousy of Don Ippolito*
A Foregone Conclusion (1875) William Dean Howells
Ferroll, Paul ambiguously presented wealthy and able murderer of his vicious wife in early novel of sensation*
Paul Ferroll (1855) Mrs Caroline Archer Clive ['V']
Ferrybridge, Lord
his wife
Gretna his son, friend to Pendennis*
Pendennis (1848) W. M. Thackeray
Fersen, Axel companion and friend to Count Adolf Ribbing*
The King With Two Faces (1897) Mary Coleridge
Fesco servant to Cataplasma
The Atheist's Tragedy (1611) Cyril Tourneur
Feshnavat, Vizier father to Noorna*

The Shaving of Shagpat (1856) George Meredith
Feste clown
Twelfth Night play (1623) William Shakespeare
Fet, Betsy thief, Fagin's* accomplice
Oliver Twist (1838) Charles Dickens
Fettes drunken old Scots medical student
ss 'The Body Snatchers'
The Wrong Box (1889) Robert Louis Stevenson and Lloyd Osbourne
Fettley, Liz, Mrs
ss 'The Wish House'
Debits and Credits (1926) Rudyard Kipling
Feuillé, Enguerrand de la Seigneur de Bristetout
ss 'A Lodging for the Night'
New Arabian Nights (1882) Robert Louis Stevenson
Fever, Jesus old Negro pygmy
Other Voices, Other rooms (1948) Truman Capote
Feverel, Sir Austen tyrannical father who applies the woman-hating 'Great Shaddock Doctrine' to the education of his family
his wife, who runs off with Somers Denzil*
Richard his son, cc, who is brought disastrously through the puppy-love stage, the Blossoming Season and Magnetic Age so as to be free from the 'Apple Disease' (temptations of Eve), but who m. Bella Mount*, and leaves; he returns to Lucy Desborough* too late
Algernon; Hippias; Richard his brothers
The Ordeal of Richard Feverel: A History of Father and Son (1859, rev. 1878) George Meredith
Feversham, Harry cc who imagines himself a coward but proves, in regaining his honour and his girl, that he is not; m. Ethne Eustace
The Four Feathers (1902) A. E. W. Mason
Fez King of
Tamburlaine play (1587) Christopher Marlowe
Fezziwig Scrooge's* old master
his wife and the three Miss Fezziwigs
A Christmas Carol (1843) Charles Dickens

ffoulkes-Corbett, Dorothea, Mrs (Aunt Dot) Anglican missionary in Turkey
The Towers of Trebizond (1956) Rose Macaulay

Fiametta
The Gondoliers opera (1899) W. S. Gilbert and Arthur Sullivan

Fibbitson, Mrs almshouse inmate
David Copperfield (1850) Charles Dickens

Fiche confidential servant
Vanity Fair (1847–8) W. M. Thackeray

Fidelia Manly's* page, heiress in disguise
The Plain Dealer play (1677) William Wycherley

Fidenza, Gian Battista 'Nostromo', cc
Nostromo (1904) Joseph Conrad (rn Josef Teodor Konrad Korzeniowski)

Fielding, Cyril principal of Government College, m. Stella Moore*
A Passage to India (1924) E. M. Forster

Fielding, George farmer turned goldminer, m. Susan Merton*
Wilhelm his father
It Is Never Too Late to Mend (1856) Charles Reade

Fielding, May m. Edward Plummer*
The Cricket on the Hearth (1845) Charles Dickens

Fielding, Mrs rich widow whom Mervyn* finally marries
Arthur Mervyn, or Memoirs of the Year 1793 (1799–1800) Charles Brockden Brown

Fiercy, Fitzwhisker, the Hon. Captain swindler posing as military swaggerer
Pantomime of Life (1837) Charles Dickens

Fierro, Martín subject of immensely popular semi-epic poem of the gaucho life
El Gaucho Martín Fierro narrative poem (two parts, 1872, 1879) José Hernández

Fife, Ramsay militant atheist neighbour of Revd Hutchins Light*
May his bovine wife
Ada his daughter, loved by Reuben Light* and then sacrificed by him to his God, the dynamo
Dynamo play (1929) Eugene O'Neill

Fika-Caka the Duke of Newcastle, Cuboy, first minister of Japan (i.e. England), in whose perineum the Atom is lodged at

the beginning of the novel; in late *roman à clef* whose authorship was once disputed but now is not
The History and Adventures of an Atom (1769) Tobias Smollett

Filby friend to the Time Traveller
The Time Machine (1895) H. G. Wells

Filch
The Beggar's Opera opera (1728) John Gay

Filcher Verdant Green's* scout
The Adventures of Mr Verdant Green (1853) Cuthbert Bede (rn Edward Bradley)

Filer friend to Cute* anxious about the improvidence of the poor
The Chimes (1844) Charles Dickens

Filgrave, Dr professional rival to Dr Thorne*
Doctor Thorne (1858) Anthony Trollope

Filippovna, Natasya cc, seduced and abandoned by Totsky*; m. Rogozhin*, who kills her
Idiot (1869) Fyodor Dostoievsky

Fillet, Dr
Sir Launcelot Greaves (1766) Tobias Smollett

Feilletoville, Marquess of
The Pickwick Papers (1838) Charles Dickens

Filmer inventor of flying-machine
Twelve Stories and a Dream (1901) H. G. Wells

Finch, Atticus defence lawyer
Jem; 'Scout' his motherless sons
To Kill a Mockingbird (1960) Harper Lee

Finchbury, Jane, Lady 'Woman with tight stays'
Dombey and Son (1848) Charles Dickens

Finching, Flora daughter of Christopher Casby*, spoiled, artless, tender-hearted
Mr F her husband
Little Dorrit (1857) Charles Dickens

Finchley, Lord 'Lord Finchley tried to mend the Electric Light/Himself. It struck him dead: And serve him right!/It is the business of the wealthy man/To give employment to the artisan'
More Peers (1910) Hilaire Belloc

Finchley, Sondra wealthy girl with whom Clyde Griffiths* falls in love ('Miss X' at his trial for murder)
Stuart her brother

her parents
An American Tragedy (1925) Theodore Dreiser

Finck, von fashionable German doctor
The Newcomes (1853–5) W. M. Thackeray

Findlayson civil engineer
ss 'The Bridge Builders'
The Day's Work (1898) Rudyard Kipling

Finio page to Camillo*
The Case is Altered play (1609) Ben Jonson

Fink, Mike 'the last of the boatmen', 'the Snapping Turtle of the Ohio', ex-scout turned boatman, real-life person, 'Casanova, together with Paul Bunyan, merged into Thor' who became legendary and fictional figure in various American works onwards from
The Crockett Almanacs† (1835–56) Anon.

Finlay, Dr cc sketches of Scottish medical life later adapted for popular radio and TV series
Beyond This Place (1953) A. J. Cronin

Finley, Heavenly
Boss Finley her politician father
Thomas Jr. her brother
Sweet Bird of Youth play (1959) Tennessee Williams (rn Thomas Lanier Williams)

Finn, Huckleberry cc
his father, drunkard
Tom Sawyer (1876); *Huckleberry Finn* (1844) Mark Twain (rn Samuel Langhorne Clemens)

Finn, Phineas cc, m Mary Flood-Jones
Malachi his father, a doctor
his mother
Matilda; Barbara two of his sisters
Phineas Finn (1869) Anthony Trollope

Finnerty, Dr
Tom Burke of Ours (1844) Charles Lever

Finney friend to Gene Forrester
A Separate Peace (1959) John Knowles

Finnis, The Misses Pansy and Penelope
Before the Bombardment (1926) Osbert Sitwell

Finsberry, Odo
ss 'Tobemory'
The Chronicles of Clovis (1911) Saki (rn Hector Hugh Munro)

Finsbury, Joseph

Masterman his brother, writer, the two last survivors of the tontine
Jacob their brother
Michael Jacob's son
Morris; John sons of Jacob adopted by Joseph
The Wrong Box (1889) Robert Louis Stevenson and Lloyd Osbourne

Finucane, Dr
Harry Lorrequer (1839) Charles Lever

Finucane, Jack Irish sub-editor on *Pall Mall Gazette*, later editor
Pendennis (1848); *The Adventures of Philip* (1862) W. M. Thackeray

Finucane, the Misses
proprietors of girls' school
Pendennis (1848) W. M. Thackeray

Fionnguisa, Michael
ss 'Marching to Zion'
Adam and Eve and Pinch Me (1921) A. E. Coppard

Fiorinda Duchess of Urbin
The Great Duke of Florence play (1636) James Shirley

Fiormonda sister to Philippo Caraffa, Duke of Pavia*
Love's Sacrifice play (1633) John Ford

Fips, Mr
Martin Chuzzlewit (1844) Charles Dickens

Firanz Prince of Shirvan
Vathek (1786) William Beckford

Firbank name of an orchid: 'a dingy lilac blossom of rarity untold'
Prancing Nigger (in England as *Sorrow in Sunlight*) (1924) Ronald Firbank

Firebird Leonora Penderton's* stallion
Reflections in a Golden Eye (1940) Carson McCullers

Fireblood thief
Jonathan Wild (1743) Henry Fielding

Firebrace, Jack young Virginian
The Virginians (1857–9) W. M. Thackeray

Firebrace, Vavasour, Sir, Baronet
his wife, a 'great Tory stateswoman'
Sybil (1845) Benjamin Disraeli

Firedamp meteorologist, friend to MacCrotchet*
Crotchet Castle (1831) Thomas Love Peacock

Firke journeyman to Eyre
The Shoemaker's Holiday (1600)

Thomas Dekker

Firkin, Mrs Miss Crawley's* maid, jealous of Becky Sharp*, m. Bowls*
Vanity Fair (1847–8) W. M. Thackeray

Firmin, Geoffrey drunken British consul in Mexico, cc
Yvonne Constable his divorced wife
Hugh his half-brother
Under the Volcano (1947) Malcolm Lowry

Firmin, Philip cc, m. Charlotte Baynes*
Laura their daughter
Dr George his father (see **Brandon**)
his mother, *née* Ringwood
The Adventures of Philip (1862) W. M. Thackeray

Firminger, Colonel
Elizabeth his daughter, in love with Robin Skyrme*
The Story of Ragged Robyn (1945) Oliver Onions

Firmly, Lord
A Citizen of the World (1762) Oliver Goldsmith

Firniss, Miss mistress of boarding school attended by Maggie Tulliver*
The Mill on the Floss (1860) George Eliot (rn Mary Anne, later Marian, Evans)

Fischer, Bette the cousin of the title; cc embroidress in gold and silver lace; cousin to Adeline Hulot*
Johann uncle to Baroness Hulot* and to Bette
La Cousine Bette (1847) Honoré de Balzac

Fish a not very stately gentleman in black
The Chimes (1844) Charles Dickens

Fish, Billy
ss 'The Man Who Would be King'
Wee Willie Winkie (1888) Rudyard Kipling

Fisher, 'Smooth' Sam, alias White, detective posing as butler
The Little Nugget (1913) P. G. Wodehouse

Fisher, Billy daydreamer, cc
Billy Liar (1959) Keith Waterhouse

Fisher, Jeremy a frog, cc
The Tale of Jeremy Fisher (1906) Beatrix Potter

Fisher, Mark author who considers converting to Islam
Pending Heaven (1930) William

Gerhardie

Fisher, Naomi mistress of Max Ebhart* and mother of his children
her mother
The House in Paris (1935) Elizabeth Bowen

Fisher, Warden symbol of God
A Bad Man (1967) Stanley Elkin

Fiske, Ann niece to Mrs Harrington*
Evan Harrington (1861) George Meredith

Fiske, John
ss 'An Anniversary'
A Beginning (1955) Walter de la Mare

Fisker, Hamilton K. m. Marie Melmotte*
The Way We Live Now (1875) Anthony Trollope

Fitch, Andrea cockney artist, m. Mrs Carrickfergus*
A Shabby Genteel Story (1840) W. M. Thackeray

Fittleworth, Earl of
Last Post (1928) Ford Madox Ford

Fitton emissary earl, and jeerer
The Staple of News play (1631) Ben Jonson

Fitzadam, Mary
Cranford (1853) Mrs Gaskell

Fitzague, Blanche, Lady medical snob
The Book of Snobs (1847) W. M. Thackeray

Fitzallard, Guy, Sir
Mary his daughter, m. Sebastian Wengrave*
The Roaring Girl play (1611) Thomas Middleton and Thomas Dekker

Fitzallan secretly married to Jane Russell*
A Fair Quarrel play (1617) Thomas Middleton and William Rowley

Fitzaquitaine, Duke of
Sybil (1845) Benjamin Disraeli

Fitzbattleaxe, Duchess of
The Duke her husband
The Book of Snobs (1847) W. M. Thackeray

Fitz-Boodle, George Savage bachelor clubman, narrator of his amorous adventures
The Fitz-Boodle Papers (1843); *Men's Wives* (1843) W. M. Thackeray

Fitzchrome, Captain
Crotchet Castle (1831) Thomas Love Peacock

FitzClare, Vincent m. Beatrice Lord*

Mary his sister
C (1924) Maurice Baring
Fitzdottrel, Fabian foolish country squire
Mistress Frances Fitzdottrel his virtuous wife
The Devil is an Ass play (1631) Ben Jonson
Fitzgerald, Brian m. Madge Frettleby*
The Mystery of a Hansom Cab (1886) F. Hume
Fitzgerald, Burgo
Can You Forgive Her? (1864) Anthony Trollope
Fitzgibbon, Laurence, the Hon.
Aspasia his sister
Phineas Finn† (1869) Anthony Trollope
Fitzmarshall, Charles see Jingle
Fitzpatrick, Brian
Harriet his wife, niece to Squire Western*
Tom Jones (1749) Henry Fielding
Fitzpiers, Edred, Dr dilletante cc, m. Grace Melbury*
The Woodlanders (1879) Thomas Hardy
Fitzpurse, Waldmar devotee to King John
Alicia his daughter
Ivanhoe (1820) Walter Scott
Fitzroy, Charles executed fictional son of Charles II in complexly plotted verse tragedy (produced 1824), set in New England
Superstition play (1826) James Nelson Baker
Fitzroy, Dorothy employer of Bridget Kiernan*
Henry her husband
Poor Women (1928) Norah Hoult
Fitzroy, William
Charlotte his wife
Lavinia his niece, m. Asa Timberlake*
In This Our Life (1942) Ellen Glasgow
Fitzsimmons, Fitzgerald, Mrs
her husband
Barry Lyndon (1844) W. M. Thackeray
Fitzwilliam, Colonel cousin to Fitzwilliam Darcy*, needs to m. a rich woman
Pride and Prejudice (1813) Jane Austen
Fizgig, Francis, Captain penniless dandy
The Great Hoggarty Diamond (1841) W. M. Thackeray
Fizkin, Horatio of Fizkin Hall
The Pickwick Papers (1837) Charles Dickens
Fizzgig, Bolaro, Don grandee of Spain

The Pickwick Papers (1837) Charles Dickens
Flack, Mrs malevolent gossip
Blue her bastard son
Riders in the Chariot (1961) Patrick White
Flaherty, Margaret ('Pegeen Mike')
The Playboy of the Western World play (1907) J. M. Synge
Flahy, Corporal
ss 'The Solid Muldoon'
Soldiers Three (1888) Rudyard Kipling
Flambeau ex-criminal friend to Father Brown*
The Innocence of Father Brown (1911) G. K. Chesterton
Flamborough, Solomon
his two daughters, the younger m. Moses Primrose*
The Vicar of Wakefield (1766) Oliver Goldsmith
Flammock, Wilkin Flemish weaver
Rose his daughter
The Betrothed (1825) Walter Scott
Flammonde cryptic character
poem 'Flammonde'
The Man Against the Sky (1916) Edwin Arlington Robinson
Flamwell, Mr
Sketches by Boz (1836) Charles Dickens
Flanagan m. Kitty Riley*
Handy Andy (1842) Samuel Lover
Flanagan, Bartle villain
Fardorougha the Miser (1839) William Carleton
Flanagan, Betty servant to Mrs Clapp*
Vanity Fair (1847–8) W. M. Thackeray
Flanders, Betty widow
Archer; Jacob her sons, the latter cc
Jacob's Room (1922) Virginia Woolf
Flanders, Moll (Betty) narrator, cc
Moll Flanders (1722) Daniel Defoe
Flanders, Sally old nurse
The Uncommercial Traveller (1860–8) Charles Dickens
Flash, Peter
Satiromastix, or *The Untrussing of the Humorous Poet* (1602) Thomas Dekker
Flash, Petronel, Sir insolvent adventurer, m. Gertrude*
Eastward Ho! play (1605) George Chapman, Ben Jonson and John Marston
Flasher, Wilkins broker

The Pickwick Papers (1837) Charles Dickens

Flashman, Harry drunken school bully; afterwards re-created in agreeable Victorian pastiche
Tom Brown's Schooldays (1857) Thomas Hughes; and onwards from *Flashman*† (1969) George Macdonald Fraser

Flask third mate
Moby-Dick, or The Whale (1851) Herman Melville

Flather, Marcus, Revd friend to Charles Honeyman*
The Newcomes (1853–5) W. M. Thackeray

Flavell Methodist preacher
Middlemarch (1871–2) George Eliot (rn Mary Anne, later Marian, Evans)

Flavin, Troy plantation overseer about to be m. to Dabney Fairchild*
Delta Wedding (1946) Eudora Welty

Flavio little yellow cat belonging to the Pope
Hadrian the Seventh (1904) Baron Corvo (rn F. W. Rolfe)

Flavius steward to Timon
Timon of Athens play (1623) William Shakespeare

Flaxman rep. for Queen of Sheba Toilet Requisites, and Gordon Comstock's* fellow lodger at Mrs Wisbeach's* house, driven from home for spending time with women in Paris when advertising Sexapeal Naturtint
Keep the Aspidistra Flying (1936) George Orwell (rn Eric Blair)

Fleabody, Olivia Q., Dr leader of woman's movement
Is He Popenjoy? (1878) Anthony Trollope

Fleance son to Banquo*
Macbeth play (1623) William Shakespeare

Fledgeby, 'Old' ex-usurer
Young Fledgeby ('Fascination') his son, also usurer (as Pubsey & Co.)
Our Mutual Friend (1865) Charles Dickens

Fleecebumpkin, John bailiff
The Two Drovers (1827) Walter Scott

Fleete victim of the 'beast'
ss 'The Mark of the beast'

Life's Handicap (1891) Rudyard Kipling

Fleetwood, Lord m. Carinthia Kirby* but abandons her; refused when he tries to re-woo her; becomes monk in Spain
The Amazing Marriage (1895) George Meredith

Fleight, Aaron Rothweil Jewish cc, soap millionaire, prospective MP; m. Augusta Macphail*
Mr Fleight (1913) Ford Madox Ford

Fleigler, Luther car salesman
Irma his wife
Appointment in Samarra (1935) John O'Hara

Fleisher, Von Humboldt gifted doomed poet, based on Delmore Schwartz
Humboldt's Gift (1975) Saul Bellow

Fleming, Agnes Oliver Twist's* mother, who was seduced by Edwin Leeford*
Rose ('Rose Maylie'*) her sister
Oliver Twist (1839) Charles Dickens

Fleming, Craig
In This Our Life (1942) Ellen Glasgow

Fleming, Henry war hero after a spell of cowardice; the ss is important in respect of his development
The Red Badge of Courage (1895); ss 'The Veteran'; *Wounds in the Rain* (1900) Stephen Crane

Fleming, Joe prizefighter, killed accidentally by John Ponta*
The Game (1905) Jack London

Fleming, Malcolm, Sir lover of Margaret Hautlieu*
Castle Dangerous (1832) Walter Scott

Fleming, Maurice alcoholic brother of Frances Harrison*
The Tree of Heaven (1917) May Sinclair

Fleming, William John
his wife, *née* Hackbut
Dahlia; Rhoda the latter, cc, m. Robert Armstrong*
Rhoda Fleming (1865) George Meredith

Flesh, Ben sufferer from multiple sclerosis
The Franchiser (1976) Stanley Elkin

Fleta a fairy
Iolanthe opera (1882) W. S. Gilbert and Arthur Sullivan

Fletcher, Dick seaman, *Fortune's Favourite*
The Pirate (1822) Walter Scott

Fletcher, Mike modern Don Juan, cc of unsuccessful novel eventually rejected by author, and usually described as 'ludicrous'

Mike Fletcher (1889) George Moore

Fletcher, Mr vulgar and ill-tempered owner of estate he once managed, upon which Christopher Blake*, rightful heir to it, is obliged to work
Will his weakling grandson
The Deliverance (1904) Ellen Glasgow

Fletcher, Phineas narrator
Abel his father, tanner
John Halifax, Gentleman (1856) Mrs Craik

Fletcher, Phineas Quaker friend to Simeon Halliday*
Uncle Tom's Cabin (1851) Harriet Beecher Stowe

Fletcher, Sam
Eppie *née* Lownie, his wife
A Window in Thrums (1889) J. M. Barrie

Fletcher, Sam
Northanger Abbey (1818) Jane Austen

Fleury, M. chef
The Admirable Crichton play (1902) J. M. Barrie

Flimnap Lord High Treasurer, Lilliput
Gulliver's Travels (1726) Jonathan Swift

Flimsy, George, Sir
his wife
Emily his seventh daughter
Jeames's Diary (1846) W. M. Thackeray

Flint, Corporal
St Patrick's Day play (1775) Richard Brinsley Sheridan

Flint, Trueman lamplighter in exclamatory American moral tale for juveniles much read for some fifty years after it appeared
Gertrude his adopted daughter (originally Amory), m. William Sullivan*
The Lamplighter (1854) Maria S. Cummins

Flintwich, Jeremiah Mrs Clennam's* confidential clerk and partner
Affery his wife
Ephraim his twin brother
Little Dorrit (1857) Charles Dickens

Flippanta Clarissa's* maid
The Confederacy play (1705) John Vanbrugh

Flite, Miss 'little mad old woman in squeezed bonnet', a ward in chancery
Bleak House (1853) Charles Dickens

Flitestone, James dead artist
ss 'The Skeleton'
Blind Love (1969) V. S. Pritchett

Flitter, Wyndham man-about-town in facetious novel of types 'halfway between Dickens and comic papers', by showman who introduced Mont Blanc to the English
The Pottleton Legacy (1849) Albert Smith

Flitton, Pamela troublemaker, m. Kenneth Widmerpool*
Books Do Furnish a Room† (1971) Anthony Powell

Flo, Aunt plump landlady of the Potwell Inn
The History of Mr Polly (1910) H. G. Wells

Flokes, Lady
The Pottleton Legacy (1849) Albert Smith

Flood, Dora brothel keeper
Cannery Row (1945) John Steinbeck

Flood, Galton cc who gradually becomes insane
his mother
his wife, whom he kills
The Murderer (1978) Roy A. K. Heath

Flood, Hugh G. cc, 'seefoodetarian', is ninety-three and wants to live to 115, in American novel full of tall stories
Old Mr Flood (1948) Joseph Mitchell

Flood, Mrs Hazel Motes'* landlady
Wise Blood (1952) Flannery O'Connor

Flood, Nora in love with Robin Vote*
Nightwood (1936) Djuna Barnes

Flood, Tomsy
Some Experiences of an Irish R.M. (1899) O. E. Somerville and Martin Ross (rn Edith Somerville and Violet Martin)

Flood-Jones, Mary m. Phineas Finn*
her mother
Phineas Finn† (1869) Anthony Trollope

Floodgay, Mrs
her husband, a Canon
Cécile their daughter
Before the Bombardment (1926) Osbert Sitwell

Flopsy Bunnies six of them
The Tale of the Flopsy Bunnies† (1909) Beatrix Potter

Flora sister of Miles*
The Turn of the Screw (1898) Henry

James
Florac, de, Comte French officer
Léonore his wife, daughter to the Chevalier de Blois
Paul their son, later Prince de Monconteur
his wife
Abbé Florac son to Paul and his wife
The Newcomes (1853–5) W. M. Thackeray
Florence, Duke of
All's Well That Ends Well play (1623) William Shakespeare
Florence, Duke of who seduces Brancha (Bianca)*
Lord Cardinal his brother
Women Beware Women play (1657) Thomas Middleton
Florence, Miss blind woman
ss 'They'
Traffics and Discoveries (1904) Rudyard Kipling
Florence, Mrs headmistress
What Katy Did at School (1873) Susan Coolidge (rn Sarah Chauncey Woolsey)
Florian
Princess Ida opera (1884) W. S. Gilbert and Arthur Sullivan
Floribel cc, murdered by her husband, Hesperus
The Bride's Tragedy play (1882) Thomas Lovel Beddoes
Florio
Count Zichi his father
Count Florio and Phyllis K. (1910) Reginald Turner
Florio a citizen of Parma
'Tis Pity She's a Whore play (1633) John Ford
Florizel Prince of Bohemia, alias Theophilus Godall
ss 'The Suicide Club'
The New Arabian Nights (1882) Robert Louis Stevenson
Florizel son of Polixenes*
A Winter's Tale play (1623) William Shakespeare
Flory, John ('Mr Porley') young timber merchant, cc
Burmese Days (1935) George Orwell (rn Eric Blair)
Flosky friend to Chris Glowry*, m. Celinda Toobad*

Nightmare Abbey (1818) Thomas Love Peacock
Floss, Dr physician attending Miss Pinkerton's* Academy
Vanity Fair (1847–8) W. M. Thackeray
Flouncey, Guy, Mrs
Tancred (1847) Benjamin Disraeli
Flower, Captain
The Hand of Ethelberta (1876) Thomas Hardy
Flower, Freda, Mrs rich widow interested in spiritualism
The Bachelors (1961) Muriel Spark
Flower, Hallie loved by Hulings*; in tale of egoism by author who was eventually described as the 'jongleur of a – regrettably – modern feudalism'
ss 'Tubal Cain'
Gold and Iron (1818) Joseph Hergesheimer
Flower, Sergeant
The Clandestine Marriage play (1776) George Colman the Elder
Flowers maid to the Rosses*
The Oriel Window (1896) Mrs Molesworth
Floyd, Andrew, Revd principal of Maresfield House
Jacob's Room (1922) Virginia Woolf
Floyd, Aurora cc novel on the then fashionable theme of bigamy which was admired by both James* and Hardy*; m. (1) James Conyers*, (2) bigamously, John Mellish*
Aurora Floyd (1863) Mary Braddon
Floyer, Robert, Sir
Cecilia (1782) Fanny Burney
Fluellen an officer
King Henry V play (1623) William Shakespeare
Flute a bellows mender
A Midsummer Night's Dream (1623) William Shakespeare
Flutter, Fopling, Sir
The Man of Mode play (1676) George Etherege
Fly parasite and inflamer of the reckonings
The New Inn, or *The Light Heart* play (1629) Ben Jonson
Flynn, Atlas young Irish labourer who fancies Mrs Tuke*
Miss Gomez and the Brethren (1971) William Trevor

Flynn, James, Father
Eliza his sister
Dubliners (1914) James Joyce
Flynn, Oweny lawyer
ss 'A Dead Cert'
The Talking Trees (1971) Sean O'Faolain
Flynn, Peter labourer, uncle of Nora Clitheroe*
The Plough and the Stars play (1926) Sean O'Casey (rn John Casey)
Flyte see **Marchmain**
Fogg the taciturn member of the firm of Dodson* and Fogg
The Pickwick Papers (1838) Charles Dickens
Fogle, Horace, Sir member of Barnes Newcome's* club
The Newcomes† (1853–5) W. M. Thackeray
Foible woman to Lady Wishfort*
The Way of the World play (1700) William Congreve
Foker, Hermann originally Voelker, kind and wealthy brewer
Henry his great-grandson, eccentric friend to Pendennis*
The Virginians (1857–9) W. M. Thackeray
Foldal, Vilhelm washed-up clerk who imagines that he is a great poet, but who challenges Borkman's* own delusions – that he will be asked, as Napoleon of finance, to return to greatness – when the latter tells him that his verse is pitiful
John Gabriel Borkman play (1896) Henrik Ibsen
Foley, George see **Macaulay, Herbert**
Foley, Peter professor of classics in small Pennsylvania college
The Huge Season (1954) Wright Morris
Foliar pantomimist in Crummles's* company
Nicholas Nickleby (1839) Charles Dickens
Follet, Jay cc of Knoxville, Tennessee
Mary his wife
Catherine; Rufus his children
his father
A Death in the Family (1957) James Agee
Folliott, Revd Dr friend to MacCrotchet*
Crotchet Castle (1831) Thomas Love Peacock
Follywit, Richard nephew to Sir Bounte-

ous Progress*
A Mad World My Masters play (1608) Thomas Middleton
Fondlewife a banker
Laetitia his wife
The Old Bachelor comedy (1793) William Congreve
Fontover, Mrs employer of Sue Bridehead*
Jude the Obscure (1896) Thomas Hardy
Fool, The to Lear*
King Lear play (1623) William Shakespeare
Foppington, Lord
A Trip to Scarborough (1777) Richard Brinsley Sheridan
Foppington, Lord just so created, formerly Sir Novelty Fashion
The Relapse, or *Virtue in Danger* play (1697) John Vanbrugh
Forbes, Father Catholic philosophical sceptic modelled on author's lifelong friend Father Terry
The Damnation of Theron Ware in England, originally as *Illumination* (1896) Harold Frederic
Forbes, Georgie enemy to Chad Buford*
The Little Shepherd of Kingdom Come (1903) John Fox Jr.
Ford, Bob first and only true love of Jim Willard*
The City and the Pillar (1948) Gore Vidal
Ford, Elmer American millionaire
Nesta his wife
Ogden their son
The Little Nugget (1913) P. G. Wodehouse
Ford, Mr gentleman of Windsor
Mistress Ford his wife
The Merry Wives of Windsor play (1623) William Shakespeare
Foresight an illiterate old fellow pretending to understand astrology, omens, dreams etc.; uncle to Angelica*
his second wife
Love for Love comedy (1710) William Congreve
Forester, Dr spy
The Ministry of Fear (1943) Graham Greene
Forester, Mr
Caleb Williams (1794) William Godwin
Forester, Philip, Sir

Jemima his wife
My Aunt Margaret's Mirror (1827) Walter Scott
Forester, Sylvan cc and educator of Haut-on*, for whom he has bought a seat in the Commons
Melincourt, or Sir Oran Haut-on (1817) Thomas Love Peacock
Forey, Helen Doria sister to Sir Austin Feverel*
Clare her daughter, m. John Todhunter*
The Ordeal of Richard Feverel: A History of Father and Son (1859, rev. 1878) George Meredith
Formalist
The Pilgrim's Progress (1678–74) John Bunyan
Forrest, Elsie
The Bachelors (1961) Muriel Spark
Forrester, Captain Roland cc Kentucky novel that struck at 'noble savage' conception of Indians but was attacked for portraying them as savage and treacherous; is saved from stake
Nick of the Woods, or The Jibbenainosay (1837) Robert Montgomery Bird
Forrester, Gene schoolboy cc
A Separate Peace (1959) John Knowles
Forrester, Mrs friend to Mary Morstan*
The Sign of Four (1890) Arthur Conan Doyle
Forrester, Pa and Ma
Lem; Mill-Wheel; Buck; Gabby; Fodder-Wing their sons
The Yearling (1938) Marjorie Kinnan Rawlings
Forster, Cacalie
Of Human Bondage (1915) W. Somerset Maugham
Forster, Zenobia dark and queenly character suggested by the feminists Margaret Fuller and Fanny Kemble
Silas her farmer husband
Priscilla her half-sister, blonde and innocent but under influence of Westervelt*; m. Hollingsworth*
The Blithedale Romance (1852) Nathaniel Hawthorne
Fort, Cassius, Colonel murdered man (based on Colonel Solomon P. Sharpe)
World Enough and Time (1950) Robert Penn Warren
Forth, James, Professor aged don, m. Be-

linda Churchill*
Belinda (1883) Rhoda Broughton
Fortunato wine connoisseur
ss 'The Cask of Amontillado'
in *Godey's Lady's Book* (1846) Edgar Allan Poe
Fortunatus cc, 'Ha, ha, so I am, for I am so full of chinckes, that a Horse with one eye may looke through and through me'
Ampedo; Andelocia his sons
Old Fortunatus play (1600) Thomas Dekker
Fortune a decayed merchant
The City Madam play (1658) Philip Massinger
Fortune, Reggie upper-class sleuth in once popular but now almost forgotten whodunnits, onwards from
Call Mr Fortune† (1920) H. C. Bailey
Fortune, Timothy, Revd
Mr Fortune's Maggot (1927) Sylvia Townsend Warner
Fosco, Count first fat villain in English literature
Eleanor his wife, sister to Frederick Fairlie
The Woman in White (1860) Wilkie Collins
Foss, Corporal attendant on Lieutenant Worthington*
The Poor Gentleman play (1802) George Colman the Younger
Foster, Amy m. Yanko Goorall*
Isaac her father
ss 'Amy Foster'
Typhoon (1903) Joseph Conrad (rn Josef Teodor Konrad Korzeniowski)
Foster, Anthony jailer of Amy Rosbart*
Janet his daughter
Kenilworth (1821) Walter Scott
Foster, Captain of the *Dreadnought*, onwards from
The Happy Return (1937) C. S. Forrester (rn C. L. T. Smith)
Foster, Eveline aunt to Dorothy Musgrave*
Beau Austin play (1892) W. E. Henley and Robert Louis Stevenson
Foster, John and Jeremiah brother shopkeepers, Monkshaven
Sylvia's Lovers (1863) Mrs Gaskell
Foster, John, Sir Warden of the Marches
The Monastery (1820) Walter Scott

Foster, Kenneth homosexual friend to Janet Smith*
Real People (1969) Alison Lurie

Foster, Lucy
Eleanor (1900) Mrs Humphry Ward

Foster, Mr 'perfectibilist' i.e. believer in the infinite progress of man
Headlong Hall (1816) Thomas Love Peacock

Fothergill, J. P. agent to the Duke of Omnium*
Framley Parsonage† (1861) Anthony Trollope

Fothergill, Miss
The Shrimp and the Anemone (1944) L. P. Hartley

Fotheringay stage name of Emily Costigan*, beautiful but stupid actress, m. Sir Charles Mirabel*
Pendennis (1848) W. M. Thackeray

Foucault, Madame Sophia Scales's* fraudulent French landlady
The Old Wives' Tale (1908) Arnold Bennett

Foulata native girl, victim of Gagool*
King Solomon's Mines (1885) Henry Rider Haggard

Foulkes, Mr friend to Mr Bastable*
Denny; Daisy his children
The Treasure Seekers (1899); *The Would-be Goods* (1901) E. Nesbit

Foulon, M. second to Stephen Monkton* in duel
ss 'Mad Monkton'
The Queen of Hearts (1859) Wilkie Collins

Fowler former tenant of Squire Cass*
Silas Marner (1861) George Eliot (rn Mary Anne, later Marian, Evans)

Fowler, Miss Mary Postgate's* employer
Wyndham her nephew, killed in an air accident*
ss 'Mary Postgate'
A Diversity of Creatures (1917) Rudyard Kipling

Fowler, Mr suitor to Harriet Byron*
Sir Charles Grandison (1754) Samuel Richardson

Fowler, Thomas narrator, journalist
The Quiet American (1955) Graham Greene

Fox, Allie modern American Robinson Crusoe*
The Mosquito Coast (1981) Paul Theroux

Fox, Bishop of Durham
Perkin Warbeck play (1634) John Ford

Fox, Brer
Uncle Remus (1880–95) Joel Chandler Harris

Fox, Charles adolescent cc
The Young Desire It (1937) Kenneth ('Seaforth') Mackenzie

Fox, Dr resourceful physician wrongly suspected of grave-robbing
Perlycross (1894) R. D. Blackmore

Fox, Kate prostitute
The Informer (1925) Liam O'Flaherty

Fox, Letty cc
Letty Fox: Her Luck (1946) Christina Stead

Fox, Madeline one-time fiancée to Martin Arrowsmith*
Arrowsmith (1925) Sinclair Lewis

Foxe, Brian
Eyeless in Gaza (1936) Aldous Huxley

Foxe-Donnell, Leo Irish patriot
Judith his mother
Julie his wife
Johno his son
A Nest of Simple Folk (1933) Sean O'Faolain

Foxey father to Sampson and Sally Brass*
The Old Curiosity Shop (1841) Charles Dickens

Foxfield, Reginald, Sir, Baronet
his mother
Let the People Sing (1939) J. B. Priestley

Foxley squire and magistrate
Redgauntlet (1824) Walter Scott

Foxstone, Lady
A Trick to Catch the Old One play (1608) Thomas Middleton

Foxy Whiskered Gentleman, The
The Tale of Jemima Puddleduck (1908) Beatrix Potter

'Foxy' drill sergeant
Stalky & Co. (1899) Rudyard Kipling

Foyle, Dennis father to Mary Brodie's* child
Hatter's Castle (1931) A. J. Cronin

Fraide, Herbert leader of the opposition
Lady Sarah his wife
John Chilcote, M.P. (1904) Katherine C. Thurston

Frail, Mrs a woman of the town, sister to Mrs Foresight*
Love for Love comedy (1710) William Congreve

Frame, John John Adam's* secretary
Holy Deadlock (1934) A. P. Herbert

Frampton, Emily cousin to Alix Sandomir*
Laurence her dead second husband
Non-Combatants and Others (1916) Rose Macaulay

Frampton, James mate, *Blackgauntlet*
The Bird of Dawning (1916) John Masefield

Frampton, Richard see Eliott, Ralph

Frampul, Frances, Lady daughter to Lord Frampul*, posing as Goodstock*
The New Inn, or *The Light Heart* play (1629) Ben Jonson

France, King of
All's Well That Ends Well play (1623) William Shakespeare

France, King of
King Lear play (1623) William Shakespeare

France, Princess of
Love's Labour's Lost play (1623) William Shakespeare

Francesca (legd.) cc verse play that was wrongly hailed as Sophoclean and Shakespearian when it was published and then produced (1902); but its author died a forgotten man
Paolo and Francesca (1899) Stephen Phillips

Francesco a gondolier
The Gondoliers opera (1889) W. S. Gilbert and Arthur Sullivan

Francesco, Don Roman Catholic priest
South Wind (1917) Norman Douglas

Franching of Peckham, friend to the Pooters*
The Diary of a Nobody (1892) George and Weedon Grossmith

Francis Maltese houseboy
The Little Girls (1964) Elizabeth Bowen

Francis, Caroline victim of the revenge, finally leading to her death, of Eliza, whose fiancée she has attracted; in 'typically sentimental didactic romance'
The Hapless Orphan, or *Innocent Victim of Revenge* (1793) 'An American Lady' (unknown)

Francis, Father
The Duenna (1775) Richard Brinsley Sheridan

Francis, Father priest who reconciles Griffith Gaunt* to his lawful wife
Griffith Gaunt, or *Jealousy* (1866); *Kate Peyton*, or *Jealousy* – later, 1873, as *Kate Peyton's Lovers* play (1867) Charles Reade

Francisca a nun
Measure for Measure play (1623) William Shakespeare

Francisco soldier
Hamlet play (1623) William Shakespeare

Françoise ever-present servant
A la recherche du temps perdu (*In Search of Lost Time*) (1913–27) Marcel Proust

Françoise servant at *pension* of Madame Smolensk*
The Adventures of Philip (1862) W. M. Thackeray

Frank Eveline Hill's lover*
ss 'Eveline'
Dubliners (1914) James Joyce

Frank proves to be Laetitia, the lost daughter of Lord Frampul; had been set up, by Prudence*, as a stale to catch Beaufort* or Latimer*
The New Inn, or *The Light Heart* play (1629) Ben Jonson

Frankenstein, Victor cc, part narrator, creator of monster, m. Elizabeth Lavenza
Alphonse his father
Caroline his mother
William; Ernest his brothers
Frankenstein (1818) Mary Shelley

Frankland, Leonard blind cc, m. Rosamond Treverton*
The Dead Secret (1857) Wilkie Collins

Frankland, Leonora seduced by Millborne*
Frances their daughter, engaged to Revd Percival Cope*
ss 'For Conscience' Sake'
Life's Little Ironies (1894) Thomas Hardy

Franklin, Desmond killer of sharks, unsuccessful rival to Mulliner*
Meet Mr Mulliner (1927) P. G. Wodehouse

Franklin, Julia heiress, m. Montraville*
Charlotte: A Tale of Truth (1791, in America as *Charlotte Temple*, 1794) Mrs

Susannah Rowson

Franks, Edward Captain of the *Young Rachel*
The Virginians (1857–9) W. M. Thackeray

Franceshina the courtesan
The Dutch Courtesan play (1603) John Marston

Fransciscus a pretended madman
The Changeling play (1653) Thomas Middleton and William Rowley

Frapp, Nicodemus baker, Chatham, cousin to Ponderevo*, called 'Uncle'
Tono Bungay (1909) H. G. Wells

Fraser tutor to Daniel Deronda*
Daniel Deronda (1876) George Eliot (rn Mary Anne, later Marian, Evans)

Fraser, Daisy prostitute
poem 'Daisy Trainor'
Spoon River Anthology verse epitaphs (1915) Edgar Lee Masters

Fraser, James
Janet his first wife
Murdo their son
Alice Murdo's wife
Ninian their son
Elsie James's second wife
The First Mrs Fraser play (1929) St John Ervine

Fraser, James cc
ss 'The French Poodle'
Unlucky for Pringle (1973) Wyndham Lewis

Fraser, Janet, Mrs *née* Ross, sister of Lady Stornaway*, cold-hearted, mercenary and vain
her ill-tempered, older husband
Mansfield Park (1814) Jane Austen

Fraser, Johnny cc popular American novel set in times of American Revolution
Drums (1925) James Boyd

Fraser, Laura
The Truth play (1907) Clyde Fitch

Fraser, Simon Master of Lovat, chief of the clan
Catriona (1893) Robert Louis Stevenson

Frasier attorney
Porgy (1925) Du Bose Hayward

Fray, Henry farm hand
Far From the Madding Crowd (1874) Thomas Hardy

Frayling, Evadne m. the reprobate Sir George Colquhoun*, with whom she remains on the condition the marriage is not consummated, m. (2) Dr Galbraith*, who first treats her for sexual frustration
The Heavenly Twins (1893) Sarah Grand (rn Frances McFall)

Frazier, Miss daughter of the 'owner'
ss 'The Ship that Found Herself'
The Day's Work (1898) Rudyard Kipling

Freckles young boy cc who believes himself to be an orphan but turns out to be son of a wealthy man, set in Limberlost Swamp of Louisiana; it achieved its astonishing popularity only in 1910 when issued with its companion, *A Girl of the Limberlost*
Freckles (1904) Gene Stratton Porter

Fred Scrooge's* nephew
A Christmas Carol (1843) Charles Dickens

freddy rat
archy and mehitabel (1927) Don Marquis

Frederic pirate apprentice, m. Mabel Stanley*
The Pirates of Penzance opera (1880) W. S. Gilbert and Arthur Sullivan

Frederick, Duke usurper
All's Well That Ends Well play (1623) William Shakespeare

Frederick, Lord see **Robinson, Hyacinth**

Free, Micky O'Malley's* Irish servant
Charles O'Malley (1841) Charles Lever

Freebody, David divorce solicitor
Holy Deadlock (1934) A. P. Herbert

Freeman ('Pinto') holiday tutor and playwright
A House of Children (1941) Joyce Cary

Freeman a good fellow
Northanger Abbey (1818) Jane Austen

Freeman, Charles, Sir Mrs Sullen's* brother
The Beaux' Strategem play (1707) George Farquhar

Freeman, Dennis playwright, based on someone not unlike Tennessee Williams*, whose success aggravates his paranoia, which fuels his creativity
The Hero Continues (1960) Donald Windham

Freeman, Lucy addressee of letters about her sexual experiences in early American novel (published anonymously) spawned by the craze for Richardson*
The Coquette: A Novel Founded on Fact

F

(1797) Mrs Hannah Foster

Freeville, Lionel, Sir an old knight
Young Freeville his son
The Dutch Courtesan play (1605) John Marston

Fremisson, Dr friend to the Stublands*
Joan and Peter (1918) H. G. Wells

French, Beatrice successful retailer of dresses for foolish women
Fanny her vulgar sister; both sisters to Ada Peachey*, and of a family whose 'minds, characters, propensities had all remained absolutely proof against such educational influences as had been brought to bear upon them'; m. Horace Lord*; dies
In the Year of Jubilee (1894) George Gissing

French, Bob racehorse trainer
ss 'I'm a Fool'
Horses and Men (1924) Sherwood Anderson

French, Mrs housekeeper to Sir Hugo Mallinger
Daniel Deronda (1876) George Eliot (rn Mary Anne, later Marian, Evans)

French, Joseph police detective in tales which had distinction of a plodding sort, onwards from
Inspector French's Greatest Case† (1924) Freeman Wills Crofts

French, Kit privateersman
Admiral Guinea play (1892) W. E. Henley and Robert Louis Stevenson

French, Mrs
Camilla; Arabella her daughters
He Knew He Was Right (1869) Anthony Trollope

Frensham, Countess of
Mr Britling Sees It Through (1916) H. G. Wells

Frenside, George literary advisor
Hudson River Bracketed (1929)
The Gods Arrive (1932) Edith Wharton

Frere, Richard scorner of convention who helps guide Lewis Arundel* to wisdom, m. Rose Arundel*
Lewis Arundel (1852) Francis Smedley

Frere, Maurice, Captain authoritarian brute, 'son of a Nobody . . . very loud on the subject of the Old English Gentleman', with vestiges of conscience awakened by Dora Vickers*, whom he m.
His Natural Life (1870–2; abridged by the author 1874; in 1885 as *For the Term of His Natural Life* – thus evading the author's irony; original text edited by Stephen Murray-Smith, 1970) Marcus Clarke

Fresco servant to Cataplasma*
The Atheist's Tragedy, or *The Honest Man's Revenge* play (1611/12) Cyril Tourneur

Frettleby, Mark
Rosanne his first wife, daughter to Ma Guttersnipe
Madge their daughter, m. Brian Fitzgerald*
The Mystery of a Hansom Cab (1886) F. Hume

Fribble a coxcomb
Miss in her Teens play (1747) David Garrick

Frica, Calekan, Mrs invites Belacqua Shuah* to an intellectual cocktail party; sings to Havelock Ellis in a deep voice, frankly itching to work that which is not seemly
ss 'A Wet Night'
More Pricks That Kicks (1934) Samuel Beckett

'Friday' friend and servant to Robinson Crusoe
Robinson Crusoe (1719) Daniel Defoe

Friechtie, Barbara ninety-year-old heroine who allegedly raised Stars and Stripes when Stonewall Jackson entered Frederick, Md. – but in the latter item she has been made into a gallant girl (in vehicle for popular actress)
poem 'Barbara Friechtie'
In War Time (1864) John Greenleaf Whittier
Barbara Friechtie play (1899) Clyde Fitch

Friendly amiable apprentice to Heartfree*
Jonathan Wild (1743) Henry Fielding

Friendly, John, Sir neighbour to Sir Tunbelly Clumsey*
The Relapse, or *Virtue in Danger* play (1697) John Vanbrugh

Frink, T. Chomondeley poet
Babbitt (1923) Sinclair Lewis

Frinton, Lady
The Last of Mrs Cheney (1925) Frederic

Lonsdale

Frion, Stephen Warbeck's* secretary
Perkin Warbeck play (1634) John Ford

Frisby, Madame milliner, m. Colonel
Altamont*
Pendennis (1848) W. M. Thackeray

Frisk, Mary see **Cutpurse, Moll**

Frith-Walter, Alan businessman, cc
  Elaine his wife
  Jack their son
  Pearl Jack's wife
Accident (1928) Arnold Bennett

Frithiof' boatswain
ss 'A Matter of Fact'
Many Inventions (1893) Rudyard Kipling

Fritz lover of Ottila Gottesheim*
Prince Otto (1885) Robert Louis
Stevenson

Frolick, Frederick, Sir cousin to Lord
Beaufort*
The Comical Revenge, or *Love in a Tub*
play (1664) George Etherege

Frome, Ethan farmer cc of grim novel: he
and Mattie Silver*, the woman he loves,
try to kill themselves by crashing a
bobsleigh into a tree, but end up cripples
  Zenobia ('Zeenie'), his wife, a whining
hypochondriac
Ethan Frome (1911) Edith Wharton

Front-de-Bouef, Reginald Norman knight
Ivanhoe (1820) Walter Scott

Frosch, Morton lawyer and friend to Stephen Monk*
The World in the Evening (1954) Christopher Isherwood

Frost ex-navy valet
ss 'Unprofessional'
Limits and Renewals (1932) Rudyard
Kipling

Frost, Miss Alvina Houghton's* governess
The Lost Girl (1920) D. H. Lawrence

Frost, Percival, Sir the King's proctor
Holy Deadlock (1934) A. P. Herbert

Froth, Lord a solemn coxcomb
  Lady Froth his wife, a great coquette,
pretender to poetry, wit and learning
The Double-Dealer play (1710) William
Congreve

Froud, Richard friend to Eddy Considine*
Without My Cloak (1931) Kate O'Brien

Frowenfeld, Joseph American apothecary
of German origin through whose eyes

most of the action of this New Orleans
historical romance is seen; m. Clotilde de
Grapions*
The Grandissimes: A Story of Creole Life
(1880) George Washington Cable

Froyd, Dr of the 'Central of Europe', who
speaks to his assistant 'quite a lot in the
Viennese language', and who is told by
Lorelei Lee* that she does not dream
('cultivate a few inhibitions and get some
sleep,' he tells her)
Gentlemen Prefer Blondes (1925) Anita
Loos

Frucht, Herr tries to cement up the daily
exploding lavatories, dies insane in the
end
D'un Château l'autre (Castle to Castle)
(1957) Louis Ferdinand Céline (rn Louis
Ferdinand Destouches)

Frugal, John, Sir a merchant
  Lady Frugal his extravagant and proud
wife
  Luke his brother
  Anne; Mary her daughters
The City Madam play (1658) Philip Massinger

Frusk, Indiana m. James Rolliver*
The Custom of the Country (1913) Edith
Wharton

Fry principal warder in Hawes's jail
It Is Never Too Late to Mend (1856)
Charles Reade

Fry, Amos ('Haymoss')
Two on a Tower (1882) Thomas Hardy

Fry, John servant to John Ridd*
Lorna Doone (1869) R. D. Blackmore

Ftatateeta Cleopatra's* nurse
Caesar and Cleopatra (1900) George
Bernard Shaw

Fu Manchu, Dr eastern fiend; head of Si-
Fan, onwards from
The Mystery of Dr Fu Manchu† (1913)
Sax Rohmer (rn Arthur Sarsfield Ward)

Fuchsheim, von, Melchior Sternfels real
name of Simplicius*
Simplicissimus (1669) Hans Jakob von
Grimmelshausen

Fudge, Poll one-eyed rebel in Shepperton
workhouse
ss 'The Sad Fortunes of the Rev. Amos
Barton'
Scenes of Clerical Life (1857) George
Eliot (rn Mary Anne, later Marian,

Evans)

Fuego, Juan de president of Nicaragua
The Napoleon of Notting Hill (1904)
G. K. Chesterton

Fugger, Melpemene ex-Sister Agatha
Professor Fugger her father
ss 'Nuns at Luncheon'
Mortal Coils (1922) Aldous Huxley

Fulano, Don magnificent black steed, cc,
shot by rascals
John Brent (1862) Theodore Winthrop

Fulbert, Canon (hist.)
Heloise and Abelard (1921) George
Moore

Fulgentinio minion to Roberto
The Maid of Honour play (1632) Philip
Massinger

Fulke Norman baron
ss 'Old Men at Pevensea'
Puck of Pook's Hill (1906) Rudyard
Kipling

Fulkerson promotes a magazine with
March* as editor
A Hazard of New Fortunes (1890)
William Dean Howells

Fullilove timber merchant
his daughter
Brother Jacob (1864) George Eliot (rn
Mary Anne, later Marian, Evans)

Fulmer unscrupulous landlord
his wife
The West Indian play (1771) Richard
Cumberland

Fulton, Pearl friend to Bertha Young*
ss 'Bliss'
Bliss and Other Stories (1920) Katherine
Mansfield (rn Katherine Mansfield Beauchamp)

Fuma native girl
Mr Fortune's Maggot (1927) Sylvia
Townsend Warner

Fun
The Alchemist play (1610) Ben Jonson

Fung-Tching
ss 'The Gate of a Hundred Sorrows'
Plain Tales from the Hills (1888) Rudyard Kipling

Fungoso son to Sordido*, one that follows
the fashion afar off, like a spy
Every Man Out of His Humour play
(1599) Ben Jonson

Furey, Michael dead adolescent once in

love with Gretta Conroy*
ss 'The Dead'
Dubliners (1914) James Joyce

Furio a gentleman attendant on Gwalter*
*The Pleasant Commedye of Patient
Grissill* play (1603) Thomas Dekker

Furlong Dublin fop
Handy Andy (1842) Samuel Lover

Furman who spits in cops' eyes
My Uncle Dudley (1942) Wright Morris

Furnace man to Lady Alworth*
A New Way to Pay Old Debts play
(1633) Philip Massinger

Furnival, Lawrence m. Molly Milner*
ss 'Miss Tarrant's Temperament'
Tales Told by Simpson (1930) May
Sinclair

Furze, Catherine cc
Mr Furze her factory-owner father
Amelia Furze her mother; in 'tragedy of
the unfulfilled'
Catherine Furze (1893) Mark Ruther-
ford (rn William Hale White)

Fuseli artist
Lolly Willowes (1926) Sylvia Townsend
Warner

Fuselli, Dan Italian-American soldier
Three Soldiers (1921) John Dos Passos

Fusilier, Agricola kills Nancanou* in duel
The Grandissimes: A Story of Creole Life
(1880) George Washington Cable

Fuzzy Wuzzy Sudanese fighter: 'So 'ere's to
you, Fuzzy Wuzzy, at your 'ome in the
Soudan;/You're a pore benighted 'eathen
but a first-class fightin' man'
poem 'Fuzzy Wuzzy'
Barrack-Room Ballads (1892) Rudyard
Kipling

Fyfe, 'Moggy' dwarf
Hobley her brother, landlord of the inn
The Story of Ragged Robyn (1945) Oliver
Onions

Fyne, John civil servant; cyclist; rambler
Mrs Fyne his feminist wife, sometimes
also described as lesbian
Chance (1913) Joseph Conrad (rn Josef
Teodor Konrad Korzeniowski)

Fynes, Ida m. Julian Silvercross*; daughter
to Lackland*
Mrs Fynes widow *née* Caryll, who
adopted her
The Old Bank (1902) William Westall

G

Gabbadeo, Maestro 'wise doctor'
Romola (1863) George Eliot (rn Mary Anne, later Marian, Evans)

Gabbett leader of mutiny
His Natural Life (1870–2; abridged by the author 1874; in 1885 as *For the Term of His Natural Life* – thus evading the author's irony; original text edited by Stephen Murray-Smith, 1970) Marcus Clarke

Gabelle, Theophile postmaster, local taxmaster
A Tale of Two Cities (1859) Charles Dickens

Gabriel of the *Jeroboam*
Moby Dick, or The Whale (1851) Herman Melville

Gabriel, His Truthfulness the Archangel
All and Everything: Beelzebub's Tales to His Grandson (1950) G. I. Gurdjieff

Gadd, Ferdinand of Bagnigge Wells Theatre
Trelawny of the Wells play (1898) A. W. Pinero

Gadny, Mrs old lady cc of notable first novel
At the Jerusalem (1967) Paul Bailey

Gadow, Madame the Lewisham's* first landlady
Love and Mr Lewisham (1900) H. G. Wells

Gadsby, Mrs widow of Captain Gadsby; formerly maid
Daniel Deronda George Eliot (rn Mary Anne, later Marian, Evans)

Gadsby, Philip, Captain m. Minnie Threegan
The Story of the Gadsbys (1888) Rudyard Kipling

Gage, Mrs postmistress
The Tree of Man (1955) Patrick White

Gagool witch doctor
King Solomon's Mines (1885) Henry Rider Haggard

Gahagan, Goliah, Major Irish adventurer

Gregory; Count Godfrey his brothers
The Adventures of Major Gahagan† (1839) W. M. Thackeray

Gailey, Sarah George Cannon's* half-sister
Clayhanger (1910); *Hilda Lessways* (1911); *These Twain* (1916) Arnold Bennett

Gaillard, Eugene m. Kate Brady
Girls in Their Married Bliss (1964) Edna O'Brien

Gaius
The Pilgrim's Progress (1678–84) John Bunyan

Gajere ex-convict, lover of Aissa*
Aissa Saved (1932) Joyce Cary

Gala, Leone cc of the bitter comedy that is being rehearsed at the beginning of *Sei personaggi in cerca d'autore*
Silia his wife
Il guioco delle parti (The Rules of the Game) (1919) Luigi Pirandello

Galatea Arethusa's* lady
Philaster (1611) Francis Beaumont and John Fletcher

Galathea cc
Galathea play (1592) John Lyly

Galazi King of the Wolves, a relative to Chaka*
Nada the Lily (1892) Henry Rider Haggard

Galbraith, Dr enlightened doctor who treats and m. Evadne Colquhoun*
The Heavenly Twins (1893) Sarah Grand (rn Frances McFall)

Gale, Roger elderly widower worried about his daughters:
Edith devoted to her five children to the exclusion of all else
Deborah schoolmistress who sacrifices her personal life for her pupils
Laura heedless hedonist; in American novel that won Pulitzer Prize
His Family (1917) Ernest Poole

Galer, Mrs washerwoman cc

Sid her son, m. Miss Carthew*
Mrs Galer's Business (1905) W. Pett Ridge
Galgenstein, G. A. M. von, Count depraved German officer in English regiment
Catherine (1840) W. M. Thackeray
Gallagher, Dan, Commandant
The Informer (1925) Liam O'Flaherty
Gallaher, Ignatius journalist
ss 'A Little Cloud'
Dubliners (1914) James Joyce
Gallanbile MP whose wife needed a cook
Nicholas Nickleby (1839) Charles Dickens
Gallegher Irish-American newsboy who solves a crime and becomes famous as an example of enterprise
Gallegher and Other Stories (1891) Richard Harding Davis
Gallegher, Johnny mill manager
Gone With the Wind (1936) Margaret Mitchell
Gallipot an apothecary
Mistress Gallipot his wife
The Roaring Girl play (1611) Thomas Middleton and Thomas Dekker
Galloway noble at the Court of England
Old Fortunatus play (1600) Thomas Dekker
Gallowglass, Viscount Bishop of Ballyshannon, son-in-law to Lord Dorking*
The Newcomes (1853–5) W. M. Thackeray
Galls, The father and son, piano tuners
Watt (1953) Samuel Beckett
Gallus (hist.) brother to Julian; executed by Constantius*
Keiser og Gallilaeer (*Emperor and Galilean*) (1873) Henrik Ibsen
Galore, Mr 'Indian nabob'
Nelly his sister
The Provost (1822) John Galt
Galt, Skinner cc
The End of My Life (1947) Vance Bourjaily
Gam, Mrs widow *née* Molloy*
Jemima Amelia her daughter, m. Dionysius Haggarty*
Men's Wives (1843) W. M. Thackeray
Gama, King
Ida his daughter, m. Hilarion*
Arac; Guron; Scynthius his sons

Princess Ida opera (1884) W. S. Gilbert and Arthur Sullivan
Gamaliel African drummer who has vision of a perfect Africa, in Canadian novel
The New Ancestors (1970) Dave Godfrey
Gambit, Dr
Middlemarch (1871–2) George Eliot (rn Mary Anne, later Marian, Evans)
Game Chicken, The prize-fighter
Dombey and Son (1848) Charles Dickens
Gamm, Jerry witchmaster
ss 'Marklake Witches'
Rewards and Fairies (1910) Rudyard Kipling
Gammon 'town traveller', dog-fancier, cc
The Town Traveller (1898) George Gissing
Gammon see **Quirk**
Gamp, Sarah, Mrs drunken midwife and nurse
her late husband
Martin Chuzzlewit (1844) Charles Dickens
Gander gentleman of a witty turn
Martin Chuzzlewit (1844) Charles Dickens
Gandish, Professor head of Drawing Academy
his wife and daughters
Charles his son
The Newcomes (1853–5) W. M. Thackeray
Gandoc the Briton
The Conquered (1923) Naomi Mitchison
Gann, James head of Gann and Blubbery, oil merchants
Juliana his wife *née* Crabb, formerly Mrs Wellesley Macarty
Caroline their daughter (Mrs Brandon in *The Adventures of Philip*)
A Shabby Genteel Story (1840) W. M. Thackeray
Gann, Rosie Driffield's* first wife
Cakes and Ale (1930) W. Somerset Maugham
Gant, Eugene see **Webber, George** the author's name for himself in his two earlier autobiographical novels
Oliver his father
Eliza his mother, a crafty miser
Ben his steady newspaperman brother
Steve his selfish brother

Look Homeward, Angel: A Story of the Buried Life (1929); Of Time and the River: A Legend of Man's Hunger in his Youth (1935) Thomas Wolfe

Gantry, Elmer crooked preacher, cc
Cleo née Benham, his wife
Elmer Gantry (1927) Sinclair Lewis

Gantz, Norman American G I, second husband of Betty Hopkiss*
Jezebel's Dust (1951) Fred Urquhart

Ganymede, Bounteous, Sir
The Roaring Girl play (1611) Thomas Middleton and Thomas Dekker

Ganz, Dr physician who helps prove Vendale's* identity
No Thoroughfare (1867) Charles Dickens

Garbage Man, The
or 'The Family Practitioner', 'The Man in the Stovepipe Hat' etc.; in experimental play produced as The Moon is a Gong (1925)
The Garbage Man: A Parade with Shouting (1926) John Dos Passos

Garbets tragic actor, friend to Costigan*
Pendennis (1848) W. M. Thackeray

Garcia
ss 'Wisteria Lodge'
His Last Bow (1917) Arthur Conan Doyle

Garden Minimus schoolboy
Mr Perrin and Mr Traill (1911) Hugh Walpole

Garden, Grace m. Henry Little*
Put Yourself in his Place (1870) Charles Reade

Garden, Revd Aubrey broad-minded cleric who runs through almost every religion in satirical novel
Anne his wife
Victoria; Maurice; Rome; Stanley; Irving; Una their children
Told By An Idiot (1923) Rose Macaulay

Gardener, Chancey see **Chance**

Gardiner, Bishop of Winchester (hist.)
Henry VIII play (1623) William Shakespeare and John Fletcher

Gardiner, Colonel commanding officer at Dundee
Waverley (1814) Walter Scott

Gardiner, Eunice schoolgirl, member of the Brodie* set
The Prime of Miss Jean Brodie (1961)

Muriel Spark

Gardiner, Mr brother to Mrs Bennet, to whom he is superior
his wife and four children
Pride and Prejudice (1813) Jane Austen

Gardner, Samuel, Revd
Frank his son
Mrs Warren's Profession play (1902) George Bernard Shaw

Gargamelle mother to Gargantua*
Gargentua, Pantagruel, Tiers Quart, Quart Part (1532–54) François Rabelais

Gargantua father to Pantagruel*
Gargantua, Pantagruel, Tiers Quart, Quart Part (1532–54) François Rabelais

Gargery, Joe blacksmith
his first wife, sister of Philip Pirrip*
Biddy his second wife
Pip his son by Biddy
Great Expectations (1861) Charles Dickens

Gargrave, Thomas, Sir
King Henry VI plays (1623) William Shakespeare

Garland, Anne m. Robert Loveday*
Martha her mother, m. Miller Loveday*
The Trumpet Major (1880) Thomas Hardy

Garland, Mary engaged to Roderick Hudson*
Roderick Hudson (1875) Henry James

Garland, Mr and Mrs kindly couple who befriend Kit Nubbles*
Abel their son
The Old Curiosity Shop (1841) Charles Dickens

Garm Ortheris'* bulldog
ss 'Garm – A Hostage'
Actions and Reactions (1909) Rudyard Kipling

Garner, George cc who finds himself involved in murder
The Second Curtain (1953) Roy Fuller

Garnet, Jeremy cc, narrator
Love Among the Chickens (1906) P. G. Wodehouse

Garnett, Prosperine
Candida play (1894) George Bernard Shaw

Garp, T. S. cc. author of the novel The World According to Bensenhaver; assassinated by one of the Ellen Jamesians (group of feminists)

his mother, whose autobiography is
called *A Sexual Suspect*
The World According to Garp (1978)
John Irving
Garron, Phil
ss 'Yoked With an Unbeliever'
Plain Tales from the Hills (1888) Rudyard Kipling
Garstein, Mr political manager
Mr Apollo: A Just Possible Story (1908)
Ford Madox Ford
Garstin, Phil mine owner and party candidate
Felix Holt (1866) George Eliot (rn Mary
Anne, later Marian, Evans)
Gart, Hermione ('Her') cc intricate feminist novel; her Christian name is too
beautiful to be spoken
Eugenia her mother
Bertrand her brother. m. Minnie, whom
she hates
Hermione (1981) H. D. (rn Hilda Doolittle)
Garter, Polly
Under Milk Wood play (1954) Dylan
Thomas
Garth, Caleb land agent, builder
Susan his wife
Christy; Aflred; Mary m. Fred Vincy*;
Jim; Ben; Letty their children
Middlemarch (1871–2) George Eliot (rn
Mary Anne, later Marian, Evans)
Garth, Dr partner to Dr Goodricke*
The Woman in White (1860) Wilkie
Collins
Garth, Miss governess and good genius of
the Vanstone* family
No Name (1862) Wilkie Collins
Garton, Robert friend to Frank Ashurst*
ss 'The Apple-Tree'
Five Tales (1918) John Galsworthy
Garvace proprietor of Port Burdock
Bazaar
The History of Mr Polly (1910) H. G.
Wells
Garvel, Archie half-brother to Beatrice
Normandy*
Tono Bungay (1909) H. G. Wells
Gascoigne ruined politician
ss 'Dr Heidegger's Experiment'
Twice-Told Tales (1837) Nathaniel
Hawthorne
Gascoigne, Henry, Revd Rector of Penni-

cote
Nancy his wife
Rex; Edwy; Warham; Anna; Lotta their
children
Daniel Deronda (1876) George Eliot (rn
Mary Anne, later Marian, Evans)
Gashe, Toby student
The Bell (1958) Iris Murdoch
Gashford hypocritical secretary to Lord
George Gordon*
Barnaby Rudge (1841) Charles Dickens
Gashleigh, Mrs
Eliza; Emily her daughters
A Little Dinner at Timmins (1852) W. M.
Thackeray
Gaspard Parisian whose child is run over
and killed by Marquis St Evremond*,
whom he murders
A Tale of Two Cities (1859) Charles
Dickens
Gasper really Camillo Ferneze*
The Case is Altered play (1609) Ben
Jonson
Gates, Martin friend to Stephen Monk*
The World in the Evening (1954) Christopher Isherwood
Gates, Robert lodge porter
The Great Hoggarty Diamond (1841)
W. M. Thackeray
Gatsby, Jay (rn Jimmy Gatz) tycoon, cc,
based in part on a bootlegger from Long
Island called Max Gerlach
The Great Gatsby (1925) F. Scott
Fitzgerald
Gattleton stockbroker
Sketches by Boz (1836) Charles Dickens
Gaulesse, Dick alias of Edward Christian*
Peveril of the Peak (1822) Walter Scott
Gaulesse, Dick see **Christian, Edward**
Gault, Selina mistress to Wolf Solent's*
father
Wolf Solent (1929) J. C. Powys
Gaunt presiding judge at unfair trial, now
mad
Winterset play (1935) Maxwell Anderson
Gaunt sailor in the torpedoed *Aurora*
The Ocean (1946) James Hanley
Gaunt see **Steyne, Marquis of**
Gaunt, Griffith alias Thomas Leicester*;
jealous bigamist, cc; m. Catherine
Peyton* and Mercy Vint
Griffith Gaunt, or Jealousy (1866); *Kate*

Peyton, or Jealousy play (1867) Charles Reade

Gaunt, John of Duke of Lancaster
King Richard II play (1623) William Shakespeare

Gauntlet, Emilia
Godfrey her brother
Sophy her cousin
Peregrine Pickle (1751) Tobias Smollett

Gauss, Richard Hosea ('Lefty') ex-preacher, crook, 'the grey streaks in his hair came from operations in prisons, performed by doctors told off to get lead out of him, and not too particular how they did it'
Love's Lovely Counterfeit (1942) James M. Cain

Gaux, Antionette (' 'Toinette') 'woman of the town'
Jacques her son
Shadows on the Rock (1932) Willa Cather

Gaveston, Piers catemite and favourite of Edward II*
Edward II play (1594) Christopher Marlowe

Gawill, Geoffrey crooked businessman
The Glass Cell (1965) Patricia Highsmith

Gawky Lieutenant
Roderick Random (1748) Tobias Smollett

Gawler coal merchant, keeper of lodging house
The Newcomes (1853–5) W. M. Thackeray

Gay, Peterkin youngest of trio of ccs, Jack Martin*, Ralph Rover* and himself, a fourteen-year-old
Coral Island† (1858) R. M. Ballantyne

Gay, Walter nephew of Sol Gills*, junior clerk in employ of Paul Dombey*, m. Florence Dombey*
Dombey and Son (1848) Charles Dickens

Gayarre dishonest trustee
The Quadroon (1856) Thomas Mayne Reid
The Octoroon play (1859) Dion Boucicault

Gayerson ('Very Young')
'Young' Gayerson his father
ss 'Venus Annodomini'
Plain Tales from the Hills (1888) Rudyard Kipling

Gazabee, Mortimer m. Lady Amelia de Courcy*
Dr Thorne (1858) Anthony Trollope

Gaze-oh, King father of Tulip Targett*
Geleley his son
The Sailor's Return (1925) David Garnett

Gazingi, Miss member of Crummles's* company
Nicholas Nickleby (1839) Charles Dickens

Geard, John Mayor of Glastonbury
Megan his wife
A Glastonbury Romance (1932) J. C. Powys

Gery, L. L.
ss 'With the Night Mail'
Actions and Reactions (1909) Rudyard Kipling

Gebbie, Mrs Catriona's* escort to Holland
her husband
Catriona (1893) Robert Louis Stevenson

Gecko fiddler, companion to Svengali*
Trilby (1894) George du Maurier

Geddes, Joshua Quaker
Rachel his sister
Redgauntlet (1824) Walter Scott

Gedge landlord of Royal Oak, Shepperton
Adam Bede (1859) George Eliot (rn Mary Anne, later Marian, Evans)

Geelan, Thomas, Father curate
Famine (1937) Liam O'Flaherty

Geierstein, Anne of
Count Albert her father, 'The Black Priest of St Paul's', wrongful holder of title
Sybilla her mother
Williewald father of Arnold Biederman and Albert
Heinrich their father
Anne of Geierstein (1829) Walter Scott

Geiger, Warren friend to Stephen Monk*
The World in the Evening (1954) Christopher Isherwood

Gellatley, Davie 'crack-brained knave'
Waverley (1814) Walter Scott

General, Mrs genteel chaperone of Mr Dorrit's* daughters
Little Dorrit (1857) Charles Dickens

General, The
Some Do Not (1924) Ford Madox Ford

Genestas, Major
Le Médecin de campagne (*The Country Doctor*) (1833) Honoré de Balzac

Genevieve fiancée of Joe Fleming* who begs him to give up boxing because she is jealous of the hold it has over him: he suggests she watch him fight, and he is killed
The Game (1905) Jack London

Geneviève, Mlle maid to Mrs Rawdon Crawley*
Vanity Fair (1847–8) W. M. Thackeray

Genslinger editor of newspaper in pay of crooked railroad bosses
The Octopus (1901) Frank Norris

Gentleman in Small Clothes, the madman
Nicholas Nickleby (1839) Charles Dickens

Geoffrey homosexual art student
A Taste of Honey play (1959) Shelagh Delaney

Geohegan, Denis the white-headed boy, cc, in pleasant comedy about group of crazy Irish; fails medical examinations, returns to acclaim
The White-headed Boy play (1921) Lennox Robinson

George cc, stolid caretaker at Charlotte's Buildings where Nelly Ambrose*, whom he eventually m., lives
A City Girl (1887) John Law (rn Margaret Harkness)

George criminal assistant to Bullivant*
Manservant and Maidservant (1947) Ivy Compton-Burnett

George history professor, cc of sex-duel comedy in tradition of Strindberg
Martha his wife
Who's Afraid of Virginia Woolf? play (1962) Edward Albee

George insolvent friend to Weller*
The Pickwick Papers (1837) Charles Dickens

George Mrs Jarley's* driver and later husband
The Old Curiosity Shop (1841) Charles Dickens

George mulatto slave of Harris*
Eliza his wife
Harry ('Jim Crow'), their son
Uncle Tom's Cabin (1851) Harriet Beecher Stowe

George one of three
Three Men in a Boat (1889) Jerome K. Jerome

George shooting-gallery proprietor
Bleak House (1853) Charles Dickens

George, M. narrator
The Arrow of Gold (1919) Joseph Conrad (rn Josef Teodor Konrad Korzeniowski)

George, Tobey army friend to George Macauley*, m. Bess Macauley*
The Human Comedy (1943) William Saroyan

George, Trooper name adopted by Rouncewell* when he ran from home
Bleak House (1853) Charles Dickens

Georgiana toadying cousin to Miss Haversham*
Great Expectations (1861) Charles Dickens

Georgiano, Black
ss 'The Red Circle'
His Last Bow (1917) Arthur Conan Doyle

Georgie Porgie
Georgina his 'native' wife
Grace his wife
ss 'Georgie Porgy'
Life's Handicap (1891) Rudyard Kipling

Gerald, Letty widow who m. Lester Kane*
Jennie Gerhardt (1911) Theodore Dreiser

Gerald, Maurice ('Maurice the Mustanger') really a knight, m. Louise Poindexter*
The Headless Horseman (1866) Thomas Mayne Reid

Geraldine beloved of Jack Wilton*
The Unfortunate Traveller, or, The Life of Jack Wilton (1594) Thomas Nashe

Gerard, Constantine Robert Moore's maternal grandfather, ruined by European unrest
Shirley (1849) Charlotte Brontë

Gerard, Lucy m. Marmaduke Heath*
Hervey her father
Lost Sir Massingberd (1864) James Payn

Gerard, Walter 'overlooker' at Trafford's Mill
Sybil his daughter, m. Charles Egremont*
Sybil (1845) Benjamin Disraeli

Gerhardt, Jennie driven from home when pregnant, becomes a 'kept woman'
Vesta her illegitimate child
William her father
Sebastian her brother

Jennie Gerhardt (1911) Theodore Dreiser

Germain, George, Lord see Brotherton

Gerrard, Mr young gentleman of the town, friend to Martin*
The Gentleman Dancing-Master play (1673) William Wycherley

Gerritt, Edna child killed by bomb or by an accident
ss 'Mary Postgate'
A Diversity of Creatures (1917) Rudyard Kipling

Gerrold a schoolmaster
The Two Noble Kinsmen play (1634) William Shakespeare and John Fletcher (?with Francis Beaumont)

Gersbach, Valentine Herzog's erstwhile best friend, lover of his ex-wife Madeline*
Herzog (1964) Saul Bellow

Gertie cc of tale of folk of Appalachia
The Dollmaker (1954) Harriette Arnow

Gertrude blind cc of French novella narrated by unnamed pastor; she dies when her sight is restored
La Symphonie Pastorale (1921) André Gide

Gertrude daughter to Touchstone*
Eastward Ho! play (1605) George Chapman, Ben Jonson and John Marston

Gertrude Hamlet's* mother
Hamlet play (1623) William Shakespeare

Gervais, Frank m. Jean Emerson*
A Lamp For Nightfall (1952) Erskine Caldwell

Gervois, Emily m. Sir Edward Beauchamp*
Sir Charles Grandison (1754) Samuel Richardson

Gessen, Adolph keeper of antique shop in Weissehäuser
ss 'The Talisman'
The Wind Blows Over (1936) Walter de la Mare

Gest, Norna cc of part of epic novel by winner (1944) of Nobel Prize
Den lange Rejse (*The Long Journey*) (1908–22) Johannes Vilhelm Jensen

Getall a box-keeper
The City Madam play (1658) Philip Massinger

Gethenites inhabitants of planet Gethen (Winter) who are androgynous

The Left Hand of Darkness (1969) Ursula Le Guin

Gething, Annis
Captain Gething her father
The Skipper's Wooing (1897) W. W. Jacobs

Getliffe, Francis Cambridge physicist, m. Katherine March*
Herbert his lawyer half-brother
The Strangers and Brothers† sequence (1940–70) C. P. Snow

Geyer, Ernestine laundry owner, best friend of Milly Ridge*, who deserts her
One Woman's Life (1913) Robert Herrick

Ghent, Julian advertising man who merges with his *Döppelganger*, Federigo*
Federigo, or The Power of Love (1954) Howard Nemerov

Ghost of Hamlet's father
Hamlet play (1623) William Shakespeare

Ghosts of Christmas Past, Present and Future, appearing to Scrooge*
A Christmas Carol (1843) Charles Dickens

Giacinta Rochester's* second mistress, unprincipled and violent
Jane Eyre (1847) Charlotte Brontë

Giacosa, Cavaliere possible father of Christina Light*
Roderick Hudson (1875) Henry James

Gianetta a *contadina*, m. Marco Palmieri*
The Gondoliers opera (1889) W. S. Gilbert and Arthur Sullivan

Gibbet highwayman
The Beaux' Strategem play (1707) George Farquhar

Gibbon, Martin Lynch
A Severed Head (1961) Iris Murdoch

Gibbons, Chris cc of notable Australian novel set in the Depression
The Go-Getter (1941) Leonard Mann

Gibbs, Alexander Maccolgie
The Cocktail Party play (1950) T. S. Eliot

Gibbs, Dr
his wife
George m. Emily Webb*; **Rebecca** their son and daughter
Our Town play (1938) Thornton Wilder

Gibbs, Ellen mistress to and nurse of Ralph Hoskin*; Mildred Lawson*, jealous of her, suggests that she slowly poisoned him

ss 'Mildred Lawson'
Celibates (1895) George Moore
Gibbs, Janet spinster
ss 'The Sad Fortunes of the Rev. Amos Barton'
Scenes of Clerical Life (1857) George Eliot (rn Mary Anne, later Marian, Evans)
Gibbs, John owner of the *Arabella*
Louisa his wife
The Lady of the Barge (1902) W. W. Jacobs
Gibbs, William hairdresser
Master Humphrey's Clock (1841) Charles Dickens
Gibby blundering and inept old friend to Elizabeth Wood*
An Advent Calendar (1971) Shena Mackay
Gibby servant to Captain Breton*
The Wonder play (1714) Susannah Centlivre
Gibley Gobbler leader of the turkeys
Uncle Remus (1880–95) Joel Chandler Harris
Gibson builder
The House With the Green Shutters (1901) George Douglas (rn George Douglas Brown)
Gibson Mr and Mrs see Nebu
Gibson, Dr
his wife, *née* Kirkpatrick
Molly their daughter
Wives and Daughters (1866) Mrs Gaskell
Gibson, Drag the 'stultifying force of the square world', threatening the town of Yellow Back Radio
Yellow Back Radio Broke Down (1969) Ishmael Reed
Gibson, Leah fiancée of Barty Josselin*
The Martian (1897) George du Maurier
Gibson, Lewis
Marise his sister
Friends and Relations (1931) Elizabeth Bowen
Gibson, Mrs wife of settler, lover of Nebu*
The Leopard (1958) Vic Reid
Gibson, Thomas jilts Camilla French*
He Knew He Was Right (1869) Anthony Trollope
Giddens, Regina *née* Hubbard, cc
Horace her husband
Alexandra their daughter

The Little Foxes play (1939) Lillian Hellman
Gidding rich American
The Passionate Friends (1913) H. G. Wells
Giddy, Patricia, Miss discoverer of gold in Anglesea
War in the Air (1906) H. G. Wells
Gideon, Arthur engaged to Jane Potter*
Potterism (1920) Rose Macaulay
Gifford, Avery indolent New Englander in satirical novel about author's own background
Betty his wife
Wickford Point (1939) John P. Marquand
Giglio legitimate King of Paflagonia, m. Rosalba*
The Rose and the Ring (1855) W. M. Thackeray
Gil-Martin the devil; and the dark side of Robert Wringhim*
The Private Memoirs and Confessions of a Justified Sinner (1824) as *The Suicide's Grave* (1828) as *Confessions of a Fanatic* in *Tales and Sketches* (1837) James Hogg
Gilbert a clerk
ss 'Old Men at Pevensea'
Puck of Pook's Hill (1906) Rudyard Kipling
Gilbert of Cranberry Moor landowner
The Monastery (1820) Walter Scott
Gilbert, Mark hosier's apprentice
Barnaby Rudge (1841) Charles Dickens
Gilbert, Mrs Eliza name under which the so improbable as to seem fictional 'bad girl', Lola Montez, later inspirational preacher (of the texts of a Revd Chauncey Burr) was buried in Brooklyn
Gilbert, Peter
his wife
The Browning Version play (1948) Terence Rattigan
Gilberts, The cannot be invited by the Middletons* to dinner because it is their turn to invite the Middletons to dinner
Sense and Sensibility (1811) Jane Austen
Gilbey
his wife
Bobby their son
Fanny's First Play play (1905) George Bernard Shaw
Gilbright, Theo one of Angelica

Deverell's* publishers
Hermione his wife
Angel (1957) Elizabeth Taylor
Gilchrist, Derek child of a famous man; no exception to the rule that such children are stupid; has eyes of cheap china blue
Patrick his father, great Irish-American historian
ss 'Children of the Great'
Unlucky for Pringle (1973) Wyndham Lewis
Gilchrist, Flora m. Vicomte de Kéroual de St Yves*
Miss Gilchrist her aunt
Ronald her brother
St Ives (1897) Robert Louis Stevenson
Gildersleeve, Lucian m. the Hon. Adela Trefoyle*
The Town Traveller (1898) George Gissing
Giles steward to Mrs Maylie*
Oliver Twist (1838) Charles Dickens
Giles unsuccessful party candidate
Middlemarch (1871–2) George Eliot (rn Mary Anne, later Marian, Evans)
Giles, George ('Giles Goat-Boy') cc
Giles Goat-Boy (1966) John Barth
Giles, Henry coroner
ss 'A Tragedy of Two Ambitions'
Life's Little Ironies (1894) Thomas Hardy
Giles, Oliver
ss 'The Three Strangers'
Wessex Tales (1888) Thomas Hardy
Gilfil, Maynard, Revd Vicar of Shepperton and Knebley, m. Caterina Sarti*
Lucy his sister, m. Arthur Heron*
ss 'Mr Gilfil's Love Story'
Scenes of Clerical Life (1857) George Eliot (rn Mary Anne, later Marian, Evans)
Gilfillian, Habakkuk ('Gifted Gilfillian') leader of the Cameronians
Waverley (1814) Walter Scott
Gill, Mr and Mrs clients of Mrs Gamp*
Martin Chuzzlewit (1844) Charles Dickens
Gill, Mrs Shirley Keeldar's* devoted housekeeper, who cheats on bills
Shirley (1849) Charlotte Brontë
Gillane, Peter
Bridget his wife
Patrick; Michael their sons

Kathleen ni Houlihan (1903) W. B. Yeats
Gillespie, Wattie old retired sawmill worker
Mirren his wife
Tom; Arnold; Walter; Meg; Grace; Bella; Kate their children
Time Will Knit (1938) Fred Urquhart
Gillett, John, Revd school chaplain
Stalky & Co.† (1899) Rudyard Kipling
Gillian, Dame Eveline Berenger's* tire-woman
The Betrothed (1825) Walter Scott
Gilliatt black assistant to Wolf Walker*, 'philosopher of darkness'
The Suicide Academy (1968); *The Rose Rabbi* (1971) Daniel Stern
Gillies prisoner in Hawes's* jail
It Is Never Too Late to Mend (1856) Charles Reade
Gilliewhackit ('Young') victim of smallpox and kidnapping
Waverley (1814) Walter Scott
Gillingham, George schoolmaster at Leddenton, friend to Philotson*
Jude the Obscure (1896) Thomas Hardy
Gillon, Ellen, Miss cc
ss 'Aunt Ellen'
Limits and Renewals (1932) Rudyard Kipling
Gills, Solomon proprietor of ship's instrument shop, *The Wooden Midshipman*, uncle to Walter Gay*
Dombey and Son (1848) Charles Dickens
Gilmore, Vincent part narrator, solicitor
The Woman in White (1860) Wilkie Collins
Gilpin draper and reluctant horseman
The Diverting History of John Gilpin poem (1782) William Cowper
Gilray
My Lady Nicotine (1890) J. M. Barrie
Gilray, Beatrice Burlap's* mistress
Point Counter Point (1928) Aldous Huxley
Gilson, John hideous schoolboy who murders an idiot dishwasher: 'I need women and because I can't buy or force them, I have to make poems for them. God knows how tired I am of using the insanity of Van Gogh and the adventures of Gauguin as can-openers'
The Dream Life of Balso Snell (1931) Nathanael West (rn Nathan Weinstein)

Gilthead a goldsmith
The Devil is an Ass play (1616) Ben Jonson
Gimblet, Brother drysalter
ss 'George Silverman's Explanation' in *All the Year Round* (1868) Charles Dickens
Gimpty crippled architect who wishes to destroy slums, in love with Kay 'Hilton'*; betrays Baby-Face Martin*
Dead End play (1936) Sidney Kingsley
Gines agent to Falkland* and incriminator of Caleb Williams*
Things as They Are, or The Adventures of Caleb Williams (1794) William Godwin
The Iron Chest play (1796) George Colman the Younger
Ginger Dick
Captains All† (1905) W. W. Jacobs
Ginger ill-tempered chestnut mare
Black Beauty (1877) Anna Sewell
Ginger Ted beachcomber, drunkard, lecher
ss 'The Vessel of Wrath'
Ah King (1933) W. Somerset Maugham
Gingos, The Eskimo family brought to Hollywood
The Day of the Locust (1939) Nathanael West (rn Nathan Weinstein)
Giorgio gondolier
The Gondoliers opera (1889) W. S. Gilbert and Arthur Sullivan
Giovanelli third-rate Italian companion of Daisy Miller*
Daisy Miller (1878) Henry James
Giovanni incestuous cc, son of Florio*
'Tis Pity She's a Whore play (1633) John Ford
Giovanni nephew to Cozimo*
The Great Duke of Florence play (1636) James Shirley
Gippings, Mrs landlady of the George
Three Men in a Boat (1889) Jerome K. Jerome
Gipps, Nancy schoolteacher
Mr Weston's Good Wine (1927) T. F. Powys
Girard, Girard magnate
Mme Girard his alcoholic wife
Malcolm (1959) James Purdy
Girder, Gibbie Cooper
Jean *née* Lightbody, his wife
The Bride of Lammermoor (1819)

Walter Scott
Girl, The Working cc of song ('You may fool the upper classes with your villainous demi-tasses/But heaven will protect the working girl') 'Heaven Will Protect the Working Girl' song (1909) Edgar Smith
Girouette, Emily society beauty who jilted Scythrop Glowry*
Nightmare Abbey (1818) Thomas Love Peacock
Gisborne of Woods and Forests
ss 'In the Rukh'
Many Inventions (1893) Rudyard Kipling
Gisquet Minister of Police
Tom Burke of Ours (1844) Charles Lever
Gissing, Alice mistress to Major Erlton*, killed during Indian Mutiny
On the Face of the Waters (1896) Flora Annie Steel
Gitano mysterious *paisano*
ss 'The Leader of the People'
The Red Pony (1937) both in *The Long Valley* (1938) John Steinbeck
Giulia a *contadina*
The Gondoliers opera (1889) W. S. Gilbert and Arthur Sullivan
Gladwin, John
ss 'John Gladwin Says'
Back o' the Moon (1906) Oliver Onions
Gladwin, Major uncle to Captain Sinclair*, in charge of Fort Detroit
The Settlers in Canada (1844) Captain Marryat
Glamour, Bob
Our Mutual Friend (1865) Charles Dickens
Glanders, Captain 50th Dragoon Guards
his wife
Anglesea his son
Pendennis (1848) W. M. Thackeray
Glansdale, William, Sir
King Henry VI plays (1623) William Shakespeare
Glanville, Louis Lady Constantine's* brother
Two on a Tower (1882) Thomas Hardy
Glanville, Mr cousin to Arabella*
The Female Quixote (1752) Mrs Charlotte Lennox
Glanville, Reginald, Sir old schoolmate and friend of Lord Pelham*, who clears

him of the charge of murdering Sir John Tirrell*
Ellen his sister m. Lord Henry Pelham*
Richard criminal counterpart to Henry Pelham*
Pelham, or The Adventures of a Gentleman (1828 rev. 1839) Edward Bulwer Lytton
Glasby, Harry pirate and traitor
The Pirate (1822) Walter Scott
Glascock, Charles eldest son of Lord Peterborough*
He Knew He Was Right (1869) Anthony Trollope
Glasher, Colonel
Lydia his wife
Henleigh; Antonia; Josephine her illegitimate children by Henleigh Grandcourt*
Daniel Deronda (1876) George Eliot (rn Mary Anne, later Marian, Evans)
Glass, Edward a marine
ss 'The Bonds of Discipline'
Traffics and Discoveries (1904) Rudyard Kipling
Glass, Franny actress
Zooey; Buddy; Seymour her brothers
Bessie their mother
Franny and Zooey (1961) J. D. Salinger
Glass, Margaret, Mistress tobacconist
Heart of Midlothian (1818) Walter Scott
Glavormelly actor
Nicholas Nickleby (1839) Charles Dickens
Gleeag surgeon and adulterer
ss 'Dayspring Mishandled'
Limits and Renewals (1932) Rudyard Kipling
Gleeson, Barney
Ellen his wife
Mary m. Martin Kilmartin*; **Ellie**; **Patrick** their children
Famine (1937) Liam O'Flaherty
Glegg retired wool-stapler
Jane his wife
The Mill on the Floss (1860) George Eliot (rn Mary Anne, later Marian, Evans)
Glen, Mr proprietor of the Dulcie Hotel
ss 'The Hitch-Hikers'
A Curtain of Green (1941) Eudora Welty
Glenallen, Earl of (William)
'Mr Lovel' his son
The Antiquary (1816) Walter Scott
Glenalmond, Lord (David Keith) friend to

Archie Weir
Weir of Hermiston (1896) Robert Louis Stevenson
Glendale, Richard, Sir loyal supporter of the Pretender
Redgauntlet (1824) Walter Scott
Glendenning, Pierre wealthy and cultivated young cc
his mother
Isabel his illegitimate sister
Pierre, or The Ambiguities (1852) Herman Melville
Glendenning, Simon
Elspeth his wife
Sir Halbert m. Mary Avenal*; **Edward** (Father Ambrose), his brother, Abbot of Kennaquahir, who becomes a monk when disappointed of the love of Mary Avenal
The Monastery; *The Abbot* (1820) Walter Scott
Glendower, Adeline heiress, one-time fiancée of Chatteris*
The Sea Lady (1902) H. G. Wells
Glenellen, Lord homosexual English peer exiled in Rome
The Judgement of Paris (1952) Gore Vidal
Glenmire, Lady sister-in-law to Mrs Jamieson*
Cranford (1853) Mrs Gaskell
Glenvarlock, Lord see **Olifaunt, Nigel**
Glick, Sammy movie tycoon who rises from the bottom
What Makes Sammy Run? (1941) Budd Schulberg
Gliddery or **Glibbery, Bob** potboy
Our Mutual Friend (1865) Charles Dickens
Glim, Revd curate at Endelstow
A Pair of Blue Eyes (1873) Thomas Hardy
Glitters, Lucy actress and sportswoman, m. Soapy Sponge*
Mr Sponge's Sporting Tour (1853); *Mr Facey Romford's Hounds* (1865) R. S. Surtees
Globson, Billy bully
The Uncommercial Traveller (1860–8) Charles Dickens
Glogwog, Chipkins, Sir aristocratic friend of the Egotistical Couple
Sketches of Young Couples (1840)

Charles Dickens

Gloriani French sculptor who correctly predicts that Roderick Hudson will 'fizzle out'
Roderick Hudson (1876) Henry James

Glorieux, le jester to Charles the Bold*
Quentin Durward (1823) Walter Scott

Glorvina Irish beauty: a self-portrait which had a huge success for a few years
The Wild Irish Girl (1806) Sydney Owenson (later Lady Morgan)

Glossin, Gilbert Ellangowan's agent, 'wily scoundrel'
Guy Mannering (1815) Walter Scott

Glossop assistant master, Stanstead School
The Little Nugget (1913) P. G. Wodehouse

Glossop, Roderick, Sir nerve specialist
Honoria his daughter
Thank You, Jeeves (1934) P. G. Wodehouse

Gloster, Duchess of (hist.)
King Richard II play (1623) William Shakespeare

Gloucester, Duke of
King Lear play (1623) William Shakespeare

Gloucester, Duke of (hist.) protector
King Henry VI plays (1623) William Shakespeare

Gloucester, Duke of (Prince Humphrey) (hist.)
King Henry V; King Henry VI plays (1623) William Shakespeare

Gloucester forger
Passages from the Diary of a Late Physician (1832) Samuel Warren

Glouster, Roberte narrator
Mayo Sergeant (1967) James B. Hall

Glover rival to Captain Wilson*
The Skipper's Wooing (1897) W. W. Jacobs

Glover, Catherine the fair maid
Simon her father
The Fair Maid of Perth (1828) Walter Scott

Glowry Scotch surgeon
Pendennis (1848) W. M. Thackeray

Glowry, Christopher owner of the abbey
Scythrop his son
Nightmare Abbey (1818) Thomas Love Peacock

Glubb, Old Brighton sailor

Dombey and Son (1848) Charles Dickens

Gluck kind brother to Hans* and Schwartz* in fable written by the author for the twelve-year-old girl he was (later) so unhappily to m.
The King of the Golden River (1850) John Ruskin

Glumboso prime minister to King Valoroso
The Rose and the Ring (1855) W. M. Thackeray

Glumdaclitch Gulliver's child nurse in Brobdingnag
Gulliver's Travels (1726) Jonathan Swift

Glumper, Thomas, Sir
Sketches by Boz† (1836) Charles Dickens

Glyde, Laura member of the Lunch Club, a ladies' literary discussion group
ss 'Xingu'
Roman Fever (1911) Edith Wharton

Glyde, Percival, Sir
Laura his wife
The Woman in White (1860) Wilkie Collins

Gnatho
The Parliament of Bees play (1641) John Day

Gobble, Judge
Sir Launcelot Greaves (1762) Tobias Smollett

Gobbo, Launcelot clownish servant
Old Gobbo his father, 'sand-blind, high-gravel blind'
The Merchant of Venice play (1623) William Shakespeare

Gobind a holy man
ss 'The Finances of the Gods'
Life's Handicap (1891) Rudyard Kipling

Gobler hypochondriac
Sketches by Boz† (1836) Charles Dickens

Gobrias father of Arbaces*
A King and No King play (1611) Francis Beaumont and John Fletcher

Goby saddler of Treddlestone
Adam Bede (1859) George Eliot (rn Mary Anne, later Marian, Evans)

Goby, Captain kindly friend to Mrs Mackenzie*
The Newcomes (1853–5) W. M. Thackeray

Godall, Theophilus see **Florizel, Prince of Bohemia**

Godbold, Ruth laundress, simple and kind

Riders in the Chariot (1961) Patrick White

Goddard, Mrs 'plain motherly' mistress of excellent old-fashioned school for young ladies
Emma (1816) Jane Austen

Godesberg, Margrave of (Karl)
Theodora his wife
A Legend of the Rhine (1845) W. M. Thackeray

Godfrey, Ella
her two daughters
ss 'The Dog Hervey'
A Diversity of Creatures (1917) Rudyard Kipling

Godsoe, John, Sergeant
ss 'A Madonna of the Trenches'
Debits and Credits (1932) Rudyard Kipling

Godwin, Dr
Adam Bede (1859) George Eliot (rn Mary Anne, later Marian, Evans)

Godwin, Richard cc
Without a City Wall (1968) Melvyn Bragg

Goering, Christina cc innovatory novel: in scarch of sainthood as distinct from her foil Frieda Copperfield* – this remarkable book is reprinted in the author's posthumous *My Sister's Hand in Mine* (1978)
Two Serious Ladies (1943) Jane Bowles

Goesler, Marie Max
Phineas Finn† (1869) Anthony Trollope

Goffe captain of the *Fortune's Favourite*
The Pirate (1822) Walter Scott

Goffe tenant farmer, Rabbit's End
Felix Holt (1866) George Eliot (rn Mary Anne, later Marian, Evans)

Gog (legd.)
Gog (1967) Andrew Sinclair

Gogan, Mary Anne Irish spinster on holiday in Italy
ss 'The Liars'
The Talking Trees (1971) Sean O'Faolain

Gogan, Mrs
Mollser her daughter
The Plough and the Stars play (1926) Sean O'Casey (rn John Casey)

Goggins, George, Dr biologist interested in mating habits, cc of novel by foremost erotologist
Come Out to Play (1961) Alex Comfort

Gogol Tuesday
The Man Who Was Thursday (1908) G. K. Chesterton

Goguelat Imperial Guardsman devoted to memory of Napoleon, of whom he delivers a fantastic biography in a candle-lit barn
Le Médecin de campagne (*The Country Doctor*) (1833) Honoré de Balzac

Goguelat killed in duel by St Ives*
St Ives (1897) Robert Louis Stevenson

Golbusto Emperor of Liliput
Gulliver's Travels (1726) Jonathan Swift

Gold, Bruce intellectual, cc
his father
Good as Gold (1979) Joseph Heller

Goldencalf, John, Sir
The Monikins (1835) James Fenimore Cooper

Goldfarb, Sara widow, compulsive eater, liver of life through soap operas, dexedrine addict, finally incarcerated schizophrenic, cc
Harry her son
Requiem for a Dream (1978) Hubert J. Selby

Golding apprentice to Touchstone*, m. Mildred*, later Deputy Alderman
Eastward Ho! play (1605) George Chapman, Ben Jonson and John Marston

Golding, Arthur miserable writer cc, jumps into Niagara Falls in mid-winter; in the author's first novel, which has been described as an 'awful performance'
Carrie his wife *née* Mitchell, based on the author's first wife, an alcoholic prostitute
Workers in the Dawn (1880) George Gissing

Golding, Emily m. James Forsyte*
The Forsyte Series (1906–33) John Galsworthy

Goldmore, Colonel from India
The Book of Snobs (1847) W. M. Thackeray

Goldring, Gertrude from Australia
Pilgrimage (1915–38) Dorothy M. Richardson

Goldsmith, Cecil college tutor
Carol his wife
Lucky Jim (1953) Kingsley Amis

Goldsmith, Henry, Mrs Esther Ansell's* benefactress
Children of the Ghetto (1892) Israel

Zangwill

Goldstein, Emmanuel enemy of the people
1984 (1949) George Orwell (rn Eric
Blair)

Goldthread, Laurence mercer of Abingdon
Kenilworth (1821) Walter Scott

Goldwire an old gentleman
Young Goldwire his son
The City Madam play (1658) Philip Massinger

Golightly, Holiday ('**Holly**') gay travelling
girl
Breakfast at Tiffany's (1958) Truman
Capote

Golightly, Lieutenant
ss 'The Arrest of Laurence Golightly'
Plain Tales from the Hills (1888) Rudyard Kipling

Gollo
Tessa his wife
Romola (1863) George Eliot (rn Mary
Anne, later Marian, Evans)

Gollop Joe Sedley's* London doctor
Vanity Fair (1847–8) W. M. Thackeray

Golloper, George, Sir
his wife
The Book of Snobs (1847) W. M.
Thackeray

Golspie, Mr
Lena his daughter
Angel Pavement (1930) J. B. Priestley

Golyadkin, Yakov Petrovich weak character whose double acts strongly until the
first Golyadkin is led to a madhouse
Dvoinik (The Double) (1846) Fyodor
Dostoievsky

Gombauld artist
Chrome Yellow (1922) Aldous Huxley

Gombold hero, pilgrim on the human
body
Head to Toe (1971) Joe Orton

Gomez
Pizarro play (1799) Richard Brinsley
Sheridan

Gomez, Butterfly Gonzalez de
Museum Pieces (1952) William Plomer

Gomez, Federico formerly Fred Culverwell
The Elder Statesman play (1958) T. S.
Eliot

Gomez, Miss Jamaican stripper saved by
Brethren of the Way in London suburb,
cc
Miss Gomez and the Brethren (1971)

William Trevor

Goneril one of the daughters of Lear*
King Lear play (1623) William Shakespeare

Gongago a Knight of Malta, General to the
Duchess of Siena
The Maid of Honour play (1632) Philip
Massinger

Gonzago, Louisa see **Mertoun, Basil**

Gonzales, Pablo
A Streetcar Named Desire play (1949)
Tennessee Williams (rn Thomas Lanier
Williams)

Gonzalo an honest councillor
The Tempest play (1623) William Shakespeare

Gooch, Mr solicitor
The Good Companions (1929) J. B.
Priestley

Good, Fluther carpenter
The Plough and the Stars play (1926)
Sean O'Casey (rn John Casey)

Good, John, Commander, RN (retd) native name **Bougwan**, one of the three
explorers (see **Quatermain**)
King Solomon's Mines (1885) Henry
Rider Haggard

Good, Matilda kindly boarding-house
keeper
The Dream (1924) H. G. Wells

Goodenough, John, Dr generous friend
Pendennis (1848) W. M. Thackeray

Goodenough, Mrs
Wives and Daughters (1866) Mrs Gaskell

Goodenough, Mrs who discloses
Henchard's past in court
The Mayor of Casterbridge (1886)
Thomas Hardy

Goodfellow, Robin 'puck' of the Shaws
Dramaticals
St Ronan's Well (1824) Walter Scott

Goodhay, J. C. rural evangelist
The Snopes trilogy (1940–59) William
Faulkner

Goodheart, Adam manservant to Sir
Ruthven Murgatroyd*
Ruddigore opera (1887) W. S. Gilbert
and Arthur Sullivan

Goodluck, Gawyn absent merchant, affianced to Dame Custance*
Ralph Roister Doister play (1566)
Nicholas Udall

Goodman friend to Valentine Vox*, forcibly locked up in lunatic asylum
Walter his evil brother
Valentine Vox, The Ventriloquist (1840) Henry Cockton

Goodman, Frank friendly cosmopolitan: one of the many guises of the unnamed cc
The Confidence Man: His Masquerade (1857) Herman Melville

Goodman, Mrs chaperone to Paula Power*
A Laodicean (1881) Thomas Hardy

Goodman, Theodora cc capable of visionary awareness of the world; 'goes mad' but may be assumed to have found fulfilment and lucidity
The Aunt's Story (1948) Patrick White

Goodman, Timothy, Revd
Hawbuck Grange (1847) R. S. Surtees

Goodrich drawing master
The Mill on the Floss (1860) George Eliot (rn Mary Anne, later Marian, Evans)

Goodricke, Dr
The Woman in White (1860) Wilkie Collins

Goodstock the Host (Lord Frampul) innkeeper
The New Inn play (1630) Ben Jonson

Goodwill keeper of the wicket-gate
The Pilgrim's Progress (1678–84) Ben Jonson

Goodwillie, Professor cc
The Professor's Love Story (1894) J. M. Barrie

Goodwin Mrs Potts'* maid and ally in frustrating wishes of Potts
The Pickwick Papers (1837) Charles Dickens

Goodwin wood-engraver, member of the Philosophers' Club
Daniel Deronda (1859) George Eliot (rn Mary Anne, later Marian, Evans)

Goodwin, Archie legman to Nero Wolfe* in detective stories onwards from
Fer-de-lance (1934) Rex Stout

Goodwin, Clara
Colonel Goodwin her father
The Adventures of Harry Richmond (1871) George Meredith

Goodwin, Lee
Sanctuary (1931) William Faulkner

Goodwood, Caspar Isabel Archer's* American suitor

The Portrait of a Lady (1881) Henry James

Goody, Mrs
Our Mutual Friend (1865) Charles Dickens

Goold, Ted knighted grocer
Daisy his wife
Prisoner of Grace (1952) Joyce Cary

Goops boneless half-human characters created as drawings, onwards from
The Lark (periodical) (1895) Gelett Burgess

Goorall, Yanko castaway, m. Amy Foster* ss 'Amy Foster'
Typhoon (1903) Joseph Conrad (rn Josef Teodor Konrad Korzeniowski)

Goose, Gibby half-witted boy
Old Mortality (1816) Walter Scott

Gorboduc King of Britain
Gorboduc play (1562) Thomas Norton and Thomas Sackville

Gorby, Sam detective
The Mystery of a Hansom Cab (1886) Fergus Hume

Gordeloup, Sophie, Madame Count Pateroff's* sister
The Claverings (1866–7) Anthony Trollope

Gordon, Colonel
Prince Otto (1885) Robert Louis Stevenson

Gordon, Emma tightrope dancer
Hard Times (1854) Charles Dickens

Gordon, Fayette adolescent cc
'Electric-Blue Damsels'
Dreams of Dead Women's Handbags (1987) Shena Mackay

Gordon, George, Lord (hist.)
Barnaby Rudge (1841) Charles Dickens

Gordon, Hugh Montgomery, Captain
Non-Combatants and Others (1916) Rose Macaulay

Gordon, John in love with and eventually m. Mary Lawrie*
An Old Man's Love (1884) Anthony Trollope

Gordon, Katherine, Lady
Perkin Warbeck play (1634) John Ford

Gordon, Maisie P. owner of, ticket seller and bouncer at the Venice Theatre in the Bowery
McSorley's Wonderful Saloon (1943) Joseph Mitchell

Gordon, Major friend to Captain Brown,
m. Jessie Brown*
Cranford (1853) Mrs Gaskell
Gordon, Squire
George his son, killed hare-coursing
Black Beauty (1877) Anna Sewell
Gordon, Stephen Mary Olivia Gertrude cc
Sir Philip her father
Lady Anne her mother
The Well of Loneliness (1928) Radclyffe
Hall
Gordon-Naysmith explorer and promoter
of 'quap'
Tono Bungay (1909) H. G. Wells
Gordyeef, Fomá cc who ruins himself
through his better impulses
Gordyeef his millionaire father
Fomá Gordyeef (1899) Maxim Gorki
Gore, 'Lawyer'
The Mill on the Floss (1860) George Eliot
(rn Mary Anne, later Marian, Evans)
Gore, Bill gang leader, shot by Smallways*
The War in the Air (1908) H. G. Wells
Goren tailor
Evan Harrington (1861) George
Meredith
Gorgon, George, Major-General, Sir
his wife, a brewer's daughter
George Augustus; Henrietta two of their
children
Lucy his niece
her mother
The Bedford Row Conspiracy (1840) W.
M. Thackeray
Goring senior constable
*Robbery Under Arms: A Story of Life
and Adventure in the Bush and in the
Goldfields of Australia* (1888, rev. 1889)
Rolf Boldrewood (rn Thomas Alexander
Browne)
Goring, Viscount (Arthur) son of the Earl
of Caversham*
An Ideal Husband play (1895) Oscar
Wilde
Goriot, Père cc, retired manufacturer of
vermicelli
Anastasia; m. Count de Restaud*;
Delphine m. Baron de Nucingen*; his
daughters, who abandon him
Père Goriot (1834) Honoré de Balzac
Gorloge, Mme sexual monster
Mort à credit (*Death on the Instalment
Plan*) (1936) Louis-Ferdinand Céline (rn

Louis-Ferdinand Destouches)
Gorman, Mrs fishwoman
Watt (1953) Samuel Beckett
Goro
Romola (1863) George Eliot (rn Mary
Anne, later Marian, Evans)
Gorton, Bill friend to Jake Barnes*
The Sun Also Rises (in England, *Fiesta*)
(1926) Ernest Hemingway
Gosford farmer
his wife
Catherine Furze (1893) Mark Ruther-
ford (rn William Hale White)
Goshawk
The Roaring Girl play (1611) Thomas
Middleton and Thomas Dekker
Goslet, Harry cc, son of an army sergeant
who believes himself to be an aristocrat
called 'Harry Le Breton'; cabinet maker;
m. Angela Messenger*
All Sorts and Conditions of Men (1882)
Walter Besant
Gosling, Giles landlord of Black Bear,
Cumnor
Cicely his daughter
Kenilworth (1821) Walter Scott
Gosport, Kate woman who embarrasses
John Leslie*
ss 'Junior'
Unlucky for Pringle (1973) Wyndham
Lewis
Gostanzo a knight
Valerio his son
Bellanora his daughter
All Fools play (1605) George Chapman
Gostray, Maria sounding-board for
Strether*; 'the reader's friend much
rather [than Strether's]' (the author's
preface)
The Ambassadors (1901) Henry James
Gotch, John, Sir
The Wonderful Visit (1895) H. G. Wells
Gotobed, Elias American politician (sena-
tor for Mickewa) puzzled by English
ways
The American Senator (1877); *The
Duke's Children* (1880) Anthony
Trollope
Goton Flemish cook at Mme Beck's*
Villette (1853) Charlotte Brontë
Gottesheim, Killian of the River Farm
Ottila his daughter
Prince Otto (1885) Robert Louis

Stevenson
Gottfried, Sir traitor
A Legend of the Rhine (1845) W. M. Thackeray
Gottlieb, August
The Human Comedy (1943) William Saroyan
Gottlieb, Max disillusioned but kindly scientist – based on the biologist Jacques Loeb
Arrowsmith (1925) Sinclair Lewis
Goudremark, Heinrich von, Baron
Prince Otto (1885) Robert Louis Stevenson
Gould, Charles mineowner cc
Mrs Gould, his wife
Nostromo (1906) Joseph Conrad (rn Josef Teodor Konrad Korzeniowski)
Gould, Humphrey idle bachelor
ss 'The Melancholy Hussar'
Life's Little Ironies (1894) Thomas Hardy
Gould, Joe lost soul, author of *An Oral History of Our Time*, eleven times as long as the Bible (but does it exist? – the answer is in the second title)
McSorley's Wonderful Saloon (1943); *Joe Gould's Secret* (1965) Joseph Mitchell
Gould, May schoolfriend to the Bartons*
A Drama in Muslin (1886) George Moore
Gould, Moses
Manalive (1912) G. K. Chesterton
Gourlay, Ailshire jester
The Antiquary (1816) Walter Scott
Gourlay, John cornbroker and carter of the village of Barbie; tyrant who fails; in novel opposed to the methods of the 'Kailyard School' of Barrie* and others
Gourlay, Mrs his feckless wife
John his son
The House With the Green Shutters (1901) George Douglas (rn George Douglas Brown)
Governor, Jack naval guest at the Haunted House
The Haunted House (1859) Charles Dickens
Gow (Smith), Henry ('Hal o' the Wind')
The Fair Maid of Perth (1828) Walter Scott
Gow, Harmon 'village oracle'

Ethan Frome (1911) Edith Wharton
Gowan, Harry indolent young artist, m. 'Pet' Meagles*
his mother
Little Dorrit (1857) Charles Dickens
Gower an officer
King Henry IV; King Henry V plays (1623) William Shakespeare
Gower chorus
Pericles play (1609) William Shakespeare
Gowing friend to the Pooters*
Diary of Nobody (1892) George and Weedon Grossmith
Gowran, 'Andy' steward of Portray Castle
The Eustace Diamonds (1873) Anthony Trollope
Gowrie, Vinson murdered hillsman
Crawford his brother, who shoots him and eventually kills himself while in jail
Intruder in the Dust (1948) William Faulkner
Grace, Ben ironically named hoodlum in hard-boiled thriller
Love's Lovely Counterfeit (1942) James M. Cain
Grace, Mrs a wench kept by Wheadle*
The Comical Revenge, or Love in a Tub play (1664) George Etherege
Gracedieu, Abel, Revd
Eunice his daughter, m. Philip Dunboyne*
Helena his adopted daughter
The Legacy of Cain (1889) Wilkie Collins
Graceless see Christian
Graciana cousin to Aurelia*, in love with Lord Beaufort*
The Comical Revenge, or Love in a Tub play (1664) George Etherege
Gradfield Budmouth architect
Desperate Remedies (1871) Thomas Hardy
Gradgrind, Thomas cc, 'logic-grinder', fanatic of the demonstrable fact, of the sort detested by Carlyle*, to whom the novel is dedicated
his wife
Louisa m. Joseph Bounderby*; **Tom** his children
Hard Times (1854) Charles Dickens
Gradman, Thomas clerk to Soames Forsyte*
The Forsyte series (1906–33) John

Galsworthy

Gradus, Jacob assassin
Pale Fire (1962) Vladimir Nabokov

Grady sailor on the *Sarah*
The Master of Ballantrae (1889) Robert Louis Stevenson

Grady servant to Captain Strong* and Colonel Altamont*
Pendennis (1848) W. M. Thackeray

Grady, Dan Irish soldier
ss 'The Mutiny of the Mavericks'
Life's Handicap (1891) Rudyard Kipling

Graeme (Avenal), Roland over-spirited young man of mysterious parentage in romances centring on period of Mary Queen of Scots' imprisonment at Lochleven; m. Catherine Seyton*
Magdalene his grandmother
The Monastery; The Abbot (1820) Walter Scott

Graeme, Alison heiress of Ballantrae, m. Henry, Lord Ballantrae*
The Master of Ballantrae (1889) Robert Louis Stevenson

Graff, Stanley salesman
Babbitt (1923) Sinclair Lewis

Grafinski treasurer, Gottesheim
Prince Otto (1885) Robert Louis Stevenson

Grafton
ss 'Piffingcap'
Adam and Eve and Pinch Me (1921) A. E. Coppard

Graham discovered by Isbister* in an apparent 200-year-old trance
When the Sleeper Wakes (1899) H. G. Wells

Graham, Cecil
Lady Windermere's Fan play (1892) Oscar Wilde

Graham, Dorothea cc in novel with sea scenes, by the author of the poem 'High Tide off the Coast of Lincolnshire'
Off the Skelligs (1872) Jean Ingelow

Graham, Helen cc who m. Arthur Huntingdon* as her second husband and leaves him for the sake of their son, but returns to nurse him at the end; afterwards m. Gilbert Markham*
The Tenant of Wildfell Hall (1848) Anne Brontë

Graham, Hugh apprentice
Master Humphrey's Clock (1841) Charles Dickens

Graham, Imogene Mrs Bowen's* protégée, entranced by Colville*
Indian Summer (1886) William Dean Howells

Graham, J. H. m. (2) Mrs Holbrook*
Emily his blind daughter, m. Philip Amory*
The Lamplighter (1854) Maria S. Cummins

Graham, John Head of his Chicago pork-packing firm
Letters from a Self-made Merchant to his Son (1903) G. H. Lorimer

Graham, Lucy see **Audley, Lady**

Graham, Mary orphan raised by Martin Chuzzlewit (Martin the Younger's grandfather)* as his daughter, m. Martin Chuzzlewit the Younger*
Martin Chuzzlewit (1844) Charles Dickens

Grainger friend to Steerforth*
David Copperfield (1850) Charles Dickens

Grammont, V. V. daughter of American oil millionaire
The Secret Places of the Heart (1922) H. G. Wells

Grampus, Alderman
his wife
Adeliza their daughter
The Professor (1837) W. M. Thackeray

Grampus, Greenland
The Impressions of Theophrastus Such (1879) George Eliot (rn Mary Anne, later Marian, Evans)

Grand Lunar Ruler of the Moon
The First Men in the Moon (1901) H. G. Wells

Grand, Digby Guards officer, narrator of hunting novel
Sir Peregrine his father
Captain Digby Grand: An Autobiography (1853) G. Whyte Melville

Grand, Guy war hero with hooks (which urgently grapple under a girl's skirt) for hands, cc
The Magic Christian (1960) Terry Southern

Grandcourt, Henleigh Mallinger selfish and tyrannical husband to Gwendolyn Harleth*, father of Lydia Glasher's* three children

Henleigh his father, formerly Mallinger"
Daniel Deronda (1876) George Eliot (rn
Mary Anne, later Marian, Evans)
Grandfather, Little Nell's* weak-charac-
tered gambler who tried to make his
grandchild's fortune by cards, Master
Humphrey's* elder brother
The Old Curiosity Shop (1841) Charles
Dickens
Grandgousier father to Gargantua*
*Gargantua, Pantagruel, Tiers Quart,
Quart Part* (1532–54) François Rabelais
Grandier, Urbain
The Devils play (1961) John Whiting
Grandison, Cardinal
Lothair (1870) Benjamin Disraeli
Grandison, Charles, Sir self-portrait of
'chivalrous gentleman'
Caroline m. Lord L*; **Charlotte** his sisters
Sir Thomas his father
Charles his cousin
Sir Charles Grandison (1754) Samuel
Richardson
Grandison, Gerald artist in Paris, m. Anne
Dunnock*
Go She Must! (1927) David Garnett
Grandison, Katherine m. Lord Montfort*
Henrietta Temple: A Love Story (1837)
Benjamin Disraeli
Grandissimes, Honoré banker
Honoré his older half-brother, a quad-
roon
Agricola his uncle, who killed Nancanou
De Grapions* over a gambling debt
The Grandissimes: A Story of Creole Life
(1880) George Washington Cable
Grandoni, Mme
Roderick Hudson (1875) Henry James
Graneangowl chaplain to Marquis of
Argyle*
The Legend of Montrose (1819) Walter
Scott
Granger, Bill
The Quiet American (1955) Graham
Greene
Granger, Edith m. as second wife Paul
Dombey, Snr*
Dombey and Son (1848) Charles Dickens
Granger, Etchingham writer cc novelist
The Inheritors, An Extravagant Story
(1901) Joseph Conrad (rn Josef Teodor
Konrad Korzeniowski) and Ford Madox
Ford

Granger, Frank American who falls in love
with his fiancée's cousin's English
ancestral home, but breaks off the engagement so that the peace of mind of its
owner, Miss Wenham*, shall not be
spoiled by her introduction into it
ss 'Flickerbridge'
The Better Sort (1903) Henry James
Grangerford, Colonel who, with his
family, shelters Huckleberry Finn
his wife
Bob; Tom; Charlotte; Sophia their children
The Adventures of Huckleberry Finn
(1884) Mark Twain (rn Samuel Langhorne Clemens)
Grannett parish overseer
Oliver Twist (1839) Charles Dickens
Grant farmer of Loranogie
The House With the Green Shutters
(1901) George Douglas (rn George
Douglas Brown)
Grant, Archibald, General
Annie his daughter, m. Lewis Arundel*
Lewis Arundel (1852) F. E. Smedley
Grant, Arthur radical, gentleman, seducer
of Nelly Ambrose*; she returns the
corpse of his baby to him, after it has died
in a charity hospital, in notable public
service novel* giving vivid picture of grim
conditions then prevailing in the slums
and amongst the poor
A City Girl (1887) John Law (rn
Margaret Harkness)
Grant, Bertha 'pale, fatal-eyed' cc of
novella
The Lifted Veil (1879) George Eliot (rn
Mary Anne, later Marian, Evans)
Grant, Donal muscular intellectual young
Scot, of upright nature
Donal Grant (1883) George Macdonald
Grant, Dr rector of Mansfield
his wife
Mansfield Park (1814) Jane Austen
Grant, Miss see **Carr**
Grant, Mrs daughter to Mr Skellhorn*
Hilda Lessways (1911) Arnold Bennett
Grant, Nan
Ben her seaman husband
The Lamplighter (1854) Maria S.
Cummins
Grant, Revd Dr 'short-necked, apoplectic'
his kindly wife

Mansfield Park (1814) Jane Austen

Grant, Revd Mr in love with Verity Cantacute*
Crump Folk Going Home (1913) Constance Holme

Grant, William of Prestongrange, Lord Advocate of Scotland
his three daughters
Miss Grant his sister and housekeeper
Catriona (1893) Robert Louis Stevenson

Grant-Menzies, Jock friend to Tony Last*
A Handful of Dust (1934) Evelyn Waugh

Grantly, Bishop of Barsetshire
Theophilus his son, archdeacon, m. Susan Harding*
Charles; Henry; Samuel; Florinda; Griselda children to Theophilus and Susan, the last-named m. Lord Dumbello
The Warden† (1855) Anthony Trollope

Granville, Juliet
The Wanderer (1814) Fanny Burney

Grapnell & Co. firm whose failure ruins Fanny Davilow*
Daniel Deronda (1876) George Eliot (rn Mary Anne, later Marian, Evans)

Gratiana
The Revenger's Tragedy (1607/8) ?Thomas Middleton; ?Cyril Tourneur

Gratiana daughter to Grissil* and Gwaltwer*
The Pleasant Commedye of Patient Grissill play (1603) Thomas Dekker

Gratiana stolen wife to Valerio*
All Fools play (1605) George Chapman

Gratiano friend to Antonio*
The Merchant of Venice play (1623) William Shakespeare

Grausis overseer of Penthea*
The Broken Heart play (1633) John Ford

Gravell, Walter
James ('Jerry') his son
ss 'Beauty Spots'
Limits and Renewals (1932) Rudyard Kipling

Graves family, the English emigrants
The Settlers in Canada (1844) Captain Marryat

Graves, Josiah bank manager
Of Human Bondage (1915) W. Somerset Maugham

Graves, Mr impotent man, and gardener of the fortunes of Ernest Louit*
Watt (1953) Samuel Beckett

Graves, Muley
The Grapes of Wrath (1939) John Steinbeck

Graviter, Edward
Loyalties play (1922) John Galsworthy

Gray disreputable fellow-conspirator with Wolfe Macfarlane*
ss 'The Body Snatcher'
The Wrong Box (1889) Robert Louis Stevenson and Lloyd Osbourne

Gray, Abe of the *Hispaniola*
Treasure Island (1883) Robert Louis Stevenson

Gray, Alice 'ancient domestic'
Habbie her husband
The Bride of Lammermoor (1819) Walter Scott

Gray, Charley ambitious banker
Point of No Return (1949) John P. Marquand

Gray, Dorian cc of 'decadent'* novel which is still widely read for its wit
The Picture of Dorian Gray (1890) Oscar Wilde

Gray, Ewan in love with Esther Sinclair*
My Mortal Enemy (1928) Willa Cather

Gray, Gideon surgeon, of Middlemas
Jean his wife
Menie their daughter
The Surgeon's Daughter (1827) Walter Scott

Gray, Jemmy prudent and provident farmer cc
John; Robin; Rose his children
ss 'Rosanna'
Popular Tales (1812) Maria Edgeworth

Gray, Jenny schoolgirl, member of the 'Brodie set'
The Prime of Miss Jean Brodie (1961) Muriel Spark

Gray, Laurence unjustly sentenced 'Convict 99' in anti-prison-conditions novel whose life extended (as a drama) for almost fifty years
Convict 99 (1898) Marie and Robert Leighton

Gray, Mrs milliner
The Mill on the Floss (1860) George Eliot (rn Mary Anne, later Marian, Evans)

Gray, Raymond ingenuous young barrister
his wife
Polly their daughter

The Book of Snobs (1847) W. M. Thackeray

Gray, Spencer see **Raymond, Geoffrey**

Graye, Cytherea cc, m. Edward Springrove*
Amos her architect father
his wife
Owen her brother
Desperate Remedies (1871) Thomas Hardy

Grayper, Mr and Mrs friends to the Copperfields*
David Copperfield (1850) Charles Dickens

Grayson, Hugh English officer and, at first, rival to Gabriel Harrison*
Walter his brother
The Yemassee (1835) William Gilmore Simms

Grazinglands gentleman from the Midlands
The Uncommercial Traveller (1860–8) Charles Dickens

Greatheart servant to the Interpreter
The Pilgrim's Progress (1678–84) John Bunyan

Greaves, Launcelot, Sir cc who is driven mad for love of Aurelia Darnel*, but is cured after being confined to a madhouse, in English variant on *Don Quixote* by one of its translators
Sir Everard his father
Jonathan his uncle
Dorothy illegitimate daughter of Jonathan, m. Thomas Clarke
Sir Launcelot Greaves (1762) Tobias Smollett

Grecco, Al (really Tony Murascho) bootlegger
Appointment in Samarra (1934) John O'Hara

Grecos, Colonel
The Firewalkers (1956) Francis King

Greech, Henry Bassington's uncle
The Unbearable Bassington (1912) Saki (rn Hector Hugh Munro)

Greedy a hungry justice of the peace
A New Way to Pay Old Debts play (1633) Philip Massinger

Green with Bushy and Bagot, creature to the King
King Richard II play (1623) William Shakespeare

Green, 'Goodhearted' sharp horse-trader
Mr Facey Romford's Hounds (1865) R. S. Surtees

Green, 'Poppet' mistress of Basil Seal*
Put Out More Flags (1942) Evelyn Waugh

Green, Anthony servant to Lady Constantine*
his wife, her maid
Two on a Tower (1882) Thomas Hardy

Green, Charles (hist.) balloonist
Sketches by Boz (1836) Charles Dickens

Green, Conrad loathsome producer
Marjorie née Manning, his wife, formerly of the Vanities Chorus
ss 'A Day With Conrad Green'
The Collected Short Stories (1941) Ring Lardner

Green, Glory starlet with whom Paul Cattleman* has an affair
The Nowhere City (1965) Alison Lurie

Green, James boon-companion to Jorrocks*
Jorrocks's Jaunts and Jollities (1838) R. S. Surtees

Green, Joe stable boy
Black Beauty (1877) Anna Sewell

Green, Kate, Mrs countrywoman
ss 'Fellow Townsman'
Wessex Tales (1888) Thomas Hardy

Green, Lily nun whom Fletcher* persuades to flee from her convent
Mike Fletcher (1889) George Moore

Green, Lucy childhood sweetheart of the Uncommercial Traveller
The Uncommercial Traveller (1860–8) Charles Dickens

Green, Mounser minor diplomat, m. Arabella Trefoil*
The American Senator (1877) Anthony Trollope

Green, Phil journalist who poses as a Jew for six months
Gentlemen's Agreement (1947) Laura Hobson

Green, Sally streetfighting girl
A Child of the Jago (1896) Arthur Morrison

Green, Saul
The Golden Notebook (1962) Doris Lessing

Green, Tom one-armed ex-soldier
Barnaby Rudge (1841) Charles Dickens

Gremio suitor to Bianca*
The Taming of the Shrew play (1623)
William Shakespeare
Grendall, Alfred, Lord
The Way We Live Now (1875) Anthony
Trollope
Grendel 1. monster, creature of a water-
hag; 2. cc of the tale told from his point of
view in American novel by scholar
Beowulf (*c.*745)
Grendel (1971) John Gardner
Grendon, Joseph Norfolk farmer
Marjorie his wife
Nancy their daughter
The Saliva Tree (1966) Brian W. Aldiss
Grenfel, Henry returned soldier whose
grandfather owned the farm upon which
the Misses Banford* and March* live;
falls in love with the latter
ss 'The Fox'
The Captain's Doll (1923) (in UK, *The
Ladybird*) D. H. Lawrence
Gresham prime minister
Phineas Finn† (1869) Anthony Trollope
Gresham, Frank, MP m. Lady Arabella de
Courcy*
Francis Newbold m. Mary Thorne*;
Augusta; Beatrice m. Revd Caleb Oriel*;
Nina their children
Dr Thorne (1858) Anthony Trollope
Gresham, Peter publisher uncle to Denham
Dobie, absorbed in 'meaningless in-
tricacy of the conventional life'
Evelyn his wife, social conformist (tells
Denham: 'Women who can't or won't
speak when they go out are a public
nuisance')
**Audrey; Catherine; Noel; Guy;
Humphrey** their children
Crewe Train (1926) Rose Macaulay
Gresley, Hester author of a novel, *An Idyll
of East London*; an emancipated
woman; cc
Lady Gresley her aunt, who dies
Revd James Gresley her clergyman
brother, who discovers *An Idyll of East
London* and burns it because it reminds
him of George Eliot*
Red Pottage (1899) Mary Cholmondeley
Gretry, Samuel wheat broker
The Pit (1903) Frank Norris
Grewgious, Hiram Rosa Bud's* guardian
Edwin Drood (1870) Charles Dickens

Grey Brother friend to Mowgli*
Jungle Books (1894–5) Rudyard Kipling
Grey, Agnes governess; cc and narrator, m.
Revd Edward Weston*
Mary her sister
Richard her father
her mother
Agnes Grey (1847) Anne Brontë
Grey, Aline lover of 'Bruce Dudley' (alias
John Stockton*); saved character*
Fred her husband, Bruce's employer
Dark Laughter (1925) Sherwood
Anderson
Grey, Caroline, Lady Barty Josselin's*
aunt
The Martian (1897) George du Maurier
Grey, Lady later Edward IV's queen
King Henry VI plays (1623) William
Shakespeare
Grey, Lord son to Elizabeth*
King Richard III play (1623) William
Shakespeare
Grey, Margaret ('**Maggie**') cc, m. Geoffrey
Trafford*, in author's best-known novel
John her uncle, a pharmacist
The Wooing O't (1873) Mrs Hector
Alexander
Grey, Matt smuggler
ss 'The Distracted Preacher'
Wessex Tales (1888) Thomas Hardy
Grey, Professor based on the philosopher
T. H. Green
Robert Elsmere (1888) Mrs Humphry
Ward
Grey, Eustace, Sir patient in madhouse
who narrates his decline in poem by
author of whom Byron* said, 'Though
Nature's sternest painter yet the best';
called by Scott* the 'British Juvenal'
'Sir Eustace Grey' poem
The Parish Register (1807) George
Crabbe
Grey, Sophia is ready to m. Willoughby*
Sense and Sensibility (1811) Jane Austen
Greybrook, Lady under whose auspices
Rita* 'comes out' in Paris
Rita (1856) Charles Aidé
Greylock, Jason unworthy lover of
Dorinda Oakley* who is cared for by her
after he has become degenerate
Barren Ground (1925) Ellen Glasgow
Greymarsh pupil at Dotheboys Hall
Nicholas Nickleby (1839) Charles

Dickens

Greymuzzle female otter
Tarka the Otter (1927) Henry Williamson

Greyslaer, Max young lawyer cc novel drawing on life of Brant and on the Kentucky Tragedy (see Beauchampe*); m. Alida de Roos
Greyslaer (1840) Charles Fenno Hoffman

Greystock, Frank cousin to Lady Eustace*, only son of Bishop of Bosborough*
The Eustace Diamonds (1873) Anthony Trollope

Greystoke, Lord cc brought up by apes (**Tarzan**) in popular series
Jane his wife
Jack his son
The *Tarzan* series (1912–32) Edgar Rice Burroughs

Gribling, Mr
ss 'Tea at Mrs Armsby's'
The Owl in the Attic (1931) James Thurber

Grice, Compson Wilfred Desert's* publisher
Flowering Wilderness† (1932) John Galsworthy

Gride, Arthur old usurer, eventually murdered in his bed
Nicholas Nickleby (1839) Charles Dickens

Gridley victim of Chancery Court, dies while evading arrest
Bleak House (1853) Charles Dickens

Gridley, Byles, Master brings home Myrtle Hazard* from near death at precipitous waterfall and is her guardian angel in novel whose plot was said to be 'so absurd that it hardly bears repetition' – but held to be acute in psychiatric detail
The Guardian Angel (1868) Oliver Wendell Holmes

Grier, Willy cc left in a garbage can
Money, Money, Money (1955) David Wagoner

Grierson, John
Hatter's Castle (1931) A. J. Cronin

Grierson, Emily, Miss eccentric spinster, courted by Homer Barron, a construction foreman who disappears
ss 'A Rose for Emily'
These Thirteen (1931) William Faulkner

Grieux, de, Chevalier young cc, narrator (to 'The Man of Quality') of the tale of his love for Manon Lescaut*; in novel which originally appeared as the seventh in a series entitled *Mémoires et aventures d'un homme de qualité* (1728–31)
Manon Lescaut (1731, rev. 1753) Abbé Prévost

Grieve, David Suvaret cc, orphan, m. (1) Lucy Purcell (who dies of cancer), (2) Dora, politically aware seamstress – in follow-up to *Robert Elsmere** which was regarded as a disappointment
Sandy; Cecile children to David and Lucy
Alexander his father, cabinet-maker
Louise his mother, a *grisette* of depraved tendencies
Louie his sister, who commits suicide
James; Jenny his grandparents
Reuben his weak uncle
The History of David Grieve (1892) Mrs Humphry Ward

Griffin cc
The Invisible Man (1897) H. G. Wells

Griffin the Pooter's* neighbour
The Diary of a Nobody (1892) George and Weedon Grossmith

Griffin, Lady rich young widow of General Griffin, m. Earl of Crabs (A. A. P)*
Matilda her daughter, m. the Hon. A. P. Deauceace*
ss 'The Amours of Mr Deauceace'
The Yellowplush Papers† (1852) W. M. Thackeray

Griffin, Miss 'model of propriety', principal of school
The Haunted House (1859) Charles Dickens

Griffin, Mr and Mrs parishioners of Revd Tuke*
Middlemarch (1871–2) George Eliot (rn Mary Anne, later Marian, Evans)

Griffin, Ray Jane Monk's* ex-lover
The World in the Evening (1954) Christopher Isherwood

Griffith usher to Queen Catherine*
King Henry VIII play (1623) William Shakespeare and John Fletcher

Griffiths, Clyde cc murderer (or is he?)
Asa his father
Elvira his mother
Hester (Esta); Julia; Frank his brother and sisters

Samuel his uncle
Elizabeth Samuel's wife
Gilbert; Myra; Bella their children
An American Tragedy (1925) Theodore
Dreiser
Griffiths, Dai miner
How Green Was My Valley (1939)
Richard Llewellyn
Griffiths, Harry Carey's* friend who goes
off with Mildred Rogers*
Of Human Bondage (1915) W. Somerset
Maugham
Griffiths, Samuel London banker
Redgauntlet (1824) Walter Scott
Grig, Lieutenant eventually General
despite being 'without two ideas'
Lord Grig his rich father
Mrs Perkins's Ball (1847) W. M.
Thackeray
Griggins funny young gentleman
Sketches of Young Gentlemen (1838)
Charles Dickens
Grildig Gulliver's* name in Brobdingnag
Gulliver's Travels (1726) Jonathan Swift
Grilla a page to Cuculus* in woman's dress
The Lover's Melancholy play (1629)
John Ford
Grimaldi a Roman gentleman
'Tis Pity She's a Whore play (1633) John
Ford
Grimble, Thomas, Sir
Nicholas Nickleby (1839) Charles
Dickens
Grimes chimney sweep, employer of Tom*
The Water Babies (1863) Charles Kings-
ley
Grimes Lady Sydenham's* lawyer
Joan and Peter (1918) H. G. Wells
Grimes, Ed brutal overseer in novel of
slavery in rural Georgia
Jubilee (1966) Margaret Walker
Grimes, Edgar bigamous crook
Decline and Fall (1928) Evelyn Waugh
Grimes, John fourteen-year-old illegiti-
mate boy who wrestles with conversion
Elizabeth his mother
Gabriel Grimes deacon, his stepfather
Deborah Gabriel's first wife
Esther Gabriel's mistress
Royal son of Gabriel and Esther
Go Tell It On The Mountain (1953)
James Baldwin
Grimes, Mrs housekeeper

Henry wharfinger, her brother-in-law
The Hole in the Wall (1902) Arthur
Morrison
Grimes, Peter sadistic cc
The Borough poem (1810) George
Crabbe
Grimley, Jane, Miss
her father, friend to the Ledburys*
Horatio her brother
The Adventures of Mr Ledbury (1844)
Albert Smith
Grimm, Percy castrator and murderer of
Joe Christmas*, acting in the name of
patriotism
Light in August (1932) William Faulkner
Grimmer, Miss partner with Miss
Drowvey*
A Holiday Romance (1868) Charles
Dickens
Grimshaw, Helen companion to Miss
Fothergill*
The Shrimp and the Anemone (1944)
L. P. Hartley
Grimshaw, Nathaniel cc m. (1) Denny
Sadgrove*, (2) Ann, his cousin
Sir James his father
Emily his mother
Daniel, Lord Grimshaw his uncle
Fanny Daniel's wife
Farewell to Youth (1928) Storm Jameson
Grimshaw, Robert cc, wealthy Londoner,
half-English, half-Greek, in love with
both Katya Lascarides* (whom he finally
m.) and Pauline Lucas*
A Call (1910) Ford Madox Ford
Grimstone Austin Ruthyn's* lawyer
Uncle Silas (1864) J. Sheridan Le Fanu
Grimstone, Aaron rich crooked builder
from the Midwest, eventually commits
suicide
Eleanor his daughter
Herbert his dissolute son; in novels
written as an answer to *The Bread
Winners**
The Money-Makers (1885) H. F. Keenan
Grimstone, Dr schoolmaster
his wife
Tom their son
Dulcie their daughter, one-time
sweetheart of Dick Bultitude*
Vice Versa (1882) F. Anstey (rn Thomas
Anstey Guthrie)
Grimstone, Jocasta, Mrs old despot

Hamilton her son
Osbert; Erica; Amy children of a dead
son
The Last and the First (1971) Ivy Comp-
ton-Burnett
Grimwig lawyer
Oliver Twist (1839) Charles Dickens
Grimwood, Eliza ('The Countess') whose
murder was never solved
Reprinted Pieces† (1838) Charles
Dickens
Grinder travelling showman
The Old Curiosity Shop (1841) Charles
Dickens
Grinderson, Gabriel clerk, partner to
Gilbert Greenhorn*
The Antiquary (1816) Walter Scott
Grindley of Corpus, tutor to Clive
Newcome*
The Newcomes (1853–5) W. M.
Thackeray
Gringoire name for the author in memoir
disguised as fiction
No Enemy: A Tale of Reconstruction
(1929) Ford Madox Ford
Grinny Granny Brer Wolf's* mother
Uncle Remus (1895) Joel Chandler
Harris
Grinsell, Lord
Middlemarch (1871–2) George Eliot (rn
Mary Anne, later Marian, Evans)
Grip raven who accompanies Barnaby
*Barnaby Rudge** (1841) Charles Dickens
Gripe rich usurer
Clarissa his wife
Corinna their daughter m. Dick Amlet*
The Confederacy play (1705) John
Vanbrugh
Gripe, Alderman seemingly precise, but a
covetous, lecherous old usurer of the city
Lady Flippant his sister, an affected
widow
Love in a Wood, or St James's Park
comedy (1672) William Wycherley
Gripp & Co. publishers
Middlemarch (1871–2) George Eliot (rn
Mary Anne, later Marian, Evans)
Grippy, Leddy cc
The Entail (1823) John Galt
Griselda cc
Grizzel; Tabitha her great-aunts
The Cuckoo Clock (1877) Mrs Moles-
worth

Grish Chunder law student
ss 'The Finest Story in the World'
Many Inventions (1893) Rudyard Kipl-
ing
Grissill daughter to Janicola*, wife to
Gwalter*, who tries her patience
*The Pleasant Commedye of Patient
Grissill* play (1603) Thomas Dekker
Griswold, Mr
Philip his son
Dead End play (1936) Sidney Kingsley
Grits, Miss plain but wealthy, m. Revd
Beilby Binny*
Vanity Fair (1847–8) W. M. Thackeray
Grizel
'The Painted Lady', her mother
Sentimental Tommy (1896) J. M. Barrie
Grizzle
Dr Syntax's* horse
Grizzle, Captain half-pay officer
The Book of Snobs (1847) W. M.
Thackeray
Grizzle, Mrs sister to Gamaliel Pickle*, m.
Commodore Trunnion*
Peregrine Pickle (1751) Tobias Smollett
Grobe, Nicholas, Revd
Alice his dead wife
Tamar their daughter
Mr Weston's Good Wine (1927) T. F.
Powys
Grobstock, Joseph 'pillar of the Syna-
gogue'
his wife
The King of Schnorrers (1894) Israel
Zangwill
Groby farmer, employer of Tess
Durbeyfield*
Tess of the D'Urbervilles (1891) Thomas
Hardy
Grogan, William telegraph operator
The Human Comedy (1943) William
Saroyan
Groneas courtier at the Laconian court
The Broken Heart play (1633) John Ford
Groom, John
Mansfield Park (1814) Jane Austen
Groombride, Lathabie, MP
ss 'Little Foxes'
Actions and Reactions (1909) Rudyard
Kipling
Grope, Albert Edward cc, narrator, jilted
by Rosalind Malley*, m. Laurette
Taube*

his mother
Albert Grope (1931) F. O. Mann
Groper, Colonel
Martin Chuzzlewit (1844) Charles Dickens
Grose, Mrs housekeeper at Bly
The Turn of the Screw (1898) Henry James
Grosvenor, Archibald idyllic poet, m. Patience*
Patience opera (1881) W. S. Gilbert and Arthur Sullivan
Grotait ('Old Smitem') gentlemanly president of Saw-Grinder's Union
Put Yourself in his Place (1870) Charles Reade
Grove, Lena
Light in August (1932) William Faulkner
Grove, Phyllis
her father
ss 'The Melancholy Hussar'
Life's Little Ironies (1894) Thomas Hardy
Grovelgrub, Revd Mr friend to Achthar*, and fellow villain
Melincourt, or Sir Oran Haut-on (1817) Thomas Love Peacock
Groves, 'Honest' James crooked landlord
The Old Curiosity Shop (1841) Charles Dickens
Grower, Mr, JP
The Mayor of Casterbridge (1886) Thomas Hardy
Grub, Gabriel drunken sexton
The Pickwick Papers (1837) Charles Dickens
Grubb partner to Smallways*
The War in the Air (1908) H. G. Wells
Grubbet, Jonathan bookseller
Waverley (1814) Walter Scott
Grubble, W. landlord of the Dedlock Arms
Bleak House (1853) Charles Dickens
Grudden, Mrs one of the Crummles* Company
Nicholas Nickleby (1839) Charles Dickens
Gureby, John Lord George Gordon's* manservant, who tried to protect him from his folly
Barnaby Rudge (1841) Charles Dickens
Gruffanuff, Jenkins rude porter turned into a brass knocker
Countess Barbara Griselda his hideous

wife
The Rose and the Ring (1855) W. M. Thackeray
Gruffydd, Merddyn, Revd minister of Chapel in love with Angharad Morgan*
How Green Was My Valley (1939) Richard Llewellyn
Grumball, Dr
Redgauntlet (1824) Walter Scott
Grumbit, Dorothy aunt to Martin Rattler*
Martin Rattler (1858) R. M. Ballantyne
Grumby, Major bushwacker, killer of Rosa Millard*
The Unvanquished (1938) William Faulkner
Grummer, Daniel old constable who arrested Pickwick* and others
The Pickwick Papers (1837) Charles Dickens
Grummidge, Dr of the Mudfog Association
The Mudfog Papers (1838) Charles Dickens
Grundy, Mrs a 'narrow minded person who keeps critical watch on the propriety of others'; 'Mrs Grundy always denies us exactly those things which we ourselves like best' says Trollope's* Julia Brabazon*
Speed the Plough play (1798) Thomas Morton
Grundy, Sam
Love on the Dole (1933) Walter Greenwood
Grunter parish clerk
his wife
Mr Weston's Good Wine (1927) T. F. Powys
Grushenska 'loose woman' redeemed
Bratya Karamazov (Brothers Karamazov) (1880) Fyodor Dostoievsky
Grushnitsky brash cadet, killed in duel by Pechorin*
Geroi Nas hego Vremeni (A Hero of Our Time) (1841) Mikhail Lermontov
Gryce, Ebenezer New York detective who was once famous, by author who established the form of the detective story; onwards from
The Leavenworth Case† (1878) Anna Katherine Green
Gryce, Miss teacher at Lowood who snores

Jane Eyre (1847) Charlotte Brontë

Gryce, Percy
The House of Mirth (1905) Edith Wharton

Gryphon, The
Alice in Wonderland (1865) Lewis Carroll (rn Charles Lutwidge Dodgson)

Guardiano
The Ward his nephew, who supplies comic relief
Women Beware Women tragedy (1657) Thomas Middleton

Guarine, Philip squire to Hugo de Lacy
The Betrothed (1825) Walter Scott

Guasconti, Giovanni student of Padua
ss 'Rappaccini's Daughter' 1844
Mosses from an Old Manse (1846) Nathaniel Hawthorne

Gubb, Hamnet
Horatio his father
The Simple Life Limited (1911) Daniel Chaucer (rn Ford Madox Ford)

Gudyill, John drunken butler
Old Mortality (1816) Walter Scott

Guendoline daughter to Corineus*, wife to Locrine*
Locrine play (1595) 'W. S.' (?George Peele; ?Robert Green)

Guermantes, Duc ('Basin') et **Duchesse** ('Oriane') members of an aristocratic and dominant family
Palamède, Baron de Charlus ('Même') the Duc's brother, inspired mainly by the author's friend, the writer Comte Robert de Montesquiou-Fezensac
Prince and Princesse de Guermantes their children
Marquise de Villeparisis aunt to the Duchesse; schoolfriend to Marcel's* grandmother
Robert, Marquis de Saint-Loup nephew to the Duc, m. Gilberte*
A la recherche du temps perdu (*In Search of Lost Time*) (1913–27) Marcel Proust

Guest head clerk to Utterson*
Dr Jekyll and Mr Hyde (1886) Robert Louis Stevenson

Guest, Maurice cc who fails to make good in art or love; one of the earliest of novels to treat homosexuality openly
Maurice Guest (1908) Henry Handel Richardson (rn Ethel Florence Lindesay Richardson Robertson)

Guest, Stephen in love with Maggie Tulliver*, m. Lucy Deane*
Laura; Miss Guest his sisters
The Mill on the Floss (1860) George Eliot (rn Mary Anne, later Marian, Evans)

Guest, William visionary narrator of Utopian novel
News From Nowhere (1891) William Morris

Guichard, Leon see **De La Touche**

Guiderius (Polydore) Cymbeline's* son
Cymbeline play (1623) William Shakespeare

Guido mentally defective son of Robin Vote* and Felix Volkbein
**Nightwood* (1936) Djuna Barnes

Guildford, Henry, Sir
King Henry VIII play (1623) William Shakespeare and John Fletcher

Guillem, Le Gros freebooter in 15th-century Aquitaine
Noémi his beautiful madcap daughter who leaves his band to join to Ogier del' Peyra*, whose son she loves
Noémi (1895) Sabine Baring-Gould

Guimarán, Pompeyo 'freethinker' who calls for confessor on his deathbed in classic Spanish novel
La Regenta (*The Regentess*, but tr. under its own title) (1884–5) Leopoldo Alas

Guinea, Philomena
The Bell Jar (1963 as *Victoria Lucas*) (1966) Sylvia Plath

Guinness, Nurse
Heartbreak House play (1917) George Bernard Shaw

Guiscard, Robert father of Behemond*
Gaita his wife
Count Robert of Paris (1832) Walter Scott

Guitar friend to Milkman Macon*
Song of Solomon (1977) Toni Morrison

Guizac, Mr Polish Catholic refugee
ss 'The Displaced Person'
A Good Man is Hard to Find (1955) Flannery O'Connor

Gules, Lord grandson to Lord Saltire*
The Book of Snobs (1847) W. M. Thackeray

Gull page to Jack Dapper*
The Roaring Girl play (1611) Thomas Middleton and Thomas Dekker

Gulla Kuttah Mullah, The bandit chief

ss 'The Lost Legion'
Many Inventions (1893) Rudyard Kipling

Gulliver, Lemuel cc, narrator
his wife
John; Betty his children
Gulliver's Travels (1726) Jonathan Swift

Gullman, Frank courtesan
A Mad World My Masters play (1608)
Thomas Middleton

Gumbo Black valet to Henry Warrington*
The Virginians (1857–9) W. M. Thackeray

Gumbril, Theodore cc
his father
Antic Hay (1923) Aldous Huxley

Gummidge, Mrs depressed housekeeper of
the boat on the beach
David Copperfield (1850) Charles Dickens

Gunch, Vergil coal dealer
Babbitt (1923) Sinclair Lewis

Gunga Dass
ss 'The Strange Ride of Morrowbie Jukes'
Wee Willie Winkie (1888) Rudyard Kipling

Gunnery, Mr teacher and benefactor of
Godwin Peak*
Born in Exile (1892) George Gissing

Gunning 'heavy, elderly, pleasant'
Last Post (1928) Ford Madox Ford

Gunpowder horse borrowed by Ichabod
Crane*
The Legend of Sleepy Hollow (1819–20)
Washington Irving

Gunter quarrelsome young medical student
The Pickwick Papers (1837) Charles Dickens

Gunville farmer
his wife
Barty their son, m. Mally Trenglos*
ss 'Malachi's Cove'
Lotta Schmidt (1867) Anthony Trollope

Gunwater steward to Sir Bounteous Progress*
A Mad World My Masters play (1608)
Thomas Middleton

Guppy, William clerk to Kenge and
Carboy, in and out of love with Esther
Summerson*
his excitable old mother
Bleak House (1853) Charles Dickens

Gurdjieff (hist.) a teacher of dancing
*All and Everything: Beelzebub's Tales to
His Grandson* (1950) G. I. Gurdjieff

Gurney, Gilbert cc
Gilbert Gurney (1836) Theodore Hook

Gurth 'son of Beowulph'
Ivanhoe (1820) Walter Scott

Gurton, Gammer
Gammer Gurton's Needle play (1575)
?William Stevenson

Gusher missionary friend to Mrs Pardiggle*
Bleak House (1853) Charles Dickens

Gustav III, King (hist.) of Sweden – who
had two distinctly different profiles
The King With Two Faces (1897) Mary
Coleridge

Guster the Snagsbys'* maidservant, perhaps called Augusta; developed fits
Bleak House (1853) Charles Dickens

Guthrie, Chris cc of what has been called
'the first truly Scottish novel since Galt'*,
m. (1) Ewan Tavendale*, farmer, (2)
Revd Robert Colquhoun*, (3) Ake
Ogilvie*
Ewan Tavendale, Jr., her son
John Guthrie her father, crofter
Jean Guthrie her mother, drudge
Will her brother
A Scots Quair trilogy: *Sunset Song*
(1932); *Cloud Howe* (1934); *Grey Granite* (1935) Lewis Grassic Gibbon (rn
James Leslie Mitchell)

Guthrie, Miss gardener
ss 'Neighbours'
A Beginning (1955) Walter de la Mare

Gutman, Caspar suave criminal in pursuit
of the Maltese Falcon
The Maltese Falcon (1930) Dashiell
Hammett

Guttersnipe, Ma mother to Rosanna
Frettleby*
The Mystery of a Hansom Cab (1886)
Fergus Hume

Guttlebury, Lord epicure
The Book of Snobs† (1847) W. M.
Thackeray

Guy, Octavius ('Gooseberry')
The Moonstone (1868) Wilkie Collins

Guzman de Alfarache rogue cc of early
Spanish picaresque novel* first tr. into
English (as *the Rogue*) in 1622
Guzman de Alfarache (1599–1605)

Mateo Alemán

Gwalter Marquis of Salucia, married to Grissil*, whose patience he tries

Gwalter their son

The Pleasant Commedye of Patient Grissill play (1603) Thomas Dekker

Gwendoline voracious sexual partner to Ferdinand* on channel crossing

Mort à credit (Death on the Instalment Plan) (1936) Louis-Ferdinand Céline (rn Louis-Ferdinand Destouches)

Gwenthyan a Welsh widow, cousin to Gwalter*

The Pleasant Commedye of Patient Grissill play (1603) Thomas Dekker

Gwenwyn (or Gwenwynwen) Prince of Powys

The Betrothed (1825) Walter Scott

Gwillin, Mrs housekeeper to the Brambles*

The Expedition of Humphrey Clinker (1771) Tobias Smollett

Gwilt, Lydia, Miss the author's most brilliantly contrived villainess, malice personified; originally maid to Ozias Midwinter's* mother

Armadale (1866) Wilkie Collins

Gwyn gentleman farmer, in poem of that name, who has no use for public opinion, but whose mistress, Rebecca*, becomes his wife

The Borough poem (1810) George Crabbe

Gwyon, Wyatt forger, ex-seminarian, cc

The Recognitions (1955) William Gaddis

H

H. cc (an unused initial in the author's name)
Black List, Section H. (1971) Francis Stuart
Habingdon, Harold puritan cc of historical novel by Anglophobe who was Van Buren's Naval Secretary
Miriam his daughter, m. Langley Tyringham* after he saves her from gibbet
The Puritan and His Daughter (1849) James Kirke Paulding
Hableton, Mrs
The Mystery of a Hansom Cab (1886) Fergus Hume
Hack Bacon's* reader and editorial manager
Pendennis (1848) W. M. Thackeray
Hackbut, Anthony
his sister, m. William Fleming*
Rhoda Fleming (1865) George Meredith
Hackbutt, Tarver
Fanny his daughter
Middlemarch (1871–2) George Eliot (rn Mary Anne, later Marian, Evans)
Hacker
Polly opera (1729) John Gay
Hackett, Mr elderly gentleman
Watt (1953) Samuel Beckett
Hackett, Tod painter cc; victim of Greener* ('her invitation wasn't to pleasure, but to struggle, sharp and hard, closer to murder than to love')
The Day of the Locust (1939) Nathanael West (rn Nathan Weinstein)
Hackitt farmer and churchwarden
his wife
ss 'The Sad Fortunes of the Rev. Amos Barton'
ss 'Mr Gilfil's Love Story'
Scenes of Clerical Life (1857) George Eliot (rn Mary Anne, later Marian, Evans)
Haddocriss, Mrs
her husband, archdeacon

Before the Bombardment (1926) Osbert Sitwell
Haden, Lily
her mother
Doris her sister
Sinister Street† (1913) Compton Mackenzie
Hadgi Swiss valet to Pickle*
Peregrine Pickle (1751) Tobias Smollett
Hadji-Asvatz-Troov Bokharian dervish
All and Everything: Beelzebub's Tales to His Grandson (1950) G. I. Gurdjieff
Hadleigh, Emilia ('Millie') witch
William her son
Edward her husband
ss 'Physic'
The Wind Blows Over (1936) Walter de la Mare
Hadwin, Mr upon whose farm Mervyn* finds a home
Eliza his daughter, with whom Mervyn falls in love
Arthur Mervyn, or Memoirs of the Year 1793 (1800) Charles Brockden Brown
Haffen, Mrs blackmailer
The House of Mirth (1905) Edith Wharton
Hagadorn, 'Jee' evangelist and abolitionist
The Copperhead (1893) Harold Frederic
Hagan, Geohegan Irish actor, later parson, m. Lady Maria Esmond*
his mother
The Virginians (1857–9) W. M. Thackeray
Hagberd, Captain
ss 'Tomorrow'
Typhoon (1903) Joseph Conrad (rn Josef Teodor Konrad Korzeniowski)
Hagenbach, Archibald von robber-knight
Anne of Geierstein (1829) Walter Scott
Hagenström, Consul the Buddenbrooks'* business rival
Buddenbrooks, Verfall einer Familie (tr. as *Buddenbrooks*) (1901) Thomas Mann
Haggage, Dr drunken debtor in

Marshalsea
Little Dorrit (1857) Charles Dickens
Haggarty, Dionysius Irish army surgeon
Jemima Amelia his slatternly and disfigured wife
Molly; Jemima their children
his mother, *née* Burke
Charles his brother
Men's Wives (1843) W. M. Thackeray
Haggerston, Mr Mr Gardiner's* lawyer
Pride and Prejudice (1813) Jane Austen
Haggerty, Paulie friend to Studs Lonigan*
The Studs Lonigan trilogy (1932–5) James T. Farrell
Haggise watchman
Bartholomew Fair play (1631) Ben Jonson
Haggistoun, Mrs chaperone to Rhoda Swartz*
Vanity Fair (1847–8) W. M. Thackeray
Haigha and Hatta messengers
Alice Through the Looking-Glass (1872) Lewis Carroll (rn Charles Lutwidge Dodgson)
Haik Secretary for War, deposes Saranson* from presidency of USA, declares war on Mexico (1939)
It Can't Happen Here (1935) Sinclair Lewis
Haines
Ulysses (1922) James Joyce
Hajji Baba Persian barber who becomes doctor and executioner in novel which led to protests from the Persian Embassy
The Adventures of Hajji Baba of Isaphan (1824); *The Adventures of Hajji Baba in England* (1828) James Justinian Morier
Haakonsson, Håkon pretender to Norwegian throne in conflict with fellow-pretender Erle Skule Bårdsson*; in author's first successful play (his tenth)
Kongs-emmnerne (*The Pretenders*) play (1863) Henrik Ibsen
Halborough, Joshua, Sr. master-millwright
Rosa m. Albert Fellmer*; **Joshua; Cornelius** his children
Selina his second wife
ss 'A Tragedy of Two Ambitions'
Life's Little Ironies (1894) Thomas Hardy
Halcombe, Marion, Mrs part-narrator, Laura Fairlie's* sister

The Woman in White (1860) Wilkie Collins
Halcro, Claud Zetland poet
The Pirate (1822) Walter Scott
Halcyon a kingfisher
Tarka the Otter (1927) Henry Williamson
Haldan, Paul idealistic socialist who fails when put to the test
Night Journey (1950) Albert Guerard
Haldimund, Ewes, Sir friend to Lord Dalgarno*
The Fortunes of Nigel (1822) Walter Scott
Haldin, Victor revolutionary student in St Petersburg
Natalie Victorovna his sister
his mother
Under Western Eyes (1911) Joseph Conrad (rn Josef Teodor Konrad Korzeniowski)
Hale Captain of the *Altair*
Gallions Reach (1927) H. M. Tomlinson
Hale, Charles ('**Fred**') murdered by Pinkie's* gang
Brighton Rock (1938) Graham Greene
Hale, Margaret cc, m. John Thornton*
Revd Richard her father
Maria her mother
Frederick her brother
North and South (1855) Mrs Gaskell
Hale, Ruth, Mrs widow, *née* Varnum*, landlady
Ethan Frome (1911) Edith Wharton
Haley slave trader
Uncle Tom's Cabin (1851) Harriet Beecher Stowe
Halford, Mr recipient of Gilbert Markham's history of the tenant
The Tenant of Wildfell Hall (1848) Anne Brontë
Hali ideal man in stilted play that runs exactly and uncannily counter to the author's novel *All About H. Hatterr*
Hali play (1950, rev. 1967) G. V. Desani
Halifax, John cc, m. Ursula March*
Muriel born blind; **Guy; Walter; Ralph; Edwin** m. Louise d'Argent*; **Maud** m. Lord Ravenel*, their children
John Halifax, Gentleman (1856) Mrs Craik
Halifax, Mrs
The Heart of the Matter (1948) Graham

Greene

Halkett, Cecilia loved by Nevile Beauchamp*, who loses her to his boring second cousin
Beauchamp's Career (1876) George Meredith

Hall, Christopher lover of Leo Proudhammer*
Tell Me How Long the Train's Been Gone (1968) James Baldwin

Hall, Cyril, Revd Vicar of Nunnely, near-sighted and simple
Margaret his sister
Pearson a lawyer relation
Shirley (1849) Charlotte Brontë

Hall, Fred Krogh's* agent
England Made Me (1935) Graham Greene

Hall, Jenny, Mrs proprietor of the Coach and Horses at Iping
The Invisible Man (1897) H. G. Wells

Hall, Maurice Christopher cc, homosexual stockbroker
Maurice (1971) E. M. Forster

Hall, Philip
Helena his wife
his mother
Sarah his sister
ss 'Interlopers at the Knap'
Wessex Tales (1888) Thomas Hardy

Hallam, Julie, Second Officer (WRNS)
The Cruel Sea (1951) Nicholas Monsarrat

Hallam, Martin m. Mary Llewellyn*
The Well of Loneliness (1928) Radclyffe Hall

Hallam, Howard, Sir
Captain Brassbound's Conversion play (1900) George Bernard Shaw

Halleck, Ben, Revd supporter of Marcia Hubbard*, whom ultimately he cannot decide whether or not to marry
A Modern Instance (1882) William Dean Howells

Haller, Harry cc of what became a campus novel of the 1960s by an early 'magic realist'
Steppenwolf (1927) Hermann Hesse

Halley, Lieutenant
ss 'The Lost Legion'
Many Inventions (1895) Rudyard Kipling

Halliday, Brother Mormon agent in

Bristol
The Uncommercial Traveller (1860–8) Charles Dickens

Halliday, Manley drunken old writer-idol of the 1920s, now movie-script writing when sober, but trying (and failing) to make a post-war comeback; based on an idea of what the author's friend Scott Fitzgerald* might have become had he survived
The Disenchanted (1951) Budd Schulberg

Halliday, Oliver ambitious to become a 'nature poet', fails in love affair with Alys Browne, who wants to be 'distinguished' by 'reading Tolstoy and playing Schumann in the late afternoon'
Happy Valley (1939) Patrick White

Halliday, Philip school friend to Frank Ashurst*
Stella m. Frank Ashurst; **Sabina; Freda** his sisters
The Apple Tree (1918) John Galsworthy

Halliday, Simeon Quaker
Rachel his daughter
Uncle Tom's Cabin (1851) Harriet Beecher Stowe

Hallijohn, George murdered by Francis Levinson*
Aphrodite his daughter, m. Joe Jiffin
Joyce her half-sister, servant to Lady Isabel Carlyle*
East Lynne (1861) Mrs Henry Wood

Hallin, Edward lecturer on economics, friend to Arthur Raeburn*
Marcella (1894) Mrs Humphry Ward

Halliwell, Captain
The Little Minister (1891) J. M. Barrie

Hallorson, Edward, Professor American archaeologist
Maid in Waiting (1931) John Galsworthy

Hallward artist
The Picture of Dorian Gray (1891) Oscar Wilde

Halm-Eberstein, Leonore, Princess prima donna, Daniel Deronda's mother
Daniel Deronda (1876) George Eliot (rn Mary Anne, later Marian, Evans)

Halpern, Mrs Jenny Stern's daughter
her husband
How Much? (1961) Burt Blechman

Halsey, Lanning in love with Tina Ralston*

ss 'the Old Maid'
Old New York (1924) Edith Wharton
Ham, Sarah ('Star Drake')
ss 'The Comforts of Home'
Everything That Rises Must Converge
(1960) Flannery O'Connor
Hamel, Isadore sculptor, m. Lucy Dormer
Ayala's Angel (1881) Anthony Trollope
Hamilton, Freddy British official in
Jerusalem
The Mandelbaum Gate (1965) Muriel
Spark
Hamilton, Guy journalist in Australian
novel-thriller
The Year of Living Dangerously (1978)
C. J. Koch
Hamilton, Melanie m. Ashley Wilkes*
Charles her brother, Scarlett O'Hara's*
first husband
Wade their son
Sarah Jane ('Miss Pittypat') their aunt
Uncle Henry
Gone With the Wind (1936) Margaret
Mitchell
Hamilton, Olive friend to Mary Love*
Nigger Heaven (1926) Carl Van Vechten
Hamilton, Samuel ('Sam') Irish neighbour
to the Trasks*
East of Eden (1952) John Steinbeck
Hamilton-Wells, Angelica cc, m. Mr
Kilroy on condition she is free to do what
she likes; she dresses as a man until
discovered to be otherwise; in once very
popular novel
Diavolo her twin
The Heavenly Twins (1893) Sarah Grand
(rn Frances McFall)
Hamlet Prince of Denmark, cc
Hamlet play (1623) William Shakespeare
Hamley, Squire
his wife
Roger; Osborne their sons
Wives and Daughters (1866) Mrs Gas-
kell
Hamlin, Jack polite and melancholy
gambler who appears in many stories,
onwards from
Gabriel Conroy (1876) Bret Harte
Hamlin, Walter satirized 'artist and poet of
highest repute' whom Miss Brown* m.
out of pity
Miss Brown (1884) Vernon Lee (rn Viola
Paget)

Hamlyn, Geoffry idealized elderly success-
ful colonist; in novel described by
Furphy* as 'exceedingly trashy and mis-
leading'
The Recollections of Geoffry Hamlyn
(1859) Henry Kingsley
Hamm son of Nagg and Nell, blind
chair-bound autocrat
Endgame play *Fin de partie* (1957)
Samuel Beckett
Hammerfield, Dr
The Iron Heel (1908) Jack London
Hammergallow, Lady of Siddermorton
The Wonderful Visit (1895) H. G. Wells
Hammerton, Mrs aunt to Andrea Fitch*
her husband, auctioneer
Vanity Fair (1847–8) W. M. Thackeray
Hammerton, William
The Knight of the Burning Pestle play
(1609) Francis Beaumont and John
Fletcher
Hammon a city gentleman
The Shoemaker's Holiday (1600)
Thomas Dekker
Hammond, Geoffrey
The Letter play (1927) W. Somerset
Maugham
Hammond, John
Jane his wife
ss 'The Stranger'
The Garden Party (1922) Katherine
Mansfield (rn Katherine Mansfield Beau-
champ)
Hammond, Mrs Arthur Machin's* land-
lady
Lynda; Ian her children
This Sporting Life (1960) David Storey
Hamolinadir sympathetic Assyrian
philosopher
*All and Everything: Beelzebub's Tales to
His Grandson* (1950) G. I. Gurdjieff
Hamps, Clara the Clayhangers'* aunt
The Clayhanger trilogy (1910–16)
Arnold Bennett
Hampton see **Montdore**
Hampton, Cedric heir presumptive to
Lord Montmore*
Love in a Cold Climate (1949) Nancy
Mitford
Hampton, Clay slow-witted cc, murderer,
Klansman, in novel dealing in depth with
the Ku Klux Klan in North Carolina
his nagging mother

his aunt
his brother
Season of Fear (1960) Guy Owen
Hamson, Chris, Mrs
These Twain (1916) Arnold Bennett
Hamson, Freddie, Dr fake specialist
The Citadel (1937) A. J. Cronin
Hanaud, Inspector famous French detective in mysteries onwards from
At the Villa Rose† (1910) A. E. W. Mason
Hand newspaper editor
Exiles play (1918) James Joyce
Hand, The
ss 'The Haunted and the Haunters'
The Haunted and the Haunters (1857) Edward Bulwer Lytton
Handbeck, J. store owner in major Alabama trilogy
The Forge (1931); *The Store* (1932); *Unfinished Cathedral* (1934) T. S. Stribling
Handcock
Some Experiences of an Irish R. M. (1899) O. E. Somerville and Martin Ross (rn Edith Somerville and Violet Martin)
Handford, Julius name used by Harmon* when viewing drowned body supposed to be his own
Our Mutual Friend (1865) Charles Dickens
Handley, Albert
The Death of William Posters† (1965) Alan Sillitoe
Hands, Israel of the *Hispaniola*
Treasure Island (1883) Robert Louis Stevenson
Handy, Abel inmate of Hiram's Hospital
The Warden (1855) Anthony Trollope
Handyman, F., Captain m. Hester Warrington*
The Virginians (1857–9) W. M. Thackeray
Hanger yeoman to Curtleaxe*
The Roaring Girl play (1611) Thomas Middleton and Thomas Dekker
Hanky, Professor
Erewhon Revisited (1901) Samuel Butler
Hanmer engineer
Middlemarch (1871–2) George Eliot (rn Mary Anne, later Marian, Evans)
Hanna, Eustace, Revd
ss 'The Record of Badalia Herodsfoot'

Many Inventions (1893) Rudyard Kipling
Hannah family servant, at first tried to turn the collapsing Jane Eyre* away
Jane Eyre (1847) Charlotte Brontë
Hannah mother to Eban*
ss 'The Talent Thou Gavest'
My People (1915) Caradoc Evans (rn David Evans)
Hannah Mrs Martin's* old retainer
Two on a Tower (1882) Thomas Hardy
Hannah, Dame m. Sir Roderic Murgatroyd*
Ruddigore opera (1877) W. S. Gilbert and Arthur Sullivan
Hannasyde
ss 'On the Strength of a Likeness'
Plain Tales from the Hills (1888) Rudyard Kipling
Hannay, Eliza cc of acidulous autobiographical novel of New Zealand suburban life
The Godwits Fly (1938) Robin Hyde (rn Iris Wilkinson)
Hannay, Richard, Major-General Sir clean-limbed reluctant British agent and narrator in classic spy romances
The Thirty-Nine Steps (1915); *Greenmantle* (1916); *Mr Standfast* (1919) John Buchan
Hannigan, Bessie
The Crock of Gold (1912) James Stephens
Hanning, Emily m. Mr Lester*
ss 'To Please his Wife'
Life's Little Ironies (1894) Thomas Hardy
Hans with Schwartz*, evil brother of three (see Gluck*) in widely read fable
The King of the Golden River (1850) John Ruskin
Hansa, Per Norwegian farmer who treks from Minnesota to settle in Dakota in 'trilogy of epic power' published in Norwegian but highly successful in translation in America: the three parts trace the history of him and his children and friends
Beret his pious wife who becomes a fanatic
Peder Victorious his son and third child
Susie *née* Doheny wife to Peder Victorious

Giants in the Earth: A Saga of the Prairie (1924–5, tr. 1927); Peder Victorious (1928, tr. 1929); Their Fathers' God (1931, tr. 1931) Ole Edvart Rölvaag

Hanson, Jeffrey friend to Arnold Middleton*
The Restoration of Arnold Middleton play (1967) David Storey

Hapgood, Nurse
The Shrimp and the Anemone (1944) L. P. Hartley

Haphazard, Abraham, Sir eminent lawyer
The Warden (1855) Anthony Trollope

Hapless, M., Miss secretary to Jane Palfry*
Antigua Penny Puce (1936) Robert Graves

Happer, Mysie
'Hob' Miller her father
Kate her aunt
The Monastery (1820) Walter Scott

Hara Singh Ressaldar
ss 'The Man Who Was'
Life's Handicap (1891) Rudyard Kipling

Harahrahhoorhy king on Saturn
All and Everything: Beelzebub's Tales to His Grandson (1950) G. I. Gurdjieff

Harbinger, Viscount (Claud Fresnay) m. Lady Barbara Caradoc
The Patrician (1911) John Galsworthy

Harborough, Mrs
Select Conversations With an Uncle (1895) H. G. Wells

Harbottle, Elijah, the Hon. Mr Justice one of Dr Hesselius'* 'cases', cc, found hanged by the neck, not suicide; 'good Christian'
Flora his wife, née Carwell
ss 'Mr Justice Harbottle'
In a Glass Darkly (1872) J. Sheridan Le Fanu

Harbottle, General
Bracebridge Hall (1823) Washington Irving

Harcourt gallant in love with Alithea Pinchwife*
The Country Wife play (1673) William Wycherley

Harcourt, Henry, Sir MP who kills himself when his career crashes, m. Caroline Waddington*
The Bertrams (1859) Anthony Trollope

Harcourt-Reilly, Henry, Sir
The Cocktail Party play (1950) T. S. Eliot

Hardcaster, Percy cc
The Revenge for Love (1937) Wyndham Lewis

Hardcastle, Lord (Michael), ('Barnabas')
The Fortune of Christina M'Nab (1901) Sarah Macnaughtan

Hardcastle, Mr country squire
Dorothy his wife
Kate their daughter
She Stoops to Conquer play (1773) Oliver Goldsmith

Hardcastle, Sally
her parents
Harry her brother
Love on the Dole (1933) Walter Greenwood

Hardcome, James m. (1) Olive Pawle, (2) Emily née Darth*
Steve his cousin, Emily Darth's first husband
ss 'The History of the Hardcomes'
Life's Little Ironies (1894) Thomas Hardy

Harden, Charles, Revd
Mary his sister
Marcella (1894) Mrs Humphry Ward

Harden, Lucia high-minded aristocrat beloved of Keith Rickman*
The Divine Fire (1905) May Sinclair

Hardey, Michael one-time MFH
Handley Cross (1843) R. S. Surtees

Hardie, Mr Edinburgh lawyer
Heart of Midlothian (1818) Walter Scott

Hardie, Richard banker
Julia née Dodd, his wife
Alfred; Jane their children
Hard Cash (1863) Charles Reade

Harding, Colonel JP
Lorna Doone (1869) R. D. Blackmore

Harding, Dickon shoeing-smith
The Story of Ragged Robyn (1945) Oliver Onions

Harding, Mr old friend to Sir Thomas Bertram*
Mansfield Park (1814) Jane Austen

Harding, Nan medical student
Little Men† (1871) Louisa M. Alcott

Harding, Septimus, Revd cc
Susan m. Theophilus Grantly*, **Eleanor** m. (1) John Bold*, (2) Francis Arabin*, his daughters
The Warden† (1855) Anthony Trollope

Harding, Warren (hist.) 'the first president

to be loved by his/bitterest enemies is dead/the only man woman or child who wrote/a single declarative sentence with seven grammatical/errors "is" dead/he's/ "dead"/if he wouldn't have eaten them Yapanese Craps/somebody might hardly never not have been/unsorry perhaps' 'XXVII' poem
W (ViVa) (1931) e. e. cummings

Harding, William friend to Martin Faber* who reconstructs, by means of a picture hung in public, Faber's murder of a woman he has tried to seduce after the latter falsely accuses him of having an affair with his wife Constance *née* Claiborne*
Martin Faber (1833, rev. as *Martin Faber, the Story of a Criminal*, 1837) William Gilmore Simms

Hardinge, Revd Mr Miles Wallingford's* guardian
Rupert; Lucy his children
Afloat and Ashore (1844) James Fenimore Cooper

Hardisty, Percy, Sir 'gentleman of the old order'
Rachel his wife
Mellicent; Polly his daughters
Men and Wives (1931) Ivy Compton-Burnett

Hardman, Mrs Mrs Pryor's* employer
Shirley (1849) Charlotte Brontë

Hardmuth, Frank villainous attorney who arranges assassination of Governor of Kentucky, and charges Whipple* with murder
The Witching Hour play (1907) Augustus M. Thomas

Hardonne, Putricides so translated (1977) from the Polish name **Patrycydes Tengier** man in state of permanent erection; in only lately recognized modern Polish classic
Nienasycenie: poweiesc (*Insatiability* (1930)) Stanislaw Ignacy Witkiewicz

Hardross, John
ss 'The Quiet Woman'
Adam and Eve and Pinch Me (1921) A. E. Coppard

Hardy, Captain
Journey's End play (1928) R. C. Sherriff

Hardy, Letitia
The Belle's Strategem play (1780)

Hannah Cowley

Hardy, Richmond, Sir
The Secret Places of the Heart (1922) H. G. Wells

Hardy, Thomas, Captain (hist.) Lord Nelson's post-captain
The Trumpet Major (1880) Thomas Hardy

Hare, Dorothy cc
Revd Charles Hare her father, Vicar of St Athelstan's, Knype Hill, Suffolk
Sir Thomas his cousin
A Clergyman's Daughter (1935) George Orwell (rn Eric Blair)

Hare, Mary elderly spinster of Xanadu
Riders in the Chariot (1961) Patrick White

Hare, Revd old friend to Lizzie Norton*
Kitty his daughter, who kills herself
ss 'John Norton'
Celibates (1895) George Moore

Hare, Richard, Mr Justice
Anne his wife
Richard; Anne; Barbara m. Archie Carlyle*
East Lynne (1861) Mrs Henry Wood

Harebrain, Dick rich fop in satire (in octosyllabics) on American education
The Progress of Dulness poem (1772–3) John Trumbull

Harebrain, Master a citizen
Mistress Harebrain his wife
A Mad World My Masters play (1608) Thomas Middleton

Haredale, Geoffrey
Reuben his elder brother
Emma his niece, m. Edward Chester*
Barnaby Rudge (1841) Charles Dickens

Harford, George (Lord Illingworth) cc, father of Gerald Arbuthnot*
A Woman of No Importance play (1893) Oscar Wilde

Hargrave, Mrs pretentious squanderer
Walter m. Helen *née* Lawrence; **Millicent** m. Ralph Hattersley*; **Esther** m. Frederick Lawrence, her children
The Tenant of Wildfell Hall (1848) Anne Brontë

Hargraves, Stephen degenerate groom and murderer, already (before exposure) whipped by Aurora Floyd* for ill-treating her dog
Aurora Floyd (1863) Mary Braddon

Harharkh, Gornahoor Beelzebub's* friend, at one time regarded as a great scientist, but now considered a has-been; his home is at Rirkh, on Saturn
Rakhoorkh his son, a conscious individual; godson of Beelzebub*
All and Everything: Beelzebub's Tales to His Grandson (1950) G. I. Gurdjieff
Hariton, Archangel
All and Everything: Beelzebub's Tales to His Grandson (1950) G. I. Gurdjieff
Harkaway, Harry, Lord
Hawbuck Grange (1847) R. S. Surtees
Harker, Chisholm ('Sard' Harker) sardonic chief officer of the 'Pathfinder' who makes a heroic journey
Sard Harker (1924) John Masefield
Harker, Jonathan cc
Minna his wife
Dracula (1867) Bram Stoker
Harkless, John reforming newspaper editor cc in romance that saw its author famous overnight
The Gentleman From Indiana (1899) Booth Tarkington
Harkness, Gary cc
End Zone (1972) Don DeLillo
Harland, Joe
Manhattan Transfer (1925) John Dos Passos
Harleigh, Henry, Sir
Passages from the Diary of a Late Physician (1832) Samuel Warren
Harlequin a poet
Los intereses creados (The Bonds of Interest) play (1908) Jacinto Benavente
Harleth, Gwendolen daughter to Mrs Davilow*, m. Henleigh Mallinger Grandcourt*
Daniel Deronda (1876) George Eliot (rn Mary Anne, later Marian, Evans)
Harley hero of the most influential of the novels of sentiment* and the apogée of the Richardsonian* influence: mortally sensitive and morally perfect, Harley dies when he learns that his love is returned
The Man of Feeling (1771) Henry Mackenzie
Harley, Adrian seedy intellectual, tutor to his cousin Richard Feverel*
Mr Justice Harley his father
his mother, née Feverel
The Ordeal of Richard Feverel: A

History of Father and Son (1859, rev. 1878) George Meredith
Harlowe, Clarissa beautiful and saintly young woman who refuses to marry Roger Solmes*, whom she despises; but she is tricked into running away with Lovelace*, whose attempts to seduce her fill most of the pages of this, the longest novel in the language
Clarissa, or The History of a Young Lady (1747–8, augmented 1749) Samuel Richardson
Harman in love with Diana Oldboy*
Lionel and Clarissa play (1768) Isaac Bickerstaffe
Harman, Isaac, Sir
Ellen his wife, née Sawbridge*, cc
The Wife of Sir Isaac Harman (1914) H. G. Wells
Harman, Joe Australian stockman, m. Jean Paget
their children
A Town Like Alice (1950) Neville Shute
Harmon, John m. Bella Wilfer*; called himself Rokesmith after being taken for dead
Old Harmon his father, Dust Contractor
Our Mutual Friend (1865) Charles Dickens
Harms, Clayton electric-sign salesman, 'Ace' Chisholm's* lodger
Eustace Chisholm and the Works (1968) James Purdy
Harnham, Edith who writes love letters for her maid Anna*
Mr Harnham her complacent husband
ss 'On The Western Circuit'
Life's Little Ironies (1894) Thomas Hardy
Haroun al Raschid caliph
Hassan play (1923) James Elroy Flecker
Harpax
Ralph Roister Doister play (1551) Nicolas Udall
Harpax centurion
Count Robert of Paris (1832) Walter Scott
Harper, Joe close friend to Tom Sawyer*
The Adventures of Tom Sawyer (1876) Mark Twain (rn Samuel Langhorne Clemens)
Harper, Mr part narrator
A Different Drummer (1962) William

Melvin Kelley
Harper, Nathanael
Major Frederick; Nathanael Locke m.
Agatha Bowen*; **Eulalie; Harriet** m.
Marmaduke Dugdale; **Mary** his children
Agatha's Husband (1853) Mrs Craik
Harpsfield, Tobias villain
The Puritan and His Daughter (1849)
James Kirke Paulding
Harrass SS doctor
Nord (*North*) (1960) Louis-Ferdinand
Céline (rn Louis-Ferdinand Destouches)
Harrel gambler; suicide; first guardian of
Cecilia Beverley*
Mrs Harrel his wife, who introduces
Cecilia to society
Cecilia (1782) Fanny Burney
Harries ('Bull') astronomer
ss 'Unprofessional'
Limits and Renewals (1932) Rudyard
Kipling
Harriet Archduchess of Roumania,
admirer of Orlando*
Orlando (1928) Virginia Woolf
Harrington, Evan cc, m. Rose Jocelyn*
Melchisedek his father, tailor
Caroline m. Major Strike*; **Harriet** m.
Andrew Cogglesby*; **Louise** m. Comte
de Saldar*, his sisters
Evan Harrington (1861) George
Meredith
Harrington, Stanley furniture manufac-
turer
his culture-vulture wife
their son and daughter
Five Finger Exercise play (1958) Peter
Shaffer
Harrington the elder
Harrington, his legitimate son who even-
tually kills himself
Harriot, his illegitimate daughter, who
dies of shock
Maria his mistress; ccs of epistolary
work, sometimes called America's first
novel, dealing with threatened incestuous
marriage between the elder Harrington's
two children
The Power of Sympathy (1789) William
Hill Brown
Harris brutal slaveowner
Uncle Tom's Cabin (1851) Harriet
Beecher Stowe
Harris greengrocer

The Pickwick Papers (1837) Charles
Dickens
Harris see Short
Harris, Jim black law student, m. Ella
Downey*
All God's Chillun Got Wings play (1924)
Eugene O'Neill
Harris, Miss fiancée of Ted*
The Lady of the Barge (1802) W. W.
Jacobs
Harris, Mr alias of Lord Highgate*
The Newcomes (1853–5) W. M.
Thackeray
Harris, Mrs mythical friend of Mrs Gamp*
Martin Chuzzlewit (1844) Charles
Dickens
Harris, Tom thirty-year-old salesman
travelling in office supplies
ss 'The Hitch-Hikers'
A Curtain of Green (1941) Eudora Welty
Harris, William Samuel one of the three
Three Men in a Boat (1889) Jerome K.
Jerome
Harrison creator of the famous *Martin
Renard* detective series and hopeful to
make 'art' of this; narrator; also trying to
write the *Life of Michael Andriaovsky**
ss 'Hic Jacet: A Tale of Artistic Con-
science'
Widdershins (1911) Oliver Onions
Harrison of British Intelligence
The Heat of the Day (1949) Elizabeth
Bowen
Harrison prefect
Stalky & Co.† (1899) Rudyard Kipling
Harrison sailor on the *Ghost*
The Sea Wolf (1904) Jack London
Harrison, Anthony wealthy timber
merchant
Frances *née* Fleming, his wife
Michael; Nicholas; John; Dorothy their
children
Bartholomew Anthony's hypochondriac
brother
Harrison, Vera wife to Bartholomew;
lover of Ferdie Cameron
Dorothy her daughter by Bartholomew;
becomes feminist and is imprisoned
Nicky her son by Bartholomew m. Phyllis
Desmond
The Tree of Heaven (1917) May Sinclair
Harrison, Colonel
Mansfield Park (1814) Jane Austen

Harrison, Dr
Amelia (1751) Henry Fielding

Harrison, Gabriel mysterious English officer who opposes the rebellion of Sanutee*; he turns out to be Governor Craven; m. Bess Matthews*
The Yemassee (1835) William Gilmore Simms

Harrison, Joseph
ss 'The Naval Treaty'
The Memoirs of Sherlock Holmes (1893) Arthur Conan Doyle

Harrison, Mary m. Arthur Jarvis*
John her brother
their parents
Cry, the Beloved Country (1948) Alan Paton

Harrowdean, Mrs friend to Mr Britling*
Oliver her husband
Mr Britling Sees It Through (1916) H. G. Wells

Harry the 'fool of quality' second son of Earl of Moreland; so regarded because he seemed less able than his brother; in influential and popular novel
The Fool of Quality (1760–77) Henry Brooke

Harry jealous narrator
ss 'The Talisman'
The Wind Blows Over (1936) Walter de la Mare

Harry of the *Hispaniola*
Treasure Island (1883) Robert Louis Stevenson

Harry see Uncleharri

Harry who objects to Jeanie's* breasts being soaked with *Flowers of Passion* scent, and isn't 'warmed up' by it
ss 'Sweat'
I Fell for a Sailor (1940) Fred Urquhart

Harsanyi, Andor pianist
The Song of the Lark (1915) Willa Cather

Hart, Dr
ss 'Mr Gilfil's Love Story'
Scenes of Clerical Life (1857) George Eliot (rn Mary Anne, later Marian, Evans)

Hart-Harris, Claud friend to Flora Poste*
Cold Comfort Farm (1932) Stella Gibbons

Harthouse, James easy-mannered parliamentary candidate at Coketown, almost seduces Louise Bounderby*
Hard Times (1854) Charles Dickens

Hartington, Sub-Lieutenant, RN befriends John Lynwood*
The Gunroom (1919) Charles Morgan

Hartletop, Lord see **Dumbello, Lord**

Hartletop, Marchioness of née Griselda Grantly*
The Dowager Marchioness
Phineas Finn† (1869) Anthony Trollope

Hartley, Adam surgeon
The Surgeon's Daughter (1827) Walter Scott

Hartley, Harry secretary to Sir Thomas Vandeleur*
ss 'The Rajah's Diamond'
The New Arabian Nights (1882) Robert Louis Stevenson

Hartley, Michael mad weaver and drunkard, shoots Robert Moore*, dies of *delirium tremens*
Shirley (1849) Charlotte Brontë

Hartman, Curtis, Revd admirer of Kate Swift*
Winesburg, Ohio (1919) Sherwood Anderson

Hartmore, Lord and Lady
The Cuckoo in the Nest (1894) Mrs Margaret Oliphant

Hartopp, Revd Mr schoolmaster
Stalky & Co. (1899) Rudyard Kipling

Hartover, John, Sir
Ellie his daughter
The Water Babies (1863) Charles Kingsley

Hartshorn, Priss graduate of Vassar
The Group (1965) Mary McCarthy

Hartsook, Ralph rural schoolteacher, cc pioneer novel notable for its transcription of Indiana local dialogue – based on experiences of author's younger brother George; m. Hannah Thompson* after being cleared of false charge of theft
The Hoosier Schoolmaster (1871) Edward Eggleston

Hartwright, Walter drawing master, part narrator
Sarah his sister
his mother
The Woman in White (1860) Wilkie Collins

Harvey family, the English emigrants
The Settlers in Canada (1844) Captain

Marryat

Harvey, Alec, Dr cc, in love with Laura Jesson*
Still Life play (1935) Noël Coward

Harvey, Grace schoolmistress cc, in love with Tom Thurnall*
her widowed mother
Two Years Ago (1857) Charles Kingsley

Harville, Captain
his less polished wife
their three children
Fanny his sister, a superior woman
Persuasion (1818) Jane Austen

Hasenclover, Dr eye specialist
The Martian (1897) George du Maurier

Haskett Alice Waythorn's* first husband, a man of lower class
ss 'The Other Two'
Roman Fever (1911) Edith Wharton

Haslam, Godfrey, Sir
Harriet his wife
Matthew m. as second husband Camilla Christy*
Jermyn; Griselda; Gregory their daughters
Men and Wives (1931) Ivy Compton-Burnett

Hassan confectioner
Hassan play (1923) James Elroy Flecker

Hassan porter
Captain Brassbound's Conversion play (1900) George Bernard Shaw

Hassein Beelzebub's* grandson, the impudent brat who dared to call men slugs
All and Everything: Beelzebub's Tales to His Grandson (1950) G. I. Gurdjieff

Hassim, Rajah friend to Lingard*, nephew of one of the greatest chiefs of Wajo
Immada his sister
The Rescue (1920) Joseph Conrad (rn Josef Teodor Konrad Korzeniowski)

Hassock, Fred entertainer, auctioneer; distant cousin of Hope Ollerton*
Let the People Sing (1939) J. B. Priestley

Hastings, George friend to Marlow*, suitor to Constance Neville*
She Stoops to Conquer play (1773) Oliver Goldsmith

Hastings, Lord
King Richard III play (1623) William Shakespeare

Hatachway, Jack, Lieutenant friend to Trunnion*

Peregrine Pickle (1751) Tobias Smollett

Hatch, Bennet
The Black Arrow (1888) Robert Louis Stevenson

Hatcher, Professor based on the author's impressions of the director of the '47 Workshop' (1905–25), George Pierce Baker, who encouraged O'Neill*, Dos Passos*, the author himself, and others
Of Time and the River: A Legend of Man's Hunger in his Youth (1935) Thomas Wolfe

Hatfield, Mr worldly and fashionable rector of Horton
Agnes Grey (1847) Anne Brontë

Hatherleigh, Ted undergraduate at Trinity
The New Machiavelli (1911) H. G. Wells

Hathi wild elephant
ss 'Kaa's Hunting'†
Jungle Books (1894–5) Rudyard Kipling

Hatt, Dickie whose wife leaves him
ss 'In the Pride of his Youth'
Plain Tales from the Hills (1888) Rudyard Kipling

Hatta see **Haigha**

Hatter, The Mad suggested by an eccentric Oxford furniture dealer called Theophilus Carter
Alice in Wonderland (1865) Lewis Carroll (rn Charles Lutwidge Dodgson)

Hatterr, H. cc prized Indian classic in English, a Eurasian born in Penang and resident for long years in India and England, inventor of a unique mixture of slang, jargon, technicalese, and rhetoric
All About H. Hatterr (1948, rev. 1972) G. V. Desani

Hattersley, Ralph rich banker, m. Millicent Hargrave*
The Tenant of Wildfell Hall (1848) Anne Brontë

Hatton 'Bishop of Woodgate', nailmaker
his virago wife and two sons
Sybil (1845) Benjamin Disraeli

Hauksbee, Lucy, Mrs 'fast', shrewd and good-hearted
ss 'Three and an Extra'†
Plain Tales from the Hills (1888) Rudyard Kipling

Hauser, Otto publisher's reader
You Can't Go Home Again (1940) Thomas Wolfe

Haut-on, Oran, Sir flute-playing Noble

Savage and MP, humorous variant on the ape as presented by the proto-anthropologist and Rousseauist* Lord Monboddo, who tried to live by his principles
Melincourt, or Sir Oran Haut-on (1817) Thomas Love Peacock

Hautia dark Polynesian queen
Mardi (1849) Herman Melville

Hautlieu, Margaret (Sister Ursula) lover of Sir Malcolm Fleming*
Castle Dangerous (1832) Walter Scott

Haverley, Miss
ss 'Only a Subaltern'
Wee Willie Winkie (1895) Rudyard Kipling

Havermann farm manager cc of popular humorous novel, written in Low German (Mencklenburger Platt) dialect, of life in Mencklenburg between 1829 and 1848, by author who was long imprisoned for taking part in a non-existent conspiracy; much enjoyed and compared with Dickens* in its translated form
Lowise his daughter, m. Franz von Rambow*
Ut mine Stromtid (An Old Story of my Farming Days) (1862–4) Fritz Reuter

Haversham Dorincourt's* family lawyer
Little Lord Fauntleroy (1886) Frances Hodgson Burnett

Havill crooked builder and architect
A Laodicean (1881) Thomas Hardy

Havisham, Miss eccentric old lady in bridal dress at Satis House, long ago jilted by man called Compeyson*, so that her mind is unhinged
Great Expectations (1861) Charles Dickens

Hawbuck, John, Sir
his wife
Hugh; Lucy his children
The Book of Snobs (1847) W. M. Thackeray

Hawdon, Captain retired military officer living under name of Nemo and making a poor living as a law writer, once lover of Lady Dedlock; father of Esther Summerson*
Bleak House (1853) Charles Dickens

Hawes brutal governor of jail
It Is Never Too Late To Mend (1856) Charles Reade

Hawes, Mrs widow with whom Sue Bridehead* lodges when pupil-teacher
Jude the Obscure (1896) Thomas Hardy

Hawk, Harry boatman
Love Among the Chickens (1906) P. G. Wodehouse

Hawk, Mulberry, Sir swaggering bully and man-about-town
Nicholas Nickleby (1839) Charles Dickens

Hawk, the Pilgrim a hawk mostly hooded and quiet; in Wisconsin author's best, most famous novel
The Pilgrim Hawk (1940) Glenway Westcott

Hawk-Eye see **Effingham**

Hawke, Gideon, Revd Ernest Pontifex's* first vicar
The Way of All Flesh (1903) Samuel Butler

Hawkes, Ben Joe cc
his family, in Sandhill, North Carolina, to which he returns for a visit
his wife and children
If Morning Ever Comes (1964) Ann Tyler

Hawkes, Dickon ('Pegtop') miller
Meg ('Beauty') his daughter
Uncle Silas (1864) J. Sheridan Le Fanu

Hawkins baker successfully sued for breach of promise by Miss Rugg*
Little Dorrit (1857) Charles Dickens

Hawkins bosun of *Fortune's Favourite*
The Pirate (1822) Walter Scott

Hawkins lawyer
The Devil's Disciple (1899) George Bernard Shaw

Hawkins, Augusta m. Revd Philip Elton*; vain and pert
Selina her elder married sister
Emma (1816) Jane Austen

Hawkins, Captain illegitimate son to Lord Privilege*
Peter Simple (1834) Captain Marryat

Hawkins, Helen
Love on the Dole (1933) Walter Greenwood

Hawkins, James, Sir
Mrs Jim his wife
ss 'William the Conqueror'
The Day's Work (1898) Rudyard Kipling

Hawkins, Jim boy ss
his mother

Treasure Island (1883) Robert Louis Stevenson

Hawkins, Mr
his son; both executed for the murder of Tyrrel*, which they did not commit
Things as They Are, or *The Adventures of Caleb Williams* (1794) William Godwin
The Iron Chest dramatization (1796) George Colman the Younger

Hawks, Andy, Captain of the Cotton Blossom Floating Palace Theatre
Parthenia Ann his wife
Magnolia their daughter m. Gaylord Ravanel*
Show Boat (1926) Edna Ferber

Hawks, Asa false prophet
Sabbath Lily his daughter
Wise Blood (1952) Flannery O'Connor

Hawkshaw, Bryan schoolfellow of Henry Esmond*
Henry Esmond (1852) W. M. Thackeray

Hawkyard, Verity religious bigot, trustee to Silverman*
ss 'George Silverman's Explanation'
in *All the Year Round* (1868) Charles Dickens

Hawley, Frank lawyer, town clerk
'**Young Hawley**' his son, law student
Middlemarch (1871–2) George Eliot (rn Mary Anne, later Marian, Evans)

Haws, Daniel part-Cherokee landlord in Chicago
Eustace Chisholm and the Works (1968) James Purdy

Hawthorn, Jerry Somerset cousin to Corinthian Tom* in two low-life London novels, by boring journalist from whom Dickens* gladly drew
Life in London, or *The Day and Night Scenes of Jerry Hawthorne Esq, and his Elegant friend, Corinthian Tom, Accompanied by Bob Logic, the Oxonian, in their Rambles and Sprees through the Metropolis* (1821); *Finish to the Adventures of Tom, Jerry and Logic in Their Pursuits Through Life In and Out of London* (1828) Pierce Egan

Hawthorne, Lucy heartless flirt who eggs on the fop Victor Campion Jr., and then drops him
The Perennial Bachelor (1925) Anne Parrish

Hawthorne, Nathaniel (hist.) cc

Pen Friends (1989) Michael Thorne

Hay, John
ss 'The Wandering Jew'
Life's Handicap (1891) Rudyard Kipling

Haydon, Robert cc
A Run Across the Island (1968) Barry Cole

Hayes, Catherine (hist.) murderess cc of novel intended to expose the mediocrity of the 'Newgate novels' then in vogue
Catherine (1840) W. M. Thackeray

Hayes, Sally teenaged friend to Holden Caulfield*
The Catcher in the Rye (1951) J. D. Salinger

Haylock, Morrison caterer
ss 'The Tie'
Limits and Renewals (1932) Rudyard Kipling

Hayman m. Susan Forsyte*
'**Dromios**'; **Giles**; **Jesse** and their two other children
The Forsyte series (1906–33) John Galsworthy

Haynes impoverished young office worker, cc novel of Trinidadian life in the 1930s; the only full-length fiction by this author, well-known for his Marxist writings and enthusiasm for cricket
Minty Alley (1936) C. L. R. James

Hayraddin, Maugrabin Quentin Durward's* guide to Liège
Quentin Durward (1823) Walter Scott

Hayston, Frank Laird of Bucklaw, m. Lucy Ashton*
The Bride of Lammermoor (1819) Walter Scott

Hayter, Charles scholar and gentleman, non-resident curate, m. Henrietta Musgrove*
his father and mother
Persuasion (1818) Jane Austen

Hayward, Duncan, Major
The Last of the Mohicans (1826) James Fenimore Cooper

Hayward, Etheridge Carey's* friend
Of Human Bondage (1915) W. Somerset Maugham

Hazard m. Penelope*
The Gamester play (1637) James Shirley

Hazard, Myrtle orphan brought from tropics to live in New England and reared by her spinster aunt; in early pioneer

study of 'multiple personality' which resembles pulp fiction in certain respects, but which contains remarkable psychological insights
The Guardian Angel (1868) Oliver Wendell Holmes

Hazard, Stephen preacher
Esther (1884) Frances Snow Compton (rn Henry Adams)

Haze, Charlotte, Mrs widow who m. Humbert Humbert*
Dolores ('Dolly' or Lolita Haze) her daughter, m. Richard F. Schiller*
Lolita (1955) Vladimir Nabokov

Haze, Cunningham chief constable
A Laodicean (1881) Thomas Hardy

Hazel, Caleb schoolmaster who appreciates sterling qualities of Chad Buford* in romance of Kentucky and the Civil War
The Little Shepherd of Kingdom Come (1903) John Fox Jr.

Hazel, Revd Mr see **Penfold, Robert**

Hazeldean, Lizzie *née* Winter, daughter of discredited minister
Charles her lawyer husband, who becomes an invalid after six years of married happiness, and who has rescued his wife's father
ss 'New Year's Day'
Old New York (1924) Edith Wharton

Hazeldean, Squire cc in novel set in village of Hazeldean by author characterized by Tennyson as 'The padded man – that wears the stays –/Who killed the girls and thrilled the boys/With dandy pathos when you wrote . . .'
My Novel, or Varieties in English Life (1850–3) Edward Bulwer Lytton

Hazelow, Tom
Adam Bede (1859) George Eliot (rn Mary Anne, later Marian, Evans)

Hazeltine, Julia niece adopted by Joseph Finsbury*, m. Gideon Forsyth*
The Wrong Box (1889) Robert Louis Stevenson and Lloyd Osbourne

Hazelwood, Charles lover of Lucy Bertram*
Sir Robert his father
Guy Mannering (1815) Walter Scott

Hazelwood, Guy college friend to Michael Fane*
Sinister Street† (1913) Compton

Mackenzie

Hazey, Mr Master of the Hard and Sharp Hunt
his wife
Anna Maria; Bill their children
Mr Facey Romford's Hounds (1865) R. S. Surtees

Hazy, Miss
Chris her nephew
Mrs Wiggs of the Cabbage Patch (1901) Alice H. Rice

He Who Gets Slapped cc, a never identified, distinguished, middle-aged stranger who suggests that he be thus addressed; in widely influential play
Tot, kto poluchaet poshchochiny (*He Who Gets Slapped*, once tr. as *The Painted Laugh*) play (1916) Leonid Andreyev

Head, Mr Georgia backwoodsman
Nelson his grandson
ss 'The Artificial Nigger'
A Good Man is Hard to Find (1955) Flannery O'Connor

Headley-Jones, Helen ('The Weasel') SDP member and do-gooder
Ruth her daughter
Barley her Golden Retriever, four years dead
Redhill Rococo (1986) Shena Mackay

Headpiece, Francis, Sir a country gentleman
Lady Headpiece his wife
Miss Betty their daughter
A Journey to London play (1728) John Vanbrugh

Headrigg, Judden
Mause his wife *née* Middlemas
Cuddie m. Jenny Dennison*; **Jenny** their children
Old Mortality (1816) Walter Scott

Headstone, Bradley schoolmaster and would-be killer in love with Lizzie Hexam*, blackmailed by Rogue Riderhood*
Our Mutual Friend (1865) Charles Dickens

Headthelot, Lord
East Lynne (1861) Mrs Henry Wood

Heale, Dr drunk and inept
Two Years Ago (1857) Charles Kingsley

Heard, Michael cousin to Salvation Yeo*
Westward Ho! (1855) Charles Kingsley

Hearn, Catherine m. Higgins Robinson*
at Gretna Green
Squire Hearn her father
Nathaniel her brother
Nathaniel's wife
ss 'The Squire's Story'
Novels and Tales (1906–19) Mrs Gaskell
Hearn, Jim fiancée to Martha*
Cranford (1853) Mrs Gaskell
Heartfree a gentleman about town
The Provok'd Wife play (1697) John
Vanbrugh
Heartfree good man
his good wife
Jonathan Wild (1743) Henry Fielding
Hearts, King, Queen and Knave of
Alice in Wonderland (1865) Lewis
Carroll (rn Charles Lutwidge Dodgson)
Heartwell a 'surly old Bachelor, pretend-
ing to slight women', secretly in love with
Sylvia*; the author's first comedy
The Old Bachelor play (1793) William
Congreve
Heaslop, Ronald son to Mrs Moore*; city
magistrate
A Passage to India (1924) E. M. Forster
Heat, Chief Inspector cc
The Secret Agent (1907) Joseph Conrad
(rn Josef Teodor Konrad Korzeniowski)
Heath, Massingberd, Sir, Baronet cc of
novel by follower of Trollope*
Sinnamenta his wife, *née* Liversedge* (m.
by gipsy rites)
Sir Wentworth his father
Marmaduke his nephew and heir, m.
Lucy Gerard*
Lost Sir Massingberd (1864) James Payn
Heath, Rosalind actress, later Countess of
Darlington
Conrad in Search of His Youth (1919)
Leonard Merrick
Heathcliff, farmer, cc, m. Isabella Linton*
Linton their son, m. Cathy Linton* (see
Earnshaw)
Wuthering Heights (1847) Emily Brontë
Heatherleigh, Dr
ss 'The Phantom Rickshaw'
Wee Willie Winkie (1888) Rudyard Kipl-
ing
Heatherstone, Patience m. Edward Bev-
erley*
her father
The Children of the New Forest (1847)

Captain Marryat
Heathfield, Alfred Dr Jeddler's* ward, m.
Grace Jeddler*, becomes village doctor
The Battle of Life (1846) Charles
Dickens
Heatleigh
ss 'A Naval Mutiny'
Limits and Renewals (1932) Rudyard
Kipling
Heaviside, Mrs ('Nannie') housekeeper to
the Seymores*
Fanny By Gaslight (1940) Michael
Sadleir
Heavyside, Charles, Captain member of
Barnes Newcome's* club
The Newcomes (1853–5) W. M.
Thackeray
Heavytop, Colonel
his wife
Vanity Fair (1847–8) W. M. Thackeray
Heccomb, Mrs Anna Quayne's* ex-gover-
ness
The Death of the Heart (1938) Elizabeth
Bowen
Hector of the Mist outlaw
The Legend of Montrose (1819) Walter
Scott
Hector slave to Gabriel Harrison*
The Yemassee (1835) William Gilmore
Simms
Hector son to Priam*
Troilus and Cressida (1623) William
Shakespeare
Hedon representing the vice of voluptu-
ousness
Cynthia's Revels, or *The Fountain of
Self-Love* play (1601) Ben Jonson
Hedzoff, K., Count captain of Valoroso's
guard
The Rose and the Ring (1855) W. M.
Thackeray
Heel, The Iron fascist organization in
control of USA for 300 years from 1912
The Iron Heel (1908) Jack London
Heeny, Mrs society masseuse
The Custom of the Country (1913) Edith
Wharton
Heep, Uriah ''umble' hypocrite, forger and
embezzler, clerk to Mr Wickfield*
his mother, teacher of hypocrisy: ''Ury,
be 'umble'
David Copperfield (1850) Charles
Dickens

Hegarty, Simon bailiff
Louisa his sister, m. John Hynes*
Famine (1937) Liam O'Flaherty
Hei, Miss sister to Phuong*
The Quiet American (1955) Graham
Greene
Heidegger, Dr aged physician who wishes
to test water from the Fountain of Youth
ss 'Dr Heidegger's Experiment'
Twice-Told Tales (1837) Nathaniel
Hawthorne
Heidlebery, Mrs comic mispronouncer in
the line of Dogberry*, anticipating Mrs
Winifred Jenkins* and Mrs Malaprop*
The Clandestine Marriage play (1766)
George Colman the Elder and David
Garrick
Heilig, Franz librarian
You Can't Go Home Again (1942)
Thomas Wolfe
Heimann, George cc, son of the Earl of
Marsden*, m. Clarice Honeywill*
Marie-Elizabeth his sister
The Marsden Case (1923) Ford Madox
Ford
Heinemann, Elizabeth inmate of home for
aged
The Poorhouse Fair (1959) John Updike
Heinrich leprous nobleman who interrupts
murderous operation on virgin which can
cure him, and is nonetheless cured and m.
her; in Middle High German poem, re-
told by Longfellow* in *Golden Legend*
and translated in *Great Short Novels of
the World* (1927); the latter title is a
modern treatment
Der arme Heinrich (Poor Heinrich) poem
(written c.1196) Hartmann von Aue
Der arme Heinrich play (1902) Gerhardt
Hauptmann
Heinrich, Herr tutor to the Britling* boys
Mr Britling Sees It Through (1916) H. G.
Wells
Heit, Colonel coroner
An American Tragedy (1925) Theodore
Dreiser
Heldar, Dick war correspondent, artist, cc,
in love with Maisie*
The Light that Failed (1890) Rudyard
Kipling
Helen
When the Sleeper Wakes (1899) H. G.
Wells

Helen girl friend to Don Birnam*
The Lost Weekend (1944) Charles
Jackson
Helen wife to Menelaus*
Troilus and Cressida play (1623) William
Shakespeare
Helena
All's Well That Ends Well play (1623)
William Shakespeare
Helena in love with Demetrius*
A Midsummer Night's Dream play
(1623) William Shakespeare
Helenus son of Priam*
Troilus and Cressida play (1623) William
Shakespeare
Helicanus a lord of Tyre
Pericles play (1609) William Shakespeare
Helkgematios Chief Governor of Purgat-
ory
*All and Everything: Beelzebub's Tales to
His Grandson* (1950) G. I. Gurdjieff
Helmer, Nora cc who leaves her compla-
cent husband
A Doll's House play (1879) Henrik Ibsen
Helmsdale, Cuthbert lustful Bishop of
Melchester
Two on a Tower (1882) Thomas Hardy
Heloise (hist.)
Heloise and Abelard (1921) George
Moore
Help rescuer of Christian* from the Slough
of Despond
The Pilgrim's Progress (1678–84) John
Bunyan
Helsing chancellor
his wife and daughter
Rupert of Hentzau (1898) Anthony
Hope
Helsing, Abraham van
Dracula (1897) Bram Stoker
Helstone, Caroline cc, shy and thoughtful,
m. Robert Moore*
James her father, a drunkard who ill
treats her mother
Revd Matthewson Helstone her uncle,
'upright falcon-like man, copper-faced';
believes all women to be fools; m. Mary
Cave
Shirley (1849) Charlotte Brontë
Helves, Captain on the steam excursion
Sketches by Boz† (1836) Charles Dickens
Hely, Walsingham attaché at British
Embassy, Paris, in love with Charlotte

Baynes*
his mother and sister
The Adventures of Philip (1862) W. M.
Thackeray
Hemington, Charles fiancé of Monica
Claverton-Ferry*
The Elder Statesman play (1958) T. S.
Eliot
Hemming, Vincent advanced thinker who
studies worldwide subjection of women
and then jilts Mary Erle* for an heiress
The Story of a Modern Woman (1894)
Ella Hepworth Dixon
Hemophil courtier at the Laconian court
The Broken Heart play (1633) John Ford
Hempel m. Sarah Turnham*
The Fortunes of Richard Mahony (1930)
Henry Handel Richardson (rn Ethel Flor-
ence Lindesay Richardson Robertson)
Hempel see **Mahony**
'Henbane' spiritual adviser to Miss Dinah
Perfect*
All in the Dark (1866) J. Sheridan Le
Fanu
Henchard, Michael hay-trusser who sells
his first wife at a fair
Susan his first wife, bought by Captain
Richard Newsom*
Elizabeth Jane Susan's daughter by
Newsom, later thought by Henchard to
be his own; m. Donald Farfrae*
The Mayor of Casterbridge (1886)
Thomas Hardy
Hencher brute whose head is pounded to
jelly by horses
The Lime Twig (1961) John Hawkes
Henderland travelling preacher
Kidnapped (1886) Robert Louis
Stevenson
Henderson 'creator' of Caxton school
Joan and Peter (1918) H. G. Wells
Henderson American millionaire travell-
ing in Africa
Henderson the Rain King (1959) Saul
Bellow
Henderson hunter aboard the *Ghost*
The Sea Wolf (1904) Jack London
Henderson, Alfred observer of the Bohem-
ian scene
Painted Veils (1920) James Huneker
Henderson, Elias the Lady of Lochleven's
chaplain
The Abbot (1820) Walter Scott

Henderson, Ethel stepdaughter of James
Chaffery*, m. George Lewisham*
Love and Mr Lewisham (1900) H. G.
Wells
Henderson, Miriam cc massive *roman
fleuve* written in stream-of-con-
sciousness* style
her parents
Sarah m. Bennett Brodie*; **Hariett** m.
Gerald Ducayne*; **Eve** her sisters
Pilgrimage 13 vols. (1915–1968)
Dorothy M. Richardson
Henderson, Ralph insurance investigator
whose letters and reports to his
employers make up this, the first true
modern (but see, e.g. Susanna and the
Elders) detective story in any language; it
began to appear in serial form in 1862
The Notting Hill Mystery (1865) Charles
Felix
Hendie music critic
Right Off the Map (1927) C. E.
Montague
Hendon, Miles later Earl of Kent, rescuer
and friend to the Prince of Wales, m.
widow of Hugh*, his villainous brother
The Prince and The Pauper (1882) Mark
Twain (rn Samuel Langhorne Clemens)
Hengo nephew to Caratach*
Bonduca play (1647) John Fletcher
Hengrave, Charles, Lord (family name
Bramsley)
his wife
Caryl cc; **Edward**; **Gilbert**; **Harry**; **Julia**
m. Tommy Holden; **Marjorie** m. Sir
Harold Ducane their children
C (1924) Maurice Baring
Henley, Frank m. Anna St Ives*; virtuous
rationalist son of steward of Anna's
father in early radical novel
Anna St Ives (1792) Thomas Holcroft
Henley, Iris goddaughter to Sir Giles
Mountjoy*, m. (1) Lord Harry Nor-
land*, (2) Hugh Mountjoy*
Blind Love (1890) Wilkie Collins and
Walter Besant (who completed the
manuscript)
Hennesey, Malachi Mr Dooley's* col-
league and confidante
Mr Dooley in Peace and in War (1898)
Peter Finlay Dunne
Hennessy, John Aloysius
Gerard m. Millicent Considine*; **Anna**

m. Denis Considine*; **Dominic** m. Louise, his children
Without My Cloak (1931) Kate O'Brien
Henning, Millicent Miss Pynsent's* neighbour
The Princess Casamassima (1866) Henry James
Henny-Penny, Sally
The Tale of Mrs Tiggy-Winkle (1905) Beatrix Potter
Henri, Frances Evans cc, daughter of English mother and Swiss father, teacher of needlework at Mlle Reuter's school, m. William Crimsworth*
Julienne, 'Tante' her aunt, who brings her up
The Professor (1857) Charlotte Brontë
Henrique, Don a grandee
The Spanish Curate play (1647) John Fletcher and Philip Massinger
Henriques poor white Portuguese
Prester John (1910) John Buchan
Henrouille, Mme
Voyage au bout de la nuit (*Journey to the End of Night*) (1932) Louis-Ferdinand Céline (rn Louis-Ferdinand Destouches)
Henry and Julia, Cousin relatives to whom the protagonist (the wife of Dr John*,) wishes to make a visit, but is forbidden by her husband, in seminal tale which the author had great difficulty in publishing
ss 'The Yellow Wallpaper'
New England Magazine (May, 1892; 1973) Charlotte Perkins Gilman
Henry IV (Bolingbroke)
King Richard II; *King Henry IV* plays (1623) William Shakespeare
Henry VII (Richmond)
King Richard III play (1623) William Shakespeare
Perkin Warbeck play (1634) John Ford (?and Thomas Dekker)
Henry, Alexandra friend to Alwyn Towers*
The Pilgrim Hawk (1940) Glenway Westcott
Henry, Chase town drunkard
poem 'Chase Henry'
Spoon River Anthology verse epitaphs (1915) Edgar Lee Masters
Henry, Frederic American ambulance driver in Italy, *Tenente* in Italian army, in love with Catherine Barkley*

A Farewell to Arms (1929) Ernest Hemingway
Henry, Mr agent to Lawrence Buxton*
The Moorland Cottage (1850) Mrs Gaskell
Henry, Senator crooked politician, Paul Madvig's* protégé
Janet his daughter
The Glass Key (1931) Dashiell Hammett
Henschil, Miss
ss 'In the Same Boat'
A Diversity of Creatures (1917) Rudyard Kipling
Henshaw, Kitt Tay boatman
The Fair Maid of Perth (1828) Walter Scott
Henshawe, Myra Driscoll
Oswald her husband
her uncle
My Mortal Enemy (1926) Willa Cather
Hentzau, Rupert of cc
The Prisoner of Zenda (1894); *Rupert of Hentzau* (1898) Anthony Hope
Hepburn, Captain cc infatuated in Vienna, where he is on duty, with Countess Johanna von Rassentlow*
his wife, who falls from the window and is killed
ss 'The Captain's Doll'
The Captain's Doll (1923) (in UK, *The Ladybird*) D. H. Lawrence
Hepburn, Philip shop owner who m. Sylvia Robson* by means of a trick but is forgiven after privations
Bella their daughter
Sylvia's Lovers (1863) Mrs Gaskell
Heraclide landlady upon whom an attempt at rape is made
The Unfortunate Traveller, or *The Life of Jack Wilton* (1594) Thomas Nashe
Herailaz famous as having been taken up alive into Heaven
All and Everything: Beelzebub's Tales to His Grandson (1950) G. I. Gurdjieff
Herb newspaper reporter
Elizabeth his daughter
Heaven's My Destination (1935) Thornton Wilder
Herbert i.e. John Ruskin, almost the only saved character* in briefly sensational satirical *roman à clef* by High Anglican Tory later attacked by Shaw*
The New Republic, or *Culture, Faith and*

Philosophy in an English Country House (1877, edition by John Lucas, 1975, lists originals of characters) William Hurrell Mallock

Herbert, Adrian
Love Among the Artists (1900) George Bernard Shaw

Herbert, Charles lover and victim of Helen Vaughan*
The Great God Pan (1894) Arthur Machen

Herbert, Charles, Major m. Sybil Anstey*
Ianthe their daughter, m. Thomson*
The Ballad and the Source (1944) Rosamond Lehmann

Herbert, Eliza
Passages From the Diary of a Late Physician (1832) Samuel Warren

Herbert, Herbert bookish recluse
Grisel his sister
The Return (1910) Walter de la Mare

Herbert, MP protested against Lord George Gordon* attending the House wearing a blue cockade
Barnaby Rudge (1841) Charles Dickens

Herbert, Niel narrator, nephew of Judge Pommeroy*
A Lost Lady (1923) Willa Cather

Herbert, Tom
East Lynne (1861) Mrs Henry Wood

Hereford, Max rich young cc of pro-Home Rule novel about the Fenian agitations, described as 'unusually powerful'; becomes Liberal MP, and m. Doreen O'Ryan*
his parents
Dermot his son
Doreen: The Story of a Singer (1894) Edna Lyall (rn A. E. Bayly)

Hereward of Hampton
Count Robert of Paris (1832) Walter Scott

Herf, Jimmy reporter cc urban novel in which the author developed his famous and influential technique
Lily his mother
Ellen *née* Thatcher, his wife
Manhattan Transfer (1925) John Dos Passos

Heriot, Eliza, Lady autocrat
Sir Robert her husband
Roberta; Angus her children
Hermia; Madeline her stepdaughters

The First and the Last (1971) Ivy Compton-Burnett

Heriot, George (hist.) goldsmith to James I
Judith his sister
The Fortunes of Nigel (1822) Walter Scott

Heriot, Tony
David; Bill his brothers, twins
Invitation to the Waltz (1932) Rosamond Lehmann

Heriot, Walter head-boy, friend to Harry Richmond*
The Adventures of Harry Richmond (1871) George Meredith

Heritage, John paper-maker and poet
Huntingtower (1922) John Buchan

Herkimer, Grandma
The Man Who Was There (1945) Wright Morris

Herkission, Archangel invented the system of Egolionopties
All and Everything: Beelzebub's Tales to His Grandson (1950) G. I. Gurdjieff

Herman of Goodalricke Preceptor of the Order of the Temple
Ivanhoe (1820) Walter Scott

Hermann King Rudolph's* majordomo
Rupert of Hentzau (1898) Anthony Hope

Hermanric Gothic chieftain in love with Antonina*
Antonina (1850) Wilkie Collins

Hermia in love with Lysander*
A Midsummer Night's Dream play (1623) William Shakespeare

Hermione Leontes'* Queen
A Winter's Tale play (1623) William Shakespeare

Hermione, Lady exposer of Lord Dalgarno's* villainy
The Fortunes of Nigel (1822) Walter Scott

Hermogenes foster-father to Leonidas*
Marriage à la Mode play (1673) John Dryden

Hermon a parasite
Gorboduc play (1652) Thomas Sackville and Thomas Norton

Hermsprong wealthy cc, lost heir born amongst the Indians of Michillmakinac and therefore a Rousseauist primitive
Hermsprong, or Man as He is not (1796) Robert Bage

Hernandez, Manuelata m. President Alvarez
Soldiers of Fortune (1897) Richard Harding Davis
Herncastle, John, Colonel uncle to Franklin Blake*
Julia his sister, m. Sir John Verinder*
The Moonstone (1868) Wilkie Collins
Herne, Mrs old crone
Lavengro (1851) George Borrow
Hernon, Patch
Kitty his wife, *née* Kilmartin
their seven children
Kate his 'wise' aunt
Famine (1937) Liam O'Flaherty
Hero Leonato's* daughter
Much Ado About Nothing play (1623) William Shakespeare
Herodsfoot, Badalia flower girl
Tom her husband
ss 'The Record of Badalia Herodsfoot'
Many Inventions (1893) Rudyard Kipling
Heron, Arthur, Revd
Lucy his wife, *née* Gilfil*
ss 'Mr Gilfil's Love Story'
Scenes of Clerical Life (1857) George Eliot (rn Mary Anne, later Marian, Evans)
Heron, Irene m. (1) Soames Forsyte* (divorced), (2) Young Jolyon Forsyte*
The *Forsyte* series (1906–33) John Galsworthy
Herrick, Nicholas owner of a school
Emily his half-sister
Pastors and Masters (1925) Ivy Compton-Burnett
Herries of Birrenswork alias of Redgauntlet*
Redgauntlet (1824) Walter Scott
Herriot, Mrs
ss 'The Story of the Gadsbys'
The Story of the Gadsbys (1888) Rudyard Kipling
Herriot, Roger executive for a musical scholarship foundation, cc
The Temptation of Roger Herriot (1954) Edward Newhouse
Herriton, Lilia widow of Charles Herriton m. Gino Carella*
Irma her daughter
Philip her brother-in-law
Harriet her intolerant sister-in-law

Where Angels Fear to Tread (1905) E. M. Forster
Herschel, John, Sir son of hist. char. who in successful 1835 hoax 'discovered' by means of new but now destroyed telescope at Cape of Good Hope a populated moon with a biped beaver that made use of fire etc.'
'Great Astronomical Discoveries Lately Made by Sir John Herschel'
New York Sun and subsequently pamphlet (1835); *The Great Moon Hoax* (1859) Richard Adams Locke
Hertford, Duke and Duchess of
ss 'Maltby and Braxton'
Seven Men (1919) Max Beerbohm
Hertoonano Christian alchemist
All and Everything: Beelzebub's Tales to His Grandson (1950) G. I. Gurdjieff
Hervey dog
ss 'The Dog Hervey'
A Diversity of Creatures (1917) Rudyard Kipling
Hervey, Clarence m. Belinda Portman* after vicissitudes
Belinda (1801) Maria Edgeworth
Hervey, Dorothy, Mrs Clarissa Harlowe's* aunt
Dolly her daughter
Clarissa Harlowe (1748) Samuel Richardson
Hervey, Gabriel (hist.) poet
Have With You to Saffron Walden, or *Gabriel Harvey's Hunt is Up* (1596) Thomas Nashe
Herz, Paul friend to Wallach*
Libby his wife
his mother
Letting Go (1962) Philip Roth
Herzbruder, Old
Young Herzbruder his son, friend to Simplicius*
Simplicissimus (1669) Hans Jakob von Grimmelshausen
Herzog, Moses cc, professor of history, writer of letters in his mind
Madeline his wife, who divorces him
June their daughter
Herzog (1964) Saul Bellow
Heseltine, John
C (1924) Maurice Baring
Hesketh, Harry m. Alicia Orgreave*
The *Clayhanger* series (1910–16)

Arnold Bennett

Hesperus
Cynthia's Revels, or *The Fountain of Self-Love* play (1601) Ben Jonson

Hesperus murderer of his wife Floribel*
The Bride's Tragedy play (1822) Thomas Lovell Beddoes

Hesselius, Martin, Dr Swedenborgian alienist who investigates series of supernatural 'cases'
In a Glass Darkly (1872) J. Sheridan Le Fanu

Hester see **Phelps, Mrs**

Heve, Dr
his brother, the vicar
The *Clayhanger* series (1910–16) Arnold Bennett

Heveland, William, ADC
Handley Cross (1843) R. S. Surtees

Hewby, Mr London architect
A Pair of Blue Eyes (1873) Thomas Hardy

Hewit, Beau
The Man of Mode play (1676) George Etherege

Hewitt, Martin early detective in short stories, onwards from
Martin Hewitt, Investigator† (1894) Arthur Morrison

Hewitt, Patience ('Patty') m. (1) Gervase Piercey, (2) Roger Pearson
Richard her father
Patience her aunt
The Cuckoo in the Nest (1894) Mrs Margaret Oliphant

Hexam, Jesse Thames 'nightbird' who finds corpse believed to be that of John Harmon*
Lizzie m. Eugene Wrayburn*; **Charley** his children
Our Mutual Friend (1865) Charles Dickens

Heydinger, Alice student at School of Science, in love with Lewisham*
Love and Mr Lewisham (1900) H. G. Wells

Heyduke, Mary, Lady
ss 'Green Tea'
In a Glass Darkly (1872) J. Sheridan Le Fanu

Heyer, Bill smallholder
South Riding (1936) Winifred Holtby

Heyling, George subject of tale of the

Queer Client
The Pickwick Papers (1837) Charles Dickens

Heyst, Axel idealist
Victory (1915) Joseph Conrad (rn Josef Teodor Konrad Korzeniowski)

Heyst, Elis teacher haunted by shame and by the shadow of Lindkvist*, his family's main creditor
Eleonora his clairvoyant sister; in play modelled around Haydn's *The Seven Last Words of Christ*
Påsk (*Easter*) play (1901) August Strindberg

Heythrop, Sylvanus shipowner (see also **Larne, Rosamund**)
Ernest; Adela his children
A Stoic (1918) John Galsworthy

Hialas Spanish agent
Perkin Warbeck play (1634) John Ford

Hibbert cc, officer on the Western Front
Journey's End play (1928) R. C. Sherriff

Hibbert, Clara
The Vortex play (1924) Noël Coward

Hibbins, Mrs reputed witch, sister to Governor Bellingham*
The Scarlet Letter (1850) Nathaniel Hawthorne

Hibou, Mlle French governess
The Virginians (1857–9) W. M. Thackeray

Hickey cheerful salesman, 'Iceman of death'
The Iceman Cometh play (1946) Eugene O'Neill

Hickey, Jerome, Dr
Some Experiences in the Life of an Irish R.M. (1899) O. E. Somerville and Martin Ross (rn Edith Somerville and Violet Martin)

Hickman, Mr fiancé of Anne Howe*
Clarissa Harlowe (1648) Samuel Richardson

Hickmot (or **Hickmer**) Australian soldier
ss 'Friend of the Family'
Debits and Credits (1926) Rudyard Kipling

Hicks see **Blood, Lydia**

Hicks, George Robert Carne's* groom
South Riding (1936) Winifred Holtby

Hicks, Hannah Martha Honeyman's* maid
The Newcomes (1853–5) W. M.

Thackeray

Hicks, Septimus one of Mrs Tibbs's boarders
Sketches by Boz† (1836) Charles Dickens

Hicksey of the Indian Police
ss 'A Conference of the Powers'
Many Inventions (1893) Rudyard Kipling

Hicksey, Bill
ss 'Bill's Paperchase'
The Lady of the Barge (1902) W. W. Jacobs

Hickson, George
Philip his nephew
The Horse's Mouth (1944) Joyce Cary

Hieronimo Marshal of Spain
Isabella his wife
Horatio their son
The Spanish Tragedy play (1592) Thomas Kyd

Higden, Betty active old woman whose mangle is operated by a lad called Sloppy
Our Mutual Friend (1865) Charles Dickens

Higginbotham, Mr wealthy old man who is saved from committing a murder by Dominicus Pike's powers of precognition
Twice-Told Tales (1834) Nathaniel Hawthorne

Higgins, Henry cc
his mother
Pygmalion play (1914) George Bernard Shaw

Higgins, Mr supposed author of a satire on Erasmus Darwin's didactic poem *The Loves of the Plants*
The Loves of the Triangles (1797) George Canning

Higgins, Mrs elderly widow
ss 'Mr Gilfil's Love Story'
Scenes of Clerical Life (1857) George Eliot (rn Mary Anne, later Marian, Evans)

Higgins, Nicholas
Bessy; Mary his daughters
North and South (1855) Mrs Gaskell

Higgins, Robinson cc, young spark, owner of the White House at Barford, burst into excess only on rare occasions; m. Catherine Hearn* at Gretna Green; is actually highwayman (hanged at Derby for murdering an old lady of Bath)
ss 'The Squire's Story'

Novels and Tales (1906–19) Mrs Gaskell

Higgs, John son of the narrator of *Erewhon** and his wife Arowhena*
Erewhon Revisited (1901) Samuel Butler

Higgs narrator and cc; m. Arowhena*
Erewhon (1872) Samuel Butler

Higgs solicitor
Vanity Fair (1847–8) W. M. Thackeray

Highgate, Lord father of Jack Belsize*, who succeeds him
The Newcomes (1853–5) W. M. Thackeray

Hightower, Gail unfrocked minister
his wife
Light in August (1932) William Faulkner

Hignett, A. L., Lieutenant-Commander
ss 'Their Lawful Occasions'
Traffics and Discoveries (1904) Rudyard Kipling

Hilarion see **Hildebrand**

Hilary uncle to Scythrop Glowry*
his wife
Nightmare Abbey (1818) Thomas Love Peacock

Hilbery, Katherine cc, granddaughter of an eminent Victorian poet whose biography she fails to finish, in part modelled on Vanessa Bell, in part on Anne Thackeray Ritchie, daughter of W. M. Thackeray; engaged to William Rodney*, m. Ralph Denham*
Night and Day (1919) Virginia Woolf

Hilda essentially innocent New England girl; art student in Rome
The Marble Faun first published in England as *Transformation* (1860) Nathaniel Hawthorne

Hildebrand, King
Hilarion his son
Princess Ida opera (1884) W. S. Gilbert and Arthur Sullivan

Hildebrandt, Sir half-brother to Theodora, Margravine of Godesberg
A Legend of the Rhine (1845) W. M. Thackeray

Hildebrod, Jacob, Duke Grand Protector of The Liberties of Alsatia
The Fortunes of Nigel (1822) Walter Scott

Hilfe, Anna refugee, m. Arthur Rowe*
Willi her brother, spy
The Ministry of Fear (1943) Graham Greene

Hill, Eveline
Harry her brother
ss 'Eveline'
Dubliners (1914) James Joyce
Hill, Fanny heroine of her own letters to a friend, describing her sexual experiences in chaste language in pornographic *tour de force* subject of many legal trials since its publication
Fanny Hill (1748–9, rev. as *Memoirs of Fanny Hill*, 1750) John Cleland
Hill, Jenny
Major Barbara play (1905) George Bernard Shaw
Hill, Mary m. Joe Rendel*
ss 'Three from Dunsterville'
The Man Upstairs (1914) P. G. Wodehouse
Hill, Tom huntsman
Jorrocks's Jaunts and Jollities (1838) R. S. Surtees
Hillary wealthy merchant
Mary his daughter, m. Henry Elliott
Diary of a Late Physician (1832) Samuel Warren
Hillcrist proud aristocrat, whose gentility 'can't stand fire'
his wife
The Skin Game play (1920) John Galsworthy
Hilliard, Archibald fortune hunter
The Money-Makers (1885) H. F. Keenan
Hillington
Mrs Dukes' Million (1977) Wyndham Lewis
Hills, Everett, DD Congregational minister
his wife
Mourning Becomes Electra play (1931) Eugene O'Neill
Hilmer, Hélène second wife of Young Jolyon Forsyte*
The *Forsyte* series (1906–33) John Galsworthy
Hilse, Old poor weaver
his blind wife, son and daughter-in-law
Die Weber (*The Weavers*) play (1892) Gerhart Hauptmann
Hilton, Jack m. Kay
Kay his mistress, in love with Gimpty*; m. Jack Hilton
Dead End play (1936) Sidney Kingsley
Hilton, Marion alcoholic prostitute,

Henry Maitland's* first wife, based on George Gissing's* first wife
The Private Life of Henry Maitland (1912) Morley Roberts
Hilton, Tim 'happily married' husband, who says: 'relationships . . . come down to men and women. There's no third sex. You have to make do with what there is. Hetero or homo. Not much variety there.'
Enemies: A Novel About Friendship (1977) Giles Gordon
Hilyer, K., Revd Vicar of Siddermorton
The Wonderful Visit (1895) H. G. Wells
Himmelfarb, Mordecai ex-professor of English, Jewish immigrant to Australia
Riders in the Chariot (1961) Patrick White
Hinchcliffe, Henry Salt chief engineer
ss 'Their Lawful Occasions'
Traffics and Discoveries (1904) Rudyard Kipling
Hindman, Alice clerk in dry-goods store
ss 'Adventure'
Winesburg, Ohio (1919) Sherwood Anderson
Hines, Eupheus mad grandfather of Joe Christmas*, murderer of Joe's father, a travelling circus man
Milly his daughter
Light in August (1932) William Faulkner
Hines, Cosmo bookseller, m. Dorothy Merlin*
The Unspeakable Skipton (1959) Pamela Hansford Johnson
Hines, Eva Buckingham narrator of novel set in Connecticut
Lucas her husband
her son
Baldur's Gate (1970) Eleanor Clark
Hines, Pattie girl over whom Romarin* and Marsden* once fought
ss 'The Accident'
Widdershins (1911) Oliver Onions
Hinkley, Ira, Revd medical student
Arrowsmith (1925) Sinclair Lewis
Hinks saddler, neighbour to Polly* at Fishbourne
The History of Mr Polly (1910) H. G. Wells
Hinton, Adelaide engaged to Edward Springrove*
Desperate Remedies (1871) Thomas

Hardy

Hinton, Jack cc, narrator, m. Louisa Bellew*
General Sir George his father
Lady Charlotte his mother
Jack Hinton (1843) Charles Lever

Hinze 'superlatively deferential' man
The Impressions of Theophrastus Such (1879) George Eliot (rn Mary Anne, later Marian, Evans)

Hipcroft, Ned m. Caroline Aspent*
ss 'The Fiddler of the Reels'
Life's Little Ironies (1894) Thomas Hardy

Hipkiss, Bessie cc, changes her name to **Campbell** m (1) Josef Rolewicz, (2) Norman Gantz
Bert Hipkiss her father
Jenny; Billy her sister and brother
Mabel Stevens her stepmother
Jezebel's Dust (1951) Fred Urquhart

Hipper, Blanche m. Loftus Wilcher*
Clarissa her sister
Herself Surprised (1941) Joyce Cary

Hippias, Uncle hypochondriacal dipsomaniac
The Ordeal of Richard Feverel: A History of Father and Son (1859, rev. 1878) George Meredith

Hippolita wife to Manfred*, false Prince of Otranto
The Castle of Otranto (1765) Horace Walpole

Hippolita wife to Richardetto*
'Tis Pity She's a Whore play (1633) John Ford

Hippolita wife to Theseus*
The Two Noble Kinsmen play (1634) William Shakespeare and John Fletcher (?with Francis Beaumont)

Hippolito
Fabritio his brother
Women Beware Women play (1657) Thomas Middleton

Hippolito friend and companion to Aurelian*
Incognita (1692) William Congreve

Hippolito son to Gratiana* and brother to Vindice*
The Revenger's Tragedy (1607/8) ?Thomas Middleton; ?Cyril Tourneur

Hippolyta Queen of the Amazons, betrothed to Theseus*
A Midsummer Night's Dream play (1623) William Shakespeare

Hippolyte porter and odd-job man, with (owing to Charles Bovary's* incompetence) a wooden leg
Madame Bovary (1857) Gustave Flaubert

Hipsley, John, Sir, Baronet
The Book of Snobs (1847) W. M. Thackeray

Hipsley, the Hon. Ginevra 'who kept white mice on whose sensibilities she experimented by means of folk-songs accompanied by the accordian'
Hudson River Bracketed (1929); *The Gods Arrive* (1932) Edith Wharton

Hire, la, Captain
Saint Joan play (1924) George Bernard Shaw

Hiren cc
The Turkish Mahomet play (1584) George Peele

Hirnam Singh
ss 'In Flood Time'
Soldiers Three (1888) Rudyard Kipling

Hirsch clerk to Moses Löwe* of Bonn
The Fitz-Boodle Papers (1843) W. M. Thackeray

Hirsch villain who kidnaps Margarita Kingsborough*
Sard Harker (1924) John Masefield

Hirsch, Dr
ss 'The Duel of Doctor Hirsch'
The Wisdom of Father Brown (1914) G. K. Chesterton

Hirte, Toby apothecary
ss 'Brother Square Toes'†
Rewards and Fairies (1910) Rudyard Kipling

His Majesty the King see **Austell**

Hist ('Hist-of-Hist) Indian maiden
The Deerslayer (1841) James Fenimore Cooper

Hitchcock engineer
ss 'The Bridge Builders'
The Day's Work (1898) Rudyard Kipling

Hittaway, Clara, Mrs daughter to Lady Fawn*
her husband, charwoman at Court of Criminal Appeals
The Eustace Diamonds (1873) Anthony Trollope

Hoang Chinese beachcomber

Moran of the Letty Lady (in England as *Shanghaied*) (1904) Frank Norris

Hoape, G. J. American millionaire
The Pretty Lady (1918) Arnold Bennett

Hoard a miser
Joyce his niece
Onesiphorus Hoard his brother
A Trick to Catch the Old One play (1608) Thomas Middleton

Hobanob, Lord
Pendennis (1848) W. M. Thackeray

Hobart, Miss friend to Miss Horne*
Sylvia Scarlett (1918) Compton Mackenzie

Hobart, Oliver m. Jane Potter*
Potterism (1920) Rose Macaulay

Hobart, Snecky
The Little Minister (1891) J. M. Barrie

Hobbes, Paul unwilling Beat in pioneer 'Beat' novel which is, not, however, in the Beat style of Kerouac's *On the Road**, which it preceded
Kathryn his Italian wife
Go (1952) John Clellon Holmes

Hobbs, Mr grocer and friend of little Fauntleroy*
Little Lord Fauntleroy (1886) Frances Hodgson Burnett

Hobden, Ralph paradigmatic old country-man
Puck of Pook's Hill† (1906) Rudyard Kipling

Hobler, Mr solicitor and cracker of jokes
Sketches by Boz† (1836) Charles Dickens

Hobomok Indian cc in one of the earliest novels to depict an Indian sympathetic-ally, written by the author – who became a noted abolitionist – at the age of twenty-two
Hobomok: A Tale of Early Times (1824) Lydia Maria Child

Hoboy an ancient; companion to Follywit
A Mad World My Masters play (1608) Thomas Middleton

Hobson, Henry Horatio tyrannical bootmaker
Maggie his eldest daughter
Hobson's Choice play (1916) Harold Brighouse

Hobson, Revd Mr chaplain to Lord Rosherville*, m. Lady Ann Milton*, daughter to Lord Rosherville
Pendennis (1848) W. M. Thackeray

Hobson, Sam
ss 'The Son's Veto'
Life's Little Ironies (1894) Thomas Hardy

Hobson, Zachariah of Hobson Bros, cloth factors
Sophia Alethea his niece, m. as second wife Thomas Newcome*
The Newcomes (1853–5) W. M. Thackeray

Hoda optimistic fat prostitute, cc and narrator of Canadian novel
Crackpot (1974) Adele Wiseman

Hodge & Smithers Liberal solicitors
The Great Hoggarty Diamond (1841) W. M. Thackeray

Hodge (also called **Roger**) foreman to Eyre
The Shoemaker's Holiday (1600) Thomas Dekker

Hodge Gammer Gurton's servant
Gammer Gurton's Needle play (1575) ?William Stevenson

Hodge, Huffle cheater and champion of Bat Burst*
The New Inn, or *The Light Heart* play (1629) Ben Jonson

Hodge, Taggert ('The Sunlight Man') magician, 'wild romantic poet with no hope of God' in American novel set in town of Batavia
The Sunlight Dialogues (1972) John Gardner

Hodgem pub vocalist
Pendennis (1848) W. M. Thackeray

Hodges, Mrs midwife
Liza of Lambeth (1897) W. Somerset Maugham

Hodgson, Captain
ss 'With the Night Mail'
Actions and Reactions (1909) Rudyard Kipling

Hoenikker, Felix dead scientist and in-ventor of ice-nine, about whom Jonah* intends to write a book
Franklin his son
Cat's Cradle (1963) Kurt Vonnegut

Hoffendahl, Diedrich revolutionary
The Princess Casamassima (1866) Henry James

Hoffer, Albert of whom Faust* is jealous
ss 'The Mortal Immortal'
Tales and Stories (1891) Mary Shelley

Höfgen, Hendrick cc, actor who is deter-

mined to be famous, renounces his communist past, and collaborates with the Nazis; based on Gustaf Gründegens, author's former brother-in-law; written 'to analyse the abject type of treacherous intellectual who prostitutes his talent for the sake of some tawdry fame and transitory wealth'; in a novel banned by Supreme Court of West Germany in 1970
Frau Bella his mother
Josy his sister
Mephisto (1936) Klaus Mann

Hogan-Yale Irish officer
ss 'The Rout of the White Hussars'
Plain Tales from the Hills (1888) Rudyard Kipling

Hogarth, John, MP
The Gates of Summer play (1956) John Whiting

Hogbary social leader, Beckenham
Tono Bungay (1909) H. G. Wells

Hogg, Mrs Malone's landlady
Shirley (1849) Charlotte Brontë

Hoggarty, Susan, Mrs rich aunt to Samuel Titmarsh*, m. Revd Grimes Wapshot*
her thirteen sisters-in-law
The Great Hoggarty Diamond (1841) W. M. Thackeray

Hogginarmo, Count of Crim Tartary
The Rose and the Ring (1855) W. M. Thackeray

Hoggins, Dr
Cranford (1853) Mrs Gaskell

Hoggins, Mary Ann m. Jeames de la Pluché
Jeames's Diary (1846) W. M. Thackeray

Hogsflesh (Mr H)
Mr H play (1813) Charles Lamb

Hohenhauer, Prince political prince who m. rejuvenated (from fifty-eight twenty-eight) Countess Zattiany* and interests her once more in Austrian politics
Black Oxen (1923) Gertrude Atherton

Hohenstockwitz, Gotthold, Dr cousin and librarian to Prince Otto*
Prince Otto (1885) Robert Louis Stevenson

Hoist a decayed gentleman
The City Madam play (1658) Philip Massinger

Hokey, Nurse
The Newcomes (1853–5) W. M. Thackeray

Holabird, Rippleton of McGurk Institute
Arrowsmith (1925) Sinclair Lewis

Holbrook, Mary cc, gradually dying from malnutrition and child-bearing
Jim her husband, miner, farmer, meatpacker; in novel set in Wyoming and elsewhere
Mazie their daughter, from the point of view of whose consciousness some of the story is told
their other children
Yonnondio: From the Thirties (1974) Tillie Olsen

Holbrook, Mrs J. H. Graham's second wife
The Lamplighter (1854) Maria S. Cummins

Holbrook, Thomas yeoman, cousin to Miss Pole*
Cranford (1853) Mrs Gaskell

Holchester, Lord father to Geoffrey Delamayn*
Man and Wife (1870) Wilkie Collins

Holdem, Dr keeper of a private lunatic asylum
Valentine Vox, The Ventriloquist (1840) Henry Cockton

Holden, John Amera's* lover
ss 'Without Benefit of Clergy'
Life's Handicap (1891) Rudyard Kipling

Holden, Tommy m. Julia Bramsley*
C (1924) Maurice Baring

Holdenough, Nehemiah Presbyterian minister
Woodstock (1826) Walter Scott

Holder, Alexander of Holder & Stevenson, bakers
Arthur his son
Mary his niece
ss 'The Beryl Coronet'
The Adventures of Sherlock Holmes (1892) Arthur Conan Doyle

Holderness, Lucas writer and swindler
Love and Mr Lewisham (1900) H. G. Wells

Holdernesse, Duke of
ss 'The Adventure of the Priory School'
The Return of Sherlock Holmes (1905) Arthur Conan Doyle

Holdfast, Aminadab
A Bold Stroke for a Wife play (1718) Susannah Centlivre

Holdhurst, Lord
ss 'The Naval Treaty'
The Memoirs of Sherlock Holmes (1894)
Arthur Conan Doyle

Holdsworth, Edward engineering colleague to Paul Manning*, jilts Phillis Holman*, and goes to Canada to a better post
Cousin Phillis (1865) Mrs Gaskell

Holdsworth, Michael inefficient farmer
Young Mike his son
Adam Bede (1859) George Eliot (rn Mary Anne, later Marian, Evans)

Holgrave 'daguerreotypist' revolutionary fellow tenant with Hepzibah Pyncheon*, m. Phoebe Pyncheon*
The House of the Seven Gables (1851) Nathaniel Hawthorne

Holiday, Burne friend to Amory Blaine* at Princeton
This Side of Paradise (1920) F. Scott Fitzgerald

Holkar Indian commander
The Adventures of Major Gahagan (1839) W. M. Thackeray

Holl, Lily m. Dick Povey*
The Old Wives' Tale (1908) Arnold Bennett

Holland, Bill
Eileen his wife
Freddy; Jane; Robin their children
A Town Like Alice (1950) Neville Shute

Holland, J. C. white middle-class cc of semi-surrealistic American novels described as resembling *Mad Magazine*; his black mistress is Kitten*
One Hundred Million Dollar Misunderstanding (1962); *Here Goes Kitten* (1964); *J. C. Saves* (1968) Robert Gover

Holland, Ruth persecuted (for going off with a married man); cc of American novel to which Babbit* may have owed something
Fidelity (1915) Susan Glaspell

Hollander a butler
The Last and the First (1971) Ivy Compton-Burnett

Holley, Percival de, Mrs
The Passing of the Third Floor Back play (1907) Jerome K. Jerome

Hollingford, Lord
Wives and Daughters (1866) Mrs Gaskell

Hollingrake, Boo (Mrs Olivia Davenport) sugar heiress, Hurtle Duffield's* first patron
The Vivisector (1970) Patrick White

Hollingsworth equivocal ex-blacksmith who wants to turn Blithedale into an institution for criminal reform
The Blithedale Romance (1852) Nathaniel Hawthorne

Hollins Irish fish-hawker and drunk, m. Maggie
The Old Wives' Tale (1908) Arnold Bennett

Hollis, Miss
ss 'The Bisara of Pooree'
Plain Tales from the Hills (1888) Rudyard Kipling

Hollis, Mr
Lady Flora his wife
Daniel Deronda (1876) George Eliot (rn Mary Anne, later Marian, Evans)

Holly, Barnabas builder's labourer, m. (1) Annie, (2) Jessy Brimsley*
Annie his first wife
Bert; Lydia; Daisy; Alice; Gertie; Kitty; Lennie his and Annie's children
South Riding (1936) Winifred Holtby

Holly, Ludwig Horace ('The Baboon') cc and narrator
She (1887) Henry Rider Haggard

Holman, Helen torch singer
Appointment in Samarra (1935) John O'Hara

Holman, Phillis cc
Revd Ebenezer her father, minister and farmer
her mother
Cousin Phillis (1864) Mrs Gaskell

Holme, Bernadine cc, consumptive at Swiss resort, in book that once brought tears to a million eyes
Zerviah her uncle
Malvina his dead wife
Ships That Pass in the Night (1893) Beatrice Harraden

Holmes, Dr
Mrs Dalloway (1925) Virginia Woolf

Holmes, Sherlock detective
Mycroft his more brilliant brother
ss 'The Empty Room'†
A Study in Scarlet (1887) Arthur Conan Doyle

Holmes, Willard fine young man cc; m.

Barbara Worth* – in popular success
The Winning of Barbara Worth (1911)
Harold Bell Wright
Holofernes schoolmaster
Love's Labour's Lost play (1623)
William Shakespeare
Holohan assistant secretary
ss 'A Mother'
Dubliners (1914) James Joyce
Holroyd, James Yorkshire bully in charge
of Camberwell power station
ss 'The Lord of the Dynamoes'
The War of the Worlds (1898) H. G.
Wells
Holsten mathematician and chemist
The World Set Free (1914) H. G. Wells
Holt, Felix watchmaker, radical, m. Esther
Lyon*
Mary his mother
Felix Holt (1866) George Eliot (rn Mary
Anne, later Marian, Evans)
Holt, Gavin midshipman, *Saltash*
The Cruel Sea (1951) Nicholas
Monsarrat
Holt, Henry, Father alias **Captain von
Holtz** (and **Holton**) Jesuit priest and
conspirator
Henry Esmond (1852) W. M. Thackeray
Holt, Jack tobacco smuggler
Pendennis (1848) W. M. Thackeray
Holton, Captain see **Holt, Henry**
Holy Joe ('Old 48') bill-poster
No. 5 John Street (1902) Richard White-
ing
Holyday, Erasmus learned dominie
Kenilworth (1821) Walter Scott
Homais disingenuous pharmacist; voluble
rationalist; quack
Madame Bovary (1857) Gustave
Flaubert
Homartyn, Lady friend to Mr Britling*
Mr Britling Sees It Through (1916) H. G.
Wells
Home [de Bassompierre], Paulina m. John
Graham Bretton*
her doting father
Villette (1853) Charlotte Brontë
Hominy, Mrs 'American philosopher and
authoress', 'The Mother of the Modern
Gracchi'
Martin Chuzzlewit (1844) Charles
Dickens
Homm, Christopher cc

Christopher Homm (1963) C. H. Sisson
Homos, Mr visitor from the Republic of
Altruria in satirical novel written under
the influence of Bellamy's *Looking Back-
ward*
his wife
A Traveller from Altruria (1894);
Through the Eye of the Needle (1907)
William Dean Howells
Hondiscio follower of Beowulf* eaten by
Grendel*
Beowulf (c.745)
Hondorp, Herbert thirty-seven-year-old
boy cc in American satire on media,
specifically TV
Golk (1960) Richard Stern
Honest, Mr old pilgrim
The Pilgrim's Progress (1678–84) John
Bunyan
Honeychurch, Lucy cousin to Charlotte
Bartlett*, m. George Emerson*
Freddy her brother
her mother
A Room With a View (1908) E. M.
Forster
Honeycombe, Will 'well-bred fine gentle-
man', expert 'in the female world' of
fashion, onwards from
The Spectator No. 2 (1711) Joseph
Addison
Honeyman, Charles vain and hypocritical
incumbent of Lady Whittlesea's* chapel,
m. Lydia Sherrick*
Martha his sister
The Newcomes (1853–5) W. M.
Thackeray
Honeythunder, Luke, Revd brow-beating
hypocritical philanthropist
his wife
Edwin Drood (1870) Charles Dickens
Honeywell, Gamaliel Bland, Judge old
judge in search of young love in sardonic
novel
The Romantic Comedians (1926) Ellen
Glasgow
Honeywell, Ruth unhappily married
woman for whom Falder* commits
forgery; in public-service* play about
inhuman conditions in British prisons
Justice play (1910) John Galsworthy
Honeywill, Clarice, m. George Heimann*
The Marsden Case (1923) Ford Madox
Ford

Honeywood the man of the title, m. Miss Richland
Sir William his uncle
The Good Natured Man play (1768) Oliver Goldsmith
Honeywood, Patty, m. Verdant Green*
Kitty her sister, m. F. Delaval*
The Adventures of Mr Verdant Green (1853) Cuthbert Bede (rn Edward Bradley)
Honeywood, Revd Dr
Elsie Venner (1861) Oliver Wendell Holmes
Honorius, Emperor (hist.)
Antonina (1850) Wilkie Collins
Honour, Mrs see **Blackmore, Mrs**
Hood, Omphale, Miss runs flower shops in West End
A Certain Man (1931) Oliver Onions
Hook, Captain one-armed pirate
Peter Pan play (1904) J. M. Barrie
Hook, John inmate of home for aged
The Poorhouse Fair (1959) John Updike
Hookham, John improvident sailor
Tom his son, friend to Duval*
Denis Duval (1864) W. M. Thackeray
Hookhorn, Philip
ss 'The Superstitious Man's Story'
Life's Little Ironies (1894) Thomas Hardy
Hoolan journalist
Pendennis (1848) W. M. Thackeray
Hooligan, Kate cc of whose middle-aged Joyce*-style monologue this novel consists
Night (1972) Edna O'Brien
Hoopdriver, J. E. cc, draper's assistant
The Wheels of Chance (1896) H. G. Wells
Hooper, Fanny ('Vandra') cc, illegitimate daughter of Mary Hopwood* and Clive Seymore*
Evelyn her daughter by Harry Somerford*
Fanny By Gaslight (1940) Michael Sadleir
Hooper, Inspector who knows a name he ought not to have known
ss 'Mrs Bathurst'
Traffics and Discoveries (1904) Rudyard Kipling
Hooper, Mrs nurse to the Desarts*
Carrots: Just a Little Boy (1876) Mrs Molesworth

Hooper, Revd Mr New England puritan minister who assumes a veil on the eve of his wedding (which does not take place) and goes to his grave in it: it is the veil that makes all men a stranger to himself, his friends and to God
ss 'The Minister's Black Veil'
The Token (1836) Nathaniel Hawthorne
Hop (''Op') yeoman of signals
ss 'The Bonds of Discipline'
Traffics and Discoveries (1904) Rudyard Kipling
Hope, Harry keeper of New York saloon which provides the setting
The Iceman Cometh play (1946) Eugene O'Neill
Hope, Jefferson
A Study in Scarlet (1887) Arthur Conan Doyle
Hope, Trelawney
ss 'The Second Stain'
The Return of Sherlock Holmes (1905) Arthur Conan Doyle
Hope, William inventor cc of author's final novel
Grace his daughter
A Perilous Secret (1885) Charles Reade
Hope-Ashburn, Myra, Lady wealthy friend to Gwyneth Cornwell*
Sir Noël her husband, gynaecologist
The Widow (1957) Francis King
Hope-Carew, Antony
ss 'The Man Who Was Unlucky With Women'
Unlucky for Pringle (1973) Wyndham Lewis
Hopeful companion to Christian*
The Pilgrim's Progress (1678–84) John Bunyan
Hopewell, Joy ('Hulga') atheist Doctor of Philosophy with an artificial leg, stolen by a Bible salesman
ss 'Good Country People'
A Good Man is Hard to Find (1955) Flannery O'Connor
Hopkins draper
Middlemarch (1871–2) George Eliot (rn Mary Anne, later Marian, Evans)
Hopkins, Captain debtor in 'last extremity of shabbiness'
David Copperfield (1850) Charles Dickens

Hopkins, Jack narrates story of child who swallowed necklace
The Pickwick Papers (1837) Charles Dickens

Hopkins, Mr greedy and untruthful middleman landlord
ss 'Rosanna'
Popular Tales (1812) Maria Edgeworth

Hopkins, Stanley, Inspector
The Return of Sherlock Holmes (1905) Arthur Conan Doyle

Hopkins, Vulture one of Boffin's* pet misers
Our Mutual Friend (1865) Charles Dickens

Hopkinson master at Grey Friars
The Newcomes (1853–5) W. M. Thackeray

Hopper, James
Lady Windermere's Fan play (1892) Oscar Wilde

Hopper, Nora engaged to George Trimmins*
her parents
Emma her aunt
Ben her uncle
ss 'The Face'
A Beginning (1955) Walter de la Mare

Hopwood, William supposed father to Fanny Hooper*
Mary his wife, mother of Fanny
Fanny By Gaslight (1940) Michael Sadleir

Horace caricature of Ben Jonson* as answer to his caricature of the author – and of Marston*, who probably had a hand in this
Satiromastix, or *The Untrussing of the Humorous Poet* play (1602) Thomas Dekker

Horace in love with Agnes*
Oronte his father
L'École des Femmes (*The School for Wives*) (1662) Molière (rn Jean-Baptiste Poquelin)

Horatio friend to Hamlet*
Hamlet play (1623) William Shakespeare

Horatio, Don
The Spanish Tragedy (1592) Thomas Kyd

Horlick, Wendell deaf superintendent of dog-pound
One Day (1965) Wright Morris

Horn, Joe American owner of store on South Pacific island
ss 'Miss Thompson'
The Trembling of a Leaf (1921) W. Somerset Maugham
Rain play (1922) (adapted) John Colton and Clemence Randolph

Horn, Van killed by cannibals
Jerry of the Islands (1917) Jack London

Hornbeck
his wife, of whom he is intensely jealous
Peregrine Pickle (1751) Thomas Smollett

Hornblow ex-smuggler
Susan his daughter, m. Captain M'Elvina*
The King's Own (1830) Captain Marryat

Hornblower nouveau-riche scoundrel
The Skin Game play (1920) John Galsworthy

Hornblower, Horatio midshipman, later admiral, in popular naval series, onwards from
The Happy Return (1937) C. S. Forrester (rn C. L. T. Smith)

Hornblower, Silas, Revd much-tattooed missionary, m. Lady Emily Sheepshanks*
Vanity Fair (1847–8) W. M. Thackeray

Hornbook, Dr hist. quack of Mauchline, the author's parish; thus exposed in satirical poem, in which Death describes him
'Death and Dr Hornbook' poem, in *Poems* (1786) Robert Burns

Horne, Miss friend to Miss Hobart*
Sylvia Scarlett (1918) Compton Mackenzie

Horner, John plumber
ss 'The Blue Carbuncle'
The Adventures of Sherlock Holmes (1892) Arthur Conan Doyle

Horner, Mr gallant alleged to be impotent
The Country Wife play (1673) William Wycherley

Horner, Revd Mr 'independent' minister, quarrelsome drunkard
ss 'Janet's Repentance'
Scenes of Clerical Life (1857) George Eliot (rn Mary Anne, later Marian, Evans)

Hornhead, Dan'l serpent-player
ss 'Absent-mindedness in a Parish Choir'
Life's Little Ironies (1894) Thomas Hardy

Horringe, Thomas, Sir, KCB ('Scree')

surgeon
ss 'Tender Achilles'
Limits and Renewals (1932) Rudyard Kipling
Horrock vet
Middlemarch (1871–2) George Eliot (rn Mary Anne, later Marian, Evans)
Horrocks butler with whom Pitt Crawley* becomes friends
his vulgar and ambitious daughter
Vanity Fair (1847–8) W. M. Thackeray
Horse, Alexandre French horse-dealer
Pending Heaven (1930) William Gerhardie
Horsefall, Zillah, Mrs nurse attending Robert Moore*, a giant dram-drinker
Shirley (1849) Charlotte Brontë
Horseman, Miss
Men's Wives (1843) W. M. Thackeray
Horseman, The Headless ghost of Sleepy Hollow
The Legend of Sleepy Hollow (1819–20) Washington Irving
Horsham, Earl of
Waste play (1907) Harley Granville Barker
Hortense Lady Dedlock's handsome French maid
Bleak House (1853) Charles Dickens
Hortensio suitor to Bianca*
The Taming of the Shrew play (1623) William Shakespeare
Horton, Chandler Von friend to Jules Farber*
You Could Live If They Let You (1974) Wallace Markfield
Hoseason, Elias Captain of the brig *Covenant*
Kidnapped (1886) Robert Louis Stevenson
Hoskin, Ralph painter who dies of love for the cold and selfish Mildred Lawson*
ss 'Mildred Lawson'
Celibates (1895) George Moore
Hoskins, Gus fellow clerk and close friend to Samuel Titmarsh*
his father, leather-seller
his sisters
The Great Hoggarty Diamond (1841) W. M. Thackeray
Hosnani, Nessim Coptic banker and conspirator
Justine his Jewish wife, cc

Falthaus Hosnani his father
Leila his intellectual mother, who loves Mountolive*
Nabouz his hare-lipped young brother
Justine† (1957–61) Lawrence Durrell
Höss, Rudolf concentration-camp commandant whose secretary Sophie Zawistowska* becomes, in order to survive
Sophie's Choice (1979) William Styron
Hossett, Christina owner of Limpid Steam Laundry, m. Albert Edward Preemby
Christina her daughter by Wilfred Devizes*
Christina Alberta's Father (1925) H. G. Wells
Hotspur (Henry Percy)
King Henry IV plays (1623) William Shakespeare
Houghton, Adelaide, Mrs
Is He Popenjoy? (1878) Anthony Trollope
Houghton, Alvina cc, m. Francesco Marasca*
James her father, draper who becomes cinema owner
Clariss her mother
The Lost Girl (1920) D. H. Lawrence
Houghton, Miss to whom Mrs O'Reilly* passes on the gossip about Zaluski*; she repeats it
The Autobiography of a Slander (1887) Edna Lyall (rn A. E. Bayly)
Houghton, Mrs satirical portrait of well-known novelist
Hotel de Dream (1976) Emma Tennant
Hounslow highwayman
The Beaux' Stratagem play (1707) George Farquhar
Houseman Aram's* accomplice and the actual criminal in crime novel written under personal influence of Godwin*
Eugene Aram (1832) Edward Bulwer Lytton
Hovenden, Anne beloved of Warland*, but m. Robert Danforth*
ss 'The Artist of the Beautiful' (1844)
Peter her brother
Mosses from an Old Manse (1846) Nathaniel Hawthorne
Hovenden, Lord m. Irene Aldwinkle*
Those Barren Leaves (1925) Aldous Huxley

How, James
Walter his son: solicitors
Justice play (1910) John Galsworthy
Howard 'short, fat and thickset',
Graham's* guardian throughout his
trance
When the Sleeper Wakes (1899) H. G.
Wells
Howard, Donald young researcher
accused of fraud
The Affair (1960) C. P. Snow
Howard, Stephen journalist
I'm Dying Laughing (1986) Christina
Stead
Howden widow, auctioneer
Heart of Midlothian (1818) Walter Scott
Howe, Anne, Miss confidante of Clarissa
Harlowe*; engaged to Mr Hickman
Annabella her mother
Clarissa Harlowe (1748) Samuel
Richardson
Howe, Governor royal governor
ss 'Howe's Masquerade
Twice-Told Tales (1842) Nathaniel
Hawthorne
Howe, Martin idealistic cc of author's first
novel
One Man's Initiation – 1917 (1920) John
Dos Passos
Howe-Nevinson, Esmé artist, m. Angelica
Deverell
Nora his sister, Angelica's companion for
thirty years
Angel (1957) Elizabeth Taylor
Howell, 'Taffy'
ss 'The Propagation of Knowledge'
Debits and Credits (1926) Rudyard Kipl-
ing
Howie, Willie
The Antiquary (1816) Walter Scott
Howler, Melchisedek, Revd Mrs
MacStinger's* spiritual adviser, ranting
preacher
Dombey and Son (1848) Charles Dickens
Howth, Margaret cc of novel exposing
poverty (in an Indiana town): written in
largely Dickensian* style; a pioneering
work by mother of Richard Harding
Davis*
Margaret Howth (1862) Rebecca Hard-
ing Davis
Hoyden, Miss
A Trip to Scarborough play (1777)

Richard Brinsley Sheridan
Hoyden, Miss daughter to Sir Tunbelly
Clumsey*
The Relapse, or *Virtue in Danger* play
(1697) John Vanbrugh
Hoyland, Algernon
Antigua Penny Puce (1936) Robert
Graves
Hoyt, Rosemary film actress
Tender is the Night (1934) F. Scott
Fitzgerald
Hrothgar descendant of Scyld* who builds
the hall, Heorot, haunted by Grendel*
Beowulf (c.745)
Hubba son to Debon*
Locrine play (1595) 'W. S.' (?George
Peele; ?Robert Green)
Hubbard, Bartley unscrupulous Boston
journalist who is divorced by his wife
(and then murdered in Arizona by one of
his victims) because of his shadiness and
philanderings
Marcia *née* Gaylord, his wife
A Modern Instance† (1882) William
Dean Howells
Hubbard, Benjamin
Oscar brothers to Regina Giddens*
Birdie Oscar's wife
The Little Foxes play (1939) Lillian Hell-
man
Hubbard, Madame
her husband
Gladys their daughter
South Riding (1936) Winifred Holtby
Hubbel, Steve
Eunice his wife
A Streetcar Named Desire play (1949)
Tennessee Williams (rn Thomas Lanier
Williams)
Hubble wheelwright
Great Expectations (1861) Charles
Dickens
Hubert de Burgh chamberlain to King
John*
King John play (1623) William Shake-
speare
Huckaback, Reuben great-uncle to John
Ridd*
Ruth his daughter
Lorna Doone (1869) R. D. Blackmore
Huckaback, Robert shopman, friend to
Titmouse*
Ten Thousand a Year (1839) Samuel

Warren
Huddle, James P.
Miss Huddle his sister
ss 'The Unrest-Cure'
The Chronicles of Clovis (1911) Saki (rn
Hector Hugh Munro)
Huddlestone, Bernard defaulting banker
Clara his daughter, m. Frank Cassilis
ss 'The Pavilion on the Links'
The New Arabian Nights (1882) Robert
Louis Stevenson
Hudibras knight and justice of the peace
who rides out in octosyllabic epigram-
matic satirical burlesque of puritans
Hudibras poem (1662–78) Samuel Butler
Hudig merchant, Almayer's* father-in-
law
Almayer's Folly (1895) Joseph Conrad
(rn Josef Teodor Konrad Korzeniowski)
Hudson, Augusta *née* Drake, lifelong
friend to Sarah Burling Ward*
Thomas her husband
Angle of Repose (1971) Wallace Stegner
Hudson, Cyrus K. American millionaire
his three wives, with all of whom he is on
friendly terms
Phyllis; Amaryllis his daughters
Count Florio and Phyllis K. (1910) Regi-
nald Turner
Hudson, Etta *née* Stackpole, old flame of
Dudley Leicester*, with whom he ap-
pears to be having an affair after his
marriage to Pauline Lucas*
A Call (1910) Ford Madox Ford
Hudson, Mrs Holmes's* landlady at Baker
Street, onwards from
The Adventures of Sherlock Holmes†
(1892) Arthur Conan Doyle
Hudson, Roderick sculptor who fails to
make good in author's first novel of
consequence
his mother
Roderick Hudson (1876) Henry James
Huett, Izz fellow dairymaid with Tess*
Tess of the D'Urbervilles (1891) Thomas
Hardy
Huff, Dr rector of Hackton
Barry Lyndon (1844) W. M. Thackeray
Hugby, F., Revd Varsity snob
his father, a haberdasher
Betsy his sister
The Book of Snobs (1847) W. M.
Thackeray

Huggins, Alfred Ezekiel crooked haulage
contractor and Methodist Preacher
South Riding (1936) Winifred Holtby
Hugh ('Maypole') wild ostler at the May-
pole Inn, hanged
Barnaby Rudge (1841) Charles Dickens
Hugh of Dallington (The Novice)
ss 'Weland's Sword'†
Puck of Pook's Hill† (1906) Rudyard
Kipling
Hugh, Canon Vicar of Pancras (Captain
Thums)
A Tale of a Tub play (1640) Ben Jonson
Hugo, Father alias Redgauntlet* when
entering monastery
Redgauntlet (1824) Walter Scott
Hulings, Alexander 'rotten lawyer' with
wider than small-town aspirations; m.
Gisela Wooddrop*
ss 'Tubal Cain'
Gold and Iron (1918) Joseph
Hergesheimer
Hulker banker
his daughter
Vanity Fair† (1847–8) W. M. Thackeray
Hull, Thomas bibliomaniac who has rid
himself of the notion that books are to be
read, in comic novel by forerunner of
Dickens*; based on collector called
Thomas Hill ('Horace he has by many
different hands/But not one Horace that
he understands')
Gilbert Gurney (1836) Theodore Hook
Hulot, Baron besotted cc, servant of the
empire; m. (2) his kitchen maid
Adeline *née* Fischer, the Baroness, his
adoring and faithful wife
Marshal Hulot his respectable elder
brother
Hortense his daughter, m. Steinbock*
Victorin his son, m. to the daughter of
Crével*
La Cousine Bette (1847) Honoré de
Balzac
Humber King of the Scythians
Locrine play (1595) W. S.' (?George
Peele; ?Robert Green)
Humberstall, R. G. A
ss 'The Janeites'
Debits and Credits (1926) Rudyard Kipl-
ing
Humbert, Humbert murderous psycho-
path

Valeria his first wife
Dolores ('**Lolita**') **Haze** his stepdaughter
Charlotte *née* Haze his second wife
Lolita (1955) Vladimir Nabokov
Humbold, Toni Virginian
Henry Esmond (1852) W. M. Thackeray
Hume, Miranda domestic tyrant
Julius her husband
Rosebery her son
Mother and Son (1954) Ivy Compton-Burnett
Humgudgeon, Corporal
Woodstock (1826) Walter Scott
Humm, Anthony President of the Brick Lane Branch of the United Grand Junction Ebenezer Temperance Association, converted fireman
The Pickwick Papers (1837) Charles Dickens
Hummel, Pavlo thief and misfit who finds a kind of home in the army and then in Vietnam
The Basic Training of Pavlo Hummel play (1973) David W. Rabe
Hummil engineer
ss 'At the End of the Passage'
Life's Handicap (1891) Rudyard Kipling
Humphrey
The Knight of the Burning Pestle play (1613) Francis Beaumont (?and John Fletcher)
Humphrey furze cutter
The Return of the Native (1878) Thomas Hardy
Humphrey, Master deformed old man
Master Humphrey's Clock† (1841) Charles Dickens
Humphrey, Squire son to Sir Francis Headpiece*
A Journey to London play (1728) John Vanbrugh
Humphreys, Alice close friend to Ellen Montgomery*
Revd John her brother
The Wide, Wide World (1850) Elizabeth Wetherell (rn Susan Bogert Warner)
Humplebee, Harry
ss 'Humplebee'
The House of Cobwebs (1906) George Gissing
Humpty-Dumpty
Alice Through the Looking-Glass (1872) Lewis Carroll (rn Charles Lutwidge

Dodgson)
Huneefa blind native woman
Kim (1901) Rudyard Kipling
Hungerford, MP
Tancred (1847) Benjamin Disraeli
Hunker American cinema magnate
Men Like Gods (1923) H. G. Wells
Hunsden, Hunsden Yorke sarcastic mill-owner, benefactor of William Crimsworth
The Professor (1857) Charlotte Brontë
Hunt Bow Street runner
Deacon Brodie play (1880) Robert Louis Stevenson and W. E. Henley
Hunt, Arabella, Mrs
Tom Jones (1749) Henry Fielding
Hunt, Laura 'murdered' cc of (filmed) thriller
Laura (1942) Vera Caspary
Hunt, Rosamund heiress
Manalive (1912) G. K. Chesterton
Hunt, Thomas Tufton, Revd blackguard; as **Tufthunt** in first-named novel
A Shabby Genteel Story (1840); *The Adventures of Philip* (1862) W. M. Thackeray
Hunter of the *Hispaniola*
Treasure Island (1883) Robert Louis Stevenson
Hunter, Frank
The Browning Version play (1948) Terence Rattigan
Hunter, Leo, Mrs author of 'Ode to an Expiring Frog'
The Pickwick Papers (1837) Charles Dickens
Hunter, Steve Hugh McVey's* partner
Poor White (1920) Sherwood Anderson
Hunter, Violet
ss 'The Copper Beeches'
The Adventures of Sherlock Holmes (1892) Arthur Conan Doyle
Huntingdon, Arthur character based on author's brother Bramwell Brontë who died of drugs and drink at thirty-one; in novel which became a scandalous bestseller of its time; m. Helen Graham*
The Tenant of Wildfell Hall (1848) Anne Brontë
Huntinglen, Earl of his wife
The Fortunes of Nigel (1822) Walter Scott
Huntley, Earl of

Perkin Warbeck play (1634) John Ford (?and Thomas Dekker)

Huntley, Gavin sex-ridden novelist and dramatic critic
Joan and Peter (1918) H. G. Wells

Huntly, Edgar sleepwalking narrator (in letters) of first novel to introduce unidealized Indians into American fiction
Edgar Huntly, or *Memoirs of a Sleepwalker* (1799) Charles Brockden Brown

Hunziger, Dawson T.
Arrowsmith (1925) Sinclair Lewis

Huon, Sir of Bordeaux
ss 'Weland's Sword'†
Puck of Pook's Hill† (1906) Rudyard Kipling

Hur, Judah Ben Jewish aristocrat eventually converted to Christianity, cc of novel immensely popular in its time
Ben Hur: A Tale of the Christ (1880) Lew Wallace

Hurd, Jim poacher charged with murder
Minta his wife
Marcella (1894) Mrs Humphry Ward

Hurlbird, Florence m. John Dowell*
The Good Soldier (1915) Ford Madox Ford

Hurree, Chunder Mookerjee Babu (R.17) in Secret Service
Kim (1901) Rudyard Kipling

Hurst, Mr husband to Charles Bingley's* sister Louisa; lives only for eating, drinking and card-playing
Pride and Prejudice (1813) Jane Austen

Hurst, Mrs Bathesheba Everdene's* aunt
Far From the Madding Crowd (1874) Thomas Hardy

Hurstpierpoint, Eulalia wealthy old flagellant
Valmouth (1919) Ronald Firbank

Hurstwood, George W. cc; married bar-manager who elopes with Carrie Meeber* and discovers failure and suicide
Sister Carrie (1900) Theodore Dreiser

Hurtle reviewer
Pendennis (1848) W. M. Thackeray

Hurtle, Winifred widow
The Way We Live Now (1875) Anthony Trollope

Hury, Jacques fiancé of Violaine Vercors*
m. Mara Vercors*

L'Annonce faite à Marie play (*The Tidings Brought to Mary*) (1912, rev. 1948) Paul Claudel

Hushabye, Hesione and **Hector**
Heartbreak House (1917) George Bernard Shaw

Huskisson, Harriet, Miss, CBE headmistress
Elsie and the Child (1924) Arnold Bennett

Huss, Job headmaster, Woldingstanton School
Gilbert his son
The Undying Fire (1919) H. G. Wells

Hussey, Johnny policeman
Bid his wife
Denis their son
A Nest of Simple Folk (1933) Sean O'Faolain

Hustler, George, Sir Commander-in-chief, India
The Newcomes (1853–5) W. M. Thackeray

Hutley, Jem storyteller otherwise known as **Dismal Jemmy**
The Pickwick Papers (1837) Charles Dickens

Hutter, Judith 'soiled enchantress' who falls in love with Natty Bumppo* who resists her because she has 'too much of the settlement about her'
Tom her father
Hetty her sister
The Deerslayer (1841) James Fenimore Cooper

Hutto, Grandma
Oliver her grandson, friend to Jody Baxter*
The Yearling (1938) Marjorie Kinnan Rawlings

Hutton, Henry
Emily his first wife
Doris his mistress, whom he later m.
ss 'The Giaconda Smile'
Mortal Coils (1922) Aldous Huxley

Huxtable theatrical agent
No Name (1862) Wilkie Collins

Huxtable, Mr member of the firm of Madras House, a shop which caters to women
his six unmarried daughters
The Madras House play (1910) Harley Granville Barker

Huxtable, Thorneycroft
ss 'The Adventure of the Priory School'
The Return of Sherlock Holmes (1905)
Arthur Conan Doyle
Hyde, Mr see **Jekyll, Dr**
Hyman, Benny publisher
I Like It Here (1958) Kingsley Amis
Hyman, Rhoda caricature of Virginia
Woolf* as alleged plagiarist from Joyce*
The Roaring Queen (1936) Wyndham
Lewis
Hymen a nymph
The Two Noble Kinsmen play (1634)
William Shakespeare and John Fletcher
(?with Francis Beaumont)
Hyndmarsh grocer, St Oggs
The Mill on the Floss (1860) George Eliot
(rn Mary Anne, later Marian, Evans)
Hynes, John
Louisa his wife, *née* Hegarty
Dr Hynes; Tony m. Mary Anne Rabbit;

Bridget their children
Julie his sister
Famine (1937) Liam O'Flaherty
Hynes, Thomsy brother to Maggie
Kilmartin*
Famine (1937) Liam O'Flaherty
Hypatia (hist.) beautiful and influential
Neoplatonic philosopher
Hypatia, or *New Foes with an Old Face*
(1853) Charles Kingsley
Hypo portrait of H. G. Wells*, whose
mistress the author had been: 'incapable
of homage'; in *roman fleuve** of 'un-
punctuated female prose'
Pilgrimage (1915–67) Dorothy M.
Richardson
Hypocrisy see **Formalist**
Hythloday, Ralph Portuguese traveller,
narrator
Utopia (1551) Thomas More

I

Iachimo friend to Philario*
Cymbeline play (1623) William Shakespeare
Iago Othello's* ancient
Emilia, his wife
Othello play (1623) William Shakespeare
Ianson, Dr
his wife and family
Agatha's Husband (1853) Mrs Craik
Ianto
Dinah his daughter
ss 'The Devil in Eden'
My People (1915) Caradoc Evans (rn David Evans)
Ibbotson, Peter originally **Gogo Pasquier,** orphaned and taken in charge by Colonel Ibbotson; taught by his lover the Duchess of Towers* to 'dream true'
Peter Ibbotson (1891) George du Maurier
Ibn Mararreh (The Hajji) chieftain
ss 'A Deal in Cotton'
Actions and Reactions (1909) Rudyard Kipling
Ickenham, Earl of (Frederick Altamont Cornwallis Twistleton)
Jane his wife, half-sister of Sir Raymond Bastable*
Pongo his nephew
Cocktail Time (1958) P. G. Wodehouse
Ida cc proto-feminist novel
Woman, or Ida of Athens (1809) Sydney Owenson (later Lady Morgan)
Ida, Countess German heiress whom Lyndon* wants to marry
Barry Lyndon (1844) W. M. Thackeray
Ida, Countess see **Gama**
Iddleston policeman
The Last Revolution (1951) Lord Dunsany
Iden, Alexander Kentish gentleman
King Henry VI plays (1623) William Shakespeare
Iden, Farmer intellectual farmer, cc, of

Coombe Oaks
his wife
Amaryllis cc, their artistic daughter
Amaryllis at the Fair (1887) Richard Jeffries
Iffley, Edgar, Sir
Anglo-Saxon Attitudes (1956) Angus Wilson
Iggiwick ('vuz-pig') hedgehog
Tarka the Otter (1927) Henry Williamson
Iggulden countryman
his son
ss 'An Habitation Enforced'
Actions and Reactions (1909) Rudyard Kipling
Ignorance 'a brisk lad'
The Pilgrim's Progress (1678–84) John Bunyan
Ignosi see **Umpopa**
Ikey boy responsible for 'supernatural' phenomena
The Haunted House (1859) Charles Dickens
Ikey Solomon Jacobs' factotum
Sketches by Boz† (1836) Charles Dickens
Ikki the porcupine
ss 'Mowgli's Brothers'†
Jungle Books (1894–5) Rudyard Kipling
Ilbury, Earl of calling himself **Mr Carisbrooke,** tenant of the Grange
Lady Mary his daughter
Uncle Silas (1864) J. Sheridan Le Fanu
Ilchester, Janet m. Harry Richmond*, her cousin
Sir Roderick, Baronet her father
her mother
Charles her brother
The Adventures of Harry Richmond (1871) George Meredith
Ilderton, Lucy confidante of Isabel Vere*
Nancy her cousin
The Black Dwarf (1816) Walter Scott
Illingsworth, Lord see **Harford, George**
Ilse, Countess actress and leader of theatri-

cal troupe which has 'failed with the people'

The Mountain Giants play (1938) Luigi Pirandello

Ilyich, Ivan man whose soliloquy is famous amongst its Russian author's shorter fiction

Smert Ivana Ilyicha (*The Death of Ivan Ilyich*) (1886) Leo Tolstoy

Ilyinsky, Olga beautiful woman loved by Oblomov*; m. Stolz*

Oblomov (1859) Ivan Goncharov

Immelmann, Art representative of CIA, military, and similar institutions, wants to obtain More's* Lapsometer as a weapon

Love Amongst the Ruins (1971) Walker Percy

Imogen Cymbeline's* daughter, wife to Posthumus*

Cymbeline play (1623) William Shakespeare

Imoinda cc

Oronooko (1688) Mrs Aphra Behn

Imray murdered by his servant

ss 'The Return of Imray'

Life's Handicap (1891) Rudyard Kipling

In-and-In-Medlay of Islington

A Tale of a Tub play (1640) Ben Jonson

Inch, Archie street-cleaning contractor who resists mechanization; becomes taxi driver; in play that failed commercially but was turned into an opera

White Wings play (1926) Philip Barry

Incubu see **Curtis, Henry, Sir**

Indian Joe murders Dr Robinson*

The Adventures of Tom Sawyer (1876) Mark Twain (rn Samuel Langhorne Clemens)

Indiana

The Conscious Lovers play (1722) Sir Richard Steele

Inesse, Master

Possibility, Master his brother

A Mad World My Masters play (1608) Thomas Middleton

Inez the King of Barataria's foster-mother

The Gondoliers opera (1889) W. S. Gilbert and Arthur Sullivan

Infadoos son of Kafa, King of the Kukuana; uncle to Twala*

King Solomon's Mines (1885) Henry

Rider Haggard

Infant, The subaltern

ss 'A Conference of the Powers'

Many Inventions (1893) Rudyard Kipling

Inflammable Gas caricature of the scientist Joseph Priestley

An Island in the Moon satirical prose fragment (written 1784–5, pub. 1907) William Blake

Ingell, Thomas, Sir, Baronet, MP magistrate

ss 'The Village that Voted the Earth Was Flat'

A Diversity of Creatures (1917) Rudyard Kipling

Ingham, Howard American novelist visiting Tunisia

The Tremor of Forgery (1969) Patricia Highsmith

Ingle, Mary, Mrs aunt to Ablard Pender*

The Last Revolution (1951) Lord Dunsany

Ingleblad, Agnes Arrowsmith's patient*

Arrowsmith (1925) Sinclair Lewis

Ingles, Arthur ruthless millionaire

Cecilia his beautiful wife, leader of high society

The Cliff-Dwellers (1893) Henry Blake Fuller

Inglesant, John cc immensely popular (Gladstone was photographed with a copy of it on his knee) religious hist. novel set in time of Charles I: finally exposed (1925) as collage of sources (Hobbes, Evelyn, Burton, Aubrey etc.) to such an extent that it was even called a literary hoax

Eustace his father

Richard his grandfather

Eustace his brother

John Inglesant (1880) John Henry Shorthouse

Inglewood, Arthur

Manalive (1818) G. K. Chesterton

Inglewood, Squire 'a whitewashed Jacobite'

Rob Roy (1818) Walter Scott

Ingloldsby, Squire Cumberland alias of Redgauntlet*

Redgauntlet (1824) Walter Scott

Ingpen, Tertius factory inspector

These Twain (1916) Arnold Bennett

Ingram, Colonel
The Iron Heel (1908) Jack London
Ingram, Theodore, Lord apathetic flirt
The Dowager Baroness his haughty
mother
Blanche; Mary his sisters
Jane Eyre (1847) Charlotte Brontë
Ingrams homosexual novelist-in-residence
Love and Friendship (1962) Alison Lurie
Iniquity the vice
The Devil is an Ass play (1616) Ben
Jonson
Innerarity, Raoul whimsical Creole clerk
The Grandissimes: A Story of Creole Life
(1880) George Washington Cable
Innes, Evelyn cc; singer who becomes a
nun
Evelyn Innes (1898)
Sister Teresa (1901) George Moore
Innes, Frank friend to and then betrayer of
Archie Weir*
Weir of Hermiston (1896) Robert Louis
Stevenson
Innocencio, Padre ironically named con-
fessor to Doña Perfecta* who persuades
her to oppose her nephew Pepe Rey* in
his quest for the hand of Rosario* in the
interests of his own niece; after murder of
Pepe Rey goes on remorseful pilgrimage
María Remedios, his niece, the treacher-
ous mother of
Jacintillo who seeks Rosario for himself
Doña Perfecta (1876) Benito Pérez
Galdós
Inquisitor, Grand
Candide (1759) Voltaire (rn François-
Marie Arouet)
Inquisitor, The
Bratya Karamazov (*Brothers Kara-
mazov*) (1880) Fyodor Dostoievsky
Insultado Spanish noble at the English
court: 'My Corocon es muy pesada, my
Anima muy atormentada, No por los
Cielos: La Piede de Espagnoll, no haze
musica in Tierra Inglesa'
Old Fortunatus play (1600) Thomas
Dekker
Interest, Moth, Sir usurer
The Magnetic Lady, or *Humours Recon-
ciled* play (1641) Ben Jonson
Interpreter, The
The Pilgrim's Progress (1678–84) John
Bunyan

Inverarity Sahib
ss 'Baa Baa Black Sheep'
Wee Willie Winkie (1888) Rudyard Kipl-
ing
Inverarity, Pierce real estate mogul, once
lover of Oedipa Mass*
The Crying of Lot 49 (1966) Thomas
Pynchon
Invern, Ulick decadent critic in novel
depicting the New York art and music
world
Painted Veils (1920) James Huneker
Iolanthe fairy, wife of Lord Chancellor and
Strephon's* mother
Iolanthe opera (1882) W. S. Gilbert and
Arthur Sullivan
Ippolit nihilist
Idiot (1869) Fyodor Dostoievsky
Ippolito, Don Italian priest and inventor,
in love with Florida Vervain*
A Foregone Conclusion (1875) William
Dean Howells
Ipps butler
ss 'The Honours of War'†
A Diversity of Creatures (1917) Rudyard
Kipling
Iqbal intelligent and non-violent young
radical cc, a Sikh imprisoned as Moslem
League member
Train to Pakistan (1956) Khushwant
Singh
Iras attendant on Cleopatra*
Antony and Cleopatra play (1623)
William Shakespeare
Caesar and Cleopatra play (1900)
George Bernard Shaw
Iredale, Philip m. Sylvia Scarlett*
Sylvia Scarlett (1918) Compton
Mackenzie
Ireton snob
ss 'A Capitalist'
The House of Cobwebs (1906) George
Gissing
Iris a spirit
The Tempest play (1623) William Shake-
speare
Irodohahoon policemen
*All and Everything: Beelzebub's Tales to
His Grandson* (1950) G. I. Gurdjieff
Irons, Batholomew, Revd 'an awakening
man'
Vanity Fair (1847–8) W. M. Thackeray
Ironside, Captain brother to Compass*, a

soldier
The Magnetic Lady, or *Humours Reconciled* play (1641) Ben Jonson
Irvine, Mrs landlady who befriends Bessie Hipkiss*
Jezebel's Dust (1951) Fred Urquhart
Irwin, Hannah companion to Clara Mowbray*, m. Biddulph
St Ronan's Well (1824) Walter Scott
Irwin, Judge upright judge who is destroyed by Stark* and Burden*, who learns too late that he is his son
All the King's Men (1946) Robert Penn Warren
Irwine, Adolphus, Revd Rector of Broxton and Vicar of Blythe and Hayslope
Anne; Kate his sisters
Adam Bede (1859) George Eliot (rn Mary Anne, later Marian, Evans)
Isaac of York father to Rebecca*
Ivanhoe (1820) Walter Scott
Isaac Sawyer's* groom
Market Harborough (1861) G. Whyte-Melville
Isaac sheriff's officer who took Mrs Bardell* to the Fleet prison
The Pickwick Papers (1837) Charles Dickens
Isabel Queen of France
King Henry V play (1623) William Shakespeare
Isabella Fabritio's* daughter
Women Beware Women play (1657) Thomas Middleton
Isabelle
The Adventures of David Simple (1744–53) Sarah Fielding
Isaev, Piotr Gavrilovitch ('Petya') lover rejected by Tatania Ostapenko*
Olga his mother
Tobit Transplanted (1931) Stella Benson
Isbister friend to Graham*, to whom he leaves his fortune
When the Sleeper Wakes (1899) H. G. Wells
Isbrand court fool, brother to Wolfram*; stabs Melveric* to death, in Victorian pastiche of Jacobean drama
Death's Jest Book, or *The Fool's Tragedy*

play (1850) Thomas Lovell Beddoes
Ishak the Caliph's minstrel
Hassan play (1923) James Elroy Flecker
Ishmael cc outcast youth with 'damp, drizzly November' in his soul; narrator
Moby-Dick, or *The Whale* (1851) Herman Melville
Isidor Joe Sedley's* Belgian servant
Vanity Fair (1847–8) W. M. Thackeray
Ismail thug who initiates Ameer Ali* into the mysteries
Confessions of a Thug (1839) Captain Meadows Taylor
Issyvoo, Herr or **Christoph** 'camera-eye' narrator
Goodbye to Berlin (1939) Christopher Isherwood
Itelo prince-champion of Arnewi tribe
Henderson the Rain King (1959) Saul Bellow
Ithamore Barabas's* slave
The Jew of Malta play (1633) Christopher Marlowe
Ithoclea favourite to Amyclas*
The Broken Heart play (1633) John Ford
Ivanhoe, Wilfred, Knight of m. Lady Rowena*
Ivanhoe (1820) Walter Scott
Ivanova, Katerina
her father, an officer who embezzled funds
Bratya Karamazov (*Brothers Karamazov*) (1880) Fyodor Dostoievsky
Ives, Alison emancipated friend to Mary Erle*
The Story of a Modern Woman (1894) Ella Hepworth Dixon
Ives, Mr sick patient who is in fact well
Love Amongst the Ruins (1971) Walker Percy
Ivory, Charles fake specialist
The Citadel (1937) A. J. Cronin
Ivy, Dick friend to Jeremy Melford*
Humphrey Clinker (1771) Tobias Smollett
Izzard member of committee which welcomed Elijah Pogrom*
Martin Chuzzlewit (1844) Charles Dickens

J

J one of the three, narrator
Three Men in a Boat (1889) Jerome K. Jerome
Jabberwock monster
Alice Through the Looking-Glass (1872) Lewis Carroll (rn Charles Lutwidge Dodgson)
Jabos, Jack Guy Mannering's* guide to Ellangowan, later postilion
Guy Mannering (1815) Walter Scott
Jabotière, Chevalier de la officer with whom Warrington* fought a duel
The Virginians (1857–9) W. M. Thackeray
Jacintha supposed wife to Octavio*
The Spanish Curate play (1647) John Fletcher and Philip Massinger
Jacinto servant to Bishop Latour*
Death Comes for the Archbishop (1927) Willa Cather
Jack boy dictator
Lord of the Flies (1954) William Golding
Jack Chad Buford's* shepherd dog
The Little Shepherd of Kingdom Come (1903) John Fox Jr.
Jack Lord Mayor who came from Hull to make his fortune
Master Humphrey's Clock (1841) Charles Dickens
Jack one of the policemen who arrested Jonas Chuzzlewit*
Martin Chuzzlewit (1844) Charles Dickens
Jack paradigmatic sailor
The Uncommercial Traveller (1860–8) Charles Dickens
Jack prisoner charged with ill-treating a woman (who died)
Sketches by Boz† (1836) Charles Dickens
Jack riverside character in pub where Pip and Magwitch are planning latter's escape
Great Expectations (1861) Charles Dickens
Jack suicide from Waterloo Bridge

ss 'Down with the Tide'
Reprinted Pieces (1858) Charles Dickens
Jack, 'Captain' companion to Colonel Jack*
Colonel Jack (1722) Daniel Defoe
Jack, 'Colonel' cc, pickpocket, pirate, narrator
Moggy his faithful wife
Colonel Jack (1722) Daniel Defoe
Jack, Black butler to Lady Tub*
A Tale of a Tub play (1640) Ben Jonson
Jack, Brother leader of Communist Brotherhood
The Invisible Man (1952) Ralph Ellison
Jack, Daddy
Uncle Remus (1880–95) Joel Chandler Harris
Jack, Esther mistress of George Webber*
Frederick her husband
Edith her sister
The Web and the Rock (1939); *You Can't Go Home Again* (1940) Thomas Wolfe
Jack, Owen
Love Among the Artists (1900) George Bernard Shaw
Jackanapes cc
Jackanapes (1879) Juliana H. Ewing
Jackie aboriginal guide who stabs and decapitates Voss*
Voss (1957) Patrick White
Jackman, James, Major Mrs Lirriper's* lodger
Mrs Lirriper's Lodgings and Legacy (1864) Charles Dickens
Jackman, Mr and Mrs
The Skin Game play (1920) John Galsworthy
Jacks, Arnold imperialist
The Crown of Life (1899) George Gissing
Jackson family, the English emigrants
The Settlers in Canada (1844) Captain Marryat
Jackson friend to cousin Feenix*

Dombey and Son (1848) Charles Dickens
Jackson of Barbox Brothers
Mugby Junction (1866) Charles Dickens
Jackson, Joby fairground showman
The Good Companions (1929) J. B. Priestley
Jackson, Miss Mrs Barton's* aunt
ss 'The Sad Fortunes of the Rev. Amos Barton'
Scenes of Clerical Life (1857) George Eliot (rn Mary Anne, later Marian, Evans)
Jackson, Mrs farmer's wife
Swallows and Amazons (1930) Arthur Ransome
Jackson, Phoenix old Negro woman going to fetch medicine for a grandson
ss 'A Worn Path'
A Curtain of Green (1941) Eudora Welty
Jackson, Samuel solicitor
The Great Hoggarty Diamond (1841) W. M. Thackeray
Jacksonini clown
Edwin Drood (1870) Charles Dickens
Jacky Australian aboriginal
It Is Never Too Late To Mend (1856) Charles Reade
Jacob (Yacubu) cook to the Company's agent, Shibi*
Aissa Saved (1932) Joyce Cary
Jacobs, Hannah beautiful young girl
Reb Shemuel her father, a rabbi
Children of the Ghetto (1892) Israel Zangwill
Jacobs, Miss pupil at the Misses Pidge's*
The Professor (1837) Charlotte Brontë
Jacobs, Solomon bailiff
Sketches by Boz† (1836) Charles Dickens
Jacomo a friar
The Jew of Malta play (1633) Christopher Marlowe
Jacques Anabaptist
Candide (1759) Voltaire (rn François-Marie Arouet)
Jadwin, Curtis speculator, m. Laura Dearborn*
The Pit (1903) Frank Norris
Jael servant to Abel Fletcher*
John Halifax, Gentleman (1823) Mrs Craik
Jafar the Caliph's Vizier
Hassan play (1923) James Elroy Flecker
Jaffe, Maud

ss 'Children of the Great'
Unlucky for Pringle (1973) Wyndham Lewis
Jagan cc, follower of Mahatma Gandhi, seller of sweets
his spoiled and westernized son
The Vendor of Sweets (1967) R. K. Narayan
Jäger, Moritz ex-weaver, now soldier
Die Weber (The Weavers) play (1892) Gerhart Hauptmann
Jaggers old Bailey lawyer employed by Magwitch*
Great Expectations (1861) Charles Dickens
Jaggers, Alley cc
Alley Jaggers† (1966) Paul West
Jago, Paul Senior Tutor, Professor of Literature; based on Canon C. E. Raven, Master of Christ's College, Cambridge
The Masters (1951) C. P. Snow
Jake cc who becomes educated through meeting educated Haitian, Ray* in post-1914–18 War novel of Harlem Black nightlife in last days of Prohibition era by Jamaican-born American poet and novelist who was major figure in Harlem Renaissance
Home to Harlem (1928) Claude McKay
Jake, Charley hedge-carpenter
'The Three Strangers'
Wessex Tales (1888) Thomas Hardy
Jakin drunken drummer boy and hero
ss 'The Drums of the Fore and Aft'
Wee Willie Winkie (1888) Rudyard Kipling
Jakin, Bob holiday friend to Tom Tulliver*
The Mill on the Floss (1860) George Eliot (rn Mary Anne, later Marian, Evans)
James coachman to the Third Viscount Castlewood*
Henry Esmond (1852) W. M. Thackeray
James IV King of Scotland
Perkin Warbeck play (1934) John Ford
James, Alfred
ss 'Alice'
Poor Women (1928) Norah Hoult
James, Grandfather maternal, grandfather of the Dewys*
Under the Greenwood Tree (1872) Thomas Hardy
James, Laura
Look Homeward, Angel (1929) Thomas

Wolfe

James, Mr of Sutton, friend to the Pooters*
his wife, a fashionable spiritualist
The Diary of a Nobody (1892) George
and Weedon Grossmith

Jameson, Bet nurse to Richard
Middlemas*
The Surgeon's Daughter (1827) Walter
Scott

Jameson, Dolores schoolmistress
South Riding (1936) Winifred Holtby

Jamf, Laszlo
Gravity's Rainbow (1973) Thomas
Pynchon

Jamie, Don younger brother to Don
Henrique*
The Spanish Curate play (1647) John
Fletcher and Philip Massinger

Jamieson, Mrs, the Hon. modelled in part
on the imperious Lady Jane Stanley
Cranford (1853) Mrs Gaskell

Jane 'domestic' employed by narrator,
jilted by William Piddingquirk*
ss 'The Jilting of Jane'
The Plattner Story (1897) H. G. Wells

Jane waitress at Bellamy's
Sketches by Boz (1836) Charles Dickens

Jane young lady encountered by the
Tuggs* at Ramsgate library
Sketches by Boz (1836) Charles Dickens

Jane, Aunt one of Wegg's* fictitious
patrons
Our Mutual Friend (1865) Charles
Dickens

Jane, Lady rapturous maiden
Patience opera (1881) W. S. Gilbert and
Arthur Sullivan

Janet 'Beautifully Janet slept/Till it was
deeply morning. She woke then/And
thought about her dainty-feathered
hen,/To see how it had kept/ . . . . /Alas,
her Chucky had died' and she 'would not
be instructed in how deep/Was the forget-
ful kingdom of death.'
'Janet Waking' poem
Chills and Fever (1924) John Crowe
Ransom

Janet Miss Betsy Trotwood's* maid,
averse to matrimony, m. a tavern keeper
David Copperfield (1850) Charles
Dickens

Janey hunchback with 144 teeth and pregnant in the hump

The Dream Life of Balso Snell (1931)
Nathanael West (rn Nathan Weinstein)

Janicola a basket maker
*The Pleasant Commedye of Patient
Grissill* play (1603) Thomas Dekker

Janki Meah
Unda his wife
ss 'At Twenty-two'
Soldiers Three (1888) Rudyard Kipling

Janoo
ss 'In the House of Suddhoo'
Plain Tales from the Hills (1888) Rudyard Kipling

Japp, Peter drunken storekeeper
Prester John (1910) John Buchan

Jaquenetta country wench
Love's Labour's Lost play (1623)
William Shakespeare

Jacques melancholy attendant on banished
Duke
As You Like It play (1623) William
Shakespeare

Jaraby, Mr old ex-public schoolboy
his wife
Basil their son, bird fancier
The Old Boys (1964) William Trevor

Jargon one of Miss Flite's* captive birds
Bleak House (1853) Charles Dickens

Jarl sailor companion to Taji*
Mardi (1849) Herman Melville

Jarley, Mrs proprietor of travelling
waxworks
George her husband
The Old Curiosity Shop (1841) Charles
Dickens

Jarman miniature painter
The Adventures of Philip (1862) W. M.
Thackeray

Jarndyce, John owner of Bleak House
Bleak House (1853) Charles Dickens

Jarrett village carpenter
Daniel Deronda (1876) George Eliot (rn
Mary Anne, later Marian, Evans)

Jarrk seal
Tarka the Otter (1927) Henry
Williamson

Jarvis, James
Margaret his wife
Arthur their son, m. Mary née Harrison
Cry the Beloved Country (1948) Alan
Paton

Jasper man to Master Penitent Brothel*
A Mad World My Masters play (1608)

Thomas Middleton

Jasper, John Edwin Drood's* uncle
Edwin Drood (1870) Charles Dickens

Jawleyford sportsman
Mr Sponge's Sporting Tour (1853) R. S. Surtees

Jay, Mr cc, Yatman's* lodger
ss 'The Biter Bit'
The Queen of Hearts (1859) Wilkie Collins

Jayne, Frank elegant essayist
Olga his Russian wife *née* Naryshkin
Told By An Idiot (1923) Rose Macaulay

Jayne, Gordon, M. D. friend to Aubrey Tanqueray*
The Second Mrs Tanqueray play (1893) Arthur Wing Pinero

Jeaffreson, Miss author of *A Child's Guide to Nietzsche*
The Marsden Case (1923) Ford Madox Ford

Jeal, Anne witch, woman
The 'Half Moon': A Romance of the Old and the New (1909) Ford Madox Ford

Jeames nauseating flunkey, footman to Lady Clavering*
Pendennis (1848) W. M. Thackeray

Jean narrator, recovering from a breakdown in a mental hospital
The Ha-Ha (1961) Jennifer Dawson

Jean servant to Gavin Dishart*
The Little Minister (1891) J. M. Barrie

Jean valet
Miss Julie play (1888) August Strindberg

Jeanie girl afraid of smelling of sweat
ss 'Sweat'
I Fell for a Sailor (1940) Fred Urquhart

Jeanne, Mlle Lady Agatha Lasenby's maid
The Admirable Crichton play (1902) J. M. Barrie

Jeavons, Molly, Lady society hostess, formerly Lady Sleaford
Ted her second husband
At Lady Molly's† (1958) Anthony Powell

Jedburgh, Lady
Lady Windermere's Fan play (1892) Oscar Wilde

Jeddler, Dr cc, philosopher who regards world as huge practical joke
Grace m. Alfred Heathfield*; **Marion** m. Michael Warden* his daughters
The Battle of Life (1846) Charles

Dickens

Jeeves, Reginald cc, Bertie Wooster's* manservant, onwards from
ss 'Extricating Young Gussie' (1915)
My Man Jeeves stories (1919); *Thank You, Jeeves* (the first novel) (1934) P. G. Wodehouse

Jefferson, Arthur, Revd
Robert's Wife play (1937) St John Ervine

Jeffrey, Mrs gossip
Mrs Galer's Business (1905) William Pett Ridge

Jeffrys, Frank cc of major novel of Australian participation in the First World War
Flesh in Armour (1932) Leonard Mann

Jehan the Crab man-at-arms
ss 'Old Men at Pevensea'
Puck of Pook's Hill (1906) Rudyard Kipling

Jehoram, Jessica arty widow
The Wonderful Visit (1895) H. G. Wells

Jekyll, Cassie m. Duncan Edgeworth*
Gretchen her mother
Revd Oscar her brother, rector
A House and Its Head (1935) Ivy Compton-Burnett

Jekyll, Dr alias **Mr Hyde** in psychological romance perhaps spoiled by author's American wife Fanny (deeply disliked by Henry James*) who made him throw the first version into the fire
Dr Jekyll and Mr Hyde (1886) Robert Louis Stevenson

Jelaluddin, Mcintosh
his native wife
as 'To be Filed for Reference'
Plain Tales from the Hills (1888) Rudyard Kipling

Jelaluddin, Mir Cambridge undergraduate in love with Joan Debenham*
Joan and Peter (1918) H. G. Wells

Jellicot, Joan senile, blind, deaf
Woodstock (1826) Walter Scott

Jello shipboard prig
Blue Voyage (1927) Conrad Aiken

Jellyby, Mrs in part, a caricature of Harriet Martineau*; devotes whole attention to colonization of Borrioboola-Gha
her husband
Caroline ('**Caddy**'); her amanuensis, m. Prince Turveydrop*; '**Peepy**' and others, their children
Bleak House (1853) Charles Dickens

Jemima sister to Polly Toodle*
Dombey and Son (1848) Charles Dickens
Jemima, Queen
The Apple Cart (1929) George Bernard Shaw
Jemmy, Dismal see Hutley, Jem
Jenatsch, Georg (hist.) Swiss patriot, murdered murderer; cc novel set in Thirty Years War by Swiss (German) author
Lucia his wife
Jürg Jenatsch (1876) Conrad Ferdinand Meyer
Jenkins steward to Sir John Flowerdale*
Lionel and Clarissa play (1768) Isaac Bickerstaffe
Jenkins, Eli, Revd
Under Milk Wood play (1954) Dylan Thomas
Jenkins, Jones
Hawbuck Grange (1847) R. S. Surtees
Jenkins, Nicholas narrator, m. Isobel Tolland*
The Music of Times series: A Question of Upbringing (1951); A Buyer's Market (1952); The Acceptance World (1955); At Lady Molly's (1957); Casanova's Chinese Restaurant (1960); The Kindly Ones (1962); The Valley of Bones (1964); The Soldier's Art (1966); The Military Philosophers (1968); Books Do Furnish a Room (1971); Temporary Kings (1973); Hearing Secret Harmonies (1975) Anthony Powell
Jenkins, Tom, Mrs keeper of a school
Tom her husband
Eunice; Eiluned their daughters
How Green Was My Valley (1939) Richard Llewellyn
Jenkins, Winifred Tabitha Bramble's* illiterate servant
The Expedition of Humphrey Clinker (1771) Tobias Smollett
Jenkinson a messenger for the Circumlocution Office
Little Dorrit (1857) Charles Dickens
Jenkinson fellow prisoner and friend to the Vicar
The Vicar of Wakefield (1766) Oliver Goldsmith
Jenkinson, Alice church-going spinster
Minnie her sister
ss 'Alice'

Poor Women (1928) Norah Hoult
Jenkinson, Mountstuart, Mrs a domineering clever widow
The Egoist (1879) George Meredith
Jenkyns, Deborah
Matilda her sister
Peter Marmaduke her brother
Cranford (1953) Mrs Gaskell
Jennett, Mrs
The Light that Failed (1890) Rudyard Kipling
Jennings pupil at Nun's house
Edwin Drood (1870) Charles Dickens
Jennings pupil at Peregrine Pickle's* boarding school
Peregrine Pickle (1751) Tobias Smollett
Jennings robemaker, friend to Dounce
Sketches by Boz (1836) Charles Dickens
Jennings Tulrumble's* secretary
The Public Life of Mr Tulrumble (1837) Charles Dickens
Jennings, Ezra hypnotist, part narrator
The Moonstone (1868) Wilkie Collins
Jennings, Miss
ss 'Mr Gilfil's Love Story'
Scenes of Clerical Life (1857) George Eliot (rn Mary Anne, later Marian, Evans)
Jennings, Mrs good-humoured, fat, merry and vulgar mother to Charlotte Palmer* and Mrs Middleton*
Sense and Sensibility (1811) Jane Austen
Jennings, Revd Mr Vicar of Kenlis
ss 'Green Tea'
In a Glass Darkly (1872) J. Sheridan Le Fanu
Jenny brickmaker's wife who exchanges her cloak for Lady Dedlock's*
Bleak House (1853) Charles Dickens
Jenny Clarissa Flowerdale's* maid
Lionel and Clarissa play (1768) Isaac Bickerstaffe
Jenny maid to the Misses Jenkyns*
Cranford (1853) Mrs Gaskell
Jenny Wren see Cleaver
Jensen, Herr
ss 'No 13'
Ghost Stories of an Antiquary (1910) M. R. James
Jenson, Anders Danish artist in Tunisia
The Tremor of Forgery (1969) Patricia Highsmith
Jephson partner to Belknap*

An American Tragedy (1925) Theodore Dreiser

Jeri petty trader in palm oil in novel set in Nigeria
Oil Man of Obange (1971) John Munonoye

Jermyn, Matthew lawyer (see also **Transome**)
his elder daughter, 'vulgarity personified'
Louisa his younger daughter
Felix Holt (1866) George Eliot (rn Mary Anne, later Marian, Evans)

Jermyn, Mr, MP
Sybil (1845) Benjamin Disraeli

Jerningham, Jerry light comedian, m. Lady Partlit*
The Good Companions (1929) J. B. Priestley

Jerningham, Ralph, Sir
Frank his son
The Merry Devil of Edmonton play (1608) ?Thomas Dekker

Jerningham, Tom confidential servant to Duke of Buckingham
Peveril of the Peak (1822) Walter Scott

Jerome, Don
The Duenna play (1775) Richard Brinsley Sheridan

Jerome, Father legal Count of Falconara
The Castle of Otranto (1765) Horace Walpole

Jerome, Thomas retired corn-factor
Susan his wife
ss 'Janet's Repentance'
Scenes of Clerical Life (1857) George Eliot (rn Mary Anne, later Marian, Evans)

Jerry attempt at a portrayal of author's friend and mentor Havelock Ellis
Palimpsest (1926) H. D. (rn Hilda Doolittle)

Jerry Irish setter pup annoyed when his master, Van Horn*, is eaten by cannibals in good but unlikely yarn
Jerry of the Islands (1917) Jack London

Jerry travelling showman with troupe of performing dogs
The Old Curiosity Shop (1841) Charles Dickens

Jerton, Kenelm
ss 'A Holiday Task'
Beasts and Super-Beasts (1914) Saki (rn Hector Hugh Monro)

Jervis, Mrs housekeeper
Pamela (1740) Samuel Richardson

Jesper, Mildred good-natured friend to Monica Madden*, ideal 'odd' (i.e. unmarried) woman, employee of Mary Barfoot*
The Odd Women (1893) George Gissing

Jessamin foot-boy to Clarissa*
The Confederacy play (1705) John Vanbrugh

Jessamine, Miss
Jessamine her niece, m. The Black Captain*
Jackanapes (1879) Juliana Ewing

Jesse a woodman,
ss 'Friendly Brook'
A Diversity of Creatures (1917) Rudyard Kipling

Jessel, Miss governess
The Turn of the Screw (1898) Henry James

Jessica daughter to Shylock*, m. Lorenzo*
The Merchant of Venice play (1623) William Shakespeare

Jesson, Laura cc, in love with Alec Harvey*, in original of movie, *Brief Encounter*
her husband
Still Life play (1935) Noël Coward

Jessop, Ernest novelist, narrator
The Marsden Case (1923) Ford Madox Ford

Jessop, Thomas, Dr
his wife
his brother, a banker
John Halifax, Gentleman (1856) Mrs Craik

Jessup, Doremus cc, liberal editor of Vermont newspaper who becomes a revolutionary
It Can't Happen Here (1935) Sinclair Lewis

Jesus Christ Divine Teacher and Sacred Individual sent from Above, whose teachings were once persecuted 'by power-possessing people who feared that if people lived by this teaching all the motives for displaying their power would disappear, and those shocks cease, the satisfaction of which evoke the tickling of their inner god Self-Love'
All and Everything: Beelzebub's Tales to His Grandson (1950) G. I. Gurdjieff

Jethway, Gertrude, Mrs a 'crazed forlorn woman'*
Felix her dead son
A Pair of Blue Eyes (1873) Thomas Hardy

Jetsome worthless protégé of Lawyer Wakem*
The Mill on the Floss (1860) George Eliot (rn Mary Anne, later Marian, Evans)

Jevons
ss 'A Friend's Friend'
Plain Tales from the Hills (1888) Rudyard Kipling

Jevons, Frances, Miss woman who lives by herself
ss 'Pish-Tush'
Unlucky for Pringle (1973) Wyndham Lewis

Jevons, Tasker provincial journalist and writer/playwright cc; in part modelled on Arnold Bennett*
Tasker Jevons: the Real Story (1916) May Sinclair

Jewby one of Snagsby's* clients
Bleak House (1853) Charles Dickens

Jewdwine, Horace priggish don eventually spurned by Lucia Harden*
The Divine Fire (1905) May Sinclair

Jewell, Arthur amateur soldier
Mr Britling Sees It Through (1916) H. G. Wells

Jewkes, Mrs evil housekeeper
Pamela (1740) Samuel Richardson

Jezebel, Lady nickname of Lady Castlewood*
Henry Esmond (1852) W. M. Thackeray

Jibbenainosay see **Bloody Nathan**

Jigger, Miss foolish, malicious and lonely school teacher at the village school
Old Crow (1967) Shena Mackay

Jike, Mrs
Love on the Dole (1933) Walter Greenwood

Jilks physician who treated Our Bore* with mutton chops and sherry
ss 'Our Bore'
Reprinted Pieces (1858) Charles Dickens

Jilks, Danby, Sir apothecary
The Newcomes (1853–5) W. M. Thackeray

Jillgall, Selina, Miss cousin to Abel Gracedieu*
The Legacy of Cain (1889) Wilkie Collins

Jim Miss Watson's* coloured boy, close friend to Tom Sawyer*
Huckleberry Finn (1884); *Tom Sawyer* (1876) Mark Twain (rn Samuel Langhorne Clemens)

Jim, 'Lord' water-clerk, formerly ship's officer, cc
Lord Jim (1900) Joseph Conrad (rn Josef Teodor Konrad Korzeniowski)

Jim, 'Shanghai' boy cc
Empire of the Sun (1984) J. G. Ballard

Jim, the Widow faithful to memory of her brute of a husband
Deephaven sketches (1877) Sarah Orne Jewett

Jew, Uncle nephew to 'Aunt Flo', wastrel
The History of Mr Polly (1910) H. G. Wells

Jimmie, Cat amputee who speeds about on his cart to peer under the dresses of women
The Narrows (1953) Ann Petry

Jimson, Gulley artist cc
his 'wives': **Sara Monday; Rozzie; Liz**
Tommy son to Jimson and Rozzie
two children to Jimson and Liz
Jenny Mud Jimson's sister
The Horse's Mouth (1944) Joyce Cary

Jingle, Alfred strolling player, calling himself Fitzmarshall, who rescues Pickwick* from irate cabman
The Pickwick Papers (1837) Charles Dickens

Jiniwin, Mrs Mrs Quilp's* mother, 'laudably shrewish in her disposition'
The Old Curiosity Shop (1841) Charles Dickens

Jinkins senior boarder at Mrs Todger's*
Martin Chuzzlewit (1844) Charles Dickens

Jinkinson barber who found relief on his deathbed by shaving his children's heads
Master Humprhey's Clock (1841) Charles Dickens

Jinks unpaid, half-fed clerk to Mr Nupkins*
The Pickwick Papers (1837) Charles Dickens

Jinkson, Giles ('The Bantam')
The Ordeal of Richard Feverel: A History of Father and Son (1859) George Meredith

Jinny one of the characters whose interior monologue* makes up this novel
The Waves (1931) Virginia Woolf

Jip Dora Spenlow's* dog
David Copperfield (1850) Charles Dickens

Jo crossing-sweeper and street Arab, Captain Hawdon's* last friend and mourner
Bleak House (1853) Charles Dickens

Joad Family fruit pickers, dust-bowl 'Oakies', forced to trek to California in search of work:
Tom ex-criminal, on parole
Noah; Winfield; Alfred; Rose of Sharon ('Rosasharron'); Rushie his brothers and sisters
Old Tom his father
Ma his mother
John his uncle
Grampa
Granma
The Grapes of Wrath (1939) John Steinbeck

Joan
Death's Jest Book, or *The Fool's Tragedy* play (1850) Thomas Lovell Beddoes

Joan of Arc (hist.) cc
King Henry VI plays (1623) William Shakespeare
Saint Joan play (1924) George Bernard Shaw

Jobba member of the Mudfog Association who invented forcing machine for bringing joint-stock railway shares to a premature premium
The Mudfog Papers (1838) Charles Dickens

Jobley, George racing man
The Good Companions (1929) J. B. Priestley

Jobling, John, Dr
Martin Chuzzlewit (1844) Charles Dickens

Jobson, Joseph clerk to Squire Inglewood*
Rob Roy (1818) Walter Scott

Jobson, Sam secretary, Edge-tool Forgers Union
Put Yourself in his Place (1870) Charles Reade

Jocelin priest-builder of spire to his cathedral, cc
The Spire (1964) William Golding

Jocelyn bitter portrait of the author's lover, Cecil Day Lewis, in book originally called *The Buried Day*, later title of his own autobiography
The Echoing Grove (1953) Rosamond Lehmann

Jocelyn, Elizabeth Mary charlady up against hard times
Frank her nephew
ss 'Miss Jocelyn'
Poor Women (1928) Norah Hoult

Jocelyn, Franks, Sir and Lady
Rose m. Evan Harrington*; **Hamilton; Seymour; Harry** their children
The Hon. Melville Sir Franks' brother, diplomat
Evan Harrington (1861) George Meredith

Jock cc, brindle terrier, in classic of doghood
Jock of the Bushveld (1907) Percy Fitzpatrick

Jody Farragut's* prison lover, who escapes
Falconer (1977) John Cheever

Joe husband to Elsie née Sprickett*
Riceyman Steps (1923); *Elsie and the Child* (1924) Arnold Bennett

Joe, Uncle stone mason
Jude the Obscure (1896) Thomas Hardy

Jogglebury carver of canes
Mr Sponge's Sporting Tour (1853) R. S. Surtees

Johansen mate of the *Ghost*
The Sea Wolf (1904) Jack London

John—, Dr physician: master of, reader to, and 'doctor' of his wife
his unnamed wife, narrator cc of 'chilling' (Howells*) early feminist tale
ss 'The Yellow Wallpaper'
New England Magazine (May, 1892; 1973) Charlotte Perkins Gilman

John a savage
Brave New World (1932) Aldous Huxley

John butler to the Pendennis* family
Pendennis (1848) W. M. Thackeray

John coachman to Theobald Pontifex*, m. Ellen
The Way of All Flesh (1903) Samuel Butler

John servant bribed to bear false witness so that Daniel Simple* can alter his father's will to his advantage
Peggy his wife, who refuses Daniel's advances, but does likewise; in novel by

sister of Henry Fielding*
The Adventures of David Simple
(1744–53) Sarah Fielding

John, Don bastard brother to Don Pedro*
Much Ado About Nothing play (1623)
William Shakespeare

John, Sir priest
The Merry Devil of Edmonton play
(1608) ?Thomas Dekker

Johnes, John, First Baron Helvellyn father
of Lady George Gaunt*
Vanity Fair (1847–8) W. M. Thackeray

Johnnie author of Gospel
*All and Everything: Beelzebub's Tales to
His Grandson* (1950) G. I. Gurdjieff

Johnny of the *Hispaniola*
Treasure Island (1883) Robert Louis
Stevenson

Johnny-the-Priest
Anna Christie play (1922) Eugene
O'Neill

Johns assistant to Dr Forester*
The Ministry of Fear (1943) Graham
Greene

Johns, Ellen girl friend to young Ewan
Tavendale*
A Scots Quair trilogy (1932–4) Lewis
Grassic Gibbon (rn James Leslie
Mitchell)

Johnson
Captain Brassbound's Conversion play
(1900) George Bernard Shaw

Johnson cc who fights against Franco for
'company and excitement' in New Zealand novel of conscience
Man Alone (1939) John Mulgan

Johnson friend to Arthur Machin*
This Sporting Life (1960) David Storey

Johnson malingerer
A Stranger and Afraid (1961) George
Turner

Johnson name adopted by Nicholas
Nickleby when acting with Crummles*
Nicholas Nickleby (1839) Charles
Dickens

Johnson one of Blimber's* pupils, who
almost choked himself to death at dinner
Dombey and Son (1848) Charles Dickens

Johnson sailor on *Ghost*
The Sea Wolf (1904) Jack London

Johnson, Emily
ss 'Mrs Johnson'
Poor Women (1928) Norah Hoult

Johnson, Harold ticket clerk
Grace his wife
The History of Mr Polly (1910) H. G.
Wells

Johnson, Harry cc, explorer in Brazil seeking his father, who has vanished into the
interior
Dead Man Leading (1937) V. S. Pritchett

Johnson, Helen, Mrs secretary-house-
keeper
ss 'Blind Love'
Blind Love (1969) V. S. Pritchett

Johnson, Jack friend to Titus Ledbury*, m.
Emma Ledbury
The Adventures of Mr Ledbury (1844)
Albert Smith

Johnson, Job London flash man who helps
to clear Glanville* of murder
*Pelham, or The Adventures of a
Gentleman* (1828, rev. 1839) Edward
Bulwer Lytton

Johnson, John election agent
Felix Holt (1866) George Eliot (rn Mary
Anne, later Marian, Evans)

Johnson, Lionel Boyd black ex-soldier and
spiritual leader of San Lorenzo, by means
of 'foma', useful lies
Cat's Cradle (1963) Kurt Vonnegut

Johnson, Lieutenant of *Saltash*
The Cruel Sea (1951) Nicholas Monsarrat

Johnson, Matilda actress engaged to Bob
Loveday*, m. Festus Derriman*
The Trumpet Major (1880) Thomas
Hardy

Johnson, Mr an extravagant rake in his
youth; now a miser and censurer of
others' pleasures; has 'no idea of a
Woman's being ruin'd in any way but
one'
Miss Nanny Johnson one of his daughters m. Mr Nokes*
The Adventures of David Simple
(1744–53) Sarah Fielding

Johnson, Mrs
Lady Susan (1871) Jane Austen

Johnson, Norman Internal Revenue agent
The Wapshot Scandal (1963) John
Cheever

Johnson, Tom 'man with a cork leg'
Dombey and Son (1848) Charles Dickens

Johnson, Tony friend to Jackanapes*
Jane his sister
their parents

Jackanapes (1879) Juliana H. Ewing
Johnstone, Willie boat owner
Guy Mannering (1815) Walter Scott
Joliffe master's mate, HMS *Harpy*
Mr Midshipman Easy (1836) Captain
Marryat
Joliffe, Colonel aged patriot
ss 'Howe's Masquerade'
Twice-Told Tales (1842) Nathaniel
Hawthorne
Joliffe, Jack diner-out
Sketches and Travels (1850) W. M.
Thackeray
Joliffe, Jocelin under-keeper at Woodstock
Lodge
Woodstock (1826) Walter Scott
Jolland school friend to Dick Bultitude
Vice Versa (1882) F. Anstey (rn Thomas
Anstey Guthrie)
Jolley, Mrs housekeeper
Riders in the Chariot (1961) Patrick
White
Jollice, Farmer
ss 'An Incident in the Life of Mr George
Crookhill'
Life's Little Ironies (1894) Thomas
Hardy
Jollifant, Inigo ex-schoolmaster, song-
writer, m. Susan Dean*
The Good Companions (1929) J. B.
Priestley
Jolliffe, Shadrack, Captain
Joanna his wife, *née* Phippard
George; Jim their sons
ss 'To Please his Wife'
Life's Little Ironies (1894) Thomas
Hardy
Jolly & Baines bankers
The Newcomes (1853–5) W. M.
Thackeray
Jolter tutor at Peregrine's school, his com-
panion abroad
Peregrine Pickle (1751) Tobias Smollett
Joltered, William, Sir President of Zoology
Section
The Mudfog Papers (1878) Charles
Dickens
Jomo
Second Skin (1964) John Hawkes
Jonah journalist
Cat's Cradle (1963) Kurt Vonnegut
Jonas Sessions, Elijah
Huw Morgan's* schoolmaster

How Green Was My Valley (1939)
Richard Llewellyn
Jones David Copperfield's boyish rival for
Miss Shepherd
David Copperfield (1850) Charles
Dickens
Jones employee of Blaze and Sparkle
Bleak House (1853) Charles Dickens
Jones private detective
The Ministry of Fear (1943) Graham
Greene
Jones, Andrew architect
ss 'Fellow Townsmen'
Wessex Tales (1888) Thomas Hardy
Jones, Athelney official detective
The Sign of Four† (1890) Arthur Conan
Doyle
Jones, Augustus, Master
Sketches and Travels (1850) W. M.
Thackeray
Jones, Bob
The Newcomes (1853–5) W. M.
Thackeray
Jones, Brutus former Pullman porter who
sets himself up as emperor on an island in
the West Indies and then retrogresses on
the evolutionary ladder
The Emperor Jones play (1920) Eugene
O'Neill
Jones, Clare lawyer, Tom Linton's* con-
federate
Roland Cashel (1850) Charles Lever
Jones, Dr attends Grace Fitzpiers*
The Woodlanders (1886) Thomas Hardy
Jones, Eric actor, lover of Cass Silenski*,
Vivaldo Moore* and Rufus Scott*
Another Country (1962) James Baldwin
Jones, H. J., Major English adventurer in
Haiti
The Comedians (1966) Graham Greene
Jones, Indefer old Welshman in dilemma as
to whom to leave his wealth
Henry his nephew, whom he dislikes
Cousin Henry (1879) Anthony Trollope
Jones, Jenny see **Waters, Mrs**
Jones, John Paul (hist.) cc
The Tory Lover (1901) Sarah Orne Jewett
Jones, Lady 'woman of virtue', mother to
Lady Darnford*
Pamela (1740) Samuel Richardson
Jones, Martha missionary
Revd Owen her brother
ss 'The Vessel of Wrath'

Ah King (1933) W. Somerset Maugham

Jones, Mildred, Mrs of mysterious social eminence
The Unspeakable Skipton (1959) Pamela Hansford Johnson

Jones, Minerva poet
poem 'Minerva Jones'
Spoon River Anthology verse epitaphs (1915) Edgar Lee Masters

Jones, Miss companion to Clare Temple*
There Were No Windows (1944) Norah Hoult

Jones, Mordecai legendary con man
The Ballad of the Flim-Flam Man† (1965, rev. 1967) Guy Owen

Jones, Mr man who Ammen* wishes, gratuitously, to kill
Mrs Jones his wife, who gives birth to a stillborn baby
King Coffin (1935) Conrad Aiken

Jones, Oliver Cromwell, Lieutenant black officer in Union army, known as 'Rau-Ru' on Hamish Bond's* plantation
Band of Angels (1955) Robert Penn Warren

Jones, Orville
his wife
Babbitt (1923) Sinclair Lewis

Jones, Philip widowed Irish Protestant landowner
Frank; Florian; Edith his children
The Landleaguers (1883) Anthony Trollope

Jones, Saddle-Sergeant comrade to John Loveday*
The Trumpet Major (1880) Thomas Hardy

Jones, Tom foundling, cc, son to Bridget Allworthy*
Tom Jones (1749) Henry Fielding

Jonsen captain of the pirates
A High Wind in Jamaica (1929) Richard Hughes

Jonson, Louisa fiancée to Charles Curzon*
Harry Lorrequer (1839) Charles Lever

Joper, Billy 'man with a glass in his eye'
Dombey and Son (1848) Charles Dickens

Jopley, Marmaduke
The Thirty-nine Steps (1915) John Buchan

Jopp, Duncan executed criminal
Weir of Hermiston (1896) Robert Louis Stevenson

Jopp, Joshua one-time manager for Henchard*, in search of revenge
The Mayor of Casterbridge (1886) Thomas Hardy

Joram assistant to Omer, Yarmouth undertaker
David Copperfield (1850) Charles Dickens

Jordan chamberlain: commands the tertia of the beds
The New Inn, or *The Light Heart* play (1629) Ben Jonson

Jordan, Malachy, Father, PP pilgrim to Lourdes
ss 'Feed My Lambs'
The Talking Trees (1971) Sean O'Faolain

Jordan, Robert cc, American fighting against Franco
For Whom the Bell Tolls (1940) Ernest Hemingway

Jordan, Thomas of Jordan's Appliances
Sons and Lovers (1913) D. H. Lawrence

Jorgan, Silas, Captain New Englander who found Raybrock's message on an island
A Message From the Sea (1860) Charles Dickens

Jorgensen, Mimi, Mrs
Christian gigolo, her second husband
The Thin Man (1934) Dashiell Hammett

Jorkens, Joseph teller of tall stories, traveller
The Travel Tales of Mr Joseph Jorkens† (1931) Lord Dunsany

Jorkins partner to Spenlow*, silent but represented as most ruthless of men
David Copperfield (1850) Charles Dickens

Jorrocks, John, MFH grocer, sportsman, cc
Julia his wife
Joe his brother
Belinda Joe's daughter, m. Charley Stobbs*
Jorrock's' Jaunts and Jollities† (1838) R. S. Surtees

Jorworth, Ap Jevan messenger sent by Gwenwyn* to Sir R. Berenger*
The Betrothed (1825) Walter Scott

Jose member of Jonsen's* crew
A High Wind in Jamaica (1929) Richard Hughes

Joseph cc twenty-seven-year-old Chicagoan, diarist
Iva his wife

Dangling Man (1944) Saul Bellow

Joseph boy prisoner tortured to death by Hawes*
It Is Never Too Late To Mend (1856) Charles Reade

Joseph servant to Heathcliff*
Wuthering Heights (1847) Emily Brontë

Joseph, Sergeant
The Mystery of a Hansom Cab (1886) Fergus Hume

Josèpha singer and tart; mistress to Hulot*
La Cousine Bette (1847) Honoré de Balzac

Josselin, Bartholomew ('Barty') cc who has a female guiding spirit, the Martian*, who makes him a famous author
Antoinette Josselin his mother (his father is Lord Runswick and he is adopted by his uncle, Lord Archibald Rowan)
Leah *née* Gibson, his wife, noble Jewess of whom the Martian at first disapproves
Martia their daughter in whom the Martian becomes incarnated
The Martian (1897) George du Maurier

Jourdain, Margery witch
King Henry VI plays (1623) William Shakespeare

Jowl, Joe gambler at The Valiant Soldier, partner to Isaac List*
The Old Curiosity Shop (1841) Charles Dickens

Jowler, Julius, Lieutenant-Colonel of the Bundelcund Invincibles
his ugly, half-caste wife
Julia their daughter, m. Chowder Loll*
The Adventures of Major Gahagan (1839) W. M. Thackeray

Jowls, Giles, Revd
Vanity Fair (1847–8) W. M. Thackeray

Joy
Jonny her son
Poor Cow (1967) Nell Dunn

Joy one of Miss Flite's* captive birds
Bleak House (1853) Charles Dickens

Joyce of the *Hispaniola*
Treasure Island (1883) Robert Louis Stevenson

Joyner, Lafayette grandfather to George Webber*
Mark ironmonger; **Maw**; **Amelia** m. John Webber* – his children
You Can't Go Home Again (1941) Thomas Wolfe

Jubberknowl, Samuel
Hawbuck Grange (1847) R. S. Surtees

Judas a corporal, a cowardly and hungry knave
Bonduca play (1647) John Fletcher

Judas devoted Apostle, now a saint: 'rendered his great objective service for which all terrestial . . . beings should be grateful' – the author agrees with Robert Graves*, the gnostic Cainites (who were reputed to possess an apocryphal *Gospel of Judas*), and a few others, on this point
All and Everything: Beelzebub's Tales to His Grandson (1950) G. I. Gurdjieff

Judd member of Voss's* expedition
Voss (1957) Patrick White

Judd, Amos Indian rajah cc, who can foresee events, brought up in ignorance of his origin in Connecticut farmhouse, in exotic American novel by author more historically important for his editorial work on *Life*
Amos Judd (1895) John Ames Mitchell

Judique, Tanis, Mrs
Babbitt (1923) Sinclair Lewis

Judkin manager, Anglo-Patagonian bank
The Wrong Box (1889) Robert Louis Stevenson and Lloyd Osbourne

Judson, Harrison, Lieutenant ('Bai-Jove Judson')
ss 'Judson and the Empire'
Many Inventions (1893) Rudyard Kipling

Judy Punch's younger sister
ss 'Baa Baa Black Sheep'
Wee Willie Winkie (1888) Rudyard Kipling

Juffles, Revd Mr
Dora his wife, *née* Warrington*
The Virginians (1857–9) W. M. Thackeray

Jug tapster
The New Inn, or *The Light Heart* play (1629) Ben Jonson

Juggernaut, Duke of
Vivian Grey (1827) Benjamin Disraeli

Juggins
Fanny's First Play play (1905) George Bernard Shaw

Juke, Laurence, the Hon. and Revd son to Lord Aylesbury*
Potterism (1920) Rose Macaulay

Jukes chief mate, the *Nan Shan*
Typhoon (1903) Joseph Conrad (rn Josef

Teodor Konrad Korzeniowski)
Jukes, Bill pirate
Peter Pan play (1904) J. M. Barrie
Jukes, Morrowbie
ss 'The Strange Ride of Morrowbie Jukes'
Wee Willie Winkie (1888) Rudyard Kipling
Jules artist without legs
Féerie pour un autre fois (*Fairy Play for Another Time*) (1952–4) Louis-Ferdinand Céline (rn Louis-Ferdinand Destouches)
Jules French sailor
ss 'The Horse Marines'
A Diversity of Creatures (1917) Rudyard Kipling
Julia a lady of Verona
Two Gentlemen of Verona play (1623) William Shakespeare
Julia cc; of this author's (first cousin to Sheridan*) greatest success
The Hunchback play (1832) James Sheridan Knowles
Julia sister to Gwalter*
The Pleasant Commedye of Patient Grissill play (1603) Thomas Dekker
Julian, Christopher music teacher, loves Ethelberta Petherwin* but m. her sister Picotee*
his father, a doctor
Faith his sister
The Hand of Ethelberta (1876) Thomas Hardy
Juliana wife to Virolet*
The Double Marriage play (1647) John Fletcher and Philip Massinger
Julie, Miss unhappy cc who gives herself to the ambitious valet, Jean*
Miss Julie play (1888) August Strindberg
Juliet cc, daughter of Capulet
Romeo and Juliet play (1623) William Shakespeare
Juliet loved by Claudio*
Measure for Measure (1623) William Shakespeare
Juliette lover to Höfgen*
Mephisto (1936) Klaus Mann
Julip, John, Uncle teacher based on a headmaster (for whom the author worked) who forged his references
The Dream (1924) H. G. Wells
Jumble, Jolly, Sir old rake turned pimp
The Soldier's Fortune play (1681)

Thomas Otway
Junior youngest son to the Duchess*, rapist
The Revenger's Tragedy (1607/8) ?Thomas Middleton; ?Cyril Tourneur
Juniper cobbler
The Case is Altered play (1609) Ben Jonson
Juniper, Brother narrator
The Bridge of San Luis Rey (1927) Thornton Wilder
Junius Roman captain in love with Bonduca's* daughter
Bonduca play (1647) John Fletcher
Juno black servant to the Seagraves*
Masterman Ready (1841–2) Captain Marryat
Jupe, Signor clown
Cecilia ('Sissy') his daughter
Hard Times (1854) Charles Dickens
Jupien 'ultimate functionary of vice'
A la recherche du temps perdu (*In Search of Lost Time*) (1913–27) Marcel Proust
Jupiter Legrand's servant who discovers the parchment when his master is bitten by a beetle
ss 'The Gold Bug' 1843
Tales (1845) Edgar Allen Poe
Jupp, Mrs Ernest Pontifex's* landlady
The Way of All Flesh (1903) Samuel Butler
Jurgen middle-aged pawnbroker restored to age twenty-one in smutty once popular tales of the land of Poictesme
Adelais his wife
Azra his mother
Coth his father
Jurgen† (1919) James Branch Cabell
Justice a roan cob
Black Beauty (1877) Anna Sewell
Justice, Beatrice music teacher
Exiles play (1918) James Joyce
Justin financier, m. Lady Mary Christian*
The Passionate Friends (1913) H. G. Wells
Justine cc, wife to Nessim Hosnani*
The *Alexandria Quartet* (1957–61) Lawrence Durrell
Justine maid and friend to the Frankensteins*, falsely accused of murder, and executed
Frankenstein (1818) Mary Shelley
Justis steward to Ernest Maltravers*
Alice (1938) Edward Bulwer Lytton

K

K cc, a confidence man amongst bureaucrats
Das Schloss (The Castle) (1926) Franz Kafka

Kaa the rock-python
ss 'Kaa's Hunting'
Jungle Books (1894–5) Rudyard Kipling

Kabnis Black teacher
ss 'Kabnis'
Cane (1923) Jean Toomer

Kadir Baksh
ss 'My Own True Ghost Story'
Wee Willie Winkie (1888) Rudyard Kipling

Kadlu eskimo
 Amoraq his wife
 Kotuko their son
 Kotuko their dog
ss 'Ququern'
The Second Jungle Book (1895) Rudyard Kipling

Kadmiel a Jew
ss 'The Treasure and the Law'
Puck of Pook's Hill (1906) Rudyard Kipling

Kaghan, Barnabas illegitimate son to Lady Elizabeth Mulhammer*, m. Lucasta Angel*
The Confidential Clerk play (1954) T. S. Eliot

Kags returned transported convict, hiding at Crachit's* house when Sikes* was there
Oliver Twist (1838) Charles Dickens

Kai Lung narrator, ingenious and ingenuous Chinaman, cc of series featuring facetious travesty of Chinese talk, onwards from
The Wallet of Kai Lung (1900) Ernest Bramah (rn Ernest Bramah Smith)

Kail, Jonathan farmhand
Tess of the D'Urbervilles (1891) Thomas Hardy

Kaimon, John cc who tries to discover himself through an outlaw karate group
Karate is a Thing of the Spirit (1971) Harry Crews

Kala Nag elephant
ss 'Toomai of the Elephants'
The Jungle Book (1894) Rudyard Kipling

Kallikrates priest of Isis reincarnated in Leo Vincey*
She (1887) Henry Rider Haggard

Kalmanuiour a three-brained (i.e. human) being of that planet with whom it is not forbidden us from Above to be frank
All and Everything: Beelzebub's Tales to His Grandson (1950) G. I. Gurdjieff

Kalon priest of the sun god
ss 'The Eye of Apollo'
The Innocence of Father Brown (1911) G. K. Chesterton

Kalonymos, Joseph Jewish merchant, friend to Charisi*
Daniel Deronda (1876) George Eliot (rn Mary Anne, later Marian, Evans)

Kamensky, Alexander Russian official
The Birds Fall Down (1966) Rebecca West (rn Cecily Fairfield)

Kamworth, Colonel
 Mary his daughter
Harry Lorrequer (1839) Charles Lever

Kane, Lester son of wealthy manufacturer who establishes Jennie Gerhardt* as his mistress; m. Letty Gerald; dies nursed by and loving Jennie
 Robert his brother
Jennie Gerhardt (1911) Theodore Dreiser

Kane, Saul redeemed drunkard
The Everlasting Mercy poem (1911) John Masefield

Kapen, Genezip cc, man who could not stand any form of captivity
Nienasycenie: poweiesc (Insatiability) (1930) Stanislaw Ignacy Witkiewicz

Karamazov, Fyodor Pavlovich twice m. widower
 Dmitry his son by his first wife, not brought up by him, cc

Ivan; Aloysha his sons by his second wife, ccs
Bratya Karamazov (Brothers Karamazov) (1880) Fyodor Dostoievsky

Kardek, Alan, Mr
All and Everything: Beelzebub's Tales to His Grandson (1950) G. I. Gurdjieff

Karenin, Marcus advanced educationist
The World Set Free (1914) H. G. Wells

Karkeet, Q. solicitor
Hilda Lessways (1911) Arnold Bennett

Karl Albert, Prince commanding officer German air fleet, shot by Bert Smallways*
The War in the Air (1908) H. G. Wells

Karmazinov mediocre Russian writer
Besy (The Possessed) (1879) Fyodor Dostoievsky

Kazbich stabs Bela*
Geroi Nas hego Vremeni (A Hero of Our Time) (1841) Mikhail Lermontov

Karolides, Constantine
The Thirty-nine Steps (1915) John Buchan

Kate daughter to Emily Frampton* by her first husband
Non-Combatants and Others (1916) Rose Macaulay

Kate impudent-looking, bewitching little cousin to Maria Lobbs*
The Pickwick Papers (1837) Charles Dickens

Kate niece to Dame Carruthers*
The Yeomen of the Guard opera (1888) W. S. Gilbert and Arthur Sullivan

Kate orphan child who visited the Skettles*
Dombey and Son (1848) Charles Dickens

Kate wife to the debtor in Solomon Jacobs's lock-up in Cursitor Street
Sketches by Boz† (1836) Charles Dickens

Kate, Catalina 'a prelapsarian Eve'
Second Skin (1964) John Hawkes

Katharine of Aragon (hist.)
King Henry VIII play (1623) William Shakespeare and John Fletcher

Katherina the shrew, daughter to Baptista*
The Taming of the Shrew play (1623) William Shakespeare

Katherine (hist.) daughter to the French king
King Henry V play (1623) William Shakespeare

Katherine attending on the princess
Love's Labour's Lost play (1623) William Shakespeare

Kathleen Claire Temple's* unpleasant maid and adversary: young and insensitive, she refuses to allow for her mistress's (i.e. Violet Hunt's) senility
There Were No Windows (1944) Norah Hoult

Katisha elderly lady, m. Ko-Ko*
The Mikado opera (1885) W. S. Gilbert and Arthur Sullivan

Katy see **Carr**

Katya Tatiana Ostapenko's* servant
Tobit Transplanted (1931) Stella Benson

Katz lawyer
The Postman Always Rings Twice (1934) James M. Cain

Kavanagh, Mat hedge-tutor, in sketches by author who received his early education from one
ss 'The Hedge School'
Traits and Stories of the Irish Peasantry (1830–33) William Carleton

Kawdle, Dr and Mrs
Sir Launcelot Greaves (1762) Tobias Smollett

Kaye, Michael idealistic young man who learns world is horrible, cc
The Lemon Farm (1935) Martin Boyd

Kean, Dan ('Firebrand')
Little Men (1871); *Jo's Boys* (1886) Louisa M. Alcott

Keane, Tom caretaker
Cathleen his daughter
Roland Cashel (1850) Charles Lever

Kear, Alroy popular novelist; caricature of Hugh Walpole*
Cakes and Ale (1930) W. Somerset Maugham

Kearney, Captain
Captain Brassbound's Conversion play (1900) George Bernard Shaw

Kearney, Matthew ('Lord Kilgoblin') cc, ruined landowner in novel admired by some critics as heralding a new and darker style in the by-then exhausted author's work
Kate his daughter
Lord Kilgoblin (1872) Charles Lever

Kearney, Mrs
ss 'A Mother'

Dubliners (1914) James Joyce
Keats, John English journalist
The Alexandria Quartet (1957–61)
Lawrence Durrell
Keawe purchaser of the bottle, m. Kokua*
ss 'The Bottle Imp'
Island Nights' Entertainments (1893)
Robert Louis Stevenson
Keck editor of the *Middlemarch Trumpet*
Middlemarch (1871–2) George Eliot (rn
Mary Anne, later Marian, Evans)
Kedgick, Captain landlord of National
Hotel
Martin Chuzzlewit (1844) Charles
Dickens
Keede, Robin, Dr freemason
ss 'In the Interests of the Brethren'†
Debits and Credits (1926) Rudyard Kipling
Keefer, Tom intellectual and liar, who
instigates mutiny but is later revealed as a
coward in bestselling novel which has
been described as tendentious
The Caine Mutiny (1951) Herman Wouk
Keegan, Father
John Bull's Other Island play (1904)
George Bernard Shaw
Keeldar, Shirley cc, cousin to Robert
Moore*, m. Louis Moore*
Charles Cave Keeldar her deceased father
Shirley (1849) Charlotte Brontë
Keeling, Abel cc Kiplingesque* Elizabethan tale
ss 'Phantas'
Widdershins (1911) Oliver Onions
Keen, Mick young butcher whose severed
finger falls into mince bought by John
Wood*
An Advent Calendar (1971) Shena
Mackay
Keene, Dr friend to Frowenfeld*
The Grandissimes: A Story of Creole Life
(1880) George Washington Cable
Keep nurse
The Magnetic Lady, or *Humours Reconciled* play (1641) Ben Jonson
Keggs butler to Lord Marshmoreton*
A Damsel in Distress (1919) P. G. Wodehouse
Keith, Isabella (hist.): 'My dear Isa, I now
sit down on my botom to answer all your
kind and beloved letters which you was
so good as to write to me'; 'I am going to

turn over a new life and am going to be a
very good girl and be obedient to Isa
Keith, here there is plenty of gooseberries
which makes my teether watter'
Letters (1863); *Journal* (1863) Marjory
Fleming (prodigy, 1803–11, commemorated by Dr Brown* of *Rab and his
Friends**)
Keith, Mr
South Wind (1917) Norman Douglas
Keith, Mrs cc of early euthanasia novel
Mrs Keith's Crime (1885) Lucy Clifford
Keith, Willie spoiled young Princeton boy
who overcomes his intellectuality to save
and then to command the *Caine* on its
final voyage
The Caine Mutiny (1951) Herman Wouk
Keith-Wessington, Agnes, Mrs
ss 'The Phantom Rickshaw'
Wee Willie Winkie (1888) Rudyard Kipling
Kelleg, Don Collar inheritor of the largest
fortune in the world
his tycoon father, whose sins he vainly
seeks to redress
An English Girl: A Romance (1907) Ford
Madox Ford
Keller journalist
ss 'A Matter of Fact'
Many Inventions (1893) Rudyard Kipling
Kello, Ralph, Sir false priest
The Corner That Held Them (1948)
Sylvia Townsend Warner
Kelly, Deborah see Rojack
Kelly, Denny twenty-nine-year-old prize
fighter who persists despite failure;
in American novel about boxing by
author whose staccato style is often reminiscent of Hemingway's*
his wife
The Circle Home (1960) Edward Hoagland
Kelly, Lizzie Timms third wife of John
Turnham*
The Fortunes of Richard Mahony (1930)
Henry Handel Richardson (rn Ethel Florence Lindesay Richardson Robertson)
Kelly, Mick fourteen-year-old cc
The Heart is a Lonely Hunter (1940)
Carson McCullers
Kelly, Oswald father to Deborah Kelly*
An American Dream (1965) Norman

Mailer

Kelway, Basil Leigh, the Hon. earnest young radical
Some Experiences of an Irish R. M. (1899) O. E. Somerville and Martin Ross (rn Edith Somerville and Violet Martin)

Kelway, Robert in love with Stella Rodney*
The Heat of the Day (1949) Elizabeth Bowen

Kemp, Dadda gaga old man
Kath; Ed his children
Entertaining Mr Sloan play (1964) Joe Orton

Kemp, Dr research worker
The Invisible Man (1897) H. G. Wells

Kemp, George Rosie Driffield's* lover
Cakes and Ale (1930) W. Somerset Maugham

Kemp, Liza cc
her mother
Liza of Lambeth (1897) W. Somerset Maugham

Kemp, Stephen child cc, narrator, of Zola-esque* novel of East End crime
Nathaniel his father, chief mate, brig *Juno*
Ellen his mother
Nathaniel ('Cap'n Kemp) his grandfather, landlord of the Hole in the Wall, Wapping
The Hole in the Wall (1902) Arthur Morrison

Kempe, Mrs village storekeeper
The Woman in White (1860) Wilkie Collins

Kendall, Sergeant detective based on a real one, Inspector Kendall
ss 'The Detective Police'
Reprinted Pieces (1858) Charles Dickens

Kendrick, Lieutenant-Commander
The African Queen (1935) C. S. Forrester (rn C. L. T. Smith)

Kenealy, Colonel
Hard Cash (1863) Charles Reade

Kenge of Kenge and Carboy, Lincoln's Inn solicitors employed by John Jarndyce* to watch over his interests
Bleak House (1853) Charles Dickens

Kenn, Revd, Dr Vicar of St Oggs, friend to Maggie Tulliver*
his invalid wife
The Mill on the Floss (1860) George Eliot

(rn Mary Anne, later Marian, Evans)

Kennedy, Charles, Dr friend to Steve Monk*
The World in the Evening (1954) Christopher Isherwood

Kennedy, Dr narrator
ss 'Amy Foster'
Typhoon (1903) Joseph Conrad (rn Josef Teodor Konrad Korzeniowski)

Kennedy, Frank Scarlett O'Hara's* second husband
Ella their daughter
Gone With the Wind (1936) Margaret Mitchell

Kennedy, Frank supervisor
Guy Mannering (1815) Walter Scott

Kennedy, Hart part-portrait of Neal Cassady, legendary Beat, who drove the bus for Kesey's Merry Pranksters
Go (1952) John Clellon Holmes

Kennedy, Quentin late owner of Huntingtower
Huntingtower (1922) John Buchan

Kennedy, Robert m. Lady Laura Standish*
Phineas Finn† (1869) Anthony Trollope

Kennet, Alderman Lord Mayor
Barnaby Rudge (1841) Charles Dickens

Kennicott, Carol tries to bring culture to Gopher Prairie
Main Street (1921) Sinclair Lewis

Kenny lesbian
Nobody Answered the Bell (1971) Rhys Davies

Kennyfeck, Mountjoy Dublin solicitor
Matilda his wife
Miss Kennyfeck; Olivia m. Revd Knox Softly* – his daughters
Roland Cashel (1850) Charles Lever

Kent, Beatrice ('Treshy') m. Lewis Raycie*
ss 'False Dawn'
Old New York (1924) Edith Wharton

Kent, Earl of
King Lear play (1623) William Shakespeare

Kent, Maria see **Beck, Modeste**

Kent, Mary m. Rollo Podmarsh*
ss 'The Awakening of Podmarsh'
The Heart of a Goof (1926) P. G. Wodehouse

Kent, Walter
Waste play (1907) Harley Granville Barker

Kentucky Cardinal bird cc of sentimental

novel with a sting
A Kentucky Cardinal (1894) James Lane Allen

Kenwigs dealer in ivory
Nicholas Nickleby (1839) Charles Dickens

Kenyon m. Hilda*, American sculptor
The Marble Faun, first published in England as *Transformation* (1860) Nathaniel Hawthorne

Keogh, Sean young farmer
The Playboy of the Western World play (1907) John Millington Synge

Keola
Lehua his wife, daughter of Kalamake*
ss 'The Isle of Voices'
Island Nights' Entertainments (1893) Robert Louis Stevenson

Kepesh, David Alan narrator, working for much of his life on a book about romantic disillusionment in the tales of Chekhov*; turns (in *The Breast*, 1972) into a breast
The Professor of Desire† (1977) Philip Roth

Kerfoot sailor on *Ghost*
The Sea Wolf (1904) Jack London

Kerick Booterin seal hunter
Patalamon his son
ss 'The White Seal'
Jungle Books (1894–5) Rudyard Kipling

Kernan drunken commercial traveller
his wife
ss 'Grace'
Dubliners (1914) James Joyce

Kerner, Johann valet to Baron de Magny*; spy
Barry Lyndon (1844) W. M. Thackeray

Kershaw, Reginald
Invitation to the Waltz (1932) Rosamond Lehmann

Kester farm manager
Sylvia's Lovers (1863) Mrs Gaskell

Ketch, John, Professor
The Mudfog Papers (1838) Charles Dickens

Ketel, Jorian servant to van Swieten
The Cloister and the Hearth (1861) Charles Reade

Ketley Sir G. Denberry-Baxter's* butler
Let the People Sing (1939) J. B. Priestley

Kettle, Lafayette Secretary of the Watertoast Institution, of presumptuous ignorance and unabashed vulgarity

Martin Chuzzlewit (1844) Charles Dickens

Kettle, Owen, Captain later Revd Sir Owen, cc, 'truculent and diverting old skipper'
his wife and daughter
Captain Kettle series (1898–1932) C. J. Cutcliffe Hyne

Kettledrummie, Gabriel fiery preacher
Old Mortality (1816) Walter Scott

Kew, Dowager Countess of (Louisa Joanna) ('Old Lady Kew') (family name Barnes) mother of Lady Ann Newcome* and Lady Fanny Canonbury*
Lady Julia her unmarried daughter
Frank, Lord Kew her grandson, m. Lady Henrietta Pulleyn*
George Frank's brother
The Newcomes (1853–5) W. M. Thackeray

Kew, Mr
his wife
Deephaven sketches (1877) Sarah Orne Jewett

Kewsy eminent QC
his wife and daughters
*The Book of Snobs** (1847) W. M. Thackeray

Keyhole, Tomlinson, Dr reviewer
Boon (1915) H. G. Wells

Keys journalist
The Cruel Sea (1951) Nicholas Monsarrat

Keyte ex-army tuckshop keeper
ss 'The Flag of their Country'
Stalky & Co. (1899) Rudyard Kipling

Kezia housemaid to Mrs Tulliver*
The Mill on the Floss (1860) George Eliot (rn Mary Anne, later Marian, Evans)

Khan, Raza head of the Actor-Gang
Mrs Dukes' Million (1977) Wyndham Lewis

Khiva Zulu servant
King Solomon's Mines (1885) Henry Rider Haggard

Khoda Dad Khan
ss 'The Head of the District'
Life's Handicap (1891) Rudyard Kipling

Khonnon brilliant Yeshiva student in the classic – Yiddish – dramatic version of much adapted Jewish (Cabbalistic) legend: Khonnon is turned away by Reb Sender* as unsuitable for his daughter

Leah*, dies of grief, and enters her as a dybbuk
his dead father, who appears as a ghost
Der Dibuk (The Dybbuk) (1918) S. Ansky (rn Shloyome Zanvil Rappoport)
Kibble, Jacob gave evidence at inquest on supposed body of Harmon*
Our Mutual Friend (1865) Charles Dickens
Kicklebury, Thomas, Sir, Baronet
his wife, gambler and snob
Clarence; Fanny; Lavinia m. Horace Milliken* – their children
The Kickleburys on the Rhine (1850) W. M. Thackeray
Kicksey, Jemima poverty-stricken sister to Lady Griffin*
ss 'The Amours of Mr Deuceace'
The Yellowplush Papers (1852) W. M. Thackeray
Kid, The narrator who registers no emotion
My Uncle Dudley (1942) Wright Morris
Kiddle, Joseph
his wife
Phoebe; Ada; Ann their daughters
Mr Weston's Good Wine (1927) T. F. Powys
Kidgerbury, Mrs occasional charlady and oldest inhabitant of Kentish Town
David Copperfield (1850) Charles Dickens
Kielland, Dagny loved by Nagel*
Mysterier† (*Mysteries*) (1892) Knut Hamsun
Kien, Professor reclusive sinologist, cc
Die Blendung (tr. as *The Tower of Babel* and then as *Auto-da-fé*) Elias Canetti
Kiernan, Bridget young servant girl
ss 'Bridget Kiernan'
Poor Women (1928) Norah Hoult
Kiffin new boy at Grimstone's*
Vice Versa (1882) F. Anstey (rn Thomas Anstey Guthrie)
Kilbarry, Lord friend and alleged relation to Barry Lyndon
Barry Lyndon (1844) W. M. Thackeray
Kilburne, Annie serious-minded cc of New England novel
Annie Kilburne (1888) William Dean Howells
Kilcarney, Marquess of m. Violet Scully*
A Drama in Muslin (1886) George

Moore
Kilgoblin, Lord see **Kearney, Matthew**
Kiljoy, Amelia Irish heiress
Barry Lyndon (1844) W. M. Thackeray
Kilkee see **Callonby**
Killigrew, Colonel
ss 'Dr Heidegger's Experiment'
Twice-Told Tales (1837) Nathaniel Hawthorne
Kilman, Doris
Mrs Dalloway (1925) Virginia Woolf
Kilmartin, Brian
Maggie his wife, *née* Hynes*
Kitty m. Patch Hermon; **Martin** m. Mary Gleeson; **Napp** m. Dan Toomey; **Michael** their children
Michael son to Martin and Mary
Famine (1937) Liam O'Flaherty
Kim see **O'Hara**
Kimble, Dr of Raveloe
his wife
Silas Marner (1861) George Eliot (rn Mary Anne, later Marian, Evans)
Kimmeens, Kitty Miss Pupford's pupil
Tom Tiddler's Ground (1861) Charles Dickens
Kimpton, Milly m. Harry Smith*
The Dream (1924) H. G. Wells
Kinbona, Merle woman of Bournehills, a representation of Barbados
The Chosen Place, The Timeless People (1969) Paule Marshall
Kinbote, Charles, Dr a Zemblian scholar
Pale Fire (1962) Vladimir Nabokov
Kinch, Horace man who suffers from dry rot, in King's Bench prison
The Uncommercial Traveller (1860–8) Charles Dickens
Kindheart, Mr friend to the uncommercial traveller
The Uncommercial Traveller (1860–8) Charles Dickens
Kindred, Jonas puritan: 'Grave Jonas Kindred . . . /Erect, morose, determined, slow'
Sarah his wife, whom he rules 'unquestion'd and alone'
Sybil his daughter; in verse tale
The Borough poem (1810) George Crabbe
Kinfauns, Baron see **Charteris**
King housemaster based on one the author disliked

Stalky & Co. (1899) Rudyard Kipling

King, Adolph Martha Quest's* first lover
Children of Violence series (1952–69) Doris Lessing

King, Barbara actress
Tell Me How Long the Train's Been Gone (1968) James Baldwin

King, Bill friend to Pulham*
H. M. Pulham Esq. (1941) John P. Marquand

King, Christian George negro who betrayed colonists to pirates on Silver Store Island
The Perils of Certain English Prisoners (1857) Charles Dickens

King, Mary very good to some, a nasty freckled little thing to others
Pride and Prejudice (1813) Jane Austen

King, Meg
Roy mad sadist, her husband
The Edge of the Paper (1963) Gillian Tindall

King, Mogul
On the Face of the Waters (1896) Flora Annie Steel

King, Reginald close friend to the Langhams*
Soldiers of Fortune (1897) Richard Harding Davies

King, Tom a 'jolly dog' always asking for a Mr Thompson
Sketches by Boz† (1836) Charles Dickens

King-Too-Toz a certain genuine learned being
All and Everything: Beelzebub's Tales to His Grandson (1950) G. I. Gurdjieff

Kingcote, Bernard neurasthenic cc, expert like his creator in 'ingenious refinement of self-torture'
Isabel Clarendon (1886) George Gissing

Kingsmill, Peter m. Roy Timberlake*
John his brother
In This Our Life (1942) Ellen Glasgow

Kingsmore, Arthur actor, m. Lady Elfride Luxellian*; grandfather to Elfride Swancourt*
A Pair of Blue Eyes (1873) Thomas Hardy

Kinraid, Charley harpooner carried off by press gang in love with Sylvia Robson*
Sylvia's Lovers (1863) Mrs Gaskell

Kinsolving, Cass Southern-born artist
Set This House on Fire (1961) William

Styron

Kint Flemish usher at M. Pelet's*
The Professor (1857) Charlotte Brontë

Kint, Mme Mme Beck's* mother
Victor her son
Villette (1853) Charlotte Brontë

Kintyre, Duke of
The New Humpty-Dumpty (1912) Daniel Chaucer (rn Ford Madox Ford)

Kinzey, Miss Harvey Cheyne's* typist
Captains Courageous (1897) Rudyard Kipling

Kiomi gipsy girl
The Adventures of Harry Richmond (1871) George Meredith

Kipe
ss 'The Yachting Cap'
Unlucky for Pringle (1973) Wyndham Lewis

Kipps, Arthur cc; illegitimate son to Margaret Euphemia Kipps and Waddy*; engaged to Helen Walsingham*; m. Ann Pornick*
Edward George his uncle
Molly Edward's wife; the guardians of Kipps during childhood
Kipps (1905) H. G. Wells

Kirby, Carinthia Jane cc, orphan, m. Lord Fleetwood*
Chillon her brother
Captain Kirby 'the Old Buccaneer', their deceased father
The Amazing Marriage (1895) George Meredith

Kirby, Skeeters ('Skeet') cc, narrator of novel which tries to emulate Twain*
Mitch Miller (1920); *Skeeters Kirby* (1923) Edgar Lee Masters

Kirillov half-mad engineer
Besy (*The Possessed*) (1879) Fyodor Dostoievsky

Kirk, Howard viciously selfish university sociologist 'historicist'
The History Man (1976) Malcolm Bradbury

Kirk, Mrs
Captain Kirk her husband
Vanity Fair (1847–8) W. M. Thackeray

Kirke Captain of the *Deliverance*, m. as second husband Magdalene Vanstone*
No Name (1862) Wilkie Collins

Kirker reporter
When a Man's Single (1888) J. M. Barrie

Kirkland, Christopher cc, narrator of novel by notable Victorian literary lady
his father, a Yorkshire vicar
his mother
The Autobiography of Christopher Kirkland (1885) Mrs Lynn Lynton

Kirkpatrick, Clare, Mrs m. Dr Gibson*
Cynthia her daughter
Wives and Daughters (1865) Mrs Gaskell

Kirkwood, Maurice cc of the last of the three 'psychiatric' novels of the author: Kirkwood has an antipathy to 'beautiful young women' because when he was an infant his lovely cousin Laura dropped him into a thorn-bush (it is she who cuddles his son and reassures him that the latter does not suffer his now cured antipathy)
A Mortal Antipathy (1885) Oliver Wendell Holmes

Kirsanov, Arkady friend to Bazarov*
Nicolai Petrovich his father, a benevolent landowner who treats his serfs well (for which they cheat him)
Pavel Petrovich his uncle, a melancholy Anglophile dandy
Otsy i deti (Fathers and Sons) (1862) Ivan Turgenev

Kirsch Joseph Sedley's* courier
Vanity Fair (1847–8) W. M. Thackeray

Kishmenhof, Professor
All and Everything: Beelzebub's Tales to His Grandson (1950) G. I. Gurdjieff

Kishwegin, Mme head of music-hall act, the Natcha-Kee-Tawara Troupe
The Lost Girl (1920) D. H. Lawrence

Kitchell, Captain brutal boss of fishing vessel, the *Bertha Millner*; kills Captain Sternerson* but drowns
Moran of the Lady Letty (in England *Shanghaied*) (1898) Frank Norris

Kitchener, Tom m. Sally Preston*
ss 'Something to Worry About'
The Man Upstairs (1914) P. G. Wodehouse

Kite, Sergeant
The Recruiting Officer play (1706) George Farquhar

Kitely jealous usurer who puts spy on his wife
Mistress Kitely
Every Man in His Humour play (1598) Ben Jonson

Kitt, Miss girl in pink on Norwood picnic
David Copperfield (1850) Charles Dickens

Kitten Deputy-Commissioner on Silver Store Island
The Perils of Certain English Prisoners (1857) Charles Dickens

Kitten prostitute; Black mistress to J. C. Holland*
One Hundred Million Dollar Misunderstanding * (1962) Robert Gover

Kitterbell, Charles nephew to Nicodemus Dumps*, whom he invited to christening of his infant son
Sketches by Boz (1836) Charles Dickens

Kittle, Maria American epistolary novel* consisting of one 17,000-word letter telling of woman captured by Indians during French and Indian War (worried that her reader might be 'worried at my silence about Mrs Kittle', the author added, 'I think we left her reposing under a tree')
History of Maria Kittle (1797) Ann Eliza Bleecker

Kittridge, Dr
Elsie Venner (1861) Oliver Wendell Holmes

Klein, Honor
A Severed Head (1961) Iris Murdoch

Klem caretakers at the uncommercial traveller's London lodgings, who 'come out of some hole when London empties itself, and go in again when it fills'
The Uncommercial Traveller (1860–8) Charles Dickens

Klesmer, Julius German-Slav musician, m. Catherine Arrowpoint*
Daniel Deronda (1876) George Eliot (rn Mary Anne, later Marian, Evans)

Klingenspohr, Stiefel von
Dorothea his wife, *née* von Speck*
The Fitz-Boodle Papers (1843) W. M. Thackeray

Kloots, Captain of the *Ter Schilling*
The Phantom Ship (1839) Captain Marryat

Knag, Miss Mme Mantalini's* forewoman
Nicholas Nickleby (1839) Charles Dickens

Kneebreeches, Mr tutor to Griselda*
The Cuckoo Clock (1877) Mrs Molesworth

Knibbs, Beck helper at Talbothays Farm
Tess of the D'Urbervilles (1891) Thomas Hardy

Knight, Henry cc, barrister, reviewer, essayist, loves Elfrida Swancourt*
A Pair of Blue Eyes (1873) Thomas Hardy

Knight, Woody retired baseball player in work by American black novelist
Ask Me Now (1980) Al Young

Knight-Bell, Mr Mudfog member who exhibited a wax preparation of the interior of a gentleman who had swallowed a key
The Mudfog Papers (1838) Charles Dickens

Knightley goldfields commissioner
Robbery Under Arms: A Story of Life and Adventure in the Bush and in the Goldfields of Australia (1888, rev. 1889) Rolf Boldrewood (rn Thomas Alexander Browne)

Knightley, George generous owner of Donwell Abbey m. Emma Woodhouse*
John his younger brother
Isabella *née* Woodhouse John's wife, sister to Emma
Henry; John; Isabella; George; Emma John and Isabella's children
Emma (1816) Jane Austen

Knightsbridge, Countess of
The Kickleburys on the Rhine (1850) W. M. Thackeray

Knockem, Dan Jordan a horse-courser and ranger of Turnbull
Bartholomew Fair play (1631) Ben Jonson

Knollys of the Arctic Research Laboratory
The Small Back Room (1943) Nigel Balchin

Knollys, Duncan Laird of Knocktarlitie, Duke of Argyle's bailie
Heart of Midlothian (1818) Walter Scott

Knollys, Monica, Lady cousin to Austin and Silas Ruthyn*
Uncle Silas (1864) J. Sheridan Le Fanu

Knott, Dorcas one-time maid, friend to Catherina Sarti*
ss 'Mr Gilfil's Love Story'
Scenes of Clerical Life (1857) George Eliot (rn Mary Anne, later Marian, Evans)

Knott, Mr

Watt (1953) Samuel Beckett

Knott, Terry, Major elderly man living with Christina Cornwell*
The Widow (1957) Francis King

Knowell, Douglas m. Martha Quest*
Children of Violence series (1952–69) Doris Lessing

Knowles London draughtsman
A Laodicean (1881) Thomas Hardy

Knowles, Floyd
The Grapes of Wrath (1939) John Steinbeck

Knox, Florence McCarthy, Mr ('Flurry') Yeates's* landlord, m. Sally Knox (below)
his grandmother
Sir Valentine Knox his uncle
Lady Knox his wife
Sally daughter to Sir Valentine and Lady Knox, m. 'Flurry' (above)
Some Experiences of an Irish R. M. (1899) O. E. Somerville and Martin Ross (rn Edith Somerville and Violet Martin)

Knox, Joel Harrison cc, unloved thirteen-year-old boy
Sanson, Edward R. his paralyzed father
Miss Mary Skully his stepmother
Randolph Amy's cousin, transvestite
Other Voices, Other Rooms (1948) Truman Capote

Knox, Mr and Mrs
Margaret their daughter
Fanny's First Play play (1905) George Bernard Shaw

Ko-Ko Lord High Executioner, m. Katisha*
The Mikado opera (1885) W. S. Gilbert and Arthur Sullivan

Kochansky, Solomon dandified Russian Jewish emigrant to Australia
his wife
Moses their son
The Unbending† (1954) Judah Waten

Kochek, Alex 'realistic' local politician
The Grand Parade (1961) Julian Mayfield

Koëldwithout, Baron family name of Baron of Grogzwig
Nicholas Nickleby (1839) Charles Dickens

Kokua wife to Keawe*
ss 'The Bottle Imp'
Island Nights' Entertainments (1893)

Robert Louis Stevenson
Kollwitz, Miss obsessive peeler of fruit;
Miss Throop's protector and companion
What a Way to Go (1962) Wright Morris
Konuzion a king and saint who invented
morality
*All and Everything: Beelzebub's Tales to
His Grandson* (1950) G. I. Gurdjieff
Kopping, Kristian 'rosy-faced Dutchman',
m. 'Tite Poulette*
ss ''Tite Poulette'
Old Creole Days (1879) George
Washington Cable
Korobochka dull-witted widow, land-
owner, whose suspicions expose
Chichikov*
Myortvye dushi (*Dead Souls*) (1842)
Nicolai Gogol
Korpenning, Bud
Manhattan Transfer (1925) John Dos
Passos
Korsoniloff, André schizophrenic pro-
fessor of philosophy in Canadian novel
Korsoniloff (1969) Matt Cohen
Kostalergi, Nina niece to Matthew
Kearney*, half-Irish and half-Greek
Lord Kilgoblin (1872) Charles Lever
Kostoglotov exiled cc in semi-autobio-
graphical novel
Rakovy Korpus (*Cancer Ward*) (1968)
Alexander Solzhenitsyn
Kotick the White Seal
ss 'The White Seal'
Jungle Books (1894–5) Rudyard Kipling
Kotuko see Kadlu
Kowalski, Stanley
Stella his wife
A Streetcar Named Desire play (1949)
Tennessee Williams (rn Thomas Lanier
Williams)
Krafft, Heinrich one of the first detailed
studies of a homosexual (the word is not
mentioned)
Maurice Guest (1908) Henry Handel
Richardson (rn Ethel Florence Lindesay
Richardson Robertson)
Krame, Peter senior midshipman, bully
The Gunroom (1919) Charles Morgan
Krant, Nicholas deputy sheriff
An American Tragedy (1925) Theodore
Dreiser
Krantz second captain
The Phantom Ship (1839) Captain

Marryat
Krapp monologuist
Krapp's Last Tape play (1958) Samuel
Beckett
Krasinsky, Julia dumb orphan
ss 'The Quiet Woman'
Adam and Eve and Pinch Me (1921) A. E.
Coppard
Kratch, Bill Notterdam's rival* and father
to his children
When the Wicked Man (1931) Ford
Madox Ford
Kratzenstein businessman
An English Girl: A Romance (1907) Ford
Madox Ford
Kreisler, Otto artist
Tarr (1918) Wyndham Lewis
Krempe, Professor
Frankenstein (1818) Mary Shelley
Krenck, Justus, Revd
Lotta his wife, missionaries
ss 'The Judgement of Dungara'
Soldiers Three (1888) Rudyard Kipling
Kretzer, Frau mother of two killed soldier
sons
her Nazi husband
Nord (*North*) (1960) Louis-Ferdinand
Céline (rn Louis-Ferdinand Destouches)
Kreymborg, Alfred (hist.) an American
editor and poet of this name (e.g. *Mush-
rooms*, 1916) did not sue the author
ss 'The Man Who Became a Woman'
Horses and Men (1924) Sherwood
Anderson
Krillet, Deborah 'the Shulamite', second
wife to Simon, falls into 'blameless love'
with husband's overseer; goes mad after
being widowed
Simeon her brutal farmer husband who
loves her passionately and sjamboks her
relentlessly
Trante; Annie Simeon's sisters
The Shulamite (1904); *The Woman
Deborah* (1910) Mrs Alice J. de C. and
Claude Askew
Kriplesing, Ralph whose rise to power,
through Coca Cola, on a West Indian
island, this novel records
his father, who becomes a *sunyasi*, a holy
man
The Mimic Men (1967) V. S. Naipaul
Kristina, Queen (hist.) characterized here
by the author, in his most ambitious

historical play, as Sweden-hating and 'reared as a man, fighting for her self-existence, against her feminine nature . . . So genuine a woman she was a woman-hater'
Kristina play (1903) August Strindberg
Kroge, Oscar H. theatre director, author of essays and elegaic odes
Mephisto (1936) Klaus Mann
Krogh, Erik great Swedish financier
England Made Me (1935) Graham Greene
Krogold legendary king fragments of whose story are introduced into the text
Mort à credit (*Death on the Instalment Plan*) (1936) Louis-Ferdinand Céline (rn Louis-Ferdinand Destouches)
Kronak, Ernest, Professor Czech refugee (alias Jeremy Bentham)
Let the People Sing (1939) J. B. Priestley
Kronberg, Thea singer
Tilly her aunt
The Song of the Lark (1915) Willa Cather
Kronbernkzion, Makary author of the *Boolmarshano* (*The Affirming and Denying Influences on Man*) and pending saint
All and Everything: Beelzebub's Tales to His Grandson (1950) G. I. Gurdjieff
Krook drunken rag-and-bone dealer, landlord to Miss Flite* and Nemo*
Bleak House (1853) Charles Dickens
Kubs and Koibs Brer Rabbit's* children
Uncle Remus (1880–95) Joel Chandler Harris
Kukshin, Madame stupid and ugly woman who talks about the rights of women without understanding anything
Otsy i deti (*Fathers and Sons*) (1862) Ivan Turgenev
Kumalo, Steven black priest cc
his wife
Abraham their son
Matthew son to John
Gertrude; John Steven's sister and brother
Cry, The Beloved Country (1948) Alan Paton
Kundoo
ss 'At twenty-two'
Soldiers Three (1895) Rudyard Kipling
Kuno thief

ss 'Nuns at Luncheon'
Mortal Coils (1922) Aldous Huxley
Kurban Sahib see Corbyn, Walter
Kurrell, Ted, Captain
ss 'A Wayside Comedy'
Wee Willie Winkie (1888) Rudyard Kipling
Kurt, Luft-Lieutenant of the *Vaterland*, Anglo-German killed in action
The War in the Air (1908) H. G. Wells
Kurtz manager of Inner Station, Belgian Congo
Heart of Darkness (1902) Joseph Conrad (rn Josef Teodor Konrad Korzeniowski)
Kusich, Abe dwarf racecourse tout; squeezes Erle Shoop's* testicles until he collapses
The Day of the Locust (1939) Nathanael West (rn Nathan Weinstein)
Kusma Proutkoff Russian equivalent to Mullah Nassr Edin*
All and Everything: Beelzebub's Tales to His Grandson (1950) G. I. Gurdjieff
Kutankumagen Russian member of Mudfog Association
The Mudfog Papers (1838) Charles Dickens
Kwakely member of Mudfog Association
The Mudfog Papers (1838) Charles Dickens
Kwan, Billy Australian-Chinese dwarf press photographer in Indonesia
The Year of Living Dangerously (1978) C. J. Koch
Kyin, U Po Sub-divisional Magistrate of Kyauktada
Burmese Days (1935) George Orwell (rn Eric Blair)
Kyle, David landlord of the George Inn, Kennaquhair
The Monastery (1820) Walter Scott
Kynaston, Harvey Fabian socialist who offers marriage to the disgraced Herminia Barton*, but is refused
The Woman Who Did (1895) Grant Allen
Kyrle, William solicitor, partner to Gilmore*
The Woman in White (1860) Wilkie Collins
Kysh friend to the narrator
ss 'Steam Tactics'
Traffics and Discoveries (1904) Rudyard

Kipling

Kyte a scrivener
 All Fools play (1605) George Chapman

Kytes, Tony m. Milly Richards*

ss 'Tony Kytes, the Arch-Deceiver'
Life's Little Ironies (1894) Thomas Hardy

L

L., Lord m. Caroline Grandison*
Sir Charles Grandison (1754) Samuel Richardson

La Berma actress
A la recherche du temps perdu (*In Search of Lost Time*) (1913–27) Marcel Proust

Labron agent for Debarry* family
Felix Holt (1866) George Eliot (rn Mary Anne, later Marian, Evans)

La Castre the indulgent father to Mirabel*
The Wild-Goose Chase play (1652) John Fletcher

Lacerteux, Germanie servant who lives a double life; the authors based the character on their own servant, whose duplicity they discovered only after her death
Germanie Lacerteux (1865) Edmond and Jules de Goncourt

Lacey, Albert suitor to Mrs Campion*
The Perennial Bachelor (1925) Anne Parrish

Lackersteen, Mr manager of a timber firm
his wife
Elizabeth their daughter, m. Mr Macgregor*
Burmese Days (1935) George Orwell (rn Eric Blair)

Lackland reformed criminal, father to Ida Fynes*
The Old Bank (1902) William Westall

La Cordifiamma, Marie actress Marie Lavington, m. Stangrave*
Two Years Ago (1857) Charles Kingsley

Lacostellerie, Count de
his wife
Pauline their daughter
Tom Burke of Ours (1844) Charles Lever

La Creevy, Miss miniature painter, 'mincing young lady of fifty'
Nicholas Nickleby (1839) Charles Dickens

Lacy, Hugh, Sir Earl of Lincoln
Rowland Lacy his nephew
The Shoemaker's Holiday play (1600) Thomas Dekker

Lacy, Hugo de Constable of Chester
Damian his nephew
Randal a distant and disreputable kinsman
The Betrothed (1825) Walter Scott

Lacy, Lord
Sir Maurice his son
The City Madam play (1658) Philip Massinger

Lacy, Miriam ('The Brushwood Girl'), m. George Cottar*
ss 'The Brushwood Boy'
The Day's Work (1898) Rudyard Kipling

Lacy, Mr Home Office jail inspector
It Is Never Too Late To Mend (1856) Charles Reade

Lacy, Rowland nephew to Earl of Lincoln*, disguises himself as **Hans Meulter**
The Shoemaker's Holiday (1600) Thomas Dekker

Ladislaw, Will cc, second cousin to Casaubon*; m. Dorothea Casaubon, *née* Brooke
Sarah his mother, daughter of Mr Dunkirk
Middlemarch (1871–2) George Eliot (rn Mary Anne, later Marian, Evans)

Ladle, Joey head cellarman of Wilding & Co.
No Thoroughfare (1867) Charles Dickens

Ladvenu, Martin, Brother
Saint Joan play (1924) George Bernard Shaw

Lady Flippant Gripe's* sister, an affected widow
Love in a Wood, or *St James's Park* comedy (1672) William Wycherley

Lady Jane large grey cat attendant to Krook*
Bleak House (1853) Charles Dickens

Ladywell, Eustace artist, suitor to Ethelberta Petherwin*
The Hand of Ethelberta (1876) Thomas

Hardy
Laertes son to Polonius*
Hamlet play (1623) William Shakespeare
Lafe lover of Dewey Dell Bundren*
As I Lay Dying (1930) William Faulkner
Lafitte, Jean pirate
Madame Delphine (1881) George Washington Cable
Lafont, Esther cc
her husband
Piers her son
The Only Child (1978) Nell Dunn
Lagnois see **Regaud**
Lagrange, Mme *pension*-keeper
The Adventures of Mr Ledbury (1844) Albert Smith
Laguerre
Polly opera (1729) John Gay
Lagune rich and gullible student of spiritualism, swindled by Chaffery*
Love and Mr Lewisham (1900) H. G. Wells
Lahens, Agnes cc who becomes a nun
Olive her mother
Major Lahens her half-mad father
ss 'Agnes Lahens'
Celibates (1895) George Moore
Laider, A. V.
ss 'A. V. Laider'
Seven Men (1919) Max Beerbohm
Laiter, Agnes
ss 'Yoked with an Unbeliever'
Plain Tales from the Hills (1888) Rudyard Kipling
Lajeunesse, Gabriel cc of poem in unrhymed hexameters; separated from Evangeline Bellefontaine* and does not meet her again until she is a sister of mercy and he is a dying old man
Basil his blacksmith father
Evangeline, A Tale of Arcadie (1847) Henry Wadsworth Longfellow
Lakamber Rajah and gunpowder smuggler
Almayer's Folly (1895) Joseph Conrad (rn Josef Teodor Konrad Korzeniowski)
Lake, Barbara is always getting Mr Cavendish into trouble
her father, a drawing master
Rose her sister
Miss Marjoribanks (1866) Mrs Margaret Oliphant
Lake, Gunter rich American banker in love with V. V. Grammont*

The Secret Places of the Heart (1922) H. G. Wells
Lake, Stanley, Captain elegant man who wishes to sell part of his wife's estate
his wife
Rachel his sister
Wylder's Hand (1864) J. Sheridan Le Fanu
Lakely editor
John Chilcote, MP (1904) Katherine C. Thurston
Lakenheath, Elizabeth, Lady aunt to Millie Uckridge*
Love Among the Chickens† (1906) P. G. Wodehouse
Lal, Chowder servant to Major Sholto*
The Sign of Four (1890) Arthur Conan Doyle
Lalun
ss 'On the City Wall'
Soldiers Three (1888) Rudyard Kipling
Lamar, Ruby
Sanctuary (1931) William Faulkner
Lamb retired butcher
his wife and daughters
The Sketch Book (1820) Washington Irving
Lamb, Charity Tom Brown's* nurse
Tom Brown's Schooldays (1857) Thomas Hughes
Lamb, Horace master of household
Charlotte wife he has m. for her money
Mortimer his cousin, Charlotte's lover
Emma Horace's aunt
Manservant and Maidservant (1947) Ivy Compton-Burnett
Lamb, Jerry farmer, m. Rita Lyons*
ss 'Feed My Lambs'
The Talking Trees (1971) Sean O'Faolain
Lamb, Leonard ('Baa-Lamb')
Middlemarch (1871–2) George Eliot (rn Mary Anne, later Marian, Evans)
Lamb, Richard English adventurer in South America
Paquita his wife
Dona Isadora her aunt
The Purple Land (1885) W. H. Hudson
Lambert, Daniel (hist.), man weighing over fifty-two stone, died 1809, who exhibited himself in London
Nicholas Nickleby (1839) Charles Dickens
Lambert, Martin, Colonel friend to War-

rington*
Molly his wife, *née* Benson
Jack priggish parson; **Charles;**
Theodosia m. George Warrington*;
Hester; Lucy their children
The Virginians (1857–9) W. M.
Thackeray
Lambert, Terence stage designer
Hemlock and After (1952) Angus Wilson
Lambert, Wilfred
The Napoleon of Notting Hill (1904)
G. K. Chesterton
Lambeth, Lord eventually refused by Bessie Alden*
his mother
his sister
An International Episode (1879) Henry
James
Lambone, Paul novelist, friend to Christina Alberta*
Christina Alberta's Father (1925) H. G.
Wells
Lambourn, Colonel paranoid friend to
Kennie Martin*
ss 'A Bit off the Map'
A Bit Off the Map (1957) Angus Wilson
Lambourne, Michael tapster's boy and
bad hat
Benedict his father
Kenilworth (1821) Walter Scott
Lambsbreath, Adam dairyman
Cold Comfort Farm (1932) Stella
Gibbons
Lambskin, Alice, Mrs attendant to Mrs
Bethune Baliol*
The Highland Widow (1827) Walter
Scott
Lammers, 'Chuck' General in U S army,
attached to NATO in Paris
Letitia his wife
Jean their daughter
Birds of America (1971) Mary McCarthy
Lammeter, Nancy m. Godfrey Cass* as
second wife
Priscilla her plain sister
her father
Silas Marner (1861) George Eliot (rn
Mary Anne, later Marian, Evans)
Lammiter
ss 'The Lang Men o' Larut'
Life's Handicap (1891) Rudyard Kipling
Lammle, Alfred unscrupulous adventurer,
m. Sophronia Akershem*

Our Mutual Friend (1865) Charles
Dickens
Lamotte, Annette m. Soames Forsyte* as
second wife
Mme Lamotte her mother
The Forsyte series (1906–33) John
Galsworthy
Lamprey friend to Hoard*
A Trick to Catch the Old One comedy
(1608) Thomas Middleton
Lamps porter at Mugby Junction
Mugby Junction (1866) Charles Dickens
Lampton, Joe cc, m. Alive Aisgill*
Room at the Top (1957) John Braine
Lancaster, Florence
David her husband
Nicky their son, engaged to Bunty Mainwaring*
The Vortex play (1924) Noël Coward
Lancaster, Kate summer visitor from
Boston to Maine seaport, friend and
companion to Helen Denis*, in distinguished local-colour* tales
Deephaven (1877) Sarah Orne Jewett
Lance army surgeon
*Vanity Fair** (1847–8) W. M. Thackeray
Lancoch, Betti
Joshua her brother
ss 'The Woman Who Sowed Iniquity'
My People (1915) Caradoc Evans (rn
David Evans)
Landau, Nathan Sophie Zawistowska's*
drug-deranged manic-depressive lover
Sophie's Choice (1979) William Styron
Landauer, Herr Jewish head of great department store
his wife
Natalie their pretty teenaged daughter
Bernhardt his nephew and partner,
liquidated by the Nazis
Goodbye to Berlin (1939) Christopher
Isherwood
Landers, Fred Anne Clephane's* guardian
The Mother's Recompense (1925) Edith
Wharton
Landless, Helena Honeythunder's* ward
Neville her brother, also his ward
Edwin Drood (1870) Charles Dickens
Landon, Edward, M P
Mary his wife
Jess; Rebecca cc; **Sylvia; Boy** their children
The Ballad and the Source (1944)

Rosamond Lehmann
Landor banker of Milby
Eustace; Benjamin lawyer; **'Belle of Milby'** his children
ss 'Janet's Repentance'
Scenes of Clerical Life (1857) George Eliot (rn Mary Anne, later Marian, Evans)
Landys-Haggart, Mrs
ss 'On the Strength of a Likeness'
Plain Tales from the Hills (1888) Rudyard Kipling
Lane manservant to Algernon Moncrieff*
The Importance of Being Earnest play (1895) Oscar Wilde
Lane, Harry the modern Joseph of Montreal
The Many Coloured Coat (1960) Morley Callaghan
Lane, Miss harassed governess
Nicholas Nickleby (1839) Charles Dickens
Langdale (hist.), vintner; premises wrecked by the Gordon rioters
Barnaby Rudge (1840) Charles Dickens
Langdale, Countess of
Castle Rackrent† (1801) Maria Edgeworth
Langdon, Bernard beloved of Elsie Venner*, but even when saved by her from death from rattlesnake bite he cannot return her love; in novel against which *Northwest Christian Advocate* of Chicago ran a series of articles warning of its ill effects
Elsie Venner: A Romance of Destiny (1861) Oliver Wendell Holmes
Langdon, Morris, Major Leonora Penderton's* lover
Alison his wife
Reflections in a Golden Eye (1940) Carson McCullers
Langer, Walter young German tutor hired by Harrington* family; in author's first stage hit
Five Finger Exercise (1958) Peter Shaffer
Langham financier
Theodore; Alice; Hope m. Robert Clay* his children
Soldiers of Fortune (1897) Richard Harding Davis
Langham, Edward Robert Elsmere's* Oxford tutor, who plants the seeds of religious doubt in his mind
Robert Elsmere (1888) Mrs Humphry Ward
Langley mistakenly called D'Anglais by Bebelle, orphan child
Somebody's Luggage (1862) Charles Dickens
Langley, David writer who passes off dead friend's material as his own
The Towers of Trebizond (1956) Rose Macaulay
Langley, Frederick, Sir proud, dark, ambitious
The Black Dwarf (1816) Walter Scott
Langley-Beard, Charles, Dr religious hypocrite
The Old Men at the Zoo (1961) Angus Wilson
Langon, Lieutenant of Irish Volunteers
The Plough and the Stars play (1926) Sean O'Casey (rn John Casey)
Langrish, Aurora, Lady
The Princess Casamassima (1866) Henry James
Languebeau Snuffe a puritan, chaplain to Belforest*
The Atheist's Tragedy, or The Honest Man's Revenge play (1611/12) Cyril Tourneur
Languish, Lydia m. Captain Jack Absolute*
The Rivals play (1775) Richard Brinsley Sheridan
Lanigan, Commander
The Moon in the Yellow River play (1932) Denis Johnston
Lanigan, James m. Caroline Considine*
Peter; John; Tony; Lucie; Nonie their children
Without My Cloak (1931) Kate O'Brien
Laniger 'man with a temper'
The Impressions of Theophrastus Such (1879) George Eliot (rn Mary Anne, later Marian, Evans)
Lanster, Emile, M. waiter
Manhattan Transfer (1925) John Dos Passos
Lanyon, Dr lawyer to whom Jekyll* reveals his secret
Dr Jekyll and Mr Hyde (1886) Robert Louis Stevenson
Lanyon, Joyce, Mrs m. Martin Arrowsmith* as second wife

Arrowsmith (1925) Sinclair Lewis

Lapell, Hubert
ss 'Hubert and Minnie'
The Little Mexican (1924) Aldous Huxley

Lapham, Silas, Colonel ruthless businessman (paint manufacturer) and social climber; cc who finally discovers morality in ruin
Persis his wife
Penelope m. Tom Corey*; **Irene** his daughters, the latter pretty and charmless
his five brothers
The Rise of Silas Lapham (1885) William Dean Howells

Lapidoth see **Cohen**

Laputa, John, Revd renegade Negro priest
Prester John (1910) John Buchan

Larch, Freda 'Second Resurrectionist'
The Good Companions (1929) J. B. Priestley

Larcom solemn butler to the Brandons*
Wylder's Hand (1864) J. Sheridan Le Fanu

Larivaudière, Lise friend to Christine*
The Pretty Lady (1918) Arnold Bennett

Lark, Tabitha organist and future aman uensis (and wife?) of Swithin St Cleeve*
Two on a Tower (1882) Thomas Hardy

Larkcom, Harry ('The Cad')
The Passing of the Third Floor Back play (1910) Jerome K. Jerome

Larkey Boy, The prizefighter, beat the Game Chicken*
Dombey and Son (1848) Charles Dickens

Larkin, Joseph eminent and respectable Christian lawyer, struck from roll of solicitors when his interest in money becomes too apparent
Wylder's Hand (1864) J. Sheridan Le Fanu

Larkins 'the eldest Miss Larkins . . . maybe about thirty'
David Copperfield (1850) Charles Dickens

Larkins, Amelia Baroski's* pupil
ss 'The Ravenswing'
Men's Wives (1843) W. M. Thackeray

Larkins, Grace, Mrs widow
Annie; Miriam m. Mr Polly*; **Minnie** her daughters
The History of Mr Polly (1910) H. G. Wells

Larkins, Jem amateur actor
Sketches by Boz† (1836) Charles Dickens

Larkspur hound bitch who wears goggles; in love with Horlick*
One Day (1965) Wright Morris

Larkyn, Mrs
ss 'Watches of the Night'
Plain Tales from the Hills (1888) Rudyard Kipling

Larkyns, Revd Mr
Charley his son, m. Mary Green*
The Adventures of Mr Verdant Green (1853) Cuthbert Bede (rn Edward Bradley)

Larne, Rosamund daughter-in-law to Silvanus Heythorp*
Phyllis; Jock her children
A Stoic (1918) John Galsworthy

Larolles, Mrs
Cecilia (1782) Fanny Burney

Larrap see **Robinson**

Larry
Anna Christie play (1922) Eugene O'Neill

Larry brute
The Lime Twig (1961) John Hawkes

Larsen, Wolf, Captain atavist cc; captain of the *Ghost*
The Sea-Wolf (1904) Jack London

Lartius, Titus Roman General
Coriolanus play (1623) William Shakespeare

La Rue, Mlle evil schoolteacher at Mme Du Pont's School for Young Ladies, who helps Montraville* seduce Charlotte Temple*; m. Colonel Crayton*
Charlotte: A Tale of Truth (1791; in America as *Charlotte Temple*, 1794) Mrs Susannah Rowson

Larue, Pierre looked like 'wily if extremely decrepit gnome', filled with enthusiasm for 'beautifully informed' young Nazis, writer of books on scandalous cultural life in European capitals (except Berlin)
Mephisto (1936) Klaus Mann

Laruelle, Jacques film maker
Under the Volcano (1947) Malcolm Lowrie

La Ruse, Count rogue
Jonathan Wild (1743) Henry Fielding

Larynx, Revd Mr Vicar of Claydyke, 'an accommodating divine'

Nightmare Abbey (1818) Thomas Love Peacock

Las Casas Pizarro's* follower
Pizarro play (1799) Richard Brinsley Sheridan

Lascar Loo's Mother
ss 'The Record of Badalia Herodsfoot'
Many Inventions (1893) Rudyard Kipling

Lascarides, Katya in love with Robert Grimshaw*, whom she finally m.
Kitty her young niece
A Call (1910) Ford Madox Ford

Lascelles, Florence, Lady loved by Ernest Maltravers*
Ernest Maltravers (1837)
Alice, or The Mysteries (1838) Edward Bulwer Lytton

Lascelles, Tattie theatrical friend to Rosalind Heath*
Conrad in Search of His Youth (1919) Leonard Merrick

Lashmars, The maternal relatives to Sophy Chapin*
ss 'A Habitation Enforced'
Actions and Reactions (1909) Rudyard Kipling

Lassman speculator
Daniel Deronda (1876) George Eliot (rn Mary Anne, later Marian, Evans)

Lasswade, Kitty, Lady cousin to the Pargiters*
The Years (1937) Virginia Woolf

Last, Tony owner of Hetton Abbey, cc
Brenda his unfaithful wife
John their son, killed in accident
A Handful of Dust (1934) Evelyn Waugh

Latch, William horse-racing man in service with Esther Waters*, her lover, father to her illegitimate son, and later her husband
Esther Waters (1894) George Moore

Latimer narrator who foresees future; m. Bertha Grant*
Alfred his half-brother
The Lifted Veil (1879) George Eliot (rn Mary Anne, later Marian, Evans)

Latimer, Darsie see **Redgauntlet, Arthur, Sir**

Latimer, Joan loved by John Adam*
Holy Deadlock (1934) A. P. Herbert

Latimer, Lord a young lord
The New Inn, or The Light Heart play

(1629) Ben Jonson

Latimer, Will
ss 'The Distracted Preacher'
Wessex Tales (1888) Thomas Hardy

Latin Grammer Master Captain Boldheart's* dire enemy
A Holiday Romance (1868) Charles Dickens

Latka, Nick unscrupulous boxing promoter
The Harder They Fall (1947) Budd Schulberg

Latour, Jean Marie cc, Bishop and later Archbishop of Agathonica
Death Comes for the Archbishop (1927) Willa Cather

La Trobe, Miss writer, director of the pageant
Between the Acts (1941) Virginia Woolf

Latta, Aaron one-time lover to Jean Miles*
Sentimental Tommy (1896) J. M. Barrie

Latta, James, Sir
Hatter's Castle (1931) A. J. Cronin

Latter, Jim, Captain Devonshire gentleman
Sir Robert his eldest brother
Aunt Latter who brings them up
Nina Woodville their cousin who loves Jim but m. Chester Nimmo*
Tom Nimmo; Sally Nimmo Nina's son and daughter by Jim
Prisoner of Grace (1952) Joyce Cary

Lattimer, Diane young woman cc, hooked on drugs and sex, of pioneer novel of Greenwich Village counter-culture, which influenced or anticipated Beat writing
Vivienne her mother
Flee the Angry Strangers (1952) George Mandel

Latude-Fernay pensioner of Lady Drew*
Tono Bungay (1909) H. G. Wells

Laughing Boy Navajo Indian silversmith and horse-trading cc of popular sentimental (and well-informed) novel
Laughing Boy (1929) Oliver La Farge

Launce servant to Proteus*
Two Gentlemen of Verona play (1623) William Shakespeare

Laura American resident in Mexico
ss 'Flowering Judas'
Flowering Judas (1930; 1935) Katherine Anne Porter

Laura schoolgirl cc of novel of life in Melbourne girls' boarding school in 1897
The Getting of Wisdom (1910) Henry Handel Richardson (rn Ethel Florence Lindesay Richardson Robertson)

Laure, Mme French actress who stabbed her husband on stage
Middlemarch (1871–2) George Eliot (rn Mary Anne, later Marian, Evans)

Laurence, Elsie young painter and dilettante, friend to Mildred Lawson*
ss 'Mildred Lawson'
Celibates (1895) George Moore

Laurence, Friar
Romeo and Juliet play (1623) William Shakespeare

Laurence, Mme friend to Mme Foucault*
The Old Wives' Tale (1908) Arnold Bennett

Laurence, Mr the host; 'in many ways a remarkable man, but unhappily one of those who are remarkable because they do not become famous – not because they do'
The New Republic, or *Culture, Faith and Philosophy in an English Country House* (1877; edition by John Lucas, 1975, lists originals of characters) William Hurrell Mallock

Laurence, Theodore ('Laurie') m. Amy March*
Bess their daughter
his grandfather
Little Women† (1868) Louisa M. Alcott

Laurentini, Lady see **Agnes, Sister**

Laurie cc, narrator
Dot her aunt (see also **ffoulkes-Corbett**)
The Towers of Trebizond (1956) Rose Macaulay

Laurie, Hubert
Night Must Fall play (1935) Emlyn Williams

Laurier wealthy young American
The War in the Air (1908) H. G. Wells

Lausch, Grandma tyrannical *grande dame* who plays an important part in the formation of the personality of Augie March*
The Adventures of Augie March (1953) Saul Bellow

Laval, Pierre (hist.) asks Destouches* to give him cyanide: is told, yes, if he will appoint him Governor of the San-Pierre and Miquelon Island (which he does)
D'un Château l'autre (*Castle to Castle*) (1957) Louis-Ferdinand Céline (rn Louis-Ferdinand Destouches)

Lavander, Lady Griselda's* godmother
The Cuckoo Clock (1877) Mrs Molesworth

La Varole servant to Lord Foppingham*
A Trip to Scarborough play (1777) Richard Brinsley Sheridan

Lavement French apothecary, employer of Roderick Random*
Roderick Random (1748) Tobias Smollett

Lavendar, Dr cc
Old Chester Tales (1898); *Dr Lavendar's People* (1903); *The Awakening of Helena Richie* (1906); *The Iron Woman* (1911) Margaretta Deland

Lavender, Edmund, Revd tutor
Barry Lyndon (1844) W. M. Thackeray

Lavengro scholar-gipsy, cc
Lavengro (1851); *Romany Rye* (1857) George Borrow

Lavenza, Elizabeth adopted daughter of Alphonse Frankenstein*, m. Victor Frankenstein*
Frankenstein (1818) Mary Shelley

LaVerne, Lenore see **Chiply, Elly**

Lavington see **Lac ordifiamma**

Lavinia daughter to Titus*
Titus Andronicus play (1623) William Shakespeare

Lavish, Miss authoress known as J. E. Prank
A Room With a View (1908) E. M. Forster

Lawford Town Clerk, Middlemas
The Surgeon's Daughter (1827) Walter Scott

Lawford, Arthur middle-aged man who changes into the character of man who killed himself 200 years ago
Sheila his wife
Alice their daughter
The Return (1910) Walter de la Mare

Lawless outlaw
The Black Arrow (1888) Robert Louis Stevenson

Lawnley, Frederick, Sir
A Simple Story (1791) Elizabeth Inchbald

Lawrence, Charles tennis player with bad

arm
The Huge Season (1954) Wright Morris
Lawrie, Mary Whittlestaff's* ward, with
whom he falls in love; m. John Gordon*
An Old Man's Love (1884) Anthony
Trollope
Lawson, Josh cc
Josh Lawson (1972) Melvyn Bragg
Lawson, Mildred cc, a cold young woman
and a pathological and malicious liar, a
portrait of Pearl Craigie (i.e. John Oliver
Hobbes*) with whom the author had had
an affair; convert to Rome (like her
original); is only happy when outside
herself
  Harold her brother, a distiller man, for
  whom she keeps house in Sutton, Surrey
  ss 'Mildred Lawson'
Celibates (1895) George Moore
Lawton, Jessica seduced by Horace Boyce*
and reduced to prostitution
The Lawton Girl (1890) Harold Frederic
Laxton
The Roaring Girl play (1611) Thomas
Middleton and Thomas Dekker
Lazarus (?hist.) indestructible cc
  Mary; Martha his sisters, trampled to
  death
  his parents, also trampled to death
Lazarus Laughed play (1927) Eugene
O'Neill
Lazarus, Abraham a Jew prosecuted by
Jiggers* for stealing plate
Great Expectations (1861) Charles
Dickens
Le Breton, Harry see Goslet, Harry
Le Fever, Lieutenant
  his son
Tristram Shandy (1767) Laurence Sterne
Le Strange, Nell bubbly narrator; m. Sir
Hugh Lancaster
Cometh Up As A Flower (1867) Rhoda
Broughton
Le Sueur, Lucetta mistress to Henchard*,
m. Donald Farfrae*
The Mayor of Casterbridge (1886)
Thomas Hardy
Le Vigan (hist.) film actor who collabor-
ated with the Nazis and eventually fled to
Argentina
D'un Château l'autre (*Castle to Castle*)
(1957) Louis-Ferdinand Céline (rn Louis-
Ferdinand Destouches)

Leak, Mrs landlady who attends witches'
sabbath
Lolly Willowes (1926) Sylvia Townsend
Warner
Leander penniless and unworthy idealist
posing as nobleman; cc Spanish comedy
Los intereses creados (*The Bonds of
Interest*) (1908) Jacinto Benavente
Leandro a young gentleman of good estate
The Spanish Curate play (1647) John
Fletcher and Philip Massinger
Leantio a factor; husband to Brancha*;
paid lover of Livia*
Women Beware Women play (1657)
Thomas Middleton
Leath, Angela beloved of Charley* the
bashful man
The Holly Tree (1855) Charles Dickens
Leath, Anna widow engaged to George
Darrow* but unable to bring herself to
m. him owing to her jealousy of his
previous intimacy with Sophie Viner*
  Owen her stepson
The Reef (1912) Edith Wharton
Leatherhead, Lanthorne a hobby-horse
seller or toyman
Bartholomew Fair play (1631) Ben
Jonson
Leatherleg shoemaker
The Staple of News play (1631) Ben
Jonson
Leaven, Robert coachman
  his wife
Jane Eyre (1847) Charlotte Brontë
Leberecht, Peter almost incestuous cc of
short and in part humorous German
novel
*Peter Leberecht, eine Geschichte ohne
Abenteuerlichkeiten* (*Peter Leberecht, a
Work Without Adventures*) (1795)
Ludwig Tieck
Lebezytnikov nihilist
Prestuplenie i Nakazanie (*Crime and
Punishment*) (1866) Fyodor Dostoievsky
Lebrun, Robert son of resort owner, in
love with Edna Pontellier*
The Awakening (1899) Kate Chopin
Lecamus, Paul visionary, in prized tale of
the supernatural
A Beleaguered City (1880) Mrs Margaret
Oliphant
Lechmore, Mrs Lionel Lincoln's* aunt
Lionel Lincoln (1825) James Fenimore

Cooper

Leclère, Black master of Bâtard*
ss 'Bâtard'
Children of the Frost (1902) Jack London

Lecoq, M. detective cc of early French police procedurals onwards from
Le Dossier no 113† (*File No. 113*) (1867) Émile Gaboriau

Lecure physician to Brunhalt*
Thierry and Theodoret play (1621) John Fletcher, Philip Massinger ?and Francis Beaumont

Ledbrain, X. statistician and expert on mathematical relationship between human and chair legs
The Mudfog Papers (1838) Charles Dickens

Ledbrook, Miss of the Crummles Company, friend to Miss Snevecelli*
Nicholas Nickleby (1839) Charles Dickens

Ledger, Felix name of cc which turns out to be a pretence, and is abandoned, in combination of fiction and criticism, by American poet
Journal of the Fictive Life (1965) Howard Nemerov

Ledsmar, Dr atheist scientist
The Damnation of Theron Ware in England, originally, as *Illumination* (1896) Harold Frederic

Lee, 'Old Bull' intended to represent the novelist William Burroughs
On the Road (1957) Jack Kerouac

Lee, Bessie nursery maid to the Reeds*
Jane Eyre (1847) Charlotte Brontë

Lee, Heinrich cc of classic German novel, partly autobiographical (but partly not), which exists in two distinct versions, the second of which is the familiar one, and which is a classic *Bildungsroman* (the earlier is not)
Der Grüne Heinrich (*Green Henry*) (1854–5, rev. 1880) Gottfried Keller

Lee, Lorelei good-looking moron who does well ('A girl can't keep on laughing all the time')
Gentlemen Prefer Blondes (1925) Anita Loos

Lee, Madeleine young widow who moves to Washington 'to touch with her own hands the massive machinery of society'. Rejects marriage offer from corrupt sena-tor
Democracy (1880) Henry Adams

Lee, Miss governess to Maria and Julia Bertram*, later to Fanny Price*
Mansfield Park (1814) Jane Austen

Lee, Mrs
The Simple Life Limited (1911) Daniel Chaucer (rn Ford Madox Ford)

Leeds, Nina cc who loses her sweetheart in the 1914–18 War in innovative play and, as nurse in military hospital, sleeps with many soldiers and becomes pregnant; m. Sam Evans*
Professor Leeds her father
Gordon her bastard son
Strange Interlude play (1927) Eugene O'Neill

Leeford, Edward Fagin's* confederate, called Monks throughout the book
Edwin betrayer of Oliver Twist's* mother; his father
Oliver Twist (1838) Charles Dickens

Leek, Henry valet to Farll* and buried in his place
Buried Alive (1908) Arnold Bennett

Lees-Noel, Aubrey, Mrs
The Patrician (1911) John Galsworthy

Leeson, Sarah mysterious servant, really Rosamond Treverton's* mother
The Dead Secret (1857) Wilkie Collins

Lefferts, Jim Elmer Gantry's* college friend
Elmer Gantry (1927) Sinclair Lewis

Legality, Mr
Civility his son
The Pilgrim's Progress (1678–84) John Bunyan

Legend, Sampson, Sir
Valentine his son, 'fallen under his father's displeasure by his expensive way of living', in love with Angelica*
Ben his younger son, 'half home-bred and half sea-bred', promised to Miss Prue*
Love for Love play (1710) William Congreve

Legeru, Sib dead poet and painter
M.F. (1971) Anthony Burgess (rn John Burgess Wilson)

Legg, Captain son to Lord Levant*
The Book of Snobs (1847) W. M. Thackeray

Leggatt narrator's chauffeur
ss 'The Horse Marines'†

A Diversity of Creatures (1917) Rudyard Kipling

Legge, 'Mother' procuress
A Glastonbury Romance (1932) John Cowper Powys

Legge-Wilson, MP
Phineas Finn† (1869) Anthony Trollope

Legrand, William impoverished Southern gentleman living in South Carolina; solves cryptogram
ss 'The Gold Bug'
Tales (1845) Edgar Allen Poe

Legrandin local snob
A la recherche du temps perdu (*In Search of Lost Time*) (1913–27) Marcel Proust

Legree, Simon cruel taskmaster; 'reconstructed' in second title
Uncle Tom's Cabin, or Life Among the Lowly (1852) Harriet Beecher Stowe
The Leopard's Spots (1902) Thomas Dixon

Leibman, Warren, Colonel friend to Christine Cornwell*
The Widow (1957) Francis King

Leicester Don Petro Rica*
Mary known as Leicester, living with her grandfather, Cornelius Corrigan*, see also **Rica**
Roland Cashel (1850) Charles Lever

Leicester, Charles, the Hon. brother to Lord Bellefield*, m. Laura Peyton*
Lewis Arundel (1852) F. E. Smedley

Leicester, Dudley friend to Robert Grimshaw*, m. Pauline Lucas*; goes into a catatonic trance
A Call (1910) Ford Madox Ford

Leicester, Earl of m. Amy Rosbart*
Kenilworth (1821) Walter Scott

Leicester, Thomas illegitimate half-brother to Griffith Gaunt*, who takes his name in order to marry Mercy Vint*
Griffith Gaunt, or Jealousy (1866); *Kate Peyton, or Jealousy* (later, 1873, as *Kate Peyton's Lovers*, play) (1867) Charles Reade

Leigh, Amyas cc, m. Ayacanora
his parents
Frank his brother, victim of the Inquisition
Thomas his uncle
Eustace Thomas's son, papist conspirator
Westward Ho! (1855) Charles Kingsley

Leigh, Aubrey American actor and journalist cc (as observer of the wickedness of the churches), by author who considered herself as equal of Shakespeare*
The Master Christian (1900) Marie Corelli

Leigh, Mrs
Charles her son
Villette (1853) Charlotte Brontë

Leighton, Patricia m. James Calder*
Wickford Point (1939) John P. Marquand

Leila a fairy
Iolanthe opera (1882) W. S. Gilbert and Arthur Sullivan

Leithen, MP cc, narrator
The Power House (1916) John Buchan

Leivers farmer
his wife
Miriam; Edgar; Maurice his children – the former two were modelled on Jessie and Alan Chambers
Sons and Lovers (1913) D. H. Lawrence

Leizer, David dying shopkeeper in obscure Russian town whose soul Anathema (the devil) decides to ruin as revenge for being debarred from heaven: he inherits a fortune, divides it, but is stoned to death because he cannot work miracles
Anathema play (1909) Leonid Andreyev

Lemaitre, Jon, Brother Inquisitor
Saint Joan play (1924) George Bernard Shaw

Lemaitre, Ursin m. Olive Caraze*
Madame Delphine (1881) George Washington Cable

Lemaitre-Vignevielle, Ursin, Captain pirate, then banker
ss 'Madame Delphine'
Old Creole Days (1879) George Washington Cable

Leman, Joseph
Clarissa Harlowe (1748) Samuel Richardson

Lemming, Brother freemason
ss 'In the Interests of the Brethren'†
Debits and Credits (1926) Rudyard Kipling

Lemon, Mrs schoolmistress
Middlemarch (1871–2) George Eliot (rn Mary Anne, later Marian, Evans)

Lemuel tells Macmann that she is dead and that he has taken her place

Molloy (1951); Malone meurt (Malone Dies) (1951) (tr. 1956); L'Innommable (1953) (The Unnamable) (tr. 1958) (trilogy) Samuel Beckett

Lemuel, Minna Jewish actress and revolutionary, loved by Sophia and Frederick Willoughby*
Summer Will Show (1936) Sylvia Townsend Warner

Lena cc, forlorn member of a travelling orchestra
Victory (1915) Joseph Conrad (rn Josef Teodor Konrad Korzeniowski)

Lena study of feeble-mindedness by pupil of William James, without her later affectations of style and manner
ss 'Lena'
Three Lives (1909) Gertrude Stein

Leneham friend to Corley*
ss 'Two Gallants'
Dubliners (1914) James Joyce

Lennox Scottish nobleman
Macbeth play (1623) William Shakespeare

Lennox, Captain m. Edith Shaw*
Henry; Janet his brother and sister
North and South (1855) Mrs Gaskell

Lennox, Lucy, Miss
Agnes her companion
ss 'The Count's Courtship'
The Riddle (1923) Walter de la Mare

Lenoir gambling prince at Rougetnoirburg
his younger brother
The Kickleburys on the Rhine (1850) W. M. Thackeray

Lenox, Dick actor, Kate Ede's* lover and then husband, who 'mutates from degenerate to innocent' as she deteriorates
A Mummer's Wife (1885) George Moore

Lensky, Lydia widow, m. Tom Brangwen*
Anna her daughter, m. Will Brangwen*
The Rainbow (1915) D. H. Lawrence

Lent
Pierce Penilesse his Supplication to the Devil (1592) Thomas Nashe

Lentrohamsinin 'Chief Culprit in the destruction of All the Very Saintly Labours of Ashiata Shiemash'*; he 'had absolutely no Being in regard to . . . information or knowledge which he had acquired'
All and Everything: Beelzebub's Tales to His Grandson (1950) G. I. Gurdjieff

Lentulus

Cataline play (1611) Ben Jonson

Lentulus man surprised at his own originality
The Impressions of Theophrastus Such (1879) George Eliot (rn Mary Anne, later Marian, Evans)

Lenville tragedian in Crummles's theatre company
his wife
Nicholas Nickleby (1839) Charles Dickens

Leo a young boy, who tells David Schearl that the Jews are Christ-killers
Call It Sleep (1934) Henry Roth

Leo, Joseph Mirah Cohen's* music master
Daniel Deronda (1876) George Eliot (rn Mary Anne, later Marian, Evans)

Leon rascally Belgian ex-valet
Huntingtower (1922) John Buchan

Leon, Raphael journalist
Children of the Ghetto (1892) Israel Zangwill

Leonard, Father slick Roman Catholic priest who influences Catherine Gaunt née Peyton* against her husband, Griffith Gaunt*
Griffith Gaunt, or Jealousy (1866) Kate Peyton, or Jealousy (later, 1873, as Kate Peyton's Lovers, play) (1867) Charles Reade

Leonard, Helen with whom Markham Sutherland* falls in love
The Nemesis of Faith (1849) J. A. Froude

Leonard, Mr school principal
Margaret his wife
their children
Look Homeward, Angel (1929) Thomas Wolfe

Leonard, Ruth mistress to Harry Angstrom*
Rabbit, Run (1960) John Updike

Leonardo servant to Bassanio*
The Merchant of Venice play (1623) William Shakespeare

Leonato governor of Messina
Much Ado About Nothing play (1623) William Shakespeare

Leonidas rightful Prince of Sicily
Marriage à la Mode play (1673) John Dryden

Léonie, Aunt to Marcel*
A la recherche du temps perdu (In Search of Lost Time) (1913–27) Marcel Proust

Leonora
Incognita (1692) William Congreve
Leonora a jilt
Joseph Andrews (1742) Henry Fielding
Leonora, Miss cc
ss 'Miss Leonora When Last Seen'
Miss Leonora When Last Seen (1963)
Peter Taylor
Leontes King of Sicilia
Hermione his Queen
A Winter's Tale play (1623) William
Shakespeare
Lepel justice visiting Hawes's* jail
It Is Never Too Late To Mend (1856)
Charles Reade
Lepido courtier
*The Pleasant Commedye of Patient
Grissill* play (1603) Thomas Dekker
Lepidus, Marcus Aemilius triumvir after
death of Julius Caesar*
Julius Caesar play (1623)
Antony and Cleopatra play (1623)
William Shakespeare
Leroy, Walter, Dr cc
Vive Le Roy (1936) Ford Madox Ford
Lescaut, Manon initially fourteen-year-old
amoral cc
Manon Lescaut (1731, rev. 1753) Abbé
Prévost
Leslie, Archie boyhood friend to David
Crawford*
Prester John (1910) John Buchan
Leslie, John cc
Perdita his wife, *née* Murdoch
ss 'Junior'
Unlucky for Pringle (1973) Wyndham
Lewis
Leslie, Kate cc, m. (ritually) General Don
Cipriano Viedma*
The Plumed Serpent (1926) D. H.
Lawrence
Leslie, Mrs poet
The Treasure Seekers (1899) E. Nesbit
Leslie, Mrs widow, close friend to Lady
Vargrave*
Alice (1838) Edward Bulwer Lytton
Leslie, Walter
Deacon Brodie play (1892) W. E. Henley
and Robert Louis Stevenson
Lesly, Ludovic le Balafré of Louis's
Scottish guard
Quentin Durward (1823) Walter Scott
L'Espanay, Mme

Camille her daughter – both murdered
ss 'The Murders in the Rue Morgue'
Prose Tales of Edgar Allen Poe (1843)
Lessways, Hilda m. (1) bigamously,
George Cannon*, (2), Edwin Clay-
hanger*
George son to Hilda and George
The *Clayhanger* series (1910–16) Arnold
Bennett
Lester, Jeeter
Ada his wife
Tom; Lizzie Bell; Clara; Ellie May; Dude
m. Bessie Rice*; **Pearl** m. Lou Bensey* –
some of their children
his mother
Tobacco Road (1932) Erskine Caldwell
Lester, Madeline in love with Aram*
Eugene Aram (1832) Edward Bulwer
Lytton
Lester, Mr m. Emily Hanning*
ss 'To Please his Wife'
Life's Little Ironies (1894) Thomas
Hardy
Lestrade, Inspector of Scotland Yard
A Study in Scarlet† (1887) Arthur Conan
Doyle
L'Estrange, Harley
My Novel (1853) Edward Bulwer Lytton
Lesworth, Gerald English soldier in Ire-
land
The Last September (1929) Elizabeth
Bowen
Letcombe-Bassett
Odtaa (1926) John Masefield
Letheridge, Lionel
ss 'Pish-Tush'
Unlucky for Pringle (1973) Wyndham
Lewis
Letitia girl waiting upon Aurelia*
The Comical Revenge, or Love in a Tub
play (1664) George Etherege
Lettcombe, Henry Branks, OBE
ss 'Aunt Ellen'
Limits and Renewals (1932) Rudyard
Kipling
Leuidulcia wife to Belforest*
*The Atheist's Tragedy, or The Honest
Man's Revenge* play (1611/12) Cyril
Tourneur
Leuknor, Stephen unscrupulous fortune-
hunter
Amelia; Lydia m. Verdley* – his sisters
The Old Bank (1902) William Westall

Levant, Lord impecunious exile
  Captain Legge his son
  The Book of Snobs† (1847) W. M.
  Thackeray
Levellier, Lord uncle and guardian to
  Carinthia and Chillon Kirby*
  The Amazing Marriage (1895) George
  Meredith
Leven, Frank
  Marcella (1894) Mrs Humphry Ward
Leventhal, Asa cc
  Mary his wife
  Max his brother
  Elena Max's wife
  The Victim (1947) Saul Bellow
Leveret, Mrs member of the Lunch Club, a
  ladies' literary discussion group, who
  usually carries her volume of *Appropriate Allusions* in her pocket (but 'Xingu' is
  not in it)
  ss 'Xingu'
  Roman Fever (1911) Edith Wharton
Leverre, Mr m. Marcia Bencombe*
  Henri his son by his first wife
  The Well Beloved (1897) Thomas Hardy
Levi, Isaac 'oriental Jew'
  It Is Never Too Late To Mend (1856)
  Charles Reade
Levi, Peter American student in Paris, cc
  Paolo his father, a lecturer
  Rosamund Brown his mother, harpsichordist
  Hans; Bob his stepfathers
  Millie his aunt
  Birds of America (1971) Mary McCarthy
Levine, Felix Polish seaman who murders
  his wife
  Levine (1956) James Hanley
Levinsky, David cc of much read novel of
  Lower East Side by Russian emigré
  The Rise of David Levinsky (1917)
  Abraham Cahan
Levinsohn solicitor to the Imperial Palace
  Hotel
  Imperial Palace (1930) Arnold Bennett
Levison, Francis, Sir murderer of
  Hallijohn*, m. Alice Challoner*
  his grandmother
  Sir Peter his great-uncle
  East Lynne (1861) Mrs Henry Wood
Levitt, Frank footpad
  Heart of Midlothian (1818) Walter Scott
Levy tried and convicted of murder in

novel in the course of which he never
appears
  About Levy (1933) Arthur Calder
  Marshall
Levy, Baron usurer
  My Novel, or Varieties in English Life
  (1850–3) Edward Bulwer Lytton
Lew, 'Piggy' drummer boy
  ss 'The Drums of the Fore and Aft'
  Wee Willie Winkie (1888) Rudyard Kipling
Lewes, Gregory secretary to Henry
  Challis*
  The Hampdenshire Wonder (1911) J. D.
  Beresford
Lewis Conrad Green's* new secretary
  ss 'A Day With Conrad Green'
  The Collected Short Stories (1941) Ring
  Lardner
Lewis French lord
  The Elder Brother play (1635) John
  Fletcher and Philip Massinger
Lewis, Cliff friend to Jimmy Porter*
  Look Back in Anger play (1956) John
  Osborne
Lewis, Cyfartha miner and boxer
  How Green Was My Valley (1939)
  Richard Llewellyn
Lewis, Dr recipient of most of Matthew
  Bramble's* letters in epistolary novel
  The Expedition of Humphrey Clinker
  (1771) Tobias Smollett
Lewis, John Aneurin librarian
  Jean his wife
  That Uncertain Feeling (1955) Kingsley
  Amis
Lewis, John numbers runner who has fled
  without paying Hubert Cooley* his
  $4,200
  The Hit (1957) Julian Mayfield
Lewis, Morgan St Mawr's* groom
  St Mawr (1925) D. H. Lawrence
Lewis, Rosemary intellectual cc from
  Cumberland
  The Silken Net (1974) Melvyn Bragg
Lewisham, George E. cc, student,
  schoolmaster, m. Ethel Henderson*
  Love and Mr Lewisham (1900) H. G.
  Wells
Lewsome medical assistant
  Martin Chuzzlewit (1844) Charles
  Dickens
Ley, Michael revenge-murderer

ss 'The Hounds of Fate'
The Chronicles of Clovis (1911) Saki (rn Hector Hugh Munro)
Leyburn, Catherine m. Robert Elsmere*
her mother
Robert Elsmere (1888) Mrs Humphry Ward
Leyburn, MP
The Mill on the Floss (1860) George Eliot (rn Mary Anne, later Marian, Evans)
Lheureux draper, usurer
Madame Bovary (1857) Gustave Flaubert
Libbard, Dr
ss 'The Giaconda Smile'
Mortal Coils (1922) Aldous Huxley
Lickcheese rent collector
Widower's Houses play (1892) George Bernard Shaw
Lickfinger master cook
The Staple of News play (1631) Ben Jonson
Lickpan, Robert Endelstow carrier
Joseph his son
A Pair of Blue Eyes (1873) Thomas Hardy
Licquorish, George Frederick editor and proprietor, *Silchester Mirror*
When a Man's Single (1888) J. M. Barrie
Lidia daughter to Charomonte*
The Great Duke of Florence play (1636) James Shirley
Light, Christina m. Prince Casamassima, loved by Roderick Hudson*; after she has separated from the Prince, becomes involved with Hyacinth Robinson* and revolutionaries
Mary her mother, née Savage
Roderick Hudson (1876); *The Princess Casamassima* (1886) Henry James
Light, Reuben shy cc who becomes a positivist preacher of electricity
Revd Hutchins Light his Fundamentalist father
his mother, who is jealous of Ada Fife* because Reuben loves her; rejects God with her dying words; in almost unplayable but readable drama set in Connecticut in late 1920s
Dynamo play (1929) Eugene O'Neill
Lightfoot, Amanda whom Judge Honeywell* is expected to marry, but does not as he wishes to avoid her 'tedious fidelity'

The Romantic Comedians (1926) Ellen Glasgow
Lightfoot, Frederick valet to Lord Clavering*
his wife, formerly Mrs Bonner, Lady Clavering's maid
Pendennis (1848) W. M. Thackeray
Lightfoot, Nance prostitute who becomes Hurtle Duffield's* mistress and inspiration of many paintings
The Vivisector (1970) Patrick White
Lightwood, Mortimer barrister, friend to Eugene Wrayburn
Our Mutual Friend (1865) Charles Dickens
Ligovsky, Mary, Princess loved by Grushnitsky*, loves Pechorin*
Geroi Nas hego Vremeni (A Hero of Our Time) (1841) Mikhail Lermontov
Liliengarten, Countess of (Rosina)
Barry Lyndon (1844) W. M. Thackeray
Lillerton, Miss remarkably inanimate woman, m. Revd Timson*
Sketches by Boz† (1836) Charles Dickens
Lillia Bianca an airy daughter to Nantolet*
The Wild-Goose Chase play (1652) John Fletcher
Lilly copying clerk, member of the Philosopher's Club
Daniel Deronda (1876) George Eliot (rn Mary Anne, later Marian, Evans)
Lilybanks, Grace, Mrs elderly widow
A Suspension of Mercy (1965) Patricia Highsmith
Lilycraft, Lady widowed sister of Squire Bracebridge*
Bracebridge Hall (1823) Washington Irving
Lilyvick uncle to the Kenwigs*
Nicholas Nickleby (1839) Charles Dickens
Limber friend to Hoard*
A Trick to Catch the Old One comedy (1608) Thomas Middleton
Limberham impotent masochist based on the Earl of Shaftesbury
The Kind Keeper, or Mr Limberham play (1680) John Dryden (?and King Charles II)
Limmason, Austin, Lieutenant
ss 'The Man Who Was'
Life's Handicap (1891) Rudyard Kipling
Limp shoemaker

Middlemarch (1871–2) George Eliot (rn Mary Anne, later Marian, Evans)

Lin Yi noted brigand
The Wallet of Kai Lung (1900) Ernest Bramah (rn Ernest Bramah Smith)

Lincoln half-brother to Ostrog*
When the Sleeper Wakes (1899) H. G. Wells

Lincoln noble at the court of England
Old Fortunatus play (1600) Thomas Dekker

Lincoln, Abraham (hist.) as young attorney, in novel based on the future president's successful defence of Duff Armstrong on a murder charge
The Graysons (1887) Edward Eggleston

Lincoln, Abraham (hist.) mad portrait of the President, by proto-fascist, as really a 'southerner'
The Southerner (1913) Thomas Dixon

Lincoln, Lionel cc of complex romance of revolutionary Boston; m. Cecil Dynever*
Sir Lionel Lincoln ('Ralph') his father, who fails to persuade his son of the justice of the rebel cause
Lionel Lincoln (1825) James Fenimore Cooper

Lindau German socialist on staff of March's* magazine
A Hazard of New Fortunes (1890) William Dean Howells

Lindkvist kindly scourge of Elis Heyst*, creditor of his family, who finally shows mercy, because once Elis's father was kind to him: 'Everything comes back'; in atypical play
Påsk (*Easter*) play (1901) August Strindberg

Lindley narrator of Poe*-like tale
ss 'The Diamond Lens' (1858)
Poems and Stories (1881) Fitz-James O'Brien

Lindley, Ernest, Revd
his wife
Mary m. Edward Massey; **Louisa** m. Alfred Durant – their daughters
ss 'Daughters of the Vicar'
The Prussian Officer (1914) D. H. Lawrence

Lindores, Lord tyrannical father
Lady Caroline ('Car') cc, forced to m. Pat Torrance*, m. (2) Edward Beaufort*
Edith her sister

Lord Rintoul her brother, murderer of Pat Torrance
The Ladies Lindores† (1883) Mrs Margaret Oliphant

Lindsey, John, Chief Inspector
Robert's Wife play (1937) St John Ervine

Lindstrum, Carl neighbour to the Bergsons and companion to Alexandra Bergson*
O Pioneers! (1913) Willa Cather

Ling
The Wallet of Kai Lung (1900) Ernest Bramah (rn Ernest Bramah Smith)

Lingard, Lina fashionable dressmaker
My Antonia (1918) Willa Cather

Lingard, Tom 'Rajah-laut', based on an adventurer and shipowner, William Lingard (d.1896) known to the author; and, later, as 'King Tom' of the brig *Lightning*
Almayer's Folly (1895); *The Rescue* (1920) Joseph Conrad (rn Josef Teodor Konrad Korzeniowski)

Linghnam, Mr
ss 'The Vortex'
A Diversity of Creatures (1917) Rudyard Kipling

Lingon, John, Revd Rector of Little Treby, brother to Arabella Transome*
Felix Holt (1866) George Eliot (rn Mary Anne, later Marian, Evans)

Linklater, Laurie yeoman of the King's Kitchen
The Fortunes of Nigel (1822) Walter Scott

Linlithgow, Countess of (Penelope) aunt to Lady Eustace
The Eustace Diamonds (1873) Anthony Trollope

Linnet, Mrs widow
Mary; Rebecca her daughters
ss 'Janet's Repentance'
Scenes of Clerical Life (1857) George Eliot (rn Mary Anne, later Marian, Evans)

Linton assistant to Pestler*, apothecary
Vanity Fair (1847–8) W. M. Thackeray

Linton, Edgar cc, m. Catherine Earnshaw*
Cathie their daughter, m. (1) Linton Heathcliff, (2) Hareton Earnshaw
Isabella his sister, m. Heathcliff*
Wuthering Heights (1847) Emily Brontë

Linton, Tom murderer
Roland Cashel (1850) Charles Lever

Lionel in love with Clarissa Flowerdale*
Lionel and Clarissa play (1768) Isaac Bickerstaffe

Lipscombe, Henry m. Mabel Blitch*
The Custom of the Country (1913) Edith Wharton

Lirazel m. Alveric
Orion their son
The King of Elfland's Daughter (1924) Lord Dunsany

Lirriper Family, The
Mrs Lirriper's Lodgings (1863) Charles Dickens

Lisa, Monna deaf old lady
Romola (1863) George Eliot (rn Mary Anne, later Marian, Evans)

Lismahago, Obidiah, Lieutenant fantastic Scottish soldier m. (1) an Indian virago, (2) Tabitha Bramble*
The Expedition of Humphrey Clinker (1771) Tobias Smollett

Lispeth hill girl betrayed by missionaries ss 'Lispeth'
Plain Tales from the Hills (1888) Rudyard Kipling

Liss, Roger Hope Ollerton's fiancé
Let the People Sing (1939) J. B. Priestley

List, Isaac Jowl's* gambling friend
The Old Curiosity Shop (1841) Charles Dickens

Listless, The Hon. Mr fop, college friend to Glowry*, a caricature of Sir Lumley St George Skeffington, a debt-ridden dramatist (1771–1850)
Nightmare Abbey (1818) Thomas Love Peacock

Literary Ladies, The Two names adopted by the Misses Codger and Toppit when they interviewed Elijah Pogram*
Martin Chuzzlewit (1844) Charles Dickens

Lithebe, Mrs Stephen Kumalo's* landlady
Cry, the Beloved Country (1948) Alan Paton

Lithenthal, Lotte second-rate actress run to fat, first lady of the Reich, modelled on Eva Braun, surrounded by 'the people's love'
Mephisto (1936) Klaus Mann

Littimer Steerforth's* servant
David Copperfield (1850) Charles Dickens

Little Billie see Bagot, William

Little Nell see Trent, Nellie

Little, Chicken boy drowned by Sula May Peace* in an accident
Sula (1974) Toni Morrison

Little, Henry workman and inventor cc; novel attacks the union practice of 'rattening', i.e. enforced membership; m. Grace Garden*
Joseph their son
James his father m. Edith Raby*
Put Yourself in his Place (1870) Charles Reade

Little, Midge warm-hearted woman
Archie husband who deserted her
David their son, journalist, m. Cressida MacPhail*
The Wedding Group (1968) Elizabeth Taylor

Little-Endians protestants
Gulliver's Travels (1726) Jonathan Swift

Littlefield, Howard, Dr
Eunice his daughter, m. Ted Babbitt
Babbitt (1923) Sinclair Lewis

Littlejohn, Eddy, Captain (Ginger) in love with Nina Blount*
Vile Bodies (1930) Evelyn Waugh

Littlewit, John a proctor
Win-the-Fight his wife
Bartholomew Fair play (1631) Ben Jonson

Liversedge, Sinnamenta m. by gipsy rites, secretly, Sir Massingberd Heath*
Rachel her mother
Lost Sir Massingberd (1864) James Payn

Livesey, Dr
Treasure Island (1883) Robert Louis Stevenson

Livia Fabritio's* daughter, who plots most of the evil
Women Beware Women play (1657) Thomas Middleton

Livingstone, Guy cc in muscular Christian novel; the author was a schoolfellow of Thomas Hughes*
Guy Livingstone, or *Thorough* (1857) George Alfred Lawrence

Livingstone, John sailor, 'judicious Christian
Heart of Midlothian (1818) Walter Scott

Liza the Darlings' maid
Peter Pan play (1904) J. M. Barrie

Llewellyn, Mary m. Martin Hallam
The Well of Loneliness (1928) Radclyffe

Hall
Lloyd, Dr Fenwick's* rival; disciple of
Mesmer
A Strange Story (1862, rev. 1863) Edward Bulwer Lytton
Lloyd, Mr apothecary called in to attend
Jane Eyre*
Jane Eyre (1847) Charlotte Brontë
Lloyd, Teddy art teacher
The Prime of Miss Jean Brodie (1961)
Muriel Spark
Llywarch, Blethyn m. Ceridwen Morgan*
How Green Was My Valley (1939)
Richard Llewellyn
Loadstone, Lady the Magnetic Lady
The Magnetic Lady, or *Humours Reconciled* play (1641) Ben Jonson
Loam, Earl of (Henry) (family name
Lazenby)
**Lady Mary; Lady Catherine; Lady
Agatha** his daughters
The Admirable Crichton play (1902)
J. M. Barrie
Lobbs, 'Old' saddler
Maria his pretty daughter
The Pickwick Papers (1837) Charles
Dickens
Lobe, Mr Albert Schearl's* boss, who
sacks him because he tried to brain him
with a hammer
Call It Sleep (1934) Henry Roth
Lobkins, Margery ('Piggy Lob') hostess of
the Mug
Paul Clifford (1830) Edward Bulwer
Lytton
Lobley servant to Tartar*
Edwin Drood (1870) Charles Dickens
Lobskini, Signor singing-master
Sketches by Boz† (1836) Charles Dickens
Locke, Alton Chartist hero who sweeps
through London sweatshops in novel
which earned its author the title of 'the
Chartist clergyman'
Alton Locke Tailor and Poet (1850)
Charles Kingsley
Locke, Townsend P. paper manufacturer
Midnight Cowboy (1966) James Leo
Herlihy
Lockert, Clyde admirer of Fran
Dodsworth*
Dodsworth (1929) Sinclair Lewis
Lockhart, Jamie cc, rapist, bandit,
merchant; m. Rosamund Musgrove*

(whom he raped)
The Robber Bridegroom (1942) Eudora
Welty
Lockhart, Keith, Sub-Lieutenant, later
Lieutenant-Commander, *Compass Rose,*
later *Saltash,* in love with Julie
Hallam*
The Cruel Sea (1951) Nicholas
Monsarrat
Lockit
Lucy his daughter
The Beggar's Opera opera (1728) John
Gay
Locksley ('Diccon bend the Bow') leader of
outlaws
Ivanhoe (1820) Walter Scott
Lockwood Heathcliff's* tenant, narrator
Wuthering Heights (1847) Emily Brontë
Lockwood porter at Castlewood
Esmond; John; Molly his children
Henry Esmond† (1852) W. M.
Thackeray
Locrine eldest son of King Brutus* of
Britain
Locrine play (1595) 'W. S.' (?George
Peele; ?Robert Green)
Loder narrator
ss 'The Cigarette Case'
Widdershins (1911) Oliver Onions
Loder, John impersonator of John
Chilcote*
John Chilcote, MP (1904) Katherine C.
Thurstone
Loder, Major gambler, scoundrel
Vanity Fair† (1847–8) W. M. Thackeray
Lodge, Farmer
Gertrude his wife
ss 'The Withered Arm'
Wessex Tales (1888) Thomas Hardy
Lodovico, Count banished nobleman
The White Devil play (1612) John
Webster
Loftie pathologist
ss 'Unprofessional'
Limits and Renewals (1932) Rudyard
Kipling
Loftis, Milton unsuccessful lawyer
Helen his bitter wife
Maudie their crippled daughter, now
deceased
Lie Down in Darkness (1951) William
Styron
Logan, 'Piggy' owner of puppet-theatre

You Can't Go Home Again (1940) Thomas Wolfe

Logan, Arabella, Mrs 'housekeeper' to George Colwan, Laird of Dalcastle*
The Private Memoirs and Confessions of a Justified Sinner (1824) as *The Suicide's Grave* (1828) as *Confessions of a Fanatic* in *Tales and Sketches* (1837) James Hogg

Loggerheads, Louise, Mrs landlady at the Dragon
Clayhanger (1910) Arnold Bennett

Loggins amateur actor under the name of Beverley, played Macbeth*
Sketches by Boz† (1836) Charles Dickens

Logic, Bob merry prankster
Life in London, or The Day and Night Scenes of Jerry Hawthorne Esq., and his Elegant Friend, Corinthian Tom, Accompanied by Bob Logic, the Oxonian, in Their Rambles and Sprees Through the Metropolis (1821); *Finish to the Adventures of Tom, Jerry and Logic in Their Pursuits Through Life In and Out of London* (1828) Pierce Egan

Logie, Maggie 'poor, simple but well thought of widow body'
ss 'Maggie Logie and the National Health'
The Dying Stallion (1967) Fred Urquhart

Loker, Tom friend to Haley*
Uncle Tom's Cabin (1851) Harriet Beecher Stowe

Loll, Chowder m. Julia Jowler
The Adventures of Major Gahagan (1839) W. M. Thackeray

Loll, Jewab Indian servant to Joseph Sedley*
Vanity Fair (1847–8) W. M. Thackeray

Loll, Mahommed General of cavalry
The Adventures of Major Gahagan (1839) W. M. Thackeray

Lollio Alibius's* man
The Changeling play (1653) Thomas Middleton and William Rowley

Lollipop, Lord younger son to the Marquis of Sillabub*
The Book of Snobs (1847) W. M. Thackeray

Lollo conjuror's assistant
Romola (1862) George Eliot (rn Mary Anne, later Marian, Evans)

Loman, James, RA

ss 'The Puzzler'
Actions and Reactions (1909) Rudyard Kipling

Loman, Willy unsuccessful salesman
Linda his wife
Ben his brother
Biff; Happy his sons
Death of a Salesman play (1949) Arthur Miller

Lomax, Charles
Major Barbara play (1905) George Bernard Shaw

Lombard, Lady (Sarah) *nouveau riche*
Lewis Arundel (1852) F. E. Smedley

Lone Sahib
ss 'The Sending of Dana Da'
Soldiers Three (1888) Rudyard Kipling

Lone, Lorn Creetur see **Gummidge**

Long Ears, the Hon. and Revd member of the Association
The Mudfog Papers (1838) Charles Dickens

Long Jack one of the crew of the *We're Here*
Captains Courageous (1897) Rudyard Kipling

Long, Adrian, Captain friend to Colonel Aubrac*
The Other Side (1946) Storm Jameson

Long, Gilbert who appears to be drawing vitality from, and driving mad, May Server*
The Sacred Fount (1901) Henry James

Long, Mrs neighbour to Mrs Bennett*
her two nieces
Pride and Prejudice (1913) Jane Austen

Long, Revd Mr rector, tutor
Lost Sir Massingberd (1864) James Payn

Long, Thomas, Sir
The Roaring Girl play (1611) Thomas Middleton and Thomas Dekker

Long-Legged Young Man, The robbed David Copperfield* of his trunk
David Copperfield (1850) Charles Dickens

Longaville French noble at the court of England
Old Fortunatus play (1600) Thomas Dekker

Longaville lord attendant to Ferdinand*
Love's Labour's Lost play (1623) William Shakespeare

Longden see **Brookenham, Nanda**

Longer, Esdras B.
ss The Lang Men o' Larut'
Life's Handicap (1891) Rudyard Kipling
Longstaffe, Pomona, Lady widow
Adolphus ('Dolly'); **Sophia** m. George
Whitstable*; **Georgiana** m. Revd Mr
Batherbolt*, curate her children
The Way We Live Now (1875) Anthony
Trollope
Longfellow, Anatole murderer of
Pettijohn*
Nigger Heaven (1926) Carl Van Vechten
Longford, Edmund student, nursed by
Milly Tetterby*, who knew him only
under the name of Denham
The Haunted Man (1848) Charles
Dickens
Longman bailiff
Pamela (1740) Samuel Richardson
Longstaff, Elsie member of the Dinky
Doos, m. Herbert Dulver*
Effie her sister
The Good Companions (1939) J. B.
Priestley
Longtree, Esther voluptuous waitress
Miss MacIntosh, My Darling (1965)
Marguerite Young
Longueville, Thomas de 'The Red Rover'
The Fair Maid of Perth (1828) Walter
Scott
Longways, Solomon old man in the
employ of Henchard*
The Mayor of Casterbridge (1886)
Thomas Hardy
Lonigan, William 'Studs' young tough cc
of famous American trilogy
Young Lonigan (1932); *The Young Man-
hood of Studs Lonigan* (1934); *Judge-
ment Day* (1935) James T. Farrell
Lonnergan, Lovetin suitor to Miss Betsy
Shannon*
Mr Facey Romford's Hounds (1865)
R. S. Surtees
Lonoff, E. I. great writer
The Ghost Writer (1979) Philip Roth
Loomis, Maybelle
Adore her eight-year-old son; stamped to
death by Homer Simpson*
The Day of the Locust (1939) Nathanael
West (rn Nathan Weinstein)
Loop Garou Kid cc, shaman-hero of
mock-cowboy-saga
Yellow Back Radio Broke Down (1969)

Ishmael Reed
Lopez
The Duenna play (1775) Richard
Brinsley Sheridan
Lopez
The Power and the Glory (1940) Graham
Greene
Lopez a curate (from the subplot in which
he figures the play gets its title)
The Spanish Curate play (1647) John
Fletcher and Philip Massinger
Lopez, Andres
For Whom the Bell Tolls (1940) Ernest
Hemingway
Lord, Cuthbert
his wife
Beatrice their daughter, m. Vincent
FitzClare*
C (1924) Maurice Baring
Lord, Stephen a retailer of pianos
Nancy his daughter, cc, m. Lionel
Tarrant*
Horace his weak son, m. Fanny French*
In the Year of Jubilee (1894) George
Gissing
Lorenheim vacuum-cleaner tout and Com-
stock's* fellow lodger
Keep the Aspidistra Flying (1936) George
Orwell (rn Eric Blair)
Lorenzo
The Merchant of Venice play (1623)
William Shakespeare
Lorenzo
The Spanish Tragedy play (1592)
Thomas Kyd
Lorenzo, Aldonza ('Dulcinea del Toboso')
*El ingenioso hidalgo Don Quijote de la
Mancha* (1605–15) Miguel de Cervantes
Lorenzo, Tomaso, Sir court painter, Crim
Tartary
The Rose and the Ring (1855) W. M.
Thackeray
L'Orge, Chevalier de
ss 'The Amours of Mr Deuceace'
The Yellowplush Papers (1852) W. M.
Thackeray
Lorimer, Rose, Dr historian
Anglo-Saxon Attitudes (1956) Angus
Wilson
Lorraine, Felix, Mrs
Vivian Grey (1827) Benjamin Disraeli
Lorraine, Hilary cc, reforming scoundrel
Alice his sister, who saves the family

honour; in romance which, it has been implied, may have influenced Hardy's *The Trumpet Major**; by author of *Lorna Doone**
Alice Lorraine (1875) R. D. Blackmore

Lorrequer, Harry cc and narrator, m. Lady Jane Callonby*
Sir Guy his uncle
Guy Sir Guy's son
Harry Lorrequer (1839) Charles Lever

Lorridaile, Constantia, Lady sister to Lord Dorincourt*, great-aunt to Lord Fauntleroy*
Sir Henry her husband
Little Lord Fauntleroy (1886) Frances Hodgson Burnett

Lorry, Jarvis confidential clerk in Tellson's* bank
A Tale of Two Cities (1859) Charles Dickens

Lorton, Augustus, Lord
Lady Windermere's Fan play (1892) Oscar Wilde

Lory servant to Young Fashion*
The Relapse, or *Virtue in Danger* play (1697) John Vanbrugh

Losberne, Mr surgeon
Oliver Twist (1839) Charles Dickens

Lossell, Elias blind, beautiful, helpless, half-idiotic cc of Dutch – but written in English – novel about sordid greed and its consequences
Hendryk; Hubert his treacherous half-brothers
God's Fool: A Koopstad Story (1892) Maarten Maartens (rn Joost van der Poorten-Schwartz)

Losson, Private
ss 'In the Matter of a Private'
Soldiers Three (1888) Rudyard Kipling

Lothair, Lord cc, m. Lady Corisande
Lothair (1870) Benjamin Disraeli

Lotus concubine to Wang Lung*
The Good Earth (1931); *Sons* (1932); *A House Divided* (1935) Pearl Buck

Loudon London factor of Quentin Kennedy's* estate
Huntingtower (1922) John Buchan

Louella
Mae her sister in 'undignified' Indiana idiom which made the author a famous humourist onwards from
Fables in Slang (1899) George Ade

Louis becomes a wealthy man, one of the characters whose interior monologue* makes up this novel
The Waves (1931) Virginia Woolf

Louis sailor on *Ghost*
The Sea Wolf (1904) Jack London

Louis XI King of France
King Henry VI plays (1623) William Shakespeare

Louit, Ernest sometime student, managing director of the House of Bando, which is designed to cure impotence
Watt (1953) Samuel Beckett

Louka servant
Arms and the Man (1894) George Bernard Shaw

Lousse woman who owns a dog which Malloy* runs over
Molloy (1951); *Malone meurt* (*Malone Dies*) (1951) (tr. 1956); *L'Innommable* (1953) (*The Unnamable*) (tr. 1958) (trilogy) Samuel Beckett

Love, Mary Black librarian in novel of Harlem life
Nigger Heaven (1926) Carl Van Vechten

Love, Tyrone Black friend to Harry Goldfarb*
Requiem for a Dream (1978) Hubert J. Selby

Loveday, John cc
Robert his brother, m. Anne Garland*
their father, miller, m. (2) Martha Garland*
The Trumpet Major (1880) Thomas Hardy

Loveday, Tom
Toddler on the Run (1964) Shena Mackay

Lovegood, manager to Sir James Chettam*
Middlemarch (1871–2) George Eliot (rn Mary Anne, later Marian, Evans)

Lovegrove, Wally drowned boy
Coming Up For Air (1936) George Orwell (rn Eric Blair)

Lovejoy, Mabel betrayed by Hilary Lorraine*, but all is finally well
Alice Lorraine (1875) R. D. Blackmore

Lovel a complete gentleman, but a melancholy guest at the inn
The New Inn, or *The Light Heart* play (1629) Ben Jonson

Lovel, Adolphus Frederick (Fred)
Cecilia his first wife, *née* Baker

Elizabeth his second wife, *née* Prior (**Bessie Bellenden,** actress)

Emma his mother, m. (2) Revd Mr Bonnington*

Frederick Popham; Cissy children to Lovel and Cecilia

Lovel the Widower† (1860) W. M. Thackeray

Lovel, Mr 'youth of genteel appearance', actually Lord William Geraldin, m. Isabella Wardour* (see **Glenallan**)

The Antiquary (1816) Walter Scott

Lovelace Dean of Brotherton

Mary his daughter, m. Lord George Germain*

Is He Popenjoy? (1878) Anthony Trollope

Lovelace, Robert aristocratic young rake whose attempts to seduce Clarissa Harlowe* are described in immensely long classic epistolary novel*; eventually killed in duel with Colonel Morden*

Clarissa (1748) Samuel Richardson

Loveless

Amanda his wife

A Trip to Scarborough play (1777) Richard Brinsley Sheridan

Loveless husband to Amanda*

The Relapse, or *Virtue in Danger* play (1697) John Vanbrugh

Lovell, Charlotte cousin to Delia Ralston*

Tina (called **Tina Ralston**) her illegitimate daughter by Clem Spender*

ss 'The Old Maid'

Old New York (1924) Edith Wharton

Lovell, Chips nephew to Lord Sleaford*, m. Patricia Tolland*

A Question of Upbringing† (1951) Anthony Powell

Lovell, Margaret widow, m. Sir William Blancove*

Rhoda Fleming (1865) George Meredith

Lovell, Sinfi gipsy girl

Panuel her father

Aylwin (1899) Theodore Watts Dunton

Lovell, Thomas, Sir

King Henry VIII play (1623) William Shakespeare and John Fletcher

Lovely, Anne in love with Fainall*

A Bold Stroke for a Wife play (1718) Susannah Centlivre

Lovemore, Charles, Sir narrator: Rivella 'was proud of having more courage than had any of our sex, and of throwing the first stone, which might give a hint for other persons of more capacity to examine the defects and vices of some men who took a delight to impose upon the world, by the pretense of public good, whilst their true design was only to gratify and advance themselves'

The Adventures of Rivella, or *The History of the Author of the Atlantis* (1714) Mrs Delarivière Manley (Also known as Mary Manley)

Loverule, Lord

Lady Arabella his wife

A Journey to London play (1728) John Vanbrugh

Lovetown, Mr and Mrs newly m. couple

Is She His Wife? (1837) Charles Dickens

Lovewell clerk to Stirling, secretly married to Fanny*

The Clandestine Marriage comedy (1766) George Colman the Elder and David Garrick

Lovewell page to Lady Brute*

The Provok'd Wife play (1697) John Vanbrugh

Lovey, Mary

Mrs Wiggs of the Cabbage Patch† (1901) Alice Hegen Rice

Lovick, Mrs guardian of Clarissa Harlowe* while she is in captivity

Clarissa Harlowe (1748) Samuel Richardson

Lovingwood, Sut rough mountaineer in popular comic Tennessee sketches

Sut Lovingwood Yarns (1867) George Washington Harris

Lovis son to Lord Bevill*, friend to Colonel Bruce*

The Comical Revenge, or *Love in a Tub* play (1664) George Etherege

Low, Mr barrister

his wife

Phineas Finn† (1869) Anthony Trollope

Lowborough, Lord m. Annabella Wilmot*

The Tenant of Wildfell Hall (1848) Anne Brontë

Lowder, Mrs aunt to Kate Croy*

The Wings of a Dove (1902) Henry James

Lowe, Moses usurer and banker

Solomon his son and partner

Solomon's wife

Emma; Minna Solomon's pretty daughters
The Fitz-Boodle Papers (1852) W. M. Thackeray

Lowestoffe, Reginald young Templar
The Fortunes of Nigel (1822) Walter Scott

Lowfield, Miss smitten with Mr Caveton
Sketches of Young Gentlemen (1838) Charles Dickens

Lowme elderly aristocrat
his wife
Robert their son
their daughters
ss 'Janet's Repentance'
Scenes of Clerical Life (1857) George Eliot (rn Mary Anne, later Marian, Evans)

Lowndes of the Indian Civil Service
ss 'At the End of the Passage'
Life's Handicap (1891) Rudyard Kipling

Lowndes, George master of words from whom HERmione* flees; portrait of Ezra Pound*, with whom the author had been in love
HERmione (1981) H. D. (rn Hilda Doolittle)

Lownie, Janet née Ogilvy
Margaret her daughter, m. Gavin Birse
A Window in Thrums (1889) J. M. Barrie

Lowten Mr Perker's* clerk, puffy-faced young man
The Pickwick Papers (1837) Charles Dickens

Lowther, Gordon music teacher
The Prime of Miss Jean Brodie (1961) Muriel Spark

Lowton, Jack law student
Pendennis (1848) W. M. Thackeray

Loyal Devasseur, Mr landlord of the inn
ss 'Our French Watering Place'
Reprinted Pieces (1858) Charles Dickens

Luba Russian émigrée
The Thinking Reed (1936) Rebecca West (rn Cecily Fairfield)

Lubin, Henry Hopkins caricature of Herbert Asquith, deposed prime minister who played bridge
Back to Methuselah play (1921) George Bernard Shaw

Luca, Fra (Bernardino di Bardi) monk, brother to Romola*
Romola (1863) George Eliot (rn Mary Anne, later Marian, Evans)

Lucas *picador* who wins Carmen's" heart
Carmen (1847) Prosper Merimée

Lucas, George
Martha his wife; both inmates of home for aged
The Poorhouse Fair (1959) John Updike

Lucas, Jean m. Bruce Wetheral*
Campbell's Kingdom (1952) Hammond Innes

Lucas, Pauline in love with Robert Grimshaw*; m. Dudley Leicester*
A Call (1910) Ford Madox Ford

Lucas, Solomon Eatanswill fancy dress dealer
The Pickwick Papers (1837) Charles Dickens

Lucas, William, Sir feels his knighthood a little too strongly, formerly in trade
Lady Lucas his wife, a very good sort of woman
Charlotte, plain but sensible, m. Mr Collins*, whom she manages well; **Marie** their daughters
Pride and Prejudice (1813) Jane Austen

Lucas-Dockery, Wilfred, Sir governor of Egdon Heath prison
Decline and Fall (1928) Evelyn Waugh

Lucass, Ernest tycoon, the greatest man from Tyneside, one-time rival to Alan Frith-Walter*
his 'hag' wife
Accident (1928) Arnold Bennett

Luce the Newcomes'* solicitor
The Newcomes (1853–5) W. M. Thackeray

Lucentio Vincentio's* son
The Taming of the Shrew play (1623) William Shakespeare

Lucero horse tamer
The Purple Land (1885) W. H. Hudson

Lucero, Father miser, defrocked priest
Death Comes for the Archbishop (1927) Willa Cather

Lucetta servant to Julia*
Two Gentlemen of Verona play (1623) William Shakespeare

Luciana sister to Adriana*
A Comedy of Errors play (1623) William Shakespeare

Lucifer
Doctor Faustus play (1604) Christopher Marlowe

Lucifer, High and Mighty Prince of Darkness Donzel del, King of Acheron . . . , His Hellhood
Pierce Penilesse his Supplication to the Devil (1592) Thomas Nashe
Lucilla
Euphues (1578–80) John Lyly
Lucina wife to Maximus*
Valentinian play (1647) John Fletcher
Lucio a fantastick
Measure for Measure play (1623) William Shakespeare
Lucius a lord
Timon of Athens play (1623) William Shakespeare
Lucius Septimius
Caesar and Cleopatra play (1900) George Bernard Shaw
Lucius Sergius uncle to Valens*
ss 'The Church that was at Antioch'
Limits and Renewals (1932) Rudyard Kipling
Lucius son to Titus Andronicus*
Young Lucius son to Lucius
Titus Andronicus play (1623) William Shakespeare
Luckett, Worth founder of pioneer family which goes from Ohio to Pennsylvania, traced in an American trilogy
The Trees (1940); *The Fields* (1946); *The Town* (1950) Conrad Richter
Lucky
Waiting for Godot play (1952) Samuel Beckett
Lucora the obstinate lady of the title; she swears chastity and can only be won when Carionil* disguises himself as a Negro
The Obstinate Lady (1657) Aston Cokayne
Lucre uncle to Witgood*
Mistress Lucre his wife
Freedom their son
A Trick to Catch the Old One play (1608) Thomas Middleton
Lucullus a lord
Timon of Athens play (1623) William Shakespeare
Lucy crippled for life in an accident
ss 'Ding Dong'†
More Pricks That Kicks (1934) Samuel Beckett
Lucy maid to Beatrix Esmond*

Henry Esmond (1852) W. M. Thackeray
Lucy maid to Lydia Languish*
The Rivals play (1775) Richard Brinsley Sheridan
Lucy servant to Millwood*, who answers her murderous mistress's question, 'How do I look today' with, 'Oh, killingly, madam! A little more red and you'll be irresistible'*
The London Merchant, or *The History of George Barnwell* play (1731) George Lillo
Lucy, Mrs a wench kept by Sir Frederick Frolick*
The Comical Revenge, or *Love in a Tub* play (1664) George Etherege
Ludlow, Johnny narrator cc of episodes reminiscent of the author's childhood in rural Worcester, regarded as by far her best (but now neglected) work
The Johnny Ludlow series (1874–89) Mrs Henry Wood
Ludovico servant and friend to Emily St Aubert*
The Mysteries of Udolpho (1794) Mrs Ann Radcliffe
Ludwig of Hombourg, Sir old Crusader
A Legend of the Rhine (1845) W. M. Thackeray
Lueli Mr Fortune's* only convert
his mother
Mr Fortune's Maggot (1927) Sylvia Townsend Warner
Luff draper, Grimsworth
Brother Jacob (1864) George Eliot (rn Mary Anne, later Marian, Evans)
Luffey redoubtable batsman
The Pickwick Papers (1837) Charles Dickens
Lufford, Charles friend to Joe Lampton*
Room at the Top (1957) John Braine
Lufton, Lady patroness to Mark Robarts*
Lord Lufton (Ludovic) her son, m. Lucy Robarts; **Justina; Lady Meredith** her children
Framley Parsonage (1861) Anthony Trollope
Lugier rough and confident tutor to Ladies, and the chief engine to entrap Mirabel*, the wild goose
The Wild-Goose Chase play (1652) John Fletcher
Lugné-Poe, Aurélian (hist.: eminent

French theatrical director) cc: 'Since it had been forbidden him, M. Lugné-Poe has respectfully abstained from making any reply, recrimination or protest against the edict of the Metropolitan Church of Art of Jesus Leader [founded solely by the author, who was its only member]. We would like to believe, although We derive little pleasure from it, that despite his lack of sincerity, the surveillance placed on him by the Church will cause him to mend his ways and abandon the spirit of perversity which is all-powerful in his soul, and cease to glorify evil, of which he is a devoted follower, By Order of the Office of Definitor'
Act of Clemency (1893) Erik Satie

Luhzin an offensive 'solid' lawyer
Prestuplenie i Nakazanie (Crime and Punishment) (1866) Fyodor Dostoievsky

Luis son of the Marquis de Telleria, religious fanatic
La Familia de Léon Roch (1878) Benito Peréz Galdós

Luiz rightful King of Barataria, attendant on the Duke of Plaza Toro*; m. Casilda*
The Gondoliers opera (1889) W. S. Gilbert and Arthur Sullivan

Lujon, Manuel wealthy Mexican ranch owner
Death Comes for the Archbishop (1927) Willa Cather

Luke i.e. Matthew Arnold
The New Republic, or Culture, Faith and Philosophy in an English Country House (1877; edition by John Lucas, 1975, lists originals of characters) William Hurrell Mallock

Luke, Walter
The Masters (1951) C. P. Snow

Luker, Septimus dealer in antiques
The Moonstone (1868) Wilkie Collins

Lukoszaite, Ona frail girl who m. Julius Rudkus* and shares his anguish as meatpacker, thief, robber – and eventually his joy in socialism
The Jungle (1906) Upton Sinclair

Lulu 1. totally amoral embodiment of feminine sexuality in German comi-tragedies which were made into an opera by Alban Berg 2. murderess and white provoker of black men

1. *Erdgeist (Earth Spirit)* play (1895)
Die Büchse der Pandora (Pandora's Box) play (1904) Frank Wedekind
2. *Dutchman* one act play (1964) Amiri Baraka (formerly LeRoi Jones)

Lumbey, Dr Mrs Kenwigs'* medical man
Nicholas Nickleby (1839) Charles Dickens

Lumkin, Dean academic type, at Convers College
Love and Friendship (1962) Alison Lurie

Lumley, Andrew art collector, friend to Charles Pitt-Heron*
The Power House (1916) John Buchan

Lumley, Captain, R. N. friend to Alfred Campbell*
The Settlers in Canada (1844) Captain Marryat

Lumley, Charles cc
Hurry On Down (1953) John Wain

Lummy Ned musical guard of the Light Salisbury coach
Martin Chuzzlewit (1844) Charles Dickens

Lumpkin, Tony Dorothy Hardcastle's son by her first marriage
She Stoops to Conquer play (1773) Oliver Goldsmith

Luna, Adeline, Mrs Olive Chancellor's* affected widowed sister
The Bostonians (1886) Henry James

Lundie, Lord law lord
ss 'The Puzzler'†
Actions and Reactions (1909) Rudyard Kipling

Lundie, Patrick, Sir champion and eventually husband of Anne Silvester*
Blanche his daughter, Anne's pupil, m. Arnold Brinkworth*
Man and Wife (1870) Wilkie Collins

Lundin, Louis, Sir town clerk of Perth
The Fair Maid of Perth (1828) Walter Scott

Lundin, Luke, Dr chamberlain to the Lady of Lochleven*
The Abbot (1820) Walter Scott

Lung, Wang Chinese peasant who becomes rich landowner
O'Lan his wife, ex-kitchen slave
their children, who in time decline
The Good Earth (1931); *Sons* (1932); *A House Divided* (1935) Pearl Buck

Lunken, Bertha German art student,

Tarr's* girl
Tarr (1918) Wyndham Lewis
Lunn, Joe cc
Scenes from Provincial Life (1950); *Scenes from Married Life* (1961) William Cooper (rn Harry Summerfield Hoff)
Lunsby, Bob butcher
Silas Marner (1861) George Eliot (rn Mary Anne, later Marian, Evans)
Lupin, Mrs landlady of the Blue Dragon, m. Mark Tapley*
Martin Chuzzlewit (1844) Charles Dickens
Lureo a poor scholar, son to Furio*
The Pleasant Commedye of Patient Grissill play (1603) Thomas Dekker
Lurgan Sahib jewel dealer based on A. M. Jacob, a china dealer in Bombay who had been a child slave, and who was a friend to Madame Blavatsky
Kim (1901) Rudyard Kipling
Luria, Alec who when he had had one woman, immediately wanted another
A Coat of Varnish (1979) C. P. Snow
Lurulu troll
The King of Elfland's Daughter (1924) Lord Dunsany
Luscombe solicitor
No Name (1862) Wilkie Collins
Luscombe, Gerald landlord who supports the Simple Life for a while
The Simple Life Limited (1911) Daniel Chaucer (rn Ford Madox Ford)
Lush, Thomas Cranmer companion and general factotum to Grandcourt*
Daniel Deronda (1876) George Eliot (rn Mary Anne, later Marian, Evans)
Lussurioso son to the Duke*
The Revenger's Tragedy (1607/8) ?Thomas Middleton; ?Cyril Tourneur
Luster black servant to the Compsons*
The Sound and the Fury (1931) William Faulkner
Luter, Joe Albert Schearl's* countryman and friend
Call It Sleep (1934) Henry Roth
Luthy, Laura
her parents
Tracy's Tiger (1951) William Saroyan
Lutyens, Captain captain of the polo team ss 'The Maltese Cat'
The Day's Work (1898) Rudyard Kipling
Luxellian, Lord (Spenser Hugo) m. (2)

Elfride Swancourt* for the sake of Kate
Kate; Mary his two daughters by his first wife
A Pair of Blue Eyes (1873) Thomas Hardy
Luxmore, Earl of (family name **Ravenel**)
William, Viscount Ravenel m. Maud Halifax*; **Lady Caroline** m. Richard Bristwood
John Halifax, Gentleman (1856) Mrs Craik
Lychnis in charge of earthlings on their arrival in Utopia
Men Like Gods (1923) H. G. Wells
Lycias a eunuch
Valentinian play (1647) John Fletcher
Lyddy, Old servant to Rufus Lyon*
Felix Holt (1866) George Eliot (rn Mary Anne, later Marian, Evans)
Lydecker, Waldo criminologist and part-narrator, based on Alexander Woollcott, in famously filmed thriller
Laura (1943) Vera Caspary
Lydgate, Tertius doctor, cc, m. Rosamund Vincy*
Sir Godwin his uncle
Captain Lydgate his cousin, son to Godwin
Middlemarch (1871–2) George Eliot (rn Mary Anne, later Marian, Evans)
Lydia Ranger's* mistress
Love in a Wood, or *St James's Park* comedy (1672) William Wycherley
Lygones father to Spaconia*
A King and No King play (1619) Francis Beaumont and John Fletcher
Lyle, Annot daughter to Sir Duncan Campbell*
The Legend of Montrose (1819) Walter Scott
Lyndall cousin to Em*
The Story of an African Farm (1883) Olive Schreiner
Lyndesay see **De Lyndesay**
Lyndon, Barry rascal, gambler and adventurer; in his own view the best, greatest and most ill-used of men; originally Redmond Barry until he takes the name of the woman he m.
The Countess of Lyndon rich foolish widow of Sir C. Barry, Barry Lyndon's wife
Bryan, Viscount Castle Lyndon their son

The Luck of Barry Lyndon (1844 in *Fraser's Magazine*) as *The Memoirs of Barry Lyndon, by Himself* (1852) W. M. Thackeray

Lyndon, the Countess of see Lyndon, Barry

Lyndsay, Edward m. Gertrude St Clair*
The Inheritance (1824) Susan Ferrier

Lyne, Angela, Mrs m. Basil Seal*
Cedric her first husband
Put Out More Flags (1942) Evelyn Waugh

Lynedon, Paul at first in love with Eleanor Ogilvie*; m. Katherine Ogilvie*
The Ogilvies (1849) Diana Craik

Lynneker, Dick cc
The Revd Lynneker his father
his mother and his four siblings
These Lynnekers (1915) J. D. Beresford

Lynwood, John midshipman, cc
The Gunroom (1919) Charles Morgan

Lyon, Esther in fact Esther Bycliff, heiress, cc, m. Felix Holt*
Revd Rufus her supposed father, m. Annette Ledru, her mother

Felix Holt (1866) George Eliot (rn Mary Anne, later Marian, Evans)

Lyons, June
Dorothy her 'bad' sister
Love's Lovely Counterfeit (1942) James M. Cain

Lyons, Laura
The Hound of the Baskervilles (1902) Arthur Conan Doyle

Lyons, Rita schoolteacher, m. Jerry Lamb*
ss 'Feed My Lambs'
The Talking Trees (1971) Sean O'Faolain

Lypiatt, Casimir artist
Antic Hay (1923) Aldous Huxley

Lysander in love with Hermia*
A Midsummer Night's Dream play (1623) William Shakespeare

Lysimachus designer
Count Robert of Paris (1832) Walter Scott

Lysimachus governor of Mitylene
Pericles play (1609) William Shakespeare

Lysippus brother to the king
The Maid's Tragedy play (1610) Francis Beaumont and John Fletcher

M

M. de C. ('**Antonio**') French spy
ss 'The Bonds of Discipline'
Traffics and Discoveries (1904) Rudyard Kipling

M., Lord uncle to Lovelace*
Clarissa Harlowe (1748) Samuel Richardson

Maartens, Katy portrait of Frieda Lawrence
The Genius and the Goddess (1955) Aldous Huxley

Maartens, Professor and Mrs
C (1924) Maurice Baring

Maas, Hendrik Dutch churchmason at Mixton, to whom Robin Skyrme* is apprenticed
The Story of Ragged Robyn (1945) Oliver Onions

Maberley, Jim
In This Our Life (1942) Ellen Glasgow

Mac Jim Nolan's* friend and mourner
In Dubious Battle (1936) John Steinbeck

MacAdam, Lady high-spirited old lady
Annals of the Parish (1821) John Galt

McAdoo, Julius, Uncle Uncle Remus-like cc of stories in first collection of author often called 'first Negro novelist'
The Conjure Woman (1899) Charles Waddell Chesnutt

McAlister, Colonel widower
Mary his daughter
The Fitz-Boodle Papers (1852) W. M. Thackeray

McAllister, Sandy ('**The Laird of Cockpen**') art student, m. Mrs Bagot*
Trilby (1894) George du Maurier

McAlpin, Sergeant
Janet his sister
The Legend of Montrose (1819) Walter Scott

MacAlpine, Jeanie landlady of inn at Aberfoil
Rob Roy (1818) Walter Scott

Macapa, Maria Mexican house cleaner
McTeague (1899) Frank Norris

Macarthy, Mr aphorist
Adam of Dublin (1920); *Adam and Caroline* (1921); *In London* (1922); *Married Life* (1924) Conal O'Connell O'Reardon (rn F. Norreys Connell)

Macarty, Wellesley, Mrs widow, *née* Crabbe, m. (2) James Gann
Isabella; Rosalind her twin daughters
A Shabby Genteel Story (1840) W. M. Thackeray

McAuden, Mrs friend to Winifred Dartie
The *Forsyte* series (1906–33) John Galsworthy

McAulay, Angus Laird of Darlin-Varach
Allan his brother
The Legend of Montrose (1819) Walter Scott

Macaulay, Herbert (alias **George Foley**), lawyer, killer
The Thin Man (1934) Dashiell Hammett

Macauley, Mrs widow
Marcus; Homer telegraph boy; **Bess** m. Tobey George; **Ulysses** her children
The Human Comedy (1943) William Saroyan

MacAusland, Libby cc, one of the graduates from Vassar
The Group (1963) Mary McCarthy

Macbeth general, king, murderer, cc
Lady Macbeth his wife, cc
Macbeth play (1623) William Shakespeare

McBryde District Superintendent of Police
A Passage to India (1924) E. M. Forster

McCabe narrator, tried and acquitted of murder
The Face on the Cutting-Room Floor (1937) Cameron McCabe (rn E. W. J. Borneman)

McCabe, Earl black ruler of San Lorenzo until coup by Papa Monzano*
Cat's Cradle (1963) Kurt Vonnegut

McCall, Larry
ss 'The Angel and the Sweep'
Adam and Eve and Pinch Me (1921) A. E.

Coppard
MacCandlish, Mrs widowed landlady of
the Gordon Arms
Guy Mannering (1815) Walter Scott
McCann, Lady
Watt (1953) Samuel Beckett
McCarron, Hoake see **Snopes**
McCarthy, Charles
James his son
ss 'The Boscombe Valley. Mystery'
The Adventures of Sherlock Holmes
(1892) Arthur Conan Doyle
McCarthy, Denis, Great-Uncle ghost
Some Experiences of an Irish RM (1899)
O. E. Somerville and Martin Ross (rn
Edith Somerville and Violet Martin)
McCaslin, Isaac sixteen-year old protago-
nist of novella set in Yoknapatawpha
County in 1880s
ss 'The Bear'
Go Down Moses (1942) William
Faulkner
McChesney, Emma saleswoman of
Featherbloom Petticoats in the Midwest:
one of the author's pioneering portraits of
women in business in stories from *Roast
Beef Medium* (1913) Edna Ferber
McChoakumchild schoolmaster employed
by Gradgrind* to install FACTS into
minds of pupils
Hard Times (1854) Charles Dickens
McClain, Curly Kansas cowpuncher cc in
the source for the musical *Oklahoma!*;
m. Laurey Williams*
Green Grow the Lilacs (1931) Lynn
Riggs
McClennan, Everett
Lily his wife
Martha his sister
Run River (1963) Joan Didion
McClour, Janet housekeeper to Murdoch
Soulis*; witch wife
ss 'Thrawn Janet'
The Merry Men (1887) Robert Louis
Stevenson
McClure, Andrew sensitive young member
of RAF
Chips With Everything play (1962)
Arnold Wesker
McClurg, Barry conservative American
financier in novel of the failure of a
marriage; m. (1) Charlotte, *née*
Wheelright (2) Countess Madeleine, *née*

de Granier, a brilliant young Fench fas-
cist
Bob his nephew
Silent Storms (1927) Ernest Poole
McCollop, Sandy student with Newcome*
at Gandish Drawing Academy
The Newcomes (1853–5) W. M.
Thackeray
McComas, Finch solicitor
You Never Can Tell (1895) George
Bernard Shaw
McCombich, Robin 'Oig' drover
Lachlan his father
Janet his aunt
The Two Drovers (1827) Walter Scott
Maccomobich, Evan Dhu foster-brother
to Fergus MacIvor*
Waverley (1814) Walter Scott
Macconochie 'old, ill-spoken, drunken
dog,' serving man
The Master of Ballantrae (1889) Robert
Louis Stevenson
McCrac, Colin m. Christina McNab*
The Fortune of Christina McNab (1901)
Sarah Macnaughtan
McCranie, Abraham ('Abe') mulatto cc of
American folk drama, 'a latter-day
Moses' and selfless visionary; lynched for
killing his legitimate half-brother;
bastard son of:
Colonel McCranie Southern gentleman
Muh Mack his old aunt
his wife
their son, a ne're-do-well who finally eggs
on the crowd to run his father off
In Abraham's Bosom play (1927) Paul
Green
McCreary, Fainy labour organizer
U.S.A. trilogy (1930–6) John Dos Passos
MacCrotchet ('Crotchet)
McCrotchet Jnr. his son, financier and
complany promoter
Lemma MacCrotchet Jnr.'s daughter
Crotchet Castle (1831) Thomas Love
Peacock
McCunn, Dickson retired grocer
Robina his wife, *née* Dickson
Huntingtower (1922) John Buchan
Macdonald, Sergius Mihailovich, Count
leader of a counter-revolution his wife
The New Humpty-Dumpty (1912)
Daniel Chaucer (rn Ford Madox Ford)
Macdonnell, Alaster 'young Colkitto'

The Legend of Montrose (1819) Walter Scott

McDowell, Eugene H. crooked estate agent in early American naturalist* novel
The Cliff-Dwellers (1893) Henry Blake Fuller

McDowell, George earnest manufacturer of aerated waters, Rotarian; has been described as an Australian Babbitt*
The Electrical Experience (1974) Frank Moorhouse

McDruggy 'fresh from Canton'
Sybil (1845) Benjamin Disraeli

Macduff nobleman of Scotland
Macbeth play (1623) William Shakespeare

McEachern, Simon Joe Christmas's* foster-father, 'representative of a wrathful and retributive Throne'
his wife
Light in August (1932) William Faulkner

MacEagh, Ranald Highland freebooter
Kenneth his grandson
The Legend of Montrose (1819) Walter Scott

McEarchern, Molly m. Jimmy Pitt*
her father, ex-police chief
A Gentleman of Leisure (1910) P. G. Wodehouse

McElvina, Captain
Susan his wife, *née* Hornblow
The King's Own (1830) Captain Marryat

McEndrick, James
Nessie his daughter
ss 'Washed in the Blood'
The Clouds are Big With Mercy (1946) Fred Urquhart

Macer, Major friend to Captain Legg*
The Book of Snobs (1847) W. M. Thackeray

MacEvoy, Janet cc, Highland landlady, later housekeeper
The Highland Widow (1827) Walter Scott

Macey parish clerk and tailor, of Raveloe
Solomon his father
Silas Marner (1861) George Eliot (rn Mary Anne, later Marian, Evans)

Macey, Mr and Mrs Mrs Maryon's* married sister and her husband, living on Silver Store Island
The Perils of Certain English Prisoners (1857) Charles Dickens

Macfadden, Adam cc, illegitimate inhabitant of slums, touched with genius, in Irish series much read in its day
Malachy his father
Adam of Dublin (1920); *Adam and Caroline* (1921); *In London* (1922); *Married Life* (1924) Conal O'Connell O'Reardon (rn F. Norreys Connell)

MacFadden, Douglas uncle to and benefactor of Jean Paget*
A Town Like Alice (1950) Neville Shute (rn Nevile Shute Norway)

McFarlane, Hugh, Dr m. Elizabeth Trant*
The Good Companions (1929) J. B. Priestley

Macfarlane, John Hector
ss 'The Norwood Builder'
The Return of Sherlock Holmes (1905) Arthur Conan Doyle

Macfarlane, Wolfe ('Toddy') famous London doctor
ss 'The Body Snatcher'
The Wrong Box (1889) Lloyd Osbourne and Robert Louis Stevenson

Macfie, Mr Sergeant, MP
Adam of Dublin (1920); *Adam and Caroline* (1921); *In London* (1922); *Married life* (1924) Conal O'Connell O'Reardon (rn F. Norreys Connell)

McGee, Travis sexually improbably well-endowed private eye, ex-crook; onwards from
The Deep Blue Goodbye† (1964) John D. Macdonald

McGeeney, Miss tweedy middle-aged woman variously disguised; ends having intercourse with Balso Snell*, who has turned into a schoolboy, in bowels of Trojan Horse
The Dream Life of Balso Snell (1931) Nathanael West (rn Nathan Weinstein)

MacGillie, Chattanach 'high-mettled' Highland chief
The Fair Maid of Perth (1828) Walter Scott

Macgillvray of the CID
The Thirty-nine Steps (1915); *The Power House* (1916) John Buchan

McGillvray, Lily Edinburgh good-time girl, pal to Bessy Hipkiss*
Jezebel's Dust (1951) Fred Urquhart

Macginnis, Buck professional kidnapper
The Little Nugget (1913) P. G. Wode-

house
McGoggin, Aurelian
ss 'The Conversion of Aurelian McGoggin'
Plain Tales from the Hills (1888) Rudyard Kipling
McGoun, Teresa Babbitt's* secretary
Babbitt (1923) Sinclair Lewis
MacGowan, Skeet pharmacist's assistant and rapist
As I Lay Dying (1930) William Faulkner
MacGown, Alexander, Sir engaged to Marjorie Ferrar*
The Silver Spoon (1926) John Galsworthy
McGraw, Dr Scots minister
Josey his third wife, *née* Mackenzie
The Newcomes (1853–5) W. M. Thackeray
MacGrawler, Peter editor of the *Asinaeum*
Paul Clifford (1830) Edward Bulwer Lytton
Macgregor (alias **James More***)
Catriona (1893) Robert Louis Stevenson
MacGregor, Aaron vet, idealist, former lover of Marguerite Wood*, pays her £100 to spend the night with him; she cheats him, but he insists she keep the money
An Advent Calendar (1971) Shena Mackay
Macgregor, Mary schoolgirl
The Prime of Miss Jean Brodie (1961) Muriel Spark
Macgregor, Mr
his wife
The Tale of Peter Rabbit† (1902) Beatrix Potter
Macgregor, Mr Deputy Commissioner, m. Elizabeth Lackersteen*
Burmese Days (1935) George Orwell (rn Eric Blair)
Macgregor, Mrs Hamlin's aunt; delightful cynical old lady
Miss Brown (1884) Vernon Lee (rn Viola Paget)
MacGregor, Robert (Robin) ('Rob Roy') cc
Helen his wife, *née* Campbell
Robert one of their sons
Rob Roy (1818) Walter Scott
MacGregor, Scott journalist who sells out for money, m. Kathleen St Peter*

The Professor's House (1925) Willa Cather
McGregor, Stumpy old man
Time Will Knit (1938) Fred Urquhart
MacGuffog *pension*-keeper at Portanferry, later under-turnkey
his wife
Guy Mannering (1815) Walter Scott
McGuffog gamekeeper
Huntingtower (1922) John Buchan
McGurk, Ross head of the Gurk Institute
Capitola his patronizing wife
Arrowsmith (1925) Sinclair Lewis
McHarg, Lloyd writer, modelled on Sinclair Lewis*
You Can't Go Home Again (1940) Thomas Wolfe
MacHeath cc, m. Polly Peachum*
The Beggar's Opera opera (1728); *Polly* opera (1729) John Gay
Machin, Arthur rugby-playing cc
This Sporting Life (1960) David Storey
Machin, Edward Henry ('Denry') cc, the card, in part based on the business man Harold Keates Hales, who believed that the author – with whom he attended school – owed him a share of the royalties
The Card (1911); *The Old Adam* (1913); *The Regent* (1913) Arnold Bennett
Machine, Frankie (Francis Majinek) heroin-addicted ex-pool-playing cc novel of Chicago slums
The Man With the Golden Arm (1949) Nelson Algren
McHull, James, the Hon.
Rhoda his wife, *née* Swartz
Macduff their son
Vanity Fair (1847–8) W. M. Thackeray
Macilente 'who, wanting that place in the world's account which he thinks his merit capable of, falls into . . . an envious apoplexy'
Every Man Out of His Humour play (1599) Ben Jonson
MacIntosh, Miss once the narrator's nursemaid
Miss MacIntosh, My Darling (1965) Marguerite Young
McIntyre overseer
Robbery Under Arms: A Story of Life and Adventure in the Bush and in the Goldfields of Australia (1888, rev. 1889) Rolf Boldrewood (rn Thomas Alexander

Browne)

McIntyre, Mrs Protestant widow running a dairy farm
ss 'The Displaced Person'
A Good Man is Hard to Find (1955) Flannery O'Connor

MacIvor, Fergus Highland chieftain
Waverley (1814) Walter Scott

McIvor, Pleasant cc of much prized hist. novel of the South, set before and during the Civil War
The Long Night (1936) Andrew Lytle

Mack, Herman cc who eats a Ford Maverick and defecates it, as revenge on the world; in American satirical novel
Car (1971) Harry Crews

Mackay, Miss headmistress
The Prime of Miss Jean Brodie (1961) Muriel Spark

McKechnie, Mr dilapidated keeper of bookshop in which Gordon Comstock* works
Keep the Aspidistra Flying (1936) George Orwell (rn Eric Blair)

McKee, Mr and Mrs
The Great Gatsby (1925) F. Scott Fitzgerald

Mackel, Ira
Mourning Becomes Electra play (1931) Eugene O'Neill

MacKellar friend to Father Buonaventure*
Redgauntlet (1824) Walter Scott

MacKellar, Ephraim servant, friend to the family, narrator
The Master of Ballantrae (1889) Robert Louis Stevenson

McKellop butler to Lord Weir*
Weir of Hermiston (1896) Robert Louis Stevenson

McKelva, Judge m. Fay Chisom*
Laurel his daughter by his deceased first wife
The Optimist's Daughter (1972) Eudora Welty

McKelvey, Charlie
Lucile his wife
Babbitt (1923) Sinclair Lewis

McKenna, Jhansi m. Corporal Slane*
Bridget her mother
'**Old Pummaloe**' sergeant, her father
ss 'A Daughter of the Regiment'
Plain Tales from the Hills† (1888) Rudyard Kipling

Mackenzie Scots detective
Raffles (1901) E. W. Hornung

Mackenzie, Flora ('**Auntie Mack**') relative to the Thomsons*
The Ballad and the Source (1944) Rosamond Lehmann

Mackenzie, Margaret cc, m. her cousin, Sir John Ball*; plain woman who is sought for her money by Samuel Rubb* and Jeremiah Maguire*
Walter; Tom her brothers, the first of whom she looks after until he dies
Sarah Tom's wife
Susanna Tom and Sarah's daughter
Miss Mackenzie (1863) Anthony Trollope

Mackenzie, Mrs ('**The Campaigner**') widow, *née* Binnie
Rosey m. Clive Newcome*; **Josey** m. Dr McCraw* her daughters
The Newcomes (1853–5) W. M. Thackeray

McKeown, Darby ('**The Blast**') piper
Tom Burke of Ours (1844) Charles Lever

Mackie, Corporal
ss 'Love o' Women'
Many Inventions (1893) Rudyard Kipling

Mackin, Mrs slipshod customer at pawnshop
Sketches by Boz† (1836) Charles Dickens

McKinley, William (hist.) assassinated President of U S A; in novel by popular juvenile local-colour* author that is still in manuscript and will probably stay that way
The Queen Bee (written 1902) Mary Catherwood

Mackintosh assistant administrator of South Sea island
ss 'Mackintosh'
The Trembling of a Leaf (1921) W. Somerset Maugham

Mackintosh friend to Dickson McCunn
Huntingtower (1922) John Buchan

Macklin gentleman ranker
ss 'The Janeites'
Debits and Credits (1926) Rudyard Kipling

Macklin, Mrs resident who screamed 'Muffins!'
Sketches by Boz† (1836) Charles Dickens

Mackridge, Mrs Lady Drew's* pensioner

Tono Bungay (1909) H. G. Wells

Mackworth
ss 'The Tie'
Limits and Renewals (1932) Rudyard Kipling

MacLain, King wandering patriarch
Snowdie Hudson his albino wife
Eugene; Randall their twin sons
The Golden Apples (1949) Eudora Welty

Maclaren Miss head housekeeper
Imperial Palace (1930) Arnold Bennett

Maclean, Mary, Lady old lady who never misses a Bath concert
Persuasion (1818) Jane Austen

McLean, Ivie m. Alie Cray*
Sentimental Tommy (1896) J. M. Barrie

McLear, Patrick supposedly a portrait of the American semi-beat poet Michael McClure
Big Sur (1962); *Desolation Angels* (1965) Jack Kerouac

Macleary, 'Luckie' mistress of inn at Tully-Veolan
Waverley (1814) Walter Scott

Macleary, John Irish-Australian sheep farmer
ss 'A propos des Bottes'
Fiery Particles (1923) C. E. Montague

McLeavy a newly widowed man (said to be based on the author's father)
Harold (Hal) his son, crook
Loot play (1966) Joe Orton

McLeod, L. Maxwell
his wife
Thea their daughter
ss 'The House Surgeon'
Actions and Reactions (1909) Rudyard Kipling

McLucre, Andrew, Bailie
Andrew his son
The Provost (1822) John Galt

Maclure, Bessie old widow
Ninian; Johnnie her sons
Peggy her granddaughter
Old Mortality (1816) Walter Scott

Maclure, Elizabeth Caldwell ('Beth') cc 'new woman' novel in which the author portrayed her husband as a sadistic doctor and vivisectionist
Dan her husband, a brutal doctor
The Beth Book (1897) Sarah Grand (rn Frances McFall)

Maclure, Nonie art student

Peggy her sister
Non-Combatants and Others (1916) Rose Macaulay

McMahon, Fay Jean nurse seven times married
Loot play (1966) Joe Orton

Macmann see Saposcat

McMann, Thomas once famous sociologist cc
Imaginary Friends (1967) Alison Lurie

Macmanus Mrs Hoggarty's* Irish agent
The Great Hoggarty Diamond (1841) W. M. Thackeray

Macmaster, Vincent friend to Tietjens*, Whig, civil servant, expert on Dante, Gabriel Rossetti, m. Edith Ethel Duchemin*
Some Do Not (1924); *No More Parades* (1925); *A Man Could Stand Up* (1926); *Last Post* (1928) Ford Madox Ford

McMillan, Duncan, Revd
An American Tragedy (1925) Theodore Dreiser

MacMurdo, Constable Cyril m. Nanie Bruce
Cocktail Time (1958) P. G. Wodehouse

McMurdo servant to Bartholomew Sholto*
The Sign of Four (1890) Arthur Conan Doyle

Macmurrachu, Meehawl farmer
Caitlin his daughter
The Crock of Gold (1912) James Stephens

McNab, Christina heiress, m. Colin McCrae*
The Fortune of Christina McNab (1901) Sarah Macnaughtan

McNaught, Moira and Jeanie Scottish twins living in village
Old Crow (1967) Shena Mackay

MacNeil, Archie shabby decaying boxer, cc Canadian novel
Each Man's Son (1951) Hugh MacLennan

McNiel milkman
Nellie his wife
Manhatten Transfer (1925) John Dos Passos

MacNulty, Julia impoverished hanger-on to Lady Eustace*
The Eustace Diamonds (1873) Anthony Trollope

McNutt, Mary shot and wounded by Paris Trout*; one of the few Negroes who is not afraid of him
Henry Ray Boxer; Thomas Boxer; Linda; Jane her children
Paris Trout (1988) Pete Dexter

MacPhadrick, Miles 'cautious man'
The Highland Widow (1827) Walter Scott

MacPhail, Alec, Dr
his wife
ss 'Miss Sadie Thompson'
The Trembling of a Leaf (1921) W. Somerset Maugham
Rain play (1922) John Colton and Clemence Randolph

Macphail, Augusta heartless woman who m. Mr Fleight* for his money and prospects
Mr Fleight (1913) Ford Madox Ford

MacPhail, Cressida Mary ('Cressie') cc, m. David Little*
Joe; Rose her parents
Harry; Rachel her grandparents
The Wedding Group (1968) Elizabeth Taylor

McPhee ship's engineer
Janet his wife
ss 'Bread Upon the Waters'†
The Day's Work (1898) Rudyard Kipling

Macpherson, Cluny chief of Clan Vourich (hist.)
Kidnapped (1886) Robert Louis Stevenson

Macpherson, Cluny dilettante poet
Mr Fleight (1913) Ford Madox Ford

McPhillip, Francis Joseph
Jack his father, bricklayer
his mother
Mary his sister
The Informer (1929) Liam O'Flaherty

MacQuedy economist, modelled on an editor of the *Scotsman* called McCulloch
Crotchet Castle (1831) Thomas Love Peacock

MacQuern, The of Balliol
Zuleika Dobson (1911) Max Beerbohm

McQumpha, Hendry
Susan his wife, *née* Duthie
Jamie; Joey; Leeby their children
A Window in Thrums (1889) J. M. Barrie

McRae, Neil poverty-stricken composer in satirical American play; dreams he is engaged to rich girl Gladys Cady* and has to work in her father's widget factory
Beggar on Horseback play with music by Deems Taylor (1924) George S. Kaufman and Marc Connelly

McRaven, Laura child cousin to the Fairchilds*
Delta Wedding (1946) Eudora Welty

McRimmon ship owner
ss 'Bread Upon the waters'
The Day's Work (1899) Rudyard Kipling

Macro, Sertorius agent for Tiberius*
Sejanus play (1605) Ben Jonson

Macrob, Neil Ray skipper of ferryboat
Kidnapped (1886) Robert Louis Stevenson

MacSarcasm, Archie, Sir
Love à la Mode play (1759) Charles Macklin

Macshane ship's surgeon, the *Thunder*
Roderick Random (1748) Tobias Smollett

McSorley, John president of an organization of gluttons
McSorley's Wonderful Saloon (1943) Joseph Mitchell

MacStinger, Mrs widowed landlady of Captain Cuttle*, m. Captain Bunsby*
The Little MacStingers her family
Dombey and Son (1848) Charles Dickens

MacSycophant, Pertinax, Sir
The Man of the World play (1781) Charles Macklin

MacTavish, Elspat 'The Woman of the Tree'
Hamish her husband
Hamish Bean their son
The Highland Widow (1827) Walter Scott

McTeague ('Mac') unlicensed dentist cc in one of the first full-blown American naturalist* novels; m. Trina Sieppe*; dies in Death Valley: chained to Schouler*, whom he has killed
McTeague (1899) Frank Norris

Macteer, Claudia narrator
Frieda her sister
The Bluest Eye (1970) Toni Morrison

McTurk, William one of the Stalky trio – a caricature of the author's school chum – who became a Fabian socialist – Beresford
Stalky and Co. (1899) Rudyard Kipling

Macumaqahn see Quartermain, Allan

McVcy, Hugh inventor cc, m. Clara Butterworth*
Poor White (1920) Sherwood Anderson

MacVittie, Ephraim partner in MacVittie & Co.
his wife
Alison their daughter
Rob Roy (1818) Walter Scott

McWaters, Miss kindly but repulsive schoolteacher
Peter Waring (1937) Forrest Reid

MacWhirr, Tom, Captain of the *Nan-Shan*
Typhoon (1903) Joseph Conrad (rn Josef Teodor Konrad Korzeniowski)

MacWhirter, Major late Bengal Cavalry
his wife, sister to Mrs Baynes*
The Adventures of Philip (1862) W. M. Thackeray

McWilliams in charge of mining railroad
Soldiers of Fortune (1897) Richard Harding Davis

Macy, Marvin violent criminal m. for ten days to Miss Amelia Evans*
The Ballad of the Sad Café (1951) Carson McCullers

Maddack, Harriet aunt to the Baines* sisters
The Old Wives' Tale (1908) Arnold Bennett

Madden, Arthur
Sylvia Scarlett (1918) Compton Mackenzie

Madden, Celia daughter of rich Irish immigrant; rejects Theron Ware*
The Damnation of Theron Ware in England, originally, as *Illumination* (1896) Harold Frederic

Madden, Elkanah, Dr
Alice; Virginia; Monica the three of his daughters who survive, the last named m. Edmund Widdowson* and dies in childbirth
The Odd Women (1893) George Gissing

Madden, Mr and Mrs butler and housekeeper to Miss Florence*
ss 'They'
Traffics and Discoveries (1904) Rudyard Kipling

Maddingham, Lieutenant-Commander, RN
ss 'Sea Constables'

Debits and Credits (1926) Rudyard Kipling

Maddison agent for Henry Crawford* on his estate
Mansfield Park (1814) Jane Austen

Maddison, Willie boy cc of this and its successors in tetralogy *The Flax of Dream*
The Beautiful Years (1921) Henry Williamson

Maddison, Phillip ('Phillip' because his father mispells his name when registering it); cousin of Willie Maddison* of *The Beautiful Years*; cc roman fleuve by British National Socialist and disciple of Richard Jeffries* *Chronicles of Ancient Sunlight: The Dark Lantern* (1951); *Donkey Boy* (1952); *Young Phillip Maddison* (1953); *How Dear is Life* (1954); *A Fox Under my Cloak* (1955); *The Golden Virgin* (1957); *Love and the Loveless: A Soldiers Tale* (1958); *A Test to Destruction* (1960); *The Innocent Moon* (1961); *It Was the Nightingale* (1962); *The Power of the Dead* (1963); *The Phoenix Generation* (1965); *A Solitary War* (1966); *Lucifer Before Sunrise* (1967); *The Gale of the World* (1969) Henry Williamson

Maddox, John
The Village Coquette opera (1836) Charles Dickens

Madelon Robinson's* ex-fiancée and killer
Voyage au bout de la nuit (Journey to the End of Night) (1932) Louis-Ferdinand Céline (rn Louis Ferdinand Destouches)

Marlely, Dr
ss 'Amos Barton'
Scenes of Clerical Life (1857) George Eliot (rn Mary Anne, later Marian, Evans)

Madgers, Winifred one of Mrs Lirriper's* maids, a Plymouth sister who m. a Plymouth brother, and who had Plymouth twins
Mrs Lirriper's Lodgings and Legacy (1864) Charles Dickens

Madigan, Maisie, Miss
Juno and the Paycock play (1925) Sean O'Casey (rn John Casey)

Madman, The narrator of the terrible story recounted in the Dingley Dell

clergyman's manuscript
The Pickwick Papers (1837) Charles Dickens

Madness one of Miss Flite's* birds
Bleak House (1853) Charles Dickens

Madras, Philip young and progressive member of the Madras House, a shop for women
Jessica his wife
Charles his father, head of the firm
The Madras House play (1910) Harley Granville Barker

Madrigal poetaster, and jeerer
The Staple of News play (1631) Ben Jonson

Madrigal, Miss companion-governess with a past
The Chalk Garden play (1955) Enid Bagnold

Madu charcoal burner
Athira his wife
ss 'Through the Fire'
Life's Handicap (1891) Rudyard Kipling

Madvig, Paul political boss of a great city, friend to Ned Beaumont*; killer
Opal his daughter
The Glass Key (1931) Dashiell Hammett

Maes, Gertrude mother to Henry Esmond*, m. Viscount Castlewood*; later a nun, Soeur Marie Madeleine
Henry Esmond (1852) W. M. Thackeray

Maffin, Jack, Captain Philip Gadsby's* close friend
ss 'The Story of the Gadsbys'
The Story of the Gadsbys (1888) Rudyard Kipling

Maggie modelled on the author's divorced wife, Marilyn Monroe
After the Fall play (1964) Arthur Miller

Maggy granddaughter of Little Dorrit's* old nurse, Mrs Bangham*; eventually employed by Mrs Pornish*
Little Dorrit (1857) Charles Dickens

Magiot, Dr communist
The Comedians (1966) Graham Greene

Magnet, Will humorous writer, m. Daphne Pope*
Marriage (1912) H. G. Wells

Magnetes a Median Lord
Tamburlaine play (1587) Christopher Marlowe

Magnus, Charlotte m. Simon March*

Lucy her sister, courted by Augie March*
The Adventures of Augie March (1953) Saul Bellow

Magnus, King
The Apple Cart (1929) George Bernard Shaw

Magnus, Peter red-haired inquisitive man, went with Mr Pickwick* to Ipswich
The Pickwick Papers (1837) Charles Dickens

Magny, General Baron Chevalier de his scapegrace grandson
Barry Lyndon (1844) W. M. Thackeray

Magog (legd.) villainous brother to Gog*
Magog (1972) Andrew Sinclair

Magsman, Toby (or Robert) narrator
Going into Society (1858) Charles Dickens

Magua ('Le Renard Subtil') traitorous Huron chief
The Last of the Mohicans (1826) James Fenimore Cooper

Maguire police sergeant
ss 'Another Temple Gone'
Fiery Particles (1923) C. E. Montague

Maguire, Jeremiah, Revd greedy and oily clergyman who lays siege to Margaret Mackenzie*
Miss Mackenzie (1863) Anthony Trollope

Magwitch, Abel cc, convict
Great Expectations (1861) Charles Dickens

Mahaina drunken friend to the Nosnibors*
Erewhon (1872) Samuel Butler

Mahbub Ali horse trader, secret service agent
Kim (1901) Rudyard Kipling

Mahmud Ali sewing man
ss 'The Debt'
Limits and Renewals (1932) Rudyard Kipling

Mahomet Singh one of the Four
The Sign of Four (1890) Arthur Conan Doyle

Mahon, Adam cc
Brides of Price (1972) Dan Davin

Mahon, Christy
Old Mahon his father, a squatter, whom he falsely claims to have murdered
The Playboy of the Western World play (1907) John Millington Synge

Mahoney, Richard Townshend aristo-
cratic Irish emigrant to Australia,
storekeeper, and doctor: successful but
finally defeated by mental illness; cc
Mary ('Polly') *née* **Turnham** his wife
Cuthbert; Lallie; Luce their children
Australia Felix (1917); *The Way Home*
(1925); *Ultima Thule* (1929); complete
version in one volume: *The Fortunes of
Richard Mahony* (1930) Henry Handel
Richardson (rn Ethel Florence, Lindesay
Richardson Robertson)
Mahood see **Basil**
Maiden, Maisie, Mrs *née* **Flaherty,** young
woman followed by Edward Ash-
burnham* from India to Nauheim, spa
in Germany
The Good Soldier (1915) Ford Madox
Ford
Maidston, Alicia m. Ablard Pender*
her mother
The Last Revolution (1951) Lord
Dunsany
Mail, Michael villager of Mellstock
Under the Greenwood Tree (1872)
Thomas Hardy
Mailsetter postmaster, Fairport
his wife
Davie their son
The Antiquary (1816) Walter Scott
Maine, Sackville coal merchant ruined by
the Sarcophagus Club
his wife
The Book of Snobs (1847) W. M.
Thackeray
Mainwaring shy Jewish photographer
who finds a market for pornography and
settles in America, in Australian novel
Janet his daughter
Danny her son
The Pure Land (1974) David Foster
Mainwaring, Bunty engaged to Nicky
Lancaster*
The Vortex play (1924) Noël Coward
Mainwaring, Joseph, Sir
Put Out More Flags (1942) Evelyn
Waugh
Mainwaring, Lydia, Mrs
The Constant Nymph (1924) Margaret
Kennedy
Mainwarings, The whose house Lady
Susan de Courcy* has to leave when both
Mr Mainwaring and his sister's suitor, Sir

James Martin*, fall in love with her
Lady Susan (1871) Jane Austen
Mainwearing head of High Cross School
Joan and Peter (1918) H. G. Wells
Mainwroth, Lord caricature of Lord
Berners*
ss 'The Love Bird'
Dumb Animal (1930) Osbert Sitwell
Mair, Professor head of section employing
Sammy Rice*
The Small Back Room (1943) Nigel
Balchin
Maisie beloved of Dick Heldar*, purport-
edly based on Florence Garrard, who
later protested
The Light that Failed (1890) Rudyard
Kipling
Maitland manservant
The Chalk Garden play (1955) Enid
Bagnold
Maitland, Annie
The Pottleton Legacy (1849) Albert
Smith
Maitland, Henry novelist and man of
letters, cc of fictional biography of
George Gissing*
The Private Life of Henry Maitland
(1912) Morley Roberts
Majendie, Walter 'moral leper' of sweet
disposition
Anne his revengeful and hypocritical
wife, in whom dutiful virtue is finally
replaced by compassion
The Helpmate (1907) May Sinclair
Makely, Mrs fashionable intellectual
A Traveller from Altruria (1894);
Through the Eye of the Needle (1907)
William Dean Howells
Malagrowther, Mungo, Sir of Girnigo
Castle
The Fortunes of Nigel (1822) Walter
Scott
Malam, JP
Silas Marner (1861) George Eliot (rn
Mary Anne, Later Marian, Evans)
Malaprop, Mrs
The Rivals play (1775) Richard Brinsley
Sheridan
Malcolm fifteen-year-old boy awaiting his
lost father, cc
Malcolm (1959) James Purdy
Malcolm, John ex-husband of Mrs Shank-
land*

Separate Tables play (1955) Terence
Rattigan
Malderton city man who lived at
Camberwell
Sketches by Boz† (1836) Charles Dickens
Maldon, Jack Mrs Strong's* idle cousin
David Copperfield (1850) Charles
Dickens
Malet, Selma actress cc of the most popu-
lar novel by Dickens's eldest grandchild
Cross Currents (1891) Mary Angela
Dickens
Malétroit, Sire de (Alain)
Blanche his niece, m. Denis de Beaulieu
ss 'The Sire de Malétroit's Door'
New Arabian Nights (1882) Robert
Louis Stevenson
Malevole banished Duke of Altofronto
disguised as Malevole, the Malcontent
Maria his wife
The Malcontent play (1604) John
Marston (additions by John Webster)
Malheureux Young Freeville's* unhappy
friend
The Dutch Courtesan play (1605) John
Marston
Malinin, Sergei
Anna his wife; White Russian refugees
Seryozha their son, m. Tatiana
Ostapenko*
Tobit Transplanted (1931) Stella Benson
Mallard Serjeant Snubbin's* elderly clerk
The Pickwick Papers (1837) Charles
Dickens
Mallard, Richard migrant to Europe
But Soft – We Are Observed! (1928)
Hilaire Belloc
Mallet, Rowland wealthy connoisseur
who becomes Roderick Hudson's*
mentor but finally denounces him as an
egoist; vainly in love with Mary Gar-
land*
Jonas his father
Cecilia his cousin
Bessie her daughter
Roderick Hudson (1875) Henry James
Malley, Rosalind jilts Grope*
Albert Grope (1931) F. O. Mann
Mallinger, Hugo, Sir
Louisa his wife
Theresa one of their three daughters
Henleigh his nephew and heir (see
Grandcourt)

Daniel Deronda (1876) George Eliot (rn
Mary Anne, later Marian, Evans)
Mallinson, Charles ('Chick') sixteen-year-
old nephew to Gavin Stevens*
Intruder in the Dust† (1948) William
Faulkner
Mallowe, Polly, Mrs friend to Mrs
Hauksbee*
ss 'The Education of Otis Yeere'
Wee Willie Winkie (1888) Rudyard Kipl-
ing
Malloy, Sam
his wife
Cannery Row (1945) John Steinbeck
Malmanash Assyrian scientist who studied
vibrations
*All and Everything: Beelzebub's Tales to
His Grandson* (1950) G. I. Gurdjieff
Malone cc
Molloy (1951); *Malone meurt* (*Malone
Dies*) (1951) (tr. 1956); *L'Innommable*
(1953) (*The Unnamable*) (tr. 1958) (tri-
logy) Samuel Beckett
Malone, Billy (Brer Rabbit)
Uncle Remus (1880–95) Joel Chandler
Harris
Malone, Gerald friend to Caryl Bramsley*,
and collector of his papers
C (1924) Maurice Baring
Malone, J. T. small-time Georgian drug-
gist dying of leukemia in novel that
centres on his final fifteen months
Martha his wife, *née* Greenlove
Ellen; Tommy their young children
Clock Without Hands (1961) Carson
McCullers
Malone, Ned
Tom Burke of Ours (1844) Charles Lever
Malone, Peter Augustus Curate of
Briarfield
Shirley (1849) Charlotte Brontë
Maloney the Areopagite Catholic mystic;
tries to crucify himself with thumbtacks
while wearing derby crowned with
thorns
The Dream Life of Balso Snell (1931)
Nathanael West (rn Nathan Weinstein)
Malpractice, Miles bright young thing
Vile Bodies (1930) Evelyn Waugh
Maltby, Hilary author, rival to Braxton*
ss 'Maltby and Braxton'
Seven Men (1919) Max Beerbohm
Maltese Cat, The polo pony

ss 'Past, Pluperfect, Prestissimo Player of the Game'
ss 'The Maltese Cat'
The Day's Work (1898) Rudyard Kipling
Malthus, Bartholomew hon. member of the Suicide Club
ss 'The Suicide Club'
New Arabian Nights (1882) Robert Louis Stevenson
Maltravers, Ernest Byronic* mystic cc, British clone of *Wilhelm Meister*
Ernest Maltravers (1837)
Alice, or The Mysteries (1838) Edward Bulwer Lytton
Maltravers, Humphrey, Sir Minister of Transportation, later Lord Metroland, m. Margot Beste-Chetwynde*
Decline and Fall† (1928) Evelyn Waugh
Malvin, Roger
Dorcas his daughter m. Reuben Bourne*
ss 'Roger Malvin's Burial' (1932)
Mosses from an Old Manse (1846) Nathaniel Hawthorne
Malvoisin, Philip de Norman nobleman
Albert his brother, Preceptor
Ivanhoe (1820) Walter Scott
Malvolio steward to Olivia*
Twelfth Night play (1623) William Shakespeare
Mamilius son to Leontes*
A Winter's Tale play (1623) William Shakespeare
Mammon, Epicure, Sir
The Alchemist play (1610) Ben Jonson
Mammy the O'Haras'* faithful slave
Gone With the Wind (1936) Margaret Mitchell
Mammy-Bammy Big Money witch-rabbit
Uncle Remus (1880–95) Joel Chandler Harris
Man from Shropshire, The see **Gridley**
Man in Black, The guide and friend to Lien chi Altangi*
A Citizen of the World (1762) Oliver Goldsmith
Manallace, James cc, popular author who takes an elborate revenge on Castorley* but then regrets it
ss 'Dayspring Mishandled'
Limits and Renewals (1932) Rudyard Kipling
Manby, Flora friend to Henry (Rico) Carrington*

St Mawr (1925) D. H. Lawrence
Mancini, Count supposed father to Consuelo* (who is in fact a lowly Corsican of mixed parentage), dissipated scrounger
Tot, kto poluchaet poshchochiny (*He Who Gets Slapped*; once tr. as *The Painted Laugh*) play (1916) Leonid Andreyev
Mandane waiting woman
A King and No King play (1611) Francis Beaumont and John Fletcher
Manders Minor fag
ss 'Slaves of the Lamp'
Stalky & Co. (1899) Rudyard Kipling
Manders, Pastor essence of conventional morality
Ghosts play (1881) Henrik Ibsen
Manderson, Sigisbee millionaire murderee
Trent's Last Case (1913) E. C. Bentley
Manderstoke, Lord (Gerry) killer of Harry Somerford
Fanny By Gaslight (1940) Michael Sadleir
Mandeville, Earl of m. Rachel Peace*; in romance of Bath in regency times
Incomparable Bellairs (1904) Agnes and Egerton Castle
Mandrake, Homunculus zany to a mountebank
Death's Jest Book, or The Fool's Tragedy play (1850) Thomas Lovell Beddoes
Mandrake, Maud (formerly Kavanagh) poet
Seamus her son by Rex Beaumont*, cc
A Bowl of Cherries (1984) Shena Mackay
Manette, Alexander, Dr cc, physician of Beauvais; imprisoned; practised in Soho
Lucie his daughter, m. Darnay*
A Tale of Two Cities (1959) Charles Dickens
Manetti, Sibilla
Romola (1863) George Eliot (rn Mary Anne, later Marian, Evans)
Manfred usurping Prince of Otranto in first of true Gothic* novels
Hippolita his wife
Conrad their sickly son; **Matilda** their daughter
The Castle of Otranto (1765) Horace Walpole
Mang the bat
ss 'Kaa's Hunting'†

Jungle Books (1894–5) Rudyard Kipling
Mangan, Boss
Heartbreak House play (1917) George
Bernard Shaw
Mangles, Sarah m. Dudley Ruthyn*
Uncle Silas (1864) J. Sheridan Le Fanu
Mango of Mango Plantain & Co.
Vanity Fair† (1847–8) W. M. Thackeray
Manilov idle day-dreaming landowner,
hence 'Manilovism'
Myortvye dushi (*Dead Souls*) (1842)
Nicolai Gogol
Manisty, Edward insufferable cousin to
Eleanor Burgoyne* m. Lucy Foster*
Eleanor (1900) Mrs Humphry Ward
Mankeltow, Captain later Lord
Marshalton
ss 'The Captive'
Traffics and Discoveries† (1904) Rud-
yard Kipling
Manley, Harry, Sir master of hounds,
'measured a man by the length of his
fork', '*aut* a huntsman *aut nullus*'
ss 'The Squire's Story'
Novels and Tales (1906–19) Mrs Gaskell
Manly 'of an honest, surly, nice humour';
in play loosely based on *Le Misanthrope**
The Plain Dealer play (1677) William
Wycherley
Manly, John coachman
Black Beauty (1877) Anna Sewell
Mann, Miss 'crabbed old maid'
Shirley (1849) Charlotte Brontë
Mann, Mrs crooked foster-mother
Oliver Twist (1839) Charles Dickens
Mannering, Guy, Colonel cc
Sophia his wife, *née* Wellwood
Julia their daughter, m. Harry Bertram*
Sir Paul; Bishop Mannering his uncles
Guy Mannering (1815) Walter Scott
Mannering, Kitty
ss 'The Phantom Rickshaw'
Wee Willie Winkie (1888) Rudyard Kipl-
ing
Mannering, Percy poet
Memento Mori (1959) Muriel Spark
Manners, Cuthbert, Dom
Sinister Street (1913) Compton
Mackenzie
Manners, Julia eloped with Alexander
Trott* in error, but m. him at Gretna
Green anyway
Sketches by Boz† (1836) Charles Dickens

Mannesah Rawdon Crawley's* chief
creditor
Vanity Fair (1847–8) W. M. Thackeray
Mannheim, Gerda German refugee
Peter her husband
The World in the Evening (1954) Chris-
topher Isherwood
Manning London journalist, neighbour to
Britling*
Mr Britling Sees It Through (1916) H. G.
Wells
Manning, Geoffrey, Sir proprietor of shoot
The Pickwick Papers (1837) Charles
Dickens
Manning, Hubert civil servant, poet, once
engaged to Ann Veronica Stanley*
Ann Veronica (1909) H. G. Wells
Manning, Paul cc, narrator, railway
engineer, in love with Phillis, but m.
Margaret Ellison*
John his father
Margaret his mother
Cousin Phillis (1864) Mrs Gaskell
Manningoe, Nancy killer of Temple (*née*
Drake*) Stevens's youngest child
Requiem for a Nun (1951) William
Faulkner
Mannion, Robert managing clerk to
Sherwin*
Basil (1852) Wilkie Collins
Mannon, Ezra, Brigadier-General (Ag-
amemnon), murdered by his wife:
Christina (Clytemnestra), who kills her-
self
Lavinia (Electra); **Orin** (Orestes) their
children
Mourning Becomes Electra play (1931)
Eugene O'Neill
Manon girl at the thieves' tavern
The Cloister and the Hearth (1861)
Charles Reade
Manresa, Mrs wealthy and vulgar guest to
the pageant
Between the Acts (1941) Virginia Woolf
Mansel, Edward, Sir Lieutenant of the
Tower
his wife
The Fortunes of Nigel (1822) Walter
Scott
Mansfield, Lord (hist.) Lord Chief Justice
at time of Gordon Riots
Barnaby Rudge (1841) Charles Dickens
Manson, Andrew, Dr cc of popular public-

service* novel; m. Christine Barlow
The Citadel (1937) A. J. Cronin

Manston, Aeneas son to Cytherea
Aldclyffe*; villain in author's first pub-
lished (and Collins*-like) novel
Eunice his lawful wife
Desperate Remedies (1871) Thomas
Hardy

Mant, May *née* Rene Iris, child actress
Caprice (1917) Ronald Firbank

Mantalini, Alfred likable blackguard who
'married on his whiskers'; good-for-
nothing spendthrift; last seen toiling at a
mangle
his wife, from whom he extracted money
by flattery
Nicholas Nickleby (1839) Charles
Dickens

Mantee, Duke gangster
The Petrified Forest play (1934) Robert
E. Sherwood

Mantrap, Gavial, Sir swindler
The Impressions of Theophrastus Such
(1879) George Eliot (rn Mary Anne, later
Marian, Evans)

Manuel foundling, twin brother to Es-
teban*
The Bridge of San Luis Rey (1927)
Thornton Wilder

Manuel sailor on the *We're Here*
Captains Courageous (1897) Rudyard
Kipling

Manuel, Dom jaded idealist in many of the
now forgotten novels of the imaginary
province of Poictesme; onwards from
Gallantry† (1907) James Branch Cabell

Manuel, Don dictator who rescues Sard
Harker and his beloved Juanita
(Margarita Kingsborough) and gives
him work
Sard Harker† (1924) John Masefield

Manylodes, Mr
The Three Clerks (1858) Anthony
Trollope

Mapen, Rose
The Ox-Bow Incident (1940) Walter
Van Tilburg Clark

Maple, Bridget aunt to Sam Crowe*; wife
to Ferret*
Sir Launcelot Greaves (1762) Tobias
Smollett

Maple, Jason cowardly fascist proprietor
of the Black Mesa Bar-B-Q in Arizona

desert
Gabby his daughter
The Petrified Forest play (1934) Robert
E. Sherwood

Maplestead, Rick cc
The Merry-Go-Round in the Sea (1965)
Randolph Stow

Maplestone, Matilda, Mrs
Julia; Matilda her daughters
Sketches by Boz† (1836) Charles Dickens

Mapple, Father deliverer of symbolic ser-
mon; character suggested by a seaman-
turned preacher, called Thompson
Moby Dick, or *The Whale* (1851) Herman Melville

Marasca, Francesco (Cicio) m. Alvina
Houghton
The Lost Girl (1920) D. H. Lawrence

Marayne, Lady m. (1) Revd Harold
Benham*, (2) Sir Godfrey, celebrated
surgeon
The Research Magnificent (1915) H. G.
Wells

Marble, Moses mate of the *John*
Afloat and Ashore (1844) James
Fenimore Cooper

Marblehall, Mr 'never did anything, never
got married until he was sixty'
Mrs Marblehall his wife, 'spent her life
trying to escape from the parlor-like jaws
of self-consciousness'; thinks her husband is named Mr Bird
ss 'Old Mr Marblehall'
A Curtain of Green (1941) Eudora Welty

Marcel cc and narrator (but seven distinct
'Is' have been distinguished in the course
of the narrative, since the author from
early on viewed personality as a multiple
phenomenon)
his father
his mother
his grandmother
Adolphe his uncle
A la recherche du temps perdu (*In Search
of Lost Time*) (1913–27) Marcel Proust

Marcella
Gorboduc play (1562) Thomas Norton
and Thomas Sackville

Marcella cc
The Duke of Milan play (1623) Philip
Massinger

Marcellus an officer
Hamlet play (1623) William Shakespeare

March Hare, The
  Alice in Wonderland (1865) Lewis
  Carroll (rn Charles Lutwidge Dodgson)
March, Augie Chicago-Jewish cc, bastard
  of an illiterate Chicago charwoman
  Georgie his mentally retarded younger
  brother
  Simon his opportunist elder brother
  Charlotte Simon's wife
  Stella Chesney his actress wife
  The Adventures of Augie March (1953)
  Saul Bellow
March, Basil
  Isabel his wife; ccs of author's first novel
  Their Wedding Trip (1871); *A Hazard of
  New Fortunes* (1890); *An Open-Eyed
  Conspiracy* (1897); *Their Silver Wedding
  Journey†* (1899) William Dean Howells
March, Charles member of Anglo-Jewish
  banking family
  Ann his wife, active communist
  Leonard his father
  Katherine his sister, m. Francis Getliffe
  Sir Philip March his uncle, the head of the
  family
  The Conscience of the Rich (1958) C. P.
  Snow
March, Colin rival in army to Barbason*
  ss 'Honours Easy'
  Fiery Particles (1923) C. E. Montague
March, Henry
  Ursula his daughter, m. John Halifax*
  John Halifax, Gentleman (1856) Mrs
  Craik
March, Hurry Harry Natty Bumppo's*
  friend
  The Deerslayer (1841) James Fenimore
  Cooper
March, Lord
  The Virginians (1857–9) W. M.
  Thackeray
March, Miss cc in love with Henry
  Grenfel*
  ss 'The Fox'
  The Captain's Doll (1923) (in UK, *The
  Ladybird*) D. H. Lawrence
March, Mr philosopher and teacher
  'Marmee' his wife
  Meg m. John Brooke; Jo m. Friedrich
  Bhaer; Beth; Amy m. Theodore Laur-
  ence, their daughters
  Aunt March his sister
  Little Women† (1868–86) Louisa M.
Alcott
Marcham, Revd Howard Episcopal
  clergyman in middle American town
  'with no real background of the spirit'
  Not by the Door (1954) James B. Hall
Marchant, T. A.
  ss 'Unlucky for Pringle'
  Unlucky for Pringle (1973) Wyndham
  Lewis
Marchbanks, Eugene
  Candida play (1894) George Bernard
  Shaw
Marchbanks, Samuel a Canadian Samuel
  Johnson* and alter ego of the author,
  who is greatly admired by some, especi-
  ally in Canada
  The Diary of Samuel Marchbanks†
  (1947) Robertson Davies
Marchdale, Peter novelist cc who meets the
  double of the heroine of the novel, *A Man
  of Words*, which he wrote under the
  pseudonym of Felix Wildmay; m.
  Beatrice, Duchess of Santangiolo*
  The Cardinal's Snuff-Box (1900) Henry
  Harland
Marchioness, The drudge, taken up by and
  eventually m. Dick Swiveller*; at school
  called Sophronia Sphynx
  The Old Curiosity Shop (1841) Charles
  Dickens
Marchmain, Marquis of (family name
  Flyte)
  Teresa his wife
  The Earl of Brideshead m. Mrs Beryl
  Muspratt*
  Lord Sebastian; Lady Julia m. Rex
  Mottram*; Lady Cordelia their children
  Brideshead Revisited (1945) Evelyn
  Waugh
Marchmill, William gun maker
  Ella his wife cc
  ss 'An Imaginative Woman'
  Wessex Tales (1888) Thomas Hardy
Marchmont a herald
  Perkin Warbeck play (1634) John Ford
Marchmont, Margaret, Mrs
  An Ideal Husband play (1895) Oscar
  Wilde
Marchmont, Miss rich crippled invalid to
  whom the young Lucy Snowe* is com-
  panion
  Villette (1853) Charlotte Brontë
Marck, William de la 'Wild Boar of

Ardennes', father to Carl Eberson*
Quentin Durward (1823) Walter Scott

Marco, Martín cc
La Colmena (The Hive) (1951) Camilo
José Cela

Marcus Andronicus brother to Titus*
Titus Andronicus play (1623) William
Shakespeare

Marcus, Hetty m. (1) Harry Smith*, (2)
Fred Sumner*, father to her children
The Dream (1924) H. G. Wells

Marden, John
ss 'The Woman in his Life'
Limits and Renewals (1932) Rudyard
Kipling

Marder, Theophilus satirist
Mephisto (1936) Klaus Mann

Mardon purchaser of Sophia Scales'*
French boarding-house
The Old Wives' Tale (1908) Arnold
Bennett

Mardon, Mary in love with Mark Rutherford*; dies young
her father, an agnostic and an influence
on Mark
The Autobiography of Mark Rutherford
(1881) Mark Rutherford (rn William
Hale White)

Mardonius
A King and No King play (1611) Francis
Beaumont and John Fletcher

Margaret (hist.) daughter to Reignier, later
wife to Henry
King Henry VI; *King Richard III* plays
(1623) William Shakespeare

Margaret sensitive orphan; m. Mr Evelyn*
Margaret (1845, rev. 1851) Sylvester
Judd

Margaret young workwoman, m. Will
Wilson*
Mary Barton (1848) Mrs Gaskell

Margaret, Dame prioress of the Bene-
dictine convent at Oby
The Corner That Held Them (1948)
Sylvia Townsend Warner

Margaret, Mad m. Sir Despard
Murgatroyd*
Ruddigore opera (1887) W. S. Gilbert
and Arthur Sullivan

Margayya cc, the financial expert, publisher of a pornographic book based on
the *Kama Sutra* called *Domestic Harmony*, written by Dr Pal*, moneylender

his spoiled son
The Financial Expert (1952) R. K.
Narayan

Margery, Dame nurse to Eveline Berenger*
The Betrothed (1825) Walter Scott

Marget, Jack priest
ss 'A Doctor of Medicine'
Rewards and Fairies (1910) Rudyard
Kipling

Margettes market gardener
his wife and son
ss 'A Friend of the Family'
Debits and Credits (1926) Rudard Kipling

Marguerite wife to St Leon*
St Leon (1799) William Godwin

Maria
Brigitte her daughter
The Power and the Glory (1940) Graham
Greene

Maria attending on the Princess
Love's Labour's Lost play (1623) William Shakespeare

Maria cc, mistress to Jordan*
For Whom the Bell Tolls (1940) Ernest
Hemingway

Maria Olivia's* servant
Twelfth Night play (1623) William
Shakespeare

Maria see **Harrington**

Maria Sir Peter Teazle's* ward
The School for Scandal play (1777)
Richard Brinsley Sheridan

Maria who tamed Petruccio*
A Woman's Prize, or The Tamer Tamed
(sequel) play (1647) John Fletcher

Marian dairymaid at Talbothays Farm
Tess of the D'Urbervilles (1891) Thomas
Hardy

Mariana an English courtesan
The Wild-Goose Chase play (1652) John
Fletcher

Mariana betrothed to Angelo*
Measure for Measure play (1623)
William Shakespeare

Mariani keeper of grog shop, 'unspeakable
scoundrel'
Lord Jim (1900) Joseph Conrad (rn Josef
Teodor Konrad Korzeniowski)

Marie-Madeleine, Soeur see **Maes,
Gertrude**

Marigold, Dr narrator

Dr Marigold's Prescriptions (1865)
Charles Dickens

Mario a Roman
Death's Jest Book, or *The Fool's Tragedy*
play (1850) Thomas Lovell Beddoes

Mario courtier
*The Pleasant Commedye of Patient
Grissill* play (1603) Thomas Dekker

Marion landlady of the Three Fish
The Cloister and the Hearth (1861)
Charles Reade

Marius young Roman noble of the time of
Marcus Aurelius, in highly influential
romance that burns with a pure, gem-like
flame
Marius the Epicurean (1885) Walter
Pater

Marius, Eugene French sea captain
Levine (1956) James Hanley

Marjoribanks, Lucilla cc, m. her cousin
Tom Marjoribanks
Dr Marjoribanks her indulgent father
Tom her cousin, proverbially unlucky,
but returns from abroad to m. Lucilla
Miss Marjoribanks (1866) Mrs Margaret
Oliphant

Mark Antony see **Antony**

Mark, Lord suitor to Kate Croy*
The Wings of the Dove (1902) Henry
James

Markby, Lady
An Ideal Husband play (1895) Oscar
Wilde

Marker, Captain shot in quarrel by
Rawdon Crawley*
Vanity Fair (1847–8) W. M. Thackeray

Marker, Mrs
Nicholas Nickleby (1839) Charles
Dickens

Markham friend to Steerforth*
David Copperfield (1850) Charles
Dickens

Markham, Gilbert cc, part narrator, m. as
third husband Helen Huntingdon*
Fergus his brother
Rose his sister
The Tenant of Wildfell Hall (1848) Anne
Brontë

Markham, Lucy m. Fred Coleman*
Frank Fairlegh (1850) F. E. Smedley

Markland, Mr and Mrs
The Woman in White (1860) Wilkie
Collins

Markleham, Mrs scheming lady called the
Old Soldier; tactless and selfish
David Copperfield (1850) Charles
Dickens

Marks partner to Tom Loker*
Uncle Tom's Cabin (1851) Harriet
Beecher Stowe

Marks, Will John Podger's* nephew
Master Humphrey's Clock (1841)
Charles Dickens

Marley, Jacob former partner to Scrooge*
whose ghost haunts him
A Christmas Carol (1843) Charles
Dickens

Marlow, Charles suitor to Kate Hardcas-
tle*
Sir Charles his father
She Stoops to Conquer play (1773)
Oliver Goldsmith

Marlow, Charlie narrator, observer,
friend, onwards from
Lord Jim† (1900) Joseph Conrad (rn
Josef Teodor Konrad Korzeniowski)

Marlowe, Philip private dick, narrator, in
influential American detective thrillers
onwards from
The Big Sleep† (1939) Raymond
Chandler

Marmeladov masochistic drunkard who is
run over and killed
his half-mad consumptive wife
Sonia his daughter by his first m., 'holy
prostitute'
his children by his second wife
*Prestuplenie i Nakazanie (Crime and
Punishment)* (1866) Fyodor Dostoievsky

Marneffe, Valerie, Mme de whore and
schemer
her complacent pimp of a husband
La Cousine Bette (1847) Honoré de
Balzac

Marner, Silas cc, linen weaver of Raveloe
Silas Marner (1861) George Eliot (rn
Mary Anne, later Marian, Evans)

Marney, Earl of (family name **Egremont**)
Arabella his wife
The Dowager Countess his mother
the Hon. Charles, MP his brother and
successor, m. Sybil Gerard*
Sybil (1845) Benjamin Disraeli

Maroola, Dain in love with Nina
Almayer*
Almayer's Folly (1895) Joseph Conrad

(rn Josef Teodor Konrad Korzeniowski)

Maroon, Captain creditor to Tip Dorrit*, horsey gentleman with tight drab legs
Little Dorrit (1857) Charles Dickens

Marple, Miss the author's second-string detective: quiet thin little old spinster, a village dweller, seventy-four in 1928, who has a nose for evil and relies on gossip, onwards from
Murder at the Vicarage† (1930) Agatha Christie

Marplot busybody who always gets it wrong
The Busie Body play (1709) Susannah Centlivre

Marpole, Jake companion to Jim Burden*
My Antonia (1918) Willa Cather

Marpole, James Captain of *Clorinda*
Henry his son
A High Wind in Jamaica (1929) Richard Hughes

Marrable, Mr and Mrs friends to the Vanstones*
No Name (1862) Wilkie Collins

Marraby, John, Sir of Brasenose
Zuleika Dobson (1911) Max Beerbohm

Marrall a term-driver, Creature of Overreach*
A New Way to Pay Old Debts play (1633) Philip Massinger

Marrowfat, Dr
A Citizen of the World (1762) Oliver Goldsmith

Marsay, Eugene ('Gene') poverty-stricken young Hungarian reporter, who becomes Communist organizer, cc
his wife, *née* Darvas*
You Can't Sleep Here (1934); *This is Your Day* (1937) Edward Newhouse

Marsden failed painter, once rival in love to Romarin*, and still, forty years after, filled with hatred for him, in sinister tale; diabetic drunkard; rolls up and 'bolts' 'pellets of bread'; has 'pitifully' hunted down 'sensation to the last inch in 'fiendishly ingenious and utterly unimaginative' manner
ss 'The Accident'
Widdershins (1911) Oliver Onions

Marsden, Charles sexless mother-centred third-rate novelist in love with Nina Leeds*
Strange Interlude play (1927) Eugene O'Neill

Marsden, The Earl of
The Marsden Case (1923) Ford Madox Ford

Marsellus, Louis vulgar materialist rich because of patent bequeathed to his wife, Rosamond *née* St Peter* by Tom Outland*, whom he despises
The Professor's House (1925) Willa Cather

Marsh see **Marshmoreton**

Marsh, Buddy owner of Kentish farm and mistress of Richmond Drew*
The Pitiful Wife (1924) Storm Jameson

Marshall, David rich Chicago merchant destroyed by his family's bourgeois expectations
Eliza his wife
Truesdale; Rosamund; Jane their three youngest children
With the Procession (1895) Henry Blake Fuller

Marshall, Emma, Nurse
A House and Its Head (1935) Ivy Compton-Burnett

Marshall, Mary gave up Dick Doubledick* on account of his wild ways but then nursed him in Brussels: when he recovered there he found himself her husband
Seven Poor Travellers (1854) Charles Dickens

Marshall, Miss friend to the Censorious Young Gentleman*
Sketches of Young Gentlemen (1838) Charles Dickens

Marshall, William see **Pembroke, Earl of**

Marshman, George and Howard
The Wide, Wide World (1850) Elizabeth Wetherell (rn Susan Bogert Warner)

Marshmoreton, John, Earl of (family name **Marsh**), m. Billie Dore
Lord Belpher; Lady Maud m. George Bevan his children
A Damsel in Distress (1919) P. G. Wodehouse

Marston, Dick narrator, m. Grace Storefield*
Ben his father
Norah his mother
Aileen his sister
Jim his brother, m. Jeanie Mossison*: members of Starlight's* gang: cattle

thieves and bank robbers in first Australian novel to present Australian-born colonials as main characters
Robbery Under Arms: A Story of Life and Adventure in the Bush and in the Goldfields of Australia (1888, rev. 1889) Rolf Boldrewood (rn Thomas Alexander Browne)

Martell follower and friend to Theodoret*
Thierry and Theodoret play (1621) John Fletcher, Philip Massinger ?nd Francis Beaumont

Marten, Edgar Jewish geologist
South Wind (1917) Norman Douglas

Martext, Oliver, Sir a vicar
As You Like It play (1623) William Shakespeare

Martha Abbess of Elcho
The Fair Maid of Perth (1828) Walter Scott

Martha aged housekeeper at Osbaldistone Hall
Rob Roy (1818) Walter Scott

Martha maid to Miss Matty Jenkins*, engaged to Jim Hearn*
Cranford (1853) Mrs Gaskell

Martha Sarah village girl
ss 'The Distracted Preacher'
Wessex Tales (1888) Thomas Hardy

Martha servant to Mrs Pendennis* and Laura Bell*
Pendennis† (1848) W. M. Thackeray

Martian, The female guiding spirit and lover to Barty Josselin*
The Martian (1897) George du Maurier

Martigny, Countess de m. Earl of Etherington*
St Ronan's Well (1824) Walter Scott

Martilla niece to Mrs Motherly*
A Journey to London play (1728) John Vanbrugh

Martin ('Madman') muddle-headed experimenter, chum to Tom Brown*
Tom Brown's Schooldays (1857) Thomas Hughes

Martin Manichean philosopher
Candide (1759) Voltaire (rn François-Marie Arouet)

Martin Miss Allen's* surly groom
The Pickwick Papers (1837) Charles Dickens

Martin servant to O'Brien*
1984 (1949) George Orwell (rn Eric Blair)

Martin servant to the Castlewoods*
Henry Esmond (1852) W. M. Thackeray

Martin, Shago black jazz singer
An American Dream (1965) Norman Mailer

Martin young milkman
Nobody Answered the Door (1971) Rhys Davies

Martin, 'Humanity' (hist.), Richard Martin, a founder of R S P C A, of 'costermonger notoriety'
Sketches by Boz† (1836) Charles Dickens

Martin, 'Pincher' cc
Pincher Martin (1956) William Golding

Martin, Amelia, Miss the Mistaken Milliner, thought she could sing
Sketches by Boz† (1836) Charles Dickens

Martin, Baby-Face gangster betrayed by Gimpty* and killed by police
Dead End play (1936) Sidney Kingsley

Martin, Betsey one-eyed (because her mother drank stout) charwoman converted to temperance
The Pickwick Papers (1837) Charles Dickens

Martin, Betty a sailor heard a supplicant in a foreign church saying 'Ah! Mihi, beate Martine!', i.e. 'All my eye and Betty Martin'
Joe Miller's Jests (1739) John Mottley (publisher)

Martin, Brother of St Illods
ss 'The Eye of Allah'
Debits and Credits (1926) Rudyard Kipling

Martin, Captain prisoner in the Marshalsea
Little Dorrit (1857) Charles Dickens

Martin, Dame 'Queen of the Revels'
Redgauntlet (1824) Walter Scott

Martin, Daniel cc
Daniel Martin (1977) John Fowles

Martin, Donald young rancher
The Ox-Bow Incident (1940) Walter Van Tilburg Clark

Martin, Dora star actress
Mephisto (1936) Klaus Mann

Martin, Dr doctor to the Pontifexes*
The Way of All Flesh (1903) Samuel Butler

Martin, Guillermo Francoist tradesman
For Whom the Bell Tolls (1940) Ernest

Hemingway

Martin, Jack companion to Ralph Rover*
Coral Island† (1858) R. M. Ballantyne

Martin, Jack the Bagman's uncle
The Pickwick Papers (1837) Charles
Dickens

Martin, James, Sir m. Lady Susan de
Courcy*
Lady Susan (1871) Jane Austen

Martin, Kennie young psychopath
ss 'A Bit off the Map'
A Bit off the Map (1957) Angus Wilson

Martin, Mr young gentleman friend to
Gerrard*
The Gentleman Dancing-Master comedy
(1673) William Wycherley

Martin, Mrs grandmother to Swithin St
Cleeve*
Giles her late husband
Two on a Tower (1882) Thomas Hardy

Martin, Philip, Revd grass-roots civil
rights leader
Etienne his estranged son
In My Father's House (1978) Ernest J.
Gaines

Martin, Phyl and Dolly
Maurice their cousin
Invitation to the Waltz (1932)
Rosamond Lehmann

Martin, Pol usher to Lady Tub*
A Tale of a Tub play (1640) Ben Jonson

Martin, Raymond, MP the 'jelly-bellied
flag-flapper'
ss 'The Flag of their Country'
Stalky & Co. (1899) Rudyard Kipling

Martin, Richard ('Shifty Dick')
Put Yourself in his Place (1870) Charles
Reade

Martin, Robert farmer, refused by Miss
Harriet Smith*, owing to interference of
Emma Woodhouse* — but ultimately
accepted
Emma (1816) Jane Austen

Martin, Sally deformed girl
ss 'Janet's Repentance
Scenes of Clerical Life (1857) George
Eliot (rn Mary Anne, later Marian,
Evans)

Martin, Sponge painter of carriages
Dark Laughter (1925) Sherwood
Anderson

Martin, Tom butcher in Fleet Prison
The Pickwick Papers (1837) Charles

Dickens

Martindale, Dorcas attends Clarissa
Harlowe* in her captivity
Clarissa Harlowe (1748) Samuel
Richardson

Martineau, Dr Harley Street specialist
The Secret Places of the Heart (1922)
H. G. Wells

Martinez, Antonio Joseph renegade priest;
landowner
Death Comes for the Archbishop (1927)
Willa Cather

Martingale, Bob, Major friend to Rawdon
Crawley*
Vanity Fair (1847–8) W. M. Thackeray

Martinon opportunist and successful sena-
tor
L'Education sentimentale (1869)
Gustave Flaubert

Martius son to Titus Andronicus*
Titus Andronicus play (1623) William
Shakespeare

Marton treacherous waiting-woman
Quentin Durward (1824) Walter Scott

Marton village schoolmaster who took
pity on Little Nell* and her grandfather
The Old Curiosity Shop (1841) Charles
Dickens

Martyn
ss 'The Rout of the Black Hussars'
Plain Tales from the Hills (1888) Rudyard Kipling

Martyn, William ('William the Conqueror'), m. Scott
her brother, in the police
ss 'William the Conqueror'
The Day's Work (1898) Rudyard Kipling

Marvell, Ralph ('The Little Fellow') sec-
ond husband to Undine Spragg*
Paul their son
Ralph's mother, née Dagonet
Urban his grandfather
Clare his sister, m. Henley Fairford*
The Custom of the Country (1913) Edith
Wharton

Marwood, Alice instrumental in setting
Mr Dombey* on right track
Dombey and Son (1848) Charles Dickens

Marwood, Mrs friend to Fainall*, 'likes
Mirabell*'
The Way of the World comedy (1710)
William Congreve

Marwood, Mrs mistress to the Fourth

Lord Castlewood*
Henry Esmond (1852) W. M. Thackeray
Marx, Bernard cc dystopia; something went wrong with his treatment while in the womb
Brave New World (1932) Aldous Huxley
Marxse, Madame lodging-house keeper
The Constant Nymph (1924) Margaret Kennedy
Mary
ss 'Marching to Zion'
Adam and Eve and Pinch Me (1921) A. E. Coppard
Mary 'The Pretty Housemaid', serving Nupkins* and then Winkle*, m. Sam Weller*; character founded on one of the author's nurses called Weller
The Pickwick Papers (1837) Charles Dickens
Mary Ann Wemmick's* maid of all work
Great Expectations (1861) Charles Dickens
Mary Anne Mrs Peacher's* favourite pupil; always held up her hand before asking a question
Our Mutual Friend (1865) Charles Dickens
Mary maid to Mrs Brandon*
The Adventures of Philip (1862) W. M. Thackeray
Mary possessed a small lamb
poem 'Mary Had a Little Lamb'
Poems for Our Children (1830) Sarah Josepha Buell Hale
Mary victim of operation by Dr Raymond*
The Great God Pan (1894) Arthur Machen
Mary, 'Sister' orphan cc of novel of Gullah Negro settlement (South Carolina)
Scarlet Sister Mary (1928) Julia Peterkin
Maryk, Steve manipulated by Keefer* into leading mutiny against Queeg*
The Caine Mutiny (1951) Herman Wouk
Maryon, Captain commander of sloop
Christopher Columbus
Marion his sister, m. Captain Carton
The Perils of Certain English Prisoners (1857) Charles Dickens
Marzo
Captain Brassbound's Conversion play (1900) George Bernard Shaw
Mash

ss 'Sandford and Merton'
The Uncommercial Traveller (1860–8) Charles Dickens
Maskelyne British intelligence officer
The Alexandria Quartet (1957–61) Lawrence Durrell
Maskery, Will wheelwright and drunkard
Adam Bede (1859) George Eliot (rn Mary Anne, later Marian, Evans)
Maskwell a villain, pretended friend to Mellefont*, in love with Cynthia*
The Double-Dealer comedy (1710) William Congreve
Maso aged servitor of the Bardi family
Romola (1863) George Eliot (rn Mary Anne, later Marian, Evans)
Mason, Bertha m. Mr Rochester*
Richard her brother
Jane Eyre (1847) Charlotte Brontë
Mason, Lady widow to Sir Joseph Mason, and reluctant forger, in what is reckoned to be one of the author's most powerful novels
Lucius her son
Joseph the eldest of Sir Joseph's four children by an earlier marriage; sullen, irascible, and an implacable enemy to his stepmother, whose inheritance he opposes
Orley Farm (1862) Anthony Trollope
Mason, Monck, Mr owner of flying machine that crossed the Atlantic in seventy-five hours in story first presented as fact
ss 'The Balloon Hoax'
Tales (1845) Edgar Allen Poe
Mason, Murray, Mr
ss 'The Two Captains'
Unlucky for Pringle (1973) Wyndham Lewis
Mason, Orville W. district attorney
An American Tragedy (1925) Theodore Dreiser
Mason, Perry lawyer-detective, onwards from
The Case of the Velvet Claws† (1933) Erle Stanley Gardner
Mason, Pierre conscientious objector cc
Behold Trouble (1944) Granville Hicks
Mason, Sarah old nurse to Colonel Newcome*
The Newcomes (1853–5) W. M. Thackeray

Mason, Warren editor and critic; eventually m. Rose Dutcher*
Rose of Dutcher's Coolly (1895) Hamlin Garland

Masoukas palm reader, gambler, adulterer, concerned man
his wife
his ailing son
A Dream of Kings (1966) Harry Petrakis

Masquerier, Bat impresario
ss 'The Village that Voted the Earth Was Flat'
A Diversity of Creatures (1917) Rudyard Kipling

Masrur Caliph's executioner
Hassan play (1923) James Elroy Flecker

Mass, Oedipa
Murcho her husband
The Crying of Lot 49 (1966) Thomas Pynchon

Massey, Edward, Revd m. Mary Lindlay
ss 'Daughters of the Vicar'
The Prussian Officer (1911) D. H. Lawrence

Massinghay, Weston Tory politician
The New Machiavelli† (1911) H. G. Wells

Masson, Dorothy secretary to Francis Chelifer*
Those Barren Leaves (1925) Aldous Huxley

Masterman consumptive socialist, friend to Sid Pornick*
Kipps (1905) H. G. Wells

Masters, Danny cc
The Escape Artist (1965) David Wagoner

Masters, Madeleine née Burkett, cc
Rickie her husband
Anthony; Colin; Clarissa their children
Dinah Dorothea Burkett her sister, m. Jo Hermann
The Echoing Grove (1953) Rosamond Lehmann

Masters, Mary ever faithful to, and m., Reginald Morton*
her father, lawyer of Dillsborough
The American Senator (1877) Anthony Trollope

Mat Malay guide
Gallions Reach (1927) H. M. Tomlinson

Matcham, John see **Sedley, Joanna**

Matcham, Mrs friend to Mrs Twysden
Rosa her daughter

The Adventures of Philip (1862) W. M. Thackeray

Matchett old family servant
The Death of the Heart (1938) Elizabeth Bowen

Matchin, Maud vulgar, pretty cc of anti-union novel (published anonymously) by politician; m. Sam Sleeny*
her father, an honest carpenter
The Bread-Winners (1884) John Hay

Mately, Dorothy thief, killed by a miraculous act of God
The Life and Death of Mr Badman (1680) John Bunyan

Matfield, Miss
Angel Pavement (1930) J. B. Priestley

Mathers, Walter racehourse owner
ss 'I'm a Fool'
Horses and Men (1924) Sherwood Anderson

Matheson, Lady
Separate Tables play (1955) Terence Rattigan

Mathews, Charles (hist.) theatre man
Sketches of Young Gentlemen (1838) Charles Dickens

Mathias
Katherine his mother
The Jew of Malta play (1633) Christopher Marlowe

Mathias lawyer
High Wind in Jamaica (1929) Richard Hughes

Mathias, Father
The Phantom Ship (1839) Captain Marryat

Matilda emissary of the devil, posing as Rosario, a young novice; seducer of Ambrosio*
The Monk (1795) Matthew G. Lewis

Matinter, The Misses guests at Bath
The Pickwick Papers (1837) Charles Dickens

Matiwan estranged wife of Sanutee* and mother to Occonestoga*
The Yemassee (1835) William Gilmore Simms

Matkah see **Sea Catch**

Matou, Rosine pert portress at Mme Beck's*
Villette (1853) Charlotte Brontë

Matters Doppelgänger of Percy Wort*
The Wort Papers (1972) Peter Mathers

Mattheson, Joshua, Sir caricature of Bertrand Russell, with whom the author had quarrelled
Women in Love (1920) D. H. Lawrence

Matthew chief clerk and partner to Adam Silvercross*
The Old Bank (1902) William Westall

Matthew of Doncaster bowyer
Anne of Geierstein (1829) Walter Scott

Matthew the town gull
Every Man in His Humour play (1598) Ben Jonson

Matthew, Inspector London detective
Guignol's band (1944) Louis-Ferdinand Céline (rn Louis-Ferdinand Destouches)

Matthews Gresbury's* page, looked as though he had always slept underground
Nicholas Nickleby (1839) Charles Dickens

Matthews, Andrew and Stella friends to Martha Quest*
The *Children of Violence* series (1952–69) Doris Lessing

Matthews, Bess m. Gabriel Harrison* (really Governor Craven)
her father, an aged puritan parson who at first refuses to allow his daughter to marry
The Yemassee (1835) William Gilmore Simms

Matuchevitz, Prince Russian ambassador
Jorrocks's Jaunts and Jollities (1838) R. S. Surtees

Matveyitch, Ivan crooked associate of Tarantyev*
Oblomov (1859) Ivan Goncharov

Matzerath, Oscar grotesque hunchback narrator of the most outstanding German post-war novel
Die Blechtrommel (The Tin Drum) (1959) Günter Grass

Mauberley, Hugh Selwyn passive aesthetic poet
Hugh Selwyn Mauberley poem (1920) Ezra Pound

Maudie Fred Booty's* girlfriend
The Combined Maze (1913) May Sinclair

Maudsley, Marian m. Viscount Trimingham*
W. H. Maudsley her father, landowner
Madeleine her mother
Marcus; Dennis her brothers
The Go-Between (1953) L. P. Hartley

Maule, Matthew carpenter
Matthew his grandfather, executed as a wizard
The House of the Seven Gables (1851) Nathaniel Hawthorne

Mauleverer, Earl of
Paul Clifford (1830) Edward Bulwer Lytton

Mauleverer, Lord
Cranford (1853) Mrs Gaskell

Mauley, Edward, Sir The Black Dwarf, wealthy victim of his treacherous friend Richard Vere*
The Black Dwarf (1816) Walter Scott

Maulnier, Colonel
The Other Side (1946) Storm Jameson

Maunders variety proprietor who kept six male and six female dwarfs in his cottage, and giants to wait on them
The Old Curiosity Shop (1841) Charles Dickens

Maurice, Robert, Sir, Baronet, MP narrator
The Martian (1897) George du Maurier

Mauruccio an old buffoon
Love's Sacrifice play (1633) John Ford

Maury, Aleck narrator cc of American novel and in several ss (sometimes as controlling intelligence rather than narrator)
Aleck Maury Sportsman (1934) Caroline Gordon; *The Collected Short Stories of Caroline Gordon* (1981)

Mauverenson, Douw cc hist. novel set in early 19th-century Mohawk Valley (N.Y. State)
In the Valley (1890) Harold Frederic

Mavering, Dan cc novel about a twice-broken engagement finally fufilled: Dan is unable to be frank about his activities because he fears the puritanism of the girl he finally m.: Alice Pasmer*
April Hopes (1887) William Dean Howells

Mavis member of gang living in bomb sites
The World My Wilderness (1950) Rose Macaulay

Maw-worm the hypocrite in adaptation from Molière* and Cibber by author who was pretty well, like Ulysses's Uncle Cyril, 'deported for a homosexual crime'
The Hypocrite play (1768) Isaac Bicker-

staffe

Mawls and Maxby pupils
ss 'Our School'
Reprinted Pieces (1858) Charles Dickens

Mawmsey grocer
Middlemarch (1871–2)George Eliot (rn Mary Anne, later Marian, Evans)

Mawworm a lieutenant and companion to Follywit*
A Mad World My Masters comedy (1608) Thomas Middleton

Max German student in love with Becky Sharp*
Vanity Fair (1847–8) W. M. Thackeray

Maximilian general
The Case is Altered play (1609) Ben Jonson

Maximus (hist.) Emperor of Britain
ss 'A Centurion of the Thirtieth'
Puck of Pook's Hill (1906) Rudyard Kipling

Maximus a distinguished warrior, perhaps one of Burbage's roles
Valentinian play (1647) John Fletcher

Maximych, Maxim the junior captain, part narrator
Geroi Nas hego Vremeni (A Hero of Our Time) (1841) Mikhail Lermontov

Maxley, James evil miser
Hard Cash (1863) Charles Reade

Maxwell family name of Lord Evandale*
Maxwell of Summertrees ('Pate-in-Peril') old Jacobite
Redgauntlet (1824) Walter Scott

Maxwell, Angus, Sir brother-in-law to Sir Gulliver Deniston*
Cynthis his wife
The World My Wilderness (1950) Rose Macaulay

Maxwell, Lord grandfather to Aldous Raeburn*
his daughter
Marcella (1894) Mrs Humphry Ward

Maxwell, Mary ('Mary Mischief') cc
Richard her father
Will; Peter ('Patie'); **Richard; David; Kennedy; Steenie** her brothers
Lady Grizel her cousin
The Raiders (1894); *The Dark o' the Moon* (1902) Samuel Rutherford Crockett

Maxwell, Mrs aunt to Helen Graham*
her husband

The Tenant of Wildfell Hall (1848) Anne Brontë

May, Ma Hla Flory's* mistress
Burmese Days (1935) George Orwell (rn Eric Blair)

May, Mr manager of James Houghton's* cinema
The Lost Girl (1920) D. H. Lawrence

Maybold, Arthur, Revd incumbent of Mellstock
his mother
Under the Greenwood Tree (1872) Thomas Hardy

Maybud, Rose m. Dick Dauntless*
Ruddigore opera (1887) W. S. Gilbert and Arthur Sullivan

Mayfill, Miss
A Clergyman's Daughter (1935) George Orwell (rn Eric Blair)

Mayflower, Phoebe Alice Lee's* maid
Woodstock (1826) Walter Scott

Mayhew, Mrs charlady
Dust Falls on Eugene Schlumberger (1964) Shena Mackay

Mayhew, Revd Mr m. Eva Lilly*
The Oriel Window (1896) Mrs Molesworth

Maylie, Mrs kindhearted woman; befriended Oliver Twist*
Harry her son, m. Rose (below)
Rose her adopted daughter
Oliver Twist (1839) Charles Dickens

Maynard college friend to Philip Firmin*
The Adventures of Philip (1862) W. M. Thackeray

Maynard, Elsie strolling player, m. Colonel Fairfax*
The Yeomen of the Guard opera (1888) W. S. Gilbert and Arthur Sullivan

Maynard, Jim engaged to Annie Bolt*
All Our Yesterdays (1930) H. M. Tomlinson

Maynard, Mr South African magistrate
Binkie his son, leader of a gang of 'hearties'
The Children of Violence series (1952–69) Doris Lessing

Maynard, Roger
his wife
Non-Combatants and Others (1916) Rose Macaulay

Maynard, Rose 'elfin child', materialized heroine of the Pinckney novels

Meet Mr Mulliner (1927) P. G. Wodehouse

Mayne, Richard, Sir (hist.) organized police force
The Uncommercial Traveller (1860–8) Charles Dickens

Mayo, Robert poetic farmer who wants to go to sea but stays to marry Ruth Atkins*; the marriage fails
Andrew his brother and rival for Ruth who goes to sea when she rejects him for Robert
Beyond the Horizon play (1920) Eugene O'Neill

Mazaro, Manuel Cuban traitor
ss 'Café des exiles'
Old Creole Days (1879) George Washington Cable

Mazey seafaring friend to Admiral Bartram*
No Name (1862) Wilkie Collins

Meacham, Miss
Separate Tables play (1955) Terence Rattigan

Meade, Dr
his wife
Darcy; Philip their sons
Gone With the Wind (1936) Margaret Mitchell

Meade, Michael owner of Imber Court
The Bell (1958) Iris Murdoch

Meadowes, Mary, Lady m. the Earl of Pastmaster*
Put Out More Flags (1942) Evelyn Waugh

Meadows, John farmer, owner of the Black Horse, in love with Susan Merton*
his mother
It Is Never Too Late To Mend (1856) Charles Reade

Meadows, Miss
ss 'The Singing Lesson'
The Garden Party (1922) Katherine Mansfield (rn Katherine Mansfield Beauchamp)

Meadows, Mrs formerly Retlow, cousin to Thomas Heard*
South Wind (1917) Norman Douglas

Meadows, Sally, Miss
Uncle Remus (1880–95) Joel Chandler Harris

Meagles, Mr and Mrs kindly old couple fond of travel

Tattycoram their adopted daughter, who ran away to Miss Wade* for a time
Minnie ('Pet') their daughter, m. Henry Gowan*
Little Dorrit (1857) Charles Dickens

Meakin, Mrs keeper of Gordon Comstock's* filthy kip in Brewer's Yard
Keep the Aspidistra Flying (1936) George Orwell (rn Eric Blair)

Mealmaker, Andrew
The Little Minister (1891) J. M. Barrie

Mealmaker, Tibbie
David her husband
A Window in Thrums (1891) J. M. Barrie

Mealy Potatoes one of Copperfield's* companions in the Murdstone* and Grinby warehouse
David Copperfield (1850) Charles Dickens

Meander a Persian Lord
Tamburlaine play (1590) Christopher Marlowe

Means, Elipalet lawyer
Jerome (1897) Mary E. Wilkins

Means, Jack employer of Hannah Thompson* who is found to be illegally bound to him
Mirandy his sister, whom he wishes Hartsook* to marry
The Hoosier Schoolmaster (1871) Edward Eggleston

Means, Tom
ss 'The Man Who Became a Woman'
Horses and Men (1924) Sherwood Anderson

Meares, Mrs
Sylvia Scarlett (1918) Compton Mackenzie

Mears, Charlie bank clerk who remembers his former lives but cannot turn his knowledge into art – and loses his power when he falls in love
ss 'The Finest Story in the World'
Many Inventions (1893) Rudyard Kipling

Meath, Larry
Love on the Dole (1933) Walter Greenwood

Meats, Henry (alias **Barnes**, alias **Brother Aloysius**) bad hat and murderer
Sinister Street (1913) Compton Mackenzie

Meaulnes, Le Grand adolescent hero of

unique French classic by author killed in 1914–18 War
Le Grand Meaulnes (The Lost Domain; The Wanderer) (1913) Alain Fournier (rn Henri Fournier)

Mecaenas friend to Octavius Caesar
Antony and Cleopatra play (1623) William Shakespeare

Medbourne a former merchant, now poor
ss 'Dr Heidegger's Experiment'
Twice-Told Tales (1837) Nathaniel Hawthorne

Media native king
Mardi (1849) Herman Melville

Medici, Francisco de Duke of Florence
Cardinal Monticelso his brother
The White Devil play (1612) John Webster

Medina Saroté with whom Nunez* falls in love
Yacob her father
ss 'The Country of the Blind'
Twelve Stories and a Dream (1903) H. G. Wells

Medina, Duke of
Agnes his daughter, m. Raymond de la Casternas
Don Lorenzo his nephew, m.(1) Antonia, (2) Virginia
The Monk (1796) Matthew G. Lewis

Medlicote, Lord patron of hospital
Middlemarch (1871–2) George Eliot (rn Mary Anne, later Marian, Evans)

Medway, Barbara m. Ferdinand Dibble*
The Heart of a Goof (1926) P. G. Wodehouse

Meeber, Carrie cc
Sister Carrie (1900) Theodore Dreiser

Meek Man, The guest to Mr Podsnap* who dared to disagree with him
Our Mutual Friend (1865) Charles Dickens

Meek, Mr and Mrs
Mr Weston's Good Wine (1927) T. F. Powys

Meek, Josiah, Revd m. Helen Green*
The Adventures of Mr Verdant Green (1853) Cuthbert Bede (rn Edward Bradley)

Meek, Mrs
George her husband
ss 'Mrs Meek'
Reprinted Pieces (1858) Charles Dickens

Meekin, Revd Mr chaplain to convicts
His Natural Life (1870–2; abridged by the author 1874; in 1885 as *For the Term of His Natural Life* – thus evading the author's irony; original text edited by Stephen Murray-Smith, 1970) Marcus Clarke

Meeks copperflue salesman
The Violent Bear It Away (1960) Flannery O'Connor

Meercraft 'projector': confidence-man
The Devil is an Ass play (1631) Ben Jonson

Meg a bawd
A Fair Quarrel play (1617) Thomas Middleton and William Rowley

Meg of the Ramme, m. George Saxton*
The White Peacock (1911) D. H. Lawrence

Meg ultimate American Jewish mom
Joseph her suffering son
A Mother's Kisses (1964) Bruce Jay Friedman

Megatherium, Lord gouty and aged
Middlemarch (1871–2) George Eliot (rn Mary Anne, later Marian, Evans)

Megatherium, The the Giant Ground Sloth seen as surviving by Mr Blettsworthy* on Rampole Island
Mr Blettsworthy on Rampole Island (1933) H. G. Wells

Megea court lady
Philaster play (1620) Francis Beaumont and John Fletcher

Meggatt, Rodney m. Janet Studdard*
Hermione their daughter
Considine his uncle
Friends and Relations (1931) Elizabeth Bowen

Meggot, Betsy, Mrs
Jane; Nancy her daughters
Mrs Perkins' Ball (1847) W. M. Thackeray

Mehalah ('Glory') passionate peasant girl in rustic novel of the Salt Marshes
Mehalah: a Story of the Salt Marshes (1880) Sabine Baring-Gould

mehitabel cat, *toujours gai*, onwards from
archy and mehitabel verse (1927) Don Marquis

Meiklewham, Saunders 'the man of law'
St Ronan's Well (1824) Walter Scott

Meister, Wilhelm son of wealthy

merchant, cc of complex *Bildungsroman Wilhelm Meisters Lehrjahre* (*Wilhelm Meister's Apprenticeship*) (1796) Johann Wolfgang Goethe

Melanctha Black-girl cc
ss 'Melanctha'
Three Lives (1909) Gertrude Stein

Melantha an affected lady
Marriage à la Mode play (1673) John Dryden

Melantius brother to Evadne*
The Maid's Tragedy play (1611) Francis Beaumont and John Fletcher

Melba popular singer, m. Malcolm*
Malcolm (1959) James Purdy

Melbury, Mr good-hearted timber merchant whose social ambitions for his daughter cause tragedy
Mrs Melbury his second wife
Grace his daughter; cc; m. Edred Fitzpiers*
The Woodlanders (1887) Thomas Hardy

Melchester, Bishop of (Cuthbert Helmsdale) hypocritical and lustful cleric
Two on a Tower (1882) Thomas Hardy

Melchisedech solicitor
Bleak House (1853) Charles Dickens

Melchitsekek, Pinchas poor poet and scholar
Children of the Ghetto (1892) Israel Zangwill

Meleander an old lord
The Lover's Melancholy play (1629) John Ford

Melema, Tito Greek scholar, adopted son to Baldassare Calvo. m. Romola de Bardi*
Romola (1863) George Eliot (rn Mary Anne, later Marian, Evans)

Melesinda
Mr H play (1806) Charles Lamb

Melford, Jerry Cambridge student, nephew to the Brambles*
Lydia his sister m. George Dennison*
The Expedition of Humphrey Clinker (1771) Tobias Smollett

'Melia nice maid at Dr Blimber's* school
Dombey and Son (1848) Charles Dickens

Melincourt, Anthelia rich young heiress abducted by Achthar* and Grovelgrub*, and about to be raped when rescued by Haut-on*
Melincourt, or Sir Oran Haut-on (1817)

Thomas Love Peacock

Melisande Zuleika Dobson's* maid
Zuleika Dobson (1911) Max Beerbohm

Melissa a bee
ss 'The Mother Hive'
Actions and Reactions (1909) Rudyard Kipling

Melissa adopted waif and friend to Chad Buford*
The Little Shepherd of Kingdom Come (1903) John Fox Jr.

Melissa m. Alonso*; cc American Gothic romance by a newspaper editor that was so popular that a teacher, Daniel Jackson, plagiarized it and profited from it; the real author sued but died before he could obtain redress
Alonso and Melissa (1811) Isaac Mitchell

Mell, Charles gaunt and sallow assistant at Salem House
David Copperfield (1850) Charles Dickens

Mellefont promised to and in love with Cynthia*
The Double-Dealer comedy (1710) William Congreve

Mellida
Antonio and Mellida play (1602); *Antonio's Revenge* play (1602) John Marston

Melliora cc, heroine-victim ('Damp not the fires thou hast rais'd with seeming Coiness! I know thou art mine . . . By Heaven, cry'd he: I will this Night be Master of my Wishes, no Matter what to Morrow may bring forth!'), in novel by successor to Manley*
Love in Excess, or *The Fatal Enquiry* (1719–20) Eliza Haywood

Mellish, E. S.
ss 'A Germ Destroyer'
Plain Tales from the Hills (1888) Rudyard Kipling

Mellish, John Yorkshire squire, m. Aurora Floyd*
Aurora Floyd (1863) Mary Braddon

Mello, Sebastian, Dr
Handley Cross (1843) R. S. Surtees

Mellon, Mrs housekeeper to Lord Dorincourt*
Little Lord Fauntleroy (1886) Frances Hodgson Burnett

Mellors man in Bowling's* firm who ap-

plies astrology to horseracing
Coming Up For Air (1936) George
Orwell (rn Eric Blair)
Mellors, Oliver educated gamekeeper in
love with Connie Chatterley*
Lady Chattlerley's Lover (1928) D. H.
Lawrence
Mellot, Claude
Sabina his wife
Two Years Ago (1857) Charles Kingsley
Mellows, J. landlord of the Dolphin's
Head, ruined by the railway
The Uncommercial Traveller (1860–8)
Charles Dickens
Melmoth, John young Irishman, cc of
pioneer Gothic novel*
Melmoth the Wanderer his ancestor
Melmoth the Wanderer (1820) Charles
Maturin
Melmotte, Marie m. Hamilton K. Fisker*
Augustus her father, swindling financier
The Way We Live Now (1875) Anthony
Trollope
Melopoyn poet
Roderick Random (1748) Tobias Smoll-
ett
Melrose, Edmund tyrannical old man with
mania for collecting curios, murdered by
one of his tenants
Netta his unhappy wife
Felicia their daughter, m. Lord Tatham*
The Mating of Lydia (1913) Mrs
Humphry Ward
Melrose, Revd Mr
ss 'Fellow Townsmen'
Wessex Tales (1888) Thomas Hardy
Meltham clever actuary who brought Jul-
ius Slinkton* to book, by posing as
Beckwith and Major Banks
Hunted Down (1860) Charles Dickens
Melveric Duke of Munsterberg
Death's Jest Book, or *The Fool's Tragedy*
play (1850) Thomas Lovell Beddoes
Melvil, Count de noble benefactor of
Ferdinand, Count Fathom*, whose
mother saves his life on the field of
Petervarad, for which service he brings
him up as his own
Renaldo his son
his daughter, whom Ferdinand plans to
seduce
*The Adventures of Ferdinand, Count
Fathom* (1753) Tobias Smollett

Melvil, John, Sir nephew to Ogleby*,
promised in marriage to Stirling's plain
elder daughter, but attracted to Fanny*
The Clandestine Marriage comedy
(1766) George Colman the Elder and
David Garrick
Melville friend to Harry Chatteris*
The Sea Lady (1902) H. G. Wells
Melville, Henry m. Anne de Travers
Bluebeard's Keys (1874) Anne
Thackeray
Melville, Herman (hist.) cc
Pen Friends (1989) Michael Thorne
Melville, Julia
The Rivals play (1775) Richard Brinsley
Sheridan
Melville, Miss niece of Tyrrel* and driven
to the grave by him because she will not
marry the odious man of his choice
Things as They Are, or *The Adventures of
Caleb Williams* (1794) William Godwin
The Iron Chest dramatization (1796)
George Colman the Younger
Melville, William, Major Laird of
Calnvreckan
Waverley (1814) Walter Scott
Melvilleson, Miss singer
Bleak House (1853) Charles Dickens
Memberge daughter to Theodoret*
Thierry and Theodoret play (1621) John
Fletcher, Philip Massinger ?and Francis
Beaumont
Members, Mark literary critic
The *Music of Time* series (1951–75)
Anthony Powell
Memsworth, Mr
The Good Companions (1939) J. B.
Priestley
Menaida, Zachary taxidermist
Oliver his son
In the Roar of the Sea (1892) Sabine
Baring-Gould
Menaphon a Persian Lord
Tamburlaine play (1590) Christopher
Marlowe
Menaphon son to Sophronos*
The Lover's Melancholy play (1629)
John Ford
Menas friend to Pompey*
Antony and Cleopatra play (1623)
William Shakespeare
Mendham, George, Revd curate, later
Vicar, of Siddermorton

The Wonderful Visit (1895) H. G. Wells
Mendoza
Man and Superman play (1903) George
Bernard Shaw
Mendoza, General villainous leader of
revolution
Soldiers of Fortune (1897) Richard
Harding Davis
Mendoza, Isaac
The Duenna play (1775) Richard
Brinsley Sheridan
Menecrates friend to Pompey*
Antony and Cleopatra play (1623)
William Shakespeare
Menelaus brother to Agamemnon*, m.
Helen*
Troilus and Cressida play (1623) William
Shakespeare
Menenius Agrippa friend to Coriolanus*
Coriolanus play (1623) William Shake-
speare
Mengan, Mrs daughter to Sir Godwin
Lydgate
Middlemarch (1871–2) George Eliot (rn
Mary Anne, later Marian, Evans)
Mengo, Alpheus, Sir distinguished surgeon
The Undying Fire (1919) H. G. Wells
Mengs, Ian landlord of the Golden Fleece
Anne of Geierstein (1829) Walter Scott
Menlove, Mrs Louis flighty and spirited
maid to Lady Petherwin
The Hand of Ethelberta (1876) Thomas
Hardy
Mennick secretary to Elmer Ford*
The Little Nugget (1913) P. G. Wode-
house
Menou, M. landlord of the Hotel Poussin
his wife
The Adventures of Philip (1862) W. M.
Thackeray
Menzies, Donald, Lieutenant
ss 'The King of the Trenches'
Blasting and Bombadiering (1967); *Un-
lucky for Pringle* (1973) Wyndham Lewis
Meon Saxon chief
ss 'The Conversion of St Wilfred'
Rewards and Fairies (1910) Rudyard
Kipling
mephistopheles Australian bad hat
It Is Never Too Late To Mend (1856)
Charles Reade
Mephistopheles cc
Doctor Faustus play (1604) Christopher

Marlowe
Mercaptan writer, friend to Theodore
Gumbril*
Antic Hay (1923) Aldous Huxley
Mercier, Leonard Vi Ransome's* lover
The Combined Maze (1913) May
Sinclair
Mercury sent by Jove to purge the courtiers
*Cynthia's Revels, or The Fountain of
Self-Love* play (1601) Ben Jonson
Mercury Sir Leicester Dedlock's* footman
Bleak House (1853) Charles Dickens
Mercutio friend to Romeo*
Romeo and Juliet play (1623) William
Shakespeare
Mercy companion to Christian*
The Pilgrim's Progress (1678–84) John
Bunyan
Merdle, Mr crooked MP and financier,
killed himself in a Turkish bath; based on
the embezzling MP John Sadleir, who
killed himself on Hampstead Heath in
1856
Little Dorrit (1857) Charles Dickens
Meredith, Chester m. Felicia Blakeney*
ss 'Chester Forgets Himself'
The Heart of a Goof (1926) P. G. Wode-
house
Meredith, Justinia, Lady *née* Lufton
Framley Parsonage (1861) Anthony
Trollope
Meredith, Owen Ap, Sir a Welsh knight
*The Pleasant Commedye of Patient
Grissill* play (1603) Thomas Dekker
Meredith, Peter cc, narrator
Lost Sir Massingberd (1864) James Payn
Meredith, Rowland, Sir matchmaking
Welsh uncle to Fowler*
Sir Charles Grandison (1754) Samuel
Richardson
Meredith, William ex-mayor of Silchester
Nell his daughter
When a Man's Single (1888) J. M. Barrie
Mergelson Sir Peter Laxton's* butler
Bealby (1915) H. G. Wells
Mergle, Miss schoolmistress
The Wheels of Chance (1896) H. G.
Wells
Merillies, Meg gipsy queen
Guy Mannering (1815) Walter Scott
Merivale, Alan schoolfriend to Michael
Fane*, m. Stella Fane*
Sinister Street† (1913) Compton

Mackenzie
Merivale, Maisie
James her son
Manhattan Transfer (1925) John Dos Passos
Meriwether, Dolly, Mrs
Gone With the Wind (1936) Margaret Mitchell
Merle, Mme Isabel Archer's* friend, ex-mistress to Gilbert Osmond*
The Portrait of a Lady (1881) Henry James
Merlin, Anthony, KC counsel for Jane Palfrey*
Antigua Penny Puce (1936) Robert Graves
Merlin, Dorothy Australian verse-dramatist, m. Cosmo Hines*
The Unspeakable Skipton (1959) Pamela Hansford Johnson
Merlin, Lord
The Pursuit of Love (1945) Nancy Mitford
Merman, Porteus
Julia his wife
The Impressions of Theophrastus Such (1879) George Eliot (rn Mary Anne, later Marian, Evans)
Merrick cousin to Clare Browell*
Right Off the Map (1927) C. E. Montague
Merrick, Alan bohemian artist who lives with Herminia Barton* but dies young of typhoid
his odious father, a Harley Street gout specialist
The Woman Who Did (1895) Grant Allen
Merrick, Mercy 'fallen woman' who changes identity with Grace Roseberry*
The New Magdalen (1873) Wilkie Collins
Merrick, Robert District Superintendent of Police (later murdered); ambisexual
his wife
The Raj Quartet (1976) Paul Scott
Merridew, Alice, Mrs friend to Mary Adam*
Holy Deadlock (1934) A. P. Herbert
Merridew, Mrs widowed sister to Sir John Verinder*
The Moonstone (1868) Wilkie Collins
Merriman American journalist

But Soft — We Are Observed! (1928) Hilaire Belloc
Merriman John Worthing's* butler
The Importance of Being Earnest play (1895) Oscar Wilde
Merriman solicitor to Sir Percival Glyde*
The Woman in White (1860) Wilkie Collins
Merritt, Eban, Squire
Lucina his daughter, m. Jerome Edwards*
Camilla his sister
Jerome (1897) Mary E. Wilkins
Merry of the *Hispaniola*
Treasure Island (1882) Robert Louis Stevenson
Merry, Charles Latin teacher
Pastors and Masters (1925) Ivy Compton-Burnett
Merrylegs performing dog belonging to Jupe*
Hard Times (1854) Charles Dickens
Merrythought
his wife
Jasper; Michael their sons
The Knight of the Burning Pestle play (1613) Francis Beaumont and John Fletcher
Merrywin headmaster of Meanwell College
Nora his wife, who drowns herself
Mort à credit (*Death on the Instalment Plan*) (1936) Louis-Ferdinand Céline (rn Louis-Ferdinand Destouches)
Merrywinkle, Mr and Mrs coddle themselves
Sketches of Young Couples (1840) Charles Dickens
Merton 'in the wine trade'
The Diary of a Nobody (1892) George and Weedon Grossmith
Merton, Emily
General Merton her father
Afloat and Ashore (1844) James Fenimore Cooper
Merton, Hetty
The Picture of Dorian Gray (1891) Oscar Wilde
Merton, Revd Mr
his wife
Caroline their eldest daughter
Alice (1838) Edward Bulwer Lytton
Merton, Susan m. George Fielding*, loved

by Wilhelm Fielding*
her father
It Is Never Too Late To Mend (1856)
Charles Reade
Merton, Sybil m. Lord Arthur Savile*
Lord Arthur Savile's Crime (1891) Oscar
Wilde
Merton, Tommy co-cc pedagogic and up-
lifting novel
his father and mother
Sandford and Merton (1783–9) Thomas
Day
Mertoun, Basil formerly Vaughan
Mordaunt his son by Louisa Gonzago*
The Pirate (1822) Walter Scott
Mervyn, Arthur young cc of American
Gothic* novel
*Arthur Mervyn, or Memoirs of the Year
1793* (1799–1800) Charles Brockden
Brown
Mervyn, Christopher, Lieutenant
ss 'The Tie'
Limits and Renewals (1932) Rudyard
Kipling
Merygreeke, Matthew
Ralph Roister Doister play (1551)
Nicholas Udall
Meryll sergeant of yeomen, m. Dame
Carruthers*
Phoebe m. Wilfred Shadbolt*; **Leonard**
his children
The Yeomen of the Guard opera (1888)
W. S. Gilbert and Arthur Sullivan
Meshach owner of sealing-wax factory
The Great Hoggarty Diamond (1841)
W. M. Thackeray
Mesheck, Aaron criminal Jew tracked
down by means of his carpet bag
ss 'The Detective Police'
Reprinted Pieces (1858) Charles Dickens
Mesiá, Don Alvaro Vetusta's (Oviedo's)
cowardly Don Juan, by whom the desper-
ate Ana Ozores* allows herself to be
seduced
La Regenta (*The Regentess* but tr. under
its own title) (1884–5) Leopoldo Alas
Mesrour name given to Miss Griffin's*
servant Tabby by the Seraglio*
The Haunted House (1859) Charles
Dickens
Messenger, Angela emancipated cc of
novel by once popular author and literary
activist whose work has fallen into obliv-

ion; heir to brewing fortune determined
to make Stepney into an earthly paradise;
m. Harry Goslet*
All Sorts and Conditions of Men (1882)
Walter Besant
Messinger, Dr explorer
A Handful of Dust (1934) Evelyn Waugh
Messua Mowgli's* foster (or real) mother
her husband
ss 'Tiger Tiger'†
Jungle Books (1894–5) Rudyard Kipling
Mesty Negro servant
Mr Midshipman Easy (1836) Captain
Marryat
Metaphor, Miles clerk to Justice
Preamble*
A Tale of a Tub play (1640) Ben Jonson
Metellus Climber conspirator against Jul-
ius Caesar*
Julius Caesar play (1623) William Shake-
speare
Methusaleh, Lord m. Emma Trotter*
Mrs Perkins's Ball† (1847) W. M.
Thackeray
Metroland, Viscount see **Maltravers,
Humphrey, Sir**
Meulter, Hans see **Lacy, Rowland**
Meunier, Charles physician, schoolfriend
to Latimer*, brings Bertha Grant* back
to life
The Lifted Veil (1859) George Eliot (rn
Mary Anne, later Marian, Evans)
Meurteuil, de, Marquise cc of French
epistolary novel
Les Liaisons dangereuses (1782)
Pierre-Ambroise-François Choderlos de
Laclos
Meyrick artist, victim of Helen Vaughan*
The Great God Pan (1894) Arthur
Machen
Meyrick, Mrs half-French, half-Scottish
Hans artist; **Amy** teacher; **Kate** artist;
Mabel musical her children
Daniel Deronda (1876) George Eliot (rn
Mary Anne, later Marian, Evans)
Micawber, Wilkins partly drawn from the
author's father
Ellen his wife
David Copperfield (1850) Charles
Dickens
Michael Mr Weston's* junior wine part-
ner
Mr Weston's Good Wine (1927) T. F.

Powys

Michaelis anarchist, 'ticket-of-leave apostle'
The Secret Agent (1907) Joseph Conrad (rn Josef Teodor Konrad Korzeniowski)

Michaelis Irish playwright who has brief affair with Connie Chatterley*
Lady Chatterley's Lover (1928) D. H. Lawrence

Michaelis, Karen cc, m. Ray Forrestier*
The House In Paris (1935) Elizabeth Bowen

Michaels, Father priest on the torpedoed *Aurora*
The Ocean (1946) James Hanley

Michel, Helen artist, widow to Maurice Michel
Raoul her stepson
Roland her son
Armand brother to Maurice
his wife
her mother-in-law
The World My Wilderness (1950) Rose Macaulay

Michele, Fra Carthusian brother
Romola (1863) George Eliot (rn Mary Anne, later Marian, Evans)

Michelson, Eliza housekeeper to Sir Percival Glyde*
The Woman in White (1860) Wilkie Collins

Michie student, ex-service corporal
Lucky Jim (1953) Kingsley Amis

Mick owner of a house
Aston his slow-witted brother who rents a room from him
The Caretaker play (1960) Harold Pinter

Micklethwaite, Tom genial mathematician
Fanny his wife, *née* Wheatley, who m. him at forty, when he could afford it
Fanny's blind, piano-playing sister
The Odd Women (1893) George Gissing

Middleburgh, Mr Edinburgh magistrate
Heart of Midlothian (1818) Walter Scott

Middlemas, Richard son to Richard Tresham* and Zilia de Moncada*
The Surgeon's Daughter (1827) Walter Scott

Middleton, Clara fiancée of Sir Willoughby Patterne*, who has some traits in common with the author's first wife; m. Vernon Whitford*

Revd Dr Middleton her father, a partial portrait of Peacock*, then the author's father-in-law, as a crusty old port-lover
The Egoist (1879) George Meredith

Middleton, Colonel narrator
The Danvers Jewels† (1887) Mary Cholmondeley

Middleton, Dr
Mr Midshipman Easy (1836) Captain Marryat

Middleton, Ellen fifteen-year-old heroine of an unusual novel: she slaps an eight-year-old cousin, causing her death by a fall, and making herself an heiress into the bargain – but she was seen, which leads to blackmail, remorse, repentance and a death-bed confession
Ellen Middleton (1844) Georgiana Fullerton

Middleton, Gerald historian unable to finish his major book on Edward the Confessor
Ingebord his wife
John journalist, ex-MP, one of their three children
Anglo-Saxon Attitudes (1956) Angus Wilson

Middleton, John, Sir good-looking man of about forty; sportsman; related to the Dashwoods*
Lady Middleton his wife, *née* Jennings, reserved, cold and correct; mother says she always gets her own way
Sense and Sensibility (1811) Jane Austen

Middleton, Revd Mr curate at Pennicote
Daniel Deronda (1876) George Eliot (rn Mary Anne, later Marian, Evans)

Midget, Miss saved character*
Outward Bound play (1924) Sutton Vane

Midget, The enigmatic and destructive figure, 'little grey jester'
Mysterier (*Mysteries*) (1892) Knut Hamsun

Midmore, Frankwell m. Connie Sperrit*
his mother
ss 'My Son's Wife'
A Diversity of Creatures (1917) Rudyard Kipling

Midwinter, Ozias creole, son of murderer, the rightful Allan Armadale*, writer
Armadale (1866) Wilkie Collins

Miff, Miss wheezy pew-opener

Dombey and Son (1848) Charles Dickens

Mifflin, Arthur juvenile lead
ss 'Deep Waters'
The Man Upstairs (1914) P. G. Wodehouse

Miggs, Miss slender, shrewish young maid of all work to Mrs Varden*
Barnaby Rudge (1841) Charles Dickens

Mignon, Modeste cc of childish religious faith but intelligence
Modeste Mignon (1846) Honoré de Balzac

Miguel sensual Mexican
The Day of the Locust (1939) Nathanael West (rn Nathan Weinstein)

Mikado of Japan, The
Nanki-Poo his son and heir
The Mikado opera (1885) W. S. Gilbert and Arthur Sullivan

Mike ancient collie who barks only when men are killed
ss 'The Hitch-Hikers'
A Curtain of Green (1941) Eudora Welty

Mikhalovna, Agatha based on a maid seduced by the author, who fed mice
Anna Karenina (1877) Leo Tolstoy

Mikulin police chief in St Petersburg
Under Western Eyes (1911) Joseph Conrad (rn Josef Teodor Konrad Korzeniowski)

Milan, Duke of see **Prospero**

Milanes friend to Leandro*
The Spanish Curate play (1647) John Fletcher and Philip Massinger

Milborough, Countess of friend to Louis Trevelyan's* mother
He Knew He Was Right (1869) Anthony Trollope

Milbran representative of a music publishing firm
The Good Companions (1939) J. B. Priestley

Mild, Lieutenant
A Laodicean (1881) Thomas Hardy

Milden, Denis friend to George Sherston*
Memoirs of a Fox-Hunting Man (1929) Siegfried Sassoon

Mildman, Samuel, Dr tutor, head of a private establishment at Helmstone
Frank Fairlegh (1850) Frank Smedley

Mildmay, William great Whig Prime Minister
Phineas Finn†(1869) Anthony Trollope

Mildred daughter to Touchstone*
Eastward Ho! play (1605) George Chapman, Ben Jonson and John Marston

'Mildred, Little' subaltern
ss 'The Man Who Was'
Life's Handicap (1891) Rudyard Kipling

Miles boy, cc
The Turn of the Screw (1898) Henry James

Miles, Henry assistant secretary in Ministry
Sarah his wife, cc, Maurice Bendrix's* lover
Mrs Bertram her mother
The End of the Affair (1951) Graham Greene

Miles, Major Lady Margaret Bellenden's brother-in-law
Old Mortality (1816) Walter Scott

Milkwash poetical young gentleman
Sketches of Young Gentlemen (1838) Charles Dickens

Mill, Alexander, Revd curate
Candida (1894) George Bernard Shaw

Millament, Mrs a fine lady, niece to Lady Wishfort*, loves Mirabell*
The Way of the World comedy (1710) William Congreve

Millar, Flora *danseuse*
ss 'The Noble Bachelor'
The Adventures of Sherlock Holmes (1892) Arthur Conan Doyle

Millard, Rosa, Miss grandmother to Bayard Sartoris*
The Unvanquished (1938) William Faulkner

Millbank industrialist
his wife
Edith m. Harry Coningsby*; **Oswald** his children
Coningsby (1844) Benjamin Disraeli

Millborne retired gentleman, seducer of Leonora Frankland*
ss 'For Conscience' Sake'
Life's Little Ironies (1894) Thomas Hardy

Miller bookseller, member of Philosophers' Club
Daniel Deronda (1876) George Eliot (rn Mary Anne, later Marian, Evans)

Miller, Daisy cc, American girl touring Italy
Mrs Miller her mother

Randolph, her brother
Daisy Miller (1878) Henry James
Miller, Emil one-time lover to Mildred Rogers*
Of Human Bondage (1915) W. Somerset Maugham
Miller, Greta
An American Tragedy (1925) Theodore Dreiser
Miller, Jane Ann, Mrs
No Thoroughfare (1867) Charles Dickens
Miller, Joseph ('Sheppey') cockney barber who follows Christ's precepts; his wife says, 'It seems so funny for a good man to become religious'
his wife
Florrie his daughter
Sheppey play (1933) W. Somerset Maugham
Miller, Miss
ss 'Miss Miller'
The Wind Blows Over (1936) Walter de la Mare
Miller, Miss mistress at Lowood
Jane Eyre (1847) Charlotte Brontë
Miller, Mitch cc of Illinois tale of two boys who, believing that Huck Finn* and Tom Sawyer* are real, try to emulate their adventures; in pastiche of Twain*
Mitch Miller (1920); *Skeeters Kirby* (1923) Edgar Lee Masters
Miller, Mrs landlady
Nancy; Betty her daughters
Tom Jones (1749) Henry Fielding
Miller, Neil young painter who destroys all his work, and feels better about it; cc of novel by disillusioned Hungarian communist who settled in America
The Hollow of the Wave (1949) Edward Newhouse
Miller, Peyton daughter to Milton and Helen Loftis*; suicide
Harry her husband, a struggling artist
Lie Down in Darkness (1951) William Styron
Miller, St Quentin author
The Death of the Heart (1938) Elizabeth Bowen
Miller, Tommy adolescent cc of author's only comedy, celebrating the 'boyhood I never had'
Ah Wilderness! play (1933) Eugene

O'Neill
Milles-Pattes midget smelling of old rat, perhaps pushed by Ferdinand* under an underground train
Guignol's band (1944) Louis-Ferdinand Céline (rn Louis-Ferdinand Destouches)
Milligan, Spike ex-burglar, friend to Jimmy Pitt*
A Gentleman of Leisure (1910) P. G. Wodehouse
Milliken, Horace
his wife, *née* Kicklebury
George; Arabella their children
Lovel the Widower† (1861) W. M. Thackeray
Milligton, William
Margaret his wife
Louis his brother
ss 'The Cartouche'
A Beginning (1955) Walter de la Mare
Mills of the Carlist cavalry
The Arrow of Gold (1919) Joseph Conrad (rn Josef Teodor Konrad Korzeniowski)
Mills teacher
Joan and Peter (1918) H. G. Wells
Mills, Julia revelled in despair, m. a 'growling old Scotch Croesus'
Reprinted Pieces (1858) Charles Dickens
Millward, Michael, Revd
Mary; Eliza his sisters
The Tenant of Wildfell Hall (1848) Anne Brontë
Millwood a murderous lady of pleasure who goes to the gallows 'loathing life and yet afraid to die'; in play by one-eyed Dissenter which has been seen as an 'exaltation of trade'; admired by Fielding* and Pope*
The London Merchant, or *The History of George Barnwell* play (1731) George Lillo
Milly married woman having an affair with Remington
The New Machiavelli (1911) H. G. Wells
Miln, General commanding the defeated Rians
Right Off the Map (1927) C. E. Montague
Milne, Alfred
Frances his wife; both teachers in national schools; unitarians who lost their faith at Cambridge, but who are finally converted

by Mr Apollo* to a belief in God
Mr Apollo: A Just Possible Story (1908)
Ford Madox Ford

Milner, Miss m. Lord Elmwood* in novel
by Roman Catholic showing the value of
a 'proper education'
Matilda her daughter, m. Rushbrook*
A Simple Story (1791) Elizabeth Inchbald

Milner, Molly m. Lawrence Furnival*
ss 'Miss Tarrant's Temperament'
Tales Told by Simpson (1930) May
Sinclair

Milsom Hervey Cheyne's* secretary
Captains Courageous (1897) Rudyard
Kipling

Milton, Ann, Lady see **Risherville, Earl of**

Milton, George Lennie's* friend; shoots
him to save him from lynching
Of Mice and Men (1937) John Steinbeck

Milton, Hetty, Mrs (pseudonym **Thomas
Plantagenet**)
Jessie her stepdaughter, Hoopdriver's*
inspiration
The Wheels of Chance (1896) H. G.
Wells

Milton, John (hist.) cc
*The Maiden and Married Life of Marie
Powell* (1849) Anne Manning
Wife to Mr Milton (1943) Robert Graves

Milton, Mona 'maternal nymphomaniac'
and mistress of Ulick Invern*
Painted Veils (1920) James Huneker

Miltoun, Lord see **Valleys**

Milvain, Jasper unimaginative, clever and
corrupt hack who wins success in novel
of the literary life; m. Amy Reardon*
Maud; Dora m. Whelpdale* his sisters,
writers for children
New Grub Street (1891) George Gissing

Milverton, Charles Augustus
ss 'The Adventure of Charles Augustus
Milverton'
The Return of Sherlock Holmes (1905)
Arthur Conan Doyle

Milvey, Frank, Revd ill-paid curate
Margaretta his cheery wife
Our Mutual Friend (1865) Charles
Dickens

Minchin, Dr
Middlemarch (1871–2) George Eliot (rn
Mary Anne, later Marian, Evans)

Mincing woman to Mrs Millimant*
The Way of the World play (1700)

William Congreve

Minderbender, Milo, Lieutenant
Catch-22 (1961) Joseph Heller

Minette, Mlle *vivandière*
Tom Burke of Ours (1844) Charles Lever

Mingott, Manson, Mrs grandmother of
Ellen Olenska*
The Age of Innocence (1920) Edith
Wharton

Minho, Gurdon novelist
The Forsyte series (1906–33) John
Galsworthy

Minim, Dick satirical portrait of a pretentious critic: 'his opinion was asked by all
who had no opinion of their own, and yet
loved to debate and decide'
The Idler (60 and 61, Saturday 9 June,
1759; Saturday, 16 June, 1759) Samuel
Johnson

Miniver, Mistress a wealthy widow
Satiromastix , or *The Untrussing of the
Humorous Poet* play (1602) Thomas
Dekker (?with John Marston)

Mink, Yussie a boy, David Schearl's*
friend and playmate
his fodder, woiks in a joolery shop in
Brooklyn
his mother, flat-breasted friend to Mrs
Schearl
Annie Yussie's sister, who wears an iron
brace on her leg
Call It Sleep (1934) Henry Roth

Minnehaha wife of Hiawatha*; means
'laughing water' in Sioux
Hiawatha poem (1855) Henry
Wadsworth Longfellow

Minnie cousin to Louisa Ames*
Mourning Becomes Electra play (1931)
Eugene O'Neill

Minnie in love with Hubert Lapell*
ss 'Hubert and Minnie'
The Little Mexican (1924) Aldous
Huxley

Minns, Augustus hero of author's first
published tale, retiring old bachelor pursued by his cousin Octavius Budden to
visit him at Stamford Hill
Sketches by Boz† (1836) Charles Dickens

Minns, Miss
Coming Up For Air (1936) George
Orwell (rn Eric Blair)

Minster, Kate heir to the Minster Iron
Works, saved from the villainous plans of

Horace Boyce*
The Lawton Girl (1890) Harold Frederic
Minter pottery manufacturer, Remington's* uncle
Gertrude; Sybil his daughters
The New Machiavelli (1911) H. G. Wells
Minty, Ferdinand seedy Old Harrovian living on his wits in Stockholm
England Made Me (1935) Graham Greene
Minx, Mistress wife to a merchant, jets it as gingerly as if she were dancing the Canaries
Pierce Penilesse his Supplication to the Devil (1592) Thomas Nashe
Mirabel the wild goose, a travelled monsieur, and a great defier of all ladies in the way of marriage, otherwise their much loose servant, at last caught by the despised Oriana*
The Wild-Goose Chase play (1652) John Fletcher
Mirabell in love with Mrs Millament*
The Way of the World comedy (1710) William Congreve
Miranda author's name for Margaret Fuller in sarcastic caricature
A Fable for Critics verse (1848) James Russell Lowell
Miranda daughter to Prospero*
The Tempest play (1623) William Shakespeare
Miriam dark exotic girl tainted by a mysterious stranger whom Donatello* flings, from the Tarpeian Rock, to his death
The Marble Faun first published in England as *Transformation* (1860) Nathaniel Hawthorne
Miriam old Jewess
Hypatia (1853) Charles Kingsley
Mirobolant, Alcide, M. celebrated chef
Pendennis (1848) W. M. Thackeray
Mirvan, Captain
Evelina (1778) Fanny Burney
Misquita, Gabral
ss 'The Gate of a Hundred Sorrows'
Plain Tales from the Hills (1888) Rudyard Kipling
Misrow groom
ss 'The War Baby'
Blasting and Bombadiering (1967); *Unlucky for Pringle* (1973) Wyndham Lewis
Miss Lonelyhearts writer of an 'Advice to

the Lovelorn' column who tries to do good and dies for it – a 'leper licker' who cannot believe in Christ
Miss Lonelyhearts (1933) Nathanael West (rn Nathan Weinstein)
Mistrust neighbour to Christian who turned back
The Pilgrim's Progress (1678–84) John Bunyan
Misty, Messrs X and XX members of the association
The Mudfog papers (1838) Charles Dickens
Mitcham, Morton of the concert party
The Good Companions (1939) J. B. Priestley
Mitchell, Fred insurance agent
Nancy his wife: neighbours to the Hollys*
Peggy their baby
South Riding (1936) Winifred Holtby
Mitchell, Harold
A Streetcar Named Desire play (1949) Tennessee Williams (rn Thomas Lanier Williams)
Mitchell, Job
The Trumpet Major (1880) Thomas Hardy
Mitchell, Morton painter, in love with Mildred Lawson*; he could hide his jealousy as he would his hand at a game of cards
ss 'Mildred Lawson'
Celibates (1895) George Moore
Mitchell, Violet chambermaid
Holy Deadlock (1934) A. P. Herbert
Mitchens, Rummy
Major Barbara play (1905) George Bernard Shaw
Mitford, Dick, Colonel friend to Sir Geoffrey Peveril*
Peveril of the Peak (1822) Walter Scott
Mith, Sergeant narrator of the Butcher's Story, based on M. Smith, a hist. detective of the time
ss 'The Detective Police'
Reprinted Pieces (1858) Charles Dickens
Mithers, Lady client of Mrs Mowcher*
David Copperfield (1850) Charles Dickens
Mitis 'is a person of no action and therefore we afford him no character'
Every Man Out of His Humour play

(1599) Ben Jonson

Mitterley, Mrs landlady
Raymond; Fern her children
Let the People Sing (1939) J. B. Priestley

Mitts, Mrs m. a one-armed pensioner
The Uncommercial Traveller (1860–8)
Charles Dickens

Mitty, Fred
his wife
Angel Pavement (1930) J. B. Priestley

Mitty, Walter cc, henpecked daydreamer
his wife
ss 'The Secret Life of Walter Mitty'
(1939)
My World – and Welcome To It (1942)
James Thurber

Mivins fellow prisoner with Pickwick*
The Pickwick Papers (1837) Charles
Dickens

Mixet, Joe friend to John Crumb*
The Way We Live Now (1875) Anthony
Trollope

Mixtus half-breed business tycoon
The Impressions of Theophrastus Such
(1879) George Eliot (rn Mary Anne, later
Marian, Evans)

Mizzler, Marquis of
The Old Curiosity Shop (1841) Charles
Dickens

M'Ling black-faced humanized beast
The Island of Dr Moreau (1896) H. G.
Wells

Mnason owner of house where Christ-
iana* lodged
The Pilgrim's Progress (1678–84) John
Bunyan

Moa (Mor) peacock
ss 'Mowgli's Brothers'†
Jungle Books (1894–5) Rudyard Kipling

Mock Turtle, The
Alice in Wonderland (1865) Lewis
Carroll (rn Charles Lutwidge Dodgson)

Mockler, Harry whose cancer is healed by
love
ss 'The Wish House'
Debits and Credits (1926) Rudyard Kipling

Mockridge, Miss
Dangerous Corner play (1832) J. B.
Priestley

Mockridge, Nance
The Mayor of Casterbridge (1886)
Thomas Hardy

Moddle, Augustus 'the youngest gentle-
man in company', boarder at Todgers*
Martin Chuzzlewit (1844) Charles
Dickens

Modjeska, Helena actress
My Mortal Enemy (1926) Willa Cather

Modus lover to Helen*
The Hunchback play (1932) James
Sheridan Knowles

Moffat parliamentary candidate
Doctor Thorne (1858) Anthony Trollope

Moffat, Elmer secretary, later railway
king, first and fourth husband of Undine
Spragg*
The Custom of the Country (1913) Edith
Wharton

Moffat, George cc, indecisive but gifted
writer of the Pre-Raphaelite school
whose career curiously anticipated that
of his creator: 'If only he would pull
himself together, and deliver one blow to
clench all the staves of the barrel'
The Benefactor (1905) Ford Madox Ford

Moffat, Sallie, Mrs friend to Meg Brooke*
Ned her husband
Little Women (1868) Louisa M. Alcott

Moffitt, Simon television personality and
zoologist
The Game (1967) A. S. Byatt

Mogford, Joseph ('Plain Joe') landlord
**Mogford, Jeremy ('Jerry the Lurker';
'Pattering Jerry')** his brother, a criminal:
'thief, swindler, begging-letter writer and
bird of prey generally'
His Natural Life (1870–2; abridged by
the author 1874; in 1885 as *For the Term
of His Natural Life* – thus evading the
author's irony; original text edited by
Stephen Murray-Smith, 1970) Marcus
Clarke

Moggeridge, Lord Lord Chancellor
Bealby (1915) H. G. Wells

Moggeridge, Revd Mr aged, workless curate
The Dream (1924) H. G. Wells

Moggridge, James
My Lady Nicotine (1890) J. M. Barrie

Moggs of Moggs' Domestic Soap
Tono Bungay (1909) H. G. Wells

Moggs, Luke head miller at Dorlcote Mill
his wife
The Mill on the Floss (1860) George Eliot
(rn Mary Anne, later Marian, Evans)

Mogyns, Alfred de, Sir *né* A. S. Muggins
Marian his wife
Alured Caradoc their son
The Book of Snobs (1847) W. M.
Thackeray
Moir, Agnes in love with Matthews
Brodie*
her mother
Hatter's Castle (1931) A. J. Cronin
Mole Crickets parasites who destroy every-
thing good
*All and Everything: Beelzebub's Tales to
His Grandson* (1950) G. I. Gurdjieff
Môle, Marquise de la shot and wounded
by Sorel*
Mathilde her daughter, seduced by Julien
Sorel
Le Rouge et le Noir (1830) Stendhal (rn
Henry Bayle)
Mole, Hannah cc, m. Samuel Blenkinsop*
Miss Mole (1930) E. H. Young
Mole, Lady de la Becky Sharp's* society
acquaintance
Vanity Fair (1847–8) W. M. Thackeray
Mole, Mr
The Wind in the Willows (1908) Kenneth
Grahame
Molina, Tony ('El Toro') boxer cc,
suggested by Primo Carnera
The Harder They Fall (1947) Budd
Schulberg
Moll old woman, lover of Macmann*
Molloy (1951); *Malone meurt* (*Malone
Dies*) (1951) (tr. 1956); *L'Innommable*
(1953) (*the Unnamable*) (tr. 1958) (tri-
logy) Samuel Beckett
Moll (hist.) the roaring girl; drunken femi-
nist cc
The Roaring Girl play (1611) Thomas
Middleton and Thomas Dekker
Molloy cc
Molloy (1951); *Malone meurt* (*Malone
Dies*) (1951) (tr. 1956); *L'Innommable*
(1953) (*The Unnamable*) (tr. 1958) (tri-
logy) Samuel Beckett
Molly housemaid to Mr Poyser*
Adam Bede (1859) George Eliot (rn
Mary Anne, later Marian, Evans)
Molly Miller Loveday's* servant
The Trumpet Major (1880) Thomas
Hardy
Molly servant to the Lambert family*, m.
Gumbo*

The Virginians (1857–9) W. M.
Thackeray
Molten, Farmer
The Sailor's Return (1925) David
Garnett
Mompert, Dr, D D bishop
his wife and daughters
Daniel Deronda (1876) George Eliot (rn
Mary Anne, later Marian, Evans)
Moncada, Alonzo Spaniard shipwrecked
in Ireland
Melmoth the Wanderer (1820) Charles
Robert Maturin
Moncada, Zilia m. Richard Tresham*
Matthias her father
The Surgeon's Daughter (1827) Walter
Scott
Monchensey, Amy, Dowager Lady
Henry, Lord Monchensey her son, cc
Ivy; Violet; Agatha her sisters
The Family Reunion play (1939) T. S.
Eliot
Monckton, Mr plausible society scoun-
drel; wishes to secure Celia Beverley's*
future
Lady Margaret his wife
Cecilia (1782) Fanny Burney
Monckton, Alfred 'mad' cc, engaged to
Miss Ada Elmslie*
his parents, of Wincot Abbey
Stephen his uncle
ss 'Mad Monkton'
The Queen of Hearts (1859) Wilkie Col-
lins
Moncrieff, Algernon m. Cecily Cardew*
The Importance of Being Earnest play
(1895) Oscar Wilde
Mond, Mustapha World Controller
Brave New World (1932) Aldous Huxley
Monday, Sara ex- 'wife' to Gulley Jimson*
The Horse's Mouth† (1944) Joyce Cary
Mondoville, Léonce de Delphine
d'Abbémar's married lover in epistolary
novel; in part inspired by the author's
lover, Benjamin Constant*
Delphine (1802) Madame de Staël
Money, Mary Ann charwoman
Far From the Madding Crowd (1874)
Thomas Hardy
Moneygawl, Isabella m. Sir Condy Rack-
rent*
Castle Rackrent (1800) Maria Edge-
worth

Moneytrap rich usurer; associate of Gripe*
Araminta his wife, intimate with Clarissa Gripe*
The Confederacy play (1705) John Vanbrugh
Monflathers, Miss headmistress of school
The Old Curiosity Shop (1841) Charles Dickens
Monikins, The four polar monkeys, two of each sex, in one of the author's few commercial and critical failures
The Monikins (1835) James Fenimore Cooper
Monimia in love with Renaldo, young Melvil*; Ferdinand fails to rape her; m. young Melvil
The Adventures of Ferdinand, Count Fathom (1753) Tobias Smollett
Moniplies, Richie serving-man to Nigel Olifaunt*
The Fortunes of Nigel (1822) Walter Scott
Monk, Joshua radical MP
Phineas Finn (1869) Anthony Trollope
Monk, Maria liar about conditions in Montreal Roman Catholic convents in allegedly non-fictional works; she died in prison while awaiting trial for theft
Awful Disclosures (1836); *Further Disclosures* (1837) Maria Monk
Monk, Mary m. Roger Forsyte*
The *Forsyte* series (1906–33) John Galsworthy
Monk, Mr
ss 'Marching to Zion'
Adam and Eve and Pinch Me (1921) A. E. Coppard
Monk, Stephen cc and narrator, m. (1) Elizabeth Wrydale*, (2) Jane Armstrong*
The World in the Evening (1954) Christopher Isherwood
Monkbarns, Laird of see **Oldbuck, Jonathan**
Monkley, James
Sylvia Scarlett (1918) Compton Mackenzie
Monks see **Leeford, Edward**
Moore, Robert Gerard master of cloth mill, an 'industrial version of the romantic hero', m. Caroline Helstone*
Gerard his father

Hortense his sister
Louis his brother, m. Shirley Keeldar*
Shirley (1849) Charlotte Brontë
Monmouth Mr Jaraby's* cat
The Old Boys (1964) William Trevor
Monmouth, Lord grandfather to Harry Coningsby*, m. Princess Lucretia Colonna*
Coningsby (1844) Benjamin Disraeli
Monogram, Damask, Sir, Baronet m. Julia Triplex*
The Way We Live Now (1875) Anthony Trollope
Monsell, Fanny m. Mark Robarts*
Framley Parsonage (1861) Anthony Trollope
Monson millionaire experimenter with flying machines
ss 'Argonauts of the Air'
The Plattner Story (1897) H. G. Wells
Monster, The amiable Negro who has been disfigured when saving a child in tale of man's inhumanity to man which Howells* thought the 'greatest short story ever written by an American'
ss 'The Monster'
Monster and Other Stories (1899) Stephen Crane
Mont, Lawrence, Sir
Emily his wife
Michael their son, m. Fleur Forsyte*
Kit; Kat Michael and Fleur's children
The *Forsyte* series (1906–33) John Galsworthy
Montagu, Paul m. Henrietta Carbury*
The Way We Live Now (1875) Anthony Trollope
Montague, Charlotte
Clarissa Harlowe (1748) Samuel Richardson
Montague, Emily cc of what is often called the first 'local-colour'* or regional* novel, because its author had lived in Canada, where it is set, and because she added local details – but the distinction really belongs to *Castle Rackrent**
The History of Emily Montague (1769) Mrs Frances Brooke
Montague, Paul m. Henrietta Carbury*
The Way We Live Now (1875) Anthony Trollope
Montairy, Lord
Victoria his wife

Lothair (1870) Benjamin Disraeli

Monteith, Mosley, Sir officer with syphilis whose child is born 'like a speckled toad', m. Edith Beale*; in novel which made a sensation because of its graphic description of the beastly Sir Mosley's syphilis
The Heavenly Twins (1893) Sarah Grand (rn Frances McFall)

Montferrers a baron; in the single play that can be attributed to its author with certainty
Charlemont his son
The Atheist's Tragedy (1611) Cyril Tourneur

Montfichet, Andrew eccentric kindhearted artist, m. Mrs Carrickfergus (same as Andrea Fitch*)
The Adventures of Philip (1862) W. M. Thackeray

Montford, Mr
An Ideal Husband play (1895) Oscar Wilde

Montfort, Lord m. Katherine Grandison*
Henrietta Temple: A Love Story (1837) Benjamin Disraeli

Montgomery medical student, assistant to Moreau*
The Island of Dr Moreau (1896) H. G. Wells

Montgomery, Ellen cc
Captain Morgan Montgomery her father
her mother
The Wide, Wide World (1850) Elizabeth Wetherell (rn Susan Bogert Warner)

Montgomery, Mrs Morris Townsend's* aunt
Washington Square (1880) Henry James

Monticue, Ethel cc, m. Bernard Clark*
The Young Visiters (1919) Daisy Ashford

Montis, Clea blonde painter
The Alexandria Quartet (1957–61) Lawrence Durrell

Montjoie French sculptor
The History of David Grieve (1892) Mrs Humphry Ward

Montjoy French herald
King Henry V play (1623) William Shakespeare

Montjoy, Diana m. (1) Ronald Ferse*, (2) Adrian Charwell*
Maid in Waiting (1931) John Galsworthy

Montmayor, Marquesa de

The Bridge of San Luis Rey (1928) Thornton Wilder

Montmorenci de Valentinois, Countess of (Blanche) née Amory
Pendennis (1848) W. M. Thackeray

Montmorency the dog
Three Men in a Boat (1889) Jerome K. Jerome

Montomorency, Hugo
Francie his wife
The Last September (1929) Elizabeth Bowen

Montoni Emily St Aubert's* aunt's villainous husband who carries her off
The Mysteries of Udolpho (1794) Mrs Ann Radcliffe

Montraville army officer, villain and seducer of Charlotte Temple* who deserts her when she is with child, in order to marry Julia Franklin
Charlotte: A Tale of Truth (1791, in America as Charlotte Temple, 1794) Mrs Susannah Rowson

Montresor revenger
ss 'The Cask of Amontillado'
in Godey's Lady's Book (1846) Edgar Allan Poe

Montreville, Adela, Mme
The Surgeon's Daughter (1827) Walter Scott

Montrose noble at the court of England
Old Fortunatus play (1600) Thomas Dekker

Montroya, Baltazar, Friar priest at Acoma, executed by Indians, for murder
Death Comes for the Archbishop (1927) Willa Cather

Monument, Polly ('Violet') working girl adopted by Lady Mildred Eldridge*
her convict father
her washerwoman mother
Claude her brother, lawyer, m. Beatrice Eldridge*
Children of Gibeon (1886) Walter Besant

Monzano, Papa dictator of San Lorenzo
Cat's Cradle (1963) Kurt Vonnegut

Moody, John servant to Sir Francis Headpiece*
A Journey to London play (1728) John Vanbrugh

Moody, Marian Grant
'Uncle Dee' her husband
Leopold their adopted son

The House in Paris (1935) Elizabeth Bowen

Moody, Tom boxing manager
Golden Boy play (1937) Clifford Odets

Moon, Adelaide m. Harold Dormer*
Antigua Penny Puce (1936) Robert Graves

Moon, Lorna mistress to Tom Moody*
Golden Boy play (1937) Clifford Odets

Moon, Michael journalist
Manalive (1912) G. K. Chesterton

Mooncalf tapster to Ursula*
Bartholomew Fair play (1631) Ben Jonson

Mooney intelligent beadle
Bleak House (1853) Charles Dickens

Mooney, Mrs landlady
Jack; Polly her children
ss 'The Boarding House'
Dubliners (1914) James Joyce

Moonshine, Saunders zealous elder and smuggler
The Bride of Lammermoor (1819) Walter Scott

Moor, Edith m. old Jolyon Forsyte*
The *Forsyte* series (1906–33) John Galsworthy

Moore, Archy slave of white descent in first of the antislavery novels; a public service* novel by lawyer and historian which influenced Stowe*
The Slave, or *Memoirs of Archy Moore* (1836) Richard Hildreth

Moore, Arthur Wellington missionary, Swan Creek, cc
The Sky Pilot (1899) R. Connor

Moore, Eddy
ss 'Three from Dunsterville'
The Man Upstairs (1914) P. G. Wodehouse

Moore, John Canadian Barbadian who returns to Barbados but is disillusioned
The Prime Minister (1971) Austin Clarke

Moore, Kathleen with whom Starr* falls in love
The Last Tycoon (1941) F. Scott Fitzgerald

Moore, Mrs
Ronald (Heaslop) by her first marriage; **Ralph; Stella** m. Cyril Fielding* her children
A Passage to India (1924) E. M. Forster

Moore, Peter close friend to Eddie Ryan*

The Silence of History (1963) James T. Farrell

Moore, Robert Gerard Anglo-French cloth-weaver, Tenant of Hollow Mill, m. Caroline Helstone*
Hortense his sister
Louis his brother, tutor to the Sympsons*, m. Shirley Keeldar*
Shirley (1849) Charlotte Brontë

Moore, Stewart, Sir
Harry Lorrequer (1839) Charles Lever

Moore, Vivaldo novelist
Another Country (1962) James Baldwin

Mopes loathsome hermit living in filth, in which he glories; based on James Lucas, the so-called Hertfordshire Hermit, an educated man who had become unbalanced on the death of his mother
Tom Tiddler's Ground (1861) Charles Dickens

Mopo assassin of Chaka, narrator
Macropha his wife
Umslopogaas his brother, founder of the People of the Axe, and later companion to Quartermain*
Nada the lily, daughter to Chaka* and Baleka*, but passed off as Mopo's
Nada the Lily (1892) Henry Rider Haggard

Mopus of Mowbray & Mopus, solicitors to Lady Eustace*
The Eustace Diamonds (1873) Anthony Trollope

Moran, Colonel Sebastian chief assistant to Moriarty*
ss 'The Empty House'
The Return of Sherlock Holmes (1905) Arthur Conan Doyle

Moran, Dan horse thief

Moran, Jacques
Molloy (1951); *Malone meurt* (*Malone Dies*) (1951) (tr. 1956); *L'Innommable* (1953) (*The Unnamable*) (tr. 1958) (trilogy) Samuel Beckett

Morano Count in love with Emily St Aubert*
The Mysteries of Udolpho (1794) Mrs Ann Radcliffe

Morbific 'non-believer in any form of contagion'
Crotchet Castle (1831) Thomas Love Peacock

Mordaunt, Revd Mr rector

Little Lord Fauntleroy (1886) Francis Hodgson Burnett

Mordax 'an intellectual worker'
The Impressions of Theophrastus Such (1879) George Eliot (rn Mary Anne, later Marian, Evans)

Mordecai, Mr
The Absentee (1812) Maria Edgeworth

Morden, William, Colonel cousin and trustee to Clarissa Harlowe; kills Lovelace* in duel
Clarissa Harlowe (1748) Samuel Richardson

Mordlin, Brother musical member of Brick Lane Ebenezer Temperance Association
The Pickwick Papers (1837) Charles Dickens

More, James see **Macgregor**

More, Thomas pseudonym of Godwin Capes* as dramatist
Ann Veronica (1909) H. G. Wells

Moreau, Fréderic cc
his widowed mother
L'Education sentimentale (1869) Gustave Flaubert

Morehouse, Bishop
The Iron Heel (1908) Jack London

Morehouse, J. Ward public relations executive
U.S.A. trilogy (1930–6) John Dos Passos

Morel violinist
A la recherche du temps perdu (*In Search of Lost Time*) (1913–27) Marcel Proust

Morel, Walter miner m. Gertrude Coppard
William; Anne m. Leonard; **Paul** clerk and artist, cc, self-portrait; **Arthur** their children
Sons and Lovers (1913) D. H. Lawrence

Morell, James Mavor, Revd cc
Candida cc, his wife, née Burgess
Candida play (1894) George Bernard Shaw

Morell, John, Sub-Lieutenant of the *Compass Rose*
Elaine his wife
The Cruel Sea (1951) Nicholas Monsarrat

Morelli, Shep gangster
The Thin Man (1934) Dashiell Hammett

Moresby, Kit cc
Port his wife
The Sheltering Sky (1949) Paul Bowles

Moreton, Joe
Robbery Under Arms: A Story of Life and Adventure in the Bush and in the Goldfields of Australia (1888, rev. 1889) Rolf Boldrewood (rn Thomas Alexander Browne)

Morfin, Mr assistant manager in offices of Dombey*, m. Harriet Carker*
Dombey and Son (1848) Charles Dickens

Morgan Ap Kerrig Woodcourt ancestor named in Mewlinnwillinwodd of Crumlinwallinwer
Bleak House (1853) Charles Dickens

Morgan, Gwilym miner
Beth his wife
Ivor m. Bronwen*; **Ianto; Davy** m. Ethelwyn; **Owen** m. Blodwen Evans; **Gwilym** m. Marged Evans; **Ceridwen** m. Blethyn Llywarch; **Angharad** m. Iestyn Evans; **Olwen; Huw** cc and narrator
How Green Was My Valley (1939) Richard Llewellyn

Morgan, James valet to Major Pendennis*; society spy
Pendennis (1848) W. M. Thackeray

Morgan, Jenny mistress to Philip Crow*
'Morgan Nelly' their daughter
A Glastonbury Romance (1932) John Cowper Powys

Morgan, Jessica sickly student, and friend to the Barmbys* and to Nancy Lord* her impoverished parents
In the Year of Jubilee (1894) George Gissing

Morgan, Miss governess to the Vincy* children
Middlemarch (1871–2) George Eliot (rn Mary Anne, later Marian, Evans)

Morgan, Organ grocer
Under Milk Wood play (1954) Dylan Thomas

Morgan, Tom of the *Hispaniola*
Treasure Island (1883) Robert Louis Stevenson

Morgenhall, Wilfred seedy old lawyer who gets his client off because his defence of him is so inadequate
The Dock Brief in *Three Plays* (1958) John Mortimer

Moriarty
ss 'In Error'
Plain Tales from the Hills (1888) Rudyard Kipling

Moriarty, James, Professor fiendish criminal, arch-rival to Holmes*
ss 'The Final Problem'†
The Memoirs of Sherlock Holmes (1894)
Arthur Conan Doyle
Morkan, Misses Kate and Julia proprietors of a musical academy
ss 'The Dead'
Dubliners (1914) James Joyce
Morland, Catherine m. Henry Tilney*
Mr Richard her father, a clergyman, 'a very respectable man'
her mother, a woman of useful plain sense
James; Richard; Harriet; George; Sarah (Sally) and five others, her brothers and sisters
Northanger Abbey (1818) Jane Austen
Morley, Gertrude belle of Muddleton engaged to Sigismund Zaluski*
her uncle
The Autobiography of a Slander (1887) Edna Lyall (rn A. E. Bayly)
Morlocks lower world inhabitants
The Time Machine (1895) H. G. Wells
Mormon (?hist.) narrator
The Book of Mormon (1879) translated out of 'the reformed Egyptian' by Joseph Smith Jr. with references by Orson Pratt Sr.
Morocco, King of
Tamburlaine play (1590) Christopher Marlowe
Morocco, Prince of unsuccessful suitor to Portia*
The Merchant of Venice play (1623) William Shakespeare
Morolt, Dennis favourite squire of Sir Raymond Berenger*
The Betrothed (1825) Walter Scott
Morona a widow
Love's Sacrifice play (1633) John Ford
Morose misanthrope who hates noise, husband to Epicene
Epicene, or The Silent Woman play (1609) Ben Jonson
Morran, Mrs Dickson McCunn's* and John Heritage's* landlady
Huntingtower (1922) John Buchan
Morringer, Ferdinand, Sir
Robbery Under Arms: A Story of Life and Adventure in the Bush and in the Goldfields of Australia (1888) rev. 1889)

Rolf Boldrewood (rn Thomas Alexander Browne)
Morris, Amanda m. William Benham*; mistress to Sir Philip Easton*
The Research Magnificent (1915) H. G. Wells
Morris, Dinah niece to Mrs Poyser*; Methodist preacher who comforts Hetty Sorrel* in prison and m. Adam Bede*;
Adam Bede (1859) George Eliot (rn Mary Anne, later Marian, Evans)
Morris, Edward defaulting bank clerk, former friend to Jack Johnson, in Dickensian-style novel by author described by Thackeray* and others as a loud-mouthed vulgarian
The Adventures of Mr Ledbury (1844) Albert Smith
Morris, George, the Hon. brother to Lord Tulla*; Tory MP
Revd Richard his cousin
Phineas Finn (1869) Anthony Trollope
Morris, Jack friend to Lord March*
The Virginians (1857–9) W. M. Thackeray
Morris, Lucy orphan; governess at home of Lady Fawn*; childhood friend to Lady Eustace*
The Eustace Diamonds (1873) Anthony Trollope
Morris, Mrs housekeeper to the Aldclyffes*
Desperate Remedies (1871) Thomas Hardy
Morris, Quincy P.
Dracula (1897) Bram Stoker
Morris, Robin cc
The Animal Game (1957) Frank Tuohy
Morris, Sergeant-Major
ss 'The Monkey's Paw'
The Lady of the Barge (1902) W. W. Jacobs
Morris, Wynne barmaid in whom all the Yorkes* are interested
Pie in the Sky (1937) Arthur Calder-Marshall
Morrison later **Mullockson, Kate**
Jeanie her sister, m. Jim Marston*
Robbery Under Arms: A Story of Life and Adventure in the Bush and in the Goldfields of Australia (1888, rev. 1889) Rolf Boldrewood (rn Thomas Alexander Browne)

Morrison senior assistant, Port Burdock
Bazaar
The History of Mr Polly (1910) H. G.
Wells
Morrison, Albert ('Albert-next-door')
his uncle, m. Margaret Ashleigh
The Treasure Seekers† (1899) E. Nesbit
Morrison, Loch a boy
Cassie his sister
The Golden Apples (1949) Eudora Welty
Morrissey friendless pimp
Mrs Eckdorf in O'Neill's Hotel (1969)
William Trevor
Morse, Ruth graduate daughter of wealthy
parents, encourages Martin Eden* but
then deserts him; seeks him out when he
becomes successful, but he rejects her
Martin Eden (1909) Jack London
Morshed, Mr midshipman
ss 'The Bonds of Discipline'†
Traffics and Discoveries (1904) Rudyard
Kipling
Morstan, Mary m. Dr Watson*
Arthur her father
The Sign of Four (1890) Arthur Conan
Doyle
Mortgage nurse to Pecunia*
The Staple of News play (1631) Ben
Jonson
Mortimer paramour to Queen Isabella*
Edward II play (1594) Christopher
Marlowe
Mortimer, Edward Earl of March (hist.)
King Henry IV; King Henry VI plays
(1623) William Shakespeare
Mortimer, Henry, Chief Inspector
Emmeline his wife
Memento Mori (1959) Muriel Spark
Mortimer, James, Dr
The Hound of the Baskervilles (1902)
Arthur Conan Doyle
Mortimer, Monte impresario
The Good Companions (1929) J. B.
Priestley
Mortis, Mrs inmate of home for aged
The Poorhouse Fair (1959) John Updike
Morton, Cyril
ss 'The Solitary Cyclist'
The Return of Sherlock Holmes (1905)
Arthur Conan Doyle
Morton, Harry 'a lad of fire, zeal and
education'
Colonel Silas his father

Morton of Millwood his uncle
Old Mortality (1816) Walter Scott
Morton, John cc, jilted by Arabella
Trefoil*, leaves her £5,000
Reginald his cousin, m. Mary Masters*
The American Senator (1877) Anthony
Trollope
Morton, Robert, Sir counsel for Ronnie
Winslow*
The Winslow Boy play (1946) Terence
Rattigan
Mortsheugh, Johnnie sexton
The Bride of Lammermoor (1819)
Walter Scott
Morville, Guy, Sir cc, m. Amy Edmon-
stone*
Archdeacon Morville his uncle
Philip m. Laura Edmonstone*; **Mary**
Verena poet; **Margaret** m. Dr Henley*;
Fanny died young his children
The Heir of Redclyffe (1853) Charlotte
M. Yonge
Mosby lover of Arden's wife
*The Lamentable and Terrible Tragedy of
Arden of Feversham in Kent* play (1592)
Anon.
Mosca parasite to Volpone*
Volpone play (1617) Ben Jonson
Moses
The School for Scandal play (1777)
Richard Brinsley Sheridan
Moses saint and genuine Sacred Individual
*All and Everything: Beelzebub's Tales to
His Grandson* (1950) G. I. Gurdjieff
Moses, Alade idealistic cc who eventually
becomes corrupt politician in Nigerian
novel
Chief the Honourable Minister (1970)
Timothy Mofolorunso Aluko
Mosgrove, Alwyn, Dr
Lady Audley's Secret (1862) Mrs
Braddon
Moss spunging housekeeper
his wife and daughter
Vanity Fair (1847–8) W. M. Thackeray
Moss unsuccessful farmer
'Gritty' his wife, sister to Edward
Tulliver*
George; Willie; Lizzie their children
The Mill on the Floss (1860) George Eliot
(rn Mary Anne, later Marian, Evans)
Moss, Ada, Miss second-rate singer at end
of her tether

ss 'Pictures'
Bliss (1920) Katherine Mansfield (rn Katherine Mansfield Beauchamp)

Moss, Adam nature lover, reluctantly captures the Kentucky Cardinal* for the sake of his capricious beloved; it dies
Kentucky Cardinal (1894) James Lane Allen

Moss, Bobby Jewish fellow student of Clive Newcome* at Gandish's
The Newcomes (1853–5 W. M. Thackeray

Moss, Duncan photographer
The Unspeakable Skipton (1959) Pamela Hansford Johnson

Mosscrop, David dissipated cc
March Hares (1896) Harold Frederic

Mossrose Jewish employee of Eglantine*, and agent for his creditors
ss 'The Ravenswing'
Men's Wives (1843) W. M. Thackeray

Mote, Hazel ('Haze') murderer and preacher of the church of truth without Jesus Christ Crucified; ('Nobody with a good car needs to be justified'); cc
Wise Blood (1952) Flannery O'Connor

Motford, Cornelia ('Kay') cc, m. H. M. Pulham
Guy her brother
H. M. Pulham, Esq (1941) John P. Marquand

Moth page to Armado*
Love's Labour's Lost play (1623) William Shakespeare

Mother of the Modern Gracchi name with which Mrs Hominy* signed her letters from Europe
Martin Chuzzlewit (1844) Charles Dickens

Motherly one that lets lodgings
A Journey to London play (1728) John Vanbrugh

Mothersole, Mrs hanged as a witch
ss 'The Ash-tree'
Ghost Stories of an Antiquary (1910) M. R. James

Moti Guj an elephant
ss 'Moti Guj – Mutineer'
Life's Handicap (1891) Rudyard Kipling

Motshill, Mr schoolmaster
How Green Was My Valley (1939) Richard Llewellyn

Mott, Geoffrey cc

The Road from the Monument (1962) Storm Jameson

Mottleville
The Mysteries of Udolpho (1794) Mrs Ann Radcliffe

Mottram of the Indian Survey
ss 'At the End of the Passage'
Life's Handicap (1891) Rudyard Kipling

Mottram, Peter Blundell's* partner
Mid-Channel play (1910) Arthur Wing Pinero

Mottram, Rex m. Lady Julia Flyte*
Brideshead Revisited (1945) Evelyn Waugh

Motts, Miss
Uncle Remus (1880–95) Joel Chandler Harris

Mouchy, Mme de Quebec acquaintance of Warrington*
The Virginians (1857–9) W. M. Thackeray

Mould undertaker
Martin Chuzzlewit (1844) Charles Dickens

Moulder, Mr outsized commercial traveller
Orley Farm (1862) Anthony Trollope

Moulin, Charlotte, Mrs Ethelberta Petherwin's* aunt
The Hand of Ethelberta (1876) Thomas Hardy

Moulton aristocratic sponger
ss 'Agnes Lahens'
Celibates (1895) George Moore

Moulton, Francis D. m. Hatty Doran*
ss 'The Noble Bachelor'
The Adventures of Sherlock Holmes (1892) Arthur Conan Doyle

Moultrie, Ag the Roarer and Greeter
A Scots Quair (1932–4) Lewis Grassic Gibbon (rn James Leslie Mitchell)

Moultrie, Mrs Mary, Elizabeth and Agnes
ss 'The House Surgeon'
Actions and Reactions (1909) Rudyard Kipling

Mounchensey, Richard, Sir
Raymond his son
The Merry Devil of Edmonton play (1608) ?Thomas Dekker

Mount Severn see **Vane**

Mount, Bella, Mrs 'enchantress' of Richard Feverel*
The Ordeal of Richard Feverel (1859)

George Meredith

Mountain, Mrs companion to Mme Esmond*
Fanny her daughter, m. Henry Warrington*
The Virginians (1857–9) W. M. Thackeray

Mountararat, Earl of
Iolanthe opera (1882) W. S. Gilbert and Arthur Sullivan

Mountclere, Lord farcical 'wicked old man' who m. Ethelberta Petherwin*
the Hon. Edgar his brother
The Hand of Ethelberta (1876) Thomas Hardy

Mountfalcon, Lord
The Ordeal of Richard Feverel: A History of Father and Son (1859) George Meredith

Mountfaucon, Susannah cc, 'museum piece', Edwardian who will not adapt herself to change
Museum Pieces (1952) William Plomer

Mountjoy, Giles, Sir banker, cc
Hugh his nephew, m. Iris Henley*
Arthur Hugh's brother, murdered for political reasons
Blind Love (1890) Wilkie Collins and Walter Besant (the latter completed the manuscript)

Mountjoy, Henrietta
Colonel Mountjoy her father
The House in Paris (1935) Elizabeth Bowen

Mountolive, David British diplomat, cc
The Alexandria Quartet (1957–61) Lawrence Durrell

Mountry, Lord m. Cynthia Drassilis*
The Little Nugget (1913) P. G. Wodehouse

Mouth, Ahmadou, Mr the prancing nigger
his ambitious wife
Miami; Edna whore; **Charlie** their children
Prancing Nigger (1924) Ronald Firbank

Mowbray, Adeline radical mother who neglects her daughter; allegedly Mary Wollstoncroft
Adeline her daughter
Adeline Mowbray, or The Mother and Daughter (1804) Amelia Opie

Mowbray, Earl of
Lady Joan; Lady Maud his daughters
Sybil (1845) Benjamin Disraeli

Mowbray, John Laird of St Ronan's
Clara his sister, m. Valentine Bulmer*
St Ronan's Well (1824) Walter Scott

Mowcher, Miss dwarf manicurist
David Copperfield (1850) Charles Dickens

Mowgli (**Nathoo** among people) boy brought up by wolves
ss 'In The Rukh'†
Many Inventions† (1893); *Jungle Books* (1894–5) Rudyard Kipling

Moxey, Christian Peak's* journalist friend
Marcella his sister
Born in Exile (1892) George Gissing

Moy-Thompson, Revd Mr headmaster
his wife
Mr Perrin and Mr Traill (1911) Hugh Walpole

Mrs Mutrie widow to railway tycoon
The Naulakha (1892) Rudyard Kipling and Wolcott Balestier

Mrs Rouse landlady of low tenement in which Haynes* is forced, by poverty, to live
Maisie her niece
Minty Alley (1936) C. L. R. James

Msimangu, Theophilus, Revd priest
Cry, the Beloved Country (1948) Alan Paton

Muck, Caesar von, Privy Councillor Nazi patron of the theatre, President of the Academy of Writers, 'truly a man of the world, sophisticated to a degree that verged on heroism', Höfgen's* admirer, author of acclaimed tragedy, *Tannenberg*
his wife
Mephisto (1936) Klaus Mann

Mucklebackit, Saunders
Maggie his dominating wife
Steenie; Patie; Jennie their children
Simon his father
Elspeth his mother, *née* Cheyne
The Antiquary (1816) Walter Scott

Mucklewrath, Habakkuk mad preacher
Old Mortality (1816) Walter Scott

Mudd killed on his first mission
Catch-22 (1961) Joseph Heller

Mudel, Adolf, Dr comic psychoanalyst
Cold Comfort Farm (1932) Stella Gibbons

Mudge, Jonas secretary of the Brick Lane Ebenezer Temperance Association

The Pickwick Papers (1837) Charles Dickens

Muff, Tarquinius
Blatheremskite his brother
Hawbuck Grange (1847) R. S. Surtees

Mufferson, Willie 'a model boy'
The Adventures of Tom Sawyer (1876) Mark Twain (rn Samuel Langhorne Clemens)

Mugford, Frederick owner of the *Pall Mall Gazette*
his wife
The Adventures of Philip (1862) W. M. Thackeray

Mugger, The crocodile
ss 'The Undertakers'
Jungle Books (1894–5) Rudyard Kipling

Muggleton, Mrs
Fanny By Gaslight (1940) Michael Sadleir

Muggs, Alfred, Sir recommended Miss Crumpton's Academy
Sketches by Boz† (1836) Charles Dickens

Muir, Lieutenant
The Pathfinder (1840) James Fenimore Cooper

Mulberry Sellers, Colonel see **Sellers, Beriah**

Mulcahy, Corporal paid agitator
ss 'The Mutiny of the Mavericks'
Life's Handicap (1891) Rudyard Kipling

Mulcare, Michael fireman on the *Oroya*
Captain Botell (1933) James Hanley

Muldoon, Roberta trans-sexual ex-football player
The World According to Garp (1978) John Irving

Mules, Revd Mr new rector of St Enedoc
In the Roar of the Sea (1892) Sabine Baring-Gould

Muleygrubs, Marmaduke staymaker of Ludgate Hill
his wife and family
Handley Cross (1843) R. S. Surtees

Mulholland, Bartly
The Informer (1925) Liam O'Flaherty

Muligrub a vintner
Mistress Muligrub his wife
The Dutch Courtesan play (1605) John Marston

Mullenberg, Amelie unruly pupil whom Francis Henri* cannot manage
The Professor (1857) Charlotte Brontë

Muller head ranger
ss 'In the Rukh'
Many Inventions (1893) Rudyard Kipling

Mullet, Professor
Martin Chuzzlewit (1844) Charles Dickens

Mulligan, Desmond poet and journalist
Men's Wives (1843) W. M. Thackeray

Mulligan, Malachi ('Buck') medical student
Ulysses (1922) James Joyce

Mulligan, Peter
The Informer (1925) Liam O'Flaherty

Mulliner butler to Mrs Jamieson*
Cranford (1853) Mrs Gaskell

Mulliner, Mr cc, narrator
Clarence his cousin
Frederick; George; Lancelot; Revd Augustine his nephews
Wilfred his brother, inventor of Mulliner's Magic Marvels
William his uncle, m. Myrtle Banks
John San Francisco Earthquake son to Uncle William and Myrtle
Meet Mr Mulliner† (1927) P. G. Wodehouse

Mullins games captain
ss 'Regulus'†
A Diversity of Creatures† (1917) Rudyard Kipling

Mullins pirate
Peter Pan play (1904) J. M. Barrie

Mullins, Sergeant
ss 'Black Jack'
Soldiers Three (1888) Rudyard Kipling

Mullion, Jenny deaf observer
Crome Yellow (1922) Aldous Huxley

Mullockson see **Morrison, Kate**

Mulqueen, Danny m. Teresa Considine*
Ignatius; Reggie; Marie-Rose; Aggie their children
Without My Cloak (1931) Kate O'Brien

Mulvaney, Terence one of the soldiers three, with Learoyd* and Ortheris*, m. Diana Shadd*
ss 'The Three Musketeers'†
Plain Tales from the Hills† (1888) Rudyard Kipling

Mumblazen, Michael heraldic expert
Kenilworth (1821) Walter Scott

Mumblecourt, Marjorie nurse to Dame Custance*

Ralph Roister Doister play (1551) Nicholas Udall

Mumby, Squire
John; Martin his sons
Mr Weston's Good Wine (1927) T. F. Powys

Munce bookmaker
Jane Clegg play (1913) St John Ervine

Muncy, Clyde writer returning from New York to Nebraska
Peggy his wife
The Home Place (1948); *The World in the Attic* (1949) Wright Morris

Munday, Mrs shopkeeper, Whortley; Lewisham's* landlady
Love and Mr Lewisham (1900) H. G. Wells

Munden, Harvey
ss 'A Lodger in Maze Pond'
The House of Cobwebs (1906) George Gissing

Muniment, Paul London socialist; political theorist; moves in 'a dry statistical and scientific air'
Rose his crippled and bedridden sister, a snob
The Princess Casamassima (1866) Henry James

Munn, Percy cc, young Kentucky lawyer and farmer
May his wife
Night Rider (1939) Robert Penn Warren

Munnings, Mrs aunt to Jim Lanigan*
Thady her husband
Without My Cloak (1931) Kate O'Brien

Munodi court noble
Gulliver's Travels (1726) Jonathan Swift

Munro, Colonel
Alice; Cora his daughters
The Last of the Mohicans (1826) James Fenimore Cooper

Munro, Grant
ss 'The Yellow Face'
The Memoirs of Sherlock Holmes (1894) Arthur Conan Doyle

Munson, Buford Negro farmer
The Violent Bear It Away (1960) Flannery O'Connor

Münster, Eugenia, Baroness morganatic wife of German prince, sister to Felix Young*, schemer
The Europeans (1878) Henry James

Munt, Dick collector of coffins

ss 'The Travelling Grave'
The Travelling Grave (1948) L. P. Hartley

Munt, Julia, Mrs aunt to Helen and Margaret Schlegel*
Howards End (1910) E. M. Forster

Munves, Mendel Jewish misfit
Homage to Blenholt (1936) Daniel Fuchs

Murascho, Tony see Grecco, Al

Murcraft
The Devil is an Ass play (1616) Ben Jonson

Murdock, Laura 'fallen woman'; cc of play very popular in its time: she understands her position when she hears a hurdy gurdy playing the song 'Bon-Bob Buddie, My Chocolate Drop'
The Easiest Way play (1908) Eugene Walter

Murdockson, Madge ('Madge Wildfire')
Donald her father
Meg her mother
Heart of Midlothian (1818) Walter Scott

Murdstone, Edward Mrs Clara Copperfield's* second husband, a harsh man who blighted lives
Jane his fittingly cruel sister
David Copperfield (1850) Charles Dickens

Murgatroyd, Major Dragoon Guards, m. Lady Angela*
Patience opera (1881) W. S. Gilbert and Arthur Sullivan

Murgatroyd, Miss founder and head of Joan and Peter's first school
Joan and Peter (1918) H. G. Wells

Murgatroyd, Ruthven, Sir disguised as Robin Oakapple
Sir Despard his younger brother, a wicked baronet, m. Mad Margaret
Sir Roderic an ancestor, m. Dame Hannah
Ruddigore opera (1887) W. S. Gilbert and Arthur Sullivan

Murietta or **Murieta, Joaquín** Robin-Hood*-like lengendary Californian or Mexican bandit; or otherwise; his head was alleged to have been preserved in alcohol; in book by gold-rusher turned journalist who probably needed cash more than facts
Life and Adventures of Joaquín Murieta (1854) John R. Ridge

Murker see Smith

Murphy cc, Dubliner, astrological speculator, killed by an exploding gas fire; burnt, his ashes placed in a paper bag, and strewn on a pub floor by Cooper*
Murphy (1938) Samuel Beckett

Murray, Rosalie m. Sir Thomas Ashby*
Matilda her sister
their parents
Agnes Grey (1847) Anne Brontë

Murray, St Elmo 'impossibly gifted and erudite young prude', tamed by Edna Earle*
St Elmo (1866) Augusta Evans Wilson

Murray-Forbes, Vincent, Vice-Admiral Sir
The Cruel Sea (1951) Nicholas Monsarrat

Murtagh Lavengro's* childhood friend
Romany Rye (1857) George Borrow

Murthwaite Indian traveller; part narrator
The Moonstone (1968) Wilkie Collins

Muscari poet
ss 'The Paradise of Thieves'
The Wisdom of Father Brown (1914) G. K. Chesterton

Muschat, Nicol 'debauched and profligate wretch'
Heart of Midlothian (1818) Walter Scott

Museau, M. governor of Fort Duquesne
The Virginians (1857–9) W. M. Thackeray

Musgrave, Ned cc
The Man of Sorrow (1808, reprinted as *The Most Unfortunate Man in the World* 1842) Theodore Hook

Musgrave, Reginald
ss 'The Musgrave Ritual'
The Memoirs of Sherlock Holmes (1894) Arthur Conan Doyle

Musgrove, Charles the elder, owner of Uppercross Hall, not much educated and not at all elegant
his wife, of substantial size
Charles his eldest son and heir, m. Mary Elliott*; Richard troublesome; Henrietta; Louisa; Harry their children
Walter younger son to Charles and Mary
Persuasion (1818) Jane Austen

Musgrove, Clement planter in 19th-century Mississippi
Rosamund his daughter, m. Jamie Lockhart*
The Robber Bridegroom (1942) Eudora

Welty

Mush, Freddy secretary to Rupert Catskill*
Men Like Gods (1923) H. G. Wells

Muskham, Jack horse breeder
Flowering Wilderness (1932) John Galsworthy

Muspratt, Beryl, Mrs admiral's widow with three children, m. Lord Brideshead*
Brideshead Revisited (1945) Evelyn Waugh

Musse, Phoebe village coquette
Mehalah (1880) Sabine Baring-Gould

Musset, Dame Evangeline satirical (and celebratory) portrait of Natalie Barney*, whose lifelong commitment was to rescue women from the 'perils of heterosexuality'; the author called this book 'a slight satiric wigging' and a 'piece of fluff'
Ladies Almanack (1928) Djuna Barnes

Mustapha, Baba uncle to Shibli Bagarag*; later King of Oolb
The Shaving of Shagpat (1956) George Meredith

Mustian, Rosacoke girl seeking happiness in too conventional terms, becomes pregnant by Wesley Beavers*, grows and learns; cc of North Carolina novel
her parents
A Long and Happy Life† (1962) Reynolds Price

Mutanhed, Lord foolish young man
The Pickwick Papers (1837) Charles Dickens

Mutimer 'early Georgian' butler to Mr Blandish*
ss 'The Spoils of Mr Blandish' (read by Boon*)
Boon (1915) H. G. Wells

Mutimer, Richard cc, artisan and fervent socialist who inherits a fortune and whose character degenerates; m. Adela Waltham*
Harry (''Arry') his drunken brother
Alice his vulgar young sister
Demos (1886) George Gissing

Mutius son to Titus Andronicus*
Titus Andronicus play (1623) William Shakespeare

Mutlar, Daisy one-time fiancée to Lupin Pooter*, m. Murray Posh*
The Diary of a Nobody (1892) George

and Weedon Grossmith

Mweta, Adamson president of new independent African state
A Guest of Honour (1971) Nadine Gordimer

My Lord sinister nameless seducer
Amelia (1752) Henry Fielding

Mybug author, m, Rennett Starkadder*
Cold Comfort Farm (1932) Stella Gibbons

Mycates King of Persia
Tamburlaine play (1592) Christopher Marlowe

Myers racing tipster
A Farewell to Arms (1929) Ernest Hemingway

Myles, Jean m. Tommy Sandys*
Sentimental Tommy (1896) J. M. Barrie

Myles, Marvin one-time fiancée to H. M.

Pulham*, m. John Ransome
H. M. Pulham, Esq (1941) John P. Marquand

Mynors, Henry suitor of Anna Tellwright*
Anna of the Five Towns (1902) Arnold Bennett

Myrtle, May professional co-respondent
Holy Deadlock (1934) A. P. Herbert

Myrtle, Mrs housekeeper to Sir Massingberd Heath*
Lost Sir Massingberd (1864) James Payn

Mysa buffalo
ss 'How Fear Came'
Jungle Books (1894–5) Rudyard Kipling

Myshkin, Prince cc, the 'idiot', an epileptic
Idiot (1869) Fyodor Dostoievsky

Mystic, Mr caricature of Coleridge
Melincourt, or Sir Oran Haut-on (1817) Thomas Love Peacock

N

Naboth
ss 'Naboth'
Life's Handicap (1891) Rudyard Kipling
Nadgett enquiry agent employed by Anglo-Bengalee Assurance Company; proved Jonas Chuzzlewit's* guilt of the attempted murder of his father
Martin Chuzzlewit (1844) Charles Dickens
Nafferton
ss 'Pig'
Plain Tales from the Hills (1888) Rudyard Kipling
Nag snake
   Nagaina his wife
   ss 'Rikki Tikki Tavi'
Jungle Books (1894–5) Rudyard Kipling
Nagel, Johan Nilsen cc, 'In the middle of the summer of 1891 the most extraordinary thing began happening in a small Norwegian coastal town. A stranger by the name of Nagel appeared . . .'
Mysterier (*Mysteries*) (1892) Knut Hamsun
Namby sheriff's officer who arrested Pickwick*
The Pickwick Papers (1837) Charles Dickens
Namgay, Doola i.e. Patsy Doolan, red-haired native of Irish decent
ss 'Namgay Doola'
Life's Handicap (1891) Rudyard Kipling
Nana Newfoundland dog, nurse to the Darling* children
Peter Pan play (1904) J. M. Barrie
Nana, Jagua ageing prostitute in Nigerian novel
Jagua Nana (1961) Cyprian Ekwensi
Nance friend to 'Tilda*
No. 5 John Street (1902) Richard Whiteing
Nancibel music student
Streets of Night (1923) John Dos Passos
Nancy cook to the Marjoribanks: no ordinary cook, gives gravy beef to the poorer off
Miss Marjoribanks (1866) Mrs Margaret Oliphant
Nancy maid to Edward Brent-Foster's aunt*, whom Lady Mary Savylle* pretends to be
The Panel (1912) (in UK, 1913, as *Ring for Nancy*) Ford Madox Ford
Nancy member of Fagin's* gang
Oliver Twist (1838) Charles Dickens
Nandy, John Edward Mrs Plornish's* father, a 'poor little reedy piping old gentleman'
Little Dorrit (1857) Charles Dickens
Nanki-Poo see **Mikado, The**
Nanni
ss 'Be This Her Memorial'
My People (1915) Caradoc Evans (rn David Evans)
Nantolet father to Rosalura* and Lillia Bianca*
The Wild-Goose Chase play (1652) John Fletcher
Narcissus
ss 'The Princess of Kingdom Gone'
Adam and Eve and Pinch Me (1921) A. E. Coppard
Narracombe, Mrs aunt to Megan David*
The Apple Tree (1918) John Galsworthy
Nasanki drunken officer who functions as author's voice in influential anti-militarist Russian novel
The Duel (1905) A. Kuprin
Nash, Bunny actress
Tell Me How Long The Train's Been Gone (1968) James Baldwin
Nash, Gabriel aesthete and talker, in part spokesman for author
The Tragic Muse (1890) Henry James
Nash, Nancy charwoman cured by Lydgate*
Middlemarch (1871–2) George Eliot (rn Mary Anne, later Marian, Evans)
Nathan majordomo at Castlewood
The Virginians (1857–9) W. M.

Thackeray

Nathan red-whiskered Jew
Sketches by Boz† (1836) Charles Dickens

Nathaniel, Sir curate
Love's Labour's Lost play (1623)
William Shakespeare

Nathoo see **Mowgli**

Native, The Major Bagstock's Indian servant
Dombey and Son (1848) Charles Dickens

Nawab Bahadur
A Passage to India (1924) E. M. Forster

Naylor, Richard, Sir Irish landowner, uncle to Lois Farquhar*
Myra his wife
Laurence Lady Naylor's nephew
The Last September (1929) Elizabeth Bowen

Nazerman, Sol Jewish pawnbroker whose family has been exterminated by Nazis
his married sister
Morton his nephew
The Pawnbroker (1961) Edward Lewis Wallant

Nazing, Walter
Annabel his wife
The Silver Spoon (1926) John Galsworthy

Neal, John letter-writing cc
Towards a Better Life (1932) Kenneth Burke

Nearchus Prince of Argos
The Broken Heart play (1633) John Ford

Neary runs a Gymnasium in Cork, former teacher to Murphy*
Murphy (1938) Samuel Beckett

Neatfoot Sir Alexander Wengrave's* man
The Roaring Girl play (1611) Thomas Middleton and Thomas Dekker

Neb Black servant to Miles Wallingford*
Afloat and Ashore (1844) James Fenimore Cooper

Neckett bailiff's man who arrested Skimpole* at Coavins' behest
Charlotte; Emma; Tom his children
Bleak House (1853) Charles Dickens

Neckland, Bert farmer
The Saliva Tree (1966) Brian W. Aldiss

Ned chimney sweep who kept a boy for the purpose of burglary
Oliver Twist (1838) Charles Dickens

Neddy one of the Fleet turnkeys
The Pickwick Papers (1837) Charles

Dickens

Needle tailor
The Magnetic Lady, or *Humours Reconciled* play (1641) Ben Jonson

Neeshawts, Dr member of the Mudfog Association
The Mudfog Papers (1838) Charles Dickens

Negget, George farmer
Lizzie his wife
ss 'Cupboard Love'
The Lady of the Barge (1902) W. W. Jacobs

Neilson Swedish philosopher on South Sea island
Sally his native wife
ss 'Red'
The Trembling of a Leaf (1921) W. Somerset Maugham

Nell, Salvation see **Sanders, Nell**

Nello Florentine barber
Romola (1863) George Eliot (rn Mary Anne, later Marian, Evans)

Nelvil, Oswald, Lord melancholy reserved Englishman, in love with Corinne* m. Lucille Edgermond*
Corinne (1807) Madam de Staël

Nemours, de, Duc in love with the Princesse de Clèves, *née* Chartres*
La Princesse de Clèves (1678) Comtesse de Lafayette

Nennius British commander
Bonduca play (1614) Francis Beaumont and John Fletcher

Nerissa waiting-maid to Portia*
The Merchant of Venice play (1623) William Shakespeare

Nerrick, Mrs landlady
Call It Sleep (1934) Henry Roth

Nesbit, Nora author of light fiction, mistress of Carey*: a partial portrait of Violet Hunt, with whom the author had had an affair
Of Human Bondage (1915) W. Somerset Maugham

Nestor Grecian commander
Troilus and Cressida play (1623) William Shakespeare

Nettingall, Misses principals of the school at Canterbury where David Copperfield's* early love, Miss Shepherd, was a pupil
David Copperfield (1850) Charles

Dickens

Neumann, Ernest narrator and cc, Jewish violinist suspected of murder of Veronika Pathzuol*, of which he is acquitted – but he discovers he did it without knowing it
As It Was Written (1885) Henry Harland

Neumiller, Otto 1881 emigrant from Germany to Dakota spanning four generations
Charles his son
Martin Charles' son and cc
Alpha Martin's wife
Beyond the Bedroom Wall: A Family Album (1975) Larry Woiwode

Nevile, Marmaduke cc, foster-brother to Nicholas Alwyn*
The Last of the Barons (1843) Edward Bulwer Lytton

Nevill friend to Scudmore*
A Woman is a Weathercock play (1612) Nathan Field

Neville one of the characters whose interior monologue* makes up this novel
The Waves (1931) Virginia Woolf

Neville, Constance
She Stoops to Conquer play (1773) Oliver Goldsmith

Neville, Edward Geraldin son to the Countess of Glenallen*
Eveline cousin to the Earl of Glenallen*, mother to Lovel*
The Antiquary (1816) Walter Scott

Neville, Fred English cavalry officer in Ireland, murdered by Kate O'Hara's* mother
An Eye for an Eye (1879) Anthony Trollope

Neville, George, Sir Catherine Peyton's* former lover, m. Mercy Vint*
Griffith Gaunt, or Jealousy (1866) Charles Reade
Kate Peyton, or Jealousy play (1867) Charles Reade

Nevin subaltern
ss 'A Conference of the Powers'
Many Inventions (1893) Rudyard Kipling

Nevin, Duncan of Nimrod Mews
Handley Cross (1843) R. S. Surtees

New, Elijah parish clerk, serpent player
ss 'The Three Strangers'
Wessex Tales (1888) Thomas Hardy

Newberry, Lizzie farmer's widow engaged in smuggling, m. Richard Stockdale*
ss 'The Distracted Preacher'
Wessex Tales (1888) Thomas Hardy

Newberry, Richard director of Crane & Newberry
The Dream (1924) H. G. Wells

Newcome, Clemency the Jeddlers' maid*, m. Benjamin Britain
The Battle of Life (1846) Charles Dickens

Newcome, Thomas weaver, m. (1) Susan (2) Sophia Alethea Hobson
Colonel Thomas Newcome son to Thomas and Susan, m. Emma, widow to Jack Casey
Brian (later Sir) m. Lady Ann Gaunt; Hobson Brian's twin brother, m. Maria twin sons to Thomas Sr. and Sophia
Clive son to Colonel Thomas and Emma, m. (1) Rosey Mackenzie, (2) Ethel Newcome, his cousin
Tommy son to Clive and Rosey
Barnes m. Lady Clara Pullcyn; Ethel m. Clive (above), her cousin children to Brian and Lady Ann
Sammie; Maria; Louisa and others, children to Hobson
The Newcomes (1853–5) W. M. Thackeray

Newent, Hilda, Mrs sister to Elizabeth Trant*
The Good Companions (1929) J. B. Priestley

Newhaven, Lord throws himself under a train
Violet his wife, who has an affair with Hugh Scarlett*
Red Pottage (1899) Mary Cholmondeley

Newman, Christopher cc
The American (1877) Henry James

Newsome, Chadwick ('Chad') young man of great virtue, cc
Mrs Newsome his mother, of Woolett, Mass., of great virtue
The Ambassadors (1903) Henry James

Newson, Richard, Captain buys Susan Henchard*
The Mayor of Casterbridge (1886) Thomas Hardy

Newton, Isaac, Sir a newt
The Tale of Jeremy Fisher (1906) Beatrix Potter

Nibby traveller in Gillingwater burners, m.

Carrie Waghorn*
The Town Traveller (1898) George Gissing
Nibrassa a counsellor of state
Love's Sacrifice play (1633) John Ford
Nibs one of Peter Pan's* band
Peter Pan play (1904) J. M. Barrie
Nicholas ('The Count') cc,
ss 'The Almond Tree'†
The Riddle (1923) Walter de la Mare
Nicholas, Bishop schemes to prevent others from achievement; also appears as ghost
Kongs-emmnerne (*The Pretenders*) play (1863) Henrik Ibsen
Nicholas, Dom fat Picardy monk
ss 'A Lodging for the Night'
New Arabian Nights (1882) Robert Louis Stevenson
Nichols, Captain dyspeptic skipper of SS *Fenton*
The Narrow Corner (1932) W. Somerset Maugham
Nichols, Ernest painter – and Charlie Keepsake, Mrs Dukes'* lodger
Mrs Dukes' Million (1977) Wyndham Lewis
Nichols, Mr
The Adventures of David Simple (1744–53) Sarah Fielding
Nick biologist
Honey his wife
Who's Afraid of Virginia Woolf? play (1962) Edward Albee
Nick of the Woods see **Bloody Nathan**
Nickits former owner of Bounderby's* country estate, until improvidence forced him to flee from England
Hard Times (1854) Charles Dickens
Nickleby, Nicholas cc, m. Madeline Bray*
Nicholas his father
his mother
Kate his sister, m. Frank Cheeryble*
Godfrey his grandfather
Godrey's wife
Ralph his great-uncle
Ralph junior his uncle, heartless usurer and villain
Nicholas Nickleby (1839) Charles Dickens
Niçois, Mme patient
D'un Château l'autre (*Castle to Castle*) (1957) Louis-Ferdinand Céline (rn Louis-

Ferdinand Destouches)
Nicola manservant
Arms and the Man (1894) George Bernard Shaw
Nicolaivitch, HH Prince Alexis
Huntingtower (1922) John Buchan
Nicolette maiden of unknown origin who turns out to be daughter of king of Carthage in 13th-century French romance
Aucassin and Nicolette
Nidderdale, Lord
The Marquis of Auld Reekie his father
The Way We Live Now (1875) Anthony Trollope
Niggardise, Dame wife to Avarice*
Pierce Penilesse his Supplication to the Devil (1592) Thomas Nashe
Nightingale ballad singer
Bartholomew Fair play (1631) Ben Jonson
Nightingale, Jack
his father
his uncle
Tom Jones (1749) Henry Fielding
Nightingale, Ronald
The Masters (1951) C. P. Snow
Nikanov, King Cockeye Johnny Russian, King of the Gipsies
McSorley's Wonderful Saloon (1943) Joseph Mitchell
Nikhil Tolstoyan cc of Bengali novel by winner of Nobel Prize
The Home and the World (1916) Rabindranath Tagore
Niles, Peter, Captain US Artillery
Hazel his sister
Mourning Becomes Electra play (1931) Eugene O'Neill
Nilghai, The war correspondent
The Light that Failed (1890) Rudyard Kipling
Nimmo
Tracy's Tiger (1951) William Saroyan
Nimmo, Chester radical politician, later Lord Nimmo, m. Nina Woodville*
Tom cabaret performer; **Sally** Nina's children by Jim Latter
Prisoner of Grace (1952) Joyce Cary
Nimrod, Apperley sporting author
Jorrocks's Jaunts and Jollities (1838) R. S. Surtees
Niner, Margaret, Miss niece to Julius

Slinkton*
Hunted Down (1860) Charles Dickens
Ninny, Innocent, Sir
his wife
Sir Abraham their son
A Woman is a Weathercock play (1612)
Nathan Field
Nioche, M.
Néonie his daughter
The American (1877) Henry James
Nipper, Susan Florence Dombey's* maid,
m. Toots*
Dombey and Son (1848) Charles Dickens
Nipson, Mrs assistant headmistress
What Katy Did at School (1873) Susan
Coolidge (rn Sarah Chauncey Woolsey)
Niv a witless lad
The King of Elfland's Daughter (1924)
Lord Dunsany
Nixon, Cristal confidential servant to Red-
gauntlet*
Redgauntlet (1824) Walter Scott
Nixon, Mr and Mrs
Watt (1953) Samuel Beckett
Nixon, Mrs servant to the Clayhangers*
The *Clayhanger* series (1910–16) Arnold
Bennett
No Zoo, Lord reputed ancestor to the
Chuzzlewit family
Martin Chuzzlewit (1844) Charles
Dickens
Noakes, Jacob friend to Festus Derriman*
The Trumpet Major (1880) Thomas
Hardy
Noakes, Percy law student
Sketches by Boz† (1837) Charles Dickens
Noaks undergraduate
Zuleika Dobson (1911) Max Beerbohm
Nobbs, Albert transvestite waiter
ss 'Albert Nobbs'
Celibate Celibates (1927) George Moore
Nobby tramp
A Clergyman's Daughter (1935) George
Orwell (rn Eric Blair)
Noble, Henrietta, Mrs sister to Mrs
Farebrother*
Middlemarch (1871–2) George Eliot (rn
Mary Anne, later Marian, Evans)
Noble, John
Ailie his wife; master and mistress of the
magnificent Rab* in much loved senti-
mental dog tale
Rab and His Friends (1855) John Brown

Noble, Maury young man about town
The Beautiful and Damned (1922) F.
Scott Fitzgerald
Nockemorf surgeon
The Pickwick Papers (1837) Charles
Dickens
Noddy 'a scorbutic youth', guest at Bob
Sawyer's* party
The Pickwick Papers (1837) Charles
Dickens
Noddy repulsive and twee gnome invented
by Enid Blyton in series of books
1925–56
Noel, Dr
ss 'The Suicide Club'
New Arabian Nights (1882) Robert
Louis Stevenson
Nog, Old the heron
Tarka the Otter (1927) Henry
Williamson
Noggs, Newman Ralph Nickleby Jr.'s
down-at-heel clerk, based on a Newman
Knott, a broken-down farmer and occa-
sional solicitor's clerk known to the
author
Nicholas Nickleby (1839) Charles
Dickens
Nogood, Boyo
Under Milk Wood play (1954) Dylan
Thomas
Nokes, Mr old man who m. Miss Nanny
Johnson* and dies of a spotted fever
The Adventures of David Simple
(1744–53) Sarah Fielding
Nolan wealthy young man with whom
Mrs Benham* elopes
The Research Magnificent (1915) H. G.
Wells
Nolan, Baruch London hosier
Felix Holt (1866) George Eliot (rn Mary
Anne, later Marian, Evans)
Nolan, Francie cc immensely popular
Wolfe*-like tale of Brooklyn
Johnny her lovable alcoholic father
Katie her tough-tender mother
A Tree Grows in Brooklyn (1943) Betty
Smith
Nolan, Gypo cc, informer
The Informer (1929) Liam O'Flaherty
Nolan, Jim communist
In Dubious Battle (1936) John Steinbeck
Nolan, Philip (hist.) cc ('Damn the United
States!') of tale written in fact to influence

the 1863 American election; by idealist Unitarian clergyman and 'local colourist'*; made into an opera in 1937; the later work is romantic but more in consonance with facts
ss 'The Man Without a Country'
If, Yes, and Perhaps (1868); *Philip Nolan's Friends* (1876) Edward Everett Hale

Noland, Lord
The Roaring Girl play (1611) Thomas Middleton and Thomas Dekker

Nolly nickname given to Oliver Twist* by Nancy*
Oliver Twist (1838) Charles Dickens

Nonentity, Dr metaphysician
A Citizen of the World (1762) Oliver Goldsmith

Noodler a pirate
Peter Pan play (1904) J. M. Barrie

Noorna Bin Noorka daughter to Vizier Feshnavat*
The Shaving of Shagpat (1856) George Meredith

Nooxhomists Babylonian group who studied smells
All and Everything: Beelzebub's Tales to His Grandson (1950) G. I. Gurdjieff

Norcross, Luella goes back to the church because religion is 'the only way out' for a murderer friend
ss 'Life Everlastin''
A New England Nun (1891) Mary Wilkins Freeman

Norfolk, Duke of (hist.)
King Henry VIII play (1623) William Shakespeare and John Fletcher

Norfolk, Duke of (hist.)
King Richard III play (1623) William Shakespeare

Norland, Harry, Lord m. Iris Henley*; murderer, swindler and terrorist
Blind Love (1890) Wilkie Collins and Walter Besant (the latter completed the manuscript)

Norland, Hubert corrupt police chief
Paris Trout (1988) Pete Dexter

Norley, Lord patron of the arts; uncle to Esmé Howe-Nevinson*
Angel (1957) Elizabeth Taylor

Norman, Helen cc loved by Arthur Golding; first religious fanatic, then aggressive agnostic

Workers in the Dawn (1880) George Gissing

Normandy, Beatrice cousin to Lady Drew*, mistress to George Carnaby*, in love with George Ponderevo*
Tono Bungay (1909) H. G. Wells

Norpois, Marquis de ex-ambassador
A la recherche du temps perdu (*In Search of Lost Time*) (1913–27) Marcel Proust

Norrie prospector
Gallions Reach (1927) H. M. Tomlinson

Norris, Arthur cc, 'gent'
Mr Norris Changes Trains (1935) Christopher Isherwood

Norris, Mr American gentleman engaged in mercantile affairs
his wife and two 'slender' daughters, who sang in every language but their own
a grandmother, 'little, sharp-eyed, quick'
Martin Chuzzlewit (1844) Charles Dickens

Norris, Mrs *née* Ward, sister to Lady Bertram*
Revd Mr Norris her husband
Mansfield Park (1814) Jane Austen

North, The Revd Mr glib, drunken conscience-stricken clergyman, 'one of the great fully realised characters in nineteenth-century fiction'
His Natural Life (1870–2; abridged by the author 1874; in 1885 as *For the Term of His Natural Life* – thus evading the author's irony; original text edited by Stephen Murray-Smith, 1970) Marcus Clarke

Northerton, Ensign
Tom Jones (1749) Henry Fielding

Northmour, R. of Graden Easter
ss 'the Pavilion of the Links'
New Arabian Nights (1882) Robert Louis Stevenson

Northumberland, Earl of (Henry Percy) (hist.)
his wife
King Richard II; *King Henry IV* plays (1623) William Shakespeare

Norton, John cc, ascetic young man
Lizzie his mother
ss 'John Norton'
Celibates (1895) George Moore

Norton, Marda house-guest at Danielstown
The Last September (1929) Elizabeth

Bowen
Norwynne, William judge
Henry his more virtuous because better educated (born in Africa) cousin; ccs of moralistic novel of sentiment* on theme of virtues of a proper (i.e. natural) education; William is obliged to sentence to death the woman whom he had seduced and abandoned (he does not then recognize her), for the attempted murder of his own child, being one of those who love 'to do everything good but that which their immediate duty requires'
Nature and Art (1796) Elizabeth Inchbald
Nosnibor, Senoj eminent inhabitant of Erewhon
his wife
Zulora; Arowhena their daughters, the latter m. the narrator
Erewhon (1872) Samuel Butler
Nostromo see **Fidenza**
Notterdam, Joseph cc, businessman
Elspeth his Scottish wife
When the Wicked Man (1931) Ford Madox Ford
Novak, Henry
Mary his daughter; both patients of Martin Arrowsmith*
Arrowsmith (1925) Sinclair Lewis
Novel 'a pert railing coxcomb'
The Plain Dealer play (1677) William Wycherley
Novotny, Sidney
his wife
The World in the Evening (1954) Christopher Isherwood
Nowak, Otto gigolo, keen on physical culture
his mother, a consumptive charlady
his father, a furniture remover
Lothar; Grete his brother and sister
Goodbye to Berlin (1939) Christopher Isherwood
Nowell, Patricia novelist, mistress to Tim Cornwell*
The Widow (1957) Francis King
Nox, George ex-public schoolboy, enemy to Mr Jaraby*
The Old Boys (1964) William Trevor
Nozdydov drunkard
Myortvye dushi (*Dead Souls*) (1842) Nikolai Gogol

Nubbles, Kit shop boy, devoted to Little Nell Trent*, m. Barbara
his mother, a laundress
The Old Curiosity Shop (1841) Charles Dickens
Nucingen, Baron de m. Delphine Goriot*
Père Goriot (1834) Honoré de Balzac
Nuflo grandfather to Rima*
Green Mansions (1904) W. H. Hudson
Nugent, Frank one of the famous five, onwards from
The Magnet† periodical (1908) Frank Richards (rn Charles Hamilton)
Nugent, Grace see **Reynolds, Grace**
Nuñez Ecuadoran mountaineer, cc
ss 'The Country of the Blind'
The Country of the Blind (1911) H. G. Wells
Nunheim, Arthur racketeer
The Thin Man (1934) Dashiell Hammett
Nunn, Jimmy comedian
his wife
The Good Companions (1929) J. B. Priestley
Nunn, Rhoda ill-tempered ('enraged') 'new woman' cc of novel important in the development of fiction dealing with women; in love with Everard Barfoot*
The Odd Women (1893) George Gissing
Nunnely, Philip, Sir proposes to Shirley Keeldar* and is refused
Lady Nunnely his mother
Shirley (1849) Charlotte Brontë
Nunsuch, Susan
Johnny her son
The Return of the Native (1878) Thomas Hardy
Nupkins, George Mayor of Ipswich, devoid of humour
The Pickwick Papers (1837) Charles Dickens
Nupton, T. K. writer
ss 'Enoch Soames'
Seven Men (1919) Max Beerbohm
Nurkeed stoker
ss 'The Limitations of Pambé Serang'
Life's Handicap (1891) Rudyard Kipling
Nurse a poor charwoman in the inn, with one eye; but is truly the Lady Frampul*, who left home melancholic, and jealous that her Lord loved her not because she brought him none but daughters

The New Inn, or *The Light Heart* play (1629) Ben Jonson

Nurse to Juliet*
Romeo and Juliet play (1623) William Shakespeare

Nurse, The sinister unnamed woman with whom Benoit* is carrying on an affair
Minty Alley (1936) C. L. R. James

Nutkin, Squirrel cc
The Tale of Squirrel Nutkin (1903) Beatrix Potter

Nuttel, Framton
ss 'The Open Window'
Beasts and Superbeasts (1914) Saki (rn Hector Hugh Munro)

Nym follower of Falstaff*, later soldier
The Merry Wives of Windsor; King Henry V play (1623) William Shakespeare

O

Oak, Gabriel cc, small farmer, then bailiff to Bathsheba Everdene*, whom he m. as second husband
Far From the Madding Crowd (1874) Thomas Hardy
Oakapple, Robin see **Murgatroyd, Ruthven**
Oakes, Boysie cowardly anti-hero, in entertainments, onwards from
The Liquidator (1964) John Gardner
Oaklands, Harry friend to Frank Fairlegh*, m. Fanny Fairlegh*
Sir John and Lady Oaklands his father and mother
Frank Fairlegh (1850) Frank Smedley
Oakley, Charles, Captain friend to Austin Ruthyn
Uncle Silas (1862) J. Sheridan Le Fanu
Oakley, Dorinda lower-middle-class woman cc who establishes a successful dairy farm on 'barren ground' that once belonged to her father, but never has children; m. Nathan Pedlar*
Rufus her idle brother
Barren Ground (1925) Ellen Glasgow
Oakley, Dorothy, Mrs
Greaves her son, m. Susan Sedgemoor*
Sir Launcelot Greaves (1762) Tobias Smollett
Oakroyd, Jess joiner and carpenter
his wife
Leonard; Lily their children
The Good Companions (1929) J. B. Priestley
Oaks, Derby, Lieutenant Sir in love with Miss Fotheringay*
Pendennis (1848) W. M. Thackeray
Oakum brutal captain of the *Thunder*
Roderick Random (1748) Tobias Smollett
Oakes, Oliver, Sir parson
The Black Arrow (1888) Robert Louis Stevenson
Oates, Sally wife of Raveloe cobbler
Jinny her daughter

Silas Marner (1861) George Eliot (rn Mary Anne, later Marian, Evans)
Oates, Stella *soi-disant* Lady of the Manor, chairwoman of parish council
Martin her browbeaten son in love with Clare Blake*; gets religion
Old Crow (1967) Shena Mackay
Obadiah servant to Walter Shandy*
Tristram Shandy (1767) Laurence Sterne
Obenreizer, Jules wine merchant's agent, embezzler, tried to murder Vendale*
No Thoroughfare (1867) Charles Dickens
Oberon King of the fairies
A Midsummer Night's Dream play (1623) William Shakespeare
Obersdorf, Kurt von young Austrian aristocrat who almost m. Fran Dodsworth*
his mother
Dodsworth (1929) Sinclair Lewis
Oberstein, Hugo spy
ss 'The Bruce-Partington Plans'
His Last Bow (1917) Arthur Conan Doyle
Oberwaltzer, Justice judge at Clyde Griffiths'* trial
An American Tragedy (1925) Theodore Dreiser
Obi cc of novel set in modern Lagos
No Longer at Ease (1960) Chinua Achebe
O'Bleary, Frederick boarder at Mrs Tibbs's*
Sketches by Boz (1836) Charles Dickens
Oblomov, Ilya Ilyitch cc, lazy and lovable man; in classic Russian novel of sloth ('Oblomovism') and purity of spirit; m. Pshenitsyana*
Andrey his child by Pshenitsyana, named after Stolz*
Oblomov (1859) Ivan Goncharov
Obregon
his wife
The Power and the Glory (1940)

Graham Greene

O'Brien Inner Party member
1984 (1949) George Orwell

O'Brien, Celeste in love with Peter Simple*
Colonel O'Brien her father, French army officer
Peter Simple (1834) Captain Marryat

O'Brien, Hyacinth, Sir idle and ill-tempered baronet MP in love with Rose Gray*
ss 'Rosanna'
Popular Tales (1812) Maria Edgeworth

O'Brien, Torlogh, Colonel cc hist. novel of 1699 conflict between Jacobites and Williamites
The Fortunes of Col. Torlogh O'Brien (1847) J. Sheridan Le Fanu

Obstinate neighbour, with Pliable*, to Christian*, and for a time his companion
The Pilgrim's Progress (1678–84) John Bunyan

O'Carroll, Marionetta orphan niece to the Hilarys*
Nightmare Abbey (1818) Thomas Love Peacock

Occonestoga Sanutee's* disinherited son who serves Gabriel Harrison*
The Yemassee (1835) William Gilmore Simms

Ochiltree, Edie traveller, beggar and 'king's bedesman'
The Antiquary (1816) Walter Scott

Ocky Milkman
Under Milk Wood play (1954) Dylan Thomas

Ocock, Henry lawyer
Agnes his wife
his father, m. Tilly Beamish*
Tom; Johnny his brothers
The Fortunes of Richard Mahony (1930) Henry Handel Richardson (rn Ethel Florence Lindesay Richardson Robertson)

O'Connor former governor of jail
It Is Never Too Late To Mend (1856) Charles Reade

O'Connor, Edward m. Fanny Dawson*
Handy Andy (1842) Samuel Lover

O'Connor, Jim 'gentleman caller'
The Glass Menagerie play (1948) Tennessee Williams (rn Thomas Lanier Williams)

O'Connor, Lieutenant
St Patrick's Day play (1775) Richard Brinsley Sheridan

O'Connor, Matthew, Dr man in woman's clothing, rouged, bewigged, nightgowned, who calls himself an 'old lady' in (second-named) novel two-thirds of which was suppressed by T. S. Eliot* when, at the behest of Edwin Muir , he published it; based on Dr Dan Mahoney, American Paris-based abortionist who had been struck off
Ryder (1928); *Nightwood* (1936) Djuna Barnes

O'Connor, Sheila schoolgirl
The Restoration of Arnold Middleton play (1967) David Storey

Octavia wife to Antony*
Antony and Cleopatra play (1623) William Shakespeare

Octavio disbanded soldier, supposedly the husband to Jacintha*
The Spanish Curate play (1647) John Fletcher and Philip Massinger

Octavius Caesar triumvir after death of Julius Caesar*
Julius Caesar; Antony and Cleopatra plays (1623) William Shakespeare

Oddy, Mr based on Henry James*, to whom the author had offered himself, but had been refused
All Souls' Night (1933) Hugh Walpole

O'Dell, Maureen painter
Eustace Chisholm and the Works (1968) James Purdy

O'Donovan, Fardorougha farmer, miser devoted to his son
Honor his wife
Connor their son
Fardorougha the Miser (1839) William Carleton

Odontsova, Anna widow, loved by Bazarov*
Katya her sister
Otsy i deti (Fathers and Sons) (1862) Ivan Turgenev

O'Dowd, Betty, Miss
Harry Lorrequer (1839) Charles Lever

O'Dowd, Michael, General Sir
Margaretta ('Peggy') his wife
Aurelia their daughter
his aged mother
Glorvina his sister, m. Captain Posky*
Vanity Fair (1847–8) W. M. Thackeray

O'Dowd, Mrs hearty Irishwoman
her drunken husband

The Tree of Man (1955) Patrick White

O'Dowda, Count
Fanny's First Play play (1905) George Bernard Shaw

O'Ferrall, Trilby cc, artist's model
Patrick her father
Trilby (1894) George du Maurier

Office, Irene, Miss 'wiser and more charitable than a virgin', yet 'had no commerce with men more intimate than a dance': Alan Frith-Walter's* perfect secretary
Accident (1928) Arnold Bennett

Offit evil labour organizer of the 'Brotherhood of Bread-Winners'; robs Farnham* and is killed by Sam Sleeny*
The Bread-Winners (1884) John Hay

O'Flaherty, Father chaplain to the Bavarian envoy
Catherine (1840) W. M. Thackeray

O'Flaherty, Major
The West Indian play (1771) Richard Cumberland

O'Flaherty, Tom army friend to Lorrequer*
Harry Lorrequer (1839) Charles Lever

Og, Angus
The Crock of Gold (1912) James Stephens

Ogden, George cc of novel set in huge Chicago block
Jessie née Bradley, his wife
The Cliff-Dwellers (1893) Henry Blake Fuller

Ogilvie, Ake peasant, poet, m. Chris Guthrie*
A Scots Quair trilogy: *Sunset Song* (1932); *Cloud Howe* (1934); *Grey Granite* (1935) Lewis Grassic Gibbon (rn James Leslie Mitchell)

Ogilvie, Allardyce, Mrs
Catriona (1893) Robert Louis Stevenson

Ogilvie, Katherine cousin to Eleanor Ogilvie* and to Isabella Worsley*; m. (1) Hugh Ogilvie, her cousin, (2) Paul Lynedon*; dies young
The Ogilvies (1849) Diana Craik

Ogilvy, Lawyer
his wife
Janet their daughter, m. Lownie
A Window in Thrums (1889) J. M. Barrie

Oglander, Grace
her father, squire of Berkley
Cripps the Carrier: A Woodland Tale

(1876) R. D. Blackmore

Ogle, Dan bad hat
The Hole in the Wall (1902) Arthur Morrison

Ogleby, Lord amorous old good-natured lord: there was a row between the co-authors when the latter refused to take this part
The Clandestine Marriage play (1766) George Colman the Elder and David Garrick

Oglethorpe, Sam friend to Jess Oakroyd*
Ted his nephew
The Good Companions (1929) J. B. Priestley

Ogmore Mrs Ogmore-Pritchard's first husband
Under Milk Wood play (1954) Dylan Thomas

O'Grady, Captain (later **Colonel**) **Philip** m. Lady Julia Egerton*
Jack Hinton (1843) Charles Lever

O'Grady, Gustavus Granby
Gustavus Horatio ('**Ratty**'); **Augusta** his son and daughter
Handy Andy (1842) Samuel Lover

O'Grady, Miss governess to the daughter of the Princess d'Ivry*
The Newcomes (1853–5) W. M. Thackeray

O'Hagan inventor
Captain Kettle series (1898–1932) C. J. Cutcliffe Hyne

O'Halloran, Count
The Absentee (1812) Maria Edgeworth

O'Halloran, May servant to Jocelyn Chadwick*
Famine (1937) Liam O'Flaherty

O'Hanlon, Patsy
Sally his wife
their three children
Famine (1937) Liam O'Flaherty

O'Hara of the Marines: Sadie Thompson's* friend; confined to barracks for drinking at the behest of Revd Davidson*
ss 'Miss Thompson'
The Trembling of the Leaf (1921) W. Somerset Maugham
Rain play (1922) John Colton and Clemence Randolph

O'Hara, Dennis, Colour-Sergeant
ss 'Black Jack'

Soldiers Three (1888) Rudyard Kipling

O'Hara, General drunken general
No More Parades (1925) Ford Madox Ford

O'Hara, Kate country girl who is seduced by Fred Neville*
her mother, who kills Neville and then goes mad
An Eye for an Eye (1879) Anthony Trollope

O'Hara, Kimball (Kim) cc
Kimball and **Annie** his parents, both dead
Kim (1901) Rudyard Kipling

O'Hara, Larry alleged portrait of American poet Lawrence Ferlinghetti
The Subterraneans (1958) Jack Kerouac

O'Hara, Scarlett cc, m (1) Charles Hamilton, (2) Frank Kennedy, (3) Rhett Butler*
Gerald; Ellen her parents
Careen; Suellen her sisters
Gone With the Wind (1936) Margaret Mitchell

O'Hara, Sean
The Revenge for Love (1937) Wyndham Lewis

Oig, Robert son to Robert Macgregor (Rob Roy)
Kidnapped (1886) Robert Louis Stevenson

Ojo one-time thief and pagan, turned mission leader
Aissa Saved (1932) Joyce Cary

Oke common-room butler
ss 'An Unsavoury Interlude'
Stalky & Co. (1899) Rudyard Kipling

O'Killigain foreman stonemason
Purple Dust play (1940) Sean O'Casey (rn John Casey)

Okolo (literally 'Voice') cc of poetic Nigerian (Ijaw) novel invariably discussed in context of the possibilities of an 'African English'
The Voice (1964) Gabriel Okara

Okonkwo self-made man, cc of novel set at the time when the Ikbo first made contact with white missionaries
Things Fall Apart (1958) Chinua Achebe

Olcott, Lucy wealthy benefactor to Mrs Wiggs*, m. Robert Redding*
Mrs Wiggs of the Cabbage Patch (1901) Alice H. Rice

Old Bricks and Mortar nickname given to

Vincent Crummles*
Nicholas Nickleby (1839) Charles Dickens

Old Man, The who brings up Chance*
Being There (1971) Jerzy Kosinski

Old Soldier, The nickname given to Mrs Markleham, Dr Strong's* mother-in-law
David Copperfield (1850) Charles Dickens

Oldacre, Jonas (alias **Cornelius**) rascally builder
ss 'The Norwood Builder'
The Return of Sherlock Holmes (1905) Arthur Conan Doyle

Oldboy, Colonel
Lady Mary his wife
Diana; Mr Jessamy their children
Lionel and Clarissa play (1768) Isaac Bickerstaffe

Oldbuck, Jonathan, Laird of Monkbarns the Antiquary
The Antiquary (1816) Walter Scott

Oldfox, Major 'an old impertinent Fop, given to scribbling'
The Plain Dealer play (1677) William Wycherley

Olding, John labourer, of Tadd's Hole
Adam Bede (1859) George Eliot (rn Mary Anne, later Marian, Evans)

Oldinport Squire of Knebley
Lady Felicia his wife
Squire Oldinport his cousin and successor
ss 'Mr Gilfil's Love Story'†
Scenes of Clerical Life (1857) George Eliot (rn Mary Anne, later Marian, Evans)

Oldtower, Ralph, Sir, Baronet honest Tory squire
his son
Grace his daughter
John Halifax, Gentleman (1856) Mrs Craik

O'Leary, Arthur cc, comic wandering Irish gentleman, friend to Harry Lorrequer*, in novel disowned by its author
Arthur O'Leary (1844) Charles Lever

Olenska, Ellen unconventional cousin to Newland Archer* in author's exposure of 1880s New York 'social code' and its trivialities
The Age of Innocence (1920) Edith Wharton

Olga Oblomov's* love who marries Stolz*
Oblomov (1859) Ivan Goncharov
Olifaunt, Nigel, Lord Glenvarloch cc, m.
Margaret Ramsay*
Randal his father
The Fortunes of Nigel (1822) Walter
Scott
Olinger
The Centaur (1963) John Updike
Oliphant, Jane m. Frederick Mulliner*
Meet Mr Mulliner (1927) P. G. Wode-
house
Olivares, Antonio wealthy Mexican
ranch-owner
Isabella his second (American) wife
Inez his daughter
Death Comes for the Archbishop (1927)
Willa Cather
Oliver a clown
Locrine play (1595) 'W. S.' (?George
Peele; ?Robert Green)
Oliver eldest son to Sir Rowland de Bois*,
m. Celia*
As You Like It play (1623) William
Shakespeare
Oliver MP for Middlemarch
Middlemarch (1871–2) George Eliot (rn
Mary Anne, later Marian, Evans)
Oliver, Bartholomew owner of Pointz Hall
Giles his son
Isa his daughter-in-law
Between the Acts (1941) Virginia Woolf
Oliver, Bill owner of a needle factory, kind
to Jane Eyre*
Rosamund his daughter, m. a rich man,
Granby
Jane Eyre (1847) Charlotte Brontë
Oliver, Doris friend to James Colet*
Gallions Reach (1927) H. M. Tomlinson
Oliver, Grammer
The Woodlanders (1887) Thomas Hardy
Oliver, Jack
Kate his wife
In This Our Life (1942) Ellen Glasgow
Oliver, Nelly supposed portrait of Frieda
Lawrence in novel by author who went
mad
Mendel (1916) Gilbert Cannan
Oliver, QC Lady Clara's counsel in the
Newcome divorce
The Newcomes† (1853–5) W. M.
Thackeray
Oliver, Mr dull government official

Mr Britling Sees It Through (1916) H. G.
Wells
Olivia Manly's* mistress
The Plain Dealer play (1677) William
Wycherley
Olivia rich countess
Twelfth Night play (1623) William
Shakespeare
Olivia, Princess wife to Prince Victor of
X*; executed
Barry Lyndon (1844) W. M. Thackeray
Olivier villain
Simplicissimus (1669) Hans Jakob von
Grimmelshausen
Olivier, Mary cc of novel of a woman
struggling to be free of family ties
her selfish and demanding mother
Mary Olivier (1919) May Sinclair
Olivier, President
ss 'The Sign of the Broken Sword'
The Innocence of Father Brown (1911)
G. K. Chesterton
Ollamoor, Wat ('Mop') musician and
dandy, father to Caroline Aspent's* child
ss 'The Fiddler of the Reels'
Life's Little Ironies (1894) Thomas
Hardy
Ollerton, Hope rolling stone; Roger
Liss's* fiancée
Let the People Sing (1939) J. B. Priestley
Ollier, Walter postman
The Horse's Mouth (1944) Joyce Cary
Ollyett journalist
ss 'The Village that Voted the Earth was
Flat'
A Diversity of Creatures (1917) Rudyard
Kipling
Olmantaboor, Brother head of a brother-
hood called The Assembly of the En-
lightened, who preached the colossal cri-
minality and sin of war
*All and Everything: Beelzebub's Tales to
His Grandson* (1950) G. I. Gurdjieff
Olympias waiting-woman to Aspatia*
The Maid's Tragedy play (1611) Francis
Beaumont and John Fletcher
O'Maera, Comfort American fan who
proposes marriage to Max Fisher*
Pending Heaven (1930) William
Gerhardie
O'Mahoney, Rachel career girl, Irish-
American opera singer
The Landleaguers (1883) Anthony

Trollope

O'Malley, Charles Irish Dragoons, cc, narrator, m. Lucy Dashwood*
  Godfrey his uncle
Charles O'Malley (1841) Charles Lever

O'Malley, Dr bibulous ship's doctor who, although married, marries Miss Charlotte Smith*; eaten by a shark
Orphan Island (1924) Rose Macaulay

O'Meagher, Josephine
  Timothy her brother, Jesuit instructor
Adam of Dublin (1920) Conal O'Connell O'Reardon (rn F. Norreys Connell)

Omer, Mr asthmatical draper, tailor and undertaker of Yarmouth who arranged funeral of Mrs Copperfield
  Minnie his daughter, m. Joram
David Copperfield (1850) Charles Dickens

Omnium, Duke of see **Palliser, Plantagenet**

Onanson, Mister who identified the disease called writing itch
All and Everything: Beelzebub's Tales to His Grandson (1950) G. I. Gurdjieff

O'Neil, Captain
  ss 'With the Main Guard'
Soldiers Three (1888) Rudyard Kipling

O'Neil, Scripps worker in pump factory
  Lucy his first wife
  Lucy ('Lousy') their daughter
  Diana his second wife
The Torrents of Spring (1933) Ernest Hemingway

Ongar, Lord vicious rich aristocrat; died of dissipation; m. Julia Brabazon*
The Claverings (1867) Anthony Trollope

Onion, Peter groom
The Case is Altered play (1609) Ben Jonson

Onnie Jay Holy see **Shoats, Hoover**

Onophrio suitor to Julia*
The Pleasant Commedye of Patient Grissill play (1603) Thomas Dekker

Onowenever, Mrs mother of an early love of the Uncommercial Traveller* (cf song by T. H. Bayley, set to music by H. Bishop, 'Oh no, we never mention her')
The Uncommercial Traveller (1860–8) Charles Dickens

Oofty-Oofty a Kanaka on the *Ghost*
The Sea Wolf (1904) Jack London

Oover, Abimelech Rhodes Scholar
Zuleika Dobson (1911) Max Beerbohm

Openshaw, John
  Joseph his father
  Elias his uncle
  ss 'The Five Orange Pips'
The Adventures of Sherlock Holmes (1892) Arthur Conan Doyle

Openwork a sempster
  Mistress Openwork his wife
The Roaring Girl play (1611) Thomas Middleton and Thomas Dekker

Ophelia daughter to Polonius*
Hamlet play (1623) William Shakespeare

Opiniam, Dr
Gryll Grange (1860) Thomas Love Peacock

O'Quilligan, Major
The Legend of Montrose (1819) Walter Scott

Orange insufferable coxcomb inseparable from Clove*
Every Man Out of His Humour play (1599) Ben Jonson

Orange, Miss friend to Miss Lemon
A Holiday Romance (1868) Charles Dickens

Orange, Robert de Hausée cc very popular novels on a Catholic theme, m. Brigit*; like his creator a Catholic convert; dies a monsignor
The School for Saints (1897); *Robert Orange* (1900) John Oliver Hobbes (rn Pearl Craigie)

Orano
Pizarro play (1799) Richard Brinsley Sheridan

Orcham, Evelyn director, Imperial Palace Hotel, m. Violet Prowler*
Imperial Palace (1930) Arnold Bennett

Orchardson, Squire rival to Robert Christianson*
  Richard his son, who carries on the feud to the next generation
God and the Man (1881) Robert Buchanan

Ordella wife to Thierry* and Queen of France
Thierry and Theodoret play (1621) John Fletcher, Philip Massinger ?and Francis Beaumont

Order man to Lady Alworth*
A New Way to Pay Old Debts play (1633) Philip Massinger

Ordith, Nicholas, Gunnery Lieutenant,

R N

The Gunroom (1819) Charles Morgan

O'Regan, Teague servant (modelled on Sancho Panza*; but also in his capacity as Irish clown transported from the English stage) to Captain Farrago*; ignorant and ambitious enemy to democracy
Modern Chivalry (1792–1805, rev. 1815, 1819)
(*A Brackenridge Reader*, edited Daniel Marder, 1970, Hugh Henry Brackenridge)

O'Reilly, Boyd Irish lawyer in charge of Olivares's estate
Death Comes for the Archbishop (1927) Willa Cather

O'Reilly, Mrs good-natured but damaging and foolish gossip of Muddleton
The Autobiography of a Slander (1887) Edna Lyall (rn A. E. Bayly)

Orellano, Gregory portrait of Bertrand Russell by one of his many lovers, who took to the novel
The Coming Back (1933) Constance Malleson

Orestes shifty Imperial Prefect whose legionaries can hardly contain pressure of intruding Goths
Hypatia, or New Foes with an Old Face (1853) Charles Kingsley

Orestes son of Agamemnon* and Clytemnestra*, and revenger for the murder of the former by the latter
The Orestia trilogy of tragedies (458BC) Aeschylus

Orestilla, Aurelia
Cataline play (1611) Ben Jonson

Orfling, The The Micawbers' maid, see **Clickett**

Orford, Ellen blind schoolmistress with sad past
'Ellen Orford'†
The Borough poem (1810) George Crabbe

Orgilus son to Crotolon*
The Broken Heart play (1633) John Ford

Orgreave, Osmond
his wife
Marian; Janet; Charlie; Johnnie; Jimmie; Alicia m. Harry Hesketh their children
The *Clayhanger* series (1910–16) Arnold Bennett

Orgueil, Mr and Mrs malevolent figures in novel in which the truth about characters is peeled off layer by layer
The Adventures of David Simple (1744–53) Sarah Fielding

Ori native chief
Vaili his daughter
Mr Fortune's Maggot (1927) Sylvia Townsend Warner

Oriana
The Inconstant play (1702) George Farquhar

Oriana fair betrothed of Mirabel*, a witty follower of the chase
The Wild-Goose Chase play (1652) John Fletcher

Oriel, Caleb, Revd Rector of Greshamsbury, m. Beatrice Gresham
Patience his sister
Doctor Thorne (1858) Anthony Trollope

Oriel, L., Revd aesthetic young curate
Pendennis† (1848) W. M. Thackeray

Orinthia
The Apple Cart play (1929) George Bernard Shaw

Orion son to Alveric* and Lirazel*
The King of Elfland's Daughter (1924) Lord Dunsany

O'Riordan, Mrs Irish widow, head housekeeper
Imperial Palace (1930) Arnold Bennett

Orlando first a man, then a woman: a joking portrait of the author's lover, Victoria Sackville-West
Marmaduke Bonthrop Shelmerdine her husband
Orlando (1928) Virginia Woolf

Orleans French prisoner at the English court
Old Fortunatus play (1600) Thomas Dekker

Orleans, Bastard of (hist.)
King Henry VI plays (1623) William Shakespeare

Orley, Miss
Robert's Wife play (1937) St John Ervine

Orlick, Dolge Joe Gargery's journeyman blacksmith, a bad character who tried to murder Pip
Great Expectations (1861) Charles Dickens

Orme, Gerald
Eleanor his wife
Jane; Margot; Dorothy; Betty; Terry

their children
Non-Combatants and Others (1916)
Rose Macaulay
Orme, Mrs charlady
The Loving Eye (1956) William Sansom
Orme, Peregrine, Sir in love with, and the
faithful friend to, and protector of Lady
Mason*
Orley Farm (1862) Anthony Trollope
Ormeau, Constantine friend to the late
Willy Trout*, and Eva Trout's* guardian
Eva Trout (1969) Elizabeth Bowen
Ormond a traveller returned from France
who feels himself free from all ethical
considerations, and who investigates his
theory of the inferiority of women when
he tries to rape Constantia Dudley*, who
kills him – in American Gothic novel
Ormond, or The Secret Witness (1799)
Charles Brockden Brown
Ormsby, Mr
Tancred (1847) Benjamin Disraeli
Oroonoko young Royal African chieftain
brought to West Indies (Surinam) by
slave-traders, who leads unsuccessful re-
bellion and is slowly tortured to death
after cutting off wife:
Imoinda's head, to save her from rape; in
early 'noble savage' novel by feminist
spy
*Oroonoko, or The History of the Royal
Slave* (1688) Mrs Aphra Behn
O'Rory, Shad political rival to Paul
Madvig*
The Glass Key (1931) Dashiell Hammett
O'Rourke, Father
ss 'The sisters'
Dubliners (1914) James Joyce
Orozembo
Pizarro play (1799) Richard Brinsley
Sheridan
Orrin schoolboy
ss 'An Unsavoury Interlude'†
Stalky & Co. (1899) Rudyard Kipling
Orsino Duke of Illyria, m. Viola*
Twelfth Night play (1623) William
Shakespeare
Orsino murderer by proxy
The Mysteries of Udolpho (1794) Mrs
Ann Radcliffe
Orson wild man of the forest, brought up
by a bear, as narrated in the old romance
Sketches by Boz† (1836) Charles Dickens

Ortheris, Stanley one of the soldiers three
ss 'Garm – a Hostage'†
Soldiers Three (1888) Rudyard Kipling
Orthodoxhydooraki Tibetan sect of Self-
tamers
*All and Everything: Beelzebub's Tales to
His Grandson* (1950) G. I. Gurdjieff
Ortiz, Jesus Nazerman's* assistant,
robber, who finally dies from a shot
intended for Nazerman, and so 'saves'
him
The Pawnbroker (1961) Edward Lewis
Wallant
Orton, 'Aussie'
ss 'A Friend of the Family'
Debits and Credits (1926) Rudyard Kipl-
ing
Ortygius Persian lord
Tamburlaine plays (1590) Christopher
Marlowe
Orville, Lord m. Evelina Anville*
Evelina (1778) Fanny Burney
O'Ryan, Doreen cc, singer, m. Max Here-
ford'
her father, imprisoned for Irish National-
ist activities
her mother
Doreen: The Story of a Singer (1894)
Edna Lyall (rn A. E. Bayly)
Osbaldistone, Frank cc, narrator, m.
Diana Vernon*
his father
Sir Hildebrand his uncle
Sir Hildebrand's wife
**Archie; Percy; Thorncliffe; John; Dick;
Wilfred; Rashleigh** Sir Hildebrand's sons
Sir Henry Hildebrand's father
William his brother
Rob Roy (1818) Walter Scott
Osborn, Captain commander of schooner
which rescues the Seagraves*
Masterman Ready (1842) Captain
Marryat
Osborne rich and ignorant merchant
Captain George his son, m. Amelia
Sedley*
Gregory son to Captain George and
Amelia
Jane; Maria m. Francis Bullock*
Osborne's daughters
Vanity Fair (1847–8) W. M. Thackeray
Osborne, Colonel Frederic, MP old friend
to the Rowley* family

He Knew He Was Right (1869) Anthony Trollope

Osborne, Lieutenant ex-schoolmaster
Journey's End play (1928) R. C. Sherriff

Osborne, Margaret *née* Piercey, widow, m. (2) Gerald Piercey*
Osy her son by her first husband
The Cuckoo in the Nest (1894) Mrs Margaret Oliphant

Osgood or Raveloe, brother-in-law to Lammeter*
his wife
Gilbert their son
Silas Marner (1861) George Eliot (rn Mary Anne, later Marian, Evans)

O'Shaughlin see Rackrent

O'Shaughnessy, Brigid client to Sam Spade*; murderess
The Maltese Falcon (1930) Dashiell Hammett

O'Shea hotel porter
Mrs Eckdorf in O'Neill's Hotel (1969) William Trevor

Osman
Captain Brassbound's Conversion (1900) George Bernard Shaw

Osmund consulting surgeon
Hard Cash (1863) Charles Reade

Osmund soldier
Vexhalia his wife
Count Robert of Paris (1832) Walter Scott

Osmund, Gilbert m. Isabel Archer*
Pansy his daughter by a previous marriage
The Portrait of a Lady (1881) Henry James

Osprey, Lady neighbour to Ponderevo*
Tono Bungay (1909) H. G. Wells

Ossipon, Alexander (**Tom**) ex-medical student, anarchist
The Secret Agent (1907) Joseph Conrad (rn Josef Teodor Konrad Korzeniowski)

Ostapenko, Tatiana Pavlovna ('**Tanya**') m. Seryozha Malinin*
Pavel; Varvara her parents
Tobit Transplanted (1931) Stella Benson

Ostrog 'The Boss'
When the Sleeper Wakes (1899) H. G. Wells

Oth hunter
The King of Elfland's Daughter (1924) Lord Dunsany

Othello Moor
Desdemona his wife
Othello play (1623) William Shakespeare

Otho, John ('**John of Burgos**')
ss 'The Eye of Allah'
Debits and Credits (1926) Rudyard Kipling

Otley, Roger, Sir Lord Mayor of London
Rose his daughter
The Shoemaker's Holiday play (1600) Thomas Dekker

O'Toole, Byron godfather to Adam Macfadden*
Adam of Dublin† (1920) Conal O'Connell O'Reardon (rn F. Norreys Connell)

O'Trigger, Lucius, Sir
The Rivals play (1775) Richard Brinsley Sheridan

Ottenburg, Frederick wealthy patron of the arts
The Song of the Lark (1915) Willa Cather

Otter, Darnley Wolf Solent's* friend
Jason his brother, a poet
Wolf Solent (1929) John Cowper Powys

Otter, Lucy art student
Of Human Bondage (1915) W. Somerset Maugham

Otter, Mr an otter
Portly his son, also an otter
The Wind in the Willows (1908) Kenneth Grahame

Ottilia, Princess in love with Harry Richmond
The Adventures of Harry Richmond (1871) George Meredith

Ottilie niece of Charlotte*
Walhlverwandschaften (*Elective Affinities*) (1809) Johann Wolfgang Goethe

Otto member of the Jonsen ship's crew
A High Wind in Jamaica (1929) Richard Hughes

Otto of Godesberg ('**Otto the Archer**')
A Legend of the Rhine (1845) W. M. Thackeray

Otto, Frederic Prince of Grunewald (alias Transome)
Amalia Seraphina his wife
Prince Otto (1885) Robert Louis Stevenson

Otway, Harry, Sir

A Room With a View (1908) E. M. Forster

Otway, Piers illegitimate cc, m. Irene Derwent*
Daniel; Alex his legitimate half-brothers their father
The Crown of Life (1899) George Gissing

Ouless, Lieutenant
ss 'His Private Honour'
Many Inventions (1893) Rudyard Kipling

Outhouse, Oliphant, Revd of St Diddulph-in-the-East, brother-in-law to Sir Marmaduke Rowley*
He Knew He Was Right (1869) Anthony Trollope

Outland, Tom Professor St Peter's* favourite student, killed in 1914–18 War; discovered an ancient Mexican cliff city
The Professor's House (1925) Willa Cather

Outram, Lance park-keeper, Martindale Castle
Peveril of the Peak (1822) Walter Scott

Overdo, Adam
Dame Overdo his wife
Bartholomew Fair play (1614) Ben Jonson

Overdone, Mistress a bawd
Measure for Measure play (1623) William Shakespeare

Overreach, Giles, Sir unscrupulous usurer; based on extortionist Sir Giles Mompesson
A New Way to Pay Old Debts play (1633) Philip Massinger

Overs, John miser
Our Mutual Friend (1865) Charles Dickens

Overstreet, Madeleine actress
Tell Me How Long The Train's Been Gone (1968) James Baldwin

Overton narrator
The Way of All Flesh (1903) Samuel Butler

Overton, Joseph Mayor of Great Winglebury, a man of the world (also appears, in *The Strange Gentleman* (play) 1836, as Owen Overton)
Sketches by Boz† (1836) Charles Dickens

Ovid
The Poetaster play (1602) Ben Jonson
Satiromastix, or *The Untrussing of the Humorous Poet* play (1602) Thomas Dekker ?and John Marston

Owen
Cherry his wife
Under Milk Wood play (1954) Dylan Thomas

Owen, Marthy
Anna Christie play (1922) Eugene O'Neill

Owen, Rhys American socialist
The Plumed Serpent (1926) D. H. Lawrence

Owen, William clergyman, m. Isabel Broderick, and changes his name to Indefer Jones*
Cousin Henry (1879) Anthony Trollope

Owlett, Jim cousin to Lizzie Newberry*; smuggler
ss 'The Distracted Preacher'
Wessex Tales (1888) Thomas Hardy

Owule old priest of Ketemfe
Aissa Saved (1932) Joyce Cary

Oxbelly, Lieutenant H M S *Rebiera*
his wife
Mr Midshipman Easy (1836) Captain Marryat

Oxenham, John seaman adventurer
Westward Ho! (1855) Charles Kingsley

Oxford, Earl of
Perkin Warbeck play (1634) John Ford

Oxford, Harry officer in the Hussars m. Constantia Durham*
The Egoist (1879) George Meredith

Ozores, Ana cc, crushed by malice and boredom
La Regenta (*The Regentess* but tr. under its own title) (1884–5) Leopoldo Alas

P

Paarenlberg, Widow m. Klaas Pool*
So Big (1924) Edna Ferber
Pablo
  Pilar his wife
  For Whom the Bell Tolls (1940) Ernest
  Hemingway
Pablo a gipsy
  The Children of the New Forest (1847)
  Captain Marryat
Pace, James Tayper settlement worker
  The Bell (1958) Iris Murdoch
Pack, 'Grubby' officer
  ss 'The Bisara of Pooree'
  Plain Tales from the Hills (1888) Rud-
  yard Kipling
Packard, Jane m. William Bates
  ss 'Rodney Fails to Qualify'
  The Heart of a Goof (1926) P. G. Wode-
  house
Packer Snagsby's* client
  Bleak House (1853) Charles Dickens
Packlemerton, Jasper murderer in Mrs
  Jarley's waxworks
  The Old Curiosity Shop (1841) Charles
  Dickens
Packles & Son theatrical agents
  Let the People Sing (1939) J. B. Priestley
Pacue page to Gasper*
  The Case is Altered play (1609) Ben
  Jonson
Padda Meon's* seal
  ss 'The Conversion of St Wilfred'
  Rewards and Fairies (1910) Rudyard
  Kipling
Paddock servant to Hannay*
  The Thirty-nine Steps (1919) John
  Buchan
Paddock, Selina bore child to 'her first
  intended', did not m. John Clark*
  ss 'Enter a Dragon'
  A Changed Man (1913) Thomas Hardy
Padella usurping King of Crim Tartary
  The Rose and the Ring (1855) W. M.
  Thackeray
Padge friend to the Pooters*

Diary of a Nobody (1892) George and
  Weedon Grossmith
Page, Clara young widow
  This Side of Paradise (1920) F. Scott
  Fitzgerald
Page, Edward, Dr
  Blodwen his sister, m. Aneurin Rees*
  The Citadel (1937) A. J. Cronin
Page, James L. foul-mouthed old farmer
  who locks his sister up
  October Light (1976) John Gardner
Page, Mary Conrad's* first sweetheart;
  later Mrs Barchester-Bailey
  Conrad in Search of his Youth (1919)
  Leonard Merrick
Paget, Gordon nursery gardener and
  Christian, partner to David Parker*
  The Middle Age of Mrs Eliot (1958)
  Angus Wilson
Paget, Jean cc, m. Joe Harman*
  Arthur; Jean her parents
  Donald her brother
  Agatha her aunt
  A Town Like Alice (1950) Neville Shute
  (rn Nevile Shute Norway)
Pahren, Emil employer, late husband of
  Christina Roche*
  Without My Cloak (1931) Kate O'Brien
Painted Jaguar ('Doffles')
  ss 'The Beginning of the Armadillos'
  Just So Stories (1902) Rudyard Kipling
Paisley, Duchess of
  Lord Arthur Savile's Crime (1891) Oscar
  Wilde
Pal, Dr 'sociologist' and author of the
  pornographic manuscript, based on the
  Kama Sutra, called *Domestic Harmony*,
  and published by Margayya*; usurer
  The Financial Expert (1952) R. K.
  Narayan
Palador Prince of Cyprus
  The Lover's Melancholy play (1629)
  John Ford
Palamon one of the two noble kinsmen,
  both being in love with Emelia*

The Two Noble Kinsmen play (1634) William Shakespeare and John Fletcher (?with Francis Beaumont)
Palate, Parson Prelate of the Parish
The Magnetic Lady, or *Humours Reconciled* play (1641) Ben Jonson
Palemon 'that sung so long until quite hoarse he grew': the writer Thomas Churchyard
Colin Clout's come home againe poem (1595) Edmund Spenser
Paley law student
Pendennis (1848) W. M. Thackeray
Palfrey, Farmer
his wife
Laetitia; Penelope their daughters
Brother Jacob (1864) George Eliot (rn Mary Anne, later Marian, Evans)
Palfrey, Jane actress (originally Price), cc, m. Marquess of Babraham, her cousin
Antigua Penny Puce (1936) Robert Graves
Palfreyman ornithologist, member of Voss's expedition
Voss (1957) Patrick White
Pallant, MP
ss 'The Village that Voted the Earth was Flat'
A Diversity of Creatures (1917) Rudyard Kipling
Pallet, Layman painter
Peregrine Pickle (1751) Tobias Smollett
Palliser, Plantagenet politician, later Duke of Omnium, sometime prime minister
Can You Forgive Her?† (1865) Anthony Trollope
Palmer a gamester
The Comical Revenge, or *Love in a Tub* play (1664) George Etherege
Palmer of Special Intelligence
But Soft – We Are Observed! (1928) Hilaire Belloc
Palmer, Charlotte, Mrs sister to Mrs Jennings*
Sense and Sensibility (1811) Jane Austen
Palmer, Mr stood smoking by his door as Boney's effigy burned
The Dynasts play (1897–1907) Thomas Hardy
Palmer, the alias of Wilfred, Knight of Ivanhoe
Ivanhoe (1820) Walter Scott
Palmer, Thomas, Mr owner of Cleveland
Charlotte his wife, *née* Jennings*
their son

Sense and Sensibility (1811) Jane Austen
Palmieri, Giuseppe gondolier, m. Tessa*
Marco his brother, gondolier, m. Gianetta*
The Gondoliers opera (1899) W. S. Gilbert and Arthur Sullivan
Palmley, Mrs poor widow
Harriet her niece
her son
ss 'The Winters and the Palmleys'
Life's Little Ironies (1894) Thomas Hardy
Palmyra daughter to Polydamus*
Marriage à la Mode play (1673) John Dryden
Palmyre former slave
The Grandissimes: A Story of Creole Life (1880) George Washington Cable
Palsworthy widow, social leader
Ann Veronica (1909) H. G. Wells
Pam, Colonel inveterate card-player
Sketches and Travels† (1850) W. M. Thackeray
Pambé Serang
ss 'The Limitations of Pambé Serang'
Life's Handicap (1891) Rudyard Kipling
Pambo, Abbot
Hypatia (1853) Charles Kingsley
Pamphilius
The Apple Cart (1929) George Bernard Shaw
Pan (hist.?) in poem whose most famous line, 'What was he doing, the great God Pan,/Down in the reeds by the river?' was thus answered by Robert Ross: 'No question for a lady to ask.'
poem 'A Musical Instrument'
Poems (1844) Elizabeth Barrett Browning
Panache, Mme aggressive history teacher at Mme Beck's*, who is dismissed
Villette (1853) Charlotte Brontë
Pancks Christopher Casby's rent collector
Little Dorrit (1857) Charles Dickens
Pandarus a pandar, uncle to Cressida*
Troilus and Cressida play (1623) William Shakespeare
Pandosto cc prose narrative from which Shakespeare* took *A Winter's Tale* – Leontes* is based on him
Pandosto, or *The Triumph of Time* (1588) Robert Greene
Pangloss, Dr tutor to Dick Dowlas*

The Heir at Law play (1797) George Colman the Younger

Pangloss, Maître over-optimistic tutor to Candide*
Candide, ou L'Optimisme (1759) Voltaire (rn François-Marie Arouet)

Pankower, Yidel, Reb tutor to David Schearl*
Call It Sleep (1934) Henry Roth

Panky, Miss shampooed every morning and in danger of being rubbed away altogether
Dombey and Son (1848) Charles Dickens

Panky, Professor
Erewhon Revisited (1901) Samuel Butler

Pansay, Theobald Jack
ss 'The Phantom Rickshaw'
Wee Willie Winkie (1888) Rudyard Kipling

Pantagruel son to Gargantua*
Gargantua, Pantagruel, Tiers Quart, Quart Part (1532–54) François Rabelais

Pantaleon, 'Don Panta' Indian friend to Guevez Abel*
Green Mansions (1904) W. H. Hudson

Panthea daughter to Arane*
A King and No King play (1619) Francis Beaumont and John Fletcher

Panther, Great Big Little redskin
Peter Pan (1904) J. M. Barrie

Panthino servant to Antonio*
Two Gentlemen of Verona play (1623) William Shakespeare

Panurge
Gargantua, Pantagruel, Tiers Quart, Quart Part (1532–54) François Rabelais

Panza, Sancho travelling companion to Don Quixote*
Don Quixote (1605–15) Miguel de Cervantes

Panzoust, de, Parvula, Lady eccentric old lady
Valmouth (1919) Ronald Firbank

Papadakis, Cora
Nick her miserly husband, murdered by her and Frank Chambers*
The Postman Always Rings Twice (1934) James M. Cain

Pape, Millicent de Bray, Mrs
Last Post (1928) Ford Madox Ford

Paperstamp, Mr caricature of Wordsworth
Melincourt, or Sir Oran Haut-on (1817) Thomas Love Peacock

Papillon special attaché to Pétain*
D'un Château l'autre (*Castle to Castle*) (1957) Louis-Ferdinand Céline (rn Louis-Ferdinand Destouches)

Paprotkin, Grischa innocent Russian victim of vicious militarism and ill luck
Der Streit um den Sergeanten Grischa (The Case of Sergeant Grischa) (1927) Arnold Zweig

Papworth, Miles, Sir 'a fast-handed Whig'
The Ordeal of Richard Feverel: A History of Father and Son (1859, rev. 1899) George Meredith

Paradine, Marmaduke ('Uncle Duke') crooked financier, brother-in-law to Paul Bultitude*
Vice Versa (1883, rev. 1894) F. Anstey (rn Thomas Anstey Guthrie)

Paragon, Mary Anne the Copperfields'* first servant; did not live up to her name
David Copperfield (1850) Charles Dickens

Paramor, Mr family lawyer
The Country House (1907) John Galsworthy

Paramore, Dr
The Philanderer play (1893) George Bernard Shaw

Parcival, Dr town philosopher
ss 'The Philosopher'
Winesburg, Ohio (1919) Sherwood Anderson

Pardiggle, Mr obtrusive and violent philanthropist
his wife
Francis one of their children
Bleak House (1853) Charles Dickens

Parflete adventurer and reprobate, m. Brigit Duboc* but vanishes before sexual consummation can occur
The School for Saints (1897); *Robert Orange* (1900) John Oliver Hobbes (rn Pearl Craigie)

Pargiter, Abel, Colonel
Eleanor; Delia; Milly; Rose; Edward; Morris; Martin his children
Celia Martin's wife
North; Peggy children to Martin and Celia
Sir Digby Abel's brother
Eugenie Digby's wife
Maggie; Sara daughters to Digby and

Eugenie
Renny husband to Maggie
The Years (1937) Virginia Woolf
Paris
Romeo and Juliet play (1623) William
Shakespeare
Paris portrait of the author's first husband,
Richard Aldington*
Helen in Egypt (1961) H. D. (rn Hilda
Doolittle)
Paris, Count Robert of
Brenhilda his wife
Count Robert of Paris (1832) Walter
Scott
Paris, Mr a vain coxcomb and rich city
heir, 'mightily affected with the french
language and fashions'
The Gentleman Dancing-Master play
(1673) William Wycherley
Paris son to Priam*
Troilus and Cressida play (1623) William
Shakespeare
Parish, Christopher tea-merchant's
employee, m. Polly Sparkes*
The Town Traveller (1898) George Gis-
sing
Parker Lady Windermere's* butler
Lady Windermere's Fan play (1892)
Oscar Wilde
Parker maid engaged to cope with the Sea
Lady
The Sea Lady (1902) H. G. Wells
Parker, David brother to Meg Eliot*, pa-
cifist and partner to Gordon Paget* in
nursery-garden business
The Middle Age of Mrs Eliot (1958)
Angus Wilson
Parker, Freddy Financial Commission,
Nicaragua; caricature of a consul at
Capri who, a homophobe, had caused the
paedophilic author much trouble on the
island
Lola his step-sister
South Wind (1917) Norman Douglas
Parker, Johnson, Mrs mother of seven
extremely fine girls, all unmarried
Sketches by Boz† (1836) Charles Dickens
Parker, Ma
ss 'The Life of Ma Parker'
The Garden Party (1922) Katherine
Mansfield (rn Katherine Mansfield Beau-
champ)
Parker, O. E. tattooed Christ

ss 'Parker's Back'
Everything That Rises Must Converge
(1965) Flannery O'Connor
Parker, Stan cc, Australian pioneer
Amy his wife
Ray; Thelma their children
The Tree of Man (1955) Patrick White
Parkes, Phil ranger in Epping Forest
Barnaby Rudge (1841) Charles Dickens
Parkin secretary, Handlers' Union
Put Yourself in his Place (1870) Charles
Reade
Parkins professor of ontography
ss 'Oh Whistle and I'll Come to You, my
Lad'
Ghost Stories of an Antiquary (1910)
M. R. James
Parkins, Rose chambermaid
Holy Deadlock (1934) A. P. Herbert
Parkinson, Montagu newspaper man
A Burnt-Out Case (1961) Graham
Greene
Parkis, Alfred private detective
Lance his young son
The End of the Affair (1951) Graham
Greene
Parkle barrister
The Uncommercial Traveller (1860–8)
Charles Dickens
Parkson Lancashire Quaker, fellow stu-
dent of Lewisham*
Love and Mr Lewisham (1900) H. G.
Wells
Parksop, Brother grandfather to George
Silverman*
George Silverman's Explanation (1868)
Charles Dickens
Parmont, Mr affectionate portrait of the
vegetarian publisher's reader and mentor
to most of the best authors of his time,
Edward Garnett
The Simple Life Limited (1911) Daniel
Chaucer (rn Ford Madox Ford)
Parnesius Roman soldier
ss 'A Centurion of the Thirtieth'†
Puck of Pook's Hill (1906) Rudyard
Kipling
Parolles follower of Bertram*
All's Well That Ends Well play (1623)
William Shakespeare
Parracombe, William sailor turned Indian
Westward Ho! (1855) Charles Kingsley
Parrenness, Duncan

ss 'The Dream of Duncan Parrenness'
Life's Handicap (1891) Rudyard Kipling

Parrot, Farmer
his wife
Bessie their daughter
ss 'Mr Gilfil's Love Story'
Scenes of Clerical Life (1857) George
Eliot (rn Mary Anne, later Marian,
Evans)

Parry, Mr
Helena his sister
Mrs Dalloway (1925) Virginia Woolf

Parsell ethnologist
Gallions Reach (1927) H. M. Tomlinson

Parsimonius the gathering Bee; in closet
play
The Parliament of Bees play (1641) John
Day

Parsloe, George
The Heart of a Goof (1926) P. G. Wodehouse

Parsons fellow apprentice of Polly* at Port
Burdock Bazaar
The History of Mr Polly (1910) H. G.
Wells

Parsons hired man who knows more about
Judge Porter* and his family than Judge
Porter does
The Deep Sleep (1953) Wright Morris

Parsons, Father Jesuit priest
Westward Ho! (1855) Charles Kingsley

Parsons, Fred one-time rival to William
Latch* for Esther Waters*
Esther Waters (1894) George Moore

Parsons, Gabriel sugar broker
Sketches by Boz (1836) Charles Dickens

Parsons, Miss matron of Kiplington High
School
South Riding (1936) Winifred Holtby

Parsons, Tom
his wife; neighbours to Winston Smith*
their seven-year-old daughter, who
betrays her father
1984 (1949) George Orwell

Partlet, Mrs
Constance her daughter, m. Dr Daly*
The Sorcerer opera (1877) W. S. Gilbert
and Arthur Sullivan

Partlit, Lady m. Jerry Jerningham*
The Good Companions (1929) J. B.
Priestley

Partridge, Benjamin schoolmaster
his wife

Tom Jones (1749) Henry Fielding

Partridge, Oswald Royalist
Children of the New Forest (1847) Captain Marryat

Parvis, Old Arson
A Message from the Sea (1860) Charles
Dickens

Pash watchmaker, member of the Philo-
sophers' Club
Daniel Deronda (1876) George Eliot (rn
Mary Anne, later Marian, Evans)

Pasmer, Alice puritan-minded high-bred cc
whose code 'makes no allowance for
human nature' m. Dan Mavering*
April Hopes (1887) William Dean
Howells

Pasquier, Gogo see **Ibbotson, Peter**

Passant, George a portrait of the author's
mentor, Herbert Howard, a homosexual
history teacher
Strangers and Brothers† (1940) C. P.
Snow

Passion, Arthur O.
Passion, Joseph J. his brother?
Mrs Dukes' Million (1977) Wyndham
Lewis

Passmore, Lucy 'white witch', victim of
Inquisition
Westward Ho! (1855) Charles Kingsley

Passnidge friend to Mr Murdstone*
David Copperfield (1850) Charles
Dickens

Pastereau, Athanasius French refugee silk-
weaver
his second wife
George his son
Henry Esmond (1852) W. M. Thackeray

Pasternak, Gene portrait of Jack Kerouac*
Go (1952) John Clellon Holmes

Pastmaster, Earl of see **Beste-Chetwynde**

Paston minister of Church in Lantern Yard
Silas Marner (1861) George Eliot (rn
Mary Anne, later Marian, Evans)

Patalamon see **Kerick Booterin**

Patch, Anthony Comstock young
American
Gloria his wife, *née* Gilbert: alcoholic ccs
of the author's second (part-autobiographical) novel (whose title is often
given incorrectly)
Adam his millionaire grandfather,
known as 'Cross Patch'
The Beautiful and Damned (1922) F.

Scott Fitzgerald

Pate-in-Peril see **Maxwell of Summertrees**

Pateroff, Count Pole; shadowy figure in the demi-monde
The Claverings (1866–7) Anthony Trollope

Pathzuol, Veronika singer, stabbed fiancée to Ernest Neumann*
her father, seducer of Neumann's mother, providing Neumann with the unconscious motive for his act
As It Was Written (1885) Henry Harland

Patience cc, dairymaid, m. Archibald Grosvenor*
Patience opera (1881) W. S. Gilbert and Arthur Sullivan

Patroclus Grecian commander
Troilus and Cressida play (1623) William Shakespeare

Patsie the commissioner's child
ss 'His Majesty the King'
Wee Willie Winkie (1888) Rudyard Kipling

Patten, Mrs rich elderly tenant of Cross Farm
ss 'The Sad Fortunes of the Rev. Amos Barton'
Scenes of Clerical Life (1857) George Eliot (rn Mary Anne, later Marian, Evans)

Patterne, Willoughby, Sir, the 'egoist'; m. Laetitia Dale*
Captain Patterne of the Marines, his cousin
Crossjay Captain Patterne's son, protégé of Vernon Whitford*
The Egoist (1879) George Meredith

Patucci, Tony sixty-year-old Napa valley winegrower seeking a mail-order bride represents himself with a photograph of his hired man, Joe*
Amy his wife
They Knew What They Wanted play (1924) Sidney Howard

Pau Amma crab
ss 'The Crab that Played with the Sea'
Just So Stories (1902) Rudyard Kipling

Paul (hist.) i.e. Saul of Tarsus, depicted as villain in both works
The Brook Kerith (1916) George Moore
King Jesus (1944) Robert Graves

Paul cc
Joan his mother

ss 'The Rocking Horse Winner'
The Lovely Lady (1932) D. H. Lawrence

Paul, Father
The Duenna play (1775) Richard Brinsley Sheridan

Paul, John bald, solemn serving-man
The Master of Ballantrae (1889) Robert Louis Stevenson

Paulina wife to Antigonus*
A Winter's Tale play (1623) William Shakespeare

Pauline cook
Vanity Fair (1847–8) W. M. Thackeray

Paulle, Queenie, Lady based on what the author then knew of Lady Diana Cooper, the socialite – they met later
The Pretty Lady (1918) Arnold Bennett

Paunceford, Squire *nouveau riche*
The Expedition of Humphrey Clinker (1771) Tobias Smollett

Pavia, Duke of
Bianca his wife, in love with Fernando*
Fiormonda his revengeful sister to plots revenge on Fernando*
Love's Sacrifice play (1633) John Ford

Pavia, Julius retired East India merchant
The Power House (1916) John Buchan

Pavia, Marquess of brother to Gwalter*
The Pleasant Commedye of Patient Grissill play (1603) Thomas Dekker

Pavillon, Hermann of Liège
Mabel his wife
Gertrude his daughter
Quentin Durward (1823) Walter Scott

Pavloussi, Hero mistress to Hurtle Duffield*
Cosmas her husband, Greek shipping magnate
The Vivisector (1970) Patrick White

Pawkie, James draper, later Provost
Sarah his wife
Jenny their daughter, m. Mr Caption
The Provost (1822) John Galt

Pawkins, Major swindler
Martin Chuzzlewit (1844) Charles Dickens

Pawle, Grammer gave Capt. Meggs's* Sunday shirt towards Boney's effigy
The Dynasts play (1897–1907) Thomas Hardy

Pawle, Olive m. James Hardcombe*
ss 'The History of the Hardcombes'
Life's Little Ironies (1894) Thomas

Hardy
Payne maid to Amelia Sedley*
Vanity Fair (1847–8) W. M. Thackeray
Payne rebel, cc, in Australian novel set in New Guinea in World War II
Young Man of Talent (1959) George Turner
Payne, Dr military surgeon
The Pickwick Papers (1837) Charles Dickens
Pazzini, La fruit seller in Milan
ss 'Mr Gilfil's Love Story'
Scenes of Clerical Life (1857) George Eliot (rn Mary Anne, later Marian, Evans)
Peabody, Dr
As I Lay Dying (1930) William Faulkner
Peabody, Olympia fiancée to Edward Brent-Foster*; perpetual grand mistress of the Boston Society for the Abolition of Vice
The Panel (1912) (in UK, 1913, as *Ring for Nancy*) Ford Madox Ford
Peace, Rachel Quaker actress, m. Lord Mandeville*
Incomparable Bellairs (1904) A. and E. Castle
Peace, Sula May cc
Plum her uncle, burnt to death by Eva, because of his emotional regression
Hannah her mother
Eva her grandmother
Sula (1974) Toni Morrison
Peach, Mrs young, dark and handsome widow, unfairly used
ss 'The Romantic Adventures of a Milkmaid'
A Changed Man (1913) Thomas Hardy
Peachey, Arthur partner in a firm of disinfectant manufacturers
Ada his wife, a hysterical and uneducated virago, *née* French*
their small boy
In the Year of Jubilee (1894) George Gissing
Peachum, Polly cc, m. Macheath*
her parents, of whom her father is a portrait of the well-known criminal, Jonathan Wild
The Beggar's Opera (1728); *Polly* operas (1729) John Gay
peacock, a (**unnamed**) 'Christ will come like that!' cc

ss 'The Displaced Person'
A Good Man is Hard to Find (1955) Flannery O'Connor
Peacock, Alec m. Violet Antrim*
The Well of Loneliness (1928) Radclyffe Hall
Peacocke, Dr and Mrs assistants at Bowick School, the 'irregularity' in whose marriage provokes a crisis
Dr Wortle's School (1881) Anthony Trollope
Peak manservant to Sir John Chester* who, on his master's death, decamped with his portable effects and set himself up as a gentleman – but got into jail and died of a fever
Barnaby Rudge (1841) Charles Dickens
Peak, Godwin cc, rationalist chemist who studies for the priesthood out of romantic ambition; in what is reckoned to be one of the author's greatest achievements
Nicholas his father
his mother
Oliver his younger brother
Charlotte his sister
Andrew his uncle, a cockney café-owner
Born in Exile (1892) George Gissing
Peake, Adrian m. Princess von and zu Dwornitzchek
Summer Moonshine (1938) P. G. Wodehouse
Peake, Enoch
The *Clayhanger* series (1910–16) Arnold Bennett
Peake, Selina m. de Jong
Simeon her father
Sarah; Abbie her aunts
So Big (1924) Edna Ferber
Pearce assistant at Shalford's
Kipps (1905) H. G. Wells
Pearce, Johnny godson to Lord Ickenham*
Cocktail Time (1958) P. G. Wodehouse
Pearce, Mrs
Pygmalion play (1914) George Bernard Shaw
Pearce, Mrs seaside landlady
Jacob's Room (1922) Virginia Woolf
Pearson, Mr mill owner, shot
Anne; Kate; Susan his daughters
Shirley (1849) Charlotte Brontë
Pearson, Roger cricketer, m. Patience Piercey*
The Cuckoo in the Nest (1894) Mrs

Margaret Oliphant

Peartree, Abel
These Twain (1916) Arnold Bennett

Peasemarsh, Albert butler, m. Phoebe Wisdom*
Cocktail Time (1958) P. G. Wodehouse

Pechorin the 'hero' of the title; young officer under the command of Maxim Maximych*; part narrator (in his journal)
Geroi Nas hego Vremeni (*A Hero of Our Time*) (1841) Mikhail Lermontov

Peckham, General
Catch-22 (1961) Joseph Heller

Peckover, Milward, Revd Rector of Kiplington
South Riding (1936) Winifred Holtby

Peckover, Mrs guardian of Mary Blythe*, whom she allows Blythe* to adopt
Jemmy her husband, circus clown
Hide and Seek (1854, rev. 1861) Wilkie Collins

Pecksniff, Seth cousin to old Martin Chuzzlewit*; architect and surveyor, hypocrite and villain – possibly intended as a caricature of the politician, Sir Robert Peel; but Samuel Cater Hall, a publisher and editor, has also been suggested
Charity a shrew; **Mercy** silly and also a hypocrite; m. Jonas Chuzzlewit* his daughters
Martin Chuzzlewit (1844) Charles Dickens

Pecunia infant of the mines
The Staple of News play (1631) Ben Jonson

Peddle and Pool solicitors of Monument Yard
Little Dorrit (1857) Charles Dickens

Pedlar, Nathan storekeeper; first employer and later husband of Dorinda Oakley*
Barren Ground (1925) Ellen Glasgow

Pedr
ss 'A Just man in Sodom'
My People (1915) Caradoc Evans (rn David Evans)

Pedringano servant to Bellimperia*
The Spanish Tragedy play (c.1592) Thomas Kyd

Pedro friend to Antonio*
The Changeling play (1653) Thomas Middleton and William Rowley

Pedro servant to Hieronimo*
The Spanish Tragedy play (c.1592) Thomas Kyd

Pedro, Don Prince of Aragon
Much Ado About Nothing play (1623) William Shakespeare

Peebles, Peter notorious litigant in case against Plainstanes*
Redgauntlet (1824) Walter Scott

Peel, Margaret university lecturer, Jim Dixon's* girl
Lucky Jim (1953) Kingsley Amis

Peel, Oliver
Dangerous Corner play (1932) J. B. Priestley

Peel-Swynnerton, Matthew friend to Cyril Povey*
The Old Wives' Tale (1908) Arnold Bennett

Peep-bo Ko-ko's* ward
The Mikado opera (1885) W. S. Gilbert and Arthur Sullivan

Peeper, Peggy
Polly opera (1729) John Gay

Peerybinkle, John carrier
Dot his younger wife
The Cricket on the Hearth (1846) Charles Dickens

Peeve editor of the *Liberal*
Men Like Gods (1923) H. G. Wells

Peffer Snagsby's* deceased partner, uncle to Mrs Snagsby
Bleak House (1853) Charles Dickens

Peggotty, Daniel old Yarmouth fisherman
Ham; Little Em'ly his nephew and niece (cousins); the latter, an orphan, eloped with Steerforth*, but was brought back
Clara ('**Peggotty**') his sister, David Copperfield's* nurse, m. Barkis*
David Copperfield (1850) Charles Dickens

Pegler, Mrs quiet respectable old shopkeeper, mother to Josiah Bounderby*, who keeps in background so as not to discredit his story of having risen from the gutter
Hard Times (1854) Charles Dickens

Peink chauffeur to Cecil Burleigh*
Men Like Gods (1923) H. G. Wells

Pelagia
Hypatia (1853) Charles Kingsley

Pelet, François headmaster of boys' school, secretly engaged to Zoraïde Reuter*,

whom he eventually m.
The Professor (1857) Charlotte Brontë
Pelham, Henry, Lord cc polished young man of hidden integrity in hugely popular novel – initially anonymous – which put an end to the fashion of wearing coloured coats – one of the most popular and capable of the 'fashionable'*, 'dandy'* or 'silver fork'* novels; also anticipated the detective-story; m. Ellen Glanville*
Pelham, or The Adventures of a Gentleman (1828, rev. 1839) Edward Bulwer Lytton
Pelham, John, Sir magistrate
ss 'Hal o' the Draft'
Puck of Pook's Hill (1906) Rudyard Kipling
Pelias foolish courtier
The Lover's Melancholy play (1629) John Ford
Pell, Solomon attorney employed by Tony Weller*
The Pickwick Papers (1837) Charles Dickens
Pellatt war correspondent
ss 'Two or Three Witnesses'
Fiery Particles (1923) C. E. Montague
Pellegrini, Rosa, Mrs
ss 'The Angel and the Sweep'
Adam and Eve and Pinch Me (1921) A. E. Coppard
Peltirogus, Horatio possible suitor for Kate Nickleby's* hand
Nicholas Nickleby (1839) Charles Dickens
Pelton, Squire
Daniel Deronda (1876) George Eliot (rn Mary Anne, later Marian, Evans)
Pelumpton, Mrs
Angel Pavement (1930) J. B. Priestley
Pelz, Benjamin portrait of the gifted poet, for a time a supporter of Hitler (but he later coined the term, 'inner emigration'), Gottfried Benn
Mephisto (1936) Klaus Mann
Pemberton, Honoria, Lady
Cecilia (1782) Fanny Burney
Pemberton, Richard
The Heart of the Matter (1948) Graham Greene
Pembroke, Agnes m. Rickie Elliot*
Herbert her brother, housemaster
The Longest Journey (1907) E. M. Forster
Pembroke, Earl of (hist.) William Marshall
King John play (1623) William Shakespeare
Pendant sycophant of Count Frederick*
A Woman is a Weathercock play (1612) Nathan Field
Pendennis, Arthur ('Pen') cc *Pendennis*, narrator of *The Newcomes* and *The Adventures of Philip*; m. Helen Laura Bell, adopted daughter of his mother
Arthur; Tom; Helen; Laura; Florence their children
Helen Pen's mother
Major Arthur Pen's uncle and guardian
The Doctor headmaster of Greyfriars
Pendennis† (1848) W. M. Thackeray
Pender, Ablard
The Last Revolution (1951) Lord Dunsany
Penderton, Leonora mistress of Major Morris Longdon*
Captain Weldon Penderton her husband
Reflections in a Golden Eye (1940) Carson McCullers
Pendleton, Jervis philanthropist, 'Daddy-Long-legs', m. Jerusha Abbott*
Daddy-Long-Legs (1912) Jean Webster
Pendragon, Admiral
ss 'The Perishing of the Pendragons'
The Wisdom of Father Brown (1914) G. K. Chesterton
Pendragon, Charles brother to Lady Vandeleur*
ss 'The Rajah's Diamond'
The New Arabian Nights (1882) Robert Louis Stevenson
Pendrel, Ralph cc who steps into portrait of an ancestor who lived in the earlier part of the 18th century; in unfinished novel
The Sense of the Past (1917) Henry James
Pendrell banker
Felix Holt (1866) George Eliot (rn Mary Anne, later Marian, Evans)
Pendyce, George in love with Helen Bellew* and with racing debts
Horace the squire of Worsted Keynes, his father
Margery his mother
The Country House (1907) John Galsworthy
Penelope Wilding's* ward, m. Hazard*

The Gamester play (1637) James Shirley

Penfeather, Mrs chief patroness of the Well
St Ronan's Well (1824) Walter Scott

Penfentenyou, A. M., the Hon. Minister of
Ways and Woodsides
ss 'The Puzzler'†
Actions and Reactions (1909) Rudyard
Kipling

Penfold, Lydia pretty and unworldly artist;
m. Claude Faversham*
Susan her sister
The Mating of Lydia (1913) Mrs
Humphry Ward

Penfold, Mrs friend to Agnes Twysden
her husband
The Adventures of Philip (1862) W. M.
Thackeray

Penfold, Robert cc, transported for a crime
he did not commit, poses as Revd Hazel;
m. Helen
Foul Play play (1868) Charles Reade and
Dion Bouicault

Pengelly blackmailer in tart atypical
thriller
Above the Dark Circus (1931) Hugh
Walpole

Penhale, William miner, friend to Basil*
Mary his wife
Susan their daughter
Basil (1852) Wilkie Collins

Penilesse, Pierce narrator (i.e. the author),
who makes his supplication
*Pierce Penilesse his Supplication to the
Devil* (1592) Thomas Nashe

Peniston, Mrs Lily Bart's* widowed aunt
The House of Mirth (1905) Edith
Wharton

Penius Roman commander
Bonduca play (1614) Francis Beaumont
and John Fletcher

Penkethman former Scotland Yard inspector, now with League of Nations
Vive Le Roy (1936) Ford Madox Ford

Penkethman, Nancy friend to Lord
Watlington
Imperial Palace (1930) Arnold Bennett

Penkin journalist; admirer of the poem
*The Love of a Bribe-Taker for a Fallen
Woman*, of which Oblomov* will have
none
Oblomov (1859) Ivan Goncharov

Penn-Raven half-evil evangelist with
power over others

Roman Bartholow poem (1923) Edwin
Arlington Robinson

Pennett, Mr George Sherston's* trustee
Memoirs of Fox-Hunting Man (1929)
Siegfried Sassoon

Penniloe, Parson portrait of the author's
father
Perlycross (1894) R. D. Blackmore

Penniman, Lavinia widowed sister to Dr
Sloper*, and his housekeeper
Washington Square (1880) Henry James

Pennington, Sarah friend to Steve Monk*
The World in the Evening (1954) Christopher Isherwood

Pennock, Sam boyhood friend to George
Webber*
You Can't Go Home Again (1942)
Thomas Wolfe

Penny, Christopher the Coward
The Passing of the Third Floor Back play
(1910) Jerome K. Jerome

Penny, Miss journalist
ss 'Nuns at Luncheon'
Mortal Coils (1922) Aldous Huxley

Penny, Robert shoemaker
Under the Greenwood Tree (1872)
Thomas Hardy

Pennyboy son, heir and suitor
Pennyboy the father, the Canter
Pennyboy the uncle, the usurer
The Staple of News play (1631) Ben
Jonson

Pennycuik, John
ss 'The Comprehension of Private
Copper'
Traffics and Discoveries (1904) Rudyard
Kipling

Pennyfeather, Paul expelled Oxford
undergraduate, teacher, and finally theology student; cc
Decline and Fall (1928) Evelyn Waugh

Penthea sister to Ithocles*, wife to
Bassanes*
The Broken Heart play (1633) John Ford

Penthièvre, de la, M. French royalist
advisor
Vive Le Roy (1936) Ford Madox Ford

Pentland, Bascom uncle to Eugene Gant*
Of Time and the River (1935) Thomas
Wolfe

Pentland, Thomas, Major
Eliza his daughter, second wife to Oliver
Gant*

Henry; William; Jim; Thaddeus; Elmer;
Greeley his sons
Look Homeward, Angel (1929) Thomas
Wolfe
Pentreath, Lord
his wife
Clementina their daughter
Daniel Deronda (1876) George Eliot (rn
Mary Anne, later Marian, Evans)
Pentstemon, Uncle 'an aged rather than
venerable figure'
The History of Mr Polly (1910) H. G.
Wells
Penury
The City Madam play (1658) Philip Mas-
singer
Penworth ambisexual schoolmaster drawn
to young Charles Fox*
The Young Desire It (1937) Kenneth
('Seaforth') Mackenzie
Peperill, Pasco uncle to Kitty Alone* who
commits arson to get insurance
Kitty Alone: A Story of Three Fires
(1895) Sabine Baring-Gould
Pepin hack writer
The Impressions of Theophrastus Such
(1879) George Eliot (rn Mary Anne, later
Marian, Evans)
Pepita
The Bridge of San Luis Rey (1927)
Thornton Wilder
Pepper ('The Avenger') Pip's page boy
Great Expectations (1861) Charles
Dickens
Pepper, Edward ('Long Ned') thief
Paul Clifford (1830) Edward Bulwer
Lytton
Peps, Parker, Dr doctor who attends Mrs
Dombey* at Paul's* birth
Dombey and Son (1848) Charles Dickens
Peralta, Don mad landowner
Demetria his daughter
The Purple Land (1885) W. H. Hudson
Perch, Mr messenger at Dombey and Son,
gossip
his wife
Dombey and Son (1848) Charles
Dickens
Percy née Leigh, Jocelyn heroine of early
American romantic blockbuster; m.
Ralph Percy
To Have and To Hold (1900) Mary
Johnston

Percy, Henry son of Northumberland
(hist.)
King Richard II play (1623) William
Shakespeare
Percy, Lady Hotspur's* wife
King Henry IV plays (1623) William
Shakespeare
Perdita daughter to Leontes*, m. Camillo*
A Winter's Tale play (1623) William
Shakespeare
Perfect, Dinah, Miss cc, old lady given to
table-rapping
All in the Dark (1866) J. Sheridan Le
Fanu
Perfecta, Doña Rey de Polentinos cc,
ironically named wealthy fanatic Roman
Catholic and Carlist, slowly becoming
insane
Rosario her daughter, eventually driven
mad by Doña Perfecta's murderous
schemes
Doña Perfecta (1876) Benito Pérez
Galdós
Perichole, Camila famous actress, mistress
to Don Andres de Ribera*
The Bridge of San Luis Rey (1927)
Thornton Wilder
Pericles Prince of Tyre
Pericles play (1609) William Shakespeare
Perigot
The Faithful Shepherdess play (c.1609)
John Fletcher
Periquello, El ('The Parrot') cc and narr-
ator of what is usually taken to be the first
Latin-American novel – strictly speaking,
this is untrue, but none before it have
shape – by an anti-clerical Mexican satir-
ist (1776–1827). 'The Parrot' is by turns
a monk, gambler, quack doctor, sexton,
civil servant, soldier, bandit and saint
El Periquillo Sarniento (tr. 1942 as *The
Itching Parrot*) (1816, incomplete;
1830–1) José Joaquin Fernández de
Lizardi
Periwinkle, Princess
The Grateful Fair play (1747) Christopher Smart
Perker, Mr solicitor employed by Pick-
wick*
The Pickwick Papers (1837) Charles
Dickens
Perkins stockbroker
his wife

Thomas their son
Mrs Perkins's Ball† (1847) W. M. Thackeray

Perkins, Jerry
Riceyman Steps (1923) Arnold Bennett

Perkins, John barrister
The Bedford Row Conspiracy (1840) W. M. Thackeray

Perkins, Tom, Revd headmaster
Of Human Bondage (1915) W. Somerset Maugham

Perkupp Pooter's* revered office principal
The Diary of a Nobody (1892) George and Weedon Grossmith

Perkyn one of Moggy Fyfe's* band
The Story of Ragged Robyn (1945) Oliver Onions

Perne, the Misses Deborah, Jenny and Haddie schoolmistresses
Pilgrimage (1915–38) Dorothy M. Richardson

Peroo a lascar
ss 'The Bridge Builders'
The Day's Work (1898) Rudyard Kipling

Perowne prefect
ss 'An Unsavoury Interlude'
Stalky & Co. (1899) Rudyard Kipling

Perowne, Wilfred, Major with whom Sylvia Tietjens* has an affair
No More Parades (1925) Ford Madox Ford

Perriam head of firm of oriental importers
Gallions Reach (1927) H. M. Tomlinson

Perrin, Vincent teacher, cc of what many have taken to be the author's best novel
Mr Perrin and Mr Traill (1911) Hugh Walpole

Perrott, Dickie child of the title
Josh his father, hanged for a murder of revenge
A Child of the Jago (1896) Arthur Morrison

Perry apothecary
Emma (1816) Jane Austen

Perseus, Mr narrator
ss 'The House Surgeon'
Actions and Reactions (1909) Rudyard Kipling

Pert, Mr youthful midshipman
White-Jacket (1850) Herman Melville

Pertinax centurion
ss 'On the Great Wall'†
Puck of Pook's Hill (1906) Rudyard Kipling

Pervaneh
Hassan play (1923) James Elroy Flecker

Pesca, Professor
The Woman in White (1860) Wilkie Collins

Peshkov, Mme
ss 'The Quiet Woman'
Adam and Eve and Pinch Me (1921) A. E. Coppard

Pestler apothecary
his wife
Vanity Fair (1847–8) W. M. Thackeray

Pestorijee Bomonjee a Parsee
ss 'How the Elephant got his Skin'
Just So Stories (1902) Rudyard Kipling

Pétain, Marshal (hist.)
D'un Château l'autre (*Castle to Castle*) (1957) Louis-Ferdinand Céline (rn Louis-Ferdinand Destouches)

Petchworth, Lady friend to Philip Pope*
Marriage (1912) H. G. Wells

Petella waiting woman to Rasalura* and Lillia Bianca*
The Wild-Goose Chase play (1652) John Fletcher

Peter 'the tall reader'
Hypatia (1853) Charles Kingsley

Peter friend to Porgy*
Porgy (1925) Du Bose Heyward

Peter Pan cc
Peter Pan play (1904) J. M. Barrie

Peter Rabbit cc
his mother
Flopsy; Mopsy; Cottontail his siblings
The Tale of Peter Rabbit† (1902) Beatrix Potter

Peter Robert Grimshaw's* dachshund, and representative of him
A Call (1910) Ford Madox Ford

Peter successor to Ben*
ss 'Little Foxes'
Actions and Reactions (1909) Rudyard Kipling

Peter, Lord imbecile peer
Sketches by Boz† (1836) Charles Dickens

Peter, Mr 'was not always understanding something'
ss 'A Long Gay Book'
G M P (1932) Gertrude Stein

Peters, D. see **De Courcy**

Peters, Ivy shady lawyer
A Lost Lady (1923) Willa Cather

Peters, William cc, known as the King's Own, as an orphan, parents unknown, entered on ship's books as William Seymour, midshipman, in love with Emily Rainscourt*
Edward his father, actually de Courcy, executed for mutiny
Ellen his mother
The King's Own (1830) Captain Marryat

Petersen, Harald whose penis was imprisoned 'in the coffin of his trousers'; m. Kay Strong*
The Group (1963) Mary McCarthy

Petersen, Sahib
ss 'Toomai of the Elephants'
The Jungle Book (1894) Rudyard Kipling

Pethel, James
Seven Men (1919) Max Beerbohm

Petherbridge, Jenny liar; 'a hurried decaying comedy jester, the face on the fool's-stick, and with a smell about her of mouse-nests'
Nightwood (1936) Djuna Barnes

Petherwin, Ethelberta *née* Chickerell*, widow, cc, m. Lord Mountclere*
Lady Petherwin her mother-in-law, widow of Sir Ralph Petherwin
The Hand of Ethelberta (1876) Thomas Hardy

Petit-Andrée assistant to Tristan l'Hermite*
Quentin Durward (1823) Walter Scott

Petitpois, Lionel, the Hon. and Revd
The Book of Snobs (1847) W. M. Thackeray

Petkoff, Paul, Major
Catherine his wife
Raina their daughter
Arms and the Man play (1894) George Bernard Shaw

Petowker, Henrietta inferior actress, member of the Crummles company, m. Lillyvick, water-rate collector, whom she left for a half-pay captain
Nicholas Nickleby (1839) Charles Dickens

Petrie, William old owner of stallion
ss 'The Dying Stallion'†
Selected Stories (1946) Fred Urquhart

Petruchio a counsellor of state
Love's Sacrifice play (1633) John Ford

Petruchio m. Katherina*
The Taming of the Shrew play (1623)

William Shakespeare
The Woman's Prize, or *The Tamer Tamed* (1647) John Fletcher

Pett, Mr intellectual cockney, ex-anarchist and ex-socialist, converted by Count Macdonald* to conservatism
The New Humpty-Dumpty (1912) Daniel Chaucer (rn Ford Madox Ford)

Pettican, Charles cousin to Mrs Sharland*
Admonition his wife
Mehalah (1880) Sabine Baring-Gould

Pettifer, Mrs friend to Janet Dempster*
ss 'Janet's Repentance'
Scenes of Clerical Life (1857) George Eliot (rn Mary Anne, later Marian, Evans)

Pettifer, Tom Captain Jorgan's* steward
A Message from the Sea (1860) Charles Dickens

Pettigrew journalist
My Lady Nicotine (1890) J. M. Barrie

Pettigrew, Mabel, Mrs nurse
Memento Mori (1959) Muriel Spark

Pettigrew, Mrs housekeeper
The Would-be-Goods (1901) E. Nesbit

Pettijohn, Randolph mean and vulgar gambler, wants Mary Love*
Nigger Heaven (1926) Carl Van Vechten

Pettitoes, Aunt aunt to Pigling Bland*
The Tale of Pigling Bland (1913) Beatrix Potter

Petulant follower of Mrs Millamant*
The Way of the World play (1700) William Congreve

Petulengro, Jasper gipsy friend to Lavengro*
Lavengro (1851) George Borrow

Peveril, Julian cc
Sir Geoffrey his father, head of family
Margaret his mother
Peveril of the Peak (1822) Walter Scott

Pew, David blind beggar
Treasure Island† (1883) Robert Louis Stevenson

Pew, Sherman young Negro with blue eyes; murdered for living in a white neighbourhood; amanuensis of Judge Fox Clane*
Clock Without Hands (1961) Carson McCullers

Peyronnette, Léonie, Madame mistress of Youma*
Youma (1890) Lafcadio Hearn

Peythroppe
ss 'Kidnapped'
Plain Tales from the Hills (1888) Rudyard Kipling
Peyton, Catherine Cumberland heiress with ill temper m. Griffith Gaunt*; accused of his murder
Griffith Gaunt, or *Jealousy* (1866); *Kate Peyton*, or *Jealousy* play (1867) Charles Reade
Peyton, Laura m. Charles Leicester*
Lewis Arundel (1852) Frank E. Smedley
Peyton, Mrs Clyde Griffiths'* landlady
An American Tragedy (1925) Theodore Dreiser
Pflugschmied American newspaper man of astonishing inaccuracy
The Marsden Case (1923) Ford Madox Ford
Phantaste representing the vice of frivolity
Cynthia's Revels, or *The Fountain of Self-Love* play (1601) Ben Jonson
Phao wolf, leader of the pack
ss 'Red Dog'
The Second Jungle Book (1895) Rudyard Kipling
Pharamond King of Spain
Philaster play (1620) Francis Beaumont and John Fletcher
Pharmacopolis Quacksalving Bee
The Parliament of Bees play (1641) John Day
Phebe shepherdess
As You Like It play (1623) William Shakespeare
Phelan, Rosie, Mrs widowed cousin to the Considines*, m. Tom Barry
Without My Cloak (1931) Kate O'Brien
Phelps, Mrs Tom Sayer's* Aunt Sally
Huckleberry Finn (1884) Mark Twain (rn Samuel Langhorne Clemens)
Phelps, Mrs wealthy widow; cc of melodrama of over-possessive mother-love
David; Robert her sons
Christina David's biologist wife
Hester Robert's girlfriend
The Silver Cord play (1926) Sydney Howard
Phenomenon, The Infant see **Crummles, Ninetta**
Phi-oo moon guardian, with Tsi-Puff*, of Cavor*
The First Men in the Moon (1901)

H. G. Wells
Phibbs haberdasher unintentionally connected with the Grimwood murder
ss 'Detective Anecdotes'
Reprinted Pieces (1858) Charles Dickens
Phil
ss 'Aunt Ellen'
Limits and Renewals (1932) Rudyard Kipling
Philammon young Christian monk in love with and swept from Christianity by Hypatia*
Hypatia, or *New Foes with an Old Face* (1853) Charles Kingsley
Philander counsellor to Porrex*
Gorboduc play (1562) Thomas Sackville and Thomas Norton
Philario friend to Posthumus*
Cymbeline play (1623) William Shakespeare
Philaster heir to the crown of Sicily
Philaster play (1620) Francis Beaumont and John Fletcher
Philautia representing the vice of self-love
Cynthia's Revels, or *The Fountain of Self-Love* play (1601) Ben Jonson
Philautus
Euphues (1578–80) John Lyly
Phylbrick butler, imposter
Decline and Fall (1928) Evelyn Waugh
Philema maid of honour
The Broken Heart play (1633) John Ford
Philibert one of the leaders of the 'honnêtes gens' opposed to the corrupt government of Quebec c.1748 (the title refers to *Le Chien d'Or*, a trading house); in historical novel that was the first popular Canadian novel, much imitated, by English-born Canadian
The Golden Dog (unauthorized 1887; 1896) William Kirby
Philip, Father sacristan
The Monastery (1820) Walter Scott
Philips, Madeleine actress
Bealby (1915) H. G. Wells
Philipson, Arthur
Seignor Philipson name adopted by his father, the exiled Earl of Oxford
Anne of Geierstein (1829) Walter Scott
Phillibrand, Maureen m. Tim Cornwell*
The Widow (1957) Francis King
Phillida

Galathea play (1592) John Lyly

Phillips, Dr Jewish society doctor, later surgeon, murderer; cc of (not incapable) anti-Semitic novel (by Jewish author, and mother to a best-selling one)
Clothilde his fat Jewish wife, murdered by him with opium
Doctor Phillips (1887) Frank Danby (rn Julia Frankeau)

Phillips, Mervyn school friend to Huw Morgan*
Ceinwen his sister
How Green Was My Valley (1939) Richard Llewellyn

Phillips, Mr breathes out port wine
his wife, sister to Mrs Bennet*
Pride and Prejudice (1813) Jane Austen

Phillips, Sam stonemason
Adam Bede (1859) George Eliot (rn Mary Anne, later Marian, Evans)

Phillips, Watkin, Sir, Baronet of Jesus College, Oxford, friend to Jeremy Melford*
The Expedition of Humphrey Clinker (1771) Tobias Smollett

Phillotson, Richard, schoolmaster, m. Sue Bridehead*
Jude the Obscure (1895) Thomas Hardy

Philo the Jew
Hypatia (1853) Charles Kingsley

Philologus
The Conflict of Conscience play (1582) Nathaniel Woodes

Philotis niece to Richardetto*
'Tis Pity She's a Whore play (1633) John Ford

Philpot geographer
Crotchet Castle (1831) Thomas Love Peacock

Phineas ('Finney') close friend to Gene Forrester*, who causes him injury and perhaps death; in minor classic of childhood
A Separate Peace (1960) John Knowles

Phippard, Joanna m. Captain Joliffe*
her mother
ss 'To Please his Wife'
Life's Little Ironies (1894) Thomas Hardy

Phipps 'callow youth' devoted to Hetty Milton*
The Wheels of Chance (1896) H. G. Wells

Phipps Lord Goring's* servant
An Ideal Husband play (1895) Oscar Wilde

Phipps of the *Daily Intelligence*
The Adventures of Philip (1862) W. M. Thackeray

Phipps, Denis
South Wind (1917) Norman Douglas

Phipps, Tristram ('Tristy')
The Revenge for Love (1937) Wyndham Lewis

Phoebe crippled daughter to Lamps*
Mugby Junction (1866) Charles Dickens

Phoebus artist
Lothair (1870) Benjamin Disraeli

Phoenix (Geronimo Trujillo) Mrs Witt's* half-breed groom
St Mawr (1925) D. H. Lawrence

Phoenixella daughter to Count Ferneze and sister to Lord Paulo* and Aurelia*
The Case is Altered play (1609) Ben Jonson

Phrynia mistress to Alcibiades*
Timon of Athens play (1623) William Shakespeare

Phunky, Mr Snubbin's* junior
The Pickwick Papers (1837) Charles Dickens

Phuong Indo-Chinese mistress to Thomas Fowler*, then to Alben Pyle*
Hei her sister
The Quiet American (1955) Graham Greene

Phydias eunuch promoted into the service of Valentinian*
Valentinian play (1647) John Fletcher

Phyllis Arcadian shepherdess, m. Strephon*
Iolanthe opera (1882) W. S. Gilbert and Arthur Sullivan

Pichot, Amédée, Captain
Tom Burke of Ours (1843) Charles Lever

Pickerbaugh, Almus, Dr Arrowsmith's* pompous and complacent supervisor when he is a public health officer at Nautilus; elected to Congress
Arrowsmith (1925) Sinclair Lewis

Pickering, Colonel
Pygmalion play (1914) George Bernard Shaw

Pickering, Joy schoolgirl, poverty-stricken ill-dressed pilferer with poetical aspirations; writer of poison pen letters

Gay her malicious younger sister, favoured by:

Mrs Pickering their cruel and ignorant mother, launderette lady

An Advent Calendar (1971) Shena Mackay

Picklan, Provost

The Provost (1822) John Galt

Pickle, Peregrine cc, adopted by Commodore Trunnion*

Gamaliel his father

Sally his mother, *née* Appleby

Gamaliel; Sally m. Charles Clover* — his brother and sister

Grizzle his aunt, m. Commodore Trunnion

Peregrine Pickle (1751) Tobias Smollett

Pickles fishmonger

A Holiday Romance (1868) Charles Dickens

Picklock man of law

The Staple of News play (1631) Ben Jonson

Pickthank witness, with Envy* and Superstition* against Christian* and Faithful*

The Pilgrim's Progress (1678–84) John Bunyan

Pickwick, Samuel cc

The Pickwick Papers (1837) Charles Dickens

Piddingquirk, William

ss 'The Jilting of Jane'

The Plattner Story (1897) H. G. Wells

Pidge, the Misses schoolteachers

The Professor (1837) W. M. Thackeray

Pidgeon attendant

Pendennis† (1848) W. M. Thackeray

Pidger former suitor to Lavinia Spenlow

David Copperfield (1850) Charles Dickens

Pie, Omicron, Sir physician

Barchester Towers (1857) Anthony Trollope

Piedmantle heraldet

The Staple of News play (1631) Ben Jonson

Pierce the drawer, knighted by Colonel Glorious Tipto*

The New Inn, or *The Light Heart* play (1629) Ben Jonson

Piercey, Gervase ('Softy') m. Patience Hewitt*

Sir Giles his father

his mother

Francis distant cousin, heir

Gerald son to Francis, m. Meg Osborne

Meg niece to Sir Giles, m. (1) Capt. Osborne, (2) Gerald Piercey

The Cuckoo in the Nest (1894) Mrs Margaret Oliphant

Piero a lord

The Revenger's Tragedy (1607/8) ?Thomas Middleton; ?Cyril Tourneur

Pierre butler to Stephen Gordon

Pauline his wife

Adèle their daughter, m. Jean

The Well of Loneliness (1927) Radclyffe Hall

Pierston (Pearston in original text), **Jocelyn** sculptor; m. Marcia Bencombe*; the 1892 version of the novel ends with his saying: 'O – no, no! I – I – it is too, too droll – this ending to my would-be romantic history! Ho-ho-ho!', but this was toned down into something even more ironic for the volume publication

The Well Beloved (1897) Thomas Hardy

Pierston, Isaac quarryman, killed in accident; secretly m. Anne Avice Caro*

The Well Beloved (1897) Thomas Hardy

Pietranara, Gina, Contessa widow, cc, in love with Fabrice de Dongo*

La Chartreuse de Parme (1839) Stendhal (rn Henri Bayle)

Piety of the Palace Beautiful

The Pilgrim's Progress (1678–84) John Bunyan

Piff, Miss passenger

Mugby Junction (1866) Charles Dickens

Piffingcap, Elmer barber, of Bagwood

ss 'Piffingcap'

Adam and Eve and Pinch Me (1921) A. E. Coppard

Pig-Baby, The

Alice in Wonderland (1865) Lewis Carroll (rn Charles Lutwidge Dodgson)

Pigeon, Frederick gullible young gambler

Vanity Fair (1847–8) W. M. Thackeray

Pigg, James huntsman

Handley Cross (1843) R. S. Surtees

Piggot, Jesse

The Oriel Window (1896) Mrs Molesworth

Piggy boy who tries, with his friend Ralph*, to set up an ordered society on desert island

Lord of the Flies (1954) William Golding

Piglet, Henry Pootel small pig
Winnie the Pooh† (1926) A. A. Milne

Pike, Dominicus itinerant tobacco-pedlar
ss 'Mr Higginbotham's Catastrophe'
Twice-Told Tales (1834) Nathaniel Hawthorne

Pilate Milkman Macon's* saintly aunt
Song of Solomon (1977) Toni Morrison

Pilate, Pontius (hist.) against the wall of whose house Jack Wilton* pissed
The Unfortunate Traveller, or The Life of Jack Wilton (1594) Thomas Nashe

Pilgrim, Billy naive optometrist who returns from Germany in the Second World War to New York and who is then kidnapped by aliens and taught that the present is eternal
his daughter
Slaughterhouse Five, or The Children's Crusade: A Duty-Dance with Death (1969) Kurt Vonnegut

Pilgrim, Dr Milby
ss 'Janet's Repentance'
Scenes of Clerical Life (1857) George Eliot (rn Mary Anne, later Marian, Evans)

Pilia Porsa bully
The Jew of Malta play (1633) Christopher Marlowe

Pilkington, Lord see **Potter, Percy**

Pilkington, Mrs housekeeper, Gauntly Hall
Vanity Fair (1847–8) W. M. Thackeray

Pilkins, Dr the Dombeys'* doctor
Dombey and Son (1848) Charles Dickens

Pillans, Alexander
The Thinking Reed (1936) Rebecca West (rn Cecily Fairfield)

Pillin, Joseph
Robert his son, in love with Phyllis Larne*
A Stoic (1918) John Galsworthy

Pilson, Georgie
Hermione; Ursula his sisters
Queen Lucia (1920) E. F. Benson

Pimpernell malicious portrait of Christopher Isherwood*, whom the author thought a coward and rotter for going to the U S A in 1939
Put Out More Flags (1942) Evelyn Waugh

Pinac fellow traveller with Mirabel*, of a lively spirit
The Wild-Goose Chase play (1652) John Fletcher

Pinch, Tom devoted assistant to Mr Pecksniff*
Ruth his pretty sister, engaged to John Westlock*
Martin Chuzzlewit (1844) Charles Dickens

Pinchwife, Jack jealous husband
Mrs Pinchwife his dissatisfied wife
Alithea his sister
The Country Wife (1673) William Wycherley

Pincini, Andreas, Signor tattooist
his wife
ss 'The Background'
The Chronicles of Clovis (1911) Saki (rn Hector Hugh Munro)

Pinckney, Leila J. writer of sentimental novels, aunt to James Rodman*
Meet Mr Mulliner (1927) P. G. Wodehouse

Pincot maid to Rachel, Lady Castlewood*
Henry Esmond (1852) W. M. Thackeray

Pine surgeon on convict ship
His Natural Life (1870–2); abridged by the author 1874; in 1885 as *For the Term of His Natural life* – thus evading the author's irony; original text edited by Stephen Murray-Smith, 1970) Marcus Clarke

Pine-Avon, Nichola, Mrs handsome pretentious widow m. Alfred Somers*
The Well Beloved (1897) Thomas Hardy

Pinecoffin
ss 'Pig'
Plain Tales from the Hills (1888) Rudyard Kipling

Pineda, Martha Brown's* mistress
Luis her husband
Angel their son
The Comedians (1966) Graham Greene

Pinesett, July m. Sister Mary*
June his twin, whose mistress Sister Mary* becomes
Scarlet Sister Mary (1928) Julia Peterkin

Pinfold, Gilbert cc, middle-aged writer and squire who hears voices – based on the author's own experience
his wife
The Ordeal of Gilbert Pinfold (1957) Evelyn Waugh

Ping Siang cruel and extortionate mandarin
The Wallet of Kai Lung (1900) Ernest Bramah (rn Ernest Bramah Smith)

Pingitzen
Tracy's Tiger (1951) William Saroyan

Pinhorn, Hester cook to Fosco*
The Woman in White (1860) Wilkie Collins

Pinhorn, Mary children's maid, m. Dick Bedford, the butler
Lovel the Widower (1860) W. M. Thackeray

Pink saddler, Treby
Felix Holt (1866) George Eliot (rn Mary Anne, later Marian, Evans)

Pinkbell butler who never appears but makes his presence felt
The Chalk Garden play (1955) Enid Bagnold

Pinkerton, Barbara, Miss head of Pinkerton's Seminary for Young Ladies
Jemima her sister
Vanity Fair | (1847–8) W. M. Thackeray

Pinkie young gang leader, m. Rose Wilson*
Brighton Rock (1938) Graham Greene

Pinnegar, Miss manageress of James Houghton's* drapery
The Lost Girl (1920) D. H. Lawrence

Pinner, Josephine and **Constantia**
ss 'The Daughters of the Late Colonel'
The Garden Party (1922) Katherine Mansfield (rn Katherine Mansfield Beauchamp)

Pio, Uncle factotum to Camila Perichole*
The Bridge of San Luis Rey (1927) Thornton Wilder

Pioche cuirassier of the guard
Tom Burke of Ours (1844) Charles Lever

Pip Negro cabin-boy who goes mad
Moby-Dick, or The Whale (1851) Herman Melville

Pip see **Pirrip**

Pipchin, Miss ill-favoured proprietress of school at Brighton
Dombey and Son (1848) Charles Dickens

Piper, Gerald, Colonel the Hon.
Charles his late brother; brothers to the late Lord Monchensey
The Family Reunion play (1939) T. S. Eliot

Pipes servant to Hawser Trunnion*
Peregrine Pickle (1751) Tobias Smollett

Pipkin, Nathaniel parish clerk in love with Maria Lobbs*
The Pickwick Papers (1837) Charles Dickens

Pippa young silk-worker cc
Pippa Passes (1841) Robert Browning

Pir Khan Holden's* servant
ss 'Without Benefit of Clergy'
Life's Handicap (1891) Rudyard Kipling

Pirate King, The
The Pirates of Penzance opera (1880) W. S. Gilbert and Arthur Sullivan

Pirelli, Cardinal cc posthumous paedophiliac novel
Concerning the Eccentricities of Cardinal Pirelli (1926) Ronald Firbank

Pirolo, Victor of the Aerial Board of Control
ss 'As Easy as A B C'
A Diversity of Creatures (1917) Rudyard Kipling

Pirrip, Philip ('**Pip**') cc, narrator, m. Estella Drummle*
Mrs Joe Gargery his sister
Great Expectations (1861) Charles Dickens

Pisanio servant to Posthumus*
Cymbeline play (1623) William Shakespeare

Pish-Tush a noble lord
The Mikado opera (1885) W. S. Gilbert and Arthur Sullivan

Pish-Tush, Mr
ss 'Pish-Tush'
Unlucky for Pringle (1973) Wyndham Lewis

Pistol Falstaff's* drinking crony, later a soldier
The Merry Wives of Windsor; King Henry IV; King Henry V plays (1623) William Shakespeare

Pitcher one of Squeers's victims
Nicholas Nickleby (1839) Charles Dickens

Pitcher, John dairyman, father to Mrs Fennell*
ss 'The Three Strangers'
Wessex Tales (1888) Thomas Hardy

Pitfall Lady Tailbush's* woman
The Devil is an Ass play (1616) Ben Jonson

Pitkin, Lemuel Captain-Carpenter*-like cc of satirical novel; poor but honest Vermont boy; becomes the 'Horst Wessel of American fascism'
A Cool Million (1934) Nathanael West (rn Nathan Weinstein)

Pitman, William Dent artist, ne'er-do-well
The Wrong Box (1889) Robert Louis Stevenson and Lloyd Osbourne

Pitsner, Mr of a music publishing firm
The Good Companions (1929) J. B. Priestley

Pitt, Jane wardrobe woman, m. Old Cheeseman
ss 'The Schoolboy's Story
Reprinted Pieces (1858) Charles Dickens

Pitt, Jimmy cc, m. Molly McEarchern*
A Gentleman of Leisure (1910) P. G. Wodehouse

Pitt-Heron, Charles
his wife
The Power House (1916) John Buchan

Pitti-Sing ward of Ko-ho*
The Mikado opera (1885) W. S. Gilbert and Arthur Sullivan

Pittle, Revd Mr
The Provost (1822) John Galt

Pittman Milby lawyer, partner to Robert Dempster*
his four daughters
ss 'Janet's Repentance'
Scenes of Clerical Life (1857) George Eliot (rn Mary Anne, later Marian, Evans)

Pittman, Jane, Miss 110-year-old black woman of whose memories, from slavery to civil rights, this novel consists
The Autobiography of Miss Jane Pittman (1971) Ernest J. Gaines

Pivart farmer at Ripple, enemy to Edward Tulliver*
The Mill on the Floss (1860) George Eliot (rn Mary Anne, later Marian, Evans)

Pizarro (hist.) Spanish conqueror of Peru, cc play adapted from Kotzebue's *Die Spanier in Peru*
Pizarro (1799) Richard Brinsley Sheridan

Placenta niece to Lady Loadstone*
The Magnetic Lady, or *Humours Reconciled* play (1641) Ben Jonson

Plaff, Lily
Pilgrimage (1915–38) Dorothy M. Richardson

Plagiary, Fretful, Sir
The Critic play (1779) Richard Brinsley Sheridan

Plaice publisher's reader
The Dream (1924) H. G. Wells

Plainstanes, Paul rival to Peter Peebles* in old lawsuit
Redgauntlet (1824) Walter Scott

Planquet, Maître master cook
Imperial Palace (1930) Arnold Bennett

Plant, C. shoemaker
The Horse's Mouth (1944) Joyce Cary

Plant, Herman Conrad Green's* dead secretary
ss 'A Day With Conrad Green'
The Collected Short Stories (1941) Ring Lardner

Plantagenet, Richard (hist.) later Duke of York
King Henry VI plays (1623) William Shakespeare

Plantagenet, Ruth the author's hazy notion of his first wife, Jan Gabrial
Lunar Caustic (1963) Malcolm Lowry

Plantagenet, Thomas see **Milton, Hetty, Mrs**

Platt apprentice with Polly* at Port Burdock
The History of Mr Polly (1910) H. G. Wells

Platt, Tom sailor on the *We're Here*
Captains Courageous (1897) Rudyard Kipling

Platte subaltern
ss 'Watches of the Night'
Plain Tales from the Hills (1888) Rudyard Kipling

Plattner, Gottfried language master at the Sussexville School
The Plattner Story† (1897) H. G. Wells

Plausible, Lord 'a ceremonious, supple, commending Coxcomb'
The Plain Dealer play (1677) William Wycherley

Plaza Toro, Duke of
his wife
Casilda their daughter, m. Luiz*
The Gondoliers opera (1889) W. S. Gilbert and Arthur Sullivan

Plef-Perf-Noof personage of Mars, 'like a Zirkliner on Karatas, or a physician on Earth'
All and Everything: Beelzebub's Tales to

His Grandson (1950) G. I. Gurdjieff

Plenty, Mr a country gentleman
The City Madam play (1658) Philip Massinger

Plessington, Hubert ex-Oxford don
'Aunt' Plessington his wife
Marriage (1912) H. G. Wells

Plessy, Lord
Middlemarch (1871–2) George Eliot (rn Mary Anne, later Marian, Evans)

Pleydell, Paulus Edinburgh Lawyer
Guy Mannering (1815) Walter Scott

Pliable neighbour, with Obstinate*, to Christian*, and for a time his companion
The Pilgrim's Progress (1678–84) John Bunyan

Plimsing house detective
Imperial Palace (1930) Arnold Bennett

Plinlimmon, Marquis of eldest son of Duke of St David's
Pendennis (1848) W. M. Thackeray

Plinth, Mrs member of the Lunch Club, a ladies' literary discussion group
ss 'Xingu'
Roman Fever (1911) Edith Wharton

Plomacy steward to Wilfred Thorne*
Barchester Towers (1857) Anthony Trollope

Plornish, Thomas plasterer, of Bleeding Heart Yard
Sally his wife
John Edward their son
Little Dorrit (1857) Charles Dickens

Plouffes, The family in book about French-Canadians by 'realistic spoofer', once 'bad boy of Canadian literature'
The Plouffe Family (1948) Roger Lemelin

Pluche, Jeames de la really James Plush, ex-footman who makes a fortune and loses it; m. Mary Ann Hoggins
James Angela; Angelina; Mary Anne their children
Jeames's Diary† (1846) W. M. Thackeray

Pluck, Mr toady to Sir Mulberry Hawk*
Nicholas Nickleby (1839) Charles Dickens

Pluffles subaltern
ss 'The Rescue of Pluffles'
Plain Tales from the Hills (1888) Rudyard Kipling

Plum, Colonel

Put Out More Flags (1942) Evelyn Waugh

Plum, George old man recollecting his past from a vantage-point of late 1940s in New Zealand novel
Plum (1978) Maurice Gee

Plumer, Mrs
George her husband, a university professor
Jacob's Room (1922) Virginia Woolf

Plummer, Caleb poor toymaker in service of Gruff and Tackleton*
Edward his son, m. May Fielding*
Bertha his blind daughter
The Cricket on the Hearth (1845) Charles Dickens

Plummer, Edwin in love with Lady Maud Marsh*
Millie his sister
A Damsel in Distress (1919) P. G. Wodehouse

Plunder one of Miss Flyte's* captive birds
Bleak House (1853) Charles Dickens

Plurabelle, Anna Livia see **Earwicker, Humphrey Chimpden**

Plush, James see **Pluche, Jeames de la**

Pluto black cat which, reincarnated, has its revenge on narrator-murderer for putting out one of its eyes, and further mistreatment
ss 'The Black Cat' (1843)
Tales (1845) Edgar Allan Poe

Plyant, Paul, Sir an uxorious foolish old knight, brother to Lady Touchwood* and father to Cynthia*
Lady Plyant his wife, insolent to her husband, and easy to any pretender
The Double-Dealer play (1710) William Congreve

Plyem, Peter, Sir parliamentary candidate for five boroughs
Heart of Midlothian (1818) Walter Scott

Plymdale wealthy manufacturer
Selina his wife
Edward their son, m. Sophy Toller*
Middlemarch (1871–2) George Eliot (rn Mary Anne, later Marian, Evans)

Plymdale, Laura, Lady
Lady Windermere's Fan play (1892) Oscar Wilde

Plyushkin miserly landowner
Myortvye dushi (Dead Souls) (1842) Nicolai Gogol

Pocahontas (rn Matoaka) (hist.); the nickname means 'playful'; helped Virginian white settlers, and m. John Rolfe*; represented in several works of fiction
The First Settlers of Virginia (1805) John Davis
The Indian Princess, or *La Belle Sauvage* play (1808) James Nelson Barker
My Lady Pocahantas (1885) J. E. Cooke
Pocahantas (1933) David Garnett
Pocher beadle
Bartholomew Fair play (1631) Ben Jonson
Pock, Francis a surgeon
All Fools play (1605) George Chapman
Pocket, Herbert Pip (Pirrip's)* friend and companion, m. Clara Barley*
Matthew his father, cousin to Miss Haversham*
Belinda his mother, hopeless and useless
Alick; Baby; Fanny; Joe his brothers and sisters
Sarah Pocket toady; relative to Miss Haversham* and to the Pocket family*
Great Expectations (1861) Charles Dickens
Pocklington, Thomas Gibbs, Sir
his wife
Our Street (1848) W. M. Thackeray
Pocock, Mrs sister to Chadwick Newsome*
Mamie her sister-in-law
The Ambassadors (1903) Henry James
Podd crooked publisher
The Marsden Case (1923) Ford Madox Ford
Podder stand-by for the All Muggleton Cricket Club; scored well off Mr Struggles's bowling
The Pickwick Papers (1837) Charles Dickens
Podger undertaker
The History of Mr Polly (1910) H. G. Wells
Podger, Uncle
Maria his wife
Three Men in a Boat (1889) Jerome K. Jerome
Podgers Lady Southdown's Brighton doctor
Vanity Fair (1847–8) W. M. Thackeray
Podgers, Dr
Hawbuck Grange (1847) R. S. Surtees

Podgers, Septimus R. chiromantist
Lord Arthur Savile's Crime (1891) Oscar Wilde
Podmarsh, Rollo m. Mary Kent*
his mother
ss 'The Awakening of Podmarsh'
The Heart of a Goof (1926) P. G. Wodehouse
Podsnap, John solid British businessman, 'who always knew what Providence meant, while it was very remarkable that what Providence meant was invariably what Mr Podsnap meant'
his wife
Georgiana his daughter
Our Mutual Friend (1865) Charles Dickens
Poe lawyer
Vanity Fair (1847–8) W. M. Thackeray
Poetaster the Poetical Bee
The Parliament of Bees play (1641) John Day
Poges, Cyril pompous English businessman
Souhaun his mistress
Purple Dust play (1940) Sean O'Casey (rn John Casey)
Pogram, Elijah symbol of all that is most ridiculous about America
Martin Chuzzlewit (1844) Charles Dickens
Pogson, Sam English traveller fleeced in Paris
his aunt
Paris Sketch Book (1840) W. M. Thackeray
Pohetohee
Polly opera (1729) John Gay
Poindexter, Louise beautiful Creole heiress, m. Maurice Gerald*
The Headless Horseman (1866) Captain Thomas Mayne Reid
Poins
King Henry IV plays (1623) William Shakespeare
Point, Jack strolling jester
The Yeoman of the Guard opera (1888) W. S. Gilbert and Arthur Sullivan
Pointdextre, Marmaduke, Sir m. Lady Sangazure*
Alexis his son, m. Aline Sangazure
The Sorcerer opera (1877) W. S. Gilbert and Arthur Sullivan

Poirot, Hercule Belgian detective with moustache loved by a vast public; onwards from
Poirot Investigates† (1925) Agatha Christie

Poitrat, Léonce accountant at clinic, with an erection 'as hard as thirty-six biceps'
Mort à crédit (Death on the Instalment Plan) (1936) Louis-Ferdinand Céline (rn Louis-Ferdinand Destouches)

Poke, Noah Connecticut sea captain who transports the monikins* in imitation of *Gulliver's Travels*
The Monikins (1835) James Fenimore Cooper

Pokingham, Lady cc of comic pornography, seduces her doctor on her deathbed
Lady Pokingham, or They All Do It (1880) Anon.

Polderdick, Captain
ss 'The King of the Trenches'
Blasting and Bombardiering (1967); *Unlucky for Pringle* (1973) Wyndham Lewis

Pole, Millicent protégée of Fleur Forsyte*
Swan Song† (1928) John Galsworthy

Pole, Miss
Cranford (1853) Mrs Gaskell

Polichinelle
Silvia his daughter and heiress
Los intereses creados (The Bonds of Interest) (1908) Jacinto Benavente

Polidacre reports herself to be dead and disguises herself as a man in order to test her husband's fidelity
The Obstinate Lady play (1657) Aston Cokayne

Polish gossip and she-parasite
The Magnetic Lady, or Humours Reconciled play (1641) Ben Jonson

Polixenes King of Bohemia
Florizel his son
A Winter's Tale play (1623) William Shakespeare

Polk-Faraday, Alex publisher-writer
Hittie his wife
A Suspension of Mercy (1965) Patricia Highsmith

Pollard, Catherine saved character* modelled on the 1930s New York Catholic philanthropist Dorothy Day
The Malefactors (1956) Caroline Gordon

Pollexfen, Hargrave, Sir, Baronet villain
Sir Charles Grandison (1754) Samuel Richardson

Pollitt, Sam egoistic idealist
Henny his wife
Louisa; Teresa their children
The Man Who Loved Children (1940) Christina Stead

Pollit see **Big Daddy**

Pollock assistant to Sierra Leone trader
ss 'Pollock and the Porrah Man'
The Plattner Story† (1897) H. G. Wells

Pollock, Guy Gopher Prairie lawyer
Main Street (1921) Sinclair Lewis

Pollock, Major
Separate Tables play (1955) Terence Rattigan

Polly waitress at the Slap Bang eating house
Bleak House (1853) Charles Dickens

Polly, Alfred cc, draper, m. Miriam Larkins*, his cousin
Lizzie his mother
The History of Mr Polly (1910) H. G. Wells

Polly, Aunt Tom's guardian – based in part on the author's mother
Tom Sawyer (1876) Mark Twain (rn Samuel Langhorne Clemens)

Polonia, Prince wealthy Italian banker
his wife
his grandfather
Vanity Fair (1847–8) W. M. Thackeray

Polonius fashionable jeweller
The Great Hoggarty Diamond† (1841) W. M. Thackeray

Polonius Lord Chamberlain, father to Laertes* and Ophelia*
Hamlet play (1623) William Shakespeare

Polperro, Second Baron family name **Trefoyle**
Third Baron his eldest son
The Hon. Adela his daughter, m. Lucian Gildersleeve*
Fourth Baron
The Town Traveller (1898) George Gissing

Polpette, M. of the Pension Bourgeoise
The Pottleton Legacy (1849) Albert Smith

Polreath, David resident of Lanrean
A Message from the Sea (1860) Charles Dickens

Polteed private detective
The *Forsyte* series (1906–33) John Galsworthy
Polwarth, Mr clergyman at Tintagel
ss 'Malachi's Cove'
Lotta Schmidt (1867) Anthony Trollope
Polydamus usurper of Sicily
Marriage à la Mode play (1673) John Dryden
Pomander, Charles, Sir 'gentleman of pleasure', friend to Ernest Vane*
Peg Woffington (1853) Charles Reade
Pomfret lady's maid at Donnithorne Chase
Adam Bede (1859) George Eliot (rn Mary Anne, later Marian, Evans)
Pomfret, Barbara cc sensation novel* of erotic school who cannot choose between John Dering* and her dead husband:
Valentine who is his cousin and who resembles him; 'she flung herself into a drift of crimson pillows . . . brooding upon the broken fire, whose lilac flames palpitated over a bed of gold-veined coals'
The Quick or the Dead (1889) Amélie Rives (later Princess Troubetzkoy)
Pomfret-Walpole boy
Mr Perrin and Mr Traill (1911) Hugh Walpole
Pomjalovsky, Nicholas friend to Eleanor Pargiter*
The Years (1937) Virginia Woolf
Pommeroy, Judge
A Lost Lady (1923) Willa Cather
Pommiere, Noël shoemaker
Shadows on the Rock (1932) Willa Cather
Pompey
Antony and Cleopatra play (1623) William Shakespeare
Pompey 'the little': dog hero of satire admired by Lady Wortley Montague
The History of Pompey the Little, or the Life and Adventures of a Lap-Dog (1751) Francis Coventry
Pompey Negro salve to Beatrix Esmond
Henry Esmond (1852) W. M. Thackeray
Pompiona daughter of the King of Moldavia*
The Knight of the Burning Pestle play (1607) Francis Beaumont (?with John Fletcher)
Pomuchelskopp evil landowner who has a

hold over von Rambow* but who is eventually chased away by his tenants
Ut mine Stromtid (An Old Story of my Farming Days) (1862–4) Fritz Reuter
Ponder, Edna Earl hotel proprietor, narrator
Daniel her uncle
Bonnie Dee Peacock Uncle Daniel's trial wife
The Ponder Heart (1953) Eudora Welty
Ponderevo, George cc, narrator, m. Marion Ramboat*
Edward his uncle and employer; inventor of Tono Bungay
Susan Edward's wife
Tono Bungay (1909) H. G. Wells
Pons, M. French master
Mr Perrin and Mr Traill (1911) Hugh Walpole
Pons, Silvain cc composer, squanderer and, eventually, gluttonous parasite
Le Cousin Pons (1847) Honoré de Balzac
Ponsonby, Inspector in charge of the search for Pru Tuke*
Miss Gomez and the Brethren (1971) William Trevor
Ponsonby, The Misses
Catherine Furze (1893) Mark Rutherford, (rn William Hale White)
Ponta, John brutal unskilled pugilist who kills Fleming* when he slips in the ring
The Game (1905) Jack London
Pontellier, Edna cc New Orleans feminist novel of adultery echoing *Madame Bovary* in Creole terms – even to the Christian name of its protagonist
Léonce her stockbroker husband
her sons
The Awakening (1899) Kate Chopin
Pontiac treacherous Indian chief
The Settlers in Canada (1844) Captain Marryat
Pontieux, Professor malicious portrait of Maurice Merleau-Ponty, who had attacked the author
The Age of Longing (1951) Arthur Koestler
Pontifex, Ernest, m. (bigamously) Ellen
Theobald his father
Christina née Allaby, his mother
Joseph; Charlotte his brother and sister
George his grandfather
Eliza; Mary; Althea his aunts

John his uncle
The Way of All Flesh (1903) Samuel Butler

Ponto Jingle's* intelligent dog
The Pickwick Papers (1837) Charles Dickens

Ponto, Major
his wife
Lieutenant Wellesley; Emily; Maria
The Book of Snobs† (1847) W. M. Thackeray

Ponts, Captain
A Woman is a Weathercock play (1612) Nathan Field

Pontypool, Lord
his wife
Dowager Lady Pontypool his mother
Pendennis (1848) W. M. Thackeray

Poodles dog
The Uncommercial Traveller (1860–8) Charles Dickens

Pooh-Bah Lord High Everything Else
The Mikado opera (1885) W. S. Gilbert and Arthur Sullivan

Pool, Klaas farmer, m. (1) Maartje, (2) Widow Paarlenberg*
Roelf; Geertje; Jozina children to Klaas and Maartje
So Big (1924) Edna Ferber

Poole crippled spy
The Ministry of Fear (1943) Graham Greene

Poole manservant to Dr Jekyll*
Dr Jekyll and Mr Hyde (1886) Robert Louis Stevenson

Poole, Grace Rochester's housekeeper
Jane Eyre (1847) Charlotte Brontë

Poole, Stanley
Angel Pavement (1930) J. B. Priestley

Poorgrass, Joseph farm hand
Far From the Madding Crowd (1874) Thomas Hardy

Pooter, Charles diarist, of Brickfield Terrace, Holloway; in minor classic of the details of 'anxious gentility'
Carrie his wife
William ('Lupin') his 'fast' son engaged to Daisy Mutlar*; m. Lilian Posh*
The Diary of a Nobody (1892) George and Weedon Grossmith

Poots apothecary and miser
Amine his daughter, m. Philip Vanderdecken*

The Phantom Ship (1839) Captain Marryat

Pope, Miss governess, a treasure
Pride and Prejudice (1813) Jane Austen

Pope, Philip coach builder
his wife
Daphne m. Will Magnet*; Marjorie m. Richard Trafford; Romola; Sydney; Theodore their children
Marriage (1912) H. G. Wells

Pope, The (hist.)
Nashe's Lenten Stuff (1599) Thomas Nashe

Popeye degenerate killer with 'vicious, depthless features like stamped tin'
Sanctuary (1931) William Faulkner

Popinjoy, Lady
The Newcomes (1853–5) W. M. Thackeray

Popjoy, Percy, The Hon
Pendennis (1848) W. M. Thackeray

Poppets, Mrs landlady
Three Men in a Boat (1889) Jerome K. Jerome

Poppins, Mary nurse, good fairy, in popular series for children onwards from
Mary Poppins (1934) Pamela L. Travers

Poppleby proprietor of dining-rooms
The Good Companions (1929) J. B. Priestley

Poppleworth chief clerk
Sons and Lovers (1913) D. H. Lawrence

Poppyseed, Miss 'an indefatigable compounder of novels'; caricature of Mrs Amelia Opie*
Headlong Hall (1816) Thomas Love Peacock

Porcello, Albany narrator and cc of tales of stunted childhood in 1890s Dunedin; published anonymously, it caused a scandal: the author was an MP, and a Labour one at that
Children of the Poor (1934); *The Hunted* (1936) John Lee

Pordage, Commissioner self-important and incompetent official
The Perils of Certain English Prisoners (1857) Charles Dickens

Pordage, Jeremy discoverer of the 're-juvenated' 18th-century earl – a disgusting ape
After Many a Summer Dies the Swan (1939) Aldous Huxley

Porgy crippled beggar on Catfish Row in seminal story of blacks on Charleston waterfront which Gershwin turned into an opera
Porgy (1925) DuBose Heyward

Porgy, Captain Falstaffian* comic character by 'Southern Cooper'*, who revelled in his low-life characters
The Partisan (1835); *Mellichampe* (1836); *Katherine Walton* (1851); *Woodcraft* (1854); *The Forayers* (1855) William Gilmore Simms

Pork Negro butler to the O'Haras*
Gone With the Wind (1936) Margaret Mitchell

Porlock, Lord see De Courcy, Countess De

Pornic Morrowbie Jukes's horse
ss 'The Strange Ride of Morrowbie Jukes'
Wee Willie Winkie (1888) Rudyard Kipling

Pornick, Sid boyhood friend to Kipps*
Fanny his wife
Anne his sister, m. Kipps
Old Pornick his father
Kipps (1905) H. G. Wells

Porrex brother to Ferrex* and son to Gorboduc*
Gorboduc play (1562) Thomas Norton and Thomas Sackville

Porson, Ronald embittered failure
The Conscience of the Rich (1958) C. P. Snow

Porteous, Old retired public schoolmaster and friend to Bowling*; sees no reason to pay any attention to Hitler
Coming Up For Air (1936) George Orwell (rn Eric Blair)

Porter, Jimmy cc
Alison his wife, based on the author's first wife
Look Back in Anger play (1956) John Osborne

Porter, Joseph, the Rt. Hon. Sir, KCB First Lord of the Admiralty
H M S Pinafore opera (1878) W. S. Gilbert and Arthur Sullivan

Porter, Howard, Judge dead cc
Mrs Porter his wife to whom he is never there; she hangs paper towels out to dry
Katherine his daughter m. Paul Webb*
The Deep Sleep (1953) Wright Morris

Porter, Lola hoydenish widow, a part-portrait of the author's lover, Jean Rhys*

When the Wicked Man (1931) Ford Madox Ford

Porthos one of the original three musketeers
Les Trois Mousquetaires (*The Three Musketeers*) (1844); *Vingt ans après* (Twenty Years After) (1845); *Le Vicomte de Bragelonne* (The Viscount of Bragelonne) (1850) Alexandre Dumas (père)

Portia (alias **Balthasar**), heiress, m. Bassanio*
The Merchant of Venice play (1623) William Shakespeare

Portia wife to Brutus*
Julius Caesar play (1623) William Shakespeare

Portman, Belinda, cc; niece to Mrs Stanhope*; m. Clarence Hervey*
Belinda (1801) Maria Edgeworth

Portman, Dr master of Brazenface College
The Adventures of Mr Verdant Green (1853) Cuthbert Bede (rn Edward Bradley)

Portman, Revd Mr Vicar of Clavering St Mary
Pendennis (1848) W. M. Thackeray

Portnoy, Alexander native of Newark, New Jersey, masturbator
Sophie his mother, *née* Ginsky
Jack his father
Hannah his sister
Portnoy's Complaint (1969) Philip Roth

Portson, R N V R peace-time stockbroker
ss 'Sea Constables'
Debits and Credits (1926) Rudyard Kipling

Portway, Elvira Robin Middleton's mistress
Lilian her grandmother, ex-actress
Anglo-Saxon Attitudes (1956) Angus Wilson

Posey, George murderous (because 'perfectibilist') cc American Civil War novel
Rozier his father, a man of 'secrecy of action and brutality of character'
Susan *née* **Buchan** his wife
Yellow Jim his Negro half-brother killed by Semmes Buchan*
Jane his half-sister; enters a convent
The Fathers (1938, rev. 1960) Allen Tate

Posh, Murray hat manufacturer, m. Daisy

Mutlar*
  Lilian his sister, m. Lupin Pooter*
  The Diary of a Nobody (1892) George
  and Weedon Grossmith
Posky, Captain m. Glorvina O'Dowd*
  Vanity Fair (1847–8) W. M. Thackeray
Post, Edward one-time fiancé to Maggie
  Campion*
  The Perennial Bachelor (1925) Anne Par-
  rish
Poste, Flora cc who visits her relatives at
  Starkadder in Sussex and reforms them;
  'something nasty in the woodshed'
  originates here
  Cold Comfort Farm (1932) Stella
  Gibbons
Posters, William
  The Death of William Posters (1965)
  Alan Sillitoe
Postgate, Mary sadistic companion whose
  'mind does not dwell' on unpleasant
  things
  ss 'Mary Postgate'
  A Diversity of Creatures (1917) Rudyard
  Kipling
Posthlewaite able and vigilant barmaid of
  the Anglers' Rest
  Meet Mr Mulliner (1927) P. G. Wode
  house
Posthumus, Leonatus husband to Imogen*
  Cymbeline play (1623) William Shake-
  speare
Potatoes fireman
  Mealy his son
  David Copperfield (1850) Charles
  Dickens
Pothinus
  Caesar and Cleopatra play (1900)
  George Bernard Shaw
Potion, Roger apothecary
  Roderick Random (1748) Tobias Smoll-
  ett
Pott, Mr editor of *Eatanswill Gazette*
  his wife
  The Pickwick Papers (1837) Charles
  Dickens
Potter city clerk
  Sketches by Boz† (1836) Charles Dickens
Potter, George 'it was sentimental slush
  that he wrote, vulgar, snobbish,
  shatteringly moral and blatantly relig-
  ious; but the public ate it' – portrait of the
  popular shop girls' journalist Godfrey

Winn, previously the author's lover for a
  short time
  Strictly Personal (autobiography) (1941)
  W. Somerset Maugham
Potter, Israel New England cc based on
  real person of that name
  Israel Potter (1855) Herman Melville
Potter, Jack, Sheriff
  his wife
  ss 'The Bride Comes to Yellow Sky'
  *The Open Boat and Other Tales of
  Adventure* (1898) Stephen Crane
Potter, Mamie soubrette
  The Good Companions (1929) J. B.
  Priestley
Potter, Muff accused of murdering Dr
  Robinson*
  Tom Sawyer (1876) Mark Twain (rn
  Samuel Langhorne Clemens)
Potter, Percy later Lord Pilkington
  his wife, 'Leila Yorke', novelist
  Revd Frank m. Peggy; **Clare**; **Johnny**;
  Jane Johnny's twin, m. Oliver Hobart*
  their children
  Potterism (1920) Rose Macaulay
Potter, Revd Dr Rector, Rosebury
  his wife
  Tom their son
  their daughters
  The Newcomes (1853–5) W. M.
  Thackeray
Potterson, Abbey, Miss hostess of the Six
  Jolly Fellowship Porters
  Job her brother
  Our Mutual Friend (1865) Charles
  Dickens
Potts, Arthur friend to Paul Pennyfeather*
  Decline and Fall (1928) Evelyn Waugh
Potts, Captain
  The Moon in the Yellow River play
  (1932) Denis Johnston
Potts, Tom reporter and editor, *Newcome
  Independent*
  The Newcomes (1853–5) W. M.
  Thackeray
Potzdoff, Captain de
  Barry Lyndon (1844) W. M. Thackeray
Pouch, Joe, Mrs soldier's widow
  Bleak House (1853) Charles Dickens
Poulengay, Bertrand de
  Saint Joan play (1924) George Bernard
  Shaw
Poulter old soldier turned schoolmaster,

Kingslorton
Middlemarch (1871–2) George Eliot (rn Mary Anne, later Marian, Evans)
Pounce, Peter, Captain usurer
Joseph Andrews (1742) Henry Fielding
Poupin, M. socialist
The Princess Casamassima (1866) Henry James
Povey, Samuel highly trusted shop assistant at Baines's, m. Constance Baines*
Cyril their son
Daniel his father, hanged for murder of his wife
Dick his nephew, m. Lily Holl*
The Old Wives' Tale (1908) Arnold Bennett
Powderell retired ironmonger
Middlemarch (1871–2) George Eliot (rn Mary Anne, later Marian, Evans)
Powell Willy Carmichael's* drinking companion
Time, Gentlemen! Time! (1930) Norah Hoult
Powell, Jotham
Ethan Frome (1911) Edith Wharton
Powell, Marie wife to John Milton*, in novel (the latter title) which scandalized academics
The Maiden and Married Life of Marie Powell (1849) Anne Manning
Wife to Mr Milton (1943) Robert Graves
Power, Frederick, Captain inseparable companion of Charles O'Malley* m. Inez Emmanuel*
Charles O'Malley, The Irish Dragoon (1841) Charles Lever
Power, Paula 'modern woman'* cc; m. George Somerset
John her dead father
Abner her sinister uncle
A Laodicean (1881) Thomas Hardy
Powerhouse jazz pianist perhaps in part modelled on Fats Waller; gets a wire, 'YOUR WIFE IS DEAD', signed 'Uranus Knockwood' but refuses to check it
ss 'Powerhouse'
A Curtain of Green (1941) Eudora Welty
Powheid, Lazarus sexton
Castle Dangerous (1832) Walter Scott
Powler, Violet housekeeper, m. Evelyn Orcham*
Imperial Palace (1930) Arnold Bennett
Powlers ancient stock, connections of Mrs

Sparsit's* late husband
Hard Times (1854) Charles Dickens
Pownceby, Mr solicitor
The Cuckoo in the Nest (1894) Mrs Margaret Oliphant
Powther, Mame blues-singing cc of novel set in the black neighbourhood of Monmouth, Connecticut
Malcolm her son
The Narrows (1953) Ann Petry
Powys, Leonora m. Edward Ashburnham*
The Good Soldier (1915) Ford Madox Ford
Poynings, George, Lord younger son to Lord Tiptoff*
Barry Lyndon (1844) W. M. Thackeray
Poynter Mary Turner's seducer, business rival to Aaron Cohen*
Aaron the Jew (1894) Benjamin L. Farjeon
Poyser, Martin, tenant of Hall Farm, uncle of Hetty Sorrel*
Rachel, his wife
Marty; Thomas; Charlotte their children
'Old Martin' his father
Adam Bede (1859) George Eliot (rn Mary Anne, later Marian, Evans)
Pozzo
Waiting for Godot play (1952) Samuel Beckett
Practice a lawyer
The Magnetic Lady, or *Humours Reconciled* play (1641) Ben Jonson
Praed
Mrs Warren's Profession play (1902) George Bernard Shaw
Prail, Elizabeth beaten, raped, kidnapped: decent woman rewarded in the New America
A Cool Million (1934) Nathanael West (rn Nathan Weinstein)
Prance, Dr 'a little medical lady'
The Bostonians (1886) Henry James
Prank, J. E. see **Lavish, Miss**
Pratchett, Mrs chambermaid, of the Bush, Australia
Somebody's Luggage (1862) Charles Dickens
Pratt, Anastasia ('Chalkline Annie') delinquent girl who introduces Joe Buck* to sex in cult novel
Midnight Cowboy (1966) James Leo Herlihy

Pratt, Dr Milby doctor
Eliza his daughter
ss 'Janet's Repentance'
Scenes of Clerical Life (1857) George
Eliot (rn Mary Anne, later Marian,
Evans)
Pratt, Helen Berlin correspondent
Mr Norris Changes Trains (1935) Christopher Isherwood
Pratt, Lola 'The Baby-Talk Lady', loved by
William Baxter
Seventeen (1915) Booth Tarkington
Pratt, Maude Coffin photographer cc
her brother and sister
Picture Palace (1978) Paul Theroux
Pratt, Miss eccentric
The Inheritance (1824) Susan Ferrier
Pratt, Miss ill-natured woman who did not
like buffo stories, comic songs, hunting
or drinking
ss 'The Squire's Story'
Novels and Tales (1906–19) Mrs Gaskell
Pratt, Mr tutor
Sense and Sensibility (1811) Jane Austen
Pray, Job Lionel Lincoln's* half-wit stepbrother
Abigail his mother
Lionel Lincoln (1825) James Fenimore
Cooper
Preamble, Justice alias Bramble, of
Maribone
A Tale of a Tub play (1640) Ben Jonson
Precedent one of Miss Flyte's* captive
birds
Bleak House (1853) Charles Dickens
Preemby, Albert Edward house agent's
clerk, m. Chrissie Hossett*
Christina Alberta cc, his nominal daughter
Christina Alberta's Father (1925) H. G.
Wells
Prendergast ex-clergyman, schoolmaster
Decline and Fall (1928) Evelyn Waugh
Prendergast, the Hon. Revd non-resident
rector of Milby
ss 'Janet's Repentance'
Scenes of Clerical Life (1857) George
Eliot (rn Mary Anne, later Marian,
Evans)
Prenderghast, Felix young schoolmaster
allegedly transformed into a peccary for
not admiring the *Sunday Times* book
reviews 'with his whole heart and soul'

The Wily Ones (1891) Gordon Giles
Prendick, Edward cc, biologist, narrator
The Island of Dr Moreau (1896) H. G.
Wells
Prentice secret service
The Ministry of Fear (1943) Graham
Greene
Prentice, Pirate
Gravity's Rainbow (1973) Thomas
Pynchon
Prescott, Dick friend to Lord Saxby*
Sinister Street (1913) Compton
Mackenzie
Prescott, Dr
Lawrence his son, m. Elmira Edwards
Jerome (1897) Mary E. Wilkins
Presly indignant poet
The Octopus (1901) Frank Norris
Prest, Henry lover to whom Lizzie
Hazeldean* prostitutes herself to obtain
money to care for her sick husband
ss 'New Year's Day'
Old New York (1924) Edith Wharton
Preston
The Vortex play (1924) Noël Coward
Preston, Edmund, the Rt. Hon.
Lady Jane his wife
The Great Hoggarty Diamond (1841)
W. M. Thackeray
Preston, Mr Lord Cumnor's* agent
Wives and Daughters (1866) Mrs Gaskell
Preston, Sally m. Tom Kitchener*
ss 'Something to Worry About'
The Man Upstairs (1914) P. G. Wodehouse
Presumption encountered by Christian*
The Pilgrim's Progress (1678–84) John
Bunyan
Pretty, Bob
ss 'A Tiger's Skin'†
The Lady of the Barge (1902) W. W.
Jacobs
Prettyman, Prince
The Rehearsal play (1671) George, Duke
of Buckingham
Prettymon, Sidney J. ('Sitting Pretty'; 'Sit')
narrator cc of novel that has been described as 'the equivalent of an Afro-American musical'
Sitting Pretty (1976) Al Young
Priam King of Troy
Troilus and Cressida play (1623) William

Shakespeare

Price, Fanny art student and eventual suicide with false faith in her own genius
Albert her brother
Of Human Bondage (1915) W. Somerset Maugham

Price, Frances, Mrs *née* Ward*, sister to Lady Bartram*
Lieutenant Price her husband
Fanny m. Revd Edmund Bartram*; **William; Susan** some of their children
Mansfield Park (1814) Jane Austen

Price, Hubert cc, artist manqué who inherits a fortune, in early novel
A Vain Fortune (1892) George Moore

Price, Myfanwy in love with Mog Edwards
Under Milk Wood play (1954) Dylan Thomas

Price, Oliver m. (1) Edith Whitebillet, (2) Edna Smith, *née* Whitebillet
Reginald; Sarah children to Oliver and Edith
Jane his sister, see **Palfrey**
his father and mother
Antigua Penny Puce (1936) Robert Graves

Price, Snobby
Major Barbara play (1905) George Bernard Shaw

Price, Willie in love with Anna Tellwright*
Anna of the Five Towns (1902) Arnold Bennett

Price, 'Tilda m. John Browdie
Nicholas Nickleby (1839) Charles Dickens

Prickshaft, Adam, Sir suitor to Mistress Miniver*
Satiromastix, or The Untrussing of the Humorous Poet play (1602) Thomas Dekker

Priddle, Retty dairymaid
Tess of the D'Urbervilles (1891) Thomas Hardy

Prie, Jaques beggar, part of the farcical sub-plot
Rachel his daughter
The Case is Altered play (1609) Ben Jonson

Priest, Judge the humorous American author's most celebrated character, empathetic old Confederate veteran given to drinking of mint juleps
Old Judge Priest† (1915) Irvin S. Cobb

Priest, Roger dentist
H. M. Pulham, Esq (1941) John P. Marquand

Prig a knavish beggar
The Beggar's Bush play (1647) John Fletcher (?Philip Massinger)

Prig, Betsey nurse, friend to Mrs Gamp*, but finally disowned by her as a 'bage creetur'
Martin Chuzzlewit (1844) Charles Dickens

Prike, Tom ne're-do-well – for whom Martin Stoner* is mistaken – guilty of an unnamed offence
ss 'The Hounds of Fate'
The Chronicles of Clovis (1911) 'Saki' (rn Hector Hugh Munro)

Prim, Obadiah Quaker guardian of Anne Lovely*
A Bold Stroke for a Wife play (1718) Susannah Centlivre

Prime, Dorothea widowed daughter of the Ray* family, a harshly evangelist woman, grimly dedicated to the Dorcas Society
Rachel Ray (1863) Anthony Trollope

Primrose, Agnes sentenced to death by her own seducer, William Norwynne*, in Rousseauist novel by friend to Godwin*
Nature and Art (1796) Elizabeth Inchbald

Primrose, Charles, Dr Vicar of Wakefield, cc, narrator; virtuous but devoid of worldly wisdom
Deborah his wife
George m. Arabella Wilmot*; **Moses** m. Miss Flamborough*; **Olivia** m. Squire Thornhill*; **Sophia** m. Sir William Thornhill* their children
The Vicar of Wakefield (1766) Oliver Goldsmith

Princess visitor to estate of Saryntsov* who says that Christianity does not require the rich to give up their estates
Boris her son, flogged for explaining the Gospels
I svet vo tme svetit (*The Light Shines in Darkness*) play (1911) Leo Tolstoy

Princhester, Bishop of see **Scrope, Edward**

Pringle Caryl Bramsley's* housemaster at Eton
C (1924) Maurice Baring

Pringle, Guy cc, lecturer in Budapest

Harriet his wife, cc
The Great Fortune† (1960) Olivia Manning
Pringle, James
ss 'Unlucky for Pringle'
Unlucky for Pringle (1973) Wyndham Lewis
Pringle, Zachariah and his family
The Ayrshire Legatees (1821) John Galt
Prior, Montagu, Captain late of the Militia
his wife
Elizabeth their eldest daughter, m. as second wife Adolphus Frederick Lovel*
Lovel the Widower (1860) W. M. Thackeray
Prior, Tom illegitimate son of Miss Midget*; wastrel condemned to good works in slums
Outward Bound play (1924) Sutton Vane
Priscilla Mrs Jellaby's* maid, given to drink
Bleak House (1854) Charles Dickens
Priscilla wooed by John Alden* on behalf of Miles Standish*; later m. him
The Courtship of Miles Standish poem (1858) Henry Wadsworth Longfellow
Prism, Laetitia, Miss governess to Cicely Cardew*, originally nurse to John Worthing*, m. Canon Chasuble*
The Importance of Being Earnest play (1895) Oscar Wilde
Pritchard, Cynlais
his wife
Dilys their daughter, murdered by Idris Atkinson*
How Green Was My Valley (1939) Richard Llewellyn
Pritchard, Sergeant
ss 'Mrs Bathurst'†
Traffics and Discoveries (1904) Rudyard Kipling
Privett, William
Betty his wife
ss 'The Superstitious Man's Story'
Life's Little Ironies (1894) Thomas Hardy
Privilege, Lord rascally uncle to Peter and Ellen Simple*
Hawkins his illegitimate son
Peter Simple (1834) Captain Marryat
Probe surgeon
A Trip to Scarborough play (1777)

Richard Brinsley Sheridan
Probert, Gareth poet
That Uncertain Feeling (1955) Kingsley Amis
Probert, Rosie
Under Milk Wood play (1954) Dylan Thomas
Proctor printer, stationer, librarian
ss 'Janet's Repentance'
Scenes of Clerical Life (1857) George Eliot (rn Mary Anne, later Marian, Evans)
Procurio, Edward 'groom of the Chambers'
The Young Visiters (1919) Daisy Ashford
Profond, Prosper, M.
The *Forsyte* series (1906–33) John Galsworthy
Prokop, Engineer cc, of Wellsian* Czech novel, who invents Krakatit, an explosive based on the principle that all matter is highly explosive but held together only until a disturbing element is introduced into it
Krakatit (1924) Karel Capek
Prong, Samuel, Revd of the Dorcas Society, for whom 'cheerfulness was a sin'
his wife
Rachel Ray (1863) Anthony Trollope
Prophilus friend to Ithocles*
The Broken Heart play (1633) John Ford
Propter, Mr portrait of a man with Ouspensky-like ideas
After Many a Summer (1939) Aldous Huxley
Prosee eminent counsel
The Pickwick Papers (1837) Charles Dickens
Prospero rightful Duke of Milan, cc
The Tempest play (1623) William Shakespeare
Pross, Miss Lucie Mannette's* companion
Solomon (alias **John Barsad**) her brother, spy
A Tale of Two Cities (1859) Charles Dickens
Prosser, Sally, Mrs political virago
ss 'The Speech'
Blind Love (1969) V. S. Pritchett
Protaldy paramour to Brunhalt*
Thierry and Theodoret play (1621) John Fletcher, Philip Massinger ?and Francis Beaumont
Proteus gentleman

Two Gentlemen of Verona play (1623)
William Shakespeare
Prothero, Mary ('Pokey')
The Group (1963) Mary McCarthy
Prothero, William friend to William
Benham*
The Research Magnificent (1915) H. G.
Wells
Protheroe doctor
Middlemarch (1871–2) George Eliot (rn
Mary Anne, later Marian, Evans)
Proudfute, Oliver bonnet maker
Maudie his wife
The Fair Maid of Perth (1828) Walter
Scott
Proudhammer, Leo black actor
Caleb his brother, a preacher
*Tell Me How Long The Train's Been
Gone* (1968) James Baldwin
Proudie, Dr Bishop of Barchester
his wife
Olivia their daughter, m. Revd Thomas
Tickler*
Framley Parsonage† (1861) Anthony
Trollope
Prout Prout i.e. Marcel Proust*
Féerie pour un autre fois (*Fairy Play for
Another Time*) (1952–4) Louis-
Ferdinand Céline (rn Louis-Ferdinand
Destouches)
Prout, Mr ('Heffy') housemaster
Stalky & Co.† (1899) Rudyard Kipling
Provis false name used by **Magwitch***
Prowd Treby watchmaker
Felix Holt (1866) George Eliot (rn Mary
Anne, later Marian, Evans)
Prowse, Tom
ss 'Communion'
Adam and Eve and Pinch Me (1921) A. E.
Coppard
Prudence chambermaid, elected sovereign
of all the sports in the inn, m. Lord
Latimer*
The New Inn, or *The Light Heart* play
(1629) Ben Jonson
Prudence; Piety; Charity of the Palace
Beautiful
The Pilgrim's Progress (1678–84) John
Bunyan
Prue, Miss a silly awkward country girl,
daughter to Foresight* by a former wife
Love for Love comedy (1710) William
Congreve

Pruffle butler to the scientific gentleman at
Clifton
The Pickwick Papers (1837) Charles
Dickens
Prufrock, Alfred cc – building on the
ironically genteelized decadence* estab-
lished by Edwin Arlington Robinson*
and the Italian *crepusculari* poets
poem 'The Love Song of Alfred J.
Prufrock'
Prufrock and Other Observations (1917)
T. S. Eliot
Pryar, Matthew snob
The Unspeakable Skipton (1959) Pamela
Hansford Johnson
Pryden, Jack former lover of Eva
Buckingham Hines*
Baldur's Gate (1970) Eleanor Clark
Pryer, Revd Mr fellow curate with Ernest
Pontifex*
The Way of All Flesh (1903) Samuel
Butler
Prynne, Amanda ex-wife of Elyot Chase*
Victor her husband
Private Lives play (1930) Noël Coward
Prynne, Hester 'scarlet woman'
Pearl her daughter
The Scarlet Letter (1850) Nathaniel
Hawthorne
Prynne, Ruth actress
Manhattan Transfer (1925) John Dos
Passos
Pryor, Mrs former governess to Caroline
Helstone*
Shirley (1949) Charlotte Brontë
Psanek, Johann Dionys, Count cc
ss 'The Ladybird'
The Captain's Doll (1923) (in UK as *The
Ladybird*) D. H. Lawrence
Pshenitsyana m. Oblomov*
Oblomov (1859) Ivan Goncharov
Psyche, Lady Professor of Humanities,
sister to Florian*, m. Cyril*
Princess Ida opera (1884) W. S. Gilbert
and Arthur Sullivan
Ptolemy, Dionysius King of Egypt
Caesar and Cleopatra play (1900)
George Bernard Shaw
Ptthmllnsprts, Professor
The Water Babies (1863) Charles Kings-
ley
Publius son to Marcus*
Titus Andronicus play (1623) William

Shakespeare

Pubsey & Co. see **Fledgeby**

Puck cc
Puck of Pook's Hill† (1906) Rudyard Kipling

Puck fairy
A Midsummer Night's Dream play (1623) William Shakespeare

Puddleduck, Jemima cc
The Tale of Jemima Puddleduck (1908) Beatrix Potter

Puddleton, Miss ('**Puddle**') governess; faithful friend to Stephen Gordon*
The Well of Loneliness (1928) Radclyffe Hall

Pudgie photographer narrator: the name by which he had been known at home, he tells Benlian*
ss 'Benlian'
Widdershins (1911) Oliver Onions

Puff
The Critic play (1779) Richard Brinsley Sheridan

Puff, Partenopox
Vivian Grey (1827) Benjamin Disraeli

Puffer, Princess old hag in East End opium den
The Mystery of Edwin Drood (1870) Charles Dickens

Puffington sportsman
Mr Sponge's Private Tour (1853) R. S. Surtees

Pug
The Devil is an Ass play (1616) Ben Jonson

Pugh, Barthelmy, Sir
The Constant Nymph (1924) Margaret Kennedy

Pugh, Mr and Mrs
Under Milk Wood play (1954) Dylan Thomas

Pugh, Mrs Miss Guthrie's* rival
ss 'Neighbours'
A Beginning (1955) Walter de la Mare

Pugstyles one of Mr Gregsbury's* constituents
Nicholas Nickleby (1839) Charles Dickens

Pulham, Henry Moulton cc, Investment Counsel, narrator, m. Cornelia Motford
George; Gladys their children
John; Mary his parents
Mary; Jim his brother and sister

H. M. Pulham Esq. (1941) John P. Marquand

Pullet gentleman farmer
Middlemarch (1871–2) George Eliot (rn Mary Anne, later Marian, Evans)

Pulleyn see **Dorking, Earl of**

Pumblechook, Uncle Joe Gargery's* uncle; hypocrite
Great Expectations (1861) Charles Dickens

Pummel valet to Theophrastus Such*
The Impressions of Theophrastus Such (1879) George Eliot (rn Mary Anne, later Marian, Evans)

Pumphrey, Professor
Babbitt (1923) Sinclair Lewis

Pumpinskill, Professor weighty member of the Association
The Mudfog Papers (1838) Charles Dickens

Pumps John Brent's horse, second in nobility only to Don Fulano*
John Brent (1862) Theodore Winthrop

Punch small boy
ss 'Baa Baa Black Sheep'
Wee Willie Winkie (1888) Rudyard Kipling

Punt, Count gambler
The Newcomes† (1853–5) W. M. Thackeray

Puntarvolo vain-glorious knight, over-Englishing his travels
Every Man Out of His Humour play (1599) Ben Jonson

Pupford, Miss teacher
ss 'Tom Tiddler's Ground'
Christmas Stories (1861) Charles Dickens

Pupker, Matthew, Sir Chairman of the United Metropolitan Improved Hot Crumpet and Muffin Baking and Punctual Delivery Company
Nicholas Nickleby (1839) Charles Dickens

Puppy wrestler (a Western man)
Bartholomew Fair play (1631) Ben Jonson

Puppy, Hannibal ('**Ball**') the High Constable's man
A Tale of a Tub play (1640) Ben Jonson

Purcell, Plucky friend to John and Amanda Ziller* who chances upon the mummified body of Christ and delivers it to them as another attraction

Another Roadside Attraction (1971) Tom Robbins

Purcell, Tom bookseller, employer to David Grieve*
Lucy his daughter, m. David Grieve, although unworthy of him
The History of David Grieve (1892) Mrs Humphry Ward

Purdue, Angela m. Wilfred Mulliner*
Meet Mr Mulliner (1927) P. G. Wodehouse

Pure, Simon preacher whom Fainall* impersonates
A Bold Stroke for a Wife play (1718) Susannah Centlivre

Purecraft, Dame widow, mother to Win-the-Fight Littlewit*
Bartholomew Fair play (1631) Ben Jonson

Purfoy, Sarah maid to Mrs Vickers*, in love with John Rex*, cc
His Natural Life (1870–2; abridged by the author 1874; in 1885 as *For the Term of His Natural Life* – thus evading the author's irony; original text edited by Stephen Murray-Smith, 1970) Marcus Clarke

Purkin, Cyril laundry manager
Imperial Palace (1930) Arnold Bennett

Purkins policeman
The Last Revolution (1951) Lord Dunsany

Purnell, Timothy, Captain
ss 'With the Night Mail'
Actions and Reactions (1909) Rudyard Kipling

Pursewarden, Percy ironist, writer
Liza his blind sister
The Alexandria Quartet (1957–61) Lawrence Durrell

Purun Dass, Sir Dewar, KCIE (Purun Bhagat)
ss 'The Miracle of Purun Bhagat'
The Second Jungle Book (1895) Rudyard Kipling

Purvis, Daisy charwoman
You Can't Go Home Again (1940) Thomas Wolfe

Putana tutoress to Anabella*
'Tis Pity She's a Whore play (1633) John Ford

Putley painter and decorator
The Diary of a Nobody (1892) George and Weedon Grossmith

Putty, James election agent
Felix Holt (1866) George Eliot (rn Mary Anne, later Marian, Evans)

Pybus, Mrs gossip
Pendennis (1848) W. M. Thackeray

Pycroft, Emanuel petty officer
ss 'The Bonds of Discipline'†
Traffics and Discoveries† (1904) Rudyard Kipling

Pycroft, Hall
ss 'The Stockbroker's Clerk'
The Memoirs of Sherlock Holmes (1894) Arthur Conan Doyle

Pyke, Johanna, Dame prioress
The Corner That Held Them (1948) Sylvia Townsend Warner

Pyke, Mr toady to Sir Mulberry Hawk*
Nicholas Nickleby (1839) Charles Dickens

Pyle, Alben the quiet American
The Quiet American (1955) Graham Greene

Pym, Cyrus, Dr
Manalive (1912) G. K. Chesterton

Pyncheon, Colonel enemy to Matthew Maule*, found dead as Maule prophesied
Gervaise his grandson
Hepzibah aged descendant
Clifford Hepzibah's brother
Phoebe cousin to Hepzibah, m. Holgrave*
Arthur Phoebe's father
Jaffrey, Judge cousin to Hepzibah
The House of the Seven Gables (1851) Nathaniel Hawthorne

Pyneweck, Lewis forger, one-time grocer of Shrewsbury, sentenced to hang by Justice Harbottle*
Flora his wife, *née* Carwell, Harbottle's mistress and, as Mrs Carwell, his housekeeper
ss 'Mr Justice Harbottle'
In a Glass Darkly (1872) J. Sheridan Le Fanu

Pynsent, George ambitious, aristocratic
Lady Diana his wife
Pendennis (1848) W. M. Thackeray

Pynsent, Miss ('Pinnie') dressmaker of modest means who brings up Hyacinth Robinson*
The Princess Casamassima (1866) Henry James

Q

Quackenboss fashionable doctor
The Newcomes (1853–5) W. M. Thackeray
Quackleben, Quentin, Dr
St Ronan's Well (1824) Walter Scott
Quaid, Silas crooked lawyer who watches his client 'as a chemist might watch the inanimate metal writhe and twist under the action of a corroding acid'
His Natural Life (1870–2; abridged by the author 1874; in 1885 as *For the Term of His Natural Life* – thus evading the author's irony; original text edited by Stephen Murray-Smith, 1970) Marcus Clarke
Quale philanthropical friend, with 'large shining knobs' for temples, to Mrs Jellaby*
Bleak House (1853) Charles Dickens
Quallon banker of Wanchester
Daniel Deronda (1876) George Eliot (rn Mary Anne, later Marian, Evans)
Quanko Samba bowler (in Mr Jingle's* West Indian matches) killed by heat
The Pickwick Papers (1837) Charles Dickens
Quantock, Daisy Mrs
Robert her husband
Queen Lucia (1920) E. F. Benson
Quarles, Philip novelist, m. Elinor Bidlake (a part-portrait of the author's first wife)
Philip their son
Sidney, Rachel his parents
Point Counter Point (1928) Aldous Huxley
Quarlous, Tom companion to Winwife*, and a gamester
Bartholomew Fair play (1631) Ben Jonson
Quartermain, Allan big-game hunter, cc, called Macumazahn by natives
King Solomon's Mines† (1885) Henry Rider Haggard
Quasimodo lovable but reviled hunchback, cc

Nôtre Dame de Paris (1831) Victor Hugo
Quaybil Sidonian port inspector
ss 'The Manner of Men'
Limits and Renewals (1932) Rudyard Kipling
Quayne, Portia cc, illegitimate sixteen-year-old girl, whose innocence is destroyed, in influential and much read novel about adolescent love
Thomas her half-brother
Anna Thomas's wife
The Death of the Heart (1938) Elizabeth Bowen
Queeg, Captain paranoiac commander of the *Caine*
The Caine Mutiny (1951) Herman Wouk
Queen, Ellery American detective in popular series
Queen, Richard, Inspector of New York Homicide Squad, his father; onwards from
The Roman Hat Mystery† (1929) Ellery Queen (rn Frederick Dannay and Manfred Lee)
Queen, Else maid at Kinraddie Manse
A Scots Quair trilogy (1932–4) Lewis Grassic Gibbon (rn Leslie Mitchell)
Queequeg Polynesian Prince, room-mate of Ishmael*
Moby-Dick or *The Whale* (1851) Herman Melville
Querini, Flavio, Count Venetian who wants to be great singer
The Unspeakable Skipton (1959) Pamela Hansford Johnson
Querry man of arid heart
A Burnt-Out Case (1961) Graham Greene
Quesnel, M. brother to Mme St Aubert*
his wife, Italian heiress
The Mysteries of Udolpho (1794) Mrs Ann Radcliffe
Quest, Martha cc
Alfred; May her parents, settled in South Africa

Douglas Knowell her husband, a civil servant
Caroline her daughter
The *Children of Violence* series: *Martha Quest* (1952); *A Proper Marriage* (1954); *A Ripple From the Storm* (1958); *Landlocked* (1965); *The Four-Gated City* (1969) Doris Lessing

Quested, Adela cc
A Passage to India (1924) E. M. Forster

Quickear policeman
The Uncommercial Traveller (1860–8) Charles Dickens

Quickly, Mistress servant to Dr Caius*
The Merry Wives of Windsor; King Henry IV; King Henry V plays (1623) William Shakespeare

Quicksilver thieving apprentice to Touchstone*
Eastward Ho! play (1605) George Chapman, Ben Jonson and John Marston

Quiggin, J. G. part-caricature of the critic and novelist Cyril Connolly
A Question of Upbringing† (1951) Anthony Powell

Quigley, Doll neighbour to the Parkers*
Bub her feeble-minded brother
The Tree of Man (1955) Patrick White

Quigley, Miss governess
The Newcomes (1853–5) W. M. Thackeray

Quigley, Failey cabinet minister
ss 'Hymeneal'
The Talking Trees (1971) Sean O'Faolain

Quijano, Alonso ('Don Quixote') cc
Don Quixote (1605–15) Miguel de Cervantes

Quilp, Daniel diabolical dwarf usurer with stained fangs which make him look like a panting dog
Betsy his pretty, timid wife, *née* Jinwin, terrified of him
The Old Curiosity Shop (1841) Charles Dickens

Quilty, Clare famous playwright murdered by Humbert Humbert*
Lolita (1955) Vladimir Nabokov

Quin, Agnes prostitute
Mrs Eckdorf in O'Neill's Hotel (1969) William Trevor

Quin, Auberon affectionate part-portrait of Max Beerbohm*
The Napoleon of Notting Hill (1904)
G. K. Chesterton

Quin, Captain m. Honoria Brady
Barry Lyndon (1844) W. M. Thackeray

Quin, James voluptuary
The Expedition of Humphrey Clinker (1771) Tobias Smollett

Quin, Widow
The Playboy of the Western World play (1907) John Millington Synge

Quinbus, Flestrin Gulliver's name in Lilliput ('man mountain')
Gulliver's Travels (1726) Jonathan Swift

Quince carpenter
A Midsummer Night's Dream play (1623) William Shakespeare

Quince, Mary maid to Maud Ruthyn*
Uncle Silas (1864) J. Sheridan Le Fanu

Quinch, Mrs
The Uncommercial Traveller (1860–8) Charles Dickens

Quincy, Quincy narrator, cc in autobiographical novel of World War Two
Confessions of a Spent Youth (1960) Vance Bourjaily

Quinion, Mr manager at Murdstone and Grinby*
David Copperfield (1850) Charles Dickens

Quinn, Harrison
Alice his wife
The Thin Man (1934) Dashiell Hammett

Quint, Emmanuel modern Christ figure accused of murder in German novel
Der Narr in Christo (The Fool in Christ) (1910) Gerhart Hauptmann

Quint, Peter ghost, malevolent valet (suggested as a portrait of George Bernard Shaw*, but this is unlikely except as a joke)
The Turn of the Screw (1898) Henry James

Quintanar, Don Víctor elderly and affable retired judge; husband to Ana Ozores*
La Regenta (*The Regentess* but tr. under its own title) (1884–5) Leopoldo Alas

Quintus son to Titus Andronicus*
Titus Andronicus play (1623) William Shakespeare

Quintus, Reggie
The Princess Zoubaroff (1920) Ronald Firbank

Quirk crooked lawyer of the firm Quirk, Gammon* and Snap*

Ten Thousand a Year (1841) Samuel Warren

Quirk, Thady steward (based on the author's father's steward, John Langan) to three generations of the Rackrents*; narrator of what is the first regional* English novel

Jason his son, a sly lawyer hated by the people

Castle Rackrent (1800) Maria Edgeworth

Quisara

The Island Princess play (1647) John Fletcher

Quiverful, Revd Mr Rector of Puddingdale *Barchester Towers* (1857) Anthony Trollope

Quixote, Don, de La Mancha cc

Don Quixote (1605–15) Miguel de Cervantes

Quodling, Mrs

Francis her illegitimate son

The Town Traveller (1898) George Gissing

Quong, Margaret 'intuitive' saved character* in first (unheeded) novel by author who later won Nobel Prize

Happy Valley (1939) Patrick White

Quorlen Tory printer, Treby Magna

Felix Holt (1866) George Eliot (rn Mary Anne, later Marian, Evans)

R

Rab 'old, gray, brindled, as big as a little Highland bull', with 'Shakespearean dewlaps'; cc
Rab and His Friends (1855) John Brown
Rab, Captain swindler, snob
The Book of Snobs (1847) W. M. Thackeray
Rabb, Fayne
Mrs Rabb her mother
HERmione (1981) H. D. (rn Hilda Doolittle)
Rabbit
Winnie the Pooh† (1926) A. A. Milne
Rabbit, Brer cc
Uncle Remus (1880–95) Joel Chandler Harris
Rabbit, Edward, Revd
his wife
Mehalah (1880) Sabine Baring-Gould
Rabbit, Mary Anne m. Tony Hynes*
James her grandfather
Famine (1937) Liam O'Flaherty
Rabbit, The White
Alice in Wonderland (1865) Lewis Carroll (rn Charles Lutwidge Dodgson)
Rabbits Eggs local character (the original of whom, at Westward Ho!, named the author 'Old Giglamps')
Stalky & Co. (1899) Rudyard Kipling
Rabbits Lady Drew's butler
Tono Bungay (1909) H. G. Wells
Raby, Guy, Squire Henry Little's* uncle m. Jael Dence*
Edith his sister m. James Little*
Put Yourself in his Place (1870) Charles Reade
Rachael millhand whom Stephen Blackpool* would have liked to marry
Hard Times (1854) Charles Dickens
Rachel actress
A la recherche du temps perdu (*In Search of Lost Time*) (1913–27) Marcel Proust
Rackrent, Patrick, Sir hard-drinking inventor of raspberry whisky, who preceded the time of the narrator, steward

Thady Quirk*
Sir Murtagh his brother and successor, furious and litigious miser
Sir Kit his brother – and successor to Murtagh, gambler with a Jewish wife who cannot understand her environment
Sir Condy distant relative and successor, m. Isabelle Moneygawl*
Castle Rackrent (1800) Maria Edgeworth
Rackstraw, Ralph able seaman, m. Josephine Corcoran*
H M S Pinafore opera (1878) W. S. Gilbert and Arthur Sullivan
Rackstraw, The Ladies Hermengilde and Yseult twin beauties
The Newcomes (1853–5) W. M. Thackeray
Radcliffe, Leonard last product of a family once aristocratic
John; Stella his parents
Elizabeth his sister
Radcliffe (1963) David Storey
Raddle, Mary Ann, Mrs fierce little woman who led her husband a dog's life
The Pickwick Papers (1837) Charles Dickens
Radfoot, George third mate on vessel which brought John Harmon* home; drugged and robbed him, but set upon and killed just afterwards – and his corpse, being dressed in Harmon's clothes, was mistaken for that of his victim
Our Mutual Friend (1865) Charles Dickens
Radford, Mrs
Clara her daughter, m. Baxter Dawes*
Sons and Lovers (1913) D. H. Lawrence
Radlett see **Alconleigh, Lord**
Raeburn nurseryman
ss 'The Rajah's Diamond'
The New Arabian Nights (1882) Robert Louis Stevenson
Raeburn, Aldous cc, later Lord Maxwell,

m. Marcella Boyce*
his aunt
Marcella (1894) Mrs Humphry Ward
Rafe man to Master Harebrain*
A Mad World My Masters play (1608)
Thomas Middleton
Raff, Captain of doubtful reputation
The Book of Snobs (1847) W. M.
Thackeray
Raffles bully, stepfather to Joshua Rigg*
(see **Featherstone, Peter**)
Middlemarch (1871–2) George Eliot (rn
Mary Anne, later Marian, Evans)
Raffles, A. J. cc, amateur cracksman,
onwards from
The Amateur Cracksman† (1899) E. W.
Hornung
Rafi King of the Beggars
Hassan play (1923) James Elroy Flecker
Ragamoffski, Gregory, Prince m. Miss
Hulker*
Vanity Fair† (1847–8) W. M. Thackeray
Raggles one-time butler turned grocer,
finally ruined
his wife, a former cook
Vanity Fair (1847–8) W. M. Thackeray
Raikes, Jack m. Polly Wheedle*
Evan   Harrington   (1861)   George
Meredith
Raikes, Sub-Lieutenant of *Saltash*
The   Cruel   Sea   (1951)   Nicholas
Monsarrat
Railsford, Mark housemaster cc
The Master of the Shell (1894) Talbot
Baines Reed
Railton-Bell, Mrs
Sybil her daughter
Separate   Tables   play   (1955)   Terence
Rattigan
Raine, Roger drunken tapster at the Peveril
Arms
his wife
Peveril of the Peak (1822) Walter Scott
Raines, Sergeant
ss 'Love o' Women'
Many Inventions (1893) Rudyard Kipl-
ing
Rainey, Fate, Mrs town gossip
Virgie his daughter
The Golden Apples (1949) Eudora Welty
Raingo, Lord a carefully only partial
portrait of the author's mentor (he gave
him space in his newspapers), Lord

Beaverbrook
Lord Raingo (1926) Arnold Bennett
Rainscourt cousin, supposed heir, of
Admiral de Courcy; murderer; suicide
Emily; Norah his daughters
The King's Own (1830) Captain Marryat
Rais, Gilles de (hist.)
St Joan play (1924) George Bernard
Shaw
Raju, Swami con-man who becomes a
saint, or, in terms of the author's Hindu
religion, discovers himself
The Guide (1958) R. K. Narayan
Rake, Lord companion to Sir John Brute*
The Provok'd Wife play (1697) John
Vanbrugh
Rakes, Fanny, Lady m. Earl of Tiptoff*
The Great Hoggarty Diamond (1841)
W. M. Thackeray
Raleigh, Walter, Sir (hist.) narrator
The Voyage of the Destiny (1979) Robert
Nye
Raleigh, James, Second-Lieutenant cc
Journey's End play (1928) R. C. Sherriff
Ralph
Doctor Faustus play (1604) Christopher
Marlowe
Ralph boy who, with Piggy*, attempts to
set up a democratic society and fails
Lord of the Flies (1954) William Golding
Ralph Brian's man
The Merry Devil of Edmonton play
(1608) ?Thomas Dekker
Ralph citizen's apprentice
The Knight of the Burning Pestle play
(1613) Francis Beaumont and John
Fletcher
Ralston *née* Lovell, Delia
James Ralston her wealthy husband
ss 'The Old Maid'
Old New York (1924) Edith Wharton
Ram second-hand bookseller
Daniel Deronda (1876) George Eliot (rn
Mary Anne, later Marian, Evans)
Rama herd-bull
ss 'Tiger Tiger'
The Jungle Book (1894) Rudyard Kipling
Ramage stockbroker, newspaper prop-
rietor
Ann Veronica (1909) H. G. Wells
Raman cc
Daisy his wife
The Painter of Signs (1976) R. K.

Narayan

Ramboat, Marion tea-gown designer, m.
(1) George Ponderevo*, (2) Wachorn
her mother
her aunt
Tono Bungay (1909) H. G. Wells

Rambow, von big landowner
Axel his son and heir
Franz his nephew, m. Lowise
Havermann*
Ut mine Stromtid (*An Old Story of my
Farming Days*) (1862–4) Fritz Reuter

Ramdez, Joe 'the Agent', shady Arab
Abdul; Suzi his children
The Mandelbaum Gate (1965) Muriel
Spark

Ramgolan Hindu sailor
Hard Cash (1863) Charles Reade

Ramorny, John, Sir Master of the House to
the Duke of Rothesay
The Fair Maid of Perth (1828) Walter
Scott

Ramos, Ishmael Columbia University
janitor who kills himself when his
football team loses
ss 'Roar Lion Roar'
Roar Lion Roar and Other Stories (1965)
Irvin Faust

Rampion, Mark partial portrait of D. H.
Lawrence*
Mary his wife
Point Counter Point (1928) Aldous
Huxley

Ramsay, David watchmaker and clock
constructor to James I
Margaret his daughter, m. Nigel
Olifaunt*
The Fortunes of Nigel (1822) Walter
Scott

Ramsay, Mrs
James her husband, professor of philo-
sophy, and in part based on the author's
father, Sir Leslie Stephen
Camilla their daughter
James their son
To the Lighthouse (1927) Virginia Woolf

Ramsden, J. St Rollo headmaster, St
Jerome's College
Before the Bombardment (1926) Osbert
Sitwell

Ramsden, Richard attempt at a portrayal
of D. H. Lawrence*, by a fellow imagist
poet

Miranda Masters (1926) John Cournos

Ramsden, Roebuck
Susan his sister
Man and Superman play (1903) George
Bernard Shaw

Ramsey, Mr client who came to offices of
Dodson and Fogg too late to settle his
debt – and had costs added
The Pickwick Papers (1837) Charles
Dickens

Ramshorn, Dr head of boys' school
Vanity Fair† (1847–8) W. M. Thackeray

Ramsummair, Ganesh, Pundit cc
The Mystic Masseur (1957) V. S. Naipaul

Rance, Albert
The Grapes of Wrath (1939) John
Steinbeck

Rand, Benjamin, Mrs believer in
Chance's* wisdom
Being There (1971) Jerzy Kosinski

Randall, William T., Captain drunkard,
bad hat
ss 'The Beach of Falesa'
Island Nights' Entertainments (1893)
Robert Louis Stevenson

Randan, Hermina de teasing caricature of
the lesbian novelist Marguerite Rad-
clyffe-Hall*, who was deeply hurt by
it
*Extraordinary Women, Theme and
Variations* (1928) Compton Mackenzie

Randolph very objectionable boy – and the
actual name, curiously, of bastard son
awarded to author by journalists
ss 'The Son's Veto'
Life's Little Ironies (1894) Thomas
Hardy

Randolph, Jim friend to George Webber*,
football star
The Web and the Rock (1929) Thomas
Wolfe

Randolph, Mr
ss 'A Naval Mutiny'
Limits and Renewals (1932) Rudyard
Kipling

Random, Roderick cc, narrator, m.
Narcissa Topehall*
Don Rodrigo his father
Charlotte his mother
Roderick Random (1748) Tobias Smoll-
ett

Randon, Varnum attempted portrait of
Randall Jarrell

Desolation Angels (1965) Jack Kerouac

Ranger, Mr young gentleman of the town in author's first play
Love in a Wood, or St James's Park play (1672) William Wycherley

Rangon
ss 'The Cigarette case'
Widdershins (1911) Oliver Onions

Rank, Father priest
The Heart of the Matter (1948) Graham Greene

Ranken, Robert m. Jenny Jimson*
The Horse's Mouth (1944) Joyce Cary

Rankin missionary
Captain Brassbound's Conversion play (1900) George Bernard Shaw

Rann the kite
ss 'Kaa's Hunting'
The Jungle Book (1894) Rudyard Kipling

Rann, Joshua shoemaker and parish clerk, Hayslope
Adam Bede (1858) George Eliot (rn Mary Anne, later Marian, Evans)

Rannock the lover
The King of Elfland's Daughter (1924) Lord Dunsany

Ransom, Basil Mississippi lawyer of conventional opinions who finally wins Verena Tarrant* from Olive Chancellor*
The Bostonians (1886) Henry James

Ransome cabin boy on the *Covenant*, murdered by Shuan*
Kidnapped (1886) Robert Louis Stevenson

Ransome, Captain fires on his own troops by order of a general who is killed, leaving him to take the blame, in American Civil War tale
ss 'One Kind of Officer'
Can Such Things Be? (1893) Ambrose Bierce

Ransome, John R. F. cc, m. Vi Usher*
Fulleylove his father
Emma his mother
The Combined Maze (1913) May Sinclair

Ranson reckless young lieutenant
ss 'Ranson's Folly'
Ranson's Folly (1902) Richard Harding Davis

Raoul, Duquette Parisian
ss 'Je ne parle pas Français'
Bliss (1920) Katherine Mansfield (rn Katherine Mansfield Beauchamp)

Raphael chemist
The Mystery of a Hansom Cab (1886) Fergus Hume

Raphaelson, Kermit midget, a painter
Laureen his wife
Malcolm (1959) James Purdy

Rapkin, Mrs Horace Ventimore's* landlady
her waiter husband
The Brass Bottle (1900) F. Anstey (rn Thomas Anstey Guthrie)

Rappaccini, Giacomo Professor of medicine whose intellectual curiosity is greater than his love for:
Beatrice his daughter, upon whom he experiments with poison
ss 'Rappaccini's Daughter' 1844
Mosses from an Old Manse (1846) Nathaniel Hawthorne

Rappit hairdresser, St Oggs
The Mill on the Floss (1860) George Eliot (rn Mary Anne, later Marian, Evans)

Rarx, Mr passenger who went mad in the long boat
The Wreck of the Golden Mary (1856) Charles Dickens

Ras ('The Exhorter') rabble-rousing West-Indian leader
The Invisible Man (1952) Ralph Ellison

Raskolnikov poor student, murderer, cc
his mother
Dunya his sister
Prestuplenie i Nakazanie (*Crime and Punishment*) (1866) Fyodor Dostoievsky

Rason, Inspector detective cc of ingenious and prized series
Hounded Down (1919) David Durham (rn Roy Vickers)
The Department of Dead Ends (1946) Roy Vickers

Rasor valet-de-chambre to Sir John Brute*
The Provok'd Wife play (1697) John Vanbrugh

Rasselas Abyssinian prince cc of stoical novel written in a romance-frame
Rasselas, Prince of Abyssinia (1759) Samuel Johnson

Rassendyll, Rudolf cc of the paradigmatic Ruritanian romance
The Prisoner of Zenda† (1894) Anthony Hope (rn Anthony Hope Hawkins)

Rassentlow, Johanna von ('**Hannele**') doll-

maker
ss 'The Captain's Doll'
The Captain's Doll (1923) (in UK as *The Ladybird*) D. H. Lawrence

Raste, Dr
Milly his wife
Eva his daughter
Riceyman Steps (1923); *Elsie and the Child* (1924) Arnold Bennett

Rastignac, Eugène de statesman
La Peau de Chagrin† (1831) Honoré de Balzac

Rat a water rat, partly inspired by the author's friend F. J. Furnivall, a scholar as well as a sculler
The Wind in the Willows (1908) Kenneth Grahame

Rat, Dr curate
Gammer Gurton's Needle play (1575) ?W. Stevenson

Ratchcali evil woman, friend to Ferdinand, Count Fathom*
The Adventures of Ferdinand, Count Fathom (1753) Tobias Smollett

Ratcliff, Mr
The Adventures of David Simple (1744–53) Sarah Fielding

Ratcliffe, Amos angelic youth
Eustace Chisholm and the Works (1968) James Purdy

Ratcliffe, Hubert humble friend and benefactor to Sir Edward Mauley*
The Black Dwarf (1816) Walter Scott

Ratcliffe, Inspector see **St Eustache, Marquis de**

Ratcliffe, James thief turned turnkey
Heart of Midlothian (1818) Walter Scott

Rathbone, Caspar illegitimate half-caste cousin to Sophia Willoughby*
Summer Will Show (1936) Sylvia Townsend Warner

Ratignolle, Adèle friend to Edna Pontellier*; 'faultless Madonna' who considers it a 'holy privilege' to efface herself; embodiment of patriarchal ideal
The Awakening (1899) Kate Chopin

Ratler, MP Liberal whip
Phineas Finn† (1869) Anthony Trollope

Ratliff, V. K. sewing machine agent
The *Snopes* trilogy (1940–49) William Faulkner

Ratner, James-julius eccentric character based in part on James Joyce* and in part

on the translator (of Céline* among others) John Rodker
The Apes of God (1930) Wyndham Lewis

Ratterer, Thomas bell-hop and drinking companion with Clyde Griffiths*
Louise his sister
An American Tragedy (1925) Theodore Dreiser

Rattray prefect
ss 'An Unsavoury Interlude'
Stalky & Co. (1899) Rudyard Kipling

Raunce, Charley butler, cc
Loving (1945) Henry Green

Raunham, John, Revd solitary bachelor
Desperate Remedies (1871) Thomas Hardy

Ravelston Comstock's* rich and kindly friend, socialist, editor of *Antichrist*, recognizes that while capitalism exists it is necessary to be corrupt
Keep the Aspidistra Flying (1936) George Orwell (rn Eric Blair)

Raven butler to Christopher Glowry*
Nightmare Abbey (1818) Thomas Love Peacock

Raven, June cc, narrator
ss 'More Friend Than Lodger'
A Bit off the Map (1957) Angus Wilson

Ravenal, Magnolia, *née* Hawkes, famous actress
Gaylord her husband, gambler and actor
Kim their daughter, also a famous actress, m. Kenneth Cameron*
Show Boat (1926) Edna Ferber

Ravender, Captain of the *Golden Mary*, who died in the long boat
The Wreck of the Golden Mary (1856) Charles Dickens

Ravenel see **Luxmore**

Ravenel, Lillie
Dr Ravenel, her father, Southern secessionist
Miss Ravenel's Conversion from Secession to Loyalty (1867) John William DeForest

Ravenshaw, Lord owner of Ecclesford in Cornwall, plays Baron Wildenheim in *Lovers' Vows*; one of the most correct men in England
Mansfield Park (1814) Jane Austen

Ravenshoe, Charles Protestant cc of popular and intricate novel by homosexual

and alcoholic brother of the more famous Muscular Christian
Densil his father
Ellen his sister
Ravenshoe (1861) Henry Kingsley
Ravenswing, The stage name of Mrs Howard Walker, *née* Crump
ss 'The Ravenswing'
Men's Wives (1843) W. M. Thackeray
Ravenswood, Edgar, Master of
Allan, Lord Ravenswood his father
Auld Ravenswood his grandfather
The Bride of Lammermoor (1819) Walter Scott
Rawkins eccentric apothecary-surgeon
The Adventures of Mr Ledbury (1844) Albert Smith
Rawkins, Simeon, Revd of Lady Whittlesea's chapel
The Newcomes (1853–5) W. M. Thackeray
Rawlins, Sal daughter to Mark Frettleby*
The Mystery of a Hansom Cab (1886) Fergus Hume
Rawson, Lieutenant
Barry Lyndon (1844) W. M. Thackeray
Ray, Shelley cc; author of *A Modern Romeo*
The World of Chance (1893) William Dean Howells
Rayber, George F. Satanic doer of good works; uncle to Tarwater*
Bernice his wife
Bishop his idiot son whom Tarwater is commanded to baptize
The Violent Bear It Away (1960) Flannery O'Connor
Raybrock, Miss postmistress at Steepways Village
Alf her brother
A Message from the Sea (1860) Charles Dickens
Raycie, Lewis who buys the 'wrong' pictures under influence of John Ruskin*
Beatrice his wife, *née* Kent*
Mr Raycie his philistine father
ss 'False Dawn'
Old New York (1924) Edith Wharton
Rivers, Condé (Condy) writer cc semi-autobiographical novel, m. Blix Bessemer*
Blix (1899) Frank Norris
Raye, Charles Bradford barrister who m.

Anna*, a maid
ss 'On The Western Circuit'
Life's Little Ironies (1894) Thomas Hardy
Rayland, Mrs nasty dominating old snob
The Old Manor House (1793) Mrs Charlotte Smith
Rayley, Paul in love with Minta Doyle*
To the Lighthouse (1927) Virginia Woolf
Raymond, Captain
Caleb Williams (1794) William Godwin
Raymond, Dr
The Great God Pan (1894) Arthur Machen
Raymond, Geoffrey alias **Spencer Gray**
Wilbur his uncle
A Damsel in Distress (1919) P. G. Wodehouse
Raymond, Tom nephew to Mrs Marlene Cooper*
The Bachelors (1961) Muriel Spark
Rayner, Daniel
Hildergarde his wife – fairly accurate portrayals of D. H. Lawrence* and his wife Frieda, as the author had known and encountered them
The South Wind of Love (1942) Compton Mackenzie
Raynor, Mrs milliner, mother to Janet Dempster*
ss 'Janet's Repentance'
Scenes of Clerical Life (1857) George Eliot (rn Mary Anne, later Marian, Evans)
Razumikhin friend to Raskolnikov*
Prestuplenie i Nakazanie (Crime and Punishment) (1866) Fyodor Dostoievsky
Razumov, Kirylo Sidorovitch cc, student in St Petersburg
Under Western Eyes (1911) Joseph Conrad (rn Josef Teodor Konrad Korzeniowski)
Reade, Richenbach
You Can't Go Home Again (1940) Thomas Wolfe
Ready, Masterman cc, old sailor who is wrecked with the Seagraves*; dies after being wounded by savage
Masterman Ready (1842) Captain Marryat
Reagan, Private
The Man Who Was There (1945) Wright Morris

Reardon, Edwin conscientious novelist and man of letters, foil to Milvain*
Amy his wife, m. Jasper Milvain*
New Grub Street (1891) George Gissing
Reba, Miss brothel keeper
Sanctuary (1931) William Faulkner
Rebecca daughter of Isaac of York, championed by Ivanhoe* – character modelled on that of 'a good Jewess' of that name – Rebecca Gratz, a German who settled in America – of whom the author had been told by Washington Irving*
Ivanhoe (1820) Walter Scott
Rebecca lazy servant to the Prices*
Mansfield Park (1814) Jane Austen
Rebecca mistress to Gwyn* ('his no vulgar taste;/The neat Rebecca – sly, observant, still;/Watching his eye, and waiting on his will') who 'honour'd still the priesthood in her fall' – he finally m. her 'And o'er his purse the lady takes control/ . . . /And fair Rebecca leads a virtuous life – /She rules a mistress, and she reigns a wife.'
The Borough poem (1810) George Crabbe
Rebow, Elijah cc, violent man who loves Mehalah Sharland* and burns her out of her home; m. Mehalah, is blinded by her, and finally drowns them both
his mad brother
Mehalah (1880) Sabine Baring-Gould
Rebura, Don
Donna Clara his wife
Donna Agnes; Philip; Martin his children
Mr Midshipman Easy (1836) Captain Marryat
Red Jacket American Indian
ss 'Brother Square Toes'†
Rewards and Fairies (1910) Rudyard Kipling
Red Knight, The
Alice Through the Looking-Glass (1872) Lewis Carroll (rn Charles Lutwidge Dodgson)
Red Man jealous murderer who kills Slim Girl*
Laughing Boy (1929) Oliver La Farge
Red Queen, The based on the real Alice's* (Alice Liddell) governess, a Miss Prickett, called by the Liddell family, Pricks
Alice Through the Looking-Glass (1872) Lewis Carroll (rn Charles Lutwidge

Dodgson
Red Reiver see **Willie of Westburnflat**
Red shanghaied American sailor on Pacific island
ss 'Red'
The Trembling of a Leaf (1921) W. Somerset Maugham
Red-haired Girl, The friend to Maisie, in love with Dick Heldar*
The Light that Failed (1890) Rudyard Kipling
Redbrook
Captain Brassbound's Conversion play (1900) George Bernard Shaw
Redburn, Jack librarian
Master Humphrey's Clock (1841) Charles Dickens
Redburn, Wellingborough young man on his first voyage
Redburn (1849) Herman Melville
Redcar, Lord coal-owner
In the Days of the Comet (1906) H. G. Wells
Reddick black man suffering from cancer of the rectum, cc
The Man Who Cried I Am (1967) John Williams
Redding, Robert
Mrs Wiggs of the Cabbage Patch (1901) Alice Hegan Rice
Redding, Rosamond schoolfriend to Katy Carr*
What Katy Did at School (1873) Susan Coolidge (rn Susan Chauncey Woolsey)
Redfern, Colonel father to Alison Porter*
Look Back in Anger play (1956) John Osborne
Redfern, George family man who is really a crook
Laburnam Grove play (1933) J. B. Priestley
Redforth, Bob related a stirring pirate yarn
A Holiday Romance (1858) Charles Dickens
Redgauntlet, Arthur Darsie, Sir brought up as **Darsie Latimer**
Sir Henry his father
his mother
Lilias his sister
Redgauntlet (1824) Walter Scott
Redherring, Remorse, Rabbi cc of novel about Sephardic Jews in 18th-century

London, by 'the Dickens of the Ghetto'
The King of Schnorrers (1894) Israel Zangwill

Reding, Charles cc whose religious agonies reflect those of the author in novel (for long unread) said to have influenced *Pendennis**
Loss and Gain (1848) John Henry Newman

Redington, Keith sailor cc of prolific author's most prized work
Nocturne (1917) Frank Swinnerton

Redlaw, Mr the haunted man
The Haunted Man (1848) Charles Dickens

Redmaynes of Lionsden neighbours to the Castlewoods*
The Virginians (1857–9) W. M. Thackeray

Redmond, Benjamin J. lawyer
The Unvanquished (1938) William Faulkner

Redmond, Rosie
The Plough and the Stars play (1926) Sean O'Casey (rn John Casey)

Redpenny medical student
The Doctor's Dilemma play (1906) George Bernard Shaw

Redruth, Tom of the *Hispaniola*
Treasure Island (1883) Robert Louis Stevenson

Redwood, Professor scientist
The Food of the Gods (1904) H. G. Wells

Redworth, Thomas long-standing faithful admirer and eventual husband of Diana Warwick*
Diana of the Crossways (1885) George Meredith

Reed, Dr m. Alice Barton*
A Drama in Muslin (1886) George Moore

Reed, Mary Jane Portnoy's girl
Portnoy's Complaint (1969) Philip Roth

Reed, Sarah Jane Eyre's* aunt, eventually repentant liar
her dead husband
John her favourite son, becomes a reprobate and kills himself
Georgiana; Eliza her daughters
Jane Eyre (1847) Charlotte Brontë

Rees, Aneurin bank manager, m. Blodwen Page
The Citadel (1937) A. J. Cronin

Rees, Attila, PC
Under Milk Wood play (1954) Dylan Thomas

Rees, Vaughan Ap, Sir suitor to Mistress Miniver*
Satiromastix, or The Untrussing of the Humorous Poet play (1602) Thomas Dekker (?with John Marston)

Reeves, Anna m. William Leadford*, as his second wife; based on the author's sometime lover and mother of his child, Amber Reeves
In the Days of the Comet (1906) H. G. Wells

Reeves, Archibald
his wife. Cousins to Harriet Byron*
Sir Charles Grandison (1754) Samuel Richardson

Reffold, Wilfred consumptive, fellow patient of Allitsen* and Bernadine Holme*
Winifred his wife
Ships That Pass in the Night (1893) Beatrice Harraden

Regan daughter to King Lear*
King Lear play (1623) William Shakespeare

Regan, Michael political boss, ruthless but honourable, based on 'Fingy' Connors of Buffalo
The Boss (1917) Edward Sheldon

Reganhart, Martha in love with Gabe Wallach*
Letting Go (1962) Philip Roth

Regnard, Baron suitor to Consuelo* with 'bulging spidery eyes'
Tot, kto poluchaet poshchochiny (*He Who Gets Slapped*, once tr. as *The Painted Laugh*) play (1916) Leonid Andreyev

Regula Baddun racehorse
ss 'The Broken Link Handicap'
Plain Tales from the Hills (1888) Rudyard Kipling

Reid labour agitator in unperformed play
The Strike at Arlingford play (1893) George Moore

Reignier, Duke of Anjou (hist.)
King Henry VI plays (1623) William Shakespeare

Reilley, Weary friend to Studs Lonigan*
Studs Lonigan trilogy (1932–5) James T. Farrell

Reilly Jocelyn Chadwick's* groom

Famine (1937) Liam O'Flaherty

Reilly, Agnes Dobell's* cook
Willie her son, gunman
The Moon in the Yellow River play (1932) Dennis Johnston

Reilly, Harry wealthy man
Appointment in Samarra (1935) John O'Hara

Reilly, Nora
John Bull's Other Island play (1904) George Bernard Shaw

Reingelder
ss 'Reingelder and the German Flag'
Life's Handicap (1891) Rudyard Kipling

Reinhart, Carlo happy cc of picaresque* series by American writer
Crazy in Berlin (1958); *Reinhart in Love* (1961); *Vital Parts* (1970); *Reinhart's Women* (1981) Thomas Berger

Reinhart, Hetty artist cc, Peter Stubland's* girl
Joan and Peter (1918) H. G. Wells

Reiver, Mrs fast and heartless Anglo-Indian
ss 'The Resistance of Pluffles'*
Plain Tales from the Hills (1888) Rudyard Kipling

Reldresal state secretary, Lilliput
Gulliver's Travels (1902) Jonathan Swift

Remedios, Jacintillo see **Innocencio, Padre**

Remington, Richard cc, forty-three-year-old philandering narrator of his autobiography: he sacrifices his political career for love of Isabel Rivers*
Margaret *née* Seddon, his high-minded wife
Arthur his father, science teacher
his mother
The New Machiavelli (1910) H. G. Wells

Remus, Uncle narrator, ex-slave
Aunt Tempy his sister
Uncle Remus (1880–95) Joel Chandler Harris

Rênal, de, M.
his wife, with whom Julien Sorel* has an affair
Le Rouge et le Noir (1830) Stendhal (rn Henri Bayle)

Renard French doctor
The Man Who Was Thursday (1908) G. K. Chesterton

Renart, Philippe
Lady Virginia ('Poots') his wife

The Thinking Reed (1936) Rebecca West (rn Cecily Fairfield)

Renata the Contessa loved by Col. Richard Cantrell*, based in part on the Venetian girl who designed the cover, Adriana Ivancich – in a book left unpraised even by the author's more enthusiastic critics
Across the River and Into the Trees (1950) Ernest Hemingway

Renato barber
The Roman Spring of Mrs Stone (1950) Tennessee Williams (rn Thomas Lanier Williams)

Renault
Venice Preserved play (1682) Thomas Otway

Rendal, Joe m. Mary Hill*
ss 'Three from Dunsterville'
The Man Upstairs (1914) P. G. Wodehouse

Rendezvous, Colonel
Mr Britling Sees It Through (1916) H. G. Wells

Renfrew, Dottie graduate of Vassar
The Group (1963) Mary McCarthy

Renisecure, Holifernes a barber's boy
The Dutch Courtesan play (1605) John Marston

Renling, Mrs wants to adopt Augie
The Adventures of Augie March (1953) Saul Bellow

Rennit, Mr private detective
The Ministry of Fear (1943) Graham Greene

Rentheim, Ella twin sister of Mrs Borkman*, whom Borkman* once rejected, although he loved her, in favour of getting his foot on the ladder
John Gabriel Borkman play (1896) Henrik Ibsen

Renzo humble peasant betrothed to Lucia* in what is often described as the greatest of all historical novels
I Promessi Sposi (*The Betrothed*) (1825–7, rev. 1840–2) Alessandro Manzoni

Repentigny, Le Gardeur de nice hero too easily led; entrapped by Bigot*; in historical novel
The Golden Dog (unauthorized 1887; 1896) William Kirby

Repton, Humphrey landscape gardener
Mansfield Park (1814) Jane Austen

Resker, Agnes
ss 'Tobemory'
The Chronicles of Clovis (1911) Saki (rn Hector Hugh Munro)
Rest one of Miss Flite's* captive birds
Bleak House (1853) Charles Dickens
Restaud, Comte de m. Anastasia Goriot*
Père Goriot (1834) Honoré de Balzac
Retlow alias **Muhlen** first husband of Mrs Meadows*
South Wind (1917) Norman Douglas
Reuben Israelite attendant on Isaac* and Rebecca*
Ivanhoe (1820) Walter Scott
Reuter, Zoraïde headmistress of girls' school, m. M. François Pelet*
her mother
The Professor (1857) Charlotte Brontë
Revel friend to the Walsinghams*
Kipps (1905) H. G. Wells
Rex, John cc dandy, convict, criminal; loved by Sarah Purfoy*
His Natural Life (1870–2; abridged by the author 1874; in 1885 as *For the Term of His Natural Life* – thus evading the author's irony; original text edited by Stephen Murray-Smith, 1970) Marcus Clarke
Rey, Pepe cc, tolerant and loving young man destroyed by forces of reaction
Doña Perfecta (1876) Benito Pérez Galdós
Reyer Anglo-French night manager
Imperial Palace (1930) Arnold Bennett
Reynard fox-hero of many (mostly French) fables and bestiaries symbolizing man who is brought to judgement for preying on society but escapes by cunning; from *c*.1200 in written form
Reynolds, Grace thought to be called Grace Nugent
The Absentee (1812) Maria Edgeworth
Reynolds, Miss pupil at Nun's House; pretended to stab herself in the hand with a pin
The Mystery of Edwin Drood (1870) Charles Dickens
Rheims, Archbishop of (hist.)
St Joan play (1924) George Bernard Shaw
Rhesos (hist.) sculptor
Aphrodite in Aulis (1931) George Moore
Rhetias a reduced courtier, servant to

Eroclea*
The Lover's Melancholy play (1629) John Ford
Rhiw, Evan
ss 'Lamentations'
My People (1915) Caradoc Evans (rn David Evans)
Rhoda one of the characters whose interior monologue* makes up this novel
The Waves (1931) Virginia Woolf
Rhys, Owen the author's notion of the American poet Witter Binner
The Plumed Serpent (1926) D. H. Lawrence
Riach second officer, *Covenant*
Kidnapped (1886) Robert Louis Stevenson
Riah, Mr ('Aaron') benevolent Jew made (by Fledgeby*) to look as if he were the grinding principal of Pubsey & Co*
Our Mutual Friend (1865) Charles Dickens
Ribbing, Adolf, Count cc ever-popular and much reprinted hist. novel by distant relative to the poet, who was also a notable poet herself
The King With Two Faces (1897) Mary Coleridge
Ribbons, Luke ex-felon, vicar's son, in love with Pearl Slattery*
The Revd Ichabod Ribbons, his father
Mrs Ribbons his mother, who lives mostly in the bath
Redhill Rococo (1986) Shena Mackay
Ribston, Mrs ('Ribby') cat, cousin to Tabitha Twitchit*
The Tale of Samuel Whiskers (1926) Beatrix Potter
Ribstone, Pepin, Sir
his wife
their son
Pendennis (1848) W. M. Thackeray
Rica, Petro, Don
Maritana; Mary m. Roland Cashel* his daughters
Roland Cashel (1850) Charles Lever
Ricardo, Mr uxorious wine-lover: the 'Watson'* to Inspector Hanaud* onwards from
At the Villa Rose (1910) A. E. W. Mason
Riccabocca, Dr Italian political exile, really a duke
My Novel, or Varieties in English Life

(1850–3) Edward Bulwer Lytton
Rice servant to Janicola*
The Pleasant Commedye of Patient Grissill play (1603) Thomas Dekker
Rice, Bessy m. Dude Lester*
Tobacco Road (1932) Erskine Caldwell
Rice, Sammy scientist cc, bomb disposer, narrator
The Small Back Room (1943) Nigel Balchin
Riceyman, T. T. deceased, uncle to Henry Earlforward*
Riceyman Steps (1923) Arnold Bennett
Rich, Brackenbury, Lieutenant
ss 'The Suicide Club'
The New Arabian Nights (1882) Robert Louis Stevenson
Rich, Mrs a wealthy widow, sister to Lord Bevill*, in love with Sir Frederick Frolick*
The Comical Revenge, or Love in a Tub play (1664) George Etherege
Richard Meg Veck's* sweetheart
The Chimes (1844) Charles Dickens
Richard, Uncle to Sir Francis Headpiece*
A Journey to London play (1728) John Vanbrugh
Richardetto quack
Hippolita his wife
'Tis Pity She's a Whore play (1633) John Ford
Richards ('Fatty') house servant
ss 'An Unsavoury Interlude'
Stalky & Co. (1899) Rudyard Kipling
Richards, Dr
How Green Was My Valley (1939) Richard Llewellyn
Richards, Milly m. Tony Kytes*
ss 'Tony Kytes, the Arch-Deceiver'
Life's Little Ironies (1894) Thomas Hardy
Richards, Mr
South Wind (1917) Norman Douglas
Richie friend to Helen Michel*
The World My Wilderness (1950) Rose Macaulay
Richie, Helena selfish woman who gradually realizes her shortcomings
The Awakening of Helena Richie (1906); *The Iron Woman* (1911) Margaretta Deland
Richland, Miss m. Honeywood*
The Good Natured Man play (1768)

Oliver Goldsmith
Richling, John Dr Sevier's* protégé; estranged from his family through marrying Northern girl
Dr Sevier (1882) George Washington Cable
Richmond, Harry cc, m. Janet Ilchester*
Augustus F. G. Roy his father, bastard of an actress and a 'royal personage' who lives a crazy life of semi-regal splendour interspersed with spells in debtor's prison; m. Marian Beltham
Anastasia Harry Richmond's mother, née Dewsbury
The Adventures of Harry Richmond (1871) George Meredith
Rickets, Mabel aged Northumbrian nurse
Rob Roy (1818) Walter Scott
Ricketts chauffeur who flirts with Eva*
The Pilgrim Hawk (1940) Glenway Westcott
Rickitts, Little junior pupil of weak constitution at Nun's House
The Mystery of Edwin Drood (1870) Charles Dickens
Rickman, Keith cockney poet modelled in part on Francis Thompson (not Ernest Dowson, as is sometimes stated) in novel of literary life which made its author famous
The Divine Fire (1905) May Sinclair
Rico rather tired portrait of D. H. Lawrence
Bid Me to Live (1960) H. D. (rn Hilda Doolittle)
Ridd, John later knighted; cc, narrator of wholesome, still popular (and much imitated) hist. romance, m. Lorna Doone*
Sarah his mother
Annie his sister
Lorna Doone (1869) R. D. Blackmore
Ridden, Highworth Foliat ('Hi') cc
Bill; Sarah his parents
Bell his sister
Odtaa (1926) John Masefield
Ridding, Mr and Mrs
Miss Mole (1930) E. H. Young
Rideout, Sampson cc, m. Delia Falkirk*, widow
Sampson Rideout, Quaker (1911) Una Silberrad
Riderhood, Rogue (Roger) waterside villain, drowned in a fight with Bradley

Headstone*
his wife, deceased
Pleasant their daughter, unlicensed pawnbroker; m. Mr Venus, taxidermist
Our Mutual Friend (1865) Charles Dickens
Ridge, Milly self-centred and selfish cc; m. (1) Jack Bragdon, (2) Edgar Duncan
One Woman's Life (1913) Robert Herrick
Ridgeon, Colenso, Sir doctor, based on woman-hating surgeon Sir Almroth Wright, who once said, 'Peace shall come about with the removal of surplus women by emigration' (but not surgery)
The Doctor's Dilemma play (1906) George Bernard Shaw
Ridler, Seton
Sir Marmaduke Ridler and Lady his parents
No. 5, John Street (1902) Richard Whiteing
Ridley Lord Barralonga's* chauffeur
Men Like Gods (1923) H. G. Wells
Ridley, John James ('J J') celebrated R A, friend to the Newcomes*
Samuel his father; butler and valet to Lord Todmorden*
his mother, ex-housekeeper
The Newcomes (1853–5) W. M. Thackeray
Ridvers, Charlie cinema owner
The Good Companions (1929) J. B. Priestley
Riebold Berman's partner
The Human Season (1960) Edward Lewis Wallant
Rieff, Morroe
To an Early Grave (1964) Wallace Markfield
Riesling, Paul artist forced to become businessman
Zilla his wife, whom he shoots
Babbitt (1922) Sinclair Lewis
Riga, Captain master of the *Highlander*
Redburn (1849) Herman Melville
Rigaud, M. alias Lagnier, alias Blandois; blackmailer, released from Marseilles prison for lack of evidence, on a charge of murdering his wife; killed in collapse of Mrs Clennam's* house
his deceased wife, widow of M. Henri Barroneau

Little Dorrit (1857) Charles Dickens
Rigby King's Proctor
Holy Deadlock (1934) A. P. Herbert
Rigby, John, MP for Tittleton
Barry Lyndon (1844) W. M. Thackeray
Rigby, Nicholas, the Rt. Hon. Lord Monmouth's political factotum
Coningsby (1844) Benjamin Disraeli
Rigg, Joshua see **Featherstone, Peter**
Rikki Tikki Tavi mongoose
ss 'Rikki Tikki Tavi'
The Jungle Book (1894) Rudyard Kipling
Riley auctioneer
Middlemarch (1871–2) George Eliot (rn Mary Anne, later Marian, Evans)
Riley, Kitty m. (1) Flanagan, (2) Tom Durfy*
Handy Andy (1842) Samuel Lover
Riley, Rabbit alias of Brer Rabbit*
Uncle Remus series (1880–95) Joel Chandler Harris
Riley, S. accountant
ss 'A Bank Fraud'
Plain Tales from the Hills (1888) Rudyard Kipling
Rima beautiful girl of the woods
Nuflo her grandfather
Green Mansions (1904) W. H. Hudson
Rimmer, Kay sister to Milly Drover*
It's a Battlefield (1935) Graham Greene
Rinaldi lieutenant and surgeon in Italian army
A Farewell to Arms (1929) Ernest Hemingway
Rinehart, B. P., Revd 'spiritual technologist'
The Invisible Man (1952) Ralph Ellison
Riney, Peter John Gourlay's* old servant
The House With the Green Shutters (1901) George Douglas
Ringert
Tracy's Tiger (1951) William Saroyan
Ringgan, Flora virtuous orphan in American bestseller of its day, thought by Elizabeth Barrett Browning* to be as good as *Uncle Tom's Cabin**
Queechy (1852) Elizabeth Wetherell (rn Susan Warner)
Ringwood, Earl
Lord Cinqbars; the Hon. Frederick; Sir John of Appleshaw his sons
the Hon. Thomas son to Lord Cinqbars
wife to Sir John

Philip; **Franklin** children to Sir John
Sir Francis brother to Earl Ringwood
Colonel Philip father to Mrs G. B. Firmin* and Mrs Troysden*
The Adventures of Philip (1862) W. M. Thackeray
Rink, Effie typist in Ponderevo's* office, and for a time his lover
Tono Bungay (1909) H. G. Wells
Rintoul, Earl of
The Little Minister (1891) J. M. Barrie
Riotor, Marie Leonie m. Sir Mark Tietjens*
Last Post (1928) Ford Madox Ford
Ripley, Tom educated psychopath and killer, devotee of the good life, cc of much valued series of superior crime fiction
Heloise his wife
The Talented Mr Ripley (1955); *Ripley Underground* (1970); *Ripley's Game* (1974); *The Boy Who Followed Ripley* (1980) Patricia Highsmith
Rippenger headmaster
Julia his wife
The Adventures of Harry Richmond (1871) George Meredith
Risingham, Earl
The Black Arrow (1888) Robert Louis Stevenson
Rita cc popular novel, m. Hubert Rochfort*
Sir Percival her father, a wastrel
her mother, who dies of smallpox
Rita (1856) Charles Aidé
Rita, Dona heiress of Henry Allegre*; cc
The Arrow of Gold (1919) Joseph Conrad (rn Josef Teodor Konrad Korzeniowski)
Ritchie-Hook, Ben, Brigadier company commander
Men at Arms (1952) Evelyn Waugh
Ritornello, Pasticcio
his three daughters
The Critic play (1779) Richard Brinsley Sheridan
Rivella popular author's name for herself in fictional, ironically layered history of her life (seduced into marriage by a bigamous cousin, left with a child to look after): 'She has very generous principles, for one of her sort; and a great deal of sense and invention' (Jonathan Swift)
The Adventures of Rivella, or The

History of the Author of the Atlantis (1714) Mrs Delariviere Manley (Also known as Mary Manley)
Rivers, Connie m. Rosasharn Joad*
The Grapes of Wrath (1939) John Steinbeck
Rivers, David in love with Belinda Churchill*
Belinda (1883) Rhoda Broughton
Rivers, Earl brother to Queen Elizabeth (hist.)
King Richard III play (1623) William Shakespeare
Rivers, Isabel assistant editor, the *Blue Weekly*
Sir Graham her father
The New Machiavelli (1911) H. G. Wells
Rivers, St John clergyman at Morton; takes in his cousin Jane Eyre*; goes to India to die; has terrifying self-control
Old Mr Rivers his dead father
Diana; Mary his sisters, governesses
Jane Eyre (1847) Charlotte Brontë
Riverton Cambridge graduate in love with Eleanor Scrope*
The Soul of a Bishop (1917) H. G. Wells
Rizzo, Enrico ('Ratso') cc, cripple from the Bronx
Midnight Cowboy (1966) James Leo Herlihy
Roanoke, Lucinda niece to Jane Carbuncle*, engaged to Sir Griffin Tewitt*
The Eustace Diamonds (1873) Anthony Trollope
Roantree, Liza
Jesse her father
ss 'On Greenhow Hill'
Life's Handicap (1891) Rudyard Kipling
Rob the Grinder see Toodle, Robin
Robarts, Mark, Revd Rector of Framley
Fanny his wife, *née* Monsell
his parents
Lucy his sister, m. Lord Lufton*
Framley Parsonage (1861) Anthony Trollope
Robbins, Captain of the *John*
Afloat and Ashore (1844) James Fenimore Cooper
Robert Wringhim man after whom Robert Wringhim (Colwan*) is named, and who is probably his real father; originally Calvinist tutor to Rabina Orde, later Lady Dalcastle*, and then to his namesake

The Private Memoirs and Confessions of a Justified Sinner (1824) as *The Suicide's Grave* (1828) as *Confessions of a Fanatic* in *Tales and Sketches* (1837) James Hogg

Robert, Count see **Paris**

Roberta farmer's daughter
Heaven's My Destination (1935) Thornton Wilder

Roberto King of Sicily
The Maid of Honour play (1632) Philip Massinger

Roberts, David leader of tin mine strikers
Strife play (1909) John Galsworthy

Roberts, John steersman on the *Jumping Jenny*
Redgauntlet (1824) Walter Scott

Roberts, Judson ex-football star
Elmer Gantry (1927) Sinclair Lewis

Robertson, George see **Staunton, George**

Robey millionaire who hires Augie March* to write a masterpiece defining the nature of man
The Adventures of Augie March (1953) Saul Bellow

Robie gardener to Miss Gilchrist*
St Ives (1897) Robert Louis Stevenson

Robin
Dr Faustus play (1604) Christopher Marlowe

Robin, Fanny servant betrayed by Troy*
Far From the Madding Crowd (1874) Thomas Hardy

Robinson ('Holy Terror') Chester's* partner
Lord Jim (1900) Joseph Conrad (rn Josef Teodor Konrad Korzeniowski)

Robinson bank manager
The Heart of the Matter (1948) Graham Greene

Robinson villain, real name Larrap
John Brent (1862) Theodore Winthrop

Robinson witty clerk in Dombey and Son
Dombey and Son (1948) Charles Dickens

Robinson, 'Red' formerly foreman, dye works
Nancy his cousin
A Glastonbury Romance (1932) J. C. Powys

Robinson, Ben storekeeper
A Lamp for Nightfall (1951) Erskine Caldwell

Robinson, Chris politician
The New Machiavelli (1911) H. G. Wells

Robinson, Dr body snatcher
The Adventures of Tom Sawyer (1876) Mark Twain (rn Samuel Langhorne Clemens)

Robinson, Hyacinth bastard orphan raised by Miss Pynsent*; cc of the author's only novel to attempt to deal with the lower classes
'Lord Frederick' his dead father – murdered by his executed French mother
The Princess Casamassima (1886) Henry James

Robinson, Léon Bardamu's* friend; shot by Madelon; has a 'weakness for independence'
Voyage au bout de la nuit (*Journey to the End of Night*) (1932) Louis-Ferdinand Céline (rn Louis-Ferdinand Destouches)

Robinson, Octavius
Violet his sister
Man and Superman play (1903) George Bernard Shaw

Robinson, Tom convict and gold prospector
It Is Never Too Late To Mend (1856) Charles Reade

Robson brother to Mrs Bloomfield*
Agnes Grey (1847) Anne Brontë

Robson, Sylvia cc of novel set in whaling town m. Philip Hepburn*
Daniel her father, farmer, hanged for attacking the press gang
her mother
Sylvia's Lovers (1863) Mrs Gaskell

Roby, Dr
Tancred (1847) Bejamin Disraeli

Roby, Mrs who invents 'Xingu' (actually the name of a Brazilian river), a topic which all the ladies of the Lunch Club, a ladies' literary discussion group, learnedly discuss; as she tells them, 'a very brilliant man . . . told me that it was best for women not to get at the source'
ss 'Xingu'
Roman Rever (1911) Edith Wharton

Roby, Thomas, MP Tory whip
Phineas Finn† (1869) Anthony Trollope

Roch beggar, friend of the peasants, in Nobel-Prize-winning series by Polish author
Chlopi (*The Peasants*) (1902–9, tr. 1925–6) Wladislaw Stanislaw Reymont

Roch, Léon young scientist cc

Maria his wife, who wishes to convert him to religion
La Familia de Léon Roch (1878) Benito Peréz Galdós

Rochcliffe, Lady Eleanore haughty beauty who 'scorned the sympathies of nature'
ss 'Lady Eleanore's Mantle' (1838)
Twice-Told Tales (1842) Nathaniel Hawthorne

Roche, Alban assistant in pet shop, in love with Prudence Tuke*
Miss Gomez and the Brethren (1971) William Trevor

Roche, Christina illegitimate farm hand, m. Emil Pahren*
Without My Cloak (1931) Kate O'Brien

Roche, Father
Famine (1937) Liam O'Flaherty

Rochecliffe, Joseph Albany, Dr alias **Joseph Albany**, practical joker, antiquarian and alleged discoverer of the material of the book
Woodstock (1826) Walter Scott

Rochefidele, Count
his wife
The American (1877) Henry James

Rochemort dapper fop, professor
Villette (1853) Charlotte Brontë

Rochester, Edward Fairfax cc, recluse, guardian of Adele Varens*; eventually m. Jane Eyre*
Bertha his mad wife
Mr Rochester his grasping deceased father
Rowland his elder brother
Jane Eyre (1847) Charlotte Brontë

Rocinante Don Quixote's* steed, a cart-horse ill-equipped to deal with high and noble adventure
Don Quixote (1605–15) Miguel de Cervantes

Rockaly magistrate
ss 'The Two Captains'
Unlucky for Pringle (1973) Wyndham Lewis

Rockminster, Countess of 'centre of fashion'
The Dowager Countess
Pendennis (1848) W. M. Thackeray

Rocque, M. swindler and killer
Louise his daughter, m. Deslauriers*
L'Education sentimentale (1869) Gustave Flaubert

Rod, Genevieve friend to John Andrews*
Three Soldiers (1921) John Dos Passos

Rodd, Martha 'prim snippet of a maid'
ss 'The Almond Tree'
The Riddle (1923) Walter de la Mare

Roddice, Hermione owner of an estate; the author's unkind portrait of Lady Ottoline Morell, who felt that it was 'so loathsome one cannot get clean after it'
Women in Love (1921) D. H. Lawrence

Roden, Mr and Mrs uncle and aunt to Caryl Bramsley*
C (1924) Maurice Baring

Roderick, Veronica rich company director's mistress
Hurry On Down (1953) John Wain

Roderigo Venetian gentleman
Othello play (1623) William Shakespeare

Rodman, James author of sensational mysteries, cousin to Mulliner*
Meet Mr Mulliner (1927) P. G. Wodehouse

Rodman, Julius English emigrant who crosses Rocky Mountains; in largely plagiarized narrative
The Journal of Julius Rodman (1840) Edgar Allan Poe

Rodney, Jim poacher, mole catcher
Silas Marner (1861) George Eliot (rn Mary Anne, later Marian, Evans)

Rodney, Stella attractive widow
Roderick her soldier son
The Heat of the Day (1949) Elizabeth Bowen

Rodrigo, Don see **Random, Roderick**

Roe travelling preacher
Adam Bede (1859) George Eliot (rn Mary Anne, later Marian, Evans)

Roederer 'licentiate' and author
Prince Otto (1885) Robert Louis Stevenson

Roehampton, Lord who was over-taxed and jeopardized his vocal chord
More Peers verse (1911) Hilaire Belloc

Roger of Salerno
ss 'The Eye of Allah'
Debits and Credits (1926) Rudyard Kipling

Roger, Father mentally deranged clergyman
The World My Wilderness (1950) Rose Macaulay

Rogers, Ben
The Adventures of Tom Sawyer (1876)
Mark Twain (rn Samuel Langhorne
Clemens)
Rogers, Jasper, Sir Chief Justice, Calcutta
Pendennis (1848) W. M. Thackeray
Rogers, Mildred (alias **Mrs Miller**) slat-
ternly cc to whom Carey* is helplessly
bound
Of Human Bondage (1915) W. Somerset
Maugham
Rogers, Milton K. Lapham's* partner
The Rise of Silas Lapham (1885) William
Dean Howells
Roget, Marie cc, Parisian beauty (the facts
were based on the real case of Mary
Cecilia Rogers) whose murder is solved
by Dupin*
ss 'The Mystery of Marie Roget'
Tales (1845) Edgar Allan Poe
Rogozhin lustful husband to Natasya
Filippovna*, whom he kills
Idiot (1869) Fyodor Dostoievsky
Rohan, Archibald, Lord
his wife, Uncle and aunt to Barty
Josselin*; his guardians
The Martian (1897) George du Maurier
Roister Doister, Ralph cc
Ralph Roister Doister play (1551)
Nicholas Udall
Rojack, Stephen Richards former con-
gressman cc
Deborah Kelly his society hostess wife
from whom he has long been separated,
and whom he murders
An American Dream (1965) Norman
Mailer
Rojas, General Vice-President, Olancho
Soldiers of Fortune (1897) Richard
Harding Davis
Roker, Tom turnkey who receives Mr
Pickwick* at the Fleet Prison
The Pickwick Papers (1837) Charles
Dickens
Rokesmith, John see **Harmon, John**
Roland cc
ss 'A Breton Innkeeper'
Unlucky for Pringle (1973) Wyndham
Lewis
Roland, Stephen father to Becky Warder*
The Truth play (1907) Clyde Fitch
Rolewicz, Josef Polish soldier, first hus-
band of Bessie Hipkiss*

Jezebel's Dust (1951) Fred Urquhart
Rolfe, John (hist.); tobacco master who m.
Pocahantas*
The First Settlers of Virginia (1805) John
Davis
The Indian Princess or *La Belle Sauvage*
play (1808) James Nelson Barker
My Lady Pocahantas (1885) J. E. Cooke
Pocahantas (1933) David Garnett
Rolla
Pizarro play (1799) Richard Brinsley
Sheridan
Rolles, Gregory Cambridge student
The Saliva Tree (1966) Brian W. Aldiss
Rolles, Simon, Revd lodger with Raeburn;
nurseryman
ss 'The Rajah's Diamonds'
The New Arabian Nights (1882) Robert
Louis Stevenson
Rolleston valet
The Admirable Crichton play (1902)
J. M. Barrie
Rolleston, Felix
The Mystery of a Hansom Cab (1886)
Fergus Hume
Rolliver, James J. m. Indiana Frusk*
The Custom of the Country (1913) Edith
Wharton
Rolliver, Mrs landlady
Tess of the D'Urbervilles (1891) Thomas
Hardy
Rollo series of twenty-eight moral tales of
a boy whose experiences on a New
England Farm and elsewhere were used
to extol the obvious virtues, onwards
from
The Rollo Books (1834) Jacob Abbott
Rolt, Helen castaway who becomes lover
of Harry Scobie*
The Heart of the Matter (1948) Graham
Greene
Romagna executed innocent radical (cf
Sacco and Vanzetti)
Bartolomeo ('**Mio**') his son, cc
Winterset play (1935) Maxwell
Anderson
Romaine, Daniel solicitor to St Yves*
St Ives (1898) Robert Louis Stevenson
Romarin painter
ss 'The Accident'
Widdershins (1911) Oliver Onions
Romashov, Sub-Lieutenant idealist
sacrificed to the ambitions of his married

lover; in important Russian novel
The Duel (1905) A. Kuprin

Rome, Adrian cc, young artist
Adrian Rome (1899) Ernest Dowson and
Arthur Moore

Rome, ⸱. ᵢrora actress
ss 'The Man in the Passage'
The Wisdom of Father Brown (1914)
G. K. Chesterton

Romeo cc, of the House of Montague*;
lover of Juliet*
Montague his father, head of his house
Lady Montague his mother
Romeo and Juliet play (1623) William
Shakespeare

Romero, Pedro Spanish bull-fighter
The Sun Also Rises (1926) Ernest
Hemingway

Romford, Facey self-made MFH, cc
Mr Facey Romford's Hounds (1865) R.
S. Surtees

Romfrey, Everard reactionary uncle of
Nevile Beauchamp* who relents only
when his nephew lies at death's door
Beauchamp's Career (1876) George
Meredith

Romilayu guide
Henderson The Rain King (1959) Saul
Bellow

Rondabale princess affianced to Alasi*
Vathek (1786) William Beckford

Rook, Tom, Captain crook and black-
guard
Revd Athanasius his father
Harriet his sister
ss 'Captain Rook'
Character Sketches (1841) W. M.
Thackeray

Rooke, Nurse a shrewd woman who gives
her services without charge
Persuasion (1818) Jane Austen

Rookwood family ccs of author's first
Gothic-historical success, reckoned to be
his most lively novel
Rookwood (1834) William Harrison
Ainsworth

Rooney, Andy cc, whose nickname gave a
term to the language; later Lord
Scatterbrain; m. his cousin Oonah
Lord Scatterbrain his father (alias
Rooney)
the Hon. Sackville his brother
Handy Andy (1842) Samuel Lover

Rooney, Paul attorney
his wife
Jack Hinton (1843) Charles Lever

Rooster, Viscount see **Dorking, Earl of**

Rooter, Alfred, Lord and Lady
C (1924) Maurice Baring

Rooth, Miriam cc, egocentric and empty –
but gifted and aware actress
The Tragic Muse (1890) Henry James

Roothing, Bobby London journalist in
love with Christina Alberta
Christina Alberta's Father (1925) H. G.
Wells

Rooum strange character with 'black and
white piebald head' possessed of mysterious scientific knowledge
ss 'Rooum'
Widdershins (1911) Oliver Onions

Rosa maid, m. Watt Rouncewell*
Bleak House (1853) Charles Dickens

Rosalba rightful Queen of Crim Tartary,
m. Prince Giglio*
The Rose and the Ring (1855) W. M.
Thackeray

Rosalind (alias **Ganymede**) daughter of the
banished Duke; m. Orlando*
As You Like It play (1623) William
Shakespeare

Rosaline attending on princess
Love's Labour's Lost play (1623)
William Shakespeare

Rosalura an airy daughter to Nantolet*
The Wild-Goose Chase play (1652) John
Fletcher

Rosanette (**'The Marshal'**) mistress to
Moreau*
L'Education sentimentale (1869)
Gustave Flaubert

Rosario see **Matilda**

Rosbart, Amy (hist.) m. Earl of Leicester
Sir Hugh her father
Kenilworth (1821) Walter Scott

Rose 'a seduced woman' who arrives with
Mr Evelyn*
Margaret (1845, rev. 1851) Sylvester
Judd

Rose Cottage, Mrs
Mae her eldest
Under Milk Wood play (1954) Dylan
Thomas

Rose i.e. Walter Pater*
The New Republic or *Culture, Faith and
Philosophy in an English Country House*

(1877; edition by John Lucas, 1975, lists originals of characters) William Hurrell Mallock

Rose neurotic murderess of her mother-in-law
Nobody Answered the Bell (1971) Rhys Davies

Rose signalman, *Compass Rose*
The Cruel Sea (1951) Nicholas Monsarrat

Rose, George Arthur Englishman who becomes Pope
Hadrian the Seventh (1904) Baron Corvo (rn Frederick Rolfe)

Rose, Gregory Nazianzen
Jemima his sister
The Story of an African farm (1883) Olive Schreiner

Rose, Hester shop assistant at the Fosters'*
Alice her mother
Sylvia's Lovers (1863) Mrs Gaskell

Rose, Otto, Revd head of Richmond Preparatory School
his wife and son
The Book of Snobs (1847) W. M. Thackeray

Rose, Revd Mr independent minister
ss 'Janet's Repentance'
Scenes of Clerical Life (1857) George Eliot (rn Mary Anne, later Marian, Evans)

Rose, Sergeant-Major
The Small Back Room (1943) Nigel Balchin

Rose, Timothy gentleman farmer, Leek Malton
Felix Holt (1866) George Eliot (rn Mary Anne, later Marian, Evans)

Roseberry, Grace
The New Magdalen (1873) Wilkie Collins

Rosedale, Simon rich and vulgar suitor of Lily Bart*, who refuses her when she changes her mind
The House of Mirth (1905) Edith Wharton

Roseilli a young nobleman
Love's Sacrifice play (1633) John Ford

Roseley, Jackson, Sir and Lady
Evan Harrington (1861) George Meredith

Rosemary girl in love with Comstock* who has not slept with him; but she does

eventually, in deservedly famous (and tender) episodes; m. Comstock
Keep the Aspidistra Flying (1936) George Orwell (rn Eric Blair)

Rosen, Anna, Countess von
Prince Otto (1885) Robert Louis Stevenson

Rosenbaum, Mr
The Treasure Seekers (1899) E. Nesbit

Rosencrantz courtier
Hamlet play (1623) William Shakespeare

Rosenthall, Nathan diamond fence
Raffles (1899–1901) E. W. Hornung

Rosetree, Harry (originally Haim Rosenbaum) factory owner
Riders in the Chariot (1961) Patrick White

Rosewater, Victor
The Thin Man (1934) Dashiell Hammett

Rosherville, Earl of
Lady Ann Milton his daughter, m. Revd Mr Hobson*
Pendennis (1848) W. M. Thackeray

Rosie child
ss 'Miss Miller'
The Wind Blows Over (1936) Walter de la Mare

Rosin, Father the minstrel
A Tale of a Tub play (1640) Ben Jonson

Ross, Colonel owner of Silver Blaze
ss 'Silver Blaze'
The Memoirs of Sherlock Holmes (1894) Arthur Conan Doyle

Ross, Duncan confederate of John Clay*
ss 'The Red-headed League'
The Adventures of Sherlock Holmes (1892) Arthur Conan Doyle

Ross, Kenneth, Captain uncle to Alan Merivale*, m. Maud Carthew*
Sinister Street (1913) Compton Mackenzie

Rosse Scottish noble
Macbeth play (1623) William Shakespeare

Rosse, Jenny
Billy her husband
ss 'A Dead Cert'
The Talking Trees (1971) Sean O'Faolain

Rossetti, Dante Gabriel (hist.)
The French Lieutenant's Woman (1969) John Fowles

Rosy, Dr
St Patrick's Day play (1775) Richard

Brinsley Sheridan

Rothschild, Father Jesuit
Vile Bodies (1930) Evelyn Waugh

Rougedragon, Rachel, Lady 'a meagre old Scotch lady'
Redgauntlet (1824) Walter Scott

Rougierre, Madam de la governess to Maud Ruthyn*; drunkard and villainess
Uncle Silas (1864) J. Sheridan Le Fanu

Rouncewell, George ('Bluffy') ex-trooper, owner of shooting-gallery, arrested on suspicion of murdering Tulkinghorn*; later released; becomes servant-companion to Sir Leicester Dedlock*
his elder brother, successful ironmaster
Watt the ironmaster's son, m. Rosa*
his mother, devoted housekeeper to the Dedlocks
Bleak House (1853) Charles Dickens

Rouncy, Miss actress friend to Miss Fotheringay*
Pendennis (1848) W. M. Thackeray

Roundhand secretary, *West Diddlesex Independent*
Ann Milly his vulgar wife
The Great Hoggarty Diamond (1841) W. M. Thackeray

Rousard elder son to D'Amville*
The Atheist's Tragedy, or The Honest Man's Revenge play (1611/12) Cyril Tourneur

Rousillon, Countess of mother to Bertram*
All's Well That Ends Well play (1623) William Shakespeare

Routh butler (alias Tuke)
his down-and-out brother
The Power House (1916) John Buchan

Routh, Joanna
Fargie her husband
Farewell, Miss Julie Logan (1932) J. M. Barrie

Rover, Ralph fifteen-year-old cc of author's best and most popular book for boys
Coral Island† (1858) R. M. Ballantyne

Rover, The Red see **Longueville, Thomas de**

Rovere, del, Mosca cc
La Chartreuese de Parme (1839) Stendhal (rn Henri Bayle)

Rowan, Laura young girl, granddaughter to Count Nikolai Diakonov*

Tania; Edward her parents
The Birds Fall Down (1966) Rebecca West (rn Cecily Fairfield)

Rowan, Richard Irish writer
Bertha his common-law wife
Archie their son
Exiles play (1918) James Joyce

Rowbotham editor, the *Wire*
When a Man's Single (1888) J. M. Barrie

Rowbotham, Denise English au pair girl let loose in an unnamed European country, who may possess the key to the country's politics, and to the problem of why the garden was ploughed up
Enemies: A Novel About Friendship (1977) Giles Gordon

Rowdon, Lord wild man in pursuit of Rita*
Rita (1856) Charles Aidé

Rowdy, John banker, of Stumpy, Rowdy & Co.
Arthur his son and partner
Lady Cleopatra Arthur's wife, *née* Stonehenge
Sketches and Travels (1850) W. M. Thackeray

Rowe, Arthur ('Digby') cc, m. Anna Hilfe*
The Ministry of Fear (1943) Graham Greene

Rowena, Lady of Hargottstandestede; descendant of Alfred the Great, m. Ivanhoe*
Ivanhoe (1820) Walter Scott

Rowens, Marilla widow
Elsie Venner (1861) Oliver Wendell Holmes

Rowland, Sergeant Sir Barnes Newcome's counsel
The Newcomes (1853–5) W. M. Thackeray

Rowley steward to Sir Oliver Surface*
The School for Scandal play (1777) Richard Brinsley Sheridan

Rowley valet to the Count de St Yves*
St Ives (1897) Robert Louis Stevenson

Rowley, Marmaduke, Sir colonial governor
his eight daughters
He Knew He Was Right (1869) Anthony Trollope

Roxy almost white slave of Percy Driscoll
Chambers her son by a Virginian gentleman adopted by Judge Driscoll* in the

belief that he is Tom Driscoll; a coward and snob who sells his mother to pay his gambling debts
The Tragedy of Pudd'nhead Wilson (1894) Mark Twain (rn Samuel Langhorne Clemens)
Roy, Richmond see **Richmond, Harry**
Roy, Rob see **MacGregor, Robert** or **Robin**
Royal
Mrs Dukes' Million (1977) Wydham Lewis
Royce, Jane, Lady
Julia her daughter
The Martian (1897) George du Maurier
Royce, Vernon master of a Cambridge college
Lady Muriel his wife
Joan their daughter
The Masters (1951) C. P. Snow
Roylance, Archibald, Sir, Baronet
Huntingtower (1922) John Buchan
Roylott, Grimesby, Dr
ss 'The Speckled Band'
The Adventures of Sherlock Holmes (1892) Arthur Conan Doyle
Ruark
Rukrooth his mother
The Shaving of Shagpat (1856) George Meredith
Rubashov, Nicholas victim of unjust trial and execution in famous account of totalitarian methods of Stalin
Darkness at Noon (1941) Arthur Koestler
Rubb, Samuel Tom Mackenzie's* dishonest partner in the oilcloth business
Miss Mackenzie (1863) Anthony Trollope
Rubelle, Mme
her husband
The Woman in White (1860) Wilkie Collins
Rubrick, Revd Mr non-juring clergyman
his four daughters
Waverley (1814) Walter Scott
Rucastle, Jephro
his wife
Alice their daughter
ss 'The Copper Beeches'
The Adventures of Sherlock Holmes (1892) Arthur Conan Doyle
Ruddiman assistant master

ss 'The Pig and Whistle'
The House of Cobwebs (1906) George Gissing
Rudge Rye grocer and smuggler
Sukey his daughter
Denis Duval (1864) W. M. Thackeray
Rudge, Mr steward to and murderer of Reuben Haredale*; hanged
Mary his wife
Barnaby his half-witted son, sentenced to hang but reprieved
Barnaby Rudge (1841) Charles Dickens
Rudkus, Julius Slav immigrant cc of scarifying public-service* novel about meat-packing industry, which led to reforms; m. Ona Lukoszaite
The Jungle (1906) Upton Sinclair
Rudolf the Fifth King of Ruritania
The Prisoner of Zenda (1894) Anthony Hope (rn Anthony Hope Hawkins)
Ruff Harry Warrington's* landlord
his wife
The Virginians (1857–9) W. M. Thackeray
Rufford, Lord wealthy aristocrat pursued by Arabella Trefoil*
The American Senator (1877) Anthony Trollope
Rufford, Nancy Leonora Ashburnham's* ward, in love and loved by Edward Ashburnham*
The Good Soldier (1915) Ford Madox Ford
Rufio
Caesar and Cleopatra play (1900) George Bernard Shaw
Rufus, William (hist.)
Satiromastix, or The Untrussing of the Humorous Poet (1602) Thomas Dekker
Rugg, Anastasia acquired a little property as a result of a successful breach of promise action against a middle-aged baker called Hawkins
her father, debt-collector, Pancks's* landlord
Little Dorrit (1857) Charles Dickens
Ruggles, Rick Curate to Ichabod Ribbons*, after children's souls through Taskforce ('I've asked God's forgiveness for losing my cool. . . . We had a good old chat')
Redhill Rococo (1986) Shena Mackay
Ruggles, Ruby m. George Crumb*

Daniel her grandfather, of Sheeps Acre farm
The Way We Live Now (1875) Anthony Trollope
Ruin one of Miss Flite's* captive birds
Bleak House (1853) Charles Dickens
Ruiz, Camilla, Mme wealthy hostess
Vitorio her son, who seduces Edna Mouth
Prancing Nigger (1924) Ronald Firbank
Rukh, Raja of suave figure in romantic melodrama with literary allusions; made very popular by the performance of George Arliss in this part
The Green Goddess play (1921) William Archer
Rumbold Fishbourne china dealer
his wife and mother-in-law
The History of Mr Polly (1910) H. G. Wells
Rumbold, George artist
Clara his pretty sister
Our Street (1848) W. M. Thackeray
Rumty see **Wilfer**
Runi South American Indian chief
Green Mansions (1904) W. H. Hudson
Runnington, Mr Charles Aubrey's* solicitor
Ten Thousand a Year (1839) Samuel Warren
Runswick, Lord father to Barty Josselin*
The Martian (1897) George du Maurier
Runt, Revd Mr chaplain to Lady Lyndon*
Barry Lyndon (1844) W. M. Thackeray
Rushbrook nephew to Lord Elmwood*
A Simple Story (1791) Elizabeth Inchbald
Rushworth, Maria née Bartram*
James her husband
Mansfield Park (1814) Jane Austen
Rushworth, Mr heavy young man; m. and then divorces Mary Bertram* when she elopes with Henry Crawford*
his pompous mother
Mansfield Park (1814) Jane Austen
Rusk, Hubert tutor to Denis Bracknel
The Bracknels (1911) Forrest Reid
Rusk, Mrs aged housekeeper to Austin Ruthyn*
Uncle Silas (1864) J. Sheridan Le Fanu
Ruskin, John (hist.); as advisor to Raycie*
ss 'False Dawn'
Old New York (1924) Edith Wharton
Rusper ironmonger, Fishbourne

his wife
The History of Mr Polly (1910) H. G. Wells
Rusport, Lady unscrupulous intriguer
Charlotte her stepdaughter, cousin to Charles Dudley*, whom she m.
The West Indian play (1771) Richard Cumberland
Russell brother of Lady Ager*
Jane his daughter, secretly married to Fitzallen*
A Fair Quarrel play (1617) Thomas Middleton and William Rowley
Russell, Lady widow of steady age and character, combining correctness of conduct with benevolence and respect for rank; close friend to Lady Elliot*
Persuasion (1818) Jane Austen
Russell, Myra cc
Maybe (1967) Burt Blechman
Rust, Ezekiel
Isabella his wife
Odtaa (1926) John Masefield
Rut physician to Lady Loadstone*
The Magnetic Lady, or Humours Reconciled play (1641) Ben Jonson
Ruth pirate maid-of-all-work
The Pirates of Penzance opera (1880) W. S. Gilbert and Arthur Sullivan
Ruth professional bridesmaid
Ruddigore opera (1887) W. S. Gilbert and Arthur Sullivan
Ruth Zionist with whom Clarel* falls in love
Clarel poem (1876) Herman Melville
Ruth, Dusky
ss 'Dusky Ruth'
Adam and Eve and Pinch Me (1921) A. E. Coppard
Ruth, Helen
ss 'A Wife of Nashville'
Collected Stories (1969) Peter Taylor
Rutherford, Edward traveller in Louisiana who saves beautiful Creole Eugénie Besançon* in novel (later adapted as successful play); m. Aurore
The Quadroon (1856) Thomas Mayne Reid
The Octoroon play (1859) Dion Boucicault
Rutherford, Mark cc of autobiographical novel of outstanding interest; minister who loses his faith

The Autobiography of Mark Rutherford (1881) Mark Rutherford (rn William Hale White)

Ruthyn, Maud cc, narrator
Austin her father
Silas her uncle
Milly; Dudley m. Sarah Mangles* Silas' children
Uncle Silas (1864) J. Sheridan Le Fanu

Rutledge, Henry Harvard professor of political theory
his alcoholic wife
his children
The Professor's Daughter (1971) Piers Paul Read

Rutledge, Job smuggler
Redgauntlet (1824) Walter Scott

Ruy Dias lover to Quisara*
The Island Princess play (1647) John Fletcher

Ryan, Eddie cc, Chicago student who loses his Catholic faith in tetralogy reckoned inferior to *Studs Lonigan*
his grandmother, *née* Hogan
Joseph Dunne his dead grandfather
The Silence of History (1963); *What Time Collects* (1964); *Lonely Future* (1966); *When Time Was Born* (1967) James T. Farrell

Rycker, André manager of a palm-oil factory
Marie his wife
A Burnt-Out Case (1961) Graham Greene

Ryde, Hillingdon, D D
Jenny his wife
Adam of Dublin† (1920) Conal O'Connell O'Reardon (rn F. Norreys Connell)

Ryder, Charles narrator, m. Lady Celia, sister to Lord Mulcaster*
John; Caroline their children
Charles's father
Jasper his cousin
Brideshead Revisited (1945) Evelyn Waugh

Ryder, Jaffe supposed portrait of American Buddhist poet Gary Snyder
The Dharma Bums (1958) Jack Kerouac

Ryder, James head attendant at the Hotel Cosmopolitan
ss 'The Blue Carbuncle'
The Adventures of Sherlock Holmes (1892) Arthur Conan Doyle

Ryder, Samson a hard, cold man
Black Beauty (1877) Anna Sewell

Ryder, Violet
Poor Women (1929) Norah Hoult

Ryecroft, Henry pseudonym for the author, whose (non-fictional) meditations these are
The Private Papers of Henry Ryecroft (1903) George Gissing

Rylett, Alf in love with Emmy Blanchard*
Nocturne (1917) Frank Swinnerton

S

Saas-Fee, Dr picture restorer
Museum Pieces (1952) William Plomer
Sabin, Mr villain and spy of mysterious
(foreign) origins, cc of the novel which
made the prolific author's name, which
once stood high among writers of espion-
age thrillers
The Mysterious Mr Sabin (1898) E.
Phillips Oppenheim
Sabina, Lily maid who nearly tempts
Antrobus* from his wife
The Skin of Our Teeth play (1942)
Thornton Wilder
Sabre, Mark idealist cc, an author unjustly
accused of murder in bestseller of its time
Mabel his wife
If Winter Comes (1921) A. S. M.
Hutchinson
Sacharissa girl graduate
Princess Ida opera (1884) W. S. Gilbert
and Arthur Sullivan
Sackbut curate and tutor
Peregrine Pickle (1751) Tobias Smollett
Sackbut, Roderick caricature of Robert
Southey
Nightmare Abbey (1818) Thomas Love
Peacock
Sackett district attorney
The Postman Always Rings Twice (1934)
James M. Cain
Sackett, Bob young New Yorker who
becomes engaged to four women at once
Saratoga, or *Pistols for Seven* play (1870)
Bronson Howard
Saddletree, Bartoline harness-maker
his wife
Heart of Midlothian (1818) Walter Scott
Sadrach of Danyrefail
Ascsah his wife
their eight children
ss 'A Father in Sion'
My People (1915) Caradoc Evans (rn
David Evans)
Sady George Esmond's Negro servant
The Virginians (1857–9) W. M.

Thackeray
Safie Arabian refugee, in love with Felix de
Lacey
Frankenstein (1818) Mary Shelley
Sagacity
The Pilgrim's Progress (1678–84) John
Bunyan
Sagely, Mrs friend to Random*
Roderick Random (1748) Tobias Smoll-
ett
Saggers, Mrs elderly inmate of Titbull's
Almshouses
The Uncommercial Traveller (1860–8)
Charles Dickens
Sahi the porcupine
ss 'Letting in the Jungle'
The Second Jungle Book (1895) Rudyard
Kipling
Sailors, Sinbad in love with Gossamer
Beynon*
Mary Ann his grandmother
Under Milk Wood play (1954) Dylan
Thomas
Saint, The see Templar, Simon
St Aldegonde, Bertram, Lord heir to a
dukedom
Lothair (1870) Benjamin Disraeli
St Amour, de, Mme keeper of Parisian
pension
Vanity Fair (1847–8) W. M. Thackeray
St Aubert, Emily pale pure maiden perse-
cuted by vicious sadist, wanting the
climax of the persecution but fearing it
and loving fearing it and keeping the
contemplation of it lusciously vague
Mona her mother
her father
The Mysteries of Udolpho (1794) Mrs
Ann Radcliffe
St Aubin, Lucy loved by William
Waverley*
Waverley (1814) Walter Scott
St Bungay, Duke of
Phineas Finn† (1869) Anthony Trollope
St Clair, Agnes m. Charles Aubrey*

Ten Thousand a Year (1839) Samuel Warren

St Clair, Gertrude cc; heiress to the estate of Rossville m. Edward Lyndsay*

Earl of Rossville her tyrannical grandfather

The Inheritance (1824) Susan Ferrier

St Clair, Neville secret beggar

his wife

ss 'The Man with the Twisted Lip'

The Adventures of Sherlock Holmes (1892) Arthur Conan Doyle

St Clare French Jesuit priest

John Inglesant (1881) J. H. Shorthouse

St Clare, Augustine son of wealthy Louisiana planter, buyer of Uncle Tom*

Marie his wife

Evangeline ('Little Eva') their daughter

Alfred twin to Augustine

Henrique Alfred's son

Uncle Tom's Cabin (1852) Harriet Beecher Stowe

St Clare, General

ss 'The Sign of the Broken Sword'

The Innocence of Father Brown (1911) G. K. Chesterton

St Cleeve, Swithin young astronomer who bigamously m. Lady Constantine*

Revd M. his deceased father who is reckoned to have m. beneath him; in *jeu d'esprit* novel

Dr Jocelyn his uncle

Two on a Tower (1882) Thomas Hardy

St Duthac Abbot of Aberbrothock

Waverley (1814) Walter Scott

St Erth, Lord

Loyalties (1922) John Galsworthy

St Eustache, de, Marquis (Wednesday; Inspector Ratcliffe)

The Man Who Was Thursday (1908) G. K. Chesterton

St Evremonde see **Darnay, Charles**

St George Julian, George innocent cc of novel about swindling

Julia his wife

George St George Julian, The Prince of Swindlers (1841) Henry Cockton

St Giles cc, hero of the gutter in savage political novel

The History of St Giles and St James (1851) Douglas Jerrold

St Ives, Anna m. Frank Henley*

Anna St Ives (1792) Thomas Holcroft

St James cc, young marquis

The History of St Giles and St James (1851) Douglas Jerrold

St Jean servant to de Florac*

The Newcomes (1853–5) W. M. Thackeray

St Jerome, Lord and Lady

Lothair (1870) Benjamin Disraeli

St Julien, Horatio stage name of Jem Larkins*

Sketches by Boz† (1836) Charles Dickens

St Leon 16th-century alchemist cc, who has found the philosopher's stone, but meets only frustration and despair

Marguerite his wife

Charles their son

St Leon: A Tale of the Sixteenth Century (1799) William Godwin

St Lys, Aubrey, Revd Vicar of Mowbray

Sybil (1845) Benjamin Disraeli

St Marys, Barbara, Lady daughter to the Earl of Bungay

A Little Dinner at Timmins (1848) W. M. Thackeray

St Maugham, Mrs old lady, keen gardener

Laurel her granddaughter

Olivia Laurel's mother

The Chalk Garden play (1955) Enid Bagnold

St Mawr Lou Witt's* stallion

St Mawr (1925) D. H. Lawrence

St Peter, Professor Godfrey unhappy historian cc

Lillian his younger and materialistic wife

Rosamond; Kathleen his daughters, the first hard and mean, the second petty

The Professor's House (1925) Willa Cather

St Simon, Robert, Lord

ss 'The Noble Bachelor'

The Adventures of Sherlock Holmes (1892) Arthur Conan Doyle

St Vincent, Gregory treacherous coward by whom Frona Welse* is taken in

A Daughter of the Snows (1902) Jack London

St Yves, Anne de Kéroual de, Count cc, French prisoner of war, narrator, m. Flora Gilchrist*

Alain his rascally cousin, spy

Count de Kéroual de St Yves his great uncle, alias **Champdivers** and **Edward Ducie**

St Ives (1897) Robert Louis Stevenson

St Pierre, Virginia educated by Clarence Hervey* to be his wife, but in love with another
Belinda (1801) Maria Edgeworth

Sait, Jack prize-fighter
The Sailor's Return (1925) David Garnett

Sakaki, Most Great Archangel sent to investigate the Cause of the Genesis of the Moon, and now one of the four Quarter-Maintainers of the whole Universe
All and Everything: Beelzebub's Tales to His Grandson (1950) G. I. Gurdjieff

Sal, Cherokee 'dissolute and irreclaimable'
Tommy her son
The Luck of Roaring Camp (1868) Bret Harte

Salanio friend to Antonio*
The Merchant of Venice play (1623) William Shakespeare

Salar salmon hero of saga, second only in the author's ouevre to *Tarka**
Salar the Salmon (1935) Henry Williamson

Salim trader, narrator
A Bend in the River (1979) V. S. Naipaul

Salisbury, Earl of (hist.)
King Henry VI plays (1623) William Shakespeare

Salisbury, Earl of (William Longsword) (hist.)
King John play (1623) William Shakespeare

Sallafranque, Marc m. Isabella Tarry
his mother
Natalie; Yolande his sisters
The Thinking Reed (1936) Rebecca West (rn Cecily Fairfield)

Sallet, Unity
ss 'Tony Kytes, the Arch-Deceiver'
Life's Little Ironies (1894) Thomas Hardy

Sally servant to Miss Honeyman*
The Newcomes (1853–5) W. M. Thackeray

Salmon, Patrico hero of a great fight with gipsies
Guy Mannering (1815) Walter Scott

Salt wool factor
Felix Holt (1866) George Eliot (rn Mary Anne, later Marian, Evans)

Salt, Jim ('Sandy Jim') carpenter
Elizabeth ('Timothy Bess') his wife
Adam Bede (1859) George Eliot (rn Mary Anne, later Marian, Evans)

Salteena, Mr 'an elderly man of forty-two', admirer of Ethel Monticue*
The Young Visiters (1919) Daisy Ashford

Salterne, Rose ('The Rose of Torridge') victim of the Inquisition
William her merchant father
Westward Ho! (1855) Charles Kingsley

Salters, Uncle of the crew of the *We're Here*
Captains Courageous (1897) Rudyard Kipling

Saltire, Lord
The Book of Snobs (1847) W. M. Thackeray

Saltpen-Jago, Honoria
ss 'A Shot in the Dark' (1913)
in *Saki, A Life of Hector Hugh Munro* (1981) by A. J. Langguth

Sam [Beckett] 'dud mystic', fellow inmate with Watt* of institution (probably a mental hospital)
Watt† (1953) Samuel Beckett

Sambo Ethiopian who changed his skin
ss 'How the Leopard Changed his Spots'
Just So Stories (1902) Rudyard Kipling

Sambo first American stage-Negro (played by white) who thus gave insulting epithet to the language
The Triumphs of Love, or *Happy Reconciliation* play (1795) John Murdoch

Samgrass history don
Brideshead Revisited (1945) Evelyn Waugh

Samoa native friend to Taji*
Mardi (1849) Herman Melville

Sampath, Mr printer, would-be film producer
Mr Sampath (1949) (In USA as *The Printer of Malgudi*, 1957) R. K. Narayan

Sampson insurance manager who narrates tale
Hunted Down (1860) Charles Dickens

Sampson, George friend to the Wilfers*; fiancé to Lavinia Wilfer; sat upon by everybody
Our Mutual Friend (1865) Charles Dickens

Sampson, Mr surgeon
Of Human Bondage (1915) W. Somerset

Maugham

Samuel Pirate King's lieutenant
The Pirates of Penzance opera (1880)
W. S. Gilbert and Arthur Sullivan

Samuels, Jake The Rogue
The Passing of the Third Floor Back play
(1910) Jerome K. Jerome

San Martino, Duchess of self-styled
South Wind (1917) Norman Douglas

Sanzzaro favourite to Cozimo, and (for
the audience) a representation of the Duke
of Buckingham, James I's unpopular
favourite
The Great Duke of Florence play (1636)
James Shirley

Sandbourne, Phil architect
Manhattan Transfer (1925) John Dos
Passos

Sanders, Nell reformed barmaid
Salvation Nell play (1908) Edward
Sheldon

Sanders, Susannah, Mrs Mrs Bardell's*
particular friend
The Pickwick Papers (1837) Charles
Dickens

Sanderson, Peggy cc
The Loved and the Lost (1951) Morley
Callaghan

Sandford, Harry farmer's son, paradigm of
a boy, unlike the selfish Tommy Merton*
Sandford and Merton (1739) Thomas
Day

Sandip terrorist and nihilist, *not* a
caricature of Gandhi, as the Marxist
critic Lukács alleged
The Home and the World (1916)
Rabindranath Tagore

Sandler, Robert radio sponsor
The Troubled Air (1951) Irwin Shaw

Sandomir, Alix cc, in love with Basil
Doyle*
Daphne her mother
Paul; Nicholas her brothers
Non-Combatants and Others (1916)
Rose Macaulay

Sandrino son to Clélia* and Fabrice de
Dongo*
La Chartreuese de Parme (1839)
Stendhal (rn Henri Bayle)

Sands, Bedwin Eastern traveller
Pendennis† (1848) W. M. Thackeray

Sands, Bernard ambisexual novelist, cc
Ella his wife

Elizabeth; James their children
Sonia wife to James
Hemlock and After (1952) Angus Wilson

Sands, Lord
King Henry VIII play (1623) William
Shakespeare and John Fletcher

Sandys, Tommy
Jean his mother, *née* Myles
Elspeth his sister
Sentimental Tommy (1896) J. M. Barrie

Sanford murdered guitar player
ss 'The Hitch-Hikers'
A Curtain of Green (1941) Eudora Welty

Sanford, Major libertine whose child Eliza
Wharton* bears
The Coquette: A Novel Founded on Fact
(1797) Mrs Hannah Foster

Sang captain of the *Rose*
Catriona (1893) Robert Louis Stevenson

Sang, Tam coach-driver of the Royal
Charlotte
The Antiquary (1816) Walter Scott

Sangazure, Lady m. Sir Marmaduke
Pointdextre*
Aline her daughter m. Alexis Pointdextre
The Sorcerer opera (1877) W. S. Gilbert
and Arthur Sullivan

Sanger, Tessa cc
her father
Kate; Paulina; Antonia m. Jacob
Birnbaum her sisters
The Constant Nymph (1924) Margaret
Kennedy

Sannie, 'Tant' Boer, m. as third husband
Piet van der Walt*
The Story of an African farm (1883)
Olive Schreiner

Sans-Pareille, Dame owner of a ship
The Bowge of Court poem (1498) John
Skelton

Sansom, Edward father to Joel Harrison
Knox*
Other Voices, Other Rooms (1948) Tru-
man Capote

Sant, Jeremiah, Comrade socialist who
murders 'Pope' Hadrian*
Hadrian the Seventh (1904) Baron Corvo
(rn Frederick W. Rolfe)

Santangiolo, Beatrice, Duchess of double
of heroine of Marchdale's* pseudonymous *A Man of Words*, m. Peter
Marchdale*
The Cardinal's Snuff-Box (1900) Henry

S

Harland

Santiago old Cuban fisherman, cc
The Old Man and the Sea (1952) Ernest
Hemingway

Santien, Placide selfish creole who redeems
himself
ss 'A No-Account Creole'
Bayou Folk (1894) Kate Chopin

Sanutee Indian chief in the author's most
popular novel, in the series called 'Border
Romances'
The Yemassee (1835) William Gilmore
Simms

Saphir, Lady rapturous maiden, m. Col-
onel Calverley*
Patience opera (1881) W. S. Gilbert and
Arthur Sullivan

Saposcat ('Sapo') turns into Macmann*
Molloy (1951); *Malone meurt (Malone
Dies)* (1951) (tr. 1956); *L'Innommable
(1953) (The Unnamable)* (tr. 1958) (trilogy) Samuel Beckett

Sapphira black slave owned by Sapphira
Colbert*
Sapphira and the Slave Girl (1940) Willa
Cather

Sapphire, Helen musician
Pending Heaven (1930) William
Gerhardie

Sappho (hist.) re-created in series of poems
by the author, as herself: she used
masculine forms, but transferred the
male 'right' of address in love to herself —
yet she pursued this project in conjunc-
tion with a male exponent of lesbian
pornography, Pierre Louÿs
Cinq petits dialogues grec poems (1901)
Natalie Barney

Sappleton, Mrs
Vera her niece
ss 'The Open Window'
Beasts and Super-Beasts (1914) Saki (rn
Hector Hugh Munro)

Sapsea, Thomas bombastic auctioneer, m.
Miss Brobity
The Mystery of Edwin Drood (1870)
Charles Dickens

Sapt, Colonel
The Prisoner of Zenda† (1894) Anthony
Hope (rn Anthony Hope Hawkins)

Saradine, Prince
ss 'The Sins of Prince Saradine'
The Innocence of Father Brown (1911)

G. K. Chesterton

Sarah the Pooters'* maid
Diary of a Nobody (1892) George and
Weedon Grossmith

Saranoff, Sergius, Major engaged to Raina
Petkoff*
Arms and the Man play (1894) George
Bernard Shaw

Saranson, Lee deposes Windrip*
It Can't Happen Here (1935) Sinclair
Lewis

Sarge poor-white-trash
Acrobat Admits (1959) Alfred Grossman

Sargent, DD Master of Boniface
Lovel the Widower (1860) W. M.
Thackeray

Sargent, Netty m. Jasper Cliff*
ss 'Netty Sargent's Copyhold'
Life's Little Ironies (1894) Thomas
Hardy

Sargent, Wilton wealthy American
ss 'An Error in the Fourth Dimension'
The Day's Work (1898) Rudyard Kipling

Sark, Lord and Lady neighbours of the
Castlewoods*
Henry Esmond (1852) W. M. Thackeray

Sarnac physiologist
The Dream (1924) H. G. Wells

Sarsefield tutor of Edgar Huntly* and
eventual unraveller of the psychotic mystery
Edgar Huntly, or *Memoirs of a Sleepwalker* (1799) Charles Brockden Brown

Sarsfield, Dominick, Sir cc, head smashed
to pieces by supernatural powers
ss 'Sir Dominick Sarsfield'
The Watcher (1894) J. Sheridan Le Fanu

Sarti, Caterina ('Tina') Italian singer
adopted by the Cheverels*, m. Maynard
Gilfil*
ss 'Mr Gilfil's Love Story'
Scenes of Clerical Life (1857) George
Eliot (rn Mary Anne, later Marian,
Evans)

Sartoris, Bayard cc, served with RAF in
1914–18 War; m. (1) Caroline White,
(2) Narcissa Benbow; killed testing an
aircraft (1920)
Bayard his grandfather
Colonel John Sartoris his great-grandfather, a violent man, m.(1) daughter to
Rosa Millard, (2) Drusilla Hawk; shot by
Redmond (or Redlaw)

John his twin, killed in 1914–18 War
Benbow his infant son by Narcissa, born on the day he is killed
Marengo Sartoris ('Ringo') Bayard's* Negro playmate and servant
Sartoris† (1929) (for full text: *Flags in the Dust*, 1973) William Faulkner

Sartoris, Lasca fascinating actress in early sympathetic novel with all-black cast
Nigger Heaven (1926) Carl Van Vechten

Sartorius
Blanche his daughter
Widowers' Houses play (1892) George Bernard Shaw

Sartorius, Ludwig, Professor the author's notion of the character of Alfred Weber, sociologist brother to the more distinguished sociologist Max Weber
Mr Noon (1924) D. H. Lawrence

Saryntsov, Nikolai Ivanovich wealthy landowner, cc of drama Shaw* felt to be the author's masterpiece; gives up his estates but fails as labourer
Marya Ivanovna his wife
his sister
their children
I svet vo tme svetit (*The Light Shines in Darkness*) play (1911) Leo Tolstoy

Sasha Russian princess loved by Orlando*
Orlando (1928) Virginia Woolf

Saskia, Princess
Eugenie her cousin
Huntingtower (1922) John Buchan

Satan the great devil
The Devil is an Ass play (1616) Ben Jonson

Satchell aged bailiff to Squire Donnithorne*
his wife
Adam Bede (1859) George Eliot (rn Mary Anne, later Marian, Evans)

Saul, Edgar mysterious cc
A Certain Man (1931) Oliver Onions

Satchel, Andrew m. Jane Vallens*
his brother and sister-in-law
ss 'Andrey Satchel and the Parson and Clerk'
Life's Little Ironies (1894) Thomas Hardy

Satchell, Stella Summersley companion to Lady Mary Justin*
The Passionate Friends (1913) H. G. Wells

Satin
The Devil is an Ass play (1616) Ben Jonson

Sattherwaite, Mrs mother to Sylvia Tietjens*
Some Do Not (1924); *No More Parades* (1925); *A Man Could Stand Up* (1926); *Last Post* (1928) Ford Madox Ford

Saturninus late Emperor of Rome
Titus Andronicus play (1623) William Shakespeare

Saul, Samuel, Revd Mr Clavering's* curate, who does most of the parish work and mortifies his flesh: 'It is not that he mortifies his flesh, but that he has no flesh to mortify'
The Claverings (1867) Anthony Trollope

Saumarez who proposes to the wrong sister in a storm
ss 'False Dawn'
Plain Tales from the Hills (1888) Rudyard Kipling

Saunders, Mr cc, 'best doctor in the Far East'
The Narrow Corner (1932) W. Somerset Maugham

Saunders, Mrs mother to Esther Waters*
her brutal husband
Esther Waters (1894) George Moore

Saunter, Mr
Lolly Willowes (1926) Sylvia Townsend Warner

Sauron the Dark Lord of Mordor
The Lord of the Rings (1954–5) J. R. R. Tolkien

Sauveterre, Fabrice, Duc de lover to Linda Talbot*
Fabrice their illegitimate son
The Pursuit of Love† (1945) Nancy Mitford

Savage, Captain
Peter Simple (1834) Captain Marryat

Savage, Eleanor Amory Blaine's* last love
This Side of Paradise (1920) F. Scott Fitzgerald

Savage, Naomi selfish and vain cc; a not too inaccurate portrait of the author's mother, Rebecca West* (his father was H. G. Wells*); part of a two-way battle that did neither much credit; Rebecca West prevented its publication in the UK until after her death
Heritage (1955) Anthony West

Savage, Richard Ellworth assistant to J. Ward Moorehouse
U.S.A. (1930–6) John Dos Passos

Savary, Colonel of the Gendarmerie Élite
Tom Burke of Ours (1844) Charles Lever

Saverne, Comte de the elder
Francis Stanislas his son, Vicomte de Barr, later Count
Clarisse wife to Francis Stanislas, *née* Viomesnil
Agnes daughter to Francis and Clarisse, m. Denis Duval*
Francis's unmarried sisters
Denis Duval (1864) W. M. Thackeray

Savile, Arthur, Lord cc, m. Sybil Merton*
Lord Arthur Savile's Crime (1891) Oscar Wilde

Savile, Lucy m. Charles Downe*
ss 'Fellow-Townsmen'
Wessex Tales (1888) Thomas Hardy

Saville, Clara m. Frank Fairlegh*
Lady Saville her mother, *née* Elliot
Frank Fairlegh (1850) F. E. Smedley

Saville, Helen friend to the Lancasters*
The Vortex play (1924) Noël Coward

Saville, Margaret, Mrs sister to Richard Walton*
Frankenstein (1818) Mary Shelley

Savio King of Paflagonia
The Rose and the Ring (1855) W. M. Thackeray

Saviola, Vincentio celebrated fencing instructor
The Monastery (1820) Walter Scott

Saviolina a court-lady
Every Man Out of His Humour play (1599) Ben Jonson

Savonarola (hist.)
Romola (1863) George Eliot (rn Mary Anne, later Marian, Evans)
ss 'Savonarola Brown'; immortal caricature of Victorian 'Shakespearean' dramatist
Seven Men (1919) Max Beerbohm

Savott, Henry, Sir, Baronet
Grace his daughter
Imperial Palace (1930) Arnold Bennett

Savoyard, Cecil
Fanny's First Play play (1905) George Bernard Shaw

Savylle, Mary, Lady the woman truly loved by Edward Brent-Foster*, who eventually m. him

The Panel (1912) (as *Ring for Nancy*, 1913, in UK) Ford Madox Ford

Sawbridge, Ellen m. Sir Isaac Harman*
The Wife of Sir Isaac Harman (1914) H. G. Wells

Sawbridge, Lieutenant HMS *Harpy*
Mr Midshipman Easy (1836) Captain Marryat

Sawdon, Tom publican
Lily his wife
South Riding (1936) Winifred Holtby

Sawyer baker murdered by his son
Robert Bolton (1838) Charles Dickens

Sawyer, Bob medical student at Guys, boon companion to Ben Allen*
The Pickwick Papers (1837) Charles Dickens

Sawyer, C., Mr Justice
The Newcomes (1853–5) W. M. Thackeray

Sawyer, John Standish hunting man, cc
Market Harborough (1861) George Whyte-Melville

Sawyer, Rosa m. Billy Wakeling*
A Town Like Alice (1950) Neville Shute

Sawyer, Tom cc
Sid his half-brother
The Adventures of Tom Sawyer† (1876) Mark Twain (rn Samuel Langhorne Clemens)

Saxby, Charles, Lord lover to Mrs Fane* and father of Michael and Stella
Sinister Street (1913) Compton Mackenzie

Saxby, Howard literary agent
Cocktail Time (1958) P. G. Wodehouse

Saxby, Long 'six-feet ten'
Dombey and Son (1848) Charles Dickens

Saxenden, Lord ('Snubby')
Maid in Waiting (1931) John Galsworthy

Saxingham, Earl of friend to Lord Vargrave*
Alice (1838) Edward Bulwer Lytton

Saxton, George m. Meg of the Ramme*
Emily; Mollie; Tom; Arthur his sisters and brothers
The White Peacock (1911) D. H. Lawrence

Saybrook, Tom declared by the author to be a portrait of the early beat writer John Clellon Holmes
On the Road (1957) Jack Kerouac

Sayer, Rose missionary, cc

The African Queen (1925) C. S. Forrester (rn C. L. T. Smith)

Sayers, Rosie fourteen-year-old child murdered by Paris Trout*
Paris Trout (1988) Pete Dexter

Sayes, Lord undergraduate
Zuleika Dobson (1911) Max Beerbohm

Saywell, Arthur, Revd country parson
Cynthia his wife
Granny ('The Mater') his mother
Cissie his sister
Lucille Yvette his daughters, the latter in love with Joe Boswell*
The Virgin and the Gipsy (1930) D. H. Lawrence

Scadder, Zephaniah real estate swindler (of Chuzzlewit*)
Martin Chuzzlewit (1844) Charles Dickens

Scaddon, Henry see **Christian, Maurice**

Scadgers, Lady Mrs Sparsit's bedridden aunt
Hard Times (1854) Charles Dickens

Scaife servant to McGillvray*
The Thirty-nine Steps† (1915) John Buchan

Scales house steward and head butler to Sir Maximus Debarry*
Felix Holt (1866) George Eliot (rn Mary Anne, later Marian, Evans)

Scales, Buck American robber and murderer
Magdelena his wife
Death Comes for the Archbishop (1927) Willa Cather

Scales, Gerald commercial traveller, m. Sophia Baines*
The Old Wives' Tale (1908) Arnold Bennett

Scaley bailiff
Nicholas Nickleby (1839) Charles Dickens

Scalognati outcast people who no longer need the human; led by Coltrone*; they perform, with Countess Ilse's* troupe, to the servants of bestial giants, 'the rulers of the world' (the then masters of Italy)
The Mountain Giants play (1938) Luigi Pirandello

Scandal free-speaking friend to Sir Sampson Legend*
Love for Love comedy (1710) William Congreve

Scanlon, Lucy loved by Studs Lonigan*
Studs Lonigan (1932–5) James T. Farrell

Scantlebury assessor of dilapidations
Obadiah his brother, asylum proprietor
In the Roar of the Sea (1892) Sabine Baring-Gould

Scape honest man ruined by roguery
Fanny; Florence; Walter his children
Vanity Fair (1847–8) W. M. Thackeray

Scapethrift Bailey's* servant
Gammer Gurton's Needle play (1575) ?W. Stevenson

Scarborough, John owner of Treton, through whose clay-workings he has become wealthy
Mountjoy his elder son, a ne'er-do-well in the Guards; declared illegitimate but then reinstated
Augustus barrister, his cold and greedy younger son
Florence his niece, m. Harry Annesley*
Mr Scarborough's Family (1883) Anthony Trollope

Scarlett, Hugh who enters into a suicide pact but cannot keep it until much later; eventually loves Rachel West*, but drowns in icy lake
Red Pottage (1899) Mary Cholmondeley

Scarlett, Michael cc
Michael Scarlett (1925) James Gould Cozzens

Scarlett, Sylvia m. Philip Iredale*
Sinister Street† (1913) Compton Mackenzie

Scarsdale, Captain 'poor brother' at Grey Friars
The Newcomes (1853–5) W. M. Thackeray

Scatcherd, Miss morose history teacher at Lowood, victimizes Helen Burns* and whips her neck
Jane Eyre (1847) Charlotte Brontë

Scatcherd, Roger, Sir, Baronet stonemason, drunkard and killer of the father of Mary Thorne*, Dr Thorne's* brother
his wife
Louis Philippe their dissipated son
Dr Thorne (1858) Anthony Trollope

Scatterbrain, Lord see **Rooney, Andy**

Schatzweiler Americanized German Jew, partner to Christopher Tietjens*
Last Post (1928) Ford Madox Ford

Schearl, David boy (aged 2–8) cc of one of the century's masterpieces about childhood

Albert his menacing and paranoid father, whose voice takes on 'a thin terrific hardness' when he is about to strike his mother, *née* Krollman

Aunt Bertha his mother's younger sister

Uncle Nathan Bertha's husband
Call It Sleep (1934) Henry Roth

Schedoni monk
The Italian (1797) Mrs Ann Radcliffe

Scheisskopf, Lieutenant who moves through the ranks to become commanding officer
Catch-22 (1961) Joseph Heller

Schiller, Richard F. m. Dolores (Lolita) Haze*
Lolita (1955) Vladimir Nabokov

Schilsky red-haired Polish violinist whose character is partly modelled on the young Richard Strauss
Maurice Guest (1908) Henry Handel Richardson (rn Ethel Florence Lindesay Richardson Robertson)

Schinderhausen, Olearius professor at Leyden
The Abbot (1820) Walter Scott

Schlangenbad, Contesse de
The Newcomes† (1853–5) W. M. Thackeray

Schlegel, Helen

Margaret her sister, ccs

Ernst their German father

Tibby their brother

Frieda their cousin
Howards End (1910) E. M. Forster

Schlemihl, Peter cc classic fairytale for adults in which he exchanges his shadow for a bottomless purse
Peter Schlemihls wundersame Geschichte (*The Strange Story of Peter Schlemihl*) (1814) Adelbert von Chamisso

Schlieffenzahn, General cruel proto-Nazi First World War German soldier, responsible for the judicial murder of Sergeant Grischa*
Der Streit um den Sergeanten Grischa (The Case of Sergeant Grischa) (1927) Arnold Zweig

Schlote, Irma sentimental German governess to Oliver Alden*

The Last Puritan (1936) George Santayana

Schmidt blackmailer of Norris*
Mr Norris Changes Trains (1935) Christopher Isherwood

Schnorp black marketeer
Gravity's Rainbow (1973) Thomas Pynchon

Schofield, John painter, friend to Michael Andriaovsky*
ss 'Hic Jacet: A Tale of Artistic Conscience'
Widdershins (1911) Oliver Onions

Schofield, Penrod twelve-year-old cc of three books, the first of which for a time rivalled Huckleberry Finn*; author of *Harold Ramorez, the Road Agent*, a blood-curdling work of fiction
Penrod (1914); *Penrod and Sam* (1916); *Penrod Jashber* (1929) Booth Tarkington

Scholey, Laurence servant attending Magnus Troil*
The Pirate (1822) Walter Scott

Schomberg hotel owner
Victory (1915) Joseph Conrad (rn Josef Teodor Konrad Korzeniowski)

Schouler, Marcus treacherous friend to McTeague*, killed by him in Death Valley
McTeague (1899) Frank Norris

Schreckenwald, Hal faithful but vicious steward to Count Albert of Geierstein*
Anne of Geierstein (1829) Walter Scott

Schreiber, Mits Aintree steward
National Velvet (1935) Enid Bagnold

Schreiderling, Colonel
his wife
ss 'The Other Man'
Plain Tales from the Hills (1888) Rudyard Kipling

Schreiner, Philip, KC counsel for Oliver Price*
Antigua Penny Puce (1936) Robert Graves

Schriften pilot of the *Ter Schilling*
The Phantom Ship (1839) Captain Marryat

Schroeder, Lina, Fräulein landlady
Mr Norris Changes Trains† (1935) Christopher Isherwood

Schulim, Reb rabbi
Call It Sleep (1934) Henry Roth

Schultz, Mrs

Mrs Wiggs of the Cabbage Patch (1901) Alice Hegen Rice

Schumann ship's doctor
Ship of Fools (1962) Katherine Anne Porter

Schutzmacher, Dr
The Doctor's Dilemma play (1906) George Bernard Shaw

Schwartz with Hans*, evil brother of three (see Gluck*) in widely read fable
The King of the Golden River (1850) John Ruskin

Schwengauer, Mattie college girl
So Big (1924) Edna Ferber

Sciben, Diogenes of Chalcot, the Great Writer
A Tale of a Tub play (1640) Ben Jonson

Scintilla pleasure-loving wife to Mixtus*
The Impressions of Theophrastus Such (1879) George Eliot (rn Mary Anne, later Marian, Evans)

Scobie ambitious soldier with a taste for power
Young Man of Talent (1959) George Turner

Scobie, Henry Deputy Commissioner of Police, cc
Louise his wife
Catherine their dead daughter
The Heart of the Matter (1948) Graham Greene

Scobie, Joshua homosexual Englishman employed by Egyptian police
The Alexandria Quartet (1957–61) Lawrence Durrell

Score, Mrs landlady of the Bugle
Catherine (1840) W. M. Thackeray

Scott of the Irrigation Department, m. William Martyn*
ss 'William the Conqueror'
The Day's Work (1898) Rudyard Kipling

Scott, David young American painter
Ship of Fools (1962) Katherine Anne Porter

Scott, Joe 'overlooker' at Robert Moore's* mill
Shirley (1849) Charlotte Brontë

Scott, Master friend to Otley*
The Shoemaker's Holiday (1600) Thomas Dekker

Scott, Roberta American girl vegetarian
Birds of America (1971) Mary McCarthy

Scott, Rufus cc black Jazz musician

Ida his sister, singer, lover of Ellis* her manager
Another Country (1962) James Baldwin

Scott, Thomas farmer, cc
Hawbuck Grange (1847) R. S. Surtees

Scott, Tom impish lad at Quilp's* wharf
The Old Curiosity Shop (1841) Charles Dickens

Scott, Undecimus ('Undy'), the Hon. shadowy figure
The Three Clerks (1858) Anthony Trollope

Scott, Weedon mining engineer who saves White Fang* and whose family and life are saved by him in return
White Fang (1905) Jack London

Scott-Brown, Surgeon-Lieutenant of the *Saltash*
The Cruel Sea (1951) Nicholas Monsarrat

Scougal, Andie captain of the *Thistle*
Catriona (1893) Robert Louis Stevenson

Scout lawyer to Lady Booby*
Joseph Andrews (1742) Henry Fielding

Scoutbush, Lord absentee Irish peer
Two Years Ago (1857) Charles Kingsley

Scragga son to Twala*, paramount chief
King Solomon's Mines (1885) Henry Rider Haggard

Scraper, Susan, Lady daughter of the Earl of Bagwig*
Scraper Buckram; Sydney her sons; and two daughters
The Book of Snobs (1847) W. M. Thackeray

Screwby servant to Sir Miles Warrington*
The Virginians (1857–9) W. M. Thackeray

Screwzer, Tommy friend to Cousin Feenix*
Dombey and Son (1848) Charles Dickens

Scrimser, Mr and Mrs Vance Weston's* grandparents, the parents of his mother; the latter's quest for perfection leads her into successful evangelism
Hudson River Bracketed (1929); *The Gods Arrive* (1932) Edith Wharton

Scrivener
Ralph Roister Doister play (1551) Nicholas Udall

Scrooge, Ebeneezer cc
A Christmas Carol (1843) Charles Dickens

Scroop, Stephen, Sir
King Richard II; *King Richard III* plays
(1623) William Shakespeare
Scrope, Edward, Bishop of Princhester
Ella his wife, daughter to Lord
Birkenholme
Eleanor eldest of their five daughters
The Soul of a Bishop (1917) H. G. Wells
Scrope, Jane owner of Philip Sparrow*
The Boke of Phyllyp Sparowe poem
(1508) John Skelton*
Scrub servant to Squire Sullen*
The Beaux' Stratagem play (1707)
George Farquhar
Scrubby likable steward who committed
suicide: on liner taking passengers (i.e.
the dead) across the Styx 'until his time
comes'
Outward Bound play (1924) Sutton
Vane
Scrymgeour artist, man of means
My Lady Nicotine (1890) J. M. Barrie
Scrymgeour, Francis Edinburgh bank clerk
ss 'The Rajah's Diamond's
The New Arabian Nights (1882) Robert
Louis Stevenson
Scuddamore, Silas Q. wealthy American
ss 'The Suicide Club'
The New Arabian Nights (1882) Robert
Louis Stevenson
Scully, William Pitt Liberal MP for Old-
borough
Sally his sister
The Bedford Row Conspiracy (1840)
W. M. Thackeray
Scuttlewig, Duke of intimate friend to the
Egotistical Young Couple*
Sketches of Young Couples (1840)
Charles Dickens
Scyld former king of Denmark
Beowulf (c.745)
Sea Catch a seal
Matkah his wife
Kotick their son
ss 'The White Seal'
The Jungle Book (1894) Rudyard Kipling
Sea Cow
ss 'The White Seal'
The Jungle Book (1894) Rudyard Kipling
Sea Rat
ss 'The White Seal'
The Jungle Book (1894) Rudyard Kipling
Sea Vitch a walrus

ss 'The White Seal'
The Jungle Book (1894) Rudyard Kipling
Seacombe, John, the Hon. uncle to
William Crimsworth*
The Professor (1857) Charlotte Brontë
Seagrave, William
his wife
William; Thomas; Caroline; Albert their
children
Masterman Ready (1842) Captain
Marryat
Seagraves, Harry corrupt lawyer with a
growing conscience
Lucy his wife
Paris Trout (1988) Pete Dexter
Seagrim, Molly
George her father, gamekeeper
Tom Jones (1749) Henry Fielding
Seal, Basil cc, m. Angela Lyne*
Cynthia, Lady Seal his mother
Barbara his sister, m. Freddy Sothill*
Put Out More Flags† (1942) Evelyn
Waugh
Seal, Martin of the BBC
Holy Deadlock (1934) A. P. Herbert
Seamstress, The with whom Carton*
travelled in the tumbril to the guillotine
A Tale of Two Cities (1859) Charles
Dickens
Searcher, Caleb
ss 'Mr Justice Harbottle'
In a Glass Darkly (1872) J. Sheridan Le
Fanu
Searing, Jerome Confederate private
ss 'One of the Missing'
In the Midst of Life (1898) Ambrose
Bierce
Searle, Clement middle-aged American
who comes to England to claim an estate
and dies
ss 'A Passionate Pilgrim'
A Passionate Pilgrim and Other Tales
(1875) Henry James
Sears, Tobias, Captain Union officer m.
Amantha Starr*; lawyer
Band of Angels (1955) Robert Penn War-
ren
Seaton, Arthur
Brian his more intellectual brother, a
writer
their parents
Saturday Night and Sunday Morning†
(1958); *Key to the Door*† (1961) Alan

Sillitoe

Seaton, Arthur
his aunt, cc
ss 'Seaton's Aunt'
The Riddle (1923) Walter de la Mare

Seaway, Anne dupe to Andreas Manston*
Desperate Remedies (1871) Thomas
Hardy

Sebastian brother to Alonso*
The Tempest play (1623) William Shakespeare

Sebastian brother to Viola*
Twelfth Night play (1623) William
Shakespeare

Sebastian younger son to D'Amville*
The Atheist's Tragedy, or *The Honest
Man's Revenge* play (1611/12) Cyril
Tourneur

Secret a bawd
The City Madam play (1658) Philip Massinger

Secret messenger to summon Christian*
The Pilgrim's Progress (1678–84) John
Bunyan

Seddon, Margaret
The New Machiavelli (1911) H. G. Wells

Sedgemoor, Susan m. Greaves Oakley*
Sir Launcelot Greaves (1762) Tobias
Smollett

Sedgett, Nic bigamist and bad hat
Rhoda Fleming (1865) George Meredith

Sedgmire, Lord Robert Carne's* father-in-
law
South Riding (1936) Winifred Holtby

Sedley, Amelia cc, m. (1) George Os-
borne*, (2) Major William Dobbin*
Georgy her son by Osborne
John her father
her mother
Joseph her brother
Vanity Fair (1847–8) W. M. Thackeray

Sedley, Joanna alias **John Matcham**, m. Sir
Richard Shelton*
The Black Arrow (1888) Robert Louis
Stevenson

Seebach, Martha maid to Mme de Saverne*
Denis Duval (1864) W. M. Thackeray

Seegrave, Superintendent of the Frizinghall
Police
The Moonstone (1868) Wilkie Collins

Seelencooper one-eyed captain, governor
of Ryde Hospital

The Surgeon's Daughter (1827) Walter
Scott

Sefton bully
ss 'The Moral Reformers'
Stalky & Co. (1899) Rudyard Kipling

Sefton, Priscilla loved by Christian Christianson* and Richard Orchardson*, m.
the former
her father, a Methodist preacher
God and the Man (1881) Robert
Buchanan

Ségouin Hungarian pianist
ss 'After the Race'
Dubliners (1914) James Joyce

Sein, Ko Ba trusted clerk
Burmese Days (1935) George Orwell (rn
Eric Blair)

Sejanus favourite of Tiberius*, cc play
based (mainly) on Tacitus which traces
his rise and fall; Shakespeare* was in the
cast of the first (1603) performance
Sejanus play (1605) Ben Jonson

Selby, George
Marianna his wife. Uncle and aunt to
Harriet Byron*
Lucy their daughter
Sir Charles Grandison (1754) Samuel
Richardson

Selby, Solomon
ss 'A Tradition of 1804'
Life's Little Ironies (1894) Thomas
Hardy

Selden escaped convict, brother to Mrs
Barrymore*
The Hound of the Baskervilles (1902)
Arthur Conan Doyle

Selden, Jim
his mother: escaping slaves
Uncle Tom's Cabin (1851) Harriet
Beecher Stowe

Selden, Lawrence loved by Lily Bart* but
without enough money
The House of Mirth (1905) Edith
Wharton

Selden, Mrs cook
Manservant and Maidservant (1947) Ivy
Compton-Burnett

Selenites inhabitants of the moon
The First Men in the Moon (1901) H. G.
Wells

Selim
Hassan play (1923) James Elroy Flecker

Selim merchant, cc

A Bend in the River (1979) V. S. Naipaul

Sellars, Poppy
Angel Pavement (1930) J. B. Priestley

Selleck, Jefferson dying businessman cc in American novel of the Midwest
Jefferson Selleck (1951) Carl Jonas

Sellers, Colonel Beriah Micawber*-like cc of novels that were dramatized as *The American Claimant* by its first author with William Dean Howells*, when his name was changed to Mulberry Sellers; based on Twain's kinsman James Lampton; the second novel (by Twain alone), based on the play, is less vivid
The Gilded Age (1873); *The American Claimant* (1892); Mark Twain (rn Samuel Langhorne Clemens); Charles Dudley Warner

Sellers, Reginald fifth-rate artist
The Man Upstairs (1914) P. G. Wodehouse

Selvaggio Knight of Arts and Industry who breaks the spell of Indolence*
The Castle of Indolence poem (1748) James Thomson

Semira
Zadig (1747–1748 as *Memnon*, the latter title being later used for another tale) Voltaire (rn François-Marie Arouet)

Semmelweis, Ignaz (hist.) physician who discovered the necessity of hygiene in obstetrics; cc of a doctoral thesis which strikingly anticipates its author's later career as a novelist under a pseudonym; it earned him the only medal for excellence that he was ever to receive
La Vie et l'oeuvre de Philippe Ignace Semmelweis (1924) Louis-Ferdinand Destouches (i.e. later, Louis-Ferdinand Céline)

Semmering, Lady Gertrude see **Casterley, Countess of**

Semphill, George, Revd who becomes a cardinal
Hadrian the Seventh (1904) Baron Corvo (rn Frederick W. Rolfe)

Semple, Jesse B. ('Simple') 'ignorant' Harlem resident; onwards from
Simple Speaks his Mind (1950) Langston Hughes

Sempronius
The Apple Cart play (1929) George Bernard Shaw

Sempronius a lord
Timon of Athens play (1623) William Shakespeare

Sen Heng
The Wallet of Kai Lung (1900) Ernest Bramah (rn Ernest Bramah Smith)

Sender, Reb wealthy and pious man who keeps turning away suitors, including Khonnon*, for the hand of his daughter: **Leah** who is possessed by a dybbuk (Khonnon's wandering soul, sent into despair because he died before his time owing to Sender's cruelty); eventually reunited with him; in Cabbalistic drama
Der Dibuk (*The Dybbuk*) (1918) S. Ansky (rn Shyloyome Zanvil Rappoport)

Sénecal socialist, policeman, murderer
L'Education sentimentale (1869) Gustave Flaubert

Sensimirinko a genuine initiate; co-founder of the brotherhood Tchaftan-touri; contacted by Ashiata Shiemash*
All and Everything: Beelzebub's Tales to His Grandson (1950) G. I. Gurdjieff

Sentiment, Popular, Mr novelist
The Warden (1865) Anthony Trollope

Sephestia, Princess cc prose romance, disguised as Samela, with lyric interludes
Menaphon (1589) Robert Greene

Septimus friend to Alcander*
The Bee (1759–60) Oliver Goldsmith

Seraglio, The group of young men
The Haunted House (1859) Charles Dickens

Seraphina heroine of Jemmy Lirriper's* tale
Mrs Lirriper's Lodgings and Legacy (1864) Charles Dickens

Serena
Porgy (1925) Du Bose Heyward

Sergeant, Mayo Gatsby*-like cc of American satirical novel
Mayo Sergeant (1967) James B. Hall

Serringe surgeon
The Relapse, or Virtue in Danger play (1697) John Vanbrugh

Server, May devitalized victim in psychological vampire story
The Sacred Fount (1901) Henry James

Service stipendiary magistrate
But Soft – We Are Observed! (1928) Hilaire Belloc

Servinton, Quintus cc in autobiographical

novel valuable for its depiction of conditions in Australian convict settlements by rich Bristol merchant turned persistent (sentenced to death; deported); forger
Quintus Servinton (1830–1) Henry Savery

Setabhai Queen of the Maharajah of Gokral Seetaren
The Naulakha (1892) Rudyard Kipling and Walcot Balestier

Seth attendant of Isaac and Rebecca*
Ivanhoe (1820) Walter Scott

Seton, Patrick medium accused of fraud
The Bachelors (1961) Muriel Spark

Seton, Sally later Lady Rosseter
Mrs Dalloway (1925) Virginia Woolf

Setter a pimp
The Old Bachelor play (1793) William Congreve

Seumas Beg
Brigid his sister; children who meet the leprechaun
The Crock of Gold (1912) James Stephens

Sevier, Dr laconic cc series of linked local colour* sketches of New Orleans life during and just after the Civil War
Dr Sevier (1882) George Washington Cable

Sevosse, Comfort 'the fool' of the title, Union Colonel, in novel – of the Reconstruction – of a vehemently Republican author who was a corrupt judge, a defender of the Negro, a critic of the Ku Klux Klan – and of Henry James* because he did not stick to veracity
A Fool's Errand (1879) 'By One of the Fools': i.e. Albion W. Tourgée

Seward, Dr
Dracula (1897) Bram Stoker

Sewis, Old half-caste butler to Squire Beltham*
The Adventures of Harry Richmond (1871) George Meredith

Seyfang, Otto
Tracy's Tiger (1951) William Saroyan

Seymore, Clive father to Fanny Hooper*
Lady Alicia his wife
Sir Everard his father
Fanny By Gaslight (1940) Michael Sadleir

Seymour, Humphrey editor of communist scandal sheet, an attempted portrait of Claude Cockburn
The Conscience of the Rich (1958) C. P. Snow

Seymour, Valerie
The Well of Loneliness (1928) Radclyffe Hall

Seymour, William see **Peters, William**

Seymour, Wilson, Sir
ss 'The Man in the Passage'
The Wisdom of Father Brown (1914) G. K. Chesterton

Seysen, Father parish priest
The Phantom Ship (1839) Captain Marryat

Sforza, Francesco, Duke of Milan (hist.), cc of romantic drama by author once considered a leading American poet, of whom O. W. Holmes* said, 'He was something between a remembrance of Count D'Orsay* and an anticipation of Oscar Wilde*'
Bianca Visconti his wife, whose family plan to kill him
Bianca Visconti verse tragedy (1839) Nathaniel Parker Willis

Sganarelle comic creation, in series of plays
L'école des maris (*The School for Husbands*) (1661); *Le Mariage forcé* (*The Forced Marriage*) (1664); *L'amour médecin* (*Love, the Doctor*) (1665); *Dom Juan ou Le Festin de pierre* (*Don Juan or the Stone Banquet*) (1665); *Le Médecin malgré lui* (*The Doctor in Spite of Himself*) (1666); *Sganarelle, ou Le Cocu imaginaire* (*The Imaginary Cuckold*) (1660) Molière (rn Jean Baptiste Poquelin)

Shaban chief eunuch
Vathek (1786) William Beckford

Shabata, Frank neighbour to the Bergsons"
O Pioneers! (1913) Willa Cather

Shackles keeper of Newgate
The Devil is an Ass play (1616) Ben Jonson

Shackles racehorse
ss 'The Broken Link Handicap'
Plain Tales from the Hills (1888) Rudyard Kipling

Shadbolt, Wilfred head jailer and assistant tormentor, m. Phoebe Meryll
The Yeomen of the Guard opera (1888) W. S. Gilbert and Arthur Sullivan

Shadd, Dinah m. Terence Mulvaney*
Sergeant Shadd her father
ss 'The Courtship of Dinah Shadd'
Life's Handicap† (1891) Rudyard Kipling

Shade, John American poet
Sybil his wife
Hazel their daughter
Pale Fire (1962) Vladimir Nabokov

Shadow servant to Fortunatus and his sons*
Old Fortunatus play (1600) Thomas Dekker

Shadow, The
ss 'The Haunted and the Haunters'
The Haunted and the Haunters (1857) Edward Bulwer Lytton

Shadowfax Gandalf's* flying horse
The Lord of the Rings (1954–5) J. R. R. Tolkien

Shadrack crazed black who witnesses Sula May Peace's* accidental killing of Chicken Little*
Sula (1973) Toni Morrison

Shafiz Ullah Khan
ss 'One View of the Question'
Many Inventions (1893) Rudyard Kipling

Shafton, Piercie, Sir 'witty and accomplished courtier'
Shafton of Wilverton his father
The Monastery (1820) Walter Scott

Shafton, Walter music-hall artist
Let the People Sing (1939) J. B. Priestley

Shagpat clothier
Kadza his wife
The Shaving of Shagpat (1856) George Meredith

Shakebag murderer, with Black Will*, of Arden*
The Lamentable and Terrible Tragedy of Arden of Feversham in Kent play (1592) Anon.

Shakespeare, William (hist.)
Nothing Like the Sun (1964) Anthony Burgess (rn John Burgess Wilson)

Shalford, Edwin proprietor, Folkestone Drapery Bazaar; Kipps's* employer
Kipps (1905) H. G. Wells

Shallard, Frank Elmer Gantry's* chief antagonist, a minister
Elmer Gantry (1927) Sinclair Lewis

Shallow justice

The Merry Wives of Windsor (play) (1623) William Shakespeare

Shallum, Mrs 'Parisianized figure'
The Custom of the Country (1913) Edith Wharton

Shaloony Irish patriot
The Newcomes (1853–5) W. M. Thackeray

Shame encountered by Faithful*
The Pilgrim's Progress (1678–84) John Bunyan

Shamlegh, The Woman of
Kim (1901) Rudyard Kipling

Shand, Ivy 'Scottish Con Girl Soaks New York Millionaire'; 'a lie, anyway'; narrator
ss 'Just What You'd Term a Simple Country Lass'
Full Score (1989) Fred Urquhart

Shandon, Charles kind-hearted ne're-do-well Irish journalist
his wife, m. (2) Jack Finucane*
Mary daughter to Charles
Pendennis† (1848) W. M. Thackeray

Shandy, Tristram cc and narrator
Walter his father, retired turkey merchant
Elizabeth his mother
Bobby his elder brother
Capt. Toby his uncle
Dinah wife to Toby
Tristram Shandy (1767) Laurence Sterne

Shankland, Ann, Mrs ex-wife to John Malcolm*
Separate Tables play (1955) Terence Rattigan

Shannon, Betsy actress
Mr Facey Romford's Hounds (1865) R. S. Surtees

Shantsee, Rumblesack another of the author's informative caricatures of the poet laureate Robert Southey (see **Sackbut** and **Feathernest**), a rebel turned conformist
Crotchet Castle (1831) Thomas Love Peacock

Sharker ship's captain
The Fortunes of Nigel (1822) Walter Scott

Sharland, Mehalah (Glory) cc, m. Elijah Rebow*
Lydia her mother
Mehalah (1880) Sabine Baring-Gould

Sharp, Becky cc, charming and unscrupulous, m. Rawdon Crawley*
her artist father
her mother, French opera dancer
Vanity Fair (1847–8) W. M. Thackeray

Sharp, Luke lawyer, religious fanatic, and, ultimately, suicide
Cripps the Carrier: A Woodland Tale (1876) R. D. Blackmore

Sharp, Mr assistant master at Salem House School
David Copperfield (1850) Charles Dickens

Sharp, Mrs maid to Lady Cheverel*
ss 'Mr Gilfil's Love Story'
Scenes of Clerical Life (1857) George Eliot (rn Mary Anne, later Marian, Evans)

Sharp, Solomon P., Colonel hist. char. see **Fort, Cassius**
Beauchampe, or The Kentucky Tragedy (1842) William Gilmore Simms

Sharpe first mate
Hard Cash (1863) Charles Reade

Sharpe, Mrs landlady (The Cheat)
The Passing of the Third Floor Back play (1910) Jerome K. Jerome

Sharpeye member of Liverpool Police
The Uncommercial Traveller (1860–8) Charles Dickens

Sharpin, Matthew
ss 'The Biter Bit'
The Queen of Hearts (1859) Wilkie Collins

Sharpitlaw, Gideon Procurator Fiscal
Heart of Midlothian (1818) Walter Scott

Shatov saved character*
his wife
Besy (The Possessed) (1879) Fyodor Dostoievsky

Shaughnessy, Galahad, Major m. Pauline d'Hemecourt*
ss 'Café des exiles'
Old Creole Days (1879) George Washington Cable

Shavem witch
The City Madam play (1658) Philip Massinger

Shaw, Edith cousin to Margaret Hale*, m. Capt. Lennox*
North and South (1855) Mrs Gaskell

Shaw, Felix cc, vicious Australian businessman

The Watch Tower (1966) Elizabeth Harrower

Shaynor, John tubercular pharmacist's assistant who almost reproduces 'The Eve of St Agnes' in drugged trance
ss 'Wireless'
Traffics and Discoveries (1904) Rudyard Kipling

Shearwater, James
Rosie his wife
Antic Hay (1923) Aldous Huxley

Sheehy, Judy
her mother
ss 'The Courtship of Dinah Shadd'
Life's Handicap (1891) Rudyard Kipling

Sheepshanks see **Southdown, Earl of**

Sheepshanks, Mr
Wives and Daughters (1866) Mrs Gaskell

Sheepskin one of Miss Flite's* captive birds
Bleak House (1853) Charles Dickens

Shelby, Arthur original owner of Uncle Tom*
Emily his wife
Mas'r George their son
Uncle Tom's Cabin (1851) Harriet Beecher Stowe

Sheldon, Dorcasina novel-reading cc of satire on the sentimental novels popular in America in the later 18th and earlier 19th centuries; it owes much to *The Female Quixote**; in a line that culminated in *Madame Bovary**
Female Quixotism: Exhibited in the Romantic Opinions and Extravagant Adventures of Dorcasina Sheldon (1801) Mrs Tabitha Tenney

Shelley, Percy Bysshe (hist.) in this once popular novel he is saved from a watery grave and comes enthusiastically to republican America
The Orphan Angel (in England as *Mortal Image*) (1926) Elinor Wylie

Shelmerdine, Marmaduke Bonthrop Orlando's* husband – portrait of Harold Nicolson, Orlando being his wife
Orlando (1928) Virginia Woolf

Shelton, Lady
Gentlemen Prefer Blondes (1925) Anita Loos

Shelton, Richard later Sir Richard; cc, m. Joanna Sedley*

Sir Harry his father
The Black Arrow (1888) Robert Louis
Stevenson
Shend man half-rescued from dissolution
ss 'The Dog Hervey'
A Diversity of Creatures (1917) Rudyard
Kipling
Shepard, Sarah McVey's* foster mother
and mentor
Poor White (1920) Sherwood Anderson
Shepherd, John, Mr lawyer
Persuasion (1818) Jane Austen
Shepherd, Miss boarder at Miss
Nettingall's school
David Copperfield (1850) Charles
Dickens
Shepherd, Revd Goode
  Mateel his daughter m. (1) Jo Erring*,
  (2) Clinton Bragg*
The Story of a Country Town (1883)
E. W. Howe
Shepherd, The one of Mrs Weller's* spirit-
ual advisors
The Pickwick Papers (1837) Charles
Dickens
Shepherdson butcher and thief
ss 'The Detective Police'
Reprinted Pieces (1858) Charles Dickens
Shepperson, Miss
ss 'A Charming Family'
The House of Cobwebs (1906) George
Gissing
Shere Khan ('Lungri') the Tiger
ss 'Mowgli's Brothers'†
The Jungle Books (1894–5) Rudyard
Kipling
Shepperton, Randy
  Margaret his sister
You Can't Go Home Again (1940)
Thomas Wolfe
Sherburn, Colonel
Huckleberry Finn (1884) Mark Twain
(rn Samuel Langhorne Clemens)
Shergold, Dr
  Emma his wife
ss 'A Lodger in Maze Pond'
The House of Cobwebs (1906) George
Gissing
Sheridan first husband of Audrey Blake*
The Little Nugget (1913) P. G. Wode-
house
Sheridan, Laura
  Laurie her brother

their mother
ss 'The Garden Party'
The Garden Party (1922) Katherine
Mansfield (rn Katherine Mansfield Beau-
champ)
Sheriff, Kate cc
The Naulakha (1892) Rudyard Kipling
and Walcot Balestier
Sheringham, Roger amateur detective who
appears in earlier books by this author
(see **Iles**) onwards from
The Poisoned Chocolates Case† (1929)
Anthony Berkeley (rn Anthony Berkeley
Cox)
Sherlock, Theodore, Revd curate, Treby
Magna
Felix Holt (1860) George Eliot (rn Mary
Anne, later Marian, Evans)
Sherrard ('The ganger')
  Margaret his wife
The Pottleton Legacy (1849) Albert
Smith
Sherrick vulgar but kindly wine merchant,
usurer
  his wife, formerly opera singer
  Julia his daughter, m. Charles Honey-
man*
The Newcomes (1853–5) W. M.
Thackeray
Sherringham, Peter stage-struck, diploma-
tist brother to Julia Dallow*, in love with
Miriam Rooth*
The Tragic Muse (1890) Henry James
Sherston, George cc
  Evelyn his aunt
Memoirs of a Fox-Hunting Man (1929)
Siegfried Sassoon
Sherwin, Margaret m. Basil*
  her father, draper and petty tyrant; her
mother
Basil (1852) Wilkie Collins
Sherwin, Vida repressed sarcastic
schoolteacher
Main Street (1921) Sinclair Lewis
Shevek physicist who has invented in-
stantaneous method of communication
The Dispossessed (1974) Ursula Le Guin
Shiell, Queely Christ-figure in Australian
novel set in Tasmania in the 1840s and
owing much to *His Natural Life**
The Tilted Cross (1961) Hal Porter
Shift a threadbare shark; one that never
was a soldier, yet lives upon lendings; his

profession is skeldring (getting money by false pretences) and odling (cheating)
Every Man Out of His Humour play (1599) Ben Jonson

Shift part played by the author himself, in his best play; character invented to ridicule Tate Wilkinson; in satire on the Methodism of George Whitefield and others
The Minor play (1760) Samuel Foote

Shillingsworth, Norman (No-name/ Nawnim)
Capricornia (1937) Xavier Herbert

Shillitoe tailor, Bursley
The Card (1911) Arnold Bennett

Shimerda, Antonia cc immigrant to Nebraska from Bohemia
her impractical, music-loving father
her vulgar mother
Yulka; Ambrosch her sister and brother
Anton (Cuzac) her husband, who legitimizes her child by Donovan*
their children
My Antonia (1918) Willa Cather

Shiner, Fred farmer-churchwarden
Under the Greenwood Tree (1872) Thomas Hardy

Shingfu aged Chinese philosopher
A Citizen of the World (1762) Oliver Goldsmith

Single, Vincent, Corporal
ss 'The Woman in his Life'
Limits and Renewals (1932) Rudyard Kipling

Shiny Villiam deputy hostler at the Rochester Bull
The Pickwick Papers (1837) Charles Dickens

Shinza, Edward African politician
A Guest of Honour (1971) Nadine Gordimer

Shipley, Hagar Currie ninety-year-old narrator, cc; daughter of a storekeeper in a Canadian prairie town
Brampton her husband
Marvin m. Doris; **John** their sons
The Stone Angel (1964) Margaret Laurence

Shirley, Dr Rector of Uppercross
his wife
Persuasion (1818) Jane Austen

Shirley, Janet
ss 'The Weeping Man'

Unlucky for Pringle (1973) Wyndham Lewis

Shirley, Peter
Major Barbara (1905) George Bernard Shaw

Shoats, Hoover religious conman calling himself Onnie Jay Holy
Wise Blood (1952) Flannery O'Connor

Shobbes friend to George Winterbourne*; unfair caricature of Ford Madox Ford*
Death of a Hero (1929) Richard Aldington

Shodbutt, Samuel caricature of Arnold Bennett*
The Roaring Queen (1936) Wyndham Lewis

Shoesmith friend to Remington*; founder of the *Blue Weekly*
The New Machiavelli (1911) H. G. Wells

Shoesmith, Tom
ss 'The Dymchurch Flit'
Puck of Pook's Hill (1906) Rudyard Kipling

Sholto, Captain
The Princess Casamassima (1866) Henry James

Shoop, Earle idiotic 'cowboy beau' of Faye Greener whose testicles are crushed
The Day of the Locust (1939) Nathanael West (rn Nathan Weinstein)

Short ('Trotters') punch-and-judy show man, whose real name is **Harris**
The Old Curiosity Shop (1841) Charles Dickens

Shorthose, Quintilian, Sir
Satiromastix, or The Untrussing of the Humorous Poet play (1602) Thomas Dekker ?and John Marston

Shortley, Mr hired man
ss 'The Displaced Person'
A Good Man is Hard to Find (1955) Flannery O'Connor

Shotover, Captain
Heartbreak House play (1917) George Bernard Shaw

Shott, Annie mother to Kim O'Hara*
Kim (1901) Rudyard Kipling

Shovel
'Ameliar' his sister
Sentimental Tommy (1896) J. M. Barrie

Shrapnel, Dr radical freethinker and republican; horsewhipped by Romfrey*
Beauchamp's Career (1876) George

Meredith

Shreve Quentin Compson's* fellow student
The Sound and the Fury (1931) William Faulkner

Shrewsbury, Earl of see **Talbot, Lord**

Shrike, William editor of a newspaper
Mary his wife, whose enormous breasts conceal a medal reading 'Awarded by the Boston Latin School, for first place in the 100 yd dash'
Miss Lonelyhearts (1933) Nathanael West (rn Nathan Weinstein)

Shropshire, Marquess of grandfather to Marjorie Ferrar*
The Silver Spoon (1926) John Galsworthy

Shropton, William, Sir m. Lady Agatha Caradoc
Ann their daughter
The Patrician (1911) John Galsworthy

Shrubfield, Mrs county *grande dame*
Before the Bombardment (1926) Osbert Sitwell

Shuah, Belacqua solipsist and peeping Tom, by nature sinfully indolent, even lazier than if he were brother to sloth herself – with an income which 'however inconsiderable, had a certain air of distinction, *being unearned*'
ss 'Sedendo et Quiescendo' (*Transition*, 21, 1932)
ss 'A Wet Night'†
More Pricks That Kicks (1934) Samuel Beckett

Shuan brutal mate of the *Covenant*
Kidnapped (1886) Robert Louis Stevenson

Shubunka crippled brothel operator in author's best novel (he went to Hollywood), set on 'Brooklyn's soggy fringe', Neptune Beach, a composite of Coney Island and Brighton Beach
Low Company (1937) Daniel Fuchs

Shuman, Zella
An American Tragedy (1925) Theodore Dreiser

Shunfield sea captain, and jeerer
The Staple of News play (1631) Ben Jonson

Shurochka Romashov's* ambitious and treacherous married lover, his murderess by a trick

The Duel (1905) Alexander Kuprin

Shushions, Mr
Clayhanger (1910) Arnold Bennett

Shute, Bernard
Cecilia his sister
Some Experiences of an Irish R. M.† (1899) O. E. Somerville and Martin Ross (rn Edith Somerville and Violet Martin)

Shuttlethwaite, Mrs
The Cocktail Party play (1950) T. S. Eliot

Shuttleworth, George
Olga Bracely his wife, prima donna
Queen Lucia (1920) E. F. Benson

Shylock cc, moneylender
The Merchant of Venice play (1623) William Shakespeare

Sib, The portrait of the novelist and loyal friend to Wilde*, Ada Leverson
The Apes of God (1930) Wyndham Lewis

Sibley, Joe portrait of the painter Whistler, who forced the author to tone it down under legal threat
Trilby (1894) George du Maurier

Sibley, Michael innocent victim in mystery in the Francis Iles* tradition
My Name is Michael Sibley (1952) John Bingham (rn Lord Clanmorris)

Sibwright, Percy neighbour to Pendennis*
The Newcomes (1853–5) W. M. Thackeray

Sibylla
Death's Jest Book, or *The Fool's Tragedy* play (1850) Thomas Lovell Beddoes

Sichcliffe, Moira perhaps, unconsciously, a witch – but who may be cured by marriage to Shend*, who once showed her consideration
Dr Sichcliffe her evil father, who never showed her consideration, and who would take up hopeless cases and insure them before sending them back into the world
ss 'The Dog Hervey'
A Diversity of Creatures (1917) Rudyard Kipling

Sicinius, Velutus tribune
Coriolanus play (1623) William Shakespeare

Sick-of-it-all writer of letters to Miss Lonelyhearts*
Miss Lonelyhearts (1933) Nathanael West (rn Nathan Weinstein)

Sidi el Assif woman sheik
Captain Brassbound's Conversion play
(1900) George Bernard Shaw
Sidney, John, Lord portrait of the author's
fellow Young England politician Lord
John Manners
Coningsby (1844) Benjamin Disraeli
Sidney, Mr farmer
his common-law wife
ss 'My Son's Wife'
A Diversity of Creatures (1917) Rudyard
Kipling
Siegfried courtier
Death's Jest Book, or *The Fool's Tragedy*
play (1850) Thomas Lovell Beddoes
Sieppe, Trina m. McTeague*, becomes a
miser; fingers are bitten off by her hus-
band before he beats her to death
her parents, uncle and aunt to Marcus
Schouler*
McTeague (1899) Frank Norris
Sievewright blacksmith in Castlewood
Nancy his daughter
Henry Esmond (1852) W. M. Thackeray
Sigglesthwaite, Agnes high school teacher
her mother
Edie her sister
South Riding (1936) Winifred Holtby
Sikes, Bill desperate and surly house-
breaker working with Fagin*; murders
his mistress, Nancy*
Oliver Twist (1839) Charles Dickens
Silas the hired man
poem 'Death of the Hired Man'
North of Boston (1914) Robert Frost
Silas, Great-Uncle bawdy country charac-
ter
Abel his son
Georgina Abel's wife
Uncle Cosmo Silas' foreign-travelling
brother
My Uncle Silas† (1939) H. E. Bates
Silas, Père devious but decent Jesuit
Villette (1853) Charlotte Brontë
Silcot, Aubrey
Emily his wife
ss 'An Anniversary'
A Beginning (1955) Walter de la Mare
Silenski, Richard novelist
Cass his wife
Another Country (1962) James Baldwin
Silenus, Otto, 'Professor'
Decline and Fall (1928) Evelyn Waugh

Silk, Ambrose portrait of the homosexual
eccentric and writer, Brian Howard
Put Out More Flags (1942) Evelyn
Waugh
Silkworm, Diaphanous, Sir a courtier
The Magnetic Lady, or *Humours Recon-
ciled* play (1641) Ben Jonson
Silla lover of Apolonius*
Pontus her father, lord and governor of
Cyprus
Silvio her brother
novela 'Of Apolonius and Silla'
Farewell to Militarie Profession (1581)
Barnabe Riche
Sillabub see Lollipop
Silton, Ben
The Man of Feeling (1771) Henry
Mackenzie
Silva, Dr Dean of Medical School
Arrowsmith (1925) Sinclair Lewis
Silva, Joe
Mourning Becomes Electra play (1931)
Eugene O'Neill
Silver Man, The
ss 'The Mark of the Beast'
Life's Handicap (1891) Rudyard Kipling
Silver, Long John in part suggested by the
overpowering personality of the author's
friend, and then enemy, the poet, editor
and imperialist, W. E. Henley
Treasure Island (1883) Robert Louis
Stevenson
Silver, Louise see d'Argent, Louise Eugénie
Silver, Mattie cousin to Zenobia Frome*,
in love with Ethan Frome*
Ethan Frome (1911) Edith Wharton
Silvercross, Julian m. Ida Eynon*
Adam his father, banker
his mother, *née* Derwent
Muriel; Harriet his sisters
The Old Bank (1902) William Westall
Silverman, George narrator cc, orphan
brought up by religious fanatics
ss 'George Silverman's Explanation'
(1868) Charles Dickens
Silvertop, George Granby, Captain m.
Lady Angela Thistlewood*, his cousin
Jeames's Diary (1846) W. M. Thackeray
Silvester, Anne governess seduced and
victimized by, and m., to Geoffrey
Delamayn*; m. (2) Sir Patrick Lundie*
Man and Wife (1870) Wilkie Collins
Silvestre, José da, Dom Portuguese

possessor of chart to the mines
King Solomon's Mines (1885) Henry Rider Haggard

Silvia daughter to the Duke of Milan
Two Gentlemen of Verona play (1623) William Shakespeare

Silvius a shepherd
As You Like It play (1623) William Shakespeare

Simcoe incumbent of Clavering St Mary
the Hon. Mrs Simcoe his wife
Pendennis (1848) W. M. Thackeray

Simeon, Willy half-witted boy who undertakes to buy can of striped paint and ends in an asylum
Coming Up For Air (1936) George Orwell (rn Eric Blair)

Simkin lawyer to the Aintree stewards
National Velvet (1935) Enid Bagnold

Simmery, Frank smart friend to Wilkins Flasher*
The Pickwick Papers (1837) Charles Dickens

Simmons beadle who dies of over-exertion when conveying an intoxicated lady to the workhouse strongroom; he left his respects
Sketches By Boz† (1836) Charles Dickens

Simmons, Miss Lady Catherine Lasenby's maid
The Admirable Crichton play (1902) J. M. Barrie

Simmons, Ned enemy to Henry Little*
Put Yourself in his Place (1870) Charles Reade

Simmons, Private
ss 'In the Matter of a Private'
Soldiers Three (1888) Rudyard Kipling

Simmons, Verena malicious gossip
Holy Deadlock (1934) A. P. Herbert

Simmons, Walter brainless jeweller
poem 'Walter Simmons'
Spoon River Anthology verse epitaphs (1915) Edgar Lee Masters

Simmons, William van driver
Martin Chuzzlewit (1844) Charles Dickens

Simms, Noble friend to Rob Angus*
When a Man's Single (1888) J. M. Barrie

Simnel, Lambert (hist.) pretender
Perkin Warbeck play (1634) John Ford

Simon ('Soft Simon') Irish farmer contented, according to the author, in the wrong way: 'precisely the species of content which leads to beggary'
ss 'Rosanna'
Popular Tales (1812) Maria Edgeworth

Simon of Penrhos
Beca his wife
ss 'The Way of the Earth'
My People (1915) Caradoc Evans (rn David Evans)

Simon, Jules jewel-thief
ss 'The Diamond Lens' (1858)
Poems and Stories (1881) Fitz-James O'Brien

Simon, Rachel cousin to the Vinneys*
Non-Combatants and Others (1916) Rose Macaulay

Simonet, Albertine first seen as a rowdy young girl on a bicycle; loved by Marcel*; suggested by several of the author's lovers and admired ones, male and female
A la recherche du temps perdu (*In Search of Lost Time*) (1913–27) Marcel Proust

Simonides King of Pentapolis
Thaisa his daughter
Pericles play (1609) William Shakespeare

Simonin, Suzanne narrator, forced into a convent
La Religieuse (*The Nun*) (1796) Denis Diderot

Simper, Harriet, Miss coquette, in love with Harebrain*, m. Brainless*; in once widely read American satirical work
The Progress of Dulness poem (1772–3) John Trumbull

Simpkin a cat
The Tailor of Gloucester (1903) Beatrix Potter

Simple encountered by Christian*
The Pilgrim's Progress (1678–84) John Bunyan

Simple, David cc, guileless hero schemed against by his beloved younger brother, m. Camilla*; second edition extensively revised by the author's brother, Henry Fielding*
The Adventures of David Simple (1744–53) Sarah Fielding

Simple, Peter naval officer
Ellen his sister
Peter Simple (1834) Captain Marryat

Simplicius so-called because he is 'simple',

as he judges only by appearances; cc of popular and highly successful German picaresque* novel, set in and just after the Thirty Years War; later the 'Huntsman of Soest'
Simplicissimus (1669) Hans Jakob von Grimmelshausen

Simpson page to Rawdon Crawley
Vanity Fair (1847–8) W. M. Thackeray

Simpson, Homer midwest hick in love with Faye Greener*; murders boy
The Day of the Locust (1939) Nathanael West (rn Nathan Weinstein)

Sims boat-pilot
A Shabby Genteel Story (1840) W. M. Thackeray

Sinclair chief officer, *Altair*
Gallions Reach (1927) H. M. Tomlinson

Sinclair Highland chief
his daughter, m. Magnus Troil*
The Pirate (1822) Walter Scott

Sinclair rich baronet, cc, narrator of latter book
The Island (1888); *No. 5 John Street* (1899) Richard Whiteing

Sinclair, Captain
The Settlers in Canada (1844) Captain Marryat

Sinclair, Emil cc influential novel originally published by author under name of Emil Sinclair
Demian (1919) Herman Hesse

Sinclair, Esther loved by Ewan Gray*
My Mortal Enemy (1928) Willa Cather

Sinclair, Mrs helps Lovelace* to kidnap Clarissa Harlowe*
Clarissa Harlowe (1748) Samuel Richardson

Sinclair, Revd Mr
The Ministry of Fear (1943) Graham Greene

Sindall counterpart to Harley*, drawn on lines of Lovelace*
The Man of Feeling (1771) Henry Mackenzie

Sing Milkman Macon's* dead grandmother
Song of Solomon (1977) Toni Morrison

Singer, John dumb man, cc
The Heart is a Lonely Hunter (1940) Carson McCullers

Singh, Hurree Jamset Ram, Nabob of Bhanipur exotic member of the famous five onwards from
The Magnet† periodical (1908) Frank Richards (rn Charles Hamilton)

Singh, Juggat farmer suspected of terrorist act, eventually killed by a train under which he throws himself, in a self-sacrificing gesture
Train to Pakistan (1956) Khushwant Singh

Singh, Rutton
Attar his brother
ss 'In the Presence'
A Diversity of Creatures (1917) Rudyard Kipling

Single Gentleman, The
The Old Curiosity Shop (1841) Charles Dickens

Singleton, Adrian friend to Dorian Gray*
The Picture of Dorian Gray (1891) Oscar Wilde

Singleton, Captain cc, pirate, narrator, m. William Walters' sister*
Captain Singleton (1720) Daniel Defoe

Singleton, Sam American painter
Roderick Hudson (1875) Henry James

Singsby village schoolmaster
Bracebridge Hall (1823) Washington Irving

Sinico, Mrs
ss 'A Painful Case'
Dubliners (1914) James Joyce

Sinker, QC
Daniel Deronda (1876) George Eliot (rn Mary Anne, later Marian, Evans)

Sinnott, Enid Mary, Mrs old deaf mute owner of Dublin hotel
Eugene m. Philomena; **Enid Mary** m. Desmond Gregan her children
Timothy John son to Eugene and Philomena
Mrs Eckdorf in O'Neill's Hotel (1969) William Trevor

Sinquier, Sarah actress, daughter of a canon
Caprice (1917) Ronald Firbank

Sir Oliver an old brown hunter
Black Beauty (1877) Mrs Anna Sewell

Sirena, Doña poor widow, matchmaker
Los intereses creados (*The Bonds of Interest*) (1908) Jacinto Benavente

Sisop the Pythagorean
An Island in the Moon satirical prose fragment (written 1784–5, pub. 1907)

William Blake

Sisson, Aaron cc amateur flautist whose flute is his 'rod' (symbolically broken by a political bomb); abandons his work at the pit for the artistic life
Aaron's Rod (1922) D. H. Lawrence

Sitnikov 'progressive' – a squeaking buffoon
Otsy i deti (Fathers and Sons) (1862) Ivan Turgenev

Sitwell, Jasper, Sir
his wife
ss 'Mr Gilfil's Love Story'
Scenes of Clerical Life (1857) George Eliot (rn Mary Anne, later Marian, Evans)

Six, Auburn
Spider Boy (1928) Carl Van Vechten

Sixsmith, Seraphine, Mrs scheming woman
Caprice (1917) Ronald Firbank

Sizzum 'sleek rascal'; leader of cavalcade of Mormons; in adventure novel by victim of Civil War
John Brent (1862) Theodore Winthrop

Skeffington, Frank, Mayor machine politician based on Mayor Curley of Boston in popular novel
The Last Hurrah (1956) Edwin O'Connor

Skeggs owner of slave depot
Uncle Tom's Cabin (1851) Harriet Beecher Stowe

Skellorn, Mr rent collector
Enoch his son
his daughter, m. Grant
Hilda Lessways (1911) Arnold Bennett

Skelmersdale village shopkeeper
ss 'Mr Skelmersdale in Fairyland'
Tales of the Unexpected† (1923) H. G. Wells

Skene, Godfrey, Lieutenant
his uncle
The Spanish Farm Trilogy (1927); *Europa's Beast: A Rich Man's Daughter* (1930) R. H. Mottram

Skettles, Barnet, Dr father of one of Mr Blimber's* pupils
Lady Skettles his wife
Master Skettles his son
Dombey and Son (1848) Charles Dickens

Skewton, Mrs, the Hon. mother to Edith Dombey*, a vain and scheming woman referred to as Cleopatra
Dombey and Son (1848) Charles Dickens

Skiffins, Mrs lady of a 'wooden appearance', m. Wemmick*
her brother, accountant and agent
Great Expectations (1861) Charles Dickens

Skill 'ancient and well approved physician'
The Pilgrim's Progress (1678–84) John Bunyan

Skimpin Buzfuz's* junior at the Bardell-Pickwick trial
The Pickwick Papers (1837) Charles Dickens

Skimpole, Harold sponger, but a delightful companion; portrait of Leigh Hunt
his wife, once a beauty, now suffering under a complication of disorders
Arethusa; Laura; Kitty his daughters: 'Beauty; Sentiment and Comedy'
Bleak House (1853) Charles Dickens

Skinner clerk at Hardie's bank
Hard Cash (1863) Charles Reade

Skinner, Dr head of Ernest Pontifex's school
his daughter
The Way of All Flesh (1903) Samuel Butler

Skinner, Mr and Mrs in charge of the experimental farm; grandparents to Albert Caddles*
The Food of the Gods (1904) H. G. Wells

Skinner, Nicholas cab-owner
Black Beauty (1877) Anna Sewell

Skionar 'transcendental poet'; friend to MacCrotchet*; caricature of Coleridge in his capacity as student of German philosophy, deplored by the author, who admired his poetry
Crotchet Castle (1831) Thomas Love Peacock

Skipper also known as **Captain** and **Edward**, cc
Gertrude his wife, who has left him for other men
Cassandra their daughter
Second Skin (1964) John Hawkes

Skipton, Daniel writer, cc
The Unspeakable Skipton (1959) Pamela Hansford Johnson

Skopje, Adele astrologer unconscious of anything in the present
One Day (1965) Wright Morris

Skrebensky, Anton son of exiled Polish baron, lover of Ursula Brangwen*
The Rainbow (1915) D. H. Lawrence

Skreigh clerk and precentor
Guy Mannering (1815) Walter Scott

Skurliewhitter, Andrew smooth-tongued villain employed by Lord Dalgarno*
The Fortunes of Nigel (1822) Walter Scott

Skylights pirate
Peter Pan play (1904) J. M. Barrie

Skyme, Robyn ('**Ragged Robin**') alias **Eccles** and **Waygood**; cc
Ned his father
John; Margaret his uncle and aunt, and adoptive parents
The Story of Ragged Robyn (1945) Oliver Onions

Skyresh, Borgolam councillor, bitter enemy to Gulliver*
Gulliver's Travels (1726) Jonathan Swift

Slackbridge socialist orator; trade union agitator; eventually sent to Coventry by his fellows
Hard Times (1854) Charles Dickens

Sladdery proprietor of a fashionable bookshop and lending library
Bleak House (1853) Charles Dickens

Slammekin, Mrs
Polly opera (1729) John Gay

Slammer, Dr fiery surgeon
The Pickwick Papers (1837) Charles Dickens

Slane, Corporal m. Jhansi McKenna
ss 'A Daughter of the Regiment'†
Plain Tales from the Hills (1888) Rudyard Kipling

Slaney, Abe gangster
ss 'The Dancing Men'
The Return of Sherlock Holmes (1905) Arthur Conan Doyle

Slang, Adolphus theatrical manager
ss 'The Ravenswing'
Men's Wives (1843) W. M. Thackeray

Slang, Lord friend to the Egotistical Young Couple*
Sketches of Young Couples (1840) Charles Dickens

Slasher surgeon
The Pickwick Papers (1837) Charles Dickens

Slater, Hermione Ravelston's* girl who sleeps with him but does not m. him as it is 'too much fag'; hates the working classes and believes they *smell*
Keep the Aspidistra Flying (1936) George Orwell (rn Eric Blair)

Slattery, Emmie poor white; m. Jonas Wilkerson*
Gone With the Wind (1936) Margaret Mitchell

Slattery, Pearl heroic and beautiful worker at Snashfold's Sweet factory, mother of four, grandmother, in comic novel of adolescent and suburban life
Jack her husband, frequent visitor of Her Majesty
Redhill Rococo (1986) Shena Mackay

Slaughter, Lieutenant fire-eating friend to Captain Waters*
Sketches by Boz† (1836) Charles Dickens

Slaughter, Olive
Mr Blettsworthy on Rampole Island (1933) H. G. Wells

Slave, The Ethiopian
ss 'The Story of the Greek Slave'
The Pacha of Many Tales (1836) Captain Marryat

Slawkenbergius, Hafen long-nosed imaginary author
Tristram Shandy (1759–67) Laurence Sterne

Sleaford, Lord former husband of Lady Molly Jeavons*
A Question of Upbringing† (1951) Anthony Powell

Sleary circus proprietor
Hard Times (1854) Charles Dickens

Sleeny, Sam assistant to Mr Matchin*; kills Offit* but is acquitted as temporarily insane; m. Maud Matchin*
The Bread-Winners (1884) John Hay

Slemp, Deacon sadist
A Cool Million (1934) Nathanael West (rn Nathan Weinstein)

Slender cousin to Shallow*
The Merry Wives of Windsor play (1623) William Shakespeare

Sletherby, Philip cc
ss 'A Shot in the Dark' (1913)
in *Saki, A Life of Hector Hugh Munro* (1981) by A. J. Langguth

Slick, Sam comic character created by Canadian Tory, most effectively in the earlier of the seven volumes devoted to him, onwards from

The Clockmaker or *The Sayings and Doings of Samuel Slick of Slickville*† (1836–40) Thomas Chandler Haliburton

Slide, Quintus editor, the *People's Banner*
Phineas Finn† (1869) Anthony Trollope

Sliderskew, Peg Gride's* housekeeper, a horrible thieving old hag; transported
Nicholas Nickleby (1839) Charles Dickens

Slightly one of Peter's* band
Peter Pan play (1904) J. M. Barrie

Slim Girl Navajo educated at white school shot by Red Man* (after being shot by Laughing Boy* but not fatally: fate's second bite at the cherry)
Laughing Boy (1929) Oliver La Farge

Slim, Simon prep-school boy captured by Ralph and Paula Fairbrother* during a game, thus fuelling resentment in the village
Old Crow (1967) Shena Mackay

Slingo horse dealer
Little Dorrit (1857) Charles Dickens

Slingstone, Countess of
Vanity Fair (1847–8) W. M. Thackeray

Slinkton, Julius murderer and swindler, modelled on the poisoner Thomas Griffiths Wainewright
Hunted Down (1860) Charles Dickens

Slipper
Some Experiences of an Irish R. M. (1899) O. E. Somerville and Martin Ross (rn Edith Somerville and Violet Martin)

Slipslop, Mrs waiting-woman
Joseph Andrews (1742) Henry Fielding

Slithers Master Humphrey's* barber
Master Humphrey's Clock (1841) Charles Dickens

Sloan, Simon boy growing up in the 1930s in New York
Teitlebaum's Widow (1970) Wallace Markfield

Sloane smooth-skinned young man, cc
Entertaining Mr Sloane play (1964) Joe Orton

Sloane, Mrs meddling woman
Arthur her husband, Liverpool docker
Ebb and Flood (1932) James Hanley

Sloboluchowicz, Erasmus caricature of the Polish dictator Marshall Pilsudski, who had a dark and sooty complexion
Nienasycenie: poweiesc (Insatiability) (1930) Stanislaw Ignacy Witkiewicz

Slocum, Aimee nasty-minded sadistic woman confounded
ss 'Lily Daw and the Three Ladies'
A Curtain of Green (1941) Eudora Welty

Slocum, Bob cc, insensitive corporation executive, mimic
Something Happened (1974) Joseph Heller

Slop, Dr man-midwife
Tristram Shandy (1767) Laurence Sterne

Slope, Obidiah, Revd chaplain to Bishop Proudie*
Barchester Towers (1857) Anthony Trollope

Sloper, Austin, Dr widower, physician
Catherine his awkward daughter, engaged to Morris Townsend*
Washington Square (1880) Henry James

Sloppy foundling; becomes a useful carpenter
Our Mutual Friend (1865) Charles Dickens

Sloth encountered by Christian*
The Pilgrim's Progress (1678–84) John Bunyan

Slothrop, Tyrone, Lieutenant a sort of metaphysical Oliver North
Gravity's Rainbow (1973) Thomas Pynchon

Slout Bumble's* predecessors as workhouse-master
Oliver Twist (1839) Charles Dickens

Slow, Mr lawyer
Miss Mackenzie (1863) Anthony Trollope

Slow-Solid the tortoise
ss 'The Beginning of the Armadillos'
Just So Stories (1902) Rudyard Kipling

Slowboy, Tilly Dot Perrybingle's* clumsy maid
The Cricket on the Hearth (1845) Charles Dickens

Slowcoach Mr Verdant Green's* tutor
The Adventures of Mr Verdant Green (1853) Cuthbert Bede (rn Edward Bradley)

Sludberry, Thomas
Sketches by Boz (1836) Charles Dickens

Sludge, Dickie 'queer, shambling, well-made urchin', guide to Edmund Tressilian*
his mother
Kenilworth (1821) Walter Scott

Sluffen master-sweep
Sketches by Boz (1836) Charles Dickens
Slug, Mr member of the Association
The Mudfog Papers (1838) Charles
Dickens
Slum poetical friend to Mrs Jarley* who
could compose to order
The Old Curiosity Shop (1841) Charles
Dickens
Slumkey, the Hon. Mr successful candi-
date for parliament, shook the hands of
twenty washed workmen and kissed all
their babies
The Pickwick Papers (1837) Charles
Dickens
Slummery a clever painter
Sketches of Young Couples (1840)
Charles Dickens
Slummintowkens members of Nupkins'*
social circle
The Pickwick Papers (1837) Charles
Dickens
Slurk editor of the *Eatanswill Independent*
and rival to Mr Pott*
The Pickwick Papers (1837) Charles
Dickens
Slush, Barnaby novelist
Death of a Hero (1929) Richard
Aldington
Sly, Christopher drunken tinker
The Taming of the Shrew (1623) William
Shakespeare
Slyme, Chevy down-at-heels connection of
the Chuzzlewit family*, said to be
perpetually round the corner
Martin Chuzzlewit (1844) Charles
Dickens
Slyter, Sidney Greene*-like detective
The Lime Twig (1961) John Hawkes
Smalder girls, The acquaintances of
Cousin Feenix*
Dombey and Son (1848) Charles Dickens
Small Porgies a large animal
ss 'The Butterfly that Stamped'
Just So Stories (1902) Rudyard Kipling
Small, Abner
Mourning Becomes Electra play (1932)
Eugene O'Neill
Small, Beverly F., Professor Levi's* ad-
visor
Birds of America (1971) Mary McCarthy
Small, Jonathan one of the Four
The Sign of Four (1890) Arthur Conan

Doyle
Small, Lennie gigantic man of small in-
tellect who does not know his own
strength
Of Mice and Men (1937) John Steinbeck
Small, Sam
Captains All† (1905) W. W. Jacobs
Small, Sam
his wife
Judy their daughter
A Town Like Alice (1950) Neville Shute
Small, Septimus m. Julia Forsyte*
The Forsyte series (1906–33) John
Galsworthy
Smallbones waif-like cc, looking like
'Famine's eldest son just arriving to years
of discretion'
Snarleyyow (1837) Captain Marryat
Smallbury, Jacob
Billy his son, both farm hands
Liddy Billy's youngest daughter, servant-
companion to Bathsheba Everdene*
Jacob's father, maltster
Far From the Madding Crowd (1874)
Thomas Hardy
Smalley, Tusker, Colonel
Lucy his wife; ccs
The Raj Quartet (1976); *Staying On*
(1977) Paul Scott
Smallin, Gorm vividly portrayed Confed-
erate deserter who hates the rich and
burns their property
Tiger Lilies (1867) Sidney Lanier
Smalls, Lily Mrs Benyon's* treasure
Under Milk Wood play (1954) Dylan
Thomas
Smallsole Master, HMS *Harpy*
Mr Midshipman Easy (1836) Captain
Marryat
Smallways, Bert cc, jack-of-all-trades, m.
Edna Bunthorne*
Tom his greengrocer brother
Jessica wife to Tom
Old Tom their father
War in the Air (1908) H. G. Wells
Smallweed, Joshua paralysed usurer and
blackmailer
his deaf and imbecile wife, whom he calls
a 'brimstone chatterer'; sister to Krook
the rag-dealer
Judy his granddaughter
Bartholomew ('Bart'; 'Chick') her twin
brother, clerk at Kenge and Carboys, a

precocious and grasping credit to the family
Bleak House (1853) Charles Dickens
Smangle in debtor's prison
The Pickwick Papers (1837) Charles Dickens
Smart, Peter cc, sensitive boy
Peter Smart's Confessions (1977) Paul Bailey
Smauker, John Mr Bantam's footman
The Pickwick Papers (1937) Charles Dickens
Smeddum tobacconist
The Provost (1822) John Galt
Smee pirate boatswain
Peter Pan play (1904) J. M. Barrie
Smee, Andrew portrait painter
The Newcomes† (1853–5) W. M. Thackeray
Smeeth, Mr
his wife
Edna; George their children
Angel Pavement (1930) J. B. Priestley
Smeraldina-Rima Belacqua Shuah's* lady-love in Vienna
ss 'Sedendo et Quiescendo' (*Transition*, 21, 1932) Samuel Beckett
Smerdyakov epileptic illegitimate son to Fyodor Karamazov*, whom he kills
Bratya Karamazov (*Brothers Karamazov*) (1880) Fyodor Dostoievsky
Smid armourer
Hypatia (1853) Charles Kingsley
Smif, Putnam soulful shop assistant in America
Martin Chuzzlewit (1844) Charles Dickens
Smiggers, Joseph Perpetual Vice-Chairman of the Pickwick Club
The Pickwick Papers (1837) Charles Dickens
Smike half-witted victim of the brutality of Squeers* who pined away
Nicholas Nickleby (1839) Charles Dickens
Smiler the whale
ss 'How the Whale got his Throat'
Just So Stories (1902) Rudyard Kipling
Smiley, George popular spycatcher in series to rival Oppenheim*
Smiley's People† (1980) John le Carré (rn David John Cornwall)
Smiley, Jim miner who bets that his frog

Dan'l Webster* can jump farther than another
ss 'The Celebrated Jumping Frog of Calveras County'
The Celebrated Jumping Frog (1867) Mark Twain (rn Samuel Langhorne Clemens)
Smiling, Mary, Mrs friend to Flora Poste*
Cold Comfort Farm (1932) Stella Gibbons
Smirke curate and tutor
Belinda his wife
Pendennis (1848) W. M. Thackeray
Smith cc of strange utopia* in which sex drive in man is extinguished
A Crystal Age (1887) W. H. Hudson
Smith detective murdered by McCabe*
The Face on the Cutting-Room Floor (1937) Cameron McCabe (rn E. W. J. Borneman)
Smith half-pay lieutenant
The Great Hoggarty Diamond (1841) W. M. Thackeray
Smith Peter Burns's* valet
The Little Nugget (1913) P. G. Wodehouse
Smith villain, real name Murker
John Brent (1862) Theodore Winthrop
Smith, Beauty villain who tries to make White Fang* more savage in order to win cash in dogfights
White Fang (1905) Jack London
Smith, Bessie real-life blues singer who became decidedly fictional in this drama wrongly attributing her death to the racist practices of a hospital
The Death of Bessie Smith play (1960) Edward Albee
Smith, Bildad
ss 'The Sad Horn Blowers'
Horses and Men (1924) Sherwood Anderson
Smith, Bob Margate draper
A Shabby Genteel Story (1840) W. M. Thackeray
Smith, Charles
his wife and subsequently widow, *née* Hamilton, friend to Anne Elliot*
Persuasion (1818) Jane Austen
Smith, Concepcion
The Pretty Lady (1918) Arnold Bennett
Smith, Culverton
ss 'The Dying Detective'

His Last Bow (1917) Arthur Conan Doyle

Smith, Harold ex-politician
Harriet his wife, *née* Sowerby
Framley Parsonage (1861) Anthony Trollope

Smith, Harriet illegitimate child placed at Miss Goddard's* m. Robert Martin*
Emma (1816) Jane Austen

Smith, Harry (the 'I' of Sarnac's* dream), m. (1) Hetty Marcus, (2) Milly Kimpton
Fanny elopes with Richard Newberry*; **Ernest** his sister and brother
Mortimer his father
The Dream (1924) H. G. Wells

Smith, Henry Martin Aluin cc, drunken down-and-out American possibly suggested by the American poet Hart Crane
his father
The Rash Act (1933); *Henry for Hugh* (1934) Ford Madox Ford

Smith, Hugh Monckton Allard cc, Englishman who looks like Henry Martin Aluin Smith*; is high up in automobile industry in Great Britain
The Rash Act (1933); *Henry for Hugh* (1934) Ford Madox Ford

Smith, Innocent
Manalive (1912) G. K. Chesterton

Smith, Iseult Eva Trout's* schoolteacher, m. Eric Able*
Eva Trout (1969) Elizabeth Bowen

Smith, Janet sensitive 'lady writer' seeking rest in Illyria, a luxurious retreat for artists, diarist
Real People (1969) Alison Lurie

Smith, Mary cc, diarist
Robert her husband
Vicky; Robin their children
Diary of a Provincial Lady (1930) E. M. Delafield

Smith, Miss Charlotte dour Scottish nurse who rules island in Pacific and dies of rage at age ninety-eight in satirical novel; m. Dr O'Malley (who is already married)
Albert Edward her son, and his nine brothers and sisters
Orphan Island (1924) Rose Macaulay

Smith, Mordecai boat owner
The Sign of Four (1890) Arthur Conan Doyle

Smith, Mrs elderly invalid living at Ash Court, upon whom her cousin Willoughby* depends
Sense and Sensibility (1811) Jane Austen

Smith, Mrs guardian of Clarissa Harlowe* in her captivity
her husband
Clarissa Harlowe (1748) Samuel Richardson

Smith, Mrs one-time governess of Anne Elliot*
Persuasion (1818) Jane Austen

Smith, Purdy m. Tilly Ocock*, *née* Beamish
Aurelia his daughter
The Fortunes of Richard Mahoney (1917–30) Henry Handel Richardson (rn Ethel Florence Lindesay Richardson Robertson)

Smith, Revd Mr Independent minister, Milby
ss 'Janet's Repentance'
Scenes of Clerical Life (1857) George Eliot (rn Mary Anne, later Marian, Evans)

Smith, Samuel real name of Horatio Sparkins*
Sketches by Boz† (1836) Charles Dickens

Smith, Septimus Warren
Lucrezia his wife
Mrs Dalloway (1925) Virginia Woolf

Smith, Stephen Fitzmaurice engaged to Elfrida Swancourt*
John; Jane his parents
A Pair of Blue Eyes (1873) Thomas Hardy

Smith, Violet
ss 'The Solitary Cyclist'
The Return of Sherlock Holmes (1905) Arthur Conan Doyle

Smith, Wayland Edmund Tressilian's confidential servant
Kenilworth (1821) Walter Scott

Smith, William Abel American presidential candidate visiting Haiti
his wife, a vegetarian and idealist
The Comedians (1966) Graham Greene

Smith, Winston cc
Katharine his wife
1984 (1949) George Orwell (rn Eric Blair)

Smithers

Sinister Street (1913) Compton Mackenzie

Smithers fellow student at South Kensington with Lewisham
Love and Mr Lewisham (1900) H. G. Wells

Smithers solicitor
The Great Hoggarty Diamond (1841) W. M. Thackeray

Smithers, Robert roaring city clerk
Sketches by Boz† (1836) Charles Dickens

Smithie Persian robe designer and maker, cousin to and employer of Marion Ramboat*
Tono Bungay (1909) H. G. Wells

Smithson, Charles amateur palaeontologist, engaged to Ernestina Freeman*
The French Lieutenant's Woman (1969) John Fowles

Smithwick and Watersby firm owning the *Golden Mary*
The Golden Mary (1856) Charles Dickens

Smivey, Chicken name given by Tigg* to Martin Chuzzlewit* on pledge ticket for his watch
Martin Chuzzlewit (1844) Charles Dickens

Smoke hunter on the *Ghost*
The Sea Wolf (1904) Jack London

Smolensk, Baronne Parisian boarding-house keeper
The Adventures of Philip (1862) W. M. Thackeray

Smollett, Captain
Treasure Island (1882) Robert Louis Stevenson

Smollett, Fabian, Dr
Florence his wife
A House and its Head (1935) Ivy Compton-Burnett

Smooth-it-away, Mr
ss 'The Celestial Railroad'
Mosses from an Old Manse (1846) Nathaniel Hawthorne

Smorltork, Count foreign visitor at the Den
The Pickwick Papers (1837) Charles Dickens

Smotherwell, Stephen executioner
The Fair Maid of Perth (1828) Walter Scott

Smouch assistant to Namby the sheriff
The Pickwick Papers (1837) Charles Dickens

Smug a smith of Edmonton
The Merry Devil of Edmonton play (1608) ?Thomas Dekker

Smythe, Isadore
ss 'The Invisible Man'
The Innocence of Father Brown (1911) G. K. Chesterton

Smythe, Richard a rationalist
The End of the Affair (1951) Graham Greene

Snaffle a livery-stable keeper
ss 'The Ravenswing'
Men's Wives (1843) W. M. Thackeray

Snagsby kindly law stationer
Bleak House (1853) Charles Dickens

Snaith, Anthony, Alderman rich and corrupt businessman
South Riding (1936) Winifred Holtby

Snake
The School for Scandal play (1777) Richard Brinsley Sheridan

Snale, Mr Independent minister who is opposed to Mark Rutherford*
The Autobiography of Mark Rutherford (1881) Mark Rutherford (rn William Hale White)

Snap see Quirk

Snap, Betsy Uncle Chill's* 'hard-favoured, yellow' old housekeeper
ss 'The Poor Relation's Story'
Reprinted Pieces (1858) Charles Dickens

Snap, Mr sheriff's officer and fence
Laetitia his daughter, pickpocket; m. Jonathan Wild*
Jonathan Wild (1743) Henry Fielding

Snarleyyow dog that bears a charmed life
Snarleyyow (1837) Captain Marryat

Snawley mean hypocrite; stepfather of two boys left with Squeers*
Nicholas Nickleby (1839) Charles Dickens

Sneer critic
The Critic play (1779) Richard Brinsley Sheridan

Sneerwell, Lady
The School for Scandal play (1777) Richard Brinsley Sheridan

Sneezum Hartley
his wife
Alicia their daughter, m. Sydney Bartleby*

A Suspension of Mercy (1965) Patricia Highsmith

Snell, Balso poet who finds Trojan Horse and travels up its alimentary canal in scatological allegory
The Dream Life of Balso Snell (1931) Nathanael West (rn Nathan Weinstein)

Snell, John landlord of the Rainbow
Silas Marner (1861) George Eliot (rn Mary Anne, later Marian, Evans)

Snell, Samuel disreputable old lawyer and indigo smuggler
Pendennis (1848) W. M. Thackeray

Snevellicci, Miss leading lady in Crummles'*
Nicholas Nickleby (1839) Charles Dickens

Snewkes suitor to Mrs Kenwig's sister
Nicholas Nickelby (1839) Charles Dickens

Snicks, Mr secretary of the Life Office
The Pickwick Papers (1837) Charles Dickens

Sniff, Mrs waitress at Mugby Junction
Mugby Junction (1866) Charles Dickens

Sniggs Mr Tulrumble's* predecessor as Mayor of Mudfog
The Public Life of Mr Tulrumble (1837) Charles Dickens

Snigsworth, Lord Twemlow's* high and mighty cousin
Our Mutual Friend (1865) Charles Dickens

Snitchey, Jonathan of Snitchey and Craggs, solicitors, sharp and kindly
The Battle of Life (1846) Charles Dickens

Snobson blackmailing clerk who gets his comeuppance
Fashion play (1845) Anne Cora Mowatt

Snodgrass, Augustus member of the Pickwick Club, great poet, m. Emily Wardle
The Pickwick Papers (1837) Charles Dickens

Snopes, Abner ('Ab') settles as sharecropper on Will Varner's* land in Frenchman's Bend in the 1890s – of obscure origin, 'just Snopeses, like colonies of rats or termites are just rats and termites'; the Snopes slowly displace the old order as represented by the Compsons* and the Sartorises*
Flem his son, president of bank in Jefferson, Mississippi, m. Eula Varner*
Mink grandson to Ab Snopes, murderer
Ike grandson to Ab Snopes, idiot who falls in love with a cow
Lump; Eck other cousins to Flem Snopes
Linda Snopes Kohl daughter to Eula and Hoake McCarron; courted by Gavin Stevens*
I. O. Snopes schoolteacher, grandson to Ab Snopes
Montgomery Ward son of I. O. Snopes and a 'gray-coloured woman', pornographer
Byron great-grandson of Ab Snopes, writer of indecent letters, m. an Indian squaw
Wallstreet Panic Snopes son to Eck Snopes (blacksmith and honest man), prosperous wholesaler – and honest like his father
Sartoris† (1929); *The Unvanquished†* (1938); *The Hamlet†* (1940) William Faulkner

Snorflerer, Dowager Lady friend to the Egotistical Young Couple*
Sketches of Young Couples (1840) Charles Dickens

Snout tinker
A Midsummer Night's Dream play (1623) William Shakespeare

Snow, Henry (alias Scarlett), friend to Sylvia Scarlett*
Juliette his wife
his six stepdaughters
Sylvia Scarlett (1918) Compton Mackenzie

Snowe, Lucy cc, narrator, companion to Paulina Home*, nursemaid and then teacher at Mme Beck's*; later runs her own small school and awaits M. Paul Emanuel*, whose return seems dubious
Villette (1853) Charlotte Brontë

Snowe, Nicholas farmer
Faith his daughter
Lorna Doone (1869) R. D. Blackmore

Snubbin, Serjeant counsel for Mr Pickwick*
The Pickwick Papers (1837) Charles Dickens

Snuffe, Langebeau puritan chaplain to Belforest*
The Atheist's Tragedy (1611) Cyril Tourneur

Snuffim, Tumley, Sir Mrs Wittitterley's*
doctor
Nicholas Nickleby (1839) Charles
Dickens
Snug joiner
A Midsummer Night's Dream play
(1623) William Shakespeare
So and So, Mr 'the well-known anti-
fascist', rather mean, shooting out
slogans
Coming Up For Air (1936) George
Orwell (rn Eric Blair)
Soames, Enoch bad poet
Seven Men (1919) Max Beerbohm
Soames, Henry motel-proprietor cc who
tries to discover meaning in face of a
heart attack that may kill him at any time
Nickel Mountain (1973) John Gardner
Sobakevich gluttonous kulak
Myortvye dushi (*Dead Souls*) (1842)
Nikolai Gogol
Sobby hitch-hiker and murderer of San-
ford*
ss 'The Hitch-Hikers'
A Curtain of Green (1941) Eudora Welty
Soby, Arnold small-college professor cc
What a Way to Go (1962) Wright
Morris
Soderball, Tiny successful businesswoman
My Antonia (1918) Willa Cather
Softly, Knox, Revd m. Olivier Kennyfeck*
Roland Cashel (1850) Charles Lever
Sogliardo an essential clown, brother to
Sordido*, yet so enamoured of the name
of a gentleman, that he will have it,
though he buys it
Every Man Out of His Humour play
(1599) Ben Jonson
Sole ex-public schoolboy
The Old Boys (1964) William Trevor
Solent, Wolf history teacher
Gerda his wife, *née* Torp
Ann Solent his mother
Wolf Solent (1929) J. C. Powys
Solinus Duke of Ephesus
A Comedy of Errors play (1623) William
Shakespeare
Solmes Lord Etherington's* confidential
servant; villainous traitor
St Ronan's Well (1824) Walter Scott
Solmes, Roger suitor to Clarissa Harlowe*
Clarissa (1748) Samuel Richardson
Solomon great-grandfather to Milkman

Macon*, escaped slave
Song of Solomon (1977) Toni Morrison
Soltyk, Louis Polish artist in Paris
Tarr (1918) Wyndham Lewis
Sombra, Don Segunda itinerant ranch
worker in Argentine classic: the leading
work in gaucho (nomadic herdsman of
the River Plate region) literature
Don Segunda Sombra (tr. as *Shadows in
the Pampas* as well as under its own title)
(1926) Ricardo Güiraldes
Somers, Alfred painter, friend and con-
fidant to Jocelyn Pierston*, m. Mrs
Pine-Avon* and descends into middle-
aged respectability
The Well Beloved (1897) Thomas Hardy
Somers, Etty cousin to the Curtises
Invitation to the Waltz (1932)
Rosamond Lehmann
Somers, Richard Lovett English poet visi-
ting Australia
Harriet his wife
Kangaroo (1923) D. H. Lawrence
Somerset, Earl of (hist.)
King Henry VI plays (1623) William
Shakespeare
Somerset, George architect, m. Paula
Power*
his father
A Laodicean (1881) Thomas Hardy
Somerton, Mr
ss 'The Treasure of Abbot Thomas'
Ghost Stories of an Antiquary (1910)
M. R. James
Somerville, Miss cousin and companion to
Lady Drew*
Tono Bungay (1909) H. G. Wells
Sommerville, Mr advocate
The Highland Widow (1827) Walter
Scott
Sondelius, Gustaf 'titanic scientist' who
dies in plague
Arrowsmith (1925) Sinclair Lewis
Sophronos brother to Meleander*
The Lover's Melancholy play (1629)
John Ford
Sophy Dr Marigold's* adopted daughter,
deaf and dumb, m. a deaf mute and went
to India
Dr Marigold's Prescriptions (1865)
Charles Dickens
Soquette seeming gentlewoman to Cata-
plasma*

The Atheist's Tragedy, or *The Honest Man's Revenge* play (1611/12) Cyril Tourneur

Soranzo a nobleman
'Tis Pity She's a Whore play (1633) John Ford

Sordido a wretched hob-nailed chuff, whose recreation is reading of almanacks
Every Man Out of His Humour play (1599) Ben Jonson

Sorel, Julien cc
Le Rouge et le Noir (1830) Stendhal (rn Henri Bayle)

Sorrel, Hetty empty-headed and vain cc found by Henry James* to be the most successful of the author's female creations
Adam Bede (1859) George Eliot (rn Mary Anne, later Marian, Evans)

Sotheby, Emmanuel village grocer
his wife
Rachel; Richard their children, the latter an artist in Paris
Go She Must! (1927) David Garnett

Sothill, Barbara, Mrs sister to Basil Seal*
Freddy her husband
Put Out More Flags (1942) Evelyn Waugh

Sotomayor de Soto, Don Guzman prisoner of Amyas Leigh*; lover and betrayer of Rose Salterne*
Westward Ho! (1855) Charles Kingsley

Souldan of Babylon (Sultan of Babylon)
Old Fortunatus play (1600) Thomas Dekker

Soulis, Murdoch, Revd Minister of Balweary
ss 'Thrawn Janet'
The Merry Men (1887) Robert Louis Stevenson

Soulsby, Sister charlatan revivalist who guides Theron Ware into pragmatic paths*
Brother Soulsby conman ('fund-raiser') in the religion game
The Damnation of Theron Ware in England, originally, as *Illumination* (1896) Harold Frederic

South West Wind, The
The King of the Golden River (1850) John Ruskin

South, Dr
Of Human Bondage (1915) W. Somerset Maugham

South, Marty in love with Winterbourne*
The Woodlanders (1879) Thomas Hardy

Southcote, Mr ingenious writer of begging letters
ss 'Begging Letter Writer'
Reprinted Pieces (1858) Charles Dickens

Southdown, Earl of family name **Sheepshanks**
Emily m. Revd Silas Hornblower*; **Jane** m. Pitt Crawley his daughters
Matilda dowager Duchess, his mother
Vanity Fair (1847–8) W. M. Thackeray

Southwold, James Royalist traitor
Children of the New Forest (1847) Captain Marryat

Sowerberry undertaker to whom Oliver Twist* is apprenticed
Oliver Twist (1838) Charles Dickens

Sowerby, Nathaniel, MP spendthrift friend to Mark Robarts*
Harriet his sister, m. Harold Smith*
Framley Parsonage (1861) Anthony Trollope

Sowndes pompous beadle
Dombey and Son (1848) Charles Dickens

Spaconia daughter to Lygones*
A King and No King play (1619) Francis Beaumont and John Fletcher

Spade, Sam the original and most convincing (based on the author's own experience working for Pinkertons) 'hardboiled' detective; onwards from
The Maltese Falcon† (1930) Dashiell Hammett

Spain, King of
The Spanish Tragedy play (1592) Thomas Kyd

Spalding American Minister at Florence
Carry; Livvy; his daughters
He Knew He Was Right (1869) Anthony Trollope

Spandrell, Maurice critic
Point Counter Point (1928) Aldous Huxley

Spank an 'approver'
Lorna Doone (1869) R. D. Blackmore

Spark, Timothy cousin to Mrs Pettican*
Mehalah (1880) Sabine Baring-Gould

Sparkes, Polly programme seller, niece to Mrs Clover*, m. Chris Parish*
Ebenezer her father, waiter
The Town Traveller (1898) George Gis-

sing

Sparkins, Horatio see **Smith, Samuel**

Sparkish, Mr
The Country Wife play (1675) William Wycherley

Sparkler, Edmund Mrs Merdle's* son by her first marriage, m. Fanny Dorrit; became a lord of the Circumlocution Office
Little Dorrit (1857) Charles Dickens

Sparks London jeweller
The Virginians (1857–9) W. M. Thackeray

Sparowe, Phyllyp bird slain at Carowe
The Boke of Phyllyp Sparowe poem (1508) John Skelton

Sparser friend to Clyde Griffiths* in Chicago
An American Tragedy (1925) Theodore Dreiser

Sparsit, Mrs Josiah Bounderby's* housekeeper
Hard Times (1854) Charles Dickens

Spartacus (hist.) Thracian cc and leader of revolt, of blank-verse play performed in 1831
The Gladiator play (1919) Robert Montgomery Bird

Spatter, Mr whose delight is to abuse people
The Adventures of David Simple (1744–53) Sarah Fielding

Spaulding, Vincent see **Clay, John**

Spavin friend to Foker*
Pendennis (1848) W. M. Thackeray

Spear, Dave
Persephone his wife
A Glastonbury Romance (1932) John Cowper Powys

Spear, Halo mentor of Vance Weston*; m. and is divorced from Lewis Tarrant*
Hudson River Bracketed (1929); *The Gods Arrive* (1932) Edith Wharton

Spearman, Rosanna second housemaid to Lady Verinder*
The Moonstone (1860) Wilkie Collins

Speed clownish servant
Two Gentlemen of Verona play (1623) William Shakespeare

Speers agent to Sir Brian Newcome*
The Newcomes (1853–5) W. M. Thackeray

Spelman, Laura cc, in study of her acceptance of her terminal cancer

The Reckoning (1978) May Sarton

Spence, Janet, Miss
ss 'The Giaconda Smile'
Mortal Coils (1922) Aldous Huxley

Spencer adventurer beloved of Bess Bridges*
The Fair Maid of the West play (1631) Thomas Hardy

Spencer legal friend to George Warrington*
The Virginians (1857–9) W. M. Thackeray

Spencer, John, Sir
Sybil his wife
Rollo; Marigold their children
Invitation to the Waltz (1932) Rosamond Lehmann

Spender, Clement ('Clem') father of Tina Ralston*
ss 'The Old Maid'
Old New York (1924) Edith Wharton

Spenlove, Dr philanthropic doctor in examination of Victorian anti-Jewish prejudice
Aaron the Jew (1894) Benjamin L. Farjeon

Spenlow, Dora m. David Copperfield*; 'child wife'
Francis of Spenlow and Jorkins, her father, David's employer
David Copperfield (1850) Charles Dickens

Spenser (hist. Hugh le Despenser) favourite of Edward II* after the execution of Gaveston*
Edward II play (1594) Christopher Marlowe

Sperrit, Connie m. Frankwell Midmore*
her father, lawyer
ss 'My Son's Wife'
A Diversity of Creatures (1917) Rudyard Kipling

Spettigue, Stephen solicitor
Charley's Aunt play (1892) Brandon Thomas

Sphynx, Sophronia see **Marchioness, The**

Spicer member of Pinkie's* gang
Brighton Rock (1938) Graham Greene

Spicer, Captain
Incomparable Bellairs (1904) A. and E. Castle

Spicer, Captain cardsharp and swindler
Frank Fairlegh (1850) F. E. Smedley

Spichcock friend to Hoard*
A Trick to Catch the Old One play
(1608) Thomas Middleton

Spidel enemy to Princess Saskia*
Huntingtower (1922) John Buchan

Spielman, Max one of the developers of
WESAC*
Giles Goat-Boy (1966) John Barth

Spielvogel, Dr Portnoy's* psychiatrist
Portnoy's Complaint† (1969) Philip
Roth

Spiker, Mr and Mrs
David Copperfield (1850) Charles
Dickens

Spilkins landlord of the Cross Keys
Felix Holt (1866) George Eliot (rn Mary
Anne, later Marian, Evans)

Spiller and Spoker artists who executed
bust of Pecksniff*
Martin Chuzzlewit (1844) Charles
Dickens

Spina, Pietro cc anti-fascist novel
Pan e vino (rev. as *Vino e pane* in 1962)
Bread and Wine (1937) Ignacio Silone

Spinach one of Miss Flite's* captive birds
Bleak House (1853) Charles Dickens

Spinachi, Lord
his children
The Rose and the Ring (1855) W. M.
Thackeray

Spinks, Elias
Under the Greenwood Tree (1872)
Thomas Hardy

Spiro, Mr editor of a popular Catholic
magazine called *Crux*
Watt (1953) Samuel Beckett

Spit dead-end kid
Dead End play (1936) Sidney Kingsley

Spitzer, Mr companion to Catherine
Cartwheel* and composer of unwritten
and unheard music
Miss MacIntosh, My Darling (1965)
Marguerite Young

Splint shipbuilder
Barry Lyndon (1844) W. M. Thackeray

Spode a journalist
ss 'The Tillotson Banquet'
Mortal Coils (1922) Aldous Huxley

Spoffard, Henry
Gentlemen Prefer Blondes (1925) Anita
Loos

Spong, Dominic friend to Ernest Bellamy*,
m. Camilla Christy* as third husband

Men and Wives (1931) Ivy Compton-
Burnett

Sponge, Soapey cockney sportsman, m.
Lucy Glitters, actress
Mr Sponge's Sporting Tour (1853) R. S.
Surtees

Spooner, H. Tidd rich young Oxford man
The Pottleton Legacy (1849) Albert
Smith

Sportin' Life
Porgy (1925) DuBose Heyward

Spots the leopard
ss 'How the Leopard Got His Spots'
Just So Stories (1902) Rudyard Kipling

Spotswood, Tyler secretary to and spokesman for crooked senator Chuck Crawford*
Number One (1943) John Dos Passos

Spottletoe, Mr and Mrs the latter, old
Martin Chuzzlewit's* niece
Martin Chuzzlewit (1844) Charles
Dickens

Spragg, Undine ruthless social-climb-
ing cc in satire on American life m.
(1) Elmer Moffat*, (2) Ralph Marvel*,
(3) Marquis of Chelles*, (4) Elmer
Moffat
The Custom of the Country (1913) Edith
Wharton

Sprague, Dr senior physician
Middlemarch (1871–2) George Eliot (rn
Mary Anne, later Marian, Evans)

Spratt universally hated manager of
Spraxton Colliery
Felix Holt (1866) George Eliot (rn Mary
Anne, later Marian, Evans)

Spray independent minister, St Oggs
The Mill on the Floss (1860) George Eliot
(rn Mary Anne, later Marian, Evans)

Sprickett, Elsie cc, charwoman, then maid
to the Earlforwards*, m. Joe
Riceyman's Steps (1923); *Elsie and the
Child* (1924) Arnold Bennett

Spring, Sam betting man
Jorrocks's Jaunts and Jollities (1838) R.
S. Surtees

Springett, Ralph
ss 'The Wrong Thing'
Rewards and Fairies (1910) Rudyard
Kipling

Springrove, Edward m. Cynthia Graye*
John his father
his mother

Desperate Remedies (1871) Thomas Hardy

Sprodgkin, Sally, Mrs
Our Mutual Friend (1865) Charles Dickens

Sprowle, Colonel and Mrs
Elsie Venner (1861) Oliver Wendell Holmes

Spruggins, Thomas candidate for the office of beadle
Sketches by Boz (1836) Charles Dickens

Spurio bastard to the Duke*
The Revenger's Tragedy (1607/8) ?Thomas Middleton; ?Cyril Tourneur

Spurrier, Ralph, Major-General, Sir Commander-in-Chief, Madras
The Newcomes (1853–5) W. M. Thackeray

Spurstowe a doctor
ss 'At the End of the Passage'
Life's Handicap (1891) Rudyard Kipling

Spyers, Jem policeman who arrested Conkey Chickweed*
Oliver Twist (1839) Charles Dickens

Squallop, Mrs Tittlebat Titmouse's* landlady
Ten Thousand a Year (1839) Samuel Warren

Square, Thomas
Tom Jones (1749) Henry Fielding

Squeamish, Mrs
Lady Squeamish her mother
The Country Wife play (1675) William Wycherley

Squeers, Wackford brutal one-eyed schoolmaster based (it is said unfairly) on a William Shaw, of Bowes; eventually transported
his wife, a fitting one for him
Master Wackford; Fanny the former greasy and odious, the latter spiteful and vixenish his children
Nicholas Nickleby (1839) Charles Dickens

Squercum, Longstaffe attorney
The Way We Live Now (1875) Anthony Trollope

Squier, Alan unsuccessful writer who asks to be shot and is
The Petrified Forest play Robert E. Sherwood

Squint, Lawyer
A Citizen of the World (1762) Oliver Goldsmith)

Squintum, Dr caricature of the methodist, George Whitefield
The Minor play (1760) Samuel Foote

Squires in charge of the bell-hops at the Green-Davidson Hotel
An American Tragedy (1925) Theodore Dreiser

Squires, Olympia sweetheart of the Uncommercial Traveller's childhood
The Uncommercial Traveller (1860–8) Charles Dickens

Squod, Phil Trooper George's* assistant at the shooting gallery
Bleak House (1853) Charles Dickens

Srinivas cc, founder of a newspaper, would-be filmscript writer
Mr Sampath (1949) (In USA as *The Printer of Malgudi*, 1957) R. K. Narayan

Stacey, Rosamund dedicated scholar; cc
The Millstone (1966) Margaret Drabble

Stack Virginian minister
The Virginians (1857–9) W. M. Thackeray

Stack, Henry Wilfrid Desert's* confidential servant
Flowering Wilderness (1932) John Galsworthy

Stackpole, Henrietta American journalist
The Portrait of a Lady (1881) Henry James

Stadger, Captain sadist
Eustace Chisholm and the Works (1968) James Purdy

Stafford Sir Hyacinth O'Brien's servant m. Rose Gray* in a ceremony 'with every simple demonstration of rural felicity'
Dorothy his mother
ss 'Rosanna'
Popular Tales (1812) Maria Edgeworth

Stafford, MP
Diary of a Late Physician (1832) Samuel Warren

Stafford, Tom suitor to Kitty Bellairs*
Incomparable Bellairs (1904) A. and E. Castle

Stagg blind owner of cellar near Barbican
Barnaby Rudge (1841) Charles Dickens

Stagg, Bill tobacco smuggler
The Hole in the Wall (1902) Arthur Morrison

Staggers a smith
The New Inn, or *The Light Heart* play

(1629) Ben Jonson

Stahr, Monroe cc, wonder-boy head of great studio, suggested in part by the producer Irving Thalberg
The Last Tycoon (1941) F. Scott Fitzgerald

Stainford, Aubrey forger
Swan Song (1928) John Galsworthy

Stakes see **Chops**

Stalkenberg, Baron von
Count Otto his brother
East Lynne (1861) Mrs Henry Wood

Stalker, Detective Inspector smart detective; based on Inspector Walker of Bow Street
ss 'The Detective Police'
Reprinted Pieces (1858) Charles Dickens

Stalky see **Corkran, Arthur**

Stamp, Victor with a chin like a box
Margaret ('Margot') his wife
The Revenge for Love (1937) Wyndham Lewis

Stanbury, Hugh close friend to Louis Trevelyan*
his mother
Priscilla; Dorothy his sisters
Jemima his aunt, of the county set which discards him
He Knew He Was Right (1869) Anthony Trollope

Stanby, Albert engaged to Mildred Lawson* but rejected by her; quasi-criminal opportunist
ss 'Mildred Lawson'
Celibates (1895) George Moore

Standish lawyer
Middlemarch (1871–2) George Eliot (rn Mary Anne, later Marian, Evans)

Standish, Elyot cc of novel set in 1930s Bloomsbury
Catherine his mother
The Living and the Dead (1941) Patrick White

Standish, Lady
A Bath Comedy† (1899) A. and E. Castle

Standish, Laura, Lady Lord Brentford's* daughter, m. Robert Kennedy*
Charles her cousin
Phineas Finn† (1869) Anthony Trollope

Standish, Miles captain of the Plymouth Colony
The Courtship of Miles Standish poem (1858) Henry Wadsworth Longfellow

Stangerson, Joseph
A Study in Scarlet (1887) Arthur Conan Doyle

Stangrave American, m. Marie de Cordifiamma*
Two Years Ago (1857) Charles Kingsley

Stanhope, Agatha ailing cc
Alison her sister, representation of Emily Dickinson, cc of play which created a sensation when it was performed
Eben her married brother
Louise his domineering wife
Alison's House play (1930) Susan Glaspell

Stanhope, Dennis Company Commander, cc
Journey's End play (1928) R. C. Sheriff

Stanhope, Vesey, Revd, DD Prebendary, Barchester
Ethelbert; Charlotte; Madeline m. Neroni* his children
Barchester Towers (1857) Anthony Trollope

Staniford, James see **Blood, Lydia**

Stanley, Ann Veronica cc, m. Godwin Capes*
Peter her father
Jim; Roddy; Alice; Gwen her brothers and sisters
Mollie her aunt
Ann Veronica (1909) H. G. Wells

Stanley, Lord
King Richard III play (1623) William Shakespeare

Stanley, Major General
Mabel m. **Frederic; Kate** his daughters
The Pirates of Penzance opera (1880) W. S. Gilbert and Arthur Sullivan

Stanley, Rose schoolgirl, member of the Brodie set
The Prime of Miss Jean Brodie (1961) Muriel Spark

Stanley, William, Sir Lord Chamberlain
Perkin Warbeck play (1634) John Ford

Stanly, Glen Pierre Glendenning's cousin
Pierre (1852) Herman Melville

Stanner, Sergeant
The Trumpet Major (1880) Thomas Hardy

Stannidge landlord
his wife
The Mayor of Casterbridge (1886) Thomas Hardy

Stant, Charlotte intelligent, penniless American, mistress to Prince Amerigo*, m. Adam Verver*
The Golden Bowl (1904) Henry James

Stanton, Adam famous surgeon, assassin of Stark*
Anne his sister, social worker and mistress to Stark
All the King's Men (1946) Robert Penn Warren

Stanton, Charles
Dangerous Corner play (1932) J. B. Priestley

Staple, Mr supporter of the Dingley Dell Cricket Club who made a speech after the great match with Muggleton
The Pickwick Papers (1837) Charles Dickens

Staples, Lawrence chief warder at Kenilworth castle
Kenilworth (1821) Walter Scott

Stapleton alias Baskerville
his wife, posing as his sister
The Hound of the Baskervilles (1902) Arthur Conan Doyle

Starbuck chief mate of the *Pequod*
Moby Dick, or The Whale (1851) Herman Melville

Stareleigh, Justice, Mr who presided over the Bardell-Pickwick case
The Pickwick Papers (1837) Charles Dickens

Stargaze an astrologer
The City Madam play (1658) Philip Massinger

Stark, Arabella
An American Tragedy (1912) Theodore Dreiser

Stark, Lysander, Colonel
ss 'The Case of the Engineer's Thumb'
The Adventures of Sherlock Holmes (1892) Arthur Conan Doyle

Stark, Willie Huey-Long-like Southern demagogue who begins as a genuine reformer and ends, assassinated by Dr Stanton*, as a populist would-be dictator with presidential ambitions
Lucy his wife
All the King's Men (1946) Robert Penn Warren

Starkadder, Judith
Amos her husband
Reuben; Seth; Elfine m. Richard Hawk-Monitor* their children
Old Mrs Starkadder ('Aunt Ada Doom')
Micah; Urk; Ezra; Caraway; Harkaway; Luke; Mark other relatives
their wives
Rennett m. Mybug*
Cold Comfort Farm (1932) Stella Gibbons

Starlight, Tom head of poaching gang
Bracebridge Hall (1823) Washington Irving

Starlight, Captain noble and Byronic English robber in Australian minor classic by conservative grazier who later became police magistrate
Robbery Under Arms: A Story of Life and Adventure in the Bush and in the Goldfields of Australia (1888, rev. 1889) Rolf Boldrewood (rn Thomas Alexander Browne)

Starr, Amantha narrator in historical novel of Kentucky in the latter half of the last century; spoiled daughter of plantation owner, and of a slave; m. Captain Tobias Sears*
Band of Angels (1955) Robert Penn Warren

Starr, Ida ex-prostitute and thief who makes good (which the author's first wife, also an ex-prostitute, did not, except as tormentor of her husband) as sempstress
The Unclassed (1882) George Gissing

Startop one of Matthew Pocket's* pupils
Great Expectations (1861) Charles Dickens

Startsov, Audrey superfluous man* in first novel of gifted Soviet author who went to the bad
Goroda i gody (*Cities and Years*) (1924) K. A. Fedin

Starveling tailor
A Midsummer Night's Dream play (1623) William Shakespeare

Starwick, Francis fastidious and affected scholar, assistant to Hatcher* and friend to Eugene Gant*, abandoned by the latter when he finds him to be a homosexual; based on author's friend, Kenneth Raisbeck, who in 1931 was strangled (probably) by a male lover
Of Time and the River: A Legend of Man's Hunger in his Youth (1935)

Thomas Wolfe

Stasia slavey ('The Slut')
The Passing of the Third Floor Back play (1910) Jerome K. Jerome

Statute first woman
The Staple of News play (1631) Ben Jonson

Staunton, George alias **Robinson** later Sir George, accomplice of Andrew Wilson*, m. Effie Deans*
'The Whistler' their son
Revd Robert his father
Heart of Midlothian (1818) Walter Scott

Stavely, Dick
Sir John his father
his mother
The Shrimp and the Anemone (1944) L. P. Hartley

Stavely, Mr and Mrs friends to the Gracedieus*
The Legacy of Cain (1889) Wilkie Collins

Stavrogin cc; brilliant man who cannot make a choice; m. Marya, a cripple
Stavrogina his mother
Besy (The Possessed) (1879) Fyodor Dostoievsky

Stead, Charles novelist, cc
his wealthy socialite wife
Brazen Prison (1971) Stanley Middleton

Steadiman, John chief mate of the *Golden Mary* who took over command after the death of Captain Ravender*
The Wreck of the Golden Mary (1856) Charles Dickens

Stedman, Ruth Quaker friend to the Hallidays*
Uncle Tom's Cabin (1851) Harriet Beecher Stowe

Steele, Charles artist
Jacob's Room (1922) Virginia Woolf

Steele, Christie landlady, the Treddles Arms
The Highland Widow (1827) Walter Scott

Steele, Lucy pretty young girl, secretly engaged to Edward Ferrars, elopes with his brother Robert*
Anne her elder sister
Sense and Sensibility (1811) Jane Austen

Steele, Tom Irishman who lost his life at Waterloo Bridge
ss 'Down With the Tide'

Reprinted Pieces (1858) Charles Dickens

Steeltrap, Simon, Sir, JP MP for Crouching Curtown
Crotchet Castle (1831) Thomas Love Peacock

Steene vet
his wife
Brother Jacob (1864) George Eliot (rn Mary Anne, later Marian, Evans)

Steenson, Steenie servant and friend to Sir Henry Redgauntlet*; grandfather to Wandering Willie*
Redgauntlet (1824) Walter Scott

Steerforth, Captain
The Ordeal of Gilbert Pinfold (1957) Evelyn Waugh

Steerforth, James eloped with Little Em'ly*; drowned
his mother
David Copperfield (1850) Charles Dickens

Steighton, Timothy clerk to Edward Crimsworth*
The Professor (1857) Charlotte Brontë

Steinbeck, Wenceslas, Count impoverished Polish pawn of Bette Fischer* and M. Marneffe*; m. Hortense Hulot*
La Cousine Bette (1847) Honoré de Balzac

Steinfeldt, Baroness suspected of poisoning the Baron von Arnheim*
Anne of Geierstein (1829) Walter Scott

Steinhart, Frau
Catherine; Lize; Fritz; Trudchen her children
Ships that Pass in the Night (1893) Beatrice Harraden

Stella
Vanessa her sister
ss 'Cardboard City'
Dreams of Dead Women's Handbags (1987) Shena Mackay

Stella, Lady
Men Like Gods (1923) H. G. Wells

Stelling, Walter, Revd curate, Kings Lorton, schoolmaster
Louisa his wife
Laura their daughter
The Mill on the Floss (1860) George Eliot (rn Mary Anne, later Marian, Evans)

Stephano drunken butler
The Tempest play (1623) William Shakespeare

Stephanos the Wrestler
Count Robert of Paris (1832) Walter Scott

Stephen country gull
Every Man in His Humour play (1598) Ben Jonson

Stephen de Suatre abbot of St Illod's
Anne of Norton his wife
ss 'The Eye of Allah'
Debits and Credits (1926) Rudyard Kipling

Stepney, Grace
Jack her husband
The House of Mirth (1905) Edith Wharton

Steptoe, Gerald
Nancy his sister
Major Steptoe; Bet their parents
The Shrimp and the Anemone (1944) L. P. Hartley

Sterling
Betty; Fanny m. Lovewell* his daughters
Miss Sterling his sister
The Clandestine Marriage play (1766) George Colman the Elder and David Garrick

Sterling, Philip prisoner of Union army (as the author had been) in Civil War novel lifted above mediocrity by its battle scenes
Tiger Lilies (1867) Sidney Lanier

Stern tall fearful man with 'pale, flowing hips': cc comic first novel on theme of American Jewish neurosis
his wife
Stern (1962) Bruce Jay Friedman

Stern, Jenny cc
How Much? (1961) Burt Blechman

Sterndale, Leon, Dr
ss 'The Devil's Foot'
His Last Bow (1917) Arthur Conan Doyle

Sternerson, Moran tough blonde who scorns femininity but yields to Wilbur* only to be killed
Captain Sternerson her father; of the *Lady Letty*, killed by Kitchell*
Moran of the Lady Letty (in England, *Shanghaied*) (1898) Frank Norris

Stetta, Violetta opera singer who figured in Mr Chuckster's* anecdotes
The Old Curiosity Shop (1841) Charles Dickens

Stettson Major a day boy
ss 'A Little Prep'
Stalky & Co. (1899) Rudyard Kipling

Stevens, Dr narrator and mentor of Mervyn*
Arthur Mervyn, or *Memoirs of the year 1793* (1799–1800) Charles Brockden Brown

Stevens, Gavin lawyer, in love with Eula Snopes* and then with her daughter Linda; m. Melisandre Backus Harriss
Judge Lemuel his father
his mother, *née* Dandridge
Max his son
his daughter
Charles ('Chick') his cousin (grandson of Judge Lemuel)
Gowan his nephew, called his cousin in *The Town*; m. Temple Drake*
Light in August and many others (1932) William Faulkner

Stevens, Mrs cc, self-portrait of American-Belgian novelist who has written well in what she calls the 'novelists of the moderate human voice' tradition (e.g. Forster*)
Mrs Stevens Hears the Mermaids Singing (1965) May Sarton

Stewart see Breck, Alan

Stewart, Charles writer to the Signet
Catriona (1893) Robert Louis Stevenson

Steyne, George Augustus, Marquess of
Lady Mary his wife
Lord Gaunt m. Lady Blanche Thistle-weed*; **George** their sons
George's wife, *née* Johnes
Plantagenet son and heir presumptive, an idiot
Vanity Fair (1847–8) W. M. Thackeray

Steynlin, Madame
South Wind (1917) Norman Douglas

Stickles, Jeremy apparitor of the King's Bench
Lorna Doone (1869) R. D. Blackmore

Stickly-Prickly hedgehog
ss 'The Beginning of the Armadillos'
Just So Stories (1902) Rudyard Kipling

Stiggins hypocritical and ranting pastor
The Pickwick Papers (1837) Charles Dickens

Stikkersee weasel
Tarka the Otter (1927) Henry Williamson

Stiles, Albert lover of Theodosia Bell* who

deserts her for another
My Heart and My Flesh (1927) Elizabeth
Madox Roberts
Stillbrook friend to Cummings*
The Diary of a Nobody (1892) George
and Weedon Grossmith
Stillbrook, Stephen detective sergeant
*Robbery Under Arms: A Story of Life
and Adventure in the Bush and in the
Goldfields of Australia* (1888, rev. 1889)
Rolf Boldrewood (rn Thomas Alexander
Browne)
Stiller, Anatol sculptor cc in Swiss (German) novel on Don Juan* theme
Julika *née* **Tschudy** his wife, a dancer
Stiller (1954) Max Frisch
Stilton, Dowager Duchess of
Vanity Fair (1847–8) W. M. Thackeray
Stiltstalking, Lancaster, Lord one of a
great and powerful family
Little Dorrit (1857) Charles Dickens
Stimson, Simon director of choir
Our Town play (1938) Thornton Wilder
Stingo narrator, would-be novelist
Sophie's Choice (1979) William Styron
Stingo, Jacob brewer
The Sailor's Return (1925) David
Garnett
Stoat, Donald
You Can't Go Home Again (1940)
Thomas Wolfe
Stobbs, Charley m. Belinda Jorrocks*
his father, a gentleman farmer
his sister
Handley Cross (1843) R. S. Surtees
Stobhall, Mrs dedicated socialist
The Simple Life Limited (1911) Daniel
Chaucer (rn Ford Madox Ford)
Stockdale, Richard m. Lizzy Newberry*
ss 'The Distracted Preacher'
Wessex Tales (1888) Thomas Hardy
Stockton, John newspaperman who
changes his name to Bruce Dudley, when
he leaves his wife to become a wheel
painter
Bernice a successful writer of cheap tales,
his wife
Dark Laughter (1925) Sherwood
Anderson
Stockton, John see **Dudley, Bruce**
Stockwell father to Young Belcourt*
The West Indian play (1771) Richard
Cumberland

Stockwool, Ruth, Mrs companion to Ann
Avice Caro*
The Well Beloved (1897) Thomas Hardy
Stoddard, Eleanor interior decorator
U.S.A. (1930–6) John Dos Passos
Stoddard, Corporal of the Wiltshires
The Plough and the Stars play (1926)
Sean O'Casey (rn John Casey)
Stofsky part-portrait of Beat poet, businessman and philanthropist, Allen Ginsberg
Go (1952) John Clellon Holmes
Stogumber, Chaplain de
Saint Joan play (1924) George Bernard
Shaw
Stohwaeser, Herr German master at Dr
Grimstone's*
Vice Versa (1882) F. Anstey (rn Thomas
Anstey Guthrie)
Stoke see **D'Urberville**
Stoke, Basil colleague of Cyril Poges*
Avril his mistress
Purple Dust play (1940) Sean O'Casey
(rn John Casey)
Stoker, J. Washbourne
Dwight; Pauline m. Lord Chuffnell* his
children
Thank You, Jeeves (1934) P. G. Wodehouse
Stokes, Captain
Pendennis (1848) W. M. Thackeray
Stokes, Leland
A Lamp for Nightfall (1952) Erskine
Caldwell
Stokes, Martin small farmer
The Village Coquette opera (1836)
Charles Dickens
Stokes, Melian portrayal of the
philosopher Bertrand Russell
Pugs and Peacocks† (1921) Gilbert
Cannan
Stokes, Mrs Titmarsh's landlady
Bob; Selina her children
The Great Hoggarty Diamond (1841)
W. M. Thackeray
Stokesay, Lionel, Professor archeologist
Gilbert his son, poet
Dollie Gilbert's widow, and lover of
Gerald Middleton*
Anglo-Saxon Attitudes (1956) Angus
Wilson
Stolz, Andrey friend to Oblomov*; m.
Olga Ilyinsky*

Oblomov (1859) Ivan Goncharov

Stone sailor in the torpedoed *Aurora*
The Ocean (1946) James Hanley

Stone, Alfred portrait of the music critic Albert Steinberg, who was a gambler
Painted Veils (1920) J. G. Huneker

Stone, Denis young poet
Crome Yellow (1922) Aldous Huxley

Stone, Jabez New Hampshire farmer who sells his soul to the devil
ss 'The Devil and Daniel Webster'
Thirteen O'Clock (1937) Stephen Vincent Benét
The Devil and Daniel Webster folk opera (1939) Stephen Vincent Benét and Douglas Moore

Stone, Karen famous actress
Tom her dead husband
The Roman Spring of Mrs Stone (1950) Tennessee Williams (rn Thomas Lanier Williams)

Stone, Major murdered by Forester*
The Ministry of Fear (1943) Graham Greene

Stone, Nettie cc of regional (Westmorland) novel which supplied material for the satirical *Cold Comfort Farm**; m. (1) Stanley de Lyndesay*, (2) Anthony Dixon*
Crump Folk Going Home (1913) Constance Holme

Stone, Sarah, Mrs
Adam Bede (1859) George Eliot (rn Mary Anne, later Marian, Evans)

Stone, Sylvanus eccentric old Professor of Natural Science writing crazy work called *Book of Brotherhood*, living in house of his daughter, Mrs Hilary Dalison*
Fraternity (1909) John Galsworthy

Stone, née Wright, Ethel woman trying to put thirty-eight (her age) out of her mind
John her husband, who grieves for his dead male friend and then leaves her
ss 'Ethel'
Poor Women (1928) Norah Hoult

Stoner, Helen stepdaughter to Dr Roylott*
Julia her dead twin sister
ss 'The Speckled Band'
The Adventures of Sherlock Holmes (1892) Arthur Conan Doyle

Stoner, Martin down-and-out in classic tale of mistaken identity

ss 'The Hounds of Fate'
The Chronicles of Clovis (1911) Saki (rn Hector Hugh Munro)

Stoney, Robert psychopath
Flee the Angry Strangers (1952) George Mandel

Stoopid servant to H. Foker*
Pendennis (1848) W. M. Thackeray

Stoply, Canon friend to the Arrowpoints*
Daniel Deronda (1876) George Eliot (rn Mary Anne, later Marian, Evans)

Storefield, George
Grace his sister
his mother and father
Robbery Under Arms: A Story of Life and Adventure in the Bush and in the Goldfields of Australia (1888, rev. 1889) Rolf Boldrewood (rn Thomas Alexander Browne)

Storks i.e. T. H. Huxley
The New Republic, or *Culture, Faith and Philosophy in an English Country House* (1877; edition by John Lucas, 1975, lists originals of characters) William Hurrell Mallock

Storm, Theodore m. Paula Arnold*
So Big (1924) Edna Ferber

Stornaway, Lord
his stupid wife, who m. him for his money
Mansfield Park (1814) Jane Austen

Storr, Bob
Eva his wife
Room at the Top (1957) John Braine

Stortford, Bishop of
Meet Mr Mulliner (1927) P. G. Wodehouse

Stossen, Mrs
her daughter
ss 'The Boar Pig'
Beasts and Superbeasts (1914) Saki (rn Hector Hugh Munro)

Stott, George ('Ginger') cricketer
Ellen Mary his wife
Victor his son, cc, the wonder
The Hampdenshire Wonder (1911) J. D. Beresford

Stoyte, Jo Californian oil magnate afraid of death, partly modelled on William Randolph Hearst
After Many a Summer Dies the Swan (1939) Aldous Huxley

Strachan, Chae farmer
Kirsty his wife

A Scots Quair trilogy: *Sunset Song* (1932); *Cloud Howe* (1934); *Grey Granite* (1935) Lewis Grassic Gibbon (rn James Leslie Mitchell)

Strachan, Noel narrator, solicitor
A Town Like Alice (1950) Neville Shute (rn Nevile Shute Norway)

Stradlater Caulfield's room-mate at Pencey
The Catcher in the Rye (1951) J. D. Salinger

Straker, Henry Tanner's chauffeur
Man and Superman play (1903) George Bernard Shaw

Straker, John
ss 'Silver Blaze'
The Memoirs of Sherlock Holmes (1894) Arthur Conan Doyle

Strang, Matthew artist cc
Rosina his commonplace wife
Billy his deformed brother
The Master (1895) Israel Zangwill

Strange, Master merchant, in love with Katherine Worldly*
A Woman is a Weathercock play (1912) Nathan Field

Stranger, Sandy schoolgirl, member of the Brodie set, becomes Sister Helena of the Transfiguration
The Prime of Miss Jean Brodie (1961) Muriel Spark

Stranger, The cc, Christ-like man
The Passing of the Third Floor Back play (1910) Jerome K. Jerome

Strap, Hugh school friend to Random
Roderick Random (1748) Tobias Smollett

Strasser-Mendana, Grace cc, widow, 'anthropologist'
Gerardo her son
A Book of Common Prayer (1977) Joan Didion

Strato
The Maid's Tragedy play (1619) Francis Beaumont and John Fletcher

Stratton, Mr
his wife
Separate Tables play (1955) Terence Rattigan

Stratton, Stephen cc, narrator
The Passionate Friends (1913) H. G. Wells

Strauchan armour-bearer
The Talisman (1825) Walter Scott

Straudenheim Strasburg shopkeeper
The Uncommercial Traveller (1860–8) Charles Dickens

Streaker housemaid who wept huge tears
The Haunted House (1859) Charles Dickens

Strephon Arcadian shepherd, son to Iolanthe* and the Lord Chancellor, m. Phyllis*
Iolanthe opera (1881) W. S. Gilbert and Arthur Sullivan

Strether, Lambert through whose sensibility all is slowly revealed in author's favourite of his novels; Strether says, 'Live all you can, it's a mistake not to'
The Ambassadors (1903) Henry James

Strether, Wulfstan great novelist hiding under the name of Buckmaster in Portugal
I Like It Here (1958) Kingsley Amis

Strett, Luke, Sir eminent doctor
The Wings of a Dove (1902) Henry James

Strickland, Charles English artist who goes to Tahiti; suggested (but no more) to author by French painter Paul Gauguin
Amy his legal wife
Ata his devoted Tahitan mistress
The Moon and Sixpence (1919) W. Somerset Maugham

Strickland, E. of the Indian police; an ambiguous, decadent 'Indianised' figure
Alice *née* Youghal his wife
Adam their son; onwards from
ss 'Miss Youghal's Sais'
Plain Tales from the Hills (1888) Rudyard Kipling

Strike, Major m. Caroline Harrington*
Evan Harrington (1861) George Meredith

Striker, Barnaby attorney
his wife
Petronilla their daughter
Roderick Hudson (1875) Henry James

Strines, Alexander
Mary his artist wife
The World in the Evening (1954) Christopher Isherwood

Stringham, Arlington
Eleanor his wife
ss 'The Jesting of Arlington Stringham'
The Chronicles of Clovis (1911) Saki (rn Hector Hugh Munro)

Stringham, Charles
*A Question of Upbringing** (1951)
Anthony Powell
Stringham, Mrs friend to Milly Theale*
The Wings of the Dove (1902) Henry
James
Stripes servant to Major Ponto*
The Book of Snobs (1847) W. M.
Thackeray
Stroeve, Dirk friend to Charles Strickland*
Blanche his wife, who falls in love with
Strickland
The Moon and Sixpence (1919) W.
Somerset Maugham
Strong, Dr Canterbury schoolmaster
David Copperfield (1850) Charles
Dickens
Strong, Edward, Captain 'The Chevalier
Strong'; friend to Sir Francis Clavering*
Pendennis (1848) W. M. Thackeray
Strong, Kay Leiland graduate of Vassar, m.
Harald Petersen*
The Group (1963) Mary McCarthy
Strongitharm, Lord
the Hon. Lenox his son
The Adventures of Philip (1862) W. M.
Thackeray
Stroope, Mrs golfing champion who occa-
sionally believes she is various titled
ladies, whose property, it being hers, she
ransacks
ss 'A Holiday Task'
Beasts and Super-Beasts (1914) Saki (rn
Hector Hugh Munro)
Strorks rhinoceros
ss 'How the Rhinoceros got his Skin'
Just So Stories (1902) Rudyard Kipling
Strother, Simon old Negro coachman, re-
tainer of the Sartoris* family
Sartoris† (1929) *William Faulkner*
Struggles member of the Dingley Dell
cricket team
The Pickwick Papers (1837) Charles
Dickens
Strumbo a clown
Locrine play (1595) 'W. S.' (?George
Peele; ?Robert Green)
Strumpher, Nick a 'square-made dwarf'
The Pirate (1822) Walter Scott
Struthers, Revd Mr
The House With the Green Shutters
(1901) George Douglas (rn George
Douglas Brown)

Stryver, Mr barrister who defends
Darnay*
A Tale of Two Cities (1859) Charles
Dickens
Stuart, Captain ex-Gordon Highlanders,
commanding the President's bodyguard
Soldiers of Fortune (1897) Richard
Harding Davis
Stuart, Nettie elopes with and m. Edward
Verral*
her father, head gardener to Mrs Verral
In the Days of the Comet (1906) H. G.
Wells
Stubb second mate, the *Pequod*
Moby Dick, or The Whale (1851) Her-
man Melville
Stubble, Ensign
Vanity Fair (1847–8) W. M. Thackeray
Stubbs English undergraduate in Paris
ss 'Providence and the Guitar'
The New Arabian Nights (1882) Robert
Louis Stevenson
Stubbs servant to Sinclair*
No. 5 John Street (1902) Richard White-
ing
Stubbs Yorkshire friend to Jorrocks*
Jorrocks's Jaunts and Jollities (1838)
R. S. Surtees
Stubbs, Jonathan youngest colonel in Brit-
ish army, m. Ayala Dormer*
Ayala's Angel (1881) Anthony Trollope
Stubbs, Robert
Eliza; Lucy his sisters
Thomas; Susan his parents
The Fatal Boots (1839) W. M. Thackeray
Stubbs, Roy
ss 'The Two Captains'
Unlucky for Pringle (1973) Wyndham
Lewis
Stubland, Peter cc, m. Joan Debenham*,
his cousin
Arthur; Dolly his parents
Joan and Peter (1918) H. G. Wells
Studdart, Colonel and Mrs
Laurel m. Edward Tilney*; **Janet** m.
Rodney Meggatt* their daughters
Friends and Relations (1931) Elizabeth
Bowen
Stuff, Nick ladies' tailor
Pinaccia his wife
The New Inn, or The Light Heart play
(1629) Ben Jonson
Stuffle lieutenant in Major Gahagan's regi-

ment
The Adventures of Major Gahagan
(1839) W. M. Thackeray
Stukeley villain who lures Beverley* to
ruin and death
The Gamester play (1753) Edward
Moore
Stultz tailors
The Newcomes† (1853–5) W. M.
Thackeray
Stumfold, Mrs
Miss Mackenzie (1863) Anthony
Trollope
Stumps, Bill
The Pickwick Papers (1837) Charles
Dickens
Sturmer, Lucy, Mrs *née* Targett
her husband
The Sailor's Return (1925) David
Garnett
Sturmthal, Melchior banner-bearer of
Berne
Anne of Geierstein (1829) Walter Scott
Sturt, Father self-sacrificing clergyman
A Child of the Jago (1896) Arthur
Morrison
Stute Fish, The
ss 'How the Whale got his Throat'
Just So Stories (1902) Rudyard Kipling
Stutfield, Lady
Lady Windermere's Fan play (1892)
Oscar Wilde
Subboys, Herbert, Sir an old knight
Beatrice; Crispinella his daughters
The Dutch Courtesan play (1605) John
Marston
Subtle
The Alchemist play (1610) Ben Jonson
Such, Theophrastus cc, narrator
Revd Theophrastus his father
The Impressions of Theophrastus Such
(1879) George Eliot (rn Mary Anne, later
Marian, Evans)
Suckling, Bob man of fashion
Vanity Fair (1847–8) W. M. Thackeray
Sudbinsky careerist official
Oblomov (1859) Ivan Goncharov
Suddhoo
ss 'In the House of Suddhoo'
Plain Tales from the Hills (1888) Rud-
yard Kipling
Suddlechop, Benjamin 'most renowned
barber in Fleet Street'

Dame Ursula his wife
The Fortunes of Nigel (1822) Walter
Scott
Suetonius (hist.)
Bonduca play (1647) John Fletcher
Suffolk, Duke of (hist.)
King Henry VIII play (1623) William
Shakespeare and John Fletcher
Suffolk, Earl of (hist.)
King Henry VI plays (1623) William
Shakespeare
Sugamo, Captain Japanese officer in
Malaya
A Town Like Alice (1950) Neville Shute
(rn Nevile Shute Norway)
Sugarman morose seller of candy on trains
The Tenants of Moonbloom (1963) Ed-
ward Lewis Wallant
Sugden, Mrs neighbour to the Oakroyds*
The Good Companions (1929) J. B.
Priestley
Suggs, Simon successful shyster lawyer in
sketch by lawyer who became a justice of
the Supreme Court
sketch 'Simon Suggs, Jr., Esq: A Legal
Biography'
*The Flush Times of Alabama and Mis-
sissippi* (1853) Joseph G. Baldwin
Sukarno, Achmed (hist.) President of In-
donesia; in Australian novel (cast as
thriller) which portrays him in the last
year of his regime, when he had lost his
earlier aspirations and became grandiose
and corrupt – and was being plotted
against by Suharto
The Year of Living Dangerously (1978)
C. J. Koch
Sukenic, Ronnie American cc, who is writ-
ing a novel about a man called Ronnie
Sukenic, who is writing a novel about . . .
Up (1968) Ronald Sukenic
Suket, Singh
ss 'Through the Fire'
Life's Handicap (1891) Rudyard Kipling
Suleiman-im-Daoud
ss 'The Butterfly that Stamped'
Just So Stories (1902) Rudyard Kipling
Sulinor ('Mango') guard-boat captain
ss 'The Manner of Men'
Limits and Renewals (1932) Rudyard
Kipling
Sullen, Squire country blockhead, son to
Lady Bountiful*

his wife
The Beaux' Stratagem play (1707)
George Farquhar
Sullivan, David lawyer in love with Hazel Carter*
The Glass Cell (1965) Patricia Highsmith
Sullivan, Mrs *née* Cooper
William her son, m. Gertrude Amory*
The Lamplighter (1854) Maria S. Cummins
Sulliwin charlady
Sketches by Boz (1836) Charles Dickens
Sumfit, Mrs cook to the Flemings*
Rhoda Fleming (1865) George Meredith
Summers, Timothy clock maker
ss 'The Three Strangers'
Wessex Tales (1888) Thomas Hardy
Summers, Will the Presenter
Summer's Last Will and Testament (1600) Thomas Nashe
Summers, Dick
The Big Sky (1947); *Fair Lane, Fair Land* (1982) A. B. Guthrie
Summerson, Esther illegitimate daughter to Lady Dedlock* and Captain Hawdon*, niece to Miss Barbary*, part narrator, m. Dr Alan Woodcourt*
Bleak House (1853) Charles Dickens
Sumner, Fred soldier; seducer of Hetty Smith*, father of her son, eventually m. her
The Dream (1924) H. G. Wells
Sunday President, Anarchist Council of European Dynamiters
The Man Who Was Thursday (1908) G. K. Chesterton
Sunderbund (Agatha), Lady rich American widow
The Soul of a Bishop (1917) H. G. Wells
Sung, Herr Chinese who runs off with Cacalie Forster
Of Human Bondage (1915) W. Somerset Maugham
Sunray lover of Sarnac*
Men Like Gods (1923) H. G. Wells
Super, Martin Canadian trapper
The Settlers in Canada (1844) Captain Marryat
Superstition witness, with Envy* and Pickthank*, against Christian* and Faithful*
The Pilgrim's Progress (1678–84) John Bunyan
Superuacuo brother to Lussurioso*

The Revenger's Tragedy (1607/8)
?Thomas Middleton; ?Cyril Tourneur
Supple, Revd Mr curate
Tom Jones (1749) Henry Fielding
Supplehouse of the *Jupiter*
Framley Parsonage (1861) Anthony Trollope
Surbiton, Lord brother to Lord Arthur Savile*
Lord Arthur Savile's Crime (1891) Oscar Wilde
Suresby, Sym servant to Gawyn Goodluck*
Ralph Roister Doister play (1552) Nicholas Udall
Surface, Oliver, Sir
Joseph; Charles his nephews
The School for Scandal play (1777) Richard Brinsley Sheridan
Surjue gentle cc, shot to death, of classic West Indian novel of Kingston slums
The Hills Were Joyful Together (1953) Roger Mais
Surrey, Earl of (hist.)
King Henry VIII play (1623) William Shakespeare and John Fletcher
Surrey, Earl of (hist.)
Perkin Warbeck play (1634) John Ford
Surrey, Earl of (hist.)
The Unfortunate Traveller, or *The Life of Jack Wilton* (1594) Thomas Nashe
Surrogate, Mr a communist
It's a Battlefield (1935) Graham Greene
Susan m. a farmer, one of the characters whose interior monologue* makes up this novel
The Waves (1931) Virginia Woolf
Susan mulatto slave
Emmeline her daughter
Uncle Tom's Cabin (1851) Harriet Beecher Stowe
Susan secretary, lover of Sammy Rice*
The Small Back Room (1943) Nigel Balchin
Susanna whose secret is that she was m. to Count Almaviva before the opera began
100 Scenes from Married Life (1976) Giles Gordon
Sussman, Kenneth public relations man for homicide bureau, changes his name to De Peters, tries to save his wife from aggressive gentiles, in novel by American black humourist

his wife
The Dick (1970) Bruce Jay Friedman
Sutherland, Markham cc of one of the most remarkable (and now neglected novels of its time; prepares for ordination but loses faith; the novel was publicly burned at Oxford
The Nemesis of Faith (1849) J. A. Froude
Sutherland, Mary
ss 'A Case of Identity'
The Adventures of Sherlock Holmes (1892) Arthur Conan Doyle
Sutpen, Thomas aspiring poor white eventually murdered by Wash Jones* when he refuses to recognize latter's granddaughter as his bastard
Ellen *née* Coldfield his wife
Henry; Judith his children by his marriage
Charles Bon his son by Eulalia Bon, part-black murdered by Henry
Clytie his daughter by a black slave
Absalom! Absalom! (1936) William Faulkner
Sutter struck-off doctor, pornographer
Rita his divorced wife, *née* Vaught*
his father, tycoon and automobile trader
his mother, anti-semite
Jamie his younger brother, dying of leukemia, mathematician
The Last Gentleman (1966) Walker Percy
Sutton, Alice, Dame nun who sings too loudly
The Corner That held Them (1948) Sylvia Townsend Warner
Sutton, Beatrice friend to Anna Tellwright*
Anna of the Five Towns (1902) Arnold Bennett
Suvretta famous musician
Gallions Reach (1927) H. M. Tomlinson
Svengali musician and evil genius
Trilby (1894) George du Maurier
Svidigaylov evil seducer of Dunya, the sister to Raskolnikov*; suicide
Prestupleni i Nakazanie (Crime and Punishment) (1866) Fyodor Dostoievsky
Svoboda, Tilly old nurse to the Landons
The Ballad and the Source (1944) Rosamond Lehmann
Swabber, Lieutenant-General
A Shabby Genteel Story (1840) W. M.

Thackeray
Swaffer a farmer
his daughter
ss 'Amy Foster'
Typhoon (1903) Joseph Conrad (rn Josef Teodor Konrad Korzeniowski)
Swallowtail, Colonel
Pendennis (1848) W. M. Thackeray
Swancourt, Elfride m. Lord Luxellian*
Revd Christopher her father, m. (2) Mrs Charlotte Troyton*
A Pair of Blue Eyes (1873) Thomas Hardy
Swann, Charles, cc, elegant and wealthy Jew, m. Odette de Crécy*
Gilberte their daughter, m. Marquis de Saint-Loup"
A la recherche du temps perdu (In Search of Lost Time) (1913–27) Marcel Proust
Swanson, Eddie car agent
Louetta his wife
Babbitt (1923) Sinclair Lewis
Swartz, Rhoda wealthy mulatto, m. James McMull
Vanity Fair (1847–8) W. M. Thackeray
Swede, A
ss 'The Blue Hotel'
The Monster (1899) Stephen Crane
Sweedlepipe, Poll Mrs Gamp's* landlord; kept a bird-fanciers' shop and did easy shaving
Martin Chuzzlewit (1844) Charles Dickens
Sweeney custom-house officer and rogue
Afloat and Ashore (1844) James Fenimore Cooper
Sweeney, Mme ('Svini') drunken nurse-maid to Mme Beck's* children, predecessor of Lucy Snowe*
Villette (1853) Charlotte Brontë
Sweet William cardsharper
The Old Curiosity Shop (1841) Charles Dickens
Sweeting, David flute-playing curate, not quite ridiculous, m. Dora Sykes*
Shirley (1849) Charlotte Brontë
Sweetwinter, Mabel miller's daughter
Bob her brother
The Adventures of Harry Richmond (1871) George Meredith
Swertha aged and avaricious housekeeper of Mertoun*
The Pirate (1822) Walter Scott

Swidger, Molly
William her husband, gatekeeper at the college
The Haunted House (1859) Charles Dickens

Swift, Kate teacher of Willard*
ss 'The Teacher'
Winesburg, Ohio (1919) Sherwood Anderson

Swigby, Joseph
Linda his wife, *née* Wellesley
A Shabby Genteel Story (1840) W. M. Thackeray

Swillenhausen, Baron von father-in-law to the baron of Grogzwig*
Nicholas Nickleby (1839) Charles Dickens

Swindon, Major
The Devil's Disciple play (1899) George Bernard Shaw

Swingler, Thomas private detective
The Old Boys (1964) William Trevor

Swint, Pluto
God's Little Acre (1933) Erskine Caldwell

Swishtail, Dr
Vanity Fair (1847–8) W. M. Thackeray

Swithin, Lucy, Mrs widowed sister to Bartholomew Oliver*
Between the Acts (1941) Virginia Woolf

Swiveller, Dick originally dissipated optimist, m. the Marchioness*
The Old Curiosity Shop (1841) Charles Dickens

Swizzle, Roger red-faced apothecary
Handley Cross (1843) R. S. Surtees

Swoshle, Henry George, Mrs
Our Mutual Friend (1865) Charles Dickens

Swosser, Captain Mrs Bayham's Badger's* first husband, naval officer
Bleak House (1853) Charles Dickens

Sybil maid to Lady Rose Otley*
The Shoemaker's Holiday (1600) Thomas Dekker

Sybilline tart who offers to provide Banks* with his sexual fantasies
The Lime Twig (1961) John Hawkes

Sycamore family solicitor to the Stub-lands*
Joan and Peter (1918) H. G. Wells

Sydenham, Oswald, VC ex-midshipman, cousin to Dolly Stubland*, with whom he is in love
Will Doll's brother (see **Debenham, Joan**)
Lady Charlotte Oswald's aunt
Joan and Peter (1918) H. G. Wells

Sydney, Henry see **Clumber, Duke of**

Sykes, Christopher mill-owner emboldened by Hollands gin
his wife
Dora m. David Sweeting*; Hannah; Harriet; Mary; John four of his six daughters and his son
Shirley (1849) Charlotte Brontë

Syllabub, Timothy hack writer
A Citizen of the World (1762) Oliver Goldsmith

Sylla's ghost
Cataline play (1611) Ben Jonson

Sylli, Signor a foolish self-lover
The Maid of Honour play (1632) Philip Massinger

Sylvia cast-off mistress of Vainlove* m. Sir Joseph Wittol*
The Old Bachelor comedy (1793) William Congreve

Sylvie little bitch at Mme Beck's; likes Paul Emanuel*
Villette (1853) Charlotte Brontë

Syme philologist, friend to Winston Smith*
1984 (1949) George Orwell

Syme, Gabriel (Thursday), poet and detective
The Man Who Was Thursday (1908) G. K. Chesterton

Symmes, Farmer rescuer of Eliza and her child
Uncle Tom's Cabin (1851) Harriet Beecher Stowe

Sympson, Mr and his family
Shirley (1849) Charlotte Brontë

Synesius Bishop of Cyrene
Hypatia (1853) Charles Kingsley

Syntax a schoolmaster
Roderick Random (1748) Tobias Smollett

T

Tabaqui jackal
ss 'Mowgli's Brothers'†
The Jungle Books (1894–5) Rudyard
Kipling

Tabitha the Temptress, pernicious court-
esan
*The Unfortunate Traveller, or The Life of
Jack Wilton* (1594) Thomas Nashe

Tacco Paduan doctor
Romola (1853) George Eliot (rn Mary
Anne, later Marian, Evans)

Tachyo Pitt the Elder
The History and Adventures of an Atom
(1769) Tobias Smollett

Tacker chief assistant to Mould˝
Martin Chuzzlewit (1844) Charles
Dickens

Tackleton venomous lecher, a harsh,
griping and mirthless man
The Cricket on the Hearth (1845)
Charles Dickens

Tadger, Brother temperance man
The Pickwick Papers (1837) Charles
Dickens

Tadman grocer
his wife
Cissie their daughter
South Riding (1936) Winifred Holtby

Tadpole political opportunist
Coningsby (1844) Benjamin Disraeli

Tadzio Polish boy who obsesses Aschenbach*
Der Tod in Venedig (*Death in Venice*)
(1913) Thomas Mann

Taffimai Metallumai little daughter to
Tegumai*
ss 'How the First Letter was Written'
Just So Stories (1902) Rudyard Kipling

Taffy see **Wynne, Talbot**

Taft, Jacob Hayslope patriarch
Adam Bede (1859) George Eliot (rn
Mary Anne, later Marian, Evans)

Tagrag, Mr merchant and former
employer of Titmouse*
Dolly his wife

Tabitha their daughter
Ten Thousand a Year (1841) Samuel
Warren

Tailbush, Lady 'the Lady Projectress'
The Devil is an Ass play (1631) Ben
Jonson

Taji young American sailor; narrator
Mardi (1849) Herman Melville

Takahira of the Aerial Board of Control
ss 'As Easy as A B C'
A Diversity of Creatures (1917) Rudyard
Kipling

Tala cousin to Count Adolf Ribbing and
loved by him
The King With Two Faces (1897) Mary
Coleridge

Talacryn, Francis, Dr Bishop of Carleon,
later a cardinal
Hadrian the Seventh (1904) Baron Corvo
(rn R. W. Rolfe)

Talakku Assyrian captain
ss 'The King of the World'
Adam and Eve and Pinch Me (1921) A. E.
Coppard

Talbot, Christian m. Linda Radlett*
Fabrice Linda's son
The Pursuit of Love (1945) Nancy Mit-
ford

Talbot, Colonel
Waverley (1814) Walter Scott

Talbot, George, Mrs see **Audley, Lady**

Talbot, Lord later Earl of Shrewsbury
(hist.)
King Henry VI plays (1623) William
Shakespeare

Talbot, Mary
Tom her husband
Cannery Row (1945) John Steinbeck

Talboys, George legal husband to Lady
Audley*
Harcourt his father
Clara his sister
Lady Audley's Secret (1862) Mary E.
Braddon

Talkapiece, Tibet maid to Dame Cu-

stance*
Ralph Roister Doister play (1552)
Nicholas Udall
Talkative
The Pilgrim's Progress (1678–84) John
Bunyan
Tall, Laban farm hand
his wife
Far From the Madding Crowd (1874)
Thomas Hardy
Tallboys gunner, HMS *Harpy*
Mr Midshipman Easy (1836) Captain
Marryat
Tallentire, Dick
ss 'The Head of the District'
Life's Handicap (1891) Rudyard Kipling
Tallentire, John casual farm labourer
Emily his wife
Joseph their son
The Hired Man (1969); *A Place in England* (1971) Melvyn Bragg
Tallow, Bob, Petty Officer coxwain of
Compass Rose
The Cruel Sea (1951) Nicholas
Monsarrat
Talmadge, Captain of General Braddock's
army
The Virginians (1857–9) W. M.
Thackeray
Tamaroo, Miss employee of Mrs Todgers
Martin Chuzzlewit (1844) Charles
Dickens
Tamburlaine Scythian shepherd, cc
Tamburlaine play (1590) Christopher
Marlowe
Tamb' Itam personal guardian of Jim in
Patu Sans
Lord Jim (1900) Joseph Conrad (rn Josef
Teodor Konrad Korzeniowski)
Tamerlane
Tamerlane play (1702) Nicholas Rowe
Tamora Queen of the Goths
Titus Andronicus play (1623) William
Shakespeare
Tancred see **Bellamont, Duke of**
Tancred, Mrs
Juno and the Paycock play (1925) Sean
O'Casey (rn John Casey)
Tangle eminent counsel
Bleak House (1853) Charles Dickens
Tangs, Timothy the elder
Tangs, Timothy the younger, his son, m.
Suke Damson*; both bottom sawyers

The Woodlanders (1887) Thomas Hardy
Tanner, John cc
Man and Superman (1903) George
Bernard Shaw
Tanpinar, Halidë Turkish woman doctor
The Towers of Trebizond (1956) Rose
Macaulay
Tanqueray, Aubrey cc
Paula his second wife, cc
Ellean his daughter by his first wife
The Second Mrs Tanqueray play (1893)
Arthur Wing Pinero
Tansey, Sara
The Playboy of the Western World play
(1907) J. M. Synge
Tansley, Charles friend to Mr Ramsay*
To the Lighthouse (1927) Virginia Woolf
Tantamount, Lucy girl with whom Walter
Bidlake* is infatuated
Point Counter Point (1928) Aldous
Huxley
Tape godmother to Prince Bull
ss 'Prince Bull'
Reprinted Pieces (1858) Charles Dickens
Taper political opportunist
Coningsby (1844) Benjamin Disraeli
Tapewell Barry Lyndon's agent
Barry Lyndon (1844) W. M. Thackeray
Tapkins, Felix gay bachelor
Is She His Wife? play (1837) Charles
Dickens
Tapley, Mark hostler at the Blue Dragon,
later servant to Martin Chuzzlewit*, m.
Mrs Lupin*
Martin Chuzzlewit (1844) Charles
Dickens
Taplin, Harry comic singer
Sketches by Boz (1836) Charles Dickens
Taplow schoolboy
The Browning Version play (1948) Terence Rattigan
Tappertit, Simon bombastic apprentice to
Gabriel Varden*
Barnaby Rudge (1841) Charles Dickens
Tappleton, Lieutenant bearer of
Slammer's* challenge to Winkle*
The Pickwick Papers (1837) Charles
Dickens
Tapwell an alehouse keeper
A New Way to Pay Old Debts play
(1633) Philip Massinger
Tarantyev 'one of the nastiest characters in
Russian fiction'; cheat

Oblomov (1859) Ivan Goncharov

Tardew agent to Lord Scoutbush*
Two Years Ago (1857) Charles Kingsley

Targe, Elsie for a brief time loved by Jocelyn Pierston*, m. Captain Popp
Colonel Targe her father, of Budmouth Regis
The Well Beloved (1897) Thomas Hardy

Targett, William cc, sailor
Tulip (Gundernay) his wife, daughter to King Gaze-oh of Dahomey
Sambo; Sheba their children
John; Harry; Francis; Lucy; Dolly his brothers and sisters
The Sailor's Return (1925) David Garnett

Tarion an officer
ss 'Consequences'
Plain Tales from the Hills (1888) Rudyard Kipling

Tarka cc, otter
Tarka the Otter (1927) Henry Williamson

Tarleton white missionary
ss 'The Beach at Falesa'
Island Nights' Entertainments (1893) Robert Louis Stevenson

Tarleton, Stuart
Brent his twin
Jim; Beatrice their parents
Tom; Boyd their brothers
their four sisters
Gone With the Wind (1936) Margaret Mitchell

Tarnapol, Peter cc
My Life as a Man (1974) Philip Roth

Tarquol son to Tarka*
Tarka the Otter (1927) Henry Williamson

Tarr, Frederick English artist
Tarr (1918) Wyndham Lewis

Tarrant, Lewis m. and is divorced from Halo Spear*; owner of *The Hour*
Hudson River Bracketed (1929); *The Gods Arrive* (1932) Edith Wharton

Tarrant, Lionel m. Nancy Lord*
his grandmother
his and Nancy's son
In the Year of Jubilee (1894) George Gissing

Tarrant, Verena 'inspirational' speaker groomed for success in the suffragette movement by Olive Chancellor*, but eventually carried off by the mediocre Ransom*, who believes woman's role is to please men
Dr Tarrant her father, a charlatan
Selah her mother
The Bostonians (1886) Henry James

Tarry, Isabella m. Marc Sallafranque*
Roy her daughter by her first husband
The Thinking Reed (1936) Rebecca West
(rn Cecily Fairfield)

Tartan, Lucy Pierre Glendinning's* fiancée
Pierre, or The Ambiguities (1852) Herman Melville

Tartar ('Tartre') Sartre
Féerie pour un autre fois (Fairy Play for Another Time) (1952–4) Louis-Ferdinand Céline (rn Louis-Ferdinand Destouches)

Tartar naval lieutenant, retired
Edwin Drood (1870) Charles Dickens

Tartar, Captain of HMS *Aurora*
Mr Midshipman Easy (1836) Captain Marryat

Tarvin, James headmaster, employer of Inigo Jollifant*
his wife
The Good Companions (1929) J. B. Priestley

Tarvin, Nicholas cc, in love with Kate Sheriff*
The Naulakha (1892) Rudyard Kipling and Wolcot Balestier

Tarwater, Francis Marion adolescent cc
Mason his mad great-uncle: bootlegger and prophet
The Violent Bear It Away (1960) Flannery O'Connor

Tarworth, Mr American realtor
ss 'The Prophet and the Country'
Debits and Credits (1926) Rudyard Kipling

Tasbrugh, Jean m. Herbert Charwell*
Alan her brother
their father, the Rector
Maid in Waiting† (1931–3) John Galsworthy

Tascher army comrade of Tom Burke*
Tom Burke of Ours (1844) Charles Lever

Tashtego American-Indian harpooner
Moby Dick, or The Whale (1951) Herman Melville

Tasker, Joseph Captain Bowers' man; en-

gaged to Selina Vickers*
Dialstone Lane (1904) W. W. Jacobs

Tasky, James Russian jockey whose name and papers Velvet Brown* uses
National Velvet (1935) Enid Bagnold

Tassel, Van Katrina much admired girl in Dutch community on the Hudson; m. Brom Bones*
ss 'The Legend of Sleepy Hollow'
The Sketch Book of Geoffrey Crayon, Gent (1820) Washington Irving

Tate, Brian, Professor short in stature, fame (which he eventually obtains) and sexual apparatus
Erica his wife
their children
The War Between the Tates (1974) Alison Lurie

Tatham, Lord rich young landowner in love with Lydia Penfold*, m. Felicia Melrose*
The Mating of Lydia (1913) Mrs Humphry Ward

Tatlin, V. Soviet constructivist in semi-surreal, learned American 'novel'
Tatlin! (1974) Guy Davenport Jr.

Tatt, Mr amateur detective
ss 'Detective Anecdotes'
Reprinted Pieces (1858) Charles Dickens

Tattle a half-witted beau
Love for Love comedy (1710) William Congreve

Tattycoram (Harriet Beadles) girl adopted by the Meagles*
Little Dorrit (1857) Charles Dickens

Taube, Laurette m. Albert Grope*
Albert Grope (1931) F. O. Mann

Taunton, Captain friend to Dick Doubledick*
Seven Poor Travellers (1854) Charles Dickens

Tausch, Herr
The Moon in the Yellow River play (1936) Denis Johnston

Tavendale, Ewan farmer, m. Christ Guthrie*
A Scots Quair trilogy: *Sunset Song* (1932); *Cloud Howe* (1934); *Grey Granite* (1935) Lewis Grassic Gibbon (rn James Leslie Mitchell)

Tavrille, Lord cousin to Lady Mary Christian*
his wife

The Passionate Friends† (1913) H. G. Wells

Taylor, Anna, Mrs widowed companion to Emma Woodhouse, m. (2) Mr Weston; a good wife but a bad governess
Anna her daughter by her first marriage
Emma (1816) Jane Austen

Taylor, Corporal fuse expert
The Small Back Room (1943) Nigel Balchin

Taylor, Douglas, Mayor crooked but straight-seeming white local leader in novel about blacks in local politics
The Grand Parade (1961) Julian Mayfield

Taylor, Jean religious octogenarian
Memento Mori (1959) Muriel Spark

Taylor, Jemmy miser of Southwark
Our Mutual Friend (1865) Charles Dickens

Taylor, Mi ex-boxer and odd-job man
Dan his father, trainer of Araminty Brown
National Velvet (1935) Enid Bagnold

Taylor, Miss see **Weston, Mrs**

TB dead-end kid
Dead End play (1936) Sidney Kingsley

Teach pirate captain of the *Sarah*
The Master of Ballantrae (1889) Robert Louis Stevenson

Teal Eye Boone's* squaw but lover of Jim Deakins*
The Big Sky (1947) A. B. Guthrie

Tearcat
The Roaring Girl play (1611) Thomas Middleton and Thomas Dekker

Tearsheet, Doll
King Henry IV plays (1623) William Shakespeare

Teazle, Peter, Sir
his wife
The School for Scandal play (1777) Richard Brinsley Sheridan

Tebab, Princess black Venus and dance-mistress who ritually whips Höfgen*
Mephisto (1936) Klaus Mann

Tebrick, Richard English gentleman
Silvia his wife, née Fox, who turns into a vixen
Lady Into Fox (1923) David Garnett

Techelles follower of Tamburlaine*
Tamburlaine play (1587) Christopher Marlowe

Tecnicus a philosopher
The Broken Heart play (1633) John Ford
Ted mate, the *Arabella*
The Lady of the Barge (1902) W. W. Jacobs
Teddy Britling's* secretary
Letty his wife, *née* Corner
Mr Britling Sees It Through (1916) H. G. Wells
Teddy small boy, owner of Rikki Tikki Tavi*
ss 'Rikki Tikki Tavi'
The Jungle Book (1894) Rudyard Kipling
Teez Negah conjuror
Haja Baba (1824) J. J. Morier
Tegg, Lieutenant, RNVR
ss 'Sea Constables'
Debits and Credits (1926) Rudyard Kipling
Tegumai Bopsulai caveman, father to Taffy*
Teshumai Tewindrow his wife
ss 'How the First Letter Was Written'†
Just So Stories (1902) Rudyard Kipling
Teioa
his wife
Mr Fortune's Maggot (1927) Sylvia Townsend Warner
Tellwright, Ephraim miser
Anna; Agnes his eldest and his youngest daughters
Anna of the Five Towns (1902) Arnold Bennett
Temperley, Jack friend to William Maddison*
his parents
Doris; Margaret his sisters
The Beautiful Years† (1921) Henry Williamson
Tempest, Leslie m. Lettice Beardsall*; based on a milkman's son, George Neville, who had been a friend to the author; Neville later published an account of him
The White Peacock (1911) D. H. Lawrence
Templar, Simon ('The Saint') modern Robin-Hood clone in crude, smoothly executed, mindless thrillers, onwards from
Meet the Tiger† (1928) Leslie Charteris
Temple, Charlotte cc, based on hist. char., Charlotte Stanley, didactic romance first

published in England (the author was originally English) and then in America, where it met with great success – by 1933 it had reached its 161st edition; designed 'for the perusal of the young and thoughtful of the fair sex'
Lucy her daughter, whose adventures are described in the sequel *Charlotte's Daughter* or *The Three Orphans* (1828), usually published as *Lucy Temple*
Charlotte: A Tale of Truth (1791; in America as *Charlotte Temple*, 1794) Mrs Susannah Rowson
Temple, Claire old literary lady, modelled on the novelist Violet Hunt*, cc of novel set in Second World War London
There Were No Windows (1944) Norah Hoult
Temple, Gus school chum to Harry Richmond*
The Adventures of Harry Richmond (1871) George Meredith
Temple, Henrietta m. Ferdinand Armine*
Henrietta Temple: A Love Story (1837) Benjamin Disraeli
Temple, Maria headmistress of Lowood, shapely, refined, just
Jane Eyre (1847) Charlotte Brontë
Temple, Mr bank clerk
The Bitter Box (1946) Eleanor Clark
Temple, Pump
Fanny his wife, *née* Figtree
The Book of Snobs (1847) W. M. Thackeray
Templer, Peter old friend to Nicholas Jenkins*
Mona his wife
Jean his sister, and one-time lover to Jenkins
*A Question of Upbringing** (1951) Anthony Powell
Templeton, Dr mesmerist
ss 'A Tale of the Ragged Mountains'
Tales of the Grotesque and Arabesque (1840) Edgar Allan Poe
Templeton, Julia m. Guy Bracebridge*
Bracebridge Hall (1823) Washington Irving
Tenbruggen Dutch merchant m. Elizabeth Chance*
The Legacy of Cain (1889) Wilkie Collins
Tenby, Edward architect, cc
Apple of the Eye (1970) Stanley Middleton

Tench
  The Power and the Glory (1940) Graham
  Greene
Tennant, Charles lover to Lady Alicia
Seymore
  Fanny By Gaslight (1940) Michael
  Sadleir
Tennant, Mrs owner of a great mansion
  Mrs Jack Tennant her daughter-in-law
  Loving (1945) Henry Green
Teppich Chancellor of Ruritania
  The Prisoner of Zenda (1894) Anthony
  Hope (rn Anthony Hope Hawkins)
Tervigersation, Duke of
  Hawbuck Grange (1847) R. S. Surtees
Terrill, Walter, Sir courtier to William
Rufus
  *Satiromastix, or The Untrussing of the
  Humorous Poet* play (1601) Thomas
  Dekker ?and John Marston
Tertius 'Emperor of China'
  ss 'Slaves of the Lamp'†
  Debits and Credits (1926) Rudyard Kipl-
ing
Teshoo Lama abbot of Suchzen
  Kim (1901) Rudyard Kipling
Tessa *contadina*, m. Giuseppe Palmieri*
  The Gondoliers opera (1889) W. S.
  Gilbert and Arthur Sullivan
Tessa *contadina*, mistress to Tito
Melema*
  Romola (1862) George Eliot (rn Mary
  Anne, later Marian, Evans)
Tester, Mrs bedmaker to Verdant Green*
  The Adventures of Mr Verdant Green
  (1853) Cuthbert Bede (rn Edward
  Bradley)
Tetley rancher
  Gerald his son
  The Ox-Bow Incident (1940) Walter
  Van Tilburg Clark
Tetterby, Adolphus struggling news-
vendor
  his family
  The Haunted Man (1848) Charles
  Dickens
Tewitt, Griffin, Sir fiancé of Lucinda
Roanoke*
  The Eustace Diamonds (1873) Anthony
  Trollope
Tha first of the elephants
  ss 'How Fear Came'
  The Second Jungle Book (1895) Rudyard

Kipling
Thaddeus (hist.) cc comparatively accu-
rate historical novel* which had a
beneficial influence on Scott* and from
which the form of the historical novel
derives; very popular amongst the young
in the last century
  Thaddeus of Warsaw (1803) Jane Porter
Thaisa daughter to Simonides*
  Pericles play (1609) William Shakespeare
Thaliard a lord of Antioch
  Pericles play (1609) William Shakespeare
Thamasta sister to Amethus*, cousin to
Palador*
  The Lover's Melancholy play (1629)
  John Ford
Thatcher, Becky Tom Sawyer's* sweet-
heart
  Judge Thatcher her father
  his wife
  Tom Sawyer† (1876) Mark Twain (rn
  Samuel Langhorne Clemens)
Thatcher, Dr physician who befriends
Rose Dutcher*
  Rose of Dutcher's Coolly (1895) Hamlin
  Garland
Theakstone, Francis, Chief Inspector of
the Detective Force
  ss 'The Biter Bit'
  The Queen of Hearts (1859) Wilkie Col-
lins
Theale, Milly invalid cc, the dove of the
title, leaves her millions to Densher*
  The Wings of a Dove (1902) Henry
  James
Theobald, Lady autocrat
  A Fair Barbarian (1881) Frances
  Hodgson Burnett
Theodoret brother to Thierry*
  Thierry and Theodoret play (1621) John
  Fletcher, Philip Massinger ?and Francis
  Beaumont
Theophile, Corporal
  Somebody's Luggage (1862) Charles
  Dickens
Thersites deformed and scurrilous Grec-
ian, with a tone anticipating that of the
French novelist Louis-Ferdinand Céline*
  Troilus and Cressida play (1623) William
  Shakespeare
Theseus brother to Emelia*
  The Two Noble Kinsmen play (1634)
  William Shakespeare and John Fletcher

(?with Francis Beaumont)

Theseus Duke of Athens
A Midsummer's Night's Dream play (1623) William Shakespeare

Thesiger, Edward, Revd Rector of St Peters, Middlemarch
his wife
Middlemarch (1871–2) George Eliot (rn Mary Anne, later Marian, Evans)

Thibault of Montigni 'the kindest soul alive'
Quentin Durward (1823) Walter Scott

Thick brute, beats Margaret Banks* to death
The Lime Twig (1961) John Hawkes

Thicket, Timothy, Sir
his sister
Roderick Random (1748) Tobias Smollett

Thiele, Captain an autocrat
Ship of Fools (1962) Katherine Anne Porter

Thierry King of France
Thierry and Theodoret play (1621) John Fletcher, Philip Massinger ?and Francis Beaumont

Thinkwell treacherous mate who in 1855 leaves shipwrecked party to its fate and prospers; his descendants go in 1922 to discover the wrecked party, and find Miss Charlotte Smith* as Queen Victoria ruling over complete reconstruction of British life in Pacific island
Orphan Island (1924) Rose Macaulay

Thirdman, Alex and Willa
Theodora their daughter
Friends and Relations (1931) Elizabeth Bowen

Thistlewood family name of **Bareacres**

Tholaway, Ben farm labourer
Adam Bede (1859) George Eliot (rn Mary Anne, later Marian, Evans)

Tholer, Thomas ('Tom Saft') half-witted farm hand
Adam Bede (1859) George Eliot (rn Mary Anne, later Marian, Evans)

Thom homeopathic practitioner
The Mudfog Papers (1938) Charles Dickens

Thomas friar
Measure for Measure play (1623) William Shakespeare

Thomas Lord Loam's* first footman

The Admirable Crichton play (1902) J. M. Barrie

Thomas servant to Sir Anthony Absolute*
The Rivals play (1775) Richard Brinsley Sheridan

Thomas the Dashwoods* manservant
Sense and Sensibility (1811) Jane Austen

Thomas, Bigger executed murderer in the author's black version of *An American Tragedy*
Native Son (1940) Richard Wright

Thomas, Brother infirmarian at St Illod's
ss 'The Eye of Allah'
Debits and Credits (1926) Rudyard Kipling

Thomas, Father credulous monk
A Burnt-Out Case (1961) Graham Greene

Thomas, George seeming friend to Prokop*; womanizer and crook
Dr Thomas his father
Annie his sister
Krakatit (1924) Karel Capek

Thomas, Mr servant
The Conscious Lovers play (1722) Richard Steele

Thomas, Rose tubercular dying prostitute in very early play
'The Web'
Thirst and Other One-Act Plays (1914) Eugene O'Neill (as Eugene G. O'Neill)

Thomas, Will lazy composer-in-residence at Convers College; 'libertine'
Love and Friendship (1962) Alison Lurie

Thomason alias assumed by Alan Breck* to help Balfour*
Kidnapped (1886) Robert Louis Stevenson

Thompkins, Idabel a wild girl
Florabel her prissy twin
Other Voices, Other Rooms (1948) Truman Capote

Thompson friend to Random* believed drowned
Roderick Random (1748) Tobias Smollett

Thompson, Frank, Revd 'examiner'
Outward Bound play (1924) Sutton Vane

Thompson, Hannah hired girl m. Ralph Hartsook*
The Hoosier Schoolmaster (1871) Edward Eggleston

Thompson, Henry, T. father-in-law to George Babbitt*
his wife
Babbitt (1923) Sinclair Lewis

Thompson, Jean attorney
his wife, *née* Lemaitre
ss 'Madame Delphine'
Creole Days (1879) George Washington Cable

Thompson, Joan, Mrs Joe Lampton's* landlady
Cedric her husband
Room at the Top (1957) John Braine

Thompson, Michael '(Management) not to be confused with Michael Thomson (Personnel), or with Thomson and Thompson in Herge's *Tintin* titles; indexed under Shaughnessy, Thomas George – the index being the key to understanding the structure of the novel'
Girl With Red Hair (1974) Giles Gordon

Thompson, Pip RAF recruit
Chips With Everything play (1962) Arnold Wesker

Thompson, Ripton school friend to Richard Feverel*
The Ordeal of Richard Feverel (1859) George Meredith

Thompson, Sadie 'loose woman' disillusioned by Revd Davidson*
ss 'Miss Thompson'
The Trembling of the Leaf (1921) W. Somerset Maugham
Rain play (1922) John Colton and Clemence Randolph

Thompson, Will husband to Rosamund Walden*
God's Little Acre (1933) Erskine Caldwell

Thompson, William see Dodd, David

Thomson, Frank, Revd
Outward Bound play (1923) Sutton Vane

Thomson, Ianthe, Mrs daughter of Mrs Jardine* by her first husband
her second husband
Maisie; Malcolm; Cherry children of Ianthe and her second husband
The Ballad and the Source (1944) Rosamond Lehmann

Thomson, Olivia ('Livvy') friend to Lois Farquhar*
The Last September (1929) Elizabeth Bowen

Thong, Miss dressmaker to the Good Companions
The Good Companions (1929) J. B. Priestley

Thorn, Frederick
East Lynne (1861) Mrs Henry Wood

Thornberry, Job British type
John Bull play (1803) George Colman the Younger

Thorne, Captain gallant Union spy in popular American play
Secret Service play (1895) William Gillette

Thorne, Dr independent honest Englishman
Revd Prebendary DD his father
Henry his profligate brother
Mary cc; his 'niece' and adoptee – actually the bastard of Henry, murdered by Roger Scratcherd*; m. Frank Gresham*
Thorne of Ullathorne
Monica sister to Thorne of Ullathorne
Dr Thorne† (1858) Anthony Trollope

Thornhill, William, Sir alias Burchell, m. Sophia Primrose*
his son, dissipated man-about-town, m. Olivia Primrose*
The Vicar of Wakefield (1766) Oliver Goldsmith

Thornton, John saves Buck* but is murdered by Indians
The Call of the Wild (1903) Jack London

Thornton, Captain
Rob Roy (1818) Walter Scott

Thornton, Frederick Bas
his wife
John; Emily; Edward; Rachel their children
A High Wind in Jamaica (1929) Richard Hughes

Thornton, John m. Margaret Hale*
his mother
Fanny his sister
North and South (1855) Mrs Gaskell

Thornton, Judge
Elsie Venner (1861) Oliver Wendell Holmes

Thornton, Tom murderer
Pelham, or The Adventures of a Gentleman (1828, rev. 1839) Edward Bulwer Lytton

Thoroughfare, Dick, Captain romantic

hero
Mrs Elizabeth Thoroughfare his mother
Niri-Esther his black wife, niece to Mrs
Yajnavalkya*
Valmouth (1919) Ronald Firbank
Thorowgood a London Merchant in play
set in 1580s prior to Armada
Maria his daughter
The London Merchant, or *The History of
George Barnwell* play (1731) George
Lillo
Thorpe, Joel Stormont brutal speculator
The Market-Place (1899) Harold
Frederic
Thorpe, Mrs
Isabella; John; Edward; William her
children
Northanger Abbey (1818) Jane Austen
Thorsen, Gunnar
Ragnhild his wife; ccs of first and best
novel, a Norwegian romance, by
Norwegian who came to America, mas-
tered English and was taken up by
Howells*
Gunnar: A Tale of Norse Life (1874)
Hljalmar Hjorth Boyesen
Thorwold governor in Melveric's* ab-
sence
Death's Jest Book, or *The Fool's Tragedy*
(1850) Thomas Lovell Beddoes
Thrasiline
Philaster play (1620) Francis Beaumont
and John Fletcher
Thraso or Polypragmus, the Plush Bee
The Parliament of Bees (1641) John Day
Thrassier a Scythian commander
Locrine play (1595) 'W. S.' (?George
Peele; ?Robert Green)
Threegan, Molly friend to Emma
Deercourt*, m. Captain Gadsby*
The Story of the Gadsbys (1888) Rud-
yard Kipling
Threl
The King of Elfland's Daughter (1924)
Lord Dunsany
Thrift, Viscount, MP
Phineas Finn (1869) Anthony Trollope
Thriplow, Mary ex-governess
Jim her late husband
Those Barren Leaves (1925) Aldous
Huxley
Throop, Miss Winifred retired headmist-
ress of a fashionable girls' school

What a Way to Go (1962) Wright Morris
Throttlebottom, Alexander modest and
retiring vice-presidential candidate m.
Diana Devereaux*
Of Thee I Sing (1932) George Kaufman,
Ira Gershwin and Morrie Ryskind
Tiger young East Indian peasant trying to
establish an identity for himself in
Trinidadian novel
A Brighter Sun (1952) Samuel Selvon
Thrum, George, Sir
his wife
ss 'The Ravenswing'
Men's Wives (1843) W. M. Thackeray
Thumb, Tom cc of farce satirizing grand-
iose plays of such as Nathaniel Lee*
Tom Thumb, A Tragedy play (1730,
rev. 1731 as *The Tragedy of Tragedies,* or
*The Life and Death of Tom Thumb the
Great*) Henry Fielding
Thumb, Tom mouse
Hunca Munca his wife
The Tale of Two Bad Mice (1904)
Beatrix Potter
Thums, Captain see Hugh, Canon
Thunder-ten-tronckh, Baron in whose
household Candide* is brought up
Cunégonde his daughter
Candide (1759) Voltaire (rn François-
Marie Arouet)
Thurbon, Victor novelist
*Pending   Heaven   (1930)   William
Gerhardie
Thurio rival to Valentine*
Two Gentlemen of Verona play (1623)
William Shakespeare
Thurnall, Tom wanderer, jack-of-all-
trades, cc
Dr Thurnall his father
Two Years Ago (1857) Charles Kingsley
Thursby, Floyd murdered accomplice of
Brigid O'Shaughnessy*
The Maltese Falcon (1930) Dashiell
Hammett
Thurtell, John (hist.) murderer
ss 'Out and Out'
Sketches of Young Gentlemen (1838)
Charles Dickens
Thwacker quartermaster
Redgauntlet (1824) Walter Scott
Thwackum, Revd Mr tutor to Tom Jones*
Tom Jones (1749) Henry Fielding
Thwaite Moffat's* protégé

The Benefactor (1905) Ford Madox Ford

Thwaites, Miss
Gaslight play (1939) Patrick Hamilton

Thye dreamer of songs
The King of Elfland's Daughter (1924)
Lord Dunsany

Thyma, Aurora Felix Aquila's* ideal lover
After London (1885) Richard Jeffries

Tib Gammer Gurton's maid
Gammer Gurton's Needle play (1575)
?W. Stevenson

Tibbets, John ('Ready Money Jack')
Jack his son, m. Phoebe Wilkins*
Bracebridge Hall (1823) Washington
Irving

Tibbs, Beau non-entity who claims friendship with great men
his wife
A Citizen of the World (1762) Oliver
Goldsmith

Tibbs, Mrs bustling little woman who kept a boarding house, and whose husband was a nonentity reduced to the polishing of boots
Sketches by Boz† (1836) Charles Dickens

Tiberius Caesar (hist.)
Lazarus Laughed play (1927) Eugene
O'Neill

Ticehurst, Will a mason
ss 'Hal o' the Draft'
Puck of Pook's Hill (1906; Rudyard
Kipling

Tickeridge, Colonel
Men at Arms (1952) Evelyn Waugh

Tickit, Mrs cook to the Meagles*
Little Dorrit (1857) Charles Dickens

Ticklepenny male nurse at Magdalen
Mental Mercyseat in London
Murphy (1938) Samuel Beckett

Tickler, Tobias, Revd m. Olivia Proudie*
Framley Parsonage† (1861) Anthony
Trollope

Tiddypot vestryman who maintained water was not a necessity of life
ss 'Our Vestry'
Reprinted Pieces (1858) Charles Dickens

Tidmarsh, Timothy, Sir, Baronet,
his wife
their six sons
Evelyn their daughter
Before the Bombardment (1926) Osbert
Sitwell

Tiernay, Maurice cc, young Irish boy,

saved from execution by personal intervention of Robespierre; organizer of Free Irish Army in Ireland
his father, guillotined during the Terror
Maurice Tiernay (1852) Charles Lever

Tietjens Strickland's* dog
ss 'The Return of Imray'
Life's Handicap (1891) Rudyard Kipling

Tietjens, Christopher cc, 'the last English
Tory'
Sir Mark, Baronet his elder brother,
Yorkshire squire, brilliant official
their father
Sylvia Christopher's unfaithful wife,
Roman Catholic, a malicious beauty
Mark their son
Some Do Not (1924); *No More Parades*
(1925); *A Man Could Stand Up* (1926);
Last Post (1928) Ford Madox Ford

Tiffany, Mr and Mrs newly rich couple: to finance her pursuit of fashion he takes to forgery, in mid-19th-century comedy successfully revived in 1958
Seraphina their daughter
Fashion play (1845) Anne Cora Mowatt

Tiffey clerk
David Copperfield (1850) Charles
Dickens

Tiflin, Jody cc, farm boy
his grandfather
ss 'The Leader of the People'
The Red Pony (1937) both in *The Long
Valley* (1938) John Steinbeck

Tiger Lily redskin
Peter Pan play (1904) J. M. Barrie

Tigg, Montague impudent adventurer;
turns up later as Tiggs Montague; murdered by Jonas Chuzzlewit*
Martin Chuzzlewit (1844) Charles
Dickens

Tiggin and Welp firm making printed calico waistcoats
The Pickwick Papers (1837) Charles
Dickens

Tiggy-Winkle, Mrs hedgehog
The Tale of Mrs Tiggy-Winkle (1905)
Beatrix Potter

Tighe, Larry
ss 'Love o' Women'
Many Inventions (1893) Rudyard Kipling

Tigner, Jimmy
ss 'Fairy Kist'

Limits and Renewals (1932) Rudyard Kipling

Tigranes King of Armenia
A King and No King play Francis Beaumont and John Fletcher

Tilbury, Edward young lawyer, lover of Alicia Bartleby*
A Suspension of Mercy (1965) Patricia Highsmith

Tilda flower girl
No. 5 John Street (1902) Richard Whiteing

Tildy Negro house-girl
Uncle Remus (1880–95) Joel Chandler Harris

Tiliot wealthy spirit merchant
Mary his wife
Felix Holt (1866) George Eliot (rn Mary Anne, later Marian, Evans)

Tillington railway clerk
ss 'The Two Captains'
Unlucky for Pringle (1973) Wyndham Lewis

Tillotson friend to Glover*
The Skipper's Wooing (1897) W. W. Jacobs

Tillotson, Comrade of Records Department
1984 (1949) George Orwell (rn Eric Blair)

Tillotson, Walter nonogenarian artist
ss 'The Tillotson Banquet'
Mortal Coils (1922) Aldous Huxley

Tilney, Edward m. Laurel Studdard*
Anna; Simon their children
Lady Elfrida Edward's mother
Friends and Relations (1931) Elizabeth Bowen

Tilney, Henry m. Catherine Morland*
General Tilney his father
Captain Fred; Eleanor his brother and sister
Northanger Abbey (1818) Jane Austen

Tiltood, Dick army friend to Sherston*
Memoirs of a Fox-Hunting Man (1929) Siegfried Sassoon

Tiltyard a feather-seller
Mistress Tiltyard his wife
The Roaring Girl play (1611) Thomas Middleton and Thomas Dekker

Timandra mistress to Alcibiades*
Titus Andronicus play (1623) William Shakespeare

Timberlake, Asa
Lavinia his wife, *née* Fitzroy
Andrew; Roy m. Peter Kingsmill; **Stanley** their children
Maggie wife to Andrew
In This Our Life (1942) Ellen Glasgow

Timberlake, Horace, Sir
The Masters (1951) C. P. Snow

Timberry, Snittle chairman at a dinner given to the Crummleses*
Nicholas Nickleby (1839) Charles Dickens

Timby-Hucks, Miss caricature of Miss Stevens, a *Times* arts feature writer whom the author disliked
Mrs Albert Grundy: Observations in Philistia (1896) Harold Frederic

Timlin, Tom, Father, PP pilgrim to Lourdes
ss 'Feed My Lambs'
The Talking Trees (1971) Sean O'Faolain

Timon noble Athenian who turned misanthrope
Timon of Athens (1623) William Shakespeare

Timorous neighbour to Christian* who turned back
The Pilgrim's Progress (1678–84) John Bunyan

Timpany 'second resurrectionist'
The Good Companions (1929) J. B. Priestley

Timpany, Dr schoolmaster
The Newcomes (1853–5) W. M. Thackeray

Timson, Charles, Revd successful aspirant for the hand (and fortune) of Miss Lillerton*
Sketches by Boz (1836) Charles Dickens

Tina, Miss timid and unattractive niece of Miss Bordereau*, in love with narrator
The Aspern Papers (1888) Henry James

Tinker Bell fairy
Peter Pan play (1904) J. M. Barrie

Tinkler housemaster
Vice Versa (1882) F. Anstey (rn Thomas Anstey Guthrie)

Tinley, Sergeant of the Wiltshires
The Plough and the Stars play (1926) Sean O'Casey (rn John Casey)

Tinman, The Flaming bully on the roads
Lavengro (1851) George Borrow

Tinto, Dick artist, later celebrated

The Bride of Lammermoor (1819) Walter Scott

Tinwell, Minnie bigamously m. to Dudebat*
The Doctor's Dilemma (1906) George Bernard Shaw

Tiny Tim see **Cratchit**

Tippins, Lady vain and garrulous old woman
Our Mutual Friend (1865) Charles Dickens

Tipto, Glorious, Sir a knight and colonel with the luck to think well of himself; talks gloriously on anything, but is seldom in the right
The New Inn, or *The Light Heart* play (1629) Ben Jonson

Tiptoff, Earl of
Lady Fanny his wife, *née* Rakes
The Great Hoggarty Diamond (1841) W. M. Thackeray

Tiptoff, Marquess of see **Lord Poynings, George**

Tiptop Crasher's* groom
Market Harborough (1861) George Whyte-Melville

Tirrell, John, Sir murderee, bestial to ladies
Pelham, or *The Adventures of a Gentleman* (1828, rev. 1839) Edward Bulwer Lytton

Tisher, Mrs widow
Edwin Drood (1870) Charles Dickens

Titania Queen of the Fairies
A Midsummer Night's Dream play (1623) William Shakespeare

'Tite Poulette m. Kristian Kopping*
ss "Tite Poulette'
Old Creole Days (1879) George Washington Cable

Titmarsh, Michael Angelo teacher
Doctor Birch and His Young Friends† (1849) W. M. Thackeray

Titmarsh, Samuel cc, narrator
Mary his wife, *née* Smith
his mother and nine sisters
The Great Hoggarty Diamond (1841) W. M. Thackeray

Titmouse, Tittlebat vulgar and vain clerk at Dowlas, Tagrag* and Bobbin, drapers; then in illicit possession of an estate worth £10,000 a year; finally lunatic; m. Lady Cecilia Dredlington*; cc of once immensely popular novel

Ten Thousand a Year (1841) Samuel Warren

Tittlemouse, Thomasina, Mrs
The Tale of Mrs Tittlemouse (1910) Beatrix Potter

Titus Andronicus cc noble Roman general
Titus Adronicus play (1623) William Shakespeare

Tiverton, Timmy 'eccentric' music-hall comedian, cc, m. Daisy Barley*
Let the People Sing (1939) J. B. Priestley

Tix, Tom bailiff
Nicholas Nickleby (1839) Charles Dickens

To-Pan tinker, or metal-man of Belsise
A Tale of a Tub play (1640) Ben Jonson

Toad, Mr cc
The Wind in the Willows (1908) Kenneth Grahame

Toagis, Mr surly retired market gardener
A Clergyman's Daughter (1935) George Orwell (rn Eric Blair)

Tobermory talking cat owned by Lady Blemley*
ss 'Tobermory'
The Chronicles of Clovis (1911) Saki (rn Hector Hugh Munro)

Tobrah little boy
ss 'Tobrah'
Life's Handicap (1891) Rudyard Kipling

Tod self-confessed thief
The Life and Death of Mr Badman (1680) John Bunyan

Todd half-caste trader who loves Dickens*
A Handful of Dust (1934) Evelyn Waugh

Todd, Almira, Mrs herbalist, cc
The Country of the Pointed Firs (1896) Sarah Orne Jewett

Todd, Captain civil-war veteran
Benton his son
Night Rider (1939) Robert Penn Warren

Todd, Ireton ('Last Trick Todd')
ss 'The Mistake of the Machine'
The Wisdom of Father Brown (1914) G. K. Chesterton

Todd, Revd Mr muscular Christian, petty thief, who is transformed by Mr Apollo* into the eighth bay tree in a garden of seven
his wife
Mr Apollo: A Just Possible Story (1908) Ford Madox Ford

Toddle, Sandy

The House With the Green Shutters (1901) George Douglas (rn George Douglas Brown)

Toddles and Poddles two of Betty Higden's minders
Our Mutual Friend (1865) Charles Dickens

Todhunter, John m. Clare Doria*
The Ordeal of Richard Feverel (1859) George Meredith

Todhunter, Mr man doomed to die who plans and carries out a successful murder, cheating the gallows at the last moment — in the best of this author's books not written under the pseudonym of Francis Iles*
Trial and Error (1927) Anthony Berkeley (rn Anthony Berkeley Cox)

Tods
ss 'Tods' Amendment'
Plain Tales from the Hills (1888) Rudyard Kipling

'Toinette hotel servant, Paris
ss 'The Amours of Mr Deuceace*'
The Yellowplush Papers (1852) W. M. Thackeray

Tollady, Mr stationer who informally adopts Arthur Golding*
Workers in the Dawn (1880) George Gissing

Tolland, Isobel sister to the Earl of Warminster*, m. Nicholas Jenkins*
Alfred, Earl of Warminster her brother, dotty peer
Priscilla her sister, m. Chips Lovell*
A Question of Upbringing (1951) Anthony Powell

Toller, Harry brewer
Sophy his daughter, m. Edward Plymdale*
Middlemarch (1871–2) George Eliot (rn Mary Anne, later Marian, Evans)

Toller, Mr and Mrs servants to Jephro Rucastle*
ss 'The Copper Beeches'
The Adventures of Sherlock Holmes (1892) Arthur Conan Doyle

Tolley commanding officer who goes by the book
Young Man of Talent (1959) George Turner

Tollifer society gigolo paid by Cowperwood* to dance attendance on his wife so that she shall not much mind what he is up to
The Titan (1914) Theodore Dreiser

Tolliver, Senator local leader
Night Rider (1939) Robert Penn Warren

Tolloller, Earl
Iolanthe opera (1882) W. S. Gilbert and Arthur Sullivan

Tolson, Victor mate and lover of Leonard Radcliffe*
Audrey his wife
Radcliffe (1963) David Storey

Tom ('Corinthian Tom')
Life in London, or The Day and Night Scenes of Jerry Hawthorne Esq, and his Elegant friend, Corinthian Tom, Accompanied by Bob Logic, the Oxonian, in their Rambles and Sprees through the Metropolis (1821)
Finish to the Adventures of Tom, Jerry and Logic in Their Pursuits Through Life In and Out of London (1828) Pierce Egan

Tom chimney sweep, later water baby, cc
The Water Babies (1863) Charles Kingsley

Tom, 'Uncle' Negro slave, cc
'Aunt Chloe' his wife
Uncle Tom's Cabin (1851) Harriet Beecher Stowe

Tom, Poor see Edgar

Tomato, Salvatore ('Sally') Mafia man in Sing-Sing
Breakfast at Tiffany's (1958) Truman Capote

Tomkins, Joseph ('Honest Joe'; Fibbet') clerk to Colonel Desborough*
Woodstock (1826) Walter Scott

Tomkins, Major the Bully
his wife, the Shrew
Vivian their daughter, the Hussy
The Passing of the Third Floor Back play (1910) Jerome K. Jerome

Tomling, Christopher engineer
ss 'The Puzzler'
Actions and Reactions (1909) Rudyard Kipling

Tomlinson rich, uneducated miller of Milby
ss 'Janet's Repentance'
Scenes of Clerical Life (1857) George Eliot (rn Mary Anne, later Marian, Evans)

Tomlinson, Augustus journalist, tutor to Paul Clifford*
Paul Clifford (1830) Edward Bulwer Lytton

Tommy dead-end kid
Dead End play (1936) Sidney Kingsley

Tomos
ss 'A Heifer Without Blemish'
My People (1915) Caradoc Evans (rn David Evans)

Tompsett coachman
The Admirable Crichton play (1902) J. M. Barrie

Toms, Cannoneer (bantam-weight champion of the world
Mr Fleight (1913) Ford Madox Ford

Toobad dearest friend to Glowry*
Celinda (alias Stella) his daughter, m. Flosky*
Nightmare Abbey (1818) Thomas Love Peacock

Toodle, Robin called Rob the Grinder
his father, a railway stoker
Polly his mother, wet nurse to Paul Dombey*
Dombey and Son (1848) Charles Dickens

Toogood 'cooperationist', a portrait of Robert Owen
Crotchet Castle (Thomas Love Peacock

Toogood, Billy, Parson
ss 'Andrey Satchel and the Parson and the Clerk'
Life's Little Ironies (1894) Thomas Hardy

Took, Peregrin (Pippin) cousin to Frodo Baggins*
The Lord of the Rings (1954–5) J. R. R. Tolkien

Tooke, Granny very old lady
Thetis her granddaughter
David her grandson, young dairyman
Valmouth (1919) Ronald Firbank

Tookey parish clerk
Silas Marner (1861) George Eliot (rn Mary Anne, later Marian, Evans)

Tooloof; Tooilan Beelzebub's* children
All and Everything: Beelzebub's Tales to His Grandson (1950) G. I. Gurdjieff

Toomai, Little
Big Toomai his father
ss 'Toomai of the Elephants'
The Jungle Book (1894) Rudyard Kipling

Toomer, Horace, Sir friend to Sir George Brumley*, a leader of the Fabian Society
The Wife of Sir Isaac Harman† (1914) H. G. Wells

Toomey, Dan m. Nappa Kilmartin
Famine (1937) Liam O'Flaherty

Toomey, Kenneth Marchal successful old homosexual writer; narrator; has many similarities to Maugham* but is not supposed to represent him
Earthly Powers (1980) Anthony Burgess (rn John Burgess Wilson)

Tootles member of Peter Pan's* band
Peter Pan play (1904) J. M. Barrie

Toots, P. Blimber's* earliest pupil, kind and weak-minded
Dombey and Son (1848) Charles Dickens

Tope verger whose grammar is not above reproach
Edwin Drood (1870) Charles Dickens

Topehall, Narcissa m. Roderick Random*
Orson her brother
her aunt
Roderick Random (1748) Tobias Smollett

Topham, Barbara aunt to Lady Castlewood*
Henry Esmond (1852) W. M. Thackeray

Topham, Lord British ambassador
The Prisoner of Zenda (1894) Anthony Hope (rn Anthony Hope Hawkins)

Toppit, Miss a literary lady
Martin Chuzzlewit (1844) Charles Dickens

Topsy black child slave, Eva St Clair's* protégée
Uncle Tom's Cabin (1851) Harriet Beecher Stowe

Torchester, Lord heir to an earldom, proposed marriage to Maggie Grey*, but is refused
The Wooing O't (1873) Mrs Hector Alexander

Torkingham, Revd Mr
Two on a Tower (1882) Thomas Hardy

Tormes, Lázaro ('Lazarillo') cc of the earliest picaresque novels
Lazarillo de Tormes (1554)

Torp, Gerda m. Wolf Solent*
her father, a stonecutter
Lob her brother
Wolf Solent (1929) John Cowper Powys

Torpenhow, Gilbert Belling very close friend to Dick Heldar*

The Light that Failed (1890) Rudyard Kipling

Torquil of the Oak, aged forester and father of eight sons
The Fair Maid of Perth (1828) Walter Scott

Torrance, Pat brute, m. Lady Caroline Lindores*; murdered by her brother Lord Rintoul*
The Ladies Lindores† (1883) Mrs Margaret Oliphant

Torre, Juanita de la see **Kingsborough, Margarita**

Torrigiano Italian builder
ss 'The Wrong Thing'
Rewards and Fairies (1910) Rudyard Kipling

Torrington, Captain friend to Henleigh Grandcourt*
his wife
Daniel Deronda (1876) George Eliot (rn Mary Anne, later Marian, Evans)

Torrismond son to the Duke of Ferrara, cc Victorian tragedy written in Jacobean style
Torrismond play (1851) Thomas Lovell Beddoes

Tortesa usurer cc in American blank verse tragedy of interest as to what could (or could not) be done in the medium at that time in that place
Tortesa, the Usurer play (1839) Nathaniel Parker Willis

Tortillion, Lord family name **Travers**
his son and daugher-in-law
Anne m. Henry Melville; **Fanny** children to his son and daughter-in-law
Bluebeard's Keys (1874) Anne Thackeray

Tortoise, Ptolemy, Alderman
The Tale of Jeremy Fisher (1906) Beatrix Potter

Tosh, Sylvia
The Little Minister (1891) J. M. Barrie

Toto see **Nebu**

Totsky wealthy womanizer
Idiot (1869) Fyodor Dostoievsky

Tott, Klas, Baron wise old lover of Queen Kristina and appointed by her as chamberlain to the *king* ('I am not queen to any king')
Kristina play (1903) August Strindberg

Tott, Laura governess

Holy Deadlock (1934) A. P. Herbert

Tottenham, Lord
The Treasure Seekers (1899) E. Nesbit

Tottle, Watkins timorous old bachelor; proposed to Miss Lillerton* but found that he had been forestalled by the Revd Timson*
Sketches by Boz (1836) Charles Dickens

Touchandgo, Miss daughter of financial swindler
Crotchet Castle (1831) Thomas Love Peacock

Touchett, Ralph cc, cousin to and in love with Isabel Archer*
The Portrait of a Lady (1881) Henry James

Touchstone clown, m. Audrey*
As You Like It play (1623) William Shakespeare

Touchstone goldsmith
Eastward Ho! play (1605) George Chapman, Ben Jonson and John Marston

Touchwood
The Impressions of Theophrastus Such (1879) George Eliot (rn Mary Anne, later Marian, Evans)

Touchwood, Senior
Mistress Touchwood his wife
Touchwood Junior their son
A Chaste Maid in Cheapside play (1630) Thomas Middleton

Touchwood, Lord uncle to Mellefont*
Lady Touchwood his wife, in love with Mellefont*
The Double-Dealer play (1710) William Congreve

Tough, Defts, Mr counsel in Peebles* vs. Plainstanes*
Redgauntlet (1824) Walter Scott

Tough, Ruby spinster
ss 'Love and Lethe'
More Pricks That Kicks (1934) Samuel Beckett

Tourvel, de, Présidente highminded m. woman seduced by Valmont*
Les Liaisons dangereuses (1782) Pierre-Ambroise-François Choderlos de Laclos

Tovesky, Marie neighbour to the Bergsons*
O Pioneers! (1913) Willa Cather

Tow-Wouse, Mr and Mrs innkeepers
Joseph Andrews (1742) Henry Fielding

Tower, Alwyn American writer
Goodbye Wisconsin (1928); *The Pilgrim Hawk* (1940) Glenway Westcott
Tower, Euthymia beautiful young athlete who saves Maurice Kirkwood* from his phobia and m. him
A Mortal Antipathy (1885) Oliver Wendell Holmes
Tower, Sergeant
The Basic Training of Pavlo Hummel play (1973) David W. Rabe
Towers, Duchess of
Peter Ibbotson (1891) George du Maurier
Towers, Tom of the *Jupiter*
The Warden (1855) Anthony Trollope
Towler servant to Sir Francis Clavering*
Pendennis (1848) W. M. Thackeray
Towler, Dick ostler
Black Beauty (1877) Anna Sewell
Town, Max portrait of the author's father, H. G. Wells*
Heritage (1955) Anthony West
Towneley college friend to Ernest Pontifex*
The Way of All Flesh (1903) Samuel Butler
Towneley, Lord and Lady
The Provok'd Husband play (1728) John Vanbrugh and Colly Cibber
Townley, Colonel, JP
Adam Bede (1859) George Eliot (rn Mary Anne, later Marian, Evans)
Townley, Miss schoolteacher, Milby
ss 'Janet's Repentance'
Scenes of Clerical Life (1857) George Eliot (rn Mary Anne, later Marian, Evans)
Townlinson, Thomas Dombey's* footman, became a grocer at Oxford Market and m. Mary Anne
Dombey and Son (1848) Charles Dickens
Townly, Colonel
A Trip to Scarborough play (1777) Richard Brinsley Sheridan
Towns, Harry successful screenwriter beset by anxieties
About Harry Towns (1974) Bruce Jay Friedman
Townsend, Arthur engaged to Marian Almond*
Morris his cousin, cc, engaged to Catherine Sloper*

Washington Square (1880) Henry James
Townsend, Pixie m. Anthony Kroesig
The Pursuit of Love (1945) Nancy Mitford
Townshend Bow Street runner
Lost Sir Massingberd (1864) James Payn
Towrowski, Count eloped with Miss Bagg*
The Book of Snobs (1847) W. M. Thackeray
Tox, Lucretia Mrs Chick's* bosom friend, but disowned by her when the latter discovered that she entertained hopes of becoming the second Mrs Dombey*
Dombey and Son (1848) Charles Dickens
Tozer, Leora m. Martin Arrowsmith* as first wife
her parents
Albert her brother
Arrowsmith (1925) Sinclair Lewis
Tpschoffski, Major see **Chops**
Trabb tailor
Great Expectations (1861) Charles Dickens
Tracy
Tracy's Tiger (1951) William Saroyan
Tracy, Reuben 'bloodless prig'; cc, m. Kate Minster
The Lawton Girl (1890) Harold Frederic
Traddles, Thomas old friend to David Copperfield*, m. Sophy; based on the author's friend Judge Talfourd
David Copperfield (1850) Charles Dickens
Tradewell an old gentleman
Young Tradewell his son
The City Madam play (1658) Philip Massinger
Trafford, Geoffrey m. Maggie Grey*
The Wooing O't (1873) Mrs Hector Alexander
Trafford, Richard Andrew brilliant scientist, m. Marjorie Pope*
Margharita; Godwin; Rachel; Edward their children
Richard's mother
Marriage (1912) H. G. Wells
Traherne, Caroline daughter to Selwyn Faramond*
The Gates of Summer play (1956) John Whiting
Traill, Archie schoolmaster, m. Isabel Desart*

Mr Perrin and Mr Traill (1911) Hugh Walpole

Traill, Rt Revd Bishop of Ealing
his wife and son
Vanity Fair (1847–8) W. M. Thackeray

Trainor druggist
poem 'Trainor, the Druggist'
Spoon River Anthology verse epitaphs (1915) Edgar Lee Masters

Trains Meercraft's* man
The Devil is an Ass play (1616) Ben Jonson

Tralala gang-raped girl
Last Exit to Brooklyn (1964) Hubert J. Selby

Trampas enemy of the Virginian*
The Virginian (1902) Owen Wister

Trampfoot member of Liverpool police
The Uncommercial Traveller (1860–8) Charles Dickens

Tranfield grace *née* Cuthbertson
The Philanderer play (1893) George Bernard Shaw

Transome temporary alias of Prince Otto*
Prince Otto (1885) Robert Louis Stevenson

Transome, Mr of Transome Court
Arabella his wife
Durfey their semi-imbecile son
Harold Arabella's son by Matthew Jermyn*
Felix Holt (1866) George Eliot (rn Mary Anne, later Marian, Evans)

Trant, Elizabeth financier and backer of the Good Companions troupe, m. Hugh McFarlane*
Hilary her nephew
The Good Companions (1929) J. B. Priestley

Trap, Jack cc, part-Aboriginal
Wilson his father
Trap (1970) Peter Mathers

Trapbois, 'Golden' usurer
Martha his daughter
The Fortunes of Nigel (1822) Walter Scott

Trapdoor
The Roaring Girl play (1611) Thomas Middleton and Thomas Dekker

Trapes, Diana
The Beggar's Opera (1728); *Polly* operas (1729) John Gay

Trapnel, Francis X. portrait of the eccentric writer Julian Maclaren-Ross
Book Do Furnish a Room† (1971) Anthony Powell

Trash, Joan a gingerbread woman
Bartholomew Fair play (1631) Ben Jonson

Trask, Adam cc, shot by his wife, Cathy *née* Ames*
Caleb; Aron their sons
Charles Adam's half-brother
East of Eden (1952) John Steinbeck

Traveller, Mr narrator
Tom Tiddler's Ground (1861) Charles Dickens

Traveller, The Uncommercial 'for the great House of Human Interest Brothers'
The Uncommercial Traveller (1860–8) Charles Dickens

Travers see **Tortillion, Lord**

Traveers, Anne, Lady widow, owner of strike-bound mine loved by organizer of strike, Reid*
The Strike At Arlingford play (1893) George Moore

Travers, Edith loves Lingard*
her suspicious husband
The Rescue (1920) Joseph Conrad (rn Josef Teodor Konrad Korzeniowski)

Traverse
The Clandestine Marriage play (1766) George Colman the Elder

Trawler, Rutherford ('Rusty') millionaire
Breakfast at Tiffany's (1958) Truman Capote

Treadaway, Curley guitar-playing apprentice to Mordecai Jones*
The Ballad of the Flim-Flam Man† (1965, rev. 1967) Guy Owen

Treadway, Camilo white racist
The Narrows (1953) Ann Petry

Treadwell, Mary divorcee
Ship of Fools (1962) Katherine Anne Porter

Treasury, Mr magnate friend to Merdle*
Little Dorrit (1857) Charles Dickens

Trebell, Henry politician (cf. Dilke or Parnell) on verge of ruin because he has a mistress
Waste play (1907, rev. 1926) Harley Granville Barker

Treble singing-master
The Provok'd Wife play (1697) John Vanbrugh

Trebonius conspirator against Julius Caesar*
Julius Caesar play (1623) William Shakespeare

Tredgold, Clay
Arrowsmith (1925) Sinclair Lewis

Tredgold, Edward
his father, estate agents
Dialstone Lane (1904) W. W. Jacobs

Tree sadler
The New Inn, or The Light Heart play (1629) Ben Jonson

Trefoil, Arabella husband-hunting cc who is left fortune by John Morton*, whom she tried to jilt; m. Mounser Green*
Lady Augustus her ambitious mother
The American Senator (1877) Anthony Trollope

Trefoyle see **Polperro, Lord**

Tregarvan, John, Sir
his wife
The Adventures of Philip (1862) W. M. Thackeray

Tregennis, Brenda
Owen; George; Mortimer her brothers
ss 'The Devil's Foot'
His Last Bow (1917) Arthur Conan Doyle

Treherne, John, Revd
The Admirable Crichton play (1902) J. M. Barrie

Trejago, Christopher almost castrated for having an affair with an Indian girl whose hands are cut off
ss 'Beyond the Pale'
Plain Tales from the Hills (1888) Rudyard Kipling

Trelawney, Squire
Treasure Island (1883) Robert Louis Stevenson

Trelawny, Rose cc well-made sentimental comedy
Trelawny of the Wells play (1898) Arthur Wing Pinero

Trellis, Daniel 'eccentric author' of novel-within-a-novel
At Swim Two Birds (1939) Flann O'Brien (rn Brian O'Nolan (Nuallain))

Trembloz, M. peasant pastor cc of Bielle in Switzerland, chastely loves Madame de Bussens*
Mme Trembloz his tyrannical mother
Les Roches blanches (The White Rocks

(1895) Édouard Rod

Tremlett, William villager
The Trumpet Major (1880) Thomas Hardy

Tremouille, La Chamberlain
The Duchess
St Joan play (1924) George Bernard Shaw

Trench, Harry, Dr
Widowers' Houses play (1892) George Bernard Shaw

Trenglos, Melachi ('Old Glos') old man, cc
Mahala (Mally) his granddaughter, m. Barty Gunville*
ss 'Malachi's Cove'
Lotta Schmidt (1867) Anthony Trollope

Trenor, George Augustus
Judy his wife
Hilda; Muriel their daughters
The House of Mirth (1905) Edith Wharton

Trent, Frederick gambler, wastrel and profligate
The Old Curiosity Shop (1841) Charles Dickens

Trent, Gwennie wardrobe mistress
Antigua Penny Puce (1936) Robert Graves

Trent, Nellie ('Little Nell') cc
Frederick her worthless brother
The Old Curiosity Shop (1841) Charles Dickens

Trent, Paul solicitor, anarchist
A Glastonbury Romance (1932) John Cowper Powys

Trent, Philip artist, reporter, investigator, cc; early epitome fo the 'human' i.e. 'realistic' detective – from whom Sayers* developed Wimsey*; onwards from
Trent's Last Case (1913) E. C. Bentley

Trepte, Regierrungsrat, Herr elderly Austrian to whom Countess von Rassentlow* becomes engaged; 'A real old Roman of the Empire'
ss 'The Captain's Doll'
The Captain's Doll (1923) (in UK as *The Ladybird*) D. H. Lawrence

Trescott, Dr who is ostracized by townsfolk for defending the Monster* who saved his child
ss 'The Monster'
Monster and Other Stories (1899) Stephen Crane

Tresham sleeping partner in Osbaldistone and Tresham
Will his son
Rob Roy (1818) Walter Scott
Tresham, Richard (alias Gen. Witherington) m. Zilia de Mncada*
Richard Middlemas their son before marriage
The Surgeon's Daughter (1827) Walter Scott
Tressilian, Edmund suitor to Amy Rosbart*
Kenilworth (1821) Walter Scott
Trevanion largest officer in the English Army
Harry Lorrequer (1839) Charles Lever
Trevelyan, Laura niece to Mrs Bonner*
Voss (1957) Patrick White
Trevelyan, Louis
Emily his wife, daughter of Sir Marmaduke Rowley*
He Knew He was Right (1869) Anthony Trollope
Trevelyan, Percy, Dr
ss 'The Resident Patient'
The Memoirs of Sherlock Holmes (1894) Arthur Conan Doyle
Trevelyan, Bunk poor tobacco farmer
Night Rider (1939) Robert Penn Warren
Treverton, Rosamond cc, m. Leonard Frankland*
her supposed parents
Andrew her eccentric uncle
The Dead Secret (1857) Wilkie Collins
Trevisa, Judith m. (1) Captain Cruel Coppinger*, (2) Oliver Menaida
Revd Peter her father, Rector of St Enodoc
Jamie her idiot twin
Dionysia her aunt, housekeeper to Coppinger
In the Roar of the Sea (1892) Sabine Baring-Gould
Trevor duellist
Diary of a Late Physician (1832) Samuel Warren
Trevor, Hugh cc of autobiographical romance by early radical novelist
Hugh Trevor (1794) Thomas Holcroft
Trevor, Victor college friend to Holmes*
ss 'The Gloria Scott'
The Memoirs of Sherlock Holmes (1894) Arthur Conan Doyle

Trewe, Robert poet
ss 'An Imaginative Woman'
Wessex Tales (1888) Thomas Hardy
Trewhella, William James ('Jaz') coal and wood merchant
Rose his wife
Kangaroo (1923) D. H. Lawrence
Triddlefitz
Ut mine Stromtid (An Old Story of my Farming Days) (1862–4) Fritz Reuter
Trig, Benira, Lord
ss 'The Three Musketeers'
Plain Tales from the Hills (1888) Rudyard Kipling
Trigorin, Kiril
The Constant Nymph (1924) Margaret Kennedy
Trilby see O'Ferrall, Trilby
Trim, Corporal servant to Tristram Shandy*
Tristram Shandy (1767) Laurence Sterne
Trim, Lord Governor of the Sago Islands
The Adventures of Philip (1862) W. M. Thackeray
Trimingham, Ninth Viscount m. Marian Maudsley*
The Go-Between (1953) L. P. Hartley
Trimmer, Mr
Sketches by Boz (1836) Charles Dickens
Trimmins, George fiancé to Norah Hopper*
his mother
ss 'The Face'
A Beginning (1955) Walter de la Mare
Trimtram servant to Chough*
A Fair Quarrel play (1617) Thomas Middleton and William Rowley
Trinculo clown
The Tempest play (1623) William Shakespeare
Tringham, Parson
Tess of the D'Urbervilles (1891) Thomas Hardy
Tringle, Emmeline aunt to Ayala Dormer*
Sir Thomas her husband, financier
Tom their son
Ayala's Angel (1881) Anthony Trollope
Trip
A Trip to Scarborough play (1777) Richard Brinsley Sheridan
Triplet, James tenth-rate dramatist-actor and scene-painter
Jane his wife

Lucy; Lysimachus; Roxalana their children
Peg Woffington (1853) Charles Reade

Triplex, Julia m. Sir Damask Monogram*
The Way We Live Now (1875) Anthony Trollope

Trippet, Tom
Catherine (1840) W. M. Thackeray

Trista, Joanna sadistic and foully behaved Belgian-Spanish pupil at Mlle Reuter's*
The Professor (1857) Charlotte Brontë

Tristan L'Hermite provost marshal of Louis's household
Quentin Durward (1823) Walter Scott

Tristram, Mr
his wife
The American (1877) Henry James

Triton, Lord philanthropist
Middlemarch (1871–2) George Eliot (rn Mary Anne, later Marian, Evans)

Trivett, Bobby a subaltern
ss 'The 'Honours of War'
A Diversity of Creatures (1917) Rudyard Kipling

Trofimovich, Stepan old liberal
Besy (The Possessed) (1879) Fyodor Dostoievsky

Troil, Ulla ('Norma of the Fitful Head')
Erland her father
Olave her uncle
Magnus Olave's son
wife to Magnus, *née* Sinclair
Minna; Brenda daughters to Magnus and his wife
The Pirate (1822) Walter Scott

Troilus son to Priam*, in love with Cressida*
Troilus and Cressida play (1623) William Shakespeare

Trollio servant to Meleander*
The Lover's Melancholy play (1629) John Ford

Troop prefect at Peter Stubland's* school
Joan and Peter (1918) H. G. Wells

Troop, Disko captain of the *We're Here*
Dan his son, friend to Harvey Cheyne jr.*
his wife
Captains Courageous (1897) Rudyard Kipling

Trotman, Captain landlord of the Cat and Fiddle
Sybil (1845) Benjamin Disraeli

Trott, Alexander young tailor; suitor to Emily Brown*; m. Julia Manners* at Gretna Green
Sketches by Boz (1836) Charles Dickens

Trotter
Fanny's First Play play (1905) George Bernard Shaw

Trotter opulent oil man
his wife and daughters
The Sketch Book (1820) Washington Irving

Trotter, Second Lieutenant
Journey's End play (1928) R. C. Sherriff

Trotter, Emma m. Lord Methusaleh*
her mother
Mrs Perkins's Ball (1847) W. M. Thackeray

Trotter, Joe manservant and friend to Jingle*
The Pickwick Papers (1837) Charles Dickens

Trotter, Nelli fishwife
St Ronan's Well (1824) Walter Scott

Trotwood, Betsey, Miss great-aunt to David Copperfield*
her scapegrace husband
David Copperfield (1850) Charles Dickens

Trounce, Sergeant
St Patrick's Day play (1775) Richard Brinsley Sheridan

Trout, Eva heiress
Jeremy her small illegitimate son
Willy her deceased father
Eva Trout (1969) Elizabeth Bowen

Trout, Paris villain
Paris Trout (1987) Pete Dexter

Trowbridge, Walt honest senator
It Can't Happen Here (1935) Sinclair Lewis

Troy, Francis, Sergeant cc, m. Bathsheba Everdene*
his mother
Far From the Madding Crowd (1874) Thomas Hardy

Troyton, Charlotte, Mrs m. Revd Christopher Swancourt*
A Pair of Blue Eyes (1873) Thomas Hardy

Truck, Thaddeus cc, great poet, Uncle Thad, 'very majestic Word-Man'
Stella his wife
ss 'Doppelgänger'
Unlucky for Pringle (1973) Wyndham Lewis

Trude, John cruel and gigantic cc who marries and mistreats a younger wife
Jael his daughter m. Richmond Drew*
David their son
Judas his son crippled when fleeing from his drunken rage
The Pitiful Wife (1924) Storm Jameson
Trueman, Adam faithful friend to Tiffany*
Fashion play (1845) Anne Cora Mowatt
Truewit manipulator of the action
Epicene, or The Silent Woman play (1609) Ben Jonson
Truffigny, M. de attaché at French Embassy
Vanity Fair (1847–8) W. M. Thackeray
Trujillo see **Phoenix**
Trull, Dolly
Polly opera (1729) John Gay
Truman and Hatchett solcitiors
Mrs Dukes' Million (1977) Wyndham Lewis
Trumbull, Borthrop auctioneer
Middlemarch (1871–2) George Eliot (rn Mary Anne, later Marian, Evans)
Trumbull, Douglas friend to Clyde Griffiths*
Jill; Gertrude; Tracy his children
An American Tragedy (1925) Theodore Dreiser
Trumbull, Tom ('Tom Turnpenny')
Redgauntlet (1824) Walter Scott
Trumpart a clown
Locrine play (1595) 'W. S.' (?George Peele; ?Robert Green)
Trumper, Tom
his wife
Hawbuck Grange (1847) R. S. Surtees
Trumpeter cc, narrator
Consider the Lilies (1968) Auberon Waugh
Trumpington, Alastair Digby Vane, Sir
Sonia his wife
Decline and Fall† (1928) Evelyn Waugh
Trumpington, Captain
ss 'The Ravenswing'
Men's Wives† (1843) W. M. Thackeray
Trumpington, Lady
The Virginians (1857–9) W. M. Thackeray
Trundle coachman
The New Inn, or The Light Heart play (1629) Ben Jonson

Trundle Wardle's* son-in-law
The Pickwick Papers (1837) Charles Dickens
Trunnion, Hawser, Commodore commanding local garrison
Grizzle his wife, *née* Pickle*
Peregrine Pickle (1751) Tobias Smollett
Truog, Maria m. Warli*
Ships that Pass in the Night (1893) Beatrice Harraden
Trupenie, Tom servant to Dame Custance*
Ralph Roister Doister play (1551) Nicholas Udall
Truscott, Jim, Inspector crooked policeman
Loot play (1966) Joe Orton
Trustie, Tristram friend to Goodluck*
Ralph Roister Doister play (1551) Nicholas Udall
Trusty, Betty, Miss untrustworthy confidante of Miss Nanny Johnson*
The Adventures of David Simple (1744–53) Sarah Fielding
Trusty, Mrs
The Clandestine Marriage play (1766) George Coleman the Elder
Tryan, Edgar, Revd curate at Paddiford Common, Milby
his sister
ss 'Janet's Repentance'
Scenes of Clerical Life (1857) George Eliot (rn Mary Anne, later Marian, Evans)
Tryphena, Aunt aunt to Conrad*
Conrad in Search of His Youth (1919) Leonard Merrick
Tsi-Puff moon guardian of Cavor*
The First Men in the Moon (1901) H. G. Wells
Tub, Squire
Lady Tub his mother
A Tale of a Tub play (1640) Ben Jonson
Tubal a Jew, friend to Shylock*
The Merchant of Venice play (1623) William Shakespeare
Tubbe, Waldo friend to George Winterbourne*
Death of a Hero (1929) Richard Aldington
Tucca, Pantilius swaggering captain who enters into a conspiracy with Crispinus* and Demetrius* to defame Horace* – subject of ridicule in second play

The Poetaster play (1602) Ben Jonson
Satiromastix, or The Untrussing of the Humorous Poet play (1602) Thomas Dekker ?and John Marston

Tuck, Thomas ('Tyburn Tom') footpad
Heart of Midlothian (1818) Walter Scott

Tucker daughter to Emily Frampton* by her first husband
Non-Combatants and Others (1916) Rose Macaulay

Tucker Edward Casaubon's* curate
Middlemarch (1871–2) George Eliot (rn Mary Anne, later Marian, Evans)

Tucker, Dan
Put Yourself in his Place (1870) Charles Reade

Tucker, Sarah upper housemaid to the Barfields*
Esther Waters (1894) George Moore

Tuckle fat and noisy footman
The Pickwick Papers (1837) Charles Dickens

Tudge, Job Felix Holt's* protégé
Felix Holt (1866) George Eliot (rn Mary Anne, later Marian, Evans)

Tudor, Alaric cc, 'robber with education'
The Three Clerks (1858) Anthony Trollope

Tudor, Father teacher at Belvedere Preparatory School
Adam of Dublin (1920) Conal O'Connell O'Reardon (rn F. Norreys Connell)

Tufthunt see Hunt, Thomas, Revd

Tufto, George Granby, Lieutenant-General, Sir
his wife
Tom his grandson
Vanity Fair (1847–8) W. M. Thackeray

Tuggridge, Albert friend to Leonard Oakroyd*
The Good Companions (1929) J. B. Priestley

Tuggs, Joseph grocer
his wife
Simon; Charlotte their children
Sketches by Boz (1836) Charles Dickens

Tugtail, Anthony
Hawbuck Grange (1847) R. S. Surtees

Tuke see Routh

Tuke, Beryl, Mrs landlady of pub awaiting demolition
her husband
Prudence her daughter, in love with

Alban Roche*
Miss Gomez and the Brethren (1971) William Trevor

Tulke prefect
ss 'The Last Term'
Stalky & Co. (1899) Rudyard Kipling

Tulkinghorn, Mr family lawyer to the Dedlocks*; murdered
Bleak House (1853) Charles Dickens

Tull, Vernon
Cora his wife
As I Lay Dying (1930) William Faulkner

Tulla, Earl of brother to George Morris*
Phineas Finn (1869) Anthony Trollope

Tullidge, Corporal
The Trumpet Major (1880) Thomas Hardy

Tulliver, Maggie cc, partly a self-portrait
Edward miller, her ignorant, obstinate, honest father
Tom whom she loves but who can understand her only in death
Elizabeth *née* Dodson, her mother
'**Gritty**' her aunt (Edward's sister) m. Moss*
The Mill on the Floss (1860) George Eliot (rn Mary Anne, later Marian, Evans)

Tulrumble, Nicholas Mayor of Mudfog
The Mudfog Papers (1838) Charles Dickens

Tunmarsh, Lord chairman of Aintree stewards
National Velvet (1935) Enid Bagnold

Tupman, Tracy companion to Pickwick*
The Pickwick Papers (1837) Charles Dickens

Tupper, George friend to Uckridge*
Uckridge† (1924) P. G. Wodehouse

Tupple clerk at Somerset House
Sketches by Boz (1836) Charles Dickens

Turfe, Tobie High Constable of Kentish Town
Sibil his wife
Awdrey their daughter, bride to John Clay*
A Tale of a Tub play (1640) Ben Jonson

Turgis
Angel Pavement (1930) J. B. Priestley

Turle, Eric lacivious poetaster and seducer of Joy Pickering*
Miriam his wife, teacher at Joy Pickering's school
An Advent Calendar (1971) Shena

Mackay
Turnbull
The Thirty-nine Steps (1915) John
Buchan
Turnbull radical MP
Phineas Finn† (1869) Anthony Trollope
Turnbull, Arphaxed farmer
Aunt Em his daughter m. Abel Jones*
Alva his son by his first wife
The War Widow (1894) Harold Frederic
Turnbull, Dr
The Mill on the Floss (1860) George Eliot
(rn Mary Anne, later Marian, Evans)
Turnbull, Michael bold borderer
Castle Dangerous (1832) Walter Scott
Turner, Bill hooligan
The Oriel Window (1896) Mrs Moles-
worth
Turner, Holman instructor at Convers
College, cc
Emmy his bored wife
Love and Friendship (1962) Alison Lurie
Turner, Jim ('Captain Flint') houseboat
owner
Swallows and Amazons (1931) Arthur
Ransome
Turner, John
his daughter
ss 'The Boscombe House Mystery'
The Adventures of Sherlock Holmes
(1892) Arthur Conan Doyle
Turner, Mary campaign worker m. John P.
Wintergreen*
Of Thee I Sing (1921) George Kaufman,
Ira Gershwin and Morrie Ryskind
Turner, Mary unwed mother saved from
suicide by Dr Spenlove*
Ruth 'Cohen' her daughter
Aaron the Jew (1894) Benjamin L.
Farjeon
Turner, Melissa in love with Chad Bu-
ford*: dies in taking journey to warn him
of his danger
The Little Shepherd of Kingdom Come
(1903) John Fox
Turner, Miss wretched English teacher at
Mme Beck's* who cannot keep order and
is dismissed
Villette (1853) Charlotte Brontë
Turner, Mrs Sherlock Holmes's* landlady
A Study in Scarlet† (1887) Arthur Conan
Doyle
Turner, Nat (hist.) narrator cc who led

black revolt in Virginia in 1831
The Confessions of Nat Turner (1967)
William Styron
Turner, Rick L. monstrous American
academic in pursuit of Wilfred Barclay*
The Paper Men (1984) William Golding
Turner, Rose girl from whom Mildred
Lawson delights in taking Morton
Mitchell*
ss 'Mildred Lawson'
Celibates (1895) George Moore
Turnham, Polly m. Richard Mahoney*
John m. (1) Emma, (2) Jinny Beamish,
(3) Lizzie Timms Kelly; **Ned**; **Jerry**;
Sarah m. Hempel her brothers and sister
Lisby her mother
Johnny; **Emma** children to John and
Emma
The Fortunes of Richard Mahoney
(1930) Henry Handel Richardson (rn
Ethel Florence Lindesay Richardson
Robertson)
Turnstall, Frank 'sharp-witted' apprentice
to Davis Ramsay*
The Fortunes of Nigel (1822) Walter Scott
Turrell, Miss Helen
Michael her illegitimate son whom con-
vention obliges her to deny and refer to as
'nephew'
ss 'The Gardener'
Debits and Credits (1926) Rudyard Kipl-
ing
Turtle, James ex-public schoolboy
The Old Boys (1964) William Trevor
Turton collector
Mary his wife
A Passage to India (1924) E. M. Forster
Turvey valet to Sir Hugh Mallinger*
Daniel Deronda (1876) George Eliot (rn
Mary Anne, later Marian, Evans)
Turveydrop, Prince dancing master, m.
Caddy Jellyby*
his father, the Model of Deportment
Bleak House (1853) Charles Dickens
Tusher, Robert, Dr Vicar of Castlewood
his wife
Thomas their son, a bishiop, m. Beatrix
Esmond*
Henry Esmond (1852) W. M. Thackeray
Tussie, Bolliver poor white squatter who
collects $10,000 life insurance on his son,
Private Tussie, and goes on a spree; in
wartime bestseller

his wife
Subrinea his daughter, loved by Anse Bushman*
Private Tussie believed killed in the war
Grandpa cc
Sid supposed grandson of Grandpa; narrator
Trees of Heaven (1940); *Taps for Private Tussie* (1943) Jesse Stuart
Twala usurping king of Kukuana tribe, killed in combat with Sir Henry Curtis*
King Solomon's Mines (1885) Henry Rider Haggard
Tweedledee
Alice Through the Looking-Glass (1872) Lewis Carroll (rn Charles Lutwidge Dodgson)
Tweedledum
Alice Through the Looking-Glass (1972) Lewis Carroll (rn Charles Lutwidge Dodgson)
Tweedy, Marion (Molly) m. Leopold Bloom*
Ulysses (1922) James Joyce
Tweeny kitchenmaid
The Admirable Crichton play (1902) J. M. Barrie
Tweeter, Tiggy absurd poetaster
The Wily Ones (1891) Gordon Giles
Tweetyman m. Marian Forsyte*
their child
The Forsyte series (1906–33) John Galsworthy
Twelvemough, Mr fashionable novelist
A Traveller from Altruria (1894) William Dean Howells
Twemlow, Martin harmless little gentleman
Our Mutual Friend (1865) Charles Dickens
Twentyman, Larry farmer in love with Mary Masters*
The American Senator (1877) Anthony Trollope
Twigger, Edward bottle-nosed Ned, a drunk
The Mudfog Papers (1838) Charles Dickens
Twin I and Twin II boys in Peter Pan's* band
Peter Pan play (1904) J. M. Barrie
Twinch, Septimus lawyer
The Pottleton Legacy (1849) Albert

Smith
Twinkleton, Miss principal of the Nun's House School at Cloisterham, a charmingly prim old maid
Edwin Drood (1870) Charles Dickens
Twisden, Jacob
Loyalties (1922) John Galsworthy
Twist, Oliver cc; workhouse boy, son to Agnes Fleming*
Oliver Twist (1839) Charles Dickens
Tyrell, Dr
Of Human Bondage (1915) W. Somerset Maugham
Twistleton see Ickenham
Twitchit, Tabitha, Mrs
Tom Kitten; Moppet; Mittens her children
The Tale of Tom Kitten† (1907) Beatrix Potter
Two Tails elephant
ss 'Her Majesty's Servants'
The Jungle Book (1894) Rudyard Kipling
Twycott, Revd Mr m. Sophy, a servant
Randolph their son
ss 'The Son's Veto'
Life's Little Ironies (1894) Thomas Hardy
Twysden, Talbot
his wife, *née* Ringwood*
Ringwood; Blanche; Agnes m. Grenville Woolcomb* their children
The Adventures of Philip (1862) W. M. Thackeray
Tybach, Twm
Madlin his wife
ss 'The Glory that was Sion's'
My People (1915) Caradoc Evans (rn David Evans)
Tybalt nephew to Lady Capulet*
Romeo and Juliet play (1623) William Shakespeare
Tyke, Walter, Revd
Middlemarch (1871–2) George Eliot (rn Mary Anne, later Marian, Evans)
Tymowski, Colonel Polish soldier
The Adventures of Philip (1862) W. M. Thackeray
Tyndar parasite
Gorboduc play (1562) Thomas Sackville and Thomas Norton
Tyrell, Dr
Of Human Bondage (1915) W. Somerset Maugham

Tyrell, James, Sir murderer of the Princes in the Tower
King Richard III play (1623) William Shakespeare
Tyrell, Sandy
Hay Fever play (1925) Noël Coward
Tyringham, Hugh cavalier who has a plantation in Virginia near to which his sworn enemy, the puritan Harold Habingdon*, flees
Langley his son; in love with and eventually m. Miriam Habingdon*; in novel demonstrating intolerance of both sides
The Puritan and His Daugher (1849) James Kirke Paulding
Tyrone, Mary drug addict
James her husband, former matinée idol

Jamie; Edmund their sons, the latter a self-portrait
Long Day's Journey Into Night play (1956) Eugene O'Neill
Tyrrel family name of **Etherington, Earl of**
Tyrrell tyrannical squire who is murdered by Falkland* (who is acquitted of it)
Things as They Are, or *The Adventures of Caleb Williams* (1794) William Godwin
The Iron Chest dramatization (1796) George Colman the Younger
Tyrrell, Thornton philosopher
Memoirs of an Infantry Officer (1930) Siegfried Sassoon
Tysefew a blunt gallant
The Dutch Courtesan play (1605) John Marston

U

Uckridge, Stanley Fetherstonehaugh cc
  Millie his wife
  Julia his aunt; onwards from
  Love Amongst the Chickens (1906) P. G.
  Wodehouse
Ugh-Lomi cc
  Eudena his mate
  ss 'A Story of the Stone Age'
  Tales of Space and Time (1899) H. G.
  Wells
Ulpius pagan votary who wishes to offer
  Antonina* up as a virgin sacrifice
  Antonina (1850) Wilkie Collins
Ulver, Delly farm girl
  Pierre (1852) Herman Melville
Ulysses Grecian commander
  Troilus and Cressida play (1623) William
  Shakespeare
Uma native wife to Wiltshire*
  ss 'The Beach of Falesa'
  Island Nights' Entertainments (1893)
  Robert Louis Stevenson
Umpopa native servant to Sir Henry
  Curtis*, later revealed as Ignosi*, rightful
  chief of the Kukuana
  King Solomon's Mines (1885) Henry
  Rider Haggard
Underhill, Updike, Dr cc of picaresque
  romance whose preface contains first
  plea for a genuinely native American
  fiction
  The Algerine Captive (1797) Royall
  Tyler
Unferth follower of Hrothgar* who taunts
  Beowulf
  Beowulf (c.745)
Under, John T. teenager from Hades
  ss 'The Diamond as Big as the Ritz'
  Tales of the Jazz Age (1922) F. Scott
  Fitzgerald
Unity servant at Endelstowe Vicarage, m.
  Martin Cannister*
  A Pair of Blue Eyes (1873) Thomas
  Hardy
Unnamable, The possibly the author 'busy

making fun of himself'
  Molloy (1951); *Maline meurt* (*Malone
  Dies*) (1951) (tr. 1956); *L'Innommable*
  (1953) (*The Unnamable*) (tr. 1958) (tri-
  logy) Samuel Beckett
Unwin 'abject' confidential maid to Lady
  Charlotte Sydenham*
  Joan and Peter (1918) H. G. Wells
Upchurch, Annabel m. Judge Honeywell*
  for his money but then deserts him for
  Dabney Birdsong*
  Bella her mother
  The Romantic Comedians (1926) Ellen
  Glasgow
Upjohn, Frank painter
  Death of a Hero (1929) Richard
  Aldington
Upjohn, John journeyman
  The Woodlanders (1887) Thomas Hardy
Uploft, George squire
  Evan Harrington (1861) George
  Meredith
Urban, Father de cc, corrupted by business
  'ethics', of novel of American Roman
  Catholic life
  Morte D'Urban (1962) J. F. Powers
Urcenze suitor to Julia*
  *The Pleasant Commedye of Patient
  Grissill* play (1603) Thomas Dekker
Urmson, Garth cursed member of New
  Hampshire family in Swedenborgian
  novel by son of more famous father
  Garth (1875) Julian Hawthorne
Urquhart, Squire wealthy historian
  Wolf Solent (1929) John Cowper Powys
Ursini, Paulo Giordano Duke of Brachiano
  Isabella his wife
  Giovanni their son
  The White Devil play (1612) John
  Webster
Ursula apostate nun at Oby
  Jackie her illegitimate son, later known as
  Jackie Pad, or Jack the Latimer, thief
  The Corner That Held Them (1948)
  Sylvia Townsend Warner

Ursula pig-woman
Bartholomew Fair play (1631) Ben Jonson
Urswick chaplain to the King
Perkin Warbeck play (1634) John Ford
Usher, Violet m. John Ransome*
her parents
The Combined Maze (1913) May Sinclair
Ussher, Miles evil and oppressive Protestant tax-man
The Macdermots of Ballycloran (1847)
Anthony Trollope
Ustane native girl
She (1887) Henry Rider Haggard
Usumcasane follower of Tamburlaine*
Tamburlaine play (1590) Christopher Marlowe
Utterson solicitor to Jekyll*
Dr Jekyll and Mr Hyde (1886) Robert Louis Stevenson
Utterword, Lady
Heartbreak House play (1917) George Bernard Shaw

$\mathcal{V}$

Vaiden, Jimmy poor white 'hard-shell Baptist' who loses his slaves when he falls into debt to Handbeck*: cc of Alabama trilogy which influenced Faulkner*
Miltiades his son, retired colonel and Klan leader, later president of town bank and would-be constructor of memorial to himself
The Forge (1931); *The Store* (1932); *Unfinished Cathedral* (1934) T. S. Stribling

Vail, Cynthia Vera Claiborne's* cousin and Tom Claiborne's* 'literary' mistress
The Malefactors (1956) Caroline Gordon

Vaillant, Joseph, Father Vicar General at Albuquerque, assistant to Jean Marie Latour*
Death Comes for the Archbishop (1927) Willa Cather

Vainlove 'capricious in his love; in love with Araminta*'
The Old Bachelor comedy (1793) William Congreve

Valancourt lover of Emily St Aubert*
The Mysteries of Udolpho (1794) Mrs Ann Radcliffe

Valborg, Erik with whom Carol Kennicott* flees to Washington
Main Street (1921) Sinclair Lewis

Valdes friend to Faustus*
Dr Faustus (1604) Christopher Marlowe ?and Samuel Rowley

Valens Roman soldier
ss 'The Church that was at Antioch'
Limits and Renewals (1932) Rudyard Kipling

Valentin, Aristide Chief of Police
ss 'The Secret Garden'
The Innocence of Father Brown (1911) G. K. Chesterton

Valentine Capitaine de Cour's* orderly, housemaid, valet, cook, steward and nurse
Somebody's Luggage (1862) Charles Dickens

Valentine dentist
You Never Can Tell play (1895) George Bernard Shaw

Valentine servant to Collonia*
The Case is Altered play (1609) Ben Jonson

Valentine young gentleman of Verona
Two Gentlemen of Verona play (1623) William Shakespeare

Valentine, Miss friend to Elizabeth Firminger*
Ragged Robin (1945) Oliver Onions

Valentine, Mr young gentleman about town
Love in a Wood, or *St James's Park* play (1672) William Wycherley

Valentini, Dr
A Farewell to Arms (1929) Ernest Hemingway

Valentinian (hist.) Valentinian III, whose story is told in the 24th chapter of Gibbon's *Decline and Fall*
Valentinian play (1647) John Fletcher

Valentinois see **Cornichon, Mme**

Valeria friend to Virgilia*
Coriolanus play (1623) William Shakespeare

Valiant-for-Truth
The Pilgrim's Progress (1678–84) John Bunyan

Vallens, Jane m. Andrew Satchel*
ss 'Andrey Satchel and the Parson and Clerk'
Life's Little Ironies (1874) Thomas Hardy

Valleys, Geoffrey, Earl of
Lady Gertrude his wife, *née* Semmering
Lord Miltoun; the Hon. Hubert; Lady Agatha m. Sir William Shropton*; **Lady Barbara** m. Lord Harbinger* their children
The Patrician (1911) John Galsworthy

Valmont, de, Vicomte cc
Les Liaisons dangereuses (1782)

Pierre-Ambroise-François Choderlos de Laclos
Valora
Tracy's Tiger (1951) William Saroyan
Valoroso King of Paflagonia
The Rose and the Ring (1855) W. M. Thackeray
Valverde servant to Pizarro*
Pizarro play (1799) Richard Brinsley Sheridan
Valvona, Doreen believer in astrology
Memento Mori (1959) Muriel Spark
Vamp, Mr caricature of Gifford, editor of the *Quarterly*
Melincourt, or *Sir Oran Haut on* (1817) Thomas Love Peacock
Van Bibber, Courtlandt law-breaking young clubman who befriends the poor; the author's idea of himself compounded with Robin Hood: it helped create an image of the suave and only apparent asinine American male: good-looking, energetic and fundamentally noble
Van Bibber and Others stories (1892); *Episodes in Van Bibber's Life* stories (1899) Richard Harding Davis
Van Brennen Philip Vanderdecken's* uncle
The Phantom Ship (1839) Captain Marryat
Van Brunt, Abraham known as Brom Bones
The Legend of Sleepy Hollow (1820) Washington Irving
Van de Bosch Dutch settler in Albany
Lydia his granddaughter, m. second Earl Castlewood*
The Virginians (1857–9) W. M. Thackeray
Van de Wayer, Mario cheerful Eton-educated hedonist and cultural butterfly
The Last Puritan (1936) George Santayana
Van Degen, Peter m. Clare Dagonet*
Thurber his father, wealthy banker
The Custom of the Country (1913) Edith Wharton
Van Dusen, S. F. X., Professor American detective
The Thinking Machine (1907); *The Thinking Machine on the Case* (in England as *The Professor on the Case*) (1908)

Jacques Futrell
Van Eyck, Margaret
Peter her father, friend to Gerard Eliasson*
The Cloister and the Hearth (1861) Charles Reade
Van Gilbert, Colonel corporation lawyer
The Iron Heel (1908) Jack London
Van Jaarsweld policeman
Cry, the Beloved Country (1948) Alan Paton
Van Kerrell, Jan Boer farmer in love with Deborah Krillet*
The Shulamite (1904) A. and C. Askew
Van Koppen, Cornelius millionaire
South Wind (1917) Norman Douglas
Van Langen German baron
his wife
Daniel Deronda (1876) George Eliot (rn Mary Anne, later Marian, Evans)
Van Osburgh, Eva, Mrs
Gwen her daughter
The House of Mirth (1905) Edith Wharton
Van Rosenbom Burgomaster of Flushing
Jorrocks's Jaunts and Jollities (1838) R. S. Surtees
Van Tassel, Katrina daugher of a rich farmer
The Legend of Sleepy Hollow (1820) Washington Irving
Van Trompe, John friend to Senator Bird*
Uncle Tom's Cabin (1851) Harriet Beecher Stowe
Van Vluyck, Miss member of the Lunch Club, a ladies' literary discussion group
ss 'Xingu'
Roman Fever (1911) Edith Wharton
Van Weyden, Humphrey narrator, aesthete rescued by Wolf Larsen* and forced to work as cabin boy; m. Maud Brewster*
The Sea Wolf (1904) Jack London
Van Winkle, Rip henpecked husband in the Kaatskill mountains who sleeps for twenty years
Dame Van Winkle his wife
Judith their daughter
Rip Van Winkle (1820) Washington Irving
Van Zyl, Adrian commando
ss 'The Captive'
Traffics and Discoveries (1904) Rudyard

Kipling

Vand, Allegra cc of Jewish American novel her nameless daughter, for whose psychological and biological father she searches
Trust (1966) Cynthia Ozick

Vandam usher at M. Pelet's*
The Professor (1857) Charlotte Brontë

Vandeleur, Thomas, Major-General, Sir
Clara his wife, *née* Pendragon
John his brother
ss 'The Rajah's Diamond'
The New Arabian Nights (1882) Robert Louis Stevenson

Vandenhuten, Jean Baptiste pupil at M. Pelet's* who is rescued from drowning by William Crimsworth*
Victor his grateful father
The Professor (1857) Charlotte Brontë

Vanderbluff
Polly opera (1729) John Gay

Vanderdecken, Philip cc, m. Amine Poots*
William his father
Catherine his mother
The Phantom Ship (1839) Captain Marryat

Vanderflint, Emmanuel Belgian officer
Teresa Diabologh his wife
Sylvia Ninon Therese Anastashia their daughter
The Polyglots (1925) William Gerhardie

Vanderlynden, Madeleine cc of trilogy (known by the title of its first book) set on a farm during the 1914–18 War in Northern France near Hazebrouk, and important for its contribution to war fiction
Jerome her father; Flemish-speaking, French-writing tenant of the 'Ferme Espagnole
Sylvie Jerome's dead wife and Madeleine's mother
Marie her elder sister
Marcel her brother
The Spanish Farm (1924); *Sixty-Four, Ninety-Four* (1925); *The Crime at Vanderlynden's* (1926); The *Spanish Farm* Trilogy (the whole slightly revised and linked) (1927) R. H. Mottram

Vandernoodt American of Dutch descent
Daniel Deronda (1876) George Eliot (rn Mary Anne, later Marian, Evans)

Vanderpool, Rosalie spoiled butterfly m.

Sir Nigel Anstruther* for his title and pays the price: he takes her cash, cuts her off from the world and her family, and deforms their son
Betty her younger sister
Ughtred her hunchbacked son by Sir Nigel
The Shuttle (1907) Frances Hodgson Burnett

Vanderwoort Dutch ship's captain, murdered by Emily Thornton*
A High Wind in Jamaica (1929) Richard Hughes

Vandremer the malarial narrator's doctor, who may not exist
Rigadon (*Rigadoon*) (1960) Louis-Ferdinand Céline (rn Louis-Ferdinand Destouches)

Vane, Ernest wealthy Shropshire squire
Mabel his wife
Peg Woffington (1853) Charles Reade

Vane, Isobel, Lady m. Carlyle* but is worked on by Levison* until she leaves him because of his alleged infidelity; later she becomes servant to Carlyle and his new wife; in Victorian blockbuster
Raymond her brother
Emma Raymond's wife
East Lynne (1861) Mrs Henry Wood

Vane, Sybil jilted by Dorian Gray*
her mother
James her brother
The Picture of Dorian Gray (1891) Oscar Wilde

Vane, William Fred his son
Lucinda his daughter m. Hugo Brayford*
Stephen the Brayford's son, conscientious objector
Lucinda Brayford (1946) Martin Beckett à Boyd

Vanecourt, Frank cc of novel by eccentric author who did not make full use of his literary gifts (not related to Mrs Margaret Oliphant*, who wrote his life)
Piccadilly (1870) Laurence Oliphant

Vanholt, Duke of
his wife
Dr Faustus (1604) Christopher Marlowe ?and Samuel Rowley

Vanringham, Tubby m. Prudence Whittaker*
Joe his brother, m. Jane Abbott*
Summer Moonshine (1938) P. G. Wode-

house

Vanslyperken, Captain brutal cc of macabre farce
Snarleyyow (1837) Captain Marryat

Vanstone, Magdalen quasi-criminal cc, m. (1) Noel Vanstone, (2) Captain Kirke*; a mistress of disguise who poses as 'Miss Bygrave'
Norah her sister, a governess, and like her, born illegitimate (although legitimized much later); m. George Bartram*, who turns out to be the Vanstone heir;
Andrew their father, m. (2) Mrs Wragge*, widow
Michael Andrew's vindictive elder brother
Noel miserly and cretinous, m. Magdalen Vanstone; **Selina** Michael's children
No Name (1862) Wilkie Collins

Vansuythen, Mrs
Major Vansuythen her husband
ss 'A Wayside Comedy'
Wee Willie Winkie (1888) Rudyard Kipling

Vanucle, Pietro artist and friend to Gerard Eliasson*
The Cloister and the Hearth (1861) Charles Reade

Vapour a tobacco-seller
A Fair Quarrel play (1617) Thomas Middleton and William Rowley

Varden, Gabriel honest locksmith on side of law and order; refuses to pick the lock at Newgate when urged to do so by the mob
Martha his wife, whose religious meagrims made his life intolerable until the riots, when she saw his virtues and reformed
Dolly their daughter, a little coquette, m. Joe Willet*
Barnaby Rudge (1841) Charles Dickens

Varens, Adèle Edward Rochester's* ward
Céline her mother, Rochester's first mistress
Jane Eyre (1847) Charlotte Brontë

Varick, Gus Alice Waythorn's* second husband, a man of a class higher than Haskett*, but not as high as Waythorn*
ss 'The Other Two'
Roman Fever (1911) Edith Wharton

Varick, Katherine friend to Jane Potter*
Potterism (1920) Rose Macaulay

Varner, Will lawyer
Eula his daughter, m. Flem Snopes*
The Hamlet† (1931) William Faulkner

Varney, Edith daughter of Confederate General for love of whom Thorne* fails to carry out his duty
Secret Service play (1895) William Gillette

Varnish, Mr
The Adventures of David Simple (1744–53) Sarah Fielding

Varnum, Lawyer
Ruth his daughter, m. Ned Hale
Ethan Frome (1911) Edith Wharton

Varrilat, Evariste, Dr
his wife
ss 'Madame Delphine'
Old Creole Days (1879) George Washington Cable

Vasek, Anastasya Russian exile in Paris
Tarr (1818) Wyndham Lewis

Vashti 'devilish' actress
Villette (1853) Charlotte Brontë

Vasquez servant to Soranzo*
'Tis Pity She's a Whore play (1633) John Ford

Vasu fanatical taxidermist, cc, plots against the temple elephant of Malgudi
The Man-Eater of Malgudi (1961) R. K. Narayan

Vathek, Caliph Faust-like hero of pseudo-Oriental fantasy by 'England's wealthiest son' (Byron) who wrote it in French, sent it to the Revd Henley, who translated it into English and published it without permission as an anonymous Arabic tale
An Arabian Tale (1786) (translated Revd Samuel Henley)
Vathek in French (1786)
The Episodes of Vathek (1912) William Beckford

Vaughan
Fanny's First Play play (1905) George Bernard Shaw

Vaughan ('Taffy') surgeon
ss 'Unprofessional'
Limits and Renewals (1932) Rudyard Kipling

Vaughan see **Mertoun, Basil**

Vaughan, Barbara Roman Catholic half-Jewish schoolteacher
The Mandelbaum Gate (1965) Muriel

Spark

Vaughan, Helen (also **Beaumont** and other aliases), *femme fatale*
Mary her mother
The Great God Pan (1894) Arthur Machen

Vaughan, Mary m. George Callender*
ss 'Deep Waters'
The Man Upstairs (1914) P. G. Wodehouse

Vaught, Kitty
The Last Gentleman (1966) Walker Percy

Vautien, Abel in love with Alissa's* sister Juliette*
La Porte étroite (Strait Is the Gate) (1909) André Gide

Vautrin ('Trompe-la-Mort') rn Jacques Collin a.k.a. Abbé Carlos Herrera (whom he had murdered); as Chief of Sûreté, Saint-Estève; criminal who becomes chief of police; partly based on the real-life ex-criminal chief of the Sûreté, Eugène François Vidocq, who was the author's friend
Le Père Goriot† (1835) Honoré de Balzac

Vaux, Nicholas, Sir
King Henry VIII play (1623) William Shakespeare and John Fletcher

Vauxhall, Lord
ss 'The Ravenswing'
Men's Wives (1843) W. M. Thackeray

Vavasour, Elsley poet, *né* John Briggs
Lucia his sister, wife to Lord Scoutbush*
Two Years Ago (1857) Charles Kingsley

Veal, Laurence, Revd
his wife
Vanity Fair (1847–8) W. M. Thackeray

Veal, Mrs friend to Mrs Bargrave*
A True Relation of the Apparition of Mrs Veal (1706) Daniel Defoe

Veck, Toby or **Trotty** little ticket porter before the church of St Dunstan's in Fleet Street
Meg his daughter, to whose wedding celebrations to Richard he awakes
The Chimes (1844) Charles Dickens

Veilchen, Annette in attendance on Anne of Geierstein*
Anne of Geierstein (1829) Walter Scott

Venables, John steward of the junior common room

Sinister Street (1913) Compton Mackenzie

Venasalvatica, Marchesa della *née* Lady Daphne Page
Adam of Dublin† (1920) Conal O'Connell O'Reardon (rn F. Norreys Connell)

Vendale, George cc
No Thoroughfare (1867) Charles Dickens

Veneada, Dr who tells his friend Hulings* that he is 'great' because he is 'unpleasant ... if for nothing else'
ss 'Tubal Cain'
Gold and Iron (1918) Joseph Hergesheimer

Veneering, Hamilton of Chicksey, Veneering and Stobbles, a drug house
Anastasia his wife, a showy couple; he brought himself a parliamentary seat, at Pocket Breeches, but eventually became bankrupt and lived in France on Anastasia's jewellery
Our Mutual Friend (1865) Charles Dickens

Vengeance, The short plump widow of grocer, friend to Mme Defarge*, leading revolutionary
A Tale of Two Cities (1859) Charles Dickens

Venice, Duke of
Othello play (1623) William Shakespeare

Venice, Duke of
The Merchant of Venice (1623) William Shakespeare

Venn, Diggory cc, 'The reddleman' m. as second husband Thomasin Yeobright*
The Return of the Native (1878) Thomas Hardy

Venner, Elsie cc of fictional study of early feminist Margaret Fuller (and an oblique attack on Calvinism), whose snake-like and schizophrenic nature is here explained by author as result of snakebite her mother received
Dudley her father
Richard her uncle
Elsie Venner: A Romance of Destiny (1861) Oliver Wendell Holmes

Venner, Tillie one of the author's portraits of the girl who would not love him, Florence Garrard

ss 'Wressley of the Foreign Office'
Plain Tales from the Hills (1888) Rudyard Kipling

Venner, Uncle
The House of the Seven Gables (1851) Nathaniel Hawthorne

Ventidius false friend to Timon*
Timon of Athens play (1623) William Shakespeare

Ventimore, Horace architect cc, who buys the brass bottle and its ill-tempered genie, m. Sylvia Futvoye
The Brass Bottle (1900) F. Anstey (rn Thomas Anstey Guthrie)

Ventnor, Charles solicitor
A Stoic (1918) John Galsworthy

Venturewell a merchant
Luce his daughter
The Knight of the Burning Pestle play (1613) Francis Beaumont and John Fletcher

Ventvogel Hottentot servant
King Solomon's Mines (1885) Henry Rider Haggard

Venus Annodomini ('Kitty')
ss 'Venus Annodomini'
Plain Tales from the Hills (1888) Rudyard Kipling

Venus, Mr taxidermist, m. pleasant Riderhood*
Our Mutual Friend (1865) Charles Dickens

Vera Pechorin's* former mistress, dying of consumption and still longing for him
her husband
Geroi Nas hego Vremeni (*A Hero of Our Time*) (1841) Mikhail Lermontov

Veranilda Gothic princess in romance set in period during the invasion by Totila
Veranilda (1904) George Gissing

Veraswami, Dr
Burmese Days (1935) George Orwell (rn Eric Blair)

Vercors, Violaine kisses the leprous Craon* in pity and is later, after becoming a recluse, murdered by her sister
Mara her sister
L'Annonce faite à Marie play (*The Tidings Brought to Mary*) (1912, rev. 1948) Paul Claudel

Verdant, Virginia, Miss cousin to Verdant Green*
The Adventures of Mr Verdant Green

(1853) Cuthbert Bede (rn Edward Bradley)

Verdi, Giuseppe (hist.) in German novel in which his desire to meet Wagner* in Venice is frustrated by the latter's death
Verdi: Roman der Oper (*Verdi: A Novel of the Opera*) (1924) Franz Werfel

Verdley, Lydia, Mrs sister to Stephen Leuknor*
The Old Bank (1902) William Westall

Verdun, Kitty ward to Stephen Spettigue*
Charley's Aunt play (1892) Brandon Thomas

Verdurin, M. and Mme successful social climbers
A la recherche du temps perdu (*In Search of Lost Time*) (1913–27) Marcel Proust

Vere, Captain commander of the *Indomitable* and, allegorically, the just God of the Bible
Billy Budd, Foretopman (1924 – definitive edition 1962) Herman Melville

Vermandero governor of the castle of Alicant
The Changeling play (1653) Thomas Middleton and William Rowley

Verges foolish officer
Much Ado About Nothing (1623) William Shakespeare

Vergil, Winter ('Daddy')
ss 'A Naval Mutiny'
Limits and Renewals (1932) Rudyard Kipling

Verily Judge Fox Clane's* black cook
Grown Boy her nephew
Clock Without hands (1961) Carson McCullers

Verinder, Julia, Lady née Herncastle, widow of Sir John
Rachel her daughter, m. Franklin Blake*
The Moonstone (1868) Wilkie Collins

Verisopht, Frederick, Lord client of Nicholas Nickleby, eventually killed in duel by Sir Mulberry Hawk*
Nicholas Nickleby (1839) Charles Dickens

Verkovensky, Pyotr son to Stepan Trofimovich*; nihilist, disciple of Stavrogin
Besy (*The Possessed*) (1879) Fyodor Dostoievsky

Verloc, Adolf spy and keeper of porno-

graphic bookshop
Winnie his wife
Steve Winnie's feeble-minded son, who is blown up
The Secret Agent (1907) Joseph Conrad (rn Josef Teodor Konrad Korzeniowski)
Vermilye, Gerard ruined man-about-town
John Halifax, Gentleman (1856) Mrs Craik
Vermont, Ophelia ('Miss Ophelia') unmarried cousin to St Clare*
Uncle Tom's Cabin (1851) Harriet Beecher Stowe
Verney, Lord
The Bath Comedy† (1899) A. and E. Castle
Vernoe unprincipled guardian to Clara Saville*
Frank Fairlegh (1850) F. E. Smedley
Vernon, Diana niece to Lady Osbaldistone*, m. Frank Osbaldistone*
Sir Frederick her father
Rob Roy (1818) Walter Scott
Vernon, Hester cc of novel about banking, one of the prolific author's best books
Catherine her elderly second cousin, cc, banker
John her deceased grandfather, consolidator of the banking house of Vernons, 'one of those men in whose hands everything turns to gold'
John her father, who 'went wrong'
Mrs John her mother
Edward her cousin, and Catherine's beloved protégé
Hester (1883) Mrs Margaret Oliphant
Vernon, Laurence
The Thinking Reed (1936) Rebecca West (rn Cecily Fairfield)
Vernon, Mrs kindly writer of letters in posthumously published epistolary novel her deceased brother, m. Lady Susan de Courcy*
her husband
Lady Susan (1871) Jane Austen
Vernon, Paddy prefect
ss 'Regulus'
A Diversity of Creatures (1917) Rudyard Kipling
Veronica wife, mother, daughter, grandmother to Ambrose*; also the first Veronica, of Jerusalem; 'All the women in Ambrose's life were called Veronica.

But not all at once.'
Ambrose's Vision: Sketches Towards the Creation of a Cathedral (1980) Giles Gordon
Verral, Edward wealthy landowner, m. Nettie Stuart*
his mother
In the Days of the Comet (1906) H. G. Wells
Vervain, Florida cc m. Henry Ferris*; in novel of which Henry James* wrote: 'it is an air played on a single string, but an air exquisitely modulated'
A Foregone Conclusion (1875) William Dean Howells
Verver, Maggie m. Prince Amerigo*
Adam her wealthy father, m. Charlotte Stant*
The Golden Bowl (1904) Henry James
Vesey, Mrs former governess to Marian Fairlie*
The Woman in White (1860) Wilkie Collins
Vespasian Black sailor on the *Agra*
Hard Cash (1863) Charles Reade
Vetch, Anastasius fiddler and gentle old radical
The Princess Casamassima (1866) Henry James
Vezzis, Miss
ss 'His Chance in Life'
Plain Tales from the Hills (1888) Rudyard Kipling
Vholes, Mr lawyer, Richard Carstone's* solicitor
Caroline; Emma; Jane his daughters, who, along with an aged father and an 102-year-old grandmother, he supports
Bleak House (1853) Charles Dickens
Viaino, Maestro mountebank
Romola (1863) George Eliot (rn Mary Anne, later Marian, Evans)
Vice
Old Fortunatus play (1600) Thomas Dekker
Vicentio Duke of Vienna
Measure for Measure play (1623) William Shakespeare
Vicenza, Isabella of m. Theodore
Frederic, Marquis of Vicenza her father
The Castle of Otranto (1765) Horace Walpole
Vickers, Ann American career woman

Ann Vickers (1933) Sinclair Lewis

Vickers, Dora cc

Captain Vickers her kindly father whose 'excess of humanity' is destroyed when he becomes commander of Tasmanian penal settlement

Mrs Sylvia Vickers her mother, genteel and empty but brave when danger threatens

His Natural Life (1870–2; abridged by the author 1874; in 1885 as *For the Term of His Natural Life* – thus evading the author's irony; original text edited by Stephen Murray-Smith, 1970) Marcus Clarke

Vickers, Selina fiancée to Joseph Tasker*
Dialstone Lane (1904) W. W. Jacobs

Vickery, 'Click' deserting sailor struck by lightning with another, unknown
ss 'Mrs Bathurst'
Traffics and Discoveries (1904) Rudyard Kipling

Victor, Brother
ss 'The Record of Badalia Herodsfoot'
Many Inventions (1893) Rudyard Kipling

Victor, Father priest
Kim (1901) Rudyard Kipling

Victoria prefect's daughter
Hypatia (1853) Charles Kingsley

Videna Queen, wife to Gorboduc*
Gorboduc play (1562) Thomas Norton and Thomas Sackville

Vidler apothecary
his daughter
The Newcomes (1853–5) W. M. Thackeray

Viedima, Cipriano, Don, General cc; ritually m. Kate Leslie*; stabs sacrificial victims &c
The Plumed Serpent (1926) D. H. Lawrence

Viel master ploughman
The King of Elfland's Daughter (1924) Lord Dunsany

Vigil, Arturo Diaz, Dr Geoffrey Firmin's doctor
Under the Volcano (1947) Malcolm Lowry

Vigil, Gregory Helen Bellew's* guardian
The Country House (1907) John Galsworthy

Vigors bully

Mr Midshipman Easy (1836) Captain Marryat

Vigors, Bert ex-soldier and market-gardener
ss 'A Friend of the Family'
Debits and Credits (1926) Rudyard Kipling

Vigot police chief
The Quiet American (1955) Graham Greene

Vilbert itinerant quack doctor
Jude the Obscure (1896) Thomas Hardy

Vile, Henry, Lord Aintree steward
National Velvet (1935) Enid Bagnold

Villamarti matador
ss 'The Bull that Thought'
Debits and Credits (1926) Rudyard Kipling

Villamayor, Justo de great poet
The Exiles (1962) Albert Guerard

Villar, Mini tough waitress whose abortion Augie March* helps to fix
The Adventures of Augie March (1953) Saul Bellow

Villars, Arthur, Revd
Evelina (1778) Fanny Burney

Villebecque, Comte de la Lord Monmouth's* steward
Flora his supposed daughter
Coningsby (1844) Benjamin Disraeli

Villiers friend to Charles Herbert*
The Great God Pan (1894) Arthur Machen

Villiers, Judith, Miss aunt to the Beverley* children
The Children of the New Forest (1847) Captain Marryat

Vincent, Arthur dissenting minister
Salem Chapel (1863) Mrs Margaret Oliphant

Vincent, Father English priest
Cry, the Beloved Country (1948) Alan Paton

Vincent, Jenkin ('Jin Vin') apprentice
The Fortunes of Nigel (1822) Walter Scott

Vincent, Mr handsome young creole in love with Belinda Portman* but with 'taste for gaming'
Belinda (1801) Maria Edgeworth

Vincey, Leo reincarnation of Kallicrates, his ancestor*
She (1887) Henry Rider Haggard

Vincey, Leo see Kallikrates

Vinci, Leonardo da (hist.), here represented as one 'who noticed lawful inexactitudes and began fully to decipher the productions of almost all branches of art'
All and Everything: Beelzebub's Tales to His Grandson (1950) G. I. Gurdjieff

Vinck, Mrs
Emma her daughter
Almayer's Folly (1895) Joseph Conrad (rn Josef Teodor Konrad Korzeniowski)

Vincy, Walter Mayor of Middlemarch
Lucy his wife
Fred cc, m. Mary Garth*; **Bob**;
Rosamond cc, m. Tertius Lydgate*;
Louise their children
Middlemarch (1871–2) George Eliot (rn Mary Anne, later Marian, Evans)

Vindice cc, the revenger, son to Gratiana*
The Revenger's Tragedy (1607/8) ?Thomas Middleton; ?Cyril Tourneur

Vine, Emma jilted by Richard Mutimer*
Demos (1886) George Gissing

Vinegar cat, Lolly Willowes'* familiar
Lolly Willowes (1926) Sylvia Townsend Warner

Viner, Father
Sinister Street (1913) Compton Mackenzie

Viner, Sophie mistress of George Darrow* (the 'reef' that wrecks their later lives); engaged to Owen Leath*, whom she has to give up
The Reef (1912) Edith Wharton

Viney ex-shipowner
The Hole in the Wall (1902) Arthur Morrison

Vining, Mr whey-faced parson tutor at Lowood who is dismissed
Jane Eyre (1847) Charlotte Brontë

Vinney, Vincent
Floss his wife
Sid his brother
Non-Combatants and Others (1916) Rose Macaulay

Vinnie homosexual
Last Exit to Brooklyn (1964) Hubert J. Selby

Vint, Mercy innkeeper's daughter m. (bigamously) Griffith Gaunt*
Griffith Gaunt, or Jealousy (1866); *Kate Peyton, or Jealousy* – later, 1873, as *Kate Peyton's Lovers* play (1867) Charles Reade

Vinteuil composer
A la recherche du temps perdu (*In Search of Lost Time*) (1913–27) Marcel Proust

Viola m. Orsino*
Twelfth Night play (1623) William Shakespeare

Violante
My Novel (1853) Edward Bulwer Lytton

Violante supposed wife to Don Henrique*
The Spanish Curate play (1647) John Fletcher and Philip Massinger

Viomesnil, Clarisse de m. Francis Saverne*
Denis Duval (1864) W. M. Thackeray

Virgilia wife to Coriolanus*
Coriolanus play (1623) William Shakespeare

Virginia a companion to Ferdinand*, upon whose stomach he tramples in a nightclub
Guignol's band (1944) Louis Ferdinand Céline (rn Louis-Ferdinand Destouches)

Virginia companion to Agnes de Medina*, m. Don Lorenzo de Medina
The Monk (1796) Matthew G. Lewis

Virginian, The unnamed hero of trash novel which, although written by a man who hardly knew the locality, sold in millions and influenced or even helped start the Western industry ('When you call me that, smile')
The Virginian (1902) Owen Wister

Virolet
Juliana his wife
The Double Marriage play (1647) John Fletcher and Philip Massinger

Virtue
Old Fortunatus play (1600) Thomas Dekker

Vitelli, Popeye executed gangster and rapist, whose features have the 'vicious, depthless quality of stamped tin'
Sanctuary† (1931) William Faulkner

Vittoria *contadina*
The Gondoliers opera (1889) W. S. Gilbert and Arthur Sullivan

Viveash, Myra
Antic Hay (1923) Aldous Huxley

Vixen the author's dog
ss 'My Lord the Elephant'†
Many Inventions† (1893) Rudyard Kipling

Vixen, Mrs
Polly opera (1729) John Gay
Vlaanderen, Pieter van Boer policeman and pillar of community who sleeps with black girl, Stephanie*, and is destroyed
Too Late the Pharalope (1953) Alan Paton
Vladimir
Waiting for Godot play (1952) Samuel Beckett
Vladimir, Mr first secretary of an unnamed embassy
The Secret Agent (1907) Joseph Conrad (rn Josef Teodor Konrad Korzeniowski)
Voiron, André, M.
ss 'The Bull that Thought'
Debits and Credits (1926) Rudyard Kipling
Volakis, Kostas originally illiterate Cretan, struggling restaurant owner in America
his slightly older wife, whom he originally married for her dowry
his murderer son, whom he finally forgives
The Odyssey of Kostas Volakis (1963) Harry Petrakis
Volanges, Mme de
Cécile her daughter
Les Liaisons dangereuses (1782) Pierre-Ambroise-François Choderlos de Laclos
Volkbein, Felix Jew trying to prove himself gentile
Nightwood (1936) Djuna Barnes
Volkov dandy
Oblomov (1859) Ivan Goncharov
Volkov, Katherine Australian pianist, inspirer of Hurtle Duffield* in old age
The Vivisector (1970) Patrick White
Volpone scoundrel magnifico cc,
Volpone play (1617) Ben Jonson
Volumnia mother to Coriolanus*
Coriolanus play (1623) William Shakespeare
Von Bork
ss 'His Last Bow'
His Last Bow (1917) Arthur Conan Doyle
Von Brunning commander of German gun-boat
The Riddle of the Sands (1903) Erskine Childers
Von Galen, Paul, Colonel m. Anna von

Leyde*
Heinrich their son
The Other Side (1946) Storm Jameson
Von Herling, Baron
ss 'His Last Bow'
His Last Bow (1917) Arthur Conan Doyle
Von Koeldwethout
Nicholas Nickleby (1839) Charles Dickens
Von Kohler, Frau Else
You Can't Go Home Again (1940) Thomas Wolfe
Von Leyde, Bertha, Baroness widow
Anna m. Paul von Galen"; **Lotte** m. Richard Gauss* her daughters
The Other Side (1946) Storm Jameson
Von Pregnitz, Kuno, Baron
Mr Norris Changes Trains (1935) Christopher Isherwood
Von Stroom supercargo
The Phantom Ship (1839) Captain Marryat
Vorticella author of a guide book
The Impressions of Theophrastus Such (1879) George Eliot (rn Mary Anne, later Marian, Evans)
Vosper butler
ss 'Keeping in with Vosper'†
The Heart of a Goof (1926) P. G. Wodehouse
Vosper, Jane procuress
John her husband
Mr Weston's Good Wine (1927) T. F. Powys
Voss, Johann Ulrich German explorer in Australia, 1845
Voss (1957) Patrick White
Vote, Robin the author's portrait of her erstwhile lover, the artist Thelma Wood, who refused to discuss the book; Robin, when ultimately unable to express herself, howls like a dog
Nightwood (1936) Djuna Barnes
Voules licensed victualler, uncle to Miriam Larkins*
his wife
The History of Mr Polly (1910) H. G. Wells
Vowle, Sandy
ss 'The Lang Men o' Larut'
Life's Handicap (1891) Rudyard Kipling
Vox, Valentine Suffolk ventriloquist, cc

very successful novel
Valentine Vox, The Ventriloquist (1840)
Henry Cockton

Vrais 'nicely faithful'; he 'listens and when
he listens he says good, good, excellent'
ss 'A Long Gay Book'
GMP (1932) Gertrude Stein

Vril not a character but a mysterious force
discovered by the inhabitants of a utopia/
dystopia in satirical (of science) speculative novel that is still of interest; gave
Bovril its name
The Coming Race (1871) Edward Bulwer
Lytton

Vuffin, Mr
travelling showman who presents a giant
and an armless, legless woman
The Old Curiosity Shop (1841) Charles
Dickens

Vulich Serbian lieutenant, honourable
gambler, blows his brains out after
Pechorin* has told him that he will die
that day (Pechorin has bet with him that
'there is no such thing as predestination')
Geroi Nas hego Vremeni (*A Hero of Our
Time*) (1841) Mikhail Lermontov

Vulmea, Tim, Private
ss 'Black Jack'
Soldiers Three (1888) Rudyard Kipling

Vulpes, Madame medium
ss 'The Diamond Lens' (1858)
Poems and Stories (1881) Fitz-James
O'Brien

Vye, Eustacia cc, gloomy irresponsible
romantic half-Corfiote beauty m. Clym
Yeobright*, lover of Damon Wildeve*
Captain Vye, her ex-sailor grandfather
The Return of the Native (1878) Thomas
Hardy

Vyry slave-child, cc of epic novel of slavery
derived from facts of the Alabama
author's own ancestry
her young mother, twenty-nine years old
when she dies in giving birth to her, her
sixteenth child by her master, John
Dutton*
Lillian one of her sisters
Jubilee (1966) Margaret Walker

Vyse, Cecil ex-fiancé to Lucy Honeychurch*
his mother
A Room With a View (1908) E. M.
Forster

W

Wabstow, Jenny
ss 'The Record of Badalia Herodsfoot'
Many Inventions (1893) Rudyard Kipling

Wachorn second husband to Marion Ramboat*
Tono Bungay (1909) H. G. Wells

Wackerbat head of a Herne Bay academy
A Shabby Genteel Story (1840) W. M. Thackeray

Wackerbath, Squirrel Horace Ventimore's* wealthy patron
The Brass Bottle (1900) F. Anstey (rn Thomas Anstey Guthrie)

Wackles, Mrs of the ladies' seminary
Melissa; Sophie m. Alick Cleggs*; **Jane** her daughters
The Old Curiosity Shop (1841) Charles Dickens

Waddington, Caroline m. (1) Sir Henry Harcourt*, (2) young George Bertram*
The Bertrams (1859) Anthony Trollope

Waddington, Henry Bysshe cc, conceited egoist
Fanny his wife
Horry their son
his mother
Mr Waddington of Wyck (1921) May Sinclair

Waddington, Miss
Before the Bombardment (1926) Osbert Sitwell

Waddy father to Arthur Kipps*
his father, who leaves Kipps a fortune
Kipps (1905) H. G. Wells

Waddy, Mary widow, landlady
The Adventures of Harry Richmond (1871) George Meredith

Wade, Eleanor m. Sir Richard Devine*
His Natural Life (1870–2; abridged by the author 1874; in 1885 as *For the Term of His Natural Life* – thus evading the author's irony; original text edited by Stephen Murray-Smith, 1970) Marcus Clarke

Wade, George chairman of rugby club
This Sporting Life (1960) David Storey

Wade, Hilda early female detective
Hilda Wade, Hospital Nurse (1900) Grant Allen

Wade, Miss discontented woman implicated in Rigaud's* theft of Mrs Clennam's* papers
Little Dorrit (1857) Charles Dickens

Wade, Richard unsuccessful California mine-owner who exchanges his mine for Don Fulano*, a steed
John Brent (1862) Theodore Winthrop

Wadman, Widow loved by Captain Shandy*
Tristram Shandy (1767) Laurence Sterne

Wagg author, wit, snob, practical joker, based on Theodore Hook*
Pendennis† (1848) W. M. Thackeray

Waghorn, Carrie refreshment-room attendant, m. Nibby*
The Town Traveller (1898) George Gissing

Wagner servant to Faustus*
Doctor Faustus play (1604) Christopher Marlowe

Wagner, Richard (unfortunately hist.)
Verdi: Roman der Oper (*Verdi: A Novel of the Opera*) (1924) Franz Werfel

Wagstaff, Mrs Edgar Tryan's* landlady
ss 'Janet's Repentance'
Scenes of Clerical Life (1857) George Eliot (rn Mary Anne, later Marian, Evans)

Wahn, Kurt dedicated communist who kills Startsov*
Goroda i gody (*Cities and Years*) (1924) K. A. Fedin

Wainsworth, Joe harness-maker in revolt against machinery
Poor White (1920) Sherwood Anderson

Wainwright, Mr surgeon
East Lynne (1861) Mrs Henry Wood

Wait, James cc
The Nigger of the 'Narcissus' (1898)

Joseph Conrad (rn Josef Teodor Konrad Korzeniowski)

Waitwell servant to Mirabell*
The Way of the World play (1700) William Congreve

Wakefield, Edward exhausted and ratty narrator
Ann his increasingly distanced wife
their children
About A Marriage (1972) Giles Gordon

Wakefield, Harry drover
The Two Drovers (1827) Walter Scott

Wakefield, Vicar of see **Primrose**

Wakeling, Billy m. Rosa Sawyer*
A Town Like Alice (1950) Neville Shute (rn Nevile Shute Norway)

Wakem, Philip deformed son of lawyer hated by Mr Tulliver*, to whom Maggie Tulliver* turns for comradeship
The Mill on the Floss (1860) George Eliot (rn Mary Anne, later Marian, Evans)

Wald, Matthew narrator of his own disastrous life in novel by Scott's* son-in-law
The History of Matthew Wald (1824) John Gibson Lockhart

Waldeck, Martin (legd.) charcoal burner ruined by gold
The Antiquary (1816) Walter Scott

Walden, Ty
Jim Leslie; Shaw; Buck; Rosamund; Jill ('**Darling Jill**') his children
Gussie Jim Leslie's wife
Griselda Buck's wife
God's Little Acre (1933) Erskine Caldwell

Waldering, Siegfried cc, soldier aristocrat of hist. novel set in time of Napoleon
At Odds (1863) Baroness von Tautphoeus

Waldman lecturer on chemistry
Frankenstein (1818) Mary Shelley

Waldo son to Otto, overseer
The Story of an African Farm (1883) Olive Schreiner

Waldo, Mr
Blodwen his wife
their son
Under Milk Wood play (1954) Dylan Thomas

Waldon Oxford scholar
Sir Charles Grandison (1754) Samuel Richardson

Waldron, Thomas, Sir squire of the village

Perlycross (1894) R. D. Blackmore

Walen, Burton editor
ss 'The Edge of the Evening'
A Diversity of Creatures (1917) Rudyard Kipling

Wales, Jack in love with Susan Brown*
Room at the Top (1957) John Braine

Walham, Lady mother to Lord Kew*
The Newcomes (1853–5) W. M. Thackeray

Wali Dad
ss 'On the City Wall'
Soldiers Three (1888) Rudyard Kipling

Walker administrator of Talua
ss 'Mackintosh'
The Trembling of a Leaf (1921) W. Somerset Maugham

Walker, Bill
Major Barbara (1905) George Bernard Shaw

Walker, Howard, Captain profligate, m. Morgiana Crump*, who supports him by singing
ss 'The Ravenswing'
Men's Wives (1843) W. M. Thackeray

Walker, Howard, Mrs see **Ravenswing, The**

Walker, James writer-in-residence in American university, cc
Stepping Westward (1965) Malcolm Bradbury

Walker, Mick boy at Murdstone and Grinby*
David Copperfield (1850) Charles Dickens

Walker, Mrs nurse
A Farewell to Arms (1929) Ernest Hemingway

Walker, Peter pedlar
Heart of Midlothian (1818) Walter Scott

Walker, Revd Mr Sub-Precentor
ss 'For Conscience' Sake'
Life's Little Ironies (1894) Thomas Hardy

Walker, Wolf Jewish cc, director of a private academy which allows potential suicides to study the implications of their planned act; in novels by American who writes on Jewish themes
The Suicide Academy (1968); *The Rose Rabbi* (1971) Daniel Stern

Walker; John; Susan; Titty; Roger; Vicky children ccs

their parents
Swallows and Amazons (1930) Arthur Ransome

Wallace, Lionel brilliant politician obsessed by visionary door
ss 'The Door in the Wall'
The Country of the Blind (1911) H. G. Wells

Wallace, Timothy
Wilkie his son
The Grapes of Wrath (1939) John Steinbeck

Wallace, William (hist.) cc early historical novel to whose patriotic fervour Scott* responded
The Scottish Chiefs (1810) Jane Porter

Wallach, Gabe cc, graduate student and instructor
his mother
Letting Go (1962) Philip Roth

Wallenrode, Earl Hungarian warrior
The Talisman (1825) Walter Scott

Wallenstein, Mr and Mrs
Wally their son
May Wally's wife
Lummox (1924) Fanny Hurst

Waller, Jack army friend to Lorrequer*
Harry Lorrequer (1839) Charles Lever

Wallinger, Joseph, Sir
his wife
Coningsby (1844) Benjamin Disraeli

Wallingford, Miles cc, narrator, in love with Lucy Hardinge*; partial self-portrait
Grace his sister
Afloat and Ashore (1844); *Miles Wallingford* (1844) James Fenimore Cooper

Wallis, Colonel Sir Walter Elliot* thinks him a fine-looking man, despite his sandy hair
Persuasion (1818) Jane Austen

Wally spoilt woman in cynical German novel which got its author a jail sentence; later rewritten
Wally die Zweiflerin (*Wally a Doubting Girl*) (1835) Karl Gutzkow

Walpole, Cutler
The Doctor's Dilemma (1906) George Bernard Shaw

Walravens, Magloire, Mme very old widow supported by Paul Emanuel*, 'hunchback, dwarfish and doting'
Villette (1853) Charlotte Brontë

Walsh, Norah streetfighting girl
A Child of the Jago (1896) Arthur Morrison

Walsh, Peter old suitor to Mrs Dalloway*
Mrs Dalloway (1925) Virginia Woolf

Walsingham, Helen one-time fiancée to Kipps*
her mother
her brother, defaulting solicitor
Kipps (1905) H. G. Wells

Walt, Piet van der m. 'Tant' Sannie*
The Story of an African Farm (1883) Olive Schreiner

Waltham, Adela m. (1) Richard Mutimer*, (2) Hubert Eldon*
Demos (1886) George Gissing

Wallis, John suicide, cc of post-death fantasy
On a Dark Night (1949) Anthony West

Walton, Miss heiress with whom Harley* is in love
The Man of Feeling (1771) Henry Mackenzie

Walton, Richard, Captain seaman; part narrator
Frankenstein (1818) Mary Shelley

Wamba Cedric's* jester
Ivanhoe (1820) Walter Scott

Wandle, Lord godfather to Aldous Raeburn*
Marcella (1894) Mrs Humphry Ward

Wang Axel Heyst's* servant
Victory (1915) Joseph Conrad (rn Josef Teodor Konrad Korzeniowski)

Wang Yu carping critic of Kai Lung's* stories
The Wallet of Kai Lung (1900) Ernest Bramah (rn Ernest Bramah Smith)

Wannop, Valentine athlete, suffragette, bluestocking, in love with Christopher Tietjens*
her mother, overworked novelist
Some Do Not (1924); *No More Parades* (1925); *A Man Could Stand Up* (1926); *Last Post* (1928) Ford Madox Ford

Wapshot, Giles, Sir
his wife and daughters
Vanity Fair (1847–8) W. M. Thackeray

Wapshot, Leander philosopher, sea captain
Sarah Coverly his wife
Coverly; Moses their sons, the first a public relations man, the second an

alcoholic
Betsey wife to Coverly
Melissa wife to Moses
Honora wealthy cousin, family matri-
arch
The Wapshot Chronicle† (1957) John
Cheever
Warbeck, Davey, Captain
The Pursuit of Love (1945) Nancy Mit-
ford
Warbeck, Gerald publisher of Fanny's Life
Fanny By Gaslight (1940) Michael
Sadleir
Warbeck, Perkin (hist.) pretender, cc
Perkin Warbeck play (1634) John Ford
Warbuckle, Bessie m. Reg Aythorne*
South Riding (1936) Winifred Holtby
Warburton, Dr
The Family Reunion play (1939) T. S.
Eliot
Warburton, Lord suitor to Isabel Archer*
The Portrait of a Lady (1881) Henry
James
Ward ('Mr Swindles') head groom to
Arthur Barfield*
Esther Waters (1894) George Moore
Ward, Agee reported missing in action: 'he
didn't like it, but he was in it'
The Man Who Was There (1945) Wright
Morris
Ward, John Calvinist cc whose austerity
brings him into conflict with his sceptical
wife; in humorous novel by Pennsylvan-
ian author
his wife
John Ward, Preacher (1888) Margaretta
Deland
Ward, Oliver engineer, inventor
Sarah Burling Ward his wife, novelist and
artist
Oliver; Betsy; Agnes their children
Lyman Oliver's son, narrator, m. Ellen
Hammond*
Rodman son to Lyman and Ellen
Angle of Repose (1971) Wallace Stegner
Warden, Henry also known as **Henry**
Wellwood
The Monastery† (1820) Walter Scott
Warden, Michael m. Marion Jeddler*
The Battle of Life (1846) Charles
Dickens
Warder, Jack friend of rival to Hugh
Wynne* who contributes a diary to hist.

novel set in American Revolutionary War
Hugh Wynne, Free Quaker (1897) S. W.
Mitchell
Wardlaw, Arthur villain who goes mad
Foul Play (1868) Charles Reade and
Dion Bouicault
Wardlaw, Mr schoolmaster
Prester John (1910) John Buchan
Wardle, Mr
his parents
Emily m. Augustus Snodgrass*;
Isabella m. Trundle* his daughters
Rachel his sister
The Pickwick Papers (1837) Charles
Dickens
Wardour, Isabella m. Mr Lovel*
Sir Arthur, Baronet her father
Sir Anthony her grandfather
Captain Reginald her brother
The Antiquary (1816) Walter Scott
Wardrop, Mr chief engineer of the *Haliotis*
ss 'The Devil and the Deep Sea'
The Day's Work† (1898) Rudyard Kipl-
ing
Ware, Cynthia cc tale by popular Ten-
nessee local colour* writer, who turned
out to be a 'frail, crippled spinster'
ss 'Drifting Down Lost Creek'
In the Tennessee Mountains (1884)
Charles Egbert Craddock (rn Mary N.
Murfree)
Ware, Randall freeman from birth,
blacksmith, husband to Vyry*
Jubilee (1966) Margaret Walker
Ware, Theron Methodist preacher cc of
American novel in which 'damnation' is
equated with self-enlightenment
Alice his wife
The Damnation of Theron Ware in Eng-
land, originally, as *Illumination* (1896)
Harold Frederic
Waring, Percy, Major in love with
Margaret Lovell*
Rhoda Fleming (1865) George Meredith
Waring, Peter narrator cc of complete
rewrite of the Ulster author's earlier
novel *Following Darkness* (1912)
David his father, a religiose village
schoolmaster in County Down
Peter Waring (1937) Forrest Reid
Waring, Robert at school with Sammy
Rice*
The Small Back Room (1943) Nigel

Balchin

Waring, Robert English overseer, m. Joan Desborough*
The Shulamite (1904) A. and C. Askew

Warland, Owen idealist watchmaker who constructs beautiful mechanical butterfly
ss 'The Artist of the Beautiful' (1844)
Mosses from an Old Manse (1846) Nathaniel Hawthorne

Warli hunchbacked postman, m. Maria Truog*
Ships that Pass in the Night (1893) Beatrice Harraden

Warming, E. cousin to Graham, the sleeper
When the Sleeper Wakes (1899) H. G. Wells

Warminster, Alfred, Earl of dotty leftist peer, brother-in-law to Nicholas Jenkins*
Isobel Tolland m. Nicholas Jenkins*; **Priscilla Tolland** m. Chips Lovell* his sisters
A Question of Upbringing† (1951) Anthony Powell

Warner cousin to Hammon*
The Shoemaker's Holiday (1600) Thomas Dekker

Warner, Alec, Dr
Memento Mori (1959) Muriel Spark

Warner, Dr
Manalive (1912) G. K. Chesterton

Warner, Sybille
The Last of the Barons (1843) Edward Bulwer Lytton

Warnham, Ernest lawyer
The Old Bank (1902) William Westall

Warre, Simon who m. Anne Delaware*, and when he finds out that she once gave herself to Algernon Dane* for cash, refuses to divorce her or to consummate the marriage – but works himself to a noble death in the tropics
The Gods, Some Mortals And Lord Wickenham (1895) John Oliver Hobbes (rn Pearl Craigie)

Warren farmer
Mary his wife
poem 'Death of the Hired Man'
North of Boston (1914) Robert Frost

Warren, Kitty, Mrs née Vavasour, cc
Mrs Warren's Profession (1902) George Bernard Shaw

Warren, Malcolm young stockbroker

detective in several superior murder mysteries onwards from
Death of My Aunt† (1929) C. H. B. Kitchen

Warren, Philip cc
The Judgement of Paris (1952) Gore Vidal

Warricombe, Sidwell daughter of wealthy manufacturer whom Peake* tries to marry by pretending to be interested in theology
her father
her mother
Born in Exile (1892) George Gissing

Warrigal half-caste boy
Robbery Under Arms: A Story of Life and Adventure in the Bush and in the Goldfields of Australia (1888, rev. 1889) Rolf Boldrewood (rn Thomas Alexander Browne)

Warrington, George
Rachel his wife, née Esmond*, to which name she reverts after his death
George; **Henry** m. Fanny Mountain* their twin sons
Theodosia wife to George
Captain Miles; **Theodosia** m. Joseph Blake*; **Hester** m. Captain Handyman*; **Mary** children to George and Theodosia
Sir Miles, Baronet uncle to the twins
Mile's wife
Miles; **Flora** m. Tom Claypole*; **Dora** m. Mr Juffles children to Sir Miles and his wife
The Virginians (1857–9) W. M. Thackeray

Wart recruit
King Henry IV plays (1623) William Shakespeare

Warwick, Diana née Merion; spiritually beautiful cc based on Caroline Norton, whose husband tried to sue Lord Melbourne for divorce
Warwick, Augustus her unimaginative barrister husband, fifteen years older than she – after his death she m. Thomas Redworth*
Diana of the Crossways (1885) George Meredith

Warwick, Earl of
Saint Joan play (1924) George Bernard Shaw

Warwick, Earl of (hist.)

King Henry VI plays (1623) William Shakespeare

Warwick, Earl of (hist.) the kingmaker; last of the barons, cc of romance set in the times of the Wars of the Roses, but reflecting its own; one of the earliest of the sympathetic portraits of the allegedly villainous Richard III*
his wife
Lady Anne their daughter
The Last of the Barons (1843) Edward Bulwer Lytton

Washington, 'Smiler' RAF recruit
Chips With Everything play (1962) Arnold Wesker

Washington, Percy
ss 'The Diamond as Big as the Ritz'
Tales of the Jazz Age (1922) F. Scott Fitzgerald

Waspe, Humphrey man to Cokes*
Bartholomew Fair play (1631) Ben Jonson

Wat the Devil Northumbrian freebooter
Rob Roy (1818) Walter Scott

Watchall man to Lady Alworth*
A New Way to Pay Old Debts play (1633) Philip Massinger

Watchett, Mrs the time-traveller's landlady
The Time Machine (1895) H. G. Wells

Watchful shepherd on the Delectable Mountain
The Pilgrim's Progress (1678–84) John Bunyan

Waterbrook agent of Wickfield*
his wife
David Copperfield (1850) Charles Dickens

Waters, Barbara loved by Francis Chelifer*
Those Barren Leaves (1925) Aldous Huxley

Waters, Esther servant girl cc, m. William Latch*
her illegitimate boy
her mother, m. Saunders* as second husband
Esther Waters (1894) George Moore

Waters, Mrs (Jenny Jones, maidservant), supposed wife to Captain Waters, and mother to Tom Jones*
Tom Jones (1749) Henry Fielding

Watkins godfather to Kate Nickleby*

Nicholas Nickleby (1839) Charles Dickens

Watkins, Charles fifty-year-old classics professor who goes into an amnesiac fugue, cc
Briefing for a Descent Into Hell (1971) Doris Lessing

Watkins, Mr
his wife
Cassandra Cleopatra their daughter
Mr Facey Romford's Hounds (1865) R. S. Surtees

Watkins, Sally nurse to Phineas Fletcher*
John Halifax, Gentleman (1856) Mrs Craik

Watkins, Utah
his wife
Under Milk Wood play (1954) Dylan Thomas

Watling, Belle mistress to Rhett Butler*; a madame
Gone With the Wind (1936) Margaret Mitchell

Watlington, Lord enormously wealthy
Imperial Palace (1930) Arnold Bennett

Watson, John, Dr (or **James**) sidekick to Sherlock Holmes* without whose narrations of them the master's exploits would be unknown; m. Mary Morstan*
A Study in Scarlet† (1887) Arthur Conan Doyle

Watson, Miss sister to Widow Douglas*
The Adventures of Tom Sawyer† (1876) Mark Twain (rn Samuel Langhorne Clemens)

Watt cc
Watt (1953) Samuel Beckett

Watt, Jean Brodie's* mistress
Deacon Brodie play (1892) Robert Louis Stevenson and W. E. Henley

Watters, Irving, Dr
Arrowsmith (1925) Sinclair Lewis

Wattey, Corporal a fen-man
The Story of Ragged Robyn (1945) Oliver Onions

Wattle, Weasel
Uncle Remus (1880–95) Joel Chandler Harris

Watts, Horne deceased but much discussed character: a portrait of the American poet Hart Crane
The Malefactors Caroline Gordon

Watts, Jim chief ERA *Compass Rose*

The Cruel Sea (1951) Nicholas Monsarrat

Watts, Leora, Mrs prostitute
Wise Blood (1952) Flannery O'Connor

Watts, Mrs nasty-minded sadistic woman confounded
ss 'Lily Daw and the Three Ladies'
A Curtain of Green (1941) Eudora Welty

Watty bankrupt
The Pickwick Papers (1837) Charles Dickens

Waule, Jane née Featherstone, rich and greedy widow
John; Eliza; Joanna; Rebecca her children
Middlemarch (1871–2) George Eliot (rn Mary Anne, later Marian, Evans)

Waverley, Edward cc
Sir Richard his father
Sir Giles his grandfather
Sir Nigel his great-grandfather
Sir Everard his uncle
Rachel his aunt
William his brother, in love with Lucy St Aubin*
Waverley (1814) Walter Scott

Wax (Rose) chambermaid
The Staple of News play (1631) Ben Jonson

Waxy solicitor
Vanity Fair (1847–8) W. M. Thackeray

Waygood see Skyrme

Wayland-Smith, Dennis, Sir opponent of yellow fiend Fu Manchu* onwards from
The Mystery of Dr Fu Manchu† (1913) Sax Rohmer (rn Arthur Sarsfield Ward)

Waymark, Osmund writer cc of author's Hogarthian second novel, a partial self-portrait, whose fantasy is to be married to a 'respectable woman'
The Unclassed (1882) George Gissing

Wayne provost of Notting Hill
The Napoleon of Notting Hill (1904) G. K. Chesterton

Waynflete, Cicely, Lady
Captain Brassbound's Conversion play (1900) George Bernard Shaw

Waythorn, George
Alice his wife, m. (1) Haskett*, (2) Gus Varick*, (3) Waythorn; in tale casting aspersions on male complacency
Lily her daughter by her first marriage
ss 'The Other Two'

Roman Fever (1911) Edith Wharton

Weak Knees with collapsible limbs and mutterings at a ghost
The Narrows (1953) Ann Petry

Weaver, Charles wealthy industrialist interested in rugby football
Diane his wife, who likes the players
This Sporting Life (1960) David Storey

Weaver, Robert friend to Eugene Gant*
Of Time and the River (1935) Thomas Wolfe

Weazel, Captain
Roderick Random (1748) Tobias Smollett

Weazleing, Lord Lord Chancellor
Phineas Finn† (1869) Anthony Trollope

Webb, Edna sister to Diane Lattimer*, dying in hospital
Carter her husband, loved by Diane Lattimer
Flee the Angry Strangers (1952) George Mandel

Webb, Mr newspaper editor
his wife
Wally; Emily their children
Our Town play (1938) Thornton Wilder

Webb, Paul m. Katherine Porter*; artist who finds out about his father-in-law
The Deep Sleep (1953) Wright Morris

Webber, Frank practical joker
Charles O'Malley (1841) Charles Lever

Webber, George cc, author; self-portrait
John; Amelia his parents
The Web and the Rock (1939); You Can't Go Home Again (1940) Thomas Wolfe

Weber, Alexander Petrovitch ('Sasha')
Tobit Transplanted (1931) Stella Benson

Webley, Everard murdered by Spandrell*
Point Counter Point (1928) Aldous Huxley

Webster, Daniel
ss 'The Devil and Daniel Webster'
Thirteen O'Clock (1937); The Devil and Daniel Webster folk opera (1939) Stephen Vincent Benét and Douglas Moore

Webster, Dan'l anti-frog-hero cc of author's first famous story, inasmuch as he allows himself to be weighted down with quail-shot and cannot jump; embellished from folk-tale of the mining camps
The Celebrated Jumping Frog (1867) Mark Twain (rn Samuel Langhorne

Clemens)

Webster, Nanny
The Little Minister (1891) J. M. Barrie

Wedderburn, C. St C. friend to Michael Fane*
Sinister Street (1913) Compton Mackenzie

Wedgecroft, Geoffrey
Waste play (1907) Harley Granville Barker

Wee Willie Winkie *see* **Williams, Percival William**

Weech, Aaron villainous fence who trains Dickie Perrott* to steal
A Child of the Jago (1896) Arthur Morrison

Weedle, Nancy
Jim her father
ss 'The Superstitious Man's Story'
Life's Little Ironies (1894) Thomas Hardy

Weedon, Tuffy, Miss guardian of Charles Stringham* during his dipsomania
A Question of Upbringing† (1951) Anthony Powell

Weeks schoolmaster
Elsie Venner (1861) Oliver Wendell Holmes

Weeks, Joe brains behind Randy Banks*
The Grand Parade (1961) Julian Mayfield

Weeks, Mrs
Gentlemen Prefer Blondes (1925) Anita Loos

Weena one of the Eloi*
The Time Machine (1895) H. G. Wells

Wegg, Silas owner of stall, friend to Venus*, hired by boffin*; one-legged blackmailer
Our Mutual Friend (1865) Charles Dickens

Weigall friend to Caryl Bramsley*
C (1924) Maurice Baring

Weir, Adam Lord of Hermiston, hanging judge, based on Robert Macqueen, Lord Braxfield
Jean his wife, whose death is described in the opening chapter
Archibald, ('Erchie') their son, cc
Weir of Hermiston (1896) Robert Louis Stevenson

Weland (Weyland Smith) smith to the Gods

ss 'Weland's Sword'†
Puck of Pool's Hill (1906) Rudyard Kipling

Welbeck, Thomas embezzler, forger, murderer, in American Gothic novel* set in Philadelphia during the plague year of 1793
Arthur Mervyn, or *Memoirs of the Year 1793* (1799–1800) Charles Brockden Brown

Welbore, Welbore, MP
Pendennis (1848) W. M. Thackeray

Welborne a prodigal
A New Way to Pay Old Debts play (1633) Philip Massinger

Welch, Edward ('Neddy') history professor
his wife
Bertrand their son
Lucky Jim (1953) Kingsley Amis

Welford, Fanny mistress to George Winterbourne*
Death of a Hero (1929) Richard Aldington

Wellburn, Tommy m. Fanny Elsing
Gone With the Wind (1936) Margaret Mitchell

Weller, Sam boots, then servant and friend to Pickwick*, m. Mary
Tony his father, coachman
his stepmother, formerly Mrs Clarke, landlady of the Marquis of Granby
The Pickwick Papers (1837) Charles Dickens

Wells, John Wellington of J. W. Wells & Co, family sorcerers
The Sorcerer opera (1877) W. S. Gilbert and Arthur Sullivan

Wellwood, Henry see **Warden, Henry**

Wellwood, Sophia m. Guy Mannering*
Guy Mannering (1815) Walter Scott

Welse, Frona superwoman cc of early novel – 'Why should she not love the body, and without shame?'
A Daughter of the Snows (1902) Jack London

Welsh, Duncan cc first novel set in rural Tennessee earlier in the century
The Innocent (1957) Madison Jones

Welwyn-Foster Rural Dean
his wife
A Clergyman's Daughter (1935) George Orwell (rn Eric Blair)

Wemmick clerk to Jaggers*
'The Aged', his father
Great Expectations (1861) Charles
Dickens
Wendell anthropologist
Streets of Night (1923) John Dos Passos
Wendigee, Julius Dutch electrician
The First Men in the Moon (1901) H. G.
Wells
Wendover, Roger man dominated – to the
exclusion of all else – by intellect, based
on Mark Pattison, also the original of
Professor James Forth* and, possibly,
Casaubon*
Robert Elsmere (1888) Mrs Humphry
Ward
Wengrave, Alexander, Sir
Sebastian his son
The Roaring Girl play (1611) Thomas
Middleton and Thomas Dekker
Wenham writer and M, confidential ser-
vant to Lord Steyne*
Vanity Fair (1847–8) W. M. Thackeray
Wentworth, Colonel
his wife, *née* Feverel*
Austin their son
*The Ordeal of Richard Feverel: A
History of Father and Son* (1859) George
Meredith
Wentworth, Frederick, Captain, RN open
and frank, engaged to Anne Elliot*, but
she breaks the engagement; eventually m.
her
Edward curate of Monksford, his brother
Persuasion (1818) Jane Austen
Wentworth, Gertrude breaks away from
her family's narrowness to m. Felix
Young*
Charlotte her sister who contents herself
with the dull Mr Brand*, originally
'chosen' by her father for Gertrude
her uncle
Clifford her brother
The Europeans (1878) Henry James
Wentworth-Williams, Sandra, Mrs
Jacob's Room (1922) Virginia Woolf
Wentz, Hjalmar settler in African state
Margot his wife
Emanuelle; Stephen their children
A Guest of Honour (1971) Nadine
Gordimer
Werner, Dr friend to Pechorin*
Geroi Nas hego Vremeni (A Hero of Our

Time) (1841) Mikhail Lermontov
Werner, Reinhard who recollects his child-
hood and youth in old age in this novella,
regarded as one of the greatest German
short narratives; by a 19th-century
master of the form; 'Immensee' means
'Bee's Lake'
Immensee (1850, rev. 1851) Theodore
Storm
Wertheim, Count de
Clotilda his daughter, m. as first wife
Francis, Earl of Castlewood*
Henry Esmond (1852) W. M. Thackeray
Werther, Jungen ('Young') cc of epistol-
ary* novel which took Europe by storm
*Die Leiden des Jungen Werthers (The
Sufferings of Young Werther)* (1774)
Johann Wolfgang Goethe
WESAC computer ruling the metaphoric
world called the University
Giles Goat-Boy (1966) John Barth
Weser Dreiburg, Princess of giantess
The Food of the Gods (1904) H. G. Wells
Wessels, Emily aunt to Laura Dearborn*
The Pit (1903) Frank Norris
Wessen, Lucy
Wilbur her brother
ss 'I'm a Fool'
Horses and Men (1924) Sherwood
Anderson
West, Arthur Cadogan
ss 'The Bruce-Partington Plans'
His Last Bow (1917) Arthur Conan
Doyle
West, C. M. V., Revd friend to Nicholas
Sandomir*
Non-Combatants and Others (1916)
Rose Macaulay
West, Dora m. Tommy Bangs*
Little Men† (1871) Louisa M. Alcott
West, John Henry six-year-old boy,
Frankie Addams's* cousin
The Member of the Wedding (1946)
Carson McCullers
West, Julian cc, wealthy young Bostonian
put into hypnotic sleep of 133 years from
which he awakes (2000 AD) into a naive,
good-hearted, broadly socialist Utopia
which sold a million (the sequel did less
well) and led to formation of the Populist
Party and possibly to some aspects of the
New Deal
Looking Backward 2000–1887 (1888);

Equality (1897) Edward Bellamy

West, Rachel cc of bestselling 'new woman' novel which has recently been reprinted
Red Pottage (1899) Mary Cholmondeley

Westbrook, Harold ('Shultzy') actor, m. Elly Chipley
Show Boat (1926) Edna Ferber

Westbury, Jack, Captain
Henry Esmond (1952) W. M. Thackeray

Western, Jasper ('Eau Douce') m. Mabel Dunham
The Pathfinder (1840) James Fenimore Cooper

Western, Roger an Indian, m. Evelyn Childs*
A Lamp for Nightfall (1952) Erskine Caldwell

Western, Squire
Sophia his daughter, m. Tom Jones*
Mrs Western his sister
Tom Jones (1749) Henry Fielding

Westervelt evil mesmerist
The Blithedale Romance (1852) Nathaniel Hawthorne

Westfield, Mr Deputy-Superintendent of Police
Burmese Days (1935) George Orwell (rn Eric Blair)

Westgate, Mrs sister to Bessie Alden*
An International Episode (1879) Henry James

Westlake, David portrait of Scott Fitzgerald*
Rilda his wife (portrait of Zelda Fitzgerald*); 'Rilda and David tortured each other because they loved one another devotedly'
Parties (1930) Carl Van Vechten

Westlake, Mr intellectual socialist suggested by William Morris
Demos (1886) George Gissing

Westlock, John Pecksniff's* pupil, m. Ruth Pinch*
Martin Chuzzlewit (1844) Charles Dickens

Westlock, Ned narrator of harsh and influential tale of Midwestern town
The Revd John his stern father
Mrs Westlock née Erring, his mother
The Story of a Country Town (1883) E. W. Howe

Westmore, Bessy mill-owner, *née*

Langhope, m. John Amherst*
Mr Langhope her father
The Fruit of the Tree (1907) Edith Wharton

Westmorland, Earl of (hist.)
King Henry IV; *King Henry V* plays (1623) William Shakespeare

Weston, Anna, Mrs (the second) *née* Taylor, governess to Emma and Isabella Woodhouse*
her husband (see also **Churchill, Frank**)
Emma (1816) Jane Austen

Weston, Edward, Revd m. Agnes Grey*
Edward; Agnes; May their children
Agnes Grey (1847) Anne Brontë

Weston, Mr amiable gentleman of Highbury, m. (1) Miss Churchill (2) Miss Taylor*
Frank his son by his first wife, m. Jane Fairfax*

Weston, Mrs (the first) *née* Churchill, mother to Frank Churchill*
Emma (1816) Jane Austen

Weston, Mr mysterious cc
Mr Weston's Good Wine (1927) T. F. Powys

Weston, Vance egocentric young writer, cc
Lorin his father, 'like one of those shrivelled Japanese flowers which suddenly expand into bloom when put in water'
Mrs Weston his mother, a 'small round-faced woman with a resolute mouth'
Pearl; May his sisters
Laura Lou *née* Tracy, his wife
Hudson River Bracketed (1929); *The Gods Arrive* (1932) Edith Wharton

Westwyn, Sophia 'the secret witness' to the death of Ormond* when he tries to rape Constantia Dudley*; leading to the latter's acquittal of a murder charge
Ormond, or The Secret Witness (1799) Charles Brockden Brown

Wetheral, Bruce Campbell cc, late Captain, RAC, narrator, m. Jean Lucas
John Henry his father
Eleanor his mother, *née* Campbell
Campbell's Kingdom (1952) Hammond Innes

Weycock, Mordred Manager, United Sugar Company
Roger his nephew
Odtaa (1926) John Masefield

Whamond, Peter

Old Peter his father
The Little Minister (1891) J. M. Barrie
Whang the miller
A Citizen of the World (1762) Oliver
Goldsmith
Wharton artist, modelled on the sculptor
Saint-Gaudens
Esther (1884) Frances Snow Compton
(rn Henry Adams)
Wharton, Eliza cc American epistolary
novel*, very popular in its time, written
in imitation of Richardson*; she is
seduced by Major Sanford* and dies in
childbirth; based on (hist.) Elizabeth
Whitman's affair with Pierpont Edwards
The Coquette: A Novel Founded on Fact
(1797) Mrs Hannah Foster
Wharton, Harry one of the famous five,
onwards from
The Magnet† periodical (1908) Frank
Richards (rn Charles Hamilton)
Wharton, Henry S., MP
Marcella (1894) Mrs Humphry Ward
Wharton, Mrs widow in Brussels who
employs Frances Henri* to mend lace
her daughter
The Professor (1857) Charlotte Brontë
Wheadle a gamester
The Comical Revenge, or *Love in a Tub*
play (1664) George Etherege
Wheedle, Mrs
Polly opera (1729) John Gay
Wheedle, Polly a maid, m. Jack Raikes
Susan her sister
Evan Harrington (1861) George
Meredith
Wheeler, Mrs follower of book called
Radiant Energy which prescribes the
eating of lettuce
Coming Up For Air (1936) George
Orwell (rn Eric Blair)
Whelpdale hack writer
New Grub Street (1891) George Gissing
Whichehalse, Hugh de, Baron
Marwood his son
Lorna Doone (1869) R. D. Blackmore
Whipple, 'Shagpoke' ex-American Presi-
dent, fascist
A Cool Million (1934) Nathanael West
(rn Nathan Weinstein)
Whipple, Clay in love with Viola
Campbell*, kills a man by accident at
Brookfield's* house; acquitted by jury

hypnotized by Brookfield*
Helen his mother
The Witching Hour play (1907) Ambrose
M. Thomas
Whistler, The 'young savage', Effie
Deans's* child
Heart of Midlothian (1818) Walter Scott
Whit, Captain a bawd
Bartholomew Fair play (1631) Ben
Jonson
Whitaker, Mrs Mrs Rushworth's* house-
keeper
Mansfield Park (1814) Jane Austen
Whitbread, Hugh
Evelyn his wife
Mrs Dalloway (1925) Virginia Woolf
White Cobra, The
ss 'The King's Ankus'
The Second Jungle Book (1895) Rudyard
Kipling
White detective, see **Fisher, 'Smooth' Sam**
White Fang three-quarters wolf; rescued
from Beauty Smith* by Weedon Scott*,
in defence of whose family he loses his
now domesticated life; in three-quarter
wolf classic
White Fang (1905) Jack London
White King, Queen and Knave, The
*Through the Looking-Glass and What
Alice Found There* (1872) Lewis Carroll
(rn Charles Lutwidge Dodgson)
White rationalist journalist
The Research Magnificent (1915) H. G.
Wells
White schoolmaster
Mr Perrin and Mr Traill (1911) Hugh
Walpole
White, Arthur
A Lamp for Nightfall (1952) Erskine
Caldwell
White, Father
ss 'Agnes Lahens'
Celibates (1895) George Moore
White, Harry womanizer, cc
Linda his wife
The Demon (1976) Hubert J. Selby
White, Helen George Willard's* girlfriend
ss 'Sophisticated'; 'Departure'
Winesburg, Ohio (1919) Sherwood
Anderson
White, J. C. American businessman: is he
Stiller*? – in Swiss (German) novel: the
question is answered unequivocally

Stiller (1954) Max Frisch
White, Mr and Mrs
Herbert their son
ss 'The Monkey's Paw'
The Lady of the Barge (1902) W. W. Jacobs
White, Mrs
Carrots (1876) Mrs Molesworth
White, Mrs Claire Temple's* cleaner, less relentless than Kathleen*
There Were No Windows (1944) Norah Hoult
White, Wylie script writer
The Last Tycoon (1941) F. Scott Fitzgerald
White-Jacket narrator of this half-autobiographical account of the cruise of the *Neversink* from Peru to Virginia
White-Jacket (1850) Herman Melville
White-tip female otter
Tarka the Otter (1927) Henry Williamson
Whitebillet, Edith m. Oliver Price*
Edna her twin, m. (1) Freddy Smith, (2) Oliver Price as second wife
Sir Reginald their father
Antigua Penny Puce (1936) Robert Graves
Whitecraft, John landlord of the Cat and Fiddle, Altringham
Peveril of the Peak (1822) Walter Scott
Whitefield, Ann
her mother
Man and Superman (1903) George Bernard Shaw
Whitefield, Mrs
Tom Jones (1749) Henry Fielding
Whitehead, Harry
ss 'I'm a Fool'†
Horses and Men (1924) Sherwood Anderson
Whitehead, Thomas 'is one and being one is one who sometime will be a quite old one'
ss 'A Long Gay Book'
GMP (1932) Gertrude Stein
Whitehouse, Betty
Gordon her husband
Freda his sister, m. Robert Caplan*
Dangerous Corner play (1932) J. B. Priestley
Whiteoaks name of English colonial landed gentry in bestselling 'sagas';

onwards from
Jalna (1927) Mazo de la Roche
Whitfield, Revd father of Jewel Bundren* and one of the monologuists in complex experimental novel* consisting of fifty-nine interior monologues
As I Lay Dying (1930) William Faulkner
Whitford, Vernon Patterne's* cousin and tutor to a poor relation; a fairly exact portrait of Leslie Stephen; m. Clara Middleton*
The Egoist (1879) George Meredith
Whitgift, Widow
her two sons
ss 'The Dymchurch Flit'
Puck of Pook's Hill (1906) Rudyard Kipling
Whitman
his wife
their two daughters
Robbery Under Arms: A Story of Life and Adventure in the Bush and in the Goldfields of Australia (1888, rev. 1889) Rolf Boldrewood (rn Thomas Alexander Browne)
Whitman, Walt (hist.) Delane's 'spark', i.e. advisory conscience, in novella
ss 'The Spark'
Old New York (1924) Edith Wharton
Whitney, Isa opium addict
ss 'The Man with the Twisted Lip'
The Adventures of Sherlock Holmes (1892) Arthur Conan Doyle
Whitstable, George m. Sophia Longe-staffe*
The Way We Live Now (1875) Anthony Trollope
Whittaker Admiralty official
The Thirty-nine Steps (1915) John Buchan
Whittaker, Betty
All Our Yesterdays (1930) H. M. Tomlinson
Whittaker, Prudence secretary to Sir Buck-stone Abbott*; m. Tubby Vanringham*
Summer Moonshine (1938) P. G. Wode-house
Whittle, Abel dim-witted farm-hand
The Mayor of Casterbridge (1886) Thomas Hardy
Whittlestaff, William the 'old man' (fifty), in love with his ward, Mary Lawrie*
An Old Man's Love (1884) Anthony

Trollope

Whorehound, Walter, Sir whose wealth depends on the childlessness of Lady Kix*
Wat; Nick his sons by Mistress Allwit*
A Chaste Maid in Cheapside play (1630) Thomas Middleton

Whybrow, Anthony see **Assher, Lady**

Whyte, Oliver
The Mystery of a Hansom Cab (1886) Fergus Hume

Wick, Robert Hanna, Second Lieutenant
ss 'Only a Subaltern'
Wee Willie Winkie (1888) Rudyard Kipling

Wickenden, Jim
his mother
Mary his adopted daughter
ss 'Friendly Brook'
A Diversity of Creatures (1917) Rudyard Kipling

Wickenham, Lord m. Allegra*
The Gods, Some Mortals and Lord Wickenham (1895) John Oliver Hobbes (rn Pearl Craigie)

Wickett, Terry uncouth chemist of integrity, Arrowsmith's* friend and, finally co-worker in research
Arrowsmith (1925) Sinclair Lewis

Wickfield, Mr lawyer
Agnes his daughter, m. as second wife David Copperfield*
David Copperfield (1850) Charles Dickens

Wickham friend to Michael Finsbury*
The Wrong Box (1889) Robert Louis Stevenson and Lloyd Osbourne

Wickham, George pretends to study law, but in fact leads a life of idleness and vice, even though he is beholden to Fitzwilliam Darcy*, enters militia, m. Lydia Bennet*, who finds no goodness in him
Old Mr Wickham his father, once a steward at Pemberley
his mother
Pride and Prejudice (1813) Jane Austen

Wickham, Mrs nurse to Paul Dombey*
Dombey and Son (1848) Charles Dickens

Wickson, Philip socialist
The Iron Heel (1908) Jack London

Wickstead murdered by Griffin*
The Invisible Man (1897) H. G. Wells

Widdows, Mrs Hannah Mole's* employer

Miss Mole (1930) E. H. Young

Widdowson, Edmund jealous husband to Monica Madden*
Mrs Luke Widdowson his widowed sister
The Odd Women (1893) George Gissing

Widgery, Douglas friend to Mrs Milton*
The Wheels of Chance (1896) H. G. Wells

Widgetts, The neighbours to Peter Stanley*
Ann Veronica (1900) H. G. Wells

Widmerpool, Kenneth financier, Labour MP, m. Pamela Flitton*, one of the great humorous creations in English fiction
A Question of Upbringing† (1951) Anthony Powell

Widow of Florence, A
All's Well That Ends Well play (1623) William Shakespeare

Wieland, Theodore mad cc based on real-life killer of Tomhannock N. Y., who destroyed his family at behest of imagined voices (see Carwin*) in initial novel by writer, often called America's first professional
Wieland, or The Transformation: An American Tale (1798) Charles Brockden Brown

Wiener jeweller at Leubronn
Daniel Deronda (1876) George Eliot (rn Mary Anne, later Marian, Evans)

Wiggen, Henry W. successful baseball pitcher cc of series
The Southpaw (1953); *Bang the Drum Slowly* (1956); *A Ticket for Seamstich* (1957); *It Looked Like for Ever* (1979) Mark Harris

Wiggle, Desborough
The Book of Snobs (1847) W. M. Thackeray

Wiggs, Mrs
Billy her husband
Mrs Wiggs of the Cabbage Patch (1901) Alice Hegen Rice

Wiglaf a companion to Beowulf*
Beowulf (c.745)

Wilberforce, Amy, Miss drunk
South Wind (1917) Norman Douglas

Wilbur, Amy 'silly, shallow, jeering' m. Maurice Garden*
Told By An Idiot (1923) Rose Macaulay

Wilbur, Ross cc inferior potboiler by gifted

author
Moran of the Lady Letty (in England, *Shanghaied*) (1898) Frank Morris
Wilcher, Thomas Loftus solicitor
Edward; Major Bill; Lucy his brothers and sister
Ann Edward's daughter, m. her cousin Robert Brown
John Bill's son, m. Puggy Brown
Robert son to Puggy and John
To Be A Pilgrim† (1942) Joyce Cary
Wilcocks, Thomas captain of the ship which rescued Gulliver*
Gulliver's Travels (1726) Jonathan Swift
Wilcox, Henry friend to Arthur Rowe*
Doris his wife
The Ministry of Fear (1943) Graham Greene
Wild, Jonathan (hist.) rogue who, in this version, picks his hangman's pocket; m. Laetitia Snap*
Jonathan Wild (1743) Henry Fielding
Wildenheim, Baron who seduces and deserts Agatha* in play adapted from Kotzbue that would be forgotten but that it was (so wrongly in the eyes of the author of the novel) given in *Mansfield Park*
Frederic his son by Agatha, who makes things right
Lovers' Vows play (1798) Elizabeth Inchbald
Wilder, Mrs friend to Stanley Timberlake*
In this our Life (1942) Ellen Glasgow
Wilderspin Bohemian painter
Aylwin (1899) Theodore Watts-Dunton
Wildeve, Damon cc, sullen failed engineer, innkeeper m. Thomasin Yeobright*, lover of Eustacia Yeobright, *née* Vye*
The Return of the Native (1878) Thomas Hardy
Wildfire, Madge see **Murdockson, Madge**
Wildfire, Nimrod Kentucky backwoodsman identified with Davy Crockett
The Lion of the West play produced 1830 (published 1954) J. K. Paulding
Wildflower, Walter boy David Schearl* thinks he knows, born in 'Europe far away: Waltush, Waltush, Wiuhlflowah,/Growin' up so high;/So are all young ladies,/An we are ready to die'
Call It Sleep (1934) Henry Roth
Wildgoose, Geoffry, Revd satirized cc

preacher of George Whitfield's Methodist theology in episodic novel
The Spiritual Quixote, or *The Summer's Ramble of Mr. Geoffry Wildgoose: A Comic Romance* (1733) Richard Graves
Wilding the gamester
his wife
The Gamester play (1637) James Shirley
Wilding, Charlotte
Jacob's Room (1922) Virginia Woolf
Wildmay, Felix see **Marchdale, Peter**
Wildrake, Roger college friend to Markham Everard*
Woodstock (1826) Walter Scott
Wilfer, Reginald ('Rumty' in the office, RW to his wife) clerk at Chicksey, Veneering and Stobbles; long-suffering little man whose life could be summed up by the remark 'What might have been is not what is'
his grandiloquent wife
Bella cc, m. John Rokesmith*; **Lavinia** m. George Sampson* his daughters
Our Mutual Friend (1865) Charles Dickens
Wilford, Stephen society rake
Frank Fairlegh (1850) Frank Smedley
Wilfred see **Ivanhoe**
Wilkerson, Jonas overseer for the O'Haras*, m. Emmie Slattery*
Gone With the Wind (1936) Margaret Mitchell
Wilkes, Ashley m. his cousin Melanie Hamilton*
Beau their son
John his father
Honey; India his sisters
Gone With the Wind (1936) Margaret Mitchell
Wilkes, Emily communist turned liberal journalist, married to Stephen Howard, in posthumous novel
I'm Dying Laughing (1986) Christina Stead
Wilkett, C. R. bacteriologist
ss 'Tender Achilles'
Limits and Renewals (1932) Rudyard Kipling
Wilkin divorce detective
Holy Deadlock (1934) A. P. Herbert
Wilkins, Cassandra
Manhattan Transfer (1925) John Dos Passos

Wilkins, Deborah Squire Allworthy's* servant
Tom Jones (1749) Henry Fielding
Wilkins, Edgar novelist
The New Machiavelli† (1911) H. G. Wells
Wilkins, Frank, Major friend to Mrs Delacroix*
The Little Girls (1964) Elizabeth Bowen
Wilkins, Herbert James Rodney Stephen Christopher
his mother
his father, author of *Herbert's Father*
ss 'Why Herbert Killed His Mother'
Truth Is Not Sober (1934) Winifred Holtby
Wilkins, Mr
A Laodicean (1881) Thomas Hardy
Wilkins, Peter cc of early speculative fiction* 'imaginary voyage' (Robinsonsade) novel whose author remained unknown until 1835; hailed by the romantics
The Life and Adventures of Peter Wilkins, A Cornish Man, Relating Particularly to His Shipwreck near the South Pole (1750; modern edition, 1973) Robert Paltock
Wilkins, Phoebe companion to Julia Templeton*, m. Jack Tibbets*
Bracebridge Hall (1823) Washington Irving
Wilkinson, Maureen friend to Middleton*
The Restoration of Arnold Middleton play (1967) David Storey
Wilkinson, Emily, Miss governess who initiates Carey* into sex
Of Human Bondage (1915) W. Somerset Maugham
Wilkinson, Peter neurotic young Englishman, lover to Otto Nowak*
Goodbye to Berlin (1939) Christopher Isherwood
Wilks actor, Professor de Worms
The Man Who Was Thursday (1908) G. K. Chesterton
Wilks, Nurse aged and tyrannical ex-nanny to Mulliner*
Meet Mr Mulliner (1927) P. G. Wodehouse
Will 'master and tutor in wickedness'
Colonel Jack (1722) Daniel Defoe
Will-Do a parson

A New Way to Pay Old Debts play (1633) Philip Massinger
Willan friend to Cyril Burnage*
Right Off the Map (1927) C. E. Montague
Willard, Jim cc, young Virginian
The City and the Pillar (1948) Gore Vidal
Willatale Queen of the Arnewi tribe
Henderson the Rain King (1959) Saul Bellow
Willcox, Henry occupant of Howards End
Charles; Paul; Eve his children
Dorothea Charles's wife
Howard's End (1910) E. M. Forster
Willems, Peter cc
An Outcast of the Islands (1896) Joseph Conrad (rn Josef Teodor Konrad Korzeniowski)
Willens, Hugo Jewish fighter against Nazism
Rain from Heaven play (1935) S. N. Behrman
Willersley friend to Remington*
The New Machiavelli (1911) H. G. Wells
Willet, John landlord of the Maypole
Joe his son, m. Dolly Varden*
Barnaby Rudge (1841) Charles Dickens
William a clown
Locrine play (1595) 'W. S.' (?George Peele; ?Robert Green)
William Quaker
his sister, m. Captain Singleton*
Captain Singleton (1720) Daniel Defoe
William son to a prison doctor
ss 'The Debt'
Limits and Renewals (1932) Rudyard Kipling
William the Conqueror see **Martyn, William**
Williams chairman of visiting justices
It Is Never Too Late To Mend (1856) Charles Reade
Williams, Arthur, Revd
Pamela (1740) Samuel Richardson
Williams, Betty, Lady widow
Sir Charles Grandison (1754) Samuel Richardson
Williams, Caleb part-narrator: ill-used young man in the service of Falkland* in novel which anticipated both detective fiction and the psychological novel
Things as They Are, or *The Adventures of Caleb Williams* (1794) William Godwin

The Iron Chest dramatization (1796) George Colman the Younger

Williams, Eliza illegitimate daughter of Col. Brandon's* sister-in-law, taken in by him as a child, and seduced by John Willoughby*, who blames her for her weakness
Sense and Sensibility (1811) Jane Austen

Williams, Farmer suitor to Olivia Primrose
The Vicar of Wakefield (1766) Oliver Goldsmith

Williams, Janey secretary
Joe her brother
U.S.A. (1930–36) John Dos Passos

Williams, Laurey pretty, spoiled orphan m. Curly McClain*
Green Grow the Lilacs (1931) Lynn Riggs

Williams, Major cc of enlightening trilogy set in the Maori Wars by New Zealand novelist
The Flying Fish (1964); *The Needle's Eye* (1965); *The Evil Day* (1967) Errol Braithwaite

Williams, Mr
ss 'The Mezzotint'
Ghost Stories of an Antiquary (1910) M. R. James

Williams, Peter evangelist
Winifred his wife
Lavengro (1851) George Borrow

Williams, Private Ellgee a silent innocent young soldier
Reflections in a Golden Eye (1940) Carson McCullers

Williams, Race first of the 'hard-boiled' detectives (dicks) in stories in Joseph T. Shaw's magazine *The Black Mask*; ('you can't make hamburgers without grinding up a little meat') stories about Williams appeared onwards from 1923 Carroll John Daly

Williams, Sam Penrod Schofield's* friend
Penrod (1914); *Penrod and Sam* (1916); *Penrod Jashber* (1929) Booth Tarkington

Williams, Slogger Tom Brown's* opponent in the big fight
Tom Brown's Schooldays (1857) Thomas Hughes

Willie of Westburnflat ('Red Reiver')
The Black Dwarf (1816) Walter Scott

Williams, Percival William ('Wee Willie Winkie')

Colonel Williams his father
ss 'Wee Willie Winkie'
Wee Willie Winkie (1888) Rudyard Kipling

Willis, Captain
Two Years Ago (1857) Charles Kingsley

Willis, Lymon hunchback and dwarf, cousin to Miss Amelia Evans*
The Ballad of the Sad Café (1951) Carson McCullers

Willis, Private m. Queen of the Fairies*
Iolanthe opera (1882) W. S. Gilbert and Arthur Sullivan

Willoughby, Clement, Sir
Evelina (1778) Fanny Burney

Willoughby, John handsome young gentleman, owner of Combe Magna in Dorset; seduces and abandons Eliza Williams*; fights duel with Colonel Brandon*; repents lastingly but does not fail to continue to enjoy himself
Sense and Sensibility (1811) Jane Austen

Willoughby, Mrs passenger on the *Oroya*
Captain Botell (1933) James Hanley

Willoughby, Sophia née Aspen, owner of Blandemer House, Dorset, cc
Frederick her husband
Augusta; Damien their children, who die of smallpox
Summer Will Show (1936) Sylvia Townsend Warner

Willowes, Laura ('Lolly') cc
Everard her father
Henry; James her brothers
Caroline Henry's wife
Sibyl James's wife
Titus son to Caroline and James
Lolly Willowes (1926) Sylvia Townsend Warner

Willson III, Dewey
A Different Drummer (1962) William Melvin Kelley

Willy Nilly postman
his wife
Under Milk Wood play (1954) Dylan Thomas

Wilmer Caspar Gutman's bodyguard
The Maltese Falcon (1930) Dashiell Hammett

Wilmington
Joan and Peter (1918) H. G. Wells

Wilmot, Annabella m. Lord Lowborough
her uncle

The Tenant of Wildfell Hall (1848) Anne
Brontë

Wilmot, Anne m. Jon Forsyte*
Francis her brother
The *Forsyte* series (1906–33) John
Galsworthy

Wilmot, Captain admiral of pirates
Captain Singleton (1720) Daniel Defoe

Wilmot, Old murderer of a traveller
his wife
The Fatal Curiosity play (1736) George
Lillo

Wilmot, Revd Mr
Arabella his daughter, m. George
Primrose*
The Vicar of Wakefield (1766) Oliver
Goldsmith

Wilshire, Jane 'aunt' (actually cousin) to
the Britlings*
Mr Britling Sees It Through (1916) H. G.
Wells

Wilson elderly manufacturer
Uncle Tom's Cabin (1851) Harriet
Beecher Stowe

Wilson see Dennison, George

Wilson servant to Sir Charles Grandison*
Sir Charles Grandison (1754) Samuel
Richardson

Wilson veteran soldier
The Red Badge of Courage (1895) Stephen Crane

Wilson, 'General' Provost of Bayswater
The Napoleon of Notting Hill (1904)
G. K. Chesterton

Wilson, Andrew ('Handie Dandie') smuggler
Heart of Midlothian (1818) Walter Scott

Wilson, Captain and owner of *Seamew*
The Skipper's Wooing (1897) W. W.
Jacobs

Wilson, Captain HMS *Harpy*
Mr Midshipman Easy (1836) Captain
Marryat

Wilson, Captain the *London Merchant*
The Settlers in Canada (1844) Captain
Marryat

Wilson, Colonel
ss 'Oh Whistle and I'll Come to You, my
Lad'
Ghost Stories of an Antiquary (1910)
M. R. James

Wilson, David 'Pudd'nhead' eccentric defence lawyer

The Tragedy of Pudd'nhead Wilson
(1894) Mark Twain (rn Samuel Langhorne Clemens)

Wilson, Davy ('Snuffy Davy')
The Antiquary (1816) Walter Scott

Wilson, Dr
ss 'Physic'
The Wind Blows Over (1936) Walter de
la Mare

Wilson, Edgar
ss 'The Man's Story'
Horses and Men (1924) Sherwood
Anderson

Wilson, Edward in love with Louise
Scobie*
The Heart of the Matter (1948) Graham
Greene

Wilson, George
Alice his wife
Jane; Jem cc, young engineering worker,
m. Mary Barton* their children
Mary Barton (1848) Mrs Gaskell

Wilson, George ('Spike') sailor
George; Grace his parents
Time Will Knit (1938) Fred Urquhart

Wilson, Ivy
'Sairy' his wife
The Grapes of Wrath (1939) John
Steinbeck

Wilson, Jabez credulous pawnbroker
ss 'The Red-headed League'
The Adventures of Sherlock Holmes
(1892) Arthur Conan Doyle

Wilson, James grocer and ironmonger,
enemy to Gourley*
his wife
The House With the Green Shutters
(1901) George Douglas (rn George
Douglas Brown)

Wilson, Joe narrator of many of the
Australian author's stories
ss 'Water Them Geraniums'†
Joe Wilson and his Mates (1901) Henry
Lawson (*The Portable Lawson* 1976)

Wilson, John, Revd oldest clergyman in
Boston
The Scarlet Letter (1850) Nathaniel
Hawthorne

Wilson, Mrs farmer's widow
Jane; Robert; Richard her children
The Tenant of Wildfell Hall (1848) Anne
Brontë

Wilson, Myrtle mistress to Tom

Buchanan*
George her husband, killer of Gatsby*
Catherine her sister
The Great Gatsby (1925) F. Scott
Fitzgerald
Wilson, Rose waitress, m. Pinkie*
her parents
Brighton Rock (1938) Graham Greene
Wilson, Scratchy old frontier gunfighter
ss 'The Bride Comes to Yellow Sky'
*The Open Boat and Other Tales of
Adventure* (1898) Stephen Crane
Wilson, William narrator, also name of his
mysterious double
ss 'William Wilson'
Tales of the Grotesque and Arabesque
(1840) Edgar Allan Poe
Wilton, Jack cc
The Unfortunate Traveller, or *The Life of
Jack Wilton* (1594) Thomas Nashe
Wiltshire, John cc, narrator, m. Uma*
ss 'The Beach of Falesa'
Islands Nights' Entertainments (1893)
Robert Louis Stevenson
Wimbush, Henry owner of Crome
Anne his niece
Crome Yellow (1922) Aldous Huxley
Wimsey, Lord Peter Death Bredon off-
shoot of Trent*, highly vulnerable aristo-
cratic private eye of the 'human' genre,
eventually married Harriet Vane*
Lady Mary Wimsey his sister m. Chief
Inspector Parker onwards from
Whose Body?† (1923) Dorothy L. Sayers
Winbrooke, George, Sir
The Man of Feeling (1771) Henry
Mackenzie
Winchell, Sergeant
The Family Reunion play (1939) T. S.
Eliot
Winchelsea, Miss high school mistress
ss 'Miss Winchelsea's Heart'
Tales of Life and Adventure† (1913)
H. G. Wells
Winchester, Bishop of (Henry Beaufort)
King Henry VI plays (1623) William
Shakespeare
Winchester, Francis, the Hon. emigrant
sheep-farmer and speculator
It Is Never Too Late to Mend (1856)
Charles Reade
Winchmore, Lieutenant RNVR
ss 'Sea Constables'

Debits and Credits (1926) Rudyard Kipl-
ing
Windermere, Arthur, Lord
Margaret his wife
Lady Windermere's Fan play (1892)
Oscar Wilde
Windibank traveller in wines masquerad-
ing as Hosmer Angel
ss 'A Case of Identity'
The Adventures of Sherlock Holmes
(1892) Arthur Conan Doyle
Windrip, Berzelius ('Buzz') fascist presi-
dent of USA
It Can't Happen Here (1935) Sinclair
Lewis
Wing, Isadora 'liberated' heroine in quest
of 'zipless fuck', in cult novels
Fear of Flying (1973); *How to Save Your
Own Life* (1977) Erica Jong
Wingate, Charles ambitious serviceman
Chips with Everything play (1962)
Arnold Wesker
Wingate, Frances cc
The Realms of Gold (1975) Margaret
Drabble
Wingfield, Amanda
Laura; Tom her children
The Glass Menagerie play (1948) Ten-
nessee Williams (rn Thomas Lanier
Williams)
Winkle, Nathaniel m. Arabella Allen
The Pickwick Papers (1837) Charles
Dickens
Winkles, Stephen, FRS Redwood's* pupil
The Food of the Gods (1904) H. G. Wells
Winlove family name of Viscount
Trimingham*
The Go-Between (1953) L. P. Hartley
Winner, Arthur, Jr. conservative middle-
aged lawyer cc of American best-selling
novel
By Love Possessed (1957) James Gould
Cozzens
Winnick, Louis oil consultant, crook
Campbell's Kingdom (1952) Hammond
Innes
Winnie the Pooh bear
Winnie the Pooh† (1926) A. A. Milne
Winslow, Ronnie cadet expelled for
stealing, in drama based on the case of
Archer Shee (who probably *was* guilty);
later vindicated
Arthur; Grace his parents

Catherine; Dickie his sister and brother
The Winslow Boy play (1946) Terence
Rattigan
Winsor, Charles
Lady Adela his wife
Loyalties play (1922) John Galsworthy
Winter
Mrs Dukes' Million (1977) Wyndham
Lewis
Winter, Adam, Dr
Arrowsmith (1925) Sinclair Lewis
Winter, Allan
Odtaa (1926) John Masefield
Winter, Jack
his mother
ss 'The Winters and the Palmleys'
Life's Little Ironies (1894) Thomas
Hardy
Winter, Lucy cc
The Small Room (1961) May Sarton
Winter, Sherman theatrical producer
Hemlock and After (1952) Angus Wilson
Winterbaum, Philip friend to Joan and
Peter
Joan and Peter (1918) H. G. Wells
Winterblossom, Philip
St Ronan's Well (1824) Walter Scott
Winterbourne young American in Italy
Daisy Miller (1878) Henry James
Winterbourne, George cc
Elizabeth his wife, *née* Paston
George; Isabel his parents
his grandparents
Death of a Hero (1929) Richard
Aldington
Winterbourne, Giles in love with Grace
Melbury*, whose reputation he saves at
the expense of his life, a 'good man who
did good things' (Marty South*)
John his father
The Woodlanders (1889) Thomas Hardy
Winterbourne, Lady sister to Lord
Maxwell
Marcella (1894) Mrs Humphry Ward
Winterfield, Graf von secretary to Prince
Karl Albert*
War in the Air (1908) H. G. Wells
Wintergreen, John P. presidential candi-
date in George Gershwin musical
lampoon of politics
Of Thee I Sing (1932) George Kaufman,
Ira Gershwin and Morrie Ryskind
Wintersloan illustrator of Will Magnet's*

work
Marriage (1912) H. G. Wells
Winton, 'Pater' schoolboy
ss 'Regulus'
A Diversity of Creatures (1917) Rudyard
Kipling
Winwife gentleman and rival to
Zeal-Of-The-Land Busy* for the hand of
Dame Purecraft*
Bartholomew Fair play (1631) Ben
Jonson
Wirt, Miss elderly governess
The Book of Snobs† (1847) W. M.
Thackeray
Wisbeach, Mrs Gordon Comstock's*
landlady, specializing in single gentlemen
Keep the Aspidistra Flying (1936) George
Orwell (rn Eric Blair)
Wisdom, Phoebe, Mrs sister to Sir Ray-
mond Bastable*, m. Albert Peasemarsh*
Cosmo her son by her first husband
Cocktail Time (1958) P. G. Wodehouse
Wiseman, Mr narrator
The Life and Death of Mr Badman
(1680) John Bunyan
Wishaw, Mrs
Evan Harrington (1861) George
Meredith
Wishfort, Lady
his daughter, m. Fainall*
The Way of the World play (1700)
William Congreve
Wisp ex-ostler turned Baptist
poem 'The Gentleman Farmer'
The Borough poem (1810) George
Crabbe
Wispe, Dido woman to Lady Tub*
A Tale of a Tub play (1640) Ben Jonson
Wister detective
Justice play (1910) John Galsworthy
Witchett, Mr secretary of local Liberal
Party
Coming Up For Air (1936) George
Orwell (rn Eric Blair)
Witgood cc of comedy to which Mas-
singer* was indebted for the plot of *A
New Way to Pay Old Debts**
A Trick to Catch the Old One play
(1608) Thomas Middleton
Witham, Arthur plumber
Albert his brother, Oxford man
The Lost Girl (1920) D. H. Lawrence
Witherden notary

The Old Curiosity Shop (1841) Charles Dickens

Witherington, General see **Tresham, Richard**

Witherow, Henry coarse and evil landlord killed by Andrew Ferguson* after he rapes Hannah Ferguson*
John Ferguson play (1915) St John Ervine

Withers narrator, friend to Arthur Seaton*
ss 'Seaton's Aunt'
The Riddle (1923) Walter de la Mare

Withers page to Mrs Skewton*
Dombey and Son (1848) Charles Dickens

Withers, Francie burnt child
Daphne, her sister, recipient of unjust leucotomy in 'tremendista'* New Zealand novel of oppressed childhood
Owls Do Cry (1957) Janet Frame

Withers, Silence, Miss Calvinist bringer up of Myrtle Hazard
The Guardian Angel (1868) Oliver Wendell Holmes

Withers, Patsy
Miss Mole (1930) E. H. Young

Witla, Eugene artist cc in partly autobiographical novel; based in part on himself, on the painter Everett Shinn, and on an editor he knew; m. Angela Blue*
Thomas his father, sewing-machine agent
Sylvia; Myrtle his sisters
The Genius (1915) Theodore Dreiser

Witt, Lou rich American, m. Sir Henry (Rico) Carrington*
her mother
St Mawr (1925) D. H. Lawrence

Witta Danish sea captain
ss 'The Knights of the Joyous Venture'
Puck of Pook's Hill (1906) Rudyard Kipling

Wittenhagen, Martin
The Cloister and the Hearth (1861) Charles Reade

Witterly, Julia employer of Kate Nickleby*
her husband
Nicholas Nickleby (1839) Charles Dickens

Wittol, Joseph, Sir foolish knight m. Sylvia*
The Old Bachelor comedy (1793) William Congreve

Witwoud, Wilfull, Sir nephew of Lady Wishfort*

Witwoud his half-brother, a follower of Mrs Millament*
The Way of the World comedy (1710) William Congreve

Woffington, Peg (hist.) actress
Peg Woffington (1853) Charles Reade

Wolf Rip Van Winkle's* dog
Rip Van Winkle (1820) Washington Irving

Wolf, Brer
Uncle Remus (1880–95) Joel Chandler Harris

Wolf, Julia ex-mistress and secretary to Clyde Wynant*
The Thin Man (1934) Dashiell Hammett

Wolfe, Nero 'the American Sherlock Holmes': obese orchid-fancier, gourmet, linguist and impolite sleuth onwards from
Fer de Lance† (1934) Rex Stout

Wolfram a knight, brother to Isbrand*
Death's Jest Book, or The Fool's Tragedy play (1850) Thomas Lovell Beddoes

Wolfram, Abbot
Ivanhoe (1820) Walter Scott

Wolfsheim, Meyer friend and patron to Gatsby*; based on a New York gangster of the time
The Great Gatsby (1925) F. Scott Fitzgerald

Wollastan free-thinking bookseller for whom Rutherford* works in London
Theresa his niece, based on George Eliot*
The Autobiography of Mark Rutherford (1881) Mark Rutherford (rn William Hale White)

Wollin, Henry
ss 'Fairy-Kist'
Limits and Renewals (1932) Rudyard Kipling

Wolsey, Cardinal (hist.)
King Henry VIII play (1623) William Shakespeare and John Fletcher

Wolsey, Hester housekeeper
Mother and Son (1954) Ivy Compton-Burnett

Wolstenholme, Charles, Sir late Attorney-General
Ten Thousand a Year (1839) Samuel Warren

Woman in the wallpaper pattern, The imprisoned alter ego, or symbol of, the narrator, the wife to Dr John —*

ss 'The Yellow Wallpaper'
New England Magazine (May, 1892; separate publication 1973) Charlotte Perkins Gilman

Won-Toller a lone wolf
The Second Jungle Book (1895) Rudyard Kipling

Wonder, John Fennil Viceroy's secretary
ss 'The Germ Destroyer'
Plain Tales from the Hills (1888) Rudyard Kipling

Wonham, Stephen half-brother to Rickie Elliot*, 'healthy and pagan'
The Longest Journey (1907) E. M. Forster

Wontner subaltern
ss 'The Honours of war'
A Diversity of Creatures (1917) Rudyard Kipling

Wood, Bob
Luke; Esther his parents
The World in the Evening (1954) Christopher Isherwood

Wood, John unqualified young man, cc
Margeurite his wife, who cheats Aaron MacGregor* of £100 paid to her for spending the night with him; but she repents
Emily; Ivan their children
Cecil his uncle, kindly but self-indulgent nurseryman, in whose dilapidated house they live, and who eats, with John, Mick Keen's* accidentally severed finger in a spaghetti bolognaise
Elizabeth John's discontented sister, teacher
An Advent Calendar (1971) Shena Mackay

Woodburn, Mrs brilliant mimic who takes everyone off in Carlingford
her husband
Miss Marjoribanks (1866) Mrs Margaret Oliphant

Woodbury, Miss
ss 'I'm a Fool'
Horses and Men (1924) Sherwood Anderson

Woodcock, Adam Falconer of Avenel
The Abbot (1820) Walter Scott

Woodcourt, Allan physician to Miss Flite*, m. Esther Summerson*
Bleak House (1853) Charles Dickens

Wooddrop, John ironmaster whose name

'is Me or nobody'; brought to his knees by Hulings*
Gisela his daughter
ss 'Tubal Cain'
Gold and Iron (1918) Joseph Hergesheimer

Woodhouse journalist
ss 'The Village that Voted the earth was Flat'
A Diversity of Creatures (1917) Rudyard Kipling

Woodhouse, Emma cc, arrogant matchmaker who is brought to see her failings, m. George Knightley*
Mr Woodhouse her valetudinarian father, whose house she runs
Isabella her sister, m. John Knightley*
Emma (1816) Jane Austen

Woodley, John
ss 'The Solitary Cyclist'
The Return of Sherlock Holmes (1905) Arthur Conan Doyle

Woodrow, George Garden proprietor of Kipps's 'superior' school
Kipps (1905) H. G. Wells

Woodruff, Mary mistress, and then loyal housekeeper, to Stephen Tarrant*
In the Year of Jubilee (1894) George Gissing

Woodruff, Sarah cc
The French Lieutenant's Woman (1969) John Fowles

Woodseer, Gower portrait of Robert Louis Stevenson*; penniless philosopher
his father, minister among the poor of Whitechapel
The Amazing Marriage (1895) George Meredith

Woodville Lieutenant of the Tower
King Henry VI plays (1623) William Shakespeare

Woodville, Frank, Lord
The Tapestried Chamber (1828) Walter Scott

Woodwell, Revd Mr Baptist minister
A Laodicean (1881) Thomas Hardy

Wool, Mrs
The Mill on the Floss (1860) George Eliot (rn Mary Anne, later Marian, Evans)

Woolcombe, Grenville rich mulatto officer in the Life Guards Green; m. Agnes Twysden*
The Adventures of Philip (1862) W. M.

Thackeray

Woolley, Ernest, The Hon.
The Admirable Crichton play (1902)
J. M. Barrie

Woolsey of Linsey Wolsey, tailors
Vanity Fair (1847–8) W. M. Thackeray

Wooster, Bertie drone, narrator
Agatha; Dahlia his dreaded aunts;
onwards from
The Man with Two Left Feet (1917) P. G.
Wodehouse

Wopsle parish clerk
Great Expectations (1861) Charles
Dickens

Worcester, Earl of
King Henry IV plays (1623) William
Shakespeare

Worldly, John, Sir
Bellafont; Katherine; Lucida
A Woman is a Weathercock play (1612)
Nathan Field

Worldly-Wiseman of the town of Carnal
Policy
The Pilgrim's Progress (1678–84) John
Bunyan

Worm
Molloy (1951); *Malone meurt* (*Malone
Dies*) (1951) (tr. 1956); *L'Innommable*
(1953) (*The Unnamable*) (tr. 1958) (trilogy) Samuel Beckett

Worm, William factotum to Mr
Swancourt*
his wife
A Pair of Blue Eyes (1873) Thomas
Hardy

Worrett, Mrs
What Katy Did at School (1873) Susan
Coolidge (rn Sarah Chauncey Woolsey)

Worsley, Gladys and Enid twins
Lennie; Victoria their parents
Sylvia Scarlett (1918) Compton
Mackenzie

Worsley, Isabella cousin to Katherine and
Eleanor Ogilvie*; selfish cc of the novel
which made the author's name
The Ogilvies (1849) Mrs Craik

Wort, William
Percy his son; both explorers
The Wort Papers (1972) Peter Mathers

Worth, Barbara foundling-to-rich-aris-
tocratic-wife heroine of low-grade
but exceedingly popular American
(1,500,000 copies in twenty-five years)

novel by muscular Christian and former
minister of Church of Disciples of Christ
The Winning of Barbara Worth (1911)
Harold Bell Wright

Worthing, John, MP Ernest; m.
Gwendolin Fairfax*
The Importance of Being Earnest play
(1895) Oscar Wilde

Worthington, Lieutenant cc
The Poor Gentleman play (1802) George
Coleman the Younger

Worthy man about town
The Relapse, or *Virtue in Danger* play
(1697) John Vanbrugh

Wortle, Jeffrey, Revd Dr, DD Rector of
Borwick and proprietor and headmaster
of Borwick School, much esteemed by
others and by himself, cc
his wife
Mary their daughter
Dr Wortle's School (1881) Anthony
Trollope

Wotton, Helen Ostrog's* niece
When the Sleeper Awakes (1899) H. G.
Wells

Wotton, Henry, Lord evil genius to Dorian
Gray*
his wife
Lady Gwendolyn his sister
The Picture of Dorian Gray (1891) Oscar
Wilde

Wracketts, Mr and Mrs socialites
The Pottleton Legacy (1849) Albert
Smith

Wragge, Mrs alias **Bygrave** widow of Dr
Wragge, m. (2) Andrew Vanstone*
'Captain' Wragge her son
Joyce his wife
No Name (1862) Wilkie Collins

Wraxall, Mr
ss 'Count Magnus'
Ghost Stories of an Antiquary (1910)
M. R. James

Wrayburn, Eugene schoolmaster, m.
Lizzie Hexam*
Our Mutual Friend (1865) Charles
Dickens

Wrench, Tom playwright, part-portrait of
author's precursor Thomas W.
Robertson
Trelawny of the Wells play (1898) Arthur
Wing Pinero

Wressley

ss 'Wressley of the Foreign Office'
Plain Tales from the Hills (1888) Rudyard Kipling

Wright, Joey K. The Satyr
The Passing of the Third Floor Back (1910) Jerome K. Jerome

Wright, Walter friend to, and biographer of, Caryl Bramsley*
C (1924) Maurice Baring

Wrigley, Ron homosexual cockney youth
Hemlock and After (1952) Angus Wilson

Wringhim, Robert narrator of second section of psychological masterpiece of the Calvinist mentality
The Private Memoirs and Confessions of a Justified Sinner (1824) James Hogg

Wrydale, Elizabeth
The World in the Evening (1954) Christopher Isherwood

Wulf
Hypatia (1853) Charles Kingsley

Wulf, Anna cc, writer of the four experimental notebooks of which this highly influential work consists
The Golden Notebook (1962) Doris Lessing

Wunsch, Professor music teacher
The Song of the Lark (1915) Willa Cather

Wyant, Dr
The Fruit of the Tree (1907) Edith Wharton

Wyat, Lucy housekeeper to Silas Ruthyn*
Uncle Silas (1864) J. Sheridan Le Fanu

Wybrow, Anthony, Captain nephew and heir to Sir Christopher Cheverel*
ss 'Mr Gilfil's Love Story'
Scenes of Clerical Life (1857) George Eliot (rn Mary Anne, later Marian, Evans)

Wycherley, the Widow
ss 'Dr Heidegger's Experiment'
Twice-Told Tales (1837) Nathaniel Hawthorne

Wychnor, Philip m. Eleanor Ogilvie*, becomes a successful author, like his creator, whose first (and successful) book this was
The Ogilvies (1849) Mrs Craik

Wyke, Muriel m. 'young' Roger Forsyte*
The *Forsyte* series (1906–33) John Galsworthy

Wykeham, Charles undergraduate

Charley's Aunt play (1892) Brandon Thomas

Wylder, Mark inheritor of the Brandon estates, cc, suddenly breaks off engagement to Dorcas Brandon*
William vicar, his brother
William's ugly wife
Wylder's Hand (1864) J. Sheridan Le Fanu

Wylie friend to Cooper*, becomes lover to and perhaps m. Miss Counihan*
Murphy (1938) Samuel Beckett

Wylie, Thomas ('Tam')
The House With the Green Shutters (1901) George Douglas (rn George Douglas Brown)

Wynant, Clyde inventor
Mimi his first wife, m. (2) Christian Jorgensen*
Dorothy cc, their daughter
Gilbert; Alice his brother and sister
The Thin Man (1934) Dashiell Hammett

Wyndham, Maria granddaughter of Mr Fletcher*, m. Christopher Blake*
The Deliverance (1904) Ellen Glasgow

Wyndwood, Eleanor beautiful woman renounced by Matthew Strang*
The Master (1895) Israel Zangwill

Wyngate, Lael (in acting version **Violet**), **Lady** wealthy and charming liberal in love with American explorer; based on Hauptmann's* rejection of Alfred Kerr, the critic who made him famous, because he was a Jew
Rain from Heaven play (1935) S. N. Behrman

Wynn, May Willie Keith's girl
The Caine Mutiny (1951) Herman Wouk

Wynne, Hugh narrator of sensational historical novel by popular American physician
Dorothea *née* Peniston, his eventual wife
Arthur his cousin, rival and enemy
Hugh Wynne, Free Quaker (1897) S. W. Mitchell

Wynne, Samuel Fawthrop proposes to Shirley Keeldar* and is rejected by reason of his profligacy and vulgarity
his father, a magistrate, owner of De Walden Hall
his two 'superlative' sisters
Shirley (1849) Charlotte Brontë

Wynne, Talbot ('Taffy') art student

Trilby (1894) George du Maurier
Wynne, Winifred m. Henry Aylwin*
  Tom her ne'er-do-well organist father
  Aylwin (1899) Theodore Watts-Dunton
Wyvern, Lord
  his wife
  Felix Holt (1866) George Eliot (rn Mary

Anne, later Marian, Evans)
Wyvern, Revd Mr
  Demos (1886) George Gissing
Wyville, Ebenezer customs man
  In the Roar of the Sea (1892) Sabine
  Baring-Gould

X

Xury ship's boy   *Robinson Crusoe* (1719) Daniel Defoe

Y

Y, Professeur imaginary interviewer in novel written to demonstrate its author's *petit truc*, little trick
Entretiens avec le Professeur Y (Interviews With Professor Y) (1955) Louis-Ferdinand Céline (rn Louis-Ferdinand Destouches)
Yacob kindly man, friend to Medina Saroté*
The Country of the Blind (1911) H. G. Wells
Yajnavalkya, Mrs masseuse of Afro-Asian stock
Valmouth (1919) Ronald Firbank
Yakstrot i.e. the Earl of Bute
The History and Adventures of an Atom (1769) Tobias Smollett
Yank cc of drama of ape-like man seeking his human self but killed by real ape in zoo
The Hairy Ape play (1921) Eugene O'Neill
Yank dying sailor on British tramp steamer
Bound East for Cardiff play (1916) Eugene O'Neill
Yardley-Orde
ss 'The Head of the District'
Life's Handicap (1891) Rudyard Kipling

Yarlett, James ('Big James') compositor
Clayhanger (1910) Arnold Bennett
Yasmin
Hassan play (1923) James Elroy Flecker
Yates, Blanche
The Thinking Reed (1936) Rebecca West (rn Cecily Fairfield)
Yates, John, the Hon. not at first much to him beyond expense and fashion, but becomes less trifling when he m. Julia Bartram*
Mansfield Park (1814) Jane Austen
Yatman, Mr
his wife
ss 'The Biter Bit'
The Queen of Hearts (1959) Wilkie Collins
Yeates, Sinclair resident magistrate
Philippa his wife
Some Experiences of an Irish R.M. (1899) O. E. Somerville and Martin Ross (rn Edith Somerville and Violet Martin)
Yeere, Otis
ss 'The Education of Otis Yeere'
Wee Willie Winkie (1888) Rudyard Kipling
Yeld, Mrs wife to the Bishop of Elmham
The Way We Live Now (1875) Anthony

Trollope
Yellowhammer a goldsmith
Maudline his wife
Moll their daughter
A Chaste Maid in Cheapside play (1630)
Thomas Middleton
Yellowless, Henry clerk in lesser orders
The Corner That Held Them (1948)
Sylvia Townsend Warner
Yellowley, Triptolemus factor of the High
Chamberlain, Orkney and Shetland
Jasper his father
The Pirate (1822) Walter Scott
Yeo, Salvation veteren mariner
Westward Ho! (1855) Charles Kingsley
Yeobright, Clym the 'native' of the title,
defeated idealist who abandons the jewel
trade to teach; m. Eustacia Vye*
Mrs Yeobright his dominating mother, in
part based on author's own
Thomasin ('Tamsin') his thoughtful
cousin m. (1) Damon Wildeve*,
(2) Diggory Venn*
The Return of the Native (1878) Thomas
Hardy
Yepanchina, Aglaya aristocratic woman,
cc
her family
Idiot (1869) Fyodor Dostoievsky
Yestreen, Adam, Revd narrator
Farewell, Miss Julie Logan (1932) J. M.
Barrie
Yillah blonde Polynesian symbolizing
Good
Mardi (1849) Herman Melville
Yitzchok, Yankele Ben m. Deborah da
Costa*
The King of Schnorrers (1894) Israel
Zangwill
Yoletta Smith's* dream-woman of the
future
A Crystal Age (1887) W. H. Hudson
Yolland, Mrs friend to Rosanna Spear-
man*
The Moonstone (1868) Wilkie Collins
Yorick dead jester
Hamlet play (1623) William Shakespeare
Yorick, Revd Mr
Tristram Shandy (1767) Laurence Sterne
York, Duke of (later Richard III)
Duchess of York, mother to Edward IV*
King Richard III play (1623) William
Shakespeare

York, Duke of cousin to the King (hist.)
King Henry V play (1623) William
Shakespeare
York, Duke of Edmund de Langlay (hist.)
King Richard II play (1623) William
Shakespeare
York, Rowland fencing master
Westward Ho! (1855) Charles Kingsley
Yorke, Hiram republican
Hesther his wife, large, cynical, portent-
ous, but a good mother; 'ponderously
hysterical' when her children cross her
Jessie picquant and pert, her father's pet;
Mark; Martin; Matthew; Rose their
children
Shirley (1849) Charlotte Brontë
Yorke, Leila see **Potter, Percy**
Yossarian, John, Captain cc
Catch-22 (1961) Joseph Heller
Youdi
Molloy (1951); *Malone meurt* (*Malone
Dies*) (1951) (tr. 1956); *L'Innommable*
(1953) (*The Unnamable*) (tr. 1958) (tri-
logy) Samuel Beckett
Youghal, Courtney young MP
The Unbearable Bassington (1912) Saki
(rn Hector Hugh Munro)
Youghal, Miss m. Strickland*
her parents
ss 'Miss Youghal's Sais'
Plain Tales from the Hills (1888) Rud-
yard Kipling
Young Couple, The Egotistical
Sketches of Young Couples (1840)
Charles Dickens
Young, Bertha
Harry her husband
her baby daughter
ss 'Bliss'
Bliss (1920) Katherine Mansfield (rn
Katherine Mansfield Beauchamp)
Young, Mildred Christian socialist
Antigua Penny Puce (1936) Robert
Graves
Youngdahl, Lee boxer-novelist-teacher
and letter-writer, cc
Wake Up, Stupid (1959) Mark Harris
Younge, Mrs Miss Darcy's* companion
Pride and Prejudice (1813) Jane Austen
Yownie, Thomas of the Gorbals Diehards
Huntingtower (1922) John Buchan
Yram jailer's daughter
Erewhon (1872) Samuel Butler

Yule, Alfred literary hack
Marian his daughter
Amy his niece, m. Edwin Reardon*
New Grub Street (1891) George Gissing
Yule, Telford
Flowering Wilderness (1932) John Galsworthy
Yum-Yum Ko-Ko's* ward, m. Nankipoo*
The Mikado opera (1885) W. S. Gilbert and Arthur Sullivan
Yundt, Karl delegate of the International Red Committee

The Secret Agent (1907) Joseph Conrad (rn Josef Teodor Konrad Korzeniowski)
Yunkum, Sahib
ss 'At Howli Thana'
Soldiers Three (1888) Rudyard Kipling
Yusef blackmailer and usurer
The Heart of the Matter (1948) Graham Greene
Yvonne daughter to Earl Dorn, m. Sir Agravaine
ss 'Sir Agravaine'
The Man Upstairs (1914) P. G. Wodehouse

Z

Zabina see Bajazeth

Zadok rapacious Jew
The Unfortunate Traveller, or *The Life of Jack Wilton* (1594) Thomas Nashe

Zahar servant to Oblomov*, as lazy as his master
Oblomov (1859) Ivan Goncharov

Zaluski, Sigismund cc, young Pole falsely accused of nihilism, atheism and assassination – so that he is falsely arrested and dies in a dungeon; in novel prompted by slanders made on the defiant author
The Autobiography of a Slander (1887) Edna Lyall (rn A. E. Bayly)

Zamor Negro servant of Barry Lyndon*
Barry Lyndon (1844) W. M. Thackeray

Zara, Queen caricature of the Duchess of Marlborough, in Tory scandal-novel peopled by monsters of vice
The Secret History of Queen Zara and the Zarazians (1705) Mrs Delariviere Manley (Also known as Mary Manley)

Zawistowska, Sophie cc, Polish ex-victim of the Nazis
Sophie's Choice (1979) William Styron

Zeenut, Maihl concubine to Mogul King*
On the Face of the Waters (1896) Flora Annie Steel

Zeggi chief of police, Yanrin
Aissa Saved (1932) Joyce Cary

Zeke, Old Brother preacher who becomes Confederate spy
Jubilee (1966) Margaret Walker

Zend ('Moonstruck')
The King of Elfland's Daughter (1924) Lord Dunsany

Zenocrate daughter to the Soldan of Egypt
Tamburlaine play (1590) Christopher Marlowe

Zephyrine, Mme
ss 'The Suicide Club'
The New Arabian Nights (1882) Robert Louis Stevenson

Zerkowe dealer in junk, m. Maria Macapa
McTeague (1899) Frank Norris

Ziba Egyptian slave
Death's Jest Book, or *The Fool's Tragedy* play (1850) Thomas Lovell Beddoes

Zigler, Naughton O. inventor
Tommy his wife
ss 'The Captive'
Traffics and Discoveries† (1904) Rudyard Kipling

Zillah servant to Heathcliff*
Wuthering Heights (1847) Emily Brontë

Ziller, John
Amanda his wife; owners of hot dog stand
Another Roadside Attraction (1971) Tom Robbins

Zimmerman headmaster
The Centaur (1963) John Updike

Zimmern, Roger cc
Imaginary Friends (1967) Alison Lurie

Zinida lion-tamer, in love with Bazano*, and mistress to Briquet*
Tot, kto poluchaet poshchochiny (*He Who Gets Slapped*; once tr. as *The Painted Laugh*) play (1916) Leonid Andreyev

Zirconderel witch
The King of Elfland's Daughter (1924) Lord Dunsany

Zorah professional bridesmaid
Ruddigore opera (1887) W. S. Gilbert and Arthur Sullivan

Zosima, Father holy father
Bratya Karamazov (*Brothers Karamazov*) (1880) Fyodor Dostoievsky

Zoyland, Will bastard to Lord P.
Nell his wife
Lady Rachel daughter to Lord P.
A Glastonbury Romance (1932) John Cowper Powys

Zubiaga, Lopez dictator
Don José his son
Odtaa (1926) John Masefield

Zuckerman, Nathan narrator, author
My Life as a Man† (1976) Philip Roth

Zuleika, Mrs

ss 'The Brushwood Boy'
The Day's Work (1898) Rudyard Kipling
Zurvan son to the Emir
The Shaving of Shagpat (1856) George
Meredith

Zuyland journalist
ss 'A Matter of Fact'
Many Inventions (1893) Rudyard Kipling

GLOSSARY OF AUTHORS AND TITLES

Anon.
Aucassin and Nicolette: Aucassin;
Nicolette
Beowulf: Aeschere; Grendel; Hondiscio;
Hrothgar; Scyld; Unferth; Wiglaf
Chuang Tzu: Chuang Tzu
Crockett Almanacs, The: Fink
Lady Pokingham, or They All Do It: Crim-
Con; Pokingham
*Lamentable and Terrible Tragedy of Arden
of Feversham in Kent, The*: Black Will;
Mosby; Shakebag

Abbot, Jacob
Rollo Books, The: Rollo

Achebe, Chinua
No Longer At Ease: Obi
Things Fall Apart: Okonkwo

Adams, Henry
Democracy: Lee

Addison, Joseph
Spectator essays: De Coverley;
Honeycombe

Ade, George
Artie: Artie
Fables in Slang: Louella

Aeschylus
The Orestia: Aegisthus; Agamemnon;
Athena; Clytemnestra; Orestes

Agee, James
Death in the Family, A: Follet

Aidé, Charles
Rita: Dacre; D'Ofort; Greybrook; Rita;
Rowdon

Aiken, Conrad
Blue Voyage: Cynthia; Demarest; Jello
King Coffin: Ammen; Jones

Ainsworth, William Harrison
Rookwood: Rookwood

Alas, Leopoldo
La Regenta: Guimaràn; Mesià; Ozores;
Quintanar

Albee, Edward
Death of Bessie Smith, The: Smith
Who's Afraid of Virginia Woolf?: George;
Nick

Alcott, Louisa M.
Jo's Boys: Bangs; Bhaer; Blake; Brooke;
Kean
Little Men: Bangs; Bhaer; Blake; Brooke;
Harding; Kean; West
Little Women: Brooke; Laurence; March;
Moffat

Aldington, Richard
Death of a Hero: Bobbe; Burnside;
Conington; Shobbes; Slush; Tubbe;
Upjohn; Welford; Winterbourne

Aldiss, Brian W.
Barefoot in the Head: Banjo; Boreas;
Brastier; Charteris
Saliva Tree, The: Aurigans; Grendon;
Neckland; Rolles

Aldrich, Thomas Bailey
Story of a Bad Boy, The: Bailey

Aleman, Mateo
Guzman de Alfarache: Guzman

Alexander, Mrs Hector
Wooing O't, The: Berry; Grey; Torchester;
Trafford

Algren, Nelson
Man With the Golden Arm, The: Machine

Allen, Grant
Hilda Wade, Hospital Nurse: Wade
Woman Who Did, The: Barton; Kynaston;
Merrick

Allen, Hervey
Anthony Adverse: Adverse

Allen, James Lane
Kentucky Cardinal, A: Kentucky Cardinal;
Moss

Allen, Walter
All in a Lifetime: Ashted
Rogue Elephant: Ashley

Allingham, Margery
Look to the Lady: Campion

Aluko, Timothy Mofolorunso
Chief The Honourable Minister: Moses

Amis, Kingsley
I Like It Here: Bowen; Hyman; Strether
Lucky Jim: Beesley; Dixon; Goldsmith;
Michie; Peel; Welch
That Uncertain Feeling: Davies; Lewis;
Probert

Amory, Thomas
*Life and Opinions of John Buncle, Esq.,
The*: Buncle

Anderson, Maxwell
Winterset: Esdras; Estralla; Gaunt;
Romagna

Anderson, Sherwood
Dark Laughter: Grey; Martin; Stockton
Horses and Men: Appleton; Bardshare;
Burt; Dudley; Edwards; French;
Kreymborg; Mathers; Means; Smith;
Wessen; Whitehead; Wilson; Woodbury

Anderson, Sherwood—*contd.*
  Poor White: Butterworth; Hunter; McVey;
    Shepard; Wainsworth
  Winesburg, Ohio: Hartman; Hindman;
    Parcival; Swift; White
Andreyev, Leonid
  Anathema: Leizer
  *Tot, kto poluchaet poshchochiny (He Who
    Gets Slapped)*: Bazano; Briquet;
    Consuelo; He Who Gets Slapped;
    Mancini; Regnard; Zinida
Ansky, S.
  Der Dibuk (The Dybbuk): Azrielke;
    Khonnon; Sender
Anstey, F.
  Brass Bottle, The: Fakrash-el-Aamash;
    Rapkin; Ventimore; Wackerbath; Vice
    Versa: Biddlecombe; Blinkhorn; Boaler;
    Bultitude; Chawner; Coggs; Grimston;
    Jolland; Kiffin; Paradine; Stohwaeser;
    Tinkler
Archer, William
  Green Goddess, The: Crespin; Rukh
Archer-Clive, Mrs Caroline
  Paul Ferroll: Ferroll
Arlen, Michael
  Green Hat, The: Fenwick
  These Charming People: Carr
Arnow, Harriette
  Dollmaker, The: Gertie
Ashford, Daisy
  Young Visiters, The: Clark; Clincham;
    Monticue; Procurio; Salteena
Askew, Claude
  with J.de C., Mrs Alice
  Shulamite, The: Krillet; Van Kerrell;
    Waring
Atherton, Gertrude
  Black Oxen: Clavering; Hohenhauer
Austen, Jane
  Emma: Abdy; Bates; Bickerton; Campbell;
    Churchill; Cole; Dixon; Fairfax;
    Goddard; Hawkins; Knightley; Martin;
    Perry; Smith; Taylor; Weston; Weston;
    Woodhouse
  Lady Susan: De Courcy; Johnson;
    Mainwarings; Martin; Vernon
  Mansfield Park: Anderson; Aylmer;
    Baddeley; Bertram; Campbell; Crawford;
    Fraser; Grant; Groom; Harding;
    Harrison; Lee; Maddison; Norris; Price;
    Ravenshaw; Rebecca; Repton;
    Rushworth; Stornaway; Whitaker;
    Yates
  Northanger Abbey: Allen; Andrews;
    Dorothy; Freeman; Morland; Thorpe;
    Tilney
  Persuasion: Alicia; Baldwin; Benwick;
    Brand; Carteret; Clay; Croft; Dalrymple;
    Elliot; Harville; Hayter; MacLean;

    Musgrove; Rooke; Russell; Shepherd;
    Shirley; Smith; Smith; Wallis; Wentworth
  Pride and Prejudice: Annesley; Bennet;
    Bingley; Bourgh; Collins; Darcy;
    Fitzwilliam; Gardiner; Haggerston;
    Hurst; King; Long; Lucas; Phillips; Pope;
    Wickham; Younge
  Sense and Sensibility: Brandon; Dashwood;
    Donovan; Ferrars; Gilberts; Grey;
    Jennings; Middleton; Palmer; Pratt;
    Smith; Steele; Thomas; Williams;
    Willoughby

Bage, Robert
  Hermsprong, or Man as He is Not:
    Hermsprong
Bagnold, Enid
  Chalk Garden, The: Madrigal; Maitland;
    Pinkbell; St Maugham
  National Velvet: Brown; Cellini; Ede;
    Schreiber; Simkin; Tasky; Taylor;
    Tunmarsh; Vile
Bailey, Paul
  At the Jerusalem: Gadny
  Peter Smart's Confessions: Smart
Baker, James Nelson
  Superstition: Fitzroy
Balchin, Nigel
  Small Back Room, The: Brine; Knollys;
    Mair; Rose; Rice; Susan; Taylor; Waring
Baldwin, James
  Another Country: Ellis; Jones; Moore;
    Scott; Silenski
  Go Tell it on the Mountain: Grimes
  Tell Me How Long the Train's Been Gone:
    Hall; King; Nash Overstreet;
    Proudhammer
Baldwin, Joseph G.
  Flush Times of Alabama and Mississippi:
    Bolus; Suggs
Ballantyne, R.M.
  Coral Island: Gay; Martin; Rover
  Martin Rattler: Fagoni; Grumbit
Ballard, J.G.
  Empire of the Sun: Jim
Balzac, Honoré de
  Illusions perdues (Lost Illusions): Chardon
  La Cousine Bette: Bianchon; Crevel;
    Fischer; Hulot; Josepha; Marneffe;
    Steinbeck
  Le Cousin Pons: Pons
  *Le Médecin de Campagne (The Country
    Doctor)*: Genestas; Goguelat
  Modeste Mignon: Mignon
  Le Peau de Chagrin: Rastignac
  Père Goriot: Goriot; Nucingen; Restaud;
    Vautrin
Banks, Mrs G. Linnaeus
  Manchester Man, The: Aspinall; Aston;
    Chadwick; Clegg

Baring, Maurice
  C: Bramsley; FitzClare; Hengrave;
  Heseltine; Holden; Lord; Maartens;
  Malone; Pringle; Roden; Rooter; Weigall;
  Wright
Baring-Gould, Sabine
  In the Roar of the Sea: Coppinger;
  Menaida; Mules; Scantlebury; Trevisa;
  Wyville
  Kitty Alone: A Story of Three Fires: Alone;
  Peperill
  Mehalah: A Story of the Salt Marshes:
  Dewitt; Dowsing; Mehalah; Musse;
  Pettican; Rabbit; Rebow; Sharland; Spark
  Noemi: Del'Peyra; Guillem
Barker, Harley Granville
  Madras House, The: Huxtable; Kent;
  Madras
  Waste: Cantelupe; Davenport; Farrant;
  Horsham; Trebell; Wedgecroft
Barker, James Nelson
  Indian Princes, The, or *La Belle Sauvage*:
  Pocahantas; Rolfe
Barnes, Djuna
  Ladies' Almanack, The: Clitoressa; Musset
  Nightwood: Flood; Guido; Petherbridge;
  Volkbein; Vote
Barnie, Natalie
  Cinq Petits Dialogues Grec: Sappho
  One Who is Legion, The: A.D.
Barrie, J.M.
  Admirable Crichton, The: Brocklehurst;
  Crichton; Fleury; Jeanne; Loam;
  Rolleston; Simmons; Thomas; Tompsett;
  Treherne; Tweeny; Wooley
  Dear Brutus: Dearth
  Farewell, Miss Julie Logan: Routh;
  Yestreen
  Little Minister, The: Babbie;
  Cruickshanks; Davidson; Dishart; Dow;
  Halliwell; Hobart; Jean; Mealmaker;
  Rintoul; Tosh; Webster; Whamond
  Mary Rose: Cameron
  My Lady Nicotine: Gilray; Moggridge;
  Pettigrew; Scrymgeour
  Peter Pan: Cecco; Cookson; Darling;
  Hook; Jukes; Liza; Mullins; Nana; Nibs;
  Noodler; Panther; Peter Pan; Skylights;
  Slightly; Smee; Tiger Lily; Tinker Bell;
  Tootles; Twin I and Twin II
  Professor's Love Story, The: Goodwillie
  Sentimental Tommy: Cathro; Cray; Grizel;
  McLean; Myles; Sandys; Shovel
  Shall We Join the Ladies?: Castro
  When a Man's Single: Abinger; Angus;
  Dowton; Kirker; Licquorish; Meredith;
  Rowbotham; Simms
  Window in Thrums, A: Duthie; Fletcher;
  Lownie; McQumpha; Mealmaker;
  Ogilvy

Barry, Philip
  White Wings: Inch
Barth, John
  Giles Goat-Boy: Giles; Spielman
  WESAC: Giles
Beaumont, Francis
  with John Fletcher
  Bonduca: Bonduca; Caratach; Hengo;
  Judas; Junius; Nennius; Penius;
  Suetonius
  King and No King, A: Arane; Arbaces;
  Bacurius; Bessus; Gobrias; Lygones;
  Mandane; Mardonius; Panthea;
  Spaconia; Tigranes
  Knight of the Burning Pestle, The:
  Hammerton; Humphrey; Greengoose;
  Merrythought; Pomponia; Ralph;
  Venturewell
  Maid's Tragedy, The: Amintor; Antiphila;
  Calianax; Cleon; Diogaras; Diphilus;
  Dula; Evadne; Lysippus; Melantius;
  Olympias; Strato
  Philaster: Arethusa; Claremont; Dion;
  Euphrasia; Galatea; Megea; Pharamond;
  Thrasiline
  Scornful Lady, The: Abigail
Beckett, Samuel
  Echo's Bones and Other Precipitates:
  Alba
  Endgame: Clov; Hamm
  Krapp's Last Tape: Krapp
  L'Innommable; Malone Meurt; and
  Molloy: Basil; Lemuel; Lousse; Malone;
  Moran; Molloy; Saposcat; Unnamable;
  Worm; Youdi
  More Pricks That Kicks: Alba; Beckett;
  Bloggs; Draffin; Frica; Lucy; Shuah;
  Tough
  Murphy: Celia; Cooper; Counihan;
  Murphy; Neary; Ticklepenny; Wylie
  'Sedendo et Quiescendo' ('Transition'):
  Smeraldina-Rima
  Waiting for Godot: Lucky; Pozzo; Vladimir
  Watt: Arsene; Erskine; Galls; Gorman;
  Graves; Hackett; Knott; McCann;
  Nixon; Sam; Spiro; Watt
Beckford, William
  Vathek: Abou Taher Achmed; Alasi;
  Barkiarokh; Firanz; Rondabale; Shaban;
  Vathek
Beddoes, Thomas Lovell
  Bride's Tragedy, The: Floribel; Hesperus
  Death's Jest Book, or *The Fool's Tragedy*:
  Adalmar; Amala; Athulf; Isbrand; Joan;
  Mandrake; Mario; Melveric; Sibylla;
  Siegfried; Thorwold; Wolfram; Ziba
  Torrismond: Torrismond
Bede, Cuthbert
  Adventures of Mr Verdant Green, The:
  Bouncer; Delaval; Filcher; Green;

Lionel and Clarissa: Harman; Jenkins;
Jenny; Lionel; Oldboy
Bierce, Ambrose
Can Such Things Be?: Ransome
In the Midst of Life: Brayton; Farquhar;
Searing
Biggers, Earl Derr
House Without a Key, The: Chan
Bingham, John
My Name is Michael Sibley: Sibley
Bird, Robert Montgomery
Gladiator, The: Spartacus
Hawks of Hawk Hollow, The: Falconer
Nick of the Woods, or The Jibbenainosay:
Forrester
Blackmore, R.D.
Alice Lorraine: Chapman; Lorraine;
Lovejoy
Cripps the Carrier: A Woodland Tale:
Cripps; Oglander; Sharp
Lorna Doone: Doone; Faggus; Fry;
Harding; Huckaback; Whichehalse
Perlycross: Crang; Fox; Penniloe; Ridd;
Snowe; Spank; Stickles; Waldron
Blake, William
Island in the Moon, An: Inflammable; Sisop
the Pythagorean
Blechman, Burt
How Much?: Halpern; Stern
Maybe: Russell
Bodkin, M. McDonnell
Paul Beck, the Rule of Thumb Detective:
Beck
Boldrewood, Rolf
*Robbery Under Arms: A Story of Life and
Adventure in the Bush and in the
Goldfields of Australia*: Barnes; Billy the
Boy; Burke; Daly; Falkland; Goring;
Knightley; Marston; McIntyre; Moreton;
Morringer; Morrison; Starlight;
Stillbrook; Storefield; Warrigal; Whitman
Boothby, Guy
Dr Nikola: Downing; Edgehill
Borchert, Wolfgang
Draussen vor der Tür (The Man Outside):
Beckmann
Borrow, George
Lavengro: Berners; Herne; Lavengro;
Petulengro; Tinman; Williams
Romany Rye: Dale; Lavengro; Murtagh
Boucicault, Dion
The Octoroon: Aurore; Gayarre;
Rutherford
Bourjaily, Vance
Confessions of a Spent Youth: Quincy
End of My Life, The: Galt
Bowen, Elizabeth
Death of the Heart, The: Brutt; Eddie;
Heccomb; Matchett; Miller; Quayne
Eva Trout: Arble; Dancey; Elsinore;

Ormeau; Smith; Trout
Friends and Relations: Gibson; Meggatt;
Studdart; Thirdman; Tilney
Heat of the Day, The: Harrison; Kelway;
Rodney
House in Paris, The: Arbuthnot; Bent;
Ebhart; Fisher; Michaelis; Moody;
Mountjoy
Last September, The: Farquar; Lesworth;
Naylor; Norton; Thomson
Little Girls, The: Beaker; Burkin; Coral;
Delacroix; Francis; Wilkins
Bowles, Jane
Two Serious Ladies: Copperfield; Goering
Bowles, Paul
Sheltering Sky, The: Moresby
Boyd, James
Drums: Fraser
Boyd, Martin
Lemon Farm, The: Kaye
Boyer, Abel (ed.)
Letters of Wit, Politicks and Morality...:
Ayloffe
Boyesen, Hljalmar Hjorth
Gunnar: A Tale of Norse Life: Thorsen
Brackenbridge, Hugh Henry
Modern Chivalry: Farrago; O'Regan
Bradbury, Malcolm
History Man, The: Kirk
Stepping Westward: Walker
Braddon, Mary Elizabeth
Aurora Floyd: Bulstrode; Conyers; Floyd;
Hargraves; Mellish
Lady Audley's Secret: Audley; Mosgrove;
Talboys
Bragg, Melvyn
Hired Man, The: Tallentire
Josh Lawson: Lawson
Place in England, A: Tallentire
Silken Net, The: Lewis
Without a City Wall: Godwin
Braine, John
Room at the Top: Aisgill; Brown;
Lampton; Lufford; Storr; Thompson;
Wales
Braithwaite, Errol
Evil Day, The; Flying Fish, The and
Needle's Eye, The: Williams
Bramah, Ernest
Max Carrados: Carlyle; Carrados
Wallet of Kai Lung, The: Chan Hung;
Chang-Ch'un; Kai Lung; Ling; Lin Yi;
Ping Siang; Sen Heng; Wang Yu
Brighouse, Harold
Hobson's Choice: Hobson
Brontë, Anne
Agnes Grey: Ashby; Bloomfield; Hatfield;
Grey; Murray; Robson; Weston
Tenant of Wildfell Hall, The: Graham;
Halford; Hargrave; Hattersley;

Brontë, Anne—*contd.*
  Huntingdon; Lowborough; Markham;
  Maxwell; Millward; Wilmot; Wilson
Brontë, Charlotte
  Jane Eyre: Bates; Briggs; Brocklehurst;
  Burns; Carter; Clara; Eshton; Eyre;
  Fairfax; Giacinta; Gryce; Hanna; Ingram;
  Lee; Lloyd; Mason; Miller; Oliver; Poole;
  Reed; Rivers; Rochester; Scatcherd;
  Temple; Varens; Vining
  Professor, The: Blemont; Brown;
  Crimsworth; Dronsart; Henri; Hunsden;
  Jacobs; Kint; Mullenberg; Pelet; Pidge;
  Reuter; Seacombe; Steighton; Trista;
  Vandam; Vandenhuten; Wharton
  Shirley: Ainsley; Armitage; Barraclough;
  Booth; Boultby; Broadbent; Cave; Donne;
  Farran; Gerard; Gill; Hall; Hardman;
  Hartley; Helstone; Hogg; Horsefall;
  Keeldar; Malone; Mann; Moore; Pearson;
  Pryor; Scott; Sweeting; Sykes; Sympson;
  Wynne; Yorke
  Villette: Agnes; Aigredpoux;
  Bassompierre; Beck; Boissec; Braun;
  Bretton; Broc; Candace; Cholmondely;
  Davies; De Hamal; Digby; Dolores;
  Emanuel; Fanshawe; Goton; Home; Kint;
  Leigh; Marchmont; Matou; Panache;
  Rochemort; Silas; Snowe; Sweeney;
  Sylvie; Turner; Vashtie; Walravens
Brontë, Emily
  Wuthering Heights: Dean; Earnshaw;
  Heathcliff; Joseph; Linton; Lockwood;
  Zillah
Brooke, Mrs Frances
  History of Emily Montague, The:
  Montague
Brooke, Henry
  Fool of Quality, The, or *The History of
  Henry Earl of Moreland*: Clinton;
  Fenton; Harry
Broughton, Rhoda
  Belinda: Churchill; Forth; Rivers
  Cometh Up as a Flower: Le Strange
Brown, Charles Brockden
  Arthur Mervyn, or *Memoirs of the Year
  1793*: Fielding; Mervyn; Stevens; Welbeck
  Edgar Huntly, or *Memoirs of a
  Sleepwalker*: Edny; Huntly
  Ormond, or *The Secret Witness*: Cleves;
  Craig; Dudley; Ormond; Sarsefield;
  Westwyn
  Wieland, or *The Transformation: An
  American Tale*: Carwin; Wieland
Brown, John
  Rab and His Friends: Noble; Rab
Brown, William Hill
  Power of Sympathy, The: Harrington
Browning, Elizabeth Barrett
  Poems: Pan

Browning, Robert
  Pippa Passes: Pippa
Brownson, Orestes
  Charles Elwood, or *The Infidel Converted*:
  Elwood
Buchan, John
  Huntingtower: Abreskov; Dougal;
  Heritage; Kennedy; Leon; Loudon;
  McCunn; McGuffog; Mackintosh;
  Morran; Nicolaivitch; Roylance; Saskia;
  Spidel; Yownie
  Prester John: Aitken; Arcoll; Colles;
  Crawfurd; Dyke; Henriques; Japp;
  Laputa; Leslie; Wardlaw
  Power House, The: Doloreine; Leithen;
  Lumley; Macgillvray; Pavia; Pitt-Heron;
  Routh
  Thirty-nine Steps, The: Alloa;
  Ammersfoot; Bullivant; Ducrosne;
  Hannay; Jopley; Karolides; Macgillvray;
  Paddock; Scaife; Turnbull; Whittaker
Buchanan, Robert
  God and the Man: Christianson;
  Orchardson; Sefton
Buck, Pearl
  Good Earth, The; *House Divided, A*; and
  Sons: Lotus; Lung
Buckingham, George, Duke of
  Rehearsal, The: Prettyman
Buckler, Ernest
  Mountain and the Valley: Cannan
Bukowski, Charles
  Ham on Rye: Chinaski
Bullins, Ed
  In New England Winter: Dawson
Bunyan, John
  Life and Death of Mr Badman, The:
  Attentive; Badman; Cox; Mately; Tod;
  Wiseman
  Pilgrim's Progress, The: Appolyon;
  Atheist; Brisk; Bubble; Christian; Demas;
  Despair; Faithful; Feeble-mind;
  Formalist; Gaius; Goodwill; Greatheart;
  Help; Honest; Hopeful; Ignorance;
  Interpreter; Legality; Mercy; Mistrust;
  Obstinate; Pickthank; Piety; Pliable;
  Presumption; Prudence; Sagacity; Secret;
  Shame; Simple; Skill; Sloth; Superstition;
  Talkative; Timorous; Valiant-for-Truth;
  Watchful; Worldly-Wiseman
Burgess, Anthony
  Beds in the East: Crabbe
  Clockwork Orange, A: Alex
  Earthly Powers: Toomey
  Enemy in the Blanket, The: Crabbe
  Inside Mr Enderby: Enderby
  M.F.: Aderyn; Emmett; Faber; Legeru
  Nothing Like the Sun: Shake
  Time for a Tiger: Crabbe
  Vision of Battlements, A: Ennis

Burgess, Gelett
  Lark, The: Goops
Burke, Kenneth
  Towards a Better Life: Neal
Burnett, Frances Hodgson
  Fair Barbarian, A: Theobald
  Little Lord Fauntleroy: Dick; Dorincourt;
  Errol; Haverhsam; Hobbs; Mellon;
  Mordaunt
  Shuttle, The: Anstruther; Dunstan;
  Vanderpool
Burnett, W.R.
  Little Caesar: Bandello
Burney, Fanny
  Cecilia, or Memoirs of an Heiress: Aresby;
  Arnott; Beverley; Briggs; De Ferrars;
  Delville; Floyer; Harrel; Larolles;
  Monckton; Pemberton
  *Evelina, or The History of a Young Lady's
  Entrance Into the World*: Anville;
  Belmont; Du Bois; Evelina; Mirvan;
  Orville
  Wanderer, The: Granville; Villars;
  Willoughby
Burns, Robert
  Poems: Hornbrook
Burroughs, Edgar Rice
  Tarzan series: Greystoke
Butler, Samuel
  Erewhon: Arowhena; Chowbok; Higgs;
  Mahaina; Nosnibor; Yram
  Erewhon Revisited: Higgs; Panky
  Way of All Flesh, The: Allaby; Ellen;
  Hawke; John; Jupp; Martin; Overton;
  Pontifex; Pryer; Skinner; Towneley
Byatt, A.S.
  Game, The: Eskelund; Moffitt
Byron, Lord George Gordon
  Don Juan: Don Juan

Cabell, James Branch
  Gallantry: Manuel
  Jurgen: Jurgen
Cable, George Washington
  Grandissimes, The: A Story of Creole Life:
  Coupé; De Grapions; Frowenfeld;
  Fusilier; Grandissimes; Innerarity; Keene;
  Palmyre
  Dr Sevier: Richling; Sevier
  Madame Delphine: Caraze; Lafitte;
  Lemaitre
  Old Creole Days: De Charleu;
  D'Hemecourt; Kopping; Lemaitre-
  vignevielle; Mazaro; Shaughnessy;
  Thompson; 'Tite Poulette; Varrilat
Cahan, Abraham
  Rise of David Levinsky, The: Levinsky
Cain, James M.
  Love's Lovely Counterfeit: Caspar;

Gauss; Grace; Lyons
  Postman Always Rings Twice, The: Allen;
  Chambers; Katz; Papadakis; Sackett
Calder-Marshall, Arthur
  Man Reprieved, A: Akens
  Pie In the Sky: Morris
Caldwell, Erskine
  God's Little Acre: Dawson; Swint;
  Thompson; Walden
  Lamp for Nightfall, A: Emerson; Gervais;
  Robinson; Stokes; Western; White
  Tobacco Road: Bensey; Lester; Rice
Calisher, Hortense
  Collected Stories: Elkin
Callaghan, Morley
  Loved and the Lost, The: Sanderson
  Many Coloured Coat, The: Lane
  Such is My Beloved: Dowling
Canetti, Elias
  Die Blendung: Kien
Cannan, Gilbert
  Mendel: Oliver
  Pugs and Peacocks: Stokes
Canning, George
  Loves of the Triangles, The: Higgins
Capek, Karel
  Krakatit: Carson; Prokop; Thomas
Capote, Truman
  Breakfast at Tiffany's: Berman; Golightly;
  Tomato; Trawler
  Other Voices, Other Rooms: Fever; Knox;
  Sansom; Thompkins
Carey, Henry
  Chrononhotthologos:
  Alddiborontiphoscophornio
Carleton, William
  Fardarougha the Miser: Fardarougha;
  Flanagan; O'Donovan
  Traits and Stories of the Irish Peasantry:
  Kavanagh
Carlyle, Thomas
  Sartor Resartus: Blumine
Carr, John Dickson
  Hag's Nook: Fell
Carroll, Lewis
  Alice in Wonderland: Alice; Dormouse;
  Duchess; Gryphon; Haigha; Hatta;
  Hearts; March Hare; Mock Turtle; Pig-
  Baby; Rabbit
  *Through the Looking-Glass and What
  Alice Found There*: Alice; Humpty-
  Dumpty; Jabberwock; Red Knight; Red
  Queen; Tweedledee; Tweedledum;
  White King Queen and Knave
Cary, Joyce
  Aissa Saved: Aissa; Bradgate; Carr; Gajere;
  Jacob; Ojo; Owule; Zeggi
  Herself Surprised: Bamforth; Hipper
  Horse's Mouth, The: Alabaster; Barbon;
  Beeder; Coker; Hickson; Jimson;

Cary, Joyce—contd.
  Monday; Ollier; Plant; Ranken
  House of Children, A: Freeman
  Prisoner of Grace: Bond; Bootham; Goold;
    Latter; Nimmo
  To Be a Pilgrim: Brown; Eeles; Wilcher
Caspary, Vera
  Laura: Hunt; Lydecker
Castle, Agnes and Egerton
  Bath Comedy, A: Standish; Verney
  Incomparable Bellairs: Mandeville; Peace;
    Spicer; Stafford
Cather, Willa
  Death Comes for the Archbishop: Allande;
    Benito; Carson; Durango; Eusabio;
    Ferrand; Jacinto; Latour; Lucero; Lujon;
    Martinez; Montroya; Olivares; O'Reilly;
    Scales; Vaillant
  Lost Lady, A: Ellinger; Herbert; Peters;
    Pommeroy
  My Antonia: Burden; Cutter; Cuzac;
    Donovan; Lingard; Marpole; Shimerda;
    Soderball
  My Mortal Enemy: Birdseye; Casey;
    Driscoll; Fay; Gray; Mokjeska; Sinclair
  O Pioneers!: Crazy Ivar; Lindstrum;
    Shabata; Tovesky
  Professor's House, The: Augusta;
    MacGregor; Marsellus; Outland; St Peter
  Sapphira and the Slave-girl: Colbert;
    Sapphira
  Shadows on the Rock: Auclaire; Charron;
    De Frontenac; DeLaval; De St Vallier;
    Gaux; Pommiere
  Song of the Lark, The: Archie; Harsanyi;
    Kronberg; Ottenburg; Wunsch
Catherwood, Mary
  Queen Bee, The: McKinley
Cela, Camilo Jose
  La Comena (The Hive): Marco
  La familia de Pascual Duarte: Duarte
Céline, Louis-Ferdinand
  D'un Chateau l'autre (Castle to Castle):
    Abetz; Bichelonne; Céline; Chateaubriant;
    Destouches; Frucht; Laval; Le Vigan;
    Niçois; Papillon; Pétain
  Entretiens avec le professeur Y (Interviews
    with Professor Y): Y
  Féerie pour un autre fois (Fairy Play for
    Another Time): Bébert; Destouches;
    Jules; Prout Prout; Tartar
  Guignol's band: Borokrom; Cascade;
    Claben; Clodovitz; de Rodiencourt;
    Matthew; Milles-Pattes; Virginia
  Mort à credit (Death on the Instalment
    Plan): Antoine; Bérenge; Des Pereires;
    Gorloge; Gwendoline; Krogold;
    Merrywin; Poitrat
  Nord (North): Harrass; Kretzer
  Rigadon (Rigadoon): Vandremer

La vie et l'oeuvre de Philippe Ignace
  Semmelweis (The Life and Works of
  Philippe Ignace Semmelweis):
  Semmelweis
Voyage au bout de la nuit (Journey to the
  End of Night): Balthazar; Bardamu;
  Henrouille; Madelon; Robinson
Centlivre, Susannah
  Bold Stroke for a Wife, A: Fainall;
    Holdfast; Lovely; Prim; Pure
  Busie Body, The: Marplot
  Wonder, The: A Woman Keeps a Secret:
    Breton; Clara; Felix; Gibby
Cervantes, Miguel de
  Don Quixote: Altisidora; Engeli; Panza;
    Quijano; Quixote; Rocinante;
Chandler, Raymond
  Big Sleep, The: Marlowe
Channing, William Ellery
  John Brown and Heroes of Harper's Ferry:
    Brown
Chapman, George
  All Fools: Gostanzo; Gratiana; Kyte; Pock
    with Ben Jonson and John Marston
  Eastward Ho!: Quicksilver; Touchstone
Charteris, Leslie
  Meet the Tiger: Templar
Chaucer, Daniel
  New Humpty-Dumpty, The: Kintyre;
    Macdonald; Pett
  Simple Life Limited, The: Bransdon; Gubb;
    Lee; Luscombe; Parmont; Stobhall
Cheever, John
  Falconer: Farragut; Jody
  Wapshot Scandal, The: Cranmer; Johnson;
    Wapshot
Chesnutt, Charles Waddell
  Conjure Woman, The: McAdoo
Chesterton, G.K.
  Innocence of Father Brown, The: Bohun;
    Brown; Flambeau; Kalon; Olivier;
    Saradine; St Clare; Smythe; Valentin
  Manalive: Gould; Hunt; Inglewood;
    Moon; Pyn; Smith; Warner
  Man Who Was Thursday, The: Bull;
    Button; De Worms; Gogol; Gregory;
    Renard; St Eustache; Sunday; Syme;
    Ward; Wilks
  Napoleon of Notting Hill, The: Barker;
    Buck; Fuego; Lambert; Quin; Wayne;
    Wilson
  Wisdom of Father Brown, The: Cowdray;
    Cray; Exmoor; Hirsch; Muscari;
    Pendragon; Rome; Seymour; Todd
Child, Lydia Maria
  Hobomok: A Tale of Early Times:
    Hobomok
Childers, Erskine
  Riddle of the Sands, The: Bartels;
    Carruthers; Davies; Von Brunning

Cholmondeley, Mary
  Danvers Jewels, The: Carr; Danvers;
    Middleton
  Red Pottage: Gresley; Newhaven; Scarlett;
    West
Chopin, Kate
  Awakening, The: Lebrun; Pontellier;
    Ratignolle
  Bayou Folk: Santien
Christie, Agatha
  Murder at the Vicarage: Marple
  Poirot Investigates: Poirot
Churchill, Winston
  Richard Carvel: Allen
Cibber, Colly
  Careless Husband, The: Easy
  Double Gallant, The: Dainty
  Love's Last Shift: Fashions
  Provok'd Husband, The: see Vanbrugh,
    John
Clark, Eleanor
  Baldur's Gate: Blake; Hines; Pryden
  Bitter Box, The: Temple
Clark, Walter Van Tilburg
  Ox-Bow Incident, The: Canby; Carter;
    Croft; Mapen; Martin; Tetley
Clarke, Austin
  Prime Minister, The: Moore
Clarke, Marcus
  His Natural Life: Bellasis; Blunt; Dawes;
    Frere; Gabbett; Meekin; Mogford;
    North; Pine; Purfoy; Quaid; Rex; Vickers;
    Wade
Claudel, Paul
  *L'Annonce faite à Marie (The Tidings
    Brought to Mary)*: Craon; Hury;
    Vercors
Clavers, Mary
  New Home, A: Clavers
Cleland, John
  Fanny Hill: Hill
Clifford, Lucy
  Mrs Keith's Crime: Keith
Clough, Arthur Hugh
  Amours du Voyage: Claude
Cobb, Irvin S.
  Old Judge Priest: Priest
Cockton, Henry
  *George St George Julian, The Prince of
    Swindlers*: St George Julian
  Valentine Vox, The Ventriloquist:
    Goodman; Holdem; Vox
Cohen, Matt
  Korsoniloff: Korsoniloff
Cokayne, Aston
  Obstinate Lady, The: Polidacre
Cole, Barry
  Run Across the Island, A: Haydon
Coleridge, Mary
  Christabel: Christabel

King With Two Faces, The: A; B; C; D;
    Fersen; Gustav III; Ribbing; Tala
Collins, Norman
  London Belongs to Me: Boon
Collins, Wilkie
  Antonina: Alaric the Goth; Antonina;
    Hermanric; Honorius; Ulpius
  Armadale: Armadale; Gwilt; Midwinter
  Basil: Basil; Bernard; Mannion; Penhale;
    Sherwin
  Blind Love: Henley; Mountjoy; Norland
  Dead Secret, The: Frankland; Leeson;
    Treverton
  Hide and Seek: Peckover
  Legacy of Cain, The: Chance; Dunboyne;
    Gracedieu; Jillgall; Stavely; Tenbruggen
  Man and Wife: Brinkworth; Delamayn;
    Dethridge; Holchester; Lundie; Silvester
  Moonstone, The: Ablewhite; Betteridge;
    Blake; Bruff; Candy; Clack; Cuff; Guy;
    Herncastle; Jennings; Luker; Merridew;
    Murthwaite; Seegrave; Spearman;
    Verinder; Yolland
  New Magdalen, The: Merrick; Roseberry
  No Name: Bartram; Bygrave; Clare; Garth;
    Huxtable; Kirke; Luscombe; Marrable;
    Mazey; Vanstone; Wragge
  Queen of Hearts, The: Bulmer; Capuchin;
    Elmslie; Foulon; Jay; Monckton;
    Sharpin; Theakstone; Yatman
  Woman in White, The: Catherick;
    Clements; Dawson; Dunthorne; Eleanor;
    Fanny; Fosco; Garth; Gilmore; Glyde;
    Goodricke; Halcombe; Hartwright;
    Kempe; Kyrle; Markland; Merriman;
    Michelson; Pesca; Pinhorn; Rubelle;
    Vesey
Colman the Elder, George
  with David Garrick
  Clandestine Marriage, The: Belford; Brush;
    Flower; Heidelberg; Lovewell; Melvil;
    Ogleby; Sterling; Traverse; Trusty
Colman the Younger, George
  Heir at Law, The: Dowlas; Pangloss
  Iron Chest, The: Falkland; Hawkins;
    Melville; Williams
  John Bull: Bulgruddery; Thornberry
  Poor Gentleman, The: Branble; Dobbins;
    Foss; Worthington
Colton, John
  Rain: Davidson; Thompson
Comfort, Alex
  Come Out to Play: Goggins
Compton, Frances Snow
  Esther: Brooke; Dudley; Hazard; Sharton
Compton-Burnett, Ivy
  House and its Head, A: Bethia; Bode;
    Burtenshaw; Edgeworth; Fellows; Jekyll;
    Marshall; Smollett
  Last and the First, The: Duff;

Compton-Burnett, Ivy—*contd.*
 Grimstone; Heriot; Hollander
 Manservant and Maidservant: Bullivant;
 George; Lamb; Selden
 Men and Wives: Bellamy; Buttermere;
 Calkin; Christy; Dabis; Dufferin;
 Hardisty; Haslam; Spong
 Mother and Son: Burke; Hume; Wolsey
 Pastors and Masters: Bumpass; Merry
Congreve, William
 Double-Dealer, The: Brisk; Carless;
 Cynthia; Froth; Maskwell; Mellefont;
 Plyant; Touchwood
 Incognita: Aurelian; Hippolito; Leonora
 Love for Love: Angelica; Foresight; Frail;
 Legend; Prue; Scandal; Tattle
 Mourning Bride, The: Almeira
 Old Bachelor, The: Araminta; Belinda;
 Bellmour; Bluffe; Fondlewife; Heartwell;
 Setter; Sylvia; Vainlove; Wittol
 Way of the World, The: Fainall; Foible;
 Marwood; Millament; Mincing;
 Mirabell; Petulant; Waitwell; Wishfort;
 Witwoud
Connell, Evan S.
 Mr Bridge and Mrs Bridge: Bridge
Connelly, Marc
 Beggar on Horseback: Cady
Connor, R.
 Sky Pilot, The: Moore
Conrad, Joseph
 Almayer's Folly: Abdulla; Almayer;
 Babalatchi; Hudig; Lakamber; Lingard;
 Maroola; Vinck
 Arrow of Gold, The: Allegre; Blunt;
 George; Mills; Rita
 Chance: Fyne
 Heart of Darkness: Kurtz
 Inheritors, The: An Extravagant Story:
 Granger
 Lord Jim: Brierly; Brown; Chester; Dain;
 De Jongh; Doramin; Jim; Mariani;
 Marlow; Robinson; Tamb'itam
 Nigger of the 'Narcissus', The: Wait
 Nostromo: Fidenza; Gould
 Outcast of the Islands, An: Willems
 Rescue, The: Hassim; Travers
 Secret Agent, The: Heat; Michaelis;
 Ossipon; Verloc; Vladimir; Yundt
 Typhoon: Carvil; Egstrom; Falk; Foster;
 Goorall; Hagberd; Jukes; Kennedy;
 MacWhirr; Swaffer
 Under Western Eyes: Haldin; Mikulin;
 Razumov
 Victory: Davidson; Heyst; Lena;
 Schomberg; Wang
Constant, Benjamin
 Adolphe: Adolphe; Eléonore
Cooke, J.E.
 My Lady Pocahantas: Pocahantas; Rolfe

Coolidge, Susan
 What Katy Did: Carr
 What Katy Did at School: Florence;
 Nipson; Redding; Worrett
Cooper, James Fenimore
 Afloat and Ashore: Drewett; Hardinge;
 Marble; Merton; Neb; Robbins;
 Sweeney; Wallingford
 Deerslayer, The: Hist; Hutter; March
 Last of the Mohicans, The: Effingham;
 Hayward; Magua; Munro
 Leatherstocking Tales, The: Bumppo;
 Chingachgook
 Lionel Lincoln: Dynever; Lechmore;
 Lincoln; Pray
 Miles Wallingford: Drewett; Wallingford
 Monikins, The: Goldencalf; Monikins;
 Poke
 Pathfinder, The: Arrowhead; Duncan;
 Dunham; Muir; Western
Cooper, William
 Scenes From Married Life and *Scenes From
 Provincial Life*: Lunn
Coppard, A.E.
 Adam and Eve and Pinch Me: Buckland;
 Cannis; Fionnguisa; Grafton; Hardcross;
 Krasinsky; Mary; McCall; Monk;
 Narcissus; Pellegrini; Peshkov;
 Piffingcap; Prowse; Ruth; Talakku
Corelli, Marie
 Master Christian, The: Leigh
Corvo, Baron
 Hadrian the Seventh: Flavio; Rose; Sant;
 Semphill; Talacryn
Cournos, John
 Miranda Masters: Ramsden
Coventry, Francis
 History of Pompey the Little, or *The Life
 and Adventures of a Lap-Dog*: Pompey
Coward, Noel
 Blithe Spirit: Arcati; Bradman; Condomint
 Brief Encounter: Beryl
 Hay Fever: Arundel; Bliss; Corydon; Tyrell
 Private Lives: Chase; Prynne
 Red Peppers: Bentley
 Still Life: Harvey; Jesson
 Vortex, The: Fairlight; Hibbert; Lancaster;
 Mainwaring; Preston; Saville
Cowley, Abraham
 Cutter of Colman Street: Cutter
Cowley, Mrs Hannah
 Belle's Stratagem, The: Doricourt; Hardy
Cowper, William
 Diverting History of John Gilpin, The:
 Gilpin
Cozzens, James Gould
 By Love Possessed: Winner
 Michael Scarlett: Scarlett
Crabbe, George
 Borough, The: Benbow; Blaney; Grimes;

Gwyn; Kindred; Orford; Wisp
Parish Register, The: Grey; Rebecca
Craddock, Charles Egbert
In the Tennessee Mountains: Ware
Craik, Mrs
Agatha's Husband: Harper; Ianson
John Halifax, Gentleman: Brithwood;
D'Argent; Fletcher; Halifax; Jael; Jessop;
Luxmore; March; Oldtower; Vermilye;
Watkins
Ogilvies, The: Lynedon; Ogilvie; Worsley;
Wychnor
Crane, Stephen
Monster and Other Stories: Monster;
Swede; Trescott
*Open Boat and Other Tales of Adventure,
The*: Potter; Wilson
Red Badge of Courage, The: Conklin;
Fleming; Wilson
Wounds in the Rain: Fleming
Creeley, Robert
Island, The: Artie
Crews, Harry
Gospel Singer, The: Fat Man
Karate is a Thing of the Spirit: Kaimon
Crockett, Samuel Rutherford
Dark O' The Moon, The: Maxwell
Raiders, The: Maxwell
Cronin, A.J.
Beyond This Place: Cameron; Finlay
Citadel, The: Barlow; Boland; Denny;
Hamson; Ivory; Manson; Page; Rees
Hatter's Castle: Brodie; Foyle; Grierson;
Latta; Moir
Crowne, John
Pandion and Amphigenia: Amphigenia
Cumberland, Richard
West Indian, The: Bellcour; Dudley;
Fulmer; O'Flaherty; Rusport; Stockwell
cummings, e.e.
W: Harding
Cummins, Maria S.
Lamplighter, The: Flint; Graham; Grant;
Holbrook; Sullivan

Danby, Frank
Doctor Phillips: Cameron; Doveton;
Phillips
d'Annunzio, Gabriele
Il fuoco (The Fire): Effrena
Davenport Jr., Guy
Da Vinci's Bicycle: Ten Stories: Da Vinci
Tatlin: Tatlin
Davies, Rhys
Black Venus: Drizzle; Eurgain
Nobody Answered the Bell: Kenny;
Martin; Rose
Davies, Robertson
Diary of Samuel Marchbanks: Marchbanks

Davin, Dan
Brides of Price: Mahon
Sullen Bell, The: Egan
Davis, John
First Settlers of Virginia, The: Pocahantas;
Rolfe
Davis, Rebecca Harding
John Andross: Andross
Davis, Richard Harding
Episodes in Van Bibber's Life: Van Bibber
Gallegher and Other Stories: Gallegher
Margaret Howth: Howth
Ranson's Folly: Cahill; Ranson
Soldiers of Fortune: Burke; Clay;
Hernandez; King; Langham;
McWilliams; Mendoza; Rojas; Stuart
Van Bibber and Other Stories: Van Bibber
Dawson, Jennifer
Ha-Ha, The: Jean
Day, John
Parliament of Bees, The: Fenerator;
Gnatho; Parsimonius; Thraso; Poetaster;
Pharmacopolis
Day, Thomas
Sandford and Merton: Barlow; Merton;
Sandford
de Goncourt, Edmond and Jules
Germanie Lacerteux: Lacerteux
de la Mare, Walter
Beginning, A: Brandt; Fiske; Guthrie;
Hopper; Milligton; Pugh; Silcot;
Trimmins
Diary of Henry Brocken: Brocken
Return, The: Bethany; Herbert; Lawford
Riddle, The: Lennox; Nicholas; Rodd;
Seaton; Withers
Wind Blows Over, The: Ada; Asprey;
Emily; Emmeline; Gessen; Hadleigh;
Harry; Miller; Rose; Wilson
De la Roche, Mazo
Jalna: Whiteoaks
De Lizardi, José Joaquin Fernàndez
*El Periquello Sarniento (The Itching
Parrot)*: Periquello
Defoe, Daniel
Captain Singleton: Singleton; William;
Wilmot
Colonel Jack: Evans; Jack; Jack; Will
Moll Flanders: Flanders
Robinson Crusoe: Crusoe; Friday; Xury
'A True Relation of the Apparition of one
Mrs Veal, the next Day after her Death,
to one Mrs Bargrave at Canterbury, the
8th September, 1705': Bargrave; Veal
DeForest, John William
*Miss Ravenel's Conversion from Secession
to Loyalty*: Ravenel
Dekker, Thomas
Old Fortunatus: Athelstane; Cornwall;
Cyprus; Fortunatus; Galloway;

Granger; Howler; Jemima; Johnson; Johnson; Joper; Kate; Larkey Boy; MacStinger; Marwood; Melia; Miff; Morfin; Native; Nipper; Panky; Peps; Perch; Pilkins; Pipchin; Robinson; Saxby; Screwzer; Skettles; Skewton; Smalder Girls; Sowndes; Toodle; Toots; Townlinson; Tox; Wickham; Withers

Dr Marigold's Prescriptions: Marie-Madeleine; Sophy

Edwin Drood: Bazzard; Billickin; Bud; Crisparkle; Datchery; Drood; Durdles; Grewgious; Honeythunder; Jacksonini; Jasper; Jennings; Landless; Lobley; Puffer; Reynolds; Rickitts; Sapsea; Tartar; Tisher; Tope; Twinkleton

George Silverman's Explanation: Parksop; Silverman

Going Into Society: Chops, Magsman

Great Expectations: Barley; Compeyson; Drummle; Estella; Gargery; Georgiana; Havisham; Hubble; Jack; Jaggers; Lazarus; Magwitch; Mary Ann; Orlick; Pepper; Pirrip; Pocket; Pumblechook; Skiffins; Startop; Trabb; Wemmich; Wopsle

Hard Times: Blackpool; Bounderby; Childers; Gordon; Gradgrind; Harthouse; Jupe; McChoakumchild; Merrylegs; Nickits; Pegler; Powlers; Rachael; Scaddon; Slackbridge; Sleary; Sparsit

Haunted House, The: Governor; Greenwood; Griffin; Ikey; Mesrour; Seraglio; Streaker; Swidger

Haunted Man, The: Redlaw; Tetterby

Holiday Romance, A: Ashford; Boldheart; Drowvey; Emilia; Grimmer; Latin Grammar Master; Orange; Pickles; Redforth

Holly Tree, The: Charley; Leath

Hunted Down: Banks; Meltham; Sampson; Slinkton

Is She His Wife?: Tapkins

Little Dorrit: Bangham; Barnacle; Casby; Chivery; Clennam; Clive; Cripples; Dawes; Dorrit; Doyce; Finching; Flintwich; General; Gowan; Haggage; Hawkins; Jenkinson; Maggy; Maroon; Martin; Meagles; Merdle; Nandy; Pancks; Peddle and Pool; Plornish; Rigaud; Rugg; Slingo; Sparkler; Stilstalking; Tattycoram; Tickit; Treasury; Wade

Martin Chuzzlewit: Brick; Bullamy; Choke; Chollop; Chuffey; Chuzzlewit; Codger; Crimple; Diver; Dunkie; Fips; Gamp; Gander; Gill; Graham; Groper; Harris; Hominy; Izzard; Jack; Jinkins; Jobling; Kedgick; Kettle; Lewsome; Literary Ladies; Lummy Ned; Lupin; Moddle; Mother of the Modern Gracchi; Mould; Mullet; Nadgett; Norris; No Zoo; Pawkins; Pecksniff; Pinch; Pogram; Prig; Scadder; Simmons; Slyme; Smif; Smivey; Spiller and Spoker; Spottletoe; Sweedlepipe; Tacker; Tamaroo; Tapley; Tigg; Toppit; Westlock

Master Humphrey's Clock: Benton; Bowyer; Gibbs; Graham; Humphrey; Jack; Jinkinson; Marks; Redburn; Slithers

Message From the Sea, A: Jorgan; Parvis; Pettifer; Polreath; Raybrook

Mrs Lirriper's Lodgings and Legacy: Jackman; Lirriper; Madgers; Seraphina

Mudfog Papers, The: Dull; Greenacre; Grummidge; Jobba; Graham; Humphrey; Knight-Bell; Kutankumagen; Kwakely; Ledbrain; Long Ears; Misty; Neeshawts; Pumpinskill; Slug; Thom; Tulrumble; Twigger

Mugby Junction: Jackson; Lamps; Phoebe; Piff; Sniff

Nicholas Nickleby: Belvawney; Belling; Bobster; Bonney; Bravassa; Bray; Browdie; Cheeryble; Crowl; Crummles; Curdle; Dabber; David; Dibabs; Digby; Dorker; Dowdles; Foliar; Gallanbile; Gazingi; Gentleman in small cl'thes; Glavormelly; Gregsbury; Greymarsh; Gride; Grimble; Grudden; Hawk; Johnson; Kenwigs; Knag; La Creevy; Lambert; Lane; Ledbrook; Lenville; Lilyvick; Lumbey; Mantalini; Marker; Matthews; Nickleby; Noggs; Old Bricks and Mortar; Peltirogus; Petowker; Pitcher; Pluck; Price; Pugstyles; Pupker; Pyke; Scaley; Sliderskew; Smike; Snawley; Snevellicci; Snewkes; Snuffim; Squeers; Swillenhausen; Timberry; Tix; Verisopht; Von Koeldwethout; Watkins; Witterly

No Thoroughfare: Dor; Ganz; Ladle; Miller; Obenreizer; Vendale

Old Curiosity Shop, The: Barbara; Brass; Cheggs; Chuckster; Codlin; Edwards; Foxey; Garland; George; Grandfather; Grinder; Groves; Jarley; Jerry; Jiniwin; Jowl; List; Marchioness; Marton; Maunders; Mizzler; Monflathers; Nubbles; Packlemerton; Quilp; Scott; Sort; Single Gentleman; Slum; Stetta; Sweet William; Swiveller; Trent; Trent; Vuffin; Wackles; Witherden

Oliver Twist: Barker; Barney; Bates; Bedwin; Blathers; Brownlow; Bumble; Chickweed; Claypole; Corney; Crackit; Dawkins; Duff; Fagin; Fang; Fet; Fleming; Giles; Grannett; Kags; Leeford; Losberne; Mann; Maylie; Nancy; Ned;

Dickens, Charles—*contd.*

Nolly; Sikes; Slout; Sowerberry; Spyers;
Twist

Our Mutual Friend: Akersham; Boffin;
Cleaver; Dancer; Eddard; Fledgeby;
Glamour; Gliddery; Goody; Handford;
Harmon; Headstone; Hexham; Higden;
Hopkins; Jane; Kibble; Lammle;
Lightwood; Mary Anne; Meek Man;
Milvey; Overs; Podsnap; Potterson;
Radfoot; Riah; Riderhood; Sampson;
Sloppy; Snigsworth; Sprodkin; Swoshle;
Taylor; Tippins; Toddles and Poddles;
Twemlow; Veneering; Venus; Wegg;
Wilfer; Wrayburn

Pantomime of Life, The: Do'em; Fiercy

Perils of Certain English Prisoners, The:
Drooce; King; Kitten; Macey; Maryon;
Pordage

Pickwick Papers, The: Allen; Baillie;
Bamber; Bantam; Bardell; Betsey;
Blotton; Boldwig; Buzfuz; Clarke;
Clubber; Cluppins; Craddock; Crookey;
Crushton; Dodson; Dowler; Dubbley;
Dumkins; Edmunds; Feilletoville; Fizkin;
Fizzgig; Flasher; Fogg; George; Goodwin;
Grub; Gunter; Harris; Heyling; Hopkins;
Humm; Hunter; Isaac; Jingle; Jinks; Kate;
Lobbs; Lowten; Lucas; Luffey; Martin;
Namby; Neddy; Nockemorf; Nupkins;
Payne; Pell; Perker; Phunky; Pickwick;
Pipkin; Podder; Ponto; Pott; Prosee;
Pruffle; Quanko; Raddle; Ramsey; Roker;
Sanders; Sawyer; Shepherd; Shiny
Villiam; Simmery; Skimpin; Slammer;
Slasher; Slumkey; Slummintowkens;
Slurk; Smangle; Smauker; Smiggers;
Smorltork; Smouch; Snicks; Snodgrass;
Snubbin; Staple; Stareleigh; Stiggins;
Struggles; Stumps; Tadger; Tappleton;
Tiggin; Trotter; Trundle; Tuckle;
Tupman; Wardle; Watty; Weller; Winkle

Public Life of Mr Tulrumble, The:
Jennings; Madman; Magnus; Mallard;
Manning; Martin; Martin; Mary;
Matinter; Mivins; Mordlin; Mudge;
Mutanhed; Sniggs

Reprinted Pieces: Bear; Bull; Dogginson;
Dornton; Demented Traveller;
Dumbledown; Dundey; Feroce; Grimwig;
Jack; Jilks; Kendall; Loyal Devasseur;
Mawls and Maxby; Meek; Mesheck;
Mills; Mith; Phibbs; Pitt; Shepherdson;
Snap; Southcote; Stalker; Steele; Tape;
Tatt; Tiddypot

Seven Poor Travellers: Doubledick;
Marshall; Taunton

Sketches by Boz: Balderstone; Barton;
Budden; Calton; Cooper; Crumpton;
Dingwall; Dobble; Dobbleton; Dounce;

Ducrow; Dumps; Evans; Evenson;
Flamwell; Gattleton; Glumper; Gobler;
Green; Helves; Hicks; Hobler; Ikey; Jack;
Jacobs; Jane; Jane; Jennings; Kate; King;
Kitterbell; Larkins; Lillerton; Lobskini;
Loggins; Mackin; Macklin; Malderton;
Manners; Maplestone; Martin; Martin;
Minns; Muggs; Nathan; Noakes;
O'Bleary; Orson; Overton; Parker;
Parsons; Peter; Potter; St Julien; Simmons;
Slaughter; Sludberry; Sluffen; Smith;
Smithers; Spruggins; Sulliwin; Taplin;
Tibbs; Timson; Tottle; Trimmer; Trott;
Tuggs; Tupple

Sketches of Young Couples: Glogwog;
Slang; Slummery; Snorflerer; Young
Couple, Egotistical

Sketches of Young Gentlemen: Balim;
Censorious Young; Gentleman; Fairfax;
Griggins; Lowfield; Marshall; Mathews;
Merrywinkle; Milkwash; Scuttlewig;
Thurtell; *Somebody's Luggage*: Cour;
Langley; Pratchett; Theophile; Valentine

Tale of Two Cities, A: Carton; Cly;
Cruncher; Darnay; D'Aulnais; Defarge;
Gabelle; Gaspard; Lorry; Manette; Pross;
Seamstress; Stryver; Vengeance

Tom Tiddler's Ground: Kimmeens;
Mopes; Traveller

Uncommercial Traveller, The: Anderson;
Antonio; Battens; Bullfinch; Carlavero;
Chips; Clergyman; Cleverly; Cocker;
Dibble; Face-Maker; Flanders; Globson;
Grazinglands; Green; Halliday; Jack;
Kinch; Kindheart; Klem; Mash; Mayne;
Mellows; Mitts; Onowenever; Parkle;
Poodles; Quickear; Quinch; Saggers;
Sharpeye; Squires; Straudenheim;
Trampfoot; Traveller

Wreck of the Golden Mary, The: Rarx;
Ravender; Smithwick; Steadiman

Village Coquette, The: Edmunds; Maddox;
Stokes

Dickens, Mary Angela

Cross Currents: Malet

Diderot, Denis

La Religieuse (The Nun): Arpajon;
Simonin

Didion, Joan

Book of Common Prayer, A: Douglas;
Stasser-Mendana

Run River: McClennan

Disraeli, Benjamin

Alroy: Alrui

Coningsby: Buckhurst; Clumber;
Coningsby; Eskdale; Millbank;
Monmouth; Rigby; Sidney; Tadpole;
Taper; Villebecque; Wallinger

Endymion: Ferrars

Henrietta Temple: A Love Story: Armine;

Grandison; Montfort; Temple
Lothair: Grandison; Lothair; Montairy;
Phoebus; St Aldegone; St Jerome
Sybil: Carey; Dandy; Devilsdust;
Egremont; Firebrace; Fitzaquitaine;
Gerard; Hatton; Marney; McDruggy;
Mobray; St Lys; Trotman
Tancred: Astarte; Baroni; Bertie and
Bellair; Bellamont; Besso; Cassilis;
Fakredeen; Flouncey; Hungerford;
Ormsby; Roby
Vivian Grey: Juggernaut; Lorraine; Puff
Diver, Maud
Captain Desmond, VC: Desmond
Dixon, Ella Hepworth
Story of a Modern Woman, The: Erle;
Hemming; Ives
Dixon, Thomas
Leopard's Spots, The: Legree
Southerner, The: Lincoln
Dos Passos, John
*Garbage Man, The: A Parade With
Shouting*: Garbage Man
Manhattan Transfer: Baldwin; Emery;
Fallic; Harland; Herf; Korpenning;
Lanster; McNiel; Merivale; Prynne;
Sandbourne; Wilkins
Number One: Spotswood
One Man's Initiation – 1917: Howe
Streets of Night: Fanshaw; Nancibel;
Wendell
Three Soldiers: Andrews; Chrisfield;
Fuselli; Rod
U.S.A.: Anderson; Dowling; McCreary;
Morehouse; Savage; Stoddard; Williams
Dostoievsky, Fyodor
Besy (The Possessed): Karmazinov;
Kirillov; Shatov; Stavrogin; Trofimovich;
Verkovensky
Bratya Karamazov (Brothers Karamazov):
Grushenska; Ivanova; Karamazov;
Smerdyadov; Zosima
Dvoinik (The Double): Golyadkin
Idiot: Filippovna; Ippolit; Myshkin;
Rogozhin; Totsky; Yepanchina
*Prestuplenie i Nakazanie (Crime and
Punishment)*: Lebezytnikov; Luhzin;
Marmeladov; Razumihkin; Raskolnikov;
Svidigaylov
Douglas, George
House with the Green Shutters, The: Allan;
Blowselinda; Gibson; Gourlay; Grant;
Riney; Struthers; Toddle; Wilson; Wylie
Douglas, Norman
North Wind: Don Francesco
South Wind: Caloveglia; Eames;
Francesco; Keith; Marten; Meadows;
Parker; Phipps; Retlow; Richards; San
Martino; Steynlin; Van Koppen;
Wilberforce

Dowson, Ernest
Adrian Rome: Rome
'Non Sum Qualis Eram': Cynara
Doyle, Arthur Conan
Adventures of Sherlock Holmes, The:
Baker; Breckenridge; Bohemia; Clay;
Doran; Holder; Horner; Hudson; Hunter;
McCarthy; Millar; Moulton; Openshaw;
Ross; Roylott; Rucastle; Ryder; St Clair;
St Simon; Stark; Stoner; Sutherland;
Toller; Turner; Whitney; Wilson;
Windibank
His Last Bow: Browner; Carfax; Eccles;
Garcia; Georgiano; Oberstein; Smith;
Sterndale; Tregennis; Von Bork; Von
Herling; West
Hound of the Baskervilles, The:
Barrymore; Baskerville; Lyons;
Mortimer; Selden; Stapleton
Lost World, The: Challenger
Memoirs of Sherlock Holmes, The:
Barclay; Brown; Burnwell; Harrison;
Holdhurst; Moriarty; Munro; Musgrave;
Pycroft; Ross; Straker; Trevelyan;
Trevor
Poison Belt, The: Challenger
Return of Sherlock Holmes, The: Adair;
Cubbit; Holdernesse; Hope; Hopkins;
Huxtable; Macfarlane; Milverton;
Moran; Morton; Oldacre; Slaney; Smith;
Woodley
Sign of Four, The: Abdullah Khan; Dost
Akbar; Forrester; Jones; Lal; Mahomet
Singh; McMurdo; Morstan; Small; Smith
Study in Scarlet, A: Drebber; Gregson;
Holmes; Hope; Lestrade; Stangerson;
Turner; Watson
White Company, The: Calverley
Drabble, Margaret
Middle Ground, The: Armstrong
Millstone, The: Stacey
Realms of Gold, The: Wingate
Dreiser, Theodore
American Tragedy, An: Alden; Belknap;
Briggs; Burleigh; Cranstone; Dickerman;
Finchley; Griffiths; Heit; Jephson; Krant;
Mason; McMillan; Miller; Oberwaltzer;
Peyton; Ratterer; Shuman; Sparser;
Squires; Stark; Trumbull
Financier, The: Butler; Cowperwood
Genius, The: Appleton; Blue; Dale; Witla
Jennie Gerhardt: Brander; Gerald;
Gerhardt; Kane
Sister Carrie: Drouet; Hurstwood; Meeber
Stoic, The: Cowperwood
Titan, The: Cowperwood; Tollifer
Dryden, John
Absalom and Achitophel: Achitophel
Don Sebastian: Dorax
Marriage à la Mode: Almathea; Argeleon;

Fox Jr., John—*contd.*
  Dean; Forbes; Hazel; Jack; Melissa;
  Turner
  Santa Maria, or *The Mysterious*
  Pregnancy: Conrad
Frame, Janet
  Owls Do Cry: Withers
Fraser, George Macdonald
  Flashman: Flashman
Frederic, Harold
  Copperhead, The: Hagadorn
  Damnation of Theron Ware, The: Forbes;
  Ledsmar; Madden; Soulsby; Ware
  In the Valley: Mauverenson
  Lawton Girl, The: Lawton; Minster; Tracy
  March Hares: Mosscrop
  Market-Place, The: Thorpe
  Mrs Albert Grundy: Observations in
  Philistia: Timby-Hucks
  Seth's Brother's Wife: Fairchild
  War Widow, The: Turnbull
Friedman, Bruce Jay
  About Harry Towns: Towns
  Dick, The: Sussman
  Mother's Kisses, A: Meg
  Stern: Stern; Frisch, Max
  Stiller: Stiller; White
Frost, Robert
  North of Boston: Silas; Warren
Froude, J.A.
  Nemesis of Faith, The: Leonard; Sutherland
Fuchs, Daniel
  Homage to Blenholt: Balkan; Munves
  Low Company: Shubunka
Fuller, Henry Blake
  Cliff-Dwellers, The: Brainard; Ingles;
  McDowell; Ogden
  With the Procession: Marshall
Fuller, Roy
  Second Curtain, The: Garner
Fullerton, Georgiana
  Ellen Middleton: Middleton
Futrell, Jacques
  Thinking Machine, The: Van Dusen
Furphy, Joseph
  Such is Life: Collins

Gaddis, William
  Recognitions, The: Gwyon
Gaines, Ernest J.
  Autobiography of Miss Jane Pittman, The:
  Pittman
  Bloodline: Copper
  In My Father's House: Martin
Galdés, Benito Pérez
  Doña Perfecta: Caballacu; Innocencio;
  Perfecta; Rey
  La Familia de Léon Roch: Luis; Roch
Gale, Zona
  Miss Lulu Bett: Deacon

Gallegos, Rómulo
  Doña Bárbara: Bárbara
Galsworthy, John
  Apple Tree, The: David; Halliday;
  Narracombe
  Country House, The: Barter; Bellew;
  Paramor; Pendyce; Vigil
  Five Tales: Ashurst; Garton
  Flowering Wilderness: Grice; Muskham;
  Stack; Yule
  Forstye series, The: Blaine; Blore; Blythe;
  Boxton; Cardigan; Charwell; Crisson;
  Croom; Danby; Dartie; Desert;
  Dumetrius; Golding; Gradman; Hayman;
  Heron; Hilmer; Lamotte; McAuden;
  Minho; Monk; Mont; Moor; Polteed;
  Profond; Small; Tweetyman; Wilmot;
  Wyke
  Justice: Cokeson; Cowley; Falder;
  Honeywell; How; Wister
  Fraternity: Dalison; Stone
  Loyalties: Canynge; Colford; Dancy; De
  Levis; Dede; Graviter; St Erth; Twisden;
  Winsor
  Maid in Waiting: Hallorson; Montjoy;
  Saxenden; Tasbrugh
  Over the River: Corven; Dornford
  Patrician, The: Casterley; Chilcox;
  Courtier; Harbinger; Lees-noel;
  Shropton; Valleys
  Silver Spoon, The: Bergfield; Ferrar;
  MacGown; Nazing; Shropshire
  Skin Game, The: Hillcrist; Hornblower;
  Jackman
  Stoic, A: Heythrop; Larne; Pillin;
  Ventnor
  Strife: Anthony; Roberts
  Swan Song: Pole; Stainford
  White Monkey, The: Bicket; Elderson;
  Greene
Galt, John
  Annals of the Parish: Balwhidder; Cayenne;
  Eaglesham; MacAdam
  Ayrshire Legatees, The: Pringle
  Provost, The: Caption; Clues; Galore;
  McLucre; Pawkie; Picklan; Pittle;
  Smeddum
Gardner, Erle Stanley
  Case of the Velvet Claws, The: Mason
Gardner, John
  Grendel: Grendel
  Liquidator, The: Oakes
  Nickel Mountain: Soames
  October Light: Page
  Sunlight Dialogues, The: Clumly
  Wreckage of Agathon, The: Agathon;
  Demodokos
Garland, Hamlin
  Rose of Dutcher's Coolly: Dutcher; Mason;
  Thatcher

Garnett, David
  Go She Must!: Grandison; Sotheby
  Lady Into Fox: Tebrick
  Sailor's Return, The: Barnes; Clall; Crock;
    Gaze-oh; Molten; Sait; Stingo; Sturmer;
    Targett
  Pocahantas: Pocahantas; Rolfe
Garnett, Richard
  Twilight of the Gods, The: Elenko
Garrick, David
  Clandestine Marriage, The: see Colman the
    Elder, George
  Miss in Her Teens: Fribble
Gaskell, Mrs
  Cousin Phillis: Dawson; Ellison;
    Holdsworth; Holma
  Cranford: Barker; Brown; Brunoni;
    Fitzadam; Glenmire; Gordon; Hearn;
    Hoggins; Holbrook; Jamieson; Jenkyns;
    Jenny; Manning; Martha; Mauleverer;
    Mulliner; Pole
  Mary Barton: Barton; Carson; Margaret;
    Wilson
  Moorland Cottage, The: Browne; Buxton;
    Henry
  North and South: Bell; Dixon; Hale;
    Higgins; Lennox; Shaw; Thornton
  Novels and Tales: Dudgeon; Hearn;
    Higgins; Manley; Pratt
  Sylvia's Lovers: Brunton; Corney; Coulson;
    Foster; Hepburn; Kester; Kinraid;
    Robson; Rose
  Wives and Daughters: Browning; Coxe;
    Cumnor; Gibson; Goodenough; Hamley;
    Hollingford; Kirkpatrick; Preston;
    Sheepshanks
Gay, John
  Beggar's Opera, The: Diver; Filch; Lockit;
    MacHeath; Peachum; Trapes
  Polly: Brazen; Cawwawkee; Coaxer;
    Culverin; Cutlace; Diver; Doxy; Ducat;
    Hacker; Laguerre; Peeper; Pohetohee;
    Slammekin; Trapes; Trull; Vanderbluff;
    Vixen; Wheedle
Gee, Maurice
  Plum: Plum
Gerhardie, William
  Pending Heaven: Bernard; Crazy; Fisher;
    Horse; O'Maera; Sapphire; Thurbon
  Polyglots, The: Diabologh; Vanderflint
Gershwin, Ira
  Lady in the Dark: Elliott
Gibbon, Lewis Grassic
  *Scots Quair, A (Cloud Howe; Grey
    Granite; Sunset Song)*: Colquhoun;
    Duncan; Guthrie; Johns; Moultrie;
    Ogilvie; Queen; Strachan; Tavendale
Gibbons, Stella
  Cold Comfort Farm: Beetle; Dolour;
    Fairford; Hart-Harris; Lambsbreath;

Mudel; Mybug; Poste; Smiling;
    Starkadder
Gide, André
  La Porte étroite: Alissa; Vautien
  La Symphonie Pastorale: Amelie;
    Gertrude
Gilbert, W.S.
  Gondoliers, The: Alhambra del Bolero;
    Annibale; Antonio; Fiametta; Francesco;
    Gianetta; Giorgio; Giulia; Inez; Luiz;
    Palmieri; Plaza Toro; Tessa; Vittoria
  H.M.S. Pinafore: Beckett; Bobsborough;
    Buttercup; Corcoran; Deadeye; Porter;
    Rackstraw
  Iolanthe: Celia; Chancellor; Fairies; Fleta;
    Iolanthe; Leila; Mountararat; Phyllis;
    Strephon; Tolloller; Willis
  Mikado, The: Katisha; Ko-Ko; Mikado of
    Japan; Peep-Bo; Pish-Tush; Pitt-Sing; Poo-
    Bah; Yum-Yum
  Patience: Angel; Bunthorne; Calverley;
    Dunstable; Ella; Grosvenor; Jane;
    Murgatroyd; Patience; Saphir
  Pirates of Penzance, The: Frederic; Pirate
    King; Ruth; Samuel; Stanley
  Princess Ida: Ada; Blanche; Chloe; Cyril;
    Florian; Gama; Hildebrand; Psyche;
    Sacharissa
  Ruddigore: Dauntless; Hannah; Margaret;
    Maybud; Murgatroyd; Ruth; Zorah
  Sorcerer, The: Daly; Partlet; Pointdextre;
    Sangazure; Wells
  Yeoman of the Guard, The: Carruthers;
    Cholmondeley; Fairfax; Kate; Maynard;
    Meryll; Point; Shadbolt
Giles, Gordon
  Wily Ones, The: Prenderghast; Tweeter
Gillette, William
  Secret Service: Thorne; Varney
Gillo, George
  Fatal Curiosity, The: Wilmot
Gilman, Charlotte Perkins
  New England Magazine: John—; Woman
    in the wallpaper pattern
Gissing, George
  Born in Exile: Gunnery; Moxey; Peak;
    Warricombe
  Crown of Life, The: Derwent; Jacks;
    Otway
  Demos: Mutimer; Vine; Waltham;
    Westlake; Wyvern
  House of Cobwebs, The: Armitage;
    Humplebee; Ireton; Munden; Ruddiman;
    Shepperson; Shergold
  In the Year of Jubilee: Barmby; Crewe;
    Damerel; French; Lord; Morgan; Peachey;
    Tarrant; Woodruff
  Isabel Clarendon: Kingcote
  New Grub Street: Milvain; Reardon;
    Whelpdale; Yule

Spiritual Quixote, or The Summer's Ramble of Mr. Geoffry Wildgoose: A Comic Romance: Wildgoose
Wife to Mr Milton: Milton; Powell

Green, Anna Katherine
Leavenworth Case, The: Gryce

Green, Henry
Loving: Albert; Edith; Raunce; Tennant

Green, Paul
In Abraham's Bosom: McCranie

Greene, Graham
Brighton Rock: Arnold; Brewer; Collconi; Corkery; Drewitt; Hale; Pinkie; Spicer; Wilson
Burnt-Out Case, A: Colin; Deo Gratias; Parkinson; Querry; Rycker; Thomas
Comedians, The: Magiot; Pineda; Smith
End of the Affair, The: Bertram; Bendrix; Miles; Parkis; Smythe
England Made Me: Davidge; Farrant; Hall; Krogh; Minty
Heart of the Matter, The: Bagster; Bowles; Halifax; Pemberton; Rank; Robinson; Rolt; Scobie; Wilson; Yusef
It's a Battlefield: Bennett; Briton; Bury; Conder; Drover; Rimmer; Surrogate
Ministry of Fear, The: Bellairs; Cost; Forester; Hilfe; Johns; Jones; Poole; Prentice; Rennit; Rowe; Sinclair; Stone; Wilcox
Power and the Glory, The: Lopen; Maria; Obregon; Tench
Quiet American, The: Dominigue; Fowler; Granger; Phuong; Pyle; Vigot

Greene, Robert
Menaphon: Sephestia
Pandosto, or The Triumph of Time: Pandosto

Greenwood, Walter
Love on the Dole: Barlow; Bull; Dorbell; Grundy; Hardcastle; Hawkins; Jike; Meath

Griffin, Gerald
Collegians, The, or The Colleen Bawn: A Tale of Garryowen: Cregan

Grimmelshausen, Hans Jakob Von
Simplicissimus: Fuchsheim; Herzbruder; Olivier; Simplicius

Groguett, Carlos
Eloy: Eloy

Grossman, Alfred
Acrobat Admits: Sarge

Grossmith, George and Weedon
Diary of a Nobody, The: Burwen-Fossilton; Franching; Gowing; Griffin; James; Merton; Mutlar; Padge; Perupp; Pooter; Posh; Putley; Sarah; Stillbrook

Guerard, Albert
Exiles, The: Andrada; Villamayor
Night Journey: Haldan

Güiraldes, Ricardo
Don segunda sombra (Shadows in the Pampas): Sombra

Gunn, Neil M.
Highland River: Beel

Gunter, Archibold Clavering
Mr Barnes of New York: Barnes

Gurdjieff, G.I.
All and Everything: Beelzebub's Tales to His Grandson: Abdil; Ahoon; Arhoonilo; Ashiata Shiemasti; Asiman; Atarnakh; Bambini; Beelzebub; Charcot; Chatterlitz; Choon-Kil-Tez; Choon-Tro-Pel; Dgloz; Eddin; Gabriel; Hadji-Asvatz-Troov; Hamolinadir; Harahrahhoorhy; Harharkh; Hariton; Hassein; Helkgematios; Herailaz; Herkission; Heroonano; Gurdjieff; Irodohahoon; Jesus Christ; Johnnie; Judas; Kalmanuiour; Kardek; Kin-Too-Toz; Kishmenhof; Konuzion; Kronbernkzion; Kusma; Lentrohamsinin; Malmanash; Mole Crickets; Moses; Nooxhomists; Olmantaboor; Onanson; Orthodoxhydooraki; Plef-Perf-Noof; Sakaki; Sensimirinko; Tooloof; Vinci

Guthrie, A.B.
Big Sky, The: Caudill; Deakins; Summers; Teal Eye
Fair Lane, Fair Land: Summers

Gutzkow, Karl
Wally di Zweiflerin (Wally a Doubting Girl): Wally

H.D.
Bid Me to Live: Rico
Helen in Egypt: Paris
hermione: Farrand; Gart; Lowndes; Rabb
Palimpsest: Jerry

Haggard, Henry Rider
King Solomon's Mines: Curtis; Foulata; Gagool; Good; Infadoos; Khiva; Quartermain; Scragga; Silvestre; Twala; Umpopa; Ventvogel
Nada the Lily: Chaka; Dingaan; Galazi; Mopo
She: Amenartas; Billali; Holly; Kallikrates; Ustane; Vincey

Hale, Edward Everett
If, Yes and Perhaps and *Philip Nolan's Friends*: Nolan

Hale, Sarah Josepha Bell
Poems for our Children: Mary

Haliburton, Thomas Chandler
Clockmaker, The, or The Sayings and Doings of Samuel Slick of Slickville: Slick

Hall, James B.
Not by the Door: Marcham
Mayo Sergeant: Glouster; Sergeant

Hall, Radclyffe
  Well of Loneliness, The: Antrim; Brockett;
    Gordon; Hallam; Llewellyn; Peacock;
    Pierre; Puddleton; Seymour
Hamilton, Patrick
  Gaslight: Alquist; Anton; Cameron;
    Thwaites
  Hangover Square: Bone
Hammett, Dashiell
  Blood Money; Dain Curse, The, and *Red
    Harvest*: Continental Op
  Glass Key, The: Beaumont; Despain;
    Henry; Madvig; O'Rory
  Maltese Falcon, The: Archer; Cairo;
    Gutman; O'Shaughnessy; Spade;
    Thursby; Wilmer
  Thin Man, The: Charles; Jorgensen;
    Macaulay; Morelli; Nunheim; Quinn;
    Rosewater; Wolf; Wynant
Hamsun, Knut
  Mysterier (Mysteries): Kielland; Midget;
    Nagel
Hanley, James
  Captain Botell: Botell; Mulcare;
    Willoughby
  Ebb and Flood: Burns; Condron; Davies;
    Sloane
  Levine: Levin; Marius
  Ocean, The: Benton; Curtain; Gaunt;
    Michaels; Stone
Hansberry, Lorraine
  Sign in Sidney Brustein's Window: Brustein
Hardy, Thomas
  Desperate Remedies: Aldclyffe; Bollen;
    Brown; Chinnery; Crickett; Gradfield;
    Graye; Hinton; Manston; Morris;
    Raunham; Seaway; Springrove
  Changed Man, A: Paddock; Peach
  Dynasts, The: Cantle; Palmer; Pawle
  Fair Maid of the West, The: Spencer
  Far From the Madding Crowd: Boldwood;
    Clark; Coggan; Everdene; Fray; Hurst;
    Money; Oak; Poorgrass; Robin;
    Smallbury; Tall; Troy
  Hand of Ethelberta, The: Belmaine;
    Blandesbury; Chickerel; Doncastle;
    Flower; Julian; Ladywell; Menlove;
    Moulin; Mountclere; Petherwin
  Jude the Obscure: Bridehead; Cartlett;
    Donn; Fawley; Fontover; Gillingham;
    Hawes; Joe; Phillitson; Vilbert
  Laodicean, A: Birch; Camperton; Cockton;
    Dare; De Stancy; Goodman; Havill; Haze;
    Knowles; Mild; Power; Somerset;
    Wilkins; Woodwell
  Life's Little Ironies: Anna; Aspent; Baxby;
    Biles; Bless; Chiles; Cliff; Cope;
    Crookhill; Darty; Dowdle; Fellmer;
    Frankland; Giles; Gould; Grove;
    Halborough; Hanning; Hardcome;

Harnham; Hipcroft; Hobson; Hookhorn;
    Hornhead; Jolliffe; Kytes; Lester;
    Millborne; Ollamoor; Palmley; Pawle;
    Phippard; Privett; Randolph; Raye;
    Richards; Sallet; Sargent; Satchel; Selby;
    Toogood; Twycott; Vallens; Walker;
    Weedle; Winter
  Mayor of Casterbridge, The: Buzzford;
    Chalkfield; Coney; Cuxsom; Fall;
    Farfrae; Goodenough; Grower;
    Henchard; Jopp; Le Sueur; Longways;
    Mockridge; Newson; Stannidge; Whittle
  Pair of Blue Eyes, A: Bicknell; Cannister;
    Glim; Jethway; Kingsmore; Knight;
    Lickpan; Luxellian; Smith; Swancourt;
    Troyton; Unity; Worm
  Return of the Native, The: Cantle; Charlie;
    Dowden; Fairway; Humphrey; Nunsuch;
    Venn; Vye; Wildeve; Yeobright
  Tess of the D'Urbervilles: Chant; Clare;
    Crick; Darch; Durbeyfield; Groby; Huett;
    Kail; Knibbs; Marian; Priddle; Rolliver;
    Tringham
  Trumpet Major, The: Bannister; Beach;
    Brett; Buck; Burden; Comfort;
    Cripplestraw; David; Derriman; Garland;
    Johnson; Jones; Loveday; Mitchell;
    Molly; Noakes; Stanner; Tremlett; Tulla
  Two on a Tower: Biles; Blore; Cecil;
    Chapman; Constantine; Fry; Glanville;
    Green; Hannah; Helmsdale; Lark;
    Martin; Melchester; St Cleeve;
    Torkingham
  Under the Greenwood Tree: Callcome;
    Day; Dewy; Endorfield; James; Mail;
    Maybold; Penny; Shiner; Spinks
  Well Beloved, The: Bencombe; Caro;
    Leverre; Pierston; Pierston; Pine-Avon;
    Somers; Stockwool; Targe
  Wessex Tales: Ballam; Barnet; Brook;
    Charlson; Clarke; Darton; Downe; Giles;
    Green; Grey; Hall; Jake; Jones; Latimer;
    Lodge; Marchmill; Martha Sarah;
    Melrose; Newberry; Owlett; Pitcher;
    Savile; Stockdale; Summers; Trewe
  Woodlanders, The: Cawtree; Charmond;
    Creedle; Damson; Fitzpiers; Jones;
    Melbury; Oliver; South; Tangs; Upjohn;
    Winterbourne
Harland, Henry
  As It Was Written: Neumann; Pathzuol
  Cardinal's Snuff-Box, The: Marchdale;
    Santangiolo
Harraden, Beatrice
  Fowler, The: Bevan
  Ships That Pass in the Night: Allitsen;
    Holme; Reffold; Steinhart; Truog; Warli
Harris, Joel Chandler
  Uncle Remus, His Songs and His Sayings:
    Benjamin Ram; Biggidy; Billy Bluetail;

Bunny Bushtail; Fox; Gibley; Grinny
Granny; Jack; Kubs and Koibs; Malone;
Mammy-Bammy; Meadows; Motts;
Rabbit; Remus; Riley; Tildy; Wattle;
Wolf

Harris, Mark
Southpaw, The: Wiggenn
Wake Up, Stupid: Youngdahl

Harris, Wilson
Da Silva da Silva's Cultivated Wilderness:
Da Silva

Harrower, Elizabeth
Watch Tower, The: Shaw

Hart, Moss
Lady in the Dark: Elliott

Harte, Bret
Gabriel Conroy: Hamlin
Luck of Roaring Camp, The: Ah Fe; Sal
Plain Language from Truthful James: Ah
Sin

Hartley, L.P.
Eustace and Hilda: Cherrington
Go-Between, The: Burgess; Colston;
Maudsley; Trimingham; Winlove
Shrimp and the Anemone, The:
Cherrington; Fothergill; Hapgood;
Grimshaw, Stavely, Steptoe
Sixth Heaven, The: Cherrington
Travelling Grave, The: Bettisher; Munt

Hauptmann, Gerhart
Der arme Heinrich: Heinrich
Der Narr in Christo (The Fool in Christ):
Quint
Die Weber (The Weavers): Baumert;
Dreissiger; Hilse; Jäger

Hawkes, John
Lime Twig, The: Banks; Hencher; Larry;
Slyter; Sybilline; Thick
Second Skin: Bub; Jomo; Kate; Skipper

Hawthorne, Julian
Garth: Urmson

Hawthorne, Nathaniel
Blithedale Romance, The: Coverdale;
Forster; Hollingsworth; Westervelt
Dolliver Romance, The: Dabney; Dolliver
House of the Seven Gables, The: Holgrave;
Maule; Pyncheon; Venner
Marble Faun, The: Donatello; Hilda;
Kenyon; Miriam
Mosses from an Old Manse: Aminadab;
Aylmer; Baglioni; Danforth; Guasconti;
Hovenden; Malvin; Rappaccini; Smooth-
it-Away; Warland
Scarlet Letter, The: Bellingham; Brackett;
Chillingworth; Dimmesdale; Hibbins;
Prynne; Wilson
Token, The: Hooper
Twice-told Tales: Gascoigne; Heidegger;
Higginbotham; Howe; Joliffe; Killigrew;
Medbourne; Pike; Rochcliffe; Wycherley

Hay, John
Bread-winners, The: Farnham; Matchin;
Offit; Sleeny

Haywood, Eliza
Love in Excess, or The Fatal Enquiry:
Melliora

Hearn, Lafcadio
Youma: Peyronnette

Heath, Roy A.K.
Murderer, The: Flood

Hecht, Ben
Eric Dorn: Brander; Dohmann; Dorn

Heller, Joseph
Catch-22: Aardvaark; Cathcart; Dreedle;
Minderbender; Mudd; Peckham;
Scheisskopf; Yossarian
God Knows: David
Good as Gold: Gold
Something Happened: Slocum

Hellmann, Lillian
Little Foxes, The: Giddens; Hubbard

Hemingway, Ernest
Across the River and Into the Trees:
Cantrell; Renata
Farewell to Arms, A: Barkley; Ferguson;
Henry; Myers; Rinaldi; Valentini;
Walker
For Whom the Bell Tolls: Agustin;
Anselmo; Berrendo; Jordan; Lopez;
Maria; Martin; Pablo
In Our Time: Adams
Men Without Women: Andreson
Old Man and the Sea, The: Santiago
Sun Also Rises: Barnes; Campbell; Cohn;
Gorton; Romero
Torrents of Spring, The: Diana; O'Neill

Henley, W.E.
with Robert Louis Stevenson
Admiral Guinea: French
Deacon Brodie: Ainslie; Brodie; Leslie;
Watt

Herbert, A.P.
Holy Deadlock: Adams; Boom; Frame;
Freebody; Frost; Latimer; Merridew;
Mitchell; Myrtle; Parkins; Rigby; Seal;
Simmons; Tott; Wilkin

Herbert, Xavier
Capricornia: Shillingsworth

Hergesheimer, Joseph
Gold and Iron: Hulings; Flower; Veneada;
Wooddrop

Herlihy, James Leo
Midnight Cowboy: Buck; Locke; Pratt;
Rizzo

Hernandez, Jose
El Gaucho Martin Fierro: Fierro

Herrick, Robert
One Woman's Life: Geyer; Ridge

Hesse, Herman
Demian: Demian; Sinclair

Kingsley, Charles
Alton Locke, Tailor and Poet: Locke
Hard Cash: Beresford
Hypatia, or New Foes with an Old Face:
Cyril; Hypatia; Miriam; Orestes; Pambo;
Pelagia; Peter; Philammon; Philo the Jew;
Smid; Synesius; Victoria; Wulf
Water Babies, The: Bedonebyasyoudid;
Cramchild; Doasyouwouldbedoneby;
Grimes; Hartover; Ptthmllnsprts; Tom
Two Years Ago: Harvey; Heale; La
Cordifiamma; Mellot; Scoutbush;
Stangrave; Tardew; Thurnall; Vavasour;
Willis
Westward Ho!: Brimblecombe; Campian;
Cary; Heard; Leigh; Oxenham;
Parracombe; Parsons; Passmore; Salterne;
Sotomayor; Yeo; York
Kingsley, Henry
Ravenshoe: Corby; Ravenshoe
Recollections of Geoffry Hamlyn, The:
Hamlyn
Kingsley, Sidney
Dead End: Angel; Dippy; Drina; Gimpty;
Griswold; Hilton; Martin; Spit; TB;
Tommy
Kipling, Rudyard
Actions and Reactions: Baxter; Beagle-Boy;
Ben; Betts; Chapin; Cloke; Conant; Din;
Farag; Garm; Gery; Groombridge;
Hodgson; Ibn Mararreh; Iggulden;
Lashmars; Loman; Lundie; McLeod;
Melissa; Moultrie; Penfentenyou;
Perseus; Peter; Purnell; Tomling
Barrack-Room Ballads: Deever;
Fuzzywuzzy
Captains Courageous: Boller; Cheyne;
Kinzey; Long Jack; Manuel; Milsom;
Platt; Troop
Collected Short Stories: Green
Day's Work, The: Bell; Boney; Buchanan;
Bukta; Cottar; Deacon; Dimbula; Emory;
Findlayson; Frazier; Hawkins; Hitchcock;
Lacy; Lutyens; Maltese Cat; Martyn;
McPhee; McRimmon; Peroo; Sargent;
Scott; Wardrop; Zuleika
Debits and Credits: Anthony; Apis;
Armine; Ashcroft; Bevin; Brownell;
Burges; Christophe; Ellis; Fettley;
Godsoe; Hickmot; Howell; Humberstall;
Keede; Lemming; Macklin;
Maddingham; Margettes; Martin;
Mockler; Orton; Otho; Portson; Roger of
Salerno; Stephen de Suatre; Tarworth;
Tegg; Tertius; Thomas; Turrell; Vigors;
Villamarti; Voiron; Winchmore
Diversity of Creatures, A: Anna;
Benzaguen; Chartres; Conroy; De Forest;
Dolbie; Dragomiroff; Eames; Ebermann;
Eden; Fowler; Gerritt; Godfrey;

Henschil; Hervey; Ingell; Ipps; Jesse;
Jules; Leggatt; Lingham; Masquerier;
Midmore; Mullins; Ollyett; Pallant;
Pirolo; Postgate; Shend; Sichcliffe;
Sidney; Singh; Sperrit; Takahira; Trivett;
Vernon; Walen; Wickenden; Winton;
Wontner; Woodhouse
Jungle Books: Akela; Baloo; Bandar-Log;
Billy; Buldeo; Darzee; Chil; Grey Brother;
Hathi; Ikki; Kaa; Kerick; Kotick; Mang;
Messua; Moa; Mowgli; Mugger; Mysa;
Nag; Petersen; Phao; Purun Dass; Rama;
Rann; Rikki Tikki Tavi; Sahi; Sea Catch;
Sea Cow; Sea Rat; Sea Vitch; Shere Khan;
Tabaqui; Teddy; Tha; Toomai; Two
Tails; White Cobra; Won-Toller
Just So Stories: Balkis; Bavian; Bi-coloured
Rock Snake; Boomer; Dingo; Djinn; Eldest
Magician; Elephant's Child; Ethiopian;
Painted Jaguar; Pau Amma; Pestorijee;
Sambo; Slow-Solid; Small Porgies; Smiler;
Spots; Stickly-Prickly; Stute Fish;
Suleiman-im-Daoud; Taffimai; Tegumai
Bopsulai
Kim: Bennett; Creighton; E23; Huneefa;
Hurree; Lurgan Sahib; Mahbub Ali;
O'Hara; Shamlegh; Shott; Teshoo; Victor
Life's Handicap: Ameera; Bahadur; Basset-
Holmer; Bertran; Bimi; Dearsley;
Dempsey; Dirkovitch; Dodd; Ephrain
Yahudi; Fleete; Georgie Porgie; Gobind;
Grady; Hay; Holden; Hummil; Imray;
Lammiter; Limmason; Longer; Lowndes;
Madu; Moti Guj; Mottram; Mulcahy;
Naboth; Namgay; Nurkeed; Pambe;
Parrenness; Pir Khan; Reingelder;
Roantree; Shadd; Sheehy; Silver Man;
Suket; Tallentire; Tietjens; Tobrah;
Vowle; Yardley-Orde
Light that Failed, The: Antirosa; Beeton;
Binat; Binkie; Broke; Heldar; Jennett;
Maisie; Nilghai; Red-Haired Girl;
Torpenhow
Limits and Renewals: Belton; Berners;
'Bunny'; Castorley; Falloux; Frost;
Gillon; Gleeag; Gravell; Harries;
Haylock; Heatleigh; Horringe;
Lettcombe; Loftie; Lucius; Mackworth;
Mahmud Ali; Manallace; Marden;
Mervyn; Phil; Quaybil; Randolph; Single;
Sulinor; Tigner; Valens; Vaughan; Vergil;
Wilkett; William; Wollin
Many Inventions: Boileau; Brander;
Brugglesmith; Challong; Cheever;
Dempsey; Dennis; Dewcy; Di'monds and
Pearls; Dowse; Eva; Fenwick; Frithiof;
Gisborne; Grish Chunder; Gulla Kuttah
Mullah; Halley; Hanna; Herodsfoot;
Hicksey; Infant; Judson; Keller; Lascar
Loo's Mother; Mackie; Mears; Mowgli;

Lewis, Sinclair
Ann Vickers: Vickers
Arrowsmith: Arrowsmith; Brumfit;
 Clawson; Duer; Fox; Gottlieb; Hinkley;
 Holabird; Hunziger; Ingleblad; Lanyon;
 McGurk; Novak; Pickerbaugh; Silva;
 Sondelius; Tozer; Tredgold; Watters;
 Wickett; Winter
Babbitt: Babbitt; Doane; Escott; Frink;
 Graff; Gunch; Jones; Judique; Littlefield;
 McGoun; McKelvey; Pumphrey;
 Riesling; Swanson; Thompson
Dodsworth: Cortright; Dodsworth;
 Lockert; Obersdorf
Elmer Gantry: Bains; Dowler; Falconer;
 Gantry; Lefferts; Roberts; Shallard
It Can't Happen Here: Haik; Jessup;
 Saranson; Trowbridge; Windrip
Main Street: Kennicott; Pollock;
 Sherwin
Lewis, Wyndham
Apes of God, The: Ratner; Sib
Blasting and Bombadiering: Beresin;
 Cantleman; Menzies; Misrow;
 Polderdick
*Cantleman's Spring Mate; The Code of a
 Herdsman and The Ideal
 Giant*: Cantleman
Mrs Dukes' Million: Beechamp; Dukes;
 Fane; Hillington; Khan; Nichols; Passion;
 Roy; Winter
Revenge for Love, The: Abershaw; Alvaro;
 Asunción; Communist; Cruze; O'Hara;
 Phipps; Stamp
Roaring Queen, The: Hyman; Shodbutt
Tarr: Soltyk; Tarr; Vasek
Unlucky for Pringle: Bannerman; Beresin;
 Blakely; Cairn; Cantleman; Charlaran;
 Crumms; Daintwich; Dean; Denning
 Fraser; Gilchrist; Gosport; Hope-Carew;
 Jaffe; Jevons; Kipe; Leslie; Letheridge;
 Meehaan; Martin; Mammiou; Miuron;
 Pish-Tush; Polderdick; Pringle; Rockaly;
 Roland; Shirley; Stubbs; Tillington;
 Truck
Lillo, George
*London Merchant, or The History of
 George Barnwell*: Lucy; Millwood;
 Thorowgood
Llewellyn, Richard
How Green Was My Valley: Bando;
 Benyon; Bronwen; Ellis the stable;
 Ethelwyn; Evans; Evans; Elias the shop;
 Griffiths; Gruffydd; Jonas Sessions;
 Jenkins; Lewis; Llywarch; Morgan;
 Motshill; Phillips; Pritchard; Richards
Lockhart, John Gibson
History of Matthew Wald, The: Wald
Some Passages in the Life of Adam Blair:
 Campbell

London, Jack
Call of the Wild, The: Thornton
Children of the Frost: Leclere
Daughter of the Snows, A: Corliss; St
 Vincent; Welse
Game, The: Fleming; Genevieve; Ponta
Iron Heel, The: Cunningham; Everhard;
 Hammerfield; Heel; Ingram; Morehouse;
 Van Gilbert; Wickson
Jerry of the Islands: Horn; Jerry
Martin Eden: Brissenden; Eden; Morse
Sea Wolf, The: Brewster; Harrison;
 Henderson; Johansen; Kerfoot; Larsen;
 Louis; Oofty-Oofty; Smoke;
 Van Weyden
Smoke Bellew: Bellew
White Fang: Scott; Smith; White Fang
Longfellow, Henry Wadsworth
Courtship of Miles Standish, The: Alden;
 Priscilla
Evangeline: Bellefontaine; Standish
Hiawatha: Minnehaha; Longus
Daphnis and Chloe: Chloe; Daphnis
Lonsdale, Frederick
Last of Mrs Cheyney, The: Cheyney;
 Frinton
Loos, Anita
Gentlemen Prefer Blondes: Beekman;
 Broussard; Dorothy; Eisman; Froyd; Lee;
 Shelton; Spoffard; Weeks
Lorimer, G.H.
*Letters from a Self-Made Merchant to His
 Son*: Graham
Lover, Samuel
Handy Andy: Casey; Dawson; Durfy;
 Dwyer; Egan; Flanagan; Furlong;
 O'Connor; O'Grady; Riley; Rooney
Lowell, James Russell
Fable for Critics, A: Miranda
Lowndes, Marie Belloc
Lizzie Borden: Borden
Lowry, Malcolm
Lunar Caustic: Plantagenet
Under the Volcano: Constable; Firmin;
 Laruelle; Vigil
Lowry, Robert
Big Cage, The: Black
Lurie, Alison
Imaginary Friends: McMann
Love and Friendship: Ingrams; Lumkin;
 Thomas; Turner
Nowhere City, The: Cattleman; Ceci;
 Einsam; Foster; Green
Real People: Berg; Smith
War Between the Tates, The: Tate
Lyall, Edna
Autobiography of a Slander, The: Cleave;
 Houghton; Morley; O'Reilly; Zaluski
Doreen: The Story of a Singer: Desmond;
 Hereford; O'Ryan

Lyly, John
Alexander and Campaspe: Campaspe
Euphues: Euphues; Lucilla; Philautus
Galathea: Galathea; Phillida
Lynton, Mrs Lynn
Autobiography of Christopher Kirkland,
The: Kirkland
Lytle, Andrew
Long Night, The: McIvor
Name for Evil, A: Brent
Velvet Morn, The: Cree
Lytton, Edward Bulwer
Alice, or The Mysteries: Cameron;
Cesarini; Darvil; De Ventadour; Ferrers;
Justis; Leslie; Lascelles; Maltravers;
Merton; Saxingham
Caxtons, The: A Family Picture: Caxton
Coming Race, The: Vril
Ernest Maltravers: Cameron; Cesarini;
Darvil; De Ventadour; Ferrers; Lascelles;
Maltravers
Eugene Aram: Aram; Houseman; Lester
Haunted and the Haunters, The: Hand;
Shadow
Last Days of Pompeii, The: Burbo
Last of the Barons, The: Alwyn; Bonville;
Nevile; Warner; Warwick
Money: Clara
My Novel, or Varieties in English Life:
Burley; Dale; Egerton; Fairfield;
Hazeldean; L'Estrange; Levy;
Riccabocca; Violante
Paul Clifford: Brandon; Clifford; Lobkins;
MacGrawler; Mauleverer; Pepper;
Tomlinson
Pelham, or The Adventures of a
Gentleman: Dawson; Glanville; Johnson;
Pelham; Thornton; Tirrell
Strange Story, A: Fenwick; Lloyd

Maartens, Maarten
God's Fool: A Koopstad Story: Lossell
Macaulay, Rose
Crewe Train: Bartlett; Chapel; Dobie;
Gresham
Non-Combatants and Others: Evie;
Frampton; Gordon; Kate; Maclure;
Maynard; Orme; Sandomir; Simon;
Tucker; Vinney; West
Orphan Island: O'Malley; Smith;
Thinkwell
Potterism: Gideon; Hobart; Juke; Potter;
Varick
Told By an Idiot: Croft; Garden; Jayne;
Wilbur
Towers of Trebizond, The: Chantry-Pigg;
Dagenham; ffoulkes-Corbett; Langley;
Laurie; Tanpinar
World My Wilderness, The: Cox;
Deniston; Dinent; Mavis; Maxwell;

Michel; Richie; Roger
What Not: A Prophetic Comedy: Chester
McBain, Ed
Cop Hater: Carella
McCabe, Cameron
Face on the Cutting-Room Floor, The:
McCabe; Smith
McCarthy, Mary
Birds of America: Bonfante; Brown;
Lammers; Levi; Scott; Smail
Group, The: Andrews; Davison; Eastlake;
Hartshorn; MacAusland; Petersen;
Prothero; Renfrew; Strong
McCullers, Carson
Ballad of the Sad Café, The: Evans; Macy;
Willis
Clock Without Hands: Clane; Malone;
Pew; Verily
Heart is a Lonely Hunter, The:
Antonapoulos; Blount; Brannon;
Copeland; Kelly; Singer
Member of the Wedding, The: Addams;
Brown; West
Reflections in a Golden Eye: Anacleto;
Firebird; Langdon; Penderton; Williams
Macdonald, John D.
Deep Blue Goodbye, The: McGee
Macdonald, George
Donal Grant: Grant
Marquis of Lossie, The: Bellair; Catanach
Phantastes: Anodos
Macdonald, Ross
Moving Target, The: Archer
Machen, Arthur
Great God Pan, The: Argentine; Clarke;
Crashaw; Herbert; Mary; Meyrick;
Raymond; Vaughan; Villiers
McKay, Claude
Home to Harlem: Jake
Mackay, Shena
Advent Calendar, An: Gibby; Keen;
MacGregor; Pickering; Wood
Bowl of Cherries, A: Almond; Beaney;
Beaumont; Cluff-Trench; Mandrake
Dreams of Dead Women's Handbags:
Gordon; Stella
Dust Falls on Eugene Schlumberger: Davis;
Fawkes; Mayhew
Old Crow: Blake; Elf; Fairbrother; Jigger;
McNaught; Oates; Slim
Redhill Rococo: Headley-Jones; Ribbons;
Ruggles; Slattery
Toddler on the Run: Loveday
Mackenzie, Compton
Extraordinary Women, Theme and
Variations: Randan
Plasher's Mead: Fane
Sinister Street: Carlyle; Carruthers;
Carthew; Castleton; Crackenthorpe;
Drake; Fane; Haden; Hazelwood;

Manners; Meats; Merivale; Ross; Saxby;
Scarlett; Smithers; Venables; Viner;
Wedderburn
South Wind of Love, The: Rayner
Sylvia and Michael: Fane
Sylvia Scarlett: Bannerman; Dorward;
Fane; Hobart; Horne; Iredale; Madden;
Meares; Monkley; Snow; Worsley
Mackenzie, Henry
Man of Feeling, The: Atkins; Harley;
Sindall; Silton; Winbrooke; Walton
Mackenzie, Kenneth (Seaforth)
Young Desire It, The: Fox; Penworth
Macklin, Charles
Man of the World: MacSycophant
MacLennan, Hugh
Each Man's Son: MacNeil
Macleod, Fiona
Spiritual Tales: Bel the Harper
Macnaughton, Sarah
Fortunes of Christina McNab, The:
Hardcastle; McCrae; McNab
Mailer, Norman
American Dream, An: Kelly; Martin;
Rojack
Mais, Roger
Hills Were Joyful Together, The: Surjue
Malamud, Bernard
Assistant, The: Alpine; Bober
Dubin's Lives: Dubin
Fixer, The: Bok
Malleson, Constance
Coming Back, The: Orellano
Mallock, William Hurrell
New Republic, or *Culture, Faith and
Philosophy in an English Country House*:
Allen; Herbert; Laurence; Luke; Rose;
Storks
Malory, Thomas
Le Morte D'Arthur: Arthur; Ban; Blaise;
Dagonet
Mandel, George
Flee the Angry Strangers: Lattimer; Stoney;
Webb
Mangione, Jerre
Ship and the Flame, The: Argento
Manley, Delarivière
Adventures of Rivella, or *The History of
the Author of The Atlantis*: Lovemore;
Rivella
*Secret History of Queen Zara and the
Zarazians, The*: Zara
*Secret Memoirs and Manners of Several
Persons of Quality of Both Sexes from
the New Atlantis, an Island in the
Mediterranean, 1709*, and *Memoirs of
Europe Towards the Close of the
Eighteenth Century*: Astrea
Mann, F.O.
Albert Grope: Grope; Malley; Taube

Mann, Klaus
Mephisto: Bruckner; Höfgen; Juliette;
Kroge; Larue; Tebab; Lithenthal; Marder;
Martin; Muck; Pelz
Mann, Leonard
Flesh in Armour: Jeffrys
Go-Getter, The: Gibbons
Mann, Thomas
Buddenbrook, Verfall einer Familie:
Buddenbrook; Hagenström
Der Tod in Venedig (Death in Venice):
Aschenbach; Tadzio
Manning, Anne
*Maiden and Married Life of Marie Powell,
The*: Powell
Manning, Olivia
Great Fortune, The: Pringle
Mansfield, Katherine
Bliss: Alice; Burnell; Fulton; Moss; Raoul;
Young
Dove's Nest, The: Fawcett
Garden Party, The: Andrews; Meadows;
Parker; Pinner; Sheridan
Prelude: Burnell; Fairfield
Manzoni, Alessandro
I Promessi Sposi (The Betrothed): Renzo
Markfield, Wallace
To an Early Grave: Braverman; Rieff
Teitlebaum's Widow: Sloan
You Could Live if They Let You: Farber;
Federman; Horton
Marlowe, Christopher
Doctor Faustus: Belzebub; Faustus;
Lucifer; Mephistopheles; Ralph; Robin;
Valdes; Vanholt; Wagner
Edward II: Edward; Gaveston; Mortimer;
Spenser
Jew of Malta, The: Barabas; Barnadine;
Bellamine; Calymatch; Del Bosco;
Ferneze; Ithamore; Jacomo; Mathias;
Pilia Porsa
Tamburlaine: Annipe; Arabia; Argier;
Bajazeth; Capolin; Ceneus; Cosroe;
Ebeza; Egypt; Fez; Magnetes; Meander;
Menaphon; Morocco; Mycates;
Ortygius; Tamburlaine; Techelles;
Usumcasane; Zenocrate
Marquand, John P.
H.M.Pulham Esq.: King; Motford; Myles;
Priest; Pulham
Late George Apley, The: Apley
Point of No Return: Gray
Wickford Point: Berg; Calder; Caraway;
Glifford; Leighton
Marquis, Don
archy and mehitabel: archy; clarence;
freddy; mehitabel
Marryat, Captain
Children of the New Forest, The:
Armitage; Beverley; Heatherstone;

Marryat, Captain—*contd.*
  Pablo; Partridge; Southwold; Villiers
  King's Own, The: Adams; Bullock;
    Debriseau; De Courcy; Hornblow;
    McElvina; Peters; Rainscourt
  Masterman Ready: Juno; Osborn; Ready;
    Seagrave
  Mr Midshipman Easy: Biggs; Bonnycastle;
    Easthupp; Easy; Joliffe; Mesty;
    Middleton; Oxbelly; Rebura; Sawbridge;
    Smallsole; Tallboys; Tartar; Vigors;
    Wilson
  Pacha of Mary Tales, The: Charis; Slave
  Peter Simple: Chucks; Hawkins; O'Brien;
    Privilege; Savage; Simple
  Phantom Ship, The: Barentz; Kloots;
    Krantz; Mathias; Poots; Schriften;
    Seysen; Van Brennen; Vanderdecken; Von
    Stroom
  Settlers in Canada, The: Angry Snake;
    Bone; Campbell; Emmersen; Gladwin;
    Graves; Harvey; Jackson; Lumley; Pontia;
    Sinclair; Super; Wilson
  Snarleyyow: Smallbones; Snarleyyow;
    Vanslyperken
Marsh, Ngaio
  Man Lay Dead, A: Alleyn; Bathgate
Marshall, Arthur Calder
  About Levy: Levy
Marshall, Paule
  Brown Girl, Brownstones: Boyce
  Chosen Place, the Timeless People, The:
    Kinbona
Marston, John
  Antonio and Mellida: Antonio; Mellida
  Dutch Courtesan, The: Faugh;
    Franceshina; Freeville; Malheureux;
    Muligrub; Subboys; Tysefew
  Eastward Ho!: see Chapman, George
  Malcontent, The: Malevole
Masefield, John
  Bird of Dawning: Bauer; Chedglow;
    Frampton
  Everlasting Mercy, The: Kane
  Odtaa: De Leyva; Elena; Letcombe-Bassett;
    Ridden; Rust; Weycock; Winter; Zubiaga
  Sard Harker: Harker; Hirsch; Manuel
Mason, A.E.W.
  At the Villa Rose: Besnard; Hanaud;
    Ricardo
  Four Feathers, The: Eustace; Feversham
Massinger, Philip
  City Madam, The: Fortune; Frugal; Getall;
    Goldwire; Hoist; Lacy; Penur; Plenty;
    Secet; Shavem; Stargaze; Tradewell
  Double Marriage, The: see Fletcher, John
  Duke of Milan, The: Marcella
  Elder Brother, The: see Fletcher, John
  Fatal Dowry, The: Charalois
  Maid of Honour, The: Adorni; Astutio;

  Aurelia; Bertoldo; Camiola; Ferdinand;
    Fulgentinio; Roberto; Sylli
  New Way to Pay Old Debts, A: Allworth;
    Amble; Furnace; Greedy; Marrall; Order;
    Overreach; Tapwell; Welborne; Will-Do;
    Watchall
  Spanish Curate, The: see Fletcher, John
  Thierry & Theodoret: see Fletcher, John
Masters, Edgar Lee
  Mitch Miller and Skeeters Kirby: Miller
  Spoon River Anthology: Fraser; Henry;
    Jones; Simmons; Trainor
Mathers, Peter
  Trap: David; Trap
  Wort Papers, The: Matters; Wort
Maturin, Charles Robert
  Melmoth the Wanderer: Melmoth;
    Moncada
Maugham, W. Somerset
  Ah King: Ginger Ted; Jones
  Cakes and Ale: Driffield; Gann; Kear;
    Kemp
  Letter, The: Hammond
  Liza of Lambeth: Blakeston; Cooper;
    Hodges; Kemp
  Moon and Sixpence, The: Strickland;
    Stroeve
  Narrow Corner, The: Blake; Nichols;
    Saunders
  Of Human Bondage: Athelney; Carey;
    Cronshaw; Forster; Hayward; Graves;
    Griffiths; Miller; Nesbit; Otter; Perkins;
    Price; Rogers; Sampson; South; Sung;
    Tyrell; Wilkinson
  Sheppey: Miller
  Strictly Personal: Potter
  Trembling of a Leaf, The: Davidson; Horn;
    Mackintosh; MacPhail; Neilson;
    O'Hara; Red; Thompson; Walker
Mayfield, Julian
  Grand Parade, The: Banks; Kockek;
    Taylor; Weeks
  Hit, The: Cooley; Lewis
Melville, Herman
  Billy Budd: Budd; Claggart; Vere
  Clarel: Ruth
  Confidence Man, The: His Masquerade:
    Goodman
  Israel Potter: Potter
  Mardi: Jarl; Media; Samoa; Taji; Yillah
  Moby Dick, or The Whale: Ahab; Bildad;
    Coffin; Daggoo; Fedallah; Flask; Gabriel;
    Ishmael; Mapple; Pip; Queequeg;
    Starbuck; Stubb; Tashtego
  Piazza Tales: Babo; Bartleby; Cereno;
    Delano
  Pierre, or The Ambiguities: Glendenning;
    Stanly; Tartan; Ulver
  Redburn: His First Voyage: Bolton;
    Redburn; Riga

White-Jacket: Chase; Claret; Cuticle; Pert;
  White-Jacket
Meredith, George
  Adventures of Harry Richmond, The:
    Bannerbridge; Beltham; Bulstead;
    Dewsbury; Eppenwelzen-sarkeld;
    Goodwin; Heriot; Ilchester; Kiomi;
    Ottilia; Richmond; Rippenger; Sewis;
    Sweetwinter; Temple; Waddy
  Amazing Marriage, The: Fleetwood;
    Kirby; Levellier; Woodseer
  Beauchamp's Career: Beauchamp; Culling;
    Denham; De Croisnel; De Rouaillat;
    Halkett; Romfrey; Shrapnel
  Diana of the Crossways: Dacier;
    Dannisborough; Dunstane; Redworth;
    Warwick
  Egoist, The: Crooklyn; Crossjay; Dale; De
    Craye; Durham; Jenkinson; Middleton;
    Oxford; Patterne; Whitford
  Evan Harrington: Belfield; Bonner;
    Cogglesby; Current; De Saldar; Fiske;
    Goren; Harrington; Jocelyn; Raikes;
    Roseley; Strike; Uploft; Wheedle;
    Wishaw
  *Ordeal of Richard Feverel, The: A History
    of Father and Son*: Bakewell; Berry;
    Blaize; Blandish; Denzil; Desborough;
    Doria; Feverel; Forey; Harley; Hippias;
    Jinkson; Mount; Mountfalcon;
    Papworth; Thompson; Todhunter;
    Wentworth
  Rhoda Fleming: Armstrong; Blancove;
    Boulby; Eccles; Fleming; Hackbut;
    Lovell; Sedgett; Sumfit; Waring
  Shaving of Shagpat, The: Abarak; Bagarag;
    Bhanavar the Beautiful; Feshnavat;
    Mustapha; Noorna bin Noorka; Ruark;
    Shagpat; Zurvan
Merimée, Prosper
  Carmen: Carmen; Lucas
Merrick, Leonard
Conrad In Search of His Youth: Adaile;
  Conrad; Heath; Lascelles; Page;
  Tryphena
Merriman, H. Seton
  Barlasch of the Guard: Barlasch
Meyer, Conrad Ferdinand
  Jürg Jenatsch: Jenatsch
Middleton, Stanley
  Apple of the Eye: Tenby
  Brazen Prison: Stead
Middleton, Thomas
  Chaste Maid in Cheapside, A: Allwit;
    Touchwood; Whorehound;
    Yellowhammer
  Mad World My Masters, A: Follywit;
    Gullman; Gunwater; Harebrain; Hoboy;
    Inesse; Jasper; Mawworm; Rafe
  Roaring Girl, The: see Dekker, Thomas

Trick to Catch the Old One, A: Foxstone;
  Hoard; Lamprey; Limber; Lucre;
  Spichcock; Witgood
  Women Beware Women: Florence;
    Guardino; Hippolito; Isabella; Leandro;
    Livia
  with William Rowley
  Changeling, The: Albius; Alsemero;
    Antonio; Delflores; Fransciscus; Lollio;
    Pedro; Vermandero
  Fair Quarrel, A: Ager; Albo; Fitzallan;
    Meg; Russell; Trimtram; Vapour
  attrib.
  Revenger's Tragedy, The: Ambiotoso;
    Antonio; Gratiana; Hippolito; Junior;
    Lussurioso; Piero; Superuacuo; Vindice
Miller, Arthur
  After the Fall: Maggie
  Death of a Salesman: Loman
Milne, A.A.
  Red House Mystery, The: Birch; Cayley
  Truth About Blayds, The: Blayds
  Winnie the Pooh: Piglet; Rabbit; Winnie
    the Pooh
Mitchell, John Ames
  Amos Judd: Judd
Mitchell, Joseph
  McSorley's Wonderful Saloon: Bardwell;
    Gordon; Gould; McSorley
  Old Mr Flood: Flood; Nikanov
Mitchell, Margaret
  Gone With the Wind: Benteen; Butler;
    Calvert; Dilcey; Elsing; Gallegher;
    Hamilton; Kennedy; Mammy; Meade;
    Meriwether; O'Hara; Pork; Slattery;
    Tarleton; Watling; Wellburn; Wilkerson;
    Wilkes
Mitchell, S.W.
  Hugh Wynne, Free Quaker: Warder;
    Wynne
Mitford, Nancy
  Love in a Cold Climate: Hampton
  Pursuit of Love, The: Alconleigh;
    Merlin; Sauveterre; Talbot; Townsend;
    Warbeck
Mitchison, Naomi
  Conquered, The: Ardorix of Curdun;
    Gandoc the Briton
  Corn King and the Spring Queen, The: Erif
    Der
Molesworth, Mrs
  Carrots: Just a Little Boy: Desart; Hooper;
    White
  Cuckoo Clock, The: Griselda;
    Kneebreeches; Lavander
  Oriel Window, The: Coles; Flowers;
    Mayhew; Piggot; Turner
Molière
  L'École des femmes (School for Wives):
    Agnes; Arnolphe; Horace

Robinson, Lennox
  White-headed Boy, The: Duffy; Ellen;
  Geohegan
Rod, Edouard
  Les roches blanches (The White Rocks):
  Bussens; Charmot; Trembloz
Rohmer, Sax
  Mystery of Dr Fu Manchu: Fu Manchu;
  Wayland-Smith
Rolfe, Frederick W.
  Hadrian the Seventh: Crowe
Ros, Amanda
  Delina Delaney: Delaney; De Maine
Ross, Martin
  Some Experiences of an Irish R.M.: see
  Somerville, E.O.
Roth, Henry
  Call it Sleep: Leo; Lobe; Luter; Mink;
  Nerrick; Pankower; Schearl; Schulim;
  Wildflower
Roth, Philip
  Ghost Writer, The: Bellette; Lonoff
  Letting Go: Herz; Reganhart; Wallach
  My Life as a Man: Tarnapol; Zuckerman
  Portnoy's Complaint: Portnoy; Reed;
  Spielvogel
  Professor of Desire, The: Kepesh
Rowe, Nicholas
  Tamerlane: Bajazet; Tamerlane
Rowley, William
  Changeling, The: see Middleton, Thomas
  Fair Quarrel, A: see Middleton, Thomas
Rowson, Susannah
  Charlotte: A Tale of Truth: Crayton;
  Franklin; La Rue; Montraville; Temple
Ruskin, John
  King of the Golden River, The: Gluck;
  Hans; Schwartz; South West Wind
Rutherford, Mark
  Autobiography of Mark Rutherford, The:
  Mardon; Rutherford; Snale; Wollaston
  Catherine Furze: Arden; Bellamy; Cardew;
  Catchpole; Colston; Crowhurst; Furze;
  Gosford; Ponsonby

Sackville, Thomas
  Gorboduc: see, Norton, Thomas
Sadleir, Michael
  Fanny By Gaslight: Beckett; Bonnet; Box;
  Cairns; Cartaret; Ferraby; Heaviside;
  Hooper; Hopwood; Manderstoke;
  Muggleton; Seymore; Tennant; Warbeck
Saki
  Beasts and Super-Beasts: Bilsiter; Jerton;
  Nuttel; Sappleton; Stroope; Stossen
  Chronicles of Clovis, The: Appin; Barfield;
  Birberry; Bishop; Clovis; Finsberry;
  Huddle; Ley; Pincini; Prike; Resker;
  Stoner; Stringham; Tobermory

Unbearable Bassington, The: Bassington;
  De Frey; Greech; Youghal
Salinger, J.D.
  Catcher in the Rye, The: Ackley; Antolini;
  Caulfield; Hayes; Stradlater
  Franny and Zooey: Coutell; Glass
Sansom, William
  Loving Eye, The: Orme
Santayana, George
  Last Puritan, The: Alden; Darnley; Schlote;
  Van de Wayer
Sapper
  Bulldog Drummond: Drummond
Saroyan, William
  Human Comedy, The: Arena;
  Beauchampe; Cabot; Ek; Eliot; George;
  Gottlieb; Grogan; Macauley
  Time of Your Life, The: Blick
  Tracy's Tiger: Luthy; Nimmo; Pingitzen;
  Ringert; Seyfang; Tracy; Valora
Sarton, May
  Faithful Are the Wounds: Cavan
  Mrs Stevens Hears the Mermaids Singing:
  Stevens
  Small Room, The: Winter
Sassoon, Siegfried
  Memoirs of a Fox-Hunting Man, The:
  Milden; Pennett; Sherston; Tiltood
  Memoirs of an Infantry Officer: Cromlech;
  Tyrrell
Satie, Erik
  'A Mammal's Notebook': critics
  Act of Clemency: Lugné-poe
Savery, Henry
  Quintus Servinton: Servinton
Sayer, Ernest Lawrence
  San Francisco Examiner: Casey
Sayers, Dorothy L.
  Whose Body?: Bunter; Wimsey
Schnitzler, Arthur
  Fräulein Else: Dorsay; Else
Schreiner, Olive
  Story of an African Farm, The: Blenkins;
  Em; Lyndall; Rose; Sannie; Waldo; Walt
Schulberg, Bud
  Harder They Fall, The: Latka; Molina
  Disenchanted, The: Halliday
  What Makes Sammy Run?: Glick
Scott, Michael
  Tom Cringle's Log: Cringle
Scott, Paul
  Raj Quartet, The: Batchelor; Merrick;
  Smalley
  Staying On: Smalley
Scott, Walter
  Abbot, The: Bradbourne; Bridget;
  Carslogie; Donald; Dryesdale; Eustace;
  Glendenning; Graeme; Henderson;
  Lundin; Schinderhausen; Woodcock
  Anne of Geierstein: Antonio; Arnheim;

Biederman; Block; Boisgelin; Bubenberg;
Cabestainy; Campo-Gasso; Colvin;
Donnerhugel; Geierstein; Hagenbach;
Matthew of Doncaster; Mengs; Philipson;
Schreckenwald; Steinfeldt; Sturmthal;
Veichen

Antiquary, The: Adhemar; Aikwood;
Blattergrowl; Breck; Caxon; Cheyne;
D'Acunha; Dousterswivel; Dryasdust;
Glenallan; Gourlay; Greenhorn;
Grinderson; Howie; Lovel; Mailsetter;
Mucklebackit; Neville; Ochiltree;
Oldbuck; Sang; Waldeck; Wardour;
Wilson

Betrothed, The: Aldrovan; Amelot;
Baldrick; Berenger; Brengwain;
Cadwallon; Dogget; Einion; Flammock;
Gillian; Guarine; Gwenwyn; Jorworth;
Lacy; Margery; Morolt

Black Dwarf, The: Armstrong; Bauldie;
Benarbuck; Earnscliff; Elliot; Ilderton;
Langley; Mauley; Ratcliffe; Willie of
Westburnflat

Bride of Lammermoor, The: Ashton;
Balderstone; Bide-the-Bent; Blackhall;
Blenkensop; Castle-Cuddy; Condiddle;
Craigengelt; Dingwall; Girder; Gray;
Hayston; Moonshine; Mortsheugh;
Ravenswood; Tinto

Castle Dangerous: Berkely; Bertram;
Erceldoun; Fleming; Greenleaf; Hautlieu;
Powheid; Turnbull

Count Robert of Paris: Achilles Tatius;
Agelastes; Bohemous of Tartentum;
Diogenes; Ederic the Forester; Engelred;
Guiscard; Harpax; Hereward;
Lysimachus; Osmund; Paris; Stephanos

Fair Maid of Perth, The: Anselm; Baliol;
Balveeny; Barber; Bonthron; Buncle;
Charteris; Clement; Craigdallie;
Croftangry; Day; Dun; Dwining; Eviot;
Glover; Gow; Henshaw; Longueville;
Lundin; MacGillie; Martha; Proudfute;
Ramorny; Smotherwell; Torquil

Fortunes of Nigel, The: Armstrong;
Barratter; Beaujeu; Christie; Colepepper;
Crambagge; Dalgarno; Heriot;
Hermione; Hildebrod; Huntinglen;
Linklater; Lowestoffe; Malagrowther;
Mansel; Moniplies; Olifaunt; Ramsay;
Sharker; Skurliewhitter; Trapbois;
Turnstall; Vincent

Guy Mannering: Allan; Archer; Baillie;
Bearcliff; Bertram; Cockburn; Dinmont;
Driver; Glossin; Hazelwood; Jabos;
Jonstone; Kennedy; MacCandlish;
MacGuffog; Mannering; Merrilies;
Pleydell; Salmon; Skreigh; Wellwood

Heart of Midlothian: Archibald; Argyll;
Balchristie; Bantext; Barron; Bickerton;

Broadwheel; Butler; Deans; Dumbledikes;
Dutton; Farbrother; Glass; Hardie;
Howden; Knollys; Levitt; Livingstone;
Middleburgh; Murdockson; Muschat;
Plyem; Ratcliffe; Saddletree; Sharpitlaw;
Staunton; Tuck; Walker; Whistler;
Wilson

Highland Widow, The: Baliol; Beauffet;
Bethune; Campbell; Lambskin; MacEvoy;
MacPhadrick; MacTavish; Sommerville;
Steele

Ivanhoe: Abdalle; Alfagi; Allan-a-Dale;
Bardon; Beaumanoir; Boabdil; Bois-
Guilbert; Bracy; Cedric of Rotherfield;
Conigsburgh; Fitzpurse; Front-de-Boeuf;
Gurth; Herman of Goodalricke; Isaac of
York; Ivanhoe; Locksley; Malvoisin;
Palmer; Rebecca; Reuben; Rowena; Seth;
Wamba; Wolfram

Kenilworth: Badger; Blount; Bowyer;
Coxe; Crane; Doboobie; Foster;
Goldthread; Gosling; Holyday;
Lambourne; Leicester; Mumblazen;
Rosbart; Sludge; Smith; Staples;
Tressilian

Legend of Montrose, The: Campbell;
Dalgetty; Evan Dhu of Lochiel;
Grancangowl; Hector of the Mist; Lyle;
Macdonnell; Maceagh; McAlpin;
McAulay; O'Quilligan

Monastery, The: Bolton; Boniface;
Catherine of Newport; Christie of
Clinthill; Doolittle; Eustace; Foster;
Gilbert of Cranberry Moor;
Glendenning; Graeme; Happer; Kyle;
Philip; Saviola; Shafton; Warden

My Aunt Margaret's Mirror: Forester

Old Mortality: Allen; Balfour of Kinloch;
Bellenden; Blane; Bothwell; Buskbody;
Dennison; Evandale; Goose; Gudyill;
Headrigg; Kettledrummie; Maclure;
Miles; Morton; Mucklewrath

Peveril of the Peak: Aldrick; Beacon;
Bigstaffe; Bridgenorth; Canter; Chiffinch;
Cholmondeley; Christal; Christian;
Clink; Cranbourne; Dangerfield;
Debbitch; Dickens; Doublefree;
Dummerar; Ellesmere; Everett;
Fenwicke; Gaulesse; Jerningham;
Mitford; Outram; Peveril; Raine;
Whitecraft

Pirate, The: Bunce; Cleveland; Derrick;
Goffe; Halcro; Hawkins; Mertoun;
Scholey; Sinclair; Strumpher; Swertha;
Troil; Yellowley

Quentin Durward: Balue; Blok; Campo-
Gasso; Charles the Bold; Crèvecoeur;
Croye; Dain; Durward; Eberson;
Glorieux; Hayraddin; Marck; Marton;
Pavillon; Petit-Andrée; Thibault of

Edgar; Fool; France; Gloucester; Goneril; Kent; Regan

King Richard II: Bagot; Bolingbroke; Bushy; Gaunt; Gloucester; Green; Northumberland; Percy; Scroop; York

King Richard III: Anne; Bourchier; Buckingham; Clarence; Dorset; Edward; Elizabeth; Grey; Hastings; Henry VII; Margaret; Norfolk; Rivers; Scroop; Stanley; Tyrell; York

Love's Labour's Lost: Costard; Armado; Dumain; Ferdinand; France; Holofernes; Jaquenetta; Katherine; Longaville; Maria; Moth; Nathaniel; Rosaline

Macbeth: Angus; Banquo; Donalbain; Duncan; Fleance; Lennox; Macbeth; Macduff; Rosse

Measure for Measure: Abhorson; Angelo; Claudio; Francisca; Juliet; Lucio; Mariana; Overdone; Thomas; Vicentio

Merchant of Venice, The: Antonio; Arragon; Bassanio; Gobbo; Gratiano; Jessica; Leonardo; Lorenzo; Morocco; Nerissa; Portia; Salanio; Shylock; Tubal; Venice

Merry Wives of Windsor, The: Bardolph; Caius; Evans; Falstaff; Fenton; Ford; Nym; Pistol, Quickly; Shallow; Slender

Midsummer Night's Dream, A: Bottom; Demetrius; Egeus; Flute; Helena; Hippolyta; Lysander; Oberon; Puck; Quince; Snout; Snug; Starveling; Theseus; Titania

Much Ado About Nothing: Antonio; Balthazar; Beatrice; Benedick; Claudio; Dogberry; Hero; John; Leonato, Pedro, Verges

Othello: Brabantio; Cassio; Desdemona; Emilia; Iago; Othello; Roderigo; Venice

Pericles: Antiochus; Cleon; Escanes; Gower; Helicanus; Lysimachus; Pericles; Simonides; Thaisa; Thaliard

Romeo and Juliet: Abram; Balthazar; Benvolio; Capulet; Escalus; Juliet; Laurence; Mercutio; Nurse; Paris; Romeo; Tybalt

Taming of the Shrew, The: Baptista; Bianca; Gremio; Hortensio; Katherina; Lucentio; Petruchio; Sly

Tempest, The: Ariel; Alonso; Antonia; Caliban; Ceres; Ferdinand; Gonzalo; Iris; Miranda; Prospero; Sebastian; Stephano; Trinculo

Timon of Athens: Alcibiades: Apemanthus; Flavius; Lucius; Lucullus; Phyrnia; Sempronius; Timon; Ventidius

Titus Andronicus: Aaron; Aemilius; Aeneas; Alarbus; Bassianus; Chiron; Demetrius; Lavinia; Lucius; Marcus Andronicus; Martius; Mutius; Publius;

Quintus; Saturninus; Tamora; Timandra; Titus Andronicus

Troilus and Cressida: Achilles; Agamenmon; Ajax; Andromache; Cassandra; Cressida; Deipholos; Diomedes; Hector; Helen; Menelaus; Nestor; Pandarus; Paris; Patroclus; Priam; Thersites; Troilus; Ulysses

Twelfth Night: Aguecheek; Antonio; Belch; Fabian; Feste; Malvolio; Maria; Olivia; Orsino; Sebastian; Viola

Two Gentlemen of Verona: Antonio; Julia; Launce; Lucetta; Panthino; Proteus; Silvia; Speed; Thurio; Valentine

Winter's Tale, A: Antigonus; Archidamus; Camillo; Cleomenes; Dion; Florizel, Hermione; Leontes; Mamilius; Paulina; Perdita; Polixenes

with John Fletcher

King Henry VIII: Abergavenny; Brandon; Bullen; Butts; Campeius; Capucius; Cranmer; Cromwell; Denny; Gardiner; Griffith; Guildford; Katharine of Aragon; Lovell; Norfolk; Sands; Suffolk; Surrey; Vaux; Wolsey

Two Noble Kinsmen, The: Arcite; Emelia, Gerrold; Hippolita; Hymen; Palamon; Theseus

Shaw, George Bernard

Apple Cart, The. Boanerges, Jemima; Magnus; Orinthia; Pamphilius; Sempronius

Arms and the Man: Bluntschli; Louka; Nicola; Petkoff; Saranoff

Back to Methuselah: Lubin

Caesar and Cleopatra: Achilles; Appolodorus; Belle Afris; Belzanor; Britannus; Caesar; Charmian; Cleopatra; Ftatateeta; Pothinus; Ptolemy; Ruio

Candida: Burgess; Garnett; Iras; Lucius; Marchbanks; Mill; Morell

Captain Brassbound's Conversion: Brassbound; Drinkwater; Hallam; Hassan; Johnson; Kearney; Marzo; Osman; Rankin; Redbrook; Sidi el Assif; Waynflete

Devil's Disciple, The: Anderson; Brudenell; Burgoyne; Dudgeon; Essie; Hawkins; Swindon

Doctor's Dilemma, The: Blenkinsop; Bonington; Cullen; Dudebat; Redpenny; Ridgeon; Schutzmacher; Tinwell; Walpole

Fanny's First Play: Bannal; Darling; Duvalet; Fanny; Gilbey; Juggins; O'Dowda; Savoyard; Trotter; Vaughan

Heartbreak House: Guinness; Hushabye; Mangan; Shotover; Utterword

John Bull's Other Island: Broadbent; Dempsey; Doran; Farrell; Keegan; Reilly

Steinbeck, John
  Cannery Row: Abbeville; Doc; Flood;
    Malloy; Talbot
  East of Eden: Abra; Albey; Ames;
    Hamilton; Traks
  Grapes of Wrath, The: Casy; Graves; Joad;
    Knowles; Rance; Rivers; Wallace; Wilson
  In Dubious Battle: Mac; Nolan
  Of Mice and Men: Milton; Small
  Red Pony, The: Gitano; Tiflin
Stendhal
  La Chartreuse de Parme; Conti; Dongo;
    Pietranara; Rovère; Sandrino
  Le Rouge et le Noir: Môle; Rênal; Sorel
Stephens, James
  Crock of Gold, The: Caitlin; Hannigan;
    Macmurrachu; Og
Stern, Daniel
  The Rose Rabbi and *The Suicide Academy*:
    Gilliatt; Walker
Stern, Richard
  Golk: Hondorp
Sterne, Laurence
  Tristram Shandy: Bridget; Le Fever;
    Obadiah; Shandy; Slawkenbergius; Slop;
    Trim; Wadman; Yorick
Stevenson, Robert Louis
  Admiral Guinea: see Henley, W.E.
  Black Arrow, The: Appleyard; Brackley;
    Hatch; Lawless; Oakes; Risingham;
    Sedley; Shelton
  Catriona: Balfour of Pilrig; Dale;
    Drummons; Duncansby; Fraser; Gebbie;
    Grant; Macgregor; Ogilvie; Sang;
    Scougal; Stewart
  Deacon Brodie: see Henley, W.E.
  Dr Jekyll and Mr Hyde: Carew; Enfield;
    Guest; Jekyll; Lanyon; Poole; Utterson
  Island Nights' Entertainments: Case;
    Keawe; Keola; Kokua; Randall; Tarleton;
    Uma; Wiltshire
  Kidnapped: Balfour of Shaws; Breck;
    Clouston; Colin of Glenure; Henderland;
    Hoseason; Macpherson; Macrob; Oig;
    Ransome; Riach; Shuan; Thomason
  Master of Ballantrae, The: Broun; Burke;
    Carlyle; Crail; Dass; Durrisdeer; Dutton;
    Grady; Graeme; MacKellar; Paul; Teach
  Merry Men, The: McClour; Soulis
  New Arabian Nights, The: Berthelini;
    Cassilis; De Beaulieu; Feuillé; Florizel;
    Hartley; Huddlestone; Malétroit;
    Malthus; Nicholas; Noel; Northmour;
    Pendragon; Raeburn; Rich; Rolles;
    Scrymgeour; Scuddamore; Stubbs;
    Vandeleur; Zephyrine
  Prince Otto: Cancellarius; Fritz; Gordon;
    Gottesheim; Goudremark; Grafinski;
    Hohenstockwitz; Otto; Rosen; Transome
  St Ives: Byfield; Chevenix; Colenso;

Dudgeon; Fenn; Gilchrist; Goguelat;
    Greensleeves; Robie; Romaine; Rowley;
    St Yves
  Treasure Island: Alan; Anderson; Arrow;
    Bones; Gray; Hands; Harry; Hawkins;
    Hunter; Johnny; Joyce; Livesey; Merry;
    Morgan; Pew; Redruth; Silver; Smollett;
    Trelawney
  Weir of Hermiston, The: Elliott;
    Glenalmond; Gregory; Innes; Jopp;
    McKellop; Weir
  with Lloyd Osbourne
  Wrong Box, The: Bloomfield; Chandler;
    Fettes; Finsbury; Gray; Hazeltine;
    Judkin; Macfarlane; Pitman; Wickham
Stevenson, William
  attrib.
  Gammer Gurton's Needle: Bailey; Cock;
    Diccon; Gurton; Hodge; Rat; Scapethrift;
    Tib
Stivens, Dal
  *Jimmy Brockett: Portrait of a Notable
    Australian*: Brockett
Stoker, Bram
  Dracula: Dracula; Harker; Helsing;
    Morris; Seward
Storey, David
  Radcliffe: Blakeley; Radcliffe; Tolson
  Restoration of Arnold Middleton, The:
    Hanson; O'Connor; Wilkinson
  This Sporting Life: Braithewaite;
    Hammond; Johnson; Machin; Wade;
    Weaver
Storm, Theodore
  Immensee: Erich; Werner
Stout, Rex
  Fer-de-Lance: Goodwin; Wolfe
Stow, Randolph
  Merry-Go-Round in the Sea, The:
    Maplestead
Stowe, Harriet Beecher
  Uncle Tom's Cabin: Adolph; Bird; Cassy;
    Cudjoe; Dinah; Emmeline; Fletcher;
    George; Haley; Halliday; Harris; Legree;
    Loker; Marks; Selden; Shelby; St Clare;
    Skeggs; Stedman; Susan; Symmes; Tan
    Trompe; Tom; Topsy; Vermont; Wilson
Stribling, T.S.
  The Forge, The Store, and *Unfinished*:
    Vaiden
Strindberg, August
  Engelbert: Engelbrektsson
  Kristina: Kristina; Tott
  Miss Julie: Jean; Julie
  Påsk (Easter): Lindkvist
Stuart, Francis
  Black List, Section H.: H.
Stuart, Jesse
  Taps for Private Tussie and *Trees of
    Heaven*: Bushman; Tussie

Batts; Benson; Bernstein; Biche; Blake;
Blinkinsop; Boyle; Brett; Claypole;
Clubber; Gumbo; Hagan; Handyman;
Hibou; Jabotière; Juffles; Lambert;
March; Molly; Morris; Mouchy;
Mountain; Museau; Nathan; Redmaynes;
Ruff; Sady; Screwby; Sparks; Spencer;
Stack; Talmadge; Trumpington; Van de
Bosch; Warrington
Yellowplush Papers, The: Blewett; Bulwig;
Dawkins; Draper; Esmond; Firebrace;
Foker; Franks; Griffin; Kicksey; L'Orge;
'Toinette

Theroux, Paul
Mosquito Coast: Fox
Picture Palace: Pratt

Thomas, A.M.
Witching Hour, The: Brookfield;
Campbell; Hardmuth; Whipple

Thomas, Brandon
Charley's Aunt: Babberley; Brassett;
Chesney; D'Alvadorez; Spettigue;
Verdun; Wykeham

Thomas, Dylan
Under Milk Wood: Benyon; Bighead;
Bread; Cat; Cut-Glass; Edwards; Evans
the Death; Garter; Morgan; Nogood;
Ocky Milkman; Ogmore; Owen; Price;
Probert; Pugh; Rees; Rose Cottage; Sailors;
Smalls; Waldo; Watkins; Willy Nilly

Thomson, James
Castle of Indolence, The: Selvaggio

Thorne, Michael
Pen Friends: Hawthorne; Melville

Thorpe, T.B.
Hive of the Bee Hunter, The: Arkansas

Thurber, James
My World – and Welcome to It: Mitty
Owl in the Attic, The: Armsby; Gribling

Thurston, Katherine
John Chilcote MP: Chilcote; Fraide;
Lakely; Loder

Tieck, Ludwig
*Peter Leberecht, eine Geschichte ohne
Abenteuerlichkeiten (Peter Leberecht, a
Work without Adventures)*: Leberecht

Tindall, Gillian
Edge of the Paper, The: King

Tolkien, J.R.R.
Lord of the Rings, The: Baggins;
Brandybuck; Sauron; Shadowfax; Took

Tolstoy, Leo
Anna Karenina: Mikhalovna
I svet vo tme svetit (The Light That Shines):
Princess; Saryntsov
*Smert Ivana Ilyicha (The Death of Ivan
Ilyich)*: Ilyich

Tomlinson, H.M.
All Our Yesterdays: Bolt; Maynard;
Whittaker

Gallions Reach: Ah Loi; Bennett; Colet;
Denny; Hale; Mat; Norrie; Oliver;
Parsell; Perriam; Sinclair; Suvretta

Toomer, Jean
Cane: Kabnis

Tourgee, Albion W.
Fool's Errand: Sevosse

Tourneur, Cyril
Atheist's Tragedy, The, or *The Honest
Man's Revenge*: Belforest; Borachio:
Fesco; Languebeau Snuffe; Leuidulcia;
Montferrars; Rousard; Sebastian; Snuffe;
Soquette
attrib.
Revenger's Tragedy, The: Ambiotoso;
Antonio; Gratiana; Hippolito; Junior;
Lussurioso; Piero; Superuacuo; Vindice

Travers, Pamela L.
Mary Poppins: Poppins

Trevor, William
Miss Gomez and the Brethren: Batt; Flynn;
Gomez; Ponsonby; Roche; Tuke
Mrs Eckdorf in O'Neill's Hotel: Eckdorf;
Gregan; Morrissey; O'Shea; Quin; Sinnott
Old Boys, The: Burdock; Cridley; Dowse;
Jaraby; Monmouth; Nox; Sole; Swingler;
Turtle

Trollope, Anthony
Ayala's Angel: Batsby; Dormer; Dosett;
Hamel; Tringle
American Senator, The: Gotobed; Green;
Masters; Morton; Rufford; Trefoil;
Twentyman
Barchester Towers: Arabin; Pie; Plomacy;
Quiverful; Slope; Stanhope
Belton Estate, The: Amedroz; Askerton;
Aylmer
Bertrams, The: Bertram; Harcourt;
Waddington
Can You Forgive Her?: Fitzgerald; Palliser
Claverings, The: Bcilby; Brabazon; Burton;
Clavering; Gordeloup; Ongar; Pateroff;
Saul
Cousin Henry: Broderick; Jones; Owen
Dr Thorne: De Courcy; Dunstable;
Filgrave; Gazabee; Gresham; Moffat;
Oriel; Scatcherd; Thorne
Dr Wortle's School: Carstairs; Peacocke;
Wortle
Eustace Diamonds, The: Benjamin; Bunfit;
Camperdown; Carbuncle; Dove; Emilius;
Eustace; Gowran; Greystock; Hittaway;
Linlithgow; MacNulty; Mopus; Morris;
Roanoke; Tewitt
Eye for an Eye, An: Neville; O'Hara
Fixed Period, The: Crasweller
Framley Parsonage: Crawley; Dumbello;
Fothergill; Lufton; Meredith; Monsell;
Proudie; Robarts; Smith; Sowerby;
Supplehouse; Tickler

Warren, Samuel—*contd.*
   Ten Thousand A Year: Aubreys; De La
   Zouch; Dredlington; Huckaback; Quirk;
   Runnington; St Clair; Squallop; Tagrag;
   Titmouse; Wolstenholme
Waten, Juda
   Unbending, The: Kochansky
Waterhouse, Keith
   Billy Liar: Fisher
Watts-Dunton, Theodore
   Aylwin: Aylwin; D'Arcy; Lovell;
   Wilderspin; Wynne
Waugh, Auberon
   Consider the Lilies: Trumpeter
Waugh, Evelyn
   Brideshead Revisited: Blanche; Cara;
   Champion; Marchmain; Mottram;
   Muspratt; Ryder; Samgrass
   Decline and Fall: Beste-Chetwynde; Fagan;
   Grimes; Lucas-Dockery; Maltravers;
   Pennyfeather; Phylbrick; Potts;
   Prendergast; Silenus; Trumpington
   Handful of Dust, A: Beaver; Grant-
   Menzies; Last; Messinger; Todd
   Men at Arms: Apthorpe; Box-Bender;
   Crouchback; Ritchie-Hook; Tickeridge
   Ordeal of Gilbert Pinfold, The: Angel;
   Drake; Pinfold; Steerforth
   Put Out More Flags: Connolly; Bentley;
   Green; Lyne; Mainwaring; Meadowes;
   Pimpernell; Plum; Seal; Silk; Sothill
   Vile Bodies: Ape; Blount; Crump; Fenwick-
   Symes; Littlejohn; Malpractice;
   Rothschild
Webb, Mary
   Precious Bane: Beguildy
Webster, Jean
   Daddy-Long-Legs: Pendleton
Webster, John
   Duchess of Malfi, The: Amalfi; Bologna;
   Bosola; Calabria
   White Devil, The: Corombona; Lodovico;
   Medici; Ursini
Weldon, Fay
   Praxis: Duveen
Wells, H.G.
   Ann Veronica: Capes; Manning; More;
   Palsworthy; Ramage; Stanley; Widgetts
   Bealby: Benshaw; Bridgett; Chickney;
   Douglas; Mergelson; Moggeridge;
   Philips
   Boon: Bathwick; Blandish; Bliss; Boon;
   Dodd; Keyhole; Mutimer
   Christina Alberta's Father: Devizes;
   Hossett; Lambone; Preemby; Roothing
   Country of the Blind, The: Wallace; Yacob
   Dream, The: Bramble; Bumpus; Good;
   Julip; Kimpton; Marcus; Moggeridge;
   Newberry; Plaice; Sarnac; Smith; Sumner
   First Men in the Moon, The: Bedford;

   Blake; Cavor; Grand Lunar; Phi-oo;
   Selenites; Tsi-Puff; Wendigee
   Food of the Gods, The: Bensington;
   Caddles; Carrington; Caterham; Cosser;
   Durgan; Redwood; Skinner; Weser
   Dreiburg; Winkles
   History of Mr Polly, The: Boomer; Flo;
   Garvace; Hinks; Jew; Johnson; Larkins;
   Morrison; Parsons; Pentstemon; Platt;
   Podger; Polly; Rumbold; Rusper; Voules
   In the Days of the Comet: Redcar; Reeves;
   Stuart; Verral
   Invisible Man, The: Bunting; Cuss; Griffin;
   Hall; Kemp; Wickstead
   Joan and Peter: Blend; Debenham;
   Fremisson; Grimes; Henderson; Huntly;
   Jelaluddin; Mainwearing; Mills;
   Murgatroyd; Reinhart; Stubland;
   Sycamore; Sydenham; Troop; Unwin;
   Wilmington; Winterbaum
   Island of Dr Moreau, The: M'Ling;
   Montgomery; Prendick
   Kipps: Bean; Bindon-Botting; Buggins;
   Chitterlow; Coote; Kipps; Masterman;
   Pearce; Pornick; Revel; Shalford; Waddy;
   Walsingham; Woodrow
   Love and Mr Lewisham: Baynes; Bonover;
   Chaffery; Dunkerley; Gadow; Heydinger;
   Henderson; Lagune; Lewisham; Lychnis;
   Munday; Parkson; Smithers
   Marriage: Alimony; Behrens; Magnet;
   Petchworth; Plessington; Pope; Trafford;
   Wintersloan
   Men Like Gods: Barnstable; Barralonga;
   Burleigh; Catskill; Crystal; Dupont;
   Hunker; Mush; Peeve; Ridley; Stella;
   Sunray
   Mr Blettsworthy on Rampole Island:
   Blettsworthy; Megatherium; Slaughter
   Mr Britling Sees It Through: Britling;
   Carmine; Corner; Dimple; Direck; Faber;
   Frensham; Harrowdean; Heinrich;
   Jewell; Manning; Oliver; Rendezvous;
   Teddy; Wilshire
   New Machiavelli, The: Bailey; Britten-
   Close; Codger; Evesham; Hatherleigh;
   Massinghay; Milly; Minter; Remington;
   Rivers; Robinson; Seddon; Wilkins;
   Willersley
   Passionate Friends, The: Christian; Justin;
   Satchell; Stratton; Tavrille
   Plattner Story, The: Jane; Monson;
   Piddingquirk; Plattner; Pollock
   Research Magnificent, The: Alexievna;
   Benham; Easton; Marayne; Morris;
   Nolan; Prothero; White
   Sea Lady, The: Bunting; Glendower;
   Melville; Parker
   Secret Places of the Heart: Caston;
   Gramont; Hardy; Lake; Martineau

Select Conversations With an Uncle:
Harborough
Soul of a Bishop: Dale; Riverton; Scrope;
Sunderbund
Tales of Life and Adventure: Bingham;
Brisher; Winchelsea
Tales of Space and Time: Eudena; Ugh-Lomi
Tales of the Unexpected: Skelmersdale
Time Machine, The: Eloi; Filby; Morlocks;
Watchett; Weena
Tono Bungay: Booch; Carnaby; Cothorpe;
Drew; Ewart; Frapp; Garvel; Gordon-
Naysmith; Hogbary; Latude-Fernay;
Mackridge; Moggs; Normandy; Osprey;
Ponderevo; Rabbits; Ramboat; Rink;
Smithie; Somerville; Wachorn
Twelve Stories and a Dream: Banghurst;
Filmer; Medina Saroté
Undying Fire, The: Barrack; Burrows; Dad;
Farr; Huss; Mengo
War in the Air, The: Bright; Bunthorne;
Butteridge; Giddy; Grubb; Gore; Karl
Albert; Kurt; Laurier; Smallways;
Winterfield
War of the Worlds, The: Elphinstone;
Holroyd
Wheels of Chance: Bechamel; Briggs;
Dangle; Hoopdriver; Mergle; Milton;
Phipps; Widgery
When the Sleeper Wakes: Asano; Graham;
Helen; Howard; Isbister; Lincoln; Ostrog;
Warming; Wotton
Wife of Sir Isaac Harman, The: Beach-
Mandarin; Brumley; Burnet; Harman;
Sawbridge; Toomer
Wonderful Visit, The: Gotch;
Hammergallow; Hilyer; Jehoram;
Mendham
World Set Free, The: Barnet; Holsten;
Karenin

Welty, Eudora
Curtain of Green, A: Carson; Clytie; Daw;
Glen; Harris; Jackson; Marblehall; Mike;
Powerhouse; Sanford; Slocum; Sobby;
Watts
Delta Wedding: Fairchild; Flavin;
McRaven
Golden Apples, The: MacLain; Morrison;
Rainey
Optimist's Daughter, The: Chisom;
McKelva
Ponder Heart, The: Earle; Ponder
Robber Bridegroom, The: Lockhart;
Musgrove
Werfel, Franz
*Verdi: Roman der Oper (Verdi: A Novel
of the Opera)*: Boito; Verdi; Wagner
Wesker, Arnold
Chips With Everything: McClure;
Thompson; Washington; Wingate

West, Anthony
Heritage: Savage; Town
On a Dark Night: Wallis
West, Nathanael
Cool Million, A: Pitkin; Prail; Slemp;
Whipple
Day of the Locust, The: Estee; Gingos;
Greener; Hackett; Kusich; Loomis;
Miguel; Shoop; Simpson
Dream Life of Balso Snell, The: Gilson;
Janey; Maloney the Areopagite;
McGeeney; Snell
Miss Lonelyhearts: Doyle; Doyle; Miss
Lonelyhearts; Sick-of-it-all; Skrike
West, Paul
Alley Jaggers: Jaggers
West, Rebecca
Birds Fall Down: Chubinov; Kamensky;
Rowan
Return of the Soldier, The: Anderson;
Baldry
Thinking Reed, The: Barnaclough;
D'Alperoussa; De Verviers; Luba; Pillans;
Renart; Sallafranque; Tarry; Vernon;
Yates
Westall, William
Old Bank, The: Fynes; Lackland; Leuknor;
Matthew; Silvercross; Verdley; Warnham
Westcott, Glenway
Goodbye Winsconsin: Tower
Pilgrim Hawk, The: Cullen; Eva; Hawk;
Henry; Ricketts; Tower
Wetherell, Elizabeth
Wide, Wide World: Humphreys;
Marshman; Montgomery
Wharton, Edith
Age of Innocence, The: Archer; Minette;
Olenska
Custom of the Country, The: Blitch;
Bowen; Chellas; Fairford; Frusk; Heeny;
Lipscombe; Marvell; Moffat; Rolliver;
Shallum; Spragg; Van Degen
Ethan Frome: Frome; Gow; Hale; Powell;
Silver; Varnum
Fruit of the Tree: Amherst; Westmore;
Wyant
Gods Arrive, The: Scrimser; Spear;
Tarrant; Weston
House of Mirth, The: Dorset; Farish;
Gryce; Haffen; Peniston; Rosedale;
Selden; Stepney; Trenor; Van Osburgh
Hudson River Bracketed: Delaney;
Frenside; Hipsley; Scrimser; Spear;
Tarrant; Weston
Mother's Recompense, The: Clephane;
Fenno; Landers
Old New York: Delane; Halsey;
Hazeldean; Kent; Lovell; Prest; Ralston;
Raycie; Ruskin; Spender; Whitman
Reef, The: Darrow; Leath; Viner

Wiseman, Adele
  Crackpot: Hoda
Wister, Owen
  Virginian, The: Balaam; Trampas;
    Virginian
Witkiewicz, Stanislaw Ignacy
  nienasycenie: poweiesc (Insatiability):
    Hardonne; Kapen; Sloboluchowicz
Wodehouse, P.G.
  Cocktail Time: Bastable; Ickenham;
    MacMurdo; Pearce; Peasemarsh; Saxby;
    Wisdom
  Damsel in Distress, A: Bevan; Byng; Dore;
    Farraday; Keggs; Marshmoreton;
    Plummer; Raymond
  Gentleman of Leisure, A: Blunt;
    McEarchern; Milligan; Pitt
  Heart of a Goof, The: Bates; Blakeney;
    Bott; Dibble; Kent; Medway; Meredith;
    Packard; Parsloe; Podmarsh; Vosper
  Little Nugget, The: Blake; Burns; Drassilis;
    Fisher; Ford; Glossop; MacGinnis;
    Mennick; Mountry; Sheridan; Smith
  Love Among the Chickens: Beale;
    Derrick; Garnet; Hawk, Lakenheath;
    Uckridge
  Man Upstairs, The: Bates; Boielle;
    Brougham; Hill; Kitchener; Mifflin;
    Moore; Preston; Rendal; Sellers;
    Vaughan; Yvonne
  Man With Two Left Feet, The: Wooster
  Meet Mr Mulliner: Biggs; Bloodenough;
    Brandon; Cartaret; Entwhistle; Franklin;
    Maynard; Mulliner; Oliphant; Pinckney;
    Posthlewaite; Purdue; Rodman;
    Stortford; Wilks
  My Man Jeeves: Jeeves
  Summer Moonshine: Bulpitt; Busby;
    Chinnery; Dwornitzchek; Peake;
    Vanringham; Whittaker
  Thank You, Jeeves: Brinkley; Chuffnell;
    Dobson; Glossop; Jeeves; Stoker
  Uckridge: Billson; Bowles; Coote;
    Corcoran; Tupper
Woiwode, Larry
  *Beyond the Bedroom Wall: A Family
    Album*: Neumiller
Wolfe, Thomas
  Look Homeward, Angel: James; Leonard;
    Pentland
  *Of Time and the River: A Legend of Man's
    Hunger in His Youth*: Hatcher; Pentland;
    Starwick; Weaver
  Web and the Rock, The: Alsop; Jack;
    Randolph; Webber
  You Can't Go Home Again: Abrahamson;
    Bendien; Edwards; Hauser; Heilig; Jack;
    Joyner; Logan; McHarg; Pennock; Purvis;
    Reade; Shepperton; Stoat; Von Kohler;
    Webber

Wood, Mrs Henry
  Danesbury House: Danesbury
  East Lynne: Carlyle; Hare; Headthelot;
    Herbert; Hallijohn; Levison; Stalkenberg;
    Thorn; Vane; Wainwright
  Johnny Ludlow series: Ludlow
Woodes, Nathaniel
  Conflict of Conscience, The: Philologus
Woolf, Virginia
  Between the Acts: Dodge; La Trobe;
    Manresa; Oliver; Swithin
  Jacob's Room: Barfoot; Coppard;
    Flanders; Floyd; Pearce; Plumer; Steele;
    Wentworth-Williams; Wilding
  Mrs Dalloway: Bradshaw; Brush; Burton;
    Dalloway; Holmes; Kilman; Parry; Seton;
    Smith; Walsh; Whitbread
  Night and Day: Datchet; Denham; Hilbery
  Orlando: Greene; Harriet; Orlando; Sasha;
    Shelmerdine
  To the Lighthouse: Bankes; Briscoe;
    Carmichael; Ramsay; Rayley; Tansley
  Waves, The: Bernard; Jinny; Louis;
    Neville; Rhoda; Susan
  Years, The: Crosby; Lasswade; Pargiter;
    Pomjalovsky
Wouk, Herman
  Caine Mutiny, The: Greenwald; Keefer;
    Keith; Maryk; Queeg; Wynn
Wright, Harold Bell
  Winning of Barbara Worth, The: Worth
Wright, Richard
  Native Son: Thomas
Wycherley, William
  Country Wife, The: Harcourt; Horner;
    Pinchwife; Sparkish; Squeamish
  Gentleman Dancing-Master, The: Gerrard;
    Martin; Paris
  Love in a Wood, or St James's Park:
    Addlepot; Gripe; Lady Flippant; Lydia;
    Ranger; Valentine
  Plain Dealer, The: Fidelia; Manly; Novel;
    Oldfox; Olivia; Plausible
Wylie, Elinor
  Orphan Angel, The: Shelley

Yeats, William Butler
  Countess Cathleen, The: Cathleen
  Green Helmet, The: Cuchulain
  Kathleen ni Houlihan: Cahel; Gillane
Yonge, Charlotte M.
  Daisy Chain, The: Anderson; Arnott
  Heir of Redclyffe, The: Edmonstone;
    Morville
Young, Al
  Ask Me Now: Knight
  Sitting Pretty: Prettymon
Young, E.H.
  Miss Mole: Blenkinsop; Corder; Mole;
    Ridding; Widdows; Withers